A Review of the Events of 1987

The 1988 World Book Year Book

The Annual Supplement to The World Book Encyclopedia

World Book, Inc.

a Scott Fetzer company

Chicago London Sydney Toronto

Printed in the United States of America.
ISBN 0-7166-0488-4
ISSN 0084-1439
Library of Congress Catalog Card Number: 62-4818

Staff

Publisher
William H. Nault

Editor in Chief
Robert O. Zeleny

Editorial Staff
Executive Editor
A. Richard Harmet

Managing Editor
Wayne Wille

Associate Editor
Sara Dreyfuss

Senior Editors
David L. Dreier
Jinger Griswold
Mary A. Krier
Barbara A. Mayes
Jay Myers
Joan Stephenson
Rod Such

Contributing Editors
Gary A. Alt
Darlene R. Stille

Research Editor
Irene B. Keller

Index Editor
Claire Bolton

Statistical Editor
Tom Klonoski

Editorial Assistant
Ethel Matthews

Art Staff
Executive Art Director
William Hammond

Art Director
Roberta Dimmer

Senior Artist, Year Book
Nikki Conner

Senior Artists
Melanie J. Lawson
Alexandra Newell

Artists
Alice F. Dole
Lucy Smith

Photography Director
John S. Marshall

Senior Photographs Editor
Sandra M. Ozanick

Photographs Editors
Barbara A. Bennett
Geralyn Swietek

Research Services
Director
Mary Norton

Researcher
Kristina Vaicikonis

Library Services
Mary Kayaian, Head

Cartographic Services
H. George Stoll, Head
Wayne K. Pichler

Product Production
Executive Director
Peter Mollman

Director of Manufacturing
Joseph C. LaCount

Research and Development Manager
Henry Koval

Pre-Press Services
Jerry Stack, Director
Lori Frankel
Madelyn Krzak
Barbara Podczerwinski

Proofreaders
Anne Dillon
Marguerite Hoye
Esther Johns
Daniel Marotta

Contents

See page 116.

See page 548.

A tear-out page of cross-reference tabs for insertion in THE WORLD BOOK ENCYCLOPEDIA appears after page 16.

Contributors

Contributors not listed on these pages are members of THE WORLD BOOK YEAR BOOK editorial staff.

Abraham, George (Doc), B.S.; Copartner, The Green Thumb. [GARDENING]

Abraham, Katherine (Katy), B.S.; Copartner, The Green Thumb. [GARDENING]

Adachi, Ken, B.A., M.A.; Literary Critic, *The Toronto Star.* [CANADIAN LITERATURE]

Adams, Charles J., B.A., Ph.D.; Professor, Institute of Islamic Studies, McGill University. [Special Report: UNDERSTANDING ISLAM]

Alexander, David T., B.Sc., M.A.; Executive Director, Numismatic Literary Guild. [COIN COLLECTING]

Alexiou, Arthur G., B.S.E.E., M.S.E.E.; Assistant Secretary, Intergovernmental Oceanographic Commission. [OCEAN]

Andrews, Peter J., B.A., M.S.; Free-Lance Writer; Biochemist. [CHEMISTRY]

Apseloff, Marilyn Fain, B.A., M.A.; Associate Professor of English, Kent State University. [LITERATURE FOR CHILDREN]

Barber, Peggy, B.A., M.L.S.; Associate Executive Director, American Library Association. [AMERICAN LIBRARY ASSOCIATION; LIBRARY]

Baum, B. Scott, B.A.; Associate Editor, American Correctional Association. [PRISON]

Bednarski, P. J., Entertainment-Media Business Reporter, *Chicago Sun-Times.* [RADIO; TELEVISION]

Berman, Howard A., M.H.L.; Rabbi, Chicago Sinai Congregation. [JEWS AND JUDAISM]

Bierman, Howard, B.E.E.; President, Paje Consultants, Inc. [COMPUTER; ELECTRONICS]

Blackadar, Alfred K., A.B., Ph.D.; Professor Emeritus, The Pennsylvania State University. [WEATHER]

Bourne, Eric, Eastern Europe Correspondent, *The Christian Science Monitor.* [Eastern European Country Articles; UNION OF SOVIET SOCIALIST REPUBLICS (Close-Up)]

Bradsher, Henry S., A.B., B.J.; Foreign Affairs Analyst. [ASIA and Asian Country Articles]

Breslin, Paul, B.A., Ph.D.; Associate Professor of English, Northwestern University. [POETRY]

Brett, Carlton E., B.A., M.A., Ph.D.; Associate Professor of Geological Sciences, University of Rochester. [PALEONTOLOGY]

Brodsky, Arthur R., B.A., M.S.J.; Senior Editor, *Communications Daily.* [COMMUNICATIONS]

Brown, Kenneth, former Editor, *United Kingdom Press Gazette.* [EUROPE and Western European Country Articles]

Bruske, Edward H., Reporter, *The Washington Post.* [COURTS; CRIME]

Bukro, Casey, B.S.J., M.S.J.; Environment Writer, *Chicago Tribune.* [ENVIRONMENTAL POLLUTION]

Buursma, Bruce, Religion Writer, *Chicago Tribune.* [RELIGION]

Campbell, Robert, B.A., M.S., M. Arch.; Architecture Critic, *The Boston Globe.* [ARCHITECTURE]

Campion, Owen F., A.B.; Editor in Chief, *The Tennessee Register.* [ROMAN CATHOLIC CHURCH]

Cardinale, Diane P., B.A.; Assistant Communications Director, Toy Manufacturers of America. [TOYS AND GAMES]

Cawthorne, David M., B.S.; Associate Editor, *Traffic World.* [Transportation Articles]

Cooney, Jane, Executive Director, Canadian Library Association. [CANADIAN LIBRARY ASSOCIATION]

Cormier, Frank, B.S.J., M.S.J.; former White House Correspondent, Associated Press. [U.S. Government Articles]

Cormier, Margot, B.A., M.A.; Free-Lance Writer. [U.S. Government Articles]

Crimmins, Eileen M., B.S., M.A., Ph.D.; Associate Professor, Andrus Gerontology Center, University of Southern California. [Special Report: THE GRAYING OF AMERICA]

Cromie, William J., B.S., M.S.; Executive Director, Council for Advancement of Science Writing. [SPACE EXPLORATION]

Dalziel, Ian W. D., Ph.D.; Professor of Geological Sciences, Institute for Geophysics, University of Texas at Austin. [WORLD BOOK SUPPLEMENT: ANTARCTICA]

Dauben, Joseph, A.B., A.M., Ph.D.; Professor of History and the History of Science, City University of New York. [WORLD BOOK SUPPLEMENT: MATHEMATICS]

DeFrank, Thomas M., B.A., M.A.; Deputy Bureau Chief and White House Correspondent, *Newsweek* magazine. [ARMED FORCES]

Dent, Thomas H., Executive Director, The Cat Fanciers' Association, Inc. [CAT]

Duffy, Robert, Political Writer, *The Toronto Star.* [TORONTO]

Dugas, Christine, M.A.; Marketing Reporter, *New York Newsday.* [ADVERTISING]

Easterlin, Richard A., M.E., A.M., Ph.D.; Professor of Economics, University of Southern California. [Special Report: THE GRAYING OF AMERICA]

Edmonds, Patricia L., B.A.; City-County Bureau Chief, *Detroit Free Press.* [DETROIT]

Elsasser, Glen R., B.A., M.S.; Correspondent, *Chicago Tribune.* [SUPREME COURT OF THE UNITED STATES]

Evans, Sandra, B.S.J.; Staff Writer, *The Washington Post.* [WASHINGTON, D.C.]

Farr, David M. L., M.A., D.Phil.; Professor of History, Carleton University, Ottawa. [CANADA; Canadian Province Articles; MULRONEY, M. BRIAN; SAUVÉ, JEANNE M.; TRUDEAU, PIERRE E.]

Fisher, Robert W., B.A., M.A.; Supervisory Economist, U.S. Bureau of Labor Statistics. [LABOR]

Fitzgerald, Mark, B.A.; Midwest Editor, *Editor & Publisher* magazine. [NEWSPAPER; PUBLISHING]

Francis, Henry G., B.S.; Executive Editor, American Contract Bridge League. [BRIDGE]

Gatty, Bob, President, Gatty Communications. [FOOD]

Goldberg, Stanley, B.S., A.M.T., Ph.D.; Consultant-Planner, Smithsonian Institution. [WORLD BOOK SUPPLEMENT: PHYSICS]

Goldner, Nancy, B.A.; Dance Critic, *The Philadelphia Inquirer.* [DANCING]

Goldstein, Jane, B.A.; Director of Publicity, Santa Anita Park. [HORSE RACING]

Gould, William, B.A.; Free-Lance Writer and Editor, England. [ENGLAND]

Grigadean, Jerry, B.S., M.Mus., Ph.D.; Producer, Grigadean Productions. [POPULAR MUSIC]

Hannan, Patrick, B.A.; Producer/Presenter, British Broadcasting Corporation Wales. [WALES]

Harakas, Stanley S., B.A., B.D., Th.D.; Professor of Orthodox Christian Ethics, Holy Cross Greek Orthodox School of Theology. [EASTERN ORTHODOX CHURCHES]

Haverstock, Nathan A., A.B.; Affiliate Scholar, Oberlin College. [LATIN AMERICA and Latin-American Country Articles]

Herreid, Clyde Freeman, A.B., M.Sc., Ph.D.; Professor of Biological Sciences, State University of New York at Buffalo. [ZOOLOGY]

Higgins, James V., B.A.; Auto Industry Reporter, *The Detroit News.* [AUTOMOBILE]

Hillgren, Sonja, B.J., M.A.; Farm Editor, United Press International. [FARM AND FARMING]

Holzer, Francine J., B.A., M.L.S.; Director, Information Services, Magazine Publishers Association. [MAGAZINE]

Horne, Donald, Professor Emeritus, University of New South Wales; former Editor, *The Bulletin.* [Special Report: AUSTRALIA'S 200TH BIRTHDAY]

Hunzeker, Jeanne M., D.S.W.; Associate Professor, Southern University at New Orleans. [CHILD WELFARE]

Jacobi, Peter P., B.S.J., M.S.J.; Professor of Journalism, Indiana University. [CLASSICAL MUSIC]

Johanson, Donald C., B.S., M.A., Ph.D.; Director, Institute of Human Origins. [ANTHROPOLOGY]

Joseph, Lou, B.A.; Senior Medical Writer, Hill and Knowlton, Inc. [DENTISTRY]

Kisor, Henry, B.A., M.S.J.; Book Editor, *Chicago Sun-Times.* [LITERATURE]

Knapp, Elaine Stuart, B.A.; Senior Editor, Council of State Governments. [STATE GOVERNMENT]

Koenig, Louis W., B.A., M.A., Ph.D., L.H.D.; Professor of Government, New York University. [CIVIL RIGHTS]

Kolgraf, Ronald, B.A., M.A.; General Manager and Publisher, *Adweek* and *Computer & Electronics Marketing.* [MANUFACTURING]

Kuersten, Joan, B.A.; Editor/Writer, National PTA. [NATIONAL PTA]

Langdon, Robert, M.A.; Visiting Fellow, Department of Pacific and SEAsian History, Australian National University. [PACIFIC ISLANDS]

Larsen, Paul A., P.E., B.S., Ch.E.; Member: American Philatelic Society; Collectors Club of Chicago; Fellow, Royal Philatelic Society, London; past President, British Caribbean Philatelic Study Group. [STAMP COLLECTING]

Lawrence, Al, A.B., M.A., M.Ed.; Associate Director, United States Chess Federation. [CHESS]

Lawrence, Richard, B.E.E.; International Economics Correspondent, *The Journal of Commerce.* [INTERNATIONAL TRADE]

Leff, Donna Rosene, B.S.J., M.S.J., M.P.P., Ph.D.; Associate Professor of Journalism and Urban Affairs, Northwestern University. [CITY]

Levy, Emanuel, B.A.; Editor, Roberts Publishing Company. [INSURANCE]

Lewis, David C., M.D.; Director, Center for Alcohol and Addiction Studies, Brown University. [DRUG ABUSE]

Liebenow, Beverly B., B.A.; Author and Free-Lance Writer. [AFRICA and African Country Articles]

Liebenow, J. Gus, B.A., M.A., Ph.D.; Rudy Professor of Political Science/African Studies, Indiana University. [AFRICA and African Country Articles]

Liscomb, Robie, B.A., M.A.; Information and Public Relations Officer, University of Victoria. [HANDICAPPED (Close-Up)]

Litsky, Frank, B.S.; Sports Writer, *The New York Times.* [Sports Articles]

Maki, John M., B.A., M.A., Ph.D.; Professor Emeritus, University of Massachusetts. [JAPAN]

Mandile, Tony, Free-Lance Writer/Photographer. [FISHING; HUNTING]

Maran, Stephen P., B.S., M.A., Ph.D.; Senior Staff Scientist, National Aeronautics and Space Administration-Goddard Space Flight Center. [ASTRONOMY]

Marty, Martin E., Ph.D.; Fairfax M. Cone Distinguished Service Professor, University of Chicago. [PROTESTANTISM]

Mather, Ian J., M.A.; Defense Correspondent, *The Observer,* London. [GREAT BRITAIN; IRELAND; NORTHERN IRELAND]

Maugh, Thomas H., II, Ph.D.; Science Writer, *Los Angeles Times.* [BIOCHEMISTRY]

McCarron, John F., B.S.J., M.S.J.; Urban Affairs Writer, *Chicago Tribune.* [CHICAGO]

Merina, Victor, A.A., B.A., M.S.; Staff Writer, *Los Angeles Times.* [LOS ANGELES]

Miller, J. D. B., M.Ec., M.A.; Professor of International Relations, Australian National University, Canberra. [AUSTRALIA]

Moores, Eldridge M., B.S., Ph.D.; Professor of Geology, University of California at Davis. [GEOLOGY]

Moritz, Owen, B.A.; Urban Affairs Editor, New York *Daily News.* [NEW YORK CITY]

Morris, Bernadine, B.A., M.A.; Fashion Critic, *The New York Times.* [FASHION]

Newcomb, Eldon H., A.B., A.M., Ph.D.; Professor and Chairman, Department of Botany, University of Wisconsin-Madison. [BOTANY]

Oatis, William N., former United Nations Correspondent, Associated Press. [UNITED NATIONS]

Pollock, Steve, B.A.; Editor, *Popular Photography.* [PHOTOGRAPHY]

Priestaf, Iris, B.A., M.A., Ph.D.; Geographer/Water Resources Specialist, David Keith Todd Consulting Engineers. [WATER]

Raeburn, Paul, B.S.,; Free-Lance Science Writer. [PHYSICS; PHYSICS (Close-Up)]

Reinken, Charles, B.B.A., M.A.; Associate Editor, *The Houston Post.* [HOUSTON]

Robinson, Walter, B.A.; Contributing Editor, *Art in America* Magazine. [ART]

Rowse, Arthur E., I.A., M.B.A.; President, Consumer News, Incorporated. [CONSUMERISM; SAFETY]

Shand, David A., B.C.A., B.Com.; First Assistant Secretary, Australian Department of Finance. [NEW ZEALAND]

Shapiro, Howard S., B.S.; Deputy New Jersey Editor, *The Philadelphia Inquirer.* [PHILADELPHIA]

Shearer, Warren W., B.A., M.A., Ph.D., J.D.; Partner, Thorpe & Shearer, Attorneys at Law; former Chairman, Department of Economics, Wabash College. [ECONOMICS]

Spencer, William, A.B., A.M., Ph.D.; Writer; Former Professor of History, Florida State University. [MIDDLE EAST and Middle Eastern Country Articles; North Africa Country Articles]

Stasio, Marilyn, B.A., M.A.; Theater Critic, *New York Post.* [THEATER; Special Report: IT'S NO MYSTERY WHY EVERYBODY LOVES A MYSTERY]

Swanton, Donald W., B.S., M.S., Ph.D., M.B.A.; Chairman, Department of Finance, Roosevelt University. [BANK; STOCKS AND BONDS]

Taylor, Doreen, Free-Lance Journalist, Writer, and Broadcaster, Scotland. [SCOTLAND]

Toch, Thomas, B.A.; Free-Lance Education Writer. [EDUCATION; EDUCATION (Close-Up)]

Trefil, James, Ph.D.; Professor of Physics, University of Virginia. [Special Report: THE DEATH OF A STAR]

Trotter, Robert J., B.S.; Senior Editor, *Psychology Today* magazine. [PSYCHOLOGY]

Tuchman, Janice Lyn, B.S., M.S.J.; Senior Editor, *Engineering News-Record.* [BUILDING AND CONSTRUCTION]

Vesley, Roberta, A.B., M.L.S.; Library Director, American Kennel Club. [DOG]

Vise, David A., B.S.; Business Reporter, *The Washington Post.* [Special Report: WILD DAYS ON WALL STREET]

Voorhies, Barbara, B.S., Ph.D.; Professor and Chair, Department of Anthropology, University of California at Santa Barbara. [ARCHAEOLOGY]

Walter, Eugene J., Jr., B.A.; Editor in Chief, *Animal Kingdom* magazine, and Curator of Publications, New York Zoological Society. [CONSERVATION; ZOOS]

Weininger, Jean, A.B., M.S., Ph.D.; Research Fellow, University of California at Berkeley. [NUTRITION]

Whitaker, Donald R., A.B.; Economist, National Marine Fisheries Service. [FISHING INDUSTRY]

Windeyer, Kendal, President, Windeyer Associates, Montreal, Canada. [MONTREAL]

Woods, Michael, B.S.; Science Editor, *The Toledo Blade.* [Energy, Mining, and Health Articles; Special Report: STORMY DEBATE OVER ACID RAIN]

Wuntch, Philip, B.A.; Film Critic, *Dallas Morning News.* [MOTION PICTURES; DEATHS (Close-Up)]

The Year
in Brief

A short essay captures the spirit of
1987, and a month-by-month listing
highlights some of the year's significant events.

See page 16

The Year
in Brief

A review of some of the major trends and events that touched many of our lives during 1987.

As so often happens during the course of a year, the spotlight shifted abruptly in 1987. For the first eight months of the year, headlines in the United States were dominated by the Iran-contra affair as Congress strove to unravel the tangles of the worst White House scandal since the Watergate era of the 1970's.

For much of the year, the Iran-contra affair shared center stage with events in the Middle East, that perennial trouble spot, as the United States Navy endeavored to protect oil tankers in the Persian Gulf from attacks by Iran.

On Monday, October 19, the White House announced that the U.S. Navy had conducted a military strike against two connected Iranian oil platforms, but that wasn't the big story on the evening news. The big story concerned the U.S. stock market, which had experienced the worst stock-price plunge in its history that day. Suddenly, the nation's supposed economic prosperity seemed shaky.

But before there was the financial crisis, there was Iran-contra. The facts began coming to light in 1986. In November of that year, it was learned that the United States had been shipping arms to Iran since 1985 and that this apparently had led to the release of three U.S. hostages held by terrorists in Lebanon. President Ronald Reagan admitted that the shipments had been made and that he had approved them, but he said this did not amount to negotiating with terrorists. Later in November, it came out that some money from the arms sale had been used, in apparent violation of U.S. law, to support *contra* rebels fighting Nicaragua's Marxist government.

Opposite page: Hardly able to believe their eyes, stockbrokers in New York City watch tensely on October 19 as stock prices on an electronic monitor tumble ever downward. By the end of the day, the United States stock market had experienced the worst one-day crash in its history, and a five-year boom in stock prices was apparently at an end.

11

In 1987, Congress set about the task of sorting things out. Hearings began in May. The star witnesses were Marine Lieutenant Colonel Oliver L. North, who headed the Iran-contra operations, and his superior on the President's National Security Council, Navy Rear Admiral John M. Poindexter. North's testimony, though it led to a brief outpouring of "Olliemania" as many Americans expressed their admiration for the earnest young officer, did not answer the central question: Did Reagan authorize the diversion of funds to the contras?

Next came Poindexter. In one brief exchange with a questioner, the answer arrived at last. The admiral said that he alone had given North the go-ahead to fund the contras. But the final report of the congressional investigators, issued in November, sharply criticized Reagan because he had "created or at least tolerated an environment" in which the illegal diversion occurred. The President, the report asserted, had failed in his constitutional duty to "take care that the laws be faithfully executed."

After the hearings ended, the President moved to reassert his leadership, but with only limited success. He was unable to persuade the Senate to accept his first-choice nominee, Judge Robert H. Bork, for an opening on the Supreme Court of the United States, and his second choice, Judge Douglas H. Ginsburg, withdrew after revelations of marijuana use. At year-end, Reagan's third nominee, Judge Anthony M. Kennedy, was awaiting Senate confirmation. But the President regained some of the old Reagan luster in a summit meeting with Soviet leader Mikhail S. Gorbachev—held in December in Washington, D.C.—at which the two heads of state signed a treaty banning medium-range land-based missiles. It was the first treaty to reduce the size of the two countries' nuclear arsenals.

Earlier in the year, Reagan took action to ensure the safe passage of oil shipments out of the Persian Gulf. In July, the United States began a policy of putting Kuwaiti oil tankers under the American flag, thus technically making them American vessels. The United States Navy was given the job of escorting the reflagged tankers through the gulf and protecting them from Iranian missiles and mines. Iran had frequently fired missiles at Kuwaiti tankers because Kuwait is an ally of Iraq, Iran's enemy in a bloody war that was in its seventh year in 1987.

By fall, the U.S. involvement in the gulf had resulted in several headline-making incidents. The Navy's October 19 attack on the Iranian oil platforms, which reportedly had been used for the launching of missiles, was made in response to a series of Iranian provocations against ships in the gulf. As always, Iran vowed to take revenge.

As the oil platforms burned, the fire went out of the U.S. stock market. The market had been erratic for several weeks, but on October 19—quickly dubbed Black Monday—the bottom fell out. In that one day, stocks lost nearly one-fourth of their value as panicky investors stampeded to sell their holdings. The U.S. stock market crash had an almost immediate global effect, triggering selling binges on the London and Tokyo stock exchanges. In the days that followed, stock prices in the United States and elsewhere rebounded somewhat, but the crash showed that the U.S. economy had problems—notably growing deficits in the budget and foreign trade—that could no longer be ignored. Most economists discounted the

Explosive mines aboard an Iranian landing craft in the Persian Gulf are inspected by United States naval personnel in September after the vessel was damaged by a U.S. Navy helicopter. The Navy took an active role in countering Iranian threats in the gulf in 1987, escorting Kuwaiti oil tankers flying the American flag and keeping sea lanes safe for international shipping.

notion that the United States might be in for a repeat of the Great Depression of the 1930's, but they said a serious recession was a possibility. Responding to such warnings, President Reagan promised to work with Congress to put the economy right.

Despite the gathering clouds in the last months of the year, Americans had good reason to celebrate in 1987. It was a bicentennial year—the 200th anniversary of the United States Constitution. The splashiest birthday party for the Constitution was held on September 17 in Philadelphia, where the venerable document was signed on the same date in 1787.

Few national constitutions have had anywhere near the staying power of the U.S. Constitution. In the Philippines, voters in February overwhelmingly approved the third constitution that nation has had since gaining its independence from the United States in 1946. Philippine President Corazon Aquino was gratified by the outcome of the vote, which confirmed her in office until 1992, but she realized that her hold on power was far from secure. Coup attempts threatened her administration in January and August. The August revolt was the more serious of the two, involving about 2,000 dissident soldiers.

President Reagan and Soviet leader Mikhail S. Gorbachev "give a hand" to each other during their December summit meeting in Washington, D.C. At the meeting, the two leaders signed a treaty banning land-based intermediate-range nuclear missiles.

Armed with brightly colored banners, South Korean students take to the streets to demand a return to democratic rule. During the year, student demonstrations often turned violent, with thousands of youths battling police and militia in Seoul and other cities in South Korea. The government finally gave in and agreed to the establishment of a new constitution and the holding of a direct presidential election in December.

Violence also rocked South Korea and Haiti in 1987. In South Korea, thousands of students, demanding a return to democratic rule, battled the police and militia. The military government of President Chun Doo Hwan gave in to those demands, and a new constitution, calling for direct presidential elections, was ratified by the nation's voters in October. On December 16, about 90 per cent of South Korea's voters turned out for the country's first open presidential election in 16 years. The ruling party's candidate, Roh Tae Woo, a former army general, won with about 37 per cent of the vote because two other candidates—Kim Young Sam and Kim Dae Jung—split most of the opposition vote.

The first presidential election in Haiti in 30 years collapsed on November 29 as armed thugs, reportedly aided by government troops, unleashed a day-long reign of terror. Thirty-four people were killed, and at least 75 were wounded. The election was rescheduled for Jan. 17, 1988.

In June 1987, Margaret Thatcher became the first British leader in 160 years to be elected to three straight terms as prime minister. (The previous three-time winner was Robert Banks Jenkinson, the Earl of Liverpool, who was prime minister from 1812 to 1827.) Thatcher's Conservative Party held a 101-seat majority in Parliament after the 1987 election, smaller than the 144-seat majority it had won in 1983 but enough to ensure continuation of her policies.

The Philippines were another trouble spot in 1987. Attempted coups threatened President Corazon Aquino's administration in January and August. Appearing in public after the August revolt, *above,* Aquino visits the tomb of the Philippines' unknown soldier.

Of all Europe's leaders, none attracted as much attention in 1987 as the Soviet Union's Mikhail S. Gorbachev. His policy of *glasnost*, or openness, was gradually transforming Soviet life, though the Soviet Union was hardly poised on the brink of democracy. Gorbachev's aim seemed strictly practical—to stimulate his nation's leaden economy by relaxing government control and improving the morale of the work force.

A fresh breeze also blew through Central America as the presidents of five Central American nations—Costa Rica, El Salvador, Guatemala, Honduras, and Nicaragua—agreed on a plan to bring peace to the region. The accord, signed on August 7, called for cease-fires in the region's civil wars, an end to outside aid for rebels, democratic reforms, and free elections. In October, Costa Rica's President Oscar Arias Sánchez, author of the plan, was awarded the Nobel Peace Prize.

Latin America suffered one of the year's worst natural disasters in early March, when the South American country of Ecuador was devastated by a series of earthquakes that left more than 300 people dead and some 4,000 missing. On October 1, an earthquake struck the Los Angeles area, causing at least seven deaths and hundreds of injuries. The Los Angeles tremor was powerful, but earth scientists said The Big One predicted for southern California was yet to come.

Two maritime disasters shocked the world in 1987. At least 188 people died after a ferry capsized in the English Channel on March 6—the greatest peacetime loss of life in the history of English Channel shipping. The vessel, *Herald of Free Enterprise*, rolled onto its side after its bow doors, which apparently had not been properly secured, suddenly swung open, allowing water to rush in.

On December 20, the passenger ferry *Dona Paz* and the oil tanker *Victor* collided, burst into flame, and sank in a busy shipping channel off Mindoro island, about 110 miles (180 kilometers) south of Manila, the Philippines. At least 1,600 people died in what was the year's worst ship disaster. Only 26 people were rescued after the collision. The Philippines' Board of Marine Inquiry on December 28 began a formal investigation into the disaster.

Symbols of freedom, hundreds of red, white, and blue balloons soar skyward during a September 17 celebration in Washington, D.C., commemorating the bicentennial of the U.S. Constitution.

Here are your
1988 YEAR BOOK
Cross-Reference Tabs

For insertion in your WORLD BOOK

Each year, THE WORLD BOOK YEAR BOOK adds a valuable
dimension to your WORLD BOOK set. The Cross-Reference
Tab System is designed especially to help youngsters and
parents alike *link* THE YEAR BOOK'S new and revised WORLD
BOOK articles, its Special Reports, and its Close-Ups to the
related WORLD BOOK articles they update.

How to Use These Tabs

First, remove this page from THE YEAR BOOK. The top Tab on
this page is ACID RAIN. Turn to the A volume of your
WORLD BOOK and find the page with the ACID RAIN article on
it. Affix the ACID RAIN Tab to that page. If your WORLD BOOK
is an older set without an ACID RAIN article in it, put the
ACID RAIN Tab in the A volume in its proper alphabetical
sequence. For most older sets of WORLD BOOK, the ACID RAIN
Tab would go on the same page as the article about ACID.

Now do the same with the remaining Tabs, and your new
YEAR BOOK will be linked to your WORLD BOOK set.

The fashion world made a big turnabout in 1987 with the revival of the miniskirt, *far left,* traditionally a symbol of good times—which Americans hoped would continue despite the stock market crash. Nobody had a better time in 1987 than beer spokesmutt Spuds MacKenzie, *left,* a hot dog if ever there was one.

Detroit on August 16 was the scene of the second-worst airline disaster ever in the United States, the crash of a Northwest Airlines plane bound for Phoenix. The twin-engine MD-80 stalled during take-off and slammed down on a nearby highway. Two motorists were killed, and only 1 person out of the 155 passengers and crew members survived—4-year-old Cecilia Cichan of Tempe, Ariz. Investigators concluded that the plane's wing flaps had been improperly positioned for take-off.

Disasters of a more personal nature disrupted the careers of several American newsmakers during the year. One of the most widely publicized episodes involved husband-and-wife television evangelists Jim and Tammy Bakker. The couple in March resigned the leadership of the PTL ministry, a $200-million TV-and-theme-park religious empire. Jim Bakker had admitted having a sexual encounter with church secretary Jessica Hahn and paying her to keep it secret. The letters *PTL* stand for two phrases, *Praise the Lord* and *People That Love.*

Sex also loomed large in the fortune of former Colorado Senator Gary Hart. He had been the front-runner for the 1988 Democratic presidential nomination until he withdrew from the race in May after trying to convince the public and the news media that his relationship with Miami model Donna Rice had been strictly professional. With Hart out of the running, the field was left to six other Democratic candidates. And then, in December, Hart unexpectedly declared himself back in the race—and again was the front-runner. Meanwhile, Vice President George H. W.

Beverly Hills Cop II, starring actor-comedian Eddie Murphy, *top,* was one of the year's biggest movies at the box office. On the popular-music scene, singer Whitney Houston, *above,* joined the top ranks of celebrities.

Irises (1889), an oil painting on canvas; courtesy of Sotheby's, Incorporated.

The prices paid for works of fine art soared in 1987. At a New York City auction in November, a buyer paid a record $53.9 million for *Irises, above,* by the Dutch postimpressionist painter Vincent van Gogh.

Bush and Senator Robert J. Dole of Kansas led the Republican pack of presidential hopefuls.

As usual, Americans seemed more interested in sports and entertainment than in politics. In February, the United States triumphed over Australia to win the America's Cup yacht races, but the bulk of U.S. sports fans seemed only minimally interested. Nor did they appear to be very excited about the Pan American Games, held in August in Indianapolis. On the other hand, they got very upset on September 22 when the players of the National Football League (NFL) went out on strike, leaving conference games to be played by hastily recruited squads of third-stringers. But the season was saved from being a total loss; the NFL regulars abandoned their contract demands on October 15 and ended the walkout.

No one person or event dominated the entertainment scene in 1987. *Beverly Hills Cop II,* with Eddie Murphy; *The Untouchables,* with Sean Connery and Kevin Costner; *Fatal Attraction,* with Glenn Close and Michael Douglas; and *Broadcast News,* with Albert Brooks, Holly Hunter, and William Hurt were the top movies. Singer Whitney Houston's star rose higher, while those of Madonna and Michael Jackson held steady in the popular-music firmament.

Two of the most unlikely new television personalities in 1987 were a dog and a disembodied head. The latter was an electronic creation named Max Headroom who—his official biography said— existed only in the circuits of a computer. Max had his own TV series for a while and was also featured in commercials for Coca-

Cola. Of more enduring popularity than Max was party animal Spuds MacKenzie, spokesmutt for Bud Light Beer.

A symbol of optimism and good times—the miniskirt—made a big comeback in 1987. The mini's return may have been connected with the stock market boom in the first half of the year. Black Monday didn't bring long dresses back out of the closet, but some jokesters suggested that if the market fell again, so would hemlines.

Rising along with skirt lengths in 1987 were the prices paid for works of art, especially still lifes by the Dutch painter Vincent van Gogh. Van Gogh's *Sunflowers* (1888), one of seven sunflower paintings he made, sold at a London auction in March for the unheard-of sum of $39.9 million. But even that price was soon dwarfed. In November, another van Gogh oil, *Irises* (1889), fetched a stratospheric $53.9 million at a sale in New York City.

If 1987 was a good year for art sellers, it was a "super" year in science: Superconductors, the Superconducting Super Collider (SSC), and a supernova all figured prominently in the news. Superconductors—materials that conduct electricity with no resistance to the current—made headlines in February. In that month, researchers at the University of Houston announced that they had achieved superconductance with a ceramic material at a temperature of −283°F. (−175°C), which meant that liquid nitrogen could be used to cool the material. All previous superconductors had required the use of much colder—and much more expensive—liquid helium. As the year progressed, scientists reported finding other ceramics that became superconductors at even higher temperatures. Suddenly, whole new technologies were in the offing.

Physicists predicted that the advances in superconductors would be applied to the SSC—a giant circular particle accelerator, or atom smasher, some 50 miles (80 kilometers) in circumference—that the federal government planned to construct in the 1990's. Twenty-five states competed for the high-tech plum in 1987.

On the night of February 23, a new star suddenly appeared in the sky above the Southern Hemisphere. Astronomers quickly determined that the bright point of light was an exploding star, or supernova, the first one visible to the unaided eye since 1604. The star blew apart some 160,000 years ago when our early ancestors were still using crude stone tools. Appearing as it did at a moment of no particular significance, the supernova served as a reminder to the self-absorbed inhabitants of planet Earth that we live in one small, anonymous corner of a vast universe. And that in the endless river of time, 1987 was but a ripple.   THE EDITORS

For details about 1987:

The Year on File—which begins on page 172—describes events of 1987 according to the country, field, or general subject area in which they occurred.

Jan. 25

Jan. 25

January

			1	2	3
4	5	6	7	8	9	10
11	12	13	14	15	16	17
18	19	20	21	22	23	24
25	26	27	28	29	30	31

4   **An Amtrak passenger train** collides with three Conrail locomotives in Chase, Md., killing 16 people in the worst accident in Amtrak's 17-year history.

5   **United States President Ronald Reagan** undergoes prostate surgery.

8   **The Dow Jones Industrial Average** (the Dow) closes above 2,000 for the first time, ending the day at 2,002.25.

13   **The Supreme Court of the United States** upholds job protection for pregnant workers.

16   **Ecuadorean President León Febres-Cordero** gains his freedom from kidnappers by ordering the release from prison of a general who led two 1986 rebellions.
China's Communist Party General Secretary Hu Yaobang resigns after accepting blame for policy mistakes in handling student unrest.

18   **André Bissonnette,** Canada's minister of state (transport), resigns pending investigation of his role in a land speculation deal.

18-30   **A strike** on the Long Island Rail Road strands an estimated 110,000 commuters in the New York City area.

20   **Ireland's coalition** government collapses over a budget dispute.

22   **Philippine government troops** fire on protesters marching on the presidential palace in Manila, killing 18.
Pennsylvania state Treasurer R. Budd Dwyer, who has been convicted in a bribery case, shoots himself to death at a televised press conference the day before his sentencing.

24   **An estimated 20,000 people** take part in a civil rights march in Cumming, Ga., in a repeat of a smaller demonstration on January 17 that had been disrupted by Ku Klux Klan members and supporters.

25   **The New York Giants** win football's Super Bowl XXI, beating the Denver Broncos 39-20.
The center-right coalition of West German Chancellor Helmut Kohl, shown above, wins reelection in parliamentary elections.

28   **Nicaragua** frees Sam N. Hall, who was arrested in December 1986 on spy charges. He is the brother of U.S. Representative Tony P. Hall (D., Ohio).

29   **Philippine rebels** apparently loyal to former President Ferdinand E. Marcos give themselves up after an unsuccessful coup attempt that began on January 27.
The United States and the European Community (EC or Common Market) settle a dispute over U.S. grain exports, averting a threatened 200 per cent U.S. tariff on some EC foods and beverages.

Feb. 23

Feb. 2

Feb. 4

February						
1	2	3	4	5	6	7
8	9	10	11	12	13	14
15	16	17	18	19	20	21
22	23	24	25	26	27	28

2   **Philippine voters** overwhelmingly approve a proposed U.S.-style constitution providing for President Corazon Aquino, shown above, to remain in office until 1992.
United Steelworkers of America members begin to return to USX Corporation steel mills, ending a work stoppage that began in August 1986, the longest in the steel industry's history.
William J. Casey resigns as director of the Central Intelligence Agency (CIA). He dies on May 6.

4   **The United States** wins the America's Cup yacht races off Fremantle, Australia.
A pay raise for members of Congress and other top federal officials goes into effect automatically after Congress fails to block it.
Congress overrides Reagan's veto of a $20-billion clean-water bill identical to the one he had vetoed in 1986.

17   **Charles Haughey's Fianna Fáil party** wins Ireland's parliamentary elections but falls short of an outright majority in Parliament.

Haughey becomes prime minister on March 10.

19   **Canadian Minister of State Roch LaSalle** resigns from the cabinet after reports of influence-peddling.

20   **Brazil** suspends interest payments on its debt to foreign commercial banks.

22   **Six industrial countries** —Canada, France, Great Britain, Japan, the United States, and West Germany—reach agreement to stabilize the U.S. dollar.
A 7,000-member Syrian peacekeeping force enters Beirut, Lebanon, at the request of Lebanese leaders.

23   **Light** from a huge *supernova* (exploding star) in the Large Magellanic Cloud reaches Earth.

25   **The National Collegiate Athletic Association (NCAA)** bans Southern Methodist University from football in 1987 because of improper payments to players.
The Supreme Court of the United States rules that judges may order strict racial quotas for job promotions to counter past discrimination.

26   **The Tower commission,** a three-member panel investigating U.S. arms sales to Iran, issues a harshly critical report.

27   **White House Chief of Staff Donald T. Regan** —criticized by the Tower commission—resigns. Former Senate Majority Leader Howard H. Baker, Jr., (R., Tenn.) replaces him.

28   **Soviet leader Mikhail S. Gorbachev** proposes a pact to eliminate U.S. and Soviet medium-range missiles from Europe, dropping demands to halt U.S. work on a space-based defense system.

March 6

March 5-6

March 19

March

1	2	3	4	5	6	7
8	9	10	11	12	13	14
15	16	17	18	19	20	21
22	23	24	25	26	27	28
29	30	31				

3   **Reagan** names William H. Webster, director of the Federal Bureau of Investigation (FBI), to replace Casey as director of the CIA. Webster takes office on May 26.

4   **Jonathan Jay Pollard,** a former Navy intelligence analyst, is sentenced to life in prison for spying for Israel.
A federal judge bans 44 textbooks from Alabama public schools on the ground that they promote what he calls "the religion of secular humanism." A federal Court of Appeals lifts the ban on August 26.

5-6   **Ecuador** is rocked by a series of earthquakes that leave more than 300 people dead and another 4,000 missing.

6   **A British ferry** capsizes in the English Channel near Zeebrugge, Belgium, killing at least 188 passengers in the worst channel disaster in history.

10   **The Roman Catholic Church** bans conception by artificial methods, including embryo transfers, artificial insemination, and surrogate motherhood.

15-16   **Finland's conservative party** gains in parliamentary elections. Conservative leader Harri Holkeri becomes prime minister on April 30.

19   **Television evangelist Jim Bakker,** shown above with his wife, Tammy Faye Bakker, resigns his ministry after admitting a 1980 sexual encounter with a church secretary.

20   **The U.S. Food and Drug Administration (FDA)** approves zidovudine, formerly known as azidothymidine (AZT), the first drug proved to prolong the lives of patients with AIDS (acquired immune deficiency syndrome).

25   **The Supreme Court** rules that employers may consider a worker's race or sex in hiring and promotion decisions.

29   **Haitian voters** overwhelmingly endorse a new constitution that reduces the power of the presidency.

30   **Vincent van Gogh's** *Sunflowers* (1888) sells for $39.9 million, nearly four times the previous record for an auctioned painting.
Indiana University wins the NCAA men's basketball championship, defeating Syracuse University 74-73.
Platoon, a 1986 film about the Vietnam War, wins the Academy Award for best picture.

31   **Pope John Paul II** arrives in Montevideo, Uruguay, beginning a two-week trip to Latin America that includes visits to Argentina and Chile.
A New Jersey judge rules that a surrogate-motherhood contract is valid, awarding custody of the child known as Baby M to her father, William Stern.

April 9-11

April 6

April 5-6

April 24

April

			1	2	3	4
5	6	7	8	9	10	11
12	13	14	15	16	17	18
19	20	21	22	23	24	25
26	27	28	29	30		

1 **Television evangelist Oral Roberts,** who declared on January 4 that God would take his life if his followers did not give him $8-million by March 31, announces success in his fund-raising.

2 **Congress** overrides Reagan's veto of an $87.5-billion highway and transit bill that permits states to raise speed limits to 65 miles (105 kilometers) per hour on rural interstate highways.

5 **A bridge** on the Governor Thomas E. Dewey Thruway collapses near Amsterdam, N.Y., killing 10 motorists.

5-6 **Canadian Prime Minister** Brian Mulroney and U.S. President Reagan hold a summit meeting in Ottawa, Canada.

6 **Sugar Ray Leonard,** shown above wearing the white trunks, wins the World Boxing Council (WBC) middleweight championship, defeating Marvelous Marvin Hagler in a split decision.

9-11 **Soviet leader Gorbachev** makes his first official visit to Czechoslovakia.

12 **Texaco Incorporated** becomes the largest firm in U.S. history to file for bankruptcy, seeking protection under the bankruptcy code to carry on a legal dispute with Pennzoil Company.

13 **China and Portugal** sign an agreement under which Portugal will return Macao to China in 1999.

17 **The United States** imposes 100 per cent tariffs on imports of Japanese personal computers, TV sets, and power tools to retaliate for Japan's alleged violation of a computer-chip trade agreement.

18 **Amintore Fanfani** takes office as prime minister of Italy, replacing Bettino Craxi, who resigned on April 9. Fanfani resigns on April 28 after losing a vote of confidence but stays on as caretaker prime minister until July 9.

19 **Rebel Argentine army officers** surrender after a four-day uprising.

22 **The U.S. Supreme Court** rules that the death penalty is constitutional despite statistics that show killers of whites are more likely to receive death sentences than are killers of blacks.

22-28 **The Sri Lankan air force** bombs Tamil rebel strongholds in seeming retaliation for terrorist attacks on April 17, 19, and 21, in which more than 350 people died.

23 **An apartment building** under construction near Bridgeport, Conn., collapses, killing 28 workers.

24 **Genetically engineered bacteria** designed to prevent frost damage are sprayed on a California field in the first authorized outdoor release of such altered bacteria.

May 28

May 17

May 8

4   **The Supreme Court** rules that states may require all-male private clubs to admit women.

5   **Congressional committees** probing the Iran-contra affair open public hearings that last until August.3.

6   **A forest fire** breaks out in northeastern China and rages until June 2, killing at least 193 people.

8   **Front-runner Gary Hart** withdraws from the race for the 1988 Democratic presidential nomination after charges that he spent a night with a woman in his wife's absence.

9   **A Polish jetliner** crashes near Warsaw, killing all 183 people aboard in Poland's worst air disaster.
Malta's conservative Nationalist Party wins a narrow victory in parliamentary elections. Party leader Edward Fenech Adami becomes prime minister on May 12.

11   **Philippine voters** elect a new legislature dominated by candidates supporting President Aquino.

14   **A military coup,** the first ever in Fiji, ousts the nation's new Indian-majority government but yields to an interim government led by the governor general.

17   **A missile-firing Iraqi warplane** attacks the Navy frigate U.S.S. *Stark* in the Persian Gulf, killing 37 crew members, whose coffins are shown above. Iraq apologizes for the attack.

22   **Canadian wheelchair athlete Rick Hansen** finishes a 26-month journey around the world that raised funds for spinal cord research.
A tornado destroys much of Saragosa, Tex., causing 30 deaths.

24   **Al Unser, Sr.,** becomes, at 47, the oldest driver to win the Indianapolis 500 automobile race.

25   **A New York state jury** acquits former Secretary of Labor Raymond J. Donovan of larceny and fraud charges.

25-27   **Soviet leader Gorbachev** makes his first official visit to Romania.

26   **South Korean President Chun Doo Hwan** dismisses Prime Minister Shinyong Lho and seven other cabinet ministers after reports of a cover-up in the January 17 death of a student in police custody.
The U.S. Supreme Court upholds a law denying bail to criminal suspects considered dangerous.

28   **West German teen-ager** Mathias Rust flies a small plane from Finland to Moscow and lands near the Kremlin. The Soviet Union fires its defense minister and its air defense chief on May 30.

31   **The Edmonton Oilers** win professional hockey's Stanley Cup, defeating the Philadelphia Flyers four games to three.

June 11

June 25

June 12

June

		1	2	3	4	5	6
7	8	9	10	11	12	13
14	15	16	17	18	19	20
21	22	23	24	25	26	27
28	29	30

1   **Lebanon's Prime Minister** Rashid Karami is assassinated when a bomb explodes in the helicopter carrying him.

2   **Economist Alan Greenspan** is nominated by Reagan to replace Paul A. Volcker as chairman of the Federal Reserve Board. Greenspan takes office on August 11.

3   **Canadian Prime Minister Mulroney** and 10 provincial leaders sign an agreement to secure Quebec's approval of Canada's 1982 constitution.

4   **South Africa's State President** Pieter Willem Botha visits Sharpeville, site of a 1960 massacre in which police gunned down 69 blacks.

8-10   **An economic summit conference** in Venice, Italy, is attended by leaders of Canada, France, Great Britain, Italy, Japan, the United States, and West Germany.

8-14   **Pope John Paul II** visits Poland.

11   **Britain's Prime Minister Margaret Thatcher** wins a third term, but with a reduced majority in Parliament.

11-30   **Panama** imposes a ''state of urgency'' in an effort to end violent antigovernment protests.

12   **Reagan,** in West Berlin, West Germany, challenges Soviet leader Gorbachev to tear down the Berlin Wall.

14   **The Los Angeles Lakers** win the National Basketball Association championship, defeating the Boston Celtics four games to two.

  Ethiopians vote in elections for their first parliament since the overthrow of Emperor Haile Selassie in 1974.

14-15   **Italy's** Christian Democrat and Socialist parties gain ground in parliamentary elections, but the Italian Communist Party loses support.

16   **Bernhard H. Goetz** is acquitted of attempted murder and assault charges in the shooting of four teen-agers who he said were trying to rob him on a New York City subway train in December 1984.

  At least 1.5 million black South Africans stay home from work on the 11th anniversary of the Soweto uprising.

  Canadian postal workers begin a rotating strike that ends with a tentative settlement on July 4.

19   **The Supreme Court** strikes down a Louisiana law that required the teaching of creationism along with evolution in public schools.

25   **Pope John Paul II** meets—despite Jewish protests—with Austrian President Kurt Waldheim, who has denied charges that he took part in Nazi war crimes.

26   **Justice Lewis F. Powell, Jr.,** retires from the United States Supreme Court.

July 4-5

July 7-14

July

			1	2	3	4
5	6	7	8	9	10	11
12	13	14	15	16	17	18
19	20	21	22	23	24	25
26	27	28	29	30	31	

1 **Reagan nominates** Appeals Court Judge Robert H. Bork to replace Powell on the Supreme Court.

4-5 **Martina Navratilova** of the United States and Pat Cash of Australia, shown above, win Wimbledon singles tennis titles.

6-7 **Sikh terrorists** in India raid three buses and kill at least 72 Hindus.

7-14 **Lieutenant Colonel Oliver L. North** testifies at the Iran-contra hearings.

11 **Australia's Prime Minister** Robert Hawke wins a third term.

13 **South Korea's President Chun** shuffles his cabinet for the second time in 1987, replacing the prime minister and seven other ministers.

15 **Taiwan's government** lifts martial law, which had been in effect since 1949.
Former National Security Adviser John M. Poindexter testifies at the Iran-contra hearings that he authorized diversion of Iran arms-sale profits to the contras and kept the information from Reagan.

17 **The Dow** closes above 2,500 for the first time, ending the day at 2,510.04.
A flash flood engulfs a bus and van carrying teen-agers from a camp near Comfort, Tex., killing 10 campers.

19 **Portugal's right wing Social Democratic Party,** which formerly ruled as part of a coalition, wins the first overall majority in parliamentary elections since democracy was restored in 1974.

20 **The United Nations (UN) Security Council** passes a unanimous resolution calling for an end to the Iran-Iraq war.
Canada's socialist New Democratic Party sweeps elections in Newfoundland, Ontario, and the Yukon Territory to fill vacant seats in Parliament.

22 **U.S. Navy warships** begin escorting Kuwaiti tankers under American flags in the Persian Gulf. One of the tankers is damaged on July 24 by an underwater mine believed planted by Iran.

24 **Reagan nominates** U.S. District Judge William S. Sessions to succeed Webster as director of the FBI. Sessions takes office on November 2.

25 **U.S. Secretary of Commerce** Malcolm Baldrige dies after being crushed by his horse in rodeo practice.

29 **Giovanni Goria,** a Christian Democrat, is sworn in as prime minister of Italy, heading a five-party center-left coalition.

31 **Fighting in Mecca,** Saudi Arabia, between Saudi police and Iranian religious pilgrims kills about 400 people, including 275 Iranians.
Tornadoes tear through Edmonton, Canada, killing 26 people.

Aug. 16

Aug. 9-30

Aug. 8-23

August

						1
2	3	4	5	6	7	8
9	10	11	12	13	14	15
16	17	18	19	20	21	22
23	24	25	26	27	28	29
30	31					

1   **Boxer Mike Tyson** wins a unanimous decision over Tony Tucker to become the first undisputed heavyweight champion of the world since 1978.

4   **The Federal Communications Commission** repeals its fairness doctrine, a policy that since 1949 required radio and TV broadcasters to air opposing sides of controversial issues.

7   **Presidents** of Costa Rica, El Salvador, Guatemala, Honduras, and Nicaragua sign a preliminary agreement designed to end conflicts in Central America, the first peace plan agreed upon by the region's leaders.

8-23   **The Pan American Games** take place in Indianapolis. Former track star Wilma Rudolph lights the flame, *above.*

9-30   **More than 300,000 South African gold and coal miners** strike for higher pay and better working conditions in the largest work stoppage in South Africa's history. The strike ends with miners accepting an offer they had previously rejected.

10   **C. William Verity, Jr.,** a retired steel executive, is nominated to replace Baldrige as secretary of commerce. Verity takes office on October 19.

13-14   **Chicago** receives a record 8.98 inches (22.8 centimeters) of rain in 13 hours, triggering widespread flooding in the city and suburbs.

15   **New Zealand voters** elect Prime Minister David R. Lange to a second term.
     Great Basin National Park is dedicated in eastern Nevada.

16   **A Northwest Airlines jetliner** crashes in Detroit, killing 156 people.

18   **A grenade attack** kills 2 members of Sri Lanka's Parliament and wounds 15 others, including Prime Minister R. Premadasa.
     A former nurse's aide, Donald Harvey of Middletown, Ohio, pleads guilty to murdering 24 people since 1983.

19   **A gunman** in Hungerford, England, kills 16 people and wounds 14 others before shooting himself to death in the worst mass murder in modern British history.

21   **Marine Sergeant Clayton J. Lonetree,** a former guard at the U.S. Embassy in Moscow, is convicted of spying for the Soviet Union. He is sentenced to 30 years in prison on August 24.

23-28   **About 50,000 Canadian railworkers** strike, shutting down Canada's two national railways, until Parliament orders them back to work.

25   **The Dow** closes at a record high of 2,722.42.

28-29   **Philippine troops** loyal to President Aquino crush a revolt by rebel soldiers in which more than 50 people are killed.

Sept. 22

Sept. 7-11

Sept. 17

September

		1	2	3	4	5
6	7	8	9	10	11	12
13	14	15	16	17	18	19
20	21	22	23	24	25	26
27	28	29	30			

1   **Pope John Paul II** meets with nine Jewish leaders concerned about the pope's June 25 audience with Austrian President Waldheim.

2   **Leaders of South Korea's opposition and ruling parties** promise direct presidential elections by December 20.

2-4   **Leaders of** 37 French-speaking nations hold a summit in Quebec City, Canada.

3   **The army of Burundi** ousts President Jean-Baptiste Bagaza in a bloodless coup.

4   **The Soviet Supreme Court** sentences West German teen-ager Mathias Rust to four years in a labor camp for landing a plane in Moscow on May 28.

6   **Argentina's ruling centrist party** loses its majority in the lower house of Congress to a party that supports the policies of former President Juan Perón.

7-11   **East German leader** Erich Honecker becomes the first East German party chief to visit West Germany.

8   **The center-right coalition** of Denmark's Prime Minister Poul Schlüter loses ground in parliamentary elections. Schlüter resigns on September 9, but at the request of Queen Margrethe II, he forms a new government the next day.

   Sweden's Prime Minister Ingvar Carlsson becomes the first Swedish prime minister to visit the White House since 1961.

10   **Pope John Paul II** arrives in Miami, Fla., for an 11-day visit to the United States and Canada.

14   **U.S. Secretary of Transportation** Elizabeth Hanford Dole announces that she will resign on October 1 to work on her husband's presidential campaign.

17   **The United States** celebrates the 200th anniversary of the signing of its Constitution with a six-hour parade in Philadelphia, shown above, and other festivities.

21   **U.S. helicopters** fire on an Iranian ship caught laying mines in the Persian Gulf, killing five Iranians in the first U.S. attack on an Iranian vessel.

22   **National Football League** players strike. They return to work on October 15 without agreement on a new contract.

23   **Senator Joseph R. Biden, Jr.,** (D., Del.) drops out of the race for the 1988 presidential nomination.

25   **The government of Fiji** is ousted by a military coup for the second time since May 14. Lieutenant Colonel Sitiveni Rabuka, who led both coups, declares himself head of government on September 30.

30   **Canadian postal workers** begin a rotating strike, their second since June 16. They return to work on October 17, the day after Parliament orders them back.

28

Oct. 25

Oct. 16

Oct. 17

October

			1	2	3
4	5	6	7	8	9	10
11	12	13	14	15	16	17
18	19	20	21	22	23	24
25	26	27	28	29	30	31

1   **A severe earthquake** rocks the Los Angeles area, causing seven deaths and more than $213 million in damage.

3   **The United States and Canada** agree to eliminate tariffs between them by 1999.

4   **Mexico's ruling party** chooses Budget Minister Carlos Salinas de Gortari as its presidential candidate, virtually assuring his election in 1988.

8   **Reagan nominates** James H. Burnley IV to replace Transportation Secretary Dole. Burnley takes office on December 3.

10   **Poland** announces sweeping economic changes, including less government control of wages and prices.

13   **Costa Rican President** Oscar Arias Sánchez wins the Nobel Peace Prize for his Central American peace plan.

14   **Premier Richard B. Hatfield** of New Brunswick, Canada, resigns after his Progressive Conservative Party loses all 58 seats in the provincial legislature to Liberals on October 13. The Liberals' Frank J.

McKenna becomes premier on October 27.

15   **The government of Burkina Faso** is overthrown in a bloody coup.
William E. Brock III announces that he will resign as U.S. secretary of labor effective on November 1 to run the presidential campaign of Senator Robert J. Dole (R., Kans.).

16   **Rescue workers** in Midland, Tex., pull 18-month-old Jessica McClure from an abandoned well where she had been trapped for more than 58 hours.
An Iranian missile hits the *Sea Isle City,* a reflagged Kuwaiti tanker, in Iran's first direct attack on a ship flying the U.S. flag.

17   **First lady Nancy Reagan** undergoes surgery for breast cancer. She leaves the hospital on October 22, shown above.

19   **The Dow** plummets 508.00 points to 1,738.74, its biggest one-day drop in history.

23   **The Senate** rejects Bork by a vote of 58 to 42, the widest margin of rejection of a Supreme Court nominee in history.

24   **The American Federation of Labor and Congress of Industrial Organizations** votes to allow the Teamsters Union to rejoin it.

25   **The Minnesota Twins** win the World Series, defeating the St. Louis Cardinals four games to three.

29   **President Reagan** nominates Judge Douglas H. Ginsburg of the U.S. Court of Appeals to the Supreme Court.
Boxer Thomas Hearns knocks out Juan Roldan to win the WBC middleweight championship, becoming the first man ever to win titles in four different weight classes.

Nov. 11

Nov. 6

Nov. 21-23

November

1	2	3	4	5	6	7
8	9	10	11	12	13	14
15	16	17	18	19	20	21
22	23	24	25	26	27	28
29	30					

1   **Chinese leader Deng Xiaoping,** 83, resigns his key posts in the Communist Party to make way for younger leaders.

3   **Reagan** nominates Ann Dore McLaughlin to succeed Brock as secretary of labor. She takes office on December 17.

5   **Secretary of Defense** Caspar W. Weinberger resigns. Frank C. Carlucci III replaces him on November 23.

6   **Noboru Takeshita** succeeds Yasuhiro Nakasone as prime minister of Japan.

7   **Tunisian Prime Minister** Zine al-Abidine Ben Ali takes control from ailing 84-year-old President Habib Bourguiba.
Ginsburg withdraws his nomination to the Supreme Court.

8   **A bomb** planted by the Irish Republican Army, an underground group, kills 11 people in Enniskillen, Northern Ireland.

10   **President Seyni Kountché** of Niger dies, and Colonel Ali Seybou succeeds him.

11   **Van Gogh's** *Irises* (1889) sells for a record $53.9 million at a New York City auction.

Reagan nominates Appeals Court Judge Anthony M. Kennedy to the Supreme Court.

13   **The FDA** approves the clot-dissolving drug *tissue plasminogen activator* (tPA), which can reduce heart-attack damage.

15   **A Continental Airlines jetliner** overturns while taking off during a snowstorm in Denver, killing 28 people.

18   **Congress** issues its final report on the Iran-contra affair, criticizing the operation for ''secrecy, deception and disdain for the law.''
A fire in a London subway station kills 31 people and injures about 80 others.

20   **The United States and Cuba** revive a 1984 agreement for the return to Cuba of some 2,600 criminals and mental patients who came to the United States in 1980.

21-23   **Cuban inmates,** fearing deportation, riot at federal prisons in Oakdale, La., and Atlanta, Ga. (shown above), seizing hostages and setting fires. The Oakdale inmates free their hostages on November 29 and the Atlanta inmates end their siege on December 4, after federal authorities agree to postpone any deportations.

25   **Chicago's Mayor Harold Washington** dies.
An opposition coalition in Suriname wins a landslide victory in parliamentary elections over candidates backed by the country's military dictatorship.

28   **A South African Airways jetliner** crashes in the Indian Ocean, killing 159 people.

29   **Haiti** cancels national elections because of violence against voters.
A Korean Air Lines jetliner disappears carrying 115 people. Officials suspect a terrorist bomb caused it to crash.

Dec. 8

December

		1	2	3	4	5
6	7	8	9	10	11	12
13	14	15	16	17	18	19
20	21	22	23	24	25	26
27	28	29	30	31		

2   **The Chicago City Council** elects Alderman Eugene Sawyer as acting mayor.

5   **Tim Brown** of the University of Notre Dame in Indiana wins the 1987 Heisman Trophy as the outstanding college football player in the United States.
Fijian President Sitiveni Rabuka steps down, returning the nation to civilian rule under President Ratu Sir Penaia Ganilau and Prime Minister Ratu Sir Kamisese Mara.

7   **A Pacific Southwest Airlines jet** crashes near Paso Robles, Calif., killing all 43 people aboard. Investigators say that a fired airline employee caused the crash.

8   **Reagan and Gorbachev** sign a treaty to eliminate their countries' medium-range nuclear missiles, the first agreement by the two powers to reduce the size of their nuclear arsenals.

9   **Riots break out** among Palestinians in the Israeli-occupied West Bank and Gaza Strip, partly in reaction to the deaths of four Palestinians in a traffic accident with an Israeli motorist. By year-end, at least 22 people have died in the riots.

13   **Belgium's ruling center-right coalition** loses most of its legislative majority to the opposition Socialists in parliamentary elections. Prime Minister Wilfried A. E. Martens resigns the next day but stays on as caretaker.

15   **Former Senator Gary Hart** (D., Colo.) reenters the 1988 presidential campaign after dropping out of the race on May 8.

16   **South Korea** holds its first direct presidential elections since 1971. The ruling party candidate, Roh Tae Woo, wins over opposition leaders Kim Young Sam and Kim Dae Jung.
Former White House aide Michael K. Deaver is convicted of lying under oath by a federal jury in Washington, D.C.
The largest Mafia trial in history ends in Palermo, Italy, with guilty verdicts against 338 of 452 defendants tried on murder, drug, and extortion charges.

19   **Gary Kasparov** of the Soviet Union retains the world championship of chess, playing Soviet challenger Anatoly Karpov to a 12-12 tie in Seville, Spain.

20   **An estimated 1,600 people** die in the collision of a passenger ship and an oil tanker off Mindoro island, the Philippines.

26   **A terrorist** throws two hand grenades into a United Service Organizations club in Barcelona, Spain, killing a U.S. Navy sailor and injuring nine other people. Catalonian separatists claim responsibility.

31   **Robert Gabriel Mugabe** takes office as Zimbabwe's first executive president.

Special Reports

Six articles and a two-part feature give special treatment to subjects of current importance and lasting interest.

See page 147.

By Charles J. Adams

Understanding Islam

One of the world's largest religions influences current events in the Middle East and throughout the world in powerful—but often misunderstood—ways.

Islam inspires many of its followers, like the Moroccan man at the left, to prayerful devotion. It drives others, like the Iranian women above, to take up arms in a militancy that some people mistakenly consider typical of the Islamic world.

Glossary

Hadith: Reports of Muhammad's sayings and deeds.

Hajj: Annual religious pilgrimage to Mecca.

Islamic resurgence: Political movements promoting the establishment of Islamic states in Muslim countries.

Jihad: Holy war.

Koran: Sacred book of Islam.

Muhammad: The prophet who founded Islam.

Mosque: Place of worship.

Muslim: Follower of Islam.

Secularism: Belief in the separation of religion and political affairs.

Sharia: Islamic law.

Shiites: Members of the second largest Muslim sect, the majority of the population of Iran and Iraq.

Sunnis: Members of the largest Muslim sect, comprising about 80 per cent of all Muslims.

The author:
Charles J. Adams is a professor of Islamic studies at McGill University in Montreal, Canada.

Westerners are often puzzled by what appear to be striking contrasts within Islam, the chief faith of Indonesia, Pakistan, Bangladesh, and nearly all of the countries in northern Africa and the Middle East. Islam is a complex religious system whose moral code forbids lying, theft, and adultery, and its followers, called Muslims, are urged never to refuse to help anyone in need. Historians credit Islam with much of the spread of knowledge during the years from A.D. 700 to 1300. And Islamic culture features a breathtaking style of art and architecture known for its tightly controlled beauty.

From its beginning, Islam has recognized no distinction between religion and politics. Even today, the majority of Muslims have as their ideal a unified community of believers acting under a single ruler devoted to upholding Islamic law. Since the 1970's that ideal has been advanced with growing insistence—and sometimes violence—by Islamic insurgent movements that see it as an alternative to the Westernizing tendencies of Muslim countries in recent times.

Although the enduring ideal remains Muslim unity, there is, in fact, much diversity in the Islamic world. Muslims live in many countries under a variety of forms of government. These countries are often in conflict with one another and have differing relationships with other nations.

Islam's ancient roots

Islam began in the Arabian city of Mecca at a time when most Arabs worshiped idols and spirits. In the early 600's, a middle-aged merchant named Muhammad had a vision while meditating on a hill above Mecca. He believed he saw the angel Gabriel, who told Muhammad that there was only one God—the God worshiped by Christians and Jews—and that Muhammad had been chosen to become a prophet, the last of a series that included Moses and Jesus.

At first bewildered and reluctant, Muhammad later came to believe he had indeed been called to deliver a divine message to his people. Muhammad began to preach to the citizens of Mecca, urging them to give up their idols and warning them of a coming day of judgment, when all people would be judged by God and sent to heaven or hell.

Most Meccans did not believe Muhammad, and some citizens plotted to kill him. Hearing of the plan, Muhammad left Mecca in 622 and traveled to the nearby city of Medina with his converts.

Muhammad's emigration from Mecca, called the Hegira, marked an important phase in his life and work. In Medina, Muhammad established himself not only as a religious reformer but also, by making a series of agreements with the city's inhabitants, as Medina's ruler. Muhammad and his followers then subdued the Arabs living in the surrounding area and attacked caravans bringing goods to and from Mecca. The Meccans tried without success to overthrow Muhammad, and in 630, Mecca surrendered without a fight.

Two years later, Muhammad died. In the few years that he preached, Muhammad had accomplished a great deal. He not only set forth the religious principles of Islam but also brought the people of Arabia under unified control for the first time in history.

After Muhammad's death, the religious community of Muslims fought battles to extend Islamic territory By 750, they ruled an area that extended from Spain to India. Conquered peoples were not forced to convert to Islam—though many did. The Arab Muslims also respected the cultural achievements of their subjects. Science and the arts flourished.

The great Muslim empire fell to Asians called Mongols in 1258. But by 1500, Turkish Muslims from central Asia had established three important Muslim empires: the Ottoman in Turkey, the Safavid in Iran, and the Mogul in India. All of the Muslims were powerful warriors, able to retain most of their conquests until modern times despite military challenges from European Christians. The most famous of these challenges were the Crusades (1096 to 1291), military expeditions intended to recapture the Holy Land, where Jesus had lived, from the Muslims.

From its beginning, then, Islam has been both a religion and a social order. Many Christians and Jews strongly believe that religion and politics should be kept separate. But combining them produced the Middle East's greatest civilization.

The Sunni-Shiite division

Throughout its history, Islam has undergone many minor divisions that produced separate sects. The most important rift occurred after Muhammad's death, when his followers disagreed about who should become the Islamic community's political leader, or *caliph* (successor to Muhammad). A minority of Muslims felt that leadership rightfully belonged to Muhammad's closest male relative, Ali. This group became known as Shiite Muslims.

The majority, however, held that any qualified male Muslim could be elected caliph. On the strength of their numbers, the majority elected a man named Abu Bakr. The majority sect became known as Sunni Muslims. Today, Sunni Muslims

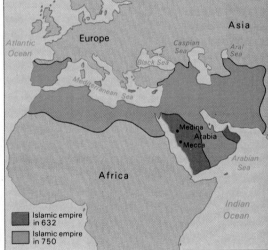

The Spread of Islam
Early converts to Islam met opposition. A Turkish painting, *top,* depicts red-robed pagans threatening an early Muslim. Arab resistance to Islam gave way within a few years, however. By Muhammad's death in 632, Muslims controlled most of Arabia, *above.* During the next 120 years, they extended their territory over much of the Middle East and northern Africa.

بِسْمِ اللهِ الرَّحْمَنِ الرَّحِيمِ

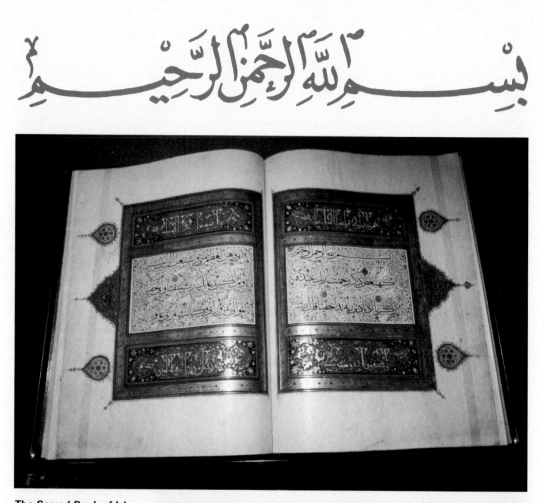

The Sacred Book of Islam
Sweeping Arabic script, *top,* spells out what may be the most-recited words in any language: "In the name of God, the compassionate, the merciful." The phrase begins and is repeated throughout the holy book of Islam, the Koran. For centuries, skilled Muslim calligraphers produced Korans of exquisite beauty such as the example from the 1500's, *above.* Today, as then, Muslim scholars intensively study the Koran, *right,* believing it the word of God.

still constitute the majority, comprising more than 80 per cent of the Muslim population.

The Sunni-Shiite political division was eventually reflected in the two sects' religious beliefs. Shiite Muslims believed that, in accordance with God's wishes, Muhammad had appointed Ali to be both political leader and Islam's spiritual leader, or *imam*. While Sunni Muslims designate many learned Muslims as imams, most Shiite Muslims believe that since the year 632 there have been only 12 imams, all descendants of Ali, the last of whom has been in hiding since about 874. These Shiite Muslims, known as Twelvers, believe that the 12th imam will someday return to initiate a reign of peace and justice that will lead to the day of judgment.

The Shiites' belief in these powerful spiritual leaders separates them from Sunni Muslims. The violent deaths of Ali and his son Husayn led to another distinction between the sects. Shiite Muslims revere Ali and especially Husayn as martyrs and take part in passionate mass displays of mourning on the anniversaries of their deaths. This highly emotional form of devotion is foreign to the more reserved Sunni Muslim majority.

Islamic teachings

Islam is based on what Muslims believe was a divine revelation to the prophet Muhammad. The revelation is recorded in the Koran, the sacred book of Islam, which comprises 114 *suras*—or chapters—of Arabic rhymed prose. Muslims believe that the Koran preserves the word of God as it was delivered to Muhammad by the angel Gabriel. The Koran contains—among other things—commands, prohibitions, warnings, and tales of earlier prophets.

For Muslims, the Koran is the absolute authority in those matters it discusses. But because it is a relatively short book—about the length of the New Testament—many subjects important to Muslims are not mentioned or are not treated in depth. To supplement the guidance of the Koran, Muslims looked to the example set by Muhammad. Pious Muslims, reasoning that Muhammad must have understood the Koran and God's will better than anyone else, collected reports about what he did and said, and what he approved or disapproved. These reports, known as the Hadith, were tested for their authenticity, classified, and assembled into books.

Even the Hadith were not comprehensive enough to help Muslims solve the problems that arose when new territories came under their control. Muslim legal experts, using the Koran and the Hadith as sources, developed a sophisticated method to determine the will of God for virtually every situation. In this way, they set down the *sharia*, or Islamic law. (The word *sharia* means the road or pathway in which God intends that people should walk.) As much a moral code as a code of law, the sharia is a set of directions for human conduct that regulates everything in Muslim life—from duties to God to social conduct, dietary habits, and personal hygiene.

"God is great, God is great," calls a muezzin, or crier, from the top of a tower known as a minaret, *right.* Five times each day, the call reminds Muslims to face Mecca and pray. At noon on Fridays, men are required to pray at houses of worship called mosques. Inside a mosque, *below,* an intricately decorated mihrab, or niche, indicates the direction of Mecca.

Islamic practices

Islam literally means *submission*, and *Muslim* is Arabic for *one who submits*. Muslims show their submission to God's will by fulfilling duties known as the "five pillars" of Islam. The first is the obligation to profess publicly that there is only one God and that Muhammad is His prophet.

The second pillar is daily prayer. Five times each day, devout Muslims around the world face in the direction of Mecca and perform a brief ritual of kneeling and reciting prayers. At noon on Fridays, they congregate in places of worship known as *mosques* to pray together and to hear a sermon.

The third duty is almsgiving. Every Muslim is obligated to give money to help the needy or for other charitable purposes.

An annual fast is the fourth pillar of Islam. Throughout Ramadan, the ninth month of the Islamic calendar, healthy adult Muslims do not eat or drink during daylight hours. Only after sundown can Muslims break their fast. During Ramadan, normal daytime work slows, and at night Muslims recite passages from the Koran and perform other religious exercises. Muslims celebrate the end of Ramadan with a three-day festival.

The fifth pillar is the *hajj*, a pilgrimage to the shrine in Mecca, which occurs during the last month of the Islamic year. Muslims believe that the shrine, called the Kaaba, was built by Abraham; Muhammad prayed there. Every Muslim who is physically able is required by Islamic teachings to make the pilgrimage at least once. While in Mecca, pilgrims perform several rituals, including circling the Kaaba seven times and then traveling to the nearby plain of Arafat to "stand in the presence of God." In commemoration of

Gold leaf covers the domed roof of a mosque in Jidda, Saudi Arabia. The building's tall minarets and central dome are features common to many mosques.

Abraham's willingness to offer his son to God, the pilgrims ritually sacrifice animals.

To these five pillars, some Muslims add a sixth, the *jihad* (holy war). While most Muslims understand *jihad* to refer to each person's inner battle against his or her own evil tendencies, some—especially political extremists—interpret *jihad* as an external struggle. They believe that participation in the military defense of Islam and Muslim territory is the duty of every able-bodied Muslim male—and, when necessary, of every Muslim.

Islam and modern politics

Muslim power, which reached its height in the 1500's, declined dramatically in the 1800's. Europe and the United States experienced the industrial and scientific revolutions, in which they became capable of the rapid production of arms and other goods. European countries grew militarily strong and began to invade Islamic lands, which were not industrialized. Russia conquered some northern Islamic territories. The Dutch took Indonesia. The French began to rule much of northern and western Africa; Italy took Libya; and Great Britain colonized India, Egypt, Malaysia, and parts of Africa. Iran and Turkey were subject to European influence in their affairs. By 1920, only Afghanistan, Yemen, and central Arabia remained completely independent.

European control of their lands deeply humiliated Muslims. The feeling intensified when Muslims realized that the only way to throw off their conquerors was to forsake their traditional ways and modernize in the European fashion. Muslim countries reluctantly imitated their enemies' military, economic, and political systems. In the process, the traditional social order based on Islamic teachings had to be abandoned.

By the mid-1900's, most emerging Muslim nations achieved some form of self-government, but they were no longer united in vast Islamic empires. Today, political thought and government in each country is a unique—and often unstable—mixture of traditional and modern ideals.

Among nations with predominantly Muslim populations, Turkey has gone the furthest toward adopting a Western pattern of social organization. Turkey's leaders have followed a philosophy of deliberate *secularism* (separation of religion from political affairs) since the Turks drove out Greek troops in the 1920's. Although 98 per cent of Turkey's citizens are Muslims, the government has restricted many cultural expressions of Islam. Even traditional Islamic dress—such as veils for women—is discouraged.

Like Turkey, Indonesia—which has the world's largest Muslim population—has adopted a government formed on Western patterns. Indonesia favors the Islamic way of life, but the country's ministry of religious affairs also assists all other religious groups in Indonesia.

The Pilgrimage to Mecca
Muslims from every sect and many nations throng Islam's holy shrine, the black-draped Kaaba, *opposite page,* in the sacred city of Mecca, Saudi Arabia. Each year, more than 2 million Muslims fulfill their religious duty to travel at least once to Mecca and perform a series of rituals that includes circling the Kaaba seven times and visiting other religious sites.

At the other extreme stand Iran and Saudi Arabia. Although Saudi leaders are vigorously pursuing a policy of modernization, both Saudi Arabia and Iran claim to be traditional Islamic states. Leaders of both nations say that the Koran is their basis for rule. The sharia is applied in the courts, and, in Saudi Arabia, enforcement agencies make sure Saudis perform their religious duties.

Between the extremes of secularism and Islamic concepts of government is a third kind of political arrangement in which the government uses Islam to gain popular support for secular policies. Libya, which has attracted much attention for its anti-Western policy and its support of terrorism, has this kind of government. When Libya's ruler, Muammar Muhammad al-Qadhafi, came to power in 1969, he seemed to be in the process of transforming Libya into an Islamic state. But in the late 1970's, his policies diverged from the traditions of Islam. In Libya today, the role of the sharia is restricted to the area of personal conduct, and the Koran is considered to have religious—but not social—relevance. Nonetheless, Qadhafi claims that his radical policies are upheld by Islam. Most outsiders agree that Qadhafi's interpretation of Islam bears little resemblance to the beliefs of Muslims elsewhere.

Another example of a government that promotes Islamic ideals but not a completely Islamic rule is Pakistan. Because Pakistan was created in 1947 as a national homeland for the Muslims of India, many Pakistanis wanted their country to be an Islamic state. The government resisted the idea but made concessions to conservative religious opinion in order to claim to be acting on the basis of Islamic principles. For example, General M. Zia-ul-Haq, president of Pakistan since 1977, created sharia courts and, because Islamic law forbids charging interest on loans, introduced an interest-free banking system. Critics charge that Zia's government uses Islam only to restrict the freedom of Pakistanis and to increase the government's control.

The example of Pakistan illustrates how the people's belief in Islam can be exploited by both sides in a political struggle. In Pakistan

Islam's influence on daily life differs vastly from one Muslim nation to another. In Iraq, a female engineer, *below,* works and dresses much like a Westerner. In contrast, many Pakistani women, *below right,* follow traditional Islamic practices that include wearing shroudlike veils whenever they venture outside their homes.

and several Middle Eastern nations, the religion provides a moral foundation for government policy. At the same time, Islam is the basis for criticism by the opponents of those in power.

Islamic resurgence

The failure of secularism to take hold in most Muslim countries reflects a rift between Middle East rulers and the masses of common people. While government leaders generally encouraged Western systems of government in the early 1900's, most Muslims deeply resented being forced to abandon their culture and take up the ways of their military enemies. In addition, the sweeping changes brought by government-sponsored modernization left many Muslims disoriented and uneasy. Because sudden wealth made rapid modernization possible, profits generated by the Middle East's oil in the mid-1900's worked to intensify the people's dissatisfaction.

In the 1970's, some Muslims began to proclaim that forsaking Islam to adopt foreign ways had caused the weakness, decline, humiliation, and unease that had plagued all Muslim countries since the 1800's. These Muslims—who make up the movements known as *Islamic resurgence*—propose instituting Islamic forms of government in Muslim nations. Islam, as they see it, is a divinely inspired way of organizing society—superior to the human inventions of Marxist socialism and democratic capitalism.

Since 1970, more than 100 Islamic resurgence groups have been founded in the Middle East. Members of these groups hope that by pursuing a revolution like the one led by Muhammad in the 600's, they will be able to create a unified Islamic state whose constitution is the sharia. Moderate resurgence groups hope to achieve their objectives using peaceful methods of persuasion. Radical groups consider it a religious duty to take up arms or use terrorist methods to achieve their ends.

Many radicals are Shiite Muslims. Their reverence for martyrs leads some to willingly sacrifice their lives in violent jihad, and

Islamic teachings are enforced to varying degrees throughout the Muslim world. In Saudi Arabia, soldiers must put down their rifles to pray as required by the Koran, *below left*. But the governments of many Muslim nations disregard the Koran's prohibition against charging interest on loans—a practice that is the foundation of modern banking. Western-style financial institutions such as the Bank of Bahrain, *below*, are fairly common.

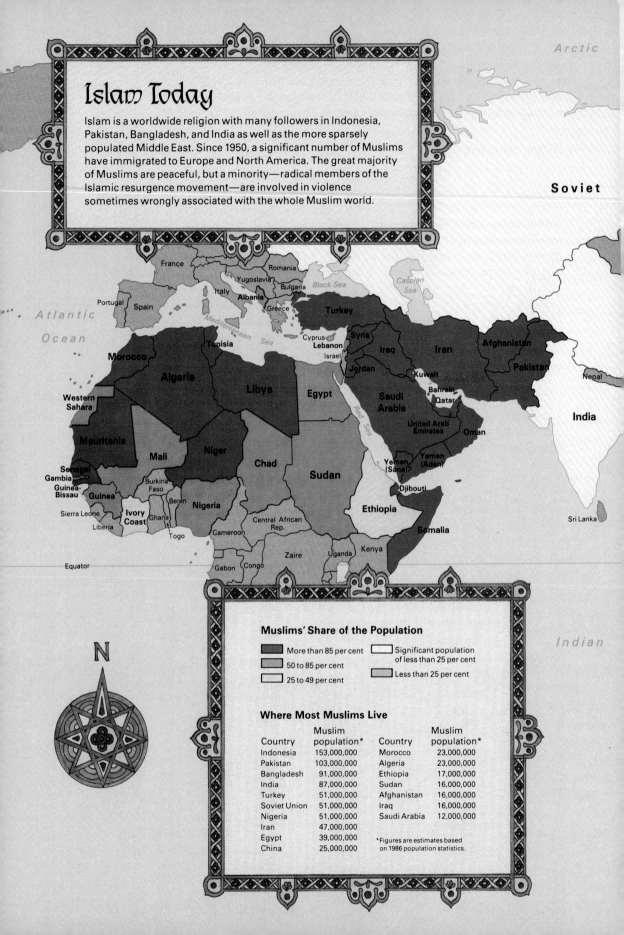

Islam Today

Islam is a worldwide religion with many followers in Indonesia, Pakistan, Bangladesh, and India as well as the more sparsely populated Middle East. Since 1950, a significant number of Muslims have immigrated to Europe and North America. The great majority of Muslims are peaceful, but a minority—radical members of the Islamic resurgence movement—are involved in violence sometimes wrongly associated with the whole Muslim world.

Muslims' Share of the Population

- More than 85 per cent
- 50 to 85 per cent
- 25 to 49 per cent
- Significant population of less than 25 per cent
- Less than 25 per cent

Where Most Muslims Live

Country	Muslim population*	Country	Muslim population*
Indonesia	153,000,000	Morocco	23,000,000
Pakistan	103,000,000	Algeria	23,000,000
Bangladesh	91,000,000	Ethiopia	17,000,000
India	87,000,000	Sudan	16,000,000
Turkey	51,000,000	Afghanistan	16,000,000
Soviet Union	51,000,000	Iraq	16,000,000
Nigeria	51,000,000	Saudi Arabia	12,000,000
Iran	47,000,000		
Egypt	39,000,000		
China	25,000,000		

*Figures are estimates based on 1986 population statistics.

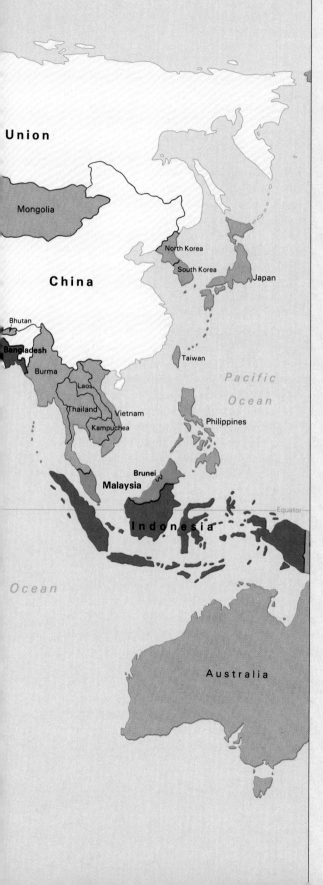

Ocean

Union

Mongolia

China

North Korea

South Korea

Japan

Bhutan

Bangladesh

Burma

Taiwan

Pacific

Ocean

Laos

Thailand

Vietnam

Kampuchea

Philippines

Brunei

Malaysia

Equator

Indonesia

Ocean

Australia

Violence in the Muslim World

The radical wing of the Islamic resurgence was responsible for the assassination of Egypt's President Anwar el-Sadat in 1981 and the bombing that killed 241 U.S. Marines in Lebanon in 1983. Fear that Iran's Islamic revolution might spread prompted Iraq to attack Iran in 1980. And the hostility between Shiite Iranians and Sunni Saudi Arabians caused a bloody riot during the 1987 pilgrimage to Mecca.

Iran and Iraq: Iranians and Iraqis battle in a war begun in 1980.

Cairo, Egypt: Minutes after this photograph was taken on Oct. 6, 1981, Egyptian President Sadat, left, was assassinated.

Mecca, Saudi Arabia: About 400 Muslim pilgrims are killed in a July 1987 riot involving Iranians, shown here on a video broadcast.

Beirut, Lebanon: A terrorist attack on U.S. Marine headquarters kills 241 Marines on Oct. 23, 1983.

makes them particularly effective warriors. The radical members of Islamic resurgence movements represent only a tiny minority of the Muslim population, but their extreme acts give them an influence far out of proportion to their numbers. Governments have been largely successful in controlling Islamic resurgence, but much of the strife in the Middle East today can be tied to these movements.

The Iranian revolution

The outstanding example of a successful Islamic revolution occurred in the predominantly Shiite nation of Iran. In 1979, Iranians overthrew their ruler, Shah Mohammad Reza Pahlavi. The revolution was supported by Iranians of every class and political opinion, including those who wanted the new government to be secular. They united under Ayatollah Ruhollah Khomeini, a Muslim religious leader. In the end, the resurgence movement dominated the revolution and declared Iran an Islamic republic, making the sharia the law of the land. Today, the legislature, the court system, and the communications media are controlled by religious scholars, who fill most important government posts. Because Iran sees the very purpose of its existence to be the promotion of Islam throughout the Middle East, it finances Islamic resurgence groups in other nations—especially those that have large Shiite Muslim minorities such as Lebanon.

In 1980, soon after the revolution, Iran was attacked by its neighbor Iraq, apparently because of an old boundary dispute. Iraq—another predominantly Shiite nation—was also motivated by a desire to overthrow Iran's Islamic republic and prevent its religious revolution from inspiring an Iraqi revolt. By late 1987, the Iran-Iraq war had entered its eighth year.

The fears of the Iraqi leaders may have been unfounded. There is little evidence that the Iraqi people have responded to Iran's revolutionary spirit. Even Saudi Arabia is generally opposed to Iran's type of Islamic republic. Conflict between the Sunni Muslims in Saudi Arabia and Iran's Shiite pilgrims erupted during the 1987 hajj, when about 400 pilgrims—many of them Iranians—were killed in a riot in Mecca.

Iranian-backed radicals are a powerful political force in Lebanon, however. Long torn by civil war, Lebanon was also occupied by Israeli troops from 1982 to 1985. Originally, the dispute between Israel and such Arab groups as the Palestine Liberation Organization (PLO) was a political struggle over power and the control of territory and did not involve Islam. But because most Arab Muslims consider Israel an extension of Western influence in the Middle East, there is a deep hostility toward Israel in all the Arab and Muslim countries. In the 1980's, Islamic resurgence movements have taken up the struggle against Israel.

The unrest caused by the Israeli invasion of Lebanon led to the emergence of radical Shiite resurgence groups in that nation. Organizations such as the Iranian-backed Hezbollah (Party of God) were devoted to pushing Westerners and Israelis out of Lebanon so that they could create an Islamic state. To accomplish this, the radicals carried out a series of military actions, bombings, kidnappings, and terrorist attacks against their opponents. In 1983, radicals bombed U.S. Marine headquarters in Beirut, Lebanon, killing 241 marines. In 1985, an Islamic resurgence group hijacked a TWA airliner. They killed 1 American passenger and held 39 passengers hostage in Beirut for more than two weeks.

It must be emphasized that the majority of Lebanese Shiite Muslims are not radicals. The largest Shiite organization, Amal (Hope), is a moderate group that supports secularism.

The Islamic resurgence also spawned violence in Egypt. President Anwar el-Sadat, who governed from 1970 until his death in 1981, was well aware of the power of resurgence movements. Sadat hoped that his concessions to moderate groups would help him gain religious support for his liberal economic policies and his attempt to make peace with Israel. But some Egyptian Muslims felt that the country's experiments with liberal democracy and Westernization were failures. Egypt's 1978 peace accord with Israel was seen as a betrayal of Arab interests. In 1981, Sadat was assassinated by Muslims linked to a radical resurgence group called Islamic Jihad.

Westerners are, on the whole, disturbed by the Islamic resurgence in Lebanon, Egypt, Iran, and elsewhere. A group in Afghanistan, however, inspires praise. Afghans who call themselves *mujahedeen* (holy warriors) came to prominence in 1978 by leading the resistance to Afghanistan's Soviet-backed government. In 1979, the Soviets invaded Afghanistan to prop up the military government, beginning a war that by December 1987 had lasted eight years. Islam inspired and mobilized the Afghans in spite of the odds against them and the terrible losses they suffered. In Afghanistan, as in Iran, the combination of national pride and Islam produced a strong military force.

The examples of several nations make it clear that violence in the Middle East cannot be blamed solely upon Islam. Despite their military history, Muslims do not believe that fighting is an end in itself. The Koran forbids senseless violence and urges people to battle only for just causes. The true origin of today's unrest is the Middle East's history of domination by foreign powers followed by sweeping but unwelcome social change. These events, not Islam, are the source of Muslims' anger.

For further reading:

Lippman, Thomas W. *Understanding Islam: An Introduction to the Moslem World.* New American Library, 1982.
Robinson, Francis. *Atlas of the Islamic World.* Facts on File, 1982.
Voll, John O. *Islam: Continuity and Change in the Modern World.* Westview Press, 1982.

By Michael Woods

Stormy Debate over Acid Rain

Is acid rain killing life in lakes, harming forests, corroding buildings, and even jeopardizing our health?

The author:
Michael Woods is science editor of *The Toledo* (Ohio) *Blade.*

When President Ronald Reagan visited Canada for a meeting with Canadian Prime Minister Brian Mulroney in April 1987, he was confronted by one of the largest crowds of demonstrators ever to protest against a foreign leader in Canada. The dominant issue for the 4,000 protesters was not nuclear weapons, foreign policy, or international trade. The focus of their anger was acid rain.

Virtually unknown to most people a decade ago, acid rain—rainfall with a high acid content due to chemicals in polluted air—has evolved from a scientific curiosity into one of the most persistent and important environmental problems of the 1980's. Acid rain has been blamed for killing aquatic life in thousands of lakes and streams around the world, stripping forest soils of nutrients, damaging farm crops, corroding stone buildings and priceless ancient monuments, and even jeopardizing human health.

Like many environmental problems, acid rain involves complex scientific and political issues. Because there are many uncertainties about the causes and effects of acid rain, electric utility and coal-mining interests say that governments should move slowly before requiring costly measures to reduce air pollution. But environmentalists cite scientific evidence suggesting that the problem is growing in intensity. They say that immediate action is needed to reduce pollutants from electric utilities that burn coal and oil, as well as pollutants from automobiles and from other sources.

And so, debate about acid rain continues—pitting scientist against scientist, region against region, nation against nation. Because the pollutants that create acid rain may be borne on air currents and cause damage far from the polluting source, the problem transcends state and national boundaries. Thus Canadians, who believe their lakes and forests are being damaged by acid rain caused by air pollutants originating in the United States, greeted President Reagan with angry chants: "Go Home Acid Rain!"

Friction between the United States and Canada over acid rain has been building since the late 1970's. In 1980, representatives of the two governments signed an agreement to attack the problem by sharply reducing pollutant emissions. After coming to power in 1981, however, the Reagan Administration backed away from the agreement, arguing that further research was needed. Reagan maintained that position when he met Mulroney at a summit conference in 1985. In 1986, Reagan and Mulroney met again and discussed a joint U.S.-Canadian report on the issue that called for a $5-billion program to explore ways to burn coal more cleanly.

But in September 1987, Canadians were angered by a report issued by a U.S. federal government study group, the National Acid Precipitation Assessment Program (NAPAP). The NAPAP report minimized the extent of the acid rain problem. Canada's Environment Minister Thomas Michael McMillan described the report as "incomplete and misleading," a judgment echoed by many scientists in both countries. Polls indicate that Canadians rank acid rain as the most important U.S.-Canadian issue.

Acid rain is also an important issue in Europe. Scandinavian countries, for example, blame the death of fish in thousands of lakes and rivers on air pollutants spewed out by industrial smokestacks in Great Britain and other parts of western Europe. In West Germany, the destruction of forestlands, believed related to acid rain and other air pollutants, is a potent political issue. *Waldsterben*—meaning *forest death*—has become a household word as once-lush firs, spruces, and pines turn yellow, shed their needles, and become skeletal. And in central Europe, many believe that acid rain has done more than the passage of centuries to wear down stone monuments and other ancient treasures.

Within the United States, acid rain is fostering sharp regional antagonism between the Northeastern and Midwestern states. Politicians from the Northeast say that acid rain caused by pollutants discharged by Midwestern electric generating stations has probably damaged thousands of lakes and streams and harmed forests in New York state and New England.

Thus, acid rain has emerged as a serious national and international issue. And while environmentalists, politicians, and electric utility and coal-mining interests argue about the need for immediate measures to curb air pollutants, most people agree on one point: Further research will help us understand acid rain and develop better ways to deal with the problem.

The term *acid rain* was first used in 1872 by Robert Angus Smith, a Scottish chemist who spent 20 years studying the chemistry of rain around the industrial city of Manchester, England. Modern scientists recognized acid rain as a potential problem in the 1950's. But it was not until the United Nations Conference on the Human Environment, held in Stockholm, Sweden, in 1972, that discussions of acid rain brought the issue into the public eye.

Today, although the public continues to use the term *acid rain*, most scientists favor a broader term—*acid deposition*. Acid deposition includes acidic snow, hail, fog, gases, and acidic dry particles, as well as acid rainfall.

Scientists measure the acidity of rain and other water solutions with a special scale that determines the concentration of hydrogen ions. Called the *pH scale* (the letters *p* and *H* stand for *power* and *hydrogen*), it ranges from 0 to 14, with a value of 7 representing a neutral solution—neither acid nor alkaline. A pH above 7 indicates an alkaline solution, such as ammonia (about 11 on the pH scale) and lye (about 13). The higher the number, the more alkaline the solution. A pH below 7 indicates an acid solution—the lower the number, the more acidic the solution.

The pH scale is a logarithmic scale, which means that an increase or decrease of 1 unit represents a tenfold change in acidity. Thus, the sulfuric acid used in automobile storage batteries (pH of about 1) is 10 times as acidic as a lemon (pH of about 2).

The pH Scale
Scientists use a measurement called the *pH scale* to grade the acidity or alkalinity of a solution. A neutral solution has a pH of 7. Values below 7 indicate acidity; values above 7 indicate alkalinity.

Sources of Acid Rain Pollutants

The gases sulfur dioxide (SO$_2$) and nitrogen oxides (NO$_x$) are the major acid-forming compounds that lead to acid rain. Transportation and industry—especially electric utilities—produce most of the SO$_2$ and NO$_x$ created by human activities.

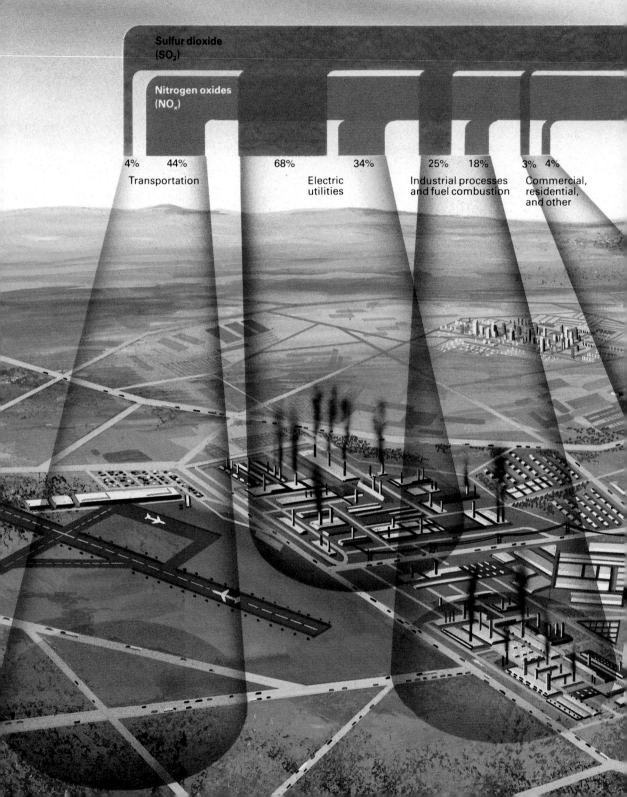

Sulfur dioxide (SO$_2$)

Nitrogen oxides (NO$_x$)

4%	44%		68%	34%	25%	18%	3%	4%
Transportation			Electric utilities		Industrial processes and fuel combustion		Commercial, residential, and other	

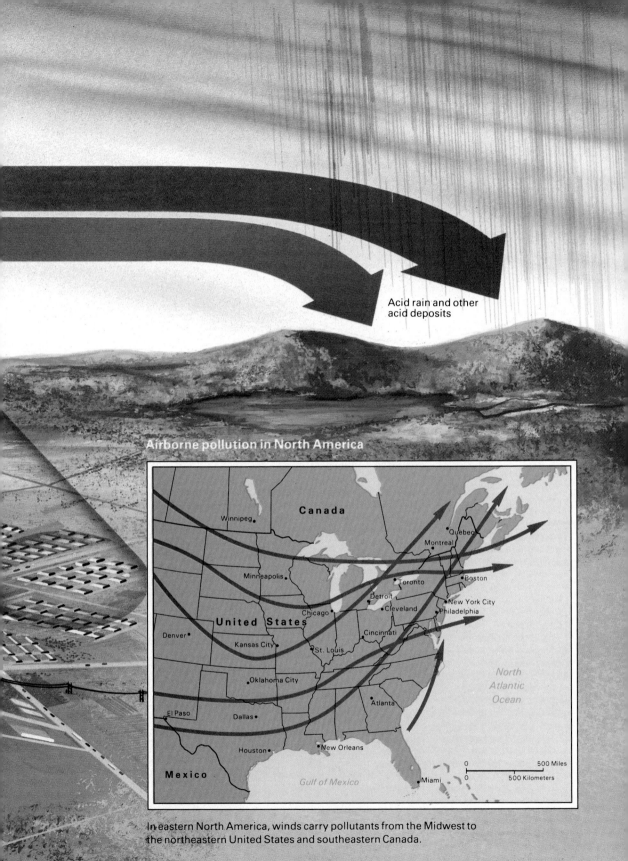

Acid rain and other
acid deposits

Airborne pollution in North America

In eastern North America, winds carry pollutants from the Midwest to
the northeastern United States and southeastern Canada.

Source: U.S. Environmental Protection Agency.

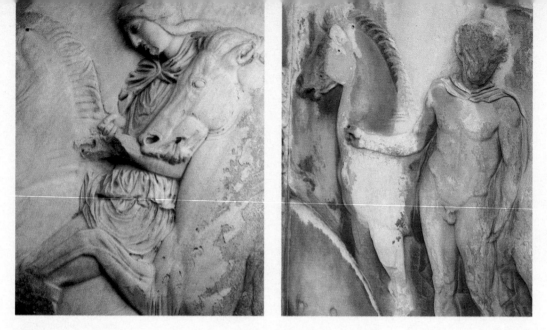

Finely sculpted details of a decorative marble panel that once graced the Parthenon, an ancient Greek temple in Athens, *above,* are well preserved today because the panel was placed in the British Museum in London in the early 1800's. But many of the features of panels remaining on the Parthenon have been lost forever, obliterated by exposure to acid deposits and other pollutants, *above right.*

All rain, even rain untouched by pollution, is at least mildly acidic because pure water combines with carbon dioxide in the air to form a weak solution of carbonic acid. Scientists generally agree that unpolluted precipitation has a pH of 5.65, and that to be called acid rain, rainfall must have a pH below 5.60—levels that are caused chiefly by the presence of sulfuric acid and nitric acid.

A number of natural processes—including volcanic eruptions, forest fires, hot springs and geysers, sea spray, and decay from organic matter—can introduce substances into the air and alter the pH of rainfall. But although these natural processes account for at least half of the global sulfur and nitrogen emissions, human beings are largely responsible for the acid rain in the Northern Hemisphere. When fossil fuels such as coal and petroleum are burned, pollutants containing sulfur dioxide and oxides of nitrogen (collectively labeled NO_x) are released.

The U.S. Environmental Protection Agency (EPA) estimates that about 20 million short tons (18 million metric tons) of NO_x were released into the atmosphere in the United States in 1985. More than 50 per cent of NO_x emissions come from industrial sources; about 44 per cent from cars, trucks, and other forms of transportation; and the rest from residential and other sources.

According to the EPA, about 27 million short tons (24 million metric tons) of sulfur dioxide were also released into the atmosphere in the United States in 1985, most coming from industrial sources. About half of the sulfur dioxide released by U.S. industry in 1985 came from electric utilities that burn coal. Coal contains sulfur, which is transformed into sulfur dioxide during combustion.

Outside the United States, emissions of sulfur dioxide and NO_x are also substantial. According to reports issued in 1981 by the Norwegian Institute for Air Research in Lillestrøm, Norway, the current annual emissions levels in Europe totaled 68 million short tons (62 million metric tons) of sulfur dioxide and more than 21 million short tons (19 million metric tons) of NO_x.

Once in the atmosphere, sulfur dioxide and NO_x are transformed into sulfuric acid and nitric acid by a series of complex chemical reactions involving sunlight, water, and other substances—a process that scientists do not fully understand. Some of the pollutants fall out of the atmosphere as gases or as dry particles called *sulfates* or *nitrates* that can acidify water and soil. Others become entrapped in water droplets in the atmosphere. The droplets, containing either dissolved acidic gases or sulfuric or nitric acid, are deposited on the earth's surface as acid rain or snow.

Tons of pollutants are discharged by coal-fired electric power plants from towering smokestacks, up to 1,000 feet (300 meters) tall. When these pollutants are released, they hitch rides on the prevailing winds and travel hundreds or even thousands of miles from their source before they fall back to earth. Ironically, these tall stacks were erected in Europe and North America in the 1960's and 1970's in an effort to relieve local pollution problems. It was believed that by dispersing pollutants high in the atmosphere, their harmful effects would be dissipated. But instead of eliminating the problem, the supertall stacks merely helped move the pollutants to other locations.

This long-range transport of the air pollutants responsible for acid rain is the cornerstone of intense political controversy in which residents of one region or country blame acid rain on another region. In North America, for example, the prevailing summer winds carry emissions from the Midwest to the northeastern United States and southeastern Canada. Both countries emit large quantities of sulfur dioxide and NO_x into the atmosphere. But because of wind patterns, the United States sends 2 to 4 times as much sulfur dioxide and 11 times as much NO_x to Canada as Canada sends to the United States, according to the EPA. Similarly, in Europe, prevailing winds carry pollutants from Great Britain and other countries and deposit them in Scandinavia.

Several reports issued by the National Academy of Sciences and other scientific groups have concluded that acid rain is a serious problem. But formulating policy to deal with acid rain—measures that could cost huge sums of money and even change national energy policies—has been complicated by the difficulties in assessing the actual hazards posed by acid rain. Electric utility and coal-mining lobbyists are quick to assert the difficulties in separating the effects of acid rain from those of other factors that can alter the ecology of lakes, streams, and forestland. For example, many land-use practices—such as timber harvesting and agriculture—sometimes harm the water quality of lakes and streams, though they generally do not cause long-term increases in acidity. Fish populations can also be altered by such factors as changes in stocking policies or

Is Acid Rain Harming Forests?

Many dying trees in West Germany's Black Forest have lost masses of needles, leaving them with sparse, scruffy crowns, *right*. Although there is no direct evidence linking acid rain with the decline of forests, many scientists believe that various pollutants, including the pollutants that cause acid rain, contribute to the problem.

Areas Vulnerable to Acid Rain

Some regions of North America (the areas colored orange-brown in the map at the right) are more sensitive than others to acid rain. Many factors, including soil chemistry and type of rock, determine the environment's capacity to neutralize acid deposits.

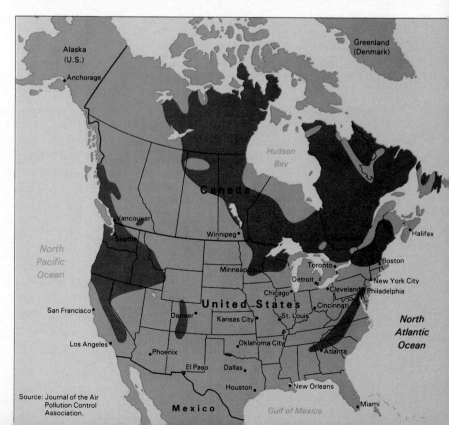

Alaska (U.S.)

Anchorage

Greenland (Denmark)

Hudson Bay

Canada

North Pacific Ocean

Vancouver

Seattle

Winnipeg

Halifax

Minneapolis

Toronto

Boston

Detroit

Cleveland

New York City

Chicago

Philadelphia

United States

Cincinnati

San Francisco

Denver

Kansas City

St. Louis

North Atlantic Ocean

Los Angeles

Phoenix

Oklahoma City

Atlanta

El Paso

Dallas

Houston

New Orleans

Miami

Mexico

Gulf of Mexico

Source: Journal of the Air Pollution Control Association.

Acid Rain and Lakes
Dipping his hand into Lake Gårdsjön in southern Sweden, ecologist Hans Hultberg comes up with a film of sooty scum containing various by-products from the burning of coal and oil. Scientists claim that thousands of lakes are acidified—and that many no longer contain fish—due to acid rain caused by wind-borne pollutants from other countries.

pollution from chemicals applied to crops that are carried by runoff into lakes and streams. But many scientists and environmentalists argue that although such factors may damage lakes, streams, and forests, their effects are usually different from those of acid rain.

In spite of the difficulty of separating acid rain's effects from other possible causes of environmental damage, a study issued in 1986 by the National Research Council (NRC), the research arm of the National Academy of Sciences, resolved one major scientific question about acid rain. It established that a definite cause-and-effect relationship exists between air pollutants such as sulfur dioxide, the formation of acid rain, and the deterioration of certain lakes in the northeastern United States.

But the NRC committee also found wide variability in the way the acidity of individual lakes has changed over time. The scientists said that many lakes in northeastern states have become less acidic since the early 1900's, while others have become more acidic than could be accounted for solely by acid rain. The NRC study concluded that decreases in acidity, or very large increases in acidity, may be due to other human activities, such as farming or forestry.

Scientists also know that some lakes have a natural ability to counteract, or buffer, the effects of acid rain. This buffering capacity is influenced by a number of factors, particularly the soil chemistry of the lake bed and surrounding area.

Speaking Out About Acid Rain

Protests calling for efforts to control acid rain take many forms, from a sign at the edge of a forest in Canada, *below left,* to a 1986 demonstration near the White House in Washington, D.C., *below right.*

When a lake has been acidified, the plants and animals that live there may be harmed. For example, studies show that when many aquatic animals are exposed to acid water, they may fail to produce eggs or they may produce eggs that fail to develop normally. Acid deposits also leach toxic metals, such as aluminum and mercury, out of the soil and transport them into lakes and streams, where they can damage fish and other organisms. Acidification can also alter communities of *phytoplankton*—tiny, free-floating plants that are a vital food source—which in turn can dramatically reduce the number and variety of fish in a lake or stream.

Aquatic life is also at the mercy of sudden, seasonal fluctuations in the acidity of lakes and streams, particularly in cold climates that receive large accumulations of acid snow. During the spring thaw, the sudden release of acid into lakes and streams when snow melts can kill aquatic life abruptly.

The impact of acid rain on forests, crops, and soils is less well documented than its effect on lakes and streams. A 1980 study by the EPA found that although some crops suffered extensive damage to foliage and reductions in yield when exposed to simulated acid rain, others sustained little apparent injury, even when exposed to extremely acid conditions.

The EPA study, like other early research on acid rain, was conducted with simulated acid rain under carefully controlled labora-

Probing Acid Rain's Effects

At a research station in West Germany, *below,* scientists examine trees exposed to acidic fog and other pollutants. In a U.S. study, trout die while confined in a stream contaminated by acid rain, *below right.*

tory conditions. But more recent field studies, measuring acid rain's actual impact on crops under more realistic conditions, have cast doubt on the extent to which acid rain actually damages crops. In September 1987, the federal government's highly criticized NAPAP report concluded that acid rain has "no consistent, demonstrable effect" on the yield of crops.

Many scientists fear that acid rain may be contributing to the mysterious decline of forests in North America and Europe. Massive episodes of tree death are spreading through the forests of East and West Germany, Poland, and other parts of Europe. Many of these forests now receive about 30 times as much acidity as they would if precipitation were falling through an unpolluted atmosphere.

Although little direct evidence links acid rain to the decline of forests, many scientists believe that acid rain and other air pollutants —particularly ozone, a form of oxygen—may be critical factors. For example, acid rain can leach toxic metals out of the soil and make them more readily available to plants, impoverish the soil by leaching out vital nutrients, leach nutrients from leaves, erode the surface layers of leaves, and kill microorganisms that are important to the health of certain plants. As a result of these various insults, trees may become more vulnerable to natural stresses such as drought, insect attacks, and extreme cold.

Scientists agree that acid rain can damage metals, surface finishes on automobiles, and materials used for buildings, statues, highways, and bridges. Such damage has intensified the debate about acid rain in such countries as Greece and Italy, where priceless ancient statuary, buildings, and monuments are being eroded by air pollution. Some of the world's greatest architectural treasures, including the Parthenon in Greece, the Colosseum in Italy, and the pyramids of Egypt, may have been damaged by acid rain.

Experts point out that because materials naturally deteriorate with time, it is difficult to separate the damage caused by natural weathering from that caused by acid rain. An acid rain study conducted in 1981 at the request of the U.S. General Accounting Office concluded that because most research had not separated the effects of acid precipitation from those of other pollutants, it was not possible to estimate acid rain's contribution to the problem. Today, a number of ongoing studies, including a 10-year study by the National Park Service, are investigating acid rain's effect on common building materials. According to the EPA, the cost of repairing or replacing U.S. structures damaged by acid deposition is estimated to be at least $5 billion a year.

Another worrisome issue involving acid rain is its impact on human health. The air pollutants that form acid rain have well-established adverse health effects. Sulfur oxides, for example, can cause acute respiratory problems in young children, elderly people, and victims of asthma and other chronic disorders. In February 1987, a number of medical experts testified before Congress that such pollutants are a threat to human health, especially to children.

Scientists also believe that human health may be threatened by acid rain's ability to dissolve toxic metals, such as mercury, aluminum, and lead, from soil and from the pipes in water distribution systems. As a result, water used for cooking and drinking may be contaminated. And people may also take in these metals if they eat contaminated fish.

The joint U.S.-Canadian report issued after Reagan and Mulroney's 1985 summit meeting found a number of instances in which acid rain apparently caused elevated levels of toxic metals in lakes. But the report found "no clear evidence" of adverse health effects caused by drinking contaminated water or eating fish caught in contaminated lakes. Similarly, the NAPAP study found no indication of an immediate health threat. The U.S.-Canadian report also described little evidence of human health problems resulting from direct contact with acid rain. Scientists know, for example, that drops of acid rain do not cause any known damage to human skin. Nor would drinking acid rain damage the gastrointestinal tract, which withstands such highly acidic foods as vinegar and lemon juice.

Despite uncertainties about the actual impacts of acid rain, intensive efforts have begun in the United States, Canada, Europe, and Japan to find remedies for the problem. Some of these efforts focus on rescuing lakes already damaged by acid rain. One approach used in Scandinavia, the United States, and Canada involves the application of lime, which is highly alkaline, to neutralize the water of acidified lakes. But liming is, at best, a temporary solution if acid rain continues to fall in a region. Other approaches, aimed at side-stepping the effects of acid rain rather than eliminating acid rain itself, include the breeding of acid-tolerant fish and crops and coating valuable artwork and structures against corrosion.

But most people agree that control efforts should focus on preventing the creation of acid deposits in the first place. In 1981, stricter standards for automobile emissions of NO_x went into effect in the United States. Comparably strict standards were scheduled to go into effect in Canada in 1988. NO_x emissions are also being reduced by electric utilities and other industrial sources as they install boilers called low NO_x burners.

The major thrust in controlling acid rain pollution, however, is directed toward reducing sulfur dioxide emissions from electric generating stations that burn coal and oil. These stations are the biggest single source of sulfur dioxide. Thanks to air pollution control efforts, sulfur discharges from U.S. electric utilities have decreased by about 19 per cent since 1975.

Sulfur dioxide emissions can be reduced in a number of different ways. For example, coal-burning electric utilities can switch to low-sulfur coal, mined in some Western states, which produces only

Control Efforts

At a power plant in Kentucky, *right,* a process called fluidized bed combustion shows promise as a way to burn coal cleanly. At a Maryland inspection station, *below,* an attendant checks automobile emissions for acid-forming pollutants.

small quantities of sulfur dioxide. But switching from high-sulfur coal, which is mined in the Midwest and northern Appalachia, would eliminate coal-mining jobs and hurt the economy of those areas. Coal-cleaning, in which high-sulfur coal is treated before burning to reduce its sulfur content by up to 40 per cent, is another option. But this process also drives up fuel costs.

Some utilities have decided to continue burning high-sulfur coal but plan to remove up to 90 per cent of sulfur dioxide given off by installing pollution control devices called *scrubbers.* These devices spray a mixture containing water and an alkaline compound, such as pulverized limestone, to react with and capture sulfur dioxide before it can pass up the smokestack in exhaust gases.

Without such controls, older coal-fired plants will continue to be the major source of NO_x and sulfur dioxide. But many groups, including electric utilities and the coal industry, lobby vigorously against tightening air pollution standards because current methods of controlling sulfur emissions are expensive. Installing scrubbers on older coal-fired power plants—a major source of pollutants—would be expensive. Scrubbers also would increase operating and maintenance costs by billions of dollars, and those costs ultimately would be paid by the consumer. Acid rain legislation calling for a substantial reduction in sulfur emissions could increase electric bills by $2 billion to $11 billion nationwide per year, according to government estimates.

Coal-burning utilities have spent about $62 billion since the early 1970's to meet federal requirements on reducing the release of sulfur dioxide, according to the U.S. Department of Energy (DOE). Because the current methods for curbing acid rain pollutants are so costly, researchers are exploring *clean coal technologies*—new ways of burning coal cleanly, with the release of little sulfur dioxide—in the hope that they will provide the ultimate answer to the acid rain problem.

Clean coal technologies include a broad spectrum of approaches. These range from advanced techniques for cleaning high-sulfur coal before combustion, to converting coal to a clean gas similar to natural gas by processing it in special devices called *gasifiers*.

One technique of great interest, a process called *fluidized bed combustion*, burns coal with high efficiency, removing more than 90 per cent of the sulfur dioxide and 50 to 75 per cent of the NO_x during the combustion process. Fluidized-bed combustors, designed as economical replacements for obsolete boilers in older power plants, burn particles of pulverized coal and limestone suspended in a stream of upward-flowing air that makes the particles behave like a fluid. Pilot-scale fluidized-bed boilers have been undergoing tests for several years, and much larger units, intended to demonstrate the commercial feasibility of fluidized bed combustion, are planned.

A report issued by the DOE in February 1987 estimated that the federal government and industry will spend more than $6 billion between 1985 and 1992 to develop and demonstrate the commercial feasibility of clean coal technologies. Some states in the Midwest also have ambitious clean coal technology programs.

If clean coal technologies fulfill their promise, the United States and other countries will be able to reduce sulfur dioxide and NO_x emissions more effectively and economically than previously possible. These technologies could eliminate many concerns about acid rain—concerns that otherwise will increase in the future, as people continue to burn fossil fuels.

But until clean coal technologies are perfected and widely adopted—an outcome that may require the pressure of legislation—many scientists and other people will continue to worry about acid rain. For the foreseeable future, as we seek answers to this complex environmental issue, acid rain will continue to claim headlines and our concern.

For further reading:

Acid Rain, an *EPA Journal* special supplement. U.S. Environmental Protection Agency, 1986.
Pawlick, Thomas. *A Killing Rain*. Sierra Club Books, 1984.
Shaw, Robert W. "Air Pollution by Particles." *Scientific American*, August 1987.

The settlers who arrived in Sydney Cove 200 years ago would not recognize the Sydney Harbour of today. A painting of the landing of the first British fleet in Sydney in 1788, *above,* captures the natural beauty of an untamed land. The Sydney Harbour of 1988, *right,* reflects the grandeur of a modern, international port.

Australia:
Past and Present

In the following 30 pages, THE WORLD BOOK YEAR BOOK presents a special two-part section in celebration of Australia's bicentennial. The first part chronicles—in works of art—the colorful history of the land "down under." In the second part, an eminent Australian journalist gives a candid account of Australia today.

Natives Dancing at Brighton, Tasmania (about 1836),
an oil painting on canvas by John Glover; Mitchell Library, Sydney

Australia's Past in Pictures

For nearly 200 years, talented
Australian artists have recorded
their nation's colorful history.

The First Australians

Australia's first inhabitants were a dark-skinned people called Aborigines who migrated to Australia about 50,000 years ago, probably from Southeast Asia.

The 960 men and women aboard the 11 British ships that dropped anchor off the southeast coast of Australia in January 1788 could not have suspected that their arrival would be remembered. Most of the people on the ships were convicts, and their new home was to be a prison colony on the shore of a vast, unexplored land. But Australians have not forgotten that these prisoners helped found their country. In 1988, Australia is throwing a bicentennial party to celebrate its beginning.

Of course, Australia's history did not begin in 1788. About 50,000 years ago, a dark-skinned people called Aborigines migrated to Australia, probably from Southeast Asia. Europeans did not discover Australia until 1606, when Dutch sailors sighted the northeast coast. In 1770, James Cook of the British Navy explored Australia's eastern coast. He claimed the area for Great Britain, naming it New South Wales. It was there in 1788 that the British established the first prison colony, which grew into the city of Sydney.

Once the colony at New South Wales was established, the exploration of Australia began in earnest. During the early 1800's, explorers opened passes through the rugged Blue Mountains west of Sydney. Settlers and freed convicts soon followed. They found that the land of New South Wales was well suited to raising sheep and cattle. Most of the land was government property, so many settlers illegally occupied government land. Some of these illegal landholders—called *squatters*—set up huge ranches called *stations* and made fortunes in wool and beef. The squatters gradually won legal title to their land, and their descendants, called the *squattocracy*, today make up some of Australia's wealthiest and most powerful families.

In 1851, prospectors discovered gold in New South Wales and the neighboring colony of Victoria. The gold rush that followed attracted immigrants, and Australia's population grew rapidly. The gold miners—who were called *diggers*—were as rough and ready as the squatters and just as determined to make their fortunes in the desolate new land.

Australia was growing fast. Six self-governing British colonies had

European Discovery

The European discovery of Australia occurred in the early 1600's, when Dutch navigators sighted the continent. Captain James Cook of the British Navy explored the eastern coast in 1770, claimed the area for Great Britain, *below,* and named it New South Wales.

Captain Cook Taking Possession of Australia (1865), an engraving based on a woodcut by John Alexander Gilfillan; National Library of Australia, Canberra

The First Fleet in Sydney Cove, January 27, 1788 (1937), an oil painting
on canvas by John C. Allcot; National Library of Australia, Canberra

been established by 1859. In 1901, the colonies formed a
nation called the Commonwealth of Australia.

World events soon tested the strength of the new nation.
In 1914, Australia entered World War I on the side of Britain, and troops from Australia and New Zealand showed outstanding courage in the landing at Gallipoli, Turkey, in 1915.
The Great Depression of the 1930's left the Australian economy temporarily in ruins. The country experienced its darkest hour during World War II, however. In 1942, Japan
bombed Darwin and threatened to invade Australia. The
threat was removed when the United States repelled Japanese forces in the Battle of the Coral Sea.

Meanwhile, a growing sense of its own identity spurred
Australia to gradually dissolve its ties with Great Britain. But
it was not until the Australia Act 1986 that the last constitutional links between the two countries were severed.

Australia's heritage has been captured by many talented
artists. On these pages are paintings that bring to life the
nation's colorful past.

The First Fleet

The first white settlers
arrived in Australia in
1788 when Britain es-
tablished a prison col-
ony there. The first
shiploads of convicts
and guards, called the
First Fleet, landed in
what is now Sydney
Harbour, *above*. The
commander of the fleet
and governor of the
colony, Arthur Phillip,
chose the site for its
deep harbor and its wa-
ter supply and named it
Sydney after Thomas
Townshend, Viscount
Sydney, a member of
the British Cabinet.

The Rum Rebellion

Officers of a British Army regiment in Sydney called the New South Wales Corps sold rum and other supplies to the early colonists at high prices. The colony's governor, William Bligh—whose crew had mutinied in 1789 when he was captain of the *Bounty*— tried to stop the liquor trade. In 1808, the army officers took over the government in an uprising that became known as the Rum Rebellion. This picture shows Major George Johnston of the New South Wales Corps announcing the arrest of Bligh. In 1809, the British government replaced Bligh, suppressed the rebellion, and recalled the regiment to Britain.

Major Johnston Announcing the Arrest of Governor Bligh (1928), an oil painting on canvas by Raymond Lindsay; Geelong Art Gallery, Geelong, Victoria, Gift of Dame Nellie Melba

Detail of *The Crossing of the Blue Mountains* (1982), an oil painting on canvas
by Bob Booth; John Sands Promotional Products, Sydney

Crossing the Blue Mountains

Only a few coastal areas of Australia were settled by the early
1800's because the rugged Blue Mountains west of Sydney
blocked expansion. In 1813, pioneers Gregory Blaxland, William Lawson, and William Charles Wentworth crossed the barrier of the Blue Mountains. Other explorers soon followed,
finding additional passes through the mountains and opening
up new lands to settlers.

Sturt's Reluctant Decision to Return (1937), an oil painting on canvas by Ivor
H. T. Hele; Historic Memorials Collection, Parliament House, Canberra

Mining Camp at Bathurst (1851), an oil painting on canvas
by E. Tulloch; Dixson Galleries, Sydney

Exploring
the New Land

Charles Sturt, a British
military officer, ex-
plored New South
Wales and South Aus-
tralia from the 1820's to
the 1840's, looking for
an inland sea. In 1844,
Sturt led an expedition
from Adelaide, South
Australia, hoping to
reach the center of the
continent. But he could
not cross the Simpson
Desert, *above,* and was
forced to turn back.

Toward Self-Government

By 1851, Australia consisted of five British colonies, each ruled by a British governor. Government House in Sydney, *right,* was the official residence of the governor of New South Wales. In 1855 and 1856, Britain granted internal self-government to all the colonies except Western Australia, which did not achieve that status until 1890. Britain continued to handle foreign affairs and defense.

Detail of a water color with ink (about 1845) by Mrs. Allan Macpherson from her sketchbook *Scenes in New South Wales;* Mitchell Library, Sydney

The Gold Rush

Prospectors found gold in 1851 in New South Wales and Victoria, starting a gold rush that caused Australia's population to soar. Hoping to make their fortune, thousands of people from overseas flocked to mining camps like the one at the left near Bathurst, New South Wales. Many of the gold seekers, successful or not, decided to stay in Australia, and the country's population soared from about 400,000 in 1850 to more than 1.1 million in 1860.

The Squatter Period

Most of the best land in Australia belonged to the British government, but settlers called *squatters* began to occupy the land illegally in the 1820's. By the 1850's, many of the squatters had grown wealthy raising sheep and cattle, and they gradually gained legal title to their land. During their leisure time, the prosperous squatters enjoyed outings like the picnic shown below at Mrs. Macquarie's Chair, a seat facing Sydney Harbour carved in rock in 1816 for Elizabeth H. Macquarie, wife of Governor Lachlan Macquarie of New South Wales.

Picnic at Mrs. Macquarie's Chair (about 1855), an oil painting
on canvas by an unknown artist; Mitchell Library, Sydney

Thomas Baines with Aborigines near the Mouth of the Victoria River, N. T. (1857), an oil painting on canvas by Thomas Baines; National Library of Australia, Canberra

Exploration Continues

Exploration of Australia's interior continued throughout the 1800's. In 1855, Sir Augustus C. Gregory led an expedition to the source of the Victoria River in the Northern Territory. The artist and explorer Thomas Baines accompanied Gregory and painted the picture of the expedition shown above.

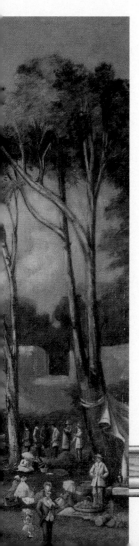

Industrial Growth

As Australia's population grew, manufacturing industries prospered because of the greater demand for goods. Industrial development quickened the growth of cities such as Melbourne, *right,* which became the financial center of Australia in the 1880's.

Detail of *Bank Place Melbourne* (about 1880), water color by Samuel T. Gill; Mitchell Library, Sydney

The Birth of a Nation

By 1901, there were six Australian colonies that joined together to form an independent nation called the Commonwealth of Australia. The federal Parliament opened at Melbourne, *below,* which served as the temporary capital until a new national capital was built at Canberra.

The Opening of the First Commonwealth Parliament in Melbourne's Exhibition Hall, 1901 (1903), an oil painting on canvas by Tom Roberts; National Library of Australia, Canberra

The Trumpet Calls (about 1915), a poster by Norman
Lindsay; Australian War Memorial, Canberra

World War I

Australia helped Britain and the other Allies
defeat Germany in World War I (1914-1918).
Posters súch as the one above helped recruit volunteers. By December 1914, three
months after the war started, more than
52,000 Australians had enlisted in a special
corps of Australian and New Zealand troops
called *Anzacs* (Australian and New Zealand
Army Corps). The Anzacs fought bravely
during the Allied landing at the Gallipoli
Peninsula in 1915 and gained a reputation
for outstanding courage.

The Great Depression

The Great Depression of the 1930's, a worldwide business slump, left the Australian economy temporarily in ruins. By 1933, during the worst of the depression, about one-third of Australia's workers had lost their jobs. The unemployed, *left,* marched through Melbourne, Sydney, and other cities demanding work.

At the Start of the March, 1932 (1944), an oil painting on hardboard by Noel J. Counihan; Art Gallery of New South Wales, Sydney

Raid over Darwin Harbour, 1942 (1975), a tempera painting on canvas and plywood by Keith Swain; Australian War Memorial, Canberra

World War II

Japanese planes bombed Darwin Harbour, *right,* in Australia's Northern Territory on Feb. 19, 1942, during World War II. More than 60 air raids followed, destroying about half the buildings in Darwin, the only area in Australia to suffer heavy damage from enemy attack. Australia and the other Allies, including Britain and the United States, defeated Germany and Japan in 1945.

Sydney Opera House (1968), an oil painting on canvas by Sir William Dobell; private collection, courtesy of the Australian Consulate General, New York City

A Great Nation

The towering concrete shells of the Sydney Opera House, *above,* completed in 1973, symbolize Australia's growth from a tiny prison colony to a great nation proud of its artistic heritage.

By Donald Horne

Australia's 200th Birthday

As they celebrate their bicentennial in 1988, Australians continue their search for a national identity and their place in the world.

Images of Australia that capture the country's beauty and character include, *clockwise from opposite page,* the distinctive Opera House in Sydney Harbour; Ayers Rock, a red-sandstone monolith in the Northern Territory; Paul Hogan, star of the movie *"Crocodile" Dundee;* and the Great Barrier Reef off the coast of Queensland.

A koala cub clings to its mother. The koala, a mammal that lives in trees, has long been a symbol of Australia.

The author:
Donald Horne is former editor of the Australian weekly *The Bulletin.* He is the author of numerous books about Australia, including the best-selling *The Lucky Country* (1964). He lives in Woollahra, New South Wales.

Australia celebrates its 200th birthday in 1988—or does it? It all depends on how you define *Australia*. If you mean the continent of Australia—rather than the nation—then Australia is much more than 200 years old. The continent now called Australia was formed between 95 million and 160 million years ago, when it began to break away from a large land mass that consisted of what are now the continents of Antarctica, Africa, Asia, Europe, North America, and South America.

If, however, you mean the time when Australia was first settled, that may have happened 50,000 years ago, when the ancestors of the present-day Aborigines, a dark-skinned people, arrived by sea, probably from Southeast Asia. On the other hand, if you mean the beginning of the European exploration of Australia, that began more than 300 years ago. In 1606, a Dutch navigator named Willem Jansz sailed along the coast of northeast Australia.

And if you mean the actual founding of the nation called Australia, then Australia is not even 100 years old. It was not until 1901 that the six Australian colonies—New South Wales, Queensland, South Australia, Tasmania, Victoria, and Western Australia—came together to form the Commonwealth of Australia.

What then does this bicentennial commemorate? It celebrates the arrival of the British in what is now Sydney, Australia's largest city, and the founding of the colony of New South Wales.

The puzzle of the 1988 celebration does not stop here, however. The people who established Australia's first British settlement in January 1788 were not like the Pilgrim Fathers who fled England 168 years earlier to establish Plymouth Colony in what is now Massachusetts. Nor did the axes that rang out among the trees of the newly named Sydney Cove belong to the traditional type of pioneers. The group that disembarked from the 11 British ships—along with 9 horses, 6 cattle, 44 sheep, 3 goats, and 28 pigs—included 570 male and 160 female convicts and 200 soldiers, some with their wives and children. What was being founded was a prison colony.

A land of contrasts

Although there is historical basis for this bicentennial, many Australians are not sure if there really is anything to celebrate. Since the late 1960's, Australians have been searching for an identity, both as a people and as an international power. And while much has been accomplished toward this end, Australians are still uncertain who they are. One reason for their confusion is that Australia is such a land of contrasts. The country's art and entertainment industries for decades promoted Australia as a land of wild, open spaces called the *bush* or the *outback*. Australia is probably best known to the rest of the world for the unusual wildlife that inhabits the bush—including such animals as the kangaroo and the koala. And when human beings are visible in this wilderness they are depicted as tough

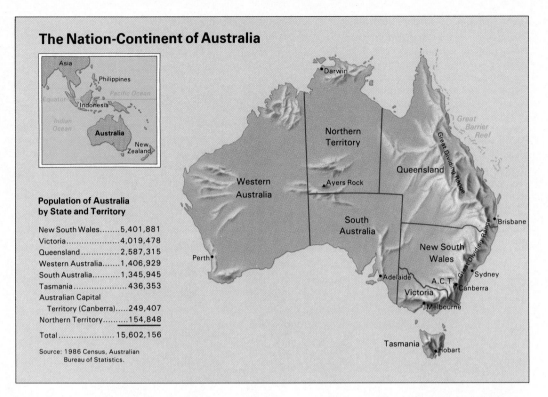

The Nation-Continent of Australia

Population of Australia by State and Territory

New South Wales	5,401,881
Victoria	4,019,478
Queensland	2,587,315
Western Australia	1,406,929
South Australia	1,345,945
Tasmania	436,353
Australian Capital Territory (Canberra)	249,407
Northern Territory	154,848
Total	15,602,156

Source: 1986 Census, Australian Bureau of Statistics.

people, like the rough-and-ready character of "Crocodile" Dundee in the 1986 hit movie of that name.

This picture of Australia is true—in part. The country does have vast open spaces. When some of its poets, painters, and filmmakers portray it as a land of huge deserts, they are not exaggerating, for about one-third of Australia is uninhabitable desert. Ayers Rock, a monolith of glowing sandstone that rises 1,000 feet (300 meters) from a semidesert plain in the Northern Territory, is a national symbol of the land's desolation. Australians call it "the Red Heart." But a more appropriate symbol of Australia is the red brick bungalow. For although Australia has by far the lowest population of any continent—except Antarctica—it is also the most suburbanized nation in the world. More than 85 per cent of its 16 million inhabitants live in urban areas.

Another of Australia's remarkable contrasts is found in its people, who are as comfortable with their macho reputation as sports fanatics and beer drinkers as with their more refined image as scholars and artists. Australians take great pride in their sporting victories. For some, the nation was reborn in 1983 when an Australian yacht won the America's Cup yacht race, breaking the United States 132-year winning streak. Besides being avid fans of boating and water sports, Australians enjoy tennis and cricket; Australian rules football, a sport invented in Australia; Rugby and soccer, two football

Australia lies between the Indian and Pacific oceans. It mainly consists of desert and grassland. Australia—the nation—is a federation of six states and two territories. Since 1945, the country's population has doubled, reaching approximately 16 million in 1987.

Australia's flag has a British Union Flag or Union Jack, five stars for the constellation Southern Cross, and a large star for the Commonwealth of Australia.

Land of Cities and Wilderness

Australia is an arid land. Because of this, approximately 95 per cent of its people live along the eastern and southwestern coasts, where there is enough rainfall to support a large population, *below.* The most populated region is the southeast, where 75 per cent of all Australians live. The rest of the country is sparsely inhabited. This uneven population distribution has created great contrasts in the Australian landscape, from sprawling cities along the coast, like Sydney, *right,* to miles of desolate land in the interior, *bottom.*

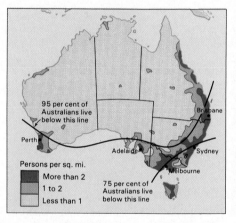

95 per cent of Australians live below this line

Perth

Brisbane

Adelaide

Sydney

Melbourne

75 per cent of Australians live below this line

Persons per sq. mi.

More than 2

1 to 2

Less than 1

games invented by the British; golf and lawn bowling; and horse racing.

In contrast, some of Australia's finest achievements have been in the laboratory—not on the football field. Australia has produced three Nobel Prize winners in science. Physician and virologist Sir Macfarlane Burnet shared the 1960 Nobel Prize for physiology or medicine for his research on organ transplants; physiologist Sir John Carew Eccles shared the 1963 Nobel Prize in the same category for his research on the transmission of nerve impulses; and chemist John Warcup Cornforth shared the 1975 Nobel Prize for chemistry for his work on the chemical synthesis of organic compounds. Australia has also proved itself a leader in developing alternative energy sources, such as wind power and sea power, and in developing *in vitro fertilization*, a process in which mammalian male and female sex cells are united in a test tube or some other artificial environment.

From Mel Gibson to Patrick White

There have been significant achievements in arts and entertainment as well. For many years, Australians looked to Great Britain for artistic inspiration. Today, Australian artists and entertainers draw influence from many other countries. More important, they believe that their own society and culture can provide them with the inspiration they need—and the financial support necessary to make a living.

Australian films have given audiences around the world glimpses of the country's landscape and people, and insight into its folklore and history. Australia has exported such films as *The Chant of Jimmie Blacksmith* (1980), an adaptation of Thomas Keneally's novel about an Aborigine's war with white society; *My Brilliant Career* (1980), the story of a young woman of the bush who must decide between marriage and a writing career; and *The Year of Living Dangerously* (1983), the story of an Australian journalist in Indonesia. These films—and others—have showcased the talents of Mel Gibson, Judy Davis, Bryan Brown, and other Australian actors.

Australian fiction has also attracted attention. The complex prose of Patrick White, winner of the 1973 Nobel Prize for literature and author of such novels as *The Tree of Man* (1955) and *Voss* (1957), and the verse and fiction of other Australian writers have found audiences in Europe, Great Britain, and the United States. There are lively schools of painting, drama, and dance. The Opera House in Sydney, with its distinctive saillike roofs, is Australia's greatest single tourist attraction.

But the greatest contrast in Australia may be in its economic life. Thanks to technological advances in agriculture, Australia's farms are among the most efficient in the world. Yet its manufacturing industries have one of the worst records for technological innovation. Most of Australia's industry is involved in manufacturing such

The Faces of Australia

In the early 1900's, most Australians—except for the Aborigines—were British or Irish immigrants or their descendants. But since the 1950's, Australia has welcomed people from all over the world. By 1985, 15 per cent of Australians were born in Europe—in such countries as Greece and Italy—and more than 3 per cent were born in the Middle East and Asia, *below.* As a result, Australia has become more ethnically diverse.

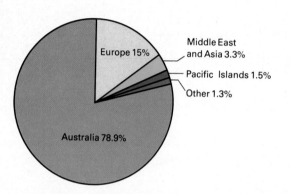

Europe 15%

Middle East and Asia 3.3%

Pacific Islands 1.5%

Other 1.3%

Australia 78.9%

Source: Australian Bureau of Statistics (1985 estimates).

Clockwise from above:
Greek children, wearing
traditional Greek cos-
tumes, attend a festival
in Sydney; an Austral-
ian street scene shows
the European—espe-
cially British and Irish—
ancestry of many Aus-
tralians; a group of Ab-
origine children in West-
ern Australia learn how
to play a didgeridoo, a
musical instrument
used in Aborigine reli-
gious ceremonies; and
Asian stores line a neighborhood street in a
Sydney suburb.

Miles of coastline encourage Australians to participate in a variety of water sports, such as windsurfing, *right*. Australians are also avid fans of Australian rules football, *far right,* a sport that was invented in Australia.

products as shoes, electronics, and appliances—using equipment and techniques imported from other countries.

Why is this? The reason may lie in Australia's history as an economic outpost of the British Empire. At that time, Australia's role was to sell raw materials—farming and mining products—to Great Britain and to buy British manufactured goods in return. When manufacturing industries were finally established in Australia, their management tended to look to other countries for technological innovation—rather than relying on or developing their own ideas. As a result, many of Australia's industries are now owned or controlled by foreign interests.

In terms of physical resources—especially minerals—Australia is one of the world's richest countries. It has major deposits of coal, bauxite (a mineral from which aluminum is made), gold, zinc, iron, copper, uranium, and even diamonds. Australia is also the largest producer of wool in the world. And even though much of its land is inhospitable, it supports highly productive wheat and cattle farms. But unlike other advanced countries rich in resources, Australia still gets almost all of its export income from mining and agricultural products—rather than from more expensive goods made from these raw materials.

The phrase "the lucky country" was used to describe this situation—in which Australian businesses were so similar to businesses in more innovative industrial societies that Australians could copy their methods without working up ideas of their own.

A nation of immigrants

When the decision was made to have a 200th birthday party, there was concern that the occasion should not seem to be devoted to just the arrival of the British in 1788, which began the forcible eviction of the Aborigines from their tribal lands. For that reason, officials chose "Living Together" as the bicentennial theme. They hoped this theme would dramatize another one of Australia's contrasts—that a country once considered by many people to be an ethnically exclusive society now embraced people from many different cultural backgrounds.

Until World War II, the single most significant thing about Australia was its connection with the British Empire. Once a year, on Empire Day, Australia celebrated its membership in what was called "the British race." But in 1942, during World War II, Australia received a shock that changed its history. Japanese troops conquered what is now Malaysia, a country northeast of Australia, and for a while the Japanese seemed on the brink of invading Australia. After the war, realizing that it could no longer rely on Britain to protect it from military invasion, and that its small population could not adequately defend such a large continent, the Australian government decided that the country must "populate or perish." It intended to increase the population with immigrants from Britain, but there were not enough British immigrants available. So, for the first time in its history, Australia encouraged immigrants from other countries.

Art and Entertainment, Australian Style

Australians are taking new pride in art and entertainment that reflects their country's spirit.

Popular cultural events include a blues festival in Sydney, *above.* Australian films, such as *Mad Max Beyond Thunderdome* (1985), *above right,* introduced worldwide audiences to Mel Gibson and other Australian actors. Many Australian artists and writers—such as operatic soprano Joan Sutherland, *right,* and Nobel Prize-winning novelist Patrick White, *far right*—have won international acclaim.

And come they did. During World War II, the population of Australia was about 7 million, mainly people of British or Irish ancestry. Today, about 21 per cent of the approximately 16 million people living in Australia were born in continental Europe and in Asia, Africa, and other parts of the world. At first, the Australian government attempted to assimilate the new immigrants that poured into the country—to make them "instant" Australians. These unreal expectations failed. Since then, the government has adopted a more tolerant and realistic program that allows for cultural diversity—provided immigrants learn to speak English, the official language, and agree to respect Australian institutions.

What is most remarkable about this new ethnic diversity is that Australia's white-only immigration policy was abandoned without the expected social discord. A law passed by Australia's first Parliament in 1901 allowed the exclusion of all non-Europeans as immigrants. It was not until 1961 that the influential magazine *The Bulletin* dropped from its masthead the slogan "Australia for the White Man." And it took another four years for the Australian Labor Party to drop the white-only policy from its platform.

Today, a little more than 2 per cent of the population was born in Asia. Most of these Asian immigrants speak English and fit easily into Australian society. But since the late 1970's, Australia has become home to thousands of Vietnamese refugees. Unlike other Asian immigrants, many of these people speak little or no English. Their arrival has spurred debate on their integration into Australian society, but so far there has been no real social friction.

Mining and agriculture are vital to Australia's economy. Mount Newman in Western Australia, *right,* is one of Australia's largest iron-ore producing areas. On an Australian sheep station, *below,* a worker rides a motorcycle—rather than a horse—to herd a flock of sheep into a pasture. Australia is one of the world's leading wool producers.

There has even been a change in attitude about the Aborigines. The Aborigines were once seen by many Australians as an inferior—and dying—race. When British colonization began, there were more than 300,000 Aborigines in Australia. Because many Aborigines were killed or forced from their land by settlers, their numbers dwindled. By 1901, there were about 80,000 Aborigines left. In the early 1900's, when it became clear that the Aborigines would not die out as a race, the government began a program designed to assimilate them into Australian society by attempting to wipe out their culture. But Aboriginal culture survived. In the 1960's, the government's assimilation policy came under attack, and a movement began to protect the Aborigines' unique way of life.

Australia has begun to give Aborigines greater control over their future. Their population is growing once again, and there are now more than 200,000 Aborigines living in Australia. They have the same civil rights as other Australian citizens. A move to restore their land rights began in 1966, but this movement has drawn great opposition from mining companies and from some conservative Australians. Even with these great strides, the death rate among Aborigines is still much higher than that of other Australians, while their levels of employment and education are quite low.

Many other minority ethnic groups in Australia are also disadvantaged. As in other countries, the lowest-paying jobs often go to immigrants who cannot speak English. Minorities are underrepresented in the leadership of labor unions and political parties. And although Australia's government has proved tolerant of its growing minority population, many native-born Australians are still prejudiced against foreigners. But these negatives should not overshadow the great progress that Australia has made in opening its doors to nonwhites.

A scientist in Sydney examines a plant that has been *cloned* (reproduced asexually). Plant clones are used to measure the effects of the environment and chemicals on genetically identical plants. These plants may one day be used to improve Australia's crop yields.

Australia's Prime Minister Bob Hawke meets with Hu Yaobang, then head of China's Communist Party, underlining Australia's determination to strengthen its economic and cultural ties with its neighbors in Asia and the Pacific.

Australia's place in the world

If Australia does have something to celebrate in 1988, it may be its growing role as an independent power in Southeast Asia. It took Australians a long time to break their dependency on Great Britain. Although the shocks of World War II demonstrated Australia's vulnerability in Southeast Asia, some Australians continued to believe in the protective force of British military power until the late 1960's, when Britain finally pulled its forces out of the area. But by that time, most Australians had come to support the 1941 declaration of John Curtin, then prime minister of Australia. In response to the Japanese military advance in World War II, he said, "I make it quite clear that Australia looks to America [for military support], free of any pangs as to our traditional links of kinship with the United Kingdom."

Since then, the belief in United States military power has been fundamental to Australia's military strategy. In 1951, Australia joined the United States and New Zealand in a collective defense agreement called the *ANZUS* treaty. Most Australians see this agreement as a basic part of Australia's strategic planning even though Australia was drawn into the Vietnam War, a conflict as widely unpopular in Australia as in the United States. In 1984, when New Zealand's government imposed a ban on U.S. ships carrying nuclear weapons within New Zealand waters, the Australian government did not support the ban. And when the United States retaliated in 1986 by ending its military cooperation with New Zealand under the ANZUS treaty, U.S. military cooperation continued with Australia.

But Australia has not just switched from one military dependency to another. There have been two developments that mark a big change in Australia's international role. One has been the development of independent military power. The belief has grown that—short of nuclear war—any military threats that may confront Australia within the foreseeable future can be handled by Australia alone, without the aid of the United States or any other outside power.

The other development reflects a change in the attitude of Australians toward their Asian neighbors. They no longer feel as threatened by their closeness to Asia as they did in the 1950's and 1960's. After the postwar collapse of European and U.S. colonial control in Asia, Australians felt deserted and uneasy. But now, many of them see the economic benefits of their position between the Indian Ocean and the South Pacific Ocean. Japan and other nearby Asian countries have become some of Australia's most promising markets. As tourists, Australians have a growing interest in Asian destinations, particularly Japan. Cultural relations have also strengthened, with notable Asian influences on some Australian artists. And aside from the influx of Asian immigrants, tens of thousands of Asian students have studied at Australian universities.

Australia in the 1980's

Australia is still growing up. The country has at last adopted its own national anthem, "Advance Australia Fair," which replaced the British anthem "God Save the Queen" in 1984. The Australia Act 1986 severed all remaining constitutional links between Great Britain and Australia, except the constitutional monarch. Australia still accepts Queen Elizabeth II as its monarch.

As Australia moves toward the year 2000, it is a much more independent, tolerant, and open society than it was 100 years ago. To many, this is a just cause for celebration. To others, however, Australia still has a long way to go to match the technological innovations of other advanced industrial societies, and to be able to meet the demands of its growing international relationships. To these Australians, the question of what is being celebrated in 1988 remains unanswered. Perhaps by the year 2001, when the country commemorates the centennial of the Commonwealth of Australia, Australians may have a more confident response to that question.

For further reading:

Carroll, John. *Intruders in the Bush: The Australian Quest for Identity.* Oxford Univ. Press, 1982.
Hughes, Robert. *The Fatal Shore.* Knopf, 1986.
Terrill, Ross. *The Australians.* Simon & Schuster, 1987.

By Eileen M. Crimmins
and Richard A. Easterlin

The Graying of America

How will the rapidly increasing number
of aged people affect the well-being
of the elderly—and the rest of society?

Grow old along with me!
The best is yet to be,
The last of life, for which the first was made.
                                    Robert Browning

The United States population is growing older.
In 1987, 12 per cent of Americans were 65 years
old or older, compared with 8 per cent in 1950.
Population experts at the U.S. Bureau of the Census expect this percentage to continue to rise
gradually, reaching 14 per cent in 2010, then to
skyrocket during the next 20 years, reaching 21
per cent by 2030. This "graying of America" has
generated concerns about whether the best really
is yet to be, about how well off tomorrow's elderly
will be. There also are questions about the impact
of an aging population on the rest of society.

A major expense always confronting the elderly
is the cost of health care. As their numbers
increase, will their Medicare federal health-
insurance benefits still be adequate? Will hospital
and medical bills drive many older people into
poverty?

One result of the growing percentage of the elderly in our society is that a shrinking percentage of working Americans will have to fund sharply higher social security and Medicare benefits. How will the necessary increases in payroll deductions affect the workers? Will they remain willing to fund the programs?

Economists wonder how the graying of America will affect the U.S. business scene. As the percentage of working Americans shrinks, will the economy become less productive? Will the United States suffer a labor shortage?

Business executives want to know how the graying will affect specific sectors of the economy. What will the elderly buy? How many of them will live by themselves? How many will live with their children or with other older people in nursing homes or retirement communities? How many of them will move to a different part of the country?

And how will the emergence of a large elderly population affect political attitudes? Will the views—and the votes—of tomorrow's elderly differ markedly from those of younger individuals? How strongly will the elderly support education, family services, and other youth-oriented programs?

No one can be sure of the answers to these questions. We can obtain valuable clues, however, by determining why the graying is underway, analyzing the manner of living of today's elderly and the individuals who will become tomorrow's elderly, and assessing what U.S. society already has done on behalf of its older people.

Why America is turning gray

The graying of America has two causes, both easy to see with the help of a few statistics. First, advances in medical care have enabled people to live longer. In the United States in 1900, the average life expectancy at birth was 47.3 years. By 1985, the latest year for which figures are available, it had climbed to 74.7 years.

Second, the U.S. birth rate rose in the mid-1900's, interrupting a long, slow decline. A dramatic increase occurred during this rise. From 1945 to 1947, the rate jumped from 20.4 births for every 1,000 people to 26.6. In 1957, the birth rate was still high—25.3— but then began to decline. The birth rate dropped to the 1933 level of 18.4 in 1966, and by 1985, it was 15.7.

The combination—fewer children being born and a longer life expectancy—led to the higher percentage of older people in U.S. society. And the population will age so dramatically between 2010 and 2030 because the unusually large number of people who were born between 1945 and 1965 will reach age 65 during those years.

The authors:
Eileen M. Crimmins is an associate professor at the Andrus Gerontology Center at the University of Southern California (USC) in Los Angeles. Richard A. Easterlin is a professor of economics at USC.

The baby boom

The years from 1945 to 1965 encompass what has been called the *baby boom* because during that period, birth rates were sharply

A Nation Growing Older

The number of elderly people in the United States will skyrocket in the next century with the aging of the *baby boomers*—the 82 million individuals born between 1945 and 1965.

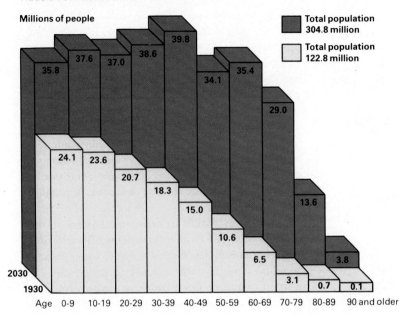

Millions of people

Total population 304.8 million

Total population 122.8 million

35.8 37.6 37.0 38.6 39.8 34.1 35.4 29.0

24.1 23.6 20.7 18.3 15.0 10.6 6.5 13.6 3.8 3.1 0.7 0.1

2030

1930

Age 0-9 10-19 20-29 30-39 40-49 50-59 60-69 70-79 80-89 90 and older

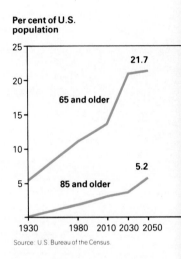

Per cent of U.S. population

25

21.7

20

65 and older

15

10

5.2

5

85 and older

1930   1980   2010 2030 2050

Source: U.S. Bureau of the Census.

higher than they were in the decades immediately before and after. The conclusion of World War II and the return of servicemen to civilian life in 1945 caused the dramatic rise in the birth rate at the beginning of the baby boom.

Behind this rise in the birth rate was a phenomenon that also accounts for much of the present behavior of *baby boomers* (the people born during the baby boom) and helps to answer our questions. This phenomenon links the size of a generation to the income potential of workers who belong to that generation. The smaller the generation, the smaller the number of people competing for jobs, and therefore the greater the workers' ability to earn money.

The relatively small size of the generations of young people reaching the labor market in the two decades before 1960 increased their earning potential. This increase in earnings, in turn, had a major impact on the birth rate. Couples did not have to wait so long to earn enough money to support a family. Consequently, young people married earlier, and fewer young wives worked to supplement their husbands' incomes. As a result, the birth rate climbed.

After 1960, however, the baby boomers began to arrive on the job market. This increasing generation size caused the earning potential of young couples to decline as more and more workers competed for the available jobs. Therefore, more young women went to work to add to family income, and childbearing was reduced or delayed. Consequently, the birth rate fell.

In the year 2030, *above left,* the U.S. population will be distributed fairly evenly among 10-year age groups ranging from birth through 69 years old. By contrast, the distribution 100 years earlier formed a stairstep pattern—population declining steadily with age. The percentage of elderly people, *above,* will soar during the years from 2010 to 2030, when the baby boomers celebrate their 65th birthdays. As the boomers continue to age, there will be a sudden increase in the percentage of people 85 and older between 2030 and 2050.

101

Experience Better than Expectations

Growing old in the United States does not seem to create as many problems as some people think it will. A poll showed that adults of all ages said certain problems were "very serious" for the elderly. But among people 65 years old and older, much lower percentages said that these problems were actually "very serious" for themselves.

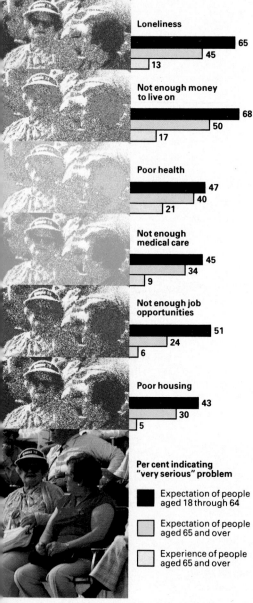

Loneliness
65
45
13

Not enough money to live on
68
50
17

Poor health
47
40
21

Not enough medical care
45
34
9

Not enough job opportunities
51
24
6

Poor housing
43
30
5

Per cent indicating "very serious" problem

■ Expectation of people aged 18 through 64

□ Expectation of people aged 65 and over

□ Experience of people aged 65 and over

Source: © National Council on the Aging. Data are for 1981.

Will tomorrow's older people have an adequate income?

Until the 1970's, the per capita income of individuals over 64 years old was substantially below that of other adults. This is no longer the case, due largely to advances in federal programs such as social security and Medicare, plus the economic success of individuals reaching retirement age. The incidence of poverty among the old has declined sharply since the 1970's and is now below the national average. Unfortunately, some older people are still in dire need—especially some widows and members of minority groups—but the gulf between the average economic condition of the elderly and that of the younger population has disappeared.

Changes in social security regulations should prevent this gulf from reappearing. Because of a change made in 1972, for example, social security benefits increase automatically to reflect the rise of the Consumer Price Index, a measure of inflation. Unless federal programs for the aged are cut sharply, the income of the older population will probably continue to grow.

People who will retire in the next two decades were born in the 1920's and 1930's, when the birth rate was declining. Their numbers were scarce as they entered the labor market during the economic boom that occurred after the end of World War II. Consequently, they have been a highly successful generation in terms of income. Many of them have saved money and have invested in private retirement programs such as company thrift plans, individual retirement accounts, stocks, and bonds. The benefits of such programs will reach a large proportion of the population for the first time as this generation retires, raising the income level of the elderly.

The baby boom generation was not so fortunate. The large size of this generation lowered baby boomers' wages and raised their unemployment rates relative to other workers.

The baby boomers have responded to their difficult circumstances, however. By remaining single or childless, having fewer children, or combining working with raising children, they have been able to keep pace with the rise in the general population's standard of living. In addition, they have

Companionship: Satisfactory for more elderly people than expected.

Contrary to expectations, old age is not a lonely time for most people. Rather than spend untold hours watching television in virtual isolation, *above left,* typical elderly individuals in the United States participate in family affairs and pursue group activities such as ceramics classes, *above.*

invested heavily in private retirement programs, so they also should be able to maintain a relatively favorable economic status after they retire.

How healthy will the elderly be?

Tomorrow's older people are likely to be healthier as well as more affluent, thanks to advances in medicine and the increasing adoption of more healthful patterns of individual behavior. Such advances and behavioral changes have already had a dramatic effect on the health of the elderly in the United States. Between 1940 and 1985, the death rate of people over 64 fell by 29 per cent.

This rapid decrease resulted in large measure from a decline in the number of deaths due to heart disease. Factors responsible for this decline included the development of new drugs and surgical treatments, changes in eating habits to reduce cholesterol intake, and—beginning in the mid-1960's—a fall-off in the percentage of individuals who smoke.

Continued improvement in diet, the pursuit of exercise programs, further reductions in smoking, stepped-up treatment of alcoholism, and increased understanding of the importance of preventive medicine will likely cut the death rate of the elderly even more. In addition, medical science almost certainly will continue to make advances in the diagnosis and treatment of diseases.

When medical care *is* needed, tomorrow's elderly will be more capable of paying for it—because of their higher incomes—than are today's elderly. And old people will continue to benefit, of course, from publicly supported health-care programs such as Medicare and Medicaid.

Money: Income for Most Is Adequate and Rising.

The average income of individuals 65 years old and older has been rising more rapidly than inflation. Since the mid-1970's, social security benefits have replaced wages and salaries as the main income source for families headed by elderly people.

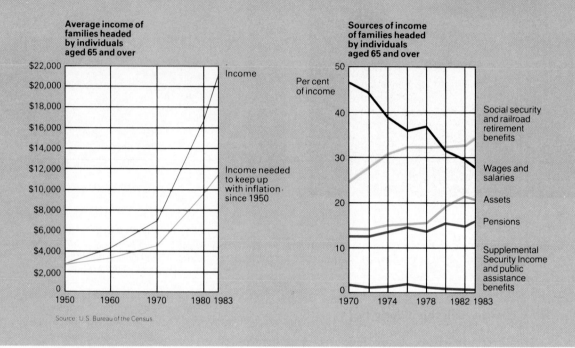

Average income of families headed by individuals aged 65 and over

Income

Income needed to keep up with inflation since 1950

Source: U.S. Bureau of the Census

Sources of income of families headed by individuals aged 65 and over

Per cent of income

Social security and railroad retirement benefits

Wages and salaries

Assets

Pensions

Supplemental Security Income and public assistance benefits

Funding the benefits

Will the cost of publicly supported programs for the elderly be too much for tomorrow's working population to handle? Social security and Medicare are funded through payroll taxes paid by workers and employers. As the number of older people grows, the cost of these programs will rise, so more and more tax revenue will be needed to pay for them.

The rates at which individuals and businesses are taxed, however, will not necessarily rise in proportion to the revenue hike. The most obvious reason for unequal increases is the growth in the nation's taxable income. Part of this growth is due to inflation, but the remainder represents *real economic growth*—increased production of goods and performance of services.

In mathematical terms, tax revenue is the product of a tax rate and taxable income. So if tax rates remain steady as taxable income increases due to inflationary and real growth, revenues will rise. Because individual social security and Medicare benefits will rise automatically in proportion to inflation but not to real growth, tax revenues will rise more rapidly than individual benefits. Thus, the

Health: Only half as common a problem as the elderly fear.

America's elderly generally enjoy good health, thanks in large measure to regular exercise—whether by purely natural means, *below left,* or with the aid of exercise equipment, *below right.*

growth of the economy will tend to compensate for the increase in the number of people receiving social security and Medicare benefits.

At present, the U.S. *gross national product* (GNP, or the total output of goods and services) is growing more rapidly than are total federal outlays for programs for the elderly. In other words, the percentage of the GNP spent on these programs is declining.

In 1982, a record high of 9.7 per cent of the GNP—nearly a dime for every dollar—went to fund programs for the elderly. This percentage will shrink to 9.1 per cent by 1990, according to John L. Palmer, a senior fellow at the Urban Institute, an independent research organization based in Washington, D.C., dealing with social and economic problems; and Stephanie G. Gould, a consultant for the Urban Institute and the World Bank, an international organi-

When the elderly require health care, good service is as available to them as it is to younger people. In fact, the elderly get an extra financial boost from Medicare—a federal health insurance program designed just for them.

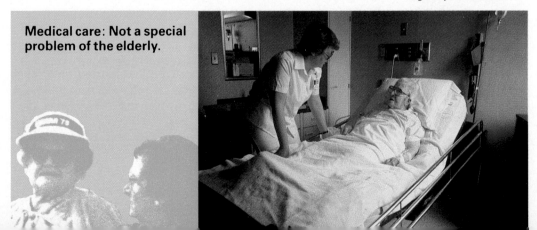

Medical care: Not a special problem of the elderly.

zation that lends money to countries to fund development projects.

Palmer and Gould expect a reversal to begin in the 1990's, however, with the outlays growing more rapidly than the GNP. They predict that, because of this reversal, the percentage of the GNP spent on programs for the elderly will rise gradually, reaching 10.2 per cent in 2010.

Then the baby boomers will begin to turn 65, accelerating the rise. By 2030, the contribution will amount to 13.0 per cent of the GNP. This figure represents a jump of 27 per cent from the figure for 2010. (In other words, 13.0 is 127 per cent of 10.2.)

The predicted jump seems to imply a need to raise the average federal tax rate by 27 per cent between 2010 and 2030 to ensure there is enough money to fund programs for the elderly. This whopping increase would mean that, for every dollar of tax an individual paid in 2010, a person with the same taxable income in 2030 would have to come up with $1.27. Whether such a hike will actually be required, however, is anybody's guess. If other federal expenditures—for national defense, agriculture, transportation, or education, for example—decreased as a percentage of the GNP, there would be less upward pressure on the tax rate.

Growth may lighten the burden

But even if the tax rate rose sharply, the burden on workers would almost certainly be lighter than if rates went up today. Because of real economic growth, per capita real income may be 75 per cent higher in 2030 than in 1987, according to Palmer and Gould. In other words, in 2030, a worker whose earnings equal the

Housing: Only 1 of 20 elderly people experiences a "very serious" problem.

Where the Elderly Live

An elderly widow who lives alone, *right,* tends her roses with a neighbor. More elderly women than men reside alone in the United States, *below right,* because most wives outlive their husbands. For the same reason, the vast majority of men aged 65 and older live with their wives.

nation's per capita income may be able to afford 75 per cent more goods and services than his or her 1987 counterpart could afford. This means, for example, that the same proportion of earnings that would buy 100 loaves of bread in 1987 might buy 175 loaves in 2030. For all practical purposes—including the shouldering of a tax burden as well as the buying of bread—the worker in 2030 might be much richer than the 1987 counterpart (because 175 is much larger than 100).

Furthermore, the proportion of young dependents—infants and children under 18 years old—to the working population may be 15 per cent lower in 2030 than it was in 1987. Clearly, such circumstances would make it considerably easier for workers to shoulder the burden of a tax increase generated by federal programs for the elderly. Realistically, then, there seems little reason for pessimism. The graying of America may create a budget problem 30 or 40 years from now, but the problem seems manageable.

The elderly and the economy

Not all visions of the impact of the graying of America are optimistic. Some analysts foresee a faltering economy, an overburdened federal budget, and even conflict between generations.

Some of the fear for the future of the U.S. economy stems from concerns about population decline, which would reduce the growth of U.S. markets and diminish opportunities for making the business investments on which a vigorous economy depends. According to even the lowest projections of the U.S. Bureau of the Census, however, the U.S. population will still be increasing in 2030.

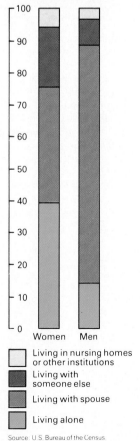

Per cent of Americans aged 65 and older

Women   Men

- Living in nursing homes or other institutions
- Living with someone else
- Living with spouse
- Living alone

Source: U.S. Bureau of the Census

107

Big Bill Coming Due

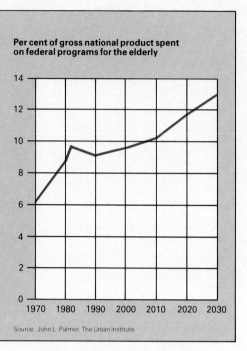

Per cent of gross national product spent on federal programs for the elderly

Source: John L. Palmer, The Urban Institute.

Spending for social security, Medicare, and other federal programs for older people will soar between 2010 and 2030 as the baby boomers born between 1945 and 1965 add their tremendous numbers to the ranks of the elderly. The total tax dollars going for such programs declined during the mid-1980's as a percentage of *gross national product* (GNP, or the nation's total output of goods and services) because the GNP grew rapidly. As more Americans grow old, however, federal outlays for programs for the elderly will grow faster than the GNP.

Another pessimistic analysis predicts that the United States will suffer a labor shortage that will retard economic growth. According to this analysis, the average retirement age will continue to decline. This decline—combined with the decrease in the birth rate already underway—will slow the growth of the work force so much that there will be too few workers for the needs of business and industry.

This concern needs to be put into historical perspective. In the two decades following World War II, the retirement age was falling and young workers were in short supply because they had been born during an era of declining birth rates in the 1920's and 1930's. Yet the economy grew rapidly. The scarcity of labor pushed wages upward, spurring businesses to invest heavily in automation and other labor-saving innovations.

The elderly as consumers

As the proportion of older Americans increases and their relative economic status improves, the demand for various goods and services will change. Most important will be the rise in the demand for health care. The elderly already spend a great deal on medical care. In 1982 and 1983, for example, about 10 per cent of the money spent by people over 64 went for health insurance, medical services, prescription drugs, and medical supplies, compared with 4.4 per cent for the general population.

The most important items on which older consumers spend *less* than the population as a whole are obvious—personal insurance and retirement investments. Currently, older people also differ from other adults in spending a larger percentage of their income on food and housing, but as their relative economic status improves, this difference is likely to diminish.

The aging of the population also affects the geographic distribution of the population. Although mobility rates among the elderly are lower than among younger people, in 1979 almost 1 out of 5 people over 64 had moved within the preceding four years. And almost half of those moves represented a substantial change in geographic location—to a different county or state, or even another country.

The redistribution of the older population has chiefly favored the so-called Sun Belt states in the South and West—most notably Florida—which offer such inducements as a warmer winter climate and lower heating costs. The areas suffering most from this redistribution were the industrial areas in the Northeastern states, particularly the cities.

Most elderly people who relocate to the South and West are retirees who can afford to leave the places where they worked—in effect, to burn bridges of financial opportunity behind them. As income continues to rise among the elderly, more of them will be able to afford such moves, so this pattern of redistribution will likely become increasingly pronounced. This implies that a growing proportion of older people will live apart from relatives, often in retirement communities with other elderly people who may share their interests.

Relocations and increases in demand for certain goods and services will boost the prosperity of various types of businesses as the population ages. Clearly, the health-care industry will be in splendid shape. Another thriving business will be the construction of retirement communities in sunny climes.

Industries associated with travel will benefit from the graying of America, if a survey conducted in 1980 by the National Council on the Aging is any indication. According to the survey, more than 50 per cent of people over 64 reported that their favorite leisure activity was travel—a shot in the arm for tomorrow's resorts, motels, airlines, and even producers of such items as recreational vehicles, luggage, and cameras. Photography finished third in the survey at 31 per cent—another boost for manufacturers of cameras, or video cameras, or whatever sophisticated device tomorrow's elderly "shutterbugs" will use. And tomorrow's travelers certainly will eat out more—a plus for the restaurant industry.

Second in the survey—at 42 per cent—was the broad category of needlepoint, weaving, and handiwork, indicating a tremendous future market for tools such as woodworking machinery and looms, and basic craft items such as yarns and beads. Tomorrow's handicrafts industry will receive further support from two additional cat-

The Elderly as Consumers
The growth of the elderly population will boost several parts of the United States market, including sectors that cater to their pleasures, such as the travel industry, *below left,* and segments that meet their needs, such as the drug industry, *below.*

egories in the survey's "top 10"—painting or drawing, and pottery or ceramics.

No industry is likely to shrink because of the graying of America, because the U.S. population almost certainly will still be increasing as late as 2030. Nevertheless, some businesses such as the production of children's apparel will likely grow less rapidly because of the declining birth rate. Even with fewer children, however, sales of children's clothing and toys will probably grow, in part because there will be more prosperous grandparents showering their grandchildren with gifts.

The elderly and politics

As business executives try to assess the future of segments of the market in which the elderly are likely to buy heavily, public policymakers are attempting to gauge the response of elderly people to programs designed to benefit other age groups. Politicians listen closely to what the elderly have to say not only because the population is growing older but also because the percentage of older people who vote is consistently higher than the overall turnout percentage. In the 1984 presidential election, for example, 67.7 per cent of people over 64 voted, compared with 59.9 per cent for all age groups—a difference of 7.8 percentage points. In the 1982 congressional election, the gap was even wider—11.4 points.

There is some evidence of increased reluctance among older people to support government spending on public programs for the young, such as education. For example, a 1983 Gallup Poll asked people of various ages whether they would vote to raise taxes for schools if requested to do so by their local school systems. Among people under 50, the number answering yes almost equaled the number answering no. Among people 50 and older, however, the vote was no by more than 2 to 1.

Viewing such evidence, some sociologists have become concerned that tensions between older people and the rest of the population will grow. Much of this evidence, however, is based on past studies that compared people who differed not only in age but also in income and education. Many attitudes previously observed among the elderly may have been largely due to their lower income and education level, rather than their age.

In the future, the financial status and education level of older people will be much closer to those of younger people. As a result, tomorrow's elderly probably will have attitudes more like those of young people. Accordingly, it is reasonable to suppose that the elderly will view spending on education and other programs for the young more favorably.

Furthermore, intergenerational conflicts in the political arena may be lessened by the growth in ties among generations. Some 30 or 40 years ago, it was common for a family to have only two or three generations alive at one time. Today, a typical family may

Political Influence
Tomorrow's elderly will have the votes to exert a major influence on government policies affecting the older population. Many of them will also express their views outside the voting booth, joining lobbying organizations and even walking picket lines like the protesters shown above.

have three or four generations alive. By 2000, the four-generation family—children, parents, grandparents, and great-grandparents—should become the average. Many of tomorrow's children will reach maturity with four surviving grandparents and at least one great-grandparent. And because of the low birth rate, there will be a relative scarcity of children, so the children will likely receive a great deal of attention from older members of the family. Increased intergenerational contact within the family may lead to a greater understanding of the special needs of the various generations.

Different generations, different histories

Information about increases in family size, educational attainment, and income levels helps us to predict in a general way the attitudes and behavior of tomorrow's elderly. But another factor—generational history—prevents us from becoming too confident about our predictions. Each generation has its own special history, and as it enters old age it brings that history with it.

Consider, for example, the experience of the generation that entered old age in the last 10 years, compared with that of the baby boomers. Those who recently retired entered the labor market during the Great Depression of the 1930's. By contrast, many baby boomers reached adulthood during the soaring inflation of the 1970's. To the former, fear of prolonged unemployment and economic hardship was always a dominant concern; to the latter, the problem of rapidly rising prices tends to be foremost.

Similarly, the lives of those currently retiring were greatly affected by World War II, a war that enjoyed almost universal popular support. The baby boom generation, however, tends to associate wars with the Vietnam War, a conflict that divided the U.S. population sharply into "doves" who opposed the war and "hawks" who supported it. Clearly, the attitudes of these two generations toward military action and the cost of national defense were affected quite differently by their differing historical experience.

These simple examples make it easy to see how historic events influence each generation, and why each generation of old people differs from the one before it in ways that may have unpredictable effects. Although the evidence suggests that the graying of America can be taken in stride, we cannot be sure.

For further reading:

Easterlin, Richard A. *Birth and Fortune*. 2nd ed. University of Chicago Press, 1987.
Kiesler, Sara B., and others, ed. *Aging*. Academic Press, 1981.
Pifer, Alan, and Bronte, Lydia, ed. *Our Aging Society*. Norton, 1986.
U.S. Senate Special Committee on Aging in conjunction with the American Association of Retired Persons, 1984. *Aging America, Trends and Projections*. U.S. Government Printing Office, 1984.
Wattenberg, Ben J. *The Birth Dearth*. Pharos, 1987.

By Marilyn Stasio

It's No Mystery Why Everybody Loves a Mystery

The Sherlock Holmes centennial reminded readers of the enduring appeal of a good detective story.

Can you identify the man with the monocle, the teen-aged girl, and other famous detectives shown here? Answers are on page 114.

"I've found it! I've found it!"

Those words introduced to the world a tall, "excessively lean" man with "sharp and piercing" eyes and a "thin, hawk-like nose" who would become the most famous detective in literature. This man, a master of disguise and an expert swordsman, could identify many different types of soil and the ash of at least 140 types of tobacco at a glance as well as decode secret messages. Yet he was ignorant of philosophy, literature, and politics, and did not know—or care—that the earth travels around the sun.

That brilliant and fascinating man was, of course, Sherlock Holmes, whose 100th anniversary was celebrated in 1987. He became the model and inspiration for every fictional detective—and probably a few real-life detectives—since then.

The British author and doctor Arthur Conan Doyle introduced the great "consulting detective" and his companion, Dr. John H. Watson, in *A Study in Scarlet*, a novel first published in the 1887 edition of *Beeton's Christmas Annual*, a London magazine. By the time of his death in 1930, Conan Doyle had written 60 adventures—4 novels and 56 short stories—featuring Holmes. The great detective's exploits have appeared in 57 languages, and his popularity grows with each new generation of mystery readers.

To celebrate Holmes's 100th anniversary in 1987, fans all over the world held workshops and commemorative dinners, including one in the British House of Commons. Holmes lovers even gathered at the Reichenbach Falls in Switzerland, the site of a deadly struggle between Holmes and archcriminal Professor James Moriarty.

The Holmes centennial took on special significance because it coincided with a recent upsurge in enthusiasm for mystery and detective fiction. According to a 1986 Gallup Poll, more than 6 of every 10 American adults have read a "whodunit," a mystery book. The poll also revealed that nearly half of these readers have also bought one of the growing number of mystery-related products, such as board games, videotapes, or computer games.

The newest wrinkle in the mystery craze is the mystery party. Held on cruise ships and at restaurants and resort hotels, these parties feature performers who act out a murder-mystery play. The guests are then challenged to play detective and to solve the "crime." Shorter versions of this entertainment can be staged at home using one of the new packaged mystery games.

Mystery fiction's increased popularity has also spilled over into television series, theater productions, and countless motion pictures. Of course, many fictional detectives, from Holmes to Dashiell Hammett's Sam Spade to Ellery Queen, have made the move from the printed page to the movie or TV screen. Current TV mystery programs include CBS's "Murder, She Wrote" and the Public Broadcasting System's "Mystery!" Recent Broadway productions have included *The Mystery of Edwin Drood*—based on an unfinished novel by British writer Charles Dickens—and *Sherlock's Last Case*. *Shear Madness*, a play in which, like *Drood*, the audience votes on the identity

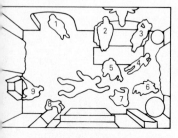

Famous Detectives
(1) Sherlock Holmes; (2) Charlie Chan; (3) Miss Marple; (4) Encyclopedia Brown; (5) Sam Spade; (6) Father Brown; (7) Hercule Poirot; (8) Nancy Drew; (9) Lord Peter Wimsey.

The author:
Marilyn Stasio writes "Mystery Alley," a syndicated newspaper column that reviews mystery and crime fiction.

of the murderer, has been running since the early 1980's in a number of cities, including Chicago and Boston. The theater recordholder, however, is *The Mousetrap*, based on a 1948 Agatha Christie novelette, which has been playing on the London stage since 1952.

What accounts for the mystery's continuing appeal to such a wide range of fans? The simplicity of the mystery's basic formula—a baffling crime is committed and a clever detective solves it—may be one reason mysteries continue to draw readers. Readers know what to expect. Yet the nearly endless variations in characters, settings, and plots keep the mystery fresh and intriguing. For example, instead of concentrating on *how* a crime was committed, the detective might spend more time trying to understand the criminal's motives or the social significance of the crime itself.

Another reason is the fun and challenge of the puzzle. "The game's afoot!" Holmes often called to Watson, and, as usual, he was right. The detective story is essentially a game, and readers can enjoy the skill and cunning of the detective while trying to beat the detective to the solution.

The detective story also satisfies us on a deeper level. Today, as in Holmes's time, crime is a serious problem. When the detective solves the crime, we feel reassured because a threat to society has been eliminated, justice has triumphed, and evil has been punished.

Movies, television, and, of course, changing times and tastes have influenced the style and even the form of the detective story since Holmes made his debut. Nevertheless, many of the basic elements that Conan Doyle used in his stories still apply today.

The first element that defines the detective story is the essential point of its plot—a crime must be committed. For the story to be satisfying, the crime should be a serious one, though not necessarily a murder. Some of Holmes's cases, for example, involve jewel thefts, missing persons, or—in "The Adventure of the Three Students"—academic cheating. Modern stories may focus on government corruption or the drug trade.

The methods used by the detective to solve the crime have also remained basically unchanged.

Who Is the Detective?

Below and on the following pages are quotations from five mystery stories featuring well-known detectives. Can you deduce the identity of the sleuths from the quotations and the accompanying clues? Answers appear on page 127.

Monsieur D

1

"The fact is, we have all been a good deal puzzled because the affair *is* so simple, and yet baffles us altogether."

"Perhaps it is the very simplicity of the thing, which puts you at fault," said my friend.

"What nonsense you *do* talk!" replied the Prefect, laughing heartily.

"Perhaps the mystery is a little *too* plain . . . A little *too* self-evident."

The upsurge in mystery fiction's popularity has spawned a variety of related activities and products. At a mystery party, *above,* guests play detective to identify the "murderer." Fans of mystery fiction have also boosted sales of mystery board games and computer and video games, *above right.*

The detective investigates the known facts, studies the clues—some of which are misleading—and questions the suspects.

Although such methods have remained fairly constant, the techniques used by detectives vary considerably. Sherlock Holmes is celebrated for his brilliant powers of observation and deduction, proving again and again that he can analyze a stranger's occupation "by [his] finger-nails, by his coat-sleeve, by his boots, by his trouser-knees. . . ." Hercule Poirot, Agatha Christie's pompous detective, boasts that he solves problems by using his own wits—his "little grey cells." Erle Stanley Gardner's lawyer-detective, Perry Mason, often breaks down a false alibi on the witness stand with shrewd questioning. In contrast, modern fictional detectives, especially police officers, rely on computers and laboratories to help crack their cases.

Another key element in mystery stories is the detective's habit of discussing the evidence with a trusted friend or colleague. This col-

league is often the kind of person the reader can identify with, and these conversations help keep the reader informed about what the detective is thinking.

There are many variations on the character of the confidant. Dashiell Hammett's detective Nick Charles relies on his wife, Nora. Earl Derr Biggers' Chinese detective, Charlie Chan, shares his thoughts with his bright young sons. There are even detectives who talk to their cats or dogs or their house plants. Nevertheless, Dr. Watson plays the role of Holmes's confidant so perfectly that, even today, detectives may refer to their friend as their "Watson."

After the discussions and a careful examination of the clues and the suspects' alibis, the detective, using exceptional powers of deduction, arrives at the solution. Often, the solution is revealed in a dramatic fashion at a gathering of all the surviving characters in the story.

Mystery buffs have made "Murder, She Wrote" starring Angela Lansbury, *top,* one of television's top-rated programs. The opportunity to vote on the identity of the murderer drew audiences to *The Mystery of Edwin Drood, above,* a Broadway musical version of the novel by Charles Dickens.

The Many Faces of Sherlock Holmes

In the first drawing of Holmes, published in the 1887 magazine in which he made his debut, *below,* Holmes's features remained a mystery. But illustrations of later stories published in *The Strand* magazine, especially those by Sidney Paget, *right,* helped to popularize the detective.

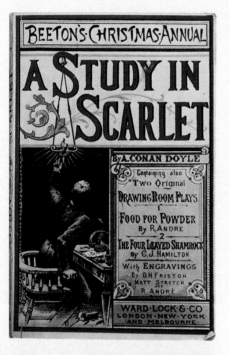

Basil Rathbone, *left*—with Nigel Bruce as Watson—and Jeremy Brett, *above* (standing), with Edward Hardwick as Watson, are among more than 100 actors who have played Holmes.

Before Conan Doyle began writing Holmes's adventures, the puzzle element of the plot was more important than the personality of the detective. The American author Edgar Allan Poe, whom scholars acknowledge as the creator of the detective story, established the importance of the puzzle-plot in three stories written between 1841 and 1844. The stories—"The Murders in the Rue Morgue," "The Mystery of Marie Rogêt," and "The Purloined Letter"—feature the detective C. Auguste Dupin. Although other Poe stories contain mystery elements, they are not considered proper detective stories because Poe violated the "fair play" rule—that is, he withheld from the reader information needed to solve the mystery.

Other early detective stories, including Wilkie Collins' *The Woman in White* (1860); Fergus Hume's *The Mystery of a Hansom Cab* (1886), and Dickens' *The Mystery of Edwin Drood* (left unfinished at his death in 1870), also downplayed the detective's personality in favor of intellectual skills and ingenious work methods. In addition, in these early stories, the process of solving the crime—discovering clues and questioning suspects—is more important than the details of the crime and the motivation of the criminals.

Conan Doyle, however, created what is now considered the classic detective story—a combination of a clever mystery-puzzle *and* a fascinating detective *and* brilliant methods of detection. By the 1920's and 1930's, a group of writers—most of them English—had developed such great command of this basic form that this period became known as the golden age of detective literature.

Along with complicated plots, the whodunits of this period can be characterized by their "polite" style. Writers of the golden age did not shy away from murder, but the violence in their books is rarely bloody. The crime is frequently committed by and among members of the educated upper classes, who keep their poise and good manners even with a murderer in their midst. In many cases, the setting is an elegant house party on a large country estate located near a picturesque village, which allows the guests to treat the murder investigation as an interesting party game—much like the mystery parties we enjoy today.

2 Who Is the Detective?

"Is there any point to which you would wish to draw my attention?"

"To the curious incident of the dog in the night-time."

"The dog did nothing in the night-time."

"That was the curious incident . . . ."

Answer on page 127.

119

During the golden age, both British and American writers refined the concept of the *series detective*—a detective such as Holmes who appears in a series of adventures. Such a character must have distinctive, colorful traits to remain interesting to readers throughout repeated appearances.

Foremost among the golden age authors was British writer Agatha Christie, who wrote 67 detective novels, 16 collections of short stories, and 16 plays. Her work has been translated into more than 100 languages, and according to her publishers, sales of her books have surpassed 400 million, making her the most widely read mystery author of all time.

Christie created two series sleuths with great personal appeal—the eccentric Belgian detective Hercule Poirot and the grandmotherly spinster Miss Jane Marple. But popular as the author's detectives are, they still take second place to her plots, which continue to amaze modern readers with their clever and complicated twists. It was Christie who perfected such devious devices as the *red herring*, a false clue designed to throw the reader off the track; and the *"unbreakable" alibi*, a seemingly unshakable defense that is eventually disproved.

Many of the other skilled authors who helped to develop the detective story during the golden age were also female and British. Dorothy L. Sayers was noted for her intellectual mysteries featuring the gentleman-sleuth Lord Peter Wimsey and the mystery writer-sleuth Harriet Vane. Margery Allingham wrote mysteries featuring the aristocratic detective Albert Campion that were greatly admired for their literary powers of description. Josephine Tey (the pen name of Elizabeth MacKintosh) is best known for *The Daughter of Time* (1951), in which a detective confined to a hospital bed "proves" that King Richard III of England did not murder his two royal nephews. The books of Ngaio Marsh, a New Zealander, feature the urbane detective Roderick Alleyn and his wife, Troy, often in vivid theatrical settings.

One of the most original characters introduced during this period was Nero Wolfe, an enormously fat detective who raises orchids, relishes gourmet food, and rarely steps out of his home to solve a case. This eccentric character, who uses an eager young assistant named Archie Goodwin to do his legwork, was the creation of the American author Rex Stout.

The Dr. Gideon Fell mysteries of American writer John Dickson Carr deserve special mention because they represent the finest examples of the *locked-room mystery* ever written. The locked-room mystery deals with a crime committed in an enclosed setting from which no entrance or exit appears possible.

Although the most common settings are rooms—or ship's cabins or train compartments— that are either sealed or guarded, the "hermetically sealed room," as Carr called it, can also be found outdoors. In *The Problem of the Wire Cage* (1939), for example, a body is discovered lying in the middle of a clay tennis court, and the only set of footprints leading across the wet clay to the body are those of the victim.

The locked-room device is the most infernally ingenious and difficult of all plot techniques. Yet Carr managed to work different versions of it into such novels as *The Three Coffins* (1935), *The Crooked Hinge* (1938), *The Emperor's Snuff Box* (1942), and—under the name Carter Dickson— *The Peacock Feather Murders* (1937) and *The Judas Window* (1938).

World War II presents a convenient cutoff point for the golden age detective story, with its emphasis on brainy detectives, tricky plots, and ingenious mystery-solving methods. The best golden age writers never entirely neglected good characterization and psychological motivation. But the postwar period saw a movement toward more realism in both the style and the content of the detective story.

At this point, the scene of influence shifted from England to the United States, where such writers as Dashiell Hammett, Raymond Chandler, James M. Cain, and Cornell Woolrich were among the pioneers of the new hard-boiled school of detective fiction.

Some of these writers actually got their start as early as the 1920's, in the new pulp magazines of that period. *Black Mask*, the most important of these pulps, published its first issue in April 1920.

1929 *The Roman Hat Mystery*, the first novel by and about a mystery writer and amateur sleuth called Ellery Queen— the pen name of Frederic Dannay and Manfred B. Lee.

1930 *The Secret of the Old Clock* by Carolyn Keene—the pen name of Harriet S. Adams—the first in the still widely read series of Nancy Drew mysteries.

1930 *It Walks by Night*, first work by John Dickson Carr, the master of the *locked-room mystery*, which deals with a crime committed in an enclosed setting.

1931 *The Strange Case of Peter the Lett*, the first of 102 police procedural novels and stories by Georges Simenon featuring the French detective Inspector Maigret.

1933 Debut of Perry Mason in *The Case of the Velvet Claws*, the first of 82 novels about the brilliant lawyer by Erle Stanley Gardner.

1934 *Fer-de-Lance* by Rex Stout, the first appearance of the enormously fat, orchid-loving detective Nero Wolfe.

1939 *The Big Sleep*, first in a series of mysteries by Raymond Chandler featuring private detective Philip Marlowe.

1952 First performance of *The Mousetrap*, the stage version of an Agatha Christie story, which is still running on the London stage.

1956 *Cop Hater*, the first of many 87th Precinct police procedurals written by Ed McBain—the pen name of Evan Hunter.

1962 *Cover Her Face*, first mystery by P. D. James, featuring the policeman-poet Adam Dalgliesh.

1964 *The Deep Blue Good-By* by John D. MacDonald, the first appearance of Travis McGee, a modern knight who specializes in rescuing people from various kinds of trouble.

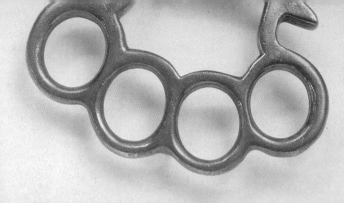

The Tough Guys

Humphrey Bogart as private eye Sam Spade and villains Peter Lorre, Mary Astor, and Sidney Greenstreet, left to right, examine a sought-after black statue in the 1941 film version of *The Maltese Falcon,* one of the most famous hard-boiled detective stories. Many hard-boiled writers, including *Maltese Falcon* author Dashiell Hammett, got their start writing for such pulp magazines as *Thrilling Detective, True Detective,* and the influential *Black Mask.*

During the 1930's, *Black Mask* was still the most influential among more than 100 imitators.

During World War II, however, mass-market paperback books gradually edged out the pulps in the popular entertainment market. Authors turned from writing short stories for the pulps to writing full-length detective novels, usually published in paperback. These rough-talking, action-packed adventures found a large and receptive readership in the millions of veterans returning home from the war. These servicemen had discovered hard-boiled fiction in the paperback novels they turned to for relief from the fighting. The popularity of movies featuring tough-guy detectives in beat-up trenchcoats also fed the market for hard-boiled fiction.

In general, this new type of mystery focused more on the nature of the crime than on the methods of detection, and for this reason the stories are more properly called *crime fiction*. More physical action than brain power was called for in the apprehension of criminals, which added more adventure—and violence—to the stories.

In "polite" mysteries, the victim was likely to be found in the drawing room, dead from a neat blow to the head or a sip of poisoned tea. The detective rarely moved beyond the immediate vicinity of the crime, catching the murderer through sheer intellectual deduction based on the clues found at the scene. In the new, hard-boiled mysteries, however, the victim was far more likely to be gunned down in a sleazy nightclub or on a city street. The police or the private detective usually had to chase down the killer under hazardous circumstances and sometimes beat a confession out of him.

The hard-boiled style of writing also marked a dramatic departure from the witty, often scholarly tone of the classical mystery. Since many of the plots were inspired by real-life crimes and well-known gangsters, the new style of writing demanded more believable characters, dialogue, and settings.

In the hands of the most gifted authors, this naturalistic style produced such acclaimed novels as Hammett's *Red Harvest* (1929) and *The Maltese Falcon* (1930) and Chandler's *The Big Sleep* (1939)

3 Who Is the Detective?

"When a man's partner is killed he's supposed to do something about it. It doesn't make any difference what you thought of him . . . when one of your organization gets killed it's bad business to let the killer get away with it."

Answer on page 127.

and *The Long Goodbye* (1953). These hard-boiled masterpieces still inspire new generations of writers, such as Elmore Leonard, the acclaimed author of *LaBrava* (1983), *Stick* (1983), *Glitz* (1985), and a number of other tough, well-crafted crime novels.

As the detective story underwent various changes, the character of the detective was also transformed. From the time of Hammett's Sam Spade and Chandler's Philip Marlowe, the detective changed from the cultured gentleman of classical detective fiction—a spokesman for the law and a staunch defender of the social order—into a loner and cynic who has no such allegiances. Personally disgusted by the crime and corruption he sees around him, he tries to restore some decency to society. But since he views law enforcers as no better than the criminals they pursue, he often finds himself operating outside the law, according to his own personal code of justice.

Such detectives invariably work as private investigators—*private eyes*—and make a virtue of their alienation from society. But despite their tendency to stay outside the rules of the law, these individualists have strong moral codes and strict consciences.

Lew Archer, for example, the hero of several fine crime novels written by American author Ross Macdonald (the pen name of Kenneth Millar), has one of the most highly developed codes of justice in all crime literature. This California-based private eye investigates murder cases that often deal with such serious matters of conscience as race relations and the environment. In *The Galton Case* (1959), *The Chill* (1964), and *The Goodbye Look* (1969), among others, Macdonald wrote sympathetically of children who rebel against their parents and get into trouble trying to find their own identity. Arthur Lyons, a contemporary California crime writer, shows a special feeling for these same issues and is considered by some as Macdonald's heir.

When the new private eyes first appeared, they seemed to work exclusively out of California. But in recent decades, tough-guy detectives have spread to Boston (in the works of Robert B. Parker), Detroit (Loren D. Estleman), Chicago (Sara

4 Who Is the Detective?

"How many wounds are there exactly?"

"I make it twelve. One or two are so slight as to be practically scratches. On the other hand, at least three would be capable of causing death."

Answer on page 127.

Paretsky, whose detective is a woman), Fort Lauderdale (John D. MacDonald), and other cities.

As the detective story became more realistic, it branched off into a new form known as the *suspense-melodrama* or *psychological-suspense story*. This type of novel closely examines the psychology of the crime and the state of mind of either the criminal or victim. Many of these novels have no detective at all, or else the detective plays a minor role.

The master of the suspense story was probably Cornell Woolrich, whose dark, mysterious studies of terror were often made into films. *The Bride Wore Black* (1940) and other books in his so-called Black Series inspired a style of moviemaking called *film noir*. Director Alfred Hitchcock turned one of Woolrich's stories into the movie *Rear Window* (1954). Modern authors who excel at this type of mystery story include Canadian-born Margaret Millar, Ruth Rendell of Britain, and Patricia Highsmith of the United States.

Since the 1960's, detective fiction has offered something for every taste. The classical mystery—now more naturalistic and more concerned with the psychological makeup of the characters—seems as popular today as it was during the golden age.

Britain's P. D. (Phyllis Dorothy) James is generally acknowledged to be the most important author currently writing in the classic style. From *Cover Her Face* (1962) to *A Taste for Death* (1986), James's novels featuring Scotland Yard Commander Adam Dalgliesh consistently honor the intricate plots and literary style of the mystery in its classic form. At the same time, James does not neglect the realistic detail and credible characterizations demanded by modern tastes. Readers particularly admire her intelligent and complex hero, who is also a published poet. In *Shroud for a Nightingale* (1971), which many consider to be James's best book, the sensitive Dalgliesh deals with remarkable compassion with the deaths of two young student nurses.

Police detectives are still a strong presence in crime fiction, but the police inspector of today is different from the scholarly gentleman of the classic detective story. Today, the detective is usu-

5 Who Is the Detective?

He glanced at the clock. "It's a quarter past three. At four o'clock I shall ask you to accompany me to my plant rooms on the roof; you'll find the orchids diverting."

Answer on page 127.

ally a hard-bitten street cop who has to deal with the roughest type of criminal and the ugliest kinds of urban crime. The detective usually appears in a type of mystery called a *police procedural*, which features detailed descriptions of police routine and station house life. Ed McBain (the pen name of Evan Hunter), whose police procedurals are set in the fictional city of Isola; Joseph Wambaugh, a former officer with the Los Angeles Police Department; and Charles Willeford, whose hero works in Miami, Fla., are among the most admired of the many authors who write this violent type of mystery story.

The mystery section of U.S. bookstores has also become much more international. Because of our common language, British authors have always found readers in the United States. But detective stories are popular in many countries—from India to the Soviet Union.

Foreign authors with a strong American following include James McClure, a South African whose police procedurals are set in that country and feature a white Afrikaner detective and his black Bantu partner, and William Marshall, who writes two lively, comic police series, one set in Hong Kong and the other in Manila, the Philippines. Janwillem van de Wetering of the Netherlands is admired for his offbeat crime adventures about Dutch police officers who work in the murder division of Amsterdam's police department. Nicolas Freeling has created two popular detectives—Piet Van der Valk of the Amsterdam police and French inspector Henri Castang. Swedish police commissioner Martin Beck, created by Maj Sjöwall and Per Wahlöö, also has loyal fans.

Probably the most famous European detective is Inspector Jules Maigret. This reserved, thoughtful officer with the Paris police department appeared in 102 detective stories written by Belgian-born author Georges Simenon. Inspector Maigret is admired for his keen psychological insights into the criminal mind and beloved by fans for the great affection he shows for his wife, his home life, and his native land.

In the United States, the enthusiasm for all forms of detective fiction has encouraged many new authors to enter the field—and to change

Youthful Sleuths

Brave and resourceful, young detectives have also done their share of clearing innocent suspects, finding missing people and papers, and cracking espionage rings. Among the most popular of these youthful sleuths are the Hardy Boys, *top;* Nancy Drew, *center,* who got a more modern image in 1986; and Encyclopedia Brown, *bottom.*

some of the older conventions to suit themselves. For example, Paretsky, Sue Grafton, and other women authors have introduced a new breed of intelligent and competent female private eyes. That same adventurous spirit has also produced some interesting ethnic detectives. Among these are the tribal police officers in Tony Hillerman's mysteries, which are set on Indian reservations in the American Southwest, and black detectives, such as Captain Ralph (Rat) Trapp, the hero of mysteries set in New Orleans by John William Corrington and Joyce H. Corrington.

Another mystery trend is the increase in amateur detectives. Nowadays, they may be anything from a bag lady in New York City to a retired stockbroker.

Of course, one of the most famous amateur detectives is Nancy Drew. Created by American writer Harriet S. Adams using the pen name Carolyn Keene, the teen-aged detective has appeared in more than 50 novels and several films. When she first appeared in print in *The Secret of the Old Clock* (1930), Nancy Drew tended to explore deserted houses and underground caves for missing manuscripts and lost chums. In 1986, however, she became much more modern. In her new series, called *The Nancy Drew Files*, the 16-year-old detective is now 18 (so that she can legally drive her blue convertible in every state) and wears $50 designer jeans. More important, the brave and independent heroine now works on more serious crimes, like record-industry piracy and espionage. Adams' father, Edward L. Stratemeyer, writing under the name Franklin W. Dixon, created the Hardy Boys.

Another popular young detective is Encyclopedia Brown, created by American writer Donald J. Sobol. This 10-year-old sleuth shows a keen respect for the intellectual process of crime detection, which is, at the heart of it, what the detective story is all about. Sherlock Holmes would probably get along very well with Encyclopedia Brown.

The style of the mystery may change over the years. Yet the mystery's great versatility, which can accommodate every kind of crime and every sort of detective, assures us of an endless supply of these addictive stories. And that's good news for every reader who loves a good mystery.

Answers to Mystery Quotations

1. C. Auguste Dupin in "The Purloined Letter" (1844) by Edgar Allan Poe.
2. Sherlock Holmes in "Silver Blaze" (1894) by Arthur Conan Doyle.
3. Sam Spade in *The Maltese Falcon* (1930) by Dashiell Hammett.
4. Hercule Poirot in *Murder on the Orient Express* (1934), also published under the title *Murder on the Calais Coach*, by Agatha Christie.
5. Nero Wolfe in *The Red Box* (1937) by Rex Stout.

For further reading:

Steinbrunner, Chris, and Penzler, Otto. *Encyclopedia of Mystery and Detection.* McGraw-Hill, 1976.
Symons, Julian. *Bloody Murder: From the Detective Story to the Crime Novel.* Viking, 1985.
Winn, Dilys, ed. *Murder Ink: Revived, Revised, Still Unrepentant.* Workman, 1984.
———. *Murderess Ink: The Better Half of the Mystery.* Workman, 1979.

The sky in the Southern Hemisphere, *right,* suddenly brightened as a supernova—an exploding star—*far right,* blazed into view on the night of Feb. 23, 1987. Astronomers from around the world flocked to observatories in Chile and Australia to study this phenomenon.

By James Trefil

The Death of a Star

Why does a star die? What happens when it dies? Astronomers are gaining new insights by studying a supernova—the explosion of a massive star—that was observed in 1987.

The author:
James Trefil is the Clarence Robinson Professor of Physics at George Mason University in Fairfax, Va.

Stars are not eternal. They are born, live out their lives, and die, just like everything else in the universe. The life spans of stars are longer than those of trees or human beings, of course, but the stars will someday disappear from the sky just as surely as the mightiest oak will fall.

When stars die, they do not go quietly. The death throes of giant stars result in spectacular explosions known as *supernovae*. A single supernova may shine for a while as brightly as an entire galaxy of a billion stars, or about a billion times brighter than our sun—a glare that is truly unimaginable. Chinese astronomers witnessed the fireworks of a supernova on July 4, 1054. The supernova was so bright that it could be seen in the daytime sky for three weeks. The ashes of that explosion are visible today through telescopes as a cloud of gas and dust known as the Crab Nebula.

Supernovae are rarely seen—only five have been observed in our galaxy, the Milky Way, in the last 1,000 years. That is one reason why there was great excitement when Canadian astronomer Ian K. Shelton detected a supernova on the night of Feb. 23, 1987. Shelton used a telescope at the Las Campanas Observatory in northern Chile. As he was developing a photograph of a section of the Large Magellanic Cloud, a small galaxy near the Milky Way that is visible from the Southern Hemisphere, he noticed a star that he had never observed before. At first he thought it was a flaw in the photographic plate. When he stepped outside the observatory and gazed up at the night sky, however, the exploding star could be easily seen with the naked eye.

The supernova in the Large Magellanic Cloud—now known as Supernova 1987A—was the first supernova visible to the unaided eye since German astronomer Johannes Kepler saw one in 1604. Although astronomers have observed supernovae in far more distant galaxies using powerful telescopes, Supernova 1987A was close enough to be seen without a telescope. So, for the first time in 383 years, astronomers were ringside spectators to a star's explosion and were able to study it with a wide range of scientific instruments.

Although relatively close compared with other galaxies, the Large Magellanic Cloud is still far enough from Earth that a long time passed before the light of this star's explosion reached us. What Shelton saw actually happened 160,000 years ago. It took that long for the light from the exploding star to reach Earth, traveling 186,282 miles (299,792 kilometers) per second. At the actual moment when this star blew up and gave off the light of 100 million suns, early human beings were using primitive stone tools and were hunting the ancestors of the woolly mammoth.

A supernova is the most spectacular stage in a star's death, but dying stars take many other forms. As a result of star death, the sky is populated with bizarre objects bearing curious names such as *red giant, white dwarf, neutron star, pulsar,* and *black hole*. As small stars die, they are transformed first into red giants and then into white dwarfs. When giant stars die, they become either rotating neutron

stars (also known as pulsars) or invisible objects called black holes. Why these changes occur is a question that has occupied astronomers for decades. Today, many astronomers believe they are on the threshold of finding the answers. Already, their understanding of these changes has shed much light on how our universe evolved and how the chemical basis of life on Earth came to be.

To understand the life cycle of a star, you have to know one important fact—that the force of gravity pulls large concentrations of matter inward. A star begins to form when gravity causes a cloud of gas and dust in space to begin contracting. The bits of gas and dust in the cloud—the raw materials of a star—are attracted toward a spot in the cloud where matter is a little more dense than elsewhere. Eventually, the material at this point becomes extremely dense, and gravity starts to pull in everything around it.

The gas and dust collect into a large sphere centered around the original point of density. The compression of the inner part, caused by the weight of the outer layers, which are pressing inward due to gravity, makes the gas at the center heat up. The temperature continues to rise until it reaches about 2,000,000°F. (1,100,000°C), at which point nuclear reactions ignite in the center of the mass. These nuclear reactions heat the star, and the outer layers become so hot they give off light. At this point, a star is born.

Astronomers believe this is how our sun was born. Our sun is considered a small star in comparison with some stars that are extraordinarily massive. But our sun is typical of most stars in the universe; large, extremely massive stars are in the minority. The size of a star determines whether its nuclear reactions will last a long time or end relatively soon.

The discovery that nuclear reactions are the energy source of stars is relatively recent. In the past, astronomers puzzled over the source of the sun's energy. Some people in the 1800's proposed that the sun was a ball of burning coal—the best-known fuel at the time. But by then, biologists and geologists who studied Earth's fossil record and rocks had shown that Earth—and therefore, the sun—had to be at least 100 million years old. A French physicist calculated that even if the sun were made of pure anthracite coal, it could generate the energy it gave off for only 10,000 years or so—hardly long enough to have allowed life to develop on Earth.

Other energy sources to power the sun were also proposed in the 1800's, but the discovery of radioactivity in 1896 provided the key to solve the riddle. Scientists learned that radioactivity was a source of energy that could last for billions of years. They also learned that radioactivity produced heat. In 1916, British astronomer Sir Arthur S. Eddington proposed that heat energy must be the force that keeps gravity from causing the sun to collapse inward and to shrink into a small object. Eddington calculated that the temperature at the center of the sun must be many millions of degrees. It was not until the 1930's, however, that physicists Hans A. Bethe of the United States and Carl F. von Weizsäcker of Germany showed how nuclear energy could power the sun and other stars. The fuel was not coal but hydrogen gas.

Once we know that a star exists by burning a fuel, we know that the star cannot live forever—even the most efficient fuel must run out someday. Much of modern astronomy is devoted to learning the precise details of how nuclear reactions keep a star alive and, ultimately, figure in its death.

Almost all the stars you see in the sky, including the sun, are stable—that is, they are not on the verge of dying. The reason for this stability lies in the energy generated by the nuclear fires in the core of a star. This energy pours outward, heating the gases in the star's outer boundaries. The pressure created by this heating counteracts the inward pull of gravity. The inward pull of gravity is still there, of course—it never stops. But as long as the nuclear reactions generate enough heat to counteract gravity, the star remains stable.

This stability cannot last forever, however. After millions or even billions of years, the star burns up its first supply of fuel, the fire dies, and the slow, unrelenting contraction that had been postponed for so long begins again. What happens at the end of a star's first fuel-burning period determines when and how the star dies and what is left behind after its death.

Let's take our sun as an example of what happens to a small star. Astronomers believe that the sun and the planets condensed out of a cloud of gas and dust about 4.6 billion years ago. When the temperatures at the sun's core reached 2,000,000°F., the reaction we call *nuclear fusion* occurred. In nuclear fusion, the *nuclei* (cores) of two or more small atoms *fuse*, or come together, to form a single large nucleus. The fused nucleus weighs less than the sum of the original nuclei, and this difference in mass is converted into energy.

In the sun, a complex series of reactions converts the nuclei of four hydrogen atoms into the nucleus of a single helium atom. All atoms consist of a heavy, positively charged nucleus surrounded by a cloud of negatively charged electrons in orbit. The nuclei, in turn, are made up of roughly equal numbers of building blocks called *protons* and *neutrons*. Both are much heavier than the electron. The proton has a positive electric charge while the neutron is, as the name suggests, electrically neutral—that is, it has neither a positive nor a negative charge.

You can compare the sun to an ordinary campfire. But instead of wood, the sun burns hydrogen, and instead of ashes, it produces helium. In both instances, we have a fuel being consumed and energy being produced. In the case of the sun, however, if the fuel were not burning, the force of gravity would cause the whole structure to collapse.

The sun consumes tremendous amounts of hydrogen—tens of millions of tons per second. Nevertheless, the sun is so big that it has burned fuel at more or less its present rate for 4.6 billion years and will continue to burn that fuel for about another 5 billion years. But, sooner or later, every star consumes its fuel. The sun is no exception to this rule, and it, too, will eventually burn all the hydrogen at its core.

When a star consumes its hydrogen, a remarkable series of events takes place. With the nuclear fires at the core extinguished, the long-thwarted force of gravity is exerted again, and the core starts to shrink. The temperature in the core increases as the pressure grows due to this shrinking. Soon, the temperature becomes so high that the helium nuclei—the "ashes" of the hydrogen fire—themselves start to undergo fusion reactions. In effect, the ashes of one fire become the fuel for the next. As a result of this new reaction, three helium nuclei are converted into a single nucleus of carbon, and a new output of energy again balances gravity. In this state of balance, helium is burned at the core, where the temperature is highest, and hydrogen is burned just outside the core, where the temperature is slightly lower. The energy from both sets of nuclear reactions stabilizes the star.

This change to burning helium at the core means the star has become what astronomers call a red giant. The red giant phase—which, for our sun, will begin about 5 billion years from now—marks the beginning of the end for stars like the sun. Astronomers call these stars red giants because they appear red in optical tele-

What Will Happen When Our Sun Dies?

Fire and then ice—that is how the world will end about 5 billion years from now, according to astronomers.

First, the sun will begin to expand as it becomes a red giant, causing dramatic climate changes on Earth, *right*. Sea levels will rise due to the melting polar caps, and violent storms will rage.

For about 2 million years, the sun will continue to expand until it fills half the sky, *right*. The oceans and atmosphere will then vanish and life as we know it will cease to exist on a scorched Earth.

Finally, the sun's nuclear fires will gradually go out. The sun will be a white dwarf, resembling a bright star in the sky, *right*. Earth will be a frozen planet.

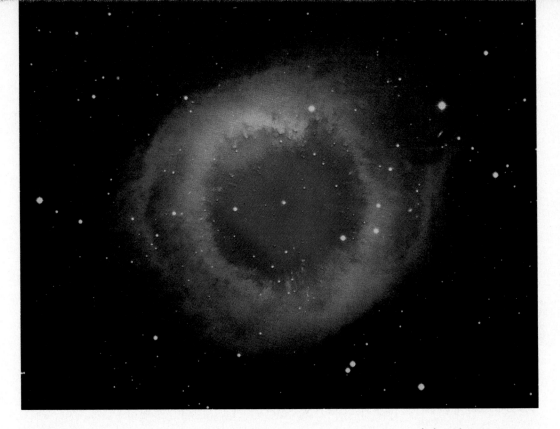

A ring of gaseous material surrounds a white dwarf star, visible as a dot at the center of the ring. The ring of material, now known as the Helix Nebula, was once part of the star but was blown off when the star ended its days as a red giant and collapsed to the size of a white dwarf.

scopes and because they become many times larger than their original size.

When the sun becomes a red giant, its outer boundary will begin to expand and Earth's climate will change dramatically. The sun's intense heat will melt the polar icecaps on Earth, causing sea levels to rise. Violent storms will rage. Gradually, Earth's atmosphere will be blown away by the force of the sun's radiation, and the intense heat will evaporate the oceans. Nothing will remain but a scorched surface of dust and rocks. At its largest, the sun will have a radius of about 67 million miles (108 million kilometers). It will be so large that it will obliterate the planets Mercury and Venus. An observer on Earth would see the sun fill half the sky, but there probably will be no such observer because life as we know it will no longer exist.

After a few hundred million years, the stopgap measure of burning helium will no longer be enough to keep the sun alive. The sun will exhaust its supply of helium fuel, ending the temporary relief from the forces of gravity, and the unrelenting contraction will start again. For relatively small stars like the sun, there isn't enough mass to create temperatures high enough to ignite another nuclear fire. The carbon atoms at the core—the ashes of the helium fire—do not get hot enough to burn. Without the heat furnished by nuclear reactions, the core begins to collapse due to gravity. The collapse will continue until the sun becomes a white dwarf.

For a star like the sun, the white dwarf stage is the end of the road. The star's nuclear fires have begun to go out, never to be

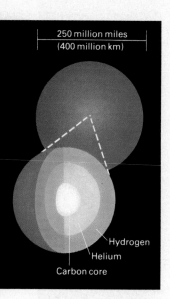

250 million miles
(400 million km)

Hydrogen
Helium
Carbon core

A small star like our sun, *above,* has nuclear reactions for about 10 billion years, first burning hydrogen gas, then helium, until only a carbon core remains.

Not all stars are small like the sun. Some are much more massive and as they evolve become even larger. They are known as supergiants, and they dwarf our sun, *below.*

rekindled. Unlike more massive stars, however, the sun will not end its life in a cataclysmic explosion. Instead, the sun will achieve a new kind of stability, though it will eventually cease to shine. The secret of the white dwarf is that the star has found another way to hold back the force of gravity, a way that does not rely on the heat of nuclear burning.

The white dwarf uses an entirely different sort of process involving electrons. Usually, every atom has electrons in orbit around its nucleus. But at temperatures as high as those in the sun, electrons do not orbit the nuclei of individual atoms. Instead, the electrons have been torn loose by collisions between rapidly moving atoms and are free to wander. Physicists call them *free electrons,* and this state of matter, where the electrons and nuclei are separated from each other, is called a *plasma.* The material in the sun is almost entirely a plasma. The free electrons in that plasma are pulled in along with the nuclei when gravity causes the sun to contract into a white dwarf.

It is impossible, however, to crowd electrons too closely together. Putting electrons into a confined space is like trying to fit cars into a parking lot. Each car gets one space, and when all the spaces are taken, no more cars can be brought in, even though the unused space between the cars may be substantial. In the same way, when you start to fill a space with electrons, you can pack only so many in before all the "parking spaces" are full.

As the sun starts to shrink after burning up its supply of helium, the electrons in the sun become increasingly crowded. Eventually, a point is reached where no more electrons can be crowded in—the "parking lot" is full. At this point, the electrons themselves exert a force called *degeneracy pressure* that counteracts gravity and stops the collapse. Once again, the star stabilizes.

But the sun's nuclear fires are slowly burning out, and the gravitational force in a star with the mass of the sun is too weak to force the electrons together. After hundreds of thousands of years, a stalemate sets in, and the star reaches its final resting place.

When this new stability is reached, the sun will be much smaller than its present size of 865,000 miles (1,392,000 kilometers) in diameter. It will, in fact, have shrunk to about the size of Earth, which

Sun

Supergiant

has a diameter of 7,926 miles (12,756 kilometers). All stars with masses up to about five times greater than that of the sun will end their lives this way, as white dwarfs. Astronomers sometimes refer to the final cinder—what a white dwarf becomes when the fires finally burn out for good—as a *black dwarf*. When the sun changes from a red giant to a white dwarf, Earth will change from a burning hot planet to a frozen lump, and so it will spend eternity.

Stars like the sun reach their final resting place in a relatively quiet manner. But the deaths of extremely large stars—those with masses more than about eight times greater than that of the sun—result in truly spectacular displays, such as supernovae. These stars differ from the sun in many ways. For one thing, because they contain so much more matter, they exert a much stronger gravitational force than does the sun. This means that the nuclear fires have to burn with extraordinary ferocity to keep the star from collapsing. So great is the demand on the fuel supply of large stars, and so quickly is their fuel consumed, that the larger a star is, the briefer its lifetime will be. The advantage of having more fuel is counteracted by the need to burn the fuel more rapidly to balance gravity. The lifetime of a large star is measured in tens of millions of years, rather than the billions of years that a star like the sun can expect to live.

In the early stages of its development, a large star has a core of helium and an outer boundary of hydrogen just as the sun does. The outer boundary resembles a shell wrapped around the core. As a large star continues to develop, however, these shells multiply and build up layer upon layer around the core. Each shell is composed of a gas that once was burned in the core of the star.

The difference between a large star and the sun becomes apparent after the helium fire has produced carbon, and all the helium at the core is gone. Unlike the sun, a large star exerts a gravitational force so strong that as the star contracts, the temperature of the core becomes high enough to ignite nuclear reactions with carbon—the ashes of the helium fire. At this point, the star is burning carbon in the core, while helium is burning in a relatively cooler shell just outside the core, and hydrogen is burning in a still cooler shell farther out.

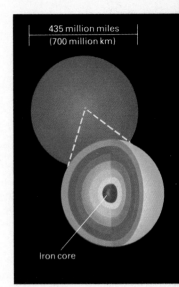

435 million miles
(700 million km)

Iron core

Supergiants, *above,* sustain nuclear reactions for only tens of millions of years because they burn their many layers of fuel quickly, resulting in an iron core that sets the stage for a supernova.

The process continues rapidly. Layers of neon, oxygen, and silicon are produced in succession and are added to the star's structure. Eventually, however, the nuclear fires start to produce iron, and this marks the end of the line for a massive star. The nucleus of an iron atom is so tightly bound that it absorbs energy, rather than releases it, when fusion occurs, so iron cannot be "burned" in the core. Iron is the ultimate nuclear ash. When iron is produced as the end product of burning in the core of a large star, no more nuclear fires can be ignited.

The other nuclear fires in the surrounding shells maintain a shaky stability in the star, but the build-up of iron cannot go on forever. The force of gravity on the core is so great that when the iron core reaches a certain critical size—when it has a mass about 40 per cent greater than that of the sun—a new nuclear reaction sets in. In essence, the electrons in the core are moving so fast that they are forced into the protons in the iron nuclei. This combining of negatively and positively charged particles turns those protons into neutrons in the process. All the electrons disappear from the core, which turns into a mass of neutrons.

The countdown to a supernova explosion has begun. With the disappearance of the electrons, which resist being packed too closely together, there is nothing left to keep the core from collapsing. Gravity takes over with a vengeance. In less than a second, the core of a star that has lived for millions of years caves in on itself. The outer layers of the star start to fall inward toward the core at high speed. Meanwhile, matter in the collapsing core has become so dense—more dense than the nucleus of an atom—that the core cannot collapse further. So, like a rubber ball that has been squeezed tight, it springs back, creating a shock wave as it rebounds. The inward-falling layers meet the shock wave of the outward-moving core, and the star tears itself apart in a titanic explosion. The material in the star is blown into space at velocities 50 times that of a rifle bullet—thousands of miles per second.

The shock wave creates temperatures high enough to trigger nuclear reactions that produce many of the heavier chemical elements, including gold and uranium. This material, too, is blown out into the space between the stars, where it may eventually collect as a cloud of gas and dust that will contract to form a new star.

What we see as a supernova is actually the outer layers of gases being blown off. These may continue to shine brightly for days or months but will eventually fade. The collapsing core left behind after the explosion becomes either a neutron star or a black hole.

A neutron star is one of the most bizarre objects in the universe. It is made almost entirely of neutrons, and it is unimaginably dense. The star is only about 12 miles (19 kilometers) in diameter—about the size of Cincinnati, Ohio—but it is so dense and massive that a teaspoonful of its gases would weigh billions of tons on Earth. When

1. As the star exhausts its fuel, its innermost layer forms an iron core. In a few days, the nuclear fires in the core go out.

2. The iron core cannot counteract the force of gravity. In a fraction of a second, the core starts to collapse.

3. The core continues to collapse until matter in the core becomes more dense than the nucleus of an atom.

Countdown to a Supernova

After shining for tens of millions of years, a massive star will exhaust its fuel and end its life in a supernova explosion.

5. The rebounding core creates a shock wave that encounters the outer layers of the star, which are collapsing inward.

4. The core cannot shrink further and in another fraction of a second, it starts to rebound.

6. About one hour later, the shock wave blows the outer layers of the star outward in a colossal explosion.

Neutron star

7. The shock wave races farther out into space, leaving behind either a neutron star or a black hole.

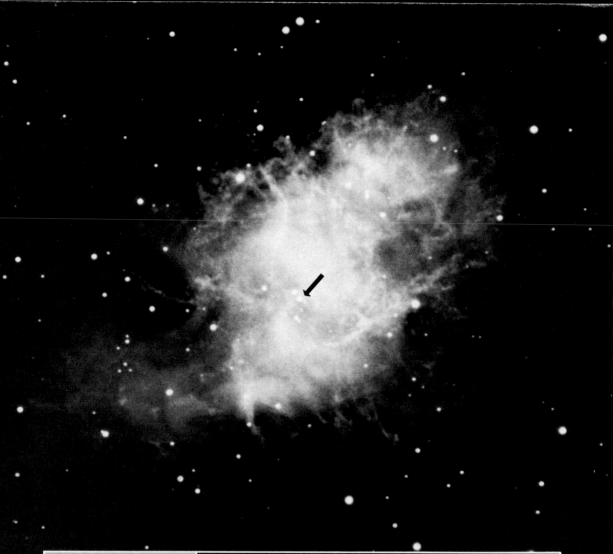

Birth of a Pulsar

The Crab Nebula, *above*, appears as a cloud of gas and dust with a pulsar (arrow) at its center. The pulsar is what remains of a star that exploded, creating the nebula. Astronomers believe the pulsar is a neutron star that emits pulses of radio waves that escape at the star's magnetic poles, *right.* Much like a lighthouse beacon, the pulsar sends out bursts of radio waves as it rotates 30 times a second.

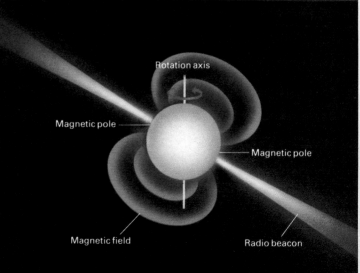

Rotation axis

Magnetic pole

Magnetic pole

Magnetic field

Radio beacon

neutrons are tightly packed together, astronomers believe that they also counteract the force of gravity—like the degeneracy pressure exerted by electrons in a white dwarf. A neutron star is much smaller than a white dwarf, however, because neutrons can be packed together much more tightly than electrons. When the neutron core in a supernova collapses, therefore, astronomers think that the collapse will eventually be halted by degeneracy pressure exerted by neutrons.

Two other things make a neutron star unique. One involves the rotation of the star; the other, its magnetic field.

Every star rotates. The sun, for example, turns on its axis every 26 days. Neutron stars turn on their axes at incredible speeds; the fastest one ever observed rotates about 650 times per second. The rapid rotation of a neutron star can be explained by comparing it to an everyday physical phenomenon. You know that when ice skaters go into a spin, they can increase the spin rate by pulling in their arms. In just the same way, when the core of a star collapses from the size of Earth to about the size of Cincinnati, it is, in effect, "pulling in its arms," and its rate of rotation increases.

Every star also has a magnetic field. A compass on the sun would line up on a north-south line just as it does on Earth. A neutron star is so concentrated that it has an enormously strong magnetic field. It is not unusual for the magnetic field at the north pole of a neutron star to be a trillion times stronger than the magnetic field at Earth's North Pole. The neutron star, then, is a rapidly rotating, extremely dense object with a powerful magnetic field.

Looking like a jumble of fence posts and wire, this radio telescope in Cambridge, England, is the device that in 1967 detected the first pulsar ever known, a rapidly rotating neutron star that sends out a beam of radiowaves every 1.3 seconds.

Until the 1960's, the existence of neutron stars had been predicted by various theories, but none had actually been seen. And the chances of observing a star about the size of Cincinnati at vast distances from Earth seemed remote. Then, in 1967, Jocelyn Bell, a graduate student working under astronomer Antony Hewish at the Mullard Radio Astronomy Observatory in Cambridge, England, discovered something in the sky that gave off short bursts of radio waves every 1.3 seconds. Stars give off radiation at a range of wavelengths, including radio wavelengths, and astronomers erect radio telescopes to receive this radiation, just as they use optical telescopes to see visible light from space. The bursts of radio waves that Bell and her colleagues received were so regular that the astronomers at first considered the possibility that they were receiving a radio communication from an intelligent civilization in outer space. Nothing in nature seemed to behave with such precise regularity. They began referring to the signal as the "LGM" for "little green men." It took some time before they realized that what they were seeing could be explained only by the theories that predicted the existence of neutron stars.

What does a rotating neutron star look like from Earth? The star is rotating so that first its north and then its south magnetic poles point in the general direction of Earth as the star rotates. Electrically charged particles tend to spiral out from the star at these north and south magnetic poles. The particles give off radio waves—waves we can detect with our radio telescopes. A neutron star is a radio version of a lighthouse. It sends out a beam of radio waves that sweeps through space, appearing to be a series of regularly spaced pulses. This beam is what Bell observed. Such a rapidly rotating neutron star came to be called a pulsar. By the late 1980's, astronomers had discovered 400 pulsars, and the existence of neutron stars had been confirmed.

Whether black holes actually exist, however, is still a subject of debate. Astronomers have not yet positively detected a black hole. But according to theories of how stars evolve, if a star is extremely massive, the end product of its supernova explosion will be a black hole. According to these theories, the star contains so much mass that even tightly packed neutrons—as in a neutron star—cannot resist the force of gravity.

The black hole represents gravity's ultimate triumph. A little smaller than a neutron star, with a diameter of less than 4 miles (6 kilometers), a black hole has so much mass packed into so small a space that no object which ventures too near can escape the pull of its gravity. Even light cannot escape from its surface. Anything that falls into a black hole remains inside. The black hole's great concentration of mass distorts the space around it so much that it causes space to curve in on itself. In effect, a black hole has pulled space in around it the way a child pulls a blanket over his or her head—except that the blanket of space which hides the star from the outside world can never be removed.

For obvious reasons, it is impossible to observe black holes directly. Nevertheless, astronomers believe they might be able to detect a black hole indirectly if one orbited a nearby companion star that was visible. Such *double-star systems*—two stars that orbit each other—are relatively common in our Galaxy. (In fact, our lone sun seems to be in a minority in this regard.) If one of the stars in a double-star system became a black hole, its gravitational force could pull matter from the other, visible star. As matter is pulled off the star, the matter would spiral in around the black hole, forming a disk of material that would be heated to temperatures of 50,000,000°F. (10,000,000°C), hot enough to give off X rays. Earth's atmosphere prevents X rays from penetrating to Earth's surface, but this radiation could be detected with X-ray telescopes launched into space.

Astronomers have not yet reported a confirmed sighting of a black hole, but one leading candidate is an invisible source of X rays known as Cygnus X-1 in the constellation Cygnus. Cygnus X-1 has a visible star companion, and the X rays it gives off are characteristic of matter being pulled into a black hole.

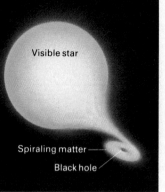

Visible star

Spiraling matter

Black hole

Although a black hole is invisible, it might be detected by observing its effect on a visible star. As shown in an artist's drawing, *above,* matter from the star would spiral into the black hole at high speeds. This would produce temperatures hot enough to give off X rays that could be detected by orbiting X-ray telescopes.

Double-star systems can also produce a supernova explosion. Many astronomers think that a single star must be about eight times more massive than the sun to end its life as a supernova. But if a white dwarf orbited a red giant in a double-star system, the gravitational force of the white dwarf could pull matter from the red giant onto its own surface, gradually accumulating enough mass to trigger a core collapse resulting in a supernova. This type of explosion, however, would destroy the star utterly, leaving nothing behind but an expanding shell of gas and dust. This appears to be what happened with two supernovae witnessed by European astronomers in 1572 and 1604.

A supernova, then, marks the death throes of a giant star or of a smaller star in a double-star system. Most of the heavy elements that have been created by the nuclear reactions in the star, along with those created in the explosion itself, are returned to the depths of space. A black hole, a neutron star, or nothing at all will be left to mark the place where the star once lived.

What is the supernova's importance to us? Astronomers believe that our Galaxy began about 10 billion or 20 billion years ago as a cloud of hydrogen and helium gas. Nothing else existed. As stars formed, some of them were large. These stars lived a short time; changed the hydrogen and helium in their interiors into heavier elements such as carbon, oxygen, and iron; and then exploded, sending these elements out into space. When new stars formed, they incorporated these heavy elements in their structure. As time went on, the Galaxy came to possess more and more of the heavy elements. By the time our sun formed, this process had been going on for quite a while. Consequently, the sun and the planets that formed around it contained a high concentration of heavy elements.

The importance of supernovae to us, then, is this: Every atom on Earth—except hydrogen and some helium—was created in a star and returned to space when that star exploded. The iron in your blood, the oxygen you breathe, and the calcium in your bones all originally emerged from supernovae.

We are all the stuff of stars.

For further reading:

Asimov, Isaac. *The Exploding Suns.* Dutton, 1985.
Bethe, Hans A., and Brown, Gerald. "How a Supernova Explodes." *Scientific American,* May 1985.
Greenstein, George. *Frozen Star.* New American Library, 1983.
Lemonick, Michael. "Supernova." *Time,* March 23, 1987.

New York
Stock Exchange

By David A. Vise

Wild Days on Wall Street

"Bulls," "bears," and wild
fluctuations in stock prices made
many people wonder in 1987 what
the stock market was all about.

"Wall Street," as my grandfather used to say, "is a two-way street." That simple phrase bears a warning to investors dazzled by visions of stock market fortunes: CAUTION—stock prices can go up, but they can also come down.

The United States stock market proved the wisdom of that warning in 1987 after defying it for five consecutive years. For a while, it looked as though stock prices might rise indefinitely. They began in August 1982 to rebound from a slump and continued to rise during the first eight months of 1987, surging to record highs. Many investors on Wall Street—the narrow thoroughfare in New York City's financial district that has become a synonym for the stock market—grew wealthier by the day. If investors sold their shares of stock, they had extra cash on hand. If they held onto their stock, shareholders felt richer and more optimistic as they watched the value of their holdings increase. A drop in the market in September and early October made some investors nervous, but most thought the downturn would be temporary and that stocks would once again soar. They were in for a shock.

On October 19, a day that was immediately christened Black Monday, the U.S. stock market experienced the biggest one-day drop in its history. Suddenly, the party on Wall Street and on for-

Arbitrager: An investor who buys and sells the same stock in two markets at the same time to profit from a difference in price.

Bear market: A period of falling stock prices and investor pessimism.

Broker: An agent who, for a commission, assists investors in the buying and selling of stocks.

Bull market: A period of rising stock prices and investor optimism.

Dow Jones Industrial Average (the Dow): An adjusted price average of 30 major stocks listed on the New York Stock Exchange. The Dow is the most widely followed stock index.

Program trading: The computer-assisted buying and selling of stocks and stock index futures in order to profit from price differences between them.

Public company: A company that is owned by a large number of stockholders and whose stock is traded freely in the stock market.

Stock: Shares in the ownership of a company.

Stock exchange: A place where stocks are bought and sold.

Stock index futures: Contracts to buy or sell a particular stock index—a group of specified stocks—by a given date and at a set price.

The author:
David A. Vise is a business reporter for *The Washington* (D.C.) *Post.* He formerly worked as an investment banker with the Wall Street firm of Goldman, Sachs & Company.

eign stock exchanges seemed to be over, and the time had come for some sober reflection. Americans wanted answers. What had caused the stock market crash, and what needed to be done to prevent another, and perhaps even more disastrous, plunge in stock prices? More to the point for the average citizen, was the economy basically sound or might a stumbling stock market lead to a business recession—or even a depression? Economists and government officials spent the remainder of 1987 debating those questions. Meanwhile, as the panic subsided on Wall Street, investors slowly regained their confidence in the stock market.

The trading—that is, the buying and selling—of stock has long been an integral part of the nation's economy. In 1792, a group of two dozen auctioneers and merchants met under a buttonwood tree in the Wall Street area to trade stocks, activity that led to the founding of what would later become the New York Stock Exchange (NYSE). Over the years, New York City has remained the hub of stock market activities in the United States.

Today, nearly 50 million Americans invest in the stock market directly by purchasing either shares of stock or shares in *mutual funds*, organizations that pool the money of their investors and select stocks for them. An even larger number of Americans, estimated at 140 million, participate in the stock market indirectly through banks, insurance companies, pension funds, and other institutions that own stock.

When corporations owned by stockholders sell new shares of stock, they usually hire large investment banking firms to handle the sales for them. The shares may be bought by individual and institutional investors throughout the world. Companies sell stock to raise money for various purposes, such as to build new plants and buy equipment. Stock sales enable a business to expand. Investors buy stock hoping to profit from a future rise in its price. They may also hope to receive *dividends* on the stock—a share of company profits typically paid four times a year to stockholders.

A share of stock is, quite literally, a certificate of partial ownership of the company. Each stockholder has the right to vote on issues affecting the company, though of course those with the most stock have the greatest say. In some corporations, even though there are thousands of stockholders, a single individual or family owns more than 50 per cent of the stock and controls the company.

Companies that have tradeable shares owned by hundreds, thousands, or even millions of investors are called *public companies*. Many public companies start as private companies owned by one or two people or by a family. It is a dream of many aspiring business people to start a company and later "go public" by selling stock.

Stock exchanges are important because they make it easy for investors to buy and sell stock in public companies. The New York Stock Exchange, nicknamed the "Big Board," is the biggest and most prestigious stock exchange in the United States. The value of all the stocks of the more than 1,500 companies listed on the NYSE is in excess of $2 trillion. The NYSE is a private company owned by its member *brokers* (agents) including such well-known investment firms as Merrill Lynch, Pierce, Fenner & Smith Incorporated; Shearson Lehman Brothers, Incorporated; Paine Webber Incorporated; and Goldman, Sachs & Company. Membership gives the holder of a "seat" on the exchange the right to buy and sell stock directly on the trading floor. Each time shares of stock pass to a new owner, the broker handling the transaction earns a commission.

The NYSE—one of three national stock exchanges in the United States—has the strictest requirements for listing a corporation's stock. To be listed on the Big Board, a company must typically have a minimum of 2,000 stockholders who own 100 or more shares; at least 1.1 million shares outstanding; and $2.5 million in income before taxes.

The two other major U.S. exchanges are the American Stock Exchange (AMEX), also in New York City, and the National Association of Securities Dealers *over-the-counter* market. Unlike the AMEX and the NYSE, the over-the-counter market has no trading floor. All of its transactions are made electronically with the aid of computer terminals displaying the latest offers to buy and sell shares. The over-the-counter market has grown considerably in the 1980's. In addition, stocks are traded at regional exchanges in Boston, Chicago, San Francisco, and other cities, and at foreign exchanges such as the London and Tokyo exchanges.

Investors who wish to buy or sell shares of stock need not go to a stock exchange, however. A simple phone call to a broker is all that is required. There are stock brokerage firms throughout the United States, many of them branch offices of the NYSE member firms. See "How Stocks Are Bought and Sold," pages 148 and 149.

A group of auctioneers and merchants met under a buttonwood tree in New York City's Wall Street area in 1792 to trade stocks, *below left.* That meeting led to the establishment of a permanent stock trading center that later became the New York Stock Exchange (NYSE). Brokers at the NYSE, *below,* throw paper into the air on Jan. 8, 1987, to celebrate as the Dow Jones Industrial Average closes at 2,002.25, passing the 2,000 mark for the first time in its history.

How Stocks Are Bought and Sold

Companies issue stock to raise capital for factory construction, the purchase of equipment, and other purposes. Stocks are bought by both individuals and large institutional investors such as banks, insurance companies, and pension funds. Investors who buy shares of a company's stock offering may later wish to sell their shares. Brokers and stock exchanges facilitate stock transactions, matching one investor's sell order with another investor's buy order. Most shares of a company's stock change hands hundreds of times after their initial sale. In the 1970's, stock exchanges became highly computerized to make stock trading faster and easier. But some types of computerized stock transactions that developed in the 1980's, particularly a procedure called *program trading*, have been blamed for causing wild swings in stock prices.

The XYZ Corporation issues 100,000 shares of stock to raise money for expansion. The XYZ stock offering is bought by both individual and institutional investors.

An individual investor who missed out on the original stock offering decides later to buy 100 shares of XYZ stock on the open market. She calls her stockbroker and puts in a buy order.

An institutional investor that purchased 10,000 shares of XYZ stock now wishes to sell the shares. An investment officer at the institution phones the order to a broker.

The individual's stockbroker handles the transaction, which is a relatively small one, by typing the order into a computer terminal connected to the central computer of the New York Stock Exchange (or another large exchange). The central computer will automatically match the customer's buy order with a sell order from another investor. The broker reports the completed sale to the client.

The institution's broker calls the brokerage firm's main trading desk, at an office near the stock exchange, to inform them of the large sell order for XYZ stock.

At the trading desk, the order is relayed by phone or computer to another broker, called a *floor broker,* on the floor of the stock exchange.

Program traders carry out computer-assisted buy and sell orders involving huge "baskets" of stocks—the stocks of dozens or hundreds of companies totaling hundreds of thousands of shares—and *stock index futures.* A stock index is a group of specified stocks, and the value of the index is based on the price of those stocks. Futures, which are traded on separate exchanges, are written agreements to buy or sell a particular stock index by a specified time and at a specified price. Program traders profit by taking advantage of price differences between futures and the stocks on which they are based. When stocks are cheaper than futures, program traders buy stocks and sell futures; when futures are cheaper, they do the opposite. After buy or sell orders from program traders reach the stock exchange, the prices of many stocks—including XYZ stock—may rise or fall rapidly.

Stock exchange

The floor broker takes the sell order to the XYZ *specialist,* a broker who is responsible for maintaining fair and orderly trading in a limited number of stocks, including XYZ stock. If not enough buyers can be found for a stock, the specialist purchases shares of the stock with his own funds in an effort to keep the price from dropping too far.

Central computer

The specialist checks a computer terminal linked to the exchange's central computer to find the *bid price* for XYZ stock—the highest price anyone is currently willing to pay for the stock—and the *offer,* the lowest price any seller will take. With that information, the floor broker determines an asking price for the client's stock, and the specialist matches the sell order with the buy order of an investor who will pay that price. The completed transaction is reported to the buyer or buyers and to the seller.

The buying and selling of shares does not necessarily involve the transfer of actual stock certificates. Although shareholders are entitled to certificates if they want them, many investors are content to receive a written statement from their broker confirming their purchase of a stock. In such cases, the actual shares are left on deposit with the brokerage firm and are registered in the firm's name. This system enables stocks to change hands quickly and easily.

Stock prices are determined by the collective judgment of investors as they seek to buy and sell shares. The market value of any given stock is the price at which buyer meets seller, and it reflects the overall supply of that stock in relation to the demand for it among investors. When demand exceeds supply, the price rises— and vice versa. In general, the most important factor increasing investors' desire to own a company's stock is the expectation that the company will be consistently profitable in the future.

Stock prices are also affected by investors' perceptions about the future of an industry. If investors are optimistic, or "bullish," about the future of the computer industry, for example, all of the major computer stocks may benefit. On the other hand, if investors are

How to Read a Stock Listing

52 Weeks		Stock	Div.	Yld %	P-E Ratio	Sales 100s	High	Low	Close	Net Chg.
High	Low									
$53\frac{1}{8}$	29	Coca Cl	1.12	3.0	14	12816	$39\frac{3}{4}$	$36\frac{1}{4}$	$37\frac{1}{2}$	+ $1\frac{1}{4}$

The stock reports in the daily newspaper contain a wealth of information. For example, this listing from Oct. 28, 1987, tells the following about the stock of the Coca-Cola Company from the previous day's trading:

52-week high and low—These figures show, in dollars, the highest and lowest prices paid for the stock during the preceding 52 weeks. Coca-Cola stock sold for a high of $53.12 (53 ⅛) per share and a low of $29. (That low occurred nine days earlier on October 19, the day the stock market plummeted.)

Stock—Coca-Cola.

Dividend—The current annual dividend (payout of profits to shareholders) of Coca-Cola stock is $1.12 per share. The annual dividend of a company's stock is based on the company's latest quarterly or semiannual declaration of profits.

Percentage yield—This figure indicates the return that investors in a stock are currently getting on their money. The yield is the annual dividend divided by the current closing price of the stock. The percentage yield of Coca-Cola's stock as of October 27 was 3.0 per cent.

Price-to-earnings (PE) ratio—This figure is obtained by dividing the stock price by the company's annual earnings per share. Many investors judge a company's financial success by its PE ratio. Above a ratio of about 15, a stock becomes increasingly questionable as an investment because the price of the stock is not justified by the company's earnings. Coca-Cola's PE ratio on October 27 was 14, a typical figure at that time for many major U.S. stocks.

Sales in 100's—This number gives the volume of shares traded (divided by 100 to save space). A total of 1,281,600 shares of Coca-Cola stock (12,816 times 100) were traded on October 27.

High, low, and closing price—These figures show, in dollars, the highest and lowest prices the stock sold for during the day's trading, and the price it was selling for when trading ended. On October 27, Coca-Cola stock sold for a high of $39.75 and a low of $36.25. It closed at $37.50.

Change—This figure gives the difference between the stock's closing price for the day and its closing price for the previous day. Coca-Cola's stock rose $1.25 in price from October 26 to October 27.

pessimistic—"bearish"—about the prospects of the domestic steel industry, then the stocks of all American steel companies may be hurt.

In addition, trends in the overall economy affect stock prices, as do national and world events. And despite all the financial analysis and computer-generated data available, human emotion is always a major factor in the stock market. It is often said that the market is driven by two competing investor emotions: greed and fear. Greed, in fact, was undoubtedly a significant factor in pushing up stock prices in the 1980's. Many market observers said that pure investor speculation—the desire to "get rich quick"—had pushed stock prices to unreasonably high levels. According to that view, the tremendous growth in the stock market was a bubble that was destined to burst sooner or later, whenever investors began to fear that the "bull" market was ending and scrambled to sell their stock.

But there were also other important reasons why stock prices made such a dramatic climb:
■ Declining interest rates—and thus a lower financial return—on bonds and various kinds of bank accounts made stocks a more attractive investment.
■ Most American corporations showed steady, if modest, growth and earnings in the 1980's, which strengthened the value and appeal of their stocks.
■ Large purchases of U.S. stocks by foreign investors, led by the Japanese, increased the demand for stocks at the same time that large buy-outs of many companies' stocks decreased the supply. (Such buy-outs are made by companies, or by powerful groups of investors, seeking to take over the company whose stock they are purchasing.)
■ Precious metals, especially gold, fell dramatically in value during the 1980's, making them less alluring than stocks as an investment.

The most widely followed measure of stock prices for the overall market is the Dow Jones Industrial Average. The Dow, as it is often called, is an adjusted stock average of 30 major NYSE-listed companies, including the International Business Machines Corporation (IBM), the American Telephone and Telegraph Company, and the General Motors Corporation. Occasionally, a company is dropped from the Dow and another company takes its place. To reflect the growing importance of service industries, for instance, the Mc-Donald's Corporation was added to the index in 1985. The Dow average is calculated by adding the per-share stock prices of the 30 companies and dividing by 0.784. The divisor, which corrects for various changes in the Dow's stocks, is refigured periodically.

In the 1980's, market observers have relied increasingly on other, broader stock indexes, such as Standard & Poor's 500 Index and the New York Composite Index, to measure price movements. Since these indexes include more stocks than the Dow—500 in the case of Standard & Poor's—they may more accurately reflect the trend of the overall stock market. Nevertheless, business analysts and professional traders continue to cite the Dow most frequently when discussing stock-price movements.

The Dow roared upward at an incredible pace during the first eight months of 1987. On January 8, the Dow passed 2,000 for the first time in its history, on July 17 it passed 2,500, and on August 25 it closed at a record high of 2,722.42. Just five years earlier, on Aug. 12, 1982—the day marking the end of the most recent "bear," or declining, market—the Dow stood at 776.92. Thus, the stock average had more than tripled during the course of the expanding bull market.

The Dow, however, did not go up smoothly; it had some bumps along the way. On a number of occasions in 1986 and 1987, the Dow jumped or dipped with alarming suddenness. On Jan. 23, 1987, for instance, the index dropped 115 points in just over an hour. These erratic movements of stock prices were due in large measure to a pair of comparatively recent developments in the market: the increasing influence of institutional investors and the computerization of stock trading.

The rise of the institutional investor has been the most visible change in the U.S. stock market in the 1980's. For decades, the market was dominated by individual investors. Today, about 75 per cent of the transactions on the NYSE involve institutions such as pension funds, banks, insurance companies, and mutual funds.

The Bull Gets Gored
The bull market that began in August 1982 lasted more than five years. In that time, the Dow Jones Industrial Average rose from a low of 776.92 to a high of 2,722.42 on Aug. 25, 1987. Less than two months later, on October 19, the bull market ended with a crash as the Dow fell 508 points—the largest one-day decline in its history. In the days and weeks that followed, the stock market was shaky, but it regained much of its lost ground.

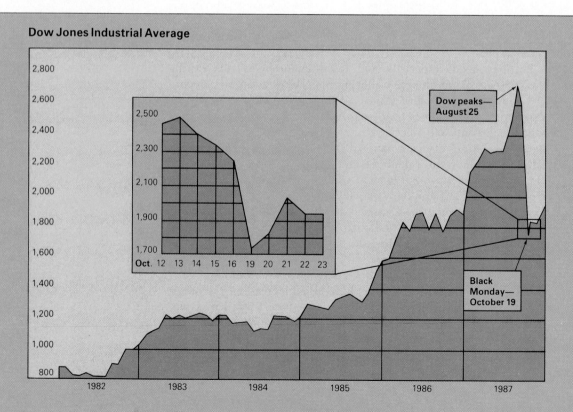

Dow Jones Industrial Average

Pension funds, in particular, have been a growing presence in the stock market. The assets of pension and retirement funds covering American workers shot up from $211 billion in 1970 to $823 billion in 1980 to $1.7 trillion in 1987. And an ever-larger share of those funds has been invested in the stock market.

Mutual funds have also played a big part in the stock market of the 1980's. Mutual funds relieve individuals of the tricky task of picking stocks by pooling the investors' money and investing it in a variety of stocks. Investors simply select a mutual fund that suits their needs. Some funds specialize in the stocks of certain kinds of companies, while others are distinguished by their degree of investment risk. Mutual funds have been highly popular in the 1980's, their investment pool growing from $41 billion in 1980 to more than $200 billion in 1987.

Institutional investors have pumped huge amounts of money into the stock market, but their investment strategies have frequently had a disruptive effect on stock prices. Playing a Wall Street version of follow-the-leader, institutions often jump into or out of stocks overnight, driving the market up or down sharply. Some market analysts complain that institutions, with their "herd instinct" and huge stock holdings, exert too much influence on the market.

Another important stock market development, the ultimate impact of which is yet to be seen, is the increased use of computers. Because they greatly simplify stock transactions, computers enable large institutional investors to trade hundreds of thousands of shares with the push of a few buttons. It is mainly through these huge, rapid transactions that institutional investors have had such a major impact on day-to-day stock prices.

The most controversial use of computers in stock transactions is a specialized application known as *program trading*. Program trading is a computer-assisted variant of *arbitrage* (pronounced *AHR buh trij* or *ahr buh TRAHZH*), a form of stock trading that takes advantage of small price differences between markets. In conventional arbitrage, a broker might note that General Motors stock is selling on the NYSE for $86 a share while at the same time it is going for $87 in

The stock market crash of 1929 combined with other weaknesses in the economy to bring on the Great Depression of the 1930's. On October 24, the first day of the crash—known as Black Thursday—worried investors gathered outside the New York Stock Exchange, *above left*. Almost exactly 58 years later, an exhausted stockbroker, *above,* reflected the fears of Wall Street as the market plummeted on Oct. 19, 1987, known as Black Monday. In 1987, however, economists expressed confidence that despite the stock market's steep decline and subsequent instability, there was little danger of the U.S. economy sinking into a depression.

In the 1980's, stock trading at exchanges around the world became closely interlinked as a result of computerization and advanced telecommunications. With the rise of this global trading, U.S. stock exchanges began to face stiff competition from major stock exchanges in other countries—such as the London Stock Exchange, *above,* and the Tokyo Stock Exchange, *above right*—for corporate stock listings.

London. By putting in a buy order in New York and a sell order in London, the arbitrager makes a quick $1-a-share profit.

Program traders deal simultaneously in large "baskets" of various stocks listed in one of the major indexes, usually the Standard & Poor's 500 Index, and contracts—called *stock index futures*—involving the same stocks. Stock index futures give investors the right to buy, or sell, the stocks that make up the index at a specified price by the end of the contract's 90-day lifetime. By purchasing such a contract, the investor bets that the price of the stocks included in the contract will rise. If that happens, the investor can pay for the contract at the current market price and sell it later at a higher price.

Program traders, for their part, are unconcerned whether stock prices go up or down. All they care about is the price gap between stock index futures and the various stocks that make up those contracts. The moment their computers tell them the price gap is big enough, they go to work, trading huge amounts of stock and futures. These whirlwind transactions ensure the traders of an arbitrage profit when the futures contracts expire.

Many Wall Street experts are critical of program trading because, even more than other forms of institutional trading, it has a huge and often negative effect on the stock market. When program traders conclude their multimillion-dollar maneuvers, stock prices can vary wildly. Program trading contributed to several severe, though temporary, drops in the Dow over the past few years. Borrowing a term from the nuclear power industry, NYSE Chairman John J. Phelan, Jr., warned in 1987 that program trading might lead to a financial "meltdown," a computer-driven collapse in stock prices.

On Black Monday—Oct. 19, 1987—a meltdown finally occurred. By the time the market closed on that day, the Dow had dropped 508 points, losing 22.6 per cent of its value. That plunge was far worse than one that occurred on another black Monday—Monday, October 28, during the historic Wall Street crash of 1929—when stock prices fell 12.8 per cent.

Although program traders may have contributed to the 1987 crash, no one at the time, Phelan included, accused them of being the main cause of it. Summing up the view of many stock market experts, the NYSE chief said the price cave-in was not caused by a single triggering event but rather was the result of a variety of stresses on the overheated U.S. financial system.

Ironically, one of the factors that led to the crash was the surging stock market itself. Between August 1982 and August 1987, investors had profited from the longest and strongest bull market in many years. But since financial markets tend to be cyclical, with booms turning into busts, it was natural that stock prices would decline at some point. What market analysts did not foresee was that the inevitable downturn would be so sudden and dramatic.

There had been warning signs, for those willing to see them. From its August peak, the Dow average had declined nearly 500 points by mid-October. On Friday, October 16, the last day of trading before Black Monday, jittery investors sent the average reeling 108 points, a record loss up to that time.

In the days leading up to Black Monday, there was a growing expectation among investors that interest rates would be going up to compensate for a possible renewal of *inflation* (rising prices). Just as falling interest rates make stocks a more desirable investment relative to bonds and bank accounts, climbing interest rates have the reverse effect. The anticipation of higher interest rates was widely cited as a factor in the stock market decline.

Wall Street leaders also pinned blame for the stock market drop on a tax proposal in Congress that would have slowed corporate takeovers. In addition, they cited the failure of Washington policy-

Program traders at a New York City brokerage firm prepare to send a massive sell order to the New York Stock Exchange. Program trading, which has been one of the most controversial uses of computers in the stock market in the 1980's, may have contributed to the Black Monday crash that occurred in October 1987.

makers to deal with the "twin deficits"—the huge federal budget deficit and the trade deficit. In 1987, both the budget shortfall and the trade deficit—an excess of imports over exports—topped $140-billion. Total federal debt exceeded a staggering $2 trillion. Investors feared that such enormous indebtedness, which required the government to borrow heavily in order to balance its accounts, jeopardized the U.S. economy. In addition, many investors said the hefty trade imbalance showed that the United States was in decline as a world economic power.

A striking aspect of the Black Monday crash was its forceful and immediate effect on stock markets elsewhere in the world, particularly in London and Tokyo. On October 20, the day after the U.S. crash, stock prices tumbled on the London and Tokyo exchanges, and in succeeding days events in each market directly affected trading in the other two. In the United States, nervous investors tuned in their radios each morning to learn what had happened on the overseas exchanges during the night. The Dow rose and fell like a ship in a rough sea.

The influence of the far-flung markets on one another was partly psychological, as investors reacted emotionally to the news of price fluctuations elsewhere in the world. But there were also more tangible links between markets, owing to the fact that the stocks of many multinational corporations such as Dow Chemical Company and IBM are traded in all of them. When stock prices of the multinationals fell in one market, they fell in the others as well. The events of October 1987 showed that the stock market, in this age of computers and instant telecommunications, was becoming one global market.

The U.S. stock market crash inevitably invited comparisons with the 1929 crash, which combined with other weaknesses in the economy to produce the Great Depression of the 1930's. Was another depression possible in the 1990's? Doomsayers pointed to a number of parallels between the eras that preceded the two stock market collapses. In both the 1920's and the 1980's, a booming stock market set price records with each passing day, and Wall Street was rocked by scandals. During the 1920's, stock prices were manipulated through trading "pools" that enriched slick insiders at the expense of unsuspecting individual investors. In the 1980's, investors were cheated by a group of investment bankers and other insiders who traded stocks on the basis of confidential information.

Both decades were marked by heavy borrowing. In the 1920's, credit was easy, and individual investors borrowed up to 90 per cent of the purchase price of stocks. In the 1980's, investors were allowed to borrow heavily to buy stock index futures, and financial fortune hunters known as *corporate raiders* borrowed as much as 90 per cent of the money needed to buy entire companies.

Other similarities abound between the 1920's and 1980's. Then, as now, Congress considered *protectionist* legislation aimed at sheltering U.S. industry from foreign competition. And in both periods, bank failures rose, energy prices fell, and income tax reform cut tax rates for individuals and hiked them for corporations.

Fortunately, there are also some important differences between today's economic situation and that of 60 years ago, particularly with regard to the stock market. Since the 1930's, increased federal regulation of market activities has provided some degree of protection against a recurrence of what happened in 1929. In 1934, Congress created the Securities and Exchange Commission (SEC) to safeguard investors by requiring public companies to make periodic disclosures of their finances. Previously, such information could be kept secret, and as a result many investors unwittingly put their money into failing companies or companies that existed only on paper. At the same time that it established the SEC, Congress gave the Board of Governors of the Federal Reserve System ("the Fed"), the agency that regulates U.S. banking and controls the nation's money supply, the authority to limit credit-fueled stock speculation. Today, investors may borrow no more than 50 per cent of a stock's purchase price. While neither the Fed nor the SEC has the authority to prop up sagging stock prices, both stand ready to take whatever action is in their power to prevent a total stock market collapse.

After Black Monday, the Fed announced that it would make cash readily available to banks, an action that facilitated stock trading and drove interest rates down slightly, thereby stimulating the stock market. This easy-money policy contrasted sharply with the agency's stance in the wake of the 1929 crash, when it tightened credit. The contraction of the money supply in the 1930's probably contributed to the depression.

The safeguards that have been built into the economy since 1929 make a depression less likely today. Still, Black Monday set off alarm bells that could not be ignored. President Ronald Reagan responded to the stock market crisis by appointing a special commission to study the crash and make recommendations for reforms.

How much of the commission's advice, expected in early 1988, would be heeded was uncertain as 1987 drew to a close, but a few members of Congress realized that strong action was needed to end the roller-coaster ride on Wall Street. A handful of legislators realized also that there was no time to dawdle. Black Monday's stock market plunge was swifter, more dramatic, and more global than anything the world had seen before. The challenge now was to make sure it wouldn't happen again.

For further reading:

Flumiani, Carlo M. *Young People's Introduction to the World of Wall Street.* The Institute for Economic and Financial Research, 1987.

Money magazine editors. *Money Guide: The Stock Market.* Andrews, McMeel, & Parker, 1987.

Seligman, Joel. *The Transformation of Wall Street.* Houghton Mifflin, 1982.

A Year in Perspective

THE YEAR BOOK casts a backward glance at the furors, fancies, and follies of yesteryear. The coincidences of history that are revealed offer substantial proof that the physical world may continually change, but human nature—with all its inventiveness, amiability, and even perversity—remains fairly constant, for better or worse, throughout the years.

See page 170.

By Sara Dreyfuss

Gala celebrations in 1887 in London, *opposite page, top,* and Philadelphia, *above,* mark the 50th anniversary of the reign of Great Britain's Queen Victoria, *opposite page, bottom,* and the 100th anniversary of the signing of the United States Constitution. The decorative floral motif in this article is adapted from a textile design by William Morris, a British artist and poet of the late 1800's.

1887: A Year in Perspective

Hollywood was established, softball was invented, and Helen Keller met her miracle worker.

"The morning was beautiful and bright with a fresh air. Troops began passing early with bands playing, and one heard constant cheering." So wrote Queen Victoria in her journal for June 21, 1887—her Golden Jubilee, marking 50 years on the British throne.

During Victoria's long reign as queen of Great Britain and Northern Ireland and empress of India, the British Empire had expanded to include about one-fourth of the world's land and people. Zulu chiefs, Indian rajahs, and other royal visitors from throughout the vast empire poured into London to celebrate the Jubilee.

Nearly a million people thronged the route of the queen's procession from Buckingham Palace to Westminster Abbey, where a thanksgiving service was held. The streets rang with cheers when Victoria appeared, riding in an open gilt carriage drawn by six perfectly matched cream-colored horses. Her advisers had urged her to wear a crown, but Victoria insisted on a black dress and bonnet like those she had worn since the death of her husband, Prince Albert, in 1861. For this joyous occasion, however, she wore white lace on her dress and diamond ornaments on her bonnet.

At 10 P.M., after a full day of festivities, beacon fires were lit on the country's highest peaks, forming a blazing chain from northeastern Scotland to southwestern Cornwall. *Harper's New Monthly Magazine* reported, "The pageant was one of the most brilliant and imposing ever seen in England." In her journal, Victoria commented, "Felt truly grateful that all had passed off so admirably."

Centennial of the Constitution

The United States also celebrated an important anniversary in 1887, the centennial of the signing of the Constitution, which had taken place on Sept. 17, 1787, in Independence Hall in Philadelphia. Thousands of visitors jammed Philadelphia for a three-day festival, held from Sept. 15 to 17, 1887. On the first day, a huge industrial parade represented the nation's trades, from shipbuilders and carriage makers to brewers and cigar makers. On the second day, the famous scarlet-coated U.S. Marine Band, conducted by John Philip Sousa, marched at the head of a military parade of 30,000 uniformed soldiers. On the third day, a vast crowd listened to speeches by President Grover Cleveland and other dignitaries in Independence Square. *Harper's Weekly* magazine called the celebration "a unique event in the history of pageantry," and *Frank Leslie's Illustrated Newspaper* declared, "Nothing could have eclipsed the spectacular brilliancy and the grand patriotic enthusiasm of the three days' national festival."

The author:
Sara Dreyfuss is Associate Editor of THE WORLD BOOK YEAR BOOK.

Unrest in Russia

Leslie's newspaper contrasted the satisfaction of Americans with the unrest in Russia: "It is easy to thrill with patriotic pride at the general prosperity of our country, the good order, the contentment

and freedom which distinguish America . . . from Russia, a cruel despotism, built upon a volcano." Russia's ruler, Czar Alexander III, held supreme power and ruled harshly. The discontent among his people, especially the middle class and university students, had become alarming.

In March 1887, a group of students led by Alexander I. Ulyanov, a 21-year-old biology student at St. Petersburg University, planned to assassinate the czar. They obtained explosives and manufactured bombs, but the police discovered the plot and arrested the students. *Leslie's* described with wonder their idealism and determination: "Most of those concerned in it [the plot] seem to have rejoiced that they were counted worthy to participate in the murderous work." The newspaper predicted, "It will be hard to stamp out such fanaticism as this by mere coercive methods."

Five of the students, including Ulyanov, were hanged in May 1887. The abortive assassination plot and the hangings deeply influenced Ulyanov's younger brother Vladimir, and the revolutionary movement proved impossible to stamp out. Thirty years later, Vladimir—who had changed his last name to Lenin—led the revolution of 1917 in which the Communists seized power in Russia. Lenin became the first dictator of the Soviet Union.

Investigating the 1887 plot to kill the czar, the police rounded up dozens of known or suspected revolutionaries. One of those arrested was a 20-year-old medical student named Józef Piłsudski, who came from what was then Russian Poland. He was charged with conspiring to assassinate the czar and was exiled to Siberia for five years. Piłsudski later led the fight for Polish independence and served as Poland's first chief of state after it became a republic in 1918.

Anne Mansfield Sullivan begins in 1887 to teach 6-year-old Helen Keller, blind and deaf since infancy, using methods later portrayed in the play and film *The Miracle Worker.*

Creation of Esperanto

One of Piłsudski's countrymen, a physician named Ludwig L. Zamenhof, saw how the language barriers among the Poles, Russians, Germans, and other peoples of Russian Poland contributed to friction. He believed that if one common language were spoken throughout the world, it would promote understanding and good feeling among nations.

Zamenhof invented a new, easy-to-learn language called Esperanto, which has only 16 rules of grammar. The first textbook of Esperanto, *Lingvo Internacia*, appeared in 1887 under the pen name Dr. Esperanto (*esperanto*, in Esperanto, means *one who hopes*). Esperanto became and is still the most widely used artificial language in the world.

Helen meets her miracle worker

A famous incident in 1887 involved a 6-year-old girl named Helen Keller, who had lost her sight and hearing as a baby. On March 3, Anne Mansfield Sullivan, a teacher from the Perkins Institution for the Blind in Boston, came to Helen's home in Tuscumbia, Ala., to work with her. Sullivan described the child as "a wild, destructive animal." Deaf, mute, and blind, Helen could be reached only by touch.

Within a month, Sullivan made a breakthrough. Holding Helen's hand in a cool stream of water, she repeatedly spelled *w-a-t-e-r* into the other hand. Helen wrote later, "Somehow the mystery of language was revealed to me. I knew then that 'w-a-t-e-r' meant the wonderful cool something that was flowing over my hand. That living word awakened my soul, gave it light, hope, joy, set it free." Keller graduated from college and lectured throughout the world to aid the blind and the deaf. Her breakthrough in 1887 was dramatized in the play and motion picture *The Miracle Worker*.

Crowding onto the wagon

The temperance movement, dedicated to curbing the use of alcoholic beverages, had wide support in 1887, especially among the middle class. Many people blamed drinking for crime, poverty, and other problems, particularly in cities. "The saloon evil has grown to such enormous proportions," *Leslie's* warned, "as not only to undermine the morals of the city, but to threaten its material prosperity, sap its social life and make good government impossible."

The temperance movement, led by such organizations as the Prohibition Party and the Woman's Christian Temperance Union (W.C.T.U.), gained considerable political power. Several states, including Iowa, Kansas, Maine, New Hampshire, and Vermont, had enacted statewide prohibition laws by 1887.

A W.C.T.U. official named Susanna Madora Salter in 1887 became the first woman mayor in the United States. Opponents of prohibition had put Salter's name on the ballot in Argonia, Kans., as a joke, never expecting her to win. Most states denied women the vote at the time, but earlier that year Kansas had authorized women to vote in school and city elections. Salter was elected mayor of Argonia on April 4, 1887, and served for one year.

Another temperance supporter was the nation's 22-year-old first lady, Frances Folsom Cleveland. *Lippincott's Monthly Magazine* reported that she wrote to one woman who joined the movement, "It is encouraging to know of every sister who wants to add her strength to the cause which happily some day will rid our land of ruined men and broken families." The W.C.T.U. saluted the President's wife for what it called her "moral heroism" in drinking only cold water at state dinners. One White House guest reported, "There were wineglasses to the right of her and wineglasses to the left of her, but still she did not falter."

Birth of the United Way

Another idealistic effort took place in Denver, where a Jewish rabbi, two Protestant clergymen, and a Roman Catholic priest joined forces in 1887 in a single fund-raising appeal. They collected about $21,700 for 22 local charities. Their cooperation was the beginning of the United Way of America, which now raises millions of dollars yearly for more than 37,000 charitable agencies throughout the United States.

The tariff issue

It seems odd today, with the federal budget deficit totaling hundreds of billions of dollars, that President Cleveland was actually troubled by a fat surplus in the U.S. Treasury. The government regularly collected more money in tariffs—taxes on imported goods—and other taxes than it could spend. For the fiscal year that ended on June 30, 1888, revenues totaled about $336 million, and expenditures only $242 million. Business suffered from a shortage of money in circulation, while huge sums lay locked up in Treasury vaults. *Harper's Weekly* warned that "paralysis" threatened the economy. "An indefinite continuation of this course," the magazine said,

Deaths of notable people in 1887 included:

Beecher, Henry Ward (1813-1887), American Protestant clergyman known for his eloquent sermons.

Borodin, Alexander (1833-1887), Russian composer.

Dix, Dorothea L. (1802-1887), American social reformer who fought for better treatment of the mentally ill.

Kirchhoff, Gustav R. (1824-1887), German physicist who pioneered in studies of the chemical composition of stars.

Krupp, Alfred (1812-1887), German industrialist who built the Krupp firm into Germany's largest arms maker.

Laforgue, Jules (1860-1887), French poet known for his ironic verses.

Lazarus, Emma (1849-1887), American poet who wrote the sonnet on the Statue of Liberty that reads, "Give me your tired, your poor . . . ."

Lind, Jenny (1820-1887), soprano known as the Swedish Nightingale.

Wheeler, William A. (1819-1887), Vice President of the United States from 1877 to 1881.

Whitworth, Sir Joseph (1803-1887), British mechanical engineer and inventor.

Wood, Ellen Price (1814-1887), British author who wrote under the name Mrs. Henry Wood, best known for her novel *East Lynne* (1861).

Woods, William B. (1824-1887), associate justice of the Supreme Court of the United States from 1881 to 1887.

"would lead to a return to a state of barter, because the government would absorb all the medium of exchange."

In President Cleveland's annual message on Dec. 6, 1887, he asked Congress to reduce the surplus by lowering tariffs, then the chief source of government revenue. He called them "the vicious, inequitable, and illogical source of unnecessary taxation." Most U.S. manufacturers wanted high protective tariffs, and a bill to lower tariffs died in Congress the next year. Cleveland had nevertheless focused attention on the problem. "The whole country will applaud the boldness and candor with which the President states what he conceives to be the dominant issue of the hour," *Leslie's* said.

Regulation of railroads

Another pressing issue was public indignation over monopolistic practices of the railroads, especially unfair rates. Congress passed the Act to Regulate Commerce (later called the Interstate Commerce Act) of Feb. 4, 1887. The new law held that railway rates must be reasonable, and it banned certain unfair practices. The act also established the Interstate Commerce Commission (ICC), the first regulatory commission in U.S. history. The ICC originally had authority only over railroads, with little power to enforce its rulings. But, said *Harper's Weekly*, "It is at least a sincere effort to begin the reform." The commission was also the first of a long line of agencies created to supervise private businesses in the public interest.

New Indian policy

One new law, the General Allotment Act of Feb. 8, 1887, became an example of good intentions gone wrong. This law broke up the land holdings of Indian tribes into small units of 40 to 160 acres (16 to 64 hectares). The government gave each unit to an individual Indian in hope of encouraging the Native Americans to become farmers. The law, known as the Dawes Act, was sponsored by Senator Henry L. Dawes of Massachusetts—"than whom," said *Leslie's*, "the Indian has no truer friend." *Leslie's* predicted that the Dawes Act would end "the idle and demoralizing existence which is enforced upon these Indians by the reservation system. Indians who own land, who are acquiring property and working for more, will

The gramophone, *above,* patented in September 1887 by German-born inventor Emile Berliner, gives better sound reproduction than the old tin-cylinder phonograph.

A sequence of photographs from *Animal Locomotion* (1887) by Eadweard Muybridge shows a dancer in motion, *below.*

An 1887 map offers residential lots for sale in a new subdivision called Hollywood, *left.*

not be a source of danger to their neighbors, and of expense to the Government."

Along with the supposed benefit to the Indians came a tempting bonus. After the Indians got their share, much land would be left over. The government intended to sell the surplus land to whites and use the money to pay for the education of Indians.

Unfortunately, the Dawes Act was a disaster for Native Americans. Many had no knowledge of farming, and others had no interest in it. Also, much of the land was unsuitable for crops. As a result, many Indians sold their land and lived off the money they received. After the money ran out, they had no means of support.

Australian-born soprano Nellie Melba, *below,* who debuts in Brussels, Belgium, in 1887, goes on to become opera's reigning queen.

Hooray for Hollywood

Out West, a Kansas real estate developer named Harvey H. Wilcox in 1886 had bought a fig orchard near Los Angeles, then a boom town of 50,000. In 1887, Wilcox turned the area into a residential subdivision called Hollywood, selling lots at $150 per acre (0.4 hectare). Then, in 1911, a small film company from New Jersey leased a Hollywood tavern as a motion-picture studio. With a sunny climate and nearby mountains and deserts to serve as backgrounds for filming, the town proved ideal for motion pictures. Other film companies followed, and Hollywood, now part of Los Angeles, became the entertainment capital of the world.

The glittering world of opera

Like today's most glamorous Hollywood stars, the opera singers of 1887 had lives of wealth and luxury, and commanded the devo-

William Randolph Hearst, a 24-year-old newspaperman, takes over *The Daily Examiner* in San Francisco in 1887 and begins to build a publishing empire that became the Hearst Corporation.

tion of their fans. The reigning prima donna was a Spanish-born soprano, Adelina Patti, the most highly paid performer of her day. *Leslie's* reported in February 1887 that Patti received $11,000 for a concert in Denver, more than the Vice President of the United States earned in a year. Clauses in all of Patti's contracts excused her from rehearsals and specified how large her name must appear on posters. An 1887 advertisement for Pears Soap carried the prima donna's endorsement: "I have found it matchless for the hands and complexion."

Otello, a new opera by the great Italian composer Giuseppe Verdi, premiered at La Scala opera house in Milan, Italy, on Feb. 5, 1887. *Leslie's* called it "a brilliant success" and reported that the audience summoned the composer for 28 curtain calls.

The Australian-born soprano Nellie Melba made her operatic debut on Oct. 13, 1887, in Brussels, Belgium. Melba's real name was Helen Porter Mitchell, but she took her stage name in honor of her hometown, Melbourne. Her debut, as Gilda in Verdi's *Rigoletto*, made her famous throughout Europe, and she eventually succeeded Patti as opera's reigning queen.

Most people in 1887 heard music only at the opera and other live performances, but an invention that year would bring music into many homes. On September 26, a German-born inventor, Emile Berliner, applied for a patent on his gramophone. Unlike the phonograph invented 10 years earlier by Thomas Edison, which used tin cylinders, Berliner's gramophone played flat disks. The disks provided better sound reproduction than cylinders, lasted longer, and could be stamped out in large quantities from a master disk.

Photography grows in popularity

Photography was a popular hobby in 1887. *The Century Illustrated Monthly Magazine* referred to "the contagion of the camera" and said, "There is something so communicable in this enthusiasm that it behooves no one to regard the phenomenon with disrespectful flippancy." Most photographs were taken on bulky glass plates that had to be changed after each exposure, but on May 2, 1887, an American clergyman named Hannibal W. Goodwin applied for a patent that revolutionized photography. Goodwin developed a celluloid film that was tough but flexible. It could be moved through a camera and used to take a series of pictures.

British-born photographer Eadweard Muybridge completed an 11-volume collection of photographs called *Animal Locomotion* in 1887. He used a series of cameras triggered in rapid succession by a clockwork device to photograph animals and people in motion—pigeons flying, horses galloping, dancers twirling, and even a mother spanking her child.

Milestones in science and medicine

The year 1887 was an important one for science. In 1864, James Clerk Maxwell, a British physicist, had predicted the existence of invisible electromagnetic waves that traveled through space at the speed of light. In 1887, the German physicist Heinrich R. Hertz performed experiments that proved Maxwell's ideas correct. Hertz's work led to the development of radio, television, and radar.

Another famous experiment in 1887 proved that a widely held theory was incorrect. Many scientists had observed that light traveled through the emptiness of outer space much as sound waves moved through air. They imagined that an invisible substance called *ether* filled all space and served as the medium through which light waves traveled, as air did for sound waves.

Two American physicists, Albert A. Michelson and Edward W. Morley, disproved the ether theory in 1887. They performed an experiment showing that light traveled at the same speed in all directions. If ether had existed, light would have traveled slower in some directions, like a swimmer moving against the current. The Michelson and Morley experiment was one of the most crucial in the history of science. It opened the way for German-born physicist Albert Einstein to formulate his theory of relativity, and—among other things—it led to the development of nuclear energy.

Important developments in medicine also took place in 1887. The National Institutes of Health, a U.S. government agency that conducts biomedical research, was born that year as a one-room laboratory on Staten Island. In Switzerland, the first contact lens, made

Master detective Sherlock Holmes makes his first appearance in 1887 in *Beeton's Christmas Annual,* a London periodical, in a novel called *A Study in Scarlet.*

of glass and covering the entire eye, was made by a glass blower at the request of ophthalmologist A. Eugen Frick.

The age of sensationalism

Newspapers in 1887 were becoming increasingly sensational in a battle to win readers. The papers tried to outdo one another with exciting reports of crimes, disasters, and scandals. They also started many reform campaigns by exposing social and political evils. Elizabeth Cochrane Seaman, a 20-year-old newspaper reporter in New York City who wrote under the pen name Nellie Bly, investigated the care of the mentally ill for *The World*. She pretended to be insane and got herself committed to the Blackwell's Island Lunatic Asylum, a mental hospital for the poor on what is now Roosevelt Island in New York City. Bly's report in *The World*, called "Ten Days in a Mad House," described how patients were poorly fed, beaten, and otherwise mistreated. It caused a public investigation of the city's mental hospitals and brought nationwide reforms.

Nellie Bly's exposé was a typical feature for *The World*, the newspaper with the largest circulation in the United States in 1887—about 250,000. Under the guidance of its Hungarian-born publisher, Joseph Pulitzer, the paper featured plentiful illustrations, exciting headlines, and human-interest stories. One *World* employee who absorbed Pulitzer's philosophy of journalism was William Randolph Hearst, the 24-year-old son of mining millionaire George

Tennis in 1887 is a genteel game played by men in white shirts and trousers and women in long dresses and hats.

Lawn Tennis (1887), a lithograph by L. Prang & Company; Granger Collection

Hearst. Young Hearst had taken a job on *The World* in 1885 after being expelled from college for playing a practical joke.

In 1887, George Hearst gave his son a San Francisco paper, *The Daily Examiner*, to run. William Randolph Hearst proceeded to remodel the *Examiner* in the image of *The World*. "We must be startlingly original," he wrote his father. Hearst hired a talented staff, spent freely on artwork and interesting features, and chartered special trains to enable reporters to cover events quickly. During the first year under his management, the *Examiner*'s circulation doubled from 20,000 to 40,000. Hearst eventually bought other newspapers and magazines and built the largest publishing empire of his day. The Hearst Corporation celebrated its 100th anniversary in 1987.

There were other important publishing events in 1887. In January, New York City publisher Louis Keller brought out the first edition of the *Social Register*, described as "a record of society, comprising an accurate and careful list of its members."

Literature, art, and sports

Sherlock Holmes, the most famous fictional detective of all time, made his appearance in 1887 in a popular novel called *A Study in Scarlet*. A Scottish physician, Arthur Conan Doyle, wrote the book to fill the time when patients failed to appear. Another popular novel that year was *She* by the British writer H. Rider Haggard. It tells the story of a white goddess in Africa who is 2,000 years old but still appears young and beautiful.

The arts were productive in 1887. American sculptor Augustus Saint-Gaudens unveiled his best-known work, a statue of Abraham Lincoln in Chicago's Lincoln Park. The city also gained two masterpieces by architect Henry Hobson Richardson—Glessner House and the Marshall Field & Company Wholesale Warehouse.

Chicago also became the birthplace of a new game, softball, in 1887. Alumni from Harvard and Yale universities had gathered at the Farragut Boat Club in Chicago on Thanksgiving Day to await the results of the Harvard-Yale football game. One of the Yale men tied a boxing glove into a ball and threw it to a Harvard man, who batted it with a stick. At the suggestion of George W. Hancock, a reporter for the Chicago Board of Trade, the men chalked base lines on the floor and began to play. Softball, often called "mush ball," caught on as a winter substitute for baseball. The new game was played indoors with a soft, 17-inch (43-centimeter) ball.

The first U.S. women's tennis championship was held at the Philadelphia Cricket Club in 1887. The winner, Ellen Hansell of Philadelphia, recalled later that the women wore long dresses, petticoats, and hats, and lobbed the ball gently back and forth.

In 1987, women's tennis had become a forceful game far different from the gentle contest of 1887, and a surplus in the U.S. Treasury was scarcely imaginable. As someone once said, "The past is a foreign country: They do things differently there."

The Year
on File

Contributors to THE WORLD BOOK
YEAR BOOK report on the major developments of 1987. The contributors' names appear at the end of the
articles they have written, and a complete roster of contributors, listing
their professional affiliations and the
articles they have written, is on pages
6 and 7.

A quiz on some events of 1987 as reported in various Year on File articles
appears on pages 174 and 175.

Articles in this section are arranged
alphabetically by subject matter. In
most cases, the article titles are the

same as those of the articles in THE
WORLD BOOK ENCYCLOPEDIA that
they update. The numerous cross-
references guide the reader to a subject or information that may be in
some other article or that may appear
under an alternative title. "See" and
"See also" cross-references appear
within and at the end of articles to
direct the reader to related information elsewhere in THE YEAR BOOK.
"In WORLD BOOK, see" references
point the reader to articles in the encyclopedia that provide background
information to the year's events reported in THE YEAR BOOK.

See "Iran-Contra Affair," page 365.

The Year on File Quiz

THE YEAR BOOK presents a quiz on some events of 1987 as reported in various articles in the Year on File. Answers appear on page 535.

1. Where did the Pan American Games take place in August?
2. What motion picture about the Vietnam War won the Academy Award for best picture?
3. What candidate, considered the front-runner for the 1988 Democratic presidential nomination, dropped out of the race in May 1987 and then changed his mind and reentered the race in December?
4. Which of the following mayors failed in his bid for reelection in 1987?
   a. Harold Washington of Chicago
   b. Richard G. Hatcher of Gary, Ind.
   c. Federico Peña of Denver
   d. W. Wilson Goode of Philadelphia
5. How many prime ministers did Italy have in 1987?
6. What two phrases do the letters *PTL* stand for?
7. What is *colorization?*
8. What embarrassing incident in May led to the dismissal of two Soviet defense officials?
9. In October, the American Federation of Labor and Congress of Industrial Organizations voted to readmit what large union that it expelled in 1957?
10. Three branches of what denomination merged in 1987 to form the fifth largest Protestant group?
11. Canadian Prime Minister Brian Mulroney and the leaders of Canada's 10 provinces signed an agreement in June to end a boycott of Canada's 1982 constitution by which province?
12. On what grounds did a federal judge ban 44 textbooks from Alabama public schools in March, only to have the ban overturned by a federal Court of Appeals in August?
13. Who became in February 1987 the first skipper to have lost and then regained the America's Cup, yachting's most prestigious trophy?
14. What television evangelist declared that God would take his life if his followers did not give him $8 million by March 31?
15. The painting below, by an artist who sold

only one painting during his lifetime, was auctioned for a record $53.9 million in November. Who was the artist?
16. What did the man above accomplish in May?
17. What West Coast city was rattled by a strong earthquake in October?
18. Which of these congressmen gave his name to the amendment limiting aid to the Nicaraguan rebels called *contras?*
   a. Senator Bob Packwood of Oregon
   b. Senator Edward M. Kennedy of Massachusetts
   c. Representative Edward P. Boland of Massachusetts
   d. Representative Jack F. Kemp of New York
19. What U.S. university was barred from football in 1987 because of improper payments to players?
20. What Georgia town became in January the site of the largest civil rights march since the 1965 rally in Selma, Ala.?
21. Match the descriptions of these ships, which made headlines in 1987, with their names:

1. U.S. Navy frigate struck by an Iraqi missile	a. *Herald of Free Enterprise*
2. British ferry that capsized in the English Channel	b. *Mobro*
3. barge carrying garbage from Islip, N.Y.	c. *Sea Isle City*
4. Kuwaiti tanker flying the U.S. flag hit by an Iranian missile	d. U.S.S. *Stark*

22. Who won the Wimbledon women's singles tennis championship in July for a sixth consecutive time, her eighth time overall?
23. A series of breakthroughs in physics in late

1986 and 1987 involved what group of materials that become excellent conductors of electricity at low temperatures?

24. Despite Jewish protests, Pope John Paul II met in June with what head of state, who has been implicated in Nazi war crimes?

25. Two Cabinet members—Transportation Secretary Elizabeth Hanford Dole and Labor Secretary William E. Brock III—resigned in the fall to work on the presidential campaign of which candidate?

26. Who in October joined a group of 11 other Supreme Court nominees that includes Clement F. Haynsworth, Jr., and G. Harrold Carswell?

27. In March, the U.S. Food and Drug Administration approved zidovudine, formerly known as azidothymidine (AZT), the first drug to combat what serious illness?

28. What explosion that happened 160,000 years ago was first detected on earth in February 1987?

29. What U.S. Cabinet member was killed in a riding accident in July?

30. Why were basketball fans in Miami and Orlando, Fla., Charlotte, N.C., and Minneapolis, Minn., cheering in April?

31. The genetically engineered bacteria sprayed on a California field in April in the first authorized outdoor release of such altered organisms were designed to do what?

32. *Glasnost* is:
    a. an opera by modern composer Philip Glass
    b. a Russian word meaning *openness*
    c. a new drug that lowers cholesterol levels in the blood

33. Who was the former world welterweight boxing champion who won the world middleweight championship in an upset victory on April 6?

34. What practice did Chrysler Chairman Lee A. Iacocca call "a lousy idea" in newspaper advertisements in July?

35. What large oil company filed for bankruptcy in April, seeking protection under the bankruptcy code to continue a legal battle with the Pennzoil Company?

36. A recall campaign was launched in 1987 against what state governor?

37. Who is the European leader shown at the left below, who in June 1987 became the first prime minister of her country to be elected to a third term since the 1800's?

38. What popular radio program, shown above, aired its last live broadcast in June?

39. Who is the track star known as the world's fastest human being after he broke the world record for the 100 meters in August?

40. Where in the South Pacific did a military coup topple the government in May and again in September?

41. What happened on Oct. 19, 1987, the day that became known as Black Monday?

42. The leader of what Middle Eastern country was assassinated in June when a bomb exploded in his helicopter?

43. What Asian country, scheduled to host the 1988 Olympic Games, was racked by antigovernment protests and labor unrest in 1987?

44. Which Democratic senator with the same name as a popular singer announced his candidacy for the presidency in May?

45. What Muslim holy city became the scene of riots that killed more than 400 people in July?

46. Who is Oliver L. North?

47. Which American city was the focal point of the national celebration of the bicentennial of the U.S. Constitution?

48. What 1987 Broadway hit is based on an 1862 novel by French author Victor Hugo?

49. What two nations whose long-time rulers fled in February 1986 approved new, democratic constitutions in February and March 1987?

50. Robert Hawke and David R. Lange were reelected in July and August, respectively, as prime ministers of which two Australasian nations?

ADVERTISING. Some of the most popular advertising in the United States in 1987 featured nonhuman characters touting a variety of products. The California Raisin Advisory Board's television commercials featuring a line of dancing, sneaker-shod raisins swinging to the 1960's song "I Heard It Through the Grapevine" continued to top advertising popularity charts in 1987. The commercials were introduced in late 1986.

Two other ad campaigns begun in 1986 that ranked high in viewer surveys in 1987 were the Coca-Cola Company's Max Headroom commercials and Anheuser-Busch's Spuds MacKenzie series. Both Max, a stuttering computer-generated character, and Spuds, the party-loving spokesdog for Bud Light beer, became 1987 celebrities. Their likenesses appeared on T-shirts, mugs, and hundreds of other products.

In a departure from its usual homespun approach, McDonald's Corporation introduced new, jazzy commercials in 1987 featuring a moon-headed man called Mac Tonight. The character wears sunglasses and white gloves, plays the piano, and sings a take-off on the popular song "Mack the Knife."

And in the fall of 1987, Coleco Industries, Incorporated, came up with a whimsical way to pitch its new Couch Potato doll in television ads featuring an assembly line of the cuddly brown potatoes. In the last shot, a young man and his new doll settle down on a couch in front of a TV set.

Taboo Broken. Some U.S. television stations and magazines lifted their ban on condom advertising in 1987. Health officials, including U.S. Surgeon General C. Everett Koop, called for the use of condoms to help halt the spread of AIDS (acquired immune deficiency syndrome). In January, San Francisco station KRON became the first major market TV station in the United States to accept condom ads, and both *Newsweek* and *The New York Times Magazine* ran condom ads in January.

Beatles to Bras. In March, Nike Incorporated, an athletic footwear manufacturer, became the first company in the United States to use an original Beatles recording in its advertising. Two record companies, EMI Records and Capitol Records, which own the original Beatles recordings, set up a licensing agreement with Nike permitting the company to use the song "Revolution" in a TV commercial for a new line of shoes. Nike reportedly paid $250,000 for the rights. But in July, Apple Records, which represents the Beatles, filed a $15-million lawsuit against Nike; Wieden & Kennedy, its advertising agency; and EMI Records and Capitol Records. The legal dispute was unresolved at year's end.

PepsiCo broke new ground in March when it placed a 30-second commercial for Diet Pepsi at the beginning of the videocassette of the hit film

Max Headroom, the Coca-Cola Company's animated pitchman for new Coke, was a hit with young—and old—consumers in 1987.

Top Gun. Although some videocassettes include advertising for other movies, this was the first time a videocassette carried a commercial message for another product. Playtex International Incorporated also made history in May 1987 when U.S. television networks began airing commercials showing live models wearing bras.

For the Advertising Industry, 1987 was a year marked by controversial—and unexpected—events. The most notable of these occurred on June 28, when WPP Group PLC, a British marketing firm, purchased JWT Group, Incorporated, of New York City for $566 million. JWT is the parent company of J. Walter Thompson Company, an advertising agency.

The WPP Group take-over followed a well-publicized management upheaval at J. Walter Thompson in January, in which Don Johnston, JWT's chairman, fired Joseph O'Donnell, chairman of J. Walter Thompson, for allegedly proposing a leveraged buy-out of JWT. Subsequent rumors of accounting improprieties, combined with JWT's dismal financial performance in 1986, made the company ripe for take-over.

Trouble in Florida. One issue that aroused the anger of both advertisers and advertising agencies in 1987 was Florida's 5 per cent tax on advertising and other services, which went into effect on July 1. To protest the tax, a number of advertisers reduced their advertising in Florida. Many major corporations also canceled conventions scheduled to be held in the state, resulting in $100 million in lost revenues. In December, the Florida legislature repealed the controversial tax.

Slow Spending. In July, Robert J. Coen, senior vice president and director of forecasting for McCann-Erickson Incorporated, an advertising agency based in New York City, predicted that spending on advertising in the United States would be sluggish through 1987. He estimated that U.S. advertising expenditures would rise 7.5 per cent during the year to $109.8 billion.

Tight Dollars. The top U.S. advertisers in 1987 continued the belt-tightening strategy that began in 1986. According to an annual study conducted by *Advertising Age* magazine, the 100 top advertisers in the United States increased their ad spending only 3.4 per cent in 1986, to $27.17 billion.

River Tragedy. A 1987 event that shocked the advertising industry was the death of five prominent U.S. advertising executives in a rafting accident on August 1. The men were riding the rapids on the Chilko River in British Columbia, Canada. Among those killed was Robert V. Goldstein, vice president of advertising at Procter & Gamble Company. Christine Dugas

In WORLD BOOK, see ADVERTISING.

AFGHANISTAN. Despite widespread resistance, the Soviet-supported government of Afghan leader Najibullah—he uses only one name—tried during 1987 to win broader political support.

Najibullah, the head of the Afghan Communist party, said on January 3 that Afghanistan's 1978 Communist revolution "is not reversible" and that those who accepted it could join in a coalition. An alliance of seven resistance groups based in Peshawar, Pakistan, rejected the invitation. The resistance also rejected a government-sponsored six-month cease-fire that began on Jan. 15, 1987. Although the cease-fire had little effect on the level of fighting, the regime later extended it until Jan. 15, 1988.

A New Constitution creating the post of an all-powerful president and commander in chief of the army was approved at a meeting in Kabul on Nov. 29 and 30, 1987, of representatives selected by Communist authorities. The gathering, called the Loya Jirgah (Grand Assembly), also elected Najibullah to the presidency.

The new Constitution also legalized other political parties besides the Communist party. But the Constitution also decreed that all political parties had to follow the program of the National Front, a Communist-controlled grouping of all authorized political activity in Afghanistan.

Afghan leader Najibullah stands before the Tomb of the Unknown Soldier in Moscow during a four-day visit to the Soviet Union in July 1987.

The Fighting. An estimated 115,000 Soviet troops and the Afghan army fought numerous guerrilla bands during 1987 without either side gaining an advantage. Guerrilla morale improved with the successful use of handheld Stinger anti-aircraft missiles. The Stingers provided some protection from Soviet helicopter gunships and fighter-bombers.

Anger over the use of the United States-made missiles, which reached the resistance through Pakistan, caused the Soviets to intensify pressure on Pakistan to stop helping the guerrillas. Air raids on Pakistani villages killed more than 260 people in February and March. Pakistani officials also blamed Afghanistan for terrorist bombings in Pakistan. United Nations-sponsored talks in Geneva, Switzerland, between Afghanistan and Pakistan in February and March and in September failed to work out a peace settlement.

Soviet Raids. The Soviet news media reported raids by Afghan guerrillas in March and April on Soviet towns near the Afghan border. The Soviets retaliated with attacks on villages in adjacent areas of Afghanistan. The raids caused concern in Moscow that the Afghan war could spill over into Soviet territory inhabited by people ethnically and religiously similar to the Afghans.   Henry S. Bradsher

See also ASIA (Facts in Brief Table). In WORLD BOOK, see AFGHANISTAN.

AFRICA. For the third consecutive year in 1987, the rains returned to most parts of Africa, though Ethiopia was again afflicted with drought. Adebayo Adedeji, executive secretary of the United Nations (UN) Economic Commission for Africa, announced in January that for the first time since 1972, African food production in 1986 had exceeded population growth. Green Revolution research on African food crops began producing results in 1987. With new strains of disease-resistant corn, rice, and *cassava* (a starchy root), the continent's farmers were obtaining dramatically increased yields per acre.

Good news in food production did not prevent certain countries, such as Angola, Ethiopia, and Mozambique, from requiring massive food aid from abroad, however. Famine in those countries was caused only partly by weather. Civil wars, government control of agriculture, lack of adequate transport, and growing rural migration to the cities also contributed.

Economic Development. Many of the reforms proposed by the UN General Assembly's special session on African economic development in 1986 were implemented in 1987. The primary emphasis was on agricultural research and the problems of the small private farmer. State farms and *collectives*—farms worked by large groups of people on a cooperative basis—were deemphasized in many

countries. Prices paid to farmers in 1987 came closer to reflecting the costs of production.

The UN special session also focused on Africa's huge foreign debt and how loans to Western and other governments can be repaid. Estimates on the size of the African debt ranged from $78 billion to $135 billion.

Two UN agencies—the World Bank and the International Monetary Fund—have played a key role in the rescheduling of debt repayment. Both agencies, however, have imposed conditions for their help, including a reduction in government spending, curbs on corruption and inefficiency, abandonment of agricultural collectivization, and cuts in food subsidies for urban dwellers.

Military Conflict. As always, many African nations in 1987 devoted the lion's share of their budget to military expenditures. The continued emphasis on soldiers and weaponry was due in part to the fact that more than half of the continent's governments are run by military leaders. In addition, many governments, civilian and military alike, faced armed challenges that could be met only with military might. In some countries, including Chad, Ethiopia, Sudan, and Uganda, civil wars have raged for almost the entire two or three decades of independence from colonial rule. These conflicts arose from two basic sources—competing political ideologies and hostility among ethnic and religious groups.

Only in Chad did internal rebellion virtually cease in 1987 as several guerrilla forces joined the government of President Hissein Habré in a common effort against Libya. Libyan troops had for years occupied the northern portion of Chad. Chad received support from France, Zaire, and other countries in opposing Libya, and throughout 1987 the war's tide ran in Chad's favor. In September, Chadian forces carried the battle into Libya itself.

In Sudan, the long-standing struggle continued between the Arab Muslims of the north and the Christians and followers of traditional religions in the south. The Sudanese People's Liberation Army, the main rebel group, in June captured the strategic town of Jekaw.

The Ethiopian regime of President Mengistu Haile-Mariam in 1987 continued to struggle with four simultaneous civil wars. The government is opposing the demands for independence or greater self-government by people in four regions of the country: Eritrea, Ogaden, Tigre, and Oromo.

In Uganda, the government of President Yoweri Museveni struggled throughout 1987 to wipe out the last pockets of rebel resistance in the north and east. The guerrillas are followers of deposed leaders Idi Amin Dada and Milton Obote and of Alice Lakwena, a rural priestess.

Jubilant Chadian troops receive a hero's welcome in the capital city of N'Djamena in January after winning a victory over Libyan forces.

South Africa continued to defy UN General Assembly resolutions that demanded the independence of Namibia (formerly South West Africa). Namibia has been under South African control since the end of World War I in 1918. South Africa extended its invasion and occupation of southern Angola in an effort to destroy the sanctuaries of guerrillas fighting for Namibian independence.

Angola was further disrupted by the rebel forces of Jonas Savimbi's National Union for the Total Independence of Angola (UNITA), which is supported by South Africa. UNITA claimed that it occupied the southeastern third of the country. In 1986 and 1987, the United States also aided UNITA, channeling weapons and other supplies into Angola from an air base in neighboring Zaire.

Mozambique was also disrupted by guerrillas allegedly supported by South Africa. The Mozambique National Resistance (Renamo)—a rebel group that is trying to overthrow the government—continued during the year to occupy more than half the rural countryside and to carry out attacks on both military and civilian convoys. In July, October, and November, more than 800 civilians—including many children—were killed in Renamo ambushes. South Africa denied Mozambique's charge that it was responsible because of its reported support for Renamo. The military forces of Malawi, Tanzania, Zambia, and Zimbabwe assisted the Mozambican army in keeping open the vital railroad links between those countries and the port cities of Mozambique.

Changes in Government. Colonel Ali Seybou was named acting president of Niger on November 10 by the country's Supreme Military Council. The appointment came just hours before Seyni Kountché, Niger's president since 1974, died of a brain tumor at a Paris hospital. Seybou was confirmed in his new office on November 14. Orderly change also occurred in Sudan in August when the 15-month-old democratic coalition of Prime Minister Sadiq el Mahdi collapsed following a break between Mahdi's Umma Party and the Democratic Unionist Party. Mahdi succeeded in forming a new government.

Other changes in African leadership were not so peaceful. President Jean-Baptiste Bagaza of Burundi was deposed in September while attending a summit meeting in Canada of heads of French-speaking countries. The coup leader, Major Pierre Buyoya, charged Bagaza with corruption, one-man rule, and a campaign of harassment against the Roman Catholic Church.

In Burkina Faso, the pro-Libyan government of President Thomas Sankara was overthrown in October during a coup led by Captain Blaise Compaoré, who had carried out a similar coup in 1983. Sankara was executed along with 12 other govern-

Facts in Brief on African Political Units

Country	Population	Government	Monetary Unit*	Foreign Trade (million U.S. $) Exports†	Imports†
Algeria	24,316,000	President Chadli Bendjedid; Prime Minister Abdelhamid Brahimi	dinar (4.7 = $1)	7,000	6,000
Angola	9,472,000	President José Eduardo dos Santos	kwanza (29.5 = $1)	1,200	1,400
Benin	4,392,000	President Mathieu Kerekou	CFA franc (279.0 = $1)	173	225
Botswana	1,202,000	President Quett K. J. Masire	pula (1.6 = $1)	653	535
Burkina Faso (Upper Volta)	8,604,000	Popular Front of the 15th of October President Blaise Compaoré	CFA franc (279.0 = $1)	110	230
Burundi	5,025,000	Committee of National Redemption President Pierre Buyoya	franc (116.1 = $1)	84	158
Cameroon	10,734,000	President Paul Biya	CFA franc (279.0 = $1)	855	1,101
Cape Verde	335,000	President Aristides Pereira; Prime Minister Pedro Pires	escudo (89.3 = $1)	2	68
Central African Republic	2,759,000	President & Prime Minister André-Dieudonné Kolingba	CFA franc (279.0 = $1)	145	140
Chad	5,395,000	President Hissein Habré	CFA franc (279.0 = $1)	113	114
Comoros	500,000	President Ahmed Abdallah Abderemane	CFA franc (279.0 = $1)	15	25
Congo	2,130,000	President Denis Sassou-Nguesso; Prime Minister Ange Edouard Poungui	CFA franc (279.0 = $1)	1,300	618
Djibouti	376,000	President El-Hadj Hassan Gouled Aptidon; Prime Minister Barkat Gourad Hamadou	franc (169.8 = $1)	96	197
Egypt	50,096,000	President Mohammad Hosni Mubarak; Prime Minister Atef Sidqi	pound (2.17 = $1)	3,200	9,000
Equatorial Guinea	345,000	President Teodoro Obiang Nguema Mbasogo; Prime Minister Cristino Seriche Bioko	CFA franc (279.0 = $1)	17	42
Ethiopia	42,403,000	President Mengistu Haile-Mariam	birr (2.1 = $1)	520	1,037
Gabon	1,232,000	President El Hadj Omar Bongo; Prime Minister Léon Mébiame	CFA franc (279.0 = $1)	2,000	900
Gambia	773,000	President Alhaji Sir Dawda Kairaba Jawara	dalasi (7.1 = $1)	59	73
Ghana	13,892,000	Provisional National Defense Council Chairman Jerry John Rawlings	cedi (173.6 = $1)	617	731
Guinea	5,845,000	President and Prime Minister Lansana Conté	franc (333.6 = $1)	537	403
Guinea-Bissau	908,000	President João Bernardo Vieira	peso (637.7 = $1)	9	57
Ivory Coast	10,826,000	President Félix Houphouët-Boigny	CFA franc (279.0 = $1)	3,500	1,600
Kenya	23,338,000	President Daniel T. arap Moi	shilling (16.7 = $1)	942	1,289
Lesotho	1,643,000	King Moshoeshoe II; Military Council Chairman Justinus M. Lekhanya	loti (1.9 = $1)	21	326
Liberia	2,410,000	President Samuel K. Doe	dollar (1 = $1)	432	366
Libya	4,202,000	Leader of the Revolution Muammar Muhammad al-Qadhafi; General People's Committee Secretary (Prime Minister) Umar Ibrahim al-Muntasir	dinar (1 = $3.53)	5,000	5,000

*Exchange rates as of Dec. 1, 1987, or latest available data.   †Latest available data.

Country	Population	Government	Monetary Unit*	Foreign Trade (million U.S. $) Exports†	Imports†
Madagascar	10,913,000	President Didier Ratsiraka; Prime Minister Désiré Rakotoarijaona	franc (1,050.0 = $1)	350	353
Malawi	7,752,000	President H. Kamuzu Banda	kwacha (2.1 = $1)	272	291
Mali	8,768,000	President Moussa Traoré; Prime Minister Mamadou Dembele	CFA franc (279.0 = $1)	175	295
Mauritania	2,069,000	President Maaouiya Ould Sidi Ahmed Taya	ouguiya (73.4 = $1)	340	250
Mauritius	1,075,000	Governor General Sir Veerasamy Ringadoo; Prime Minister Aneerood Jugnauth	rupee (12.3 = $1)	442	463
Morocco	24,290,000	King Hassan II; Prime Minister Azzedine Laraki	dirham (7.6 = $1)	2,200	3,800
Mozambique	15,330,000	President Joaquím Alberto Chissano; Prime Minister Mario da Graca Machungo	metical (396.4 = $1)	90	525
Namibia (South West Africa)	1,175,000	Administrator-General Luis Pienaar	rand (1.9 = $1)	no statistics available	
Niger	6,688,000	Supreme Military Council President Ali Seybou; Prime Minister Hamid Algabid	CFA franc (279.0 = $1)	251	309
Nigeria	105,623,000	President Ibrahim Babangida	naira (4.4 = $1)	12,600	8,300
Rwanda	6,809,000	President Juvénal Habyarimana	franc (73.4 = $1)	131	299
São Tomé and Principe	102,000	President Manuel Pinto da Costa	dobra (33.0 = $1)	9	20
Senegal	7,085,000	President Abdou Diouf	CFA franc (279.0 = $1)	525	805
Seychelles	68,000	President France Albert René	rupee (5.2 = $1)	5	90
Sierra Leone	3,678,000	President Joseph S. Momoh	leone (29.8 = $1)	137	167
Somalia	5,790,000	President Mohamed Siad Barre	shilling (120.2 = $1)	108	407
South Africa	34,944,000	State President Pieter Willem Botha	rand (1.9 = $1)	9,200	10,400
Sudan	23,498,000	Supreme Council President Ahmed al Mirghani; Prime Minister Sadiq el Mahdi	pound (2.5 = $1)	557	1,235
Swaziland	713,000	King Mswati III; Prime Minister Sotja Dlamini	lilangeni (1.9 = $1)	174	322
Tanzania	25,085,000	President Ali Hassan Mwinyi; Prime Minister Joseph Warioba	shilling (75.6 = $1)	225	1,000
Togo	3,307,000	President Gnassingbé Eyadema	CFA franc (279.0 = $1)	191	233
Tunisia	7,616,000	President Zine al-Abidine Ben Ali; Prime Minister Hedi Baccouche	dinar (1 = $1.27)	1,600	2,900
Uganda	15,908,000	President Yoweri Museveni; Prime Minister Samson Kisekka	shilling (53.7 = $1)	352	325
Zaire	33,265,000	President Mobutu Sese Seko; Prime Minister Mabi Mulumba	zaire (123.8 = $1)	1,913	1,383
Zambia	7,384,000	President Kenneth David Kaunda; Prime Minister Kebby Musokotwane	kwacha (7.7 = $1)	788	513
Zimbabwe	9,174,000	Executive President Robert Gabriel Mugabe	dollar (1.6 = $1)	1,100	930

United States Secretary of State George P. Shultz joins in a traditional Masai dance in Kenya in January during a six-nation African tour.

ment leaders. Compaoré said Sankara was corrupt and neglected economic development.

In addition to organized military opposition, real or rumored threats to existing governments were reported elsewhere. In March, President Joseph S. Momoh of Sierra Leone accused former Vice President Francis Minah and other civilians of attempting a coup. After the discovery of a large cache of arms, the plotters were arrested. In Somalia, the regime of President Mohamed Siad Barre arrested four senior military officers in June following rumors of a coup. June also brought the latest act in the continuing saga of coup attempts against Ghana's leader, Jerry John Rawlings. The revolt led to a number of arrests.

In southern Africa, an internal power struggle followed the 1986 coronation of the young King Mswati III of Swaziland. Conflicts within the government and the royal family led to the arrest in May of 13 provincial leaders on charges of treason and inciting rebellion.

Elections. Balloting for national, regional, and local offices was held in many African nations in 1987. In the Central African Republic, Comoros, Ethiopia, Gabon, Liberia, Malawi, and Seychelles, the ruling party either was unopposed or encountered only token opposition. The ruling party in Zaire, dissatisfied with electoral returns, nullified the results and scheduled new elections.

In contrast, the August elections in Mauritius, a tiny island nation in the Indian Ocean, found 31 parties competing, both individually and in coalitions. Although the popular vote among the two leading coalitions was close, the Alliance coalition of Prime Minister Aneerood Jugnauth captured 39 of the 62 contested seats in parliament. The only other contested election in black Africa occurred in Gambia. Staving off a challenge by a former minister of economic planning, President Alhaji Sir Dawda Kairaba Jawara received 59 per cent of the vote.

In South Africa, elections on May 6 strengthened the ruling National Party in the all-white chamber of the three-house Parliament.

Although multiparty systems have survived in a number of black African nations and were being restored in Senegal and other countries during the early 1980's, the move to create single-party states increased in 1987. The Central African Republic outlawed all opposition parties in February. In August, the Zimbabwe African National Union-Patriotic Front (ZANU-PF) used its majority in Parliament to eliminate the legislative seats reserved for the minority whites. Prime Minister Robert Gabriel Mugabe and chief opposition leader Joshua Nkomo agreed in December to unite their parties and establish a single-party state with Mugabe as executive president. In Kenya and other nations with a single-party system, harassment of dissidents continued.

Domestic Violence. Disturbances over economic, social, and political conditions threatened the stability of several African countries in 1987. In South Africa, government crackdowns on blacks opposing the policy of *apartheid* (racial segregation) led to further deaths in 1987 as well as strikes in major industries. Racially motivated violence also rocked Madagascar, where many Indians and Pakistanis were killed or injured in February.

Religion was at the center of violence in Nigeria. Religious tensions there have been growing since 1986, when Nigeria joined the Organization of the Islamic Conference, an international body that promotes unity among Islamic countries. In March, religious riots broke out in several cities in the Muslim north, leading to the death of a number of Christians.

Religion was also the source of violence in Angola, where cult groups in February attacked government forces. In Uganda, the followers of priestess Alice Lakwena, convinced that they could not be harmed by bullets, were killed by government troops. The September coup in Burundi was preceded by several months of harassment of the Roman Catholic Church. Deposed President Jean-

Baptiste Bagaza had banned weekday church services, closed church schools, and detained a number of priests.

Student rioting threatened the stability of Ghana, Madagascar, Nigeria, Senegal, Sierra Leone, and Sudan in 1987. Some of the riots were to protest inadequate living conditions, but others were expressions of outrage against government policies. Labor union members clashed with police in Burkina Faso early in the year over government-controlled wages and food prices.

AIDS. The World Health Organization (WHO), a UN agency, reported in 1987 that Africa has been more seriously affected by AIDS (acquired immune deficiency syndrome) than any other world region. WHO officials estimated that as many as 2 million Africans south of the Sahara were infected. Groups with the highest rates of infection were heterosexuals, urban dwellers, and the educated elite. Many children were also infected.   J. Gus Liebenow and Beverly B. Liebenow

See also the various African country articles. In WORLD BOOK, see AFRICA.

AGRICULTURE. See FARM AND FARMING.

AIDS. See HEALTH AND DISEASE; PUBLIC HEALTH.

AIR FORCE. See ARMED FORCES.

AIR POLLUTION. See ENVIRONMENTAL POLLUTION.

ALABAMA. See STATE GOVERNMENT.

ALASKA. See STATE GOVERNMENT.

ALBANIA. This small Communist state—which for years has cut itself off from contacts with most other countries—continued to pursue its own brand of "openness" in both foreign and domestic affairs during 1987.

West Germany Recognized. A major step, taken on Sept. 15, 1987, was the diplomatic recognition of West Germany. For three years, Albania had insisted that it would not recognize West Germany until that nation agreed to pay it *war reparations*—money intended to compensate for a devastation of territory. Nazi Germany had occupied Albania in 1943, during World War II.

In 1987, Albania agreed to defer the reparations issue. In effect, West Germany will compensate Albania by increased trade and the exchange of West German high technology for Albanian oil and minerals. West Germany already was second only to Italy in trade with Albania.

Other Foreign Affairs. East Germany agreed to help build rail links between Albania's mining centers and the port of Durrës on the Adriatic Sea. Albania established relations with Canada in September 1987. On August 30, the government of Greece formally ended a state of war maintained with Albania since 1940.

In October, Albania announced that it would attend a conference of Balkan states, including Bulgaria, Greece, Romania, and Turkey, scheduled

Former Central African Republic leader Jean-Bédel Bokassa enters a Bangui courtroom on June 12, when he was convicted of murder and sentenced to death.

One of a series of deadly tornadoes rips through Edmonton, Canada, and its suburbs on July 31, killing 26 people and injuring hundreds of others.

for 1988. Albania had refused to take part in such meetings since they began in the 1970's.

Domestic Policy took a new turn with the naming of younger, professionally qualified people to the People's Assembly (parliament). On the economic front, managers of government-owned industries and farms were allowed more flexibility in making decisions concerning production and the use of profits. The government also increased inducements for farmers to raise more livestock and crops on their tiny, privately owned plots.

Albania progressed with major projects in its Five-Year Plan for 1986 through 1990, including the expansion and modernization of export industries, and the construction at Koman of the nation's largest hydroelectric power plant. Albania also planned to apply Western technology to its petroleum and chrome industries, which have fallen short of their potential because of financial neglect and overcentralized management.

Friction with Yugoslavia continued because of an ongoing dispute over the status of Kosovo, a province of Yugoslavia. Most residents of Kosovo are ethnic Albanians, many of whom want to upgrade Kosovo to a republic within Yugoslavia. Albania supports demands for this enhancement of Kosovo's status. Eric Bourne

See also EUROPE (Facts in Brief Table). In WORLD BOOK, see ALBANIA.

ALBERTA. Savage tornadoes ripped through the suburbs of Edmonton on July 31, 1987, killing 26 people, injuring nearly 300 others, and leaving hundreds homeless. Many victims lived in a trailer park devastated by the storm. The Insurance Bureau of Canada estimated damage at $150 million, making the storm the most costly natural disaster in Canada's history. (All monetary amounts in this article are Canadian dollars with $1 = U.S. 77 cents as of Dec. 31, 1987.)

A Large Financial Institution, the Principal Savings and Trust Company, went into bankruptcy in August, the 11th Alberta financial institution to become insolvent since 1983. The firm was a victim of losses suffered in the depressed property market that followed the collapse of the oil boom in the early 1980's. The Canadian Commercial Bank of Edmonton and the Northland Bank of Calgary had failed from the same causes in 1985.

The failure of these institutions was seen as a heavy blow to the province's financial reputation. The provincial government had encouraged the establishment of banks and trust companies to free Alberta from its financial dependence on central Canada. Ironically, in the latest collapse, the Principal Savings and Trust Company's assets were acquired by the Metropolitan Life Insurance Company, which has its Canadian headquarters in Ottawa, Ont.

Tax Hike. Hard-hit by depressed prices for oil and grains, Alberta taxpayers faced almost $1 billion in tax increases in the provincial budget, which was presented on March 20. The increases were designed to reduce the province's $3.3-billion budget deficit. Since 1985, revenues from oil and gas had dropped by 64 per cent.

A provincial tax on gasoline was reintroduced, and increased taxes were imposed on hotel rooms, insurance, vehicle licenses, tobacco, and alcohol. Personal income taxes and corporate taxes were increased. Under the new taxes, an Alberta family of four with an income of $40,000 would pay an extra $340 per year to finance the attack on the deficit. The budget also called for spending to be cut by 4.4 per cent.

Sales Tax Avoided. The financial planning of the Progressive Conservative administration of Premier Donald Getty carefully avoided introducing a provincial sales tax to increase revenues. Alberta thus remained the only province in Canada without a direct provincial levy on purchases.

The Progressive Conservatives, elected to power in 1986, held 61 seats in the Alberta legislature. The New Democratic Party held 16 seats, the Liberal Party had 4 seats, and the Representative Party held 2 seats.   David M. L. Farr

In WORLD BOOK, see ALBERTA.

ALGERIA celebrated 25 years of independence from France in July 1987. Aside from economic success, Algeria's major accomplishment in its first 25 years as a nation was the establishment of a stable political system based on the National Liberation Front, Algeria's only legal political party. A census taken in April, however, revealed that 50 per cent of Algerians were born after independence and were more concerned about jobs, school, and other personal problems than politics.

Fundamentalism. Like other Muslim countries in 1987, Algeria had its problems with Islamic fundamentalism. In April, the government released 186 people, most of them students, who had been jailed in November 1986 for rioting in Constantine and other cities to protest government plans to introduce compulsory Islamic studies in the schools. The government had ordered the studies to placate Islamic fundamentalists. But in July, a state security court in Médéa sentenced four fundamentalists to death for subversion and five others to life sentences. An additional 202 defendants were given shorter terms. It was the largest mass trial in Algerian history. In the Special Reports section, see UNDERSTANDING ISLAM.

Regional Affairs. President Chadli Bendjedid continued to push his country's role as a regional power in 1987. In June, he visited Mauritania and

Yasir Arafat, chairman of the Palestine Liberation Organization, meets the press during an April meeting of the Palestine National Council in Algeria.

dedicated a new Algerian-built oil refinery at Nouadhibou. Algeria also mended fences with Libya and Tunisia. Algerian negotiators obtained compensation from Libya for wages lost by Tunisian workers expelled from Libya in 1985 because they refused to become Libyan citizens.

But relations with Morocco remained cool. The two countries broke off relations in 1976 after Algeria recognized the Polisario Front guerrillas as the government of Western Sahara, which Morocco controls. A meeting between Bendjedid and Morocco's King Hassan II on May 4, 1987, produced no agreement on the Western Sahara conflict other than an exchange of prisoners.

The Economy. Faced with continuing trade deficits and lowered oil revenues, the government intensified its efforts to make the economy more flexible and efficient. In July, the Council of Ministers issued regulations allowing government-owned enterprises to determine their own budgets, growth plans, prices, and investments. An agricultural reform program approved in October was designed to break up some 200 large farms into small ones, affecting 45 per cent of Algeria's agricultural land. In November, Bendjedid abolished the Planning Ministry as a further step away from state socialism. William Spencer

See also AFRICA (Facts in Brief Table). In WORLD BOOK, see ALGERIA.

An American Library Association poster featuring actress Phylicia Rashad—Clair Huxtable on TV's "The Cosby Show"—urges people to read.

AMERICAN LIBRARY ASSOCIATION (ALA). The American Library Association in 1987 broke attendance records at its annual conference for the third consecutive year. More than 17,200 participants attended the meeting, held in San Francisco from June 27 to July 6.

Outgoing President Regina U. Minudri, director of the Berkeley (Calif.) Public Library, introduced the keynote speaker, Theodore Roszak, a history professor at California State University in Hayward and author of *The Cult of Information: The Folklore of Computers and the True Art of Thinking* (1986). Librarians, Roszak said at the meeting, "can offer what no machine can—a living mind, a human presence."

Margaret E. Chisholm, director of the Graduate School of Library and Information Science at the University of Washington in Seattle, took office as the new ALA president. F. William Summers, dean of the School of Library and Information Studies at Florida State University in Tallahassee, was elected ALA vice president and president-elect.

Video in Libraries. The Carnegie Corporation of New York, a philanthropic foundation in New York City, awarded a $560,000 grant to the ALA in 1987 for a project designed to increase the use of videocassettes by libraries in the United States. The ALA planned to use the Carnegie grant to buy video equipment for selected libraries and to help those and other libraries expand their collections of educational and cultural videos.

Service Awards. World Book, Incorporated, awards two major grants each year to advance the development of library service. In 1987, the Government Documents Round Table, a group concerned with free access to government information, received a $5,000 grant to assist it in compiling a computer database listing federal documents that have been discontinued. The second $5,000 award went to the ALA's Office for Library Personnel Resources to support a conference on recruiting members of minority groups to librarianship. Stephen H. Fuller, chairman and chief executive officer of World Book, accepted a special citation at the ALA annual conference honoring World Book for its contribution of the awards for more than 25 years.

Children's Books. The 1987 Newbery Medal for the most distinguished contribution to American children's literature published in 1986 was awarded to Sid Fleischman, author of *The Whipping Boy*. Illustrator Richard Egielski was awarded the 1987 Caldecott Medal for the best American picture book, *Hey, Al*. Peggy Barber

See also CANADIAN LIBRARY ASSOCIATION; LIBRARY; LITERATURE FOR CHILDREN. In WORLD BOOK, see AMERICAN LIBRARY ASSOCIATION.

ANGOLA. The armed conflict that has plagued Angola since independence in 1975 entered its 12th year in 1987. The government of President José Eduardo dos Santos continued to fight rebels.

The Marxist dos Santos regime—the ruling party is called the Popular Movement for the Liberation of Angola (MPLA)—received massive aid from the Soviet Union and Cuba in 1987. The Soviets supplied tanks, trucks, and other equipment valued at more than $1 billion. An estimated 37,000 Cuban troops defended strategic sites and provided technical aid to the Angolan army. Revenues from U.S.- and French-operated oil refineries in the Cabinda area were used to subsidize the Cuban troops. The MPLA forces and the Cubans carried out a September assault against rebel strongholds near the town of Mavinga.

The Main Rebel Force opposing the MPLA is the National Union for the Total Independence of Angola (UNITA), led by Jonas Savimbi. The UNITA forces, who control the southeastern third of Angola, receive supplies from South Africa and operational support from 7,000 South African combat troops. The South Africans are in Angola to pursue guerrillas of the South West Africa People's Organization (SWAPO), a Namibian rebel group that is trying to liberate Namibia from South Africa.

UNITA in 1987 also received $15 million in military aid from the United States, including Stinger antiaircraft missiles. Hoping to secure diplomatic support from Zaire and other mineral-exporting countries in southern Africa, Savimbi agreed to stop UNITA attacks on the Benguela Railroad, which links Zaire and the Angolan port city of Lobito.

United States negotiations with MPLA leaders in April, July, and September failed to end the war. The MPLA refused to negotiate with UNITA.

Declining Economy. An estimated 650,000 Angolan farmers fled combat areas in 1987, causing a collapse in agricultural production. As food became scarce, famine, malnutrition, and infant mortality rose dramatically. The war had also destroyed the mining industry by 1987.

In August, dos Santos blamed many of Angola's economic problems on corruption, poor management of government companies, and excessive socialist planning. During the year, he introduced an austerity program that included cuts in government spending and the encouragement of private initiative.   J. Gus Liebenow and Beverly B. Liebenow

See also AFRICA (Facts in Brief Table). In WORLD BOOK, see ANGOLA.

ANIMAL. See CAT; CONSERVATION; DOG; ZOOLOGY; ZOOS.

Guerrillas ride in a truck through "Free Angola"—an area under their control—as they prepare to battle government troops in 1987.

ANTHROPOLOGY. A surprising discovery in Tanzania and research on ancient teeth, both reported in 1987, suggest that the earliest human ancestors were more primitive and apelike than anthropologists had believed.

The discovery of several hundred fragments of a 1.8-million-year-old *hominid* skeleton at Olduvai Gorge in northern Tanzania, reported in May 1987, yielded surprising new insights about the earliest direct human ancestor. (Hominids include modern human beings and our closest human and prehuman ancestors.)

The specimen, known as Olduvai Hominid 62 (OH 62), was found by anthropologist Timothy D. White of the University of California at Berkeley on an expedition led by anthropologists Donald C. Johanson of the Institute of Human Origins in Berkeley and Fidelis T. Masao of the National Museums of Tanzania in Dar es Salaam. From the shape of OH 62's upper jaw, the anthropologists determined that the skeleton was that of a *Homo habilis*, believed to have been the earliest direct human ancestor. *Homo habilis*, who lived from about 2 million to 1.6 million years ago in Africa, walked upright and had a relatively large brain.

This discovery of some of the oldest stone tools with *Homo habilis* fossils has led scientists to conclude that *Homo habilis* was the first hominid to make tools. These tools represent an important advance in hominid development, since *Australopithecus*, the apelike creature from which *Homo habilis* evolved, apparently did not make tools.

The discovery of OH 62 is especially important because it is the first time scientists have found both skull bones and limb bones from the same *Homo habilis* individual. Previous fossils identified as belonging to *Homo habilis* consisted of skull bones and teeth. Anthropologists have also found a few limb bones that may have belonged to *Homo habilis*. Johanson and Masao believe the new-found fossils are from the same individual because the bones were found close together and are the same color. In addition, there was no duplication of bones, as would have been the case if more than one individual had been found.

Measurements of OH 62's thighbones—a good indicator of height—revealed that the creature stood about 3 feet 3 inches (100 centimeters) tall. Because of the skeleton's small size, the anthropologists concluded that OH 62 was a female. Heavy wear on a wisdom tooth indicated that OH 62 was about 30 years old when she died.

Johanson and his colleagues were surprised to discover that OH 62's upper arm bones were relatively long compared with her thighbones. In fact, OH 62's hands, like those of modern African

The arm bones of a 1.8-million-year-old skeleton found in Tanzania in May suggest that the human ancestor *Homo habilis* was more apelike than humanlike.

apes such as the chimpanzee, would have hung nearly to her knees. (In contrast, modern human legs are relatively longer and our hands extend only to midthigh.) This finding suggests that *Homo habilis*, like many modern apes, lived partly in the trees, perhaps eating and sleeping there and fleeing there for safety.

The discovery of OH 62's primitive body structure has also raised questions about the evolutionary speed at which early apelike hominids became larger and more humanlike. Anthropologists had believed that *Homo habilis* had the same humanlike body structure as *Homo erectus*, the successor of *Homo habilis*, who first appeared about 1.6 million years ago. OH 62, however, suggests that the transition from the apelike body of *Homo habilis* to the humanlike body of *Homo erectus* occurred relatively rapidly, within about 200,000 years. Johanson theorized that increasing intelligence and the greater use of tools could explain the rapid change in body structure.

Infancy in Early Hominids. A study of tooth development in early hominids, reported in April 1987, suggests that a prolonged period of infancy, a uniquely human characteristic, is a fairly recent development in hominid evolution. The study, by anthropologist Holly B. Smith of the University of Michigan in Ann Arbor, challenges the long-held theory that early hominids matured slowly.

Smith's study, an update of research published in September 1986, examined tooth formation in the jaws of 15 early hominid children, including several types of australopithecines as well as *Homo habilis* and *Homo erectus*. She then compared the dental development in these hominids with the patterns in modern human beings and modern apes. In apes, which mature quickly, teeth erupt sooner than they do in human beings, who mature slowly. Smith concluded that the pattern of dental development in early hominids was more apelike than humanlike.

Human beings, whose brains quadruple in size after birth, require a longer period of social and intellectual nurturing than apes, whose brains only double in size. Scientists have long thought that a prolonged period of infancy developed early in hominid evolution, by at least 2 million years ago.

If early hominid infants developed quickly, however, they were probably more primitive than scientists had believed. Even *Homo habilis*, who had a relatively large brain, may have been more apelike than humanlike, a suggestion that complements findings about OH 62's apelike body. If early hominids had a short infancy, other humanlike behavior, such as food sharing and the division of labor, may also have developed later than scientists had believed.   Donald C. Johanson

See also ARCHAEOLOGY. In WORLD BOOK, see ANTHROPOLOGY; PREHISTORIC PEOPLE.

ARCHAEOLOGY. A 1,200-year-old cache of jade, flint, and shell artifacts was found on March 5, 1987, at the ancient Maya city of Copán in western Honduras. The cache was discovered beneath an altar at the foot of a temple-pyramid by archaeologist David Stuart, a student at Princeton University in New Jersey. The artifacts included two large jade statues, three elaborate flint spearheads chipped to represent the profiles of Maya faces, several stingray spines, and a spiny oyster shell. The shell contains a substance that might be dried blood.

Archaeologists working at the site believe that the cache was a ceremonial offering buried when the temple-pyramid was dedicated in A.D. 756, at the height of the Maya's artistic achievement. Maya ceremonies often included bloodletting, for which stingray spines were used. The scientists speculated that if the substance in the oyster shell is blood, it is probably that of Smoke-Shell, who was the Maya ruler at that time.

Ancient Egyptian Tomb. The discovery of a 3,300-year-old tomb in Egypt's Valley of the Kings was announced in February 1987 by archaeologist Kent R. Weeks of the University of California at Berkeley. The tomb was discovered using a magnetometer, an instrument that records the intensity of a magnetic field. The magnetic intensity recorded at the tomb differed from that of the surrounding bedrock.

According to preliminary analysis, the underground tomb, which consists of a number of chambers, was the burial place of several sons of Ramses II, who ruled Egypt from about 1290 to 1224 B.C. The central chamber, which is nearly filled with rubble, has been badly damaged by water seepage and, perhaps, looters. Archaeologists hope that the tomb's other chambers are undamaged. If the tomb contains well-preserved artifacts, it could be as spectacular a find as that of the tomb of King Tutankhamen, discovered in 1922.

Ancient Egyptian Boat. A space-age drill enabled scientists from Boston University's Center for Remote Sensing in October 1987 to view a dismantled 4,600-year-old Egyptian boat on a television screen without uncovering the chamber in which it was buried. The chamber, near the Great Pyramid at Giza, Egypt, was discovered using a ground-penetrating radar device that allows scientists to identify buried structures. A similar boat, also dismantled, was found in a nearby pit in 1954. Egyptian and American scientists working at the site also retrieved samples of the air inside the chamber. They hoped that analysis of the air would provide clues to the atmosphere at the time the chamber was sealed.

To enter the chamber, the scientists used a specially designed drill, based on technology developed for lunar exploration, that prevented fresh

An archaeologist excavates the remains of Fort Mose, north of St. Augustine, Fla., believed to be the oldest settlement of free blacks in the United States.

air from entering the pit. After collecting air samples, the scientists lowered a camera into the chamber. The camera revealed piled-up sections of a boat that the archaeologists believe was intended to carry the spirit of King Khufu, called Cheops by the Greeks, in the afterlife. They also found inscriptions on the wall of the chamber.

Preliminary analysis of the air samples, however, revealed that it was stale, an indication that the chamber had not remained airtight. After examining the chamber, the scientists sealed the drill hole, leaving the chamber intact.

Free Black Settlement. The discovery of what is believed to be the oldest settlement of free blacks in the United States was announced in February 1987 by archaeologist Kathleen A. Deagan of the Florida State Museum in Gainesville. The remains of a fort, named Fort Mose, were found about 2 miles (3 kilometers) north of St. Augustine, Fla. The fort, which was occupied between 1738 and 1763, was part of the defensive system for St. Augustine, which then belonged to Spain. The fort was defended by black slaves who had escaped from the British colonies in what are now North and South Carolina. The Spaniards offered the blacks protection in return for their help against British attacks.

The archaeologists were guided to Fort Mose by a map of the fort made by the British in 1740.

The ongoing excavation at the site is expected to provide much detail about the daily life of the fort's inhabitants.

Buddha's Bones. Relics of Siddhartha Gautama, the founder of Buddhism, were found in several underground chambers beneath a collapsed temple pagoda in China, archaeologists announced in April 1987. The relics are believed to be the ashes of Buddha's finger bones, according to inscriptions on tablets also found in the chambers. Chinese records indicate that the bones were buried in the chamber in A.D. 874. Scientists are unsure of how the relics came to China from India, where Buddha preached.

Dating the Minoans' End. The catastrophic volcanic eruption that destroyed the Aegean island of Thira (also spelled Thera) and the flourishing Minoan civilization there occurred in 1645 B.C., 150 years earlier than scientists had believed, according to research published by Danish scientists in August 1987. The most commonly accepted date for the explosion of Thira, now known as Santorini, has been 1500 B.C. Many scholars believe that the legend of Atlantis, described by the Greek philosopher Plato in the 300's B.C., referred to the volcanic eruption on Thira and the end of Minoan civilization.

The scientists based their findings on an analysis of the acidity in cores of ice drilled near the center of southern Greenland. The layers of ice in a core can be dated in much the same way as tree rings. In one layer of the Greenland ice, dated to 1645 B.C., the scientists found high levels of sulfuric acid, which was formed from sulfur dioxide in volcanic ash. They concluded that the ash came from the eruption of Thira. The new findings agree with radiocarbon dates obtained from plant material buried on Thira at the time of the eruption. Other dating methods have produced a later date for the eruption, however.

Ancient Dog Cemetery. A 2,500-year-old cemetery containing the graves of several hundred dogs—both full-grown animals and puppies—was found at Tel Ashqelon, the remains of an ancient city about 30 miles (50 kilometers) south of Tel Aviv-Yafo, Israel, according to a report by U.S. scientists published in August 1987. The dogs, which were all of the same breed—similar to a greyhound or whippet—were buried individually with great care.

The dogs were buried over a 50-year period, which ruled out an epidemic as the cause of death. In addition, skeletal evidence suggested that the animals died of natural causes and so were not sacrificed during religious rites. The most likely explanation is that the burial ground was part of a kennel for hunting hounds.   Barbara Voorhies

In WORLD BOOK, see AEGEAN CIVILIZATION; ARCHAEOLOGY; EGYPT, ANCIENT; MAYA.

ARCHITECTURE.

Rapid, uncontrolled construction of new buildings in suburbs—especially clusters of office buildings called *office parks*—emerged as a leading story in United States architecture in 1987. The Urban Land Institute, a respected planning association, and the National Trust for Historic Preservation, the nation's leading preservation group, made such suburban sprawl the topic of major conferences. Experts from both groups warned that rapid, unregulated suburban growth would be a major U.S. problem in the 1990's. Two areas often cited as suffering ill effects from hasty, unplanned building are Tysons Corner, Va., a suburb of Washington, D.C., and traffic-choked Orange County outside Los Angeles.

Noteworthy Buildings of 1987 included two major museums. An addition to the Tate Gallery in London opened in September and quickly proved controversial. British architects James Stirling and Michael Wolford designed the new wing in bright colors and bold patterns that, in the opinion of many critics, detracted from the artworks displayed inside. Even more controversial was the new Musée d'Orsay in Paris, a museum created from a magnificent former railroad station, the Gare d'Orsay. Into the huge, glass-vaulted space of the station, Italian architectect Gae Aulenti inserted stone structures, serving as galleries, that resembled Egyptian temples. The Musée d'Orsay opened in December 1986 and by early 1987 had stirred great controversy. Critics thought the stone galleries clashed with the light, open architecture of the station, and visitors found the arrangement of galleries confusing.

In New York City, however, a vast development called Battery Park City won nearly unanimous praise. The project began to assume final form with the completion of the World Financial Center, a group of four office towers by Cesar Pelli and Associates of New Haven, Conn. The development, located on 92 acres (37 hectares) of newly created filled land in the Hudson River, includes apartment towers and retail space as well as office buildings. Pelli also designed one of the project's chief attractions, a glass-enclosed public plaza called the Winter Garden. Many critics compared Battery Park City favorably with Rockefeller Center. They praised the project's master plan and design guidelines, developed by Cooper, Eckstut Associates of New York City, and the landscaping by Hanna/Olin Limited of Philadelphia.

Also notable was the Mississauga City Hall in a suburb of Toronto, Canada. The new city hall, built from a competition-winning design by the firm of Jones & Kirkland, called to mind the shapes of prairie farm buildings.

Two of architect Cesar Pelli's four office towers for the World Financial Center face a plaza in the new Battery Park City project in New York City.

In Houston, Italian architect Renzo Piano designed a long, low building sided with gray clapboard to house the Menil Collection of art. The building opened in June 1987 to considerable acclaim (see ART).

Probably the most talked-about architectural project in the United States—at least among architects—was the resort village of Seaside under construction in northwestern Florida. Developer Robert Davis and designers Andres Duany and Elizabeth Plater-Zyberk of Miami were creating an exquisite village of pastel cottages, lanes, and squares modeled on the seafront towns of the past.

Competitions—in which many architects submit designs for a new building, with the winner picked by a jury—continued to be important and often controversial. Most notable was the competition for a new town hall in The Hague, the Netherlands. The jury chose Dutch architect Rem Koolhaas, only to be overruled by The Hague's City Council, which preferred the entry submitted by Richard Meier of New York City. In Los Angeles, the firm of SITE Projects Incorporated won a competition for renovation of a downtown park in Pershing Square. Their proposal featured an undulating landscape with ridges of earthwork to buffer street noise and conceal parking ramps.

Arata Isozaki of Japan and James Stewart Polshek of New York City teamed to win the right to design a new wing of the Brooklyn Museum in New York City. Michael Dennis and Jeffrey Clark of Boston won a competition for a new student center and campus plan for Carnegie-Mellon University in Pittsburgh, Pa.

A New TV Series, "America by Design," ran on public television in October and November. Historian Spiro Kostof, hosting the five-part series, presented architecture less as an art than as the product of social and technological forces.

Major Exhibitions of 1987 included "New Architecture: Foster, Rogers, Stirling" at the Royal Academy in London, showing the work of three British architects—Norman Foster, Richard Rogers, and James Stirling—who have achieved world prominence. At the Museum of Modern Art in New York City, an exhibition called "Mario Bellini: Designer" displayed work of Italian designer Bellini, noted for his sleek furniture and household products.

The 100th anniversary of the birth of the Swiss-French architect Le Corbusier, whose real name was Charles-Édouard Jeanneret-Gris, occurred in October. Many exhibitions and symposiums throughout the world focused on Le Corbusier, a central figure in the Modern movement in architecture.   Robert Campbell

In WORLD BOOK, see ARCHITECTURE; LE CORBUSIER.

ARGENTINA. President Raúl Alfonsín of Argentina was credited with averting the threat of a military coup in April 1987. Alfonsín personally intervened to put down a rebellion begun by a military officer who had been summoned to stand trial for human rights abuses against dissidents in the late 1970's. (Military leaders took over Argentina's government in 1976. In a campaign to rid the country of terrorism, they violated many of the people's civil rights. A civilian government took office in 1983.)

The officer was joined by others in the military who were angered over continued prosecutions of lower-ranking officers after 10 top-ranking officers were convicted in 1986 of human rights abuses. The 1987 rebellion began when army Major Ernesto Guillermo Barreiro refused to obey a court summons on April 15. He was immediately discharged. Dressed in battle fatigues and heavily armed, he sought refuge at an infantry base in Córdoba, where officers sympathetic to his plight refused to arrest him.

President Alfonsín called his cabinet into session and convened a vacationing Congress. On April 16, he told Congress that he would not negotiate with the rebelling officers, declaring that Argentines "do not want to return to being the pariahs of the world." A crowd estimated at 100,000 stood outside the chamber, cheering.

Barreiro fled the country on April 17, but meanwhile, troops at a base near Buenos Aires had joined the mutiny and were demanding an end to trials of lower-ranking officers, arguing that they had merely followed orders in putting down a leftist rebellion in the 1970's. An estimated 9,000 people disappeared during the military's campaign against the left.

Alfonsín decided to take a direct hand in ending the rebellion. In a dramatic appearance on the balcony of the presidential palace on April 19, Alfonsín told Argentines that he would go to the base to persuade the officers to surrender. When he returned nearly four hours later, a crowd of 200,000 people cheered as he announced: "The house is in order, and there is no bloodshed."

In the aftermath of the rebellion, Alfonsín retired nearly half of the generals in command of troops and installed a new army chief of staff, General José D. Caridi. On May 13, Alfonsín presented a bill to Congress that would free hundreds of middle- and low-ranking officers from prosecution for having obeyed the orders of their superiors. Congress passed the "due obedience" law in May, but grievances remained within Argentina's armed forces, including complaints over low pay and shortages of equipment.

Economy. The Argentine economy continued to falter in 1987. On July 20, the government announced the sale of its stake in eight petrochemi-

Rebel Argentine soldiers at a military base outside Buenos Aires are challenged in April by civilians chanting pro-democracy slogans.

cal companies to private interests, as part of a program to cut spending on poorly administered state enterprises. But the sale failed to generate confidence in the economy or help offset its decline. Inflation amounted to more than 100 per cent in the first nine months of 1987, and the country's trade surplus was expected to fall to $900 million, from $2.1 billion in 1986.

On September 6, Argentine voters expressed their anger over the economy at the polls where President Alfonsín's Radical Civic Union won only 37 per cent of the vote, down from 52 per cent in the 1983 presidential elections. As a result, the party lost its majority in Congress, though it remained the single largest party within that body. Alfonsín's party also lost four governorships, including control of the province of Buenos Aires, which was reclaimed by the Peronist opposition that supports the policies of Juan Perón, president from 1946 to 1955 and again in 1973 and 1974.

In October, President Alfonsín announced new economic austerity measures, including a wage and price freeze, to ease the burden imposed by the country's foreign debt, which amounted to $53 billion. Nathan A. Haverstock

See also LATIN AMERICA (Facts in Brief Table). In WORLD BOOK, see ARGENTINA.

ARIZONA. See STATE GOVERNMENT.

ARKANSAS. See STATE GOVERNMENT.

ARMED FORCES. The United States dramatically expanded its military presence in the Persian Gulf in 1987 in an effort to counter growing Soviet influence in the region and to assist pro-American Arab nations that were increasingly threatened by Iran. In the gulf, U.S. forces engaged in limited combat operations for the first time since warplanes conducted bombing raids against Libya in the spring of 1986.

In May 1987, the Administration of President Ronald Reagan decided to provide 11 Kuwaiti oil tankers with U.S. naval escorts and allow the tankers to display the U.S. flag. American officials hoped the action would deter Iranian attacks on the shipping vessels of neutral countries. The reflagged Kuwaiti tanker *Bridgeton* struck an underwater mine during the first convoy in July, however, prompting a major build-up of U.S. military presence in the gulf. By the end of the year, the U.S. Navy had more than 30 warships in or near the gulf.

On September 21, U.S. Army helicopters operating in the Persian Gulf from the deck of a Navy frigate attacked an Iranian ship that was laying mines in international waters. The attack killed five Iranian sailors and wounded four. On October 8, U.S. helicopters seized two Iranian gunboats and sank a third after the boats fired on an American patrol helicopter. In an Iranian attack

A fire—the aftermath of an accidental Iraqi missile attack—burns aboard the U.S.S. *Stark* in the Persian Gulf. The May tragedy killed 37 sailors.

on October 16, the reflagged tanker *Sea Isle City* was heavily damaged by a Chinese-made Silkworm missile. The United States retaliated by demolishing two connected Iranian offshore oil platforms.

Stark Tragedy. Thirty-seven U.S. sailors aboard the U.S.S. *Stark,* a Navy destroyer patrolling the Persian Gulf, were killed on May 17 when the ship was struck by two Exocet missiles fired by an Iraqi Mirage jet. Iraq apologized for the attack, claiming that the pilot of the jet had mistaken the *Stark* for an Iranian warship. United States Navy investigators and a congressional committee sharply criticized the *Stark's* officers for not using defensive countermeasures that might have prevented the tragedy. In July, the *Stark's* captain and weapons officer were allowed to resign to avoid court-martial.

Arms Control. On November 24, the United States and the Soviet Union reached agreement on a treaty to eliminate intermediate nuclear forces (INF). The accord, which had taken six years of intensive negotiations, marked the first agreement between the nuclear superpowers to reduce the size of their nuclear arsenals instead of merely limiting their growth.

The treaty required the United States to scrap about 360 Pershing II and ground-launched cruise missiles in Europe, while the Russians were to dismantle nearly 700 missiles. Verification pro-

visions to ensure compliance over the three-year phase-in period included on-site inspection of missile sites by teams of experts. The INF agreement was signed by President Reagan and Soviet leader Mikhail S. Gorbachev at a summit meeting in Washington, D.C., on December 8. But major differences remained between the two sides on strategic arms negotiations.

New Weapons. In the absence of an agreement on strategic arms, the United States moved forward on a variety of new weapons systems. Testing proceeded on the MX land-based intercontinental missile; a single-warhead mobile missile known as Midgetman; the Trident II submarine-launched ICBM (intercontinental ballistic missile); submarine-launched cruise missiles; and ASAT (antisatellite), a system designed to destroy enemy surveillance satellites in outer space.

Espionage. A military court found Marine Sergeant Clayton J. Lonetree guilty of espionage in August and sentenced him to 30 years in prison. Lonetree was the central figure in a scandal involving several Marine guards at the U.S. Embassy in Moscow. The guards allegedly gave Soviet agents access to politically sensitive areas of the embassy complex in exchange for sexual favors. Lonetree was found guilty of conspiring with Soviet agents, disclosing the identity of U.S. intelligence officials, and giving Soviets floor plans of the U.S. embassies in Moscow and Vienna. He appealed the conviction. The Marine Corps dropped espionage charges against Marine Corporal Arnold Bracy, citing insufficient evidence. Four other Marines were charged with lesser offenses.

Jonathan Jay Pollard, a civilian intelligence analyst for the U.S. Navy, pleaded guilty to selling secrets to Israel and was sentenced to life imprisonment in March. His wife, Anne Henderson Pollard, was sentenced to five years as an accessory.

Conventional Weapons. In September, the Pentagon awarded a contract to Rockwell International Corporation to develop the X-31, an experimental jet fighter that would be able to outmaneuver any other aircraft in existence or under development. Testing continued on a nonnuclear cruise missile that could be launched with extreme accuracy from submarines, and on Stealth aircraft able to avoid detection by enemy radar. The Army began work on a new family of armored vehicles and a laser pistol that could destroy infrared sensors on enemy tanks and aircraft.

Defense Budget. For the seventh consecutive year, the Reagan Administration submitted a record peacetime budget for the Department of Defense. The request, which was submitted on January 5 for the 1988 fiscal year beginning Oct. 1,

1987, was for $303.3 billion in spending authority, an increase of $21.6 billion over the fiscal 1987 allocation.

The single largest budget item was a $5.2-billion request for research and development of the Strategic Defense Initiative (SDI), a space-based antimissile defense system popularly known as "Star Wars." The Pentagon also asked for $5.4 billion for F-16 and F-18 jet fighters, $5 billion for a new Trident submarine and Trident II missiles, $2.3-billion for the Midgetman strategic missile, $2.1-billion for Aegis missile cruisers, $1.9 billion for the MX missile, $1.8 billion for Los Angeles-class attack submarines, and $1.6 billion for the M-1 tank.

Personnel Developments. United States military troop strength stood at 2,173,085 on October 31, a decrease of 3,928 from the previous year.

The Supreme Court of the United States in June significantly strengthened the right of the military to prosecute service members. The court ruled that military personnel could be court-martialed for crimes that were unrelated to their military duties or that occurred off base. Another June decision prohibited military personnel from suing their superiors for damages after alleged violations of their constitutional rights. In October, the Pentagon issued directives barring military

Defense Secretary Caspar W. Weinberger, left, is greeted by a congressman before a January defense-budget hearing. Weinberger resigned in November.

commanders from interfering with the careers of officers' spouses.

Resignations and Appointments. Secretary of Defense Caspar W. Weinberger resigned his post on November 5. He was replaced by National Security Adviser Frank C. Carlucci III on November 23. In one of his first official actions, Carlucci on December 4 ordered the armed forces to cut about $33 billion from the budget for the 1989 fiscal year. (See CARLUCCI, FRANK C., III.) Admiral William J. Crowe, Jr., was reappointed to a second two-year term as chairman of the Joint Chiefs of Staff in June. After six controversial years as secretary of the Navy, John F. Lehman, Jr., resigned in April and was succeeded by James H. Webb, Jr., an assistant secretary of defense. General Paul X. Kelley retired as commandant of the Marine Corps and was succeeded by General Alfred M. Gray, Jr. General John A. Wickham, Jr., retired as Army chief of staff in June and was succeeded by General Carl E. Vuono. General John R. Galvin was appointed supreme commander of the North Atlantic Treaty Organization (NATO) forces in Europe. He replaced General Bernard W. Rogers. Thomas M. DeFrank

In WORLD BOOK, see the articles on the branches of the armed forces.

ARMY. See ARMED FORCES.

ART prices soared to unheard-of levels in 1987. Vincent van Gogh, a visionary Dutch postimpressionist painter who committed suicide at age 37 in 1890, sold only one painting during his lifetime. In 1987, three paintings by van Gogh sold at separate art auctions for astonishing multimillion-dollar prices. On March 30, van Gogh's *Sunflowers* (1888) sold at Christie's auction house in London for $39.9 million, nearly four times the previous record for an auctioned painting.

On June 29, 1987, van Gogh's *The Bridge at Trinquetaille* (1888) sold for $20.2 million at Christie's in London. The professional art world had no sooner become used to these record prices when van Gogh's *Irises* (1889) sold at Sotheby's auction house in New York City on November 11 for an extraordinary $53.9 million.

The Booming Market for Art resulted in million-dollar price tags for works by a range of artists during 1987, including Paul Cézanne, Thomas Eakins, Paul Gauguin, Wassily Kandinsky, Gustav Klimt, Amedeo Modigliani, Claude Monet, Jackson Pollock, Pierre August Renoir, and James McNeill Whistler. Pablo Picasso's *Souvenir du Havre* (1912) sold for $7.5 million at Sotheby's in London on December 1, the highest price ever paid for a work by the Spanish artist. *The Laundresses* (1870's) by Edgar Degas sold for $13.7 million at

Vincent van Gogh's *Irises* (1889) sells for $53.9 million at a New York City auction in November, setting a new auction record for a painting.

Visitors at the A. S. Pushkin State Museum of Fine Arts in Moscow get their first look at the work of Russian-born painter Marc Chagall in September.

Christie's in London on November 30, a record price for a work by a French impressionist.

Old Masters. A number of major 1987 museum exhibitions brought together artworks that had been scattered for centuries. The Metropolitan Museum of Art in New York City showed some 70 paintings by Francisco Zurbarán, a Spanish master of the 1600's known for his deeply religious depictions of saints and martyrs. The Zurbarán exhibition ran from Sept. 22 to Dec. 13, 1987.

The Montreal Museum of Fine Arts in Canada mounted an exhibition called "Leonardo da Vinci: Engineer and Architect" from May 8 to Nov. 22, 1987. The exhibition featured not fine art but rather notebooks and 14 operating models of Leonardo's inventions, including an ingenious but unworkable flying machine. The many designs in the exhibition confirmed Leonardo's reputation as the most versatile genius of the 1400's.

Other Cultures, far from our own time and place, were explored in a number of 1987 blockbuster shows. "The Age of Sultan Süleyman the Magnificent" documented the artistic achievements of the Ottoman Empire of the 1500's with more than 200 examples of *calligraphy* (ornamental handwriting), illustrated manuscripts, arms and armor, textiles, rugs, and precious objects. The exhibition opened at the National Gallery from February 1 to May 17 and then appeared at the Art

Institute of Chicago from June 14 to September 7 and at the Metropolitan Museum from Oct. 4, 1987, to Jan. 17, 1988.

"Treasures of the Holy Land: Ancient Art from the Israel Museum" featured 200 art objects dating from prehistoric times to the A.D. 1400's, including some of the Dead Sea Scrolls, the oldest known manuscripts of the Bible. The exhibition opened in the United States at the Metropolitan Museum from Sept. 26, 1986, to Jan. 4, 1987, and also appeared at the Los Angeles County Museum of Art from April 9 to July 5, 1987, and at the Museum of Fine Arts in Houston from Oct. 30, 1987, to Jan. 17, 1988.

European Moderns on view in U.S. museums during 1987 included Jean Arp, Paul Klee, and Berthe Morisot. "The Universe of Jean Arp" celebrated the centennial of the birth of one of France's foremost abstract artists. The exhibition presented 130 of Arp's collages, wood and cardboard reliefs, and sculptures. The show appeared at the Minneapolis (Minn.) Institute of Arts from March 14 to May 17, 1987; the Boston Museum of Fine Arts from July 1 to September 13; and the San Francisco Museum of Modern Art from Dec. 3, 1987, to Jan. 31, 1988.

Klee, a Swiss-born painter known for his graphic wit and color harmonies, was the subject of a comprehensive retrospective of some 300

A new building, designed by Italian architect Renzo Piano to admit natural light, houses the Menil Collection of art, which opened in June in Houston.

works mounted by the Museum of Modern Art (MOMA) in New York City from Feb. 4 to May 5, 1987. The exhibition also appeared at the Cleveland Museum of Art from June 24 to August 16.

The first U.S. retrospective of Morisot, a little-known woman French impressionist of the 1800's, appeared at the National Gallery from Sept. 6 to Nov. 29, 1987. The show gave many museum-goers their first look at Morisot's vibrant paintings of the world of women and children, rendered in glowing colors and feathery brushstrokes. The show was to travel to the Kimbell Art Museum in Fort Worth, Tex., and the Mount Holyoke College Art Museum in South Hadley, Mass., during 1988.

American Painters were also the focus of important 1987 art shows. The Metropolitan Museum's "American Paradise: The World of the Hudson River School" went on view from Oct. 4, 1987, to Jan. 3, 1988. The exhibition featured the spectacular wilderness scenes of Thomas Cole, Frederick Edwin Church, Albert Bierstadt, and other members of the Hudson River School, a group of landscape painters of the 1800's.

The great modern American artist Georgia O'Keeffe, who died in 1986 at the age of 98, became the subject of a major museum retrospective consisting of more than 100 oils, water colors, pastels, and drawings. The exhibition of O'Keeffe's spare Southwestern landscapes, symbolist still lifes,

and abstractions opened at the National Gallery from Nov. 1, 1987, to Feb. 21, 1988. The show was due to travel to Chicago, Dallas, and New York City during 1988 and 1989.

The Studio Museum in Harlem assembled 200 paintings, sculptures, and photographs in "Harlem Renaissance: Art of Black America." The exhibition mapped the flowering of black culture in the Harlem section of New York City in the 1920's and 1930's. After appearing at the Studio Museum from Feb. 12 to Aug. 30, 1987, the show was due at eight other museums in 1988 and 1989.

New Regional Art. The lively Chicago art scene checked in with "Surfaces," a show of paintings made since 1970 by 25 Chicago painters, at the Terra Museum of American Art from Sept. 1 to Nov. 15, 1987.

"Berlinart: 1961-1987" showcased the thriving art scene in West Berlin, West Germany. The show featured approximately 175 works by 55 artists, including examples of the emotionally charged paintings from the Berlin neoexpressionist school. "Berlinart" went on view at MOMA from June 4 to September 8 and subsequently at the San Francisco Museum of Modern Art from Oct. 15, 1987, to Jan. 3, 1988.

The Museum of Fine Arts in Houston presented the first major U.S. show of contemporary Hispanic art, featuring about 180 works by 39

American artists of Hispanic descent from May 2 to August 16. The exhibition was to appear at the Corcoran Gallery of Art in Washington, D.C., from October 1987 to January 1988, and at other museums in the United States and Mexico.

The Museum Boom continued as several leading museums in 1987 inaugurated new facilities with special exhibitions. On September 28, the Smithsonian Institution opened two new museums on the National Mall in Washington, D.C., in a $73.2-million, 360,000-square-foot (33,400-square-meter) museum complex that lies almost entirely underground. One of the new museums, the Arthur M. Sackler Gallery, opened with seven exhibitions highlighting the nearly 1,000-item collection of Asian and Near Eastern art given to the nation by Sackler, a psychiatrist and avid art collector who died in May. The Smithsonian's National Museum of African Art, home of the nation's collection of 6,000 African art objects, opened with five shows. Also in Washington, D.C., the privately funded National Museum of Women in the Arts opened its first permanent home in April in a 1907 Renaissance Revival building.

In Houston, a museum called the Menil Collection opened in June 1987 in an elegant $21-million, 100,000-square-foot (9,300-square-meter) building by Italian architect Renzo Piano. It houses some 10,000 art objects collected by oil heiress Dominique de Menil and her husband.

In Chicago, the Art Institute unveiled its renovated Galleries of European Art in May after a three-year, $6.6-million project that restored the original elegance of the galleries' 1893 floor plan and decorative details. Chicago also saw the opening in April of the new home of the Terra Museum, which moved from the Chicago suburb of Evanston to a new 60,000-square-foot (5,600-square-meter) facility in two renovated buildings in Chicago's downtown shopping area.

In New York City, the Metropolitan Museum opened its new $26-million Lila Acheson Wallace Wing for art of the 1900's on Feb. 3, 1987. The three-level, 110,000-square-foot (10,200-square-meter) wing is named after the cofounder of *Reader's Digest* magazine, who was its biggest donor.

Wyethmania, a wave of enthusiasm for American realist painter Andrew Wyeth, swept the United States in 1987. "Andrew Wyeth: The Helga Pictures," a collection based on 1986's press sensation—Wyeth's secret trove of paintings and drawings of a blond model, Helga—went on view at the National Gallery from May 24 to Sept. 27, 1987. It toured to the Museum of Fine Arts in Boston from Oct. 28, 1987, to Jan. 3, 1988, and was due in Houston, Los Angeles, San Francisco, and Detroit through January 1989.   Walter Robinson

In WORLD BOOK, see ART AND THE ARTS; PAINTING; SCULPTURE.

ASIA. Unusually bad weather afflicted Asia during 1987, increasing hardships for some of the world's poorest people. From India across Southeast Asia and up to northeastern China, droughts and floods reduced food crops and caused suffering and death.

Residents of towns and cities suffered less because governments distributed domestic food stocks to prevent urban shortages. Some countries imported food to ensure adequate supplies.

Villagers took the brunt of the hardships. Even in times of good weather, millions of Asian villagers survive on meager rations as they struggle to grow enough food or earn enough money to adequately feed themselves. In 1987, many villagers saw their fields parched into barrenness or their crops swept away by floods. Their wells dried up or were contaminated by floodwaters. Their jobs disappeared because farmers did not need day laborers and shopkeepers had few customers. Few if any Asians starved, but many suffered malnutrition that made them more vulnerable to deadly diseases and hindered the physical and mental growth of children.

Harvest Shortfalls. Monsoon rains were late and scant across three-quarters of India, leaving many areas too dry for planting. Officials expected food-grain output to be 18 million metric tons (20 million short tons) below normal. Reserves of 23 million metric tons (25 million short tons) were available, but there were distribution problems. Parts of eastern India flooded in late summer, and adjacent Bangladesh had its worst floods in many decades. Some 25 million people were affected in Bangladesh, and at least 1,000 people died. Food production was down 20 per cent, increasing the need for foreign aid.

Both Thailand and Indonesia harvested less rice than normal but encountered no major problems. Indochina was hard-hit, however. Kampuchea's worst drought in more than a decade cut its September rice harvest to almost nothing and curtailed planting for the main winter crop. With its rice output about 25 per cent below normal, Kampuchea appealed for international aid. So did Laos, where the rice yield was down more than 40 per cent. In Vietnam—where malnutrition is common even in good weather—the rice harvest was short of target by 1 million metric tons (1.1 million short tons). Observers blamed the shortfall on drought as well as flawed economic policies.

New Constitutions. Afghanistan, South Korea, and the Philippines adopted new constitutions in 1987. The Communist regime in Afghanistan convened a *Loya Jirgah* (Grand Assembly) of regional and tribal leaders on November 29 to ratify a constitution that gave strong powers to the president. The Loya Jirgah named as president Afghanistan's Communist party boss, Najibullah.

Members of an Indian peacekeeping force stationed in Sri Lanka proudly display weapons surrendered by guerrillas during a brief August cease-fire.

After being governed by a series of constitutions written by the political faction in power, South Korea adopted on October 27 its first constitution created by agreement between the government and the opposition. The new Constitution strengthened democratic institutions and called for direct presidential elections. The ruling party candidate, Roh Tae Woo, won the first presidential election held under the new Constitution on December 16.

On February 2, citizens of the Philippines voted to ratify a constitution that restored the system of government set aside in 1972, when then-President Ferdinand E. Marcos declared martial law. The new Constitution established a strong presidency and a two-chamber congress.

New Leaders were selected in several Asian countries in 1987 in addition to Afghanistan and South Korea. Zhao Ziyang assumed China's top job on November 2, when he became general secretary of the Communist Party. Noboru Takeshita became prime minister of Japan on November 6. And in Vietnam on June 18, six months after Truong Chinh turned over leadership of the Communist Party to Nguyen Van Linh, Truong Chinh relinquished the Vietnamese presidency to Vo Chi Cong.

Sir David Wilson on April 9 became governor of Hong Kong for the difficult transition period before China assumes control of the British colony in 1997. Portugal on April 13 signed an agreement to turn over Macao to China on Dec. 20, 1999.

Economic Reform in Burma. Burma sought in 1987 a way out of an economic decline caused by "the Burmese way to socialism"—policies that included self-imposed isolation from world trade. The nation—which had once been the world's largest rice exporter—suffered a severe rice shortage in 1987. Although drought contributed to the shortage, another factor was strict official control of the rice trade, which caused many farmers to refuse to work during the spring planting season.

U Ne Win, chairman of the military-dominated Socialist Programme Party that rules the country, conceded on August 10 that his policies might be flawed. For the first time since 1962, the government on September 1 lifted trade restrictions on rice and other staple foods. On September 5, officials announced that large-denomination currency notes were no longer of value. The move was intended to destroy profits from the black market, where much of Burma's trade took place, and to eliminate counterfeiting by provincial rebels. The action compounded public distress over Burma's deteriorating economic conditions, however, and led to the first rioting since protests were sparked by the country's failing economy in 1974.

Facts in Brief on Asian Countries

Country	Population	Government	Monetary Unit*	Foreign Trade (million U.S. $) Exports†	Imports†
Afghanistan	17,375,000	People's Democratic Party General Secretary and Revolutionary Council President Najibullah; Prime Minister Sultan Ali Keshtmand	afghani (54.4 = $1)	778	902
Australia	16,297,000	Governor General Sir Ninian Martin Stephen; Prime Minister Robert Hawke	dollar (1.4 = $1)	22,900	26,000
Bangladesh	109,471,000	President Hussain Muhammed Ershad; Prime Minister Mizanur Rahman Choudhury	taka (30.1 = $1)	934	2,600
Bhutan	1,507,000	King Jigme Singye Wangchuck	ngultrum (12.7 = $1)	15	69
Brunei	244,000	Sultan Sir Hassanal Bolkiah	dollar (2 = $1)	3,100	640
Burma	39,778,000	President U San Yu; Prime Minister U Maung Maung Kha	kyat (6.0 = $1)	317	602
China	1,096,584,000	Communist Party General Secretary Zhao Ziyang; Acting Premier Li Peng; Central Military Commission Chairman Deng Xiaoping	yuan (3.71 = $1)	31,300	39,500
India	803,975,000	President R. Venkataraman; Prime Minister Rajiv Gandhi	rupee (13.0 = $1)	8,300	15,000
Indonesia	172,975,000	President Suharto; Vice President Umar Wirahadikusumah	rupiah (1,650 = $1)	18,600	10,300
Iran	49,098,000	President Ali Khamenei; Prime Minister Mir Hosein Musavi-Khamenei	rial (66.8 = $1)	7,800	10,000
Japan	121,671,000	Emperor Hirohito; Prime Minister Noboru Takeshita	yen (133 = $1)	175,600	129,500
Kampuchea (Cambodia)	6,676,000	People's Revolutionary Party Secretary General & Council of State President Heng Samrin (Coalition government: President Prince Norodom Sihanouk; Vice President Khieu Samphan; Prime Minister Son Sann)	riel (4 = $1)	10	30
Korea, North	21,478,000	President Kim Il-song; Premier Yi Chong-ok	won (1 = $1.06)	1,380	1,720
Korea, South	42,621,000	President Chun Doo Hwan; Prime Minister Kim Chung-Yul	won (791.5 = $1)	34,800	31,200
Laos	3,850,000	Acting President Phoumi Vongvichit; Prime Minister Kaysone Phomvihan	kip (35 = $1)	36	98
Malaysia	16,614,000	Paramount Ruler Sultan Iskandar Yang di-Pertuan Agong; Prime Minister Mahathir bin Mohamed	ringgit (2.5 = $1)	15,400	12,300
Maldives	197,000	President Maumoon Abdul Gayoom	rufiyaa (7 = $1)	23	52
Mongolia	2,052,000	People's Great Khural Presidium Chairman Jambyn Batmonh; Council of Ministers Chairman Sodnom Dumaagiyn	tughrik (3.4 = $1)	no statistics available	
Nepal	17,649,000	King Birendra Bir Bikram Shah Dev; Prime Minister Marich Man Singh Shrestha	rupee (20.6 = $1)	162	460
New Zealand	3,372,000	Governor General Sir Paul Reeves; Prime Minister David R. Lange	dollar (1.5 = $1)	5,750	6,200
Pakistan	108,591,000	President M. Zia-ul-Haq; Prime Minister Mohammed Khan Junejo	rupee (17.5 = $1)	3,100	5,600
Papua New Guinea	3,997,000	Governor General Sir Kingsford Dibela; Prime Minister Paias Wingti	kina (1 = $1.14)	920	969
Philippines	58,712,000	President Corazon Aquino; Vice President Salvador Laurel	peso (21.1 = $1)	4,600	5,200
Singapore	2,669,000	President Wee Kim Wee; Prime Minister Lee Kuan Yew	dollar (2.0 = $1)	22,800	26,300
Sri Lanka	17,370,000	President J. R. Jayewardene; Prime Minister R. Premadasa	rupee (29.8 = $1)	1,400	2,000
Taiwan	20,242,000	President Chiang Ching-kuo; Prime Minister Yu Kuo-hua	new Taiwan dollar (29.4 = $1)	30,400	21,600
Thailand	54,345,000	King Bhumibol Adulyadej; Prime Minister Prem Tinsulanonda	baht (25.5 = $1)	7,100	9,200
Union of Soviet Socialist Republics	286,230,000	Communist Party General Secretary Mikhail S. Gorbachev; Supreme Soviet Presidium Chairman Andrei A. Gromyko; Council of Ministers Chairman Nikolai I. Ryzhkov	ruble (1 = $1.69)	86,956	82,922
Vietnam	62,996,000	Communist Party General Secretary Nguyen Van Linh; Council of State Chairman Vo Chi Cong; Council of Ministers Chairman Pham Hung	dong (78.5 = $1)	763	1,823

*Exchange rates as of Dec. 1, 1987, or latest available data.   †Latest available data.

ASIA

Refugees. Across Asia, refugees continued to flee wars and other problems in 1987. The government of Afghanistan claimed that in response to its program of reconciliation, 80,000 Afghans living as refugees in Pakistan had returned home. But according to Pakistan—which is a haven for more than 3 million Afghans, the world's largest group of refugees—more Afghans fled Afghanistan in 1987 than returned to it.

Greater numbers of refugees left Vietnam by boat in 1987 than in 1986, when more than 11,000 Vietnamese crossed the South China Sea to seek refuge in Malaysia and Thailand. The arrival of Vietnamese refugees concerned many nations in Southeast Asia, because several countries were still reluctant hosts to the remnants of earlier waves of desperate migrants.

At midyear, more than 118,000 refugees lived in camps in Thailand. An additional 250,000 Kampucheans were denied refugee status, though they camped just inside the Thai border. Other countries in the region housed 24,000 more. In August, Hong Kong sent back to China 855 of 7,200 Vietnamese refugees who had first settled on state farms in China but who since June had sought a better life in Hong Kong.

Warfare. Despite diplomatic talks that sought to resolve some problems, Asia had more border conflicts and internal wars during 1987 than did any other region of the world.

The two largest wars were in Afghanistan and Kampuchea. In Afghanistan, rebels battled the Soviets—who invaded Afghanistan in 1979—and the Soviet-supported military government. The resistance reported high morale after acquiring new antiaircraft missiles from abroad, but neither side claimed to see any prospect of winning the war. In Kampuchea, guerrillas fought the Vietnamese army and the government it supported. There, too, no end to the conflict was in sight. The Communist rulers of both Kampuchea and Afghanistan called for national reconciliation—but on terms that would leave power in Communist hands. The anti-Communist resistance in both countries rejected the offers.

Fighting flared along Kampuchea's border with Thailand. When China sought to dissuade Vietnam from occupying Kampuchea, skirmishes occurred along the Vietnam-China border.

In early 1987, India and Pakistan conducted military exercises in border areas, temporarily raising tensions. In October, the two countries fought a limited but heated battle on a glacier in the Karakoram Range.

India and China rushed troops to their ill-defined and disputed frontier in the eastern Hima-

India's Prime Minister Rajiv Gandhi, at right, shakes hands with Pakistan's President M. Zia-ul-Haq in New Delhi during Zia's February visit to India.

Wearing a ceremonial uniform, Sir David Wilson salutes an honor guard upon his arrival in Hong Kong on April 9 to take the post of governor.

laya in the spring, stirring fears of a repeat of their 1962 border war. Both nations wanted to avoid war, however, and during the summer, soldiers pulled back from a close confrontation. Diplomatic talks in November failed to resolve their long-standing border dispute.

Indian soldiers saw combat in Sri Lanka during the year. By agreement with the government of Sri Lanka, Indian troops entered the island nation on July 30 to supervise the disarming of Tamil separatist guerrillas. The guerrillas refused to cooperate, however, and in October, the Tamil separatists fought the Indians for control of the town of Jaffna.

A Communist rebellion continued to ravage the Philippines in 1987. And in Indonesia, guerrillas on the former Portuguese island of Timor maintained their resistance to Indonesian control.

U.S. Recognizes Mongolia. After a quarter-century of occasional talks, the United States on January 27 extended diplomatic recognition to Mongolia, an isolated Soviet ally in eastern Asia. The Soviet Union announced in June that it had withdrawn troops from that nation. The move was intended to help improve Soviet relations with China. Press reports, however, said that 60,000 Soviets remained in Mongolia.   Henry S. Bradsher

See also the various Asian country articles. In WORLD BOOK, see ASIA.

ASTRONOMY. The first supernova visible to the unaided eye in 383 years topped the list of astronomical discoveries in 1987. Among the other discoveries were images of giant arcs and the existence of what may be planets around other stars.

The Explosion of a Star. Canadian astronomer Ian K. Shelton discovered a *supernova*, the powerful explosion of a massive star, while photographing the night sky at Las Campanas Observatory in northern Chile on Feb. 23, 1987. The supernova appeared in the southern sky and was so bright that it could be seen without a telescope. Because it was in the southern sky, it could not be viewed from the continental United States or Canada.

Supernova 1987A, as it was named, was the brightest supernova since one in our galaxy, the Milky Way, was seen in 1604. It was the nearest supernova to Earth since one in the constellation Cassiopeia erupted about 1680.

Supernova 1987A was spotted in the Large Magellanic Cloud, a small galaxy about 160,000 *light-years* from Earth. A light-year, the distance light travels in a year, is equal to about 5.9 trillion miles (9.5 trillion kilometers). Within hours of Shelton's discovery, the National Aeronautics and Space Administration pointed a telescope on the *International Ultraviolet Explorer* (IUE), an orbiting observatory, at the supernova.

The IUE's observations revealed that the supernova occurred in a *blue supergiant* star. This finding was a major surprise because astronomers had thought that supernovae occur only in *red supergiant* stars, not in blue supergiants. Red supergiants were thought to be the last stage in the lives of massive stars, preceding their explosion as supernovae. Blue supergiants were thought to be the precursors to red supergiants. Now, astronomers theorize that under certain conditions, a star may reach a second blue supergiant phase shortly before it explodes as a supernova.

During 1987, observatories in South America, Australia, and South Africa focused optical and radio telescopes on Supernova 1987A, while a telescope mounted in a jet aircraft, the Kuiper Airborne Observatory, recorded its light at infrared wavelengths.

In May, physicists flew to Australia to launch high into Earth's atmosphere the first of many balloons carrying scientific instruments designed to detect gamma rays breaking through the material ejected from the star. They also checked readings from a gamma-ray sensor mounted in the *Solar Maximum Mission Observatory* satellite. Astronomers believe the gamma rays will reveal the creation in the supernova of heavy chemical elements and radioactive isotopes such as cobalt 56. According to the theory of how a supernova occurs, the heavy chemical elements are forged in the intense heat and pressure of a shock wave that blows off the

A 1984 picture of a nearby galaxy, *top*, shows the star (arrow) that may have exploded as the supernova, *above*, seen on Earth in February 1987.

outer layers of the star. The shock wave is a result of the collapse of the dense core of the star.

The collapse of the core was signaled by a powerful outburst of subatomic particles known as *neutrinos* that were detected in laboratories located in underground mines in Kamioka, Japan, and Fairport Harbor, Ohio. Neutrinos pass almost unhindered through ordinary matter and travel at or near the speed of light—186,282 miles (299,792 kilometers) per second. The neutrinos from Supernova 1987A reached Earth hours before the actual light from the supernova because the neutrinos left the collapsing core of the exploding star before the shock wave reached the outer layers of the star and thus before the explosion became visible. The collapse of the core is thought to have produced a small, rapidly spinning and highly magnetized object known as a *pulsar*. In the Special Reports section, see THE DEATH OF A STAR.

Giant Luminous Arcs that appeared to be the largest single structures astronomers ever observed were reported by astronomers Roger Lynds of the National Optical Astronomy Observatories in Tucson, Ariz., and Vahe Petrosian of Stanford University in California. On January 7, the astronomers announced the discovery of three such arcs, each about 500,000 light-years long and shining with the power of 100,000 billion suns.

After analyzing the light from one of the arcs, Lynds and Petrosian reported in November that the giant arcs were almost certainly the images of distant galaxies that have been formed and distorted by a *gravitational lens*. A gravitational lens is a massive object or objects with a gravitational field that bends the light rays from a more distant object and thereby creates an image of that object.

The Great Attractor. What may be a huge supercluster of galaxies far beyond the constellations Hydra and Centaurus was dubbed the "great attractor" in April by astronomer Alan Dressler of the Mount Wilson and Las Campanas observatories' headquarters in Pasadena, Calif. The existence of such a cluster is still unproved, but Dressler and his colleagues believe it is the likely source of the powerful gravity that is making the Milky Way, the Andromeda galaxy, and thousands of other galaxies in our local region of the universe move uniformly in its direction at a speed of about 600 kilometers (375 miles) per second.

The space between galaxies is constantly enlarging due to the general expansion of the universe, but astronomers have found that galaxies in our region also exhibit a streaming motion, like a ripple moving across a rushing river. They theorize that this motion must be caused by an unseen supercluster of galaxies—the "great attractor."

Other Solar Systems. In June, Canadian astronomers announced the best evidence yet for the existence of planets circling stars other than our sun.

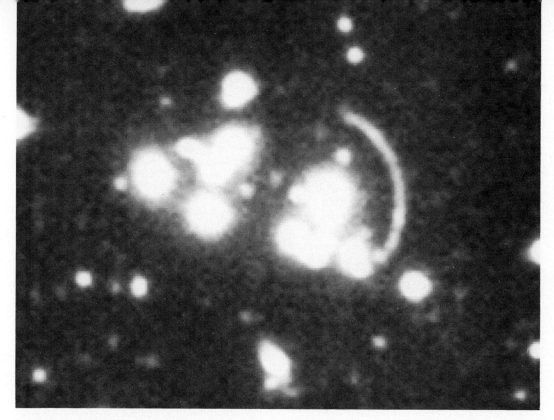

An enormous arc as bright as 100,000 billion suns, one of three reported in January, is thought to be the distorted image of a distant galaxy.

Bruce Campbell of Dominion Astrophysical Observatory in Victoria, British Columbia, and Gordon A. H. Walker and Stephenson Yang of the University of British Columbia in Vancouver reported on their search for planets around 16 nearby stars that resemble our sun. They measured small changes in the motions of the stars. If there is a planet orbiting a star, then the force of gravity will cause both star and planet to orbit around a common center of mass. The more massive the planet, the faster the star moves.

The astronomers inferred the presence of planets from the motions of the stars. If the planets exist, they probably could not be seen directly from Earth with existing telescopes because they would be too dim and would be lost in the glare of starlight. The strongest hints for the possible existence of these planets came from the stars Epsilon Eridani and Gamma Cephei. The astronomers believe these stars have planets about two to three times the mass of Jupiter, which is the largest planet in our solar system. The reddish star Epsilon Eridani is relatively close to Earth—only 11 light-years away—and astronomers who have searched for signs of intelligent life elsewhere in the universe have long regarded it as a star likely to have planets.   Stephen P. Maran

See also SPACE EXPLORATION. In WORLD BOOK, see ASTRONOMY.

AUSTRALIA. Australian voters reelected Robert Hawke, leader of the Australian Labor Party (ALP), to his third consecutive term as prime minister on July 11, 1987. The ALP won a majority in the House of Representatives, but the party once again failed to obtain a majority in the Senate.

The campaign was marked by considerable division among the opposing National and Liberal parties. Sir Johannes Bjelke-Petersen, National premier of Queensland, was behind much of the fighting between the parties. In April, he was successful in breaking the 38-year-old National-Liberal coalition and in discrediting leaders of both parties in an attempt to replace them as a contender for prime minister. His attempt failed, but Bjelke-Petersen's influence greatly reduced the credibility of both opposition parties, and he resigned as premier on December 1.

It was Hawke's desire to gain a majority in the Senate that prompted him on May 27 to dissolve both houses of Parliament and call for an election five months ahead of schedule. On April 3, the Senate had rejected Hawke's "Australia Card" legislation for the second time. The proposed law, designed to reduce tax evasion and welfare cheating, would have required all citizens to present a special card when they started new jobs, opened bank accounts, sold houses, or completed other financial transactions. Although opinion polls

A sailor snares a protester near a navy launch
carrying Prime Minister Hawke in Sydney Harbour
in June. Hawke was campaigning for reelection.

tablished a "two-tiered" wage system on March 10.
The system's first tier gave a general wage increase
to the 7.6 million workers under its jurisdiction.
The second tier allowed individual unions to seek
additional increases in certain industries in return
for higher productivity and other improvements.

Australia's appetite for imports continued to exceed its capacity to pay for them with exports. In
August, the government reported that the country's trade deficit was $A 402 million, up sharply
from $A 159 million in June. Exports of wool,
gold, iron ore, and diamonds sold well, but grains,
sugar, and coal experienced overproduction and a
decline in prices. Meat exports were substantial,
due in part to new overseas markets for lamb, but
the beef trade was threatened in August, when the
United States government rejected beef shipments
due to possible pesticide contamination.

Defense. On March 19, Kim Beazley, minister
for defense, presented a *white paper* (policy statement) that proposed a "layered" defense system.
The system is designed to stop and—if necessary—confront invaders from the north by improving Australia's detection and surveillance system; increasing the strength and flexibility of its
submarines; and stationing more ground troops in
Darwin, a city in Australia's Northern Territory.

Foreign Policy. Australia's foreign policy in 1987
centered on political upheavals in the South Pacific. The mounting tension in New Caledonia
over independence posed a problem for Australia.
New Caledonia is an island territory of France located about 1,200 miles (1,900 kilometers) northeast of Australia. The islanders—called Kanaks—
have been fighting for independence from France.
Australia and its partners in the South Pacific
Forum supported the Kanaks. This support
brought heavy criticism from France and the island's French settlers in 1987. On January 9,
France expelled Australia's consul-general from
New Caledonia due to his contacts with Kanaks.
Australia and France later patched up the matter,
but difficulties over New Caledonia continued
throughout the year.

In 1987, the Australian government denounced
what it called attempts by Libya to spread revolt
and terrorism in the South Pacific. On April 7,
Prime Minister Hawke condemned Libya for its
increasing presence in the area. On May 19,
Hawke ordered the immediate closing of the Libyan Embassy in Canberra.

Aborigines. Controversy rose during the year
over the 1988 bicentennial celebration of the first
British settlement in Australia. Some Aborigine
activists argued that Aborigines should boycott bicentennial events because the coming of white settlers to Australia led to the destruction of Aborigine society through brutality, disease, and the
seizure of tribal lands.

showed a majority of Australians were in favor of
the Australia Card legislation before the election,
the opposition parties successfully mounted a campaign against it in August and September. The
campaign—along with a lack of a majority in the
newly elected Senate—forced the government to
abandon the legislation.

The Economy. After two troubled years, the
Australian economy took a slight upward turn in
1987. The Australian dollar, which began the year
at $A 1 = U.S. 65 cents, rose to about U.S. 70
cents by midyear and to about 72 cents by the end
of the year. Inflation rates fell from 9.8 per cent
at the end of 1986 to 9.3 per cent in June 1987.
Treasurer Paul Keating predicted inflation would
fall to 7 per cent by December.

Interest and unemployment rates also fell
slightly during 1987, but the country's growing
foreign debt and large trade deficit remained serious problems. On May 13, Keating revealed the
government's austere economic program for fiscal
1987-1988. Keating's "minibudget" was designed
to cut the federal deficit by 2 per cent or $A 4-
billion. The program called for cuts in defense,
welfare, and health spending, and sales of several
government enterprises to private groups.

To sever the tie between wage increases and inflation, the Conciliation and Arbitration Commission, Australia's federal labor relations board, es-

Pope John Paul II drew criticism by meeting in June with Austria's President Waldheim, who was linked to atrocities committed during World War II.

The progress of the Aborigines remained precarious in 1987. A. Clyde Holding, the minister for Aboriginal affairs, said on May 27 that as a result of a movement to restore tribal lands to Aborigines, the Aborigines had secured titles to 12 per cent of the country. In contrast, American Indians in the United States own only about 4 per cent of the land. Holding also pointed out that although there have been improvements in education and housing for Aborigines, their life expectancy is still 20 years less than that of whites, and their unemployment rate is much higher.

Other News. The year was marked by intense activity among the four or five major Australian financial groups that control most of the country's mass media. This was due to legislation introduced in April that banned companies or individuals from owning both newspapers and television stations in any of the state capitals. The legislation did allow media groups to own television stations that together covered up to 75 per cent of the national audience.

In October, John Fairfax Limited, one of Australia's largest media groups, purchased the U.S. magazine *Ms.* from Gloria Steinem and Patricia Carbine, the magazine's founders.　　J. D. B. Miller

See also Asia (Facts in Brief Table). In the Special Reports section, see Australia: Past and Present. In World Book, see Australia.

AUSTRIA formed a coalition government of its two largest parties on Jan. 14, 1987, with Franz Vranitzky, a Socialist, remaining in office as chancellor and Alois Mock, leader of the People's Party, becoming vice chancellor. The previous government, a coalition of the Socialists and the right wing Freedom Party, had collapsed in September 1986. Parliamentary elections in November 1986 left the Socialists and the People's Party in a virtual deadlock.

Bruno Kreisky, the Socialist Party's elder statesman and a former chancellor, resigned as honorary president of that party on Jan. 19, 1987, in protest against Vranitzky's leadership and Mock's appointment as foreign secretary. Demonstrators who were angry because the new cabinet had no minister of the environment protested as the cabinet was sworn in on January 21.

United States Bars Waldheim. The United States on April 27 barred Kurt Waldheim, president of Austria and former secretary-general of the United Nations, from entering the United States because of his activities as an officer in the German army during World War II. The U.S. Department of Justice said that evidence collected was sufficient to establish "that Kurt Waldheim assisted or otherwise participated in the persecution of persons because of race, religion, national origin, or political opinion."

Waldheim claimed that he played only a minor, noncombatant role in the German army after being wounded in 1941. In a broadcast to the Austrian nation on April 28, 1987, Waldheim said he had a clear conscience and added, "You can trust me."

At a rally in Innsbruck on May 4, Waldheim announced that he would institute legal action against the U.S. Justice Department "to deal legally with these monstrous lies." Three days later, he initiated legal proceedings against Edgar M. Bronfman of Montreal, Canada, president of the World Jewish Congress, for slander after accusations that Waldheim was "part and parcel of the Nazi killing machine."

Vatican Visit. Jewish organizations protested when Waldheim visited Pope John Paul II in the Vatican on June 25. Diplomats noted that the visit to the Vatican was Waldheim's first official trip to a foreign country since his election in June 1986. See ROMAN CATHOLIC CHURCH.

After Waldheim returned to Vienna, Austria's capital, on June 28, 1987, the Socialists called for him to resign. Parliament supported this call by a vote of 268 to 217, but Waldheim remained in office at year's end.   Kenneth Brown

See also EUROPE (Facts in Brief Table). In WORLD BOOK, see AUSTRIA; WALDHEIM, KURT.

AUTOMOBILE. The mid-1980's sales boom of the United States automobile industry came to an end in 1987. Automakers looked ahead somewhat gloomily to a period of excess production capacity, intense price competition, and an increasingly crowded domestic car market. These factors—along with shifting economic circumstances—led to dramatic changes in the industry in 1987, including the sale of the fourth largest automaker in the United States and a move by Japanese companies into the U.S. luxury-car market.

U.S. Sales. Total sales of imported and domestic new cars and trucks were forecast at less than 15 million for 1987, a decline of 8 to 10 per cent from the 1986 record of 16.3 million. Falling sales and a weakening economy led many forecasters to predict a further 10 per cent sales decline in 1988.

The downturn came as a surprise to most industry experts, who had been predicting strong sales through 1989. A few, however, felt that the slowdown in 1987 was natural because the industry had witnessed sales growth for four consecutive years—from 1983 through 1986. This had been the U.S. auto industry's longest cyclical sales upturn since the early 1960's.

AMC Sold. In a bold move, Chrysler Corporation announced on March 9, 1987, that it had bought American Motors Corporation (AMC) for

General Motors unveils an experimental solar-powered car called Sunraycer on September 10. In November, the car won a race across Australia.

at least $1.1 billion. The move was approved by AMC's board on May 20. AMC, formed in 1954 by merging Nash-Kelvinator Corporation and Hudson Motor Car Company, ceased to exist as a separate entity. The fourth largest U.S. automaker, it became Chrysler's Jeep/Eagle Division.

Although the move was a financial risk for Chrysler, officials said they gained considerably with the purchase. The acquisition expanded Chrysler's production and sales base. In the face of expected price wars and market turmoil in the 1990's, Chrysler said its enlarged sales base had a better chance of making a solid profit. The AMC purchase also gave Chrysler the well-known and profitable Jeep brand name.

Renault Impact. Chrysler's purchase had wide implications. The sale also involved the French automaker Regie Nationale des Usines Renault. Renault had purchased a majority share in AMC in 1980, at a time when it viewed the United States as its largest potential market outside Europe. But with the sale of its AMC holdings, Renault withdrew from the U.S. market.

To many industry experts, Renault's move reflected the difficulty European automakers have in competing in the U.S. market. Their position was not helped by the decline in the value of the U.S. dollar in 1987. This factor made foreign cars more expensive in the United States.

Volkswagen Decline. Renault was not the only European automaker to suffer setbacks in the United States during the year. Volkswagen of America, the U.S. subsidiary of the West German automaker, had its share of problems in 1987. On November 20, Volkswagen announced that it would close its assembly plant in New Stanton, Pa., in 1988, ending its 10-year experiment as a U.S. manufacturer. Suffering from high prices and a declining share of the U.S. small-car market, Volkswagen will import all its cars into the United States from other nations in the future.

Japanese Hit. If European automakers were hurt by the weakening U.S. dollar, they were not alone. Japanese automakers also felt the pinch. Export sales of Japanese cars to the United States softened for the first time since 1978. Some Japanese automakers feared that their 1987 U.S. exports would end up well below the annual quota of 2.3 million cars set by the Japanese government. As 1987 ended, there was speculation that Japan's Ministry of International Trade and Industry would cut the quota below 2.3 million.

Most Japanese companies responded to the sales decline by expanding their U.S. assembly and manufacturing operations. They also unveiled plans to enter more profitable, higher-priced U.S. markets.

Mazda Motor Corporation on October 9 opened its first U.S. car-assembly plant in Flat Rock, Mich.

An employee of a U.S. automobile parts supplier puts a bar code on a car-door crate. More auto suppliers used the inventory code in 1987.

On September 17, Honda Motor Company announced plans to build a second plant in Maryville, Ohio. And the Toyota Motor Company said on November 9 that it would add production of major components—such as engines, transmissions, and axles—to its car-assembly plant under construction in Georgetown, Ky.

To further offset soft sales, Japanese companies made moves into the U.S. luxury-car market. Toyota and Nissan Motor Company both announced plans to sell large, eight-cylinder luxury cars by 1989 or 1990. In August, Toyota unveiled its new luxury division called Lexus. Nissan's new upscale line, revealed in July, is called Infiniti.

South Korea Victory. The decline in Japanese imports was a boon to South Korea, whose fledgling auto industry burst onto the world scene in spectacular fashion in 1987. South Korean exports to the United States were expected to exceed 300,000 cars by year-end. Hyundai Motor Company's Excel model, the first South Korean car shipped to U.S. markets, was 1987's biggest seller. But other Korean-built cars also experienced growing sales during the year. These included Daewoo Motor Company's Pontiac LeMans, which it builds for General Motors Corporation (GM); Kia Motors' Festiva, a joint venture between Mazda and Ford Motor Company; and Mitsubishi Motor Corporation's Precis.

Labor. The U.S. auto industry focused much of its attention during the year on the United Auto Workers (UAW), which began negotiations in July to renew union contracts at GM and Ford. The automakers and the UAW appeared ready for a major collision. The union wanted to stop the decade-long decline in employment caused by growing import sales, more efficient manufacturing techniques, and the practice of *outsourcing,* or transferring work to other companies or other countries. At the same time, Ford and GM said they needed even greater efficiency in labor cost to survive in the highly competitive environment expected in the 1990's.

But differences were resolved peaceably. On September 17, Ford and the UAW reached an agreement in which hourly workers won unprecedented job guarantees. Ford agreed to protect UAW workers against layoffs except during sales declines. GM followed suit on October 8, agreeing to a similar three-year contract. See LABOR.

Overproduction. During 1987, GM continued to address the overcapacity problem that had dragged down its profits. The company closed its Norwood, Ohio, plant on August 26 and its Flint, Mich., body-assembly plant on December 10. Nine more plants were scheduled to close by 1990. The entire U.S. auto industry was burdened by too many plants, experts warned.   James V. Higgins

In WORLD BOOK, see AUTOMOBILE.

AUTOMOBILE RACING. Only 11 days before the 1987 Indianapolis 500, the most important automobile race in the United States, Al Unser, Sr., did not have a car to drive. After a series of improbable events, he won the race, becoming the oldest driver, at 47, to win it and only the second to win it four times. Bobby Rahal won the Championship Auto Racing Teams (CART) series for Indianapolis-type cars for the second straight year, and Dale Earnhardt won the Winston Cup series for late-model sedans, also for the second straight year. Internationally, Nelson Piquet of Brazil won the World Drivers' Championship in a series of Grand Prix road and street races for the Formula One cars.

Indianapolis 500. Unser's contract with Roger Penske's racing team expired after the 1986 season, and Penske decided to enter only two cars at Indianapolis in 1987—to be driven by Danny Sullivan and Rick Mears. But when Danny Ongais approached Penske and brought a sponsor with him, Penske entered a third car and hired Ongais to drive it. Meanwhile, Unser was unsuccessful in finding a car to drive. But after Ongais crashed in practice on May 13, Penske hired Unser to replace him in the May 24 race.

The record crowd of 400,000 watched 47-year-old Mario Andretti of Nazareth, Pa., start from the pole and lead for more than 170 of the 200 laps. But on the 180th lap, raw fuel flooded Andretti's engine and knocked him out of the race. Colombian Roberto Guerrero then led for two laps until he stalled coming out of a pit stop. During Guerrero's troubles, Unser took the lead and beat Guerrero by 5 seconds.

Indy Cars. CART ran a 14-race series from April to November for Indianapolis-type cars. Rahal, who won six races in 1986 in a March-Cosworth, switched to a Lola-Cosworth and finished with three victories and five second places. Rahal, of Dublin, Ohio, won $1,261,098 to $937,074 for 25-year-old Michael Andretti and $922,162 for Andretti's father, Mario.

NASCAR (the National Association for Stock Car Auto Racing) conducted its Winston Cup 29-race series from February to November, almost all on oval tracks. Earnhardt, of Kannapolis, N.C., won 6 of the first 8 races and 11 overall and led in earnings with $2,069,243. The most important NASCAR race was the opener, the Daytona 500 on February 15 in Daytona Beach, Fla. Bill Elliott of Dawsonville, Ga., won in a Ford Thunderbird.

Formula One. The world championship was decided in a series of 16 races from April to November in Europe, the United States, Canada, Mexico, Brazil, and Australia. Formula One cars are lighter, sleeker versions of Indianapolis-type cars.

The series produced a season-long battle between Piquet and Nigel Mansell of Great Britain.

Al Unser, Sr., raises four fingers, signifying his fourth victory in the Indianapolis 500 in May 1987, which tied A. J. Foyt's record.

Piquet finished the season with 73 points to 61 for Mansell and 57 for Ayrton Senna of Brazil, who drove a Lotus-Honda. Although Mansell won six races, Piquet was steadier, with three first-place finishes and seven second-place finishes. Alain Prost of France, in a McLaren-Porsche, won three races and finished the season with 28 career victories, breaking Jackie Stewart's record of 27.

Piquet and Mansell were teammates on the British-based Williams-Honda team. Piquet signed with Lotus to drive in 1988 for more than $4 million.

Other Races. Porsche 962's won the leading 24-hour endurance races. The winning drivers were Derek Bell of Great Britain, Hans Stuck of West Germany, and Al Holbert of Warrenton, Pa., on June 13 and 14 in the 24 Hours of Le Mans in France. Bell, Holbert, Al Unser, Jr., of Albuquerque, N. Mex., and Chip Robinson of Oldwick, N.J., won the 24 Hours of Daytona on January 31 and February 1 in Florida.

On September 5 in Indianapolis, Joe Amato of Old Forge, Pa., became the first top-fuel drag driver to better 280 miles per hour (mph) or 450 kilometers per hour (kph) when he reached a speed of 283.13 mph (455.65 kph) during a quarter-mile run. On October 1 in Ennis, Tex., Darrell Gwynn of Miami, Fla., covered a quarter-mile in 5.084 seconds, the fastest ever.   Frank Litsky

In WORLD BOOK, see AUTOMOBILE RACING.

AVIATION. Flight delays, near-collisions, and other safety problems plagued the United States aviation industry in 1987. On July 8, the National Transportation Safety Board (NTSB) in Washington, D.C., revealed that errors by air-traffic controllers increased 50 per cent in June 1987 over June 1986. Days later, on July 15, the U.S. Department of Transportation (DOT) in Washington, D.C., reported that it received nearly as many consumer complaints over flight delays, lost baggage, and other problems in the single month of June 1987 as it did during the first six months of 1986. These figures, along with reports that near-collisions between airplanes—both in the air and on the runway—were increasing, raised serious questions about air transportation. The DOT took a number of actions aimed at correcting the problems.

On August 29, the DOT announced that six major U.S. airlines had agreed to try to reduce flight delays at the four busiest U.S. airports or face fines of up to $1,000 for each flight arriving late by 15 minutes or more. American Airlines, Delta Air Lines, United Airlines, USAir, Continental Airlines, and Eastern Airlines said they would modify schedules at Hartsfield International Airport in Atlanta, Ga.; Dallas-Fort Worth International Airport; Chicago-O'Hare International Airport; and Logan Airport in Boston. According to the agreements, flights had to arrive or depart within 30 minutes of published schedules at least 50 per cent of the time by November 1 and 75 per cent of the time by April 1, 1988.

On August 21, the DOT proposed a regulation that would require all commercial and commuter aircraft with more than 20 passenger seats to install collision-warning equipment over the next three to five years. The equipment warns pilots if another plane is approaching. If there is a possibility of collision, the system advises the pilot what action to take.

The DOT also proposed on August 22 extending the traffic restrictions currently in place at the nation's 23 busiest airports to 9 additional airports. The restrictions require all planes—no matter how small—to be in contact with air-traffic controllers and to obey the controllers' orders when flying near these airports. The nine airports expected to be added to the restricted list were Dulles International near Washington, D.C.; Baltimore-Washington International; Charlotte-Douglas International in North Carolina; Tampa International and Orlando International in Florida; Memphis International; Salt Lake City International in Utah; William P. Hobby Airport in Houston; and Phoenix Sky Harbor International.

Largest Fine. On February 10, the DOT announced that Eastern Airlines agreed to pay a fine of $9.5 million for safety violations. It was the largest penalty ever imposed against an airline.

Sales and Mergers. On October 30, the DOT approved USAir Group's move to purchase Piedmont Aviation for $1.59 billion. The merger created the nation's fifth largest airline.

Delta Air Lines and Western Airlines got the go-ahead in 1987 to merge. A federal court in San Francisco had blocked the merger, pending resolution of a union dispute. But on April 1, Justice Sandra Day O'Connor of the Supreme Court of the United States unblocked the merger, and on April 6 the full court refused to overturn her ruling. The merger created the fourth largest U.S. airline.

People Express Incorporated, an airline that pioneered discount fares in the United States, ceased to exist on February 1 after it merged with Continental Airlines. Texas Air, Continental's parent company, agreed in September 1986 to take over People Express.

On February 18, UAL Incorporated, the parent company of United Airlines, changed its name to the Allegis Corporation and announced plans to link United with its other travel services. But on June 9, Allegis said it would sell its Hertz rental car operation, its Westin hotel chain, and other interests and shift its focus to its aviation operations.

Airbus Industrie's French-built A320 airliner made its debut in 1987. The 150-seat plane is expected to enter commercial service in 1988.

Steve Kelley, © 1987 *San Diego Union*

Chinese Plans. In February, China announced plans to establish six independent airlines by 1988 that will operate international and domestic flights. Three of the airlines—China International Airway, China Eastern Airway, and China Southern Airways—had been organized by year-end. All six airlines will be government-owned but will be able to negotiate and sign contracts with foreign airlines and with tour and cargo agencies.

Crashes. Several major aviation accidents made headlines in 1987. On August 16, a Northwest Airlines jet crashed shortly after take-off from Detroit Metropolitan Airport, killing 156 people. The death toll made it the second-worst aviation disaster in United States history, exceeded only by a 1979 crash in Chicago that killed 273 people. On October 16, the NTSB released recordings of the flight crew's conversation indicating that the pilot did not extend the plane's wing flaps into their proper position at take-off.

On May 9, a Polish airliner bound for New York City crashed and burned outside Warsaw, killing all 183 people aboard. It was the worst aviation disaster in Poland's history.

On November 28, a South African Airways jumbo jet crashed into the Indian Ocean near Mauritius. All 159 people aboard the jet died in the crash, which was the worst aviation accident in South African history.

On November 15, a Continental Airlines jetliner overturned while taking off from Denver's Stapleton International Airport during a snowstorm. At least 28 people died in the crash.

Aircraft Sales. In June, the Boeing Company announced that it had sold a total of 1,842 B-737 planes, making the B-737 the best-selling plane in history. The B-737 has been popular because it can be operated by a crew of two, which cuts labor costs. Most planes require crews of three.

Tension heated up in 1987 between Airbus Industrie, a European aircraft consortium, and two U.S. aircraft companies—Boeing and the Mc-Donnell Douglas Corporation.

In April, Airbus made history when it received a $2.5-billion order from Northwest Airlines for up to 20 of a proposed line of long-range jetliners with four engines, called the A340. Northwest also took an option on 10 planned medium-range jets with two engines called the A330. Although Airbus aircraft have been leased by U.S. airlines, this was Airbus' first direct sale to a U.S. airline. Then, on June 5, Airbus formally announced that it would develop and build both the A340 and the A330. The long-range A340 would compete with McDonnell Douglas' MD-11 plane and Boeing's 747 aircraft.   David M. Cawthorne

See also TRANSPORTATION. In WORLD BOOK, see AVIATION.

AWARDS AND PRIZES presented in 1987 included the following:

Arts Awards

ACADEMY OF MOTION PICTURE ARTS AND SCIENCES. "Oscar" Awards: **Best Picture,** *Platoon.* **Best Actor,** Paul Newman, *The Color of Money.* **Best Actress,** Marlee Matlin, *Children of a Lesser God.* **Best Supporting Actor,** Michael Caine, *Hannah and Her Sisters.* **Best Supporting Actress,** Dianne Wiest, *Hannah and Her Sisters.* **Best Director,** Oliver Stone, *Platoon.* **Best Original Screenplay,** Woody Allen, *Hannah and Her Sisters.* **Best Screenplay Adaptation,** Ruth Prawer Jhabvala, *A Room with a View.* **Best Cinematography,** Chris Menges, *The Mission.* **Best Film Editing,** Claire Simpson, *Platoon.* **Best Original Score,** Herbie Hancock, *'Round Midnight.* **Best Original Song,** Giorgio Moroder and Tom Whitlock, "Take My Breath Away." **Best Art Direction,** *A Room with a View.* **Best Costume Design,** *A Room with a View.* **Best Makeup,** *The Fly.* **Best Sound,** *Platoon.* **Best Sound Effects Editing,** *Aliens.* **Best Visual Effects,** *Aliens.* **Best Documentary Feature,** *Artie Shaw: Time Is All You've Got* and *Down and Out in America* (tie). **Best Documentary Short Subject,** *Women—For America, for the World.* **Best Animated Short Film,** *A Greek Tragedy.* **Best Live-Action Short Film,** *Precious Images.* **Best Foreign-Language Film,** *The Assault* (Netherlands). See MATLIN, MARLEE; NEWMAN, PAUL.

AMERICAN ACADEMY AND INSTITUTE OF ARTS AND LETTERS. Gold Medal for Belles Lettres and Criticism, historian Jacques Barzun. **Gold Medal for Painting,** Isabel Bishop. **Award for Distinguished Service to the Arts,** violinist Isaac Stern.

AMERICAN DANCE FESTIVAL. Samuel H. Scripps-American Dance Festival Award, Alvin Ailey, American dancer and choreographer.

AMERICAN FILM INSTITUTE. Life Achievement Award, actor Jack Lemmon.

AMERICAN INSTITUTE OF ARCHITECTS. Honor Awards, City of Chicago Department of Public Works, Bureau of Architecture, and Murphy/Jahn of that city, for the O'Hare International Airport Rapid Transit Extension; Clark & Menefee, Charleston, S.C., and the Charleston Architectural Group for the Middleton Inn in that city; Davis, Brody & Associates, New York City, for the New York Public Library restoration; Frank O. Gehry & Associates, Venice, Calif., for ICS/ERL, a complex of computer science and engineering classrooms at the University of California at Irvine; Frank O. Gehry & Associates for the Norton residence, Venice, Calif.; Michael Graves of Princeton, N.J., for Michael C. Carlos Hall at Emory University, Atlanta, Ga.; Michael Graves for the Humana Building, Louisville, Ky.; Grondona/Architects, San Diego, for Claudia's, a storefront bakery in that city; Hammond Beeby and Babka Incorporated, Chicago, for the Conrad Sulzer Regional Library in that city; Steve Izenour with Christine Matheu and Venturi, Rauch and Scott Brown, Philadelphia, for a house on Long Island Sound, Stony Creek, Conn.; Fay Jones & Associates Architects, Fayetteville, Ark., for the Reed house, Hogeye, Ark.; R. M. Kliment & Frances Halsbrand Architects, New York City, for the Computer Science Building at Columbia University in that city; Kohn Pedersen Fox Associates PC, New York City, for the Procter & Gamble General Offices Complex, Cincinnati, Ohio; Richard Meier & Partners, New York City, for the Museum für Kunsthandwerk, Frankfurt, West Germany; Charles W. Moore and Chad Floyd of Centerbrook, Essex, Conn., for the Hood Museum of Art at Dartmouth College, Hanover, N.H.; Payette Associates of Princeton, N.J., and Venturi, Rauch and Scott Brown for the Lewis Thomas Laboratory at Princeton University; Antoine Predock Architect, Albuquerque, N. Mex., for the Fuller

house, Scottsdale, Ariz.; the Restoration Committee of the Frank Lloyd Wright Home and Studio Foundation, Oak Park, Ill., for the restoration of the Frank Lloyd Wright Home and Studio there; Skidmore, Owings & Merrill, New York City, for the National Commercial Bank, Jidda, Saudi Arabia; Tigerman, Fugman, McCurry of Chicago for a private residence in western Connecticut.

AMERICAN MUSIC AWARDS. Pop/Rock Awards: Female Vocalist, Whitney Houston. **Male Vocalist,** Lionel Richie. **Duo or Group,** Huey Lewis and the News. **Single,** "There'll Be Sad Songs," Billy Ocean. **Album,** *Whitney Houston,* Whitney Houston. **Female Video Artist,** Madonna. **Male Video Artist,** Billy Ocean. **Video Duo or Group,** Huey Lewis and the News. **Video Single,** "Dancing on the Ceiling," Lionel Richie.

Soul Music/Rhythm and Blues Awards: Female Vocalist, Whitney Houston. **Male Vocalist,** Lionel Richie. **Duo or Group,** New Edition. **Single,** "Nasty," Janet Jackson. **Album,** *Whitney Houston,* Whitney Houston. **Female Video Artist,** Janet Jackson. **Male Video Artist,** Lionel Richie. **Video Duo or Group,** Kool & the Gang. **Video Single,** "Greatest Love of All," Whitney Houston.

Country Music Awards: Female Vocalist, Barbara Mandrell. **Male Vocalist,** Willie Nelson. **Duo or Group,** Alabama. **Single,** "Grandpa," The Judds. **Album,** *Greatest Hits,* Alabama. **Female Video Artist,** Reba McEntire. **Male Video Artist,** George Jones. **Video Duo or Group,** Alabama. **Video Single,** "Grandpa," The Judds.

CANNES INTERNATIONAL FILM FESTIVAL. Golden Palm Grand Prize, *Under Satan's Sun* (France). **Special Jury Prize,** *Repentance* (Soviet Union). **Jury Prize,** *Brightness* (Mali) and *Shinran* (Japan). **Best Actor,** Marcello Mastroianni, *Dark Eyes.* **Best Actress,** Barbara Hershey, *Shy People.* **Best Director,** Wim Wenders, *The Wings of Desire.*

CAPEZIO DANCE AWARD. Dancer and actor Fred Astaire; choreographer Bob Fosse; ballet dancer Rudolf Nureyev; television producer Jac Venza, creator of the "Dance in America" series.

HYATT FOUNDATION. Pritzker Architecture Prize, Japanese architect Kenzo Tange.

JOHN F. KENNEDY CENTER FOR THE PERFORMING ARTS, Honors, singer Perry Como; actress Bette Davis; entertainer Sammy Davis, Jr.; violinist Nathan Milstein; choreographer Alwin Nikolais.

MACDOWELL COLONY. Edward MacDowell Medal, composer Leonard Bernstein.

NATIONAL ACADEMY OF RECORDING ARTS AND SCIENCES. Grammy Awards: Record of the Year, "Higher Love," Steve Winwood. **Album of the Year,** *Graceland,* Paul Simon. **Song of the Year,** "That's What Friends Are For," Burt Bacharach and Carole Bayer Sager, songwriters. **Best New Artist,** Bruce Hornsby and the Range. **Music Video, Short Form,** "Dire Straits: Brothers in Arms," Dire Straits. **Music Video, Long Form,** *Bring on the Night,* Sting.

Pop Awards: Pop Vocal Performance, Female, *The Broadway Album,* Barbra Streisand. **Pop Vocal Performance, Male,** "Higher Love," Steve Winwood. **Pop Vocal Performance by a Duo or Group,** "That's What Friends Are For," Dionne & Friends. **Pop Instrumental Performance,** "Top Gun Anthem," Harold Faltermeyer and Steve Stevens.

Rock Awards: Rock Vocal Performance, Female, "Back Where You Started," Tina Turner. **Rock Vocal Performance, Male,** "Addicted to Love," Robert Palmer. **Rock Vocal Performance by a Duo or Group,** "Missionary Man," Eurythmics. **Rock Instrumental Performance,** "Peter Gunn," Art of Noise.

Rhythm and Blues Awards: Rhythm and Blues Vocal Performance, Female, *Rapture,* Anita Baker. **Rhythm and Blues Vocal Performance, Male,** "Living in America," James Brown. **Rhythm and Blues Vocal Performance by a**

Duo or Group, "Kiss," Prince and the Revolution. **Rhythm and Blues Instrumental Performance,** "And You Know That," Yellowjackets. **Rhythm and Blues Song,** "Sweet Love," Anita Baker, Luis A. Johnson, and Gary Bias, songwriters.

Country Awards: Country Vocal Performance, Female, "Whoever's in New England," Reba McEntire. **Country Vocal Performance, Male,** *Lost in the Fifties Tonight,* Ronnie Milsap. **Country Vocal Performance by a Duo or Group,** "Grandpa," The Judds. **Country Instrumental Performance,** "Raisin' the Dickens," Ricky Skaggs. **Country Song,** "Grandpa," Jamie O'Hara, songwriter.

Jazz Awards: Jazz Fusion Performance, Vocal or Instrumental, *Double Vision,* Bob James and David Sanborn. **Jazz Vocal Performance, Female,** *Timeless,* Diane Schuur. **Jazz Vocal Performance, Male,** "'Round Midnight," Bobby McFerrin. **Jazz Vocal Performance by a Duo or Group,** *Free Fall,* 2 + 2 Plus. **Jazz Instrumental Performance, Solo,** *Tutu,* Miles Davis. **Jazz Instrumental Performance, Group,** *J Mood,* Wynton Marsalis. **Jazz Instrumental Performance, Big Band,** *The Tonight Show Band with Doc Severinsen.*

Classical Awards: Classical Album, *Horowitz: The Studio Recordings, New York 1985,* Vladimir Horowitz. **Classical Orchestra Recording,** *Liszt: A Faust Symphony,* Sir Georg Solti conducting the Chicago Symphony Orchestra. **Opera Recording,** *Bernstein: Candide,* John Mauceri conducting the New York City Opera Chorus and Orchestra. **Choral Performance,** *Orff: Carmina Burana,* James Levine conducting the Chicago Symphony Chorus and Orchestra.

NATIONAL ACADEMY OF TELEVISION ARTS AND SCIENCES. Emmy Awards, Comedy: Best Series, "The Golden Girls." **Lead Actor,** Michael J. Fox, "Family Ties." **Lead Actress,** Rue McClanahan, "The Golden Girls." **Supporting Actor,** John Larroquette, "Night Court." **Supporting Actress,** Jackée Harry, "227."

Drama Awards: Best Series, "L.A. Law." **Lead Actor,** Bruce Willis, "Moonlighting." **Lead Actress,** Sharon Gless, "Cagney & Lacey." **Supporting Actor,** John Hillerman, "Magnum, P.I." **Supporting Actress,** Bonnie Bartlett, "St. Elsewhere."

Other Awards: Drama or Comedy Special, *Promise.* **Miniseries,** "A Day in the Life." **Variety, Music, or Comedy Program,** *The 1987 Tony Awards.* **Lead Actor in a Miniseries or Special,** James Woods, *Promise.* **Lead Actress in a Miniseries or Special,** Gena Rowlands, *The Betty Ford Story.* **Supporting Actor in a Miniseries or Special,** Dabney Coleman, *Sworn to Silence.* **Supporting Actress in a Miniseries or Special,** Piper Laurie, *Promise.*

NATIONAL SOCIETY OF FILM CRITICS AWARDS. Best Film, *The Dead.* **Best Actor,** Steve Martin, *Roxanne.* **Best Actress,** Emily Lloyd, *Wish You Were Here.* **Best Supporting Actor,** Morgan Freeman, *Street Smart.* **Best Supporting Actress,** Kathy Baker, *Street Smart.* **Best Director,** John Boorman, *Hope and Glory.* **Best Screenplay,** John Boorman, *Hope and Glory.* **Best Cinematography,** Philippe Rousselot, *Hope and Glory.*

NEW YORK DRAMA CRITICS CIRCLE AWARDS. Best New Play, *Fences,* August Wilson. **Best New Foreign Play,** *Les Liaisons Dangereuses,* Christopher Hampton. **Best Musical,** *Les Misérables.*

NEW YORK FILM CRITICS CIRCLE AWARDS. Best Film, *Broadcast News.* **Best Actor,** Jack Nicholson, *Broadcast News, Ironweed,* and *The Witches of Eastwick.* **Best Actress,** Holly Hunter, *Broadcast News.* **Best Supporting Actor,** Morgan Freeman, *Street Smart.* **Best Supporting Actress,** Vanessa Redgrave, *Prick Up Your Ears.* **Best Director,** James L. Brooks, *Broadcast News.* **Best Screenplay,** James L. Brooks, *Broadcast News.* **Best Foreign-Language Film,** *My Life as a Dog* (Sweden).

ANTOINETTE PERRY (TONY) AWARDS. Drama Awards: Best Play, *Fences.* **Leading Actor,** James Earl Jones, *Fences.* **Leading Actress,** Linda Lavin, *Broadway Bound.* **Featured**

Actor, John Randolph, *Broadway Bound.* **Featured Actress,** Mary Alice, *Fences.* **Direction,** Lloyd Richards, *Fences.*

Musical Awards: Best Musical, *Les Misérables.* **Leading Actor,** Robert Lindsay, *Me and My Girl.* **Leading Actress,** Maryann Plunkett, *Me and My Girl.* **Featured Actor,** Michael Maguire, *Les Misérables.* **Featured Actress,** Frances Ruffelle, *Les Misérables.* **Direction,** Trevor Nunn and John Caird, *Les Misérables.* **Book for a Musical,** Alain Boublil and Claude-Michel Schönberg, *Les Misérables.* **Score for a Musical,** Claude-Michel Schönberg (music) and Herbert Kretzmer and Alain Boublil (lyrics), *Les Misérables.* **Choreography,** Gillian Gregory, *Me and My Girl.*

Best Reproduction of a Play or Musical, *All My Sons.*

UNITED STATES GOVERNMENT. National Medal of Arts, painter Romare H. Bearden; J. William Fisher, founder of the Gramma Fisher Foundation, which supports American opera; singer Ella Fitzgerald; oil executive and art patron Armand Hammer; art patron Frances A. Lewis; retail executive and art patron Sydney Lewis; poet Howard Nemerov; choreographer Alwin Nikolais; sculptor Isamu Noguchi; composer William Schuman; poet and novelist Robert Penn Warren.

WOLF FOUNDATION. Wolf Prizes: Arts, Polish-born American violinist Isaac Stern; Polish composer Krzysztof Penderecki.

Journalism Awards

AMERICAN SOCIETY OF MAGAZINE EDITORS. National Magazine Awards: General Excellence, Circulation over 1 Million, *People Weekly;* **Circulation of 400,000 to 1 Million,** *Elle;* **Circulation of 100,000 to 400,000,** *Common Cause;* **Circulation Under 100,000,** *New England Monthly.* **Personal Service,** *Consumer Reports.* **Special Interests,** *Sports Afield.* **Reporting,** *Life.* **Public Interest,** *Money.* **Design,** *Elle.* **Pho-**

President Ronald Reagan gives the National Medal of Arts, honoring artistic excellence, to jazz singer Ella Fitzgerald in June.

John Larroquette of NBC's "Night Court" in September kisses the statuette representing his third straight Emmy for best supporting actor.

tography, *National Geographic*. **Fiction**, *Esquire*. **Essays and Criticism**, *Outside*. **Single-Topic Issue**, *Bulletin of the Atomic Scientists*.

LONG ISLAND UNIVERSITY. George Polk Memorial Awards: National Reporting, Andrew Wolfson and Daniel Rubin, *The* (Louisville, Ky.) *Courier-Journal*, for stories on the safety record of military air charters. **Local Reporting,** Sally Jacobs, *The Raleigh* (N.C.) *News and Observer*, for stories leading to the indictment of a federal prison guard in connection with the suffocation of an inmate. **Regional Reporting,** Alex Beasley and Rosemary Goudreau, *The Orlando* (Fla.) *Sentinel*, for a series on medical malpractice insurance. **Foreign Reporting,** *Newsweek* magazine for its coverage of terrorism in the Middle East. **Environmental Reporting,** *High Country News*, Paonia, Colo., for its series on water resources in the West. **Financial Reporting,** Peter G. Gosselin, *The Boston Globe*, for his reports on fraudulent practices by the First Commodity Financial Corporation. **Science Reporting,** *Science Times*, the weekly science section of *The New York Times*. **National Television Reporting,** Bill Moyers, CBS News, for *The Vanishing Family—Crisis in Black America*, a documentary on unwed teen-aged parents. **Local Television Reporting,** Lee Coppola, WKBW-TV, Buffalo, N.Y., for a report on the operations of a business school. **International Television Reporting,** David Fanning and Martin Smith for *Who's Running the War?*, an account of supply channels to Nicaraguan rebels produced for the Public Broadcasting System series "Frontline."

Career Award, James Reston, columnist for *The New York Times*. **Book,** *The Paper: The Life and Death of The New York Herald Tribune*, Richard Kluger.

THE SOCIETY OF PROFESSIONAL JOURNALISTS, SIGMA DELTA CHI. Sigma Delta Chi Distinguished Service Awards, Newspaper Awards: General Reporting, Circulation More than 100,000, Thomas J. Maier and Rex Smith,

Newsday, Long Island, New York, for a series charging that the Suffolk County police rely heavily on confessions to prosecute murder cases; **General Reporting, Circulation Less than 100,000,** Kent Steward, *The Hays* (Kans.) *Daily News*, for a story chronicling the last year in the life of an elderly woman; **Editorial Writing,** Richard Doak, *The Des Moines* (Iowa) *Register*, for editorials on farm policy; **Washington Correspondence,** Alfonso Chardy, *The Miami* (Fla.) *Herald*, for stories on how the National Security Council and the Central Intelligence Agency illegally assisted the rebels in Nicaragua; **Foreign Correspondence,** Juan O. Tamayo, *The Miami Herald*, for articles on terrorism; **News Photography,** Kim Komenich, *San Francisco Examiner*, for photographs of the downfall of Philippine President Ferdinand E. Marcos; **Editorial Cartooning,** Michael Keefe, *The Denver Post;* **Public Service in Newspaper Journalism, Circulation More than 100,000,** *The Seattle Times*, for a series on the manufacture of nuclear weapons; **Public Service in Newspaper Journalism, Circulation Less than 100,000,** *The* (Wilkes-Barre, Pa.) *Times Leader*, for a series charging the directors of a Luzerne County educational agency with wasteful spending.

Magazine Awards: Magazine Reporting, Ken Case, *Third Coast*, for an exposé of unscrupulous activities by an Austin, Tex., banker; **Public Service in Magazine Journalism,** *Money*, for an article about the financial and safety practices of blood banks.

Radio Awards: Radio Reporting, Frederick J. Kennedy and Philip John Till, National Broadcasting Company (NBC) News, for reports on the 1986 U.S. bombing raid against Libya; **Public Service in Radio Journalism,** NBC News, for a documentary on the impact of cocaine trafficking; **Editorializing on Radio,** Steve Smith, KNX-AM, Los Angeles, for a commentary calling for protection for policyholders when insurance companies go bankrupt.

Television Awards: Television Reporting, "The CBS Evening News," for reports on the war in Afghanistan; **Public Service in Television Journalism, Stations in the Top 50 Markets,** WCCO-TV, Minneapolis, Minn., for an investigation uncovering evidence of the innocence of a convicted rapist; **Public Service in Television Journalism, All Other Stations,** WBRZ-TV, Baton Rouge, La., for a documentary about the murder of a key witness in a federal drug case; **Editorializing on Television,** Michael Tuck, KGTV, San Diego, for a series about misuse of a city credit card by a San Diego councilman.

Research About Journalism: *The American Journalist: A Portrait of U.S. News People and Their Work*, David H. Weaver and G. Cleveland Wilhoit.

UNIVERSITY OF GEORGIA. George Foster Peabody Broadcasting Awards, NBC Radio News for its coverage of the 1986 U.S. attack on Libya; Canadian Broadcasting Corporation radio network for *Paris: From Oscar Wilde to Jim Morrison;* Connecticut Public Radio for its science series "One on One"; CBS News "Newsmark" for *Where in the World Are We?*, a documentary dealing with Earth's geography; WHAS Radio News, Louisville, Ky., for an educational program about schizophrenia; The Fine Arts Society of Indianapolis for pioneering classical music on radio in that city; WTMJ-TV, Milwaukee, for exposing the poor driving records of some school-bus drivers; WFAA-TV, Dallas, for its investigation of the football program at Southern Methodist University; KPIX-TV, San Francisco, for its "AIDS Lifeline" public service campaign; CBS News "Sunday Morning" for its broadcast of pianist Vladimir Horowitz's trip to the Soviet Union; McNeil/Lehrer Productions and the British Broadcasting Corporation for "The Story of English"; WQED/Pittsburgh for "Anne of Green Gables"; American Broadcasting Companies (ABC) Entertainment and Churchill Films for *The Mouse and the Motorcycle;* Thames Television International and D. L. Taffner Limited for *Unknown Chaplin;* WQED/Pittsburgh and the National Geographic

Society for "The National Geographic Specials"; CBS News "CBS Reports" for *The Vanishing Family—Crisis in Black America;* John F. Kennedy Center for the Performing Arts for *The 1986 Kennedy Center Honors: A Celebration of the Performing Arts;* Thames Television International and WGBH-TV, Boston, for the "Masterpiece Theatre" series "Paradise Postponed"; NBC Entertainment for "The Cosby Show"; CBS Entertainment and Garner-Duchow Productions for *Promise,* a drama about a man who assumes responsibility for his schizophrenic brother; Jim Henson and the Muppets, for outstanding television entertainment; WSB-TV, Atlanta, Ga., for a dramatization of the childhood of civil rights leader Martin Luther King, Jr.; WCCO-TV, Minneapolis, Minn., for its public service campaign promoting safe driving; WCVB-TV, Boston, for its public service campaign against racial, religious, and ethnic discrimination; ABC News for "This Week with David Brinkley"; Dorothy Stimson Bullitt, King Broadcasting, Seattle, for her contributions to broadcasting.

Literature Awards

ACADEMY OF AMERICAN POETS. Lamont Poetry Selection, *The River of Heaven,* Garrett Kaoru Hongo. **Walt Whitman Award,** *The Weight of Numbers,* Judith Baumel.

AMERICAN LIBRARY ASSOCIATION. Newbery Medal, *The Whipping Boy,* Sid Fleischman. **Caldecott Medal,** *Hey, Al,* Richard Egielski, illustrator.

ASSOCIATION OF AMERICAN PUBLISHERS. National Book Awards: Fiction, *Paco's Story,* Larry Heinemann. **Nonfiction,** *The Making of the Atomic Bomb,* Richard Rhodes.

BOOKER PRIZE. *Moon Tiger,* Penelope Lively.

CANADA COUNCIL. Governor General's Literary Awards, English-Language: Fiction, *The Progress of Love,* Alice Munro. **Poetry,** *The Collected Poems of Al Purdy,* Alfred Purdy. **Drama,** *Doc,* Sharon Pollock. **Nonfiction,** *Northrop Frye on Shakespeare,* Northrop Frye.

French-Language: Fiction, *Les silences du corbeau,* Yvon Rivard. **Poetry,** *L'écouté,* Cécile Cloutier. **Drama,** *La visite des sauvages,* Anne Legault. **Nonfiction,** *Le réalisme socialiste: Une esthétique impossible,* Régine Robin.

CANADIAN LIBRARY ASSOCIATION. Book of the Year for Children Award, *Shadow on Hawthorne Bay,* Janet Lunn. **Amelia Frances Howard-Gibbon Illustrator's Award,** *Moonbeam on a Cat's Ear,* Marie-Louise Gay, author and illustrator.

COLUMBIA UNIVERSITY. Bancroft Prizes in American History, *A Vigorous Spirit of Enterprise,* Thomas M. Doerflinger; *Roots of Violence in Black Philadelphia, 1860-1900,* Roger Lane.

INGERSOLL FOUNDATION. Ingersoll Prizes: T. S. Eliot Award for Creative Writing, Mexican poet and essayist Octavio Paz. **Richard M. Weaver Award for Scholarly Letters,** German-born philosopher Josef Pieper.

NATIONAL BOOK CRITICS CIRCLE. National Book Critics Circle Awards, Fiction, *Kate Vaiden,* Reynolds Price. **General Nonfiction,** *War Without Mercy: Race and Power in the Pacific War,* John W. Dower. **Biography/Autobiography,** *Tombee: Portrait of a Cotton Planter,* Theodore Rosengarten. **Poetry,** *Wild Gratitude,* Edward Hirsch. **Criticism,** *Less than One: Selected Essays,* Joseph Brodsky. **Citation for Excellence in Reviewing,** Richard Eder, for book reviews in the *Los Angeles Times.*

PEN AMERICAN CENTER. Faulkner Award, *Soldiers in Hiding,* Richard Wiley.

RITZ PARIS HEMINGWAY AWARD. *A Summons to Memphis,* Peter Taylor.

ROYAL SOCIETY OF CANADA. Pierre Chauveau Medal, Benoît Lacroix, University of Montreal. **Sir William Dawson Award,** Gérard Dion, Laval University, and F. Kenneth Hare, University of Toronto. **Jason A. Hannah Medal,** Toby Gelfand. **Innis-Gérin Medal,** Anthony D.

Marlee Matlin says "thank you" in sign language in March after becoming the first deaf performer to win the Academy Award for best actress.

Scott, University of British Columbia. **Lorne Pierce Medal,** Rudy Wiebe.

YALE UNIVERSITY LIBRARY. Bollingen Prize in Poetry, Stanley Kunitz.

Nobel Prizes. See NOBEL PRIZES.

Public Service Awards

AMERICAN INSTITUTE FOR PUBLIC SERVICE. Thomas Jefferson Awards, Joan W. Bailey, founder of the Clover Caring Center, Charlotte, N.C., which distributes food, clothing, and household items to the needy; Justice William J. Brennan, Jr., of the Supreme Court of the United States; Elizabeth Brown, founder of the Honolulu, Hawaii, chapter of Toughlove, a national program for parents of problem teen-agers; Irving Brown, senior adviser to the president of the American Federation of Labor and Congress of Industrial Organizations; Fred Doescher, a volunteer in the Pittsburgh, Pa., Meals-on-Wheels program, which delivers hot meals to elderly shut-ins; Steven Jobs, cofounder of Apple Computer Incorporated; Howard Jones, founder of the Opportunities Industrialization Center, Durham, N.C., which teaches job skills to the unemployed; Jim Knocke, founder of the St. Jude's Job Network, Atlanta, an organization that provides job placement and training; Ginetta Sagan, founder of the Aurora Foundation, a human-rights organization.

FOUR FREEDOMS FOUNDATION. Four Freedoms Medal, former Speaker of the House Thomas P. O'Neill, Jr. **Freedom of Speech Medal,** Herbert Block, editorial cartoonist of *The Washington Post.* **Freedom of Worship Medal,** Leon H. Sullivan, pastor of Zion Baptist Church, Philadelphia, and author of a code of conduct for companies doing business in South Africa. **Freedom from**

Want Medal, philanthropist Mary W. Lasker. **Freedom from Fear Medal,** former United States diplomat George F. Kennan.

MARTIN LUTHER KING, JR., CENTER FOR NONVIOLENT SOCIAL CHANGE. Martin Luther King, Jr., Peace Prize, Philippine President Corazon Aquino for leading a popular revolt that overthrew President Ferdinand E. Marcos without a civil war.

NATIONAL ASSOCIATION FOR THE ADVANCEMENT OF COLORED PEOPLE. Spingarn Medal, broadcasting executive Percy Sutton.

TEMPLETON FOUNDATION. Templeton Prize for Progress in Religion, Stanley L. Jaki, Hungarian-born monk and physicist, for his writings on science and religion.

UNITED STATES GOVERNMENT. Presidential Medal of Freedom, former U.S. ambassador to Great Britain Anne L. Armstrong; former Chief Justice of the United States Warren E. Burger; business executive Justin W. Dart (posthumous); U.S. Court of Appeals Judge Irving R. Kaufman; comic actor Danny Kaye (posthumous); retired U.S. Army General Lyman L. Lemnitzer; former Director of Central Intelligence John A. McCone; Frederick Douglass Patterson, founder of the United Negro College Fund; Nathan Perlmutter, executive director of the Anti-Defamation League; Russian-born conductor and cellist Mstislav Rostropovich; physician and Project HOPE founder William B. Walsh; composer Meredith Willson (posthumous).

Pulitzer Prizes

JOURNALISM. Public Service, Andrew Schneider and Matthew Brelis, *The Pittsburgh* (Pa.) *Press,* for a series about dangerous medical problems and drug addiction among airline pilots and crews. **General News Reporting,** *Akron* (Ohio) *Beacon Journal,* for coverage of an attempted take-over at Goodyear Tire and Rubber Company. **Investigative Reporting,** Daniel R. Biddle, H. G. Bissinger, and Fredric N. Tulsky, *The Philadelphia Inquirer,* for articles about corruption and incompetence in Philadelphia courts; John Woestendiek, *The Philadelphia Inquirer,* for uncovering evidence of the innocence of a convicted murderer. **Explanatory Journalism,** Jeff Lyon and Peter Gorner, *Chicago Tribune,* for a series on gene therapy. **Specialized Reporting,** Alex S. Jones, *The New York Times,* for a profile of the divided Bingham newspaper family of Kentucky. **National Reporting,** *The Miami Herald,* for its articles on the Iran-contra affair; *The New York Times,* for its coverage of the aftermath of the *Challenger* explosion. **International Reporting,** Michael Parks, *Los Angeles Times,* for coverage of the unrest in South Africa. **Feature Writing,** Steve Twomey, *The Philadelphia Inquirer,* for a profile of life aboard the U.S. Navy aircraft carrier *America.* **Commentary,** Charles Krauthammer, The Washington Post Writers Group, for his columns on national issues. **Criticism,** Richard Eder, *Los Angeles Times,* for book reviews. **Editorial Writing,** Jonathan Freedman, *The* (San Diego) *Tribune,* for editorials urging passage of the 1986 immigration reform law. **Editorial Cartooning,** Berke Breathed, The Washington Post Writers Group, for his "Bloom County" cartoon strip. **Spot News Photography,** Kim Komenich, *San Francisco Examiner,* for photographs of the downfall of Philippine President Marcos. **Feature Photography,** David Peterson, *The Des Moines* (Iowa) *Register,* for photographs of Iowans hard-hit by the farm crisis.

LETTERS. Biography, *Bearing the Cross: Martin Luther King, Jr., and the Southern Christian Leadership Conference,* David J. Garrow. **Fiction,** *A Summons to Memphis,* Peter Taylor. **General Nonfiction,** *Arab and Jew: Wounded Spirits in a Promised Land,* David K. Shipler. **History,** *Voyagers to the West: A Passage in the Peopling of America on the Eve of the Revolution,* Bernard Bailyn. **Drama,** *Fences,* August Wilson. **Poetry,** *Thomas and Beulah,* Rita Dove.

MUSIC. Music Award, "The Flight into Egypt," John Harbison.

SPECIAL CITATION. Joseph Pulitzer, Jr., former chairman of the Pulitzer Prize Board.

Science and Technology Awards

COLUMBIA UNIVERSITY. Louisa Gross Horwitz Prize, Günter Blobel, Rockefeller University.

GAIRDNER FOUNDATION. Gairdner Foundation International Awards, René G. Favaloro, Clinica Guemes, Buenos Aires, Argentina; Robert C. Gallo, National Cancer Institute, Bethesda, Md., and Luc Montagnier, Pasteur Institute, Paris; Walter J. Gehring, University of Basel, Switzerland, and Edward B. Lewis, California Institute of Technology (Caltech), Pasadena; Eric R. Kandel, Columbia University; Michael Rossmann, Purdue University.

ALBERT AND MARY LASKER FOUNDATION. Albert Lasker Basic Medical Research Award, Susumu Tonegawa, Massachusetts Institute of Technology (M.I.T.), Cambridge; Philip Leder, Harvard Medical School, Boston; Leroy E. Hood, Caltech. **Albert Lasker Clinical Medical Research Award,** Mogens A. Schou, Århus University Psychiatric Institute, Denmark.

ROYAL SOCIETY OF CANADA. Thomas W. Eadie Medal, Alexander McLean, University of Toronto. **McLaughlin Medal,** Henry G. Friesen, University of Manitoba. **Willet G. Miller Medal,** Harold Williams, Memorial University. **Rutherford Medal in Chemistry,** Grenfell N. Patey, University of British Columbia. **Rutherford Medal in Physics,** A. John Berlinsky, McMaster University. **John L. Synge Award,** James G. Arthur, University of Toronto. **Henry Marshall Tory Medal,** Keith L. Laidler, University of Ottawa.

UNITED STATES GOVERNMENT. National Medal of Science, Philip H. Abelson, *Science* magazine; Anne Anastasi, Fordham University; R. Byron Bird, University of Wisconsin; Raoul H. Bott, Harvard University; Michael E. DeBakey, Baylor College of Medicine; Theodor O. Diener, U.S. Department of Agriculture; Harry Eagle, Albert Einstein College of Medicine; Walter M. Elsasser, Johns Hopkins University; Michael H. Freedman, University of California at San Diego; William S. Johnson, Stanford University; Har Gobind Khorana, Massachusetts Institute of Technology; Paul C. Lauterbur, University of Illinois; Rita Levi-Montalcini, Laboratory of Cell Biology, Rome; George E. Pake, Xerox Corporation; H. Bolton Seed, University of California at Berkeley; George J. Stigler, University of Chicago; Walter H. Stockmayer, Dartmouth College; Max Tishler, Wesleyan University; James A. Van Allen, University of Iowa; Ernst Weber, Polytechnic Institute of New York.

National Medal of Technology, Joseph V. Charyk, Communications Satellite Corporation; W. Edwards Deming, New York University; John E. Franz, Monsanto Corporation; Robert N. Noyce, Intel Corporation.

UNIVERSITY OF SOUTHERN CALIFORNIA. John and Alice Tyler Ecology-Energy Prize, Richard Evans Schultes, former director of the Botanical Museum, Harvard University; geographer Gilbert F. White.

WOLF FOUNDATION. Wolf Prizes: Agriculture, Theodor O. Diener, United States Department of Agriculture. **Chemistry,** Sir David C. Phillips, Oxford University; David M. Blow, Imperial College of Science and Technology, University of London. **Mathematics,** Kiyoshi Ito, Kyoto University, Japan; Peter D. Lax, New York University. **Medicine,** Pedro Cuatrecasas, Glaxo, Incorporated, Research Triangle Park, N.C.; Meir Wilchek, Weizmann Institute of Science, Rehovot, Israel. **Physics,** Herbert Friedman, Naval Research Laboratory, Washington, D.C.; Bruno B. Rossi, Massachusetts Institute of Technology; Riccardo Giacconi, Space Telescope Science Institute, Baltimore.

Sara Dreyfuss

BABBITT, BRUCE EDWARD (1938-   ), a former governor of Arizona, formally declared his candidacy for the 1988 Democratic presidential nomination on March 10, 1987.

Babbitt was born in Los Angeles on June 27, 1938. He attended the University of Notre Dame in Indiana and received a bachelor's degree in geology in 1960. In 1962, while doing graduate work in geophysics, Babbitt decided to leave science for public service. He received a master's degree in geophysics from the University of Newcastle, England, in 1963 and a law degree from Harvard Law School in 1965.

From 1965 to 1967, Babbitt was an attorney for the U.S. Office of Economic Opportunity. He then practiced law in Phoenix from 1967 to 1975 and was elected attorney general of Arizona in 1974.

Babbitt became governor upon the death of Governor Wesley Bolin in March 1978. Later that year, Babbitt was elected to his first full term. In 1982, he was reelected with 63 per cent of the vote. During his term, Arizona's rates of growth in population and economy were among the highest in the United States.

Babbitt and his wife, Harriet (Hattie), a trial lawyer, have two sons. Joan Stephenson

BAHAMAS. See LATIN AMERICA.

BAHRAIN. See MIDDLE EAST.

BALLET. See DANCING.

BANGLADESH in 1987 suffered what President Hussain Muhammed Ershad called the nation's most devastating flood in 70 years. Some annual flooding in Bangladesh is a normal result of monsoon rains. But 1987 brought the most rainfall in 75 years, greater than normal runoff from deforested areas in Nepal and India, and continued silting of the Ganges and Brahmaputra rivers, which decreased the volume of water carried to the Bay of Bengal. The resulting floods affected some 25 million Bangladeshis.

Cooperation by the government, the army, and volunteer agencies kept the official death toll at about 1,000 people. Unofficial estimates of the deaths ranged up to 5,000.

Property Damage was estimated at $1.5 billion. About 3 million metric tons (3.3 million short tons) of grain—20 per cent of the normal yearly production—were lost. The flooding also increased the need for foreign aid. Even before the floods, both exports and imports had dropped off. The government encouraged foreign investors to set up joint-venture industries in Bangladesh that took advantage of the country's cheap labor, but the attempts had limited success.

Government Opposition. Ershad opened the year's first parliamentary session on January 24 by saying that he was fully committed to multiparty democracy. But Ershad, who was a general when

Residents of Sirajganj, Bangladesh, lead a cow to safety in August during Bangladesh's most devastating flood in several decades.

he took power in 1982, also said that the armed forces had a role in "establishing a democratic setup" in Bangladesh and should protect its democracy. The main alliance of opposition parties, who want a return to civilian rule in Bangladesh, walked out when Ershad began speaking.

In July, the main alliance—headed by the Awami League under Hasina Wajed—and another opposition alliance headed by the Bangladesh Nationalist Party under Khaleda Zia formed a united front to encourage strikes and protests demanding Ershad's resignation. On November 10, the front launched a drive against Ershad that led to a week of violence in which 11 people were killed. The government arrested over 5,000 people, including Wajed and Zia.

Continuing Agitation—and the threat of a three-day general strike called for November 29—caused Ershad to declare a state of emergency on November 27. The action suspended individuals' legal rights. Strikes and demonstrations continued. On December 6, Ershad dissolved parliament and said he would try to hold new parliamentary elections within three months. Wajed and Zia, who were released from arrest on December 10, refused to cooperate with the government to end the agitation or schedule elections.   Henry S. Bradsher

See also ASIA (Facts in Brief Table). In WORLD BOOK, see BANGLADESH.

BANK. Dangers threatened the United States banking system in 1987, though the nation achieved a peacetime record of five consecutive years of economic growth. A 22.6 per cent fall in average stock prices on October 19 and increasing uncertainty about the health of some state economies created serious problems for banks. A post-depression record 184 banks failed in 1987.

Money Supply. The narrowly defined index of money supply, *M1,* which represents the amount of U.S. currency in circulation and in checking and NOW accounts, began 1987 at $748 billion. The M1 growth rate had been 16.5 per cent per year through 1986 as the Federal Reserve System (the Fed) increased bank reserves fairly quickly. In 1987, however, growth slowed to less than 1 per cent, and M1 finished the year at only $752.2 billion. A more broadly defined index, *M2,* which represents M1 plus the amount of money in savings accounts, certificates of deposit (CD's), and money-market mutual funds, began 1987 at $2,800 billion and rose at only 3.2 per cent to end the year at $2,897.1 billion.

Stock Market Nose Dive. The Fed temporarily reversed its policy of slowing growth of the money supply after October 19—when the Dow Jones Industrial Average dropped 508 points—to avoid any repeat of the snowballing financial collapse that led from a stock market crash in 1929 to the

breakdown of the U.S. banking system during the Great Depression. Between 1930 and 1933, more than half of all U.S. banks failed, and the money supply decreased by one-third.

Before 1933, the year Congress created the Federal Deposit Insurance Corporation (the FDIC), a bank failure meant the loss of depositors' money and the wealth it represented. Even the rumor of a bank's insolvency could set off a "run" on the bank, as panicky depositors tried to withdraw their money. Because more than 80 per cent of an average bank's assets consist of loans that cannot be quickly converted into cash, even a financially sound bank can be pushed into bankruptcy by a run if it cannot borrow more cash from the Fed. The Federal Reserve Act of 1913, which created the Fed, had given the system the duty to be the lender of last resort in a crisis, but in the early 1930's the Fed refused to save the banking system.

Today, most economists blame the Fed for helping to cause the Great Depression, and officials at the Fed in 1987 clearly remembered this. Alan Greenspan, the chairman of the Fed's Board of Governors, announced after the 1987 market plunge that the Fed would prevent any shortage of bank reserves.

Interest Rates. The Fed's policy caused an immediate drop in interest rates during the week of October 19. The three-month Treasury bill rate, which held steady at 5.6 per cent through the first seven months of 1987, began rising at the end of July and passed 7 per cent on October 16. One week later, the rate dropped to 6 per cent, and it ended the year at 5.7 per cent.

The 90-day CD rate was 6.2 per cent in January and climbed gradually past 7 per cent in early May before falling slightly. The CD rate fluctuated between 6.6 and 6.8 per cent in July and August. From the end of August to October 16, the rate rose to 8.8 per cent and then fell to 8.2 per cent after the stock market crash. The rate was 6.5 per cent at the end of the year.

The prime rate—what banks announce as the rate they charge their best corporate customers on short-term loans—was 7.5 per cent from September 1986 to the end of March 1987. Then it began a slow rise, reaching 9.25 per cent in early October. On October 17, some banks announced their intention to increase their prime rate to 9.5 per cent. But the rates fell after October 19, and by year-end the prime rate stood at 8.75 per cent.

Inflation. The Consumer Price Index (CPI)—a measure of the average level of retail prices—rose less than 2 per cent in 1986 and only 3.7 per cent in 1987. As a result, the Fed feared damage to the banking system more than the possibility of renewed inflation.

Record Bank Failures. In addition to the 184 banks that failed in 1987, 17 savings and loan as-

Alan Greenspan fields questions from reporters in June after being named to replace Paul A. Volcker as chairman of the Federal Reserve Board.

sociations (S&L's) were closed. Most failures were caused by defaulted loans.

Bank and S&L failures no longer make depositors poor; instead, they put a burden on government deposit insurers. From 1985 through 1987, five state deposit insurers collapsed when all their assets had to be used to pay depositors' claims. On March 12, 1987, Utah became the latest state insurer to admit defeat.

The assets of even the FDIC and the other federal deposit insurance agency—the Federal Savings and Loan Insurance Corporation (FSLIC)— look small compared with the size of potential claims. By late February, FSLIC assets derived from insurance premiums paid by S&L's had dropped to $2 billion, though claims of more than $4 billion were expected. Because of the projected shortfall, some failing S&L's that had lost virtually all their capital due to loan losses were nonetheless allowed to remain open. These institutions—called the "living dead" by some observers—would have been closed or merged with healthy S&L's if the FSLIC had the cash to do so. On August 10, President Ronald Reagan signed the Competitive Equality Banking Act of 1987, which helped shore up the FSLIC by allowing it to raise $10.8 billion by issuing long-term bonds.

The FDIC, with assets of $18 billion, was in a better position than the FSLIC but still expected losses of $2 billion by year-end. The strength of the FDIC and FSLIC lies not in their assets, however, but in the Fed's willingness to loan them money as needed. State insurance agencies do not have this source of revenue.

The Latin-American Debt Crisis, a problem that first grabbed headlines in 1982, was neither better nor worse in 1987. At the end of 1986, Argentina, Brazil, and Mexico—which have all been slow in repaying their debts—owed U.S. banks about $255 billion. On Feb. 20, 1987, Brazil stopped paying interest as well as principal on its U.S. debt. But a significant trade surplus allowed restructuring of the debt to delay action on the crisis for another year.

Volcker Resignation. Paul A. Volcker, who was appointed chairman of the Board of Governors of the Fed by President Jimmy Carter in 1979, refused reappointment on June 2, 1987. Volcker's main accomplishment while at the Fed was helping lower the inflation rate to less than 4 per cent. This made Americans more willing to save money—which could in turn help to slow the inflation rate in the future.

Alan Greenspan, who had served as chief economic adviser to President Gerald R. Ford, succeeded Volcker on August 11. See GREENSPAN, ALAN. Donald W. Swanton

In WORLD BOOK, see BANK.

BASEBALL

BASEBALL. On the field, the Minnesota Twins overcame preseason odds of 150-1 and won the 1987 World Series, defeating the St. Louis Cardinals. Off the field, major league owners faced charges of conspiring against free agency and failing to hire enough black managers.

The division races were exciting, and the regular-season attendance of 52,008,918 was almost 10 per cent higher than the previous record of 47,500,347 set in 1986. The 4,458 major league home runs in 1987 were the most ever, bettering the previous record of 3,813 in 1986. The Toronto Blue Jays hit 10 home runs in one game, a record. The major leagues tested the balls used during the season and reported that they were no livelier than in previous years.

Regular Season. The American League West was considered a weak division because of the won-lost records of its teams. Minnesota finished just 8 games above .500 with a record of 85-77, defeating the Kansas City Royals by 2 games and the Oakland Athletics by 4. Still, Minnesota boasted the best home record in the majors, finishing the regular season with a 56-20 record at home and never losing there in the play-offs.

In the American League East, Toronto led the Detroit Tigers by 3½ games with a week to go, but Toronto lost its last 7 games, including a 3-game

Minnesota pitcher Frank Viola, Most Valuable Player in the World Series, hurls against St. Louis in the series, which Minnesota won.

series in Detroit on the final weekend of the season. Detroit won the division by 2 games.

Minnesota's division title was its first since 1970, and Detroit was favored in the league championship series held from October 7 to 12. Minnesota won the first 2 games of that series at home and 2 of the next 3 at Detroit, taking the play-offs, 4 games to 1.

In the National League East, St. Louis beat the Mets by 3 games and the Montreal Expos by 4. In the West, the San Francisco Giants finished 6 games ahead of the Cincinnati Reds. For San Francisco, which lost 100 games two seasons before, this was the first division title since 1971. It was the third in six years for St. Louis.

In the championship play-offs from October 6 to 14, San Francisco took a 3-2 lead in games. Facing elimination, St. Louis won the next 2 games and captured the play-offs, 4 games to 3.

World Series. Although St. Louis was missing first baseman Jack Clark and third baseman Terry Pendleton due to injuries, it was favored in the World Series from October 17 to 25 because of its greater play-off experience and speed. Minnesota had good starting pitchers in Frank Viola and Bert Blyleven and a strong reliever in Jeff Reardon, but its defense was questionable.

Minnesota won the first two games at home, 10-1 and 8-4, behind Viola and Blyleven. Then the teams moved to St. Louis for three games, and the Cardinals won them all—3-1, 7-2 (over Viola), and 4-2 (over Blyleven). The final two games were in Minnesota, and the Twins won both, 11-5 and 4-2. Viola won the deciding game and was voted the series' Most Valuable Player.

Stars. Outfielder Tony Gwynn of the San Diego Padres won the National League batting championship with .370, the league's highest average since Stan Musial's .376 in 1948. Third baseman Wade Boggs of the Boston Red Sox (.363) won his fourth American League batting title in five years.

There were batting streaks of 39 games by designated hitter Paul Molitor of the Milwaukee Brewers, in the American League, and of 34 games, a major league rookie record, by catcher Benito Santiago of San Diego in the National League. First baseman Mark McGwire of Oakland led the American League with 49 home runs, a major league record for rookies. Santiago and McGwire were voted the rookies of the year.

First baseman Don Mattingly of the New York Yankees tied a major league record with home runs in eight consecutive games and set a new record with six grand slams in one season. Nolan Ryan, the Houston Astros' 40-year-old pitcher, led the majors with 270 strikeouts and the National League with a 2.76 earned-run average.

Hall of Fame. Three retired players were voted into the National Baseball Hall of Fame in Coop-

Final Standings in Major League Baseball

American League

Eastern Division

	W.	L.	Pct.	G.B.
Detroit Tigers	98	64	.605	
Toronto Blue Jays	96	66	.593	2
Milwaukee Brewers	91	71	.562	7
New York Yankees	89	73	.549	9
Boston Red Sox	78	84	.481	20
Baltimore Orioles	67	95	.414	31
Cleveland Indians	61	101	.377	37

Western Division

	W.	L.	Pct.	G.B.
Minnesota Twins	85	77	.525	
Kansas City Royals	83	79	.512	2
Oakland Athletics	81	81	.500	4
Seattle Mariners	78	84	.481	7
Chicago White Sox	77	85	.475	8
California Angels	75	87	.463	10
Texas Rangers	75	87	.463	10

Offensive Leaders

Batting Average—Wade Boggs, Boston	.363
Runs Scored—Paul Molitor, Milwaukee	114
Home Runs—Mark McGwire, Oakland	49
Runs Batted In—George Bell, Toronto	134
Hits—Kirby Puckett, Minnesota	207
Stolen Bases—Harold Reynolds, Seattle	60
Slugging Percentage—Mark McGwire, Oakland	.618

Leading Pitchers

Games Won—Roger Clemens, Boston, and Dave Stewart, Oakland (tie)	20
Win Average (15 decisions or more)—John Cerutti, Toronto (11-4)	.733
Earned Run Average (162 or more innings)—Jimmy Key, Toronto	2.76
Strikeouts—Mark Langston, Seattle	262
Saves—Tom Henke, Toronto	34
Shutouts—Roger Clemens, Boston	7

Awards*

Most Valuable Player—George Bell, Toronto
Cy Young—Roger Clemens, Boston
Rookie of the Year—Mark McGwire, Oakland
Manager of the Year—Tom Kelly, Minnesota

National League

Eastern Division

	W.	L.	Pct.	G.B.
St. Louis Cardinals	95	67	.586	
New York Mets	92	70	.568	3
Montreal Expos	91	71	.562	4
Philadelphia Phillies	80	82	.494	15
Pittsburgh Pirates	80	82	.494	15
Chicago Cubs	76	85	.472	18½

Western Division

	W.	L.	Pct.	G.B.
San Francisco Giants	90	72	.556	
Cincinnati Reds	84	78	.519	6
Houston Astros	76	86	.469	14
Los Angeles Dodgers	73	89	.451	17
Atlanta Braves	69	92	.429	20½
San Diego Padres	65	97	.401	25

Offensive Leaders

Batting Average—Tony Gwynn, San Diego	.370
Runs Scored—Tim Raines, Montreal	123
Home Runs—Andre Dawson, Chicago	49
Runs Batted In—Andre Dawson, Chicago	137
Hits—Tony Gwynn, San Diego	218
Stolen Bases—Vince Coleman, St. Louis	109
Slugging Percentage—Jack Clark, St. Louis	.597

Leading Pitchers

Games Won—Rick Sutcliffe, Chicago	18
Win Average (15 decisions or more)—Dennis Martinez, Montreal (11-4)	.733
Earned Run Average (162 or more innings)—Nolan Ryan, Houston	2.76
Strikeouts—Nolan Ryan, Houston	270
Saves—Steve Bedrosian, Philadelphia	40
Shutouts—Rick Reuschel, San Francisco; Bob Welch, Los Angeles (tie)	4

Awards*

Most Valuable Player—Andre Dawson, Chicago
Cy Young—Steve Bedrosian, Philadelphia
Rookie of the Year—Benito Santiago, San Diego
Manager of the Year—Bob (Buck) Rodgers, Montreal

*Selected by Baseball Writers Association of America.

---

erstown, N.Y. They were outfielder Billy Williams, who played 16 seasons with the Cubs and 2 with Oakland from 1959 to 1976; pitcher Jim (Catfish) Hunter, who played for Oakland and the Yankees between 1965 and 1979; and third baseman Ray Dandridge, who played from 1933 to 1948 in the Negro Leagues.

Free Agents. Following the 1985 season, 62 players whose contracts had expired declared themselves free agents. Few received offers from other teams, and only four signed with new teams.

The Major League Players Association accused the club owners of plotting together unfairly to withhold offers and filed a grievance. On September 21, arbitrator Thomas T. Roberts ruled in favor of the players. Roberts said he planned to hold hearings to consider remedies for the players involved.

Another arbitrator was hearing a similar grievance for players who became free agents after the 1986 season. Those players included Detroit pitcher Jack Morris and Chicago Cubs outfielder Andre Dawson. In 1987, Morris received no offer from another team and won $1,850,000 in salary arbitration. Dawson, who earned $1,055,000 from Montreal in 1986, also received no offer. He told the Cubs he would sign with them for any salary they chose. They gave him a base salary of $500,000, and he rewarded them in 1987 by leading the majors in runs batted in with 137 and tying for first in home runs with 49. He was named the National League's Most Valuable Player, the first ever from a last-place team.

Blacks. On April 6, Al Campanis, executive vice president and director of player development for the Los Angeles Dodgers, suggested on national television that blacks lack "some of the necessities" to be major league managers and general managers. Two days later, he resigned under pressure. In June, Commissioner of Baseball Peter V. Ueberroth hired Harry Edwards, a black sociologist, as a part-time consultant to find blacks and Hispanics to fill managerial and front-office positions. Subsequently, five teams fired their managers and seven changed general managers, but none found a black replacement.

Balls and Bats. For years, it was believed that some pitchers secretly scraped balls to alter their flight. In 1987, Joe Niekro of Minnesota was caught with an emery board in his pocket and Kevin Gross of Philadelphia with sandpaper glued to his glove. Both were suspended for 10 days.

Bats can be altered by drilling a hole in the barrel and filling it with cork, making the bat lighter and easier to swing. Suspected bats were seized and X-rayed. Outfielder Billy Hatcher of Houston was the only player found using an altered bat, and he was suspended for 10 days.   Frank Litsky

In WORLD BOOK, see BASEBALL.

BASKETBALL. The national college basketball titles for the 1986-1987 season went to the Indiana University men and the University of Tennessee women. Among the professionals, the Los Angeles Lakers regained the National Basketball Association (NBA) title from the Boston Celtics, their usual rival in the annual play-off finals.

College Men. The college season ran from November 1986 to March 1987. Louisville and North Carolina were the preseason favorites. The University of Nevada at Las Vegas, however, was ranked first for most of the season in the separate weekly polls of the Associated Press panel of writers and broadcasters and the United Press International board of coaches.

The best regular-season records among major colleges belonged to Nevada-Las Vegas (33-1), DePaul (26-2), Temple (31-3), North Carolina (29-3), New Orleans (25-3), Iowa (27-4), Alabama (26-4), Georgetown (26-4), Indiana (24-4), and Purdue (24-4).

The National Collegiate Athletic Association (NCAA) chose 64 teams for its men's tournament held from March 12 to 30, 1987. Louisville, which won the title the year before, had an 18-14 record during the regular season and was not among the 64 teams invited.

Nevada-Las Vegas, which led the nation in scoring (92.6 points per game), was seeded first in its

National Basketball Association Standings

Eastern Conference

Atlantic Division

	W.	L.	Pct.	G.B.
Boston Celtics	59	23	.720	
Philadelphia 76ers	45	37	.549	14
Washington Bullets	42	40	.512	17
New Jersey Nets	24	58	.293	35
New York Knicks	24	58	.293	35

Central Division

Atlanta Hawks	57	25	.695	
Detroit Pistons	52	30	.634	5
Milwaukee Bucks	50	32	.610	7
Indiana Pacers	41	41	.500	16
Chicago Bulls	40	42	.488	17
Cleveland Cavaliers	31	51	.378	26

Western Conference

Midwest Division

Dallas Mavericks	55	27	.671	
Utah Jazz	44	38	.537	11
Houston Rockets	42	40	.512	13
Denver Nuggets	37	45	.451	18
Sacramento Kings	29	53	.354	26
San Antonio Spurs	28	54	.341	27

Pacific Division

Los Angeles Lakers	65	17	.793	
Portland Trail Blazers	49	33	.598	16
Golden State Warriors	42	40	.512	23
Seattle SuperSonics	39	43	.476	26
Phoenix Suns	36	46	.439	29
Los Angeles Clippers	12	70	.146	53

Individual Leaders

Scoring

	G.	F.G.	F.T.	Pts.	Avg.
Michael Jordan, Chicago	82	1,098	833	3,041	37.1
Dominique Wilkins, Atlanta	79	828	607	2,294	29.0
Alex English, Denver	82	965	411	2,345	28.6
Larry Bird, Boston	74	786	414	2,076	28.1
Kiki Vandeweghe, Portland	79	808	467	2,122	26.9
Kevin McHale, Boston	77	790	428	2,008	26.1
Mark Aguirre, Dallas	80	787	429	2,056	25.7

Rebounding

	G.	Tot.	Avg.
Charles Barkley, Philadelphia	68	994	14.6
Charles Oakley, Chicago	82	1,074	13.1
Buck Williams, New Jersey	82	1,023	12.5
James Donaldson, Dallas	82	973	11.9

region. The other top-seeded teams were Indiana, North Carolina, and Georgetown. But on March 21, Syracuse upset North Carolina, 79-75, in the East regional final in East Rutherford, N.J., and Providence upset Georgetown, 88-73, in the Southeast regional final in Louisville, Ky.

The four regional champions were Nevada-Las Vegas, Indiana, Syracuse, and Providence. They advanced to the Final Four in New Orleans. There, in the national semifinals on March 28, Indiana overcame early foul trouble to defeat Nevada-Las Vegas, 97-93, and Syracuse stopped Providence's long-range shooting and won, 77-63. That set up an exciting final on March 30 between Indiana and Syracuse.

Syracuse led favored Indiana by 3 points with 38 seconds left. With 5 seconds remaining, Indiana took the lead on a baseline jump shot by guard Keith Smart. Then, Derrick Coleman, Syracuse's freshman forward, threw a desperate floor-length inbounds pass, only to have Smart intercept it and save Indiana's 74-73 victory.

In the championship game, Smart scored 21 points, including Indiana's last 6 points and 12 of its last 15, and was voted the Most Valuable Player in the Final Four. The national title was the third for Indiana under coach Bobby Knight.

The College Player of the Year was David Robinson, Navy's 7-foot 1-inch (216-centimeter) center. He ranked first in the nation in blocked shots (4.5 per game), third in scoring (28.2 points), and fourth in rebounds (11.8). Other consensus all-Americans were forwards Danny Manning of Kansas and Reggie Williams of Georgetown and guards Steve Alford of Indiana and Kenny Smith of North Carolina. Robinson later signed a $26-million, eight-year contract with the San Antonio Spurs of the NBA, though he first had to serve two years in the United States Navy.

Women. Texas ranked first after the regular season for the fourth straight year. After an 85-78 loss to Tennessee on Dec. 14, 1986, in Austin, Tex., it won its last 25 games.

In the NCAA's 48-team tournament in Austin, the Final Four were Texas (31-1), Long Beach State (33-2), Louisiana Tech (29-2), and Tennessee (26-6). The semifinals on March 27 produced two upsets as Louisiana Tech beat Texas, 79-75, and Tennessee eliminated Long Beach State, 74-64. In the final on March 29, 1987, Tennessee won, 67-44, with a tenacious defense that stopped Louisiana Tech's inside game and ended Tech's 19-game winning streak.

After the season, the women made a significant rules change for the 1987-1988 season. They voted to award 3 points for a field goal of at least 19 feet 9 inches (6.02 meters), the same rule the men instituted in the 1986-1987 season.

NBA Season. The 23 teams played 82 regular-season games each from October 1986 to April 1987. Attendance at NBA games rose 7.6 per cent to a record high of 12,065,351.

The division winners were the Lakers (65-17) by 16 games, the Celtics (59-23) by 14, the Atlanta Hawks (57-25) by 5, and the Dallas Mavericks (55-27) by 11. They joined 12 other teams in the play-offs.

Play-Offs. The Lakers eliminated the Denver Nuggets, 3 games to 0; the Golden State Warriors, 4-1; and the Seattle SuperSonics, 4-0. The Celtics beat the Chicago Bulls, 3-0; the Milwaukee Bucks, 4-3; and the Detroit Pistons, 4-3.

In the third game of the Boston-Detroit series, forward Larry Bird of Boston and center Bill

With five seconds left, Keith Smart of Indiana University scores the winning basket over Syracuse on March 30 to give Indiana the NCAA title.

225

The 1986-1987
College Basketball Season

College Tournament Champions

NCAA (Men) Division I: Indiana
        Division II: Kentucky Wesleyan
        Division III: North Park (Illinois)
NCAA (Women) Division I: Tennessee
        Division II: New Haven (Connecticut)
        Division III: Wisconsin-Stevens Point
NAIA (Men): Washburn (Kansas)
      (Women): Southwest Oklahoma State
NIT: Southern Mississippi
Junior College (Men): College of Southern Idaho
          (Women): Northeast Mississippi

College Champions

Conference	School
Atlantic Coast	North Carolina (regular season)
	North Carolina State (tournament)
Atlantic Ten	Temple*
Big East	Georgetown—Pittsburgh— Syracuse (tie, regular season)
	Georgetown (tournament)
Big Eight	Missouri*
Big Sky	Montana State (regular season)
	Idaho State (tournament)
Big South	Baptist*
Big Ten	Indiana—Purdue (tie)
Colonial Athletic	Navy*
East Coast	Bucknell*
Eastern College Athletic-North	Northeastern*
Eastern College Athletic-Metro	Marist*
Gulf Star	Stephen F. Austin State
Ivy League	Pennsylvania
Metro	Louisville (regular season)
	Memphis State (tournament)
Metro Atlantic	St. Peter's (regular season)
	Fairfield (tournament)
Mid-American	Central Michigan*
Mid-Continent	Southwest Missouri State*
Mid-Eastern	Howard (regular season)
	North Carolina A & T (tournament)
Midwestern City	Evansville—Loyola (tie; regular season)
	Xavier (tournament)
Missouri Valley	Tulsa (regular season)
	Wichita State (tournament)
Ohio Valley	Middle Tennessee (regular season)
	Austin Peay (tournament)
Pacific Coast Athletic	Nevada-Las Vegas*
Pacific Ten	UCLA*
Southeastern	Alabama*
Southern	Marshall*
Southland	Louisiana Tech*
Southwest	Texas Christian (regular season)
	Texas A & M (tournament)
Southwestern Athletic	Grambling (regular season)
	Southern (tournament)
Sun Belt	Western Kentucky (regular season)
	Alabama-Birmingham (tournament)
Trans America Athletic	Arkansas-Little Rock (regular season)
	Georgia Southern (tournament)
West Coast Athletic	San Diego (regular season)
	Santa Clara (tournament)
Western Athletic	Texas-El Paso (regular season)
	Wyoming (tournament)

*Regular season and conference tournament champions.

Laimbeer of Detroit got into a fistfight. They were ejected from the game, and the league fined them a total of $7,000. In the fifth game, center Robert Parish of Boston punched Laimbeer three times and was suspended for the next game, which Boston lost.

The championship round from June 2 to 14 matched the Lakers and the Celtics for the third time in four years. It was the Lakers' sixth trip to the finals in eight years. The quicker and fresher Lakers were favored, especially since the Celtics were slowed by injuries to Parish, forward Kevin McHale, and guard Danny Ainge.

The Lakers, coached by Pat Riley, took a 3-1 lead in games, but the Celtics won the fifth game at home, 123-108. The Lakers then returned home and won the sixth game, 106-93, and the championship series, 4 games to 2.

This was the Lakers' fourth title in the eight seasons since Earvin (Magic) Johnson joined them. The 6-foot 9-inch (206-centimeter) guard was voted the Most Valuable Player in the regular season and again in the play-offs.

The Stars. During the regular season, Johnson averaged a career high of 23.9 points per game and led in assists (12.2 per game) for the fourth time in five years. In the play-off finals, he averaged 26.2 points, 13 assists, and 8 rebounds per game.

Michael Jordan, Chicago's 6-foot 6-inch (198-centimeter) guard, easily won the scoring title by averaging 37.1 points per game. He became the first player since Wilt Chamberlain in 1963 to score 3,000 points in one season. Jordan and Johnson were chosen as the guards on the all-star team, along with McHale and Bird of Boston at forward and Akeem Olajuwon of the Houston Rockets at center. Forward Chuck Person of the Indiana Pacers was voted Rookie of the Year.

At age 37, forward Julius Erving of the Philadelphia 76ers, one of the sport's most spectacular players, played his final season. In his last home game, he became the third NBA player in history—along with Chamberlain and Kareem Abdul-Jabbar—to score more than 30,000 career points.

Expansion. On April 22, the NBA decided to expand, awarding four new franchises for $32.5 million each. The league admitted Charlotte, N.C., and Miami, Fla., for the 1988-1989 season and Orlando, Fla., and Minnesota (playing in Minneapolis) for the 1989-1990 season. League officials had planned to admit only three teams, but when they could not decide between Miami and Orlando, they took both cities. Minnesota previously had an NBA franchise until the Minneapolis Lakers moved from that city to Los Angeles for the 1960-1961 season.

Frank Litsky

In WORLD BOOK, see BASKETBALL.

BELGIUM faced possible political chaos after a national election in December 1987 failed to resolve a long-running dispute involving the country's two languages. Most Belgians belong to one of two ethnic groups—the Flemings, who speak Dutch, and the Walloons, whose language is French.

Belgium's Constitution divides the country into language regions. By law, officials of political units in each region must pass tests of their knowledge of that region's language. The mayor of a group of villages refused to meet this requirement in the fall of 1986, touching off the dispute.

The Happart Affair. The villages involved are officially Flemish, but most of their residents speak French and refuse to speak Dutch. The mayor, José Happart, refused to take a test of his knowledge of Dutch.

Belgium's highest court dismissed Happart from office in October 1986, but local officials reinstated him. The conflict split the Christian Social Party, led by Prime Minister Wilfried A. E. Martens, along ethnic lines, and brought the collapse of his center-right coalition government.

Martens tried for a year to work out a compromise, but finally resigned on Oct. 15, 1987. King Baudoin I accepted Martens' resignation and scheduled a national election for December 13. Martens stayed on as caretaker prime minister.

Election Setback. The election reduced the coalition's majority in the 212-seat House of Representatives—the more powerful of the two houses of Parliament—from 18 seats to 8. Although this is a substantial margin, political observers said that Martens would have trouble rebuilding his coalition because of the ethnic friction.

Channel Tragedy. The worst peacetime disaster in the history of English Channel shipping occurred on March 6 when the British-owned ferry *Herald of Free Enterprise* sank outside the harbor of Zeebrugge, Belgium. Belgium mounted a rescue operation that saved 348 people. In the ensuing weeks, however, 188 bodies were recovered and 5 people were listed as missing.

Soccer Fans Extradited. Great Britain extradited 25 soccer fans to Belgium on September 9 to face manslaughter charges stemming from a riot that occurred during a game played at Heysel Stadium in Brussels, Belgium, on May 29, 1985. The fans were supporters of an English soccer team. As a result of the riot, 38 people died, most of them fans of the other team.   Kenneth Brown

See also EUROPE (Facts in Brief Table). In WORLD BOOK, see BELGIUM.

BELIZE. See LATIN AMERICA.
BENIN. See AFRICA.
BHUTAN. See ASIA.

A Belgian farmer drops a firecracker into an empty milk can in May during a protest in Brussels against proposed cuts in farm subsidies.

BIOCHEMISTRY

BIOCHEMISTRY. The first partial map of the human *genome*—the genetic makeup of human beings—was announced in October 1987 by researchers at Collaborative Research, Incorporated, of Bedford, Mass., and the Massachusetts Institute of Technology (M.I.T.) in Cambridge. Genes, which determine all inherited traits, are composed of *deoxyribonucleic acid* (DNA). The map consists of 404 genetic *markers*, distinctive fragments of DNA that are often inherited in patterns correlated with a tendency to develop particular diseases.

The researchers predicted that their genome map would speed the search for the genetic defects that cause many inherited diseases. The map was also described as a first step in a massive project that many biologists are trying to launch—a detailed biochemical analysis of the entire human genome.

Meanwhile, scientists in 1987 identified genetic markers associated with several diseases. Such markers make possible prenatal identification of fetuses with these diseases or with a strong susceptibility to these diseases. The illnesses for which markers were identified include colon cancer, premature menopause, Alzheimer's disease, neurofibromatosis (elephant man's disease), and cystic fibrosis. Researchers also identified a marker for a mental illness called manic-depressive disorder, providing the first strong evidence that a tendency to develop a mental disorder may be inherited (see MENTAL ILLNESS).

AIDS Vaccine. Human trials of a vaccine against AIDS (acquired immune deficiency syndrome)—the first such trials authorized in the United States—were begun in October by MicroGeneSys, Incorporated, of West Haven, Conn. The vaccine contains a protein found on the outer coat of the virus that causes AIDS. The United States Food and Drug Administration (FDA) approved human tests of a second experimental AIDS vaccine in November.

New Antibiotic. A chance observation that surgical wounds in laboratory frogs do not become infected while healing has led to the discovery of a new family of antibiotics. Molecular biologist Michael Zasloff of the National Institutes of Health in Bethesda, Md., reported in July that the frogs' skin contains two substances that kill an unusually wide variety of bacteria, protozoa, and fungi. Zasloff predicted that these substances, which he called *magainins* (the Hebrew word *magain* means *shield*), could be tested—probably on burn victims—in as little as two years.

Genetic Engineering. After four years of regulatory and legal delays, the first authorized release into the open air of bacteria altered by genetic engineering techniques occurred in California in April. Researchers from the University of California at Berkeley and Advanced Genetic Sciences,

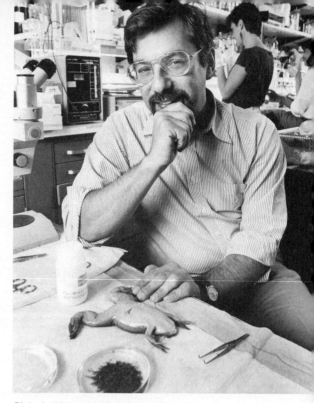

Biologist Michael Zasloff of the National Institutes of Health discovered a new family of antibiotics by studying an African frog.

Incorporated, of Oakland sprayed a strawberry patch in the San Francisco suburb of Brentwood and a potato field in Tulelake, 350 miles (560 kilometers) to the north, with the bacteria. The genetically altered strain of bacteria was designed to protect the plants from frost damage at temperatures just below freezing.

When sprayed on crops, the altered bacteria displace naturally occurring bacteria that encourage the formation of ice crystals. As a result, the temperature at which the treated plants freeze and suffer damage is slightly reduced.

Despite vandalism by environmental activists who uprooted many of the plants, the scientists said the tests were successful. The researchers reported that the genetically engineered bacteria protected the plants and did not spread beyond the test plots. Several companies also conducted field studies in 1987 that tested plants genetically engineered to provide resistance to herbicides and to insect pests called cutworms. These tests, too, were successful.

Patenting Animals. The U.S. Patent and Trademark Office ruled in April that inventors could patent new forms of animals created through genetic engineering techniques. Experts predicted that the patent ruling would stimulate the growth of the animal biotechnology industry. Many researchers have been working to make farm animals more resistant to disease or more productive by inserting desirable genes into their chromosomes. The ruling also touched off a vigorous debate about the morality of altering animal genes. Many opponents vowed to lobby Congress to reverse the ruling.

New Products. On November 13, the FDA approved the marketing of a genetically engineered drug called *tissue plasminogen activator* (tPA), a protein that can reduce the damage of heart attacks by dissolving harmful blood clots. The drug, manufactured by Genentech Incorporated of South San Francisco, Calif., was expected to cost at least $2,000 per dose.

Although tPA was the only new genetically engineered product approved in 1987, a March report by the Office of Technology Assessment, an advisory agency of Congress, said that more than 80 hormones, enzymes, proteins, and other biological products for therapeutic use in human beings were being developed by the biotechnology industry. Others believed to be near FDA approval included *erythropoietin,* a kidney hormone that stimulates the production of red blood cells, and *atrial natriuretic factor,* a heart hormone that lowers blood pressure.   Thomas H. Maugh II

In WORLD BOOK, see BIOCHEMISTRY.

BIOLOGY. See BIOCHEMISTRY; BOTANY; PALEONTOLOGY; ZOOLOGY.

BOATING. The United States regained the America's Cup, yacht racing's most prestigious trophy, in 1987. The winning yacht was *Stars & Stripes,* sailed by Dennis Conner of San Diego.

The United States had held the cup for 132 years until it was lost in 1983 for the first time ever. In that series, *Australia II* defeated the American defender, *Liberty,* four races to three, off Newport, R.I. Conner, who sailed *Liberty,* immediately began a campaign to regain the cup.

Thirteen yachts from six nations competed for the role of challenger. Four Australian yachts vied for the role of defender. The trials and the cup races were held off Fremantle on the western coast of Australia. The craft were about 65 feet (20 meters) long and belonged to the 12-Meter class. The term *12-Meter* does not refer to the length of the yachts but to a complicated formula involving length, sail area, and hull measurement—characteristics that affect a yacht's speed.

In the challengers' finals, *Stars & Stripes* defeated the yacht *New Zealand,* four races to one. Alan Bond, the successful challenger in 1983, attempted to become the defender this time with *Australia IV.* But Kevin Parry's *Kookaburra III,* sailed by Iain Murray, defeated *Australia IV,* 5-0, to become the defender.

The four-of-seven-race finals lasted from January 31 to February 4 over an eight-leg course cov-

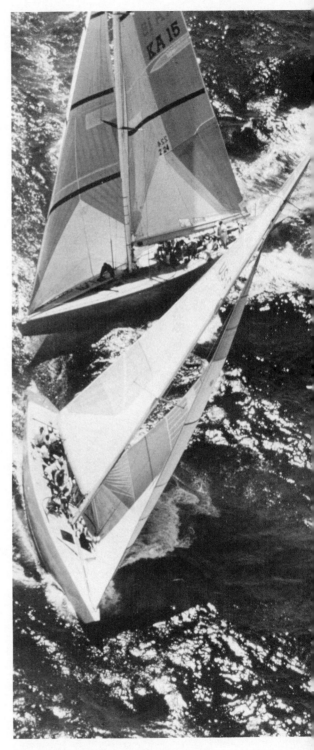

Stars & Stripes, the U.S. challenger, leads *Kookaburra III* of Australia in the final America's Cup race in February. *Stars & Stripes* won.

ering about 24 nautical miles (44 kilometers). *Stars & Stripes* swept *Kookaburra III* in four races.

The San Diego Yacht Club planned a 1991 defense with 12-Meter sloops. But Michael Fay of New Zealand's Mercury Boat Club issued a challenge for a one-on-one series in 1988 in yachts twice the size of the 12-Meter boats. When the San Diego Yacht Club rejected the challenge as invalid, Fay sued and won. In December 1987, the San Diego club accepted the challenge to race in August or September 1988 using the larger yachts.

Other Yachts. On May 7, 1987, Philippe Jeantot of France, in the 60-foot (18-meter) sloop *Crédit Agricole III*, won a round-the-world solo race in the record time of 134 days. The race started and ended in Newport. In the Southern Ocean Racing Conference's six-race winter series in Florida and the Bahamas, the overall winner was the 42-foot (13-meter) *Sprint*, owned by John Stevens of Grosse Pointe, Mich.

Powerboats. In September, Chip Hanauer of Seattle, in *Miller American*, won his sixth straight Gold Cup for unlimited hydroplanes, breaking Gar Wood's record of five straight through 1921. Jim Kropfeld of Cincinnati, Ohio, in *Miss Budweiser*, took the series title. Al Copeland of New Orleans won his fourth straight national high-point title for offshore superboats. Frank Litsky

In WORLD BOOK, see BOATING; SAILING.

BOLIVIA. Víctor Paz Estenssoro, Bolivia's president, was credited with Bolivia's economic recovery in 1987. The economy was expected to grow 2.2 per cent, its first increase in seven years.

Paz Estenssoro managed the turnabout by reducing the federal budget deficit from 30 per cent of the gross national product (GNP)—the total value of all goods and services produced—to 3.5 per cent during his two years in office. He also raised tax revenues to 14 per cent of GNP from only 1 per cent. For Bolivians, the best news was that inflation was holding steady at a 12.5 per cent annual rate, as against 24,000 per cent in 1985.

On Jan. 1, 1987, Bolivia introduced a new currency, the *boliviano*, which replaced the peso. With renewed international confidence in Bolivia's economy, the nation worked out an agreement with its creditors in July under which it bought back almost $1 billion in debt at a big discount with funds provided by foreign governments.

Paz Estenssoro's party, the Revolutionary Nationalist Movement, lost heavily in municipal elections on December 6. The chief winners were the Revolutionary Leftist Movement and the rightist Nationalist Democratic Alliance. Nathan A. Haverstock

See also LATIN AMERICA (Facts in Brief Table). In WORLD BOOK, see BOLIVIA.

BOOKS. See CANADIAN LITERATURE; LITERATURE; LITERATURE FOR CHILDREN; POETRY; PUBLISHING.

BORK, ROBERT HERON (1927-   ), President Ronald Reagan's controversial choice for Supreme Court justice, became the 12th nominee to the Supreme Court of the United States to be rejected outright by the U.S. Senate. The Senate voted on Oct. 23, 1987, against confirmation by 58 to 42, the widest margin of rejection ever for a Supreme Court nomination. See SUPREME COURT OF THE UNITED STATES.

Born on March 1, 1927, in Pittsburgh, Pa., Bork attended the University of Chicago, where he received a bachelor's degree in 1948 and a law degree in 1953. After working for a Chicago law firm, Bork began teaching law at Yale University in New Haven, Conn., in 1962 and kept his association with the law school until 1981.

From 1973 to 1977, Bork served as solicitor general in the U.S. Department of Justice. During the Watergate scandal, President Richard M. Nixon named Bork acting attorney general after Attorney General Elliot L. Richardson and his deputy resigned because they refused Nixon's order to fire Watergate special prosecutor Archibald Cox. Bork then carried out the firing. In 1982, Bork was appointed to the U.S. Court of Appeals for the District of Columbia circuit.

Bork has two sons and a daughter by his first marriage to Claire Davidson, who died in 1980. In 1982, Bork married Mary Ellen Pohl. Rod Such

BOTANY. Plant pathologist Gary Strobel of Montana State University in Bozeman received widespread publicity and criticism in August 1987 for conducting an unauthorized experiment in which he injected elm trees with a genetically altered bacterium to protect them from Dutch elm disease. In nature, the fungus that causes the disease is spread when bark beetles carry the fungal spores on their bodies from infected to healthy American elm trees. The disease, first observed in the Netherlands in 1919, became known in the United States in 1930.

In his experiment, Strobel used the bacterium *Pseudomonas syringae*, which is known to produce an agent that inhibits the fungus. Using genetic engineering techniques, Strobel developed a mutant strain of the bacterium that produces more of the antifungal agent than the unaltered strain.

The Altered Bacterium apparently protected elm trees against the disease, since trees injected with the bacterium and the fungus remained healthy, while trees injected with only the fungus died within six weeks. But Strobel had acted without the Environmental Protection Agency (EPA) permit needed to release a genetically altered organism into the environment. Many members of the scientific community condemned his flouting of EPA regulations. In September, Strobel destroyed the treated elm trees.

Botanist Gary Strobel of Montana State University cuts down an elm tree—used in an unauthorized test of genetically altered bacteria—in September.

Genetic Engineering of Cereal Crops. In recent years, rapid progress has been made in developing ways to alter plants by the introduction of foreign genes that act as the blueprint for desirable traits. For example, in one common method of introducing genes into plants, a bacterium called *Agrobacterium tumefaciens*, which infects some plants, is used to carry genetic material into those plants. For poorly understood reasons, however, this technique and others have not been applied successfully to plants called *monocots*, which include maize (corn), wheat, rice, and other cereal crops.

In January 1987, researchers reported progress in using genetic engineering techniques to alter the genetics of cereal grains. Scientists in Great Britain and Switzerland reported that they had been able to use *Agrobacterium* to introduce genetic material into maize. This accomplishment surprised many scientists, who believed that the technique would not work with monocot species, which are not naturally infected by *Agrobacterium*. And scientists in West Germany found that when genetic material was injected into young floral shoots of rye plants, it occasionally altered the genetic traits of the pollen produced on the shoots. Researchers agreed that these developments were highly encouraging.   Eldon H. Newcomb

In WORLD BOOK, see BOTANY.

BOTSWANA. See AFRICA.

BOWLING. The younger generation swept the three most important tournaments on the Professional Bowlers Association of America (PBA) tour for men in 1987. The Ladies Pro Bowlers Tour (LPBT) was hurt when most of its leading players broke away and formed a rival Ladies Touring Players Association (LTPA).

The Men's Tour. The PBA's 34 tournaments from January to December carried prize money totaling almost $5.5 million. The richest and most significant tournaments were the $500,000 United States Open from January 4 to 10 in Tacoma, Wash.; the $260,000 PBA national championship from March 22 to 28 in Toledo, Ohio; and the $250,000 Firestone Tournament of Champions from April 21 to 25 in Akron, Ohio. Pete Weber, 24, of St. Louis, Mo., was the star of those tournaments. He finished first in the Firestone tournament and second in the U.S. Open.

In the U.S. Open, Del Ballard, Jr., 23, of Richardson, Tex., won the final game from Weber, 247-209, and earned the record winner's purse of $100,000. In the PBA championship, Randy Pedersen, 24, of Santa Maria, Calif., beat Amleto Monacelli of Venezuela, 233-222, in the final. In the Firestone tournament final, Weber defeated Jim Murtishaw of Vista, Calif., 222-190.

Weber's victory in the Firestone tournament was his 10th on the tour. That tournament lifted his career earnings in 7 years as a professional to $733,331, surpassing the $731,003 earned by his 57-year-old father, Dick Weber, over 28 years.

The year's leading money winners were Weber with $175,491, Ballard with $162,795, and Pete McCordic of Houston with $153,281. McCordic's earnings included a $100,000 bonus for rolling a perfect 300 game on January 31 during the Greater Los Angeles Open in Torrance, Calif. Mark Roth of Spring Lake Heights, N.J., earned $93,195 during the year, raising his career total to $1,278,041 and breaking Earl Anthony's career earnings record of $1,274,021.

The Women's Tour was fragmented because the leading bowlers were dissatisfied with the LPBT. So a new group was established in 1987, and where there had been one women's tour struggling for prize money and television exposure, there were now two. There were only about 50 full-time touring professionals, so both tours filled in with part-time professionals and guests.

The LPBT conducted 14 tournaments, most of them broadcast on cable television. Its leading winner, with $55,095, was Betty Morris of Stockton, Calif. Lisa Wagner of Palmetto, Fla., with $43,205, led the LTPA tour. Members of both tours competed in the U.S. Open in Mentor, Ohio, in April. Carol Norman of Ardmore, Okla., won the record $40,000 winner's purse.   Frank Litsky

In WORLD BOOK, see BOWLING.

BOXING. Heavyweight Mike Tyson and middleweights Sugar Ray Leonard and Thomas Hearns scored major victories in 1987. Tyson, of Catskill, N.Y., became the first heavyweight since Leon Spinks in 1978 to be recognized as the world champion by all of boxing's major governing bodies. Leonard, of Potomac, Md., came out of a 2½-year retirement in April, took Marvelous Marvin Hagler's middleweight title, and retired again. Six months later, on October 29, Hearns, of Detroit, knocked out Juan Roldan of Argentina in Las Vegas, Nev., in four rounds, in a middle-weight title fight. In doing so, Hearns became the first man ever to win titles in four weight divisions.

Tyson. In 1986, Tyson won the World Boxing Council's (WBC) heavyweight title. In 1987, he won the World Boxing Association (WBA) and International Boxing Federation (IBF) titles in a 16-month heavyweight series sponsored by Home Box Office (HBO), a cable television network.

In Las Vegas bouts, Tyson won the WBA title by outpointing James (Bonecrusher) Smith of Lillington, S.C., on March 7, and the IBF title by outpointing Tony Tucker of Cincinnati, Ohio, on August 1. He also won a title defense with a technical knockout of Pinklon Thomas of Philadelphia in the sixth round on May 30.

Only Michael Spinks, of St. Louis, Mo., seemed to have a chance against Tyson, but Tyson's handlers did not appear anxious to make that match. The IBF stripped Spinks of his heavyweight title in February when he refused to make a mandatory defense as part of the HBO series. Instead, for a $4-million guarantee, Spinks fought Gerry Cooney, of Huntington Station, N.Y., on June 15 in Atlantic City, N.J., and won a technical knockout in the fifth round.

Leonard. The April 6 fight in Las Vegas between Leonard and Hagler was a promoter's dream. Hagler, from Brockton, Mass., was 32 years old, the champion since 1980 and unbeaten since 1976. Leonard was 31, a former welterweight champion who had retired after eye surgery, returned for one fight, and retired a second time.

When the fighters signed, Hagler held the WBC, WBA, and IBF titles. The WBA vacated its title in February, however, because Hagler would not fight its leading contender. The IBF said that it would not recognize Leonard as champion because of his boxing inactivity and eye surgery.

Still, the Hagler-Leonard fight captivated the public and set boxing records for gross receipts ($60 million) and live gate ($7.9 million). Although Hagler was favored, Leonard was faster and surprisingly strong and won a 12-round split decision. In May, he retired again.   Frank Litsky

In WORLD BOOK, see BOXING.

BOY SCOUTS. See YOUTH ORGANIZATIONS.
BOYS CLUBS. See YOUTH ORGANIZATIONS.

World Champion Boxers
World Boxing Association

Division	Champion	Country	Date won
Heavyweight	James Smith	U.S.A.	1986
	Mike Tyson	U.S.A.	March '87
Junior heavyweight	Evander Holyfield	U.S.A.	1986
Light heavyweight	Marvin Johnson	U.S.A.	1986
	Leslie Stewart	Trinidad	May '87
	Virgil Hill	U.S.A.	Sept. '87
Middleweight	Marvelous Marvin Hagler	U.S.A.	1980
	Sumbu Kalambay	Italy	Oct. '87
Junior middleweight	Mike McCallum	Jamaica	1984
	Julian Jackson	U.S. Virgin Islands	Nov. '87
Welterweight	vacant		Jan. '87
	Mark Breland	U.S.A.	Feb. '87
	Marlon Starling	U.S.A.	Aug. '87
Junior welterweight	Patrizio Oliva	Italy	1986
	Juan Martin Coggi	Argentina	July '87
Lightweight	Edwin Rosario	Puerto Rico	1986
	Julio Cesar Chavez	Mexico	Nov. '87
Junior lightweight	Brian Mitchell	South Africa	1986
Featherweight	Stevie Cruz	U.S.A.	1986
	Antonio Esparragoza	Venezuela	March '87
Junior featherweight	Victor Callejas	Puerto Rico	1984
	Louie Espinoza	U.S.A.	Jan. '87
	Julio Gervacio	Dominican Republic	Nov. '87
Bantamweight	Bernardo Pinango	Venezuela	1986
	Takuyama Muguruma	Japan	March '87
	Park Chang Yong	South Korea	May '87
	Wilfredo Vasquez	Puerto Rico	Oct. '87
Junior bantamweight	Khaosai Galaxy	Thailand	1984
Flyweight	Hilario Zapata	Panama	1986
	Fidel Bassa	Colombia	Feb. '87
Junior flyweight	Myung-Woo Yuh	South Korea	1985

World Boxing Council

Division	Champion	Country	Date won
Heavyweight	Mike Tyson	U.S.A.	1986
Cruiserweight	Carlos DeLeón	Puerto Rico	1986
Light heavyweight	Dennis Andries	Great Britain	1986
	Thomas Hearns	U.S.A.	March '87
	Donny La Londe	Canada	Nov. '87
Middleweight	Marvelous Marvin Hagler	U.S.A.	1980
	Sugar Ray Leonard	U.S.A.	April '87
	Thomas Hearns	U.S.A.	Oct. '87
Super welterweight	Duane Thomas	U.S.A.	1986
	Lupe Aquino	Mexico	July '87
	Gianfranco Rosi	Italy	Oct. '87
Welterweight	Lloyd Honeyghan	Great Britain	1986
	Jorge Vaca	Mexico	Nov. '87
Super lightweight	Tsuyoshi Hamada	Japan	1986
	Rene Arredondo	Mexico	July '87
	Roger Mayweather	U.S.A.	Nov. '87
Lightweight	Hector Camacho	Puerto Rico	1985
	José-Luis Ramirez	Mexico	July '87
Super featherweight	Julio Cesar Chavez	Mexico	1984
	vacant		Nov. '87
Featherweight	Azumah Nelson	Ghana	1984
Super bantamweight	Samart Payaharoon	Thailand	1986
	Jeff Fenech	Australia	May '87
Bantamweight	Miguel Lora	Colombia	1985
Super flyweight	Gilberto Roman	Mexico	1986
	Santos Laciar	Argentina	May '87
	Jesus Rojas	Colombia	Aug. '87
Flyweight	Sot Chitalada	Thailand	1984
Light-flyweight	Jung-Koo Chang	South Korea	1983
Strawweight	Hiroki Ioxa	Japan	Oct. '87

BRAZIL. President José Sarney revealed on Sept. 4, 1987, that Brazilian scientists had succeeded in enriching uranium, thus joining the group of nations capable of producing nuclear weapons. Sarney denied, however, that Brazil had any ambition to actually make such weapons.

In September, Brazil's first radiation accident raised serious doubts about the government's ability to manage Brazil's nuclear capability. The accident, described by the World Health Organization as the worst radiation accident in the Western world, occurred at Goiânia in central Brazil. A family that operated a scrapyard opened an abandoned piece of hospital equipment filled with cesium 137, a radioactive substance. Several people handled the shiny bluish substance and spread it through the neighborhood, thus exposing themselves and others to potentially lethal doses of radiation. By early December, 4 people had died and about 30 others were hospitalized with radiation sickness.

Several Brazilian scientists criticized the nation's Commission for Nuclear Energy for failing to establish safeguards that could have prevented the accident and for failing to set guidelines for handling radiation emergencies. Critics said the incident might further erode public support for the government's ambitious nuclear energy program.

The Economy. For most of 1987, the Sarney administration was unable to devise an acceptable plan for paying off Brazil's staggering foreign debt. On February 20, Sarney announced that Brazil would unilaterally impose a moratorium on interest payments on $67 billion in medium- and long-term debt. United States banks, which hold the bulk of Brazil's debt, protested angrily. Brazil's total debt was then about $108 billion.

The moratorium proved to be the prelude to the resignation of Finance Minister Dilson Funaro on April 26. His successor, Luiz Carlos Bresser Pereira, an economist, struggled unsuccessfully in the ensuing months to resolve the debt impasse. Emergency measures announced on June 12 failed to cope with spiraling inflation, which was then estimated at about 1,000 per cent.

In September, Bresser Pereira campaigned in Washington, D.C., for a radical plan to resolve the debt crisis. But his proposal, under which Brazil would convert $67 billion of debt into tradeable, below-market-rate bonds, was rejected by U.S. Secretary of the Treasury James A. Baker III. In frustration, Bresser Pereira resigned on December 18.

Mounting Opposition. Increasingly, President Sarney was forced to turn to his military backers as support for his administration waned among the Brazilian people. On March 7, Brazilian navy sailors were called in to unload grain and cargo ships at 30 ports where some 40,000 merchant

marines had been on strike since late February. The strike threatened Brazil's export trade and imports of vital foodstuffs.

On March 10, heavily armed troops occupied 10 oil refineries operated by Petrobras, the state oil company, to thwart a threatened strike. The troops were withdrawn four days later, when union leaders agreed to negotiate their demands, which included a 150 per cent wage increase. By March 24, 500,000 bank employees—representing 90 per cent of all bank employees—were out on strike. On March 31, police used tear gas and clubs to disperse demonstrators outside the Bank of Brazil in Brasília, injuring 30 people.

The frustration on economic issues extended to the countryside, where farmers expressed their anger over depressed prices for their harvests by blockading roads. Land reform suffered a serious loss on September 8 when Marcos Freire, a popular Cabinet minister, was killed in an air force jet that exploded shortly after take-off from the mining town of Carajas in the northern state of Pará. Freire was credited with forcefulness in pushing a land redistribution program. Under the program, about 1.4 million families would receive land taken from owners who were not cultivating it and planned to sell it. Nathan A. Haverstock

See also LATIN AMERICA (Facts in Brief Table). In WORLD BOOK, see BRAZIL.

BRIDGE. The United States won a double victory in bridge at Ocho Rios, Jamaica, in October 1987, capturing both the Bermuda Bowl world open team championship and the Venice Cup world women's team championship. In the Bermuda Bowl, the Americans defeated Great Britain, 354-290. Playing for the United States were Bob Hamman and Bobby Wolff, both of Dallas; and Californians Chip Martel of Davis, Lew Stansby of Castro Valley, Mike Lawrence of Berkeley, and Hugh Ross of Oakland.

In the Venice Cup competition, the United States defeated France 251-219. On the winning team were Lynn Deas and Juanita Chambers, both of Schenectady, N.Y.; Beth Palmer of Silver Spring, Md.; Katherine Wei of Houston; Judi Radin of New York City; and Cheri Bjerkan of Highland Park, Ill.

The World Bridge Federation, the game's governing body, began a campaign in 1987 to bring the Soviet Union into world bridge.

Jaggy Shivdasani of India became the first non-American to win the Spingold Knockout Team Championship, one of the American Contract Bridge League's three top team events, in Baltimore in July. He also won another major team event, the Reisinger Board-a-Match Teams, in Anaheim, Calif., in November. Henry G. Francis

In WORLD BOOK, see BRIDGE.

An access shaft is dug in northern France prior to work on the "Chunnel"—a tunnel under the English Channel to link France and Great Britain.

BRITISH COLUMBIA. Premier William N. Vander Zalm's Social Credit government followed a conservative economic agenda in 1987. His administration, elected in 1986, told the legislature that their major goal was to restrain the government from interfering with the private sector.

Believing that strikes had tarnished British Columbia's image, the government in April proposed sweeping revisions to the province's labor laws. The proposed legislation gave power to an industrial relations commissioner to monitor all labor disputes and to recommend ending those threatening the health and safety of residents or affecting the province's economy.

Opponents viewed the bill as an effort to destroy the labor unions. A massive 24-hour general strike by public employees and union members on June 1 closed down public transportation, schools, offices, factories, mines, and lumber mills but failed to check the passage of the bill.

On July 11, the Canadian federal government and British Columbia signed an agreement creating a new national park, South Moresby National Park. The park will be located in the distinctive wilderness area of South Moresby Island, which is part of the Queen Charlotte Islands off the coast of British Columbia.   David M. L. Farr

In WORLD BOOK, see BRITISH COLUMBIA.

BRUNEI. See ASIA.

BUILDING AND CONSTRUCTION. Spending for new construction in the United States in 1987 was expected to rise to about $392 billion, according to an August forecast by the U.S. Department of Commerce. That figure topped the $388.8 billion spent for new construction in 1986. According to the Commerce Department, the private sector was expected to spend an estimated $319 billion of the 1987 total for new construction, with the remaining $73 billion funded by federal, state, and local governments.

New Contracts. Although spending figures reflect the actual value of projects completed in a particular year, contracts awarded during the year are a more accurate indication of future activity. At midyear, construction economists at McGraw-Hill Incorporated—a leading source of data about the construction industry—expected new contracts awarded in 1987, excluding residential work, to total $149 billion, down 7 per cent from the $160-billion awarded for new contracts in 1986. The dip in overall contract awards came despite modest gains of 2 to 6 per cent in heavy construction of dams, wastewater-treatment plants, and waterways. Slight drops in transportation sector contracts and major slides in nonresidential building contracts were the major sources of the decline.

New contracts in the commercial building sector plunged in 1987. McGraw-Hill economists pre-

The world's largest floating hotel, built in a Japanese shipyard for North Sea oil workers, begins its three-month journey to Norway in May.

dicted that contracts for office buildings and banks would fall 19 per cent by the end of 1987 from the $22 billion awarded in 1986. They estimated that contracts for stores and shopping centers would be down 5 per cent in 1987, from $13 billion in 1986.

Apartments. Experts predicted that new contracts for apartments in 1987 would also take a nosedive, down 18 per cent from $29 billion in contracts awarded in 1986. The market—stripped of a favorable tax treatment known as passive losses—was staging a major retreat, according to McGraw-Hill economists.

Family Housing. Fueled by high demand, the first quarter of 1987 was strong for single-family housing starts. But in April, a surge of fixed-rate mortgages back into the 10 to 11 per cent range led to a decline in the market. In September, McGraw-Hill economists expected the number of starts of one- and two-family units in 1987 to total 740,000, down from 785,000 units in 1986. But despite the decline in the number of units, the monetary value of starts may have equaled or exceeded the value of 1986 starts, because of a trend toward building more expensive houses.

Accidents. Two major accidents in 1987—the collapse of a highway bridge and of a building under construction—prompted the construction industry to reflect on quality and professionalism.

The first accident, the collapse on April 5 of a bridge on the Governor Thomas E. Dewey Thruway in New York, killed 10 people and intensified concern about the adequacy of bridge inspection, particularly underwater. The 540-foot (165-meter) bridge spanned Schoharie Creek, about 40 miles (64 kilometers) west of Albany. New York state authorities and the Federal Highway Administration (FHWA) concluded that *scour*—the wearing away of the soil beneath the pier footings of the bridge by severe floodwaters—was the leading cause of the disaster. As a result, the FHWA recommended that stricter standards be used for bridge foundation design, setting piers and footings below predicted scour depths.

The second accident involved a 13-story building under construction in Bridgeport, Conn., which collapsed on April 23, killing 28 workers. The building, called L'Ambiance Plaza, was being constructed using a technique called the *lift-frame method*. This technique involves casting concrete slabs on the ground and then jacking them up on columns to their final elevation, where they are secured. An investigation, conducted by the National Bureau of Standards for the Occupational Safety and Health Administration (OSHA), determined that the collapse was triggered when one of the brackets holding a concrete slab to its jack failed as the slab was being lifted. OSHA officials imposed a record total of $5.11 million in fines on the contractors of L'Ambiance Plaza.

Rehabilitating Structures. Construction began in 1987 to strengthen the 3,240-foot (988-meter) suspension bridge that spans the River Severn Estuary in southwest England. The Severn Bridge's 1960 design featured streamlined box-shaped girders as the towers that support the suspension cables. This design resulted in a 30 per cent cost savings compared with designs using conventional steel trusses to build the towers, but its safety was questioned in 1970 when a bridge supported by box-girder towers collapsed in Australia.

A review of bridge design in Great Britain finally led to a program to rehabilitate the Severn Bridge. The rehabilitation was underway in 1987 and included repairing and strengthening miles of welding in the steel bridge deck, replacing more than 1.4 miles (2.3 kilometers) of hangers that support the deck, and strengthening the 445-foot (136-meter) towers.

In another major rehabilitation project, Grand Central Terminal in New York City got a new copper roof in 1987—the first phase of the restoration of the landmark railway station. For years, water had seeped through leaky seams and holes in the building's ornamental *frieze*—a sculptured band around the top of the roof. The frieze was cleaned and repaired by expert craftworkers, and a waterproof membrane was installed behind it. Then copper sheeting was fastened around strips of wood and clamped to produce an airtight seal.

Parisian Landmark. A new, cube-shaped landmark began to take shape in Paris in 1987. Targeted for completion by July 14, 1989—the 200th anniversary of the French Revolution—the structure will become the centerpiece for an area of skyscrapers called La Defense.

The structure, nicknamed The Cube, is 364 feet (111 meters) tall and consists of two 35-story office towers rising from a 5-story base, and connected by a 3-story top section that spans a distance of 230 feet (70 meters). The top section will initially be used for an exhibition celebrating France's bicentennial.

Earthquake Resistance. The earthquake resistance of buildings in the Los Angeles area was tested on Oct. 1, 1987, as the city rode out a severe earthquake that killed seven people and injured dozens of others and caused more than $213 million in damage. A number of buildings collapsed, and others were damaged beyond repair. But the earthquake held few surprises for the construction industry. Unreinforced masonry buildings affected by the strongest tremors suffered the greatest damage, while most buildings designed to recent building codes held up well.   Janice Lyn Tuchman

In WORLD BOOK, see BRIDGE; BUILDING; CONSTRUCTION.

BULGARIA followed Soviet leader Mikhail S. Gorbachev's policy of *perestroika* (restructuring) throughout 1987, proposing sweeping changes in all spheres of political, economic, and social life. Bulgaria, however, presented its program of perestroika—with some justification—as an outgrowth of its own experiments with reform originating in the 1960's.

Bulgaria's leader Todor Zhivkov told the Communist Party Central Committee on July 28 and 29, 1987, that the organization of the nation's economy, government, and Communist Party was obsolete. He called for new structures designed to meet contemporary needs.

Zhivkov said that the primary change in the economy would be the introduction of "self-management." The state would continue to own all business enterprises in Bulgaria's Communist economy, but the enterprises would become more independent of the nation's central planners. Each business would make its own production and sales decisions, raise capital through banks that the government would create, elect its own management, and distribute its "profits" as it wished.

Zhivkov also hinted at constitutional changes, including a "strengthening" of the National Assembly (parliament) and the nomination of opposing candidates for election. At present, all candidates run unopposed.

Changes in Government. On August 18, the National Assembly merged Bulgaria's units of regional government—28 districts—into 9 provinces. It also merged several major departments and established five new ministries.

The Economy fell short of its target in the first half of 1987. With unusual openness, the government revealed that many businesses were "in dire financial straits." Whether the government would close these businesses under new regulations directed against enterprises that lose money, however, remained to be seen.

Foreign Affairs. Bulgaria continued to support all Soviet foreign policy initiatives but was extremely active in seeking improved contacts with the West during 1987. High-level officials visited Bulgaria from France, Great Britain, Italy, the United States, and West Germany.

Zhivkov visited West Germany from June 2 to 5 to discuss trade and cooperation. In Brussels, Belgium, Bulgaria's trade minister conferred with Western ambassadors about relations with the European Community, or Common Market, and even the possibility of signing the General Agreement on Tariffs and Trade, the chief pact governing international commerce.   Eric Bourne

See also EUROPE (Facts in Brief Table). In WORLD BOOK, see BULGARIA.

BURKINA FASO. See AFRICA.

BURMA. See ASIA.

BURNLEY, JAMES HORACE, IV (1948-), took office as secretary of transportation on Dec. 3, 1987, succeeding Elizabeth Hanford Dole. Burnley had been acting secretary of transportation since Dole resigned on October 1.

Burnley was born in High Point, N.C., on July 30, 1948. He earned a bachelor's degree in 1970 from Yale University in New Haven, Conn., and a law degree from Harvard Law School in Cambridge, Mass., in 1973.

From 1973 to 1975, Burnley worked as an associate in the law firm of Brooks, Pierce, McLendon, Humphrey & Leonard in Greensboro, N.C. He then became a partner in the firm of Turner, Enochs, Foster, Sparrow & Burnley, also in Greensboro.

Burnley left the firm in 1981 to become director of the Volunteers in Service to America (VISTA) program. He was named associate deputy attorney general at the Department of Justice in 1982.

In November 1983, Burnley became deputy secretary of transportation. As chief adviser to the secretary, he played a role in airline safety policies and in the deregulation of the railroad, aviation, and trucking industries.

Burnley and his wife, Jane, have two children. The family lives in Falls Church, Va.   Mary A. Krier

BURUNDI. See AFRICA.

BUS. See TRANSIT.

BUSH, GEORGE H. W. (1924-), 43rd Vice President of the United States, in 1987 formally announced his candidacy for the 1988 Republican presidential nomination. Polls of Republican voters showed that Bush was their top choice for the nomination. The Vice President declared his candidacy in Houston on October 12 after returning from a European tour.

During that tour, on September 28, Bush stood with Lech Walesa, the Polish labor leader, in Warsaw and strongly endorsed the outlawed Solidarity labor union. Bush's travels in Poland were intended to appeal to Polish-American voters, such as Detroit-area automobile workers. But on October 2 in Brussels, Belgium, Bush praised Soviet military tank mechanics and joked that if they ran out of work, "send them to Detroit because we could use that kind of ability." Bush later apologized, saying no insult to U.S. auto workers was intended.

Seeking to distance himself from the Iran-contra affair, Bush told journalists at a February 12 news conference in Lansing, Mich., that he had expressed "certain reservations" about "certain aspects" of the secret sale of U.S. arms to Iran in 1986.   Frank Cormier and Margot Cormier

In WORLD BOOK, see BUSH, GEORGE H. W.

BUSINESS. See BANK; ECONOMICS; LABOR; MANUFACTURING.

CABINET, UNITED STATES. Four major changes occurred in President Ronald Reagan's Cabinet in 1987, and a former Cabinet official was cleared of criminal charges. A jury in New York City in May found former Secretary of Labor Raymond J. Donovan not guilty of larceny and fraud charges. After being indicted in 1984, Donovan resigned his Cabinet position in 1985. He was the first Cabinet member ever indicted for a crime while in office. Donovan and seven codefendants, including several executives in a construction company coowned by Donovan, were accused of attempting to defraud the New York City Transit Authority of $7.4 million between 1979 and 1984.

In July 1987, Secretary of Commerce Malcolm Baldrige, a champion rodeo rider, died of injuries received when a horse he was riding fell on him. Baldrige had served in the Cabinet since the beginning of the Reagan Administration in 1981.

In September 1987, Secretary of Transportation Elizabeth Hanford Dole said she would resign on October 1 to work in the presidential campaign of her husband, Senator Robert J. Dole (R., Kans.). In October, Secretary of Labor William E. Brock III announced that he, too, planned to resign, effective November 1, to manage Dole's presidential campaign.

In November, Secretary of Defense Caspar W. Weinberger, who had served in his post longer than any secretary of defense since Robert S. McNamara in the 1960's, announced his resignation. Weinberger reportedly resigned because he was tired after seven years of service and because his wife, Jane, was ill.

In August, Reagan named C. William Verity, Jr., former chairman of Armco Incorporated, a steel manufacturer, to succeed Baldrige. In October and November, Reagan announced three other appointments. He chose James H. Burnley IV, deputy secretary of transportation, to move up to the post of secretary. Reagan named Ann Dore McLaughlin to succeed Brock as secretary of labor. McLaughlin had been press secretary to the secretary of the treasury and later undersecretary of the interior. McLaughlin, who took office in December, became the only woman in the Cabinet.

To replace Weinberger, Reagan tapped his national security adviser, Frank C. Carlucci III. Carlucci had previously held a variety of important government positions under both Democratic and Republican administrations.   Rod Such

See also BURNLEY, JAMES H., IV; CARLUCCI, FRANK C., III; MCLAUGHLIN, ANN DORE; VERITY, C. WILLIAM, JR. In WORLD BOOK, see CABINET.

CALIFORNIA. See LOS ANGELES; STATE GOV'T.

CAMBODIA. See KAMPUCHEA.

CAMEROON. See AFRICA.

CAMP FIRE. See YOUTH ORGANIZATIONS.

CANADA

The Progressive Conservative government of Prime Minister M. Brian Mulroney, heir to the largest parliamentary majority in Canadian history in 1984, continued to fall in public favor during 1987. Opinion polls in September showed that only 27 per cent of decided voters supported the government, a far cry from the 50 per cent approval rating enjoyed by the Progressive Conservatives (PC's) when they first took office.

The prime minister's critics regarded him as untrustworthy and fiercely partisan. Mulroney was also criticized for frequently rewarding friends and political favorites with government positions.

Despite the criticism, the PC's could claim major accomplishments in 1987, including a booming economy. The Mulroney government had succeeded in bringing Quebec into the constitution—a move that the province had rejected in 1982—and had proposed a sweeping reform of Canada's personal and corporate taxation system. It had also negotiated a free trade agreement with the United States.

The PC government lost two seats in special federal elections held on July 21 to fill empty seats in Parliament. The election results left the PC's with 208 of the 282 seats in the House of Commons. The Liberals held 40 seats, and the New Democratic Party (NDP) had 33 seats. The remaining seat was held by an independent.

Cabinet Changes. The 40-member Mulroney cabinet—the largest in Canadian history—lost 2 of its Quebec members with the resignations of André Bissonnette, minister of state for transport, and Roch LaSalle, a minister of state. Bissonnette, who resigned in January at the request of the prime minister, and LaSalle, who offered his resignation voluntarily in February, were alleged to have been involved in personal and party financial scandals. Bissonnette was charged in August with fraud and accepting a bribe over a land deal.

Opposition Parties. The Liberals and the NDP, the two opposition parties in Parliament, experienced varying fortunes during the year. The once-powerful Liberal Party of Pierre E. Trudeau, prime minister from 1968 to 1979 and 1980 to 1984, was seriously divided on policy questions. Party members could not agree on a number of major issues, including the constitutional changes negotiated by Mulroney, free trade with the

Canadian Rick Hansen propels himself along a Rocky Mountain road in March during his world tour to raise funds for spinal cord research.

United States, and the testing of cruise missiles in northern Canada. Trudeau's successor as Liberal Party leader, John N. Turner, seemed unable to assert leadership over the various factions. In a public opinion poll in September, Liberal support stood at 32 per cent.

The NDP seemed to be the principal beneficiary of the public's disenchantment with the PC's, scoring a 39 per cent approval rating in the September poll. Edward Broadbent, NDP leader, was easily the most popular political figure in Canada, according to the opinion polls.

Immigration and Refugee Bills, prompted by an unprecedented flood of immigrants claiming refugee status, were introduced in February. The bills were designed to establish a new process for determining genuine refugees—people fleeing persecution—and to discourage the illegal transport of would-be immigrants to Canada. Many aliens were believed to be abusing the system by avoiding normal immigration procedures.

One such case occurred on July 12, when 174 Sikhs from northern India were landed from a small freighter on a lonely stretch of Nova Scotia's coast. They were admitted to Canada while their claims for refugee status were investigated. The bills were passed in the Commons in the August session, after vigorous protests by church and hu-

manitarian groups. Sent to the Senate, they received a thorough examination that was still underway at year-end.

Death Penalty. On June 30, Canada's House of Commons ended any prospect of a return of the death penalty, perhaps for many years to come. All the party leaders spoke against a motion to restore capital punishment. The motion was defeated by a vote of 148-127. The death penalty had been abolished in Canada in 1976.

Native Rights. A federal and provincial conference held in Ottawa, Ont., on March 26 and 27 failed to produce an agreement to establish rights to self-government for native peoples in the constitution. Leaders of organizations representing 575,000 native peoples—Indian, Inuit (Eskimo), and mixed-race people—insisted on an "inherent," or unconditional, right to self-government, stemming from their centuries on the land. But the federal government and most of the provinces would consider self-rule only if specific rights were defined by negotiation. Four provinces and the native groups turned down a federal draft amendment designed to reach a compromise, and the conference ended without an agreement.

Meech Lake Accord. Another meeting involving the federal and provincial governments met with more success than the native rights conference.

Demonstrators protest United States policy on acid rain during U.S. President Ronald Reagan's visit to Ottawa, Ont., in April.

On April 30 at Meech Lake, Quebec, the federal government and the provincial leaders met to consider a set of conditions put forward by Quebec under which the province would formally accede to the 1982 constitution. Quebec, under separatist Prime Minister René Lévesque, had rejected the constitution in 1982. Lévesque's successor, Robert Bourassa, had prepared new terms for the consideration of the federal government and the other provinces.

An agreement was reached at the April meeting, and the parties met again on June 3 to draft a final version of the Meech Lake accord, which was signed by Mulroney and the 10 provincial premiers. A key provision of the accord called for the recognition in the constitution of Quebec as a "distinct society" within Canada, with the right to pass laws to protect its French language and culture.

Other terms of the agreement included a new amending formula requiring unanimous consent of Ottawa and all the provinces for changes in federal institutions such as Parliament and the Supreme Court of Canada; a provision granting the provinces power to nominate candidates for the Senate and the Supreme Court, with the federal government's consent necessary to appoint them; a provision giving a province the right to decline involvement in new federally funded social programs and receive compensation from the federal government for a provincial program with the same objectives; and increased powers over immigration policy by the provinces. The accord called for the prime minister and the provincial premiers to hold at least two annual meetings—one to discuss constitutional matters and the other to deal with economic issues.

The Meech Lake accord required approval by the House of Commons and each provincial legislature. Quebec was the first province to approve the accord by a debate and vote on June 23. It was followed by Saskatchewan on September 23 and Alberta on December 7. The federal Parliament approved the agreement on October 27.

The Economy performed at a strong pace during 1987, growing during the second quarter at a seasonally adjusted annual rate of 6.1 per cent—one of the best records among Western industrialized nations. Canada's gross domestic product—the value of all goods and services produced within Canada's borders, regardless of ownership—stood at $547.2 billion (not adjusted for inflation) by the end of June. (All monetary amounts in this article are Canadian dollars with $1 = U.S. 77 cents as of Dec. 31, 1987.) Domestic consumer demand was a key element in growth because export trade remained volatile.

In November, the unemployment rate fell to 8.2 per cent, the lowest level since 1981. Inflation rose in the early part of the year but began to level off

The Ministry of Canada*
In order of precedence

Martin Brian Mulroney, prime minister

George Harris Hees, minister of veterans affairs and minister of state (senior citizens)

Charles Joseph Clark, secretary of state for external affairs

Flora Isabel MacDonald, minister of communications

John Carnell Crosbie, minister of transport

Donald Frank Mazankowski, deputy prime minister, president of the Queen's Privy Council for Canada, government House leader, and president of the Treasury Board

Elmer MacIntosh MacKay, minister of Revenue Canada

Jake Epp, minister of national health and welfare

John Wise, minister of agriculture

Ramon John Hnatyshyn, minister of justice and attorney general of Canada

David Edward Crombie, secretary of state and minister responsible for multiculturalism

Robert R. De Cotret, minister of regional industrial expansion and minister responsible for science and technology

Henry Perrin Beatty, minister of national defence

Michael Holcombe Wilson, minister of finance

Harvie Andre, minister of consumer and corporate affairs

Otto John Jelinek, minister of state (fitness and amateur sport)

Thomas Edward Siddon, minister of fisheries and oceans

Charles James Mayer, minister of state (grains and oilseeds)

William Hunter McKnight, minister of Indian affairs and northern development

Thomas Michael McMillan, minister of the environment

Patricia Carney, minister for international trade

Benoît Bouchard, minister of employment and immigration

Michel Côté, minister of supply and services

James Francis Kelleher, solicitor general of Canada

Marcel Masse, minister of energy, mines and resources

Barbara Jean McDougall, minister of state (privatization), minister responsible for the status of women, and minister responsible for regulatory affairs

Gerald S. Merrithew, minister of state (forestry and mines)

Monique Vézina, minister of state (transport)

Stewart McInnes, minister of public works

Frank Oberle, minister of state (science and technology)

Lowell Murray, leader of the government in the Senate and minister of state (federal-provincial relations)

Paul Wyatt Dick, associate minister of national defence

Pierre Cadieux, minister of labour

Jean Charest, minister of state (youth)

Thomas Hockin, minister of state (finance)

Monique Landry, minister for external relations

Bernard Valcourt, minister of state (small business and tourism)

Gerry Weiner, minister of state (immigration)

Doug Lewis, minister of state and minister of state (Treasury Board)

Pierre Blais, minister of state (agriculture)

*As of Dec. 31, 1987.

Premiers of Canadian Provinces

Province	Premier
Alberta	Donald Getty
British Columbia	William N. Vander Zalm
Manitoba	Howard Pawley
New Brunswick	Frank J. McKenna
Newfoundland	Brian Peckford
Nova Scotia	John Buchanan
Ontario	David Peterson
Prince Edward Island	Joseph A. Ghiz
Quebec	Robert Bourassa
Saskatchewan	Grant Devine

Commissioners of Territories

Northwest Territories	John H. Parker
Yukon Territory	J. Kenneth McKinnon

Canada, Provinces, and Territories Population Estimates

	1986 census	1987 estimate
Alberta	2,375,278	2,403,781
British Columbia	2,889,207	2,918,677
Manitoba	1,071,232	1,080,552
New Brunswick	710,422	713,228
Newfoundland	568,349	568,485
Northwest Territories	52,238	53,643
Nova Scotia	873,199	878,438
Ontario	9,113,515	9,215,586
Prince Edward Island	126,646	127,501
Quebec	6,540,276	6,560,878
Saskatchewan	1,010,198	1,018,785
Yukon Territory	23,504	23,575
Canada	**25,354,064**	**25,563,129**

City and Metropolitan Population Estimates

	Metropolitan Area 1986 census	City 1986 census
Toronto	3,427,168	612,289
Montreal	2,921,357	1,015,420
Vancouver	1,380,729	431,147
Ottawa-Hull	819,263	
Ottawa		300,763
Hull		58,722
Edmonton	785,465	573,982
Calgary	671,326	636,104
Winnipeg	625,304	594,551
Quebec	603,267	164,580
Hamilton	557,029	306,728
St. Catharines-Niagara	343,258	
St. Catharines		123,455
Niagara Falls		72,107
London	342,302	269,140
Kitchener	311,195	150,604
Halifax	295,990	113,577
Victoria	255,547	66,303
Windsor	253,988	193,111
Oshawa	203,543	123,651
Saskatoon	200,665	177,641
Regina	186,521	175,064
St. John's	161,901	96,216
Chicoutimi-Jonquière	158,468	
Chicoutimi		61,083
Jonquière		58,467
Sudbury	148,877	88,717
Sherbrooke	129,960	74,438
Trois-Rivières	128,888	50,122
Thunder Bay	122,217	112,272
Saint John	121,265	76,381

in the summer, as bumper crops brought down food prices. In November, the inflation rate stood at 4.2 per cent. The Canadian dollar gained from its 1986 levels—about U.S. 72 cents—to reach U.S. 77 cents in December. Interest rates rose in the third quarter. The Bank of Canada rate, which sets chartered bank rates, stood at 8.7 per cent in early December.

Labor. A precedent-setting settlement was reached in a strike between the Canadian Auto Workers union and Chrysler Canada Limited on September 17. The company agreed to a six-year pension agreement that would provide 90 per cent protection against inflation, up to 6 per cent a year, for pensions of any workers who retire. The

union announced it would present the other automakers with the same pension demand.

Budget. The federal budget, presented on February 18, called for $110 billion in spending. The budget took a conservative line, indicating that the government planned no changes in its economic policies. The deficit for the 1988 fiscal year, which began on April 1, was estimated at $29.3 billion, $2.7 billion less than the 1987 deficit. There were modest increases in indirect taxes on tobacco products, snack foods, gasoline, and airline tickets.

Tax Reform. On June 18, Finance Minister Michael Holcombe Wilson unveiled the government's plan for comprehensive tax reform. Beginning in 1988, there would be only 3 personal income tax brackets—taxed at 17, 26, or 29 per cent of taxable income—reduced from 10 brackets. The plan called for phasing out a range of tax exemptions and deductions and replacing them with tax credits. Almost 1 million Canadians would end up paying no income tax, and another 1.2 million would pay less tax under the new system. Although corporate tax rates would be decreased, more corporations—banks, trust companies, and insurance companies—would be required to pay tax.

Wilson's announcement was the first phase in a tax-reform process. The second phase of the plan called for changes in sales taxes, now collected by both the federal and provincial governments.

Free Trade Agreement. After 17 months of negotiations, a comprehensive free trade agreement between Canada and the United States was reached on October 3. On December 7, negotiators worked out the final details of the pact, which was released on December 11. It was signed on Jan. 2, 1988. The pact was subject to the approval of the Canadian Parliament and the U.S. Congress, and the agreement was expected to meet much resistance in both legislatures.

The Canadian negotiating team had broken off talks on Sept. 23, 1987. But high-level discussions resumed on September 28 in a round of meetings in Washington, D.C.

The principal thrust of the agreement was a plan to eliminate all tariffs over a 10-year period, beginning on Jan. 1, 1989. Other provisions touched on service industries, energy trade, and regulations governing U.S. investment in Canada. A U.S.-Canadian arbitration panel was to be set up to deal with trade disputes.

The popularity of a free trade agreement steadily waned in Canada during 1987. By late September, only about 50 per cent of the Canadians polled felt it would benefit Canada by improving employment and incomes. The big Canadian labor unions were adamantly opposed to free trade, but business in Canada gave the plan its full support.

U.S. President Ronald Reagan visited Ottawa on April 5 and 6, his third annual summit meeting

Pickets gather at a railroad yard in Scarborough, Ont., in August, just before a one-week strike by nearly 50,000 railway workers officially begins.

with Prime Minister Mulroney. In a speech to the joint houses of Parliament, Reagan gave strong endorsement to free trade.

Reagan also promised to deal with a long-standing dispute over the ownership of the Northwest Passage through the Arctic Islands. Canada claims sovereignty in the channel, but the United States insists it is an international waterway. Both countries were concerned with reports of Soviet submarines in those ice-bound waters. On Jan. 11, 1988, the United States signed an agreement with Canada promising to seek Canadian permission before sending United States icebreakers through the Northwest Passage. But the agreement stopped short of recognizing Canada's claim to the channel.

On another contentious issue—acid rain—Reagan offered his critics little satisfaction, except to admit that the United States produced half of the air pollutants that lead to the formation of acid rain. Acid rain has been blamed for damaging lakes and forests in North America and elsewhere. Reagan reaffirmed his country's interest in pursuing a long-term study to discover ways of burning coal more cleanly. In September 1987, a report of a scientific panel convened by the Reagan Administration said that acid rain had not caused significant damage to the environment. The report's findings were hotly challenged by the Canadian government, as well as by many U.S. and Canadian scientists. In the Special Reports section, see STORMY DEBATE OVER ACID RAIN.

Canada Hosted two large international conferences in late 1987. The first meeting, organized by La Francophonie, a group of French-speaking nations, met in Quebec City, Que., in September. The meeting was attended by representatives of 37 French-speaking countries, including President François Mitterrand of France. Projects in education, energy, agriculture, and the sharing of scientific information were discussed and launched.

The second meeting hosted by Canada, the 28th Heads of Government Conference—a gathering of leaders of the 47 Commonwealth nations—was held in Vancouver, B.C., in October. The main topic of the meeting was South Africa's policy of *apartheid* (racial segregation). The representatives decided to create a committee of foreign ministers to examine the effectiveness of sanctions.

Economic Summit. Mulroney attended the 13th annual economic summit of the seven major non-Communist industrialized countries, held in Venice, Italy, from June 8 to 10. Although few concrete decisions were made at the gathering, there was agreement on the need to coordinate economic policies, reduce agricultural subsidies, and continue diplomatic efforts to persuade the South African government to soften apartheid.

Federal Spending in Canada

Estimated Budget for Fiscal 1987-1988*

	Millions of dollars†
Transfer payments:	
To other levels of government:	
Health insurance	6,843
Post-secondary education	2,366
Fiscal transfer payments	5,902
Canada Assistance Plan	4,192
Territorial governments	697
Other	1,296
To persons:	
Old age security	10,258
Guaranteed income supplement	3,753
Spouse's allowance	582
Government's contribution to	
unemployment insurance	2,785
Family allowances	2,562
Other	1,540
Subsidies:	
Western Grain Transportation Act	724
Agricultural Stabilization Act	363
Petroleum incentives payments	130
Western Grain Stabilization Act	99
Other	261
Other transfer payments:	
Development assistance	2,258
Employment and immigration programs and	
employment initiatives	1,677
Indians and Inuit	1,354
Regional industrial expansion	890
Other	2,333
Public debt charges	28,200
Payments to Crown corporations	
Canada Mortgage and Housing Corporation	1,667
Canadian Broadcasting Corporation	881
VIA Rail Canada Inc.	500
Canada Post Corporation	375
Atomic Energy of Canada Limited	169
Other	1,026
Operating and capital expenditures:	
National defense	10,340
Other departments and agencies	
Salaries, wages and other personnel costs	10,007
Other	4,111
Total	**110,141**

*April 1, 1987, to March 31, 1988.
†Canadian dollars; $1 = U.S. 77 cents as of Dec. 15, 1987.

Spending Since 1982

Billions of dollars

Fiscal year

Source: Treasury Board of Canada.

Defense. An important defense policy statement issued by the Canadian government on June 5 reaffirmed Canada's faith in the North Atlantic Treaty Organization (NATO) but dropped a commitment to reinforce NATO's northern flank in Norway in the event of a military crisis in Europe. Instead, the study called for concentrating Canada's presence in southern West Germany, where 7,000 Canadian troops are stationed. A second brigade, based in Canada, would be positioned to reinforce the first one if needed.

The study also outlined a 15-year budget of $183 billion to provide new military equipment. The equipment would include 10 nuclear-powered submarines for Arctic and coastal patrols, as well as new frigates and a surveillance system to be used under Arctic ice.

Facts in Brief: Population: 25,563,129. Government: Governor General Jeanne M. Sauvé; Prime Minister M. Brian Mulroney. Monetary unit: the Canadian dollar. Value of foreign trade (in Canadian dollars): exports, $115,900,000,000; and imports, $104,900,000,000. David M. L. Farr

See also the Canadian provinces articles; CANADIAN LIBRARY ASSOCIATION (CLA); CANADIAN LITERATURE; L'HEUREUX-DUBÉ, CLAIRE; McKENNA, FRANK J.; MONTREAL; SAUVÉ, JEANNE M.; TORONTO; TRUDEAU, PIERRE E. In WORLD BOOK, see CANADA.

CANADIAN LIBRARY ASSOCIATION (CLA) in 1987 presented several briefs to the Canadian government on issues important to the library community. In June, the CLA expressed its concerns about proposed pornography legislation, pointing out the negative effects that the law would have on libraries. The CLA argued that if the law were passed, libraries would be forced to make major changes in staffing and in the way library materials are selected and organized to ensure that libraries would not be held criminally liable for circulating obscene material. The CLA also joined other organizations in objecting to the government's sweeping definition of pornography.

In October, the CLA expressed concerns about a proposed amendment to the Copyright Act, originally passed in 1924, that would permit the formation of copyright licensing bureaus. Libraries would have to negotiate with these bureaus for the privilege of making photocopies of published material. CLA members also conducted a letter-writing campaign urging the government to continue subsidizing the postal rate for library books.

CLA Organization. A presidential commission on the CLA's organization chaired by Basil Stuart-Stubbs, chairman of the School of Librarianship at the University of British Columbia in Vancouver, presented its report to the CLA Council in March 1987. The report recommended wide-ranging changes in the structure and programs of the CLA, including the consideration of a plan to link the CLA and provincial library associations more closely. A number of the commission's recommendations were adopted. For example, the CLA established a group to monitor developments in information technology.

Annual Meeting. Vancouver was the site of the CLA's annual meeting, which was held from June 11 to 17, 1987, and attended by more than 1,800 delegates. The conference theme, "Merchants of Light," was addressed by the keynote speaker, Canadian broadcaster Lister Sinclair. William R. Converse, chief librarian of the University of Winnipeg in Manitoba, took office as the new CLA president. Associate Librarian Vivienne I. F. Monty, head of the Government and Business Library at York University in Toronto, became first vice president and president-elect.

Awards. John E. Dutton, director of the Calgary (Alta.) Public Library, won the 1987 CLA Outstanding Service to Librarianship Award. Janet Lunn was awarded the CLA Book of the Year for Children Award for *Shadow on Hawthorne Bay*. The Amelia Frances Howard-Gibbon Illustrator's Award went to Marie-Louise Gay for *Moonbeam on a Cat's Ear*.   Jane Cooney

In WORLD BOOK, see CANADIAN LIBRARY ASSOCIATION.

CANADIAN LITERATURE had a record year in 1987, with publication of nearly 2,300 books. Although many of the new books were cookbooks and other instructional guides such as sports and self-help publications, Canadian publishers issued some 600 books in the fields of fiction, history, business, essays, poetry, memoirs, and biographies in 1987.

Biographies and Memoirs. *The Politics of the Imagination*, Sandra Djwa's biography of F. R. Scott, an influential poet, lawyer, and civil libertarian, and David G. Pitt's *E. J. Pratt: The Master Years*, the story of a fine poet and teacher, were among the important literary biographies of 1987. Farley Mowat's *Virunga* examined the controversial life of Dian Fossey, a scientist who was murdered in 1985 while she was working to save the endangered mountain gorillas of central Africa. Scott Young's *Gordon Sinclair* was an account of an irrepressible celebrity who made his name in broadcasting and journalism.

Possibly the most intriguing autobiography of 1987 was novelist Sylvia Fraser's *My Father's House*, an account of her childhood and adolescence, during which she was sexually abused by her father. Charles Ritchie, well known for the four books of diaries describing his experiences as a high-ranking diplomat, contributed *My Grandfather's House*, a witty collection of reminiscences. Pierre Berton,

a journalist and popular historian, also recalled his youthful years in the first volume of his memoirs, *Starting Out*.

George Woodcock, a distinguished critic and author of more than 50 books, wrote the second volume of his autobiography, *Beyond the Blue Mountains*. P. K. Page, best known as a poet, contributed *Brazilian Journal*, a memoir of her experiences as a diplomat's wife in South America.

Memoirs of three well-known public figures appeared in 1987. Criminal lawyer Edward L. Greenspan told of his successes and failures in *Greenspan: The Case for the Defense*. Knowlton Nash examined his career as a television newscaster for the Canadian Broadcasting Corporation in *Prime Time at Ten*. Scientist and broadcaster David Suzuki wrote of the stages of his life in *Metamorphosis*.

Fiction. Many critics agreed that the outstanding work of Canadian fiction in 1987 was Michael Ondaatje's *In the Skin of a Lion*, a novel that gave a voice to the nameless immigrants who helped build the city of Toronto, Ont. Roch Carrier's *Heartbreaks Along the Road* explored political chicanery and human gullibility in the province of Quebec. Perhaps the best first novel of 1987 was Marion Quednau's *The Butterfly Chair*, an account of a young woman trying to come to terms with the murder-suicide of her parents.

The outstanding short-story collection of 1987 was Jane Urquhart's *Storm Glass*, a book that combined a poet's metaphorical feeling for language with a classicist's sense of form. Other fine story collections included Josef Skvorecky's *The Mournful Demeanor of Lieutenant Boruvka*, Rohinton Mistry's *Tales from Firozsha Baag*, Eric McCormack's *Inspecting the Vaults*, and W. P. Kinsella's *Red Wolf, Red Wolf*.

Brian Moore's *The Color of Blood* depicted an unnamed European country split by political and religious intrigue. Notable mystery novels included Eric Wright's *A Body Surrounded by Water*, Anna Porter's *Mortal Sins*, K. G. E. Konkel's *The Glorious East Wind*, and Peter Robinson's *Gallows View*.

History and Politics. Peter C. Newman continued his best-selling saga of the Hudson's Bay Company with the second volume in the series, *Caesars of the Wilderness*. Reference books that provided valuable insights into Canada's past included *The Illustrated History of Canada*—written by six of Canada's foremost historians and edited by R. Craig Brown—and the first volume of the *Historical Atlas of Canada*, edited by R. Cole Harris. *The Oxford Illustrated Literary Guide to Canada* by Albert and Theresa Moritz linked some 500 places to the writers and characters associated with them.

Two books, Reg Whitaker's *Double Standard* and Victor Malarek's *Haven's Gate*, tackled the subject of Canada's often controversial immigration strategies. *Justice Delayed*, by David Matas and Susan

Charendoff, attacked the sluggish search for Nazi war criminals known to be living in Canada. Among many books that dealt with politics and politicians were Claire Hoy's *Friends in High Places*, a study of patronage in Prime Minister Brian Mulroney's federal government; Rod McQueen's *Blind Trust*, an account of the inquiry into the alleged conflict of interest on the part of former federal cabinet minister Sinclair Stevens; and John Sawatsky's *The Insiders*, an analysis of the powerful lobbying industry in Canada.

Canadian journalists produced several notable books in 1987. Jack Cahill's *Words of War* provided a firsthand account of the Vietnam War, and Bryan Johnson's *Four Days of Courage* gave an on-the-spot report on the fall of President Ferdinand E. Marcos of the Philippines. *The Arctic Imperative*, by John Honderich, argued for a coherent policy to establish Canadian sovereignty in the North.

Poetry. Douglas LePan's *Weathering It* was a selection of poems from his 40-year career. New collections from other major poets included George Bowering's *Delayed Mercy and Other Poems*, Gwendolyn MacEwen's *Afterworlds*, Patrick Lane's *Selected Poems*, Ralph Gustafson's *Winter Prophecies*, Irving Layton's *In My Father's House*, and Raymond Souster's *The Eyes of Love*.

Essays and Criticism. Novelist Adele Wiseman's essay collection, *Memoirs of a Book-Molesting Childhood*, provided personal and lively views on reading, writing, and the flourishing of Canadian women writers. Geoff Hancock's *Canadian Writers at Work* featured interviews with 10 important authors, including Margaret Atwood, Mavis Gallant, and Alice Munro. George Woodcock's *Northern Spring* was a collection of 17 well-argued essays on the maturing of Canadian literature after 1960.

Awards. The Governor General's Literary Awards for books published in 1986 went to Alice Munro for *The Progress of Love* (English fiction); Alfred Purdy for *The Collected Poems of Al Purdy: 1956-1986* (English poetry); Northrop Frye for *Northrop Frye on Shakespeare* (English nonfiction); Sharon Pollock for *Doc* (English drama); Yvon Rivard for *Les silences du corbeau* (French fiction); Cécile Cloutier for *L'écouté* (French poetry); Régine Robin for *Le réalisme socialiste: Une esthétique impossible* (French nonfiction); and Anne Legault for *La visite des sauvages* (French drama).

Liedewy Hawke won the Canada Council Translation Prize for her English translation of *Hopes and Dreams: The Diary of Henriette Dessaulles, 1874-1881*. Pierre Desruisseaux and François Lanctôt won for their French translation of George Woodcock's *Gabriel Dumont*. W. P. Kinsella received the Stephen Leacock Memorial Award for humor for *The Fencepost Chronicles*.   Ken Adachi

In WORLD BOOK, see CANADIAN LITERATURE.

CAPE VERDE. See AFRICA.

CARLUCCI, FRANK CHARLES, III (1930-   ), succeeded Caspar W. Weinberger as secretary of defense on Nov. 23, 1987. Carlucci had been President Ronald Reagan's national security adviser. See CABINET, UNITED STATES.

Born on Oct. 18, 1930, in Scranton, Pa., Carlucci was the grandson of an immigrant Italian stonecutter and the son of an insurance broker. He graduated from Princeton University in New Jersey with a bachelor's degree in 1952 and attended Harvard Business School in Cambridge, Mass., for postgraduate studies.

After serving in the United States Navy and holding various jobs in business, Carlucci joined the Foreign Service in 1956. He remained with the service until 1969.

In 1969, a friend from Princeton, Donald H. Rumsfeld, appointed Carlucci assistant director of operations for the Office of Economic Opportunity. In 1971, Carlucci succeeded Rumsfeld as director. Carlucci has been a deputy director at the Office of Management and Budget, the Department of Health, Education, and Welfare, the Department of Defense, and the Central Intelligence Agency, under both Democratic and Republican administrations.

Carlucci married Marcia Myers, his second wife, in 1976 and has three children, two by his first marriage. He is an avid tennis player.   Rod Such

CARTER, JAMES EARL, JR. (1924-   ), the 39th President of the United States, met in Moscow on July 1, 1987, with Soviet leader Mikhail S. Gorbachev. The Soviet news agency Tass said Gorbachev emphasized to Carter his interest in promoting a broad Middle East peace.

Carter, an architect of the 1978 Israel-Egypt peace agreement while in the White House, made a five-nation Middle East tour in March. Speaking at a meeting of business leaders and diplomats in Cairo, Egypt, Carter voiced sharp criticism of President Ronald Reagan, who defeated him in the 1980 election. Carter asserted that Reagan was too inclined to seek military, rather than negotiated, solutions to problems in Central America and the Middle East. Carter also visited Algeria, Israel, Syria, and Jordan.

In June, Carter and his wife, Rosalynn, toured U.S. cities promoting a new book, *Everything to Gain*, that they wrote together. On April 15, their daughter, Amy, 19, was acquitted of charges stemming from a 1986 protest in Amherst, Mass., against the Central Intelligence Agency. Her activism reportedly interfered with her studies. She was suspended from Brown University in Providence, R.I., after finishing her sophomore year in May and announced in December that she would not return.   Frank Cormier and Margot Cormier

In WORLD BOOK, see CARTER, JAMES EARL, JR.

The world's first test-tube kittens were born in April as part of a study on using *in vitro* fertilization to save endangered cat species.

CAT. The cat—already the most popular domestic pet in the United States—became even more popular in 1987. Statistics released by Market Research Corporation of America showed that at least one cat is kept as a pet in 3 of every 10 households. The total feline population in the United States was estimated at 57.8 million.

In August, veterinarian Paul D. Pion and other researchers at the University of California at Davis discovered a link between nutritionally deficient cat foods and heart disease in cats. Adding the nutrient taurine to cat food could prevent the deaths of thousands of cats each year, they said.

The Cat Fanciers' Association 1987 National Best Cat was Grand Champion Bar-B Rerun, a black Persian male bred and owned by Barbara K. Thal of Davie, Fla. A blue-eyed, white Persian male, Grand Champion Windborne Angel's Got Blue Eyes, was the association's National Best Kitten for 1987. Angel's breeder, Vicki Dickerson, and his owners, Dickerson and Clifford and Barbara Farrell of Salinas, Calif., repeated their 1986 win in this category. Grand Champion and Grand Premier Chinquapin Baubles Bangles and Beads, a sable Burmese spay, was named 1987 Best Altered Cat. Baubles was bred and owned by Ann E. Bickman and Linda M. Swope, both of Smyrna, Ga.   Thomas H. Dent

In WORLD BOOK, see CAT.

CENSUS. On Jan. 1, 1988, the population of the United States was about 244.4 million, 2.2 million more than a year earlier, according to estimates by the U.S. Bureau of the Census. The southern and western Sun Belt regions continued to record the largest population gains.

On July 23, 1987, the Census Bureau reported that among metropolitan areas with populations of at least 1 million, the biggest gains between 1980 and 1986 were in Phoenix (26 per cent), Dallas-Fort Worth (25 per cent), Atlanta, Ga. (20 per cent), San Antonio (19 per cent), Tampa-St. Petersburg, Fla. (19 per cent), San Diego (18 per cent), and Sacramento, Calif., and Houston (17 per cent each). The largest population losses were in industrialized and economically depressed areas such as Detroit; Pittsburgh, Pa.; and Cleveland.

Hispanic Population. A Census Bureau report issued in September revealed that the Hispanic population in the United States had increased by 30 per cent since 1980, compared with a gain of 6 per cent for the non-Hispanic population. The bureau estimated that 23 per cent of the increase in the Hispanic population was due to the inclusion of nearly 1 million Hispanic illegal aliens. The study also found that as a group, Hispanics—who totaled 18.8 million—were younger, poorer, less educated, and growing more rapidly in numbers than any other U.S. ethnic group.

Women and Earnings. On September 3, the Census Bureau reported that full-time women workers earned 70 per cent as much as men earned in 1986, up from 62 per cent in 1979. It was the first significant increase in decades and largely reflected movement by women into some higher-paying occupations. But the study also revealed that people working in female-dominated professions earned less than workers in sexually integrated or male-dominated professions.

Women and Marriage. In a report on marriage rates of college-educated women issued in January, the Census Bureau sharply disagreed with a controversial 1986 study by demographers at Harvard University in Cambridge, Mass., and Yale University in New Haven, Conn. The Census Bureau said that a white, college-educated woman still single at age 30 has a 58 per cent to 66 per cent chance of eventually marrying, and that at age 40, her chances of marrying would be 17 per cent to 23 per cent. In contrast, the Harvard-Yale study had predicted that 30-year-old women had only a 20 per cent chance of marrying, and that the odds dropped to a mere 1.3 per cent by age 40. Expert opinions differed on the relative validity of the two studies. Frank Cormier and Margot Cormier

See also POPULATION. In WORLD BOOK, see CENSUS.

CENTRAL AFRICAN REPUBLIC. See AFRICA.

CHAD. President Hissein Habré in 1987 pursued a combined policy of forgiveness toward former political foes and ethnic balance in staffing the government. Tensions subsided among the more than 200 ethnic groups in Chad. Since the mid-1960's, the country has been in a constant state of civil war with roughly 11 armed factions trying to gain power. Late in 1986, the leaders of some of the warring groups pledged their loyalty to Habré, and several were given high government posts.

Chadian Unity was partly due to the improved skills of Habré's soldiers in fighting former President Goukouni Oueddei, Habré's long-time opponent. Libya provided both troops and arms to support Goukouni, while Habré's forces were aided by France, which ruled Chad until 1960. In addition to sending 2,500 troops to Chad in 1987, France supplied Habré with $200 million in military and economic aid. The United States in 1987 gave the Habré government $70 million worth of ground-to-air missiles and other equipment.

In October 1986, having defeated Goukouni's forces in several battles, Habré launched an all-out offensive against the rebels and Libyan troops. During the fighting, many of Goukouni's troops turned on the Libyans and switched their allegiance to Habré. Libya's ruler, Muammar Muhammad al-Qadhafi, immediately withdrew his support of Goukouni and jailed him in Tripoli.

President Ronald Reagan welcomed Chad's President Hissein Habré to the White House in June and pledged continued U.S. aid for the African nation.

In March 1987, Habré's forces recaptured the town of Faya-Largeau from the Libyans and overran a Libyan air base at Wadi Doum. After other battles in June and August, the fleeing Libyans left behind Soviet-supplied planes, tanks, and equipment worth more than $500 million.

The Conflict Worsened in August. Libyan planes attacked Habré's positions with bombs and—according to the Chadians—chemical weapons, including poison gas. Much of the fighting was in the Aozou Strip, a 42,000-square-mile (109,000-square-kilometer) region in northern Chad that Libya has occupied since 1973, asserting historic and legal claims to the territory.

In a bold move aimed at retaking the Aozou Strip, the Chadians in September attacked a Libyan air base at Matan as Sarra. France—hoping to avoid direct military contact with Libya—urged Habré to settle the Aozou dispute through diplomacy. He agreed, and on September 11 the Organization of African Unity arranged a cease-fire between Chad and Libya.

Grinding Poverty. With a $78 per-capita annual income, Chad is one of the world's poorest nations. The price of cotton, its main export, has fallen by 50 per cent on world markets since the 1970's. J. Gus Liebenow and Beverly B. Liebenow

See also AFRICA (Facts in Brief Table). In WORLD BOOK, see CHAD.

CHEMISTRY. The development of military aircraft that cannot be detected by radar took an unexpected turn in August 1987 when chemist Robert R. Birge of Carnegie-Mellon University in Pittsburgh, Pa., reported the discovery of chemicals that absorb rather than reflect radar beams. Such chemicals, if used in paint applied to an airplane, would make the craft "invisible" to radar. The experts, however, have not discovered how to use the chemicals in paint without destroying their ability to absorb radar beams.

Military researchers have tried for years to find ways to prevent radar from detecting aircraft. The United States reportedly has already built experimental Stealth fighters—jets whose wing shape and special coating make them less obvious to radar. But radar scans of varying wavelengths could spot these aircraft.

The new chemicals, called *Schiff base salts*, can convert radar beams of various wavelengths into heat, so the beams do not bounce back to detectors. A paint containing a mixture of such chemicals could absorb a wide range of wavelengths, foiling even radar systems that used varying wavelengths.

Suprisingly, the research leading to the discovery of the chemicals was not a defense project. Rather, Birge was studying the chemistry of vision. He used the Schiff base salts as a model for *rhodopsin*, a pigment found in the retina of the eye. Rhodopsin changes its structure when it absorbs light.

Appetite Control. A chemist at the Monell Chemical Senses Center in Philadelphia has discovered a chemical that may help dieters by reducing their craving for food. Michael J. DiNovi revealed in April 1987 that a noncaloric carbohydrate called *2,5-AM* suppressed the appetites of laboratory rats. The carbohydrate is chemically similar to fructose, a sugar found in corn syrup. Rats that ate 2,5-AM before meals reduced their overall intake of food significantly.

Strangely, DiNovi found that 2,5-AM can also stimulate rats' appetites, depending upon when they consume it. Rats normally are active at night. In the morning, when they usually rest, they get their energy from sugar stored in their blood. Rats fed 2,5-AM in the morning apparently could not use their stored energy, so they ate to obtain more energy, increasing their overall food intake.

DiNovi has not shown that 2,5-AM works in human beings. But if it does, it could not only decrease the appetites of dieters but also stimulate people who have poor appetites to eat more—individuals suffering from liver disease, for example, and patients undergoing drug treatment for cancer.

Ozone Hole Verdict. Natural weather processes have teamed up with artificial chemicals to pro-

A new plastic containing cornstarch may help solve waste-disposal problems. It disintegrates in water and can be eaten by bacteria in soil.

duce a hole in the atmospheric layer of *ozone* (an oxygen compound) above Antarctica, according to a September 1987 report by Robert T. Watson, a research scientist at the National Aeronautics and Space Administration (NASA) Office of Earth Science and Applications in Washington, D.C. Watson's report may end a decade-long debate over the danger of *chlorofluorocarbons* (CFC's), compounds that are used widely in refrigeration fluids and insulation.

Ozone in the upper atmosphere shields us from ultraviolet radiation, a cause of skin cancer and other diseases. In 1974, chemist F. Sherwood Rowland, now of the University of California at Irvine, suggested that CFC's could react chemically with the ozone, thereby destroying the ozone layer.

In 1985, scientists noted a loss of ozone in the atmosphere above Antarctica. The discovery of this ozone "hole" energized the debate on CFC's and led NASA to collect samples of Antarctic air in August and September 1987. Watson directed the collection project.

The clearest indicator that CFC's are partly responsible for the ozone hole was the presence of more than 100 times the expected amount of chlorine monoxide, a compound created when CFC undergoes a chemical change. Chemists suspect that, of all the compounds involved in the creation of the ozone hole, chlorine monoxide is the most damaging.

Dissolving Gallstones. The 20 million Americans who suffer from *gallstones*, hard objects that form in the gall bladder or bile duct, may benefit from a new chemical compound reported in April 1987. Medicinal chemist Ashok K. Batta and his colleagues at the University of Medicine and Dentistry of New Jersey in Newark said that the substance, called *ursocholic acid*, dissolves gallstones.

The usual treatment for gallstones is to remove the gall bladder, requiring major surgery. Another treatment—for patients who are too sick for surgery—is to use drugs to dissolve the gallstones. Unfortunately, the drugs are expensive and typically take one to two years to effectively remove the stones.

In tests conducted in Italy, ursocholic acid completely dissolved gallstones in 4 of 10 people in just six months. Furthermore, the new compound is chemically simpler than the traditional drugs and therefore would cost much less to produce.

One problem with ursocholic acid is that 30 per cent of it is washed out in the urine before it reaches the gallstones. Batta and his co-workers have focused their efforts on improving the compound. They have already reduced the amount of ursocholic acid wasted by the body to less than 10 per cent.
Peter J. Andrews

In WORLD BOOK, see CHEMISTRY.

CHESS. World chess champion Gary Kasparov of the Soviet Union held onto his title in 1987, playing countryman and former world champion Anatoly Karpov to a 12-12 tie. Under the rules, Karpov would have had to win the match outright to regain the title. At the end of the 24-game match on December 19, Kasparov had won 4, Karpov had won 4, and 16 games had been drawn. The match was held in Seville, Spain.

Earlier in 1987, a worldwide series of competitions qualified Yasser Seirawan of Seattle, Nigel Short and Jonathan Speelman of Great Britain, and six other players for *candidates' elimination matches.* This series of play-offs, scheduled to begin in January 1988 in St. John, Canada, will eliminate all but one player. This player will challenge Kasparov for the world championship in 1990.

Other Tournaments. Joel Benjamin of New York City and Nick deFirmian of San Francisco became United States cochampions on Nov. 18, 1987, in Estes Park, Colo. Seirawan won the New York Open, held from April 7 to 19 in New York City. More than 1,000 players from 25 countries competed in this tournament—the largest open chess tournament ever held. Former Soviet champion Boris Gulko, now of Silver Spring, Md., won the World Open, held from June 26 to July 5 in Philadelphia. Lev Alburt of New York City won the U.S. Open Championship, held from August 2 to 14 in Portland, Ore.

Younger Players. United States youngsters won an unprecedented four world championships at the International Youth and Peace Chess Festival, held from July 6 to 22 in San Juan, Puerto Rico. John Viloria, 9, of Yonkers, N.Y., won the under-10 world championship. Eight-year-old Susan Urminska of Kapaa, Hawaii, captured the girls' under-12 world championship. Jessica Ambats, 13, of New York City tied Cathy Haslinger of Great Britain for the girls' under-14 world title.

Patrick Wolf, 19, of Belmont, Mass., won the U.S. Junior Invitational Championship, played from June 15 to 24 in New York City. Seventeen-year-old Andrew Serotta of Lansdale, Pa., captured the U.S. Junior Open championship, held on July 24 and 25 in Philadelphia.

More than 1,800 young U.S. chess players competed in national team chess championships in 1987. Dalton School of New York City won the elementary school team championship, held on April 11 and 12 in Terre Haute, Ind. On May 2 and 3 in Buena Park, Calif., Hunter School of New York City became champions for the eighth grade and below, while Metcalf School of Burnsville, Minn., won the championship for the ninth grade and below. Bellarmine High School of San Jose won the high school championship, held from April 24 to 26 in Pulaski, Va.
Al Lawrence

In WORLD BOOK, see CHESS.

CHICAGO. Harold Washington, the city's first black mayor, died of a heart attack on Nov. 25, 1987. His unexpected death at age 65 came less than eight months after an April 7 mayoral election in which Washington, a Democrat, became the first Chicago mayor since Richard J. Daley to win a second term. Nowhere was Washington's passing mourned more fervently than in Chicago's black community, where he had become a symbol of the growing political power of blacks.

Before funeral services for Washington had been completed, his allies and opponents in the City Council were scrambling to choose an acting mayor. Most black council members backed Timothy C. Evans, chairman of the council's finance committee, who promised to carry on Washington's "reform agenda." They were outmaneuvered, however, when the council's white Democratic members threw their support behind a smaller faction of blacks who favored Eugene Sawyer, a black councilman who, his critics said, was identified with the Daley-era political "machine."

Sawyer, 53, was elected acting mayor by a 29-19 council vote after a raucous, all-night council session that lasted into the early hours of December 2. Many observers in Chicago predicted that Sawyer and Evans will oppose each other in a special mayoral election scheduled for 1989.

Budget and Taxes. Sawyer's first major accomplishment as acting mayor was obtaining council approval on Dec. 16, 1987, of a record $2.7-billion municipal budget for 1988. Passage was assured only after Sawyer scaled back an increase of $87 million in property-tax revenue that had been called for in Washington's spending plan.

Schools. In September, Chicago public-school teachers began a strike that lasted 19 school days, the longest in the city's history. Teachers returned to classes on October 6 after the Board of Education promised them a 4 per cent pay raise in the 1987-1988 school year and another 4 per cent increase in the following school year. School administrators admitted, however, that they did not have funds to cover the raises and would have to seek financial help from the Illinois legislature.

During the year, many Chicago parents and politicians demanded reforms to improve the city's public schools. Those demands became louder in late October, after the release of a national report showing that half of the city's public high schools ranked in the bottom 1 per cent of schools in the United States on the American College Testing program (ACT), an aptitude test required by many colleges.

Population and Economy. Studies in 1987 indicated that Chicago's population had stabilized af-

Chicago Mayor Harold Washington exults in April after being elected to a second four-year term, but he died less than eight months later.

ter a long decline. From 1980 to 1985, the number of city dwellers increased by 2,531 to 3,007,603—the first increase in about 30 years. In 1985 whites composed 39 per cent of the population; blacks, 41 per cent; Hispanics, 16 per cent; and Asians and "others," 4 per cent.

Scandals. A dozen people, including eight current or former city officials, were indicted in November as a result of a three-year federal probe into the financial management of Chicago public-service agencies. The officials were charged with defrauding the city by directing city business to a local automobile-supply company in return for cash kickbacks, vacation trips, and campaign contributions. The probe, Operation Lantern, was expected to lead to further indictments.

Meanwhile, other federal probes continued. On May 14, prosecutors announced the indictment of nine local officials including the chief clerk of the Cook County Circuit Court, Morgan M. Finley, former mayoral aide Clarence McClain, and two aldermen. All allegedly took payoffs from a federal informant. On June 8, a 10th judge was convicted of bribe-taking in the federal government's three-year-old Operation Greylord probe of corruption in the county courts. Two more judges pleaded guilty to Greylord-related charges of tax fraud on December 16.   John F. McCarron

See also CITY. In WORLD BOOK, see CHICAGO.

Children in the Chicago suburb of Palatine listen as SAM—*S*afety *A*lways *M*atters—the robot warns them to be on their guard against strangers.

CHILD WELFARE. The Centers for Disease Control (CDC) in Atlanta, Ga., reported in June 1987 that 516 cases of AIDS (acquired immune deficiency syndrome) had been reported in children under 13 years old in the United States since 1981. About 80 per cent of the afflicted children are black or Hispanic, and most live in cities.

Children with AIDS range from severely ill, hospitalized infants to children living at home or in foster care. Most were born with AIDS, having contracted it in the womb from their mothers.

Legislation. The Child Abuse Prevention, Adoption, and Family Services Act of 1987 was approved by the United States House of Representatives on June 8, 1987, with strong support from both Democrats and Republicans. The bill authorizes the continuation and expansion of various child welfare programs, including efforts to curb family violence and child abuse and neglect. At year-end, the Senate had not acted on the bill.

Jailed Juveniles. Two groups of prominent jurists in 1987 urged states to abolish the detention of juveniles in adult jails. The Conference of Chief Justices, made up of state supreme court chief justices, and the Council of Judges of the National Council on Crime and Delinquency adopted resolutions urging states to meet the December 1988 deadline set by the federal government for moving juveniles to separate detention facilities.

A University of Illinois study completed in 1987 revealed that the suicide rate for juveniles held in adult jails is eight times higher than the suicide rate among those held in juvenile detention facilities. The study found that juveniles held in adult facilities are often taunted, molested, or injured by older inmates.

The U.S. Office of Juvenile Justice and Delinquency Prevention set aside $1 million in 1987 to help states meet the December 1988 deadline. By the end of 1987, only nine states had established separate facilities for all juvenile detainees.

Children in Poverty. The number of impoverished families with children in the United States increased by 35 per cent from 1979 to 1987, according to a report issued in September 1987 by the Center on Budget and Policy Priorities. The center, a private research group in Washington, D.C., said 5.5 million American families with children currently live in poverty—defined in 1986 as an annual income of less than $11,203 for a family of four—compared with 4.1 million such families in 1979. The report said the increase was due mainly to reduced federal support for cash-assistance programs such as Aid to Families with Dependent Children.   Jeanne M. Hunzeker

In WORLD BOOK, see AIDS; CHILD WELFARE.

CHILDREN'S BOOKS. See LITERATURE FOR CHILDREN.

CHILE. A visit to Chile by Pope John Paul II in early April 1987 underscored the demands of many Chileans for democratic elections after 14 years of military rule. At a news conference before his visit, the pope criticized the military regime of President Augusto Pinochet Ugarte as "dictatorial." During his visit, the pope emerged from a meeting with Pinochet and called for the restoration of democracy in the "not distant future." He also went out of his way to console victims of the regime's brutality, including Carmen Gloria Quintana, 19, who was reportedly set on fire by soldiers during street disturbances in 1986.

Clashes between police and demonstrators erupted as the pope celebrated an outdoor Mass before 1 million people in Santiago on April 3. One civilian was killed, and 109 police officers and more than 300 civilians were injured, during the pope's three-day visit to the capital.

Seven leftist political parties announced on June 26 that they were forming a United Left coalition to press for elections in Chile.

When Communist-led labor unions called a general strike on October 7, most Chileans avoided demonstrations. Chile's largest opposition party, the Christian Democrats, has renounced tactics that might lead to bloodshed.   Nathan A. Haverstock

See also LATIN AMERICA (Facts in Brief Table). In WORLD BOOK, see CHILE.

U.S. Secretary of State George P. Shultz, seated at center, watches a ceremony honoring the philosopher Confucius on a visit to China in March 1987.

CHINA. The ruling Chinese Communist Party elected new leaders on Nov. 2, 1987, after a year of political turmoil in which party conservatives challenged the modernization policies of China's most powerful figure, Deng Xiaoping (Teng Hsiao-p'ing in the traditional Wade-Giles spelling). The election was a victory for Deng. Party officials installed his protégé, Zhao Ziyang, as general secretary of the Chinese Communist Party and ousted many of Deng's opponents.

The Year of Turmoil began with a demonstration by 1,000 students at the China Science and Technology University in Hefei (Ho-fei), the capital of Anhui (Anhwei) Province, on Dec. 5, 1986. The students wanted freedom to nominate their own candidates for the Provincial People's Congress instead of having to endorse the Communist Party's choices. The demand for more democracy quickly spread to other universities in a dozen cities in China. The protest also broadened into calls for other forms of political liberalization.

The Communist Party newspaper, *People's Daily,* initially gave some support to the student protests. It was unclear whether reformers associated with Deng were encouraging the students in order to show support for greater liberalization, or whether Deng's conservative opponents were trying to discredit reform by showing that it would lead to a weakening of party power.

By early January, however, party officials had become concerned about the demonstrations and warned that protests could endanger China's "national unity." Elderly party leaders who had opposed Deng's moves away from centralized control of the economy launched an offensive. They charged that the demonstrations were a denial of the socialist system and an advocacy of capitalism. The party viewed such attacks as threats to Deng's ability to continue his reform program.

China's key decision-making body—the Politburo of the Communist Party Central Committee—and some other senior officials met on January 16. During the meeting, Hu Yaobang—whom Deng in 1980 named to be party general secretary, and thus to run the party and the country—admitted errors and was forced to resign. Most observers viewed Hu as a scapegoat for Deng's policies. China's premier, Zhao Ziyang, was immediately named acting general secretary.

Dissent Within the Party. Attacking what they termed "bourgeois liberalism," the conservatives in February and March 1987 campaigned against any further relaxation of the government's economic control and the party's political control. They also tried to stop a diminishment of the power of local party officials. The conservative campaign hindered Deng and Zhao's efforts to restructure China's economy along less Marxist and

253

more productive lines and to give workers more freedom from the party's control of employment.

Zhao tried to compromise in a March 25 speech that opened a session of the National People's Congress, China's party-controlled parliament. Zhao defended practical economic reforms but called for tighter controls on intellectual and artistic expression.

During the summer, the party leadership continued to debate. By autumn, the conservatives appeared to have lost ground, seemingly because they could not offer an alternative program for overcoming China's continuing economic problems—which Deng and Zhao wanted to tackle by fostering individual initiative in a careful, controlled move toward limited capitalism.

The Showdown between the factions occurred at the first Communist Party Congress in five years, which was held in Beijing (Peking) from October 25 to November 1. Nearly 2,000 delegates representing 46 million Communist Party members attended.

Zhao gave the keynote speech, in which he defended modernization programs, telling the assembled Chinese Marxists to "widen your vision, develop new concepts, and enter a new realm." Although public ownership would continue to dominate China's economy, he said, under the reforms, private enterprise could expand. Zhao also introduced a major reform of personnel policies that allowed the party to fill only political job openings, while competitive examinations would be the basis for professional appointments.

Election Results. The Congress closed with the election of a new 175-member Central Committee, which guides the party between congresses. The delegates reelected the party's leadership, confirming Deng and Zhao's policies.

After years of fighting elderly conservatives, Deng had stressed that party leaders should be younger and better educated. The delegates responded as he wished. Deng, 83, and many other elderly leaders were not reelected to the committee. Although the ouster of older committee members enabled Deng to maneuver most of his conservative opponents out of office, his own retirement was a symbolic gesture. Deng had arranged for a change in party rules so that, even without belonging to the Central Committee, he could remain head of the party's military commission. This job, and Deng's ties to Zhao and other protégés, ensured his continuing power.

The new Central Committee met on November 2 and elected Zhao general secretary. The committee also named 17 of its members to the Politburo and selected Zhao, party secretary Hu Qili,

Zhao Ziyang toasts a group of reporters on November 2 in Beijing (Peking) soon after being elected general secretary of the Chinese Communist Party.

and Deputy Premiers Li Peng, Qiao Shi, and Yao Yilin for the Politburo Standing Committee, which handles daily business.

The average age of the new Politburo Standing Committee members was about 64, 13 years younger than the average age of the previous members. In the Central Committee as a whole, the average age of members was about 55, down about 4 years.

Those dropped from leadership posts included President Li Xiannian, 81, one of several comrades of Mao Zedong (Mao Tse-tung)—China's leader from 1949 to 1976—who were not reelected. Two other party greats, economist Chen Yun, 82, and National People's Congress Chairman Peng Zhen, 85, lost their positions of influence. Delegates elected all three men to a Central Advisory Commission, but a party report made clear that the three were not expected to interfere in the work of the new, younger leaders.

Hu Yaobang won partial rehabilitation by being named to the Politburo and reelected to the Central Committee, while many of those responsible for his January dismissal lost their seats.

Li Peng was named acting premier, succeeding Zhao, on November 24. Li was virtually assured of becoming China's premier at the next meeting of the National People's Congress in 1988. Although committed to economic reform, Li was believed to be a moderate who would move cautiously.

The drive to rejuvenate China's leadership also extended to its top military command. On November 27, military chief of staff Yang Dezhi, 77, was replaced by 62-year-old Chi Haotian. Two other elderly top officers were also replaced.

Economic Problems plagued China throughout 1987. On October 29, Zhao said that in 1978 China's entire economy was controlled by the government. He estimated that only 50 per cent was under government control in 1987 and predicted that in 1989 or 1990 only 30 per cent of the country's economic activity would be so controlled.

Government officials worried that economic planning based on a projected population of 1.2 billion in the year 2000 would be inadequate because too many Chinese were violating the official policy of "one couple, one child." The birth rate was rising as peasants grew wealthier and became more willing to pay fines for having more children than official policy decreed.

Officials also worried about inflation—which had undermined China's pre-1949 government and led to Mao's victory. Until the government began a program of economic reform in 1978, prices of many basic goods had remained unchanged for 20 years. But from 1979 to 1987, the official price index rose 35.8 per cent—and the unofficial indicators were higher. Although personal income rose also, officials feared accelerating inflation.

The problem was complicated by the need to reform China's pricing structure so that prices gave a better indication of true value. This was, however, a difficult job that officials were hesitant to tackle.

Riots in Tibet displayed that region's strong anti-Chinese feelings—despite being under China's firm control since 1959, when Tibet's Buddhist spiritual leader, the Dalai Lama, fled into exile in India. On Sept. 27, 1987, in Lhasa, the capital of Tibet, more than 20 Buddhist monks marched around the Jokhang temple, their holiest shrine, shouting demands for Tibetan independence. Police broke up the protest. About 35 monks demonstrated again on October 1. When police clubbed some of them, hundreds of Tibetans rioted. The police opened fire. At least six Tibetans and four Chinese died. Police suppressed another protest on October 6, but riots were reported in several other Tibetan towns.

Chinese authorities accused the Dalai Lama of causing the trouble. On a September visit to the United States, the Dalai Lama had appealed for China to withdraw its occupying army from Tibet and negotiate with Tibetans on their country's future. China insisted that most Tibetans appreciated the benefits it provided them.

A Devastating Forest Fire burned 1.5 million acres (0.6 million hectares) in northeast China from May 6 to June 2. The fire killed 193 people, injured 226, and left 56,000 homeless. The Communist Party blamed the disaster on its secretary in the Forestry Ministry, Yang Zhong, and fired him on June 10.

Weaponry. China conducted on June 5 its first nuclear test since 1984. The explosion occurred underground in the desert area of Xinjiang (Sinkiang) in western China.

The United States announced on October 22 that it had halted plans to sell China high technology goods that were under U.S. export controls. The decision followed a dispute over Iran's use of Chinese-made Silkworm missiles to attack ships flying the U.S. flag in the Persian Gulf. United States officials claimed that China sold the missiles to Iran. A U.S. Senate resolution warned that continued sales could "seriously jeopardize U.S.-China relations." Chinese leaders denied providing the missiles to Iran.

Police Torture. Amnesty International—a human rights organization based in London—said on September 8 that police use of torture was widespread in China, despite government efforts to limit it. Henry S. Bradsher

See also ASIA (Facts in Brief Table). In WORLD BOOK, see CHINA.

CHURCHES. See EASTERN ORTHODOX CHURCHES; JEWS AND JUDAISM; PROTESTANTISM; RELIGION; ROMAN CATHOLIC CHURCH.

CITY. United States cities in 1987 continued to experience two different trends—low-income areas that slipped deeper into poverty and a flourishing downtown renovation. Federal policies—including tax changes that become effective in 1988 and the continued phase-out of federal aid to the cities—left urban areas in a state of uncertainty, especially as they tried to grapple with the effects of the stock market crash in October 1987. Experts predicted the biggest impact would occur in housing, as worried consumers postponed house and condominium purchases and developers delayed investment decisions.

Population Trends. San Diego and Dallas joined the list of U.S. cities with at least 1 million residents in 1986, according to estimates by the U.S. Bureau of the Census in October 1987. Six cities joined the list of U.S. cities with populations of more than 100,000, bringing the total to 182.

New York City remained the nation's largest city, with an estimated 7,262,700 residents. Los Angeles was second largest with 3,259,300 people, followed by Chicago with 3,009,530, and Houston with 1,728,910. Although the top four cities increased their population between 1984 and 1986, Philadelphia and Detroit—the fifth and sixth largest cities—lost residents.

With lawsuits pending, the Census Bureau on Oct. 30, 1987, refused to adjust its upcoming 1990 census figures to include people who may be omitted from the count. Several major cities objected; claiming that cities suffer most from undercounting when federal aid is based on population.

Poverty. Census data released in July 1987 showed a slight decrease in the proportion of Americans living in poverty in 1986. According to the report, the 1986 poverty rate—the proportion of the population with incomes below the government's official poverty level of $11,203 for a family of four in 1986—was 13.6 per cent, down from 14 per cent in 1985.

Census Bureau officials reported that "income inequality" between the richest and the poorest Americans continued to increase, however. The richest 20 per cent had 46.1 per cent of total U.S. income, and poorest 20 per cent had only 3.8 per cent of the total income.

For the first time in 1986, families headed by women accounted for more than half of all poor families. The number of poor families headed by a husband and wife declined to 3.1 million, while the number of poor families that are headed by a woman increased to 3.6 million. Poverty rates for children under the age of 6 declined slightly during 1986 to 22 per cent. The proportion of black children in families living in poverty was 45.6 per cent; and for Hispanic children, 40.7 per cent. For white children, the poverty rate was 17.7 per cent.

Democrat Annette G. Strauss gives a thumbs-up victory signal after becoming the first woman elected mayor of Dallas on April 18, 1987.

Homeless. The problem of the growing number of homeless people in U.S. cities continued in 1987. In the 1970's, state and local governments began releasing mentally ill people from medical facilities into outpatient care programs. Many of these people were unable to cope and ended up on the streets. The U.S. Department of Housing and Urban Development estimated the number of homeless people in the United States at 250,000 to 350,000 in 1984, its most recent estimate, while other groups put the number at 2 million to 3 million people.

New York City in 1987 instituted a controversial policy that would enforce the hospitalization of severely mentally ill homeless people. The American Civil Liberties Union challenged the plan. The administration of New York City Mayor Edward I. Koch went to court in November to defend the policy.

On July 22, President Ronald Reagan signed a law authorizing $443 million in aid to the homeless in fiscal 1987 and $616 million for fiscal 1988 beginning on Oct. 1, 1987. The law provides funds for emergency food and shelter.

Housing. Experts disagreed on whether *gentrification*—the renovation of older, run-down housing into higher-priced housing—was beneficial for cities. A debate surfaced in 1987 about the wisdom of converting industrial and commercial buildings, such as warehouses, into homes. In Manhattan, a borough of New York City, for example, loft housing pushed out several factories, thus reducing employment in the area. In Chicago, businesses in an area north of downtown that was once a strip of light industry and warehouses joined to oppose zoning the area for residential use.

Innovations in public housing during the year offered some solutions to a continuing urban problem. One of the most unusual housing projects was built near Seattle. The King County Housing Authority developed Vantage Glen, a development of 164 mobile homes that are landscaped and set into the ground. The units were sold for $25,000 to $35,000 with below-market-rate mortgages to the low-income elderly. A federal grant and tax-exempt county bonds helped finance the $8-million project.

In Dallas, about one-third of the city's public housing was scheduled for demolition after a federal judge approved a settlement in April in favor of a group of low-income people who had sued the federal government and the local housing authority. Their suit charged that blacks were assigned to housing units only in west Dallas, while whites were distributed throughout the city. The settlement called for razing virtually all of the 2,600 units in a west Dallas neighborhood and scattering the units' residents to other neighborhoods. Displaced residents would be given federally funded vouchers to pay for new housing costs that exceed 30 per cent of their income.

Segregation. An October 1987 study by the Milwaukee Urban League and the University of Wisconsin in that city reported that Milwaukee is the most segregated United States city. Using 1980 census data, researchers found that 97.5 per cent of blacks in Milwaukee lived in the central city area. Chicago, which experts often cite as the most segregated American city, ranked 13th, with 83.8 per cent of blacks in Chicago living in the central city area.

Another study released in October 1987 showed that black and Hispanic students in 438 Los Angeles-area public high schools scored lower than white students in reading, writing, and mathematics. The University of Chicago study found that poor school performance was related to a student's racial background and family income. Statewide test scores indicated that the lowest scores were recorded in schools with the largest numbers of poor and minority students.

Elections. Mayoral elections occurred in several large cities in November 1987. In a bitter contest, Philadelphia's first black mayor, Democrat W. Wilson Goode, narrowly defeated former Mayor Frank L. Rizzo, who ran as a Republican.

Democrat Carrie Saxon Perry became the first black woman mayor of a Northeastern city when

50 Largest Cities in the World

Rank	City	Population
1.	Mexico City	10,061,000
2.	Seoul, South Korea	9,645,932
3.	Tokyo	8,353,674
4.	Moscow	8,275,000
5.	Bombay, India	8,227,332
6.	New York City	7,262,700
7.	São Paulo, Brazil	7,033,529
8.	Shanghai	6,880,000
9.	London	6,767,500
10.	Jakarta, Indonesia	6,503,449
11.	Cairo, Egypt	6,133,000
12.	Hong Kong	5,930,000
13.	Beijing (Peking)	5,760,000
14.	Teheran, Iran	5,734,199
15.	Tianjin (Tientsin), China	5,300,000
16.	Karachi, Pakistan	5,208,170
17.	Bangkok, Thailand	5,153,902
18.	Rio de Janeiro, Brazil	5,093,232
19.	Delhi, India	4,884,234
20.	Leningrad, Soviet Union	4,295,000
21.	Santiago, Chile	4,225,299
22.	Lima, Peru	4,164,597
23.	Shenyang (Shen-yang), China	4,130,000
24.	Bogotá, Colombia	3,982,941
25.	Pusan, South Korea	3,516,807
26.	Ho Chi Minh City, Vietnam	3,419,978
27.	Sydney, Australia	3,364,858
28.	Wuhan (Wu-han), China	3,340,000
29.	Calcutta, India	3,305,006
30.	Madras, India	3,276,622
31.	Los Angeles	3,259,300
32.	Guangzhou (Canton), China	3,220,000
33.	Madrid, Spain	3,188,297
34.	Berlin (East and West), East and West Germany	3,062,979
35.	Chicago	3,009,530
36.	Yokohama, Japan	2,992,644
37.	Baghdad, Iraq	2,969,000
38.	Lahore, Pakistan	2,952,689
39.	Buenos Aires, Argentina	2,908,001
40.	Melbourne, Australia	2,832,893
41.	Rome	2,830,569
42.	Istanbul, Turkey	2,772,708
43.	Chongqing (Ch'ung-ch'ing), China	2,730,000
44.	Pyongyang, North Korea	2,639,448
45.	Osaka, Japan	2,636,260
46.	Harbin, China	2,590,000
47.	Hanoi, Vietnam	2,570,905
48.	Chengdu (Ch'eng-tu), China	2,540,000
49.	Bangalore, India	2,476,355
50.	Kiev, Soviet Union	2,409,000

Sources: 1986 Bureau of the Census estimates for cities of the United States; censuses or government estimates for cities of other countries.

50 Largest Cities in the United States

Rank	City	Population*	Per cent change in population since 1980	Mayor†
1.	New York City	7,262,700	+2.5	Edward I. Koch (D, 1/90)
2.	Los Angeles	3,259,300	+9.8	Thomas Bradley (NP, 6/89)
3.	Chicago	3,009,530	+0.1	Eugene Sawyer (D‡)
4.	Houston	1,728,910	+7.3	Kathryn J. Whitmire (NP, 1/90)
5.	Philadelphia	1,642,900	−2.7	W. Wilson Goode (D, 1/92)
6.	Detroit	1,086,220	−9.7	Coleman A. Young (D, 1/90)
7.	San Diego	1,015,190	+16.0	Maureen F. O'Connor (D, 1/89)
8.	Dallas	1,003,520	+10.9	Annette G. Strauss (NP, 5/89)
9.	Phoenix	914,350	+12.8	Terry Goddard (D, 12/89)
10.	San Antonio	894,070	+13.1	Henry G. Cisneros (D, 4/89)
11.	Baltimore	752,800	−4.3	Kurt L. Schmoke (D, 12/91)
12.	San Francisco	749,000	+10.3	Art Agnos (NP, 1/92)
13.	Indianapolis	719,820	+2.7	William H. Hudnut III (R, 12/91)
14.	San Jose	712,080	+13.1	Thomas McEnery (D, 12/90)
15.	Memphis	652,640	+1.0	Richard C. Hackett (I, 12/91)
16.	Washington, D.C.	626,000	−1.9	Marion S. Barry, Jr. (D, 1/91)
17.	Jacksonville	610,030	+12.8	Thomas L. Hazouri (D, 7/91)
18.	Milwaukee	605,090	−4.9	Henry W. Maier (D, 4/88)
19.	Boston	573,600	+1.9	Raymond L. Flynn (D, 1/92)
20.	Columbus, Ohio	566,030	+0.1	Dana G. Rinehart (R, 1/92)
21.	New Orleans	554,500	−0.6	Sidney J. Barthelemy (D, 5/90)
22.	Cleveland	535,830	−6.6	George V. Voinovich (R, 11/89)
23.	Denver	505,000	+2.5	Federico Peña (D, 6/91)
24.	El Paso	491,800	+15.6	Jonathan W. Rogers (NP, 4/89)
25.	Seattle	486,200	−1.5	Charles Royer (NP, 1/90)
26.	Nashville, Tenn.	473,670	+4.0	William H. Boner (D, 9/91)
27.	Austin, Tex.	466,550	+25.2	Frank C. Cooksey (NP, 5/88)
28.	Oklahoma City, Okla.	446,120	+10.4	Ronald J. Norik (D, 4/91)
29.	Kansas City, Mo.	441,170	−1.5	Richard L. Berkley (NP, 4/91)
30.	Fort Worth, Tex.	429,550	+11.5	Bob Bolen (NP, 4/89)
31.	St. Louis, Mo.	426,300	−5.9	Vincent L. Schoemehl, Jr. (D, 4/89)
32.	Atlanta, Ga.	421,910	−0.7	Andrew J. Young, Jr. (D, 1/90)
33.	Long Beach, Calif.	396,280	+9.6	Ernie Kell (D, 7/88)
34.	Portland, Ore.	387,870	−2.2	J. E. Clark (NP, 11/88)
35.	Pittsburgh, Pa.	387,490	−8.6	Richard S. Caliguiri (D, 1/90)
36.	Miami, Fla.	373,940	+3.6	Xavier L. Suarez (NP, 11/89)
37.	Tulsa, Okla.	373,750	+7.9	Dick Crawford (D, 5/88)
38.	Honolulu, Hawaii	372,330	+1.2	Frank Fasi (R, 1/89)
39.	Cincinnati, Ohio	369,750	−4.1	Charles J. Luken (D, 11/89)
40.	Albuquerque, N. Mex.	366,750	+10.4	Ken Schultz (NP, 12/89)
41.	Tucson, Ariz.	358,850	+6.0	Thomas J. Volgi (D, 12/91)
42.	Oakland, Calif.	356,960	+5.2	Lionel J. Wilson (D, 7/89)
43.	Minneapolis, Minn.	356,840	−3.8	Donald M. Fraser (D, 1/90)
44.	Charlotte, N.C.	352,070	+7.9	Sue Myrick (R, 11/89)
45.	Omaha, Nebr.	349,270	+1.9	Bernie Simon (NP, 6/89)
46.	Toledo, Ohio	340,680	−3.9	Donna Owens (R, 12/89)
47.	Virginia Beach, Va.	333,400	+27.2	Robert G. Jones (D, 6/88)
48.	Buffalo, N.Y.	324,820	−9.2	James D. Griffin (D, 12/89)
49.	Sacramento, Calif.	323,550	+17.3	Anne Rudin (NP, 12/89)
50.	Newark, N.J.	316,300	−3.9	Sharpe James (D, 7/90)

*1986 estimates (source: U.S. Bureau of the Census).
†The letters in parentheses represent the mayor's party, with D meaning Democrat, R Republican, I Independent, and NP nonpartisan. The date is when the term of office ends (source: mayors' offices).
‡Chosen acting mayor on Dec. 2, 1987, following the death of Mayor Harold Washington on November 25. Will serve at least until April 1989.

General revenue‡	Total debt outstanding‡	Unemployment rate§	Cost of living index#	Per capita income**	Sales tax rate††
$23,048,000,000	$12,127,073,000	5.5%	142.9	$15,076	8.25%
2,334,000,000	3,372,291,000	6.6	115.7	14,526	6.5
2,166,000,000	1,506,108,000	6.6	114.2 est.	14,655	8
1,175,000,000	2,273,200,000	9.3	102.1	14,517	8
1,983,000,000	2,294,981,000	5.0	118.0	13,746	6
1,393,000,000	911,886,000	9.5	109.5 est.	13,943	4
626,000,000	817,544,000	4.9	116.8	13,474	6
670,000,000	807,308,000	6.7	110.8	15,861	8
690,000,000	1,002,953,000	5.4	109.1	13,199	6.5
392,000,000	1,857,246,000	8.3	98.5	11,540	7.5
1,335,000,000	999,930,000	4.5	105.7	13,563	5
1,747,000,000	1,250,883,000	4.1	126.2 est.	19,592	6.5
540,000,000	421,831,000	5.1	97.6	12,997	5
459,000,000	381,337,000	4.7	111.7	17,577	7
643,000,000	655,913,000	6.0	101.2	11,575	7.75
2,877,000,000	2,119,578,000	3.3	121.9 est.	17,724	6
529,000,000	2,714,000,000	5.7	103.6 est.	14,184	5
471,000,000	512,000,000	4.8	116.4 est.	12,168	5
1,090,000,000	616,000,000	2.2	123.0 est.	15,932	5
355,000,000	753,000,000	5.1	103.3	12,609	5.5
582,000,000	796,000,000	9.2	98.7	12,389	9
424,000,000	390,000,000	5.9	101.7	14,216	6.5
740,000,000	670,000,000	6.7	103.5	15,783	7.1
208,000,000	345,000,000	11.0	98.6	8,745	7
444,000,000	637,000,000	5.8	107.8	14,787	7.9
577,000,000	1,177,000,000	4.8	100.4 est.	12,125	7.75
357,000,000	1,515,000,000	6.9	106.1	13,483	8
318,000,000	390,000,000	5.9	97.5	13,201	6
443,000,000	430,000,000	6.1	105.2 est.	13,821	6.225
270,000,000	515,000,000	7.5	105.3 est.	14,138	7.25
465,000,000	406,000,000	7.3	96.0	13,991	6.1
501,000,000	1,019,000,000	4.5	107.5	13,848	5
437,000,000	423,000,000	6.6	115.0 est.	14,526	6.5
309,000,000	506,000,000	5.1	108.5	13,247	0
308,000,000	378,000,000	7.1	96.1	12,680	6
239,000,000	237,000,000	6.4	107.4 est.	13,249	5
339,000,000	848,000,000	7.6	103.7 est.	12,962	7
450,000,000	234,000,000	3.6	149.8 est.	13,709	4
357,000,000	200,000,000	5.9	102.2	12,905	5.5
346,000,000	818,000,000	6.3	103.0	12,305	5
275,000,000	627,000,000	5.1	104.3	11,626	7
374,000,000	717,000,000	5.3	114.5 est.	16,365	7
524,000,000	1,574,000,000	3.9	113.7 est.	15,189	6.5
225,000,000	297,000,000	4.0	99.0	12,430	5
184,000,000	173,000,000	4.9	95.6	13,156	5.5
235,000,000	189,000,000	7.0	102.3	12,629	6
358,000,000	324,000,000	4.7	103.2	12,177	4.5
495,000,000	254,000,000	5.3	97.8	12,626	8
179,000,000	126,000,000	5.6	110.1	12,831	6
286,000,000	157,000,000	4.8	124.4	16,274	6

‡Figures are for 1984-1985 fiscal year (source: U.S. Bureau of the Census).
§July 1987 figures for metropolitan areas (source: U.S. Bureau of Labor Statistics).
#The higher the number, the higher the cost of living. Entries marked *est.* are YEAR BOOK estimates. Based on a survey done in spring 1986 (source: American Chamber of Commerce Researchers Association).
**1984 figures for metropolitan areas (source: U.S. Bureau of Economic Analysis).
††Total sales tax rate, including state, county, school district, and special district taxes (source: Tax Foundation, Inc.).

she was elected mayor of Hartford, Conn., on November 3. In Baltimore, prosecutor Kurt L. Schmoke, a 37-year-old Democrat, became that city's first elected black mayor with 79 per cent of the vote. In Charlotte, N.C., Republican Sue Myrick unseated that city's first black mayor, Democrat Harvey Gantt. Five-term Mayor Richard G. Hatcher of Gary, Ind., was defeated in a primary election in May. His opponent in the primary, Democrat Thomas V. Barnes, also a black, won the mayoral election in November. Mayors reelected in 1987 included Indianapolis' William H. Hudnut III, Houston's Kathryn J. Whitmire, Boston's Raymond L. Flynn, Denver's Federico Peña, and Miami's Xavier L. Suarez. Harold Washington, who was reelected mayor of Chicago on April 7, died of a heart attack on November 25. Alderman Eugene Sawyer was elected acting mayor on December 2 by a bitterly divided City Council.

Women won more mayoral elections in 1987. They held the office in 15 per cent of the cities with a·population of more than 30,000. In 1975, they held only 4 per cent of all mayoral offices in these cities. Cities with women at the helm included Houston; Toledo, Ohio; Corpus Christi, Dallas, and Galveston, Tex.; and Tampa, Fla.

AIDS. As of Nov. 9, 1987, eight United States cities had reported at least 1,000 cases of AIDS (acquired immune deficiency syndrome) since 1981. New York City led with 11,178 cases, followed by San Francisco with 4,321, Los Angeles with 3,758, and Houston with 1,521, according to the Centers for Disease Control in Atlanta, Ga. During the year, urban health officials were concerned about the disproportionate incidence of AIDS among blacks and Hispanics.

Clean Air. In December 1987, Congress approved an extension of deadlines under the federal Clean Air Act. The extension gave more than 60 cities, including New York City and Los Angeles, until Aug. 31, 1988, to reduce ozone and carbon monoxide pollution. After that date, the cities face a federal ban on new sources of ozone pollution, such as factories.

Funds Ended. On September 30, the federal government eliminated its revenue-sharing program, which in the fiscal year 1986 distributed $4.5 billion to 39,000 municipalities. The program's end caused financial problems in many small and midsized cities and resulted in higher taxes and a loss or reduction of many city services.

Cleveland Celebrates. Cleveland ended an almost 10-year-long financial crisis in June 1987 when it paid off the last of its $110-million deficit. City government officials celebrated by burning facsimiles of the notes on which the city defaulted in December 1978.　　　　Donna Rosene Leff

See also ELECTIONS and articles on individual cities. In WORLD BOOK, see CITY.

CIVIL RIGHTS. In its annual report on human rights throughout the world, released on Feb. 19, 1987, the United States Department of State severely criticized the Soviet Union and other Communist or Soviet-backed countries for continued abuses. The report said that despite the release of prominent dissidents from Soviet labor camps, thousands of other dissidents remained imprisoned or confined in psychiatric institutions. The report also condemned the "persecution" and "harassment" of minority groups within the Soviet Union and the restrictions on Russian Jews wishing to emigrate.

The report did not take into account 140 Soviet political prisoners pardoned on February 10, in what was believed to be the largest such release since 1956. The Soviets freed another 150 dissidents on Feb. 17, 1987. On February 20, they released Jewish dissident Iosif Z. Begun, jailed in 1983 for allegedly anti-Soviet writings about the plight of Soviet Jews. Earlier in February, demonstrators protesting Begun's imprisonment were shoved and punched by Moscow police. On June 30, the Supreme Soviet of the U.S.S.R., the national legislature, passed a law giving citizens an unprecedented right of legal appeal against officials violating their rights.

Soviet-bloc countries experienced demonstrations for human rights in 1987. On March 15, about 1,500 Hungarians marched through Budapest for three hours in a call for democracy and against Soviet domination. On January 7, Charter 77, a Czechoslovak human rights group, marked its 10th anniversary by issuing a document calling on citizens to assert their legal rights and on the government to permit basic freedoms. Human rights and peace activists from 13 countries held a three-day meeting in an unfinished church in Warsaw, Poland, in May, despite government harassment and condemnation.

Nicaragua. *La Prensa,* the opposition newspaper closed down by the Nicaraguan government in June 1986, resumed publication on Oct. 1, 1987, free of censorship. *La Prensa's* return to the newsstand was part of a peace accord approved in August by Nicaragua and four other Central American countries. On September 22, the government announced an end to censorship of the media. On September 23, Nicaragua's President Daniel Ortega lifted a 21-month ban on Radio Católica, the country's Roman Catholic radio station, but the station was not allowed to broadcast news.

Asia. In South Korea, opposition to the government of President Chun Doo Hwan was galvanized by disclosures that a student at Seoul National University, Park Chong Chol, had been tortured and killed by police on January 14 while being questioned about the whereabouts of a campus radical leader. It was the first time Chun's

Protected by National Guardsmen, an estimated 20,000 demonstrators take part in a civil rights march in Cumming, Ga., on January 24.

government, which had often been accused of police brutality, had acknowledged such abuses.

Prospects for impending constitutional changes seemed to be crushed when Chun in April ordered a halt to debate on constitutional reform until after the 1988 Summer Olympics, which are to be held in Seoul. At the same time, Chun announced he would retain the present system of choosing the president by electoral college. Opponents denounced this method as a step toward rigging the election in the government's favor. Under pressure from three weeks of street demonstrations, Chun relented. On July 1, he approved a series of constitutional changes, including direct popular vote in presidential elections. On December 16, South Korea held its first direct presidential election since 1971.

In January 1987, the Chinese government cracked down on public demonstrations in the face of widespread rallies by students demanding greater democracy and freedom of expression. The conservative backlash also led to the firing of university professors and newspaper editors and the resignation on January 16 of Communist Party General Secretary Hu Yaobang.

Civil Rights March. An estimated 20,000 people marched through Cumming, Ga., near Atlanta, on January 24 in one of the largest civil rights demonstrations since 1965. The march was a response to the disruption of an interracial "walk for brotherhood" held a week earlier in Cumming, the county seat of Forsyth County, which has no black residents. At that march, several hundred members of the Ku Klux Klan and Klan sympathizers had thrown stones and bottles and shouted epithets at marchers. Although counterdemonstrators also appeared at the second march, nearly 2,300 police officers and members of the Georgia National Guard protected the marchers and prevented violence.

Howard Beach. Three white teen-agers were convicted of manslaughter in December 1987 for their involvement in an attack on three black men in the Howard Beach section of New York City in December 1986. One of the black men, Michael Griffith, died after being struck by an automobile as he fled from his attackers onto a highway. A fourth defendant was acquitted in 1987, and seven other teen-agers awaited trial for attempted murder and other charges.

Affirmative Action. On Feb. 25, 1987, the Supreme Court of the United States approved the use of temporary racial quotas for both promotions and hiring in cases where there has been severe discrimination against blacks in the past. The ruling upheld an Alabama program that required the state police to promote equal numbers of blacks and whites.

On March 25, the Supreme Court ruled that employers may take gender into account when determining promotions even if there is no proven history of sex discrimination. The case involved a male employee of the Santa Clara County (Calif.) Transportation Agency, who claimed that a less qualified woman had been promoted over him. The agency had promoted the woman in an effort to create a more balanced work force.

Death Penalty. On April 22, the Supreme Court upheld Georgia's death penalty system despite statistical evidence that people convicted of killing whites receive the death penalty far more frequently than people convicted of killing blacks.

Advances for Women. A study by Rutgers The State University of New Jersey in Camden reported on May 26 that the number of women in state legislatures has grown in every election since 1969. The 7,461 state legislators in 1987 included 1,157 women—or 15.5 per cent, compared with 301 or 4 per cent in 1969.

More than 12,000 female and minority employees of San Francisco were awarded a total of $35.4 million in special raises under a comparable pay agreement reached on March 18, 1987. The wages of the affected employees had been lower than those of white men in jobs requiring comparable skills. In 1987, 13 states began to adjust their employees' compensation, based at least partly on the concept of comparable worth.

Barriers to membership by women in private all-male clubs were weakened on May 4 when the Supreme Court ruled that Rotary Clubs had no constitutional right to ban women from the organization. The case arose when Rotary International, a service organization, tried to revoke the charter of the Rotary Club of Duarte, Calif., for admitting three women as members. The court upheld a California appeals court ruling that a state law barring discrimination by business establishments applied to Rotary Clubs because the organization was often used for business purposes and by nonmembers. The ruling did not outlaw all-male private clubs, however.

In June, Lions International, another international service club, voted to admit women as members. Kiwanis International followed suit in July.

Protecting AIDS Victims. The Supreme Court ruled on March 3 that a 1973 law barring discrimination against the handicapped in federally aided programs also applies to people with contagious diseases. Although the case involved a teacher with tuberculosis, the ruling was expected to benefit victims of AIDS (acquired immune deficiency syndrome). The justices stated, however, that the federal law does not protect people who pose a real risk of infection to others or whose disease prevents them from doing their job.   Louis W. Koenig

In WORLD BOOK, see CIVIL RIGHTS.

CLASSICAL MUSIC. The experiences of the Detroit Symphony Orchestra served as an example of the ups-and-downs of United States musical institutions in 1987. In the spring, its directors announced that by the fall of 1988, the ensemble would return to a rebuilt Orchestra Hall, said to be the most acoustically perfect orchestral hall in the United States. The symphony had left the hall for bigger quarters 50 years ago.

Restoration was underway when, in September 1987, shortly after the start of the performance season, orchestra members went on strike. The musicians wanted a 20 per cent salary increase, while management asked them to take an 11 per cent cut. On December 14, the musicians ratified a new three-year contract providing a pay raise of about 16 per cent in several steps.

Budget Squeeze. Rising costs combined with increasingly scarce funds from both public and private sources left the fiscal condition of many musical organizations hovering between serious and critical. The Rochester (N.Y.) Philharmonic had a brief work stoppage in October over wages. The Omaha (Nebr.) Symphony was silent all spring. The Oakland (Calif.) Symphony Orchestra went out of business, though its players created a season of their own, beginning in July. So, too, did members of the San Antonio Symphony after they were asked to take a 40 per cent pay cut.

The San Francisco Opera canceled its already short summer season for financial reasons. The Seattle Opera Association, world-renowned for its presentations of German composer Richard Wagner's *The Ring of the Nibelung*, announced that its 1988 performance would be canceled. The Colorado Opera Festival in Colorado Springs also suspended its 1987-1988 season.

Upbeat News. But there was positive news to balance the financial negatives on the music scene. In Houston, the Symphony Orchestra celebrated a year in the black. Houston's new Gus S. Wortham Theater Center, a $70-million, two-theater showcase, had a ceremonial concert opening in May and a dramatic opera opening in October, when the Houston Grand Opera presented a new production of Italian composer Giuseppe Verdi's *Aïda*. The Lyric Opera of Chicago ended a two-year fund-raising campaign by exceeding its $25-million goal. In Austin, Tex., a new company, the Lyric Opera, was formed. In Pittsburgh, Pa., the Opera, the Civic Light Opera, and two local dance companies took up residence in a new home, the former Stanley Theater, now refurbished as the Benedum Center for the Performing Arts.

A June gala opened the Alice Busch Opera Theatre, the new home of the Glimmerglass Opera, near Cooperstown, N.Y. And in Tampa, Fla., the Tampa Bay Performing Arts Center opened in September.

A cast of hundreds take part in an extravagant staging of Giuseppe Verdi's opera *Aïda* in May at a 3,000-year-old temple beside the Nile River in Egypt.

Premieres. Not only were there new theaters, but there also were new musical creations for them and for other halls around the world. The most publicized debut occurred in Houston with the official premiere in October of John Adams' *Nixon in China*, an opera about President Richard M. Nixon's groundbreaking 1972 visit to China. Adams peopled his first opera with Richard and Pat Nixon, Henry A. Kissinger, and Chinese leaders Mao Zedong (Mao Tse-tung in the traditional Wade-Giles spelling) and Zhou Enlai (Chou Enlai). Although praised by some critics, the opera was judged to be "worth a few giggles but hardly a strong candidate for the standard repertory" by *The New York Times.*

Two operas with literary sources also had prominent debuts in 1987. Milan's La Scala opera house in January introduced Flavio Testi's *Riccardo III*, based on William Shakespeare's *Richard III*, to mixed critical and audience reaction. In West Germany, the Munich Opera Festival turned in July to the tale of the Trojan women carried off by the Greeks after the burning of Troy. Composer Aribert Riemann used this famous story as the basis for *Troades*, a two-hour opera in one act.

Other Opera Premieres in 1987 included David Winkler's *All's Well That Ends Well* at New York City's Marymount Manhattan Theatre in January; Malcolm Fox's *The Iron Man*, performed by chil-

dren at the State Opera of South Australia in Adelaide in April; and Gordon Getty's *Plump Jack*, a piece about Shakespeare's comic character Sir John Falstaff performed in concert by the San Francisco Symphony in June.

Revivals. Other unusual presentations included the revival in Philadelphia by the American Music Theater Festival of Harry Partch's *Revelation in the Courthouse Park* (1961) featuring the composer's 43-note scale and unusual handmade instruments; the first U.S. performance of British composer Stephen Oliver's *Beauty and the Beast* by Opera Theater of St. Louis, Mo., in June; and Philip Glass's *Satyagraha* (1980) by Chicago's Lyric Opera.

Orchestral Debuts. The symphonic world also had its share of premieres. The Philadelphia Orchestra entered into the spirit of the 200th anniversary of the U.S. Constitution by commissioning six works, including *Transfigured Notes* by Milton Babbitt, Concerto for Orchestra by Stephen Stucky, and *Revelations* by Nicholas Thorne.

William Bolcom's Symphony No. 4 was among the important new works of 1987. The St. Louis Symphony Orchestra premiered the work in March.

Elliott Carter's first orchestral composition in a decade, *A Celebration of Some 100 × 150 Notes*, had its first performance by the Houston Symphony in April. It was one of 21 new fanfares commissioned by the orchestra for the Texas sesquicentennial.

Time magazine called John Harbison's Symphony No. 2 "luminous." It was premiered by the San Francisco Symphony in May, a month after Harbison won the Pulitzer Prize for music. The symphony's "New and Unusual Music" series was highlighted by the introduction in December of *The W. of Babylon* by Charles Wuorinen.

Special Events. The Vienna Philharmonic performed all of German composer Ludwig van Beethoven's symphonies and concertos at New York City's Carnegie Hall in March. In May, tenor Placido Domingo led a cast from the Opera Company of Verona, Italy, in a grand performance of *Aïda* at Luxor, Egypt, on the site of a 3,000-year-old temple beside the Nile River.

"Sound Celebration"—held to mark the 50th anniversary of the Louisville (Ky.) Orchestra—brought together composers and performers of new music for 10 days of concerts and discussions. And in November, tenor Luciano Pavarotti, cellist Yo-Yo Ma, and a host of other musicians gathered at Carnegie Hall in a "Music for Life" concert to raise money for the care of victims of AIDS (acquired immune deficiency syndrome).

Concerts in Cremona, Italy, honored violin maker Antonio Stradivari on the 250th anniversary of his death. Concerts, recordings, and a biography marked the 50th anniversary of the death of American composer George Gershwin. And a gala concert in Chicago on October 9 celebrated the 75th birthday of Chicago Symphony conductor Sir Georg Solti. Earlier in 1987, he won his 25th Grammy Award, more than any other performer in the history of that recording prize.

Conductors. British conductor Raymond Leppard took over the Indianapolis Symphony Orchestra as music director. Romanian conductor Sergiu Comissiona became music director of the New York City Opera, and Greek conductor Spiros Argiris will direct the Spoleto Festivals in Italy and Charleston, S.C.

Don Giovanni. Although considerable attention was paid to Verdi's opera *Otello* during 1987—its 100th anniversary—even more went to Austrian composer Wolfgang Amadeus Mozart's *Don Giovanni*, which was 200 years old. Although Prague, Czechoslovakia, the city of its premiere, ignored the occasion, a major new production conducted by Austria's Herbert von Karajan was presented in Salzburg, Austria. Perhaps the strangest salute came at the PepsiCo Summerfare festival in Purchase, N.Y., where a group of six singers called Companias Divas of Mexico presented *Donna Giovanni*. In another production, director Peter Sellars transferred the story to New York City's Spanish Harlem and made it a ghetto drama featuring prostitution and drugs.   Peter P. Jacobi

In WORLD BOOK, see CLASSICAL MUSIC; OPERA.

CLOTHING. See FASHION.

COAL. United States coal production was expected to reach record levels in 1987, according to the annual estimate issued by the National Coal Association (NCA), an industry group, on June 23. The NCA forecast output at 897 million short tons (814 million metric tons), an increase of 9 million short tons (8 million metric tons) over 1986 and about 1 million short tons (0.9 million metric tons) more than the previous record in 1984.

United States coal consumption in 1987 was expected to reach 892 million short tons (809 million metric tons), about 2 million short tons (1.8 million metric tons) more than in 1986. Electric utilities were expected to use 694 million short tons (630 million metric tons) of coal, equaling the consumption record set in 1985.

The NCA also predicted that the United States would export about 65 million short tons (59 million metric tons) of coal in 1987, a decline of about 6 million short tons (5 million metric tons) from 1986. The organization blamed the slump in exports on increased foreign competition and a growing worldwide surplus of coal. The NCA predicted that the coal glut would worsen as China continued to develop its extensive coal resources.

Chinese Mine. China opened the Antaibo coal mine, its largest open-pit coal mine, in September 1987 after two years of construction. The $650-million mine, developed by China and the Los Angeles-based Occidental Petroleum Corporation, is in Shanxi (Shansi) province in northern China.

Surface Protection. The Supreme Court of the United States on March 9 ruled that states can require coal-mining companies to leave millions of tons of coal in the ground in order to protect the land above underground mines. The decision upheld a Pennsylvania law requiring mining companies to leave enough coal in the ground to prevent the land and buildings above mines from sinking. Mine owners argued that the law unfairly deprived them of property without just compensation. The Supreme Court, however, said there was no evidence that the law made coal mining unprofitable, adding that states have the right to protect the environment.

Exemption Eliminated. President Ronald Reagan on May 7 signed legislation that eliminated a loophole in a 1977 federal law intended to reduce environmental damage caused by strip mining. Under the Surface Mining Control and Reclamation Act of 1977, operators of strip mines of 2 acres (0.8 hectare) or less were not required to restore land damaged by mining. The exemption was intended to shield small, family-owned mines from the high costs of land restoration and other environmental requirements. But some large mining companies had abused the provision by dividing large tracts into 2-acre plots, which they left unrestored when they finished mining.

Turkish Power Plant. Queensland, a big coal-producing state in northeastern Australia, on January 19 agreed to help build a $1-billion coal-fired power plant at Yumurtalik in southern Turkey. Queensland expected to sell the plant about $100-million worth of coal annually.

Labor Disputes. Coal miners in the Australian states of Queensland, New South Wales, and Tasmania staged a series of strikes in 1987 to protest a restructuring of Australia's coal industry. Australian coal companies, citing coal surpluses, rising costs, and foreign competition, closed six mines, resulting in the loss of more than 1,000 jobs.

Coal miners in Great Britain on September 21 began a limited ban on overtime work to protest a new disciplinary code issued by British Coal, the government agency that operates British mines. The National Union of Mineworkers opposed several provisions of the code, including the use of industrial tribunals to resolve disputes over the firing of miners. The union opposed the tribunals because employers would not be bound by the tribunals' decisions and so would be free to ignore judgments in favor of fired miners.   Michael Woods

See also ENERGY SUPPLY; ENVIRONMENTAL POLLUTION; MINING. In the Special Reports section, see STORMY DEBATE OVER ACID RAIN. In WORLD BOOK, see COAL.

COIN COLLECTING. After a design competition, the United States Treasury in April 1987 chose a $5 gold coin designed by Marcel Jovine of Closter, N.J., and a silver dollar designed by Patricia Verani of Londonderry, N.H., to commemorate the bicentennial of the U.S. Constitution. The face value of the coins was traditional and bore no relation to the prices charged for them. The silver dollar cost $26; the $5 gold piece cost $215.

Diane Wolf of New York City, a member of the federal Commission of Fine Arts, began a campaign in February to redesign all five circulating U.S. coins—the cent, nickel, dime, quarter, and half dollar. Four of the present U.S. coins have been in use for about 40 years, and federal law limits the use of a specific coin design to 25 years.

New Canadian Coin. Canada in May released a new 11-sided *aureate* (gold-colored) $1 coin depicting the common loon, a water bird found in Canada and the Northern United States. The coin, made from an aureate nickel alloy bonded to a nickel core, will replace Canada's $1 bill.

Coin Dealers Accused of Fraud. The Federal Trade Commission (FTC) in 1987 brought civil charges against two large coin dealers in the United States that allegedly defrauded customers. The FTC said the companies—Rare Coin Galleries of America in Boston and Security Rare Coin &

Monique Vézina, then Canada's minister of supply and services, introduces a new Canadian $1 coin at the Royal Canadian Mint in Winnipeg, Man., in April.

A rescue worker surveys the scene of a mud slide that killed at least 205 people when it struck a slum area outside Medellín, Colombia, in September.

Bullion Corporation in Minneapolis, Minn.—had inflated the value of coins they sold. Another company, New England Rare Coin Galleries in Boston, agreed to refund $1.5 million to customers but did not admit guilt.

The complaints against these companies inspired rare-coin industry trade groups such as the American Numismatics Association and the Professional Numismatists Guild to begin exploring the possibility of certification for coin dealers. To become certified, dealers would have to demonstrate that they price coins fairly.

Auction Prices. At a February sale in Los Angeles, an extremely rare silver proof 1885 *trade dollar* sold for $87,500. Trade dollars were minted officially from 1873 to 1883 for trade with the Orient. A limited number of proof trade dollars were produced illegally by mint officials in 1884 and 1885.

At another California auction, in West Hollywood in March, a gold octodrachm picturing King Antiochus III of Syria, who ruled Greek provinces in Asia from 223 to 187 B.C., sold for $140,000. The coin is believed to be the only one of its kind.

Gold and Silver prices were relatively stable in 1987. Silver, which had sold for $5 to $6 in 1986, climbed to $8.90 per troy ounce (31 grams) in early 1987 before settling back to $6.70. Gold was $486 per troy ounce at year-end.   David T. Alexander

In WORLD BOOK, see COIN COLLECTING.

COLOMBIA. Carlos Enrique Lehder Rivas, a top Colombian drug trafficker, was arrested by Colombian police and military personnel on Feb. 4, 1987, as part of a joint campaign against illegal drugs by the United States and Colombia. Under a 1979 extradition treaty, Lehder Rivas was flown to the United States, where he was wanted on narcotics charges.

It was apparent, however, that the power of Colombia's drug kingpins remained unchecked when Colombia's Supreme Court on June 25, 1987, declared unconstitutional a law ratifying Colombia's extradition treaty with the United States. The Supreme Court justices had received death threats and were under heavy security.

On December 30, a Colombian judge released Jorge Luis Ochoa Vásquez, who was wanted in the United States on drug charges. The United States protested to Colombia about the release.

Political violence in Colombia escalated in 1987, with reports of about 1,200 political killings. On October 11, Jaime Pardo Leal, leader of the Patriotic Union, Colombia's main leftist party, was assassinated. Some observers feared that a right wing terror campaign loomed.   Nathan A. Haverstock

See also LATIN AMERICA (Facts in Brief Table).

In WORLD BOOK, see COLOMBIA.

COLORADO. See STATE GOVERNMENT.

COMMON MARKET. See EUROPE.

COMMUNICATIONS. Jan. 1, 1987, was a milestone in the reshaping of United States telecommunications—the third anniversary of the breakup of the American Telephone and Telegraph Company (AT&T). In 1974, the Department of Justice filed an antitrust suit against AT&T. In 1982, AT&T agreed to divest itself of its 22 Bell System local telephone companies, settling the suit.

United States District Judge Harold H. Greene modified the agreement slightly, and, on Jan. 1, 1984, AT&T combined the 22 phone companies into seven independent firms called regional holding companies (RHC's). Jan. 1, 1987, was so important because one of the terms of the breakup was that the Justice Department would review the modified final judgment every three years and tell Greene whether any of the restrictions placed on the RHC's should be changed.

On February 2, the department recommended lifting restrictions forbidding the RHC's from manufacturing telecommunications equipment, providing information services such as computer databases, and supplying long-distance service. AT&T, congressional critics, and consumer activists, however, condemned the department's recommendations. The RHC's themselves objected to the proposal to allow them to provide long-distance service. The Justice Department withdrew this proposal on April 27, recommending instead that Greene consider RHC requests to enter the long-distance business on a case-by-case basis.

On Sept. 10, 1987, Greene ruled that restrictions forbidding the RHC's from manufacturing equipment and providing long-distance service would remain in force. He explained that the essential condition present at the time of the breakup—that the RHC's controlled almost all local telephone traffic—still existed, and that the RHC's could misuse this control to discriminate against potential competitors.

Greene partially lifted the ban preventing the RHC's from providing information services. He ruled that the RHC's could transmit data for information-service companies but could not produce the content. He also abolished the requirement that RHC's obtain the court's permission to enter businesses outside telecommunications.

New Chief at FCC. Mark S. Fowler on January 16 announced his resignation as chairman of the Federal Communications Commission (FCC). He left office on April 17, after serving for six years, and was succeeded by Commissioner Dennis R. Patrick. Fowler's last major act as chairman was to preside over a controversial plan increasing the monthly line charge for residential subscribers from $2 to $3.50 by April 1989.

Profit Policy Proposal. Patrick proposed on August 4 that the FCC change the manner in which it controls the profits of AT&T and local phone companies. Under procedures followed for decades, the FCC first computed a rate of return due to each firm—based on that firm's cost of doing business—and the firm set prices to earn that return. Patrick proposed that the FCC set a cap on prices and let the firm adjust its costs accordingly.

Deregulation Trade-Offs. Several state governments in 1987 approved measures to lighten regulatory requirements placed on AT&T and local telephone companies. The model for many of these measures was the *social contract* proposed by V. Louise McCarren, head of Vermont's Public Service Board. Under a social contract, a company agrees to freeze basic rates in return for a substantial deregulation of other services. Vermont tentatively approved a social contract with New England Telephone Company in 1986.

Another alternative was the *price incentive* rule, in which a state retains the rate-of-return regulation, but allows telephone companies that exceed an authorized benchmark return to keep some of the extra funds. New York announced such a plan in February 1987.

Colorado and Minnesota established a third method. These states deregulated some telephone services offered by competing firms but kept basic services under traditional rules.

In WORLD BOOK, see COMMUNICATION.

COMOROS. See AFRICA.

COMPUTER. In 1987, manufacturers of computers saw bright signs of recovery from the sales slump of recent years. Although industry annual growth rates fell from 62 per cent in the early 1980's to 18 per cent in 1986, analysts predicted growth of 25 to 30 per cent in 1987. They also became aware of a major shift in the industry structure as computer manufacturers turned away from building large, expensive mainframe computers and toward making smaller personal computers. The number of mainframe-manufacturing firms dropped from a high of six in the 1960's to only three by 1987. These were International Business Machines Corporation (IBM), Burroughs Corporation, and Control Data Corporation.

New IBM Models. In April 1987, IBM introduced its Personal System/2 (PS/2) model, hoping its sales would compensate for the 17 per cent drop in sales of IBM mainframe equipment.

The original PS/2 computer line included five machines built around 16-bit microprocessor chips and three top-of-the-line models designed around a powerful 80386 microprocessor, a 32-bit chip made by Intel Corporation of Santa Clara, Calif. (A bit is a 0 or 1, the basic "letters" of the computer "alphabet." The more bits a chip can handle at once, the faster the computer operates. A 32-bit chip can handle 2 million to 3 million instructions per second.)

An operable but outdated small computer meets its fate in Tokyo, where such machines become obsolete in as little as six months.

In August, IBM introduced another new machine, the Model 25, which is 40 per cent smaller yet twice as fast as the IBM Personal Computer (PC), and inexpensive by IBM standards. The Model 25 was designed for home and educational use and is versatile enough to be used by both young children learning to read and business executives preparing complex reports. The Model 25 is equipped with a *mouse*—a hand-operated device that moves the cursor around on the screen. Prices for the Model 25 range from $1,350 for a monochrome monitor to $1,695 for a full-color monitor.

After the introduction of its PS/2 line, IBM moved to protect against the development of PS/2 "clones," cheaper computers that run IBM-compatible programs. In July, Chips and Technologies, Incorporated, of Milpitas, Calif., introduced computer chips that would allow clone makers to compete with the new IBM line. IBM responded with lawsuits and threats of lawsuits while it awaited patents on the PS/2 parts.

Aggressive Apple. Apple Computer, Incorporated, of Cupertino, Calif., in March introduced a new generation of personal computers, the Macintosh SE and the Macintosh II. The SE uses a 16-bit microprocessor, while the Macintosh II contains a 32-bit microprocessor. Both machines can be adapted to run IBM software.

Apple then began an aggressive marketing campaign aimed at businesses, particularly promoting the Macintosh's desk-top publishing capabilities. Desk-top publishing software combines text and graphics and lays out pages for reports, magazines, newsletters, and even books.

Soon after their introduction, the new Macintosh models became best sellers in the industry. The profits enabled Apple in April to declare its first cash dividend on stock.

In August, Apple unveiled Hypertext, new software for organizing Macintosh computer files into "stacks." Hypertext also allows users to customize commercially available software.

Other New Models. Tandy Corporation of Fort Worth, Tex., previewed four new machines in August, with emphasis on quality performance at low prices. Its Model 4000, with the Intel 80386 microprocessor, at $4,299 was priced more than 35 per cent lower than comparable models from IBM and Compaq Computer Corporation of Houston.

Compaq, in September 1986, became the first manufacturer to introduce a computer with the 80386 chip. In September 1987, Compaq introduced the two fastest and most powerful microcomputers in the world—the Deskpro 386-20 and the Portable 386.

Other personal computers using the Intel 80386 chip were introduced during the year by American Telephone & Telegraph Company and NCR Corporation of Dayton, Ohio.

Adapting to Ada. A programming language called Ada received strong support in 1987. The U.S. Department of Defense (DOD) insists that systems designers use Ada to prepare programs that govern military aircraft and missile systems. Software costs for sophisticated military and defense projects run into the hundreds of millions of dollars. In past years, although program contractors were strongly urged to include Ada as part of their systems package, as many as 70 per cent of the contractors requested and received waivers on the basis of extended delays or cost overruns. Not any more, warned the DOD in 1987, as it tightened its mandate to standardize computer language and reduce software development expenses. As a result, analysts expect the market for Ada programming expertise to rise from $130-million in 1987 to $500 million by 1990.

Supercomputers grew faster and more powerful in 1987. Supercomputers, 25 or more times more powerful than the largest mainframes, are used mainly by mathematicians, scientists, and aircraft and automobile designers.

Intel Corporation in August introduced its second generation of scientific supercomputers, which it claims are 10 times faster than the first generation. Each supercomputer contains up to 128 Intel 80386 microprocessors.

The Japanese announced their first supercomputer in May. The machines are made by NEC Corporation of Japan and sold by Honeywell, Incorporated, of Minneapolis.

The world's most advanced supercomputer system, built by the National Aeronautics and Space Administration, was dedicated in March at Ames Research Center in Mountain View, Calif. The system was designed to simulate weather patterns, the evolution of galaxies, and wind-tunnel tests of aerodynamic designs. It can perform up to 1.72 billion computations per second. The heart of the system is a Cray-2 supercomputer made by Cray Research, Incorporated, of Minneapolis.

In October, Control Data Corporation unveiled two new supercomputers with price tags that were half of those for Cray's least expensive model. One of the Control Data supercomputers costs less than $1 million.

Fax for PC's. A low-cost JT Fax machine for IBM PC's and clones was introduced in mid-1987 by Asher Technologies Corporation of Roswell, Ga. Facsimile (fax) transmission is a fast, cost-effective way to send documents. The Asher Fax machine costs $395, and a portable model is available for $495.   Howard Bierman

See also ELECTRONICS. In WORLD BOOK, see COMPUTER.

CONGO. See AFRICA.

CONGRESS OF THE UNITED STATES. With both the Senate and the House of Representatives firmly controlled by the Democrats in 1987, Congress and the Republican Administration of President Ronald Reagan engaged in a yearlong test of wills over the federal budget. The fiscal tug of war finally produced a budget by a single vote. In the early hours of December 22, following a month of negotiations, the House approved, 209 to 208, the biggest spending bill in history: $603.9 billion in spending authority for the 1988 fiscal year that began on Oct. 1, 1987.

The measure, which the Senate approved 59 to 30 on the same day, replaced 13 separate spending bills that Congress had hoped to enact before the start of the fiscal year. It was one of two bills designed to reduce the projected 1988 deficit of $180 billion by $33.2 billion. That goal was fixed after the conclusion of bipartisan "summit" negotiations on the budget following the October 19 stock market collapse. The second bill included $9 billion in tax increases, mostly affecting wealthy individuals and corporations, plus assorted spending cuts.

In its final days before adjournment, Congress voted $8.1 million in humanitarian aid to the *contra* rebels fighting the Marxist government of Nicaragua; passed a two-year $30.6-billion housing bill that would fund housing-assistance programs for low-income Americans; scrapped a 1952 law that permitted the government to bar foreigners holding unpopular political views from entering the United States; authorized $20.1 billion for air-traffic control and other aviation projects; and agreed to a $4-billion rescue of the Farm Credit System, a government-supervised, farmer-owned system of banks, through the sale of federally backed bonds. Strong opposition to contra aid by House Democrats came within one vote of derailing the session-ending budget compromise.

Tests of Strength. Congressional Democrats sought—and won—early tests of strength with the President, who had been weakened by the Iran-contra affair, an arms-sale scandal that cast a cloud over the Reagan Administration in late 1986 and 1987 (see IRAN-CONTRA AFFAIR). Democrats risked nothing by embracing sure-thing programs popular with Republicans, such as a clean-water bill. And Reagan showed himself equally adept at posturing by wielding a veto pen that had no punch behind it because the vetoes were sure to be overridden.

Under the leadership of its new Speaker, James C. Wright, Jr. (D., Tex.), the House on January 8 voted 406 to 8 to pass a $20-billion clean-water bill that Reagan had vetoed in 1986. The measure, extending the Clean Water Act of 1972 and providing funds for sewage-treatment plants, sailed through the Senate on a 93 to 6 vote on January 21. Arguing that the bill was "loaded with waste," Reagan vetoed it nine days later. The House gave the President his first legislative defeat of the year on February 3, voting 401 to 26 to override his veto. The Senate assured enactment of the bill the next day by voting 86 to 14 to override.

The second test of strength involved a six-year, $87.5-billion highway and mass transit bill that passed the House 407 to 17 on March 18. Also approved was companion legislation permitting states to raise the speed limit on rural sections of interstate highways from 55 to 65 miles (88 to 105 kilometers) per hour. Although Reagan vowed to veto the bill, which contained $4 billion more than he wanted, the Senate passed it two days later, 79 to 17. Visiting the Capitol on May 2, Reagan met with 13 Republican senators who were on record as favoring an override of his veto. "I beg you to vote with me on this," he said. None of the 13 were swayed, however, and on April 2 the Senate overrode the veto 67 to 33, exactly the two-thirds majority needed.

But Reagan won a veto battle in June after both the Senate and House gave lopsided approval to a bill affecting the Federal Communications Commission (FCC). The legislation directed the FCC to continue enforcing the Fairness Doctrine, a regulation requiring broadcasters to air conflicting views on key public issues. The FCC in 1985 is-

Members of the United States House of Representatives

The House of Representatives of the second session of the 100th Congress consisted of 258 Democrats and 177 Republicans (not including representatives from American Samoa, the District of Columbia, Guam, Puerto Rico, and the Virgin Islands) when it convened in January 1988, compared with 258 Democrats and 177 Republicans when the first session of the 100th Congress convened. This table shows congressional district, legislator, and party affiliation. Asterisk (*) denotes those who served in the 99th Congress; dagger (†) denotes "at large."

Alabama
1. H. L. Callahan, R.*
2. William L. Dickinson, R.*
3. Bill Nichols, D.*
4. Tom Bevill, D.*
5. Ronnie G. Flippo, D.*
6. Ben Erdreich, D.*
7. Claude Harris, D.

Alaska
†Donald E. Young, R.*

Arizona
1. John J. Rhodes III, R.
2. Morris K. Udall, D.*
3. Bob Stump, R.*
4. Jon Kyl, R.
5. Jim Kolbe, R.*

Arkansas
1. Bill Alexander, D.*
2. Tommy Robinson, D.*
3. John P. Hammerschmidt, R.*
4. Beryl F. Anthony, Jr., D.*

California
1. Douglas H. Bosco, D.*
2. Wally Herger, R.
3. Robert T. Matsui, D.*
4. Vic Fazio, D.*
5. Nancy Pelosi, D.
6. Barbara Boxer, D.*
7. George Miller, D.*
8. Ronald V. Dellums, D.*
9. Fortney H. (Pete) Stark, D.*
10. Don Edwards, D.*
11. Tom Lantos, D.*
12. Ernest L. Konnyu, R.
13. Norman Y. Mineta, D.*
14. Norman D. Shumway, R.*
15. Tony Coelho, D.*
16. Leon E. Panetta, D.*
17. Charles Pashayan, Jr., R.*
18. Richard H. Lehman, D.*
19. Robert J. Lagomarsino, R.*
20. William M. Thomas, R.*
21. Elton Gallegly, R.
22. Carlos J. Moorhead, R.*
23. Anthony C. Beilenson, D.*
24. Henry A. Waxman, D.*
25. Edward R. Roybal, D.*
26. Howard L. Berman, D.*
27. Mel Levine, D.*
28. Julian C. Dixon, D.*
29. Augustus F. (Gus) Hawkins, D.*
30. Matthew G. Martinez, D.*
31. Mervyn M. Dymally, D.*
32. Glenn M. Anderson, D.*
33. David Dreier, R.*
34. Esteban E. Torres, D.*
35. Jerry Lewis, R.*
36. George E. Brown, Jr., D.*
37. Alfred A. McCandless, R.*
38. Robert K. Dornan, R.*
39. William E. Dannemeyer, R.*
40. Robert E. Badham, R.*
41. William D. Lowery, R.*
42. Daniel E. Lungren, R.*
43. Ronald C. Packard, R.*
44. Jim Bates, D.*
45. Duncan L. Hunter, R.*

Colorado
1. Patricia Schroeder, D.*
2. David Skaggs, D.
3. Ben Nighthorse Campbell, D.
4. Hank Brown, R.*
5. Joel Hefley, R.
6. Daniel Schaefer, R.*

Connecticut
1. Barbara B. Kennelly, D.*
2. Samuel Gejdenson, D.*
3. Bruce A. Morrison, D.*
4. Christopher Shays, R.
5. John G. Rowland, R.*
6. Nancy L. Johnson, R.*

Delaware
†Thomas R. Carper, D.*

Florida
1. Earl Hutto, D.*
2. Bill Grant, D.
3. Charles E. Bennett, D.*
4. Bill Chappell, Jr., D.*
5. Bill McCollum, R.*
6. Kenneth H. (Buddy) MacKay, D.*
7. Sam M. Gibbons, D.*
8. C. W. Bill Young, R.*
9. Michael Bilirakis, R.*
10. Andy Ireland, R.*
11. Bill Nelson, D.*
12. Thomas F. Lewis, R.*
13. Connie Mack III, R.*
14. Daniel A. Mica, D.*
15. E. Clay Shaw, Jr., R.*
16. Lawrence J. Smith, D.*
17. William Lehman, D.*
18. Claude D. Pepper, D.*
19. Dante B. Fascell, D.*

Georgia
1. Lindsay Thomas, D.*
2. Charles F. Hatcher, D.*
3. Richard B. Ray, D.*
4. Pat Swindall, R.*
5. John Lewis, D.
6. Newt Gingrich, R.*
7. George Darden, D.*
8. J. Roy Rowland, D.*
9. Edgar L. Jenkins, D.*
10. Doug Barnard, Jr., D.*

Hawaii
1. Patricia Saiki, R.
2. Daniel K. Akaka, D.*

Idaho
1. Larry Craig, R.*
2. Richard H. Stallings, D.*

Illinois
1. Charles A. Hayes, D.*
2. Gus Savage, D.*
3. Marty Russo, D.*
4. Jack Davis, R.
5. William O. Lipinski, D.*
6. Henry J. Hyde, R.*
7. Cardiss Collins, D.*
8. Dan Rostenkowski, D.*
9. Sidney R. Yates, D.*
10. John Edward Porter, R.*
11. Frank Annunzio, D.*
12. Philip M. Crane, R.*
13. Harris W. Fawell, R.*
14. J. Dennis Hastert, R.
15. Edward R. Madigan, R.*
16. Lynn M. Martin, R.*
17. Lane A. Evans, D.*
18. Robert H. Michel, R.*
19. Terry L. Bruce, D.*
20. Richard J. Durbin, D.*
21. Melvin Price, D.*
22. Kenneth J. Gray, D.*

Indiana
1. Peter J. Visclosky, D.*
2. Philip R. Sharp, D.*
3. John Patrick Hiler, R.*
4. Dan R. Coats, R.*
5. James Jontz, D.
6. Danny L. Burton, R.*
7. John T. Myers, R.*
8. Frank McCloskey, D.*
9. Lee H. Hamilton, D.*
10. Andrew Jacobs, Jr., D.*

Iowa
1. Jim Leach, R.*
2. Thomas J. Tauke, R.*
3. David R. Nagle, D.
4. Neal Smith, D.*
5. Jim Ross Lightfoot, R.*
6. Fred Grandy, R.

Kansas
1. Pat Roberts, R.*
2. James C. Slattery, D.*
3. Jan Meyers, R.*
4. Dan Glickman, D.*
5. Bob Whittaker, R.*

Kentucky
1. Carroll Hubbard, Jr., D.*
2. William H. Natcher, D.*
3. Romano L. Mazzoli, D.*
4. Jim Bunning, R.
5. Harold (Hal) Rogers, R.*
6. Larry J. Hopkins, R.*
7. Carl C. (Chris) Perkins, D.*

Louisiana
1. Robert L. Livingston, R.*
2. Corrinne C. (Lindy) Boggs, D.*
3. W. J. (Billy) Tauzin, D.*
4. Charles (Buddy) Roemer, D.*‡
5. Thomas J. (Jerry) Huckaby, D.*
6. Richard Hugh Baker, R.
7. James A. (Jimmy) Hayes, D.
8. Clyde C. Holloway, R.

Maine
1. Joseph E. Brennan, D.
2. Olympia J. Snowe, R.*

Maryland
1. Roy P. Dyson, D.*
2. Helen Delich Bentley, R.*
3. Benjamin L. Cardin, D.
4. Thomas McMillen, D.
5. Steny H. Hoyer, D.*
6. Beverly B. Byron, D.*
7. Kweisi Mfume, D.
8. Constance A. Morella, R.

Massachusetts
1. Silvio O. Conte, R.*
2. Edward P. Boland, D.*
3. Joseph D. Early, D.*
4. Barney Frank, D.*
5. Chester G. Atkins, D.*
6. Nicholas Mavroules, D.*
7. Edward J. Markey, D.*
8. Joseph P. Kennedy II, D.
9. John Joseph Moakley, D.*
10. Gerry E. Studds, D.*
11. Brian J. Donnelly, D.*

Michigan
1. John Conyers, Jr., D.*
2. Carl D. Pursell, R.*
3. Howard E. Wolpe, D.*
4. Fred Upton, R.
5. Paul B. Henry, R.*
6. Bob Carr, D.*
7. Dale E. Kildee, D.*
8. Bob Traxler, D.*
9. Guy Vander Jagt, R.*
10. Bill Schuette, R.*
11. Robert W. Davis, R.*
12. David E. Bonior, D.*
13. George W. Crockett, Jr., D.*
14. Dennis M. Hertel, D.*
15. William D. Ford, D.*
16. John D. Dingell, D.*
17. Sander M. Levin, D.*
18. William S. Broomfield, R.*

Minnesota
1. Timothy J. Penny, D.*
2. Vin Weber, R.*
3. Bill Frenzel, R.*
4. Bruce F. Vento, D.*
5. Martin O. Sabo, D.*
6. Gerry Sikorski, D.*
7. Arlan Stangeland, R.*
8. James L. Oberstar, D.*

‡Rep. Charles (Buddy) Roemer was scheduled to resign his House seat to take office as governor of Louisiana on March 14, 1988.

Mississippi
1. Jamie L. Whitten, D.*
2. Mike Espy, D.
3. G. V. (Sonny) Montgomery, D.*
4. Wayne Dowdy, D.*
5. Trent Lott, R.*

Missouri
1. William L. (Bill) Clay, D.*
2. Jack Buechner, R.
3. Richard A. Gephardt, D.*
4. Ike Skelton, D.*
5. Alan D. Wheat, D.*
6. E. Thomas Coleman, R.*
7. Gene Taylor, R.*
8. Bill Emerson, R.*
9. Harold L. Volkmer, D.*

Montana
1. Pat Williams, D.*
2. Ron Marlenee, R.*

Nebraska
1. Doug Bereuter, R.*
2. Hal Daub, R.*
3. Virginia Smith, R.*

Nevada
1. James H. Bilbray, D.
2. Barbara F. Vucanovich, R.*

New Hampshire
1. Robert C. Smith, R.*
2. Judd Gregg, R.*

New Jersey
1. James J. Florio, D.*
2. William J. Hughes, D.*
3. James J. Howard, D.*
4. Christopher H. Smith, R.*
5. Marge Roukema, R.*
6. Bernard J. Dwyer, D.*
7. Matthew J. Rinaldo, R.*
8. Robert A. Roe, D.*
9. Robert G. Torricelli, D.*
10. Peter W. Rodino, Jr., D.*
11. Dean A. Gallo, R.*
12. Jim Courter, R.*
13. H. James Saxton, R.*
14. Frank J. Guarini, D.*

New Mexico
1. Manuel Lujan, Jr., R.*
2. Joe Skeen, R.*
3. William B. Richardson, D.*

New York
1. George J. Hochbrueckner, D.
2. Thomas J. Downey, D.*
3. Robert J. Mrazek, D.*
4. Norman F. Lent, R.*
5. Raymond J. McGrath, R.*
6. Floyd H. Flake, D.*
7. Gary L. Ackerman, D.*
8. James H. Scheuer, D.*
9. Thomas J. Manton, D.*
10. Charles E. Schumer, D.*
11. Edolphus Towns, D.*
12. Major R. Owens, D.*
13. Stephen J. Solarz, D.*
14. Guy V. Molinari, R.*
15. Bill Green, R.*
16. Charles B. Rangel, D.*
17. Ted Weiss, D.*
18. Robert Garcia, D.*
19. Mario Biaggi, D.*
20. Joseph J. DioGuardi, R.*
21. Hamilton Fish, Jr., R.*
22. Benjamin A. Gilman, R.*
23. Samuel S. Stratton, D.*
24. Gerald B. Solomon, R.*
25. Sherwood L. Boehlert, R.*
26. David O'B. Martin, R.*
27. George C. Wortley, R.*
28. Matthew F. McHugh, D.*
29. Frank Horton, R.*
30. Louise M. Slaughter, D.
31. Jack F. Kemp, R.*
32. John J. LaFalce, D.*
33. Henry J. Nowak, D.*
34. Amory Houghton, Jr., R.

North Carolina
1. Walter B. Jones, D.*
2. Tim Valentine, D.*
3. Martin Lancaster, D.
4. David E. Price, D.
5. Stephen L. Neal, D.*
6. Howard Coble, R.*
7. Charlie Rose, D.*
8. W. G. (Bill) Hefner, D.*
9. J. Alex McMillan III, R.*
10. Cass Ballenger, R.
11. James McClure Clarke, D.

North Dakota
†Byron L. Dorgan, D.*

Ohio
1. Thomas A. Luken, D.*
2. Willis D. Gradison, Jr., R.*
3. Tony P. Hall, D.*
4. Michael G. Oxley, R.*
5. Delbert L. Latta, R.*
6. Bob McEwen, R.*
7. Michael DeWine, R.*
8. Donald E. Lukens, R.
9. Marcy Kaptur, D.*
10. Clarence E. Miller, R.*
11. Dennis E. Eckart, D.*
12. John R. Kasich, R.*
13. Donald J. Pease, D.*
14. Thomas C. Sawyer, D.
15. Chalmers P. Wylie, R.*
16. Ralph Regula, R.*
17. James A. Traficant, Jr., D.*
18. Douglas Applegate, D.*
19. Edward F. Feighan, D.*
20. Mary Rose Oakar, D.*
21. Louis Stokes, D.*

Oklahoma
1. James M. Inhofe, R.
2. Mike Synar, D.*
3. Wesley W. Watkins, D.*
4. Dave McCurdy, D.*
5. Mickey Edwards, R.*
6. Glenn English, D.*

Oregon
1. Les AuCoin, D.*
2. Robert F. Smith, R.*
3. Ron Wyden, D.*
4. Peter A. DeFazio, D.
5. Denny Smith, R.*

Pennsylvania
1. Thomas M. Foglietta, D.*
2. William H. (Bill) Gray III, D.*
3. Robert A. Borski, Jr., D.*
4. Joseph P. Kolter, D.*
5. Richard T. Schulze, R.*
6. Gus Yatron, D.*
7. W. Curtis Weldon, R.
8. Peter H. Kostmayer, D.*
9. E. G. (Bud) Shuster, R.*
10. Joseph M. McDade, R.*
11. Paul E. Kanjorski, D.*
12. John P. Murtha, D.*
13. Lawrence Coughlin, R.*
14. William J. Coyne, D.*
15. Don Ritter, R.*
16. Robert S. Walker, R.*
17. George W. Gekas, R.*
18. Doug Walgren, D.*
19. William F. Goodling, R.*
20. Joseph M. Gaydos, D.*
21. Thomas J. Ridge, R.*
22. Austin J. Murphy, D.*
23. William F. Clinger, Jr., R.*

Rhode Island
1. Fernand J. St Germain, D.*
2. Claudine Schneider, R.*

South Carolina
1. Arthur Ravenel, Jr., R.
2. Floyd Spence, R.*
3. Butler Derrick, D.*
4. Liz J. Patterson, D.
5. John McK. Spratt, D.*
6. Robert M. (Robin) Tallon, D.*

South Dakota
†Tim Johnson, D.

Tennessee
1. James H. Quillen, R.*
2. John J. Duncan, R.*
3. Marilyn Lloyd, D.*
4. James H. Cooper, D.*
5. Bob Clement, D.
6. Bart Gordon, D.*
7. Donald K. Sundquist, R.*
8. Ed Jones, D.*
9. Harold E. Ford, D.*

Texas
1. Jim Chapman, D.*
2. Charles Wilson, D.*
3. Steve Bartlett, R.*
4. Ralph M. Hall, D.*
5. John W. Bryant, D.*
6. Joe Barton, R.*
7. Bill Archer, R.*
8. Jack Fields, R.*
9. Jack Brooks, D.*
10. J. J. (Jake) Pickle, D.*
11. J. Marvin Leath, D.*
12. James C. Wright, Jr., D.*
13. Beau Boulter, R.*
14. Mac Sweeney, R.*
15. Eligio (Kika) de la Garza, D.*
16. Ronald Coleman, D.*
17. Charles W. Stenholm, D.*
18. Mickey Leland, D.*
19. Larry Combest, R.*
20. Henry B. Gonzalez, D.*
21. Lamar Smith, R.
22. Tom DeLay, R.*
23. Albert G. Bustamante, D.*
24. Martin Frost, D.*
25. Michael A. Andrews, D.*
26. Richard Armey, R.*
27. Solomon P. Ortiz, D.*

Utah
1. James V. Hansen, R.*
2. Wayne Owens, D.
3. Howard C. Nielson, R.*

Vermont
†James M. Jeffords, R.*

Virginia
1. Herbert H. Bateman, R.*
2. Owen B. Pickett, D.
3. Thomas J. (Tom) Bliley, Jr., R.*
4. Norman Sisisky, D.*
5. Dan Daniel, D.*
6. James R. Olin, D.*
7. D. French Slaughter, R.*
8. Stanford E. (Stan) Parris, R.*
9. Frederick C. Boucher, D.*
10. Frank R. Wolf, R.*

Washington
1. John Miller, R.*
2. Al Swift, D.*
3. Don Bonker, D.*
4. Sid Morrison, R.*
5. Thomas S. Foley, D.*
6. Norman D. Dicks, D.*
7. Mike Lowry, D.*
8. Rod Chandler, R.*

West Virginia
1. Alan B. Mollohan, D.*
2. Harley O. Staggers, Jr., D.*
3. Robert E. Wise, Jr., D.*
4. Nick J. Rahall II, D.*

Wisconsin
1. Les Aspin, D.*
2. Robert W. Kastenmeier, D.*
3. Steven Gunderson, R.*
4. Gerald D. Kleczka, D.*
5. Jim Moody, D.*
6. Thomas E. Petri, R.*
7. David R. Obey, D.*
8. Toby Roth, R.*
9. F. James Sensenbrenner, Jr., R.*

Wyoming
†Dick Cheney, R.*

Nonvoting Representatives
American Samoa
Fofo I. F. Sunia, D.*

District of Columbia
Walter E. Fauntroy, D.*

Guam
Ben Blaz, R.*

Puerto Rico
Jaime B. Fuster, D.*

Virgin Islands
Ron de Lugo, D.*

Members of the United States Senate

The Senate of the second session of the 100th Congress consisted of 54 Democrats and 46 Republicans when it convened in January 1988. Senators shown starting their term in 1987 were elected for the first time in the Nov. 4, 1986, elections. Others shown ending their current terms in 1993 were reelected to the Senate in the 1986 balloting. The second date in each listing shows when the term of a previously elected senator expires.

State	Term	State	Term	State	Term
Alabama		**Louisiana**		**Ohio**	
Howell T. Heflin, D.	1979–1991	J. Bennett Johnston, Jr., D.	1972–1991	John H. Glenn, Jr., D.	1974–1993
Richard C. Shelby, D.	1987–1993	John B. Breaux, D.	1987–1993	Howard M. Metzenbaum, D.	1976–1989
Alaska		**Maine**		**Oklahoma**	
Theodore F. Stevens, R.	1968–1991	William S. Cohen, R.	1979–1991	David L. Boren, D.	1979–1991
Frank H. Murkowski, R.	1981–1993	George J. Mitchell, D.	1980–1989	Don Nickles, R.	1981–1993
Arizona		**Maryland**		**Oregon**	
Dennis DeConcini, D.	1977–1989	Paul S. Sarbanes, D.	1977–1989	Mark O. Hatfield, R.	1967–1991
John McCain III, R.	1987–1993	Barbara A. Mikulski, D.	1987–1993	Bob Packwood, R.	1969–1993
Arkansas		**Massachusetts**		**Pennsylvania**	
Dale Bumpers, D.	1975–1993	Edward M. Kennedy, D.	1962–1989	John Heinz, R.	1977–1989
David H. Pryor, D.	1979–1991	John F. Kerry, D.	1985–1991	Arlen Specter, R.	1981–1993
California		**Michigan**		**Rhode Island**	
Alan Cranston, D.	1969–1993	Donald W. Riegle, Jr., D.	1976–1989	Claiborne Pell, D.	1961–1991
Pete Wilson, R.	1983–1989	Carl Levin, D.	1979–1991	John H. Chafee, R.	1976–1989
Colorado		**Minnesota**		**South Carolina**	
William L. Armstrong, R.	1979–1991	David F. Durenberger, R.	1978–1989	Strom Thurmond, R.	1956–1991
Timothy E. Wirth, D.	1987–1993	Rudy Boschwitz, R.	1978–1991	Ernest F. Hollings, D.	1966–1993
Connecticut		**Mississippi**		**South Dakota**	
Lowell P. Weicker, Jr., R.	1971–1989	John C. Stennis, D.	1947–1989	Larry Pressler, R.	1979–1991
Christopher J. Dodd, D.	1981–1993	Thad Cochran, R.	1978–1991	Thomas A. Daschle, D.	1987–1993
Delaware		**Missouri**		**Tennessee**	
William V. Roth, Jr., R.	1971–1989	John C. Danforth, R.	1976–1989	James Sasser, D.	1977–1989
Joseph R. Biden, Jr., D.	1973–1991	Christopher S. (Kit) Bond, R.	1987–1993	Albert A. Gore, Jr., D.	1985–1991
Florida		**Montana**		**Texas**	
Lawton Chiles, D.	1971–1989	John Melcher, D.	1977–1989	Lloyd M. Bentsen, D.	1971–1989
Bob Graham, D.	1987–1993	Max Baucus, D.	1978–1991	Phil Gramm, R.	1985–1991
Georgia		**Nebraska**		**Utah**	
Sam Nunn, D.	1972–1991	J. James Exon, D.	1979–1991	Edwin Jacob Garn, R.	1974–1993
Wyche Fowler, Jr., D.	1987–1993	David K. Karnes, R.	1987–1989	Orrin G. Hatch, R.	1977–1989
Hawaii		**Nevada**		**Vermont**	
Daniel K. Inouye, D.	1963–1993	Chic Hecht, R.	1983–1989	Robert T. Stafford, R.	1971–1989
Spark M. Matsunaga, D.	1977–1989	Harry M. Reid, D.	1987–1993	Patrick J. Leahy, D.	1975–1993
Idaho		**New Hampshire**		**Virginia**	
James A. McClure, R.	1973–1991	Gordon J. Humphrey, R.	1979–1991	John W. Warner, R.	1979–1991
Steven D. Symms, R.	1981–1993	Warren B. Rudman, R.	1980–1993	Paul S. Trible, Jr., R.	1983–1989
Illinois		**New Jersey**		**Washington**	
Alan J. Dixon, D.	1981–1993	Bill Bradley, D.	1979–1991	Daniel J. Evans, R.	1983–1989
Paul Simon, D.	1985–1991	Frank R. Lautenberg, D.	1982–1989	Brock Adams, D.	1987–1993
Indiana		**New Mexico**		**West Virginia**	
Richard G. Lugar, R.	1977–1989	Pete V. Domenici, R.	1973–1991	Robert C. Byrd, D.	1959–1989
J. Danforth Quayle, R.	1981–1993	Jeff Bingaman, D.	1983–1989	John D. Rockefeller IV, D.	1985–1991
Iowa		**New York**		**Wisconsin**	
Charles E. Grassley, R.	1981–1993	Daniel P. Moynihan, D.	1977–1989	William Proxmire, D.	1957–1989
Tom Harkin, D.	1985–1991	Alfonse M. D'Amato, R.	1981–1993	Robert W. Kasten, Jr., R.	1981–1993
Kansas		**North Carolina**		**Wyoming**	
Robert J. Dole, R.	1969–1993	Jesse A. Helms, R.	1973–1991	Malcolm Wallop, R.	1977–1989
Nancy Landon Kassebaum, R.	1978–1991	Terry Sanford, D.	1986–1993	Alan K. Simpson, R.	1979–1991
Kentucky		**North Dakota**			
Wendell H. Ford, D.	1974–1993	Quentin N. Burdick, D.	1960–1989		
Mitch McConnell, R.	1985–1991	Kent Conrad, D.	1987–1993		

sued a report saying that the doctrine, which dated from the 1940's, was no longer necessary because the large number of radio and television stations in the United States now ensured a diversity of views. After Reagan vetoed the bill, the Senate on June 23, 1987, returned it to committee, in effect sustaining the veto.

Welfare Reform. On December 16, the House overcame fierce Republican opposition to approve, 230 to 194, the most ambitious welfare system overhaul in decades. The measure stressed job training for welfare recipients, particularly teen-aged parents, and would cost $5 billion over five years, plus an extra $700 million for the federal food-stamp program. The Senate was not scheduled to act on welfare reform until 1988.

Political Campaign Spending. Efforts by Senate Democrats to make campaign-financing reforms a major goal for 1987 were abandoned on September 15 after proponents fell nine votes short of the number needed to shut off a Republican filibuster against the measure. Democrats had pushed for campaign spending ceilings to help overcome the Republican Party's fund-raising edge in many congressional races. Senate Republicans, on the other hand, wanted to place stricter limits on contributions from labor unions and political action committees, both of which they deemed most helpful to Democrats.

Congress Gets a Raise. Political posturing in Congress was never more evident than in early 1987, when the lawmakers debated giving themselves a pay raise. Reagan proposed on January 5 that the pay of Senate and House members be raised to $89,500 from $77,400. Except for occasional cost-of-living adjustments, salaries had not been increased since 1969. The raise was to take effect on February 4 unless voted down before then by both houses of Congress.

Amazingly, the members of Congress found a formula for both getting their raise and proclaiming to their constituents that they did not really want it. On Dec. 29, 1986, the Senate had voted $50 million in emergency aid for the homeless and attached an amendment disapproving the pay raise. The House passed the measure by voice vote on Feb. 4, 1987, but the provision rejecting the salary hike was meaningless because the raise had taken effect earlier the same day.

Presidential Politics forced the first shakeup of the House Republican leadership since 1980. On June 4, 1987, Representative Dick Cheney of Wyoming was unanimously elected chairman of the House Republican Conference. He took over the position—the third-ranking Republican post in the House—from Representative Jack F. Kemp of New York, who quit to focus on his campaign for the 1988 Republican presidential nomination. Until his election to the conference chairmanship,

Cheney had been head of the House Republican Policy Committee, a post he relinquished to Representative Jerry Lewis of California.

Senate Republicans voted 24 to 17 on Jan. 20, 1987, to designate Senator Jesse A. Helms of North Carolina as senior Republican on the Senate Foreign Relations Committee, displacing Senator Richard G. Lugar of Indiana. Helms, who had been in the Senate four years longer than Lugar, decided to assert his claim to seniority on the committee.

House Democrats also had an internal squabble. On January 7, they stripped Representative Les Aspin of Wisconsin of the chairmanship of the House Armed Services Committee. Aspin, who had come under fire from both conservative and liberal Democrats for his stands on various issues, promised to become "more open" and accessible to his House colleagues. On January 22, Aspin regained the committee chairmanship, defeating Representative J. Marvin Leath of Texas.

Six senators announced during the year that they would not seek reelection in 1988. They were Democrats Lawton Chiles of Florida, William Proxmire of Wisconsin, and John C. Stennis of Mississippi—all of them committee chairmen—and Republicans Daniel J. Evans of Washington, Robert T. Stafford of Vermont, and Paul S. Trible, Jr., of Virginia.

Reps in Hot Water. Several Democratic House members encountered legal and ethical difficulties in 1987. Ten-term Democratic Representative Mario Biaggi of New York was indicted in a New York City federal court on March 16, charged with trying to obtain government contracts for a Brooklyn ship-repair company. On September 22, a jury acquitted him of bribery and conspiracy but convicted him on less serious charges, including accepting an illegal gratuity—free vacations in Florida—and obstructing justice. Biaggi was sentenced on November 5 to 30 months in prison and fined $500,000. He still faced trial on a June 3 indictment accusing him of violating federal anti-racketeering laws.

Seven-term Democratic Representative Harold E. Ford of Tennessee was indicted on April 24 on federal conspiracy and fraud charges involving dealings with convicted bank swindler C. H. Butcher, Jr., who was also indicted. Ford was charged with receiving money from Butcher in return for political favors.

In September, a federal tax court ruled that Democratic Representative James A. Traficant, Jr., of Ohio owed the government about $180,000 in back taxes, penalties, and interest. Traficant, who denied any wrongdoing and vowed to appeal, was accused of avoiding taxes on $108,000 received from two organized-crime factions in 1980, when he was sheriff of Mahoning County, Ohio.

To mark the bicentennial of the U.S. Constitution, 55 members of Congress hold a ceremonial session at Philadelphia's Independence Hall on July 16.

Other Ethics Issues. A group of conservative House Republicans pressed for the creation of a bipartisan commission to look into what they termed a "pattern of corruption" involving at least 10 Democratic representatives and to recommend changes in the way the House polices itself. After an emotional debate, the House defeated the proposal 297 to 77 in June. Representative Newt Gingrich (R., Ga.), a principal sponsor of the commission idea, said the House Committee on Standards of Official Conduct "seems to protect the institution rather than police it."

The standards committee on September 23 accused four House Democrats—Richard H. Stallings of Idaho, Charlie Rose of North Carolina, William H. Boner of Tennessee, and Austin J. Murphy of Pennsylvania—of violating House rules. The committee said Stallings wrongly borrowed $4,800 from his campaign fund to buy a car. It charged that Rose converted $63,000 in campaign funds to his personal use. The committee accused Boner, who resigned his seat in 1987 after being elected mayor of Nashville, Tenn., of "conduct reflecting discreditably on the House" in his handling of 1984 campaign funds. And it accused Murphy of placing a "ghost" employee on the House payroll and of allowing another person, not named, to cast votes for him on three days when he was absent.

The House voted 324 to 68 on December 18 to reprimand Murphy, who denied any wrongdoing. It was the first disciplinary action against a House member since 1984.

After questions were raised about the personal finances of House Speaker Wright, he announced on Oct. 16, 1987, that he was placing assets worth $187,317 in a *blind trust*—a trust fund managed by other people—"in order to devote my full energies and undivided attention to the responsibilities of the speakership."

Deaths. The Democratic edge in the Senate of 55 seats to 45 at the start of the 1987 session was whittled down to 54-46 following the death on March 6 of Democratic Senator Edward Zorinsky of Nebraska. Governor Kay A. Orr appointed a fellow Republican, businessman David Karnes, to fill the vacancy.

Representative Stewart B. McKinney, a Connecticut Republican, died of pneumonia brought on by AIDS (acquired immune deficiency syndrome) on May 7. He was the first member of Congress known to have died of AIDS. His physician said he thought McKinney contracted AIDS from blood transfusions. Frank Cormier and Margot Cormier

See also UNITED STATES, GOVERNMENT OF THE. In WORLD BOOK, see CONGRESS OF THE UNITED STATES.

CONNECTICUT. See STATE GOVERNMENT.

CONSERVATION. In January 1987, the United States Congress passed a $20-billion Clean Water Act that provided $18 billion for the construction of sewage-treatment plants and $2 billion for the cleaning of waterways. President Ronald Reagan, who vetoed an identical bill in 1986, vetoed the 1987 act on January 30. On February 4, Congress overrode the presidential veto.

Sea Otters Protected. In 1987, officials from the U.S. Fish and Wildlife Service (FWS) began to establish a new colony of sea otters off the California coast. Although sea otters were almost exterminated by Russian fur traders in the 1700's and 1800's, the species recovered, and today about 1,650 thrive in a 225-mile (360-kilometer) stretch of California coastal waters between Santa Cruz and Morro Bay. But offshore oil drilling in the area has given conservationists reason to fear for the otters' long-range survival. A major oil spill could wipe out the entire colony.

In the mid-1980's, the FWS developed a plan to establish a second sea otter colony at a safer location near San Nicolas Island, 75 miles (120 kilometers) southwest of Los Angeles. Commercial divers who harvest shellfish that otters eat protested that the introduced species would destroy their livelihood. But the FWS obtained the necessary approvals from California authorities in July,

and by August 28 had captured 24 sea otters—the first in a test group of 70—and released them in their new territory. If the group establishes itself, another 180 animals will be relocated.

Wildlife Imperiled. On March 23, the Canadian government announced that it had approved resumption of large-scale seal hunting, in which up to 57,000 seals per year can be killed. International protests and a European boycott of Canadian seal pelts had virtually eliminated the large-scale hunts in the early 1980's. The newly revised regulations prohibit hunters from killing baby seals or nursing-mother seals and require that the animals be shot rather than clubbed to death. Worldwide animal welfare organizations continued to oppose the seal hunt.

Each year, as many as 47,000 sea turtles drown after becoming entangled in nets cast by American shrimp-fishing crews. All five turtle species commonly found in U.S. waters are endangered. On July 15, the National Marine Fisheries Service required that most shrimp boats use turtle excluder devices (TED's), which allow the reptiles to escape from shrimp nets. Busloads of Louisiana shrimpers traveled to Washington, D.C., in March to protest the regulation, however, claiming that TED's are inefficient and cause a 10 to 20 per cent loss of netted shrimp. According to the shrimpers, the

Destined for Michigan, where the moose population needs bolstering, a moose is airlifted out of a park in Ontario, Canada, in February.

The Newest National Park

Sagebrush deserts, green meadows, and snow-capped mountains await visitors at Great Basin National Park, the newest United States national park. The new park was a personal triumph for National Park Service Director William Penn Mott, Jr., who had campaigned to create a Great Basin national park since the 1930's. At its dedication on Aug. 15, 1987, Mott declared, "Great Basin is now a jewel in the crown which makes up the national park system."

The park's name is misleading because relatively few of its 77,109 acres (31,205 hectares) actually occupy the desert known as the Great Basin. The park lies in eastern Nevada near the Utah border. Much of its acreage straddles the rugged mountains of the South Snake Range. The combination of desert and mountain terrain provides scenery of stunning beauty and diversity.

The outstanding scenic feature of the park is Wheeler Peak, the highest mountain in the Snake Range. Wheeler soars 13,063 feet (3,982 meters) above sea level. Near the summit of the mountain is the southernmost glacier in the United States.

On the slopes of Wheeler Peak stand gnarled groves of Great Basin bristlecone pine, the oldest living things on earth. Some of these evergreen trees are more than 4,000 years old. Aspen, fir, spruce, and mountain mahogany also grow in the park. Mesquite, sagebrush, and yucca dot its desert areas. Mule deer roam the mountain forests, and golden eagles are numerous overhead.

Because the park's elevation ranges from Wheeler Peak's 13,063 feet to barely 6,200 feet (1,900 meters) at the Snake Creek, visitors can see a wide range of environments by traveling a short distance. Habitats in the park range from arid deserts and lush meadows at the lower elevations to alpine tundra at the highest.

Other scenic attractions in Great Basin park include Lexington Arch, a towering rock formation, and Lehman Caves, the largest series of limestone caverns in the Western United States. Inside the caves, huge columns of variously colored limestone reach from floor to ceiling. Park headquarters and a visitors' center stand at the entrance to the caverns.

The U.S. government established Great Basin National Park at relatively low cost by elevating to national park status several areas already under federal management. The new park was created from the former Lehman Caves National Monument, Wheeler Peak Scenic Area, and a portion of Humboldt National Forest. Great Basin was the first national park to be established south of Alaska since 1972 and the first ever for Nevada.

Perhaps the most striking feature of Great Basin National Park is its isolation. The nearest town is Baker, Nev., with a population of about 50. The park lies nearly 300 miles (480 kilometers) from Las Vegas, and visitors to Great Basin must travel about 75 miles (120 kilometers) from the nearest interstate highway. Those who make the trip, however, will find spectacularly varied terrain and some of the last unspoiled wilderness in the West.

Sara Dreyfuss

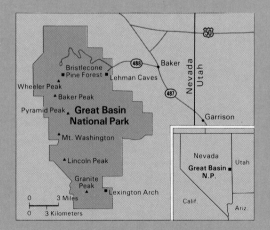

Great Basin National Park opened in August in Nevada, *left*, and includes the oldest living things on earth, Great Basin bristlecone pine trees, *right*.

loss of shrimp plus the cost of the TED's will result in a $61.9-million loss to the shrimping industry. The shrimpers, backed by Louisiana politicians, planned to challenge the ruling in court.

On April 19, FWS biologists captured the last California condor living in the wild and transported it to the San Diego Wild Animal Park. The California condor population has declined so sharply that captive breeding is the species' only hope for survival, according to FWS officials. The last 27 California condors now live at the San Diego Wild Animal Park and the Los Angeles Zoo. Biologists hope that they can build up the condor population and then return the birds to the wild.

In February, scientists at the Wyoming Fish and Game Department captured another member of a near-extinct species, the black-footed ferret. During 1985 and 1986, disease and starvation severely reduced the only known population of the ferret. Hoping that captive breeding would save the species from extinction, scientists took all the ferrets that could be captured to a breeding facility in Laramie, Wyo. The ferret captured in February 1987 brought the total known population of the species to 18. In June, the ferrets boosted conservationists' hopes by giving birth to eight baby ferrets, seven of which survived.

Threats to Marine Mammals. In summer 1987, the Japanese government announced plans to conduct whaling in the Antarctic Ocean despite the International Whaling Commission's strong disapproval. Conservation groups around the world also condemned the plan. Officials in Japan contended that the hunt was for purposes of scientific research only. They planned to kill 825 minke whales and 50 sperm whales by year's end.

In July and August, bottle-nosed dolphins that were dead or dying washed ashore along the east coast of the United States from New Jersey to Virginia. As the number of dead dolphins grew almost daily—eventually approaching 400—marine pathologists investigated the cause of the deaths. On August 19, they announced that a common bacterium normally found in coastal waters had become deadly to the dolphins. The scientists speculated that a virus, a naturally occurring poison, industrial pollutants, or an immune system disorder might have weakened the dolphins, making them susceptible to infection by usually harmless bacteria.

Wildlife Protection. In July, members of the Convention on International Trade in Endangered Species of Wild Fauna and Flora met for two weeks in Ottawa, Canada. Delegates from 86 nations discussed regulation of the world's $5-billion annual trade in threatened wildlife and related products. The convention banned the sale of the hyacinth macaw, the Corsican swallowtail butterfly, the Orsini's viper, and the star cactus. They

also restricted the sale of a wide variety of creatures ranging from arrow poison frogs to hummingbirds.

Some restrictions were relaxed. Representatives allowed Peru and Chile to sell vicuña wool, but only if the animals were sheared—and not killed —during wool removal. In a difficult decision, delegates voted to continue allowing African countries with surplus elephants to sell ivory. Poachers are killing more than 100,000 African elephants yearly.

The Fourth World Wilderness Congress, which was held in Denver in September, opened with the presentation of a comprehensive inventory of the world's major wilderness areas, many of which are threatened by human development. The inventory identified some 32 million square miles (83 million square kilometers) of wilderness in 28 countries and Antarctica. Delegates urged governments around the world to grant formal protection to their wild lands. Fewer than 20 per cent of the earth's wilderness areas have been granted such protection.

On August 15, federal and Nevada officials dedicated Great Basin National Park, the 49th national park in the United States and Nevada's first. See Close-Up.   Eugene J. Walter, Jr.

See also ENVIRONMENTAL POLLUTION; WATER; ZOOLOGY. In WORLD BOOK, see CONSERVATION.

CONSTITUTION OF THE UNITED STATES. On Jan. 1, 1987, the United States kicked off a yearlong 200th birthday celebration for its Constitution with fireworks in Philadelphia. The high point of the celebration came on September 17, the anniversary of the signing of the Constitution, when Philadelphia staged a huge parade and other festivities. See PHILADELPHIA (Close-Up).

The Celebration gave many Americans a chance to praise the Constitution. In a ceremony on May 25 in Philadelphia, Governor Robert P. Casey of Pennsylvania noted that the Constitution has ". . . room for 50 different state constitutions and 150 million different versions of life, liberty, and the pursuit of happiness." And on September 17, President Ronald Reagan told thousands of people gathered near Independence Hall in Philadelphia that the ". . . genius of our constitutional system is its recognition that no one branch of government alone could be relied on to preserve our freedoms."

Assessing the Constitution. The bicentennial celebration gave others the opportunity to assess the Constitution and the political system it established. In January 1987, the Committee on the Constitutional System, a group of about 200 elected officials and constitutional analysts, issued a report stating that there are flaws in the U.S. political system that make the nation unable to respond effectively to today's problems. The report, designed to stimulate debate on the Constitution, proposed changes to correct these flaws.

One problem, according to the committee, is the inability of the President and Congress to work together to develop national policies. While the sharing of power by the executive, legislative, and judicial branches of the government is a safeguard against tyranny, the group said, the separation of powers has produced a government that arrives at more stand-offs than solutions.

Among the changes the committee suggested was lengthening terms of office in the House of Representatives to four years and in the Senate to eight years, with all members of Congress to be elected in presidential election years. This would more closely link the fate of presidential and congressional candidates, as well as cut the cost and time of campaigns. Another proposal would allow members of Congress to serve in the Cabinet or in other executive positions.

Convention Call. No additional states in 1987 passed resolutions calling for a constitutional convention to write an amendment requiring a balanced federal budget. Thirty-two states have passed such resolutions, but 34 states are needed for Congress to call a convention.   Mary A. Krier

In WORLD BOOK, see CONSTITUTION OF THE UNITED STATES.

CONSUMERISM. The collapse of worldwide securities markets in October 1987 was expected to eventually hold down prices for consumer goods and services in the United States. But for most of 1987, inflation pressures built at a faster rate than had been seen since 1984. By the end of 1987, the Consumer Price Index (CPI), the measurement of changes in the cost of goods and services, showed a 3.7 per cent increase since January. This rise was much higher than the 1.9 per cent CPI increase for 1986.

Gasoline and heating- and cooking-fuel prices rose faster than prices for other consumer goods, increasing 17.5 and 14.4 per cent respectively in 12 months. Rates for home mortgages were also high, averaging 11.6 per cent in October—their highest rate in two years. Energy prices were erratic, however, rising 1.7 per cent in August and dropping 0.5 per cent in September.

Health care costs, which increased 6.4 per cent during the first nine months of 1987, continued to rise faster than most other costs. This increase led to a jump in health insurance premiums, including government Medicare premiums, which rose by 38 per cent on Jan. 1, 1988.

Automobile Prices also headed upward at a steady pace. Despite weak buyer demand—which prompted U.S. automakers to offer rebates and discount financing for much of the 1987 model

year—prices for most 1988 model cars were raised substantially. Numerous automobile advertisements claimed the contrary, however. On September 28, *The Wall Street Journal* reported that although General Motors Corporation (GM) touted big savings on 1988 models, prices had actually increased. GM had included many former options—such as power steering and AM/FM stereo—in the standard prices of its 1988 models and then discounted the options below its 1987 prices. According to the *Journal*, base prices were actually 6 to 8 per cent higher. GM also grouped its other options into packages to encourage buyers to purchase more than just one or two. Other automakers adopted similar sales tactics and renewed rebate programs in 1987.

Deregulated Industries. The costs of telephone, transportation, and banking services increased in 1987, reflecting a trend in several deregulated industries. As prices for these services rose, their availability often decreased, especially in rural areas, which can rarely support the strong competition deregulation was designed to foster.

These problems were most keenly felt by air travelers in 1987. As airline companies continued to merge, discount fares became less common. According to a federal survey, prices for air travel out of large cities dropped by about 33 per cent immediately after the industry was deregulated in the early 1980's, but the cost of flights out of smaller cities rose by 16 per cent. In the mid-1980's, fares in large cities often have been higher than they were before deregulation.

Fare hikes and cutbacks in service also occurred in the intercity bus and truck transportation industries. The U.S. Department of Transportation reported in 1987 that more than 3,000 small U.S. communities had lost bus service since deregulation began in 1982.

Legislation. In 1987, consumer groups regained some of the political clout they enjoyed in the 1960's and 1970's. The 1986 elections increased the number of consumer-oriented legislators in both federal and state governments. In Congress, the changed atmosphere led to pressure to reinstitute federal regulation of several industries.

In August, U.S. President Ronald Reagan signed into law the Competitive Equality Banking Act of 1987. Under one provision of the act that takes effect in September 1988, a bank cannot delay access to funds deposited by check for more than two intervening days if the check is drawn on a local bank or more than six intervening days if the check is drawn on an out-of-state bank. In 1990, the limit will be reduced to one day for local checks and four days for others.

The banking act also allowed the Federal Savings and Loan Insurance Corporation to borrow up to $10.8 billion over the next three years to

Chrysler Corporation Chairman Lee A. Iacocca shows an advertisement in July apologizing for Chrysler's disconnecting of odometers on 60,000 vehicles.

close or merge weak savings and loan institutions. Many such organizations teetered on the brink of financial collapse in 1987. Another new law, which took effect in December 1987, required lenders to cap interest rates on adjustable mortgages, including home-equity loans.

In October, a Senate committee held hearings on reinstituting federal regulation of some areas of the commercial airline industry. The Senate considered requiring the Reagan Administration to hire an additional 1,000 air-traffic controllers and requiring airlines to publish information about their service and flight-delay records. During the hearings, pilots representing the Air Line Pilots Association testified that they had been forced to fly unsafe, inadequately maintained planes. A spokesperson for Eastern Airlines—one of the airlines accused of making cutbacks in maintenance—called the pilots' testimony "safety scare tactics."

Fraud and Price Fixing. Federal agencies charged with buyer protection stepped up their activities in 1987. In June, the U.S. Department of Justice charged Chrysler Corporation with fraud. A federal grand jury in St. Louis, Mo., indicted the automaker for turning back odometers on more than 60,000 cars and trucks that had been driven as much as 400 miles (600 kilometers) and then sold as new. The practice came to light in Missouri

when Chrysler employees stopped for speeding told police their cars' odometers and speedometers were not connected. Chrysler faced a maximum fine of $120 million if convicted of fraud. In December, Chrysler pleaded no contest to the charges and agreed to pay at least $16.4 million to settle suits filed by states and individuals. In July, the company offered to extend the affected vehicles' warranties for an additional two years or 20,000 miles (32,000 kilometers).

The Federal Trade Commission (FTC) tried with limited success to prevent price fixing at five title-insurance companies that accounted for about half the title-insurance business in the United States. In January, an FTC administrative law judge, Morton Needelman, supported charges against title-insurance companies in Connecticut and Wisconsin but rejected charges against firms in six other states on the ground that price-fixing was allowed there.

In August, the FTC accused three national travel agencies of misleading consumers. A federal judge prohibited the firms—which were based in Indianapolis and in Naperville, Ill.—from offering phony discounts on vacations in Hawaii and elsewhere.   Arthur E. Rowse

See also AUTOMOBILE; AVIATION; BANK; SAFETY. In WORLD BOOK, see CONSUMERISM.
COSTA RICA. See LATIN AMERICA.

COURTS. The lingering specter of Nazism un- leashed a flood of emotions in 1987 as courts in France and Israel sought justice for crimes com- mitted during World War II (1939-1945).

In Lyon, France, former Nazi officer Klaus Bar- bie went on trial on May 11, charged with crimes against humanity. Barbie had served as head of the Gestapo (the Nazi secret police) in Lyon from 1942 to 1944. Having fled to South America in 1951, Barbie was taken into French custody in 1983 following his expulsion from Bolivia.

The French government accused Barbie of hav- ing participated in roundups of French Jews who were sent to their deaths in Nazi extermination camps. He was also charged with having tortured French resistance fighters. Barbie, who boycotted much of his trial, denied responsibility for the de- portation of French Jews. He acknowledged wag- ing a campaign against the French resistance, but he maintained that this activity was a justifiable act of war. The court panel of three judges and nine jurors rejected Barbie's defense. He was convicted on July 4 and sentenced to life in prison.

"Ivan the Terrible"? In a courtroom in Jerusa- lem, Israel, survivors of Nazi concentration camps broke down in tears as they testified against ac- cused war criminal John Demjanjuk. Survivors identified Demjanjuk as the executioner called "Ivan the Terrible" at the Treblinka extermina- tion center in German-occupied Poland, where he allegedly helped kill more than 850,000 men, women, and children.

Demjanjuk had immigrated to the United States after World War II. The United States extradited him to Israel in 1986.

Demjanjuk admitted that he had been captured by Nazi troops while serving as a Soviet soldier. But he testified that his arrest was a case of mis- taken identity, maintaining that he had been a prisoner of war in German hands during the time he allegedly worked at Treblinka. At year-end, the 10-month-old trial continued without a verdict.

Mafia Trial. The largest Mafia trial in history ended on December 16 in Palermo, Italy, with guilty verdicts against 338 of 452 defendants on murder, drug, and extortion charges. The jury ordered lengthy prison terms for those con- victed, including life imprisonment for 19 top Mafia leaders.

The trial began in February 1986 with 474 de- fendants. During the proceedings, 12 of the ac- cused were dropped from the case and 10 died.

Bhopal Ruling. An Indian judge on Dec. 17, 1987, ordered Union Carbide Corporation to pay about $270 million as interim relief to victims of the 1984 gas leak in Bhopal, India. The Indian

An expert explains the operation of Treblinka, a World War II death camp, at the trial of accused Nazi John Demjanjuk, which began in February in Israel.

government has charged that Union Carbide's negligence caused the leak and is seeking $3 billion in damages in a case that is still pending. Union Carbide claims the accident resulted from sabotage.

Frozen-Embryo Case. A California court ruling in late 1987 resolved the fate of two embryos frozen since 1981. The embryos, which had been conceived using the eggs and sperm of a Los Angeles couple, Elsa and Mario Rios, had been in legal limbo since the couple's death in a plane crash in 1983. The embryos had remained frozen in liquid nitrogen in Melbourne, Australia, where the laboratory conception took place. The California court declared that any children born as a result of the embryos' implantation into another woman would have no claim on the Rioses' estate. The decision led government officials in the Australian state of Victoria to give the go-ahead for the embryos to be implanted.

Baby M Case. A New Jersey judge's ruling against the biological mother in a child custody dispute stirred a nationwide debate on the issue of surrogate parenting. The controversial case over the custody of the child known as Baby M (for Melissa) pitted William Stern and his wife, Elizabeth, against Mary Beth Whitehead, a 30-year-old housewife who had agreed to be artificially inseminated by William Stern and bear a child for the couple for a $10,000 fee. Shortly after the child was born, Whitehead changed her mind. She refused the fee and sought to keep the baby.

The trial, which began in January 1987, took place under Judge Harvey R. Sorkow of Bergen County Superior Court. After hearing testimony from both sides, the judge awarded custody of the child to her biological father on March 31. Because there were no laws or previous court rulings in New Jersey on surrogacy, Sorkow based his ruling on the principles of contract law and on the best interests of the child.

Textbook Rulings Overturned. In a pair of decisions that came within days of each other, federal appellate courts reversed rulings that had been favorable to Christian fundamentalist parents. On August 24 in Cincinnati, Ohio, the U.S. Court of Appeals for the Sixth Circuit reversed a lower court decision that had allowed a group of parents in Hawkins County, Tennessee, to remove their children from public school reading classes. The classes used textbooks that offended the parents' religious beliefs. The Appeals Court found that neither the textbooks nor the classes violated First Amendment guarantees of religious freedom.

On August 26, a federal Court of Appeals in Atlanta reversed a lower court ruling that had banned 44 history, social studies, and home economics textbooks from Alabama public schools. The court overturned the March 4 ruling of Judge W. Brevard Hand of the Federal District Court in Mobile, Ala., who had found that the books violated the First Amendment requirement of religious neutrality by promoting the "religion of secular humanism." Hand had ruled that the books' lack of information on Christianity and other religions served to promote a godless set of principles that themselves constituted a religion. The Court of Appeals held that the omission of religion did not violate the First Amendment.

Longest Jury Trial Ends. The longest jury trial in U.S. history ended on October 22, more than 3½ years after it began, when a jury in Belleville, Ill., found that Monsanto Company, a chemical manufacturer, had failed to warn residents of a Missouri town of the dangers of a 1979 chemical spill. The spill resulted when a railroad tank car ruptured in Sturgeon, Mo., leaking chemicals used to make wood preservatives. The spill contained less than a teaspoon (4.9 milliliters) of dioxin, a toxic chemical. The 65 plaintiffs claimed that they suffered illnesses because of the dioxin and that Monsanto failed to advise them of the danger presented by the spill. The jury awarded the plaintiffs $16.2 million in punitive damages. Monsanto planned to appeal. Edward H. Bruske

See also CRIME; SUPREME COURT OF THE U.S. In WORLD BOOK, see COURT; LAW.

With his wife at his side, former Labor Secretary Raymond J. Donovan meets the press in New York City in May after being acquitted of fraud and larceny.

CRIME. Tales of espionage in the United States Embassy in Moscow unfolded in 1987. Charges that U.S. Marine Corps guards stationed in Moscow and other European locations had for years engaged in forbidden relationships with Soviets rocked the Marines and shook government confidence in the security of its foreign installations.

On Jan. 10, 1987, the Marine Corps disclosed that a 25-year-old Marine guard had been arrested in December 1986 on charges of spying. Sergeant Clayton J. Lonetree, the first Marine ever charged with spying, was accused of allowing Soviet agents access to sensitive areas of the U.S. Embassy in Moscow—a charge later dropped due to lack of evidence. He was also accused of passing information to an agent of the KGB (the Soviet intelligence agency). United States officials said that Lonetree had been romantically involved with a Russian woman employed at the embassy, who introduced him to the KGB agent.

On March 24, the Marine Corps revealed that a second Marine guard, Corporal Arnold Bracy, 21, had been arrested on suspicion of spying because of his unauthorized contacts with Soviet women. The investigation subsequently widened to include other Marines who had similar secret relationships with Soviets at various U.S. installations in Europe.

But the investigation began to unravel when Bracy and other Marines withdrew their reported confessions to agents of the Navy investigative service. Bracy withdrew statements that he had acted as an accomplice to Lonetree in giving Soviet agents access to the embassy. He also accused military investigators of forcing him to confess and of falsifying the results of a lie-detector test he had taken in March. In June, charges against Bracy were dropped. In September, Marine Sergeant Robert S. Stufflebeam, 24, the second-ranking guard at the U.S. Embassy in Moscow, was acquitted of charges that he had improper contacts with Soviet women, but he was convicted of failure to properly carry out his duties.

Military prosecutors began general court-martial proceedings against Lonetree in July. On August 21, Lonetree was convicted of espionage and related charges. Three days later, he was sentenced to 30 years in prison, but he appealed.

Israel Spy Case. Jonathan Jay Pollard, who worked as a civilian counterintelligence analyst for the U.S. Navy, was sentenced on March 4 to life in prison on spy charges. Pollard had pleaded guilty to selling Israel more than 1,000 documents containing classified U.S. intelligence information. His wife, Anne Henderson Pollard, was sentenced to five years for acting as an accomplice.

Crime on Wall Street. In 1987, Wall Street was stunned by new revelations of insider stock trading—the buying and selling of stocks based on confidential information—and charges of illegal profits made by advance knowledge of corporate take-overs. Investor Ivan F. Boesky, who agreed in November 1986 to pay a $50-million fine and give up $50 million in illegal profits from insider stock deals, cooperated with federal investigators and implicated other traders and investment firms. In December 1987, he was sentenced to three years in prison.

On February 12, three top Wall Street traders were arrested and charged with involvement in a multimillion-dollar scheme to swap secrets in corporate take-over transactions. The charges were dropped after the U.S. Attorney's office requested a delay while it sought additional evidence.

On February 13, investment banker Martin A. Siegel pleaded guilty to insider trading charges and agreed to repay the government more than $9 million. And in June, the U.S. Securities and Exchange Commission charged the investment firm of Kidder, Peabody & Company with making nearly $14 million in insider deals through Boesky and fined the firm $25.3 million.

Special Prosecutors in Washington, D.C., pressed several investigations in 1987 involving current and former high-ranking members of President Ronald Reagan's Administration. Prosecutor Lawrence E. Walsh pursued charges of wrongdoing against officials involved in a plan to sell military arms to Iran and divert profits from the sales to the *contras* (rebel troops) in Nicaragua. Among those being investigated were former National Security Advisers Robert C. McFarlane and Rear Admiral John M. Poindexter, and Marine Lieutenant Colonel Oliver L. North. See IRAN-CONTRA AFFAIR.

In July, a federal grand jury indicted Lyn Nofziger, former senior political adviser to President Reagan, on six counts of violating ethics laws. Nofziger was accused of illegal lobbying of government officials on behalf of Wedtech Corporation, a military contractor in New York City. Wedtech was the subject of several ongoing criminal investigations in 1987. The Wedtech inquiry also was examining the legality of actions taken by U.S. Attorney General Edwin Meese III.

Drug Trafficking. Efforts by United States agencies to curb drug trafficking at its overseas sources brought mixed results in 1987. Law-enforcement officials in Colombia arrested Colombian Carlos Enrique Lehder Rivas, reputed to be one of the world's most notorious and violent cocaine traffickers. Lehder Rivas was captured on February 4 and extradited to the United States for trial. And on November 20, at a warehouse near Miami, Fla., U.S. customs agents seized 6,292 pounds (2,854 kilograms) of cocaine that had been hidden in boards shipped from Costa Rica. The seizure, which had an estimated street value of more than $340 million, was the largest in U.S. history.

On December 30, a Colombian judge ordered the release from prison of Jorge Luis Ochoa Vásquez, reportedly an associate of Lehder Rivas. The United States, which had requested that Ochoa Vásquez be transferred there for trial on drug charges, protested to Colombia.

Organized Crime. The U.S. government's crackdown on organized crime suffered several setbacks in 1987, including the acquittal on March 13 of John Gotti, reputed boss of New York City's most powerful crime family. Gotti was found not guilty of charges covering 69 specific crimes, including racketeering, murder, and *loan-sharking* (moneylending at extremely high interest rates).

Donovan and Biaggi. Former U.S. Secretary of Labor Raymond J. Donovan was found not guilty on May 25 of charges that forced him from office in March 1985. Donovan had been accused of participating in a scheme to steal $7.4 million from funds earmarked for a New York City Transit Authority subway project while he was an official of a New Jersey construction firm.

Representative Mario Biaggi (D., N.Y.) was convicted on September 22 of obstruction of justice and other charges in connection with allegations that he used his influence to obtain no-bid contracts for a New York City ship-repair company. Biaggi was acquitted of more serious charges of bribery and conspiracy. On November 5, Biaggi was sentenced to 30 months in prison and a $500,000 fine. He appealed the conviction.

LaRouche Indicted. Prosecutors took sweeping actions against a group led by political extremist and perennial presidential candidate Lyndon H. LaRouche, Jr. LaRouche followers were accused of using phony fund-raising tactics to make as much as $30 million to support the organization. On June 30, LaRouche was indicted by a federal grand jury on a charge of obstruction of justice. The indictment accused LaRouche and top officials of his organization of trying to block a federal investigation of credit-card fraud. In December, LaRouche aide Roy Frankhauser was convicted of conspiring to cover up the fraud.

Howard Beach. An incident in the Howard Beach neighborhood of Queens, a borough of New York City, prompted an examination of race relations in the New York City area. The incident, which occurred in December 1986, involved a group of white teen-agers armed with clubs who allegedly chased a young black man onto a highway, where he was struck by an automobile and killed. Twelve teen-agers were indicted on Feb. 10, 1987, on charges ranging from rioting to second-degree murder. On December 21, three defendants were convicted of manslaughter and one was acquitted. The eight other defendants still awaited trial.   Edward H. Bruske

In WORLD BOOK, see CRIME.

CUBA. Tit for tat reprisals marked the first four months of United States-Cuban relations in 1987. To protest a December 1986 flight of a U.S. spyplane over Cuban military maneuvers, Cuba barred U.S. diplomats on the island from using chartered planes to bring in mail and supplies. In retaliation, the Administration of President Ronald Reagan on February 1 abruptly reassigned the head of its mission in Havana, pointedly leaving the post unfilled for the first time since limited diplomatic relations were restored in 1977.

On April 29, the U.S. House of Representatives voted overwhelmingly to further strengthen the U.S. trade embargo against Cuba. Then, on May 5, the Cuban government arrested two people on charges of spying for the U.S. Central Intelligence Agency. The two were a female Cuban exile, who is a U.S. citizen, and her brother, who was employed by the Cuban government. During the year, Cuban television broadcast a series of reports about U.S. espionage in Cuba.

Defector. On May 28, Brigadier General Rafael del Piño Díaz, a Cuban Air Force officer and a hero of the Cuban resistance to the U.S.-backed Bay of Pigs invasion in 1961, defected to the United States. Piño Díaz, who flew his wife and three children in a small airplane from Cuba to a U.S. Navy base in Florida, was considered an ex-

Nicaraguan President Daniel Ortega, left, confers with Cuban President Fidel Castro on the Central American peace plan in August in Havana, Cuba.

pert on Cuban military operations in Africa and elsewhere.

Political Prisoner. On May 29, Cuban authorities freed Roberto Martín Pérez Rodríguez, 53, Cuba's longest-held political prisoner. Pérez Rodríguez served nearly 28 years for his alleged role in a plot to overthrow Cuban President Fidel Castro. He was freed at the request of Panamanian leader General Manuel Antonio Noriega Morena.

Talks. In May, U.S. and Cuban officials met in Havana. Agreement was reached on restoring chartered flights between the two countries. Cuba released about 30 political prisoners in August and September. Also in September, the United States named John J. Taylor, a veteran diplomat, to head its mission in Havana.

On November 20, the United States and Cuba revived a 1984 immigration agreement. Over 20,000 Cubans per year would be allowed to immigrate to the United States. The agreement also called for the return to Cuba of about 2,600 Cubans, many of them criminals and mental patients, who came to the United States in a 1980 boat lift. Fearing deportation, Cuban inmates rioted at federal prisons in Oakdale, La., and Atlanta, Ga. (see PRISON).   Nathan A. Haverstock

See also LATIN AMERICA (Facts in Brief Table). In WORLD BOOK, see CUBA.

CYPRUS. See MIDDLE EAST.

CZECHOSLOVAKIA got a new leader on Dec. 17, 1987, when Gustáv Husák resigned as Communist Party general secretary and was replaced by Miloš Jakeš (pronounced *MEE lohsh YAH kehsh*). Jakeš, 64, formerly the party's secretary for economic affairs, had long been seen as likely to take over the top post from the 74-year-old Husák. The change brought in a younger man but indicated no essential change in policy. Husák, who had predicted that the posts of party secretary and head of state would be separated, remained as president of Czechoslovakia.

Earlier, there were hints of Soviet impatience at Czechoslovakia's apparent reluctance to embark on internal reform despite Husák's endorsement, on March 18, of changes advocated by Soviet leader Mikhail S. Gorbachev. These changes included *perestroika* (economic restructuring) and *glasnost* (openness in the flow of information). Gorbachev visited Czechoslovakia for follow-up talks with Husák April 9 to 11.

Husák's formal endorsement of the Soviet reforms marked some turnabout for a Czechoslovak leadership that had always followed a rigidly orthodox Communist policy. Husák had come to power in 1969, the year after the Czechoslovak government under Alexander Dubček tried to implement sweeping reforms. The Soviet bloc crushed Dubček's reform movement by force in 1968, as troops from the Soviet Union and four of its allies invaded Czechoslovakia. In 1969, the already much-purged Czechoslovak Communist Party dismissed Dubček and installed Husák.

New Reforms. On July 17, 1987, Czechoslovakia introduced measures containing elements of the 1968 reforms—curbs on centralized control of business enterprises and a requirement that enterprises show a "profit," rather than subsidize their losses. Both these elements were part of Gorbachev's perestroika concept.

Politically, however, the new measures fell short of the 1968 reforms, which had provided for directors to be nominated and elected by workers. According to the 1987 measures, the employees of a business enterprise would elect a council, which, in turn, would elect a director. The council, however, could elect only an individual on a government list. And, in compiling this list, the government would give more consideration to individuals' "high political and moral qualities" than to their professional ability.

Economic Problems. The economy grew less than 2 per cent during the first six months of 1987, compared with a target of 3.1 per cent. A major problem was a mounting trade deficit with the Soviet Union.   Eric Bourne

See also EUROPE (Facts in Brief Table). In WORLD BOOK, see CZECHOSLOVAKIA.

DANCING. On Sept. 30, 1987, the Joffrey Ballet unveiled what had always been considered an impossibility—a reconstruction of Russian dancer Vaslav Nijinsky's choreography for *The Rite of Spring*. Most dance historians agree that the 1913 premiere of *The Rite of Spring* by Russian director Sergei Diaghilev's Les Ballets Russes in Paris was a landmark of modern culture. Today, the ballet is known through its score by Russian composer Igor Stravinsky. Nijinsky's original choreography was quickly forgotten because the ballet was performed only eight times. At its premiere, the violent, unconventional nature of the ballet caused the audience to riot and throw objects at Stravinsky and the dancers.

The 1987 re-creation, performed at the Dorothy Chandler Pavilion in Los Angeles, was the result of extensive research by Millicent Hodson, an American dance historian. The set, originally designed by Nicholas Roerich, who also did the costumes, was reconstructed by Hodson's husband, art historian Kenneth Archer.

Hodson's task was especially difficult because she had no dance-notation score to work from. Her sources were firsthand written accounts of the choreography, drawings, and notations on various musical scores, and, most important, the memories of the few surviving dancers who were associated with Diaghilev's troupe.

Robert Swinston and Catherine Kerr perform in *Fabrications,* one of three new works by Merce Cunningham that premiered during the 1986-1987 season.

Another so-called lost ballet, George Balanchine's *Mozart Violin Concerto,* was presented by the Tulsa (Okla.) Ballet Theater on September 27. It was the first time the work had been presented in its entirety in North America. The ballet was staged by Esmeralda Agoglia, an Argentine dancer who had performed in the work's 1942 premiere in Buenos Aires, Argentina.

Bolshoi Tour. The most exciting event for U.S. dance enthusiasts in 1987 was the visit of Moscow's Bolshoi Ballet, the company's first trip to the United States since 1979. The troupe brought only one new production, *The Golden Age,* by the Bolshoi's artistic director Yuri Grigorovich.

Critical reception of the troupe was mixed. Even those who admire Grigorovich's work felt that he dominated the repertory. There was much praise for the Bolshoi's latest star, Irek Mukhamedov. Yet several critics felt that the troupe was too dependent on the talents of a few dancers. The tour was a sellout, however.

The Moscow Ballet, a smaller company from the Soviet Union, made its U.S. debut in September. The troupe was led by Vyacheslav Gordeyev, one of the Bolshoi's biggest stars in the 1970's. In addition to the traditional Russian repertory, the group performed an excerpt from Balanchine's 1960 ballet *Donizetti Variations.* This was the first time a Soviet company had performed anything

by the Russian-born choreographer, who left his homeland as a young man.

French Ballet. The burgeoning dance scene in France was recognized in 1987. Maguy Marin's unusual production of *Cinderella* to a score by Russian composer Sergei Prokofiev became the sleeper hit of the year when the Lyon Opéra Ballet performed the work at New York City's City Center in January and again in May. Most of the action is in pantomime and everyday movement rather than dance. Although the dancers wear masks and awkward costumes that tend to dehumanize them, Marin's staging and dramatic set—a life-sized dollhouse—produced a work haunting for its evocation of innocence and touching for its portrayal of the hero and heroine's yearning for love. In October, two of Marin's darker pieces, *Babel Babel* and *Eden,* inaugurated the dance component of the Brooklyn Academy of Music's Next Wave Festival.

The Regional Ballet Movement in the United States showed further signs of consolidation in 1987. Since 1980, the trend has been for a larger successful dance company to absorb a smaller faltering one. The smaller organization provides a second home city for performing and a second funding base. In July, the Pacific Northwest Ballet in Seattle announced a second-city relationship with the Minnesota Dance Theatre in Minneapo-

Members of Moscow's Bolshoi Ballet soar across the stage in *The Golden Age*
in July during the company's first visit to the United States since 1979.

lis. This take-over was made possible by the 1986
firing of the Minnesota's founder and director,
Loyce Houlton, by the company's board.

The marriage between the Pennsylvania Ballet
and Milwaukee Ballet Company in June 1987 was
the first of its kind, however. The venture joined
two vigorous organizations, with each retaining its
full identity. The resulting Pennsylvania and Milwaukee Ballet under director Robert Weiss will
share dancers and repertory and spend equal
amounts of time in Philadelphia and Milwaukee.

Ballet in the West. Both the San Francisco Ballet
and the Pacific Northwest Ballet made great artistic strides in 1987. Under the direction of Icelan-
dic-born dancer Helgi Tomasson since 1985, the
San Francisco Ballet won national attention in
February 1987 when it premiered works by two
highly regarded choreographers—*New Sleep* by
William Forsythe and *Schumann Symphony* by Canada's James Kudelka. In addition to his adventurous programming, Tomasson was praised for in-
stilling finer classical style in the company and
bringing an international flavor to the roster.

The Pacific Northwest Ballet has also attracted
dancers from major troupes throughout the
world. Besides performing in the Western United
States, the troupe made a rare appearance on the
East Coast at the Kennedy Center for a week in
April, where it received good reviews.

Chicago Change. Dancers of the Chicago City
Ballet were laid off in November after Henry D.
Paschen, the company's chief sponsor, withdrew
his financial support. His action followed the
ouster of his wife, Maria Tallchief—the founder
of the company—as artistic director. Tallchief had
opposed the decision by the company's board of
directors earlier in the year to fire artistic co-direc-
tor Paul Meija. Meija later became director of the
Fort Worth Ballet in Texas. In September, Daniel
Duell, a principal dancer with the New York City
Ballet, had filled the vacancy at the Chicago City
Ballet.

Modern Dance. The larger modern dance companies—those of Alvin Ailey, Paul Taylor, Merce
Cunningham, Martha Graham, and Alwin Nikolais—all produced new works by their respective
choreographers. The Martha Graham Dance
Company opened a three-week season at the City
Center on October 6 with a star-studded gala. Rudolf Nureyev and Mikhail Baryshnikov danced the
leading roles in Graham's *Appalachian Spring,* and
Maya Plisetskaya, former Bolshoi ballerina, performed *Incense,* a 1906 dance by Ruth St. Denis.
In November 1987, Plisetskaya became artistic director of Spain's National Ballet. On October 13,
Graham premiered *Persephone,* her 177th dance,
set to Stravinsky's Symphony in C. Nancy Goldner

In WORLD BOOK, see BALLET; DANCING.

DEATHS in 1987 included those listed below, who were Americans unless otherwise indicated. An asterisk (*) indicates that the person has a biography in THE WORLD BOOK ENCYCLOPEDIA.

Abbott, Douglas C. (1899-March 17), Canada's minister of finance from 1946 to 1954 and a justice on the Supreme Court of Canada from 1954 to 1973.
Abel, I. W. (Iorwith Wilbur Abel) (1908-Aug. 10), a founder of the United Steelworkers of America and its president from 1965 to 1977.
Adams, John Quincy (1922-July 21), insurance executive and descendant of two United States Presidents.
Alfrink, Bernard Cardinal (1900-Dec. 17), Roman Catholic archbishop of Utrecht, the Netherlands, from 1955 to 1976.
Andrews, Eamonn (1922-Nov. 5), Irish-born host of the British Broadcasting Corporation's (BBC) version of the celebrity guest show "This Is Your Life."
***Anouilh, Jean** (1910-Oct. 3), French playwright known for the gloom and cynicism of his dramas.
Armstrong, O. K. (Orland Kay Armstrong) (1893-April 15), Republican congressman from Missouri from 1951 to 1953; contributing editor of *Reader's Digest*.
***Astaire, Fred (Frederick Austerlitz)** (1899-June 22), elegant motion-picture dancer. See Close-Up.
Astor, Mary (Lucile Langhanke) (1906-Sept. 25), sophisticated actress who starred in *The Maltese Falcon* (1941).
Bailey, Sherwood (1923-Aug. 6), former child actor who played Spud in the "Our Gang" motion pictures of the 1930's.
Baird, Bil (William B. Baird) (1904-March 18), puppeteer who, with his wife, Cora, created such popular television puppets as Charlemane the Lion and Slugger Ryan.
Baldrige, Malcolm (1922-July 25), U.S. secretary of commerce from 1981 until his death.
***Baldwin, James Arthur** (1924-Nov. 30), black author who wrote eloquently about racial prejudice.
Barnett, Ross R. (1898-Nov. 6), Democratic governor of Mississippi from 1960 to 1964.
Barrow, Errol Walton (1920-June 1), prime minister of Barbados from 1961 to 1976 and again since 1986.
Bass, Alfie (1921-July 15), British comic actor.
Bennett, Michael (Michael B. Di Figlia) (1943-July 2), choreographer and director of the Broadway hit *A Chorus Line* (1975).
Bergman, Jules (1929-Feb. 12), science editor for American Broadcasting Companies (ABC) News.
Betts, Huck (Walter M. Betts) (1897-June 13), pitcher for the Philadelphia Phillies and the Boston Braves from 1920 to 1935.
Bishop, Jim (1907-July 26), newspaper columnist and author of the best seller *The Day Lincoln Was Shot* (1955).
Bissell, Patrick (1957-Dec. 29), dancer with the American Ballet Theatre.
Blakeley, Colin (1930-May 7), actor, born in Northern Ireland, noted for his supporting roles in British theater, films, and television.
Bolger, Ray (1904-Jan. 15), dancer, singer, and actor best known as the Scarecrow in *The Wizard of Oz* (1939).
Bonura, Zeke (Henry J. Bonura) (1908-March 9), first baseman for the Chicago White Sox from 1934 to 1937, who had a lifetime batting average of .307.
Bramwell-Booth, Catherine (1883-Oct. 3), British leader of the Salvation Army; granddaughter of founder William Booth.
Brannum, Hugh (1910-April 19), actor who played Mr. Green Jeans on TV's "Captain Kangaroo."
***Brattain, Walter H.** (1902-Oct. 13), physicist who shared the 1956 Nobel Prize in physics for inventing transistors.
Brenan, Gerald (Edward FitzGerald Brenan) (1894-Jan. 19), British writer known for his studies of Spain.

Jackie Gleason, Ralph on TV's "Honeymooners"

René Lévesque, prime minister of Quebec

John Huston, legendary film director

Jacqueline du Pré, British cellist

Brewer, Jim (1937-Nov. 16), baseball pitcher whose 16 years in the major leagues included 11 years as a star reliever for the Los Angeles Dodgers.
Brown, Clarence (1890-Aug. 17), director of the films *National Velvet* (1944) and *The Yearling* (1947).
Bryant, Boudleaux (1920-June 25), songwriter who with his wife, Felice, wrote such Everly Brothers hits as "Bye Bye Love" (1957) and "Devoted to You" (1958).
Burgess, Sir John (1912-Feb. 10), chairman of Great Britain's Reuters news agency from 1959 to 1968.
Burnham, James (1905-July 28), founding editor of the conservative *National Review* magazine in 1955.
***Burns, Arthur F.** (1904-June 26), Austrian-born economist who served as chairman of the Board of Governors of the U.S. Federal Reserve System from 1970 to 1978.
Burns, Haydon (1922?-Nov. 22), Democratic governor of Florida from 1965 to 1967.
Burton, Sala (1925-Feb. 1), Polish-born Democratic congresswoman from California since 1983.
Butterfield, Paul (1942-May 4), harmonica player who led the Butterfield Blues Band.
***Caldwell, Erskine** (1903-April 11), author best known for his novels about Southern life, including *Tobacco Road* (1932) and *God's Little Acre* (1933).
Campbell, Archie (1914-Aug. 29), country humorist who appeared at the Grand Ole Opry in Nashville, Tenn., and on television's "Hee Haw."
Carlson, Frank (1893-May 30), Republican representative from Kansas from 1935 to 1947, governor of that state from 1947 to 1950, and senator from 1950 to 1969.

DEATHS

Carney, Charles J. (1913-Oct. 7), Democratic representative from Ohio from 1970 to 1979.

Carroll, Madeleine (Marie-Madeleine Bernadette O'Carroll) (1906-Oct. 2), British-born film star.

Carter, Tim Lee (1910-March 27), physician; Republican representative from Kentucky from 1965 to 1980.

Casey, William J. (1913-May 6), director of the Central Intelligence Agency from 1981 to 1987.

Caspary, Vera (1899-June 13), novelist who wrote *The White Girl* (1929) and the mystery *Laura* (1942).

Chamoun, Camille N. (1900-Aug. 7), president of Lebanon from 1952 to 1958.

Chenier, Clifton (1925-Dec. 12), Cajun-style accordion player.

Chevrier, Lionel (1903?-July 8), Canada's minister of transport from 1945 to 1954 and president of the St. Lawrence Seaway Authority from 1954 to 1957.

Chouinard, Julien (1929-Feb. 6), justice on the Supreme Court of Canada since 1979.

Coco, James (1929-Feb. 25), pudgy actor who starred on Broadway in *Last of the Red Hot Lovers* (1969).

Cohen, Wilbur J. (1913-May 18), secretary of health, education, and welfare in 1968 and 1969.

Cole, W. Sterling (1904-March 15), Republican representative from New York from 1935 to 1957.

Collins, J. Lawton (1896-Sept. 12), U.S. Army general nicknamed "Lightning Joe" during World War II (1939-1945).

Cotton, Henry (1907-Dec. 22), top British golfer from the 1930's to the 1950's.

Cox, Allan V. (1926-Jan. 27), geophysicist; member of the SCIENCE YEAR Editorial Advisory Board from 1977 to 1980.

Curtis, Charlotte M. (1928-April 16), first woman editor in the top ranks of *The New York Times*.

Dana, Viola (Virginia Flugrath) (1897-July 10), silent-film star.

Daniels, Dominick V. (1908-July 17), Democratic congressman from New Jersey from 1959 to 1977.

Darrell, Peter (1929-Dec. 1), British ballet dancer, choreographer, and artistic director of the Scottish Ballet.

Daugherty, Duffy (Hugh D. Daugherty) (1915-Sept. 25), Michigan State University football coach from 1954 to 1972.

Davis, Edith L. (1896-Oct. 26), mother of first lady Nancy Reagan.

De Angeli, Marguerite (1889-June 16), writer and illustrator of children's books who won the Newbery Medal in 1950 for *The Door in the Wall*.

*De Broglie, Louis V. (1892-March 19), French physicist who won the 1929 Nobel Prize in physics for his theory about the wave nature of electrons.

Delaney, James J. (1901-May 24), Democratic congressman from New York from 1945 to 1947 and again from 1949 to 1979.

Dempster, Hugh (1900-April 30), British actor.

Den Uyl, Joop (Johannes M. den Uyl) (1919-Dec. 24), prime minister of the Netherlands from 1973 to 1979.

Derringer, Paul (1906-Nov. 17), baseball pitcher whose 15 years in the major leagues included 9 years with the Cincinnati Reds from 1933 to 1942.

Dickson, Lovat (1902-Jan. 2), Australian-born British writer and publisher; director of Macmillan & Company from 1941 to 1964.

Donnellan, Thomas A. (1914-Oct. 15), Roman Catholic archbishop of Atlanta, Ga., from 1968 to 1987.

Donner, Frederic G. (1902-Feb. 28), chairman of General Motors Corporation from 1958 to 1967.

Dorn, Francis E. (1911-Sept. 17), Republican representative from New York from 1953 to 1961.

Duncan-Sandys, Lord (Duncan E. Sandys) (1908-Nov. 26), British Cabinet minister.

Dunton, A. Davidson (1912-Feb. 7), Canadian journalist and educator; president of Carleton University in Ottawa, Ont., from 1958 to 1972.

*Du Pré, Jacqueline (1945-Oct. 19), British cellist.

Dutton, Red (Mervyn A. Dutton) (1898-March 15), Canadian-born hockey player and member of the Hockey Hall of Fame.

Egan, Richard (1921-July 20), leading man in many action films.

Eisele, Donn F. (1930-Dec. 1), former Apollo astronaut.

Ellmann, Richard (1918-May 13), literary scholar; biographer of Irish novelist James Joyce.

Fairfax, Sir Warwick Oswald (1901-Jan. 14), Australian newspaper publisher.

Folsom, James E. (1908-Nov. 21), Democratic governor of Alabama from 1947 to 1951 and from 1955 to 1959.

*Ford, Henry, II (1917-Sept. 29), head of the Ford Motor Company from 1945 until 1980.

Fosse, Bob (Robert L. Fosse) (1927-Sept. 23), choreographer and director who won an Academy Award in 1972 for the film *Cabaret*.

Fraser, Bill (1908-Sept. 5), British character actor.

Fraser, Sir Hugh (1936-May 5), Scottish businessman; former owner of Harrods department store.

Fuqua, Samuel G. (1901?-Jan. 27), admiral in the U.S. Navy and Medal of Honor recipient.

Gerhardsen, Einar H. (1897-Sept. 19), prime minister of Norway from 1945 to 1951 and from 1955 to 1965.

Gingold, Hermione (1897-May 24), British-born actress who became a familiar guest on TV talk shows in the United States.

Harold Washington, mayor of Chicago

Rashid Karami, prime minister of Lebanon

Danny Kaye, versatile actor and comedian

Clare Boothe Luce, writer and congresswoman

Gleason, Jackie (Herbert J. Gleason) (1916-June 24), entertainer who played Ralph Kramden on the 1950's TV series "The Honeymooners."

Goh, Cho San (1948-Nov. 28), Singapore-born ballet dancer and choreographer.

Goodell, Charles E. (1926-Jan. 21), Republican who represented New York in the U.S. House of Representatives from 1959 to 1968 and in the Senate from 1968 to 1971.

Gordon, Walter L. (1906-March 21), Canada's minister of finance from 1963 to 1965.

Green, Edith S. (1910-April 21), Democratic representative from Oregon from 1955 to 1975.

Green, Freddie (1911-March 1), jazz guitarist who played with the Count Basie Band for almost 50 years.

Greene, Sir Hugh Carleton (1910-Feb. 19), director general of the BBC from 1960 to 1969; brother of novelist Graham Greene.

Greene, Lorne (1915-Sept. 11), Canadian-born star of TV's "Bonanza" from 1959 to 1973.

Greenwood, Joan (1921-Feb. 27), British motion-picture actress known for her distinctive husky voice.

Gross, H. R. (Harold Royce Gross) (1899-Sept. 22), Republican representative from Iowa from 1949 to 1975.

Gubbrud, Archie (1910?-April 26), Republican governor of South Dakota from 1961 to 1965.

Guldahl, Ralph (1911-June 11), top professional golfer of the 1930's.

Haley, Sir William (1901-Sept. 6), director general of the BBC from 1944 to 1952 and editor of *The Times* of London from 1952 to 1966.

Hammer, Ireene Wicker (Irene Seaton) (1900-Nov. 17), star of "The Singing Lady" children's radio show from 1931 to 1975.

Handl, Irene (1901-Nov. 29), British comic actress.

Harlow, Bryce N. (1916-Feb. 17), aide to Presidents Dwight D. Eisenhower and Richard M. Nixon.

Hartman, Elizabeth (1943-June 10), actress nominated for an Academy Award for her role in *A Patch of Blue* (1966).

Hayes, Woody (Wayne Woodrow Hayes) (1913-March 12), Ohio State University football coach from 1951 to 1978.

Hayworth, Rita (Margarita Cansino) (1918-May 14), actress known as Hollywood's "Love Goddess" who starred in *Gilda* (1946) and *Miss Sadie Thompson* (1953).

*****Heifetz, Jascha** (1901-Dec. 10), Lithuanian-born violinist.

Heinz, Henry John, II (1908-Feb. 23), chairman of the H. J. Heinz Company food products firm.

*****Heller, Walter W.** (1915-June 15), economist who served as chairman of the Council of Economic Advisers from 1961 to 1964.

Herman, Babe (Floyd C. Herman) (1903-Nov. 27), first baseman and center fielder with the Brooklyn Dodgers from 1926 to 1931.

*****Herman, Woody** (1913-Oct. 29), jazz clarinetist and bandleader whose biggest hit was "Woodchoppers' Ball" (1939).

*****Hess, Rudolf** (1894-Aug. 17), last survivor of the German Nazi leaders convicted of war crimes at Nuremberg in 1946.

Hitchcock, Henry-Russell (1903-Feb. 19), architectural historian.

Holiday, Jimmy (1934?-Feb. 15), composer of such popular hits as "Put a Little Love in Your Heart" (1969) and "All I Ever Need Is You" (1971).

Howser, Dick (1937-June 17), manager of baseball's Kansas City Royals from 1981 to 1986.

*****Huston, John** (1906-Aug. 28), Hollywood film director who made *The Maltese Falcon* (1941), *The African Queen* (1951), and *Prizzi's Honor* (1985). He became an Irish citizen in 1964.

Woody Hayes, Ohio
State football coach

Geraldine Page, Oscar-winning actress

Henry Ford II, head
of Ford Motor Company

I. W. Abel, leader
of steelworkers' union

Imlach, Punch (George Imlach) (1918-Dec. 1), Canadian coach who directed the Toronto Maple Leafs from 1958 to 1969; member of the Hockey Hall of Fame.

Jackson, Travis (1903-July 27), shortstop for baseball's New York Giants from 1922 to 1936; member of the National Baseball Hall of Fame.

Jochum, Eugen (1902-March 26), German orchestra conductor who founded the Bavarian Radio Symphony Orchestra.

Johnson, Gus (1938-April 28), forward for basketball's Baltimore Bullets (now the Washington Bullets) from 1963 to 1972.

Johnston, Richard B. (1930-Jan. 8), U.S.-born Canadian archaeologist.

Jonathan, Leabua (1914-April 5), prime minister of Lesotho from 1965 to 1986.

Kabalevsky, Dmitri (1904-mid-February), Russian composer.

Karami, Rashid (1921-June 1), prime minister of Lebanon who held office 10 times from 1955 to 1987.

*****Kaye, Danny (David Daniel Kominski)** (1913-March 3), versatile comedian and actor.

*****Kaye, Nora (Nura Koreva)** (1920-Feb. 28), ballerina; charter member of the American Ballet Theatre.

Kaye, Sammy (1910-June 2), bandleader whose slogan was "Swing and Sway with Sammy Kaye."

Kazen, Abraham, Jr. (1919-Nov. 29), Democratic representative from Texas from 1967 to 1985.

Keate, James Stuart (1913-March 1), Canadian newspaper publisher.

He Already Danced Like an Angel

Bouquets of tributes followed the death of dancer and actor Fred Astaire on June 22, 1987. President Ronald Reagan called him "an American legend," and composer Irving Berlin told the press, "There hasn't been such a talent as his." In fact, Astaire had been showered with praise all his life. In 1934, when songwriter Cole Porter listed what he considered the best things in the world in "You're the Top," he included "You're the nimble tread/Of the feet of Fred/Astaire."

Astaire was born Frederick Austerlitz in Omaha, Nebr., on May 10, 1899. His father was a beer salesman. His mother had show-business ambitions for Fred and his sister, Adele, who was 18 months older. The children's mother enrolled them in dancing school and, when Fred was 7 years old and Adele was 8, she took them to New York City for professional training. Soon the two youngsters were touring as a brother-and-sister vaudeville act under the name of Astaire.

Astaire and his sister became Broadway stars in the 1920's, but Hollywood executives considered Fred too thin to be a leading man in motion pictures. According to legend, a studio talent scout once dismissed Astaire's chances with

Fred Astaire and Ginger Rogers make dancing look easy in the "Pick Yourself Up" number from their hit motion picture *Swing Time* (1936).

a memo that read, "Can't act. Can't sing. Balding. Dances a little."

Astaire finally became a Hollywood star at the age of 34 in *Flying Down to Rio* (1933). He and Ginger Rogers played supporting roles to the film's stars Dolores Del Rio and Gene Raymond, but audiences left the theaters praising Astaire and Rogers. They starred together in nine other feature films, including such classics as *The Gay Divorcée* (1934), *Top Hat* (1935), *Swing Time* (1936), and *Shall We Dance?* (1937).

Dapper and trim, Astaire was always a gentleman. He made intricate dance routines look effortless. His dancing was smooth, relaxed, and so light-footed that it seemed almost possible when, thanks to trick photography, he danced up the walls and across the ceiling in *Royal Wedding* (1951). When Astaire had to dance with a partner whose gracefulness did not match his own, he could gallantly make her look like his equal.

But when Astaire danced with Rogers, he became something more than an elegant gentleman—he became a passionate lover. He pursued her in their dance numbers with an ardor that delighted movie audiences. The most frequently quoted comment about the dancing duo was that Fred gave Ginger class, while Ginger gave Fred sex appeal.

By the end of the 1930's, audiences for the Astaire-Rogers musicals began to decline, but Astaire's popularity held steady. His dancing triumphs continued, in tandem with Eleanor Powell in *Broadway Melody of 1940*, Rita Hayworth in *You'll Never Get Rich* (1941), Leslie Caron in *Daddy Long Legs* (1955), Cyd Charisse in *Silk Stockings* (1957), and Barrie Chase in a series of warmly received television specials. Astaire stayed so youthful that it did not seem inappropriate when he co-starred with Audrey Hepburn in *Funny Face* (1957), though she was almost 30 years younger than he.

In the late 1950's, Astaire began to do character parts in nonmusical films. He was poignant in *On the Beach* (1959), a drama about the aftermath of nuclear war. Astaire's last musical was Francis Ford Coppola's 1968 version of *Finian's Rainbow*.

Despite the praise showered on Astaire, he received only one Academy Award nomination. He was nominated as best supporting actor for his portrayal of an elegant con man in *The Towering Inferno* (1974). He was a sentimental favorite, but Robert De Niro won the award for his role in *The Godfather, Part II*. The television cameras bore down on Astaire's face when De Niro's name was called. The veteran actor did not miss a beat. He turned to his daughter, said "I'm so glad," and led the applause. Philip Wuntch

Kid Thomas (Thomas Valentine) (1896-June 16), jazz trumpeter and long-time leader of New Orleans' Preservation Hall jazz band.

King, Cecil H. (1901-April 17), British publisher who controlled more than 200 magazines and newspapers, including the *Daily Mirror.*

Kishi, Nobusuke (1896-Aug. 7), prime minister of Japan from 1957 to 1960.

Kneip, Richard F. (1933-March 9), Democratic governor of South Dakota from 1971 to 1978.

Kohlberg, Lawrence (1927-Jan. 17?), Harvard University professor of education whose theory of the six stages of moral development is used worldwide.

Kountché, Seyni (1931-Nov. 10), president of Niger since he seized power in a coup in 1974.

Lake, Arthur (Arthur Silverlake) (1905-Jan. 9), actor who played Dagwood Bumstead in more than two dozen *Blondie* films.

***Landon, Alfred M.** (1887-Oct. 12), Republican governor of Kansas from 1933 to 1937 and candidate for President in 1936.

Lansdale, Edward G. (1908-Feb. 23), retired U.S. Air Force major general; expert on guerrilla warfare.

Lash, Joseph P. (1909-Aug. 22), Pulitzer Prize-winning author of *Eleanor and Franklin* (1971).

Laurence, Margaret (1926-Jan. 5), Canadian novelist; author of *The Stone Angel* (1964) and *A Jest of God* (1966).

Leloir, Luis Federico (1906-Dec. 3), Argentine chemist who won the Nobel Prize in 1970 for his discovery of *sugar nucleotides,* compounds involved in the storage of energy by living things.

Le Roy, Mervyn (1900-Sept. 13), Hollywood producer and director for more than 40 years.

Lescoulie, Jack (1912-July 22), first announcer for TV's "Today" show in the 1950's.

***Lévesque, René** (1922-Nov. 1), prime minister of Quebec from 1976 to 1985.

Levi, Primo (1919-April 11), Italian Jewish author who survived the Nazi death camp at Auschwitz.

Levine, Joseph E. (1905-July 31), motion-picture producer.

Levine, Philip (1900-Oct. 18), Russian-born serologist who discovered the Rh factor in blood.

Lewis, Wilfrid B. (1908-Jan. 10), British-born Canadian physicist who developed Canada's Candu nuclear reactor.

Liberace (Wladziu Valentino Liberace) (1919-Feb. 4), flamboyant pianist and entertainer.

Licht, Frank (1916-May 30), Democratic governor of Rhode Island from 1969 to 1973.

Livingston, Jerry (Jerry Levinson) (1909?-July 20), composer of "Mairzy Doats" (1944).

***Lobel, Arnold** (1933-Dec. 4), illustrator and author of children's books who won the 1981 Caldecott Medal for his book *Fables* (1980).

Locke, Bobby (1917-March 9), South African golfer who won the British Open four times between 1949 and 1957.

Lubell, Samuel (1911-Aug. 16), Polish-born public opinion analyst.

Luboff, Norman (1917?-Sept. 22), director of the famous Norman Luboff Choir.

***Luce, Clare Boothe** (1903-Oct. 9), editor, playwright, congresswoman, and diplomat.

MacBeth, Donald (1950?-March 1), Canadian-born jockey who won the first Breeders' Cup thoroughbred horse race in 1984.

MacLean, Alistair (1922-Feb. 2), British adventure novelist who wrote *The Guns of Navarone* (1957).

Madden, Ray J. (1892-Sept. 28), Democratic representative from Indiana from 1943 to 1977.

Mamoulian, Rouben (1897-Dec. 4), Russian-born stage and film director who helped found the Directors Guild of America.

Arthur F. Burns,
chairman of the Fed

Bayard Rustin,
civil rights leader

Rita Hayworth,
Hollywood "Love Goddess"

Liberace, flamboyant
pianist and entertainer

Mariucci, John (1916-March 23), defenseman with the Chicago Black Hawks from 1940 to 1948; member of the U.S. Hockey Hall of Fame.

Marquand, Richard (1937-Sept. 4), British director of the film *Return of the Jedi* (1983).

Martin, John Bartlow (1915-Jan. 3), journalist, author, and political speechwriter.

Martin, Quinn (1922-Sept. 5), TV producer.

Marvin, Lee (1924-Aug. 29), rugged actor who won an Oscar in 1965 for his performance in *Cat Ballou.*

Masson, André (1896-Oct. 28), French surrealist painter.

Maysles, David (1932-Jan. 3), filmmaker who, with his brother Albert, made such documentaries as *Salesman* (1969) and *Gimme Shelter* (1970).

McCree, Wade H., Jr. (1920-Aug. 30), solicitor general of the United States from 1977 to 1981.

McKinney, Stewart B. (1931-May 7), Republican congressman from Connecticut since 1971.

McLaren, Norman (1914-Jan. 26), Scottish-born Canadian filmmaker.

McLean, Sir Kenneth Graeme (1896-June 5), British lieutenant general who helped plan the Allied invasion of Europe during World War II.

McMahon, Don (1930-July 22), pitcher for seven major-league baseball teams from 1957 to 1974.

McNamara, Kevin (1926-April 8), Roman Catholic archbishop of Dublin.

***Medawar, Sir Peter B.** (1915-Oct. 2), British zoologist who shared the 1960 Nobel Prize for physiology or medicine for his work on the body's rejection of transplanted tissues.

Mikes, George (1912-Aug. 30), Hungarian-born British author of *How to Be an Alien* (1946).

Milford, Theodore R. (1895-Jan. 19), British clergyman who founded the Oxfam relief agency.

Miller, Julius Sumner (1909-April 14), physicist who portrayed Professor Wonderful on TV's "The Mickey Mouse Club" in the 1950's.

Minsky, Morton (1902?-March 23), last of the four Minsky brothers who ran a famous chain of burlesque theaters in New York City.

Mitchell, Dale (1921-Jan. 5), outfielder with the Cleveland Indians from 1946 to 1956.

Moore, Gerald (1899-March 13), British pianist and recital accompanist.

Moorhead, William S. (1923-Aug. 3), Democratic representative from Pennsylvania from 1959 to 1981.

Morano, Albert P. (1908-Dec. 16), Republican representative from Connecticut from 1951 to 1959.

Muntz, Earl W. (1914-June 20), automobile dealer and electronics manufacturer known as "Madman Muntz."

Murchison, Clinton W., Jr. (1924-March 30), oil millionaire and former owner of the Dallas Cowboys football team.

*Myrdal, Gunnar (1898-May 17), Swedish sociologist and economist who shared the 1974 Nobel Prize in economics.

Negri, Pola (Barbara Apollonia Chalupiec) (1899?-Aug. 1), Polish-born silent-film star.

Rudolf Hess, last of the top Nazis

Margaret Laurence, eminent Canadian novelist

Ray Bolger, the scarecrow in *Oz*

Andy Warhol, a founder of pop art

Nix, Robert N. C., Sr. (1905-June 22), Democrat who was Pennsylvania's first black U.S. representative, serving from 1958 to 1979.

Nixon, Donald (1914-June 27), hotel executive; brother of former President Richard M. Nixon.

Nixon, Edgar D. (1899-Feb. 25), black civil rights leader who helped organize the 1955 bus boycott in Montgomery, Ala.

*Northrop, John H. (1891-May 27), biochemist who shared the 1946 Nobel Prize in chemistry for his work on the purification and crystallization of enzymes.

Oboler, Arch (1909-March 19), top radio scriptwriter of the 1930's and 1940's who created the series "Lights Out."

O'Boyle, Patrick A. (1896-Aug. 10), Roman Catholic cardinal; first archbishop of Washington, D.C.

O'Konski, Alvin E. (1904-July 8), Republican congressman from Wisconsin from 1943 to 1973.

Page, Geraldine (1924-June 13), winner of the Academy Award for best actress in 1986 for *The Trip to Bountiful*.

Peller, Clara (1902?-Aug. 11), Russian-born actress who uttered the famous line "Where's the beef?" in TV commercials for a hamburger chain.

Perlmutter, Nathan (1923-July 12), national director of the Anti-Defamation League of B'nai B'rith.

Phillips, Channing E. (1928-Nov. 11), Protestant clergyman and civil rights leader.

Piret, Edgar L. (1910-Oct. 1), Canadian-born chemist who developed the quick-drying process used to make K-rations for the U.S. armed forces.

Plaza Lasso, Galo (1906-Jan. 28), president of Ecuador from 1948 to 1952; secretary-general of the Organization of American States from 1968 to 1975.

Poage, Bob (William R. Poage) (1899-Jan. 3), Democratic congressman from Texas from 1937 to 1978.

Preston, Robert (Robert Preston Meservey) (1918-March 21), musical comedy star who played the title role in *The Music Man* on Broadway in 1957 and on film in 1962.

Proulx, Adolphe (1927-July 22), Canadian archbishop of the Roman Catholic diocese of Gatineau-Hull, Que.

Provensen, Martin E. (1916-March 27), illustrator of children's books who, with his wife, Alice, won the 1984 Caldecott Medal for *The Glorious Flight*.

Pyle, J. Howard (1906?-Nov. 29), Republican governor of Arizona from 1951 to 1955.

Rich, Buddy (Bernard Rich) (1917-April 2), legendary jazz drummer.

Robison, Howard W. (1915-Sept. 26), Republican representative from New York from 1958 to 1975.

Rogers, Carl R. (1902-Feb. 4), psychologist who developed client-centered therapy, a method that encourages troubled individuals to take the lead in their treatment.

Rorke, Hayden (1910-Aug. 19), actor who played the space agency psychiatrist on TV's "I Dream of Jeannie" from 1965 to 1970.

Rosenberg, Edgar (1925?-Aug. 14), German-born husband and manager of comedian Joan Rivers.

Rosenthal, Harold D. (1917-March 19), British opera critic.

Rowan, Dan (1922-Sept. 22), co-star of the 1960's comedy series "Rowan & Martin's Laugh-In."

*Rustin, Bayard (1910-Aug. 24), civil rights leader; chief organizer of the 1963 March on Washington.

Rutherford, Angelo (1953?-Jan. 30), former child actor who portrayed Willie Porter on the 1960's TV series "Gentle Ben."

Sackler, Arthur M. (1913-May 26), psychiatrist, art collector, and philanthropist.

Sampson, Will (1934?-June 3), Creek Indian actor who played the mute Chief Bromden in *One Flew Over the Cuckoo's Nest* (1975).

Sankara, Thomas (1950?-Oct. 15), president of Burkina Faso (formerly Upper Volta) since a 1983 coup.

Schidlof, Peter (1922-Aug. 16), Austrian-born violist of the Amadeus Quartet.

Scott, Randolph (1898-March 2), actor who starred in many Western movies, including *Santa Fe* (1951) and *Ride the High Country* (1962).

***Segovia, Andrés** (1893-June 2), Spanish classical guitarist.

Selkirk, George A. (1908-Jan. 19), Canadian-born outfielder for the New York Yankees from 1934 to 1942.

Sewell, Luke (James L. Sewell) (1901-May 14), catcher for the Cleveland Indians from 1921 to 1932 and manager of the St. Louis Browns from 1941 to 1946.

Shapiro, Samuel H. (1907-March 15), Democratic governor of Illinois in 1968 and 1969.

Shawn, Dick (Richard Schulefand) (1923-April 17), comic actor who played Adolf Hitler in *The Producers* (1968).

Silkin, John E. (1923-April 26), British Labour Party leader and Cabinet minister.

Singh, Charan (1902-May 29), prime minister of India in 1979 and 1980.

Sirk, Douglas (Claus Detlev Sierck) (1900-Jan. 14), Danish-born film director known for such melodramas as *Magnificent Obsession* (1954) and *Imitation of Life* (1959).

Snedden, Sir Billy Mackie (1926-June 26), former leader of Australia's Liberal Party.

Soames, Lord (Arthur C. J. Soames) (1920-Sept. 16), last British governor of Rhodesia (now Zimbabwe).

***Soyer, Raphael** (1899-Nov. 4), Russian-born realist painter.

Stanford-Tuck, Robert R. (1916-May 5), one of Great Britain's most decorated World War II pilots.

Stewart, Michael (1929-Sept. 20), Tony Award-winning author of the Broadway hits *Bye Bye Birdie* (1960) and *Hello, Dolly!* (1964).

Stewart, Slam (Leroy Stewart) (1914-Dec. 9), jazz bassist.

Sullivan, Maxine (Marietta Williams) (1911-April 7), jazz and folk singer.

Susskind, David (1920-Feb. 22), TV producer and interviewer.

***Taylor, Maxwell D.** (1901-April 19), U.S. Army general and chairman of the Joint Chiefs of Staff from 1962 to 1964.

Taylor, Ralph W. (1872?-May 15), last survivor of the charge up San Juan Hill in the Spanish-American War of 1898.

Tosh, Peter (Winston H. MacIntosh) (1944-Sept. 11), Jamaican reggae music artist.

Trapp, Maria von (1905-March 28), Austrian-born singer whose story was told in the 1965 film *The Sound of Music*.

Trend, Lord (Burke St. John Trend) (1914-July 21), secretary to the British Cabinet from 1963 to 1973.

Trifa, Valerian (1914-Jan. 28), Romanian-born archbishop of the Romanian Orthodox Episcopate of America who was deported from the United States in 1984 for concealing his Nazi past.

Troughton, Patrick G. (1920?-March 28), British actor who played Dr. Who on the BBC TV series of that name from 1966 to 1969.

Tudor, Antony (William Cook) (1908-April 19), British-born choreographer of the American Ballet Theatre.

Vernon, Jackie (Ralph Verrone) (1924?-Nov. 10), television and nightclub comedian.

Walston, Bobby (1929?-Oct. 7), end and place-kicker for football's Philadelphia Eagles from 1951 to 1962.

***Warhol, Andy** (1930?-Feb. 22), artist who helped found the pop art movement.

***Washington, Harold** (1922-Nov. 25), first black mayor of Chicago.

Andrés Segovia, Spanish classical guitarist

James Baldwin, writer about racism

Lee Marvin, movie tough guy

William J. Casey, director of the CIA

Wei, Charles C. (1914?-Feb. 20), Chinese-born shipping executive and contract bridge champion who devised the popular Precision Club system of bidding.

Wells, Sarajane (1913?-Jan. 10), radio actress who played Betty Fairfield on "Jack Armstrong, All-American Boy" and Mary Rutledge on "The Guiding Light."

Wheeler, Hugh (1912-July 26), British-born novelist who wrote the books for the musicals *A Little Night Music* (1973) and *Sweeney Todd* (1979).

Williams, Anna (1873-Dec. 27), 114-year-old Welsh woman thought to be the world's oldest living person in 1987.

***Williams, Emlyn** (1905-Sept. 25), Welsh actor and playwright who wrote *The Corn Is Green* (1938).

Wilson, Earl (1907-Jan. 16), columnist who covered entertainment for the *New York Post* from 1942 to 1983.

Wittig, Georg (1897-Aug. 26), West German chemist who shared the 1979 Nobel Prize for chemistry.

Worrell, Eric (1924-July 13), Australian naturalist who founded the Australian Reptile Park at Gosford, New South Wales.

Wydler, John W. (1924-Aug. 4), Republican representative from New York from 1963 to 1981.

Young, Dick (1917-Aug. 31), nationally syndicated sports columnist.

Yourcenar, Marguerite (1903-Dec. 17), French-born writer and scholar.

Zorinsky, Edward (1928-March 6), Democratic senator from Nebraska since 1977.   Sara Dreyfuss

DELAWARE. See STATE GOVERNMENT.

DEMOCRATIC PARTY leaders were stunned on Dec. 15, 1987, by the announcement that former Senator Gary Hart of Colorado was reentering the race for the 1988 Democratic presidential nomination. Earlier in the year, Hart had been strongly favored in all polls until a personal scandal forced him to drop out of the race.

Hart withdrew on May 8, five days after *The Miami* (Fla.) *Herald* reported that a young woman, Miami model Donna Rice, had spent the night with him in his Washington, D.C., town house. Hart, who earlier had challenged the news media to prove rumors that he was a womanizer, initially denied the rendezvous.

Hart explained in December that he was reentering the race because, "I have a sense of new direction and a set of new ideas that our country needs that no one else represents." Many political observers believed his decision was partly due to the failure of any other candidate to pull ahead of the pack. During Hart's absence, the other six candidates—similar in age, experience, and outlook—had each struggled to create an image that would separate him from the others.

The acknowledged front-runner in the public opinion polls before Hart's reentry had been Jesse L. Jackson, a black civil rights leader from Illinois. Jackson was making a determined effort to broaden his appeal beyond the black community, which gave him strong support in the 1984 presidential primary campaigns. Others in the race were Governor Michael S. Dukakis of Massachusetts, former Governor Bruce E. Babbitt of Arizona, Senators Albert A. Gore, Jr., of Tennessee and Paul Simon of Illinois, and Representative Richard A. Gephardt of Missouri. (See the individual biographies on each of the presidential candidates.)

Out of Race. Another noteworthy aspect of the Democratic line-up was the absence of a candidate who had been expected to make a strong showing in the primary elections in 1988: Governor Mario M. Cuomo of New York. Almost as stunning as Hart's reentry was Cuomo's declaration in February that he would not be a candidate. Cuomo said he thought it would be in the best interests of his family, his state, and the Democratic Party that he not seek the presidency. Other prominent Democrats who decided not to run included Governor Bill Clinton of Arkansas, former Governor Charles S. Robb of Virginia, Representative Patricia Schroeder of Colorado, and Senators Sam Nunn of Georgia, Bill Bradley of New Jersey, and Dale Bumpers of Arkansas.

A misstep destroyed the campaign of Senator Joseph R. Biden, Jr., of Delaware. Biden withdrew

As his aides look on, former Senator Gary Hart announces in May that he is withdrawing from the presidential race, but he reentered it in December.

on September 23 after he admitted plagiarizing a law school paper in 1965 and using, without credit, the language and theme of a British politician's autobiographical campaign speech in his own presidential quest.

Wooing the South. On Feb. 10, 1987, the Democratic Party's site selection committee voted 44 to 13 for Atlanta over Houston as the location of its 1988 nominating convention. The convention will be held in Atlanta's Omni Center from July 18 to 21, 1988.

Before the rebirth of Hart's campaign, Jackson had been widely expected to lead the Democratic pack in the March 8, 1988, "Super Tuesday" primaries in 15 mostly Southern states. But in October 1987, Senator Gore made a calculated effort to energize his lagging campaign, boost his appeal in the South, and distinguish himself from his rivals by picturing them as weak and indecisive on foreign and defense policy. Polls indicated that Gore's tactic was successful, though his differences with the other candidates may have been exaggerated.

Debates Planned. An early feature of the Democratic presidential campaign was the planning of 70 debates or joint appearances before mid-March 1988. Democratic National Committee Chairman Paul G. Kirk, Jr., said such events would be good for the party by giving lesser-known candidates a forum and putting the focus of the campaign on issues rather than on personalities. But the candidates themselves insisted on limits. After participating in three debates and a joint appearance in one week in September, Dukakis said, "I can't do four debates a week and conduct a campaign."

The Democratic and Republican national committees agreed to jointly sponsor three debates in September and October 1988 between their presidential nominees and one between the vice presidential nominees. The League of Women Voters, sponsor of presidential debates for over 25 years, accused the parties of "stealing" the debates.

Other Actions. On Oct. 22, 1987, Democratic leaders opened an office of voter participation within the party's national committee. Their aim was to increase the numbers of voters in 1988 to 100 million, up from 92 million in 1984.

In January 1987, House Democrats elected five-term Representative Beryl Anthony, Jr., of Arkansas to be chairman of the Democratic Congressional Campaign Committee. He succeeded Representative Tony Coelho of California, who had transformed the nearly defunct committee into a powerful fund-raising tool that helped preserve Democratic majorities in the House of Representatives. Coelho resigned to become House Democratic whip.   Frank Cormier and Margot Cormier

See also ELECTIONS; REPUBLICAN PARTY. In WORLD BOOK, see DEMOCRATIC PARTY.

DENMARK. A general election on Sept. 8, 1987, left Denmark in political chaos. The four parties that ruled the nation via a center-right minority coalition lost seats in the Folketing (parliament), finishing with 70 of that body's 179 seats. The Conservatives led the government parties with 38 seats, with the Liberals, the Center Democrats, and the Christian People's Party winning 32. An allied centrist party, the Radical Liberals, won 11 seats, while a group of opposition parties led by the Social Democrats won 85. The right wing Progress Party got 9 seats, and a left wing group called Common Course won the remaining 4.

The election cast the Progress Party, with its 9 seats, in a pivotal role. An alliance of the four coalition parties, the Radical Liberals, and the Progress Party would hold 90 seats—a majority in the Folketing and therefore enough to support a government. Parties on both the left and right, however, disapproved of the Progress Party for its strong antitax views and its opposition to Denmark's traditionally liberal welfare-state policies. The Radical Liberals refused to participate in an alliance that would include the Progress Party.

The leader of the Social Democrats, Anker Jørgensen, invited the Radical Liberals to join the opposition group to form a government. The Radical Liberals declined the invitation.

On September 9, Prime Minister Poul Schlüter revived his four-party minority coalition government and hoped for Radical Liberal support. Radical Liberal leader Niels Helweg Petersen said that his party's members of the Folketing would "consider each proposal from the government as it is put forward."

Downturn Expected. Schlüter called the election on August 18, four months before his term of office was scheduled to end. The election came as Denmark faced an economic crisis that threatened its extensive welfare system. The country had a total foreign debt of $38.4 billion, and both Denmark's exports and its agricultural output were down from 1986 levels.

Greenland Stalemate. The left wing coalition government of Greenland collapsed in March following a dispute over the modernization of the North Atlantic Treaty Organization's early-warning radar system at the United States military base in Thule. Elections held on May 26 failed to change the political situation. The center-left Siumut Party of Prime Minister Jonathan Motzfeldt kept its 11 seats in the 27-seat parliament. The main opposition, the center-right Atassut Party, also retained 11 seats.

Greenland is a province of Denmark but established its own government to control internal affairs in 1979.   Kenneth Brown

See also EUROPE (Facts in Brief Table). In WORLD BOOK, see DENMARK; GREENLAND.

DENTISTRY. More people in the United States are keeping their natural teeth than ever before, according to a national survey released in May 1987 by the National Institute of Dental Research in Bethesda, Md. The survey, conducted in 1985 and 1986, found that only 14.6 per cent of Americans between the ages of 55 and 64 have lost their teeth. In a similar survey conducted between 1960 and 1962, 36.3 per cent of the adults in that age group were toothless. The 1987 report also found a similar decrease in toothlessness among adults between the ages of 65 and 74.

The American Dental Association in Chicago attributed the drop in toothlessness to *fluoridation* (the addition of *fluorides*, chemicals that prevent tooth decay, to water supplies), advances in dental technology, and regular dental checkups.

Pain-Relief Spray. In March 1987, researchers at the University of Medicine and Dentistry of New Jersey in Newark and Tufts University School of Dentistry in Boston reported that a painkiller called *butorphanol* gave quick pain relief to dental patients when administered as a nasal spray after treatment. Butorphanol is currently given to patients as an injection because it is not as effective in tablet or capsule form.

In their study, the researchers gave butorphanol nasal spray to 75 patients who experienced pain after surgery on impacted wisdom teeth. The investigators then monitored the intensity of the pain—as well as the amount of pain relief—in each patient at various intervals. The researchers found that the patients experienced pain relief as quickly as 15 minutes after receiving the spray.

According to the researchers, the nasal spray may provide an alternative painkiller for patients who cannot take other pain-relieving drugs. But the researchers noted that butorphanol nasal spray caused drowsiness, dizziness, and nausea in some patients, the same side effects seen in patients given butorphanol by injection.

Screw-In Teeth? A tiny fixture, similar to a screw, has been developed to secure artificial teeth to the bone beneath gum tissues, according to a September 18 report by researchers of the State University of New York at Buffalo and Roswell Park Memorial Institute, also in Buffalo. The fixture, made of titanium, is 3.5 millimeters (about ⅛ inch) long.

According to the researchers, the fixture is implanted into the bone where an artificial tooth is to be placed. The artificial tooth is then fitted with a tiny post, which is inserted into the fixture. The fixture could also be used to hold posts that support dentures. The researchers are still testing the fixture's overall effectiveness. Lou Joseph

In WORLD BOOK, see DENTISTRY.

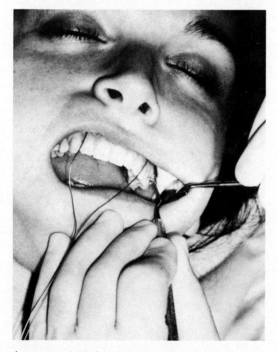

In a new method of dental anesthesia, electrodes placed in the patient's mouth transmit a weak electric current that relieves pain.

DETROIT in 1987 witnessed a major air disaster, an unprecedented agreement between an automaker and a union, a teachers' strike, and the continued redevelopment of decaying parts of the city. Crime continued to dominate Detroit-area headlines, including the slayings of three policemen in a suburban motel, an alleged arson fire that killed three fire fighters, and the gunshot deaths of at least 34 young people.

Airliner Crashes. On August 16, a Northwest Airlines jet taking off from Detroit Metropolitan Airport stalled and crashed in a fireball on a nearby road. The crash took 156 lives, including 2 on the ground. The only surviving passenger was a 4-year-old girl, Cecilia Cichan of Tempe, Ariz. The crash was the second worst accident in United States aviation history, exceeded only by a 1979 Chicago crash that killed 273.

Federal investigators determined that the jet's wing flaps had not been set properly for take-off. In mid-October, the investigators announced that the plane's warning systems, which should have alerted the pilots about the flaps, might have failed because of an electrical short circuit.

Auto Workers Contract. In September, the United Auto Workers union (UAW) and Ford Motor Company conducted the most amiable contract negotiations in memory. For the first time ever, the UAW extended its workers' contracts

After five trouble-plagued years of construction, Detroit's People Mover elevated train wends its way through the city's downtown area in July.

past the September 14 strike deadline and kept bargaining with Ford, the automaker it chose as its negotiating target in 1987. Less than three days later, the two sides agreed to a pact that the UAW said gave its members a "historic" assurance of job security and that Ford officials said would permit the company to improve efficiency. In October, the UAW settled for roughly the same contract terms with General Motors Corporation.

The automobile industry lost a historic figure in 1987. On September 29, Henry Ford II, who for 35 years had headed the company his grandfather founded, died of pneumonia at age 70.

School Strike. About 182,000 Detroit public school students received an unexpected vacation starting on August 31, when the district's 11,500 teachers went on strike. Classes resumed three weeks later, after teachers settled for a 6.5 per cent raise for the 1987-1988 school year and—if the school system can find the money—raises totaling 13 per cent over the next two years.

Crime. Efforts to stem Detroit's crime epidemic continued in 1987. After the April shooting death of a local high school football star, rallies were held throughout the city asking students to pledge that they would not carry weapons. But the violence continued, and by early November, more than 300 youths under age 17 had been injured—34 of them fatally—in gun-related incidents.

In July, three policemen from the suburb of Inkster were ambushed and then killed with their own guns after they went to a motel to serve a warrant on a woman and her three sons. After being apprehended by other officers, the family members said they were embittered by a "racist" society that thwarted their ambitions.

In March, three Detroit firemen died in a huge warehouse fire apparently set by an arsonist.

Redevelopment. The 14-year-old administration of Detroit Mayor Coleman A. Young continued its efforts to redevelop the city, especially along the riverfront, on the northbound artery of Woodward Avenue, and on the city's east side. During the year, city officials launched a $20-million renovation of the Detroit City Airport and announced plans for a new office tower near the expanding Cobo Hall convention center—the first new office project downtown since the Renaissance Center was built a decade ago. But the Cobo Hall expansion failed to spur the new hotel construction city officials had predicted.

The People Mover monorail system began operating in July after five years of construction plagued by setbacks, including work stoppages and cracked support beams. City officials hoped the 2.9-mile (4.7-kilometer) system, which loops through the central business district, would help spur downtown redevelopment.   Patricia L. Edmonds

See also CITY. In WORLD BOOK, see DETROIT.

DISASTERS

DISASTERS. The worst natural disaster of 1987 occurred in Ecuador, where a series of earthquakes on March 5 and 6—and the flooding and mud slides that followed—caused at least 300 confirmed deaths. An additional 4,000 people were believed dead.

The year's worst disaster at sea happened on December 20, when the Philippine passenger ship *Dona Paz*, loaded with Christmas travelers, collided with the oil tanker *Victor*. Both ships burst into flames and sank in the shark-infested waters off Mindoro island. Officials estimated that the death toll was at least 1,600.

Among the year's other major disasters were three aviation accidents. A Polish jetliner on its way to New York City crashed on May 9, just minutes after take-off from Warsaw, Poland. All 183 people aboard died in the crash, Poland's worst air disaster ever. On August 16, a Northwest Airlines passenger jet had just taken off from Detroit on its way to Phoenix when it crashed in flames. The crash killed 154 of the 155 people aboard the plane and 2 motorists on the ground. The death toll made it the second-worst airline disaster in United States history, exceeded only by a 1979 Chicago crash that killed 273 people. A South African Airways jumbo jet crashed into the Indian Ocean near Mauritius on Nov. 28, 1987. All 159 people aboard the jet died in the worst aviation disaster in South African history.

Disasters that resulted in 30 or more deaths in 1987 included the following:

Aircraft Crashes

Jan. 3—Near Abidjan, Ivory Coast. A Brazilian jetliner crashed shortly after take-off, killing 50 of the 51 people aboard.

May 9—Near Warsaw, Poland. A LOT Polish Airlines jetliner crashed in flames shortly after take-off, killing 183 people in Poland's worst air disaster.

June 26—Near Baguio, Philippines. A Philippine Airlines plane hit a mountain, killing all 50 people aboard.

July 30—Near Mexico City. A cargo plane crashed on a busy highway, killing 54 people.

Aug. 16—Detroit. A Northwest Airlines jetliner crashed in flames shortly after take-off, causing 156 deaths.

Aug. 31—Off Phuket Island, Thailand. A Thai Airways jet plunged into the Andaman Sea, and all 83 people aboard were killed.

Oct. 15—Mount Crezzo, Italy, near Lake Como. All 37 people aboard an Italian airliner died after it crashed in the foothills of the Alps.

Nov. 28—Indian Ocean, near Mauritius. A South African Airways jumbo jet crashed into the ocean, killing all 159 people aboard in South Africa's worst air disaster.

Dec. 8—Near Lima, Peru. A navy plane carrying Peru's top soccer team crashed into the Pacific Ocean, killing 42 of the 43 people aboard.

Bus and Truck Crashes

Late January—Assam state, India. About 60 Hindu pilgrims died after their bus fell into a river.

March 15—Near Soroti, Uganda. An overloaded bus hit a truck and then plunged off a bridge into a river, causing 101 deaths.

Mid-June—Near Patiala, India. More than 60 people drowned after a crowded bus crashed through the side of a bridge and hurtled into a canal.

Aug. 7—Uttar Pradesh state, India. At least 68 people drowned after their bus plunged into a canal.

Oct. 20—Moro, Pakistan. A train crashed into a bus at a railroad crossing, killing at least 50 bus passengers.

Nov. 13—Mexico City. A bus skidded into a lake, causing 40 deaths.

Dec. 11—Cairo, Egypt. A train collided with a bus full of schoolchildren, killing 64 of them.

Earthquakes

March 5-6—Napo province, Ecuador. A series of earthquakes caused flooding and deadly mud slides that left about 300 people dead and 4,000 missing.

Nov. 26—Pantar island, Indonesia. An earthquake caused landslides and a tidal wave that left at least 42 people dead and many more missing.

Explosions and Fires

March 15—Harbin, China. An explosion at a linen mill killed at least 47 workers.

May 6-June 2—Heilongjiang (Heilungkiang) province, China. A forest fire caused at least 193 deaths.

Sept. 26—Near Surabaya, Indonesia. A crowded bus exploded in flames, burning 41 passengers to death.

Nov. 18—London. A fire at the King's Cross subway station killed 31 people.

Mine Disasters

March 26—Near Zamora, Ecuador. Between 30 and 50 miners died in a cave-in at a gold mine.

April 9—Ermelo, South Africa. A methane gas explosion at a coal mine killed 34 miners.

Aug. 31—Near Welkom, South Africa. An underground explosion sent a crowded elevator hurtling down a gold-mine shaft, and at least 50 miners were killed.

Shipwrecks

Jan. 16—Off Cebu island, Philippines. At least 50 participants in a Roman Catholic festival drowned after the boat carrying them sank.

March 6—Zeebrugge, Belgium. An English Channel ferry capsized after leaving the harbor, killing at least 188 people in the worst peacetime channel disaster ever.

May 8—Near Nantong (Nan-t'ung), China. A ferry collided with a tugboat and sank in the Yangtze River, drowning about 95 people.

July 11—Off Negros island, Philippines. Eight bodies were found and an additional 64 people were feared dead after a ferry sank in rough seas.

Oct. 6—Off Nagua, Dominican Republic. More than 100 refugees hoping to reach Puerto Rico drowned or were killed by sharks after a boat carrying them overturned in shark-infested waters.

Oct. 15—Near Narayanganj, Bangladesh. A ferry sank in the Sitalakhya River, drowning up to 100 people.

Oct. 26—Northern Bangladesh. A ferry sank after hitting a silt island in the Ganges River, killing an estimated 110 people.

Nov. 28—Bangladesh. A river ferry collided with a larger cargo vessel and sank, leaving 100 people missing and feared drowned.

Dec. 20—Off Mindoro island, Philippines. At least 1,600 people died after a passenger ship collided with an oil tanker and both vessels sank.

Storms and Floods

Late January—São Paulo, Brazil. At least 75 people died in floods.

Feb. 1—Villa Rica, Peru, near Tingo María. Torrential

298

Investigators examine wreckage of a Northwest Airlines jetliner that crashed on take-off from Detroit on August 16, killing 156 people.

rains caused a river to overflow its banks and wash away part of Villa Rica, leaving more than 100 people dead and about 250 missing.

Feb. 7-8—Vanuatu. Typhoon Uma caused at least 49 deaths.

April-June—China. Widespread floods triggered by heavy rains killed at least 356 people.

May 22—Saragosa, Tex. A tornado destroyed most of the town and killed 30 people.

July 9—Near Kazipet, Andhra Pradesh state, India. A flash flood swept two cars of a passenger train into a river and killed at least 53 people.

July 15-16—Southern South Korea. Typhoon Thelma caused floods, mud slides, and stormy seas that killed at least 123 people and left about 212 missing.

July 24-26—Northern Iran. Flooding killed about 150 people in Neyshabur and nearby villages, 140 people in Teheran, and 55 in Arak.

July 27—Seoul, South Korea. Heavy rains triggered flash floods and landslides that caused at least 74 deaths.

July 28—Zhejiang (Chekiang) and Jiangsu (Kiangsu) provinces, China. Typhoon Alex killed 68 people.

Aug. 2-early September—Bangladesh. Flooding set off by heavy monsoon rains caused more than 1,000 deaths due to drowning, collapsed buildings, and flood-spawned epidemics.

Aug. 13—Philippines. Typhoon Betty battered Luzon and nearby islands, killing 48 people.

Sept. 9-11—Fujian (Fukien) and Zhejiang (Chekiang) provinces, China. Typhoon Gerald caused 95 deaths.

Sept. 25-29—Natal province, South Africa. As many as 250 people died in floods caused by five days of record heavy rains.

Oct. 23-26—Philippines and Taiwan. Typhoon Lynn caused at least 7 deaths in the Philippines and left 42 people dead and 18 missing in Taiwan.

Nov. 25-26—Luzon island, Philippines. Typhoon Nina killed at least 658 people.

Train Wrecks

Feb. 17—Itaquera, Brazil, near São Paulo. A commuter train switched tracks into the path of an oncoming train, killing at least 46 people.

July 2—Kasumbalesha Shaba, Zaire, near Lubumbashi. A trailer-truck crashed into a train, killing 128 people.

Aug. 7—Kamensk-Shakhtinskiy, Soviet Union. A runaway locomotive rammed a passenger train, causing dozens of fatalities.

Oct. 19—Near Jakarta, Indonesia. A commuter train crashed head-on into another train, killing 155.

Other Disasters

Jan. 1-18—Northern Europe. One of the worst cold spells on record caused nearly 265 deaths, including 77 in the Soviet Union and 38 in Great Britain.

March 9—Near Lima, Peru. Landslides triggered by heavy rains left at least 100 people dead.

May 4—Western Sumatra Island, Indonesia. Tons of earth and rock, loosened by heavy rains, swamped two villages and caused at least 118 deaths.

July 20-29—Southern Europe. A heat wave caused at least 1,000 deaths in Greece and about 50 in Italy.

Sept. 6—Near Maracay, Venezuela. Mud slides left at least 400 people dead.

Sept. 27—Near Medellín, Colombia. A landslide buried a shantytown and killed at least 205 people.

Nov. 29—Los Maitenes, Chile. An avalanche buried a construction camp, leaving 60 workers feared dead.

Dec. 5—Peru. Mud slides swept through five villages in the Andes, killing more than 100 people.   Sara Dreyfuss

DJIBOUTI. See AFRICA.

DOG. On Feb. 10, 1987, in New York City's Madison Square Garden, Judge Louis Auslander of Lake Forest, Ill., selected a German shepherd dog, Champion Covy Tucker Hill's Manhattan, as best-in-show at the Westminster Kennel Club's 111th annual show. It was the first time a German shepherd dog won the top prize. The champion, known as "Hatter," is owned by Shirlee Braunstein of Woodmere, N.Y., and Jane Firestone of Southern Pines, N.C.

In 1986, the American Kennel Club (AKC) registered 1,106,399 dogs. Cocker spaniels, poodles, and Labrador retrievers led the list of the most popular registered breeds. Golden retrievers were in fourth place, followed by German shepherd dogs, chow chows, beagles, miniature schnauzers, dachshunds, and Shetland sheepdogs. The Finnish spitz became eligible for AKC registration for the first time in August 1987. In July, Kenneth A. Marden of Titusville, N.J., succeeded William F. Stifel of Irvington, N.Y., as president of the AKC.

In 1987, communities throughout the United States passed antidog laws aimed at the American Staffordshire terrier and other "pit bull" dogs. The AKC joined other dog-related organizations in opposing breed-specific laws and encouraged the enactment of legislation that deals with the problem of vicious dogs of any breed.   Roberta Vesley

In WORLD BOOK, see DOG.

DOLE, ROBERT JOSEPH (1923-   ), United States senator from Kansas, announced his bid for the 1988 Republican presidential nomination on Nov. 9, 1987. He pledged to work for a balanced federal budget by cutting federal spending but said the cuts would not hurt "vulnerable Americans."

Dole was born on July 22, 1923, in Russell, Kans. He attended the University of Kansas in Lawrence from 1941 to 1943 before World War II interrupted his education. He joined the Army in 1943 and earned two Bronze Stars. Battle wounds left him with a paralyzed right arm.

After retiring from the Army in 1948, Dole returned to college. He earned a bachelor's degree and a law degree from Washburn Municipal University (now Washburn University of Topeka) in Kansas in 1952.

Dole's political career began in 1950, when at the age of 26 he was elected to one term in the Kansas legislature. From 1953 to 1960, he served as Russell County prosecuting attorney. Dole was elected to the U.S. House of Representatives in 1960 and to the Senate in 1968.

In 1975, Dole married his second wife, Elizabeth Hanford, who served as secretary of transportation from 1983 to 1987.   Mary A. Krier

In WORLD BOOK, see DOLE, ROBERT J.

DOMINICAN REPUBLIC. See LATIN AMERICA.

DROUGHT. See WATER; WEATHER.

DRUG ABUSE. A national survey of high school seniors conducted by the University of Michigan's Institute of Social Research in Ann Arbor, Mich., and released in January 1988, revealed considerable drug use among the students surveyed. The study, conducted in 1987, found that 66 per cent of the students had used alcohol within the month before the survey and that 37.5 per cent had consumed five or more drinks in one bout of drinking during the two weeks before the survey. In addition, 36 per cent of the students had used marijuana in the year before the survey, and 4.3 per cent had used cocaine in the month before they were polled.

The study also revealed that marijuana use had continued to decline from its peak in 1978. Daily use of the drug dropped from 10.7 per cent of those surveyed in 1978 to 3.3 per cent in 1987. Cocaine use has remained high for the last several years, but use of the drug declined in 1987. The proportion of high school seniors who use cocaine by smoking it—including those who use a highly addictive smokable form of cocaine called *crack*—also dropped during the year.

Alcohol Abuse. A 1987 Gallup Poll found that alcohol abuse affects the lives of a vast number of Americans. The poll found that 4 out of every 10 people had been damaged—or knew someone who had been damaged—due to drinking. The poll also revealed that 1 out of 5 teen-agers reported an alcohol problem at home.

Medical Research. According to two studies reported in May 1987 by research teams based at Harvard Medical School in Boston and the National Cancer Institute in Bethesda, Md., even moderate drinking of alcoholic beverages significantly increases the risk of breast cancer in women. Some health experts advised women with other known risk factors—including obesity and a family history of breast cancer—to abstain from drinking alcohol.

Researchers at the University of California at San Francisco reported in April 1987 that more than 10 per cent of cocaine users who were treated at a San Francisco hospital during a seven-year period suffered psychiatric or neurological problems linked to cocaine use. These problems included seizures, strokes, anxiety, depression, serious mental disturbances, and headaches.

AIDS (acquired immune deficiency syndrome) and its association with intravenous (IV) drug abuse was a major public health concern in 1987. Researchers reported at a conference on AIDS held in Washington, D.C., in June 1987 that although recent evidence suggested that the rate of new infection resulting from sexual contact had slowed somewhat, the spread of AIDS among IV drug abusers continued unabated.   David C. Lewis

In WORLD BOOK, see DRUG ABUSE.

DRUGS. The United States Food and Drug Administration (FDA) in Washington, D.C., on Sept. 1, 1987, approved a new prescription drug that reduces levels of cholesterol in the blood more effectively than any other medication. High cholesterol levels can increase the risk of heart attacks. The drug, called lovastatin, was developed by Merck Sharp & Dohme Research Laboratories of West Point, Pa., and is sold under the trade name Mevacor.

Lovastatin is the first of a new family of anticholesterol drugs that actually block the production of cholesterol by the liver. According to health experts, lovastatin not only is more potent in reducing cholesterol levels than previous medications, but also is easier to take and has fewer side effects. Physicians emphasized that lovastatin works best when the patient also follows a low-cholesterol diet.

Heart Attack Drug. The FDA on November 13 approved a new drug for use in the emergency treatment of heart attacks. Called *tissue plasminogen activator* (tPA), it reduces the damage caused by a heart attack by dissolving harmful blood clots and restoring normal blood flow to the heart muscle. If administered within the first six hours of a heart attack, it can often halt the attack or prevent serious damage to the heart. Produced by genetic engineering technology, tPA is sold by Genentech, Incorporated, of South San Francisco, Calif., under the trade name Activase.

AIDS Vaccines. On March 19, French researcher Daniel Zagury of the Pierre and Marie Curie University in Paris announced that he had injected himself and several volunteers with an experimental vaccine against AIDS (acquired immune deficiency syndrome). The vaccine, developed by scientists at the National Institutes of Health in Bethesda, Md., was intended for animal tests.

Another experimental AIDS vaccine—developed by MicroGeneSys, Incorporated, a small genetic engineering firm in West Haven, Conn.—received FDA approval for human tests on August 17. The FDA said that several other private companies in 1987 had applied for permission to begin testing experimental AIDS vaccines on human volunteers.

AIDS Drug OK'd. The first drug effective in prolonging the lives of some AIDS patients received FDA approval on March 20. The medication, zidovudine (formerly called azidothymidine or AZT), was developed by Burroughs Wellcome Company of Triangle Research Park, N.C., and given the trade name Retrovir. The drug works by inhibiting reproduction of the AIDS virus. Health officials emphasized that zidovudine does not cure AIDS and noted that it has potentially severe side effects. Another drawback is the cost of the drug—an estimated $5,500 to $8,500 per year per patient.

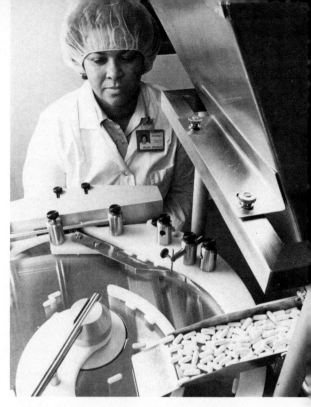

A worker at Burroughs Wellcome Company monitors production of zidovudine (formerly called AZT). The FDA approved the AIDS drug on March 20.

Alzheimer's Breakthrough? Public clamor for a controversial and highly publicized drug used to treat Alzheimer's disease led the U.S. government to announce a nationwide study of the medication in August, only to halt the study in October. Alzheimer's disease is a brain disorder that causes progressive severe memory loss and the inability to perform simple functions.

In late 1986, a research team at the University of California at Los Angeles reported that tetrahydroaminoacridine (THA) produced dramatic memory improvement in 17 Alzheimer's patients. Some scientists questioned the value of the 1986 research, especially since it was based on an extremely small sampling. The study, announced by the National Institute on Aging on August 6, would have tested THA's effectiveness in 300 Alzheimer's patients at 17 medical centers throughout the United States. But on October 23, the FDA requested a temporary suspension of the study to check on possible toxic side effects of THA.

IL-2 Treatment. On May 7, the FDA decided to expand the use of experimental cancer treatments using *interleukin-2* (IL-2), a protein that activates the body's disease-fighting immune system. Previously, IL-2 treatments had been available to only small numbers of patients. The new ruling made IL-2 treatments available at 52 cancer centers in the United States. The IL-2 treatments are intended for patients who have certain advanced cancers for which no other treatment exists.

Experimental Drugs. Otis R. Bowen, U.S. secretary of health and human services, announced on May 21 a program that makes experimental drugs more readily available to desperately ill or dying patients. Patients who have diseases for which no comparable alternative treatment exists can decide whether to risk taking a promising experimental drug that has not been fully tested for safety and effectiveness. In the past, physicians could not prescribe drugs for such conditions until the drug underwent lengthy tests and won FDA approval.

Hope for MS Victims. Medical researchers at the Albert Einstein College of Medicine in New York City reported on August 12 that a new experimental drug appears to slow—and may even reverse—the nerve damage that cripples victims of *multiple sclerosis* (MS). MS is a disease of the nervous system that can cause paralysis and other disabilities.

The experimental drug, called Cop 1, was developed in Israel. A two-year study found it beneficial, particularly in patients who were in the early stages of MS and had not suffered severe crippling. The researchers cautioned that it could take several years to establish Cop 1's effectiveness and safety as a treatment for MS.   Michael Woods

See also DRUG ABUSE; MEDICINE. In WORLD BOOK, see DRUG.

DUKAKIS, MICHAEL STANLEY (1933-   ), governor of Massachusetts, formally declared his candidacy for the 1988 Democratic presidential nomination on April 29, 1987. In his campaign, Dukakis stressed his record as governor, claiming that the economic improvement enjoyed by Massachusetts in the last decade reflected his leadership abilities. He embraced many traditional liberal views, including a woman's right to an abortion and more aid for education, housing, and jobs.

Dukakis, the son of Greek immigrant parents, was born on Nov. 3, 1933, in Brookline, Mass. He graduated from Swarthmore College in Pennsylvania in 1955, earning highest honors in political science. After serving in the U.S. Army in Korea from 1955 to 1957, he entered Harvard Law School and received his law degree in 1960. From 1963 to 1971, Dukakis served in the Massachusetts House of Representatives. He was elected governor in 1974 but failed in his 1978 bid for reelection. He then served as a lecturer at Harvard University's John F. Kennedy School of Government from 1979 to 1982 and made successful runs for governor in 1982 and 1986.

Dukakis married Katharine (Kitty) Dickson in 1963. Kitty Dukakis is director of the Public Space Partnerships Program, an environmental program at the Kennedy School of Government. The couple has three children.   Joan Stephenson

DU PONT, PIERRE SAMUEL, IV (1935-   ), campaigned during 1987 for the 1988 Republican presidential nomination after becoming the first declared candidate on Sept. 16, 1986. In his campaign, du Pont advanced a variety of ideas that set him apart from his conservative rivals. He favored, for example, a private savings option to social security, and the granting of coupons called *education vouchers* to parents, who would use them to pay for their children's education at either public or private schools.

Pierre du Pont, nicknamed Pete, was born in Wilmington, Del., on Jan. 22, 1935, a member of the family that founded the gigantic chemical firm E. I. du Pont de Nemours & Company. He received an engineering degree from Princeton University in New Jersey in 1956, served in the United States Navy from 1957 until 1960, and in 1963 obtained a law degree from Harvard Law School in Cambridge, Mass. He worked as an engineer for the family firm from 1963 to 1969.

After serving in the Delaware legislature from 1969 to 1971, he was a member of the U.S. House of Representatives from 1971 to 1977. Du Pont served as governor of Delaware from 1977 to 1985.

Du Pont's wife, Elise, is an attorney and a former assistant administrator of the Agency for International Development. The du Ponts have four children.   Jay Myers

EASTERN ORTHODOX CHURCHES. Centuries of tradition were broken in 1987 when Patriarch Demetrios of Constantinople, Turkey, the leading figure of the Orthodox world, traveled extensively to visit leaders of other Orthodox churches. In May, he visited the patriarchates of Alexandria, Egypt, and Jerusalem, Israel, and in August he visited the patriarchates of Moscow; Belgrade, Yugoslavia; and Bucharest, Romania.

Patriarch Demetrios' stop in Moscow was significant because the Russian Orthodox Church was planning a 1988 celebration of the 1,000th anniversary of the introduction of Christianity to Russia. During his visit, he met with Patriarch Pimen, Metropolitan of Moscow and All Russia.

In November, Patriarch Demetrios visited the Church of Greece in Athens. He ended his year of travels with three visits in December designed to establish a closer relationship among the world's churches. He met with Pope John Paul II at the Vatican in Rome, and with Robert A. K. Runcie, archbishop of Canterbury, in England. He also went to Geneva, Switzerland, to visit the World Council of Churches, an organization of Eastern Orthodox and Protestant churches.

Crisis in Greece. A serious rift between Greece's Socialist government and the Greek Orthodox Church occurred in 1987. On April 3, the Greek Parliament passed a measure that would have

British Prime Minister Margaret Thatcher tours
St. Sergius Monastery in Zagorsk during a
visit to the Soviet Union in March.

stripped the church of its extensive land holdings throughout Greece and given potential control over church councils to government appointees. The measure provoked widespread protests and a sharp division between Archbishop Seraphim, primate of Greece, and Prime Minister Andreas Papandreou. On November 3, the archbishop and the prime minister reached a compromise that was satisfactory to the church.

Other Events. On March 8, Parthenios III was elected patriarch of the patriarchate of Alexandria. He succeeded Patriarch Nicholas VI, who died in July 1986.

In May 1987, Archbishop Iakovos, primate of the Greek Orthodox Archdiocese of North and South America, participated in groundbreaking ceremonies for a new administration building at the Ecumenical Patriarchate of Constantinople. The building, funded in part by his archdiocese, replaces a structure destroyed in a 1941 fire.

Holy Cross Greek Orthodox School of Theology in Brookline, Mass., ended its 50th anniversary year in September by hosting the Third International Conference of Orthodox Theological Schools. September also was the start of the 50th anniversary of St. Vladimir's Orthodox Theological Seminary in Crestwood, N.Y.   Stanley S. Harakas

In WORLD BOOK, see EASTERN ORTHODOX CHURCHES.

ECONOMICS. Despite the single largest decline of stock prices in history on Oct. 19, 1987, the United States economy remained surprisingly strong throughout the year. In November, the economy began the sixth year of its current expansion, the longest peacetime period of sustained growth in U.S. history.

The gross national product (GNP)—the total value of all goods and services produced—grew by slightly more than 3 per cent during 1987 in *constant dollars* (dollars adjusted for inflation) to more than $4 trillion. The inflation rate as measured by the Implicit Price Deflator—also called the Implicit Price Index or GNP Deflator—was slightly more than 3 per cent. Consumer prices rose by about 3.7 per cent. These encouraging signs were reinforced by the fact that total civilian employment rose above 112 million near year-end, the largest total ever and nearly 1 million higher than the 1986 total.

Industrial production rose by 5.4 per cent, and the long decline in manufacturing employment ended in 1987 as employment in that sector rose slightly over 1986 levels. Between June and October, 1987, 300,000 new manufacturing jobs were created. The unemployment rate continued to drop in 1987, averaging about 6 per cent for the year.

Unemployment rates among experienced wage and salary workers also decreased, reaching approximately 5.5 per cent at year-end. More than 50 per cent of the unemployed managed to find work within seven weeks. The *long-term unemployed* (those out of work for more than 26 weeks) made up 15 per cent of the unemployed—about the same rate as in 1986. Nearly 2 of every 3 Americans over the age of 16 sought work in 1987, and about 94 per cent found jobs.

Stock Market Crash. Responding to these forces, the U.S. stock market surged to new highs in all major indexes. The highs were reached in August and were part of a five-year bull market that began in August 1982, when the Dow Jones Industrial Average (the Dow, the best-known index of stock prices) was below 800. From that point to its peak, the Dow average increased by about 300 per cent. From January to September 1987, the Dow increased about 36 per cent. After dropping in September and early October, the Dow plummeted a record 508 points on October 19, wiping out about $500 billion in stock value. At year-end, however, market averages were a little higher than when the year began.

A variety of factors apparently were behind the crash, including the concern of foreign markets about the value of the U.S. dollar, the relatively high ratio between the prices of stocks and their earnings, and a general feeling that the market was due for a correction—that is, a brief pause in

Congressional leaders join President Ronald Reagan to announce a compromise agreement reached in November to reduce the federal budget deficit.

its ascent. Together, these elements created a sell psychology made worse by modern trading techniques that rely on computer programs. Many observers believe that computer trading tends to intensify the normal swings of the market. Whatever the reasons, a record was established for a single-day fall, and this in itself introduced new doubts about the strength of the economy in 1988.

Prior to October 19, stock market analysts and economists almost unanimously predicted that 1988 would be a prosperous year with growth in the economy running between 2 to 3 per cent after adjusting for inflation. After October 19, however, these estimates dropped by about 1 percentage point, and some analysts actually predicted a recession in 1988.

Several basic reasons underlay the uncertainty about economic growth in 1988. These included the sizable U.S. budget deficit; the deficit in the U.S. balance of trade, which reached $156 billion in 1986; serious financial problems among many of the developing countries, especially Latin-American nations that owe billions of dollars to U.S. banks; and the continued unwillingness of the American people to save sufficiently to meet demands for investment funds and government requirements for financing the deficit. Complicating this entire picture was the continuing decline of the dollar.

Balance of Trade. The U.S. trade deficit—caused by an excess of imports over exports—means that other countries have large holdings in U.S. dollars. Foreign investors have used these dollars to buy U.S. securities—primarily Treasury bills and bonds—and real estate. Consequently, over the last several years, the United States has become a *debtor nation*—that is, the United States owes more to other countries than other countries owe the United States. Payment of the net interest and dividends owed to foreign countries has reduced the capacity of the United States to buy.

Many economists believe that the primary cause of the trade deficit was an overvalued U.S. dollar. Nations no longer redeem their currencies for gold. As a result, each country's currency has a price in relation to every other country's currency. For example, if U.S. $1 is equal in value to 2 West German Deutsche marks, 1 Deutsche mark is worth U.S. 50 cents. Anyone possessing $1 could purchase 2 marks and use those marks to purchase goods in West Germany. Also, a German possessing 2 marks could buy $1 and purchase something in the United States for that amount. If $1 is worth 3 marks, however, this would enable the U.S. citizen holding $1 to purchase 3 marks' worth of goods in West Germany, and a West German would need 3 marks to purchase goods worth $1 in the United States.

Selected Key U.S. Economic Indicators

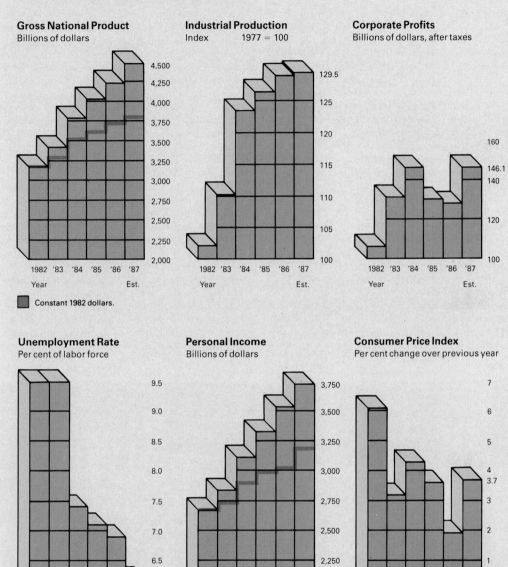

Gross National Product
Billions of dollars

4,500
4,250
4,000
3,750
3,500
3,250
3,000
2,750
2,500
2,250
2,000

1982 '83 '84 '85 '86 '87
Year   Est.

■ Constant 1982 dollars.

Industrial Production
Index   1977 = 100

129.5
125
120
115
110
105
100

1982 '83 '84 '85 '86 '87
Year   Est.

Corporate Profits
Billions of dollars, after taxes

160
146.1
140
120
100

1982 '83 '84 '85 '86 '87
Year   Est.

Unemployment Rate
Per cent of labor force

9.5
9.0
8.5
8.0
7.5
7.0
6.5
6.2
6.0

1982 '83 '84 '85 '86 '87
Year   Est.

Personal Income
Billions of dollars

3,750
3,500
3,250
3,000
2,750
2,500
2,250
2,000

1982 '83 '84 '85 '86 '87
Year   Est.

■ Constant 1982 dollars.

Consumer Price Index
Per cent change over previous year

7
6
5
4
3.7
3
2
1
0

1982 '83 '84 '85 '86 '87
Year   Est.

The most frequently used measure of the nation's total economic performance is the gross national product (GNP). The GNP measures the value in current prices of all goods and services produced by a country in a year. Constant dollars show the amounts adjusted for inflation. The unemployment rate is the percentage of the total labor force that is unemployed and actively seeking work. The consumer price index (CPI) measures inflation by showing the change in prices of selected goods and services consumed by urban families and individuals. Industrial production is a monthly measure of the physical output of manufacturing, mining, and utility industries. Personal income is current income received by individuals, nonprofit institutions, and private trust funds before taxes. Corporate profits are quarterly profit samplings from major industries.

All 1987 figures are *Year Book* estimates based on data from The Conference Board.

Under the latter condition, there would be a strong incentive for Americans to buy West German goods and a strong disincentive for West Germans to buy American goods. If this also applied to other countries' currencies, then the tendency could become overwhelming for the United States to purchase more than it sold, and the dollar would be considered overvalued. This is exactly the condition that prevailed for several years until 1986, and many economists believe this has been the primary cause for the failure of U.S. exports to keep up with imports.

Dollar's Decline. To some extent, however, the situation has been corrected since 1985 by a 40 per cent decline in the value of the U.S. dollar in relation to the currencies of other industrialized nations. The results are beginning to show in a narrowing of the trade deficit.

Budget Deficit. As for the federal government's budget deficit, a compromise between Congress and the Administration of President Ronald Reagan, which was reached in late November 1987, promised to reduce the budget originally proposed by $30 billion. But at the end of 1987, the prospects of a balanced budget by 1990 seemed as distant as ever.

In comparison with the budgetary deficits found in many industrialized countries, the U.S. deficit— equal to about 3 per cent of the GNP—is not large. The growth of the U.S. economy over the past few years has been the greatest in the Western world. Inflation rates have been modest. Employment has been high in the United States, in contrast with many other Western countries where unemployment has been greater and the number of jobs has remained stagnant.

The situation in the developing countries and in the Communist bloc has been even gloomier. Inflation has been rampant in most of Latin America, and it is commonly believed that the economies of the Soviet Union and its Eastern European satellites have been weakened by excessive military spending.

Although the U.S. economy compared favorably with those in the rest of the world in 1987, Americans continued to express concern about their economic future. Part of the reason may have been that not all sectors of the U.S. economy performed as well as the economy as a whole in 1987. In particular, heavy manufacturing has suffered most from the inroads of foreign competition. The end of the recent speculative boom in land prices has brought many Midwestern farmers into acute economic distress, especially those who borrowed substantial sums to buy more land, thinking that land prices would continue to rise.

A summit meeting in June in Venice, Italy, brings together the leaders of seven major industrial nations for their annual talk on the world economy.

EDUCATION continued to be an important political issue in the United States in 1987. On July 25, the National Governors' Association issued a report calling for a stronger educational system to provide a foundation for American competitiveness in the world economy. The report, *Jobs, Growth, and Competitiveness*, said that tomorrow's workers will not be able to compete using yesterday's skills.

In a September debate sponsored by the University of North Carolina, nine Democratic and Republican 1988 presidential candidates discussed such issues as federal spending on education and the use of education vouchers—coupons that families could use to send their children to their choice of public or private schools. Most candidates supported proposals to increase accountability in education. Such proposals place greater responsibility on educators for the success or failure of their schools. In a September speech at the National Press Club in Washington, D.C., U.S. Secretary of Education William J. Bennett addressed the same issue, saying that greater accountability was "essential to carrying forward the movement for education reform" in the 1980's.

Comparing Schools. In March 1987, a blue-ribbon panel appointed by Bennett and chaired by former Tennessee Governor Lamar Alexander called for marked expansion of the National Assessment of Educational Progress (NAEP) to facilitate the evaluation and comparison of U.S. schools. The NAEP was created by Congress in 1969 to provide "report cards" on a representative number of U.S. students. The panel recommended that an expanded NAEP publicize student test scores on a state-by-state basis. The NAEP was also urged to measure achievement in additional subjects, test more private school students, and include in its surveys 17-year-olds who have left school.

In the past, the NAEP conducted its surveys in such a way that state-by-state comparisons were impossible. State education officials encouraged this method of testing because some officials feared comparisons would undermine their states' authority to pursue their own educational programs. They also argued that poor performances by some states—which could reflect differences in state income or population composition—might lead to unfair criticism of those states. In the face of the recent demands for more accountability in education, however, the Council of Chief State School Officers, an organization that represents senior state education officials, reversed its position on how the NAEP compiles data.

In August 1987, the U.S. Department of Education proposed that Congress enact a law to change the NAEP as recommended by Bennett's panel. In September, the NAEP received a $572,000 federal grant to develop the first assess-

Marty Lowe, *The Wall Street Journal;*
permission, Cartoon Features Syndicate

"I'm not afraid of ghosts or monsters—
It's the national debt that scares me."

More important may have been the shock to American expectations. Americans are not accustomed to finding their goods not competitive. The fall of the U.S. dollar relative to other currencies is also considered bad, though many economists believe that such a reduction is the only way to restore the fortunes of U.S. exporters and close the deficit in the balance of payments.

Protectionism. The impact of the October 19 stock market crash at least temporarily postponed Congress's consideration of *protectionist* legislation—high tariffs and other trade barriers that protect domestic industries from foreign competition. Congress was wary of adopting measures similar to laws passed in 1929 and 1930 that many economists believe worsened the Great Depression.

As 1987 ended, the major factors that would affect the U.S. economy in 1988 seemed to bear little resemblance to those that existed in 1930. In the absence of any severe shocks to the financial system, many economists expected the U.S. economy to continue its expansion.   Warren W. Shearer

See also INTERNATIONAL TRADE; MANUFACTURING; STOCKS AND BONDS; and individual country articles. In the Special Reports section, see WILD DAYS ON WALL STREET. In WORLD BOOK, see ECONOMICS.

ECUADOR. See LATIN AMERICA.

U.S. Schools Get an F in Humanities

Two best sellers and a widely publicized government report sharply criticized United States schools in 1987. The critiques focused on cultural education and predicted dire results for U.S. society if reforms are not made.

E. D. Hirsch, Jr., a professor of English at the University of Virginia in Charlottesville, wrote *Cultural Literacy: What Every American Needs to Know.* The book was published in April and quickly became a best seller, with 200,000 copies sold by mid-October.

Cultural Literacy faults U.S. schools for neglecting to help students become "culturally literate"—that is, for failing to teach them about the important people, events, and works of literature that have shaped modern culture. An appendix, "What Every American Needs to Know," contains a list of nearly 5,000 dates, events, places, famous people, book titles, and phrases that Hirsch believes should be familiar to any truly literate American. The list includes such entries as *black holes, Paul Revere, Iliad,* and *Humpty-Dumpty.*

According to Hirsch, educators disregard cultural literacy because many are primarily concerned with teaching students skills and believe that the subject matter used in such lessons is relatively unimportant. But Hirsch warns that the schools' failure to convey important cultural information may undermine the teaching of such basic skills as reading and writing. Knowl-

edge of the cultural context in which words are used is crucial to the development of these skills, Hirsch argued. "Literacy is far more than a skill," he wrote. "It requires large amounts of specific information. To grasp the words on a page, we have to know a lot of information that isn't down on the page."

A second critique of school curriculums, *The Closing of the American Mind: How Higher Education Has Failed Democracy and Impoverished the Souls of Today's Students,* by Allan Bloom, a professor of social thought at the University of Chicago, was published in April. Like *Cultural Literacy,* Bloom's book was a best seller. By mid-November, 445,000 copies had been sold.

The Closing of the American Mind attacks U.S. universities and colleges for failing to instruct students in the important traditions of Western thought, including such classics as the works of English playwright William Shakespeare, Greek philosopher Plato, and Italian poet Dante Alighieri. Bloom blames the schools' failure on the belief of many educators in *relativism,* which asserts that all ideas have equal value. Bloom argues that widespread belief in relativism leads educators to disregard the notion that there are principles and facts that all students should learn. According to Bloom, Americans who are unaware of this cultural information are like "ignorant shepherds living on a site where great civilizations once flourished."

In August, Lynne V. Cheney, chairperson of the U.S. National Endowment for the Humanities (NEH), joined the chorus of critics with the publication of *American Memory: A Report on the Humanities in the Nation's Public Schools.* The study, which was mandated by Congress, analyzes preliminary results of an NEH-funded survey of 17-year-old American students. Tested on history and literature, the students performed poorly. Two-thirds, for example, were unable to identify the time of the Civil War within a half-century, and nearly one-third did not know Christopher Columbus reached the New World before 1750. The students' knowledge of literature was equally poor.

Cheney blames the students' ignorance on the same culprit Hirsch cites—teachers who emphasize the process of learning rather than subject matter. The problem, according to Cheney, is "the belief that we can teach our children *how* to think without troubling them to learn anything worth thinking about."

Some educators took issue with the charges made by Hirsch, Bloom, and Cheney. The educators faulted all three authors for ignoring the importance of contemporary curriculums that address topics pertaining to minority groups and women.   Thomas Toch

Three publications condemning U.S. students' ignorance of cultural traditions sparked the interest of many readers in 1987.

ment to compare students in each state. The project, a mathematics test for students in 4th, 8th, and 12th grades, was planned for 1990.

Helping Poor Students. A great deal of attention was focused on economically disadvantaged students in 1987. In early September, the Committee for Economic Development, an association of corporate leaders and university presidents, released *Children in Need*, a report that outlined strategies for improving the education of students in low-income families, many of whom live under conditions of economic hardship that inhibit their ability to do well in school. Experts estimate that up to 30 per cent of U.S. students live under such conditions. The committee called for a greater emphasis on educational programs for disadvantaged students in their early years and for restructuring schools to make them more supportive of such young people. The committee also urged the development of programs that motivate disadvantaged students to stay enrolled in school and encourage dropouts to return to the classroom.

Individuals, corporations, and other institutions launched initiatives on behalf of disadvantaged students in 1987. In early October, Ohio State University announced a "Young Scholars Program," which is designed to encourage minority elementary school students to remain in school through high school and go on to college. Ohio State plans to provide the students with tuition incentives, summer workshops, and tutoring.

Teaching Profession. Efforts to professionalize public-school teaching continued in 1987. A major development was the establishment in May of the National Board for Professional Teaching Standards, Incorporated, a national teacher-certification panel created by the Carnegie Forum on Education and the Economy. The certification panel planned to issue national credentials to teachers who meet high standards in subject knowledge and teaching ability. The board is the first national organization to license teachers. In mid-October, James A. Kelly, a former high school history teacher and former Ford Foundation officer, was named president of the certification board.

In August, the Rochester, N.Y., school system and the Rochester Teachers' Association reached agreement on an unprecedented collective-bargaining contract that pays the system's teachers salaries much higher than the national average. Under the contract, salaries for teachers without experience will jump 52 per cent, to $28,935, by the 1989-1990 school year. The contract also establishes a career ladder that enables teachers to work toward earning leadership roles in their schools and salaries as high as $70,000. The agreement also eliminated a long-standing, union-backed policy of granting transfers from one school to another solely on the basis of seniority.

Calls for Curriculum Reform. Several reports published in 1987 criticized U.S. schools for failing to teach students the historical, philosophical, literary, and other cultural information they need to be competent citizens (see Close-Up). In addition, groups from across the political spectrum urged schools to place greater emphasis on teaching students moral and civic responsibilities. In April, for example, People for the American Way, a civil liberties organization, sponsored a conference on "Values, Pluralism, and Public Education." Both conservative and liberal conference participants agreed that the teaching of such values as honesty and reliability should be a more prominent part of school curriculums.

AIDS. Repercussions of the AIDS (acquired immune deficiency syndrome) epidemic reached U.S. schools in 1987. On March 16, the U.S Public Health Service publicized its long-awaited national plan for educating schoolchildren about AIDS. The plan encouraged educators to teach students to avoid AIDS by abstaining from sexual activity until marriage. According to the plan, the federal government will provide schools with guidelines for AIDS instruction.

In mid-October, the U.S. Department of Education released the first official federal publication on AIDS education in schools. The handbook, *AIDS and the Education of Our Children: A Guide for Parents and Teachers*, urged parents and educators to emphasize that "appropriate moral and social conduct" is the only sure way to prevent the spread of the fatal disease. The publication also warned that advising students of the protection condoms give against AIDS could "suggest to teen-agers that they are expected to engage in sexual intercourse." Many educators criticized such statements as naive, and the handbook quickly became controversial.

A few school systems struggled to cope with the difficulties that arose when students contracted AIDS or picked up the AIDS virus. In some cases, students remained in school without incident. In other instances, the presence of an infected student in a public school became a divisive, even violent, issue. In August, residents of Arcadia, Fla., made bomb and death threats against the family of Clifford and Louise Ray, whose three hemophiliac sons had been exposed to AIDS through blood transfusions and wished to attend a public elementary school. On August 28, the family's home was destroyed by fire. The family then moved to Sarasota, Fla., where the boys attended public school without harassment.

Religion, Courts, and the Schools. Three important federal judicial decisions involving the rights of fundamentalist Christian students were handed down in 1987. In Mobile, Ala., in March, U.S. District Judge W. Brevard Hand became the first on

An 8-year-old watches striking Chicago teachers walk the picket line in September. The strike kept Chicago schools closed for 19 school days.

the federal bench to rule that the promotion of moral behavior without reference to God or religious faith, sometimes called *secular humanism*, is itself a religion. According to Judge Hand, teaching secular humanism in public schools violated the First Amendment prohibition against the government's establishment of religion. The judge ordered 44 textbooks removed from the Alabama public schools on the grounds that they promoted the "religious belief system" of secular humanism.

The ruling supported the position of some fundamentalist Christians, who had long argued that secular humanism is a religion that places human values above any divine authority. The Alabama Board of Education appealed the ruling, however, and on August 26, the 11th U.S. Circuit Court of Appeals in Atlanta, Ga., unanimously overturned Judge Hand's decision. According to the higher court, the textbooks did not promote any religion.

In June, the Supreme Court of the United States ruled unconstitutional a Louisiana law that required public schools teaching evolution to also teach *creationism* (the belief that, perhaps only thousands of years ago, the earth and all forms of life were created essentially as they are today). In a 7 to 2 decision, the Supreme Court found that the law violated the First Amendment.

In August, the Sixth U.S. Circuit Court of Appeals ruled that a Tennessee school system could require children in seven families to use textbooks that their fundamentalist Christian parents claimed were antireligious. The appeals court found a difference between requiring a child to read such material and requiring a child to believe it. The decision overturned the October 1986 ruling of a lower federal court, which said that the parents had a legal right to keep their children out of reading classes that used the books and could be reimbursed for the cost of private reading lessons for the youngsters.

Enrollments and Funding. In 1987, total enrollment in U.S. elementary and secondary schools increased for the third consecutive year. At the start of the 1987-1988 school year, 45.7 million students were enrolled in public and private schools—an increase of 400,000 from the previous year. College enrollment declined marginally during the same period, however. Slightly more than 12 million students were enrolled in schools of higher education at the beginning of the 1987-1988 school year.

The total U.S. education bill was estimated at $308 billion for 1987-1988, an increase of nearly $30 billion over the previous year. Spending at the elementary and secondary levels was estimated at $184 billion, a $14-billion increase over 1986-1987.   Thomas Toch

In WORLD BOOK, see EDUCATION.

EGYPT. Elections for the People's Assembly, Egypt's legislature, held on April 6, 1987, underscored the steady advance of democracy under the regime of President Mohammad Hosni Mubarak. The elections were originally scheduled for 1988. But they were advanced in response to a decision by Egypt's Supreme Court to hear a suit challenging the constitutionality of the 1984 election law under which the existing Assembly had been elected. Opposition politicians opposed the law because it, in effect, barred independent candidates from running for office. In January 1987, the Assembly passed a new law allowing independents to run. In February, Mubarak dissolved the Assembly and scheduled new elections.

Mubarak's National Democratic Party retained power by winning 346 of the Assembly's 448 elective seats. An alliance of three opposition parties—the Socialist Labor Party, the Liberal Socialist Party, and the officially outlawed but tolerated Muslim Brotherhood—won 60 seats. The New Wafd Party, previously the main opposition party, won 35 seats. Independents won the remaining 7 seats. Two small parties failed to win the 8 per cent of votes required to be seated.

In October, Mubarak's nomination by the Assembly for a second six-year term was approved in a national referendum. Mubarak, the only candidate, won 97 per cent of the vote.

Fundamentalism. The democratization of Egyptian politics helped keep most Islamic fundamentalist groups in Egypt working within the system. But extremists continued their activities. In May, 37 members of Islamic Jihad, an underground group, were arrested and charged with plotting to overthrow the regime. The incident led Egypt to break diplomatic relations with Iran, charging that Iran had funded the group. The one remaining Iranian diplomat in Cairo was expelled.

The Economy. In May, the International Monetary Fund, an agency of the United Nations, agreed to lend Egypt $327 million over an 18-month period, which provided some relief for the cash-strapped Egyptian economy. Also in May, the Club of Paris, a group of Western creditor nations, agreed to allow Egypt to reschedule $12 billion in foreign debt over a 10-year period. The government, in turn, agreed to reduce subsidies on basic commodities and to work to reduce its chronic budget deficit.

The 1987 budget, approved in May, cut spending. The expected $312-million deficit was 13 per cent less than in 1986. But with population increasing by 1 million per month and 35 per cent of revenues going for interest on its national debt, Egypt faced an uphill struggle.   William Spencer

See also MIDDLE EAST (Facts in Brief Table). In the Special Reports section, see UNDERSTANDING ISLAM. In WORLD BOOK, see EGYPT.

ELECTIONS. Three governorships were up for grabs in the United States in 1987, and the incumbent Democratic Party retained all three. In November 3 elections, millionaire political novice Wallace Wilkinson was elected governor of Kentucky by nearly a 2 to 1 margin over Republican State Representative John Harper. Governor Martha Layne Collins was ineligible to succeed herself. In Mississippi, Ray Mabus, the state auditor, defeated Jack Reed, a Republican businessman, by 53 to 47 per cent. Governor William A. Allain did not seek a second term.

Edwin W. Edwards, the governor of Louisiana who was acquitted in a 1986 political corruption trial, abandoned his quest for a fourth term after running second to U.S. Representative Charles E. (Buddy) Roemer III, a fellow Democrat, in an October 24 bipartisan primary. Edwards conceded the office to Roemer rather than face him in a runoff election.

Governor Recall. Strenuous efforts were made in Arizona in 1987 to force an election in the spring of 1988 on the issue of recalling Republican Governor Evan Mecham. Petitions with 390,000 signatures demanding a recall were presented at the State Capitol on November 2. Among Mecham's controversial actions was the cancellation of a holiday honoring civil rights leader Martin Luther King, Jr.

Mayorships. In November 3 elections, Democratic Mayor W. Wilson Goode of Philadelphia narrowly defeated former Mayor Frank L. Rizzo, a Democrat who turned Republican. In Hartford, Conn., Democratic state legislator Carrie Saxon Perry defeated Republican Philip L. Steele to become the first black woman to lead a major Northeastern city. Lawyer Kurt L. Schmoke, a Democrat, became the first elected black mayor of Baltimore, crushing Republican Samuel Culotta.

But in Charlotte, N.C., Republican Sue Myrick upset Mayor Harvey Gantt, a two-term Democrat who was the city's first black mayor. Republican Mayors Kathy Whitmire of Houston; William H. Hudnut III of Indianapolis; and Donna Owens of Toledo, Ohio, were reelected, as was Democrat Raymond L. Flynn of Boston. And in a November 10 runoff, Republican Mayor Xavier L. Suarez of Miami, Fla., easily beat former Mayor Maurice A. Ferre. State legislator Art Agnos was elected mayor of San Francisco on December 8, defeating John L. Molinari, city supervisor. Mayor Dianne Feinstein was ineligible for another term.

In Earlier Elections, Richard G. Hatcher, the first black mayor of Gary, Ind., was defeated in seeking nomination to a sixth term on May 5, 1987. Beating him in the Democratic primary was Thomas V. Barnes, assessor of Indiana's Calumet Township, who is also black. Barnes easily won the general election on November 3.

Federico Peña, a Democrat and Denver's first Hispanic mayor, narrowly won reelection in a June 16 runoff over Republican Don Bain, a corporate attorney. Democratic Mayor Henry G. Cisneros of San Antonio was reelected on April 4 with 67 per cent of the vote. Annette G. Strauss, sister-in-law of former Democratic National Chairman Robert Strauss, became the first woman to be elected mayor of Dallas in an April 18 runoff. She captured 56 per cent of the vote to defeat businessman Fred Meyer. On the same day, Betty Turner became the first woman mayor of Corpus Christi, Tex., by defeating Hispanic activist Tony Bonilla, 58 to 42 per cent, in a runoff.

Harold Washington, a Democrat and Chicago's first black mayor, won a second term in office on April 7, defeating three white opponents. His margin over his closest rival and most bitter political foe, Cook County Democratic Chairman Edward R. Vrdolyak—who ran as Illinois Solidarity Party candidate—was 54 to 42 per cent. Aldermanic elections gave Washington a clear majority in the City Council.

But Washington's four-year term was cut short on November 25 when he died unexpectedly of a heart attack. On December 2, at 4:01 A.M., Alderman Eugene Sawyer was elected acting mayor during an all-night, special City Council session. See Chicago.

Mayor Recalled. On January 13, voters in Omaha, Nebr., recalled Mayor Michael Boyle for alleged abuse of power by a margin of 56 to 44 per cent. Boyle, mayor since 1981, was in his second term. He became the target of a recall drive in October 1986 after he fired Police Chief Robert Wadman on grounds of insubordination.

House. One Democrat and one Republican won in special elections for seats in the House of Representatives in 1987. In California's Fifth Congressional District, Democratic Party activist Nancy Pelosi easily won a special election runoff on June 2 to succeed Democrat Sala Burton, who died on February 1. In Connecticut's Fourth District, Republican Christopher Shays defeated Democrat Christine Niedermeier, a fellow state representative, in a special election on August 17 to succeed Republican Stewart B. McKinney, who died on May 7.

Better Late Than Never. In a final bit of unfinished business from the 1986 elections, U.S. Representative John Patrick Hiler, a Republican, was declared the winner of a recount in Indiana's Third Congressional District on January 22. He defeated Democratic challenger Thomas W. Ward by 47 votes.   Frank Cormier and Margot Cormier

See also Congress of the United States; Democratic Party; Republican Party; State Government. In World Book, see Elections.

ELECTRIC POWER. See Energy Supply.

ELECTRONICS. Semiconductor chips, the foundation of many electronic devices, were the focus of a trade dispute between Japan and the United States during 1987. In March, the United States accused Japan of violating a trade agreement signed in July 1986 by "dumping" computer chips on the world market below cost. This unfair pricing hurt the U.S. semiconductor industry. In retaliation, the United States imposed 100 per cent tariffs on Japanese televisions, personal computers, and other electronic products. In November, the United States eased the tariffs, saying Japan had stopped its unfair trade practices.

The trade dispute created a shortage of electronic chips in the United States. The shortage of dynamic random-access memory (DRAM) chips for computers was particularly critical because most of these chips are manufactured in Japan. In late 1987, the Japanese Ministry of International Trade and Industry increased the production quota for Japanese suppliers from 4 million DRAM's per month to 7 million.

A Better Semiconductor was the focus of much research during 1987. Silicon is the material most commonly used for making semiconductor chips, but engineers were reaching the physical limits of silicon for the molding of complex solid-state circuits. Researchers in the United States and Japan

A computer chip introduced by IBM in January stores 1 million bits of data in two-thirds the area of the million-bit chip it replaced.

experimented with gallium arsenide, which can switch electronic circuits on and off five times faster than can silicon.

Optical computer chips that transmit signals as pulses of light were also under development at several U.S. universities during 1987. A protein molecule that changes color in response to light serves as the on-off switch.

Chips made of *superconductors* (materials that conduct electricity without resistance) became the focus of a whole new technology after the discovery in late 1986 and early 1987 of materials that become superconducting at relatively high temperatures. Earlier superconductors had to be kept too cold to be much use. See PHYSICS (Close-Up).

Sharper Images. Victor Company of Japan (JVC) introduced a new type of videocassette recorder (VCR) at the Consumer Electronics Show held in Chicago in June. The new technology, called *super VHS*, creates clearer, sharper video images by producing 430 horizontal lines to create the video picture. A conventional VCR produces 240 lines on the television screen. Prices for the super-VHS machines were $1,200 and up. To take advantage of the high resolution produced by the super-VHS machine, the unit must be connected to a high-resolution TV set.   Howard Bierman

See also COMPUTER. In WORLD BOOK, see ELECTRONICS.

EL SALVADOR. As 1987 drew to a close, several volatile developments heightened political tensions in El Salvador. On November 23, President José Napoleón Duarte accused the country's best-known rightist politician, Roberto D'Aubuisson, of masterminding the 1980 assassination of Roman Catholic Archbishop Oscar Arnulfo Romero. A week earlier, two civilian spokesmen for leftist rebels, Rubén Zamora and Guillermo Ungo, ended their political exile and arrived in the capital city, San Salvador, despite threats against their lives. Their return and the charges against D'Aubuisson raised fears of a new outbreak of political killings.

President Duarte said he based his charges against D'Aubuisson and a former aide, Alvaro Rafael Saravia, on the testimony of a man who said he drove the getaway car for the archbishop's assassin. Duarte said the driver testified that he was present when Saravia reported to D'Aubuisson that his orders to kill the archbishop had been carried out. Soon after the charges, Saravia was arrested in the United States and held for extradition to El Salvador. As a member of the National Assembly, D'Aubuisson cannot be prosecuted.

D'Aubuisson has long been widely regarded as the head of the right wing death squads responsible for thousands of political killings. He has denied such charges. Archbishop Romero had been outspoken against the death squads.

Negotiations. Before the threat of new violence emerged, President Duarte met on October 4 with negotiators representing leftist guerrillas for the first time in nearly three years. The meeting stemmed from the signing of a peace accord by five Central American presidents on August 7. Both sides at the meeting pledged themselves to a negotiated settlement of the civil war.

Fighting in the guerrilla war was intense early in 1987. On March 31, rebel forces destroyed an important government military base at El Paraíso near the Honduran border, killing nearly 70 government troops and the first U.S. military adviser to die in combat.

Refuge. Alarmed by the possible impact of a new U.S. immigration reform law, President Duarte appealed to U.S. President Ronald Reagan on April 10 to provide temporary refuge to the estimated 400,000 to 600,000 Salvadorans who had sought refuge illegally in the United States since 1982. Duarte said that El Salvador's economic crisis was somewhat relieved by the nearly $600 million sent annually to El Salvador by Salvadorans working in the United States. President Reagan denied his request on May 14.   Nathan A. Haverstock

See also LATIN AMERICA (Facts in Brief Table). In WORLD BOOK, see EL SALVADOR.

EMPLOYMENT. See ECONOMICS; LABOR.

ENDANGERED SPECIES. See CONSERVATION.

ENERGY SUPPLY. The United States on May 11, 1987, urged the 20 other member nations of the International Energy Agency (IEA) to intensify efforts to stockpile petroleum to soften the effects of a possible future energy crisis. John S. Herrington, secretary of the U.S. Department of Energy (DOE), said that large emergency stockpiles of petroleum will provide some energy security for IEA countries, most of which are heavily dependent on imported oil. The IEA was formed in 1974 to coordinate efforts of Western oil-importing nations to diversify fuel sources, increase energy efficiency, and otherwise cope with a severe crisis in world energy supplies that existed at that time.

Speaking at an IEA meeting in Paris, Herrington said that some member countries were lagging behind the goal of creating a 90-day strategic stockpile of oil. He said the United States, which has a 100-day supply of oil in underground caverns along the Gulf of Mexico, would triple the rate at which it is filling its so-called Strategic Petroleum Reserve.

U.S. Energy Output. The DOE on September 28 reported that the United States produced 2.0 per cent less energy during the first half of 1987 than during the same period in 1986. Energy consumption remained unchanged, however. The United States produced about 32 quadrillion British thermal units (B.T.U.'s) of energy and consumed

Giant windmills generate electricity in West Germany's first wind-energy park. The park, located on the North Sea coast, opened on August 24.

about 38 quadrillion B.T.U.'s. (A B.T.U. is a unit for measuring heat.) Imports of all forms of energy were 14.5 per cent higher during the first half of 1987. Imports of petroleum rose 8.3 per cent, while imports of natural gas were up 25.1 per cent from 1986 levels.

Act Repealed. President Ronald Reagan on May 21 signed a bill that eliminated government restrictions on the kinds of fuel that can be burned by industries and other large energy users. The bill repealed the Powerplant and Industrial Fuel Use Act of 1978. Enacted in response to the energy crisis of the 1970's, the Powerplant Act had prohibited large energy users from burning oil or natural gas in new boilers. Under the new law, these energy users are free to use the cheapest available fuel.

Versatile Vehicles. A presidential task force recommended on July 14 that the U.S. government buy at least 5,000 "flexible-fueled" motor vehicles. The vehicles would be capable of running on gasoline or on alternative fuels such as *methanol* (wood alcohol), produced from natural gas, coal, or wood. The task force encouraged more extensive use of alternative fuels such as methanol, *ethanol* (grain alcohol), and compressed natural gas to ease urban air pollution. Officials noted that such fuels burn more cleanly than gasoline and would decrease U.S. dependence on imported oil.

Plant for Sale. The DOE began seeking potential buyers for the Great Plains coal gasification plant on October 9. The plant is the only commercial facility in the United States for converting coal to clean-burning, synthetic natural gas. It was built in 1984 near Beulah, N. Dak., for $2 billion by a group of five energy companies that believed energy prices would continue rising. Prices fell, however, making the plant uneconomical and forcing the firms to default on more than $1.5 billion in federal loans in 1985. Energy Department officials said the plant is currently profitable, converting about 16,000 short tons (14,500 metric tons) of coal each day into 142 million cubic feet (4 million cubic meters) of synthetic natural gas.

Wind Power. Researchers at the DOE on April 30 announced the completion of the most comprehensive assessment ever performed of wind-energy resources in the United States. The study estimated potential wind-power resources in each state and included data on seasonal variations in wind, the percentage of land suitable for wind-energy development, and other factors. It also identified major regions—such as many coastal areas, the Great Lakes, and much of the Great Plains—that are suitable sites for *wind turbines* (devices that are turned by wind to generate energy). Officials predicted that the data will be of value to wind-energy developers and electric utilities.

Nuclear Plant Go-Ahead. The U.S. Nuclear Regulatory Commission (NRC) on October 29 eliminated the major obstacle preventing the start-up of two controversial nuclear power plants on the East Coast. State and local governments had prevented the Shoreham nuclear power station on Long Island, New York, and the Seabrook station in New Hampshire from operating by refusing to cooperate in developing emergency evacuation plans. Government officials had insisted it would be impossible to evacuate the heavily populated areas near the plants. Shoreham is 75 miles (120 kilometers) northeast of New York City, and Seabrook is about 40 miles (60 kilometers) north of Boston. The lack of evacuation plans had prevented the NRC from licensing the stations.

But in its October announcement, the NRC said it would consider licensing such plants provided the owners had developed adequate plans for responding to an accident or other emergency. The NRC noted that it no longer would permit state and local governments to prevent licensing of substantially completed plants by refusing to participate in emergency-planning efforts.

Maine Says Nay. On November 3, voters in Maine rejected for the third time in seven years a referendum that would have forced the closing of the state's only nuclear power plant. The plant—Maine Yankee in Wiscasset—generates 27 per cent of the state's electricity.

Nuclear Output. As of July 1987, nuclear power plants supplied 16.0 per cent of the United States electricity needs, compared with 14.8 per cent in July 1986, according to the DOE. By the end of June 1987, there were 105 operating nuclear reactors in the United States with a total generating capacity of 96.1 million kilowatts.

Chernobyl Trial. The Supreme Court of the Soviet Union on July 29 sentenced the former director of the Chernobyl nuclear power station and two top aides to 10 years in a labor camp. The officials were found guilty of violating safety regulations prior to the 1986 explosion that led to the world's worst nuclear-plant accident. Three other officials received lesser sentences.

U.S.-Canada Pact. The United States and Canada on October 3 reached an agreement on a free trade pact that included provisions encouraging sales of electricity, oil, uranium, and other energy resources between the two countries. The provisions called for greater U.S. access to Canadian energy supplies and greater Canadian access to U.S. energy markets.

The United States also agreed to export to Canada up to 50,000 barrels per day of Alaskan oil and to eliminate restrictions on processing Canadian uranium for U.S. nuclear power plants. Both countries said they would consult with each other before issuing new energy regulations or taking

action that could hinder the "freest possible bilateral trade in energy." The pact, which was signed on Jan. 2, 1988, awaited the approval of the U.S. Congress and the Canadian Parliament.

Energy Development. The government of India in April announced an ambitious plan to produce about 20 per cent of its energy needs from nonconventional sources such as sunlight, *biomass* (plant material), wind, and small hydroelectric power plants. India's Department of Nonconventional Energy Sources said the project would cost $40 billion and be completed in the year 2001.

The plan calls for the establishment of decentralized energy systems throughout India that meet local demands for firewood, cooking gas, and power to run irrigation pumps. Energy-rich materials would be harvested—in the form of firewood—from "energy plantations," and recovered from sewage sludge and municipal waste. The program also would involve the purchase of improved wood-burning stoves to replace the inefficient stoves currently in use in many homes. The project would be financed through a renewable energy development agency established by the Indian government.   Michael Woods

See also COAL; PETROLEUM AND GAS. In the Special Reports section, see STORMY DEBATE OVER ACID RAIN. In WORLD BOOK, see ENERGY SUPPLY.

ENGINEERING. See BUILDING AND CONSTRUCTION.

ENGLAND. Early in the morning of Oct. 16, 1987, the worst storm in more than 275 years roared across southeastern England, killing 19 people and toppling walls, trees, and power lines. Winds in some areas reached 110 miles (177 kilometers) per hour, and heavy rains caused flooding. London was blacked out, and about 3 million homes in the southeast were without electricity for up to two weeks. An estimated 15 million trees were blown down in the counties of Essex, Kent, Suffolk, and Sussex. British weather forecasts just hours before the storm failed to mention it.

On November 18, a fire at a subway station in London killed 31 people and injured about 80 others. The blaze started near the end of the evening rush hour at King's Cross Station, the city's busiest underground station.

Nuclear Issues. On January 26, the British government received the go-ahead to build a nuclear plant using a pressurized water reactor (PWR) design at Sizewell in Suffolk. The approval came from Sir Frank Layfield, who headed an investigation of the government's plans for the PWR, called Sizewell B. The study found that the PWR design would be the most cost-effective method of providing needed electric power.

Local protests convinced the British government on May 1 that it should cancel plans to set up nuclear waste test dumps in the counties of Bedford-

London bobbies ride 2 of the 200 bicycles purchased by the city's police department in 1987 to help officers respond to calls more quickly.

shire, Essex, Humberside, and Lincolnshire. The Nuclear Industry Radioactive Waste Executive agency was then faced with the task of selecting new sites.

Elections. In a year that saw a June parliamentary general election return the Conservative Party of Prime Minister Margaret Thatcher to power for a record-tying third consecutive term, Oxford University had its own election. On March 14, Roy Jenkins, former Labour Party finance minister and former leader of the Social Democratic Party, was elected Oxford's chancellor. Ironically, in the general election on June 11, Jenkins lost his Scottish seat in the House of Commons.

The Royal Year was an eventful one for the children of Queen Elizabeth II. On January 12, her youngest son, Prince Edward, resigned from the Royal Marines amid a storm of controversy. In June, he masterminded a televised charity contest featuring hilarious outdoor games between teams headed by himself; Prince Andrew and his wife, Sarah; and Princess Anne. Also in June, the queen bestowed on Princess Anne the title of Princess Royal. A rumored rift between Charles, Prince of Wales and heir to the British throne, and his wife, Diana, made headlines in 1987.

Sports. The Football League, the professional soccer league in England and Wales, celebrated its 100th anniversary in 1987. The league celebrated its anniversary with a 3-0 win over the Rest-of-the-World team on August 8 in Wembley Stadium.

It was also the 200th anniversary year of the Marylebone Cricket Club (MCC), the organization that administers the laws of cricket from its headquarters at Lord's Cricket Ground in London. From August 20 to 25, the MCC team participated in a high-scoring five-day match with the Rest-of-the-World team at Lord's. But like so many of the year's summer events, the final day's play was canceled due to rain, and the match ended in a draw.

In soccer, Everton won the 1987 Football League championship on February 7 for the ninth time in its history. On May 16, Coventry City beat Tottenham Hotspur by a score of 3-2 to gain its first win in the Football Association Cup Final.

At the All-England Lawn Tennis Championships at Wimbledon on July 5, an English mixed-doubles pair, Jeremy Bates and Jo Durie, brought off a surprise win over Australians Darren Cahill and Nicole Provis. It was the first all-British triumph in the mixed doubles at Wimbledon since 1936. Oxford University won the 133rd Boat Race on March 28 with a four-length victory over Cambridge University. On July 19, England's Nick Faldo won the 116th British Open Golf Championship at the Muirfield Course in Gullane, Scotland.   William Gould

See also GREAT BRITAIN. In WORLD BOOK, see ENGLAND.

ENVIRONMENTAL POLLUTION. The garbage barge *Mobro*, loaded with 3,186 short tons (2,890 metric tons) of trash, became a symbol in 1987 of the growing waste-disposal dilemma in the United States. The barge, which left New York City on March 22, sailed about 6,000 miles (9,700 kilometers) in search of a place to dump the waste. It was turned away by at least six U.S. states and the countries of Mexico, Belize, and the Bahamas before it finally returned to the New York City area, where the rubbish was burned in September.

The barge became world famous in the 155 days it sailed from port to port, dramatizing a serious environmental issue that had gained little previous public recognition. Waste-management experts pointed to the garbage barge as a compelling example of the need to deal with the growing refuse heap. Each American produces about 5 pounds (2.3 kilograms) of garbage a day—making a total of about 220 million short tons (200 million metric tons) a year nationally.

Although more than 90 per cent of the waste in the United States was buried in municipal landfills in 1987, the number of such landfills had declined 50 per cent since 1979. The U.S. Conference of Mayors estimated in 1987 that more than half of the nation's cities would run out of landfill capacity in less than 10 years. Waste-disposal costs in the United States have risen as haulers have had to travel farther to find disposal sites. Moreover, many landfills present serious health risks by leaking toxic compounds into ground-water supplies. Waste-management experts stress that alternatives to landfills must include various solutions, such as recycling, waste reduction, and incineration.

Air Pollution. According to the U.S. Environmental Protection Agency (EPA), more than 70 areas of the United States failed to meet a Dec. 31, 1987, deadline for reducing ozone or carbon monoxide—or both—to levels specified in the 1970 Clean Air Act. In December, Congress extended the deadline to Aug. 31, 1988.

Ozone, the major component of smog, is a form of molecular oxygen containing three atoms as opposed to the two atoms found in normal atmospheric oxygen. High levels of ozone can irritate the breathing passages. The chemical forms in the lower atmosphere when sunlight acts upon certain compounds released by the combustion and vaporization of gasoline, fuel oil, and other fossil fuels. Excessive levels of carbon monoxide stem primarily from the burning of fossil fuels. High concentrations of this pollutant can cause headaches and dizziness and are particularly dangerous to people with heart or lung disorders.

Under the Clean Air Act, areas that fail to meet the August 1988 deadline could face both discretionary and mandatory sanctions. Mandatory sanctions involve a ban on the construction of new industrial facilities that would create more air pollution. According to a proposal made in November 1987 by EPA Administrator Lee M. Thomas, the agency could delay imposing the construction ban for up to five years, provided an area submitted plans that would bring its emissions into compliance.

Discretionary sanctions include withholding federal sewage-treatment grants and highway funds. Under the November proposal, the EPA would invoke discretionary sanctions only if a noncomplying area did not make reasonable efforts to reduce its emissions by 3 per cent each year.

Protecting the Ozone Shield. Twenty-four nations, including the United States, in September signed an agreement in Montreal, Canada, to freeze and then reduce their consumption of *chlorofluorocarbons* (CFC's), a group of chemicals that are believed to damage the fragile layer of ozone in the upper atmosphere. Although excessive ozone in the lower atmosphere is a serious form of air pollution, the ozone layer in the upper atmosphere provides a critical shield against sunlight's harmful ultraviolet radiation. Deterioration of this shield could lead to an increase in skin cancer and could damage crops and wildlife, according to scientists. The Montreal pact is to take effect in 1989, at which time the participating nations will freeze their consumption of CFC's at 1986 levels. The participating nations pledged to reduce their consumption of CFC's by 1999 to half the 1986 levels. CFC's are widely used as refrigerants, insulating materials, solvents, and, in many countries, as propellants in aerosol sprays.

Radon. In August 1987, the EPA released the results of the largest survey of indoor concentrations of radon gas in the United States. The survey found excessive levels in 21 per cent of the 11,600 homes tested in 10 states.

Radon is an invisible, odorless, radioactive gas produced by the decay of uranium in rock and soil. Scientists estimate that 5,000 to 20,000 lung cancer deaths a year in the United States might be linked to radon trapped inside houses.

The survey findings, according to the EPA, indicate that radon might be a problem in virtually every state. The 10 states surveyed were Alabama, Colorado, Connecticut, Kansas, Kentucky, Michigan, Rhode Island, Tennessee, Wisconsin, and Wyoming.

Superfund. The EPA in July added 99 sites to its list of hazardous waste dumps to be cleaned up under the Superfund program. These additions brought the number of Superfund sites, which represent the worst toxic waste dumps in the United States, to 951. The new entries included 32 federal facilities, marking the first time the EPA has included federal installations on the list of most-hazardous waste sites.

In another Superfund first, the EPA and several private companies reached agreement in June to share the expense of cleaning up a toxic waste site in La Marque, Tex. In all previous Superfund cleanups, the government footed the bill and then sued the polluters to recover the costs.

Oil Plan Attacked. Nine environmental groups filed suit in August to block the U.S. Department of the Interior's five-year plan for opening vast areas of the outer continental shelf to oil and gas exploration. The plan, which went into effect on July 2, would open huge tracts off the coasts of California, Oregon, Washington, Florida, and Massachusetts for exploration. The suit charged that the plan offers inadequate protection of marine and coastal environments and that it would threaten various coastal industries, including fishing and tourism.

Clean Water Issues. On February 4, Congress enacted the Clean Water Act by overriding a presidential veto. The bill, which provided $18 billion in sewer and water-treatment construction funds, had been vetoed by President Ronald Reagan in January. The President had criticized the bill as a "budget-buster."

In other action concerning water pollution, the Environmental Protection Agency on June 24 announced the final standards for the maximum allowable levels of vinyl chloride, benzene, carbon tetrachloride, and five other hazardous chemicals in drinking water. These standards, which take effect on Jan. 9, 1989, were the first issued under the Safe Drinking Water Act amendments of 1986. Standards regulating an additional 75 chemicals were to be issued by the EPA in 1989. Environmental groups, including the Natural Resources Defense Council, attacked the first eight standards as too lax.

On Oct. 22, 1987, the EPA issued proposed standards for the filtration and disinfection of drinking water drawn from rivers and lakes. The proposals, which would affect some 3,000 water systems supplying over 21 million people, would cost an estimated $2 billion. Consumers would bear the cost in increased water bills.

Asbestos Cleanup Continues. The EPA in October issued a final warning to school systems that they must inspect their buildings for the presence of asbestos. Plans for removing or enclosing the cancer-causing fibers must be filed by October 1988, and remedial action must begin by July 1989. School systems that fail to comply with these regulations face fines of up to $5,000 a day for each violation.   Casey Bukro

See also CONSERVATION; WATER. In the Special Reports section, see STORMY DEBATE OVER ACID RAIN. In WORLD BOOK, see ENVIRONMENTAL POLLUTION.

EQUATORIAL GUINEA. See AFRICA.

ETHIOPIA. Hunger in Ethiopia has been a world concern since the early 1970's, and 1987 was no exception. A drought in mid-1987 raised the grim possibility of another famine in 1988.

But drought was not the only problem. Armed rebellion against the central government made it difficult for farmers to plant and harvest crops. And the forced *villagization* scheme—replacing small family landholdings with collective and government-run farms—instituted by the Marxist regime of President Mengistu Haile-Mariam has been costly in terms of lost lives, uprooted families, and falling agricultural production.

The threat to Ethiopia caused by Somalia's long-time claim to the Ogaden region in eastern Ethiopia lessened in 1987. Peace negotiations between the two nations, started in 1986, continued in 1987. Ethiopia was still disrupted by civil war, however, as rebels in four regions of the country sought independence or self-rule. The roughly 250,000 Ethiopian troops, black Africa's largest army, are supported by more than 25,000 Cubans and other personnel from Communist nations.

A February *referendum* (direct vote) on a new constitution led to the creation in September of a Soviet-style Communist Party under President Mengistu.   J. Gus Liebenow and Beverly B. Liebenow

See also AFRICA (Facts in Brief Table). In WORLD BOOK, see ETHIOPIA.

EUROPE. Arms talks dominated European politics in 1987. In February, Soviet leader Mikhail S. Gorbachev offered to discuss the elimination from Europe of medium-range nuclear missiles known as *intermediate nuclear forces* (INF). In April, the Soviets submitted a draft treaty offering to remove both shorter-range and longer-range INF missiles—an offer that became known as the *double-zero option*.

The Soviets surprised the West by calling for the scrapping of 72 Pershing IA missiles stationed in West Germany. That country was in charge of the Pershing rockets, while the United States controlled the warheads. The Soviets had never before called for the elimination of the Pershing IA's as part of an arms deal with the United States, regarding the missiles as West German property. West German Chancellor Helmut Kohl did not want to include the Pershings in a double-zero deal, but he later agreed to do so.

The European Community (EC or Common Market) came no nearer to solving its monetary problems in 1987. The EC started the year near bankruptcy and failed to resolve a budget crisis.

President Reagan, his back to the Berlin Wall during a June 12 speech, challenges the Soviet leader: "Mr. Gorbachev, tear down this wall."

The main reason for the failure was British Prime Minister Margaret Thatcher's refusal to help unless the EC changed its financial policies, including the payment of subsidies to farmers.

Thatcher won a third term in June, strengthening her position in Europe. (EC nations are Belgium, Denmark, France, Great Britain, Greece, Ireland, Italy, Luxembourg, the Netherlands, Portugal, Spain, and West Germany.)

A Middle East Crisis caused dissension in the West during the year. Ships carrying oil through the Persian Gulf became victims of attacks by Iran and Iraq, which have been at war since 1980. International sea lanes in the gulf became dangerous because of mines believed laid by Iran.

On July 31, Thatcher refused a request by United States President Ronald Reagan to send minesweepers into the gulf. She changed her mind, however, after a U.S.-owned tanker struck a mine in the Gulf of Oman—the waters between the Persian Gulf and the Indian Ocean—on August 10. Both Great Britain and France ordered minesweepers to the scene on August 11. Italy and the Netherlands later followed suit.

Troubles in Belgium. One of the world's worst maritime disasters occurred on March 6 just off the English Channel port of Zeebrugge, Belgium, when the British-owned ferry *Herald of Free Enterprise* sank. Belgian rescue teams saved 348 passengers, but 188 people were killed, and 5 people were listed as missing.

Inmates in a crowded Belgian prison rioted in September in protest against the better treatment they believed a group of 26 British prisoners was due to receive. The British prisoners were soccer fans facing manslaughter charges for their part in a 1985 riot in a stadium in Belgium. Thirty-nine fans, most of them Italians, died as a result of the riot. To assure Great Britain that the 26 British prisoners would be treated well in prison, Belgian authorities broadcast television pictures of the comfortable cells in which the British prisoners would be held. When Belgian prisoners saw the TV pictures, they became angry and rioted.

Disarmament Talks. Gorbachev offered on February 28 to discuss the elimination from Europe of all long-range INF, which have an approximate range of 600 to 3,400 miles (1,000 to 5,500 kilometers). Long-range INF include Soviet SS-20 missiles and U.S. Pershing II's. The Soviets formally presented Gorbachev's proposal on March 2, in Geneva, Switzerland—scene of ongoing arms talks between the Soviet Union and the United States since 1985. Washington reacted favorably to the proposal, but the North Atlantic Treaty Organization (NATO) was lukewarm. (The members of NATO are Canada, Iceland, Norway, Turkey, and the United States, plus all the EC nations except Ireland.)

On April 14, Gorbachev extended the offer to include short-range INF, which have an approximate range of 300 to 600 miles (500 to 1,000 kilometers) and include Soviet SS-23 missiles and the Pershing IA's in West Germany. The new offer disturbed Great Britain and France. These two nations feared that their missiles would be included in a double-zero deal between the United States and the Soviet Union.

West Europeans were concerned that the scrapping of the British and French missiles—and the Pershing IA's on West German soil—would leave Western Europe vulnerable to Soviet-bloc tanks and artillery. The United States indicated that if its European allies could not agree to the double-zero option, then the United States would make a separate deal with the Soviets.

West Germany Agrees. After weeks of internal debate, West Germany's government on June 1 gave a go-ahead to a double-zero offer that would not affect the Pershing IA's. The West Germans asked the United States and the Soviet Union to negotiate a step-by-step dismantling of medium-range missiles, however, beginning with those that have the shortest range.

NATO agreed to a double-zero deal on June 11. The new accord prompted France and West Germany to discuss the creation of a joint fighting force, with the hope that it might lead to the creation of a West European army.

On August 26, Kohl offered to dismantle the Pershing IA's with "the final dismantling" of U.S. and Soviet INF. He insisted, nevertheless, that the Pershings would never be part of a U.S.-Soviet pact. On December 8, the United States and the Soviet Union signed a treaty eliminating their shorter-range and longer-range INF missiles.

EC Budget Crisis. The EC faced a budget deficit of almost $6 billion in 1987. In January, Jacques Delors, president of the European Commission, the EC's executive branch, toured the capitals of EC member nations to try to persuade EC leaders that the organization needed to reform its financial structure. Delors produced a plan basing each country's contribution on its *gross national product* (the total output of goods and services). Under the present system, the EC receives 1.4 per cent of each nation's value-added tax, a kind of sales tax.

The EC also had to resolve an internal quarrel between the commission and the European Parliament—the EC's legislature. At the end of 1986, Parliament refused to endorse the EC's $39-billion 1987 budget. In addition, Parliament called for extra funds for development aid for the Third World, but the EC's finance ministers refused to approve such aid.

Budget Compromise. During a stormy meeting, Thatcher told Delors to cut the deficit by cutting costs, especially through reform of the Common

Facts in Brief on European Countries

Country	Population	Government	Monetary Unit*	Foreign Trade (million U.S. $)	
				Exports†	Imports†
Albania	3,248,000	Communist Party First Secretary and People's Assembly Presidium Chairman Ramiz Alia; Prime Minister Adil Çarçani	lek (5.6 = $1)	345	335
Andorra	44,000	The bishop of Urgel, Spain, and the president of France	French franc & Spanish peseta	no statistics available	
Austria	7,488,000	President Kurt Waldheim; Chancellor Franz Vranitzky	schilling (11.6 = $1)	17,100	20,800
Belgium	9,886,000	King Baudouin I; Prime Minister Wilfried A. E. Martens	franc (34.8 = $1)	53,300 (includes Luxembourg)	55,800
Bulgaria	9,328,000	Communist Party General Secretary & State Council Chairman Todor Zhivkov; Prime Minister Georgi Atanasov	lev (1 = $1.21)	13,800	14,100
Czechoslovakia	15,835,000	Communist Party General Secretary Miloš Jakeš; President Gustáv Husák; Prime Minister Lubomir Strougal	koruna (8.5 = $1)	17,840	17,940
Denmark	5,144,000	Queen Margrethe II; Prime Minister Poul Schlüter	krone (6.4 = $1)	17,100	18,200
Finland	4,910,000	President Mauno Koivisto; Prime Minister Harri Holkeri	markka (4.1 = $1)	13,540	13,140
France	55,206,000	President François Mitterrand; Prime Minister Jacques Chirac	franc (5.6 = $1)	100,900	107,300
Germany, East	16,606,000	Communist Party Secretary-General & State Council Chairman Erich Honecker; Prime Minister Willi Stoph	mark (1.65 = $1)	23,900	22,200
Germany, West	60,839,000	President Richard von Weizsäcker; Chancellor Helmut Kohl	Deutsche mark (1.65 = $1)	174,000	145,400
Great Britain	56,672,000	Queen Elizabeth II; Prime Minister Margaret Thatcher	pound (1 = $1.81)	101,000	109,100
Greece	10,100,000	President Christos Sartzetakis; Prime Minister Andreas Papandreou	drachma (130.5 = $1)	8,500	10,100
Hungary	10,827,000	Communist Party First Secretary János Kádár; President Károly Németh; Prime Minister Károly Grósz	forint (46.9 = $1)	13,500	13,000
Iceland	248,000	President Vigdís Finnbogadóttir; Prime Minister Thorsteinn Palsson	krona (36.5 = $1)	814	904
Ireland	3,716,000	President Patrick J. Hillery; Prime Minister Charles Haughey	pound (punt) (1 = $1.60)	10,390	10,050
Italy	57,240,000	President Francesco Cossiga; Prime Minister Giovanni Goria	lira (1,220 = $1)	78,400	90,500
Liechtenstein	30,000	Prince Franz Josef II; Prime Minister Hans Brunhart	Swiss franc	no statistics available	
Luxembourg	368,000	Grand Duke Jean; Prime Minister Jacques Santer	franc (34.2 = $1)	53,300 (includes Belgium)	55,800
Malta	390,000	President Paul Xuereb; Prime Minister Edward Fenech Adami	lira (1 = $3.10)	400	757
Monaco	29,000	Prince Rainier III	French franc	no statistics available	
Netherlands	14,647,000	Queen Beatrix; Prime Minister Ruud Lubbers	guilder (1.86 = $1)	67,900	64,900
Norway	4,174,000	King Olav V; Prime Minister Gro Harlem Brundtland	krone (6.42 = $1)	18,700	14,500
Poland	38,462,000	Communist Party First Secretary & President Wojciech Jaruzelski; Council of Ministers Chairman Zbigniew Messner	zloty (311.7 = $1)	17,800	17,400
Portugal	10,270,000	President Mário Soares; Prime Minister Aníbal Cavaço Silva	escudo (134.5 = $1)	5,700	7,100
Romania	23,560,000	Communist Party General Secretary & President Nicolae Ceauşescu; Prime Minister Constantin Dăscălescu	leu (8.3 = $1)	12,200	10,400
San Marino	24,000	2 captains regent appointed by Grand Council every 6 months	Italian lira	no statistics available	
Spain	39,934,000	King Juan Carlos I; President Felipe González Márquez	peseta (111.3 = $1)	24,000	28,000
Sweden	8,338,000	King Carl XVI Gustaf; Prime Minister Ingvar Carlsson	krona (5.98 = $1)	30,500	28,500
Switzerland	6,551,000	President Pierre Aubert	franc (1.35 = $1)	27,400	30,700
Turkey	53,547,000	President Kenan Evren; Prime Minister Turgut Ozal	lira (969.1 = $1)	7,958	11,344
Union of Soviet Socialist Republics	286,230,000	Communist Party General Secretary Mikhail S. Gorbachev; Supreme Soviet Presidium Chairman Andrei A. Gromyko; Council of Ministers Chairman Nikolai I. Ryzhkov	ruble (1 = $1.69)	86,956	82,922
Yugoslavia	23,652,000	President of the Presidency Lazar Mojsov; Federal Executive Council President Branko Mikulić	dinar (1,251.9 = $1)	10,600	12,200

*Exchange rates as of Dec. 1, 1987, or latest available data.   †Latest available data.

Vacationers visiting the Parthenon on March 9 throw snowballs as Athens, Greece, endures its heaviest snowfall since 1953.

Agricultural Policy (CAP), which fixes production targets and price supports. The CAP uses about 70 per cent of the EC budget. On Feb. 13, 1987, EC finance ministers drafted a budget compromise that they believed the European Parliament would accept. The compromise budget included $34 million—half the amount requested by Parliament—for aid to Third World developing nations and the poorer EC countries.

The EC also drew up long-term plans, based on Delors's proposals, to avoid annual budget crises and overspending on agriculture. The European Parliament accepted the compromise on February 19.

The European Commission reported on March 4 that the EC had "sunk into a morass of budgetary malpractices" bringing it to "the brink of bankruptcy." The commission urged the EC to raise its annual budget to $60 billion by 1992.

Britain Stands Firm. Britain maintained its firm stance on EC financing at a summit meeting in Brussels, Belgium, on June 29 and 30, 1987. Britain said it would not tolerate increased revenues or regional expenditures until the EC curbed overspending, especially on agriculture.

Trade Disputes. The EC and the United States faced the threat of a trade war in 1987. In January, the United States demanded that the EC compensate it for the loss of U.S. grain sales to Spain.

That nation had joined the EC in January 1986 and, in accordance with EC regulations, had increased its grain purchases from other EC nations.

The United States demanded a payment of $400 million and the imposition on Jan. 30, 1987, of 200 per cent duties on some foods and beverages imported from EC nations. Among the products listed were canned ham, cheeses, olives, white wine, cognac, and gin.

The EC retaliated by threatening to impose extra tariffs of up to $61 per metric ton (1.1 short tons) on U.S. corn, bread flour, pasta, and rice. The new president of the EC, Sir Henry Plumb of Great Britain, warned on January 23 that the United States would get a "bloody nose" in any trade war. The dispute, which became known as "the pasta war," continued until August 7, when the two sides reached a compromise agreement.

Threat by Japan. A flood of Japanese products into Britain prompted the EC to consider trade sanctions against Japan in March. At that time, the United States was threatening to impose protectionist measures against Japan. These measures would have caused Japan to cut its exports to the United States and to increase its exports to EC nations. On April 10, the EC decided to restrict imports of whatever Japanese goods might be diverted from the United States if that nation imposed the measures.

At an economic summit conference of seven industrialized nations in Venice, Italy, in June, the United States announced that it would reduce trade sanctions against Japan, and the finance ministers of the countries at the summit agreed to stabilize exchange rates for their currencies. These moves prevented an escalating trade war.

Currency Crisis. The strength of the West German Deutsche mark, particularly against the French franc, started a European currency crisis at the beginning of 1987. Representatives of the eight nations of the European Monetary System (EMS)—founded in 1979 to stabilize exchange rates—held an emergency meeting in Brussels on January 9. (All the EC members except Britain, Greece, Portugal, and Spain are in the EMS.)

The weakness of the French franc had pushed the system to the breaking point. In an attempt to drive down interest rates in West Germany, the EMS increased the value of the mark and the Dutch guilder by 3 per cent and the Belgian and Luxembourger franc by 2 per cent, relative to the other EMS currencies. Counting this revaluation, the value of the Deutsche mark had grown since 1979 by 22 per cent against all EMS currencies, and by 45 per cent against the French franc.

European stock markets followed Wall Street in crashing to low levels in October. Financiers blamed the U.S. budget and trade deficits.

Birthday for EC. On June 28, 30,000 visitors celebrated the EC's 30th birthday in Brussels. The EC grew out of the Treaty of Rome, signed in 1957. Belgium staged a three-day party at which European Currency Unit (ECU) banknotes were used for the first time. This currency is used at present only in financial dealings such as those between banks, but the ECU is intended to replace a confusing variety of national currencies in consumer transactions.

The Single European Act, a revision of the Treaty of Rome, took effect on July 1, after Ireland—the final holdout against the act—gave its assent. Irish voters had approved the act in a *referendum* (vote of the people) on May 26. The act restricts the use of the veto by member nations, sets up a permanent secretariat for political cooperation, and enhances the power of the European Parliament, which is elected by the direct vote of the citizens of the member nations.

More Applications. Turkey applied for membership in the EC on April 14, and the North African country of Morocco followed suit on July 20. The EC is unlikely to admit either nation. Greece will likely object to the admission of Turkey, its neighbor and archrival. Morocco's location outside Europe may make it ineligible to join.   Kenneth Brown

See also the various European country articles. In WORLD BOOK, see EUROPE.

EXPLOSION. See DISASTERS.

FARM AND FARMING. Most economic indicators showed that the United States agricultural economy, which in the early 1980's had suffered the worst crisis since the Great Depression of the 1930's, began to turn around in 1987. Buoyed by near-record government subsidies, national farm income climbed to a record high. In fiscal year 1987 (Oct. 1, 1986, to Sept. 30, 1987), the value of U.S. agricultural exports rose for the first time since 1981. And after declining dramatically since 1982, the value of farmland inched upward. But the upswing by-passed some farmers whose debts were so burdensome that subsidies could not rescue them.

U.S. Agricultural Exports rose for two reasons. First, the 1985 farm law—which established U.S. farm programs for the next five years—had lowered the floor on price supports. This reduced farm prices, making U.S. products more competitive. Second, the U.S. dollar fell against the currencies of other nations in 1987, also making U.S. products cheaper. As a result, in 1987, exports rose by nearly 6 per cent to $27.9 billion. Exports had fallen to $26.3 billion in fiscal 1986.

Increases in cotton, livestock products, fruits, and vegetables accounted for most of the gain. Pushed down by government policies, the prices of most other commodities also fell.

The lower prices contributed to a rise in the volume of farm exports for the first time since 1980. Export shipments rose 18 per cent to 129 million metric tons (142 million short tons) in 1987.

The value of U.S. agricultural imports fell by a slight 1.4 per cent to $20.7 billion. This yielded a positive agricultural trade balance with the rest of the world of $7.2 billion, compared with a record $26.6 billion in 1981.

Farm Income. The long-awaited expansion in exports contributed to a record national net farm income of from $44 billion to $46 billion. But farmers were heavily dependent on direct government payments of $14 billion to $16 billion. All government farm income and price support expenditures cost taxpayers $23 billion in 1987, down slightly from the 1986 record of $25.8 billion.

Farmers also benefited from an unprecedented decline in expenses for the third consecutive year. Farmers planted fewer acres, delayed machinery purchases, and reduced fertilizer use.

Farmland Values stabilized and began to rise in 1987, after falling by more than 60 per cent since 1982 in the hardest-hit Midwestern states. Land values in that region rose by 3.3 per cent in the third quarter of 1987, the third consecutive quarterly increase.

The good economic news slowed the number of farmers going out of business. The Department of Agriculture estimated there were 2.17 million

Agricultural Statistics, 1987

World Crop Production
(million units)

Crop	Units	1986-1987*	1987-1988*†	% U.S. 1987-1988
Coarse grains‡	Metric tons	833	798	27
Corn	Metric tons	474	446	41
Wheat	Metric tons	529	501	11
Rice (rough)	Metric tons	466	444	1
Barley	Metric tons	182	186	6
Soybeans	Metric tons	98	102	52
Cotton	Bales§	70	77	18
Coffee	Bags#	79	101	0.2
Sugar (centrifugal)	Metric tons	103	101	6

*Crop year. †Preliminary.
‡Corn, barley, sorghum, rye, oats, millet, and mixed grains.
§480 pounds (217.7 kilograms) net.
#132.3 pounds (60 kilograms).

Output of Major U.S. Crops
(millions of bushels)

Crop	1986-1987*	1987-1988*†
Corn	8,253	7,060
Sorghum	942	741
Wheat	2,092	2,105
Soybeans	1,940	1,960
Rice (rough)‡	134	129
Potatoes‡	362	386
Cotton§	9.7	14.6
Tobacco#	1,163	1,230

*Crop year. †Preliminary.
‡1 million hundredweight (45.4 million kilograms).
§1 million bales (480 million pounds) (217.4 million kilograms).
#1 million pounds (454,000 kilograms).

U.S. Production of Animal Products
(millions of pounds)

	1986-1987*	1987-1988*†
Beef	23,588	22,508
Pork	14,389	15,715
Total red meat‡	38,732	38,975
Eggs§	5,804	5,770
Turkey	3,829	4,072
Total milk#	1,420	1,435
Broilers	15,513	16,282

*Crop year. †Preliminary.
‡Beef, pork, veal, lamb, and mutton.
§1 million dozens.
#100 millions of pounds (45.4 million kilograms).

American farms as of June 1, 1987—a loss of 38,500 since 1986. But the rate of decline had slowed since the previous year, when 62,800 farms were lost.

U.S. Production. The 1987 harvest of corn—the major U.S. crop—fell to 7.06 billion bushels, down 14 per cent from 1986. The drop resulted from a government program, designed to trim excessive surpluses, that required farmers to idle a portion of their acreage to qualify for subsidies. Favorable weather produced a record national average corn yield of 119.4 bushels per acre (0.4 hectare).

The U.S. wheat and soybean harvests were both up 1 per cent from 1986, and cotton production rose 51 per cent. Grain sorghum production was down 21 per cent; rice, 4 per cent; and peanuts, 3 per cent. Beef production fell 4 per cent. Pork production rose 1 per cent, and poultry production jumped 10 per cent.

World Production. World wheat production fell 5 per cent from a record high in 1986. Largely because of a smaller U.S. crop, corn production fell 6 per cent. Production of coarse grains, which include corn, fell 4 per cent.

Rice production fell 5 per cent. Soybean production was up 4 per cent, setting a record, and cotton production climbed 11 per cent. Both beef and pork production fell less than 1 per cent, and poultry production rose by 6 per cent.

Subsidized Exports. Despite complaints from competing grain-exporting nations such as Australia and Canada, the United States subsidized some of its agricultural exports to match the subsidized prices offered by the European Community (EC or Common Market).

To encourage the Soviet Union to fulfill the terms of its five-year grain agreement with the United States, the U.S. government subsidized 4 million metric tons (4.4 million short tons) of U.S. wheat sold to the Soviets in April. Later in the year, the United States offered to subsidize another 4.75 million metric tons (5.24 million short tons). Vying for China's business, the U.S. government subsidized 2 million metric tons (2.2 million short tons) of wheat sold to China and then offered to subsidize another 1 million metric tons (0.9 million short tons).

Generic Certificates. Government-owned commodities also went to American farmers, who were given coupons called *generic certificates* in place of cash for a portion of their subsidies. Farmers can trade the certificates for cash or any surplus commodity they want. Government economists called the program, which operated for its first full year in 1987, the most significant agricultural policy development in at least a decade.

Idled Cropland. To qualify for the certificates and other government benefits, farmers were required to idle grain and cotton acreage as the government attempted to balance supply with demand. By 1987, farmers had idled nearly 68.5 million acres (27.7 million hectares), 23.5 million acres (9.5 million hectares) more than in 1986 and second only to a 1983 record of 78 million acres (31.6 million hectares). Land used for crops in 1987 totaled 330 million acres (133.5 million hectares). Three-fourths of the land idled in 1987 was included in the government program linking acreage reduction and crop subsidies.

The rest was idled under a conservation program that paid farmers to take the most highly erodible land out of production for 10 years. Nearly 16 million acres (6.5 million hectares) were enrolled in the conservation program for the 1987

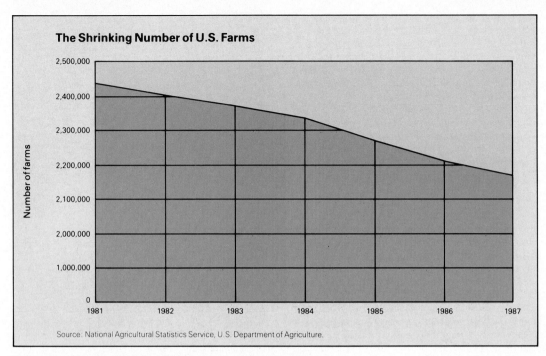

The Shrinking Number of U.S. Farms

Source: National Agricultural Statistics Service, U.S. Department of Agriculture.

The number of farms in the United States has dropped throughout the
1980's. Farm bankruptcies accounted for most of the decrease.

crop season. Additional enrollments raised the total to 23 million acres (9.3 million hectares) by the end of 1987.

Farm Loans. The Farm Credit System, a federally supervised farmer-owned network of banks, registered a small profit of $4 million in the third quarter of 1987, after losing $4.8 billion since 1985. It was the first quarterly profit in 2½ years for the system, the largest U.S. lender to farmers. But because some of the network's banks remained in severe financial trouble, Congress voted in December to pay part of the interest on $4 billion in bonds issued by the system to bail out the banks.

Research. To address an expected long-term acreage surplus, a Department of Agriculture task force called for an effort to diversify U.S. agriculture within 25 years by developing enough new farm and forest products to occupy 150 million acres (61 million hectares). As part of that effort, the U.S. government and the newspaper industry cooperated on a project that successfully used a fiber plant called *kenaf*, also known as *ambary,* to produce paper for newspapers.

Advances in methods to detect the presence of fertilizer and chemicals leaching through the soil into ground water led to increased federal and state monitoring to determine the scope of the problem. By 1987, more than 20 different pesti-

cides were found in wells that provide drinking water in more than 20 states.

Genetic Science. In 1987, after overcoming legal challenges and receiving federal regulatory approval, U.S. scientists for the first time performed government-approved field tests of genetically engineered microorganisms. (Genetic engineering is the insertion of genes from one organism into the genetic material of another organism.)

In two experiments, genetically engineered frost-inhibiting bacteria were released into the environment. In June, Advanced Genetic Sciences Incorporated of Oakland, Calif., reported that the bacteria, released in April, had protected strawberry plants against frost damage. A scientist at the University of California at Berkeley conducted a similar experiment with potato plants in April.

Experiments with genetically engineered plants proliferated in 1987. For example, the Monsanto Company of St. Louis, Mo., tested tomato plants that had been genetically altered with a protein that enables the plants to ward off attacks by hornworms and fruit worms. Researchers at Washington University in St. Louis working with Monsanto scientists also developed genetically engineered tomato plants that are tolerant of a plant disease—tobacco mosaic virus.   Sonja Hillgren

See also FOOD. In WORLD BOOK, see AGRICULTURE; FARM AND FARMING.

FASHION. The big news in fashion in 1987 was the resurgence of the short skirt. For some time, fashion designers had insisted that "anything goes" when it came to the length of hemlines. Most women had accepted this approach, and some alternated long skirts with short ones. Other women concentrated on the length they preferred.

When the fashion collections for fall 1987 were unveiled in the spring, however, it was clear that designers were surprisingly unanimous in their support for the short hemline. Designers in all fashion centers—London; Milan, Italy; New York City; and Paris—endorsed short skirts.

The new hemlines bared the knees and sometimes went to midthigh. The most popular skirt lengths measured 19 to 21 inches (48 to 53 centimeters) from the waistband to the hem. The shorter lengths were the fashion choice for teenagers, but women of all ages began revealing their knees.

Some journalists suggested that the overwhelming agreement among designers on hemlines was a plot to promote short skirts in an effort to sell more clothes. To other observers, including major retailers, such unanimity was proof that a fashion change was inevitable.

Although the new shorter styles were designed for fall, women jumped the gun. Many began rolling up their waistbands or turning up the hemlines on their longer outfits to accommodate the new trend before the shorter fashions hit the stores. Those who were successful in finding short skirts began wearing them in the spring season. By fall, the trend had gathered momentum.

Retailers did not get completely carried away by the new trend, however. Most provided a choice of longer styles for women, especially businesswomen concerned about the appropriateness of wearing short skirts in the office. The continued presence of longer fashions in 1987 also assured women that there would not be a repeat of the disaster in the 1970-1971 fashion season, when the miniskirt was suddenly replaced by the midiskirt.

Softer Shapes. Along with the shorter skirts came a change in the shape of clothes in 1987. Oversized silhouettes, popular for several years, gave way to narrower, curving, and more traditionally feminine clothes. Exaggerated shoulder pads moved out of the mainstream as women turned to softer clothes for daytime wear as well as for evening.

Giorgio Armani, Gianni Versace, and Valentino, in Italy, and Emanuel Ungaro, Yves Saint Laurent, and Karl Lagerfeld at Chanel, in Paris, endorsed this new look. Alistair Duncan Blair and Jasper Conran brought a calmer look to British fashion, which long had a reputation for wild, uninhibited designs.

Designer Christian Lacroix's 1987 couture line featured ultrafeminine dresses with short skirts gathered in poufs and shawllike *fichu* bodices.

Lacroix Goes Solo. Christian Lacroix, a 36-year-old designer, opened his own couture house in 1987. Lacroix, who had worked for Jean Patou since 1983, attracted an avid following for his ultrafeminine clothes in imaginative fabrics. Lacroix made the move shortly after the showing of his collection in January, which brought him worldwide attention.

Lacroix's first collection under his own name was introduced at the beginning of the fall showings in July 1987. It brought him immediate acclaim. Lacroix's imaginative clothes showed a strong peasant influence. Ladylike and faintly nostalgic, with shawllike *fichu* bodices and flouncy skirts, they captured the essence of Provence, a region in the south of France, where Lacroix was born. The clothes differed greatly from the tough chic of the broad-shouldered, sleek-skirt era that they replaced.

Scaasi Success. Feminine clothes were also a hit with U.S. designers in 1987. Arnold Scaasi, a designer of couture clothes for more than 20 years, had a big success with his soft styles. Scaasi's ready-to-wear collection also gained momentum. His successes put him alongside Geoffrey Beene, Calvin Klein, Donna Karan, Bill Blass, and Oscar de la Renta as one of the influential American designers in 1987.   Bernadine Morris

In WORLD BOOK, see CLOTHING; FASHION.

FINLAND. Nonsocialist parties led by the conservative National Coalition Party won a national election on March 15 and 16, 1987. Conservative leader Ilkka Suominen said the elections called for "fresh winds of change" after his party gained 9 seats in the 200-seat Eduskunta (parliament), to finish with a total of 53 seats. The conservative share of the vote rose by 1 percentage point to 23.3 per cent. The Social Democrats—leaders of the coalition that governed Finland—declined by 2.5 percentage points and lost 1 seat but remained the largest party with 24.3 per cent of the vote and 56 seats. Other nonsocialist parties—the Center Party, the Swedish People's Party, and the Christian League—gained seats, but the Finnish Rural Party lost 8 of its 17 seats.

New Government. As a result of the election, the conservatives participated in a coalition government for the first time since 1966. President Mauno Koivisto asked Harri Holkeri of the National Coalition Party, director of Finland's Central Bank, to head the new government as prime minister and to form a four-party government of conservatives, Social Democrats, and members of the Swedish People's Party and the Rural Party. The new government took over on April 30, with the outgoing Socialist prime minister, Kalevi Sorsa, assuming the post of foreign minister.

Neighborliness. A "know-your-neighbor" drive was started in January by the Finnish-Soviet Society, the National Board of Education, and 70 other organizations when it was learned that less than 1 per cent of Finnish schoolchildren were electing to study the Russian language. Although Finland shares an 800-mile (1,300-kilometer) border with the Soviet Union, studies showed that 60 per cent of Finnish 18-year-olds had a negative attitude toward the Soviet Union and favored Western culture, including football and hamburgers.

Trade Surplus. Finland's trade arrangement with the Soviets is based on barter, rather than on the sale of goods for money. The value of bartered goods is supposed to balance out over periods of five years. In 1986, however, the Finns had a trade surplus of $825 million, so Finland threatened to cut exports to the Soviet Union.

In January 1987, Soviet Council of Ministers Chairman Nikolai I. Ryzhkov visited Helsinki, Finland's capital, and worked out a compromise. The Soviets agreed to export much more oil to Finland, enabling the Finns to maintain the levels of their exports to the Soviet Union.

Trade with the West increased by 4 per cent in the first half of 1987, compared with the first half of 1986. The forest industry accounts for more than one-third of Finland's exports.　Kenneth Brown

See also EUROPE (Facts in Brief Table). In WORLD BOOK, see FINLAND.

FIRE. See DISASTERS.

FISHING. George Cochran of North Little Rock, Ark., in August 1987 won first prize of $50,000 in the 17th annual Bass Anglers Sportsman Society (BASS) Master Classic. The tournament took place on the Ohio River near Louisville, Ky. Cochran's three-day catch of 15 pounds 5 ounces (6.9 kilograms) was the lightest ever to win a BASS Classic. Rick Clunn of Montgomery, Tex., the all-time BASS money winner, received the $12,000 second prize.

In the $300,000 United States Bass Open in July at Lake Mead on the Arizona-Nevada border, Larry Hopper of Santa Ana, Calif., caught 23.65 pounds (10.7 kilograms) to take the $50,000 first prize. The $17,000 second-place award went to Dave Gliebe of Chandler, Ariz., for his catch of 22.75 pounds (10.3 kilograms).

In November, O. T. Fears III of Sallisaw, Okla., won the $100,000 prize in the Red Man All American Bass Championship, held on the Arkansas River near Little Rock, with a total catch of 28 pounds 5 ounces (12.8 kilograms). James Allen of Crystal Springs, Miss., received the second-place prize.

Linda England of Old Hickory, Tenn., won $20,000 in the 11th annual Bass N' Gal Classic held in October on Lake Eufaula in Alabama. Her winning total weighed 27 pounds 8 ounces (12.5 kilograms). Burma Thomas of Rainsville, Ala., won second prize.

A Record 58.9 Million Americans over the age of 6 fished in 1985, according to the latest nationwide survey conducted by the U.S. Fish and Wildlife Service. Adult anglers (aged 16 and over) numbered 46.6 million—more than 1 in 4 adult Americans. The amount spent totaled $28.2 billion and averaged $604 per adult angler.

The Sale of Billfish became illegal in Massachusetts on Aug. 1, 1987, following a ruling by the Massachusetts Marine Fisheries Advisory Commission. The commission also established a limit of one fish per boat trip for white, blue, or striped marlin, and for Atlantic sailfish.

Because sport anglers feared that commercial fishing might wipe out the marlin population, they applauded the commission's decision. In 1986, recreational fishers released about 500 of the 602 white marlin caught off the Massachusetts coast.

Fish Aid. The 50 states and other jurisdictions received a record $140 million in federal funds in 1987 as a result of the Dingell-Johnson program begun in 1950. The funding comes from taxes on sales of fishing equipment, motorboat fuel, and pleasure boats. It pays for such projects as the acquisition of lakes and public access rights for fishing, the development and improvement of access facilities, the improvement of fish habitats, and fishery research.　Tony Mandile

In WORLD BOOK, see FISHING.

FISHING INDUSTRY. Heavy commercial fishing in the Antarctic region, primarily by the Soviet Union, has dramatically reduced fish stocks in the area, according to United States government officials. William E. Evans, assistant administrator of the United States Department of Commerce's National Marine Fisheries Service, said in March 1987 that substantial decreases in Antarctic fish populations could adversely affect other marine life in the area.

Catches in the South Georgia region, about 1,000 miles (1,600 kilometers) east of the tip of South America, reached a peak of about 500,000 metric tons (550,000 short tons) in the 1979-1980 season. But less than 75,000 metric tons (82,700 short tons) were taken in 1985.

Fish Catch. The estimated 1987 world catch of seafood was 91 million metric tons (100 million short tons)—up 2 per cent from the 89.2 million metric tons (98 million short tons) taken in 1986. The value of fish entering international trade in 1986 was about $22.9 billion, an increase of more than 20 per cent over the 1985 figure. The United States fish catch in 1986 totaled 2.7 million metric tons (3 million short tons) and was valued at $2.8-billion. Experts estimated that commercial landings in 1987 would be close to the 1986 catch.

Consumption. Per capita consumption of seafood in the United States should reach 16 pounds (7.3 kilograms) per year by 1990, according to a report issued in April by economist Kenneth Roberts of the Louisiana Cooperative Extension Service at Louisiana State University in Baton Rouge. In recent years, consumption has increased at an annual rate of 2.5 per cent.

Fish Oil. Citing evidence that menhaden fish oil is safe for human consumption, the National Fish Meal and Oil Association, an organization of fish-oil processors, in January 1987 asked the U.S. Food and Drug Administration (FDA) to permit its use in food products in the United States. Most of the approximately 36 million gallons (136 million liters) of menhaden oil produced annually in the United States is exported. Approval of the petition by the FDA would open a promising new market for menhaden oil for U.S. producers.

U.S.-Japanese Pact. Japan agreed in March to make it easier for U.S. processors of Pacific pollack and herring to sell their products in Japan. According to U.S. fishing industry representatives, the agreement marked the first time American-processed fish would be permitted in Japan without strict trade barriers. Experts predicted that the pact would increase U.S. fish exports by $85 million in 1987.   Donald R. Whitaker

In WORLD BOOK, see FISHING INDUSTRY.

FLOOD. See DISASTERS.

FLORIDA. See STATE GOVERNMENT.

FLOWER. See GARDENING.

FOOD. The United States food industry maintained stable prices in 1987. Ample supplies, continued high demand, and a low inflation rate combined to hold food prices to a 4.2 per cent increase—slightly higher than the overall rise in the Consumer Price Index—the most widely used measure of inflation. American consumers spent only 16.7 per cent of disposable income—the amount left for spending after taxes—on food in 1987, one of the world's lowest rates.

Farmers. Prospects for American farmers brightened in 1987, though 10 to 15 per cent of U.S. farmers remained burdened by excessive debt. Land values slowly increased, and net cash farm income was projected to hit record levels, particularly for livestock farmers. But the good news was offset by the continued surplus produced by farmers and by the fact that one-third to one-half of net cash farm income came from direct government payments.

World Food Stocks experienced a 6 per cent decrease from 1986 levels, but supplies—particularly meat—remained more than adequate to satisfy demand. Although food supplies were abundant, more than 400 million people remained underfed worldwide, due to poverty, lack of proper distribution channels, and poor management.

Developing countries continued to expand their agricultural output in 1987. India, for example, became an exporter of food, and several other countries moved in that direction. But some regions experienced local problems—including a monsoon in parts of Asia and a threat to harvests in five African countries from infestations of locusts and grasshoppers—that threatened agricultural output.

Agriculture. Early plantings and good weather led to bountiful harvests in the United States in 1987, though overall production declined by 7 per cent from 1986 levels because fewer acres were planted. Wheat and soybean crops fared slightly better than in 1986, while yields of rice, peanuts, and dry beans experienced marginal declines. Lower production led to a moderate depletion of United States stockpiles, though an abundance of crops remained on hand.

Eating Out remained a way of life. Americans spent an average of about 40.5 per cent of their 1987 food budgets on food prepared away from home. Diners spent as much on food away from home in the first six months of 1987 as they did in the entire year in 1980. Sales in the food service industry rose to $197.5 billion, a 6.4 per cent growth over 1986, and menu prices rose 4 per cent. Fast-food eateries continued to pace the food-service industry, accounting for nearly 40 per cent of industry growth.

Ethnic and regional cuisines were popular, particularly Italian, Mexican, Asian, and Cajun foods.

Robert Hageman, *The Wall Street Journal,* permission, Cartoon Features Syndicate

"Grazing"—sampling a variety of items—became a growing trend among diners. Take-out and home-delivery services expanded significantly as many time-conscious consumers preferred to eat at home but not prepare food themselves.

Grocery Store Sales totaled $219.5 billion, an increase of 5.5 per cent, for a real growth rate (over and above the inflation rate) of 2.5 per cent over 1986 sales figures. Food prices at grocery stores climbed 3.2 per cent.

New grocery stores were generally larger, typically about 43,800 square feet (4,070 square meters). Store closings outpaced store openings, and the number of acquisitions of existing stores by new owners was twice the 1986 figure.

Consumption. Americans sent mixed signals in their choice of foods. Heightened awareness of nutrition and its relation to health caused Americans to eat leaner meats, more poultry and fish, more pasta, and reduced-calorie and low-fat products. According to the U.S. Department of Agriculture (USDA), the per capita consumption of poultry was expected to exceed that of beef by the end of 1987. The USDA also reported that Americans ate more vegetables than ever before, especially fresh produce. At the same time, however, such items as gourmet candy and superpremium ice cream—ice cream with a high butterfat content—soared in popularity.

Health Claims and Packaging. In August, the Food and Drug Administration (FDA) published a proposed rule to allow health claims on food packages as a means of informing the public about diet and its relation to health. Some food companies already made health claims for such items as margarine and high-fiber cereal. The FDA rule would require that any health claim for a food must be substantiated by generally accepted scientific evidence and must emphasize the importance of a total diet. But critics pressed for changes in the rule to protect consumers from potentially misleading labels. The rule was not expected to be made final until at least 1988.

Diet and Health. Health and nutrition experts have long recommended a diet lower in fat and cholesterol and higher in fiber than is currently eaten by most Americans. In March, the National Cancer Institute in Bethesda, Md., began a two-year joint consumer-education project with Giant Food, Incorporated, a supermarket chain based in Landover, Md. Giant Food provided information in its stores on food shopping, preparation, and healthful eating habits. The aim of the project was to determine if such information affected food purchases and induced shoppers to consume more fiber and less fat in their diets. Bob Gatty

See also FARM AND FARMING; NUTRITION. In WORLD BOOK, see FOOD; FOOD SUPPLY.

FOOTBALL

FOOTBALL. A 24-day strike interrupted the National Football League's (NFL) 1987 season, wiping out games on the last weekend in September and leading to games among hastily assembled replacement teams on the next three weekends. But the regular players returned, the season was completed, and the play-offs were held on schedule.

At the finish, the best team was the Washington Redskins of the National Football Conference. The Redskins defeated the Denver Broncos of the American Football Conference, 42-10, in Super Bowl XXII on Jan. 31, 1988, in San Diego.

In college football, Miami of Florida became the unofficial national champion. In a game between the only major teams still undefeated and untied (Syracuse had been tied by Auburn earlier in the day), Miami upset top-ranked Oklahoma, 20-14, on Jan. 1, 1988, in the Orange Bowl in Miami.

Professional. The five-year collective-bargaining agreement between the NFL Management Council, representing club owners, and the NFL Players Association, the players' union, expired on Aug. 31, 1987. The players' main goal in a new agreement was *free agency*. Free agency would have meant that when their individual contracts expired, players could sign with any club without that club being required to compensate their previous team. The 1,585 players had salaries ranging from $50,000 to $1.1 million a year. The average was $230,000.

Negotiations stalled, and the players struck on September 22 after the second game of the scheduled 16-game season. In 1982, when the players struck for 57 days, no games were played. This time, the owners lined up replacement teams, mostly with players cut in training camp. A few of the regular players announced that they would cross picket lines and continue playing.

The owners canceled the games of September 27 and 28, the third weekend of the season. When they resumed the schedule with replacement teams, more regulars drifted back.

Faced with a collapse of the strike, the union sought arbitration and failed. On October 15, the union decided to return to work without a collective-bargaining contract or a back-to-work agreement, but it filed a federal antitrust suit against the league to seek free agency.

The players reported for work that afternoon, a Thursday. The owners told them they could not play that weekend and would not be paid for that week because the deadline for regular players to return that week was Wednesday. The players accused the league of a double standard because nonroster players could be added as late as Saturday. The players filed a complaint with the Na-

Striking players from the Los Angeles Raiders yell at their replacements, who were bused to the Los Angeles Memorial Coliseum in October to play Kansas City.

National Football League Final Standings

American Conference

Eastern Division

	W.	L.	T.	Pct.
Indianapolis Colts	9	6	0	.600
Miami Dolphins	8	7	0	.533
New England Patriots	8	7	0	.533
Buffalo Bills	7	8	0	.467
New York Jets	6	9	0	.400

Central Division

	W.	L.	T.	Pct.
Cleveland Browns	10	5	0	.667
Houston Oilers	9	6	0	.600
Pittsburgh Steelers	8	7	0	.533
Cincinnati Bengals	4	11	0	.267

Western Division

	W.	L.	T.	Pct.
Denver Broncos	10	4	1	.700
Seattle Seahawks	9	6	0	.600
San Diego Chargers	8	7	0	.533
Los Angeles Raiders	5	10	0	.333
Kansas City Chiefs	4	11	0	.267

National Conference

Eastern Division

	W.	L.	T.	Pct.
Washington Redskins	11	4	0	.733
Dallas Cowboys	7	8	0	.467
St. Louis Cardinals	7	8	0	.467
Philadelphia Eagles	7	8	0	.467
New York Giants	6	9	0	.400

Central Division

	W.	L.	T.	Pct.
Chicago Bears	11	4	0	.733
Minnesota Vikings	8	7	0	.533
Green Bay Packers	5	9	1	.367
Tampa Bay Buccaneers	4	11	0	.267
Detroit Lions	4	11	0	.267

Western Division

	W.	L.	T.	Pct.
San Francisco 49ers	13	2	0	.867
New Orleans Saints	12	3	0	.800
Los Angeles Rams	6	9	0	.400
Atlanta Falcons	3	12	0	.200

Individual Statistics (American Conference)

Leading Scorers, Touchdowns

	TDs.	Rush	Rec.	Ret.	Pts.
Johnny Hector, N.Y. Jets	11	11	0	0	66
Earnest Byner, Cleveland	10	8	2	0	60
Curt Warner, Seattle	10	8	2	0	60
Albert Bentley, Indianapolis	9	7	2	0	54
Robb Riddick, Buffalo	8	5	3	0	48
Mark Duper, Miami	8	0	8	0	48
Larry Kinnebrew, Cincinnati	8	8	0	0	48
Steve Largent, Seattle	8	0	8	0	48

Leading Scorers, Kicking

	PAT	FG	Longest	Pts.
Jim Breech, Cincinnati	25-27	24-30	46	97
Dean Biasucci, Indianapolis	24-24	24-27	50	96
Tony Zendejas, Houston	32-33	20-26	52	92
Rich Karlis, Denver	37-37	18-25	51	91
Gary Anderson, Pittsburgh	21-21	22-27	52	87
Norm Johnson, Seattle	40-40	15-20	49	85
Pat Leahy, N.Y. Jets	31-31	18-22	42	85
Chris Bahr, L.A. Raiders	27-28	19-29	48	84
Nick Lowery, Kansas City	26-26	19-23	54	83
Tony Franklin, New England	37-38	15-26	50	82

Leading Quarterbacks

	Att.	Comp.	Yds.	TDs.	Int.
Bernie Kosar, Cleveland	389	241	3,033	22	9
Dan Marino, Miami	444	263	3,245	26	13
Dave Krieg, Seattle	294	178	2,131	23	15
Bill Kenney, Kansas City	273	154	2,107	15	9
Marc Wilson, L.A. Raiders	266	152	2,070	12	8
Jim Kelly, Buffalo	419	250	2,798	19	11
John Elway, Denver	410	224	3,198	19	12
Ken O'Brien, N.Y. Jets	393	234	2,696	13	8
Jack Trudeau, Indianapolis	229	128	1,587	6	6
Warren Moon, Houston	368	184	2,806	21	18

Leading Receivers

	No. Caught	Total Yds.	Avg. Gain	TDs.
Al Toon, N.Y. Jets	68	976	14.4	5
Steve Largent, Seattle	58	912	15.7	8
Andre Reed, Buffalo	57	752	13.2	5
Chris Burkett, Buffalo	56	765	13.7	4
Ronnie Harmon, Buffalo	56	477	8.5	2
Carlos Carson, Kansas City	55	1,044	19.0	7
Ernest Givins, Houston	53	933	17.6	6
Kellen Winslow, San Diego	53	519	9.8	3
Earnest Byner, Cleveland	52	552	10.6	2
Bill Brooks, Indianapolis	51	722	14.2	3

Leading Rushers

	No.	Yds.	Avg.	TDs.
Eric Dickerson, Indianapolis	283	1,288	4.6	6
Curt Warner, Seattle	234	985	4.2	8
Mike Rozier, Houston	229	957	4.2	3
Marcus Allen, L.A. Raiders	200	754	3.8	5
Sammy Winder, Denver	196	741	3.8	6
Kevin Mack, Cleveland	201	735	3.7	5
Earnest Jackson, Pittsburgh	180	696	3.9	1
Christian Okoye, Kansas City	157	660	4.2	3
Albert Bentley, Indianapolis	142	631	4.4	7
Troy Stradford, Miami	145	619	4.3	6

Leading Punters

	No.	Yds.	Avg.	Longest
Ralf Mojsiejenko, San Diego	67	2,875	42.9	57
Harry Newsome, Pittsburgh	64	2,678	41.8	57
Scott Fulhage, Cincinnati	52	2,168	41.7	58
Mike Horan, Denver	44	1,807	41.1	61
Kelly Goodburn, Kansas City	59	2,412	40.9	55

Individual Statistics (National Conference)

Leading Scorers, Touchdowns

	TDs.	Rush	Rec.	Ret.	Pts.
Jerry Rice, San Francisco	23	1	22	0	138
Mike Quick, Philadelphia	11	0	11	0	66
Charles White, L.A. Rams	11	11	0	0	66
Mark Bavaro, N.Y. Giants	8	0	8	0	48
Dalton Hilliard, New Orleans	8	7	1	0	48
J. T. Smith, St. Louis	8	0	8	0	48
Herschel Walker, Dallas	8	7	1	0	48

Leading Scorers, Kicking

	PAT	FG	Longest	Pts.
Morten Andersen, New Orleans	37-37	28-36	52	121
Roger Ruzek, Dallas	26-26	22-25	49	92
Mike Lansford, L.A. Rams	36-38	17-21	48	87
Kevin Butler, Chicago	28-30	19-28	52	85
Paul McFadden, Philadelphia	36-36	16-26	49	84
Ray Wersching, San Francisco	44-46	13-17	45	83
Ed Murray, Detroit	21-21	20-32	53	81
Raul Allegre, N.Y. Giants	25-26	17-27	53	76
Chuck Nelson, Minnesota	36-37	13-24	51	75
Ali Haji-Sheikh, Washington	29-32	13-19	41	68

Leading Quarterbacks

	Att.	Comp.	Yds.	TDs.	Int.
Joe Montana, San Francisco	398	266	3,054	31	13
Phil Simms, N.Y. Giants	282	163	2,230	17	9
Neil Lomax, St. Louis	463	275	3,387	24	12
Jim McMahon, Chicago	210	125	1,639	12	8
Steve DeBerg, Tampa Bay	275	159	1,891	14	7
Randall Cunningham, Philadelphia	406	223	2,786	23	12
Bobby Hebert, New Orleans	294	164	2,119	15	9
Wade Wilson, Minnesota	264	140	2,106	14	13
Danny White, Dallas	362	215	2,617	12	17
Jay Schroeder, Washington	267	129	1,878	12	10

Leading Receivers

	No. Caught	Total Yds.	Avg. Gain	TDs.
J. T. Smith, St. Louis	91	1,117	12.3	8
Roger Craig, San Francisco	66	492	7.5	1
Jerry Rice, San Francisco	65	1,078	16.6	22
Herschel Walker, Dallas	60	715	11.9	1
Pete Mandley, Detroit	58	720	12.4	7
Gary Clark, Washington	56	1,066	19.0	7
Mark Bavaro, N.Y. Giants	55	867	15.8	8
Henry Ellard, L.A. Rams	51	799	15.7	3
Neal Anderson, Chicago	47	467	9.9	3
Mike Quick, Philadelphia	46	790	17.2	11
Mike Renfro, Dallas	46	662	14.4	4

Leading Rushers

	No.	Yds.	Avg.	TDs.
Charles White, L.A. Rams	324	1,374	4.2	11
Rueben Mayes, New Orleans	243	917	3.8	5
Herschel Walker, Dallas	209	891	4.3	7
Gerald Riggs, Atlanta	203	875	4.3	2
Roger Craig, San Francisco	215	815	3.8	3
Stump Mitchell, St. Louis	203	781	3.8	3
Joe Morris, N.Y. Giants	193	658	3.4	3
Darrin Nelson, Minnesota	131	642	4.9	2
George Rogers, Washington	163	613	3.8	6
Neal Anderson, Chicago	129	586	4.5	3
Walter Payton, Chicago	146	533	3.7	4

Leading Punters

	No.	Yds.	Avg.	Longest
Rick Donnelly, Atlanta	61	2,686	44.0	62
Jim Arnold, Detroit	46	2,007	43.6	60
Sean Landeta, N.Y. Giants	65	2,773	42.7	64
Dale Hatcher, L.A. Rams	76	3,140	41.3	62
Don Bracken, Green Bay	72	2,947	40.9	65
Steve Cox, Washington	63	2,571	40.8	77

The 1987 College Football Season

1987 College Conference Champions

Conference	School
Atlantic Coast	Clemson
Big Eight	Oklahoma
Big Sky	Idaho
Big Ten	Michigan State
Ivy League	Harvard
Mid-American	Eastern Michigan
Ohio Valley	Eastern Kentucky—Youngstown State (tie)
Pacific Coast	San Jose State
Pacific Ten	Southern California
Southeastern	Auburn
Southland	Northeast Louisiana
Southwest	Texas A & M
Southwestern	Jackson State
Western Athletic	Wyoming
Yankee	Maine—Richmond (tie)

Major Bowl Games

Bowl	Winner	Loser
All-American	Virginia 22	Brigham Young 16
Aloha	UCLA 20	Florida 16
Amos Alonzo Stagg (Div. III)	Wagner (N.Y.) 19	Dayton (Ohio) 3
Bluebonnet	Texas 32	Pittsburgh 27
Blue-Gray	South 12	North 10
California	Eastern Michigan 30	San Jose State 27
Cotton	Texas A & M 35	Notre Dame 10
Fiesta	Florida State 31	Nebraska 28
Florida Citrus	Clemson 35	Penn State 10
Freedom	Arizona State 33	Air Force 28
Gator	Louisiana State 30	South Carolina 13
Hall of Fame	Michigan 28	Alabama 24
Holiday	Iowa 20	Wyoming 19
Hula	West 20	East 18
Independence	Washington 24	Tulane 12
Liberty	Georgia 20	Arkansas 17
Orange	Miami 20	Oklahoma 14
Palm (Div. II)	Troy State (Ala.) 31	Portland State (Ore.) 17
Peach	Tennessee 27	Indiana 22
Rose	Michigan State 20	Southern California 17
Senior	North 21	South 7
Sugar	Auburn 16 (tie) Syracuse 16 (tie)	
Sun	Oklahoma State 35	West Virginia 33
NCAA Div. I-AA	Northeast Louisiana 43	Marshall (W. Va.) 42
NAIA Div. I	Cameron (Okla.) 30	Carson-Newman (Tenn.) 2
NAIA Div. II	Pacific Lutheran (Wash.) 16 (tie) Wisconsin-Stevens Point 16 (tie)	

All-American Team (as picked by AP)

Offense
Tight end—Keith Jackson, Oklahoma
Wide receivers—Ernie Jones, Indiana; Marc Zeno, Tulane
Tackles—Dave Cadigan, Southern California; Stacy Searels, Auburn
Guards—Mark Hutson, Oklahoma; John McCormick, Nebraska
Center—Ignazio Albergamo, Louisiana State
Quarterback—Don McPherson, Syracuse
Running backs—Craig Heyward, Pittsburgh; Thurman Thomas, Oklahoma State
Place kicker—David Treadwell, Clemson
Return specialist—Tim Brown, Notre Dame

Defense
Ends—Darrell Reed, Oklahoma; John Roper, Texas A & M
Tackles—Chad Hennings, Air Force; Daniel Stubbs, Miami
Linebackers—Kurt Crain, Auburn; Dante Jones, Oklahoma; Paul McGowan, Florida State; Chris Spielman, Ohio State
Backs—Bennie Blades, Miami; Rickey Dixon, Oklahoma; Deion Sanders, Florida State
Punter—Tom Tupa, Ohio State

Player Awards
Heisman Trophy (best player)—Tim Brown, Notre Dame
Lombardi Award (best lineman)—Chris Spielman, Ohio State
Outland Award (best interior lineman)—Chad Hennings, Air Force

tional Labor Relations Board, which upheld them on December 10 and ordered the league to pay the striking players between $21 million and $25-million in lost wages and incentive bonuses for that weekend.

The season was shortened to 15 games, and the strike games counted in the final standings. The San Francisco 49ers, the Redskins, and the San Diego Chargers had 3-0 records during the strike, and San Francisco and Washington qualified for the play-offs. The 1987 Super Bowl champion New York Giants, the Philadelphia Eagles, the Kansas City Chiefs, and the Minnesota Vikings were 0-3 during the strike, and of those four, only the Vikings made the play-offs.

For the season, nonstrike attendance of 59,611 per game was close to the record. Nonstrike television ratings were close to 1986 levels.

Play-Offs. The division winners were San Francisco (13-2), the Chicago Bears (11-4), Washington (11-4), Denver (10-4-1), the Cleveland Browns (10-5), and the Indianapolis Colts (9-6). They advanced to the play-offs with four wild-card teams—the New Orleans Saints (12-3), the Houston Oilers (9-6), the Seattle Seahawks (9-6), and Minnesota (8-7). The Saints gained the play-offs for the first time in their 21-year history, and the Colts for the first time since 1977 when the team played in Baltimore.

The play-offs began with the two wild-card games on Jan. 3, 1988, and both resulted in upsets. Minnesota routed New Orleans, 44-10, and Houston eliminated Seattle, 23-20, in overtime.

In the division play-offs on January 9 and 10, Washington upset Chicago, 21-17; Minnesota upset San Francisco, 36-24; Denver trounced Houston, 34-10; and Cleveland eliminated Indianapolis, 38-21. In the conference championship games on January 17, Washington defeated Minnesota, 17-10, and Denver beat Cleveland, 38-33.

In the Super Bowl, Washington recovered from a 10-point deficit by scoring 35 points in the second quarter, a play-off record for most points scored in one quarter. Redskins quarterback Doug Williams threw four touchdown passes and set a Super Bowl record with 340 passing yards (311 meters), earning the Most Valuable Player award.

The Pro Football Hall of Fame in Canton, Ohio, added seven retired players—fullbacks Larry Csonka and John Henry Johnson, quarterback Len Dawson, wide receiver Don Maynard, offensive guard Gene Upshaw, center Jim Langer, and defensive tackle Joe Greene. The seven were inducted on Aug. 8, 1987.

Canada. The Canadian Football League endured deep financial problems because of an economic slump, poor marketing, and increased competition from Canadian baseball and hockey teams and NFL telecasts. The Montreal Alouettes went out of business on June 24, just before the season opened, and the eight surviving teams lost a total of U.S. $6.2 million during the year.

The Edmonton Eskimos won the Grey Cup championship game by beating the Toronto Argonauts, 38-36, on November 29 in Vancouver, B.C. Jerry Kauric kicked the deciding 49-yard (45-meter) field goal with 45 seconds remaining.

College. When the regular season ended in December, Oklahoma, Miami, and Syracuse were the only undefeated and untied teams in the National Collegiate Athletic Association's (NCAA) Division I-A for major colleges. Each had an 11-0 record. Florida State, Nebraska, and San Jose State were 10-1, and Auburn and Louisiana State were 9-1-1. At the opposite end, Columbia extended its losing streak to 41 games, surpassing the previous record of 34 for major colleges.

After the regular season, the wire-service polls ranked Oklahoma first in the nation, Miami second, Florida State third, and Syracuse fourth. Syracuse's only chance to win the national championship was for Oklahoma and Miami to tie. But first Syracuse had to beat Auburn in the Sugar Bowl in New Orleans on New Year's Day. Instead, the game ended in a 16-16 tie when Win Lyle of Auburn kicked a 30-yard (27-meter) field goal with one second left. That night, Miami upset Oklahoma, and the wire services and other selectors promptly named Miami the national champion.

Oklahoma led the major colleges in six of the eight leading categories, including total offense and defense, rushing offense, and passing defense. The team also led in scoring offense with an average of 43.5 points per game, and scoring defense, allowing their opponents an average of 7.5 points per game.

Writers and broadcasters voted the Heisman Trophy as the nation's outstanding player to Tim Brown, the Notre Dame flanker and kick returner. Quarterback Don McPherson of Syracuse was second, and Gordie Lockbaum of Holy Cross, a wide receiver and defensive back, was third.

On February 25, for the first time ever, the NCAA canceled a school's football season because of repeated rules violations. It penalized Southern Methodist University in Dallas after unidentified athletic officials from the school had paid $61,000 to players in violation of rules.

The NCAA barred Southern Methodist from playing in 1987 and allowed it only seven games (none at home) in 1988. It said the school could give no football scholarships in 1987 and only 15 in 1988. It allowed Southern Methodist players to transfer to other colleges without losing a year of eligibility, and most did. Southern Methodist later canceled the 1988 season, too, saying it could not be competitive. Frank Litsky

In WORLD BOOK, see FOOTBALL.

FORD, GERALD RUDOLPH (1913-   ), the 38th President of the United States, appeared personally before the Senate Judiciary Committee at televised hearings on Sept. 15, 1987. Assuming a role that was unprecedented for a former President, Ford introduced Robert H. Bork, President Ronald Reagan's nominee for a vacancy on the Supreme Court of the United States. In October, however, the committee and the full Senate rejected the Bork nomination. See SUPREME COURT OF THE UNITED STATES.

In the fall, Ford joined former Presidents Jimmy Carter and Richard M. Nixon in filming endorsements of the U.S. space program. Ford and Nixon also participated in a July 22 memorial tribute in Washington, D.C., to Arthur F. Burns, a former chairman of the Federal Reserve System's Board of Governors, who died in June.

Ford's wife, Betty, 69, underwent coronary artery by-pass surgery on November 20 at the Eisenhower Medical Center near their home in Rancho Mirage, Calif. On December 30, she had surgery to repair sutures from the heart operation.

Besides appearing in occasional pro-am celebrity golf tournaments, Ford remained active on the boards of directors of several major corporations. Frank Cormier and Margot Cormier

In WORLD BOOK, see FORD, GERALD R.

FOUR-H CLUBS. See YOUTH ORGANIZATIONS.

FRANCE. An unprecedented power-sharing arrangement, formed as a result of a national election in March 1986, faced a crisis in January 1987. According to the arrangement, France's top two leaders were members of opposing political parties for the first time since the founding of the Fifth Republic in 1958. François Mitterrand, a Socialist, was president, while the prime minister was Jacques Chirac, a member of the conservative Rally for the Republic (RPR) party.

The first test of the relationship was a wave of industrial unrest over wage restraints that began in mid-December 1986 with a strike by employees of the state-owned railway company. On Jan. 6, 1987, workers at the state-owned electrical utility struck, causing occasional blackouts throughout France. Chirac said on January 6 that if an agreement was not reached to end unrest, there might be "no way out except to call an election."

The strikes crumbled as a result of Chirac's firm stand. On January 10 and 11, rail workers began to vote to return to work, and the electrical workers settled for a wage hike of about 3 per cent.

Election Rumors. Political observers speculated that France soon would hold another national election. In addition to the labor problems, the government faced mounting pressure on the franc; signs of war in the former French African colony of Chad; a failure to free French hostages

French riot police stand guard in January at a railway station in Paris during a strike that paralyzed most of France's rail traffic.

held in Beirut, Lebanon; and renewed threats and attempted bombing attacks by terrorists. In Chirac's view, Mitterrand was doing little to help solve the nation's problems.

Nationality Law. More than 10,000 people paraded in Paris on March 15 to protest a bill that would reform the French nationality code. The bill would abolish the right to French citizenship automatically bestowed on individuals who are born in France but whose parents are not citizens of France. After the protest, Minister of Justice Albin Chalandon promised to revise the bill.

Rebel Minister. Another political crisis occurred on June 3, when Chirac told his minister of culture and communications, François Léotard, to stop acting like a political militant or leave the government. Léotard, who leads the small Republican Party, one of the main parties in the coalition that governs France, had threatened to run against Chirac in the 1988 presidential elections. Léotard decided to stay in the government. Had he resigned, taking some of his party's ministers with him, the government might have collapsed.

Relations with Iran neared the breaking point on July 13, when the French insisted that Wahid Gordji, an Iranian who had taken refuge in the Iranian Embassy in Paris, give himself up for police questioning about his suspected involvement in 1986 terrorist bombings in Paris.

In retaliation, Iranian authorities announced that they would try Paul Torri, France's consul in their capital, Teheran, for espionage. The French cordoned off the Iranian Embassy, and the French Embassy in Teheran was blockaded by Iran. On July 17, France severed diplomatic relations with Iran and prevented a group of 13 Iranians, including three diplomats, from leaving the country by crossing the border into Switzerland.

The standoff ended on November 29, when France allowed Gordji to return to Iran. Iran, in turn, released Torri.

In the fall, a scandal involving illegal arms sales to Iran rocked France's Socialist Party. A Defense Ministry report made public in November said that the Luchaire Armaments Company, a French arms maker, had sold artillery shells to Iran from 1983 to 1986 despite an embargo on arms sales to that country. Officials of the Socialist government then in power concealed the sales, and Luchaire reportedly gave some proceeds from the sales to the Socialist Party. Kenneth Brown

See also EUROPE (Facts in Brief Table). In WORLD BOOK, see FRANCE.

FUTURE FARMERS OF AMERICA (FFA). See YOUTH ORGANIZATIONS.

GABON. See AFRICA.

GAMBIA. See AFRICA.

GAMES. See TOYS AND GAMES.

GARDENING. In September 1987, the United States first international floral exposition, called AmeriFlora '92, was officially sanctioned by the International Association of Horticulture Producers. The festival will be held in 1992 in Columbus, Ohio, which is acting as host for the 500th anniversary celebration of Christopher Columbus' landing in the New World. AmeriFlora '92 will be launched in April 1992 by an indoor floral and garden show that is expected to include exhibitors from 25 to 30 nations. President Ronald Reagan's Christopher Columbus Quincentenary Jubilee Commission named the festival as one of the five focal points of the national celebration.

Saving the American Chestnut. Most of the American chestnut trees in North America were wiped out by a fungus disease called *chestnut blight* that entered the United States in the 1890's. In September 1987, the first U.S. patent ever issued for a chestnut tree was granted for a hybrid called the Revival Chestnut—a tree that appears to be blight-resistant and to possess the appearance of the stately American chestnut.

Creating the Revival Chestnut involved crossbreeding Chinese chestnut trees, which have a natural resistance to the blight, with some of the surviving specimens of the American chestnut. Then, by a process called *backcrossing*—crossing the hybrids with pure American chestnut trees—plant breeders obtained new hybrids that were genetically more like the American chestnut than the original hybrids. Plant breeders predict that by continued backcrossing, they will be able to produce a tree that is almost a genetic replica of the pure American chestnut while retaining the Chinese chestnut's resistance to blight.

Supersweet Corn. The year 1987 was one of great improvement in sweet corn varieties and acceptance of those varieties by home gardeners and commercial growers. These improved varieties have up to 25 per cent more sweetness and hold their taste much longer than previous types. The sweetest varieties, called *supersweet*, require growing conditions that include wide spacing and warm soil, making them unsuitable for most home gardens. Home gardeners turned to related varieties called *sugar extenders* or *sugar enhancers*, which are more appropriate for home gardens.

Year of the Tomato. The National Garden Bureau, an educational service of the seed industry, declared 1987 as the Year of the Tomato. According to data collected by the National Gardening Association, the tomato was the most popular item in home gardens in the United States, with 85.4 per cent of all food-gardening households growing them. George (Doc) Abraham and Katherine (Katy) Abraham

In WORLD BOOK, see GARDENING.

GAS AND GASOLINE. See ENERGY SUPPLY; PETROLEUM AND GAS.

GEOLOGY. An earthquake measuring 5.9 on the Richter scale struck the Los Angeles area on Oct. 1, 1987. (The *Richter scale* is a scale for indicating the magnitude of earthquakes on which quakes of 4.5 and above are potentially destructive.) The quake, which caused seven deaths and more than $213 million in damages, occurred along a previously unidentified *fault* (crack in the earth's crust) about $7\frac{1}{2}$ miles (12 kilometers) beneath the surface.

Geologists had believed that the faults along which major earthquakes occur nearly always extend all the way to the earth's surface. Most quakes also occur along faults where adjacent *tectonic plates*—huge slabs making up the earth's outer crust—are moving past each other. The October quake, however, occurred along a *thrust fault*—a fault created when a block of crust becomes so highly compressed that one section of the block is thrust horizontally over another block.

Surprise Earthquake Zone. An area of the Pacific Northwest in the United States and Canada thought to be relatively free of earthquakes has actually experienced many major quakes in the past, according to research reported in April by geologists Thomas H. Heaton and Stephen H. Hartzell of the United States Geological Survey (USGS) in Pasadena, Calif. In a geologic survey of the region, the scientists found changes in the landscape typical of those caused by large earthquakes. No such quakes have occurred in the past 150 years.

Earth's Hot Center. The earth's core is hotter than the surface of the sun, according to an April report by scientists from several U.S. universities. The scientists based their conclusion on the temperature of iron melted under pressures found at the core. (Iron is believed to be the chief element in the earth's core.) The scientists calculated the temperature at the core to be about 12,420°F. (6,880°C), several thousand degrees hotter than previously estimated.

Reigning Champion. Mount Everest is still the world's tallest mountain, according to measurements reported in October by Italian scientists. Earlier in 1987, a U.S. scientist announced that K2—or Mount Godwin Austen—another mountain in the Himalaya, was taller than Everest. The newest measurements, however, using satellite surveying techniques and traditional land-based measuring techniques, indicated that Everest's peak is 29,108 feet (8,872 meters) above sea level—840 feet (256 meters) higher than K2.

Volcanoes and Climate. Evidence supporting the long-held theory that large volcanic eruptions can significantly change the world's climate was reported in May by geologists Thomas P. Miller of the USGS in Anchorage, Alaska, and Robert L. Smith of the USGS in Sacramento, Calif. Scientists believe such changes occur when sulfur dioxide spewed into the atmosphere by a volcano com-

Twisted rail lines indicate the strength of an earthquake that struck New Zealand's North Island on March 2, injuring at least 25 people.

bines with water, forming droplets of sulfuric acid. The droplets affect the amount of sunlight reaching the earth and the amount of heat radiating from the earth into space. But scientists have been unable to confirm the link between eruptions and climatic change because knowledge of past volcanic eruptions is often sketchy at best.

Miller and Smith's study of volcanic eruptions in the Aleutian Islands off the coast of Alaska filled in some of the gaps in the volcanic record. They identified and dated 12 large eruptions in the region, 11 of them previously unknown. The scientists believe that 10 of the eruptions were large enough to have caused climatic changes.

Tibetan Geology. One of the first geologic expeditions to northern Tibet has revealed new information about one of the most geologically intriguing and unknown areas on earth. Geologists Peter Molnar and B. Clark Burchfiel of the Massachusetts Institute of Technology in Cambridge reported in January that the Plateau of Tibet is not a single block of crust, as previously thought, but consists of at least two blocks. The scientists discovered that the plateau is made up in part of a 200-million-year-old *suture belt*—a region containing the remains of an ocean that disappeared when two continents collided.   Eldridge M. Moores

In WORLD BOOK, see GEOLOGY.

GEORGIA. See STATE GOVERNMENT.

GEPHARDT, RICHARD ANDREW (1941-   ), a United States congressman from Missouri since 1976, declared his candidacy for the 1988 Democratic presidential nomination on Feb. 23, 1987. In his campaign, he stressed his support of *protectionism,* the use of trade barriers to protect U.S. industries from foreign competition.

Gephardt was born in St. Louis, Mo., on Jan. 31, 1941. He attended Northwestern University in Evanston, Ill., where he received a degree in speech in 1962. He received a law degree from the University of Michigan Law School in 1965.

After law school, Gephardt joined a St. Louis law firm. He soon entered politics, working as a precinct captain in St. Louis. He served on the St. Louis Board of Aldermen from 1971 to 1976.

In 1976, Gephardt made a successful bid for Congress. With Senator Bill Bradley (D., N.J.), he sponsored a tax simplification proposal that led to sweeping tax revision in 1986.

Gephardt has a reputation as a tireless worker and a consensus builder. But his critics charge that he changes his position on issues to gain political advantage. He once favored constitutional amendments to bar school busing and abortion. But he no longer supports such amendments, though he remains personally opposed to abortion.

Gephardt and his wife, Jane, were married in 1966. They have three children.   Joan Stephenson

GERMANY, EAST. East Germany's Communist Party Secretary-General Erich Honecker made a historic visit to Bonn, the capital of West Germany, on Sept. 7 and 8, 1987. No East German head of state had ever visited West Germany before. Previous attempts to organize such a visit had failed because of East-West tensions and the Soviet Union's refusal to allow a trip.

After the talks, representatives of the two Germanys signed cooperation agreements and said that the relationship between their states was "a stabilizing factor for constructive East-West relations." Chancellor Helmut Kohl of West Germany agreed to pay a return visit to East Germany.

Many Issues Discussed. Kohl and Honecker had a "frank exchange" on human rights. The two leaders jointly urged the United States and the Soviet Union to seize the opportunity for an agreement to eliminate medium-range missiles from Europe and called for verifiable agreements on limiting conventional forces, strategic missiles, and chemical and space weapons.

At a banquet, Kohl urged that "the whole German people must be free to choose reunification." But Honecker replied, "Socialism and capitalism cannot be united any more than fire and water."

The Leaders Agreed to increase youth exchanges and to discuss the formation of a joint commission to boost inter-German trade. They also pledged to cooperate in nuclear reactor safety, science and technology, and environmental protection, including the control of pollution of the Elbe River, which flows through both countries.

Signs of Accord. The growing accord between the two Germanys had been evident earlier in 1987. At the end of March, the Soviets and East Germans conducted military maneuvers 18 miles (29 kilometers) from the West German border. The East Germans invited two West German Army officers to watch the maneuvers.

On July 17, East Germany announced a general amnesty for "most prisoners." West German authorities suggested that 2,000 political prisoners would be released by year-end.

Political observers expected East Germany would allow more than 1 million East Germans to visit relatives in West Germany in 1987. In 1986, 570,000 East Germans made such visits.

Berlin Celebrates. Soviet leader Mikhail S. Gorbachev visited East Berlin on May 27 to celebrate the 750th anniversary of the founding of Berlin. Gorbachev remained in East Berlin on May 28 and 29 to attend a summit meeting of the Warsaw Pact, the Soviet bloc military alliance.   Kenneth Brown

See also EUROPE (Facts in Brief Table). In WORLD BOOK, see GERMANY.

Erich Honecker, left, the first East German head of state to visit West Germany, reviews troops with West German leader Helmut Kohl in September.

GERMANY, WEST

GERMANY, WEST. Chancellor Helmut Kohl's three-party center-right coalition won national elections on Jan. 25, 1987, though his Christian Democratic Union (CDU) and its affiliate in the state of Bavaria, the Christian Social Union (CSU), polled 4.5 percentage points less of the vote than in the previous election in 1983. The CDU-CSU combination won 44.3 per cent of the vote, while the liberal Free Democratic Party (FDP), the third partner in the coalition, gained 2.1 percentage points to poll 9.1 per cent. The biggest winner was the environmentalist Green Party, which gained 2.7 points to win 8.3 per cent of the vote.

Kohl's Plans. On March 18, Kohl told parliament what his policies would be during the next four years. He forecast more cooperation with the Soviet Union and concrete results in arms control. He warned, however, that nuclear disarmament would increase the problem of imbalance in nonnuclear forces in Europe. The Warsaw Pact, the Soviet bloc's military alliance, has more such forces than does its Western counterpart, the North Atlantic Treaty Organization (NATO). Chancellor Kohl said his goal remained "freedom and unity for all Germans."

Missiles Deal. Kohl's government was divided on the future of 72 aging Pershing IA nuclear missiles based on German soil. The Pershing rockets are under the control of West Germany, but the United States controls the nuclear warheads.

The Soviet Union wanted to include the missiles in a program to eliminate all Soviet and United States medium-range nuclear weapons from Europe. Kohl feared, however, that giving up the Pershings would expose West Germany to the Warsaw Pact's short-range, "battlefield" nuclear weapons and superior nonnuclear forces.

On June 4, the Bundestag (the more powerful of the two houses of parliament) approved Kohl's exclusion of the Pershings from proposals to eliminate medium-range weapons, 232 votes to 189. After intense lobbying by NATO countries, however, Kohl offered on August 26 to scrap the Pershings if the Soviets and the Americans reached an accord on banning medium-range weapons. The two superpowers signed such a treaty on December 8.

Brandt Resigns. Willy Brandt resigned as chairman of the Social Democrat Party (SDP) on March 23, after holding that post for 23 years. Other leaders of the party had criticized Brandt's leadership and his nomination of Margarita Mathiopoulos as the party's first press spokeswoman. Mathiopoulos was a citizen of Greece and was not a member of the SDP. The party chose Hans-Jochen Vogel to succeed Brandt.

A voter in Wiesbaden walks past a poster of Chancellor Helmut Kohl as West Germany gears up for national elections on January 25. Kohl's coalition won.

SDP-Greens Alliance Falls. West Germany's first coalition state government of the SDP and the Greens collapsed on February 9, when Holger Börner, Social Democrat premier of Hesse, fired his environment minister, a Green, in a dispute over a nuclear fuel plant. The collapse prompted a state election on April 5. The SDP lost heavily in the election. The Greens gained, but not enough to offset the SDP losses. As a result, the CDU and the FDP formed Hesse's first center-right government.

Hostage Crisis. Kohl faced a tough decision in February—whether to allow a suspected Lebanese terrorist, Mohammed Ali Hamadei, to be extradited to the United States. The United States had indicted Hamadei for the June 1985 hijacking of a Trans World Airlines jet and the murder of a passenger—a U.S. Navy diver. Terrorists holding two West German hostages in Beirut said they would kill the two if West Germany extradited Hamadei. The West German government announced on June 24, 1987, that it would not extradite Hamadei, but would try him in West Germany on charges of air piracy and murder.   Kenneth Brown

See also EUROPE (Facts in Brief Table). In WORLD BOOK, see GERMANY.

GHANA. See AFRICA.

GIRL SCOUTS. See YOUTH ORGANIZATIONS.

GIRLS CLUBS. See YOUTH ORGANIZATIONS.

GOLF. Each of the four 1987 Grand Slam tournaments for men went down to the final hole. None of the four were won by the favored contenders. Larry Mize of Columbus, Ga., won the Masters; Scott Simpson of San Diego won the United States Open; Nick Faldo of England took the British Open; and Larry Nelson of Columbus, Ga., captured the Professional Golfers' Association (PGA) championship.

Jane Geddes, Ayako Okamoto of Japan, and Betsy King won often on the Ladies Professional Golf Association (LPGA) tour. Chi Chi Rodriguez of Puerto Rico was the most frequent winner on the PGA senior tour.

The three major tours offered record purses in 1987—$31.5 million for the PGA Tour's 46 tournaments, $11 million for the LPGA's 36, and $8.7-million for the senior tour's 37. The Hertz Corporation, which sponsored the Hertz Bay Hill Classic in Orlando, Fla., offered $1 million for a hole in one on the 17th hole of the final round on March 15, and Dan Pooley made one with a No. 4 iron.

Grand Slam. The Masters, held from April 9 to 12 in Augusta, Ga., was a homecoming for Mize, who was born and raised a few miles from the course. He birdied the last hole for a 72-hole score of 285. That tied him with Greg Norman of Australia and Severiano Ballesteros of Spain.

On the first hole of a three-man, sudden-death play-off, Ballesteros took a bogey 5 and was eliminated. On the second hole, Mize, 90 feet (27 meters) off the green and 140 feet (43 meters) from the hole, chipped in with a sand wedge for a birdie. Norman then missed a 50-foot (15-meter) birdie putt, and Mize won.

In the U.S. Open, played from June 18 to 21 in San Francisco, Simpson one-putted six of the last nine holes, and his 277 beat Tom Watson by 1 stroke. Watson missed forcing a play-off when his 45-foot (14-meter) uphill putt on the last hole stopped 2 inches (5 centimeters) short of the cup.

In the British Open, held from July 16 to 19 at the Muirfield course in Gullane, Scotland, Faldo parred every hole on the final round, and his 279 beat Paul Azinger and Rodger Davis by 1 stroke. Azinger had led by 3 strokes with nine holes left, but he then made four bogeys, including two on the last two holes.

In the PGA championship, held from August 6 to 9 in Palm Beach Gardens, Fla., Nelson and Lanny Wadkins tied at 287, the highest winning score since the tournament first was decided by *medal play*—the lowest score—in 1958. On the first play-off hole, Nelson sank a 6-foot (2-meter) putt for par. Wadkins then slid a 5-foot (1.5 meter) par putt past the hole.

PGA Tour. The season ended with the richest tournament ever, the $2-million Nabisco Championships of Golf from October 29 to November 1 in San Antonio for the 30 top players in 1987. Watson's 268 beat Chip Beck by 2 strokes and Norman by 3.

Although Curtis Strange finished last, 25 strokes behind Watson, he took the season money-winning title with $925,941, a tour record. Azinger, who could have won the earnings title with a second-place finish in the Nabisco, finished fourth in the tournament. Azinger won the point competition for Player of the Year. He and Strange won three tournaments each.

LPGA Tour. Geddes won five tournaments, while Okamoto and King won four each. Okamoto was the first non-American to become the LPGA Player of the Year and led in earnings with $466,034 to $460,385 for King.

In the major tournaments, Geddes won the LPGA championship, King the Nabisco Dinah Shore tournament, Laura Davies of England the U.S. Women's Open, and Jody Rosenthal the Du Maurier Classic. Nancy Lopez' 35th tournament victory in February automatically placed her in the LPGA Hall of Fame.

Senior Tour. The colorful, 51-year-old Rodriguez won seven tournaments. Bruce Crampton won five tournaments, and Gary Player and Bob Charles won four each.   Frank Litsky

In WORLD BOOK, see GOLF.

GORE, ALBERT ARNOLD, JR. (1948-   ), Democratic senator from Tennessee, announced his candidacy for the presidency of the United States on June 29, 1987. Gore was the first Vietnam veteran to seek the presidency, and if elected he would be the youngest President ever. He said his top priorities would include reducing the federal budget deficit and reaching an arms-control agreement with the Soviet Union.

Gore, the son of former Senator Albert A. Gore, Sr. (D., Tenn.), was born on March 31, 1948, in Washington, D.C. He graduated with honors from Harvard University in Cambridge, Mass., in 1969.

From 1971 to 1976, after serving with the U.S. Army in Vietnam for two years, Gore studied religion and law at Vanderbilt University in Nashville. During the same period, he worked as a newspaper reporter and homebuilding contractor.

Gore was elected to the U.S. House of Representatives in 1976. In the House, he became known as an effective investigator, leading congressional probes of hazardous-waste dumping and other issues. In 1984, Gore was elected to the Senate, receiving the most votes ever cast for a candidate in a Tennessee election.

Gore and his wife, the former Mary E. Aitcheson, have four children. Mary Gore, nicknamed Tipper, has led a campaign against sexually explicit lyrics in rock music.   David L. Dreier

GORIA, GIOVANNI GIUSEPPE (1943-   ), a Christian Democrat, became prime minister of Italy on July 29, 1987, heading a five-party coalition. Goria came to power after a national election in June failed to resolve a problem that plagues Italian governments—the need to forge coalitions of parties that have widely varying political philosophies in order to amass enough support in Parliament to pass legislation. See ITALY.

A difference with a minor partner in Goria's coalition—the Liberal Party—prompted Goria to resign on November 14. The Liberals claimed that the government had broken a promise to emphasize spending cuts in setting the national budget. After resigning, Goria offered the Liberals a compromise, which they accepted on November 18, and Goria reestablished his government.

Goria was born on July 30, 1943, in Asti. He obtained a degree in economics from the University of Turin, then worked at a savings bank in Asti. He was first elected to Parliament in 1976, and, in 1981, he became budget undersecretary. He was appointed treasury minister in 1982.

Goria helped shape an economic policy that led to a rise in productivity and a sharp decline in inflation. Opponents criticize him, however, for major increases in government spending.

The new prime minister and his wife, Eugenia, have two children.   Jay Myers

GRAF, STEFFI (1969-   ), of West Germany, displayed her formidable forehand and fast feet in 1987 and, at 17, became the youngest tennis player to win the French Open. Graf defeated Martina Navratilova, 6-4, 4-6, 8-6, to take the women's singles title on June 6 in Paris.

Graf was born on June 14, 1969, in Brühl, West Germany, a small town near Heidelberg. Her parents, Peter and Heidi Graf, operated a tennis school. Graf began playing tennis at the age of 4. Coached by her father, she turned professional at 13, the youngest player to be ranked by the Women's International Tennis Association at that time. In 1984, Graf won a gold medal in tennis at the Summer Olympic Games in Los Angeles.

In 1985, Graf was a finalist or semifinalist in seven tournaments. In 1986, she won her first professional tournament, and then, in 1987, won eight tournaments, including her first grand slam at the French Open. She was a finalist at Wimbledon, England, in July and at the United States Open in Flushing Meadow in New York City in September, losing both times to Navratilova. In August, Graf was ranked number one in women's tennis—replacing Navratilova—after defeating Chris Evert in the Virginia Slims of Los Angeles tournament. It was the first time since 1980 that neither Navratilova nor Evert had held the top ranking. See TENNIS.   Rod Such

GREAT BRITAIN. Prime Minister Margaret Thatcher ended a period of intense political speculation on May 11, 1987, by calling a general election for June 11. Her sense of timing was vindicated when her Conservative Party gained a landslide victory in the election. The victory made Thatcher the first British prime minister to win three consecutive general elections since Robert Banks Jenkinson, the Earl of Liverpool, who was prime minister from 1812 to 1827. See THATCHER, MARGARET HILDA.

The Conservatives won 375 seats, giving them a majority of 101 seats in the House of Commons, only 43 fewer than after their landslide victory in 1983. The Labour Party won 229 seats, only 21 more than in 1983, making this its second biggest defeat since 1918. The centrist Alliance, a coalition of the Liberal Party and the Social Democratic Party (SDP), lost 5 seats, finishing with 22 seats.

The most surprising feature of the election was the sophisticated campaign mounted by the Labour Party. Labour's imagemakers changed the party's symbol from the traditional red banner to a red rose, and hired Hugh Hudson, director of the Oscar-winning 1981 film *Chariots of Fire,* to produce its television commercials. The campaign was widely admired as an example of powerful propaganda, and it worried Conservative campaign managers.

In the end, the campaign failed to disguise the unpopularity of many of Labour's policies. Labour lost votes because its defense policy advocated that Britain abandon its nuclear weapons. Voters also were unable to believe that the high-spending programs proposed by the Labour Party could be accomplished without big tax increases. What some observers called Labour's "Loony Left" did not help its campaign either. This group included party extremists who ran the councils of many of London's boroughs. Their policies appeared to combine financial extravagance with support for minority groups at the expense of the majority.

Voters instead opted for Thatcher's policies of careful budgeting, low inflation, and steady eco-

Margaret Thatcher waves to crowds in London in June after being elected to her third consecutive term as Britain's prime minister.

nomic growth. The Conservative policies of privatizing government-owned industries by selling stocks to the public and of allowing tenants of council housing to buy the homes they rented proved vote-getters. But the Conservatives did not triumph throughout Great Britain. In Scotland, where they were perceived as the "English" party, they lost 11 seats. In England's industrial north and in South Wales, where unemployment is high, the Labour Party held on to its seats.

Investors line up outside a London office to buy shares in Rolls-Royce during the British government's sale of the aircraft company in May.

Alliance Upheaval. The election had a traumatic effect on the Liberal-SDP Alliance. Three of SDP's four founding members—Roy Jenkins, Shirley Williams, and William Rogers—lost their seats in Parliament.

After the election, the Alliance began a bitter debate over whether the SDP and the Liberal Party should merge. Liberal leader David Steel proposed the merger. He argued that voters had been confused by the Alliance's double leadership in the election. But SDP leader David Owen, the only founding member of SDP who managed to keep his parliamentary seat, announced that he would oppose any merger.

On August 6, two-thirds of SDP members voted in favor of merger negotiations. But Owen and a minority of SDP members said they would refuse to join a merged party, and Owen stepped down immediately as SDP leader. The SDP majority elected Robert Maclennan, a Scottish lawyer, as its new leader and head of the party's negotiating team. On September 17, Liberal members voted overwhelmingly in favor of merger. The negotiations were expected to lead to a new merged party by the spring of 1988.

Thatcher's Program. On June 13, Prime Minister Thatcher reshuffled her Cabinet. The most notable change was the reinstatement of Cecil Parkinson as secretary of state for energy. Parkinson re-

signed from the Cabinet in 1983 after he admitted that his secretary was pregnant with his child.

Thatcher's plan for her third term included a campaign to help Britain's blighted inner cities, and more sales of government-owned properties, including water utilities. Her proposed community charge caused the most debate, however. The proposal would replace the local property tax with a tax levied equally on all adults. The opposition labeled the proposed charge a "poll tax" and said it would benefit the wealthy but hurt poor people and renters.

***Spycatcher* Drama.** Prime Minister Thatcher remained determined in 1987 to stop Peter Wright, a former MI5 agent (British counterintelligence officer), from publishing his memoirs in Britain. The government held the position that intelligence officers had a lifelong duty to remain silent.

Wright, 71, was retired and living in Australia, where he was beyond the reach of British law. The British government, however, went to court in Australia to have his book, *Spycatcher: The Candid Autobiography of a Senior Intelligence Officer,* banned in that country. Britain lost the case when the New South Wales Supreme Court ruled on March 13 that Australian security was not threatened by the book and that the British government had secretly cooperated with other authors writing about British security services. Britain appealed to the New

South Wales Court of Appeal, lost again on September 24, and then announced that it would appeal to the Australian High Court. On September 29, the Australian High Court refused the government's plea to ban *Spycatcher* until the appeal was heard, and the book was then published in Australia. *Spycatcher* had already become a best seller in the United States, where the British government did not try to stop the publication.

The ban on *Spycatcher* continued in Britain, however, because the government had obtained injunctions preventing British newspapers from publishing excerpts of the book. On December 21, the High Court in London refused to make the ban permanent but granted another temporary injunction at least until January 1988. The controversy was complicated by politically explosive charges in the book. Wright's principal allegation was that Sir Roger Hollis, former head of MI5 who is now dead, had been a Soviet agent.

Archer Wins Case. In another sensational court battle in 1987, Jeffrey Archer, former deputy chairman of the Conservative Party and best-selling novelist, won libel damages of 500,000 pounds ($800,000) against a London newspaper, *The Star,* on July 24. The newspaper had alleged that Archer had sex with a London prostitute in September 1986 and paid her to keep quiet.

Fiji Revolt. In an unprecedented move, Queen Elizabeth II attempted to stop Fiji from becoming a republic after Lieutenant Colonel Sitiveni Rabuka seized power on Sept. 25, 1987. Fiji was a member of the Commonwealth, a group of nations that consider the monarch of Great Britain their head of state. The queen warned she would consider any move against Governor General Ratu Sir Penaia Ganilau, her representative in Fiji, a treasonable act. Nonetheless, Rabuka declared Fiji a republic on October 6, ending 113 years of allegiance to the British Crown. On December 5, Rabuka stepped down as head of government and said Ganilau had been named president.

The Royal Family. It was a mixed year for Britain's royal family. Prince Charles won praise for his campaign to raise the nation's consciousness about inner-city poverty. After visiting slums in London on July 1, he criticized the government's lack of attention to urban problems.

Prince Edward, Queen Elizabeth's youngest son, bucked a royal family tradition on January 12 when he resigned from the Royal Marines. Edward said he preferred to go into television.

Charles and Diana, the Prince and Princess of Wales, made headlines when the press reported in October that the couple had spent 39 days apart. The separation fueled rumors of marital problems between the prince and princess.

Ferry Disaster. On March 6, the *Herald of Free Enterprise,* a British ferry, capsized while crossing

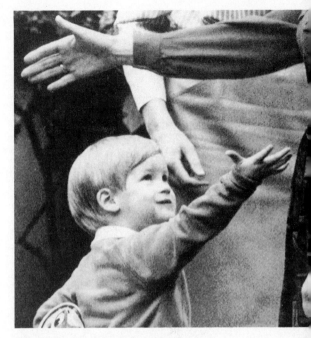

Prince Harry, son of the Prince and Princess of Wales, reaches out for his teacher's hand on his first day of school on September 16.

the English Channel from the Belgian port of Zeebrugge to Dover, England. The accident killed 188 of the approximately 540 passengers and crew aboard. An official report issued on July 24 said that the ferry had left port with its bow doors open, allowing water to pour into the car decks.

Shooting Spree. On August 19, 27-year-old Michael Ryan, a member of a local gun club, shot and killed 16 people, including his mother, in the quiet country town of Hungerford in Berkshire. After police surrounded him in a local school, he shot himself. Ryan had been able to buy guns with ease, including a handgun and a Chinese-made AK-47 semiautomatic rifle he used in the massacre, the worst in modern British history. Home Secretary Douglas Hurd announced on September 22 that he would ban the sale of all multiple-fire weapons as well as shortened-barrel guns.

Printing Strike Ended. The 13-month strike by three printing unions in London ended on February 6. The unions struck after Rupert Murdoch, owner of four British newspapers, moved his printing operation to a computerized plant. Union leaders ended the strike after attorneys said that legal action by Murdoch could bankrupt the unions.   Ian J. Mather

See also ENGLAND; IRELAND; NORTHERN IRELAND; SCOTLAND; WALES. In WORLD BOOK, see GREAT BRITAIN.

Greek textile workers in Athens protest in February against the government's anti-inflation program, which virtually froze their wages.

GREECE confronted Turkey over oil rights in the Aegean Sea in March 1987. Warships from both countries steamed toward three islands off the Turkish coast on March 27 after Turkey announced it had issued licenses for oil prospecting in the Aegean seabed.

At an emergency meeting of the North Atlantic Treaty Organization (NATO) in Brussels, Belgium, on March 27, NATO Secretary-General Lord Carrington appealed to the two sides to "avoid recourse to force at all costs." Both Greece and Turkey are members of NATO.

The dispute arose because the two nations have not agreed on the ownership of the seabed, which likely contains substantial oil deposits. Greece has more than 2,000 islands in the Aegean Sea, with a territorial limit of 6 nautical miles (11 kilometers) around each. Greece maintains, however, that it has a right to extend the limit to 12 nautical miles (22 kilometers). Turkey has said that an attempt to extend the limit would be an act of war.

Following negotiations inspired by the NATO appeal, Greece and Turkey reached a temporary agreement on March 28. Turkey agreed not to explore for oil in disputed waters, and Greece agreed to halt its exploration.

U.S. Bases. The oil dispute soured Greek relations with the United States. During negotiations for renewal of U.S. military bases in Greece, Greece accused the United States of supporting Turkey in this dispute and in an ongoing disagreement over Cyprus. (That island has been divided between ethnic Greeks and ethnic Turks since 1974. In 1983, the Turkish Cypriots declared their part of the island an independent nation, the Turkish Republic of Northern Cyprus.)

Anti-Austerity Strikes. The year 1987 started with a series of strikes protesting the Socialist government's austerity program, designed to reduce the demand for consumer goods, thereby curbing inflation and cutting imports. This program had led to a virtual freeze in pay for Greek workers, yet the inflation rate was a lofty 17 per cent.

Church and State. Parliament passed legislation on April 3 authorizing the government to seize land owned by the Greek Orthodox Church and give it to farm cooperatives. The measures also would place valuable church property in urban areas under the control of committees dominated by people who were not members of the clergy. The church objected to the proposed makeup of the urban committees. In September, the government compromised with the church, allowing the committees to be appointed by bishops, rather than by local public officials. In November, the government made further concessions, and an agreement was reached.   Kenneth Brown

See also EUROPE (Facts in Brief Table). In WORLD BOOK, see CYPRUS; GREECE.

GREENSPAN, ALAN (1926-   ), was sworn in as chairman of the Board of Governors of the Federal Reserve System, usually called the Fed, on Aug. 11, 1987. In that capacity, he became responsible for managing the supply of money in the United States. Greenspan succeeded Paul A. Volcker, who resigned after serving as Fed chief for eight years. Greenspan was expected to continue Volcker's strong stand against inflation by keeping a tight rein on the nation's money supply.

Greenspan was born on March 6, 1926, in New York City. He studied economics at New York University (NYU), earning a bachelor's degree in 1948 and a master's degree in 1950.

From 1954 to 1974, Greenspan was chairman and president of Townsend-Greenspan & Company, a New York City economic consulting firm. He resumed that position in 1977 after serving for three years as chairman of President Gerald R. Ford's Council of Economic Advisers. Also in 1977, he received a doctorate in economics from NYU. In 1981, Greenspan was named chairman of the National Commission on Social Security Reform, a post he held for two years.

Greenspan was married briefly and is now divorced.   David L. Dreier

GRENADA. See LATIN AMERICA.

GUATEMALA. See LATIN AMERICA.

GUINEA. See AFRICA.

HAIG, ALEXANDER MEIGS, JR. (1924-   ), declared his candidacy for the 1988 Republican presidential nomination on March 24, 1987. Among the Republican candidates, he was the most critical of the Administration of President Ronald Reagan for what he considered an ineffective foreign policy. And unlike his competitors, Haig said that congressional Democrats should not be blamed exclusively for the highly unbalanced federal budgets of the Reagan presidency. "This deficit is a Republican deficit," he declared.

Haig was born on Dec. 2, 1924, in Philadelphia. He graduated from the United States Military Academy at West Point, N.Y., in 1947 and served in the Army until 1979.

From 1969 to 1973, Haig was a member of the National Security Council. In 1973 and 1974, he was White House chief of staff for Presidents Richard M. Nixon and Gerald R. Ford. He then became supreme commander of North Atlantic Treaty Organization (NATO) forces. After leaving the Army, Haig served as president and chief operating officer of United Technologies Corporation, an aircraft manufacturer.

Haig became Reagan's first secretary of state in 1981 but resigned on June 25, 1982. He then founded a business-consulting firm, with which he remained active in 1987. Haig and his wife, Patricia, have three children.   Jay Myers

HAITI. Haiti's scheduled presidential election was canceled on Nov. 29, 1987, after voting was disrupted by violent attacks on polling places that left more than 24 people dead. The provisional military government of National Council President Henri Namphy dissolved the independent, civilian electoral council that was charged with supervising the elections. And in response, the Administration of President Ronald Reagan suspended nearly all United States military and economic aid to Haiti. The Namphy government appointed a new electoral council in December and said it would try again to hold an election on Jan. 17, 1988.

According to eyewitnesses and journalists, the attacks on polling places in Port-au-Prince were carried out by former members of the Tontons Macoutes, the bodyguards of the deposed dictator Jean-Claude (Baby Doc) Duvalier. In some cases, policemen and soldiers participated.

Violence had threatened Haiti's elections for most of 1987. In March, voters adopted a new Constitution that prohibited former officials of the Duvalier dictatorship from running for public office for a 10-year period. In early November, the electoral council disqualified several former Duvalier associates, and several election officials were assaulted.   Nathan A. Haverstock

See also LATIN AMERICA (Facts in Brief Table). In WORLD BOOK, see HAITI.

HANDICAPPED. The United States government in June 1987 formed a panel to write new rules to prevent discrimination against physically impaired air travelers. At hearings on the issue in September, blind passengers and wheelchair users testified that airline policies affecting the handicapped are inconsistent and inconsistently applied.

One thorny issue involved prohibitions against seating blind travelers near emergency exits. Airlines said that such policies were necessary for safety, an assertion challenged by blind travelers.

Passengers who use wheelchairs told the panel that they also experienced discrimination. They urged that airlines be required to provide onboard wheelchairs narrow enough to maneuver in a plane's aisle.

The panel, which included representatives from the disabled community, the air travel industry, and the U.S. Department of Transportation, hoped to complete the new rules by early November. After a period of public comment, the Transportation Department will issue final regulations.

Disability Claims. A Social Security Administration regulation that has been used to deny hundreds of thousands of disability claims in recent years was upheld by the Supreme Court of the United States on June 8. The regulation denies disability benefits to people who suffer from medical impairments that would not prevent them

Around the World in a Wheelchair

On May 22, 1987, Rick Hansen, a 29-year-old Canadian paraplegic, propelled his wheelchair into Vancouver, Canada, completing a 25,000-mile (40,000-kilometer) around-the-world journey. As Hansen triumphantly wheeled through the city where his tour began 26 months earlier, tens of thousands of onlookers cheered.

Hansen's feat, which was designed to raise awareness of the potential of the disabled and to establish a trust fund for spinal cord research, was called the Man in Motion World Tour. The 34-country journey took Hansen—accompanied by a six-person crew that included a physical therapist—across the United States and through Europe, the Middle East, New Zealand, and Australia. After traveling through China, South Korea, and Japan, Hansen wheeled up the east coast of the United States and crossed Canada. He was showered with flowers in Poland, met Pope John Paul II at the

Vatican in Rome, and was cheered by 800,000 Chinese in the city of Tianjin (Tientsin). During the tour, romance blossomed between Hansen and physical therapist Amanda Reid, and they were married in Vancouver on Oct. 10, 1987.

Hansen grew up in Williams Lake in central British Columbia. He was an all-around high school athlete when, in 1973, his spinal cord was damaged in a truck accident, leaving him paralyzed from the waist down. He first had the idea of a wheelchair tour around the world shortly after his discharge from a Vancouver rehabilitation center in 1974.

Even before his world tour, Hansen had achieved an impressive array of athletic accomplishments, including victories in 19 international wheelchair marathons. He was named Canada's National Disabled Athlete of the Year in 1979, 1980, and 1982. In 1983, he and hockey star Wayne Gretzky shared the Lou Marsh Trophy as Canada's Outstanding Athletes of the Year.

The Man in Motion World Tour began on March 21, 1985, as about 300 well-wishers saw Hansen off from a Vancouver shopping center. In spite of Hansen's athletic background, he was troubled by illness and pain throughout the grueling tour, during which he wheeled an average of 50 miles (80 kilometers) a day. Intense pain developed in his shoulders and fingers, and his constricted posture in the wheelchair led to bladder and digestive problems. Twice, he collapsed due to fatigue.

As Hansen persevered, donations from corporations, individuals, schools, and community groups flooded the Man in Motion World Tour offices. By August 1987, twice the original fund-raising goal had been reached—for a total of more than $20 million Canadian (about $15 million in U.S. currency). The money will be invested, and half the interest earned will be donated to spinal cord research. The other half of the earned interest will be used to foster public awareness of the needs of disabled people and to fund rehabilitation programs and wheelchair sports.

Hansen hoped the tour would not only raise publicity and money but also enhance the self-respect of disabled people and give encouragement to those struggling with a disability. Everywhere he went, he brought a message that inspired many people—"Be all you can be with what you have." In the words of sixth-grader Tammy Corness of Surrey, British Columbia, who has cerebral palsy, "Every time I have to climb the stairs or do something I might not be able to do, I think of Rick. When I think of Rick and his determination, it gives me determination too."

Robie Liscomb

Surrounded by well-wishers, disabled Canadian athlete Rick Hansen wheels the last few yards of his round-the-world journey on May 22.

from performing most jobs. In particular, the regulation has been used to deny claims of older workers who cannot perform physical labor.

The June ruling was seen as only a partial defeat for disability claimants, however. The court interpreted the regulation narrowly and criticized the government for using the regulation improperly against qualified applicants. The impact of the court's ruling was expected to depend on how broadly the decision is interpreted by the government and lower courts.

Contagious-Disease Ruling. In a decision seen as potentially important for workers suffering from AIDS (acquired immune deficiency syndrome), the Supreme Court ruled on March 3, 1987, that federal law protects people with contagious diseases from discrimination. The court said that employers who receive federal funds may not discriminate against people who are physically or mentally impaired by contagious disease, unless the employees pose a significant risk of infection to others or are unable to do their work. The court's decision involved a teacher who was fired after several hospitalizations for tuberculosis. Groups concerned about discrimination against victims of AIDS regarded the ruling as an important victory.   Joan Stephenson

In WORLD BOOK, see HANDICAPPED.

HARNESS RACING. See HORSE RACING.

HART, GARY WARREN (1936-   ), stunned the United States political world on Dec. 15, 1987, when he announced that he was reentering the race for the 1988 Democratic presidential nomination. The former U.S. senator from Colorado withdrew from the race on May 8, after a Miami, Fla., newspaper reported that he had spent part of a weekend at his home with model Donna Rice. Hart at first denied the report, but as evidence of their relationship accumulated, the scandal eroded his support. In explaining his move to rejoin the race, Hart said he had a "set of new ideas" that "no one else represents."

Hart was born on Nov. 28, 1936, in Ottawa, Kans. He received bachelor's degrees from Bethany Nazarene College in Bethany, Okla., in 1958 and from Yale University Divinity School in 1961. In 1964, he graduated from Yale Law School.

After working as a lawyer for the U.S. departments of Justice and of the Interior, Hart set up private practice in Denver. In 1972, he served as director of Senator George S. McGovern's (D., S. Dak.) presidential campaign.

Hart was elected to the U.S. Senate in 1974 and 1980. In 1986, he retired from the Senate to run for President. He also joined the Denver law firm of Davis, Graham and Stubbs.

Hart and his wife, Lee, were married in 1958. They have two children.   Mary A. Krier

HAUGHEY, CHARLES JAMES (1925-   ), became prime minister of Ireland on March 10, 1987, when the Dail (parliament) elected him to the position by a one-vote margin. He succeeded Prime Minister Garret FitzGerald, head of the Fine Gael party. In a general election held in February, Haughey's Fianna Fáil party won enough seats to make Haughey prime minister, but not enough for a majority in parliament. See IRELAND.

Haughey previously served as prime minister from December 1979 to June 1981, when he lost the post to FitzGerald. He became prime minister again in March 1982 but lost the support of parliament less than eight months later. In December 1982, FitzGerald became prime minister.

Haughey was born on Sept. 16, 1925, in Castlebar, County Mayo, Ireland. He studied accounting and law at University College in Dublin before being elected to parliament in 1957. He became minister of justice in 1961, minister of agriculture in 1964, and minister of finance in 1966. Haughey resigned as finance minister in 1970, when he was charged with conspiring to smuggle arms into Northern Ireland for the Irish Republican Army. He was later acquitted. From 1977 to 1979, he was minister of health and social welfare.

Haughey married Maureen Lemass in 1951. They have four children.   Mary A. Krier

HAWAII. See STATE GOVERNMENT.

HEALTH AND DISEASE. Scientists on June 18, 1987, reported the first clear evidence that reducing levels of *cholesterol* (fatty substances) in the blood can slow or even reverse *atherosclerosis*, the type of heart disease that causes most heart attacks. Atherosclerosis occurs when cholesterol and other substances build up and eventually clog blood vessels that carry oxygen and nutrients to the heart.

The new findings, reported by researchers at the University of Southern California School of Medicine in Los Angeles, were heralded by the National Heart, Lung, and Blood Institute (NHLBI) in Bethesda, Md. The institute's director, Claude J. M. Lenfant, said many patients may be able to reverse their heart disease by a combination of drugs and low-cholesterol diets.

Officials of the NHLBI said that millions of people around the world could benefit from cholesterol-lowering regimens. They specifically recommended such regimens as a preventive measure for people who have had *coronary by-pass surgery*, a procedure in which veins are used to by-pass blocked portions of the *coronary arteries* (arteries that supply blood to the muscular tissue of the heart). Taking cholesterol-lowering drugs and following a low-cholesterol diet could help prevent the formation of new fatty deposits in the by-pass, officials said.

347

New AIDS Virus. On May 6, French scientists reported that a second virus is capable of causing AIDS (acquired immune deficiency syndrome). Researchers at the Pasteur Institute in Paris said the new virus, called *human immunodeficiency virus type 2* (HIV-2), appeared to be found only in western Africa. Human immunodeficiency virus type 1 currently is believed to cause AIDS in North America and Europe.

Alcohol and Cancer. Two separate studies reported on May 7 presented evidence that even moderate consumption of alcoholic beverages by women increases their risk of developing breast cancer. Based on the findings of these studies, cancer authorities recommended that women with other risk factors for breast cancer—such as obesity or a family history of the disease—reduce their alcohol consumption.

One of the studies, conducted at Harvard Medical School in Boston, examined the eating and drinking habits of 89,000 women. The researchers found that women who take even one alcoholic drink a day have a 50 per cent greater risk of developing breast cancer than women who do not drink. The other study, conducted at the National Cancer Institute (NCI) in Bethesda, involved more than 7,000 women. The NCI researchers found that three drinks per week increase the risk of breast cancer by 50 to 100 per cent.

Defective Genes. New evidence that Alzheimer's disease is hereditary—caused by defective genes that damage the brain with advancing age—was reported on May 23. Alzheimer's disease causes memory loss and impaired intellectual functioning in an estimated 2.5 million Americans.

Scientists from the Mount Sinai School of Medicine in New York City studied about 380 parents, brothers and sisters, and children of Alzheimer's disease victims. They found that the overall risk of developing the disease is four to five times higher among close relatives of patients than it is in the general population. The researchers concluded that 50 per cent of the immediate family members of Alzheimer's patients may develop the disease.

Low-Level Poisoning. Studies published on April 23 in *The New England Journal of Medicine* suggested that low levels of toxic substances may be more harmful than previously believed. One study, conducted by scientists at the Harvard Medical School and other institutions, found that exposure to even very low levels of lead prior to birth slows the mental development of an infant during the first year of life. The main sources of lead are automobile exhaust and lead-based paint that flakes off walls in older, run-down buildings.

The other study, conducted by the National Institute for Occupational Safety and Health, found that factory workers had a higher risk of developing *leukemia* (a cancer of the blood) when exposed to *benzene* (an industrial chemical) at levels currently permitted by the U.S. government. The researchers said that under the current federal exposure limits, workers may face a 70 per cent greater risk of developing leukemia.

Salmonella Rise. A study issued by the National Academy of Sciences (NAS) on May 12 concluded that chicken and other poultry contaminated with *Salmonella* bacteria may be causing millions of cases of *Salmonellosis*—a type of food poisoning—each year. The NAS, which advises the U.S. government on science and technology, reported that the U.S. Department of Agriculture's poultry inspectors do not detect *Salmonella* bacteria. They recommended improving inspection techniques.

Centennial Celebrated. One of the world's foremost medical research establishments—the National Institutes of Health (NIH) in Bethesda—observed its 100th anniversary in 1987. The NIH, an agency of the U.S. government, began in 1887 as a small laboratory on Staten Island in New York City. Today, it consists of 12 institutes staffed by 15,000 people. The NIH's annual budget of $6 billion funds almost 40 per cent of all medical research in the United States.   Michael Woods

See also DRUGS; MEDICINE; NUTRITION; PUBLIC HEALTH. In WORLD BOOK, see HEALTH; DISEASE.

HOBBIES. See COIN COLLECTING; STAMP COLLECTING; TOYS AND GAMES.

HOCKEY. The Edmonton Oilers returned to the top of the National Hockey League (NHL) in the 1986-1987 season. The team achieved the best regular-season record and then won the Stanley Cup play-offs. Its captain, Wayne Gretzky, was again the league's Most Valuable Player (MVP).

In 80 regular-season games, the Oilers' explosive offense carried them to a division title with 106 points. The other division winners were the Philadelphia Flyers with 100 points, the Hartford Whalers with 93, and the St. Louis Blues with 79.

Play-Offs. The division winners led 16 of the 21 teams into the play-offs. Edmonton easily advanced to the finals by eliminating the Los Angeles Kings, 4 games to 1; the Winnipeg Jets, 4-0; and the Detroit Red Wings, 4-1. Philadelphia gained the finals by defeating the New York Rangers 4-2; the New York Islanders, 4-3; and the Montreal Canadiens—the Stanley Cup defenders—4-2.

Edmonton took a 3-1 lead in games in the play-off finals, which began on May 17, but Philadelphia won the next two games. The Oilers won 3-1 in the seventh and decisive game on May 31.

Gretzky's Year. This was the eighth NHL season for the 26-year-old Gretzky, and for a record eighth time he was voted the Hart Trophy as the league's MVP. He won the Ross Trophy as scoring champion for the seventh straight season, also a record, leading the league in goals (62), assists

National Hockey League Standings

Prince of Wales Conference

Charles F. Adams Division

	W.	L.	T.	Pts.
Hartford Whalers	43	30	7	93
Montreal Canadiens	41	29	10	92
Boston Bruins	39	34	7	85
Quebec Nordiques	31	39	10	72
Buffalo Sabres	28	44	8	64

Lester Patrick Division

	W.	L.	T.	Pts.
Philadelphia Flyers	46	26	8	100
Washington Capitals	38	32	10	86
New York Islanders	35	33	12	82
New York Rangers	34	38	8	76
Pittsburgh Penguins	30	38	12	72
New Jersey Devils	29	45	6	64

Clarence Campbell Conference

James Norris Division

	W.	L.	T.	Pts.
St. Louis Blues	32	33	15	79
Detroit Red Wings	34	36	10	78
Chicago Black Hawks	29	37	14	72
Toronto Maple Leafs	32	42	6	70
Minnesota North Stars	30	40	10	70

Conn Smythe Division

	W.	L.	T.	Pts.
Edmonton Oilers	50	24	6	106
Calgary Flames	46	31	3	95
Winnipeg Jets	40	32	8	88
Los Angeles Kings	31	41	8	70
Vancouver Canucks	29	43	8	66

Scoring Leaders

	Games	Goals	Assists	Pts.
Wayne Gretzky, Edmonton	79	62	121	183
Jari Kurri, Edmonton	79	54	54	108
Mario Lemieux, Pittsburgh	63	54	53	107
Mark Messier, Edmonton	77	37	70	107
Doug Gilmour, St. Louis	80	42	63	105
Dino Ciccarelli, Minnesota	80	52	51	103
Dale Hawerchuk, Winnipeg	80	47	53	100
Michel Goulet, Quebec	75	49	47	96
Tim Kerr, Philadelphia	75	58	37	95
Ray Bourque, Boston	78	23	72	95
Ron Francis, Hartford	75	30	63	93

Leading Goalies

(25 or more games)	Games	Goals against	Avg.
Brian Hayward, Montreal	37	102	2.81
Patrick Roy, Montreal	46	131	2.93
Ron Hextall, Philadelphia	66	190	3.00
Daniel Berthiaume, Winnipeg	31	93	3.17

Awards

Calder Trophy (best rookie)—Luc Robitaille, Los Angeles

Hart Trophy (most valuable player)—Wayne Gretzky, Edmonton

Lady Byng Trophy (sportsmanship)—Joe Mullen, Calgary

Masterton Trophy (perseverance, dedication to hockey)—Doug Jarvis, Hartford

Norris Trophy (best defenseman)—Ray Bourque, Boston

Ross Trophy (leading scorer)—Wayne Gretzky, Edmonton

Selke Trophy (best defensive forward)—Dave Poulin, Philadelphia

Smythe Trophy (most valuable player in Stanley Cup)—Ron Hextall, Philadelphia

Vezina Trophy (most valuable goalie)—Ron Hextall, Philadelphia

Philadelphia Flyers' goalie Ron Hextall, right, defends his net, but the Edmonton Oilers won the seventh game and took the Stanley Cup in May.

(121), and total points (183). During the play-offs, Gretzky broke Jean Beliveau's career play-off record of 176 points.

Gretzky was named as center on the NHL all-star team. The other all-stars were Jari Kurri of Edmonton and Michel Goulet of the Quebec Nordiques at wing, Ray Bourque of the Boston Bruins and Mark Howe of Philadelphia on defense, and Ron Hextall of Philadelphia in goal.

International. The world championships from April 17 to May 3 in Vienna, Austria, ended in a bitter dispute. Sweden defeated Canada, 9-0, in the final game and won its first title. The favored Soviet Union protested that Canada had intentionally lost by such a wide margin to deprive the Soviets of the title, which was based on most goals.

The Soviet national team and an NHL all-star team split the two games of the Rendez-Vous 87 series from February 11 to 13 in Quebec City, Canada. The Soviets met some of those same NHL stars in the Canada Cup series in August and September. The finals in that series between the Soviets and the Canadian team resulted in some of the most exciting hockey ever played, according to many observers. The two teams split the first two games, both of which ended in overtime with identical 6-5 scores. Canada then won the final game, 6-5.   Frank Litsky

In WORLD BOOK, see HOCKEY.

HONDURAS. The United States continued to beef up its military presence in Honduras and supplied additional arms and equipment to Honduran forces in 1987. On May 12, the White House announced that the United States would sell 10 F-5E jet fighters and 2 F-5F trainers to Honduras, at a total cost of $72 million. In providing the advanced model aircraft, the White House ignored the Senate Foreign Relations Committee, which on April 23 had voted to ban sales of supersonic jets to Central American nations.

United States air, naval, and land forces carried out large-scale maneuvers in Honduras from April 1 to May 10, followed on May 13 by a combined air and sea assault maneuver near Trujillo on the Honduras-Nicaragua border. Code-named Operation Solid Shield, the combined maneuver was intended to simulate a U.S. response to a Honduran request for assistance in repelling invaders from Nicaragua. The maneuver involved some 40,000 U.S. troops and included a simulated evacuation of the U.S. naval base at Guantánamo Bay in Cuba in case Cuba retaliated against the base for an attack on Nicaragua.

Profiteering. Amid the military build-up, there were reports of war profiteering and corruption within the Honduran military. On March 31, General Walter López Reyes, former chief of the Honduran armed forces, charged that the U.S. Central Intelligence Agency (CIA) had bribed Honduran politicians to win their support for Nicaraguan *contras*—rebels fighting the Nicaraguan government—who have operated from bases in Honduras. There were also allegations by junior officers that some of their superiors were profiteering on the resale to the contras of military equipment supplied by the United States to Honduras.

Contra Bases. Uneasiness among Hondurans over the presence of the contras continued in 1987. Hondurans feared that either the situation would lead to war with Nicaragua or the contras might pose an armed menace to Honduras if they lost U.S. support. Because of those fears, Honduran President José Azcona del Hoyo demanded in 1986 that the contras evacuate their Honduran bases by April 1987. In February, Azcona said that all the contras had infiltrated back into Nicaragua, but Nicaragua denied the claim.

Torture. In May, a 29-year-old former sergeant in the Honduran Army charged that the army's high command maintained a network of secret jails at which nearly 200 suspected leftists were tortured and killed between 1980 and 1984. The former sergeant said the CIA was aware of the network and the killings. His charges were confirmed by U.S. and Honduran officials, according to *The New York Times.* Nathan A. Haverstock

See also LATIN AMERICA (Facts in Brief Table). In WORLD BOOK, see HONDURAS.

HORSE RACING. In January 1987, Lady's Secret was named 1986 Horse of the Year. The contenders for 1987 Horse of the Year were Ferdinand, winner of the $3-million Breeders' Cup Classic; Theatrical, winner of the $2-million Breeders' Cup Turf; and Java Gold.

Breeders' Cup Day, with a total purse of $10-million for seven races, was held at Hollywood Park in Inglewood, Calif., on November 21. In its fourth year, it again brought together some of the best thoroughbreds in the world. Theatrical narrowly defeated Trempolino—winner of Europe's premier race, the Prix de l'Arc de Triomphe in Longchamp, France. Europe's outstanding miler, Miesque, won the $1-million Breeders' Cup Mile.

The Classic featured the first competitive meeting of two Kentucky Derby winners since 1979. Ferdinand had won the 1986 derby, and Alysheba won the 1987 derby on May 2. In the Classic, Ferdinand outdueled Alysheba in a photo finish, giving jockey William Shoemaker and trainer Charles Whittingham their first Breeders' Cup victory.

For the third straight year, D. Wayne Lukas trained winners of two Breeders' Cup races—Sacahuista in the $1-million Distaff and Success Express in the $1-million Juvenile. Lukas-trained Lady's Secret became the top thoroughbred filly or mare money-winner when she won an allowance

Major Horse Races of 1987

Race	Winner	Value to Winner
Belmont Stakes	Bet Twice	$329,160
Breeders' Cup Sprint	Very Subtle	450,000
Breeders' Cup Juvenile Fillies	Epitome	450,000
Breeders' Cup Distaff	Sacahuista	450,000
Breeders' Cup Mile	Miesque	450,000
Breeders' Cup Juvenile	Success Express	450,000
Breeders' Cup Turf	Theatrical	900,000
Breeders' Cup Classic	Ferdinand	1,350,000
Breeders' Cup Steeplechase	Gacko	125,000
Budweiser Irish Derby	Sir Harry Lewis	483,339
Epsom Derby (England)	Reference Point	433,500
Grand National Steeplechase (England)	Maori Venture	104,183
Japan Cup (Japan)	Le Glorieux	824,401
Kentucky Derby	Alysheba	618,600
Melbourne Cup (Australia)	Kensei	637,870
Preakness	Alysheba	421,100
Prix de l'Arc de Triomphe (France)	Trempolino	650,000
Rothmans International Stakes (Canada)	River Memories	456,900

Major U.S. Harness Races of 1987

Race	Winner	Value to Winner
Cane Pace	Righteous Bucks	$174,462
Hambletonian	Mack Lobell	523,150
Little Brown Jug	Jaguar Spur	124,729
Meadowlands Pace	Frugal Gourmet	451,250
Woodrow Wilson Pace	Even Odds	711,250

Alysheba surges ahead of Bet Twice, right, to win the Kentucky Derby in May.
But in June, Bet Twice won the Belmont Stakes to deny Alysheba the Triple Crown.

race at Monmouth Park, N.J., on July 21 and her earnings reached $3,021,425.

Other Races. After the Kentucky Derby, Alysheba won a second leg of the Triple Crown when he took the Preakness on May 16 at Pimlico in Baltimore. But the third leg and a $5-million bonus eluded Alysheba when Bet Twice won the Belmont Stakes at Elmont, N.Y., on June 6. Bet Twice, who placed second in both the derby and the Preakness, won a $1-million bonus for earning the most points for placings in the Triple Crown.

Java Gold's bid for Horse of the Year was based in the East, where the 3-year-old won the Traverse Stakes, Whitney Handicap, and Marlboro Cup among six victories in eight starts. He did not compete, however, for the Triple Crown and was injured prior to the Breeders' Cup.

Harness Racing. Mack Lobell, winner of the Hambletonian, took more than a second off the trotting record as he ran a mile in 1 minute 52⅕ seconds on September 21. He also equaled the world mile record of 1 minute 57⅖ seconds on a half-mile track at Rosecroft Raceway in Maryland on October 31.

Quarter Horse Racing. Elans Special won the All-American Futurity at Ruidoso Downs, N. Mex., on September 7.   Jane Goldstein

In WORLD BOOK, see HARNESS RACING; HORSE RACING.

HOSPITAL. A new federal law that went into effect on Oct. 1, 1987, requires thousands of hospitals in the United States to encourage donations of kidneys, livers, hearts, and other organs needed for transplants. Under the law, hospitals must identify potential organ donors—usually patients who have suffered severe head injuries in accidents and are "brain dead"—and inform their families of the option to donate the patient's organs.

The law, designed to increase the availability of organs for transplantation, also requires hospitals to notify local agencies that arrange for removal, preservation, and distribution of organs when a patient is a potential organ donor.

Resuscitation Guidelines. The Joint Commission on Accreditation of Hospitals (JCAH) on June 4 said that hospitals must establish formal policies that determine when physicians and nurses can refrain from reviving a terminally ill patient whose heart or breathing has stopped. The commission, which is based in Chicago, said that 40 per cent of United States hospitals and nursing homes lack formal guidelines on withholding resuscitation from hopelessly ill patients.

The guidelines would be used to determine when to administer life-sustaining aid in a terminally ill patient. The JCAH said the guidelines must define the role of the patient's family in any medical decision to withhold resuscitation.

351

Occupancy Rate in U.S. Hospitals

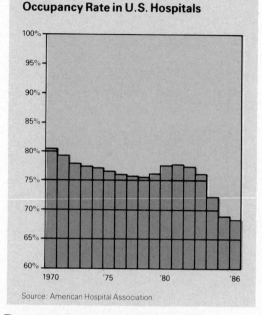

Source: American Hospital Association.

The occupancy rate—the percentage of occupied beds—in U.S. hospitals has declined since 1982, causing some hospitals to reduce staff size.

On September 3, the JCAH changed its name to the Joint Commission on Accreditation of Healthcare Facilities. The change reflects the commission's growing role in establishing standards for health care institutions other than hospitals.

Hospital Sale. Hospital Corporation of America, the largest U.S. hospital chain, announced on May 31 that it would sell 104 of its 229 hospitals to its employees. The chain, which is based in Nashville, agreed to the sale after resisting a take-over attempt by three Texas businessmen who wanted to buy the firm for $3.8 billion. The chain's employees formed a new company called HealthTrust that completed the purchase on September 17 for $2.1 billion.

AIDS Hospital Closed. The first U.S. hospital devoted solely to the treatment of patients suffering from AIDS (acquired immune deficiency syndrome) announced on August 6 that it would close because of financial problems. The Institute for Immunological Disorders in Houston reported that it had lost more than $8 million since it opened in 1986. Officials said many of the AIDS patients treated at the 150-bed facility had no medical insurance and were unable to pay for lengthy hospital stays that sometimes cost as much as $1,200 per day.   Michael Woods

In WORLD BOOK, see HOSPITAL.

HOUSING. See BUILDING AND CONSTRUCTION.

HOUSTON. The economy of Houston seemed to stabilize in 1987 after a two-year decline. By March, the unemployment rate was 9 per cent, down from a record high of 10.7 per cent in May 1986.

Still, thousands of Houston-area businesses filed for bankruptcy reorganization during the year, and more than two dozen banks failed. On February 23, two large investment research and advisory companies lowered their ratings of Houston's bonds. To shore up the city's finances, the Houston City Council cut the municipal budget by 3 per cent on July 29.

Economic Diversification. There were hopeful signs in 1987 that Houston's economy was moving away from its traditional reliance on the oil industry. On December 1, for example, it was announced that McDonnell Douglas Corporation would build $1.9 billion worth of components in the Houston area for a planned U.S. space station. The work will add some 1,000 jobs to the area.

A study released in September by a Washington, D.C.-based statistical research firm forecast 5,600 new jobs by the year 2000 for Harris County, of which Houston is the county seat. On November 2, the county government announced a tax reduction program for businesses that expand or relocate in the county. The Houston City Council was considering a similar action.

New Arts and Convention Facilities. On May 9, the city's elite turned out in force for the gala opening of the $70-million Gus S. Wortham Theater Center. The center, which will house the city's ballet and opera companies, was the site of a nationally televised debate among major Democratic presidential candidates on July 1. The $105-million George R. Brown Convention Center, which opened on September 26, hosted a similar Republican debate on October 28. The Menil Collection, a $25-million art museum with a collection of some 10,000 artworks, opened on June 7.

Mayor Reelected. Kathryn J. Whitmire was elected to her fourth consecutive term as Houston's mayor on November 3. Whitmire received 73.5 per cent of the vote in an easy victory over six opponents. On the same day, Harris County voters approved legalized horse-race betting by 57.2 to 42.8 per cent. Opponents of horse racing portrayed it as a moral issue, while those in favor saw it as an economic boon to the county.

Schools Get Bad Grade. On July 9, the state downgraded the Houston Independent School District's accreditation from the first to the second rank of Texas' five-level ranking system. The action was a blow to city boosters who have been trying to lure new businesses to Houston. The city's schools got another black eye in November, when the results of a statewide skills test were announced. Houston students scored lowest among students in the state's eight major urban areas.

Houston's dazzling new George R. Brown Convention Center, one of the largest convention facilities in the United States, opened in September.

Law Enforcement. *The Houston Post* in 1987 disclosed that internal investigations by the Houston Police Department had covered up police misconduct. Police Chief Lee P. Brown pledged to reform the department's record-keeping procedures so that abuses would be harder to conceal.

Transit Plan Unveiled. On October 23, Houston's Metropolitan Transit Authority approved a $2.5-billion, 10-year plan for upgrading the city's transportation system. The scheme included an 18-mile (29-kilometer) rail system and $556 million in street improvements. A public vote on the plan was scheduled for January 1988.

Newspapers Sold. Both of Houston's major newspapers changed hands in 1987. On March 12, the Hearst Corporation bought the *Houston Chronicle* from Houston Endowment, a charitable foundation. On September 10, MediaNews Group Incorporated announced that it was buying *The Houston Post* from the Toronto Sun Publishing Corporation, a Canadian company that had owned the *Post* since 1983.

Oilers to Stay. Kenneth S. (Bud) Adams, owner of the Houston Oilers, threatened to move his National Football League team to Jacksonville, Fla. But in October, after the city announced plans for increased seating in the Astrodome, Adams said the franchise would stay.   Charles Reinken

See also CITY. In WORLD BOOK, see HOUSTON.

HOUSTON, WHITNEY (1963-   ), made popular music history in 1987 when she became the first female singer to have an album listed number one on its debut on *Billboard* magazine's sales chart. Houston's popularity was so great that the album, *Whitney*, containing the hit song, "I Wanna Dance with Somebody," became an instant number one without having to climb the chart to that position.

Houston was born on Aug. 9, 1963, in Newark, N.J., to a musical family. Her mother, Emily (Cissy) Drinkard Houston, is a gospel and rhythm and blues singer. Popular singer Dionne Warwick is a cousin of Houston's. At age 11, Houston made her solo debut at the New Hope Baptist Church in Newark.

In February 1985, Houston released her first record album, titled *Whitney Houston*. It became the best-selling debut album in history, reaching worldwide sales of 13 million by July 1987. A single from that album—"Saving All My Love for You"—brought her a Grammy Award in February 1986 as best pop female vocalist. The album also won seven American Music Awards. Many other songs from her two albums became top hits as singles, including "Greatest Love of All" and "How Will I Know."

Houston is also a fashion model, having modeled for such magazines as *Vogue, Seventeen,* and *Cosmopolitan.*   Rod Such

HUNGARY got two new leaders, a severe economic program, and two new forms of taxation in 1987. The economy continued to stagnate throughout the year. The growth rate was only 1 per cent, with agriculture lagging behind production targets. Hungary's foreign debt exceeded $10 billion, the biggest per capita debt in the Soviet bloc.

New Officials. Hungary's leader since 1956, Communist Party First Secretary János Kádár, initiated changes involving the highest posts in the government. They brought notable, younger officials to the forefront in apparent preparation for Kádár, 76, to relinquish the top post.

Károly Grósz, 57, became prime minister, and 64-year-old Károly Németh was promoted to president. Political observers saw Grósz, a determined reformer, as most likely to succeed Kádár.

The Economic Program got underway on July 20 with a step termed by Kádár as "not pleasant." The government raised the price of fuel oil by 29 per cent; flour and bread, 19 per cent; electricity, 18 per cent; and natural gas, 17 per cent. The main purpose of the price hikes was to adapt the economy to basic market criteria of production costs and profitability.

Other details of the economic plan included more independence for government-owned business enterprises, the withdrawal of government subsidies from enterprises that lose money, and new forms of taxation.

New Taxes. Since the 1970's, the government had levied an income tax on only the small private sector of Hungarians working for themselves. On Sept. 19, 1987, the National Assembly (parliament) approved an income tax for individuals who work in state-run businesses and services and a West European-style value-added tax (VAT)—a kind of indirect sales tax—of 25 per cent.

The new income tax—the first of its kind in a Soviet-bloc nation—involved several tax brackets, with tax rates of 60 per cent in the highest brackets. The National Assembly scheduled the income tax and VAT to take effect on Jan. 1, 1988.

The new measures were designed to reduce Hungary's high budget deficits and to slow the pace of inflation by taking cash out of the economy. Also, the new taxes, combined with reductions in taxes on businesses, would relieve highly profitable enterprises of excessive taxation. High tax rates—about 90 per cent—had given business managers little incentive to improve their firms.

Out of Business. The regime's other moves included declaration of the first bankruptcies under a law calling for the liquidation of failing enterprises, and the establishment of retraining and employment agencies. Layoffs began at a score of major enterprises by mid-1987.   Eric Bourne

See also EUROPE (Facts in Brief Table). In WORLD BOOK, see HUNGARY.

HUNTING. The states and territories of the United States and the Commonwealth of Puerto Rico in 1987 received about $108 million in federal aid for wildlife restoration projects as a result of the Pittman-Robertson Act of 1937. Such funding comes primarily from taxes on hunting equipment and is distributed in proportion to the land area and number of hunting licenses issued in each region. Alaska and Texas each received more than $5 million in Pittman-Robertson funds in 1987.

Hunters Strike Back. The Wildlife Legislative Fund of America (WLFA), based in Columbus, Ohio, launched a $1.7-million program, "Protect What's Right," in 1987. According to the WLFA, the program will mobilize hunting clubs throughout the United States and provide them with the verbal tools to battle antihunting groups. Organizations endorsing the program include the National Rifle Association of America, Ducks Unlimited, the National Turkey Federation, the National Trappers Association, and the North American Hunting Club.

Record Ram. A backpacker in Oregon found the carcass of a huge Rocky Mountain bighorn ram that apparently died of a virus sometime in the spring of 1987. The $14\frac{1}{2}$-year-old sheep, known as Old Scarface because of a large wound on his nose and a missing right eye, had been a favorite target of big-game hunters for many years.

Now, Scarface has officially gone on record as the largest ram ever found in the United States. Measurements of the length, spread, and circumference of his horns outclassed those of the previous titleholder, a Wyoming ram killed by a hunter in 1883.

Science to Help Wardens? Researchers at the University of Wyoming, supported by a $29,300 grant from the Wyoming Game and Fish Department, in 1987 began research on the development of a technique to determine accurately if and how long meat has been frozen. According to Tom D. Moore, a forensic and analytical specialist, such a technique would help in prosecuting some individuals accused of breaking hunting laws. The game department's laboratory in Laramie, Wyo., gets at least 10 queries a year from game wardens concerning the age of frozen meat in the possession of hunters suspected of hunting illegally.

Waterfowl Plan. Ducks Unlimited, the 600,000-member world leader in waterfowl conservation, contributed the first funds to the $1.2-billion North American Waterfowl Management Plan, a joint U.S.-Canadian project established in 1986. Ducks Unlimited put up $1 million for wetlands conservation projects to preserve waterfowl habitats in Canada. The Canadian Wildlife Service has promised to match any funds raised in the United States.   Tony Mandile

In WORLD BOOK, see HUNTING.

ICE SKATING. The two Americans who won world figure-skating championships in 1986 lost them in 1987. Two other Americans won two World Cup titles each in speed skating and became favorites for the 1988 Winter Olympics in Calgary, Canada.

Figure Skating. The world championships, held from March 9 to 14 in Cincinnati, Ohio, attracted 132 skaters from 24 nations. The defending singles champions were Brian Boitano of Sunnyvale, Calif., and Debi Thomas of San Jose. Boitano finished second to Brian Orser of Orillia, Canada, among the men. Thomas was second to Katarina Witt of East Germany among the women.

In men's singles, Orser had finished second the three previous years. After the 1987 compulsory figures and short program, he was assured of the title if he won the concluding free-skating program. In the free skating, Boitano attempted to become the first skater in history to complete a quadruple jump successfully in competition, but he had to put his hand on the ice to keep from falling. Then he made a bad landing on a triple flip, and his chances were gone.

Witt was the women's champion in 1984 and 1985 before losing to Thomas in 1986. This time, Witt finished fifth in the compulsory figures and needed a let-down by Thomas. It came when Thomas almost fell in the short program on a double axel. Thomas skated well in the free program despite painful tendinitis in both heels. Witt skated better.

Soviet skaters finished first and second in the other two world-championship events. Ekatrina Gordeeva and Sergei Grinkov won the pairs, and Natalya Bestemianova and Andrei Bukin won the ice dancing.

Speed Skating. American skating, which had slumped since Eric Heiden's five gold medals in the 1980 Winter Olympics, revived. Bonnie Blair of Champaign, Ill., won the women's 500-meter and 1,000-meter titles in the two-month World Cup series, and Nick Thometz of Minnetonka, Minn., took the same titles for men. In addition, each skater broke the world record for 500 meters on two occasions in March—36.55 and 36.23 seconds by Thometz and 39.43 and 39.28 seconds by Blair.

Karin Enke Kania of East Germany won her sixth women's world sprint title and her fourth world overall championship at the world championships held on February 1 and 2 in Ste. Foy, Canada. Blair finished second in the sprints.

The men's world champions were Akira Kuroiwa of Japan (sprint) and Nikolai Gulyaev of the Soviet Union (overall).   Frank Litsky

In WORLD BOOK, see ICE SKATING.

ICELAND. See EUROPE.

IDAHO. See STATE GOVERNMENT.

ILLINOIS. See CHICAGO; STATE GOVERNMENT.

Katarina Witt of East Germany reclaims her singles title in the world figure-skating championships in Cincinnati, Ohio, in March.

IMMIGRATION. A major new United States immigration law, the product of a decade of effort and controversy in Congress, began to take effect on May 5, 1987—six months after it was signed by President Ronald Reagan. Chief among the law's provisions was a one-year amnesty program for illegal aliens who could prove that they had resided continuously in the United States since Jan. 1, 1982, or earlier.

On May 5, 1987, the U.S. Immigration and Naturalization Service (INS) began distributing and processing applications from thousands of illegal aliens who sought temporary legal-resident status. Those obtaining temporary legal status would be eligible after 18 months to apply for permanent legal status and after another five years to apply for American citizenship.

The INS estimated that about 3.9 million illegal aliens would meet the requirements of the amnesty program. But in November 1987, halfway through the amnesty period, fewer than 1 million people had applied for legal status.

Advocate Groups for Immigrants complained that INS policies would divide thousands of families in which some members would be eligible for amnesty while others would be subject to deportation. On October 8, INS Commissioner Alan C. Nelson announced a liberalization of regulations.

If parents were eligible for amnesty but their children were not, Nelson said, the children would not be deported. In cases where only one parent was eligible, deportation of children would be considered on a case-by-case basis.

Employer Sanctions. The law also provided for civil and criminal penalties against employers who knowingly hire illegal aliens. This provision officially took effect on June 1, and the INS began to enforce the law in August. INS Commissioner Nelson said there had been a 30 per cent decline during the 1987 fiscal year in the number of illegal aliens apprehended at the Mexican border—a drop to 1.1 million arrests from 1.6 million a year earlier. But Border Patrol officials noted a surge in the number of illegal aliens apprehended beginning in June.

Cuban Agreement. On November 20, the U.S. Department of State said it had reached an agreement with Cuba that would allow the deportation of about 2,500 of the 125,000 Cubans who arrived in the United States in 1980. Most of the 2,500 are criminals or mental patients.

After hearing of the agreement, Cuban prisoners rioted in Oakdale, La., and Atlanta, Ga. See PRISON.   Frank Cormier and Margot Cormier

In WORLD BOOK, see IMMIGRATION.

INCOME TAX. See TAXATION.

Illegal aliens jam the Mexican Consulate in Chicago in May, seeking documents needed to obtain legal status under a new U.S. immigration law.

INDIA. Prime Minister Rajiv Gandhi's government was troubled during 1987 by waning political support, continuing religious and separatist violence, the worst drought in 125 years, and other serious problems.

The ruling Congress Party lost three state-assembly elections in 1987 despite Gandhi's personal campaigns on behalf of its candidates. On March 23, a coalition led by the Congress Party in Kerala was replaced by a Communist-led alliance, and the ruling Communist-dominated coalition in West Bengal increased its majority. In Haryana, in the Hindi-speaking heartland of Indian politics, the Congress Party government was ousted by a local alliance on June 18. In Jammu and Kashmir on March 23, the Congress Party, in alliance with a local group, won the state-assembly election but was accused of vote fraud.

Opposition to Gandhi grew within the Congress Party, though Gandhi's strong support in Parliament ensured his continued control of the party. The opposition centered on charges of corruption. Gandhi denied any wrongdoing.

On January 24, Gandhi changed the appointment of Vishwanath Pratap Singh from finance minister to defense minister. According to Indian media, Gandhi made the switch because Singh's drive to end government corruption had endangered some of Gandhi's friends. Singh resigned the defense post on April 12 and began publicly campaigning against corruption—in effect challenging Gandhi's leadership. Gandhi on July 16 expelled from the Congress Party three former ministers and close colleagues. On July 19, Gandhi expelled Singh, and a fifth party member resigned. On October 2, Singh and others opposed to Gandhi announced the creation of the People's Front. The People's Front joined on November 28 with three political parties—Janata, Lok Dal, and Congress (Socialist)—to try to remove Gandhi from office.

In a letter dated March 9, President Zail Singh accused Gandhi of failing to keep him informed of official business. Zail Singh and Gandhi backed away from creating a constitutional crisis, however, and Zail Singh did not seek reelection when his five-year term ended in July. Gandhi's choice for the presidency, Vice President R. Venkataraman, was overwhelmingly elected president on July 16.

Sikh Rebellion. Punjab state was torn by violence as a militant minority of India's Sikh religious community continued to demand the formation of a separate Sikh nation. On May 11, Gandhi dismissed the entire state government for failing to deal with Sikh terrorists who, he said, "run a parallel administration in the state." Gandhi imposed direct rule on Punjab from the central government based in New Delhi, India's capital.

Balancing empty waterpots on their heads, women of Mehsana, India, wait in line for drinking water during India's severe 1987 drought.

The body of India's former Prime Minister Charan Singh is carried on the shoulders of Indian military officers in his May 31 funeral in New Delhi.

But violence continued—often involving Sikh extremists killing Hindus. From January through September, more than 900 Indians were killed. Particularly chilling incidents occurred on July 6 and 7, when Sikh gunmen stopped buses in Punjab and adjacent Haryana and killed at least 72 Hindu passengers. In September, the police director of Punjab claimed that 40 of the 100 most wanted Sikh terrorists had been shot or captured. The militants said that the police had killed many innocent Sikh youths.

Strife Between Hindus and Muslims also plagued India in 1987. In Meerut, on May 22 and 23, a landlord-tenant dispute led to several days of riots and killings. The violence was fed by long-held grudges over a Muslim mosque that Hindus claimed had been built on the site of an ancient Hindu shrine. At least 100 and perhaps as many as 500 Indians—mostly Muslims—were killed in the riots. Observers accused Hindu police of rounding up and coldly killing many Muslims.

Three New Indian States were created in 1987. On February 20, Mizoram, whose separatist guerrillas made peace with the Indian government in 1986, became India's 23rd state, and Arunachal Pradesh became the 24th. On May 30, Goa became India's 25th state.

Other Developments. In a Rajasthan village on September 4, an 18-year-old widow burned to death on her husband's funeral pyre. The act, *suttee*, is a Hindu custom that has been illegal since 1829. The dead woman's father-in-law and three others were arrested for murder and for encouraging a suicide, but hundreds of thousands of Hindu pilgrims traveled to the cremation site to honor the widow's act.

In January, India and Pakistan engaged in army maneuvers along the Punjab border, but tensions eased without a clash. From September 23 to 25, Indian troops fought Pakistan over disputed Kashmir territory. The soldiers battled on the Siachen Glacier, more than 20,000 feet (6,000 meters) above sea level. In October, an Indian peacekeeping force trying to disarm Tamil guerrillas in Sri Lanka fought India's biggest battle since its 1971 war with Pakistan.

Drought. Three-quarters of India did not receive the usual monsoon rainfall during May, June, July, and August. The drought cut food production dramatically. The government avoided widespread famine by using stores of surplus grain—the result of India's much-improved agriculture. On September 11, Gandhi imposed austerity measures to save money for drought relief by cutting bureaucratic allowances and imposing special taxes. Henry S. Bradsher

See also Asia (Facts in Brief Table); Sri Lanka. In World Book, see India.

INDIAN, AMERICAN. Self-rule by native peoples continued to be an important issue in the United States and Canada in 1987. In January, the U.S. Bureau of Indian Affairs (BIA) said that it planned to turn over responsibility for Indian schools to state governments or tribes. The federal government would still help pay for the schooling, but tribes or states would run the schools.

According to Ross O. Swimmer, assistant secretary of the interior for Indian affairs, many of the 181 schools owned or operated by the BIA were substandard. About 10 per cent of Indian children attended schools operated by the BIA in 1987; the rest were in public schools or schools operated by tribal governments.

The plan was criticized by Suzan Shown Harjo, executive director of the National Congress of American Indians, which represents 150 tribal governments. Harjo said that the transfer of the schools to the states ignored tribal wishes.

Plan for Tribal Authority. In October, Swimmer and U.S. Secretary of the Interior Donald P. Hodel proposed a plan calling for a fundamental shift in the relationship between the U.S. federal government and the 500 Indian tribes in the United States. The proposal, aimed at promoting greater self-determination by Native Americans and less reliance on the government, was submit-

ted to the Subcommittee on Interior and Related Agencies of the U.S. House of Representatives Appropriations Committee. The plan called for dispersing responsibility for developing and managing Indian programs among the tribes, rather than administering them through the BIA.

Native American leaders have long criticized the federal bureaucracy for discouraging responsibility and initiative by the tribes, while failing itself to meet the needs of native peoples. Under Swimmer and Hodel's proposal, many Indian programs would be financed by a system of direct grants to the tribes. Swimmer said that such a system would allow the tribes to design their own programs, and either operate the programs themselves or contract them to the BIA or another agency.

Health Rules. In October, the U.S. Department of Health and Human Services announced that tighter eligibility rules would take effect in March 1988 for people receiving treatment from the federal government's Indian Health Service. Under the new regulations, an eligible person must be of Indian or native Alaskan descent and a member of a federally recognized tribe, and must reside within an area designated by the Health Service.

Native Rights Conference. A conference held in Ottawa, Canada, on March 26 and 27 failed to produce an agreement establishing rights to native

Indians favoring self-government for Canada's native peoples demonstrate in Ottawa, Ont., on March 26, 1987, prior to a national meeting on the issue.

self-government in the Canadian constitution. At the meeting, Canada's Prime Minister Brian Mulroney and provincial premiers met with leaders of organizations representing Canada's native peoples, including Indian, Inuit (Eskimo), and people of mixed ancestry.

The main point of contention was the native leaders' insistence on an unconditional, "inherent" right to self-rule that would give native peoples broad powers of self-government in land and resource ownership, language and culture, and political jurisdiction. But leaders of the federal government and most of the provinces would agree to self-rule only if specific rights were defined by negotiation. The conference ended without an agreement after native leaders and four provinces rejected a draft amendment.

Territorial Agreement Stalled. In March, native leaders in Canada were unable to make final a plan to divide the Northwest Territories into an eastern and a western territory. The Inuit generally live in the eastern parts of the territories, while the western parts are inhabited by the Dene Indians, *métis* (persons of mixed Indian and white ancestry), and whites. Final negotiations stalled when a dispute over the location of the boundary could not be resolved.   Joan Stephenson

In WORLD BOOK, see INDIAN, AMERICAN.

INDIANA. See STATE GOVERNMENT.

INDONESIA held general elections on April 23, 1987. The preceding three-week campaign was the most peaceful in the country's history, and election day brought a 91 per cent voter turnout, one of the largest in Indonesia's history.

Election Results. President Suharto's Golkar Party—Indonesia's ruling coalition of government and business leaders with strong ties to the armed forces—increased its share of the vote for seats in the House of Representatives. House members serve five-year terms, during which they usually approve the government's policies. In the 1982 elections, Golkar won 64 per cent of the vote. In 1987, the party won 73 per cent, capturing 299 of 400 elective seats. Suharto later appointed 100 members of the armed forces to the House, which is part elective and part appointive. Golkar also won control of all 27 Indonesian provinces for the first time.

The United Development Party, which represented Muslim leaders and others, saw its share of the vote drop from 28 per cent in 1982 to 16 per cent in 1987 and its number of House seats fall from 94 to 61. The Indonesian Democratic Party, a coalition of nationalists and Christians, increased its share of ballots from 8 per cent to 11 per cent and its House seats from 24 to 40. Successful Democratic candidates included Megawati Sukarno, a daughter of the late President Sukarno.

Supporters of Golkar, Indonesia's ruling party, wave a sign indicating their party's number-two spot on the ballot list for April 23 elections.

Other Developments. The government shut down the independent Jakarta newspaper *Prioritas* on June 29, after the paper called attention to corruption and economic problems in Indonesia. The government claimed *Prioritas* published inaccurate and one-sided stories.

Two commuter trains collided head-on on October 19 in a suburb south of Jakarta, the capital. The crash killed 155 people and injured more than 260, including many schoolchildren. It was Indonesia's worst train wreck in history.

Economy. Suharto reported in his Independence Day speech on August 15 that the domestic economy was growing at a rate of 3.2 per cent after several years of slower growth. The worldwide decline in the prices of oil and gas—Indonesia's main exports—did not affect the economy as much as experts had feared because sales of other exports increased. Domestic spending declined because 41 per cent of the country's earnings from exports were used to pay Indonesia's foreign debt—the largest in Asia.

Inflation was estimated at 8 per cent in 1987, down from 9 per cent in 1986. Prolonged drought forced the government to import corn to substitute for normal rice crops, however, and threatened to push up food prices. Henry S. Bradsher

See also Asia (Facts in Brief Table). In WORLD BOOK, see INDONESIA.

INSURANCE. Most financial indicators for the property and casualty insurance industry during the first nine months of 1987 showed significant improvement over the same period in 1986 and were projected to remain positive for the rest of the year. The industry reported a consolidated net after-tax income of $11.3 billion for the first nine months of 1987, according to the Insurance Services Office (ISO) and the National Association of Independent Insurers, the industry's official statistical organizations. The 1987 income was 24.2 per cent higher than the $9.1-billion net income for the same period in 1986.

The jump in profits was even more impressive than the statistics indicated because insurers paid $2.5 billion in taxes for the 1987 period, while they received a tax credit of $0.3 billion one year earlier. Another positive factor was that the underwriting loss for January through September 1987—$7.3 billion—was well below the $12.4-billion figure for the first nine months of 1986. Net investment income of $17.3 billion for the 1987 period was up 7.5 per cent compared with $16.1-billion one year earlier.

Premium Growth-Rate Decrease. The percentage of increase in earned premiums had a disappointing showing in 1987, however. Even though earned premiums for the first nine months of 1987 reached $144.9 billion, exceeding the $132.0-

billion underwritten in the 1986 period, the growth rate was only 9.8 per cent, compared with 24.0 per cent for comparable periods in 1986 and 1985. Sean Mooney, economist and senior vice president of the Insurance Information Institute, predicted in October that the increase for 1987 would be about 10 per cent, compared with 22 per cent for 1986.

The decline in the earned premium growth rate could be traced to several sources. First, commercial policyholders' insurance rates, which shot up in 1986 in response to the liability crisis of the mid-1980's, leveled off in 1987 and even began to fall as the competitive spirit began to return to the insurance industry. In addition, reports indicated that some potential policyholders who were unable to find a willing insurer or unable to afford the high cost of coverage decided to "go bare," that is, to do without insurance.

A third and more important factor was the expansion of "alternative risk transfer mechanisms," methods of insuring against loss without using a traditional insurance company. These mechanisms include captive insurers, self-insurers, and risk-retention groups. Daniel J. McNamara, president of the ISO, estimated in October that alternative risk mechanisms represented 30 per cent of the commercial insurance market—a share worth nearly $50 billion in premiums annually.

Captive Insurers, which are wholly owned by major industrial firms or groups, are not a new phenomenon, but the use of these entities developed with greater intensity in 1987. One factor in the increase was the revised federal Risk Retention Act, which became law in late 1986. The original act allowed companies to form groups to insure themselves against product liability losses. The revision allows such groups to insure themselves against any liability risk. These captive insurers need to be licensed in only one state and may operate nationally without regulatory interference by other states. Industry sources and regulators expressed much apprehension about the viability and stability of the alternative insurers.

Other Developments. The 508-point drop in the Dow Jones Industrial Average on October 19 resulted in a drop of $10 billion in policyholders' surplus, according to McNamara. He saw the plunge as a potentially constructive event, in that it gave second thoughts to those insurers who seemed bent on returning to "reckless insurance-pricing practices."

By the end of November, insured losses from catastrophes such as windstorms and hurricanes—including the October Los Angeles earthquake—reached a relatively low $722 million, compared with $871.5 million in such insured losses for all of 1986. Emanuel Levy

In WORLD BOOK, see INSURANCE.

INTERNATIONAL TRADE. The world economy grew an estimated 2.8 per cent in 1987, slowing down for the third consecutive year. Growth rates among major industrial nations varied. Canada, Great Britain, Italy, Japan, and the United States reported higher growth during the year, but growth in France and West Germany declined.

The economic growth of most developing nations was also slower in 1987 than in 1986. Once again, Asian nations moved ahead faster than nations in Africa, Latin America, and the Middle East, growing about 6 per cent. Africa's economic growth rate improved slightly, averaging about 1.5 per cent, but Latin America's fell to about 2.5 per cent, mainly because of a sharp decline in Brazil's growth rate. In the Middle East, economies contracted despite a modest rise in oil prices.

Industrial nations continued to control inflation, which averaged about 3 per cent in 1987. The United States and Canada experienced a moderate rise in inflation, but in Japan and in much of Western Europe, inflation declined. Among developing nations, inflation approached 40 per cent, higher than in 1986, when the average was less than 30 per cent. This jump was due largely to soaring prices in Argentina, Brazil, and Mexico.

Trade Imbalances. Huge trade and payments imbalances among major nations—especially Ja-

pan, the United States, and West Germany—caused concern during the year. Even though the value of the U.S. dollar fell against other major currencies—an action that tends to make U.S.-made products cheaper in international markets—the United States incurred another record deficit, of more than $150 billion, in its *international payments* (transactions in merchandise, services, trade, and corporate fund transfers). By the end of 1987, the U.S. foreign debt, which reflected this deficit, was estimated at about $400 billion. This was by far the largest debt of any nation.

Japan and West Germany, on the other hand, once again amassed exceptionally large international payments surpluses in 1987. Combined, these surpluses totaled about $125 billion.

These payments imbalances continued to force the value of the U.S. dollar to drop. The dollar declined during 1987 by an average of 17 per cent against other major currencies. This decline created uncertainties about exchange rates. Many financial experts also felt the declining dollar could lead to a rise in U.S. inflation.

Dollar Decline. The U.S. dollar and other key currencies were relatively stable in 1987 until October 15, when a dispute erupted between United States Treasury Secretary James A. Baker III and West German financial authorities. Baker, dis-

Visitors try out an Apple Macintosh computer in Moscow in June at a trade show featuring computers manufactured in the United States.

turbed by interest-rate increases in West Germany, hinted that he would not object to the dollar's falling in value if West Germany did not reduce its interest rates. A few days later, on October 19, the New York Stock Exchange crashed and brought more downward pressure on the dollar (see STOCKS AND BONDS). Baker later disclosed that he would risk a further decline in the dollar if it was needed to help avoid an economic recession.

Venice Summit. At the 13th annual economic summit—held in Venice, Italy, from June 8 to 10—the leaders of Canada, France, Great Britain, Italy, Japan, the United States, and West Germany emphasized the need for exchange rate stability. They said that their governments would coordinate their economic policies more closely to foster balanced and noninflationary economic growth. In an attempt to renew confidence in the U.S. economy—and the dollar—President Ronald Reagan and Congress agreed on November 20 to reduce the United States federal budget deficit by $30.2-billion in fiscal 1988 and by $45.8 billion in fiscal 1989. The commitment for fiscal 1988 was met on Dec. 22, 1987, when Congress passed and Reagan signed a $603.9-billion spending bill that would reduce the deficit by $33.2 billion.

Foreign Debt. The total foreign debt of developing nations rose in 1987 to an estimated $1.1-trillion, and debt payments continued to impede their economic growth. Several countries—most notably Brazil—refused to pay the interest on their commercial bank debt. But on November 6, Brazil agreed to pay its overdue interest to creditor banks after the banks said they would help finance those payments.

Most developing countries were helped somewhat by the increased prices of many of their primary commodity exports, such as metals. Even so, most of these countries remained unable to obtain new commercial bank credits.

Bankers and developing nations during 1987 explored new approaches to reducing debt. Heavily indebted developing nations were offered the prospect of more foreign aid at the annual meeting of the World Bank and the International Monetary Fund (IMF)—two United Nations organizations—in Washington, D.C., from September 29 to October 1. The United States agreed to negotiate with other World Bank members to increase lending resources for the bank. Major industrial nations subsequently agreed to triple to more than $12 billion a special IMF loan fund for the world's poorest nations.

Trade Agreements. On October 3, the United States and Canada announced a wide-ranging trade agreement that would eliminate all tariffs between the two countries within 10 years. The agreement, which was signed on Jan. 2, 1988, calls for the establishment of a U.S.-Canadian arbitra-

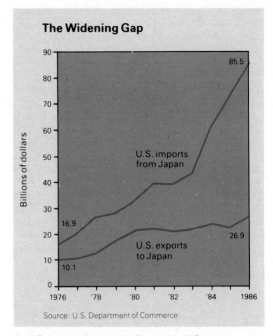

The Widening Gap

Billions of dollars

U.S. imports from Japan

16.9 ... 85.5

U.S. exports to Japan

10.1 ... 26.9

Source: U.S. Department of Commerce

As U.S. imports from Japan far outstrip U.S. exports to Japan, the trade imbalance between the two countries continues to widen.

tion board to resolve trade disputes. The agreement was subject to the approval of Canada's Parliament and the United States Congress.

On Nov. 6, 1987, the United States and Mexico signed a much more limited trade accord. The two countries agreed to consult on mutual trade problems and to possibly negotiate future agreements in trade and investment.

During 1987, the United States resolved a grain trade dispute with the European Community (EC or Common Market), but clashed with Japan over electronic products. On April 17, the U.S. government announced that it had imposed 100 per cent tariffs on $300 million worth of imported Japanese products because Japan had failed to honor an agreement to buy more U.S. computer chips and to stop underpricing its chip exports to other countries. On November 2, the U.S. Department of Commerce reported that Japanese firms had stopped underpricing, and the United States lifted some of the tariffs.

Congressional Action. The U.S. House of Representatives in April and the Senate in July voted on—and passed—their own versions of comprehensive trade legislation. They had not agreed on a final bill by year-end.   Richard Lawrence

See also ECONOMICS. In WORLD BOOK, see INTERNATIONAL TRADE.

IOWA. See STATE GOVERNMENT.

IRAN. In 1987, the regime of Ayatollah Ruhollah Khomeini pressed ahead in its savage war with Iraq. Iran's relations with other countries, both in the Middle East and in the West, were also frequently adversarial. In September, Iran rejected a United Nations Security Council resolution, passed unanimously, that called for a cease-fire and peace negotiations to end the war with Iraq.

Ground War. Beginning in January, Iranian ground forces launched a series of offensives aimed at Al Basrah, a key southern city in Iraq. The Iranians advanced to within 9 miles (14 kilometers) of the city before being thrown back with losses estimated at 70,000. Other assaults during the spring fared no better. In March, Iran, supported by Kurdish guerrillas opposed to the Iraqi government, mounted an attack on Iraqi positions in northern Iraq. But the Iranians gained only a few hundred yards, at a cost of 30,000 casualties.

War in the Gulf. A shift in the focus of the war to the Persian Gulf thereafter not only widened the conflict but also alarmed nearby Arab states. Using Silkworm missiles apparently acquired from China and fast patrol boats, Iranian forces launched attacks on oil tankers bound for Kuwait and other gulf states and laid mines along shipping lanes. Iranian saboteurs also damaged oil installations as far away as Oman.

Regional Conflicts. In March, Tunisia broke relations with Iran, accusing the Khomeini regime of backing a plot to overthrow its government. Egypt severed relations with Iran in May, also accusing Iran of fomenting antigovernment activity.

The worst incident, however, occurred on July 31, when Iran and Saudi Arabia became embroiled in a bloody conflict in Mecca, Saudi Arabia, during the annual Islamic pilgrimage. Despite warnings by the Saudis not to use the pilgrimage for political purposes, thousands of Iranians staged a public protest. About 400 people died, most in a panic-stricken retreat, when Saudi security agents attempted to disperse the crowd.

Disputes with the West. France broke relations with Iran in July after French accusations of an Iranian diplomatic interpreter's involvement in terrorist incidents led to the French Embassy in Teheran and the Iranian Embassy in Paris being cordoned off by armed guards. France and Iran ended the siege of each other's embassies in late November, after France released the Iranian interpreter. In August, the French imposed a boycott on Iranian oil.

Iran and Great Britain began to expel each other's diplomats after an Iranian diplomat was arrested in May for shoplifting in Manchester, England. Eventually, the two countries expelled all but one of the other's representatives.

In October, the United States banned Iranian imports and tightened restrictions on American exports to Iran. The move was made because of U.S. anger over Iranian attacks on commercial shipping in the Persian Gulf.

Execution. In September, Mehdi Hashemi, the head of the agency responsible for promoting Iran's revolution abroad, was executed for treason and other crimes. Hashemi had helped expose the sale of arms to Iran by the United States in 1986. He was an aide of Ayatollah Hussein Ali Montazeri, Khomeini's designated successor.

The Economy. The war with Iraq, along with lower oil prices, continued to affect economic progress. The budget, approved by the Majlis (parliament) in March 1987, forecast a deficit of $19.5 billion, with 24 per cent of expenditures—$55.5 billion—going for war costs.

Iranians continued to feel the economic effects of the war, including 20 per cent inflation, shortages of basic goods, and strict rationing. In July, the government launched on all-out assault on profiteering, corruption, and black market activities. Although Iraqi raids periodically damaged Iran's oil installations, oil production remained steady during the year at 1.7 million to 2 million barrels per day.   William Spencer

See also IRAN-CONTRA AFFAIR; IRAQ; MIDDLE EAST (Facts in Brief Table). In the Special Reports section, see UNDERSTANDING ISLAM. In WORLD BOOK, see IRAN.

IRAN-CONTRA AFFAIR. Two United States congressional committees spent almost all of 1987 jointly investigating the Iran-contra affair—the trading of arms for hostages with Iran and the diversion of some profits from the arms sales to finance *contra* rebels fighting the Marxist government of Nicaragua. The deals, set up by members of President Ronald Reagan's National Security Council (NSC), occurred in 1985 and 1986.

In a 472-page majority report released on Nov. 18, 1987, the Iran-contra committees concluded that President Reagan failed in his constitutional duty to "take care that the laws be faithfully executed." The committees also alleged that the Reagan Administration broke several laws, including the Boland Amendment, legislation passed in 1982 and in 1984 that banned the use of federal funds for the contras. It was named after U.S. Representative Edward P. Boland (D., Mass.), one of its sponsors.

The majority report said "the common ingredients of the Iran and contra policies were secrecy, deception and disdain for the law." The report was signed by 3 Republican senators and all 15 Democrats on the Senate and House select committees that held televised public hearings on the controversy during May, June, and July. All the committee members agreed there was no evidence that Reagan knew about the diversion of funds to

the contras, but the majority report held that "if the President did not know what his national security advisers were doing, he should have."

Minority Report. Two Republican senators and all six Republicans on the House committee filed a minority report on November 18 that called the majority findings "hysterical." While conceding that Reagan and his staff "made mistakes," the minority report said that there was "no Administration-wide dishonesty and coverup."

No Condemnation. The majority report insisted that fundamental constitutional and legal issues were involved in the Iran-contra affair and said that those involved in the arms deal "viewed the law not as setting boundaries for their actions, but

Marine Lieutenant Colonel Oliver L. North, who headed the Iran-contra operations, is sworn in before the congressional investigating committees on July 7.

raising impediments to their goals." Noting that Reagan made a number of public statements that turned out to be incorrect after the scandal came to light in November 1986, the majority said the President had not yet condemned the conduct of senior aides who "lied, shredded documents, and covered up their actions" to support policies they believed were embraced by Reagan.

Still to be heard from by the end of the year was special counsel Lawrence E. Walsh, who was inves-

Former National Security Adviser John M. Poindexter testifies in July before congressional probers investigating the Iran-contra affair.

profits to the contras without telling the President. Convinced Reagan would "think it was a good idea" to shift money to the contras, Poindexter said, he acted on his own so that Reagan could deny knowledge of the diversion if it came to light.

But the star witness at the hearings was former Poindexter aide Marine Lieutenant Colonel Oliver L. North. North was the key NSC figure involved in carrying out the arms-for-hostages and contra-aid programs. In July, North testified that at one point he and other collaborators decided that he would be the "fall guy"—the person to take the blame—if the secret dealings came to light. But, according to North, it was later decided that Poindexter might have to fill that role.

During his six days of televised testimony, the charismatic North became a national celebrity. To some, he was a hero, even though he testified to lying to Congress and to shredding key documents with the help of his secretary, Fawn Hall.

Where's the Money? The congressional inquiry found that arms sales to Iran yielded about $16-million in profits, of which only $3.8 million went to the contras. More than $6 million was spent or deposited in accounts set up for North's collaborators. Frank Cormier and Margot Cormier

See also NORTH, OLIVER LAURENCE; PRESIDENT OF THE UNITED STATES.

tigating possible criminal wrongdoing by Reagan aides and associates. He was expected to produce indictments in early 1988.

Tower Report. The November congressional report was tougher on Reagan than one issued on Feb. 26, 1987, by a three-member bipartisan commission he had appointed to look into the affair. Former Senator John G. Tower (R., Tex.) headed the commission. The 300-page report was, however, highly critical of Reagan's detached management style. Tower said Reagan "clearly didn't understand" what was going on, and "was poorly advised and poorly served" by key aides.

Reagan's Response. On March 4, just days after the Tower report was released, Reagan said in a televised speech that he had violated his own policy of not bargaining with terrorists by trading arms for hostages. Previously, he had denied that any such trade had occurred. "My heart and my best intentions still tell me that is true," he said in his March speech, "but the facts and evidence tell me it is not." Reagan rejected advice from some associates that he apologize for the scandal. Instead, he said that "as President, I cannot escape responsibility."

Congressional Hearings. During the congressional hearings, Rear Admiral John M. Poindexter insisted that, as Reagan's national security adviser, he authorized the secret diversion of arms sales

IRAQ. The unrelenting war betweeen Iraq and Iran moved into its eighth year in September 1987, with no relief in sight for hard-pressed Iraqi ground forces. In January, Iranian troops followed up earlier advances with a massive assault on the key southern Iraqi city of Al Basrah. The attack was halted by superior Iraqi artillery and air power within about 14 kilometers (9 miles) of the city. Nevertheless, the Iranians continued to hammer Iraqi lines through the spring, despite an estimated 70,000 casualties.

On the northern front, Iranian forces allied with Kurdish guerrillas opposed to the Iraqi government seized territory near Kirkuk in March, also with huge casualties. But nowhere along the long battlefront were the Iranians able to make any significant breakthroughs.

Air War. As in previous years, the stalemate on the ground led to a resumption of Iraqi air raids on Iranian cities as well as on military targets. Although Iraq lost 10 per cent of its air force to Iranian antiaircraft missiles in the spring offensives, it retained almost total air superiority and was able to raid cities such as Teheran and Qom deep inside Iran. Heavy civilian casualties, however, led Iran to retaliate with missile strikes on Iraqi cities. In one such attack on Baghdad, Iraq's capital, in October, a missile exploded near a school, killing 32 people and injuring 218, nearly all children.

The Persian Gulf: Center of Turmoil

In March, Amnesty International, a human rights organization based in London, strongly protested the reported mutilation and murder of 57 Kurdish children by the Iraqi government. The organization said that the victims had been among 300 to 500 Kurdish children taken by the Iraqi government in 1985 to pressure members of their families—suspected Kurdish guerrillas—to surrender.

The Economy benefited from Iraq's ability to transport oil exports by pipeline across Turkey or Saudi Arabia rather than through the war-racked Persian Gulf. During 1987, oil exports expanded steadily, reaching 2.8 million bpd in December. A 60 per cent increase in other exports along with $10.9 billion in oil revenues enabled the government to balance its budget, eliminating a $3.5-billion deficit remaining from 1986. Heavy arms expenditures—some $23.9 billion from 1981 to 1985—continued to increase Iraq's foreign debt, however. By mid-May, the debt had climbed to $27 billion.

In July, a new sulfur plant went into operation at Mishraq. It will increase yearly sulfur exports by 30 per cent to 650,000 metric tons (717,000 short tons), making Iraq the world's eighth largest producer of sulfur. William Spencer

See also IRAN; MIDDLE EAST (Facts in Brief Table). In WORLD BOOK, see IRAQ.

Tanker War. During the summer, Iraq mounted a major effort to cripple the Iranian economy with air strikes on shipping in the Persian Gulf, intended to shut off Iranian oil exports. The campaign was halted for 45 days in July and August to demonstrate Iraq's compliance with a United Nations Security Council resolution calling for a cease-fire and a negotiated end to the war. But when Iran refused to comply with the resolution, Iraq resumed the raids on August 29.

In September, Iraqi jets carrying Exocet missiles made five attacks on Iran-bound tankers within a 36-hour period, the heaviest assault since the tanker war began in 1984. Iraqi raids on Iranian oil terminals and tankers in August and September resulted in a 600,000-barrel-per-day (bpd) drop in production.

Despite the war costs and the daily arrival of coffins carrying the bodies of soldiers killed at the front, Iraqi morale remained high. So did the popularity of President Saddam Hussein.

Kurdish Affairs. In May, the government issued a new administrative statute for the Kurdish Autonomous Region in northeastern Iraq. The statute granted the region political autonomy and permitted the use of the Kurdish language along with Arabic in the government and schools. The Kurds were also given control over regional budget allocations and management.

IRELAND. Prime Minister Garret FitzGerald, leader of the Labour Party and Fine Gael (Gaelic People) minority coalition, called for a general election on Jan. 20, 1987, after the coalition collapsed over proposed welfare cuts. In a four-week campaign dominated by the issue of Ireland's disastrous economy, Fine Gael stuck to its uncompromising package of financial austerity. In particular, the package called for cuts in unemployment benefits, increased gas and tobacco taxes, and higher health service charges. The opposition Fianna Fáil (Soldiers of Destiny) promised economic growth.

When the election was held on February 17, the voters gave power to Fianna Fáil, but only by a slim margin. Although Fianna Fáil won 81 seats in the Dáil, Ireland's parliament, it was 3 seats short of an overall majority. Fine Gael lost 17 seats, finishing with 51 seats in its worst performance in 30 years. The Progressive Democrats, a party founded in 1985, did unexpectedly well, winning 14 seats, mainly from Fine Gael. Labour won 12 seats, down 2, while the Workers Party went from 2 seats to 4. Four seats went to independents. Sinn Féin, the political wing of the outlawed Irish Republican Army, failed to win a seat.

On March 10, Charles Haughey, Fianna Fáil leader, was elected Taoiseach (prime minister) by one vote. See HAUGHEY, CHARLES JOSEPH.

Charles Haughey waves to crowds after his Fianna Fáil party wins Ireland's February 17 election. He became prime minister on March 10.

Economy. Ireland's devastated economy was the major issue in 1987. Virtually all the country's income tax revenue went toward paying the interest on a huge national debt, which has doubled to 24 billion Irish pounds (about U.S. $30 billion). Unemployment in 1987 was 19 per cent, and many young people left Ireland to find work elsewhere.

During the year, Haughey abruptly reversed his stance on many of the policies on which he had won the election. He accepted the controversial Anglo-Irish Agreement (an agreement that gives Ireland a voice in the affairs of Northern Ireland), though he previously criticized it. On the economic front, a program of fiscal discipline substantially lowered public spending and borrowing.

Act Passed. In a *referendum* (vote of the people) held on May 27, Irish voters overwhelmingly endorsed the Single European Act, which updated the founding treaty of the European Community (EC or Common Market), a group of 12 Western European nations, including Ireland, that work to unite their economic resources into a single economy. The referendum was held after the Irish Supreme Court ruled in April that the act clashed with Ireland's Constitution and could be changed only by referendum.   Ian J. Mather

See also NORTHERN IRELAND. In WORLD BOOK, see IRELAND.

IRON AND STEEL. See STEEL INDUSTRY.

ISRAEL. The 20th anniversary of Israel's June 1967 victory over the armies of three Arab neighbors—Egypt, Jordan, and Syria—found Israelis bitterly divided and still searching for peace with their neighbors. Among the Arab countries, only Egypt by 1987 had recognized Israel as a sovereign state. The situation was unlikely to change while Arab territories and their Palestinian Arab population remained under Israeli occupation.

Conference Stalemate. The growing polarization of Israelis over the fate of the occupied West Bank and Gaza Strip was reflected in the inability of the government to take decisive action. Israelis who were willing to allow some form of Palestinian self-determination in the occupied territories in return for a peace treaty were bitterly opposed by those who wanted to hold onto the territories as integral parts of Israel.

Foreign Minister Shimon Peres pressed for an international peace conference sponsored by the United States and the Soviet Union. He met secretly with King Hussein I of Jordan in April 1987 and reportedly reached agreement on the terms of such a conference.

But Peres' hopes were dashed when the conservative Likud bloc headed by Prime Minister Yitzhak Shamir—the other half of Israel's ruling coalition government—refused to go along. Shamir declared himself unalterably opposed to an in-

Israeli security forces fire tear gas at Arab protesters in December, during
the worst unrest in the Israeli-occupied West Bank and Gaza Strip since 1967.

ternational conference, saying it would bring pressure on Israel to give up parts of its territory.

Peres then attempted to win support in the
Knesset (parliament) for early elections—not due
until the fall of 1988—and a chance to proceed
with the conference. But the effort failed.

Scandals within the government undermined
public confidence in Israel's leaders in 1987. The
sentencing in March of Jonathan Jay Pollard, an
American Jew who had pleaded guilty to passing
United States defense secrets to Israel, created a
serious rift between the U.S. Jewish community
and Israel. American Jews were particularly upset
when the Israeli government promoted an Israeli
Air Force officer indicted in the United States for
his role in the spy operation. The officer later
gave up his promotion. They were also angered by
Israel's refusal to cooperate with U.S. investigators. In May, two committees set up by the Israeli
government to investigate Israel's role in the Pollard affair cleared the country's leaders of any
knowledge or involvement in the case.

In May, Shin Bet, Israel's intelligence and security agency, was rocked by scandal for the second
time in a year. In May 1986, Shin Bet agents were
accused of fatally beating two Palestinian bus hi-
jackers in 1984. The 1987 scandal involved a Muslim lieutenant in the Israeli Army who had been
given an 18-year prison sentence in 1980 for alleg-

edly aiding Palestinian guerrillas in southern Lebanon. In May 1987, Israel's Supreme Court ruled
that Lieutenant Izat Nafsu had been unjustly convicted on the basis of perjury and harsh interrogation methods by Shin Bet.

The Economy. A continued austerity program
brought inflation down to 18 per cent in 1987 as
Israelis learned to live with less. One result was
cancellation in August of the U.S.-financed Lavi
jet fighter project, with the loss of several hundred
jobs. The United States had pressured Israel to
scrap the project after cost estimates reached $68
million per aircraft.

Education also suffered uder the austerity program. In a rare show of unity, both Arab and Jewish university students staged a protest against a
decision by Israel's Cabinet in May to increase university tuition fees by 50 per cent for students who
do not serve in the Israeli Army. Israeli Arabs,
who are exempt from Israel's military draft, condemned the increase as discriminatory. The government later reversed itself.

December Unrest. Tensions between Israelis and
Arabs in the West Bank and Gaza Strip exploded
in December into the worst outbreak of violence
in the occupied territories since 1967. The unrest
began after four Palestinians died in a collision
with an Israeli Army truck. Rumors that the crash
was in retaliation for the stabbing of an Israeli in

Gaza's main square triggered violent protests in Gaza and the West Bank beginning on December 9. By late December, at least 22 Palestinians had been killed by Israeli security forces in battles with rock- and firebomb-throwing youths. The Israeli Army arrested more than 1,000 demonstrators in an effort to end the conflict.

Continuing Violence. The December violence was only the worst of the occasional unrest throughout the year. A hunger strike staged in April by Palestinians in Israeli jails to protest prison conditions spilled over into rioting in the West Bank. The disturbances led the government to close Birzeit University—a center of Palestinian resistance to the Israeli occupation of the West Bank—for the rest of the academic year.

In June, the anniversary of the 1967 occupation was marked by violence between Palestinians and ultranationalist Jewish settlers in the West Bank. Thirteen settlers were jailed briefly.

Constitution. In October, a group of Israeli legal scholars drafted a written constitution for the nation. Israel currently has no written constitution. The constitution would combine elements of the British and U.S. systems, with separation of powers, a judiciary able to veto legislation, and equal protection for religious groups.   William Spencer

See also MIDDLE EAST (Facts in Brief Table). In WORLD BOOK, see ISRAEL.

ITALY. A bitter political deadlock ended on July 29, 1987, when Giovanni Goria, a Christian Democrat, was sworn in as the head of Italy's 47th government since the end of World War II in 1945. At 43 years of age, Goria became Italy's youngest prime minister. His government was a coalition of the same five parties that had governed the country since 1981—Christian Democrats, Socialists, Republicans, Social Democrats, and Liberals. See GORIA, GIOVANNI GIUSEPPE.

Craxi Crisis. The deadlock began in February 1987, when Socialist Prime Minister Bettino Craxi was supposed to hand over the leadership to a Christian Democrat under a power-sharing deal arranged in 1986. Craxi declared the agreement invalid but finally stepped down on March 3.

Craxi's exit set the scene for tough bargaining by the political parties. President Francesco Cossiga asked Giulio Andreotti, a Christian Democrat who had served five times as prime minister, to form a government. The Socialists refused to serve under him, however, and he abandoned attempts to forge a coalition on March 25.

Cossiga next offered the Communists an opportunity to form a coalition government. They failed, so Craxi's government continued to serve in a caretaker role.

An early national election became inevitable on April 8, when the Christian Democrats withdrew

Italy's new Prime Minister Giovanni Goria, right, takes the oath of office in Rome's Quirinal Palace on July 29.

16 of their ministers from the government. Craxi's government resigned on the following day. Christian Democrat Oscar Luigi Scalfaro, Craxi's interior minister, then tried to form a government but also failed.

Fanfani Government. Finally, Amintore Fanfani, a Christian Democrat who had served five times as prime minister, succeeded in forging a coalition. Fanfani's government took office on April 18, but it collapsed on April 28 when it lost a vote of confidence in Parliament. Cossiga dissolved Parliament on the same day and scheduled a national election for June 14 and 15.

Little Change. The election had little effect on the balance of power among the parties. The Christian Democrats, the largest party, won 34.3 per cent of the vote, up from 32.9 per cent in the last election in 1983. The Socialists jumped 2.9 percentage points, from 11.4 per cent in 1983 to 14.3 per cent in 1987. The Communists plummeted from 29.9 per cent to 24.6 per cent. Cossiga asked Goria to form a government on July 13.

Porn Parliamentarian. Pornographic film star Ilona Staller—known as *Cicciolina* (Little Buxom One)—attracted a great deal of attention during the election campaign. She ran for the Chamber of Deputies (one of the two houses of Parliament) as a member of the small Radical Party, to stress that party's commitment to civil liberties. She won election as a deputy from Rome.

A Dispute with the Vatican began on February 26, when the government confirmed that it had issued an arrest warrant for Archbishop Paul Marcinkus, a close associate of Pope John Paul II. The government charged Marcinkus with fraudulent bankruptcy.

Marcinkus is chairman of the Institute for Religious Works (IOR), which functions as the bank for the Vatican. The charge grew out of a scandal involving the 1982 bankruptcy of Banco Ambrosiano, a bank in Italy. Marcinkus was charged with being an accessory to the fake bankruptcy that led to the bank's collapse.

The Vatican refused to hand over the archbishop. Government lawyers then tried to find a way to get around the 1929 Treaty of the Lateran, which protects individuals within the walls of Vatican City. On March 28, the government announced that it would seek the extradition of Marcinkus, but the Vatican warned the government not to interfere with its sovereignty. Vatican lawyers claimed that the warrants for Marcinkus and two other IOR officials were invalid because they were members of the "central entity" of the Vatican. On July 17, Italy's highest court threw out the arrest warrants.
Kenneth Brown

See also EUROPE (Facts in Brief Table). In WORLD BOOK, see ITALY; VATICAN CITY.

IVORY COAST. See AFRICA.

JACKSON, JESSE LOUIS (1941-   ), a Baptist minister and civil rights activist, formally announced his candidacy for the 1988 Democratic presidential nomination on Oct. 10, 1987. Jackson's campaign centered on concerns of workers. Polls in summer and early fall of 1987 showed Jackson to be the Democratic front-runner. But many commentators said that Jackson—the only black in the race—would have to struggle to be considered a mainstream candidate.

Jackson was born on Oct. 8, 1941, in Greenville, S.C. In 1963, he graduated from North Carolina Agricultural and Technical State University in Greensboro, N.C. He attended Chicago Theological Seminary for two years before joining civil rights leader Martin Luther King, Jr., to work for voting rights for blacks in Alabama. From 1966 to 1971, Jackson directed the economic arm of the Southern Christian Leadership Conference. In 1968, he was ordained a Baptist minister.

From 1971 to 1983, Jackson was national president of Operation PUSH, a volunteer human-rights organization that he founded. In 1984, Jackson became president of the National Rainbow Coalition, a political organization.

Jackson married the former Jacqueline Brown in 1964. They have five children.   Jinger Griswold

In WORLD BOOK, see JACKSON, JESSE LOUIS.

JAMAICA. See WEST INDIES.

JAPAN. Noboru Takeshita became Japan's 17th postwar prime minister on Nov. 6, 1987, by winning the confirmation of Japan's Diet (parliament) required by the Constitution. One of his rivals for the post, Takako Doi, head of the Japan Socialist Party, was Japan's first woman candidate for prime minister. See TAKESHITA, NOBORU.

Takeshita had been the secretary-general of the ruling Liberal Democratic Party (LDP) and leader of the party's largest faction. He was assured of election when he was named president of the LDP on October 20 by Prime Minister Yasuhiro Nakasone. The prime minister's appointment of his successor was unusual, prompted by the failure of Takeshita and his two principal rivals for the party presidency to agree on a single candidate. Having Nakasone name a successor was deemed preferable to undergoing a hotly contested election that might damage the party's unity and prestige.

Takeshita was regarded as an effective behind-the-scenes politician, but many observers doubted his potential for strong national leadership. Some predicted that Takeshita would not be reelected prime minister after his two-year term as LDP president ended in 1989.

Nakasone, who had served as prime minister since 1982 and was considered by many observers Japan's most effective postwar prime minister, was expected to continue playing an important role in

A tax protester hits an effigy of Japan's Prime Minister Yasuhiro Nakasone
in March, after Nakasone proposed a tremendously unpopular sales-tax hike.

Japan's political affairs. Under Nakasone, Japan became a world economic power and a more assertive participant in international affairs. Nakasone placed more emphasis on foreign policy than his post-World War II predecessors did. He pursued close ties with the United States, developing a particularly friendly relationship with U.S. President Ronald Reagan.

Delicate U.S. Relations. Handling relations with the United States—particularly in the area of economics—continued to be one of the Japanese government's most difficult problems, especially when the troubled U.S. economy was reflected in Japan.

The sudden dive of U.S. stock prices on October 19 had an immediate impact on the Japanese stock exchange. On October 20—only five days after the Nikkei Dow Jones Average hit a high of 26,646 yen—the average fell 3,836.48 yen, almost 15 per cent. The drop was five times as steep as any previous one-day decline. The market rapidly recovered, registering a record single-day gain of 2,037.32 yen on October 21, more than half the previous day's loss. One week later, the total value of the Tokyo stock market showed a loss of 14 per cent as compared with a more than 33 per cent loss on the New York Stock Exchange.

The value of the yen grew to a record 121 yen to U.S. $1 on December 31 in spite of efforts by the Bank of Japan to prop up the dollar. Japanese

leaders blamed the dollar's weakness on the U.S. government's failure to deal with the huge U.S. budget and foreign trade deficits.

Japanese influence in the U.S. economy continued to grow in 1987. In April, the level of Japanese investment in the United States reached $135-billion, second only to the amount of British investment. More than $60 billion in U.S. government securities were held by Japanese investors, who were, in effect, financing the U.S. budget deficit. Japan's importance as a source of capital for U.S. companies was illustrated in October, when a group of Japanese financial companies agreed to buy $350 million worth of new securities in the BankAmerica Corporation, the third largest U.S. bank. Japanese firms also made major real estate acquisitions in New York City, Los Angeles, and other American cities in 1987.

Balance of Trade. The falling value of the dollar—which raised import prices and lowered export prices in the United States—did not have the expected effect of reducing the United States unfavorable balance of trade with Japan. Japan reported that its surplus from trade with the United States reached a record $51 billion in 1986 and would show little change in 1987. The U.S. estimate of the 1986 surplus was $58 billion.

Trade friction with the United States continued to increase in 1987. On April 17, President Reagan imposed a $300-million punitive tariff on Japanese goods in retaliation for Japan's alleged dumping of semiconductor chips on the U.S. market. The tariff was relaxed and virtually lifted on November 2 when U.S. government officials became satisfied that the dumping had stopped.

But Americans complained that Japanese markets were not as open to them as U.S. markets were to the Japanese. The United States also criticized Japan's failure to open its markets to American industries. The Japanese continued to restrict bidding on construction contracts for an $8.3-billion airport to be built near Osaka. On August 8, however, Japanese and United States officials reached an agreement allowing U.S. computer manufacturers to bid freely on Japanese contracts for supercomputers.

In Washington, D.C., in early May and in New York City on September 21, Prime Minister Nakasone conferred with President Reagan on ways to ease trade tensions. They agreed to act cooperatively but reached no specific solutions to the difficulties.

A specific remedy came on October 2, however, when Japan's defense minister announced in Washington, D.C., that Japan had dropped plans to develop and build its own fighter plane and would instead purchase American-built fighters such as the General Dynamics F-16. The purchase could significantly reduce the trade imbalance.

Illegal Sales to Soviets. News reports on April 30 revealed that in 1982 and 1983 a subsidiary of the Toshiba Corporation illegally sold to the Soviet Union sophisticated machine tools capable of producing virtually noiseless submarine propellers. United States officials claimed the tools allowed Soviets to build submarines that were hard to detect. Some Toshiba executives resigned, and others were arrested and found guilty of illegally selling high technology to the Soviet Union. The Japanese government took measures to eliminate illegal trade with the Soviet Union.

Employment and GNP. In January, the Japanese work force was 57.2 million, an increase of 240,000 in one year. Japan's unemployment rate reached a record high of 3 per cent in January, however. Unemployment stayed at that level until July, when it fell to 2.7 per cent.

On May 29, the government introduced a comprehensive $43-billion program to stimulate Japan's domestic economy and thus increase the demand for imports. Officials hoped the plan would help increase the gross national product (GNP)—the value of goods and services produced—by 2 per cent and expand the import market by about 5 per cent in the 1987 fiscal year. The program allocated $36 billion for new public works, including antidisaster projects, highways, educational facilities, housing, and a range of local government projects. The increase in Japan's GNP for the fiscal year 1987 was projected at 3.2 per cent. In the fiscal year 1986, the growth rate was 2.4 per cent.

Other Domestic Economic News. On April 1, 1987, the government's 115-year-old Japanese National Railways (JNR) ceased operations. It was replaced by a national network of six private passenger-train companies and one freight company. The JNR's staggering debt of $250 billion, excessive overstaffing, and operation of unprofitable local lines made the reorganization necessary.

Because the strong yen resulted in lower prices for farming supplies, Japanese farm organizations agreed in May to a reduction of about 5 per cent in the government's rice subsidy, which had not been decreased in more than 30 years. The subsidy had artificially inflated the prices consumers paid for rice and created a vast oversupply.

The government announced on January 23 that it had formally dropped its self-imposed limit on defense spending of 1 per cent of the GNP. Japan adopted the spending cap in 1976. The $23-billion defense budget for fiscal year 1987 equaled 1.004 per cent of the year's projected GNP. The defense budget for 1986 through 1991 was projected at 1.04 per cent of the GNP.   John M. Maki

See also ASIA (Facts in Brief Table). In WORLD BOOK, see JAPAN.

JEWS AND JUDAISM. Great contrasts characterized the major developments in the world's Jewish community in 1987. There was dissension—and unity—between Jews in the United States and Israel, and tension—and reconciliation—between Jews and the Roman Catholic Church.

Pollard Issue. On March 4, 1987, Jonathan Jay Pollard, a Jewish citizen of the United States and a former U.S. Navy intelligence analyst who had pleaded guilty to charges of spying for Israel, was sentenced to life in prison. The case caused conflict within the Jewish community.

American Jews were torn between their support for Israel and their anger at what many felt was the Israeli government's betrayal of its friendship with the United States. Following Israel's formal apology to the United States on March 6, some Jewish leaders said they hoped this episode would lead to greater openness between American Jews and Israel.

Roman Catholic Relations. Controversy arose on June 25, 1987, when Pope John Paul II met with Austria's President Kurt Waldheim in an official audience at the Vatican in Rome. Waldheim, who had been a lieutenant in the German army in World War II, has been accused of taking part in deporting and executing Jews and other civilians in Europe. Jewish leaders, as well as most of the Jewish community, were angered and hurt that an

Jews in Rome protest Pope John Paul II's June 25 meeting with Austria's President Kurt Waldheim, who had been linked to Nazi war crimes.

alleged war criminal would be welcomed by the pope. Many Roman Catholic Americans, including leading bishops, shared these concerns. The Vatican said the pope's meeting with Waldheim was based on the church's historic ties with predominantly Roman Catholic Austria.

On September 1, nine Jewish leaders from the United States met with the pope at his summer residence in Castel Gandolfo, Italy. They engaged in a frank discussion of the Waldheim visit. The Jewish delegation expressed the disappointment the Jewish community felt over what they viewed as the Vatican's insensitivity to Jewish feelings about the Holocaust (the Nazis' mass slaughter of Jews). The pope responded by affirming his friendship and support and acknowledged his personal understanding of the suffering experienced under the Nazis. He did not, however, justify or apologize for his visit with Waldheim.

The pope again met with a group of U.S. Jewish leaders on September 11 in Miami, Fla., during a visit to the United States. He said that Catholics "recognize and appreciate the spiritual treasures of the Jewish people and their religious witness to God." Using the Hebrew term for the Holocaust—*Shoah*—the pope spoke of the church's sorrow over "the ruthless and inhuman attempt to exterminate the Jewish people in Europe." Jewish and Catholic leaders said the Miami meeting was positive, with each group showing a genuine desire to understand the other's position. They also emphasized that the conflicts between Jews and the Vatican in 1987 in no way detracted from the great progress made in recent years in Jewish-Catholic relations in the United States.

Soviet Jews. Although Soviet leader Mikhail S. Gorbachev's new policy of *glasnost* (openness) led to some improvement in the conditions of Soviet Jews in 1987, concern over their plight continued during the year. The Soviet government in March permitted Jews in the United States to send 5,000 Hebrew-Russian Bibles and prayer books to congregations in Moscow that do not have access to religious books and supplies. In September, the government allowed the first public library of Jewish books in the Soviet Union to open.

But glasnost did not seem to help the estimated 200,000 to 400,000 Jews who want to leave the Soviet Union. Of these, approximately 11,000 are *refuseniks,* Jewish activists who have formally applied for visas but have not received them. Many have been waiting for as long as 15 years and have endured loss of jobs and constant abuse. The Soviet Union granted visas to 8,011 Jews during 1987. Although this was a significant increase over the 914 visas issued in 1986, it was still far below the record number of 51,320 Soviet Jews released in 1979.   Howard A. Berman

In WORLD BOOK, see JEWS; JUDAISM.

JORDAN. After 35 years in power, King Hussein I continued in 1987 to guide Jordan with a steady hand and to stay on good terms politically with all the country's neighbors. During the year, Hussein held a number of secret meetings with Israel's Foreign Minister Shimon Peres. Both leaders sought to find an acceptable formula for an international Arab-Israeli peace conference. But Hussein was unable—or unwilling—to ensure Jordanian and Palestinian participation on terms agreeable to the more conservative members of Israel's coalition government.

Arab Affairs. In February, Hussein permitted the Palestine Liberation Organization (PLO) to reopen its offices in Amman, Jordan's capital. The offices had been closed since July 1986, when the king canceled an agreement with PLO leader Yasir Arafat. The agreement had called for the formation of a joint Jordanian-PLO delegation to hold direct peace talks with Israel.

In September and October 1987, Hussein made state visits to Syria, Libya, and the Persian Gulf states to drum up support for an Arab League summit held in Amman from November 8 to 11. He said the summit was necessary to establish a unified Arab policy toward Iran and an Arab-Israeli peace conference, though such a conference would take place under international auspices.

U.S. Relations. Hussein managed to stay on good terms with the United States, though he sharply criticized the Administration of President Ronald Reagan for what he called its inept Middle East policy. In February, he turned down an invitation to visit the United States, citing outrage over the Administration's secret arms sales to Iran. Earlier that month, reportedly under pressure from pro-Israeli members of Congress, the Administration had withdrawn a proposal to upgrade Jordan's antiaircraft missile system. In July, 2,300 U.S. troops carried out a week of joint maneuvers with the Jordanian Army. It was the largest joint exercise ever by the two countries.

The Economy. The budget approved by Jordan's Senate in January was the first to exceed the billion-dinar (about $2.8-billion) mark. Jordan's economic performance during 1987 was so good that some economists cited the country in September as one of the three best prospects in the region for foreign business.

In October, Jordan's first chemical fertilizer plant went into production. Its output of 12,000 metric tons (13,200 short tons) a year will meet all domestic needs. William Spencer

See also MIDDLE EAST (Facts in Brief Table). In the Special Reports section, see UNDERSTANDING ISLAM. In WORLD BOOK, see JORDAN.

JUDAISM. See JEWS AND JUDAISM.

JUNIOR ACHIEVEMENT. See YOUTH ORGANIZATIONS.

KAMPUCHEA. Amid continuing warfare, key players in the struggle for control of Kampuchea (formerly called Cambodia) took part in intensive diplomatic maneuvers during 1987. Those involved included Kampuchea's Communist government; Vietnam, which propped up that government with 140,000 soldiers; and an opposition coalition of Kampuchean Communists and non-Communists, including about 60,000 guerrillas.

Prince Norodom Sihanouk, nominal head of the opposition coalition and a former chief of state, announced that he would begin a one-year leave from coalition leadership on May 7, 1987. Sihanouk acted in protest after members of one faction in the coalition—the Communist Khmer Rouge—killed two guerrilla soldiers from Sihanouk's own faction. His announcement followed a report by Amnesty International—a London-based human-rights organization—that charged both the Khmer Rouge and the government with torturing prisoners and other abuses. The Khmer Rouge was responsible for mass murders when it ruled Kampuchea from 1975 to 1979.

Movement Toward Peace. The Kampuchean government announced a new "policy of national reconciliation" on Aug. 27, 1987. The government said it would meet with all factions except Khmer Rouge leader Pol Pot and his close associates. Another official statement on October 8 said that Vietnamese troops would leave Kampuchea as foreign countries ceased to aid Kampuchean guerrillas. Elections would then be held and a new ruling coalition set up. The government offered Sihanouk "a high position" in the new coalition. The Soviet Union, which indirectly subsidized Vietnam's costly war to maintain control of Kampuchea, endorsed this offer on October 17. The United Nations General Assembly voted 117 to 21 on October 14 to urge a Vietnamese withdrawal.

Kampuchean Prime Minister Hun Sen met with Sihanouk near Paris in December. The two discussed the possibility of a political reconciliation and called for more talks in 1988.

Other Developments. Hun Sen said on October 19 that he was waiting for the United States—which did not officially recognize his government—to ask directly for the return of the remains of United States soldiers missing since the 1970-1975 war in Kampuchea.

Along Kampuchea's border with Thailand, Vietnamese and Thai troops fought at Chong Bok pass from January into July. Inside Kampuchea, guerrillas fought throughout the year.

Drought cut rice production to about 1 million metric tons (1.1 million short tons), little more than half the amount needed. Henry S. Bradsher

See also ASIA (Facts in Brief Table). In WORLD BOOK, see KAMPUCHEA.

KANSAS. See STATE GOVERNMENT.

KEMP, JACK FRENCH (1935-   ), a United States representative from New York, announced on April 6, 1987, his candidacy for the 1988 Republican presidential nomination. He pledged a commitment to full employment—without inflation.

Kemp was born on July 13, 1935, in Los Angeles. After graduating from Occidental College in Los Angeles in 1957, he embarked on a 13-year career in professional football, playing quarterback for the Pittsburgh Steelers, San Diego Chargers, and Buffalo Bills. He served as special assistant to the governor of California in 1967 and was special assistant to the chairman of the Republican National Convention in 1969.

A member of the House of Representatives since 1971, Kemp was coauthor of the Kemp-Roth tax bill, which, when signed into law by President Ronald Reagan in 1981, cut tax rates by 25 per cent. Kemp also cosponsored the Kemp-Kasten tax plan, which became part of the Tax Reform Act of 1986.

Kemp is an outspoken supporter of President Reagan's "Star Wars" space defense system. He also supports the Reagan Administration's aid to *contra* rebels fighting the Marxist government in Nicaragua.

Kemp married Joanne Main in 1958. They have four children.   Mary A. Krier

KENTUCKY. See STATE GOVERNMENT.

KENNEDY, ANTHONY McLEOD (1936-   ), a federal appeals court judge, was nominated to the Supreme Court of the United States by President Ronald Reagan on Nov. 11, 1987. Kennedy was Reagan's third nominee to fill the vacancy created when Justice Lewis F. Powell, Jr., retired in June. The earlier nominees were Robert H. Bork, who was rejected by the Senate on October 23, and Douglas H. Ginsburg, who withdrew on November 7. Legal experts describe Kennedy's decisions on the bench as conservative, but more moderate than those of Bork or Ginsburg. See SUPREME COURT OF THE UNITED STATES.

Kennedy was born on July 23, 1936, in Sacramento, Calif., where his father was a lawyer. The young Kennedy earned a bachelor's degree in political science in 1958 at Stanford University in California and a law degree in 1961 at Harvard Law School in Cambridge, Mass. After his father died in 1963, he took over the older man's law practice. In 1975, President Gerald R. Ford appointed Kennedy to the U.S. Court of Appeals for the Ninth Circuit in California.

Since 1965, Kennedy has taught part-time at the McGeorge School of Law at the University of the Pacific in Sacramento.

Kennedy and his wife, Mary, an elementary-school teacher, were married in 1963. They have three children.   Sara Dreyfuss

KENYA. Overpopulation and charges of human rights abuses against the government of President Daniel T. arap Moi threatened Kenya's economic and political stability in 1987.

With a 4 per cent annual rate of increase, Kenya's population—more than 23 million in 1987—may double by 2010, causing food and housing shortages and high unemployment. In 1987, the government acted to avert such a crisis, including increasing family-planning services.

Amnesty International—a worldwide human-rights organization—and members of the United States Congress in 1987 joined Kenyan journalists, business executives, and lawyers in criticizing Moi's human rights record. Charges against Moi's government included the detention of suspects without trial, the torture and mysterious deaths of prisoners, and the harassment of critics. Those alleged abuses caused strained relations between Kenya and the United States.

Kenya's relations with Uganda and Libya also deteriorated in 1987. Beginning in March, the Moi government deported thousands of Ugandans for allegedly spying or causing unrest. In April, claiming that Libya was training Kenyan dissidents as guerrillas, Kenya expelled five Libyan diplomats.   J. Gus Liebenow and Beverly B. Liebenow

See also AFRICA (Facts in Brief Table). In WORLD BOOK, see KENYA.

KOREA, NORTH. On April 23, 1987, officials in Communist North Korea launched a seven-year economic development plan. The new plan emphasized using foreign trade to help achieve less ambitious goals than those proposed in earlier, relatively unsuccessful plans.

In August, after years of frustrated efforts to collect payments on North Korea's international debt, two Western banking syndicates declared the country was in default on $773 million in loans. The declaration—and the threat of having its foreign assets seized—prodded North Korea into signing a new 12-year agreement for the repayment of its foreign debts.

On July 23, the North Korean government proposed a plan for drastic troop reduction in both North and South Korea. North Korea said it would begin by releasing 100,000 troops from its armed forces, which the government said comprised a total of 520,000 soldiers. United States officials estimated North Korea's troop strength at 830,000, however, and said the 100,000 released were simply diverted to construction projects. One such project was a 150,000-seat stadium in the capital, Pyongyang, that North Korea hoped would be used for some events of the 1988 Summer Olympic Games.   Henry S. Bradsher

See also ASIA (Facts in Brief Table); KOREA, SOUTH. In WORLD BOOK, see KOREA.

Protests ripped South Korea during 1987. In Seoul in May, police erect
a net to protect against rocks and firebombs thrown by students.

KOREA, SOUTH. In South Korea's first direct presidential election since 1971, Roh Tae Woo was elected president on Dec. 16, 1987. Roh (pronounced *Noh*) was to take office on Feb. 25, 1988 (see ROH TAE WOO). The election climaxed a tumultuous year of political demonstrations, labor unrest, and the unexpected adoption of a new, more democratic Constitution.

The Year of Protest was foreshadowed in 1986, when opponents of President Chun Doo Hwan's army-backed government agitated for direct election of the next president by the people rather than by a government-dominated electoral college. Chun's opponents renewed their efforts after Park Chong Chol, a 21-year-old student at Seoul National University, died during police torture on Jan. 14, 1987. Five police officials were arrested in an investigation of torture during interrogations of antigovernment activists. Roh, then chairman of the ruling Democratic Justice Party (DJP), responded to demonstrators angry over Park's death by saying that "pro-Communist radicals and destructionists" were only pretending to call for democratization. Helmeted police firing tear-gas canisters broke up protests during Park's funeral.

Continuing demonstrations led on April 8 to a split in the main opposition party, the New Korea Democratic Party (NKDP). Some members wanted to consider a compromise in their demands for constitutional reform. Those who did not favor compromise followed Kim Dae Jung and Kim Young Sam, who, along with 66 of the party's 90 members of the National Assembly, formed a new Reunification Democratic Party (RDP). Kim Young Sam was elected RDP president on May 1. Chun's government had technically banned Kim Dae Jung from politics.

President Chun responded on April 13 by announcing the suspension of talks between the DJP and the NKDP on constitutional changes. He said that his successor would be chosen by the electoral college and that changes in future elections would not be discussed until after the 1988 Summer Olympic Games were held in Seoul, the capital.

As charges mounted that senior government officials were protecting those responsible for Park's death, Chun fired Prime Minister Shinyong Lho and seven other ministers on May 26, 1987. Chun named Lee Han Key, a specialist in international law, as prime minister and assembled a new cabinet.

The ruling DJP nominated Roh on June 10 as its presidential candidate to succeed Chun. Despite the government's roundup and arrest of some 2,600 student radicals and opposition politicians in early June, opponents openly showed their anger over Roh's nomination, mounting the worst street disturbances since Chun came to power with the help of Roh, then his fellow general, in 1980. As the street violence continued and rock-hurling youths were met with tear gas and police clubs, Roh expressed fears that South Korea's middle class was turning against the government. Under pressure, Chun met with Kim Young Sam on June 24 and proposed a resumption of talks on constitutional changes. This failed, however, to end the agitation, in which an estimated 830,000 people took part.

Unexpected Reforms. Roh dramatically changed the situation with a June 29 statement conceding the basic demands of the demonstrators. He proposed several government changes, including speedy amendment of the Constitution to permit direct presidential elections in December and a peaceful transfer of power in February 1988; legal revisions to ensure free and fair competition for the presidency; amnesty for Kim Dae Jung so that he could compete for the presidency; freedom for all political prisoners except those accused of treason and violent crimes; and freedom of the press.

Officials indicated that the proposal had been worked out between Chun and Roh, with Roh to take public credit for them. Chun publicly accepted the proposal on July 1, thus ending the street protests. Chun removed all members of the ruling party from the cabinet on July 13 to make the government more politically neutral until the presidential elections were held. Lee was replaced by an acting prime minister, Kim Chung-Yul.

Members of the National Assembly from the DJP and RDP worked together to write South Korea's ninth constitution—and the first one written by bipartisan consensus rather than imposed by those in power. The framers agreed to limit presidents to one five-year term, rather than a seven-year term, and to enhance the Assembly's powers. The Assembly approved the Constitution on October 12, and it was ratified on October 27 by 93 per cent of voters in a national referendum.

Labor Unrest erupted as democratization unleashed workers' pent-up demands. Some 2,000 strikes occurred in July and August. The average South Korean industrial employee worked 54½ hours a week for about $60 under hazardous conditions that made South Korea's workplace accident rate one of the world's highest. The government had banned labor unions other than company unions in smaller businesses and prohibited outsiders from assisting union members.

Although the strikes were illegal, the government did not crack down. Chun's efforts to maintain order, however, led on August 22 to the death of a shipyard worker hit by a tear-gas canister. Dissidents unsuccessfully tried to turn the worker's funeral into a nationwide strike. Labor unrest gradually subsided in September as companies conceded some worker demands.

A Five-Way Presidential Campaign developed in the autumn. Roh sought the support of the governing elite, the military establishment, and big business. He met in Washington, D.C., on September 14 with United States President Ronald Reagan in an effort to show his acceptability to the United States—South Korea's ally and military protector. Reagan praised the move toward democratization but avoided endorsing Roh.

Kim Jong Pil competed with Roh for the vote of government supporters. Kim was prime minister from 1971 to 1975. Chun had confiscated Kim's wealth in 1980, accusing him of corruption.

The opposition vote in the Dec. 16, 1987, election was divided between Kim Dae Jung and Kim Young Sam. Each man urged the other to withdraw, but each insisted that he had earned the right to be president. Both drew large crowds during their campaigns. Shin Jeong Yil, a member of a minor political party, also joined the race.

Official election results gave Roh 35.9 per cent of the vote; Kim Young Sam 27.5 per cent; and Kim Dae Jung 26.5 per cent. Kim Jong Pil and Shin Jeong Yil shared about 10 per cent of the vote. Roh's party was accused of vote fraud, but the charges were not substantiated. Henry S. Bradsher

See also ASIA (Facts in Brief Table). In WORLD BOOK, see KOREA.

KUWAIT. See MIDDLE EAST.

LABOR. The United States experienced its lowest unemployment rate in almost 10 years during 1987. Low inflation and the continued growth of the economy pushed the unemployment rate down to 6 per cent, the lowest rate since 1978, according to the U.S. Department of Labor. When translated to the workplace, this meant that only about 6 out of 100 Americans looking for work were unable to find it. Low inflation helped keep wage increases moderate. The broadest measure of wage change—the U.S. Bureau of Labor Statistics Employment Cost Index—showed an increase of 3.4 per cent from September 1986 to September 1987.

Collective Bargaining. Despite the growth of the U.S. economy since 1982, the vulnerability of some industries to foreign and domestic competition caused employers in those industries to continue seeking wage and benefit concessions from workers in 1987. Other employers in 1987 offered employees profit-sharing and onetime payments, such as year-end bonuses, that were tied to productivity and profit, instead of wage increases. In some cases, workers accepted pay or benefit reductions to aid ailing companies. Other workers focused on ways to protect their jobs.

Approximately 3.1 million workers in 1987 were covered by major collective-bargaining agreements—contracts applying to 1,000 workers or

Teamsters President Jackie Presser, left, and AFL-CIO President Lane Kirkland smile after the AFL-CIO readmits the Teamsters in October.

more. During the first nine months of the year, these settlements provided annual wage increases of 2.3 per cent over the life of the contracts. The last time these contracts were negotiated, they yielded wage increases of 2.5 per cent.

Steel Strike Resolved. The longest steel strike in U.S. history ended on Feb. 2, 1987, after the United Steelworkers of America and USX Corporation, the largest U.S. steel producer, agreed to a new four-year contract. The strike began on Aug. 1, 1986.

The agreement, which was ratified by union members on Jan. 31, 1987, provided savings for USX and profit-sharing for the workers. The union agreed to an average $1.12 an hour wage cut, a reduction in paid holidays from 10 days to 7, and a cut in Sunday premium pay.

The union won, however, a profit-sharing plan in which USX will distribute to workers 10 per cent of its first $200 million in pretax profits and 20 per cent of its profits over $200 million. USX also agreed to modernize its Monongahela Valley Works near Pittsburgh, Pa.

Comparable Worth. On March 18, the city of San Francisco, the Service Employees Union, and other unions reached a comparable worth agreement. The agreement gave pay adjustments valued at $35.4 million to women and minority workers whose wages were lower than male workers in comparable jobs that required similar skill, education, and performance requirements. The workers also received a 4.5 per cent pay increase in July, with another 5 per cent increase scheduled for July 1988.

A similar agreement, valued at $68 million, was granted to New York state employees in May. Approximately 35,000 women and 17,000 minority workers received an average wage raise of $800 annually.

Longshoring. In July, the West Coast Longshoremen and the Pacific Maritime Association agreed to a contract that freezes wages in the first contract year. The pay of cargo-handling workers, however, was changed to include a new rate that replaces "overtime" pay. In the past, workers were paid overtime for the last two hours of an eight-hour day. Under the new agreement, this overtime would be included in a new rate of $19.43 an hour. This rate is more than the previous straight-time pay of $17.27 an hour, but is less than the previous overtime rate of $25.90 an hour. The new straight-time hourly rate would rise to $19.83 in 1988 and to $20.33 in 1989.

Postal Pact. The United States Postal Service reached contract agreements with three postal unions, representing a total of 650,000 workers, in 1987. On July 14, the Postal Service and the Mail Handlers Union agreed on a 1.6 per cent annual

Changes in the United States Labor Force

	1986	1987
Total labor force	119,547,000	121,587,000
Armed forces	1,706,000	1,737,000
Civilian labor force	117,841,000	119,850,000
Total employment	111,307,000	112,439,000
Unemployment	8,240,000	7,411,000
Unemployment rate	7.0%	6.1%
Change in real earnings of production and nonsupervisory workers (private nonfarm sector)*	+ 1.3%	− 0.9%
Change in output per employee hour (private nonfarm sector)†	+ 0.5%	+ 1.2%

*Constant (1977) dollars, 1986 change from December 1985 to December 1986; 1987 change from October 1986 to October 1987 (preliminary data).

†Annual rate for 1986; for 1987, change is from third quarter 1986 to third quarter 1987 (preliminary data).

Source: U.S. Bureau of Labor Statistics.

pay hike over the next three years. A week later, on July 21, the Postal Service reached agreements with the American Postal Workers Union and the National Association of Letter Carriers. These contracts provided 7 per cent wage increases over the contracts' 40-month life. Cost-of-living adjustments were retained. The bargaining round was marked by squabbling and rivalry among the three unions, including charges that the settlement by the Mail Handlers Union was a "sellout."

Automobile Industry. The United Auto Workers (UAW) reached contract agreements with Ford Motor Company and General Motors (GM) Corporation in 1987 that were unprecedented in the amount of job security they offered workers. The UAW and Ford agreement, reached on September 17, included a new guaranteed employment program that is intended to protect UAW employees from layoffs, except during production slowdowns due to market conditions. UAW employees at Ford received a 3 per cent hike and performance bonuses that equaled 3 per cent of pay.

The Ford contract also included a profit-sharing plan, in which employees could receive 7.5 per cent of profits above 1.8 per cent of sales, up to a limit of 2.3 per cent of sales. Cost-of-living increases—1 cent more for every 0.26 percentage point rise in the Consumer Price Index (the measurement of changes in the cost of goods and serv-

ices)—were retained. On October 8, GM agreed to a similar three-year contract.

Football. On September 22, the National Football League Players Association, representing more than 1,500 professional football players, went on strike against the National Football League (NFL). The players were protesting the NFL's policy of free agency. Free agency allows a player to change teams—without any restrictions—when his contract with one team expires.

The players' current contract said that once a player has completed his contract with one team he can accept offers from any other. But it gives the team that held the player's contract the right to meet any other team's offer to keep the player. The contract also said that a team that loses a player to another team must be compensated for the loss by receiving comparable players. Although the football players agreed to these provisions in a previous contract negotiation in exchange for minimum pay and benefit increases, the players said this policy has had a negative effect on offers made to migrating players.

In response to the strike, the NFL hired substitute players to play in scheduled games. The players' association ended the strike on October 15, and players returned to work with the free-agent issue unresolved. The players filed a lawsuit in a federal court in Minneapolis, Minn., against the NFL. The suit charged that the NFL's bargaining posture violates federal antitrust laws.

Sanitation on the Farm. On April 28, the U.S. Department of Labor issued new regulations that require people who employ 11 or more farm workers to provide those workers with safe drinking water, toilets, and hand-washing facilities. The regulations will affect more than 471,000 workers.

Drug Testing. The Administration of President Ronald Reagan on February 19 announced that a random drug-testing program would be set up for U.S. government employees. The Department of Transportation was the first civilian government agency to carry out the order in 1987. Meanwhile, on October 31, the U.S. Senate approved a bill that would require all transportation employees who are responsible for passenger safety to undergo drug and alcohol tests.

Labor groups objected to both measures, calling them unconstitutional. Some transportation unions decided to tackle the issue head-on by negotiating drug-testing agreements with railroad and trucking companies during the year.

Minimum Wage. The Reagan Administration firmly opposed bills introduced in Congress in 1987 that would raise the national minimum wage from $3.35 an hour to $4.65 an hour by 1990. The Administration argued that the increase would throw "vulnerable groups," such as teenagers and members of minority groups, out of work. Proponents of the increase argued that a higher minimum wage was needed to help the working poor.

Union News. The American Federation of Labor and Congress of Industrial Organizations (AFL-CIO) on October 24 voted unanimously to readmit the Teamsters Union as an affiliated member. The Teamsters were expelled from the AFL-CIO in 1957 for alleged corruption.

Air-traffic controllers in the United States voted on June 11 to form a new union, the National Air Traffic Controllers Association (NATCA). The union replaced the Professional Air Traffic Controllers Organization, which was dissolved in 1981 after President Reagan fired most of its members for participating in an illegal strike. NATCA, which is expected to work closely with the Federal Aviation Administration in rebuilding the nation's air-traffic control system, is an affiliated member of the Marine Engineers' Beneficial Association.

Acquittal. A New York State Supreme Court jury on May 25 acquitted former Secretary of Labor Raymond J. Donovan and seven codefendants on charges of defrauding New York City in a subway construction project. Donovan, who resigned his post in 1985, was the first Cabinet official to be indicted while in office. Robert W. Fisher

See also ECONOMICS. In WORLD BOOK, see LABOR FORCE; LABOR MOVEMENT.

LAOS. On Sept. 11, 1987, Laos appealed to the thousands of Laotians who had fled the country after the Communist take-over in 1975 to show their love for their homeland by sending more money to make "an even greater contribution to the construction and development of the country." The appeal was made at the end of a three-day meeting of the Lao Front for National Reconstruction in the capital city of Vientiane. The Front was established in 1979 to attract support for the Communist regime in Laos.

In other action at the meeting, the Front's 300 delegates on September 9 adopted rules stating that the Front was under the leadership of the Lao People's Revolutionary Party, the country's Communist organization. Kaysone Phomvihan, the party's general secretary and prime minister of Laos, told the delegates that the country's population had grown 2.4 per cent annually since 1977. During the same period, income per person rose 60 per cent and industrial production increased 450 per cent. He said that illiteracy had been almost wiped out.

A long-standing border dispute with Thailand flared up again on August 7 and 8. Since 1984, the two countries have argued over ownership of three border villages. Henry S. Bradsher

See also ASIA (Facts in Brief Table). In WORLD BOOK, see LAOS.

LATIN AMERICA. The presidents of five Central American nations—Costa Rica, El Salvador, Guatemala, Honduras, and Nicaragua—signed a peace agreement on Aug. 7, 1987, in Guatemala City, Guatemala, bringing hope for an end to political violence in that troubled region. The accord was fashioned by Costa Rica's President Oscar Arias Sánchez, who was awarded the 1987 Nobel Peace Prize in recognition of his efforts.

Media attention focused on military provisions of the accord. The agreement called for an "effective cease-fire" between government and rebel forces in El Salvador, Guatemala, and Nicaragua; an end to foreign aid for rebel groups; and a ban on the use of foreign sanctuaries for rebels. The accord also called for each country to put into effect such political measures as regular elections, freedom of the press and political organization, amnesty for rebels who lay down their arms, and a dialogue with unarmed opposition groups.

Other aspects of the accord that received little attention from the media may prove equally important in laying the groundwork for long-range stability in Central America. For example, the pact called for the creation of national reconciliation commissions to monitor compliance with the accord, and the holding of elections to select members of a Central American parliament. The elections to the proposed parliament were to be held simultaneously throughout Central America in the first half of 1988.

Even before the plan was scheduled to take effect on Nov. 7, 1987, several nations took steps to comply with some of its provisions. On October 7, Guatemala convened talks in Madrid, Spain, with rebel leaders to negotiate settlement of a guerrilla struggle that has smoldered intermittently for 26 years. Also in October, the government of El Salvador renewed talks with guerrilla forces that had been suspended since the first face-to-face meeting of rebels and government officials in 1984. Nicaragua declared a unilateral one-month cease-fire in three regions on October 9 and later released about 985 political prisoners and loosened up on government press censorship.

U.S. Reaction. The Administration of United States President Ronald Reagan initially reacted to the peace plan as "fatally flawed." But as support for it grew, the Administration gave it a second look. Speaker of the House James C. Wright, Jr. (D., Tex.), predicted that the award of the Nobel Peace Prize to Arias meant failure for Reagan's push for $270 million in additional military and economic aid for the *contra* rebels fighting the Nicaraguan government. Wright argued that the peace accord should be given a chance to work before Congress considered renewed military aid.

In late December, the Administration and the Democratic-controlled Congress reached a com-

The presidents of five Central American nations announce agreement on
a regional peace plan in August in Guatemala City, Guatemala.

promise that provided $8.1 million in nonmilitary
aid for the contras. Included in that figure was
$4.5 million to cover shipping costs for weapons
previously purchased by the contras. Military shipments were to be suspended for a week in January
1988 to determine if the regional peace accord
was making progress.

Meanwhile, Central America remained heavily
armed, with more than 150,000 troops on the side
of governments in El Salvador, Guatemala, Honduras, and Nicaragua. Additional thousands were
fighting under rebel banners in those countries,
except for Honduras, where large numbers of
U.S. troops staged military maneuvers in 1987.

Cuba in OAS? The presidents of eight Latin-
American nations, meeting in Acapulco, Mexico,
from November 26 to 29, proposed major changes
to reinforce the importance of the Organization of
American States (OAS). In particular, Brazilian
President José Sarney and Mexican President Miguel de la Madrid Hurtado called for the Cuban
government to be readmitted to the OAS. The
OAS is an association of 31 Latin-American nations and the United States. It seeks regional cooperation and a peaceful solution to inter-American conflicts.

The Cuban government was expelled from the
OAS in 1962 as the United States and other Latin-
American countries sought to isolate the Commu-

nist regime. Since then, however, even many
conservative Latin-American governments have
adopted friendlier relations with Cuba, as reflected in remarks made by Sarney. He said that
Cuba's presence in the OAS and other regional organizations in the Western Hemisphere was "in-
dispensable" to their functioning. De la Madrid
said that the issue of readmitting Cuba was expected to be taken up in 1988, when the OAS ob-
serves its 40th anniversary.

The Acapulco meeting also called for a ceiling
on the repayment of Latin America's colossal foreign debt. In a document issued at the end of the
conference, the presidents of the eight nations
said that Latin America's estimated $400-billion
debt "should be adjusted to the capacity of each
country to pay." The statement called for limits on
interest rates charged by foreign lenders and declared that Latin America could never achieve sustained economic growth until there is "a turnabout
in the massive transference of financial resources
abroad." The other nations represented at the
conference were Argentina, Colombia, Panama,
Peru, Uruguay, and Venezuela.

Women in the Work Force. In a September report, the Inter-American Development Bank described an extraordinary transformation of Latin
America's labor force in recent years. Women
were entering the Latin-American work force

Facts in Brief on Latin-American Political Units

Country	Population	Government	Monetary Unit*	Foreign Trade (million U.S. $) Exports†	Imports†
Antigua and Barbuda	83,000	Governor General Sir Wilfred Ebenezer Jacobs; Prime Minister Vere C. Bird, Sr.	dollar (2.7 = $1)	41	134
Argentina	31,965,000	President Raúl Alfonsín	austral (3.5 = $1)	8,400	4,100
Bahamas	246,000	Governor General Sir Gerald C. Cash; Prime Minister Lynden O. Pindling	dollar (1 = $1)	296	891
Barbados	272,000	Governor General Sir Hugh Springer; Prime Minister Lloyd Erskine Sandiford	dollar (2 = $1)	352	552
Belize	172,000	Governor General Minita Gordon; Prime Minister Manuel Esquivel	dollar (2 = $1)	90	128
Bolivia	6,918,000	President Víctor Paz Estenssoro	boliviano (2.1 = $1)	673	582
Brazil	144,427,000	President José Sarney	cruzado (63.6 = $1)	25,100	12,700
Chile	12,668,000	President Augusto Pinochet Ugarte	peso (230.6 = $1)	3,700	3,000
Colombia	30,577,000	President Virgilio Barco Vargas	peso (259.6 = $1)	3,600	4,100
Costa Rica	2,710,000	President Oscar Arias Sánchez	colón (65.5 = $1)	994	1,126
Cuba	10,314,000	President Fidel Castro	peso (1 = $1.36)	6,500	8,600
Dominica	74,000	President Clarence Seignoret; Prime Minister Mary Eugenia Charles	dollar (2.7 = $1)	29	57
Dominican Republic	6,675,000	President Joaquín Balaguer	peso (4.5 = $1)	735	1,500
Ecuador	10,013,000	President León Febres-Cordero	sucre (250 = $1)	2,100	1,700
El Salvador	6,089,000	President José Napoleón Duarte	colón (4.9 = $1)	772	1,052
Grenada	119,000	Governor General Sir Paul Godwin Scoon; Prime Minister Herbert Blaize	dollar (2.7 = $1)	22	63
Guatemala	9,165,000	President Vinicio Cerezo	quetzal (1 = $1)	1,200	1,300
Guyana	1,006,000	President Hugh Desmond Hoyte; Prime Minister Hamilton Green	dollar (8.8 = $1)	214	209
Haiti	5,697,000	National Council President Henri Namphy	gourde (5 = $1)	207	338
Honduras	4,801,000	President José Azcona del Hoyo	lempira (2 = $1)	933	873
Jamaica	2,427,000	Governor General Sir Florizel Glasspole; Prime Minister Edward Seaga	dollar (5.3 = $1)	569	999
Mexico	84,964,000	President Miguel de la Madrid Hurtado	peso (2,350 = $1)	21,866	13,460
Nicaragua	3,622,000	President Daniel Ortega	córdoba (1,957 = $1)	218	840
Panama	2,322,000	President Eric Arturo Delvalle; Commander in Chief of the Panamanian Defense Forces General Manuel Antonio Noriega Morena	balboa (1 = $1)	410	1,340
Paraguay	4,007,000	President Alfredo Stroessner	guaraní (313.1 = $1)	350	730
Peru	21,254,000	President Alan García Pérez; Prime Minister Guillermo Larco Cox	inti (20 = $1)	2,400	2,200
Puerto Rico	3,197,000	Governor Rafael Hernández Colón	U.S. $	no statistics available	
St. Christopher and Nevis	44,000	Governor General Clement Arrindell; Prime Minister Kennedy Alphonse Simmonds	dollar (2.7 = $1)	31	47
St. Lucia	126,000	Governor General Sir Allen Montgomery Lewis; Prime Minister John Compton	dollar (2.7 = $1)	50	107
St. Vincent and the Grenadines	130,000	Governor General Joseph Lambert Eustace; Prime Minister James Mitchell	dollar (2.7 = $1)	42	65
Suriname	398,000	Commander of the National Army Désiré D. Bouterse; Acting President L. F. Ramdat-Misier; Prime Minister Jules Albert Wijdenbosch	guilder (1.8 = $1)	314	299
Trinidad and Tobago	1,239,000	President Noor Mohamed Hassanali; Prime Minister A. N. R. Robinson	dollar (3.6 = $1)	2,000	1,400
Uruguay	3,081,000	President Julio María Sanguinetti	new peso (267.3 = $1)	960	708
Venezuela	20,116,000	President Jaime Lusinchi	bolívar (7.5 = $1)	12,300	8,200

*Exchange rates as of Dec. 1, 1987, or latest available data.   †Latest available data.

faster than men. Between 1950 and 1980, the number of men holding salaried jobs increased about 94 per cent, but the number of women holding such jobs increased by 300 per cent. In Venezuela and Mexico, the change was astonishing, as women doubled their representation in the work force during the 1970's. "The significance of the increase in the women's labor force cannot be overstated," the bank's report concluded. "Women are increasingly occupying positions at all levels of society and at a rate faster than previously anticipated."

The report also highlighted advances in education in Latin America. Enrollment at primary school and secondary school levels increased nearly 700 per cent between 1950 and 1985. Total attendance in 1985 reached 89 million students, out of a possible total enrollment of 117 million. This meant that 76 per cent of eligible children were enrolled in schools in 1985, compared with only 28 per cent in 1950. Female students made up only 25 per cent of all students in 1950, but they represented 45 per cent of total enrollment in 1985.

U.S. Pressure on Dictators. In 1987, the Reagan Administration brought pressure openly on several Latin-American dictatorships. The U.S. Department of Justice weighed the possibility of in-

dicting Panamanian strongman Manuel Antonio Noriega on charges of drug trafficking. The U.S. ambassador in Paraguay publicly spoke out in favor of new leadership in a country that has been dominated by a single man—President Alfredo Stroessner—since 1954, longer than any other nation in the Western Hemisphere.

In Chile, U.S. envoys met openly with opponents of President Augusto Pinochet Ugarte, who has resisted holding free elections. In Suriname, the United States sided with the Netherlands in withholding economic aid until Suriname's Commander of the National Army Désiré D. Bouterse permitted elections in November that will presumably lead to the restoration of civilian rule.

United States support of Haiti's military leader, however, backfired when the November presidential elections were canceled because of violence that appeared to be supported by the military. The United States suspended economic and military aid to Haiti in retaliation for the failure of National Council President Henri Namphy to ensure peace at the polls.

Soviet Trade. The Soviet Union's Foreign Minister, Eduard A. Shevardnadze, toured Brazil, Argentina, and Uruguay from September 27 to October 8, drumming up trade deals. Shevardnadze assured his hosts that the Soviets did not seek to

Ecuadoreans examine the wreckage caused by an earthquake that struck in March, killing at least 300 people and perhaps as many as 4,000.

displace the United States in an area of traditional U.S. influence but sought only to expand Soviet trade opportunities.

In February, the Soviets contracted to buy 50,000 short tons (45,000 metric tons) of sugar from the Dominican Republic in each of the next three years at 8 cents per pound (0.45 kilogram), just above the depressed world price. The Soviet purchase helped take up the slack when the United States, despite protests from Caribbean sugar producers, cut back on U.S. sugar imports from Latin America on January 1. The Dominicans lost nearly half of their U.S. sugar quota.

Elsewhere in Latin America, the Soviets have quietly helped Argentina become a nuclear power by supplying fuels and services that Western nations, in compliance with several treaties, refused to sell. Argentina also began buying Soviet-made turbines for hydroelectric power plants and railroad locomotives, using profits made by selling grain and beef to the Soviets.

In 1987, the Soviet Union sought closer economic ties with Brazil, Latin America's largest economy, by selling Brazil badly needed oil and offering to help develop its computer industry. The Soviets also sought landing rights in Brazil for Aeroflot—the Soviet airline. Major projects in the works included a Soviet offer of $60 million in equipment in exchange for half the output from a large manganese-iron ore mine in the Amazon region of Brazil.

Hispanics in the United States. The U.S. Bureau of the Census reported on September 10 that Hispanics have increased their numbers within the United States by 30 per cent since 1980—five times as fast as the rest of the population. According to the Census Bureau, Hispanics numbered 18.8 million, or 7.9 per cent of the U.S. population, in 1987. The census figures also revealed that Hispanics were on the average younger than the rest of the population and thus had higher birth rates. Hispanics were also generally poorer than most other Americans.

According to the U.S. Immigration and Naturalization Service, 56.5 per cent of New York City's foreign-born residents are of Hispanic origin—excluding Puerto Ricans, who are U.S. citizens. Dominicans are the most numerous foreign-born group in New York City, followed by Jamaicans and Guyanese.

Hispanics have become a dominant political and economic force in Florida's Dade County, which includes the city of Miami. The city's Hispanic population, mostly comprising Cuban refugees, has prospered. In 1987, Miami had 30 Latin-owned banks and 1,500 Latin lawyers. Eight Spanish-language radio stations served the 30 per cent of the Hispanic population for whom Spanish is the primary language.

Pan American Games. The 10th Pan American Games, a quadrennial, Olympic-style competition for Western Hemisphere athletes, were held in Indianapolis from August 8 to 23. Nearly 4,500 athletes took part in 31 sports, together with 2,000 coaches, trainers, and officials from 38 nations. The United States won the most medals—168 gold, 118 silver, and 83 bronze. Cuba was second in medals, with 75 gold, 52 silver, and 48 bronze. Cuba's 600 athletes, coaches, and officials represented the largest contingent from the island to visit the United States since 1959.

To honor the Latin guests, the Indianapolis Museum of Art staged a landmark exhibit of Latin-American art covering the period between 1920 and 1987. The show, called "Art of the Fantastic," later toured museums in New York City, Miami, and Mexico City.

Special Olympics. Following the Pan American Games, about 380 mentally retarded athletes from Latin America competed at the Seventh International Special Olympics, held July 31 to August 8 at the University of Notre Dame and St. Mary's College in Notre Dame, Ind.   Nathan A. Haverstock

See also articles on the various Latin-American countries. In WORLD BOOK, see LATIN AMERICA and articles on the individual countries.

LAW. See CIVIL RIGHTS; COURTS; CRIME; SUPREME COURT OF THE UNITED STATES.

LEBANON. The return of Syrian forces to Beirut in February 1987 to restore order was one of the few bright spots in a disastrous year for Lebanon. The Syrians moved in, at the request of Lebanese leaders, after street battles between various factions and militias brought the country close to anarchy.

The Syrians quickly restored order in West Beirut and disarmed the militias. But clashes with the Hezbollah (Party of God) militia—a Shiite Muslim organization backed by Syria's ally Iran—left 20 Shiites dead. After the clashes, Syrian forces did not attempt to expand their control to the Beirut suburbs, which are centers of Shiite power.

Siege Lifted. In April, the Syrians also lifted a siege of two Palestinian refugee camps in southern Beirut by Amal (Hope), the largest Shiite militia. Amal had refused to allow deliveries of food to the camps. In September, Amal and the Palestine Liberation Organization (PLO) formally agreed to end three years of fighting. But battles between the two groups continued to erupt as Amal remained determined to prevent the PLO from reestablishing its power base in Lebanon.

Peace Plan. In March, the Syrians issued yet another plan for political reform in Lebanon. It differed in a number of ways from a plan proposed in late 1985. That plan had been blocked by Lebanon's dominant Maronite Christians because it

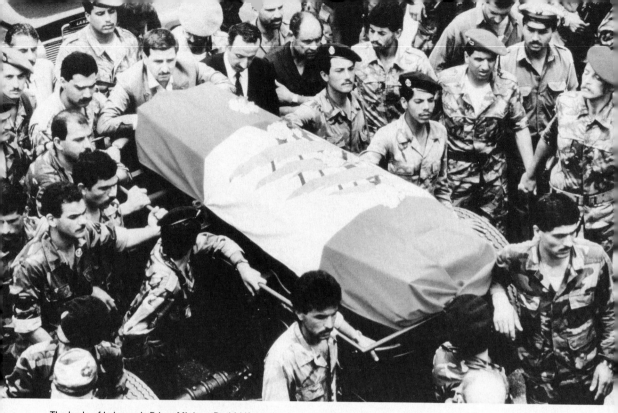

The body of Lebanon's Prime Minister Rashid Karami, who was killed in June, is escorted at his funeral in Tripoli by Lebanese soldiers.

would have weakened their power. But because the Syrians were unable to extend their authority over all of Lebanon, their new plan stood little chance of acceptance.

Hostages. Lebanon remained a dangerous place for foreigners, even those of long residence. In January, three American teachers and an Indian professor were seized at gunpoint on the campus of Beirut University College. A terrorist group calling itself Islamic Jihad (Holy War) for the Liberation of Palestine claimed responsibility. The group demanded the release of a hijacking suspect held in West Germany and some 400 Palestinians jailed in Israel as the price for their hostages' freedom.

Also in January, two West German citizens were kidnapped. In October, one of the West Germans was released, reportedly in exchange for a payment of $2.5 million and an agreement by the West German government not to extradite the hijacking suspect to the United States, where he could be sentenced to death.

After the kidnappings in January, the U.S. Department of State issued severe restrictions on travel to Lebanon. United States passports would not be valid there, and violators would face up to five years in prison and $2,000 in fines.

At year-end, Lebanese groups held 26 foreign hostages, 8 of them Americans. Among the miss-

ing was Terry Waite, an emissary of the archbishop of Canterbury. Waite had disappeared in January while on a mission sponsored by the Church of England to free hostages.

Assassinations. On June 1, the chronic Lebanese violence reached into high government circles with the assassination of Prime Minister Rashid Karami. He was killed by a bomb hidden in the cockpit of a military helicopter in which he was traveling. Karami had resigned in May to protest the lack of progress toward implementation of the Syrian peace plan, but his resignation had not been accepted by President Amine Gemayel. After the assassination, the president named Salim al-Huss, like Karami a Sunni Muslim, as acting prime minister.

Karami was not the only high official killed during the year. Gemayel's Islamic affairs adviser died during a violent demonstration by Shiite Muslims in Beirut protesting the deaths of Iranian pilgrims in Mecca, Saudi Arabia, in July, during the annual pilgrimage (see SAUDI ARABIA).

South Lebanon, along the Israeli border, remained relatively quiet for most of 1987. Israeli planes raided Palestinian refugee camps near Sidon several times in May after an upsurge of PLO attacks across the border. In July, a seaborne raid by Israeli commandos into Lebanon killed seven Lebanese Shiite militiamen. It was the first such raid since the 1982 Israeli invasion of Lebanon. In December, the Israeli Army advanced more than 1 mile (1.6 kilometers) into the Bekaa Valley in southern Lebanon in battles with guerrillas.

The Economy—or what was left of it—reflected Lebanon's collapsing political sysem. The government did not issue a 1987 budget until October. The cabinet met in April for the first time in seven months, but members could not agree on measures to deal with the worsening financial crisis. Labor leaders called a general strike in November to protest a cabinet proposal for a 40 per cent increase in the minimum wage, noting that the inflation rate was 350 per cent.

In July, the Lebanese pound, worth 7.7 to U.S. $1 in 1984, dropped to 184 to U.S. $1, and in December, it reached a record low of 480 to U.S. $1. In November, Lebanon's central bank suspended trading, leaving many Lebanese destitute. All that stood between Lebanon and bankruptcy was its reserves—$4 billion in gold and $500 million in currency, enough to cover imports for 25 months. But a cabinet proposal to sell 20 per cent of the gold reserves was opposed by the country's finance minister, who said gold sales would further erode public confidence in the currency.   William Spencer

See also MIDDLE EAST (Facts in Brief Table). In WORLD BOOK, see LEBANON.

LESOTHO. See AFRICA.

L'HEUREUX-DUBÉ, CLAIRE (1927-   ), a member of the Quebec Court of Appeal, on April 14, 1987, became the first French-Canadian woman to be appointed to the Supreme Court of Canada. She succeeded Supreme Court Justice Julien Chouinard, who died on February 6.

L'Heureux-Dubé was born in Quebec City, Que., on Sept. 7, 1927. She attended Collège Notre-Dame de Bellevue and Laval University Law Faculty, both in that city, graduating *cum laude* in 1951. Although more than half of the lawyers now graduating from Quebec law schools are women, when L'Heureux-Dubé began to practice, she was one of a mere handful of women lawyers in Quebec City. From 1952 to 1973, she worked with a Quebec City law firm, and is considered an expert on family law.

L'Heureux-Dubé was appointed to the Superior Court of Quebec in 1973 and to the Quebec Court of Appeal in 1979. She is described as a tireless worker who has helped sensitize her colleagues to women's issues. Experts disagreed over whether the new Supreme Court justice would be liberal or conservative. Most believed, however, that in issues involving the state versus individual rights, L'Heureux-Dubé would side with the individual.

L'Heureux-Dubé was married to Arthur Dubé, a university professor who died in 1978. She has two children.   Joan Stephenson

LIBERIA. The special relationship that Liberia has long had with the United States—the country was founded by Americans in the 1800's as a home for freed black slaves—was severely tested in 1987. In February, the U.S. General Accounting Office charged that the military government of President Samuel K. Doe could not account for $66.5 million in U.S. aid it received from 1980 to 1985. The Doe government was also having trouble repaying a number of loans from U.S. banks.

In February, Doe agreed to allow a group of U.S. financial experts to work with Liberian officials in 1988. The American advisers will assist in planning the national budget as well as in collecting and spending government revenues.

Despite objections from the U.S. Congress, the Administration of President Ronald Reagan gave Liberia another $40 million in aid in 1987. The Doe regime's minting of $5 coins fueled inflation and threatened Liberia's use of the U.S. dollar as its official currency.

The Doe government continued its harassment of the press, students, teachers, unions, and Christian ministries. Restrictions on opposition parties permitted Doe's party to make a clean sweep of legislative and mayoral elections held in February 1987.   J. Gus Liebenow and Beverly B. Liebenow

See also AFRICA (Facts in Brief Table). In WORLD BOOK, see LIBERIA.

LIBRARY. The Congress of the United States and President Ronald Reagan officially designated 1987 as "The Year of the Reader." Libraries and literacy organizations throughout the United States responded with programs and celebrations to focus attention on the importance of reading.

On Oct. 14, 1987, the American Library Association and the National Commission on Libraries and Information Science, a federal planning agency, launched a national campaign to put a library card in the hands of every child in the United States. The campaign, built around the theme "The Best Gift You'll Ever Give Your Child," was a response to a challenge from Secretary of Education William J. Bennett, who said that every school should have a library and every child should have and use a library card.

Librarian of Congress. In September, Daniel J. Boorstin resigned as the 12th librarian of Congress, a position he had held since 1975. The noted historian and author made many contributions during his tenure in the post, including improvements to the library's physical facilities. Historian James H. Billington, Boorstin's successor as head of the world's largest library, was sworn in on Sept. 14, 1987. Billington, a specialist in Soviet culture, was formerly director of the Woodrow Wilson International Center for Scholars at the Smithsonian Institution in Washington, D.C.

James H. Billington, right, is sworn in as librarian of Congress by Chief Justice William H. Rehnquist, left, in September as President Reagan looks on.

Library Funding. In 1987, for the sixth consecutive year, Reagan proposed the elimination of library funds from the federal budget. Federal contributions represent about 5 per cent of public library revenue. Funds to help support academic libraries were also scheduled for elimination. In August, however, the House of Representatives voted 336-89 to restore and increase library funding for fiscal year 1988. Senate action was still pending.

Spending by U.S. public libraries rose 10.7 per cent in 1986 to approximately $3.45 billion, according to an annual survey reported in August 1987 by the Library Research Center at the University of Illinois at Urbana-Champaign. It was the largest increase in the last 10 years. The center estimated the total public library circulation of books and other materials in 1986 at 1.15 billion, unchanged from 1985.

Despite these signs of financial health, librarians in 1987 struggled to meet service demands. The rapid decline of the U.S. dollar against foreign currencies—which increases the cost of books and magazines published in other countries—and escalating prices of scholarly journals hit academic libraries especially hard.   Peggy Barber

See also AMERICAN LIBRARY ASSOCIATION; CANADIAN LIBRARY ASSOCIATION. In WORLD BOOK, see LIBRARY.

LIBYA. The military machine of Leader of the Revolution Muammar Muhammad al-Qadhafi suffered a severe defeat in neighboring Chad in 1987, as Libyan forces were driven from that country after a 14-year occupation. In January, Chadian forces captured Fada, the administrative capital of northern Chad, and in March they seized Wadi Doum, a key Libyan air base in Chad. In the battles, Libya lost not only 2,000 men but also most of its huge arsenal of Soviet-supplied weaponry. In April, Libyan forces withdrew from all of northern Chad to bases in the Aozou Strip, a 43,000-square-mile (111,300-square-kilometer) border area claimed by both countries.

But Chadian President Hissein Habré was not ready to accept anything but total victory. In August, his forces drove the Libyans out of the Aozou Strip, killing 650 Libyans. Although unable to match Chadian mobility or tactics, Libya had total air superiority, and daily bombing raids destroyed the town of Aozou. On September 11, the Organization of African Unity (OAU) arranged a cease-fire. Later that month, Chad and Libya agreed to accept OAU mediation to determine the ownership of the Aozou Strip.

Qadhafi Still in Command. The Chad debacle badly tarnished Qadhafi's political luster abroad, but it had little effect on his power at home. There were some rumblings of dissent in the armed forces, however. In March, five air force men diverted a transport plane bound for Chad to Cairo, Egypt, where they received asylum. But the defeats and international hostility served only to unite the Libyan people behind their leader.

Regional Contracts. In 1987, Qadhafi continued his efforts to unite Libya with other Arab countries as part of his long-term goal of establishing a unified Arab nation. In June, he visited Algeria and urged its government to agree to a federal union of "Algibya." Initially, the visit produced nothing but a medal for Qadhafi. But in late October, Libya's Foreign Minister Ali Treiki said that the two countries had agreed in principle on "political unity."

In June, Qadhafi sent a series of videocassettes to other Arab leaders urging them to prepare their people to resist the "inevitable" invasion of the Arab homeland by the Western powers. Resistance, he said, should include rapid population growth, the development of nuclear weapons, and expanded production of consumer goods.

PLO Reconciliation. Qadhafi played an important role in the unification of various factions of the Palestine Liberation Organization (PLO) at an April meeting of the Palestine National Council. A long-time opponent of PLO Chairman Yasir Arafat, Qadhafi changed his position in an attempt to obtain a PLO commitment to an international conference on the Arab-Israeli conflict.

Libyan leader Muammar Muhammad al-Qadhafi salutes crowds in Tripoli on September 1, the 18th anniversary of the coup that brought him to power.

The Economy. Sharply reduced oil revenues, from a high of $22 billion in 1980 to $5 billion in the 1986-1987 fiscal year, brought belt-tightening and unaccustomed shortages to the Libyan people. The 1987 budget, approved by the General People's Congress in March, set development expenditures at $4.5 billion, well below the spending of previous years.

Rationing of fuel and basic food commodities was introduced for the first time since the 1969 revolution. All new housing and road construction projects were canceled. Both agricultural production and output of manufactured goods remained stagnant because of a lack of workers. Most foreign workers and technicians, on whom the Libyan economy had depended heavily, had been expelled by Libya or asked to leave by their own government.

The Great Man-Made River project, intended to make Libya self-sufficient in food production, moved ahead on schedule, however. In August, work began on the 2,500-mile (4,000-kilometer) pipeline that will carry water northward from underground reservoirs in the Sahara to farmland along the Mediterranean coast.   William Spencer

See also AFRICA (Facts in Brief Table); CHAD. In the Special Reports section, see UNDERSTANDING ISLAM. In WORLD BOOK, see LIBYA.

LIECHTENSTEIN. See EUROPE.

LITERATURE. An almost unparalleled bounty of literature was harvested in the United States in 1987. Books dealing with contemporary affairs and notable volumes of fiction were especially abundant.

In the category of contemporary affairs, books on espionage stirred controversy on both sides of the Atlantic. Peter Wright's *Spycatcher*, the autobiography of a high-ranking British counterintelligence agent, was notable partly because its publication was forbidden in Great Britain and many copies of the book were spirited there from the United States. Similarly, Bob Woodward's *VEIL: The Secret Wars of the CIA 1981-1987*, examining the clandestine operations of the Central Intelligence Agency (CIA) under Director William J. Casey, infuriated many readers in high places.

Australian Phillip Knightley's *The Second Oldest Profession* argued brilliantly that spy networks exist to perceive threats to a country, but instead often imagine or create such threats. Another book on espionage, *The Red and the Blue* by British author Andrew Sinclair, was an engrossing study of Soviet recruitment of students at England's Cambridge University between 1921 and 1935. The story of one of these students, Anthony Blunt—an especially effective Soviet spy after World War II—was ably told by Barrie Penrose and Simon Freeman in *Conspiracy of Silence*.

Toni Morrison wrote one of the finest American novels of 1987, *Beloved*, a haunting tale of a woman who flees from slavery in Kentucky.

In *Cloak & Gown*, Robin W. Winks told how Yale University provided a rich nursery of agents for U.S. intelligence agencies between 1939 and 1961. William E. Burrows' *Deep Black* explored the United States expensive but effective gathering of intelligence from satellites in orbit.

The Crimes of Patriots by Jonathan Kwitny alleged that members of the CIA operated an Australian bank to finance fraudulent and illegal schemes, including drug smuggling. Howard Blum's *I Pledge Allegiance* was a flawed but valuable study of the case of John A. Walker, Jr., a retired U.S. Navy warrant officer convicted of selling secrets to the Soviets.

In other areas of contemporary affairs, Mikhail S. Gorbachev's *Perestroika: New Thinking for Our Country and the World* was the Soviet leader's outline for the restructuring of Soviet society. It was received in the West with guarded optimism. Events in Cental America were explored in a number of books, led by Peter Davis' *Where Is Nicaragua?*, notable for its sensitive appraisal of people as well as political events.

Many books exploring the peril of AIDS (acquired immune deficiency syndrome) appeared in 1987. Among these was Randy Shilts's *And the Band Played On: Politics, People, and the AIDS Epidemic*, a thoughtful exploration of political and social aspects of the rapidly spreading disease.

Several former student radicals of the 1960's looked back on their youth. James E. Miller's *Democracy Is in the Streets* was a fine account of the events surrounding the birth of the student anti-war movement. Todd Gitlin's *The Sixties* was a masterly, unsentimental overview of the period.

A number of books explored faults in American education. Among them were Allan Bloom's best-selling *The Closing of the American Mind*, subtitled *How Higher Education Has Failed Democracy and Impoverished the Souls of Today's Students*, and E. D. Hirsch, Jr.'s *Cultural Literacy*, which urged that schools return to a basic core curriculum. See EDUCATION (Close-Up).

Robert Sam Anson's *Best Intentions* examined the deep-seated social problems that led to the slaying of a promising young black prep-school student by a white policeman in New York City. William Julius Wilson's *The Truly Disadvantaged* further examined these problems, contending that economic shifts since the 1964 Civil Rights Act have increased the numbers of the impoverished minority called the "underclass."

Fiction from the United States. The year's most acclaimed American novel was Toni Morrison's *Beloved*, a haunting tale of an escaped slave mother who kills her baby daughter rather than let slave chasers take the infant. Not far behind was Philip Roth's *The Counterlife*, the fifth and most eloquent in a series of novels exploring the tribulations of a Jewish writer in America. Nobel laureate Saul Bellow proved that his imaginative powers had not diminished in his novel *More Die of Heartbreak*.

Ward Just's *The American Ambassador* was a fine novel of generational struggle over morals and justice between a young American terrorist and his father, a high-ranking diplomat. Cynthia Ozick offered a searingly beautiful work about the legacy of a Polish-Jewish author in Sweden in *The Messiah of Stockholm*.

Walker Percy's technological thriller *The Thanatos Syndrome* satirized what he saw as a tendency to idolize behavioral science. Larry Heinemann's vivid, eerie *Paco's Story* explored the life of a wounded Vietnam veteran and won the National Book Award for fiction. Also notable was *That Night*, Alice McDermott's second novel, a brief, lyrical celebration of childhood in suburbia.

The journalist Tom Wolfe turned out a deft first novel, *The Bonfire of the Vanities*, a satire of money-grubbing in New York City. Other accomplished first novels came from Robert Boswell, Michael Dorris, Mary Gardner, and Stephen McCauley.

Steven Stern proved that fiction in the Jewish-American immigrant tradition was still vigorous in *Lazar Malkin Enters Heaven*, a collection of tales set in Stern's native Memphis, Tenn. Other promi-

Peter Taylor and Ernest Hemingway's granddaughter Mariel smile as he receives the Ritz Paris Hemingway Award in April for his novel *A Summons to Memphis*.

nent short-story collections were turned out by Frederick Barthelme, Mavis Gallant, Isabel Huggan, Sue Miller, Anne Phillips, and John Updike.

English-Speaking Countries. South Africans writing in English exported several important novels. Among them were *Foe*, by J. M. Coetzee, an engrossing retelling of Daniel Defoe's 1719 classic *Robinson Crusoe* from the point of view of a woman castaway, and Nadine Gordimer's *A Sport of Nature*, a hopeful fantasy of South Africa's future.

Australian writers contributed two interesting novels, Sumner Locke Elliott's *Waiting for Childhood* and Thomas Keneally's *The Playmakers*. From England came D. M. Thomas' *Sphinx*, Eva Figes' *The Seven Ages*, Julian Barnes's *Staring at the Sun*, Margaret Drabble's *The Radiant Way*, and Russell Hoban's *The Medusa Frequency*.

The best of the Latin-American translations was Ariel Dorfman's *The Last Song of Manuel Sendero*, a scorching satire of Chilean politics. Spain offered Juan Goytisolo's *Landscapes After the Battle*, and Portugal was represented by José Saramago's *Baltasar and Blimunda*.

Biography. Among the best literary biographies in 1987 were David Herbert Donald's *Look Homeward*, a long, brilliant portrait of novelist Thomas Wolfe. Kenneth S. Lynn's *Hemingway* contended that the source of Ernest Hemingway's "manly" fiction was a troubled masculinity caused by a domineering mother. Martin Stannard's *Evelyn Waugh: The Early Years 1903-1939* convincingly declared the English novelist a literary master.

Ronald Hayman's *Sartre: A Life* sought explanations for the often contradictory writings of the French philosopher Jean-Paul Sartre, while Annie Cohen-Solal's accomplished biography of the same title concentrated on Sartre's life.

Important figures in the fields of music and art were explored. Joseph Horowitz' *Understanding Toscanini* argued convincingly that the career of the late Italian conductor Arturo Toscanini was largely based on canny merchandising of the most popular classical music. Joan Peyser's *Bernstein* was a gossipy and controversial psychobiography of conductor Leonard Bernstein. Colin Simpson's *Artful Partners* explored art critic Bernard Berenson's relationship with the rascally art dealer Joseph Duveen. Ernest Samuels' *Bernard Berenson*, though an "official" biography, displayed its subject "warts and all."

Among political biographies, Doris Kearns's *The Fitzgeralds and the Kennedys* ably examined the intertwining of two Boston families that produced a President of the United States. Richard Gid Powers' *Secrecy and Power* closely examined the life of J. Edgar Hoover and his iron rule of the Federal Bureau of Investigation from 1924 to 1972. Stephen E. Ambrose's *Nixon* explored in a detached and objective way the often contradictory career of Richard M. Nixon before his presidency.

Other important biographies included *George C. Marshall: Statesman, 1945-1959,* by Forrest C. Pogue; *Wilbur and Orville: A Biography of the Wright Brothers,* by Fred Howard; and *Many Masks: A Life of Frank Lloyd Wright,* by Brendan Gill.

Autobiography. The year's best work in this category was *Little Wilson and Big God,* by British novelist Anthony Burgess (John Burgess Wilson). Burgess described his life to the age of 42 and the Roman Catholicism against which he rebelled. *The Enigma of Arrival* told how the Trinidad-born Indian writer V. S. Naipaul came to terms with his adopted England despite its colonial history. American author Arthur Miller looked back on a long and interesting life as a playwright and political figure in *Timebends.*

One of the year's most fascinating books was *Berlin Diaries, 1940-1945.* It told how White Russian Princess Marie Vassiltchikov, trapped in Germany by World War II, worked in the Nazi foreign ministry and witnessed the unsuccessful plot to assassinate Adolf Hitler in 1944.

Two noted critic-novelists published their memoirs in 1987. Richard Gilman's *Faith, Sex, Mystery* was the deeply affecting story of a Jewish atheist's conversion to and departure from Roman Catholicism. Mary McCarthy told of her life as a precocious child with bracing honesty in *How I Grew.*

Jonathan Raban's *Coasting* was an English journalist's engaging account of a year's introspective voyage in a small boat around the English coast. Bruce Chatwin's remarkable *Songlines* told of his immersion in Australian Aboriginal ways. Nien Cheng, a Chinese expatriate in the United States, told in *Life and Death in Shanghai* of her harrowing persecution by Red Guards during the Cultural Revolution terror of the 1960's.

Letters. Among the year's important volumes of correspondence were *The Collected Letters of Joseph Conrad: 1861 to 1897, Volume I,* edited by Frederick R. Karl and Laurence Davies. The *Frank Lloyd Wright Letters Trilogy,* edited by Bruce Brooks Pfeiffer, and *Don't Tread on Me: The Selected Letters of S. J. Perelman,* edited by Prudence Crowther, also were noteworthy.

History. In a curiously lackluster year in this genre, a few books stood out. *The Making of the Atomic Bomb* by Richard Rhodes was a massive yet engrossing study of the people and machines that brought the world into the nuclear age. It won the National Book Award for nonfiction.

Robert Hughes's *The Fatal Shore* dealt brilliantly and colorfully with the opening of Australia by convicts from England. Other significant histories were David Abraham's *The Collapse of the Weimar Republic,* Jean Levi's *The Chinese Emperor,* Nell Irvin Painter's *Standing at Armageddon: The United States, 1877-1919,* and Fritz Stern's *Dreams and Delusions: The Drama of German History.*

Science and Medicine. Among the year's most interesting books in this category was James Gleick's *Chaos: Making a New Science,* which chronicled the growth of the curious mathematical study of disorder and unpredictability. Melvin Konner's shocking *Becoming a Doctor* was an indictment of the grueling manner in which medical students are trained. Charles E. Rosenberg's *The Care of Strangers* was a perceptive history of the United States hospital system.

Best Sellers. Hardcover best sellers of the year included Scott Turow's courtroom mystery *Presumed Innocent,* Tom Clancy's *Patriot Games,* Stephen King's *Misery,* Ravi Batra's *The Great Depression of 1990,* Bernie S. Siegel's *Love, Medicine & Miracles,* and Tip O'Neill's *Man of the House.*

Among paperback best sellers were *The Road Less Traveled,* by M. Scott Peck; *The Bourne Supremacy,* by Robert Ludlum; *Women Who Love Too Much,* by Robin Norwood; *It,* by Stephen King; and *Fatherhood,* by Bill Cosby.   Henry Kisor

In the Special Reports section, see IT'S NO MYSTERY WHY EVERYBODY LOVES A MYSTERY. See also AWARDS AND PRIZES (Literature Awards); CANADIAN LITERATURE; LITERATURE FOR CHILDREN; POETRY; PUBLISHING. In WORLD BOOK, see LITERATURE.

LITERATURE FOR CHILDREN. Many books about the Constitution of the United States were published in 1987, the 200th anniversary of that document, along with an abundance of picture books and books for preschoolers. Some outstanding books of 1987 were:

Picture Books

Piggins by Jane Yolen, illustrated by Jane Dyer (Harcourt Brace Jovanovich). Bright, detailed illustrations add to the mystery of a disappearing diamond pendant. Ages 4 to 8.

Old Henry by Joan W. Blos, illustrated by Stephen Gammell (Morrow). When Henry moves into a dilapidated house, he has problems with his neighbors. Superb illustrations. Ages 5 to 8.

Humphrey's Bear by Jan Wahl, illustrated by William Joyce (Holt). A boy's adventures with his teddy bear and dramatic paintings make this an excellent bedtime story. Ages 4 to 8.

The Enchanted Book: A Tale from Krakow by Janina Porazińska, translated by Bożena Smith, illustrated by Jan Brett (Harcourt Brace Jovanovich). A miller's three daughters are caught by an enchanter. Striking paintings with Polish folk motifs. Ages 5 to 9.

26 Letters and 99 Cents by Tana Hoban (Greenwillow). The alphabet and counting with coins are taught with bright illustrations. Ages 3 to 7.

Mufaro's Beautiful Daughters: An African Tale by John Steptoe (Lothrop, Lee & Shepard Bks.). One daughter, hoping to marry the king, tries to get to the city before her sister does. Lush, dramatic paintings depict the African setting. Ages 6 to 9.

Eyes of the Dragon by Margaret Leaf, illustrated by Ed Young (Lothrop, Lee & Shepard Bks.). A village official insists that an artist add eyes to a dragon painting, with disastrous results. Haunting illustrations. Ages 4 to 8.

Owl Lake by Tejima (Philomel). Striking color woodcuts depict an owl's activities one night. Ages 2 to 6.

Death of the Iron Horse by Paul Goble (Macmillan/Bradbury). Young Cheyenne Indians derail a freight train—the "iron horse" feared by their people—and enjoy the contents. Vivid paintings illustrate a tale based on fact. Ages 5 to 9.

Prince Boghole by Erik Christian Haugaard, illustrated by Julie Downing (Macmillan). Three princes try to win the hand of a princess in this lavishly painted tale. Ages 6 to 9.

What the Mailman Brought by Carolyn Craven, illustrated by Tomie De Paola (Putnam). When Will is home sick, mysterious packages begin to arrive. Humorous paintings. Ages 5 to 8.

The Castle Builder by Dennis Nolan (Macmillan). A boy's sand castle becomes the subject of a fantasy. Superb black-dot illustrations. Ages 6 and up.

The Angel and the Soldier Boy by Peter Collington (Knopf). Two tiny toys become part of a pirate adventure in a wordless book with oversized color illustrations. Ages 3 to 7.

The Ridiculous Story of Gammer Gurton's Needle adapted by David Lloyd, illustrated by Charlotte Voake (Clarkson N. Potter). Diccon the Bedlam, a troublemaker, causes chaos in a rollicking tale with funny water-color illustrations. All ages.

Aster Aardvark's Alphabet Adventures by Steven Kellogg (Morrow). The reader romps through the alphabet with hilarious illustrations and alliterations. Ages 4 and up.

Possum Magic by Mem Fox, illustrated by Julie Vivas (Abingdon). Beautiful water colors depict Australian wildlife and foods. Glossary and map included. Ages 4 to 8.

Can You Catch Josephine? by Stéphane Poulin (Tundra). Daniel's cat comes to school and the chase begins. Humorous pictures. Ages 4 to 7.

In Coal Country by Judith Herdershot, illustrated by Thomas B. Allen (Knopf). The life of a coal-mining family is well told and effectively illustrated. Ages 7 to 11.

The Devil and Mother Crump by Valerie Scho Carey, illustrated by Arnold Lobel (Harper & Row). A comical tale of an ornery old woman who bests the Devil and angels. Ages 8 and up.

Knots on a Counting Rope by Bill Martin, Jr., and John Archambault, illustrated by Ted Rand

Hey, Al, written by Arthur Yorinks and illustrated by Richard Egielski, won the 1987 Caldecott Medal for children's picture books.

(Holt). Striking paintings show an Indian grandfather telling his blind grandson about the boy's birth and growth. Ages 4 to 8.

Paper John by David Small (Farrar, Straus & Giroux). John creates objects—even his house—out of paper, but a small devil comes and causes an uproar. Inventive. Ages 4 to 7.

The Z Was Zapped by Chris Van Allsburg (Houghton Mifflin). In an unusual alphabet book in 26 acts, the letters face hazards. Ages 8 and up.

Poetry and Songs

The Voyage of the Ludgate Hill: Travels with Robert Louis Stevenson by Nancy Willard, illustrated by Alice Provensen and Martin Provensen (Harcourt Brace Jovanovich). Stevenson's freighter trip to New York City is humorously told in verse. A funny mixture of animals is shown. Ages 7 to 12.

Cat Poems selected by Myra Cohn Livingston, illustrated by Trina Schart Hyman (Holiday House). Cat lovers will enjoy this varied collection with its expressive black-and-white illustrations. Ages 4 and up.

Dinosaurs selected by Lee Bennett Hopkins, illustrated by Murray Tinkelman (Harcourt Brace Jovanovich). Eighteen poems in various moods are dramatically illustrated. Ages 6 and up.

Annabel Lee by Edgar Allan Poe, illustrated by Gilles Tibo (Tundra). Haunting airbrush paintings

Sid Fleischman's *The Whipping Boy* won the 1987 Newbery Medal for "the most distinguished contribution to American literature for children."

capture the narrator's love for—and loss of—Annabel Lee. Ages 12 and up.

Click, Rumble, Roar: Poems About Machines selected by Lee Bennett Hopkins, photographs by Anna Held Audette (Crowell). Poems about such subjects as a car wash, power shovel, and tractor form a delightful collection. Excellent photographs. Ages 5 to 10.

This Delicious Day: 65 Poems selected by Paul B. Janeczko (Orchard Bks.). Fresh, original poems about people, animals, and feelings. All ages.

Roomrimes by Sylvia Cassedy, illustrated by Michele Chessare (Crowell). Rich, imaginative poems for each letter of the alphabet. All ages.

Fantasy

The Tricksters by Margaret Mahey (Macmillan/Margaret K. McElderry). Three brothers mysteriously appear near the Hamiltons' seaside New Zealand home, with alarming results. Ages 12 and up.

Dr. Dredd's Wagon of Wonders by Bill Brittain, illustrated by Andrew Glass (Harper & Row). The villagers are in trouble when Calvin runs away from his evil master, Dr. Dredd. Ages 9 to 12.

Who's Afraid? And Other Strange Tales by Philippa Pearce (Greenwillow). Supernatural tales of people, places, and objects are effectively written. Ages 12 and up.

Redwall by Brian Jacques, illustrated by Gary Chalk (Putnam/Philomel). The abbey mice and their friends try to save Redwall Abbey from Cluny the Scourge—a one-eyed rat—and his horde. Ages 12 and up.

The Naked Bear edited by John Bierhorst, illustrated by Dirk Zimmer (Morrow). Varied, often humorous folktales of the Iroquois Indians have interesting introductions and good pen-and-ink drawings. Ages 10 and up.

They Dance in the Sky: Native American Star Myths by Jean Guard Monroe and Ray A. Williamson, illustrated by Edgar Stewart. Eight sections of several short tales have good pencil drawings. Ages 10 and up.

Through the Hidden Door by Rosemary Wells (Dial). Barney, in trouble at boarding school, is befriended by Snowy, who shows him a secret cave with strange contents. Riveting. Ages 10 to 14.

Fiction

Edith Herself by Ellen Howard (Atheneum/Jean Karl). Edith, growing up in the 1890's, must adjust to epilepsy and to living with her sister after her mother dies. Ages 12 and up.

Fat: A Love Story by Barbara Wersba (Harper & Row). Rita, fat all of her 16 years, gets a job delivering cheesecake and falls hopelessly in love. Ages 12 and up.

Fell by M. E. Kerr (Harper & Row). Life becomes complicated when John Fell agrees to an unusual proposition. Ages 12 and up.

Isaac Campion by Janni Howker (Greenwillow). Isaac's life is shaped by the death of his brother and his father's bitterness. Ages 12 and up.

Moon Lake Angel by Vera Cleaver (Lothrop, Lee & Shepard Bks.). Resourceful Kitty, deserted by both parents, plots revenge against her mother. Ages 10 and up.

Rabble Starkey by Lois Lowry (Houghton Mifflin). Rabble and her mom find a loving home until problems arise. Ages 12 and up.

The Ruby in the Smoke by Philip Pullman (Knopf). Sally Lockhart tries to solve the mystery of her father's death in this tale of murder in London in the 1800's. Ages 12 and up.

The Goats by Brock Cole (Farrar, Straus & Giroux). As a prank, Laura and Howie are left nude on an island. Ages 12 and up.

Children of Christmas by Cynthia Rylant, illustrated by S. D. Schindler (Orchard Bks.). Six unusual stories about loneliness and love at Christmas. Ages 8 and up.

Sons from Afar by Cynthia Voigt (Atheneum). James hopes he will understand himself better when he finds his father, but the results of the search are unexpected. Ages 12 and up.

Shadow on Hawthorne Bay by Janet Lunn (Scribner). Mary's extrasensory perception leads her from Scotland to Canada, where she encounters numerous problems. Ages 12 and up.

M. E. and Morton by Sylvia Cassedy (Harper/Crowell). Mary Ella, extremely bright, and her slow brother find a friend who turns their lives upside down. Ages 12 and up.

Hatchet by Gary Paulsen (Macmillan/Bradbury). A survival story of a boy who uses a hatchet to cope with the wilderness. Ages 12 and up.

Devil Storm by Theresa Nelson (Orchard Bks.). A gripping fictional account of the 1900 hurricane that devastated Galveston, Tex., and the nearby Bolivar Peninsula. Ages 10 to 12.

Class Clown by Johanna Hurwitz, illustrated by Sheila Hamanaka (Morrow). Lucas gets into trouble at school and decides to try to behave. Humorous. Ages 7 to 9.

Pig-Out Inn by Lois Ruby (Houghton Mifflin). Dovi helps her mom run a diner and care for a young boy, abandoned by his father, and finds many surprises in a small town. Ages 12 and up.

People, Places, Animals, and Projects

Maggie by My Side by Beverly Butler (Dodd, Mead). The blind author describes her experiences with one of her guide dogs. Full of fascinating information. Ages 11 and up.

Handtalk Birthday: A Number & Story Book in Sign Language by Remy Charlip and Mary Beth Miller, illustrated by George Ancona (Macmillan/Four Winds). Through amusing color photographs, children can learn hand signs for words and numbers. Ages 5 and up.

Shh! We're Writing the Constitution by Jean Fritz, illustrated by Tomie De Paola (Putnam). A readable, often humorous account of the problems the Founding Fathers faced creating the U.S. Constitution. Ages 8 and up.

Into a Strange Land: Unaccompanied Refugee Youth in America by Brent and Melissa Ashabranner (Dodd, Mead). Fine photographs illustrate this interesting and moving book about the problems faced by refugee children sent alone to the United States. Bibliography and index. Ages 12 and up.

The American Revolutionaries: A History in Their Own Words 1750-1800 by Milton Meltzer (Crowell). A fascinating account beginning with an immigrant's description of the horrors of the voyage from England to Philadelphia. Included are the Bill of Rights and an index. Ages 12 and up.

From Flower to Flower: Animals and Pollination by Patricia Lauber, photos by Jerome Wexler (Crown). A clear description of pollination with superb photographs. Ages 7 to 11.

There Once Was a Time by Piero Ventura (Putnam). A history of people—including their work, living conditions, clothing, and travel—from ancient times to the present is profusely illustrated in color. Ages 10 and up.

Icebergs and Glaciers by Seymour Simon (Morrow). Clear, simple prose and excellent color photographs explain how glaciers and icebergs form and behave. Ages 6 to 9.

A Visit to Washington, D.C. by Jill Krementz (Scholastic Hardcover). Matt Wilson, 6, tells of his favorite spots and the usual attractions. Excellent color photographs. Ages 4 to 8.

The Alamo by Leonard Everett Fisher (Holiday House). The story of the famous landmark is accompanied by dramatic illustrations. Index. Ages 10 and up.

Harold Roth's Big Book of Horses by Margo Lundell (Grosset & Dunlap). The reader learns all about various kinds of horses, how they are trained, and what they do. Clear simple text with wonderful color photographs. Ages 6 to 11.

Awards in 1987 included:

The Newbery Medal for the best American children's book was awarded to Sid Fleischman for *The Whipping Boy.* The Caldecott Medal for "the most distinguished American picture book for children" went to Richard Egielski for *Hey, Al.* Lothrop was cited by the Mildred L. Batchelder Award for its publication of *No Hero for the Kaiser* by Rudolf Frank.   Marilyn Fain Apseloff

In WORLD BOOK, see CALDECOTT MEDAL; LITERATURE FOR CHILDREN; NEWBERY MEDAL.

LOS ANGELES. An earthquake struck the Los Angeles area on the morning of Thursday, Oct. 1, 1987, causing at least seven deaths, hundreds of injuries, and property damage estimated at more than $213 million. The quake, the third largest to hit Los Angeles in the last 50 years, was centered in the San Gabriel Valley, about 10 miles (16 kilometers) east of downtown Los Angeles.

The earthquake damaged thousands of buildings throughout the Los Angeles area, knocked out electrical power to 500,000 homes and businesses, and forced the temporary closing of two freeways. Many residents—an estimated 2,000 within the city limits alone—were displaced from their homes. The fatalities included a 23-year-old student at California State University at Los Angeles who was killed when the wall of a campus parking garage collapsed. At least three deaths were attributed to heart attacks.

On October 4, an aftershock caused additional property damage, but no deaths were reported. The earthquake and aftershock were the strongest and most damaging to hit the Los Angeles area since 1971, when a quake killed 64 people and caused $500 million in property damage.

Pope Visits City. An estimated 250,000 people lined the streets of a Los Angeles parade route to see Pope John Paul II on September 15 as the pontiff arrived for a two-day visit. The pope later celebrated Mass before more than 100,000 people in the Los Angeles Memorial Coliseum.

Helping the Homeless. In an effort to aid the growing homeless population in Los Angeles, the city opened an "urban campground" on June 15 in the downtown area. The 12-acre (4.9-hectare) campsite, on land owned by the Southern California Rapid Transit District, became a temporary home for an estimated 2,600 men, women, and children. The campers erected tents, cardboard shelters, and other makeshift dwellings at the site.

Despite attempts by activists to keep the campground open, the city closed it on September 25. Mayor Thomas Bradley and other city officials said the site had been intended only as an emergency response to the homeless problem, not a permanent solution. Meanwhile, the Los Angeles City Council on August 28 approved the purchase of 102 used mobile homes to house the homeless.

Freeway Violence resulted in the death of 4 people and the wounding of 16 others in the Los Angeles area during the summer and early fall. Nearly 100 incidents of roadway violence, many involving guns, were reported to the Los Angeles Sheriff's Department during that period. Law-enforcement officials said the rash of violence was most likely caused by drivers' frustration with increasingly congested roads.

On September 26, California Governor George Deukmejian signed into law several state bills

Rubble covers vehicles in Los Angeles in October after an earthquake that caused at least seven deaths and an estimated $213 million in damage.

aimed at cracking down on freeway aggression. The bills increased the penalties for shootings and other forms of violence and put more California Highway Patrol officers on the freeways.

Schools. In a move to ease overcrowding in classrooms, the Los Angeles Board of Education voted on October 12 to put all schools in the Los Angeles Unified School District on a year-round schedule. A week later, the school board reversed itself and postponed action until 1988.

In 1987, about 25 per cent of the district's 592,000 students attended schools operating on a year-round calendar. At those schools, the student body is divided into groups that follow different schedules—while some students are in school, others are on vacation.

Police Tax. In the June 2 city election, Los Angeles voters overwhelmingly rejected a proposal to raise the property tax in several inner-city districts to pay for additional police officers in those areas. The measure, which had stirred opposition from community leaders who felt that their neighborhoods were being unfairly singled out, lost by a 6 to 1 margin.   Victor Merina

See also CITY. In WORLD BOOK, see LOS ANGELES.

LOUISIANA. See STATE GOVERNMENT.
LUXEMBOURG. See EUROPE.
MADAGASCAR. See AFRICA.

Peter G. Diamandis led a group of officers of the CBS magazines division who bought the division from CBS Inc. in July for $650 million.

MAGAZINE advertising revenues in the United States increased in 1987 by about 5.5 per cent over 1986, reaching a record $5.4 billion. The number of advertising pages also rose in 1987, totaling nearly 156,000, an increase of 3.1 per cent.

The combined circulation per issue of all consumer magazines surveyed by the Audit Bureau of Circulations (ABC) in the United States climbed to 336.5 million during the first six months of 1987, up 3.4 per cent over the same period in 1986. The ABC is an independent company that issues circulation figures, verified by auditors, for magazines and other publications.

An annual survey conducted by the Magazine Publishers Association (MPA) and Price Waterhouse indicated that U.S. magazines were more profitable in 1986 than in 1985. The magazines showed a pretax operating profit of 11.0 per cent, compared with 9.7 per cent in 1985.

According to a survey conducted in the spring of 1987 by Mediamark Research, Incorporated, about 94 per cent of all U.S. adults read magazines and they read about 10 different issues per month. The average magazine reader is in his or her late 30's, has at least a high school education, is married, and has a household income above the national average.

Awards. The MPA named George V. Grune, chairman of the board and chief executive officer of the Reader's Digest Association, Incorporated, to receive the 1987 Henry Johnson Fisher Award, the industry's most prestigious honor. The Kelly Award for outstanding magazine advertising was presented to McKinney, Silver, and Rockett, an advertising agency in Raleigh, N.C., for its North Carolina travel and tourism advertising campaign.

The American Society of Magazine Editors presented its National Magazine Awards in April. Winners were *Consumer Reports* for personal service, *Sports Afield* for special interests, *Life* for reporting, *Money* for public interest, *Elle* for design, *National Geographic* for photography, *Esquire* for fiction, *Outside* for essays and criticism, and *Bulletin of the Atomic Scientists* for single-topic issue.

In the category of general excellence, which is presented in four groups according to circulation size, the winners were *New England Monthly* (less than 100,000); *Common Cause* (100,000 to 400,000); *Elle* (400,000 to 1,000,000); and *People Weekly* (more than 1 million).

New Magazines aimed at the affluent appeared in 1987, bearing such names as *Millionaire*, *MBA*, *Condé Nast's Traveler*, *Veranda*, and *Tiffany*. Other new magazines covered a wide variety of special interests, from *Baby Times* and *Cooking Light* to *Southern Travel* and *Video Digest*. Murdoch Magazines, with French publisher Hachette Publications, launched a film magazine called *Premiere*.

Changes. *Ms.* celebrated its 15th anniversary and was sold to Australian publisher John Fairfax Limited. Time Incorporated sold its science magazine *Discover* to Family Media, Incorporated, for $26 million.

The largest magazine transaction of 1987 was the purchase of the CBS magazines division from CBS Inc. by the officers of the division, headed by Peter G. Diamandis. The sales price was $650 million. The flagship magazine of both the old CBS division and the new Diamandis Communications, Incorporated, is *Woman's Day.* Soon after the CBS purchase, Diamandis Communications sold four of its special interest magazines—*Field & Stream, Home Mechanix, Skiing,* and *Yachting*—to Times Mirror Magazines for $167.5 million.

Gottlieb to *New Yorker*. Samuel I. Newhouse, Jr., whose family acquired *The New Yorker* magazine in 1985, announced on Jan. 13, 1987, that Robert A. Gottlieb would succeed William Shawn as editor of that magazine. Gottlieb was president and editor in chief of Alfred A. Knopf, a subsidiary of Random House—also a Newhouse property. Shawn succeeded Harold Ross, *The New Yorker*'s founding editor, in 1952.   Francine J. Holzer

See also PUBLISHING. In WORLD BOOK, see MAGAZINE.

MAINE. See STATE GOVERNMENT.

MALAWI. See AFRICA.

MALAYSIA. Prime Minister Mahathir bin Mohamed defeated an unusual challenge to his leadership on April 24, 1987, when he was narrowly reelected president of the United Malays National Organization (UMNO). Because UMNO is the largest party in Malaysia's ruling coalition, its president automatically becomes prime minister.

Mahathir's bid for a third three-year term had been opposed by party members who charged that his administration was corrupt. Tunku (Prince) Razaleigh Hamzah, Malaysia's minister of trade and industry, ran against Mahathir with the support of UMNO Deputy President Musa Hitam. Such dissension within the ruling party is rare. In fact, Mahathir was unopposed in his two previous bids for the UMNO presidency. But in 1987, almost half of the 1,479 party delegates voted for the opposition. Mahathir won by only 43 votes.

After the election, the UMNO remained split, and the losers threatened to fight Mahathir again. On April 28, Razaleigh and Foreign Minister Rais Yatim resigned their Cabinet posts. On April 30, Mahathir fired three other ministers and four deputy ministers who had sided with Razaleigh.

Racial Tensions developed in October between the Malay ethnic majority and the large Chinese ethnic minority. Protests were sparked when the government appointed teachers who did not speak the Mandarin Chinese dialect to work in Chinese primary schools. Beginning on October 27, the government closed three newspapers and arrested 106 people under a law that permitted detention without trial. Those arrested were mostly ethnic Chinese, including the leader of Malaysia's main opposition party. Mahathir said he acted to prevent racial riots, but critics accused him of violating democratic principles.

In March and April, 653 ethnic Chinese guerrillas surrendered to the Thai army at the Malaysia-Thailand border. The Thais granted amnesty to those who surrendered and gave them land to farm. The guerrillas were members of the Communist Party of Malaysia.

Economic Conditions improved in 1987. In 1985, falling world prices for Malaysia's main exports—palm oil, crude oil, rubber, cocoa, timber, and tin—caused the economy to contract by 1 per cent. In 1986, the economy grew by only 1 per cent. But in 1987 prices began to rise for raw-material exports, especially oil, whose price almost doubled. Exports of manufactured goods rose by one-third. As a result, the government expected a 2 per cent growth rate in 1987.   Henry S. Bradsher

See also ASIA (Facts in Brief Table). In WORLD BOOK, see MALAYSIA.

MALDIVES. See ASIA.

MALI. See AFRICA.

MALTA. See EUROPE.

MANITOBA. The New Democratic Party administration of Premier Howard Pawley, helped by a bustling economy, enacted a vigorous legislative program in 1987. This program included the passage of a controversial amendment to Manitoba's Human Rights Code that guaranteed the civil rights of homosexuals and creating a new system of arbitration in labor disputes. The labor legislation allowed an arbitrator in a dispute to impose the final offer of the union or the employer.

The provincial budget, presented on March 16, raised taxes for high-income earners, making Manitoba families with an income of $150,000 the highest-taxed group in Canada. (All monetary amounts in this article are Canadian dollars with $1 = U.S. 77 cents as of Dec. 31, 1987.) In addition, a flat tax of 2 per cent—designed to by-pass the deductions and exemptions of the federal tax system—was imposed on the net income of all Manitoba taxpayers.

In April, the 52-year-old Pawley, formerly a small-town lawyer, was ordered to pay $10,000 in damages for defaming the leader of a citizens' group protesting the government's 1984 plan to extend French-language services in the province. In its ruling, the court said that Pawley had gone beyond "fair comment" in his remarks about the complainant.   David M. L. Farr

In WORLD BOOK, see MANITOBA.

MANUFACTURING. After years of stagnation, plant closings, and layoffs, United States manufacturers enjoyed a boom year in 1987. The turnaround was significant because in recent years U.S.-made goods have suffered from a reputation for shoddy quality and high cost. Industry had bloated payrolls and outdated manufacturing plants and machinery. Foreign competition was stiff, and U.S. managers focused mainly on domestic sales rather than selling to emerging global markets. Even when attempts were made to market overseas, the overvalued U.S. dollar kept American products from being competitive.

The face of U.S. manufacturing has changed considerably over the last 20 years. The United States lost its leadership position in the production of mass commodity items, such as textiles, shoes, consumer electronics, and, recently, even some mass-produced semiconductor memory chips.

But U.S. manufacturers finally reacted to these developments in the 1980's, and the first positive results were seen in 1987. Older plants were shut down, and modern, more efficient facilities were opened. For example, according to *Time* magazine, General Electric Company shut down 30 aging plants from 1981 to 1986, while opening 20 new factories. The big three automakers—General Motors Corporation (GM), Ford Motor Company, and Chrysler Corporation—also continued to shut down older plants and to retool and open new facilities with advanced production techniques that incorporate computer-integrated manufacturing and robotics.

Modernization affected the steel industry, too. "For the first time in 30 years, we have lower costs of producing steel for our customers in the United States than the Japanese industry has in providing steel to their customers in Japan," Chairman David M. Roderick of USX Corporation (formerly United States Steel Corporation) told *Time.* USX was actually able to sell "20,000 tons of hot-rolled bands to an Osaka [Japan] tube company at a price 12 per cent below that of Japanese producers," Roderick said.

A major reason U.S. manufacturers were able to sell their goods overseas was the 35 per cent fall in the value of the dollar during 1986 and 1987. The drop in the dollar's value made U.S. goods less expensive, in many cases, than the goods of producers overseas. The declining dollar finally helped make a small dent in the daunting U.S. trade deficit, which reached $156 billion in 1986. In the first half of 1987, U.S. exports were up nearly 15 per cent over the first half of 1986. The export wave was led by chemicals, paper products, and lumber, which are extremely price-sensitive.

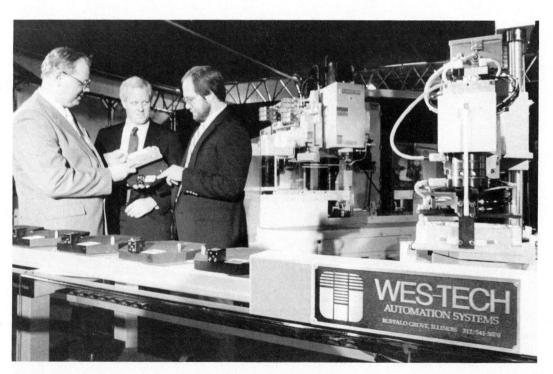

Executives examine the components of a completely automated "minifactory"— touted as the factory of the future—that was exhibited in June in Chicago.

An employee of Levi Strauss & Company in El Paso, Tex., unloads a gigantic washing machine that can wash 500 pairs of jeans at a time.

Total manufacturing shipments through the first nine months of 1987 were $1.8 trillion, up 5.1 per cent over 1986. Industrial production rose at a brisk annual rate of 8.7 per cent in the third quarter. Production rose 0.4 per cent in November, but much of the rise was due to automobile production, and many of the automobiles produced remained unsold on dealer lots. Chrysler and GM continued to close plants, and even Volkswagen announced it would close its Pennsylvania plant, the first opened in the United States by a foreign auto manufacturer. At the same time, however, three Japanese automakers—Honda, Toyota, and Nissan—announced plans to build new plants in the United States.

Employment. Increased sales meant more jobs. More than 423,000 civilian jobs were created in the third quarter of 1987 alone. Most new jobs continued to be in the service sector, but manufacturing jobs also rose significantly. There were 19.2 million manufacturing jobs in October 1987. Between June and October, 300,000 new jobs were created as U.S. manufacturers geared up to produce more goods for export markets. About 2 million manufacturing jobs had been lost in the streamlining of the 1981 to 1984 period out of a total industrial work force of 20.3 million. But by 1987, half of the eliminated manufacturing jobs had been recovered.

Factories Were Humming. Manufacturing capacity, which had been at 79.1 per cent in October 1986, improved to 81.7 per cent in November 1987. That was more like the average 81.5 per cent utilization figure of the 1960's and 1970's. Some facilities, such as paper and plastics factories, were operating at almost full capacity—96 per cent—to meet domestic and overseas demand.

New Factory Orders were up 1.3 per cent in October 1987, compared with October 1986. According to the Department of Commerce, orders for *durable goods* (goods expected to last three or more years) and *nondurable goods* (goods expected to last less than three years) rose to an adjusted $209.7 billion in November 1987. Orders were especially strong for automobiles, ships, tanks, and civilian aircraft.

Productivity in U.S. manufacturing plants also improved in 1987. American workers continued to produce more per hour than workers in any other country. Overall output per worker-hour—including farm and service industries—increased by 3.5 per cent in 1986 and was up by an annual rate of 2.6 per cent in the third quarter of 1987.

Manufacturing productivity was up at a 4.5 per cent annual rate. The main reasons for the increase were improved quality control, plant modernization, and low wage increases—an average of less than 3 per cent a year—for factory workers.

But the U.S. lead in productivity was slipping, and Japan was gaining, according to *Industry Week* magazine. Japanese plants use more advanced production techniques with four times as many robots as U.S. plants—40,000 versus 10,000. And Japanese plants are generally more modern—10 years old on average, compared with an average age of 17 years in the United States. Finally, Japanese plants have lower administrative costs because a greater proportion of their workers are directly engaged in production, rather than overseeing production. The ratio of white-collar to blue-collar workers in the United States is 14 to 1; in Japan, the ratio is 8 to 1.

Machine Tool Orders rebounded smartly during the second half of 1987. Orders were up 29 per cent in September over August, to $183.1 million. In October, tool orders surged 46.2 per cent from September to $267.3 million. This October 1987 figure was 48.4 per cent over that of October 1986, according to the National Machine Tool Builders Association.

Machine tools are power-driven tools used to cut or shape metal. They are used heavily by the automobile, aerospace, and other manufacturing industries and are an indicator of future *capital investment* (spending on new factories and equipment). Total orders for the first 10 months of 1987 were $1.74 billion, down 6.3 per cent from 1986. The decline was due to ongoing competition

A worker at a Goodyear Tire & Rubber company plant in Ohio looks over tank tracks built for the U.S. Army's new M1 supertank.

from imports. Machine tool imports accounted for 55 per cent of the U.S. market in 1986.

Research and Development (R & D). The United States spends more money on R & D than any other country. The R & D expenditures in Japan, however, account for 3 per cent of Japan's gross national product (GNP)—the value of all goods and services produced—while the U.S. figure is only 2.5 per cent. The largest nongovernmental R & D spenders are GM ($4.1 billion), Ford ($4.0 billion), International Business Machines Corporation ($3.9 billion), American Telephone and Telegraph Company ($2.3 billion), and General Electric ($1.3 billion), according to *Business Week* magazine.

Double-digit annual increases in R & D spending were common in the 1970's. In 1987, the increase will be only an estimated 7.28 per cent, according to the National Science Foundation. The federal government accounted for $60.35 billion in R & D spending, including increased expenditures for the Strategic Defense Initiative, also known as "Star Wars." Private industry accounted for $58.57 billion in research. Universities, colleges, and nonprofit groups accounted for $4.1-billion.

Capital Investment. A major indicator of business confidence in the economy is spending on capital investment. This includes expenditures on all types of equipment, from furnaces to new factories to computers. According to the Department of Commerce, capital spending in 1987 was only 1.4 per cent above 1986. Two problems affecting this spending were high interest rates, which made borrowing for plants and equipment expensive, and the 1986 Tax Reform Act, which took away tax benefits previously available to businesses investing in new equipment.

Black Monday. When the U.S. stock market lost 22.6 per cent of its value in one day on Oct. 19, 1987, it sent shock waves throughout the economy. Although the economy was strong before the crash, the impact on manufacturing remained to be seen. Some economists feared that a slowdown in consumer spending due to reduced personal wealth and uncertainty over the future could lead to a recession.

On the other hand, the opportunity that arose in 1987 to compete overseas due to the devaluation of the dollar and a more accessible global market made the future look brighter. Products made in the United States were attractive once again. For one year at least, manufacturing was back with renewed vigor. Ronald Kolgraf

In WORLD BOOK, see MANUFACTURING.

MARINE CORPS, U.S. See ARMED FORCES.
MARYLAND. See STATE GOVERNMENT.
MASSACHUSETTS. See STATE GOVERNMENT.

MATLIN, MARLEE (1965-), received the Academy of Motion Picture Arts and Sciences Award for best actress on March 30, 1987. Matlin won the award for her first film performance. She portrayed Sarah Norman, a stubborn and withdrawn deaf woman, in the romantic drama *Children of a Lesser God*. Matlin was the first deaf actress to win an Oscar.

Matlin was born in Morton Grove, Ill., a Chicago suburb, on Aug. 24, 1965. At the age of 18 months, she contracted roseola, a childhood illness that left her almost completely deaf. When Matlin was 8 years old, she began acting in sign-language productions at the Center on Deafness in Des Plaines, Ill. Her first role was Dorothy in *The Wizard of Oz*. She also starred in the center's productions of *Annie*, *Peter Pan*, and *Mary Poppins*.

After graduation from a program for the hearing impaired at John Hersey High School in Arlington Heights, Ill., Matlin studied criminal justice at William Rainey Harper Junior College in Palatine, Ill. When she was 18, she played a minor part in *Children of a Lesser God* at Chicago's Immediate Theater. Matlin won the lead in the film version after a casting director saw a videotape of her performance. Her second film, *Walker*, opened in November 1987. Jinger Griswold

MAURITANIA. See AFRICA.
MAURITIUS. See AFRICA.

McKENNA, FRANK JOSEPH (1948-   ), a 39-year-old criminal lawyer and leader of the Liberal Party in New Brunswick, Canada, took office as premier of the province on Oct. 27, 1987. In elections on October 13, McKenna's party had won a stunning victory over the Progressive Conservative Party of Premier Richard P. Hatfield. See NEW BRUNSWICK.

During his campaign, McKenna criticized the Meech Lake accord of June 3—an agreement between the federal government and the provinces that led to Quebec's formal acceptance of the 1982 Canadian constitution—and said that he would work to persuade the other premiers that changes in the agreement were needed. After the election, he declared that his first priority would be the creation of jobs in New Brunswick.

McKenna was born in Apohaqui, N.B., on Jan. 19, 1948. He graduated from St. Francis Xavier University in Antigonish, N.S., in 1970. After a year of graduate work in political science at Queen's University at Kingston in Ontario, he entered the University of New Brunswick in Fredericton, receiving a law degree in 1974.

McKenna entered the New Brunswick legislature in the 1982 election. He won the Liberal Party leadership in 1985.

In 1972, McKenna married Julie Friel. They have three children.　　　　　Joan Stephenson

McLAUGHLIN, ANN DORE (1941-   ), became United States secretary of labor on Dec. 17, 1987. She succeeded William E. Brock III, who resigned effective November 1. She is only the second woman to head the Labor Department, after Frances Perkins from 1933 to 1945.

McLaughlin, the former Ann Lauenstein, was born in Newark, N.J., on Nov. 16, 1941. She received a bachelor of arts degree from Marymount College in Tarrytown, N.Y., in 1963. After working for the American Broadcasting Companies, Incorporated (ABC), in New York City, she returned to Marymount in 1966 as director of alumnae relations.

McLaughlin obtained her first political appointment in 1971 when she became the communications director of President Richard M. Nixon's reelection committee. In 1973, she was appointed director of the office of public affairs at the Environmental Protection Agency (EPA). She left the EPA in 1974 and in 1977 started her own public relations firm.

McLaughlin returned to government work in 1981 as the assistant secretary for public affairs at the Department of the Treasury. In 1984, she became an undersecretary of the interior.

McLaughlin married John J. McLaughlin, an editor of the conservative journal *National Review*, in 1975.　　　　　Barbara A. Mayes

MEDICINE. On Sept. 5 and 6, 1987, in one of the rarest and most complicated operations ever performed, a 70-member surgical team at Johns Hopkins Hospital in Baltimore successfully separated 7-month-old Siamese twin boys joined at the back of the head.

The boys, Patrick and Benjamin Binder, were born on February 2 in Ulm, West Germany. The twins shared a broad band of flesh, skull, and brain tissue and an important blood vessel that drains blood and fluid from the brain. They were attached in such a way that they would be bedridden for life, unable to sit, stand, or walk.

In the 22-hour operation, surgeons separated the twins, using special techniques that divided the shared tissue. Following the surgery, the infants were heavily sedated. The drug-induced coma was intended to prevent complications that could cause permanent brain damage. By year-end, the twins were conscious and in stable condition.

Three-Way Transplants. Johns Hopkins also was the site of the United States first "living donor" heart transplant on May 12. The transplant involved a complex, carefully coordinated series of operations on three different patients.

It all began when surgeons transplanted the heart and lungs of an accident victim into a patient suffering from *cystic fibrosis,* an inherited disease that causes some cells to secrete thick mucus, damaging the lungs and other organs. Surgeons believed that transplanting both heart and lungs would be more effective than transplanting only the lungs. Because the cystic fibrosis patient's heart was healthy, surgeons were able to transplant it into a victim of heart disease.

This was not the first three-way transplant, however. On May 14, officials at Harefield Hospital in Middlesex, England, announced that two similar—but unpublicized—three-way transplants were performed earlier. One took place in late April; the other occurred in early May.

Youngest Heart Recipient. A 3-hour-old boy from Surrey, Canada, near Vancouver, became the world's youngest heart transplant recipient on October 16. The baby, Paul Holc, was diagnosed before he was born as having a fatal heart malfunction called *hypoplastic left heart syndrome.* Physicians at Loma Linda University Medical Center in Loma Linda, Calif., delivered the baby by Caesarean section when a donor heart became available from another Canadian baby, who was born without a brain. It was necessary to perform the transplant operation as quickly as possible after Paul was born because his condition could have deteriorated rapidly, according to Elmar P. Sakala, the university's chief of obstetrics.

Transplant for Parkinson's. Surgeons at Vanderbilt University Medical Center in Nashville, Tenn., on April 9 transplanted adrenal gland tissue into the brain of a woman with Parkinson's disease. This was the first such transplant performed in the United States.

Parkinson's disease is a progressive nerve disorder that causes tremors, loss of muscle control, and other symptoms. The disease is believed to be the result of a deficiency of *dopamine*, a chemical that transmits nerve impulses, in the brain. The adrenal glands, located near the kidney, produce hormones that are chemically similar to dopamine.

The transplant followed an April report in *The New England Journal of Medicine* indicating that patients with Parkinson's disease who received adrenal cell transplants in October 1986 had shown a marked improvement. The 1986 transplants were performed in Mexico City, where the technique was developed.

Benefits of Mammograms. A major American Cancer Society (ACS) study concluded on Sept. 17, 1987, that *mammograms,* X rays of the breast that are recommended for women over age 50 as a test for cancer, can save the lives of younger women as well. The study found that regular mammograms can detect extremely small, localized breast cancers in women between the ages of 40 and 49.

If detected early, breast cancer can be treated more effectively, increasing the patient's chances for survival. The ACS said the benefits of routine mammograms were already well established for women over age 50 and that the new study helped to eliminate any uncertainties about the benefits of routine mammograms for younger women.

The value of routine mammograms was dramatized in October, when the procedure detected a small cancerous tumor in the left breast of first lady Nancy Reagan. She underwent surgery on October 17, and physicians said her prospects for a full recovery were excellent because the cancer had been found and treated early.

Cause of Muscular Dystrophy Found. Researchers at the Howard Hughes Medical Institute of Children's Hospital in Boston reported on December 23 that they had identified the cause of Duchenne muscular dystrophy (DMD), the most common form of the muscle-wasting disease muscular dystrophy. According to the researchers, a protein called *dystrophin,* normally made by muscle cells, is missing in DMD victims. The protein probably plays a role in muscle contraction. The Muscular Dystrophy Association in New York City called the discovery "the most important step" ever taken on the way to a treatment for the disease.

Cancer Fight Effective? A study released on April 15 concluded that government health officials had overstated the progress made in treating cancer. The study, conducted by the General Accounting Office (GAO), the congressional auditing and investigative agency, said that between 1950

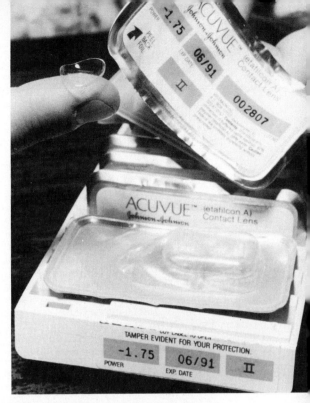

Johnson & Johnson unveils Acuvue, a disposable contact lens, on July 14. The contacts can be worn up to a week before being discarded.

and 1982 there was little or no improvement in the survival rate for most common cancers.

The GAO examined cancer statistics compiled by the National Cancer Institute (NCI) in Bethesda, Md., that seemed to indicate a significant decrease in cancer deaths in the United States. But the GAO found that the billions of dollars used to fund cancer research had resulted in less progress than that claimed by the NCI. The study found that the NCI statistics appeared to show advances because of a number of possible distorting factors. These ranged from changes in compiling statistical data to earlier detection of more easily curable cancers. Vincent T. DeVita, Jr., NCI director, criticized the GAO report and insisted that significant progress had been made in fighting cancer.

Regular Examinations. The American Heart Association (AHA) in Dallas on June 8 issued its first set of comprehensive recommendations on routine physical examinations that can help prevent heart and blood-vessel disease. The AHA said that routine medical examinations for people who appear healthy should begin at age 20 and be repeated at least every 5 years until age 60. People between the ages of 60 and 75 who have no symptoms of cardiovascular disease should have medical checkups every 2½ years. Healthy adults need annual examinations only after they reach age 75, according to the AHA.

The first medical examination should include the patient's body weight, blood pressure, and the levels of cholesterol, fats, and sugar in the blood. Those tests should be repeated every five years. An additional blood pressure reading should be taken midway between each checkup. The AHA also recommended an *electrocardiogram* (a record of the electrical impulses produced by the heart) at ages 20, 40, and 60, and a chest X ray at 40. The AHA advised additional testing for smokers.

Diagnosis Guidelines. The American College of Physicians and Blue Cross and Blue Shield, a health insurance organization, on April 1 issued new guidelines for the appropriate use of tests to diagnose disease. The guidelines advise physicians when to order chest X rays, electrocardiograms, and 13 other common laboratory tests. Blue Cross and Blue Shield said the guidelines could lower health care costs by $6 billion per year.

Costs Rise. Health care costs in the United States rose 8.4 per cent in 1986, according to the Health Care Financing Administration (HCFA) in fall 1987. Although this was the second lowest increase in 20 years, it was still significantly more than the overall inflation rate in the United States. Americans spent $458 billion on health care in 1986, according to the HCFA.   Michael Woods

See also DRUGS; HEALTH AND DISEASE; PUBLIC HEALTH. In WORLD BOOK, see MEDICINE.

Exposure to bright artificial light can relieve a type of depression called *seasonal affective disorder,* researchers reported in 1987.

MENTAL ILLNESS. Scientists reported strong evidence in 1987 that some forms of mental illness are hereditary—caused by defects in genes that can be passed from parents to their children. On February 26, three separate groups of researchers concluded that some people inherit a predisposition to manic-depressive illness, a condition that affects an estimated 1 out of every 100 people worldwide. Manic-depressive individuals experience extreme mood swings, alternating between periods of elation and frantic activity and periods of extreme depression and lassitude.

One of the research projects, conducted at the University of Miami in Coral Gables, Fla., involved a 10-year study of manic depression in three generations of an Amish family in Pennsylvania. The researchers traced the disease to a defect in a single gene. The two other research groups found a similar inherited predisposition to manic-depressive illness but linked it to a different gene. Mental health authorities predicted that the findings could lead to new approaches in diagnosing and treating manic-depressive illness.

Schizophrenia Findings. On May 12, researchers at the University of British Columbia in Vancouver, Canada, reported preliminary evidence that a gene or genes could cause schizophrenia, the most common serious mental disorder. Victims suffer delusions, hallucinations, and other symptoms.

The Vancouver researchers traced the approximate location of a gene in a man and his nephew who both suffered from schizophrenia. Because the two shared physical similarities, researchers suspected a hereditary link in the disease.

Another group of mental health researchers on April 30 challenged the long-held belief that schizophrenics never recover from their illness. Although generations of psychiatrists and psychologists have believed that schizophrenics have little chance of recovery, a series of studies conducted at Yale University in New Haven, Conn., and at the University of Pittsburgh found that various degrees of recovery are the rule rather than the exception. The new findings involved about 1,300 patients who were examined at intervals of 20, 30, or 40 years after initial diagnosis. The results indicated that 50 to 66 per cent of the patients had either recovered or improved significantly.

Help for AIDS Patients. A report published on May 1 by the American Psychiatric Association (APA) in Washington, D.C., recommended improving mental health care for patients with AIDS (acquired immune deficiency syndrome). Public health specialist Michael E. Faulstich of the University of Alabama School of Medicine in Birmingham headed the APA study and reported that up to 40 per cent of AIDS patients experience symptoms of emotional illness.

According to the report, AIDS patients often have symptoms of depression, anxiety, and other emotional difficulties. The report also said that AIDS can cause abnormalities in the central nervous system, resulting in mental retardation and hallucinations. The APA report suggested that medication, psychotherapy, and other measures could help relieve excessive anxiety and depression among AIDS patients and improve their ability to cope with the disease.

Cutting Health Cost. A massive study of health insurance claims filed by almost 44,000 families in the United States concluded on October 1 that treatment of mental and emotional disorders can reduce overall health care costs. The study, published by the APA, found that many patients who needed treatment for mental disorders increased their use of other health services for up to three years before obtaining mental health treatment.

The study reported that 33,000 individuals who received mental health care from 1980 to 1983 showed an especially sharp increase in costs for other health care services during a six-month period immediately prior to receiving treatment for their mental disorder. But once treatment began, total costs dropped continuously over the next three years. Michael Woods

See also PSYCHOLOGY. In WORLD BOOK, see MENTAL ILLNESS.

MEXICO. On Oct. 4, 1987, Mexico's ruling Institutional Revolutionary Party (PRI) named Carlos Salinas de Gortari, minister of budget and planning, as its presidential candidate in elections scheduled for July 1988. Salinas de Gortari's victory was considered a near-certainty. The PRI never lost a presidential election since it was formed in 1929.

At 39, Salinas de Gortari is the PRI's youngest candidate in some 50 years and, if elected, would be the first economist to hold the Mexican presidency. As minister of budget and planning, he served as a key economic policymaker under current President Miguel de la Madrid Hurtado. Salinas de Gortari was regarded as a chief architect of the economic austerity measures imposed on Mexico following the collapse of world oil prices in the early 1980's. Following that collapse, Mexico's foreign debt and inflation rate grew at an alarming rate.

De la Madrid's choice of Salinas de Gortari as his successor was widely seen as a way of continuing the austerity program. The belt-tightening measures were popular with business leaders but were increasingly resented by the Mexican workers who had to bear their brunt. Mexican workers reached a new wage agreement with the government in December, however, averting the threat of a general strike.

On December 14, Mexico devaluated its controlled rate for the peso by about 20 per cent, bringing it closer to the rate at which the peso was selling on the free market. The government also announced that import tariffs would be cut in half, from 40 per cent to 20 per cent, to ease consumer prices.

Opposition Gains Strength. Although the PRI is Mexico's dominant party, two other political parties have been gaining strength. The conservative National Action Party (PAN), a strong advocate of free enterprise, named industrialist Manuel Ortega Clouthier as its presidential candidate in November. PAN is particularly strong in northern Mexico, where it has elected several mayors, and the party garnered 16 per cent of the vote in the 1982 presidential elections.

In September, the newly formed Mexican Socialist Party, created in March by a coalition of five left wing parties, chose Herberto Castillo, a civil engineer and the former leader of the Mexican Workers Party, as its presidential candidate. In previous elections, left wing parties never won more than 10 per cent of the vote.

Smuggling. During 1987, newspaper reports revealed that a lively trade in smuggled goods has developed between the United States and Mexico. The smuggled goods include television sets, videocassette recorders, and other consumer electronic items that are flown secretly from the United States into Mexico. The Mexican government has slapped high tariffs on imported electronic products to conserve precious hard-currency reserves, making it difficult for most consumers to afford these goods except on the black market. Alberto Konik Tacher, director of Mexican customs operations, said that Mexican officials confiscated contraband worth an estimated $65 million in 1986.

Mexico has also become headquarters for a lucrative illicit trade in rare and endangered wildlife species. Some 50,000 rare parrots annually are smuggled into the United States, where they fetch up to $2,500 apiece. In the summer of 1987, Mexican conservation groups denounced the "plundering" of endangered bird, reptile, and feline species. They said that the "indifference" of Mexican authorities to this illegal trade had reached "scandalous levels."

Pollution Curbs. In January, the Mexican government announced a series of measures aimed at curbing smog in Mexico City, widely regarded as one of the world's most polluted cities. The measures included regulating exhaust emissions on many of the city's 3 million automobiles. Beginning in 1988, all cars sold in Mexico must have emission-control systems. Nathan A. Haverstock

See also LATIN AMERICA (Facts in Brief Table). In WORLD BOOK, see MEXICO.

MICHIGAN. See DETROIT; STATE GOVERNMENT.

MIDDLE EAST

United States involvement in the quagmire of Middle Eastern politics deepened in 1987. An Iraqi missile attack on a U.S. naval vessel, the frigate U.S.S. *Stark*, on May 17 killed 37 crew members and served as the catalyst for direct American involvement in the Iran-Iraq war. By year-end, the United States had more than 30 vessels in or near the Persian Gulf.

The warships represented a new U.S. policy of protecting tanker traffic from Iranian attacks to ensure the delivery of vital oil supplies to Europe and Japan. A strong U.S. naval presence also was intended to demonstrate U.S. commitment to protecting the Arab states of the gulf region in the face of Iranian threats. But the U.S. intervention and the subsequent arrival in the gulf of warships from several European countries increased the possibility that the conflict would widen.

Regional Tension. Although the Iran-Iraq war remained the main focus of Middle East tension, mounting friction elsewhere in the region contributed to the general political instability. Unrest among Palestinians in the Israeli-occupied West Bank and Gaza Strip exploded in December into violence that left at least 22 Palestinians dead.

Within Israel, disagreements between the two blocs that make up the coalition government stalled progress toward a peace settlement with Arab states. Hopes for an international peace conference were scuttled by the opposition of Israel's Prime Minister Yitzhak Shamir.

Another source of Middle Eastern tension was members of Islamic resurgence groups, who want Islamic forms of government installed in Muslim nations. Inspired by the Iranian revolution, these Muslims either challenged or were perceived as threats by a number of secular regimes, including those of Tunisia, Syria, and Algeria. Only in Egypt were they allowed to join in the political process and take part in national elections.

The Iran-Iraq War entered its eighth year with peace between the two regional powers seemingly as remote as ever. Iran launched a series of massive ground assaults on the key southern Iraqi city of Al Basrah in January. The Iranians advanced to within 9 miles (14 kilometers) of the city before they were stopped, at a cost of an estimated 70,000 casualties. Ground action was limited to artillery exchanges until December, when heavy

U.S. sailors inspect mines on the *Iran Ajr,* an Iranian minelaying ship captured and destroyed in the Persian Gulf by U.S. forces in September.

406

Iranians in Teheran demonstrate against
Saudi Arabia and the United States after
275 Iranians died in a riot in Mecca in July.

But Iranian speedboats attacked neutral shipping in a blow-for-blow retaliation for the raids.

Particularly deadly were mines laid down by Iran in gulf shipping lanes. And even U.S. military protection did not guarantee safe passage. On July 24, the *Bridgeton*, one of two reflagged tankers in the first convoy being escorted through the gulf, struck a mine. The ship suffered only minor damage, however.

After the incident, the United States, Great Britain, and other countries rushed minesweepers to the area. In September, U.S. warships blew up the *Iran Ajr*, an Iranian vessel, after it was spotted laying mines. But the Iranians laid mines faster than an international minesweeping force could pluck them out of the water.

Silkworm missiles, apparently supplied to Iran by China, seriously damaged a number of vessels, including the reflagged Kuwaiti tanker *Sea Isle City* in October. The tanker, the first American-registered vessel to be hit, was not under escort by U.S. warships when struck.

UN Action. Increasing international concern over the conflict prompted the United Nations (UN) to intervene in July. The Security Council on July 20 unanimously approved Resolution 598 calling for an immediate cease-fire, withdrawal of both sides to recognized international boundaries, the return of prisoners, and a negotiated peace settlement.

Iraq immediately accepted the resolution and halted its attacks on gulf shipping. But Iran waffled, continuing to insist that the UN must condemn Iraq for starting the war. Faced with Iranian procrastination on the resolution, the Iraqis resumed their air raids in August.

The Security Council, however, failed to pass a second resolution, advocated by the United States, calling for economic sanctions and an arms embargo if the two countries failed to stop fighting. China, Iran's main arms supplier, and the Soviet Union both opposed the measure.

Arab Unity. The Iranian threat to the Arab gulf states, particularly such smaller countries as Kuwait and Bahrain, led the Arab world to undertake strenuous efforts to unite against the regime of Iranian leader Ayatollah Ruhollah Khomeini. Most Arab countries supported Saudi Arabia in a bitter dispute with Iran over the death of 275 Iranians during the annual religious pilgrimage to Mecca in July. The Iranians died in a melee that broke out when Saudi security forces tried to disperse thousands of Iranian pilgrims holding an illegal political demonstration.

Most Arab leaders also supported UN Resolution 598, and at an Arab League summit conference in Amman, Jordan, in November, all 21 members of the league called for an immediate cease-fire. Even Syria, allied with Iran and a bitter

fighting broke out along Iraq's southern border.

With the ground war stalemated for most of the year, action shifted to the air and sea. Iraq, holding near-total air superiority, concentrated its air attacks on Iran-bound oil tankers in the Persian Gulf and Iranian oil installations and industrial plants. Iran retaliated by firing missiles at targets in Baghdad and other Iraqi cities and by threatening sabotage in Kuwait and other Arab oil-producing states that support Iraq.

U.S. Intervention. Although the attack on the *Stark* was the catalyst for U.S. intervention in the gulf, it was the threat to Kuwait that prompted the move. Pressure for U.S. intervention mounted during the first half of 1987 as Iranian speedboats attacked Kuwaiti tankers. By June, 16 Kuwaiti vessels had been attacked. As a result, in June, the United States agreed to *reflag* (reregister as American vessels) 11 Kuwaiti tankers and provide them with U.S. naval escorts through the gulf.

An earlier request from Kuwait to the Soviet Union had resulted in the Soviets leasing tankers to Kuwait and the promise of Soviet naval protection. But the Administration of President Ronald Reagan was determined to block any further Soviet penetration in the gulf.

Iraq hoped that its raids on Iranian ships and oil facilities would seriously disrupt Iran's oil export capacity and thus affect its military power.

Facts in Brief on Middle Eastern Countries

Country	Population	Government	Monetary Unit*	Exports†	Foreign Trade (million U.S. $) Imports†
Bahrain	483,000	Amir Sheikh Isa bin Sulman Al-Khalifa; Prime Minister Sheikh Khalifa bin Sulman Al-Khalifa	dinar (1 = $2.65)	2,800	2,800
Cyprus	688,000	President Spyros Kyprianou (Turkish Republic of Northern Cyprus: Acting President Rauf R. Denktaş)	pound (1 = $2.26)	561	1,470
Egypt	50,096,000	President Mohammad Hosni Mubarak; Prime Minister Atef Sidqi	pound (2.17 = $1)	3,200	9,000
Iran	49,098,000	President Ali Khamenei; Prime Minister Mir Hosein Musavi-Khamenei	rial (66.8 = $1)	7,800	10,000
Iraq	17,306,000	President Saddam Hussein	dinar (1 = $3.31)	7,450	9,500
Israel	4,284,000	President Chaim Herzog; Prime Minister Yitzhak Shamir	shekel (1.57 = $1)	6,300	9,400
Jordan	3,945,000	King Hussein I; Prime Minister Zaid Rifai	dinar (1 = $2.89)	789	2,733
Kuwait	1,870,000	Amir Sheikh Jabir al-Ahmad al-Sabah; Prime Minister & Crown Prince Sheikh Saad Al-Abdullah Al Sabah	dinar (1 = $3.60)	8,000	7,000
Lebanon	2,828,000	President Amine Gemayel; Acting Prime Minister Salim al-Huss	pound (480 = $1)	482	2,200
Oman	1,350,000	Sultan Qaboos bin Said	rial (1 = $2.60)	5,000	3,400
Qatar	332,000	Amir & Prime Minister Sheikh Khalifa bin Hamad Al Thani	riyal (3.6 = $1)	2,600	1,100
Saudi Arabia	12,566,000	King & Prime Minister Fahd ibn Abd al-Aziz Al Saud	riyal (3.75 = $1)	37,000	34,000
Sudan	23,498,000	Supreme Council President Ahmed al Mirghani; Prime Minister Sadiq el Mahdi	pound (2.5 = $1)	557	1,235
Syria	11,857,000	President Hafiz al-Assad; Prime Minister Mahmoud az-Zoubi	pound (3.9 = $1)	1,600	3,600
Turkey	53,547,000	President Kenan Evren; Prime Minister Turgut Ozal	lira (969.1 = $1)	7,958	11,344
United Arab Emirates	1,465,000	President Sheikh Zayid bin Sultan Al-Nahayyan; Prime Minister Sheikh Rashid ibn Said al Maktum	dirham (3.67 = $1)	9,800	6,600
Yemen (Aden)	2,316,000	Supreme People's Council Presidium Chairman Haydar Abu Bakr al-Attas; Council of Ministers Chairman Yasin Sa'id Nu'man	dinar (1 = $2.97)	10	1,200
Yemen (Sana)	7,073,000	President Ali Abdallah Salih; Prime Minister Abdel Aziz Abdel Ghani	rial (8.99 = $1)	316	762

*Exchange rates as of Dec. 1, 1987, or latest available data.   †Latest available data.

foe of the Iraqi regime, backed the resolution. The league also condemned Iran's occupation of Iraqi territory and aggression against Kuwait.

Egypt and Israel. Another consequence of the new Arab unity was reconciliation with Egypt, ostracized since it signed a peace treaty with Israel in 1979. Although the league stopped short of readmitting Egypt to full-fledged membership— mainly because of opposition from Syria—member states were encouraged to restore diplomatic relations. By mid-November, all the gulf states plus four other league members had renewed ties with Egypt.

Ironically, Egypt's return to the Arab fold coincided with the 10th anniversary of the journey by Egypt's President Anwar el-Sadat to Israel that had resulted in the 1979 peace treaty. That anniversary, carefully ignored in Egypt, also brought few smiles to Israel. Many Israelis felt that peace with Egypt had not been worth the price of losing the Sinai Peninsula with its empty land and rich oil resources. The Sinai, seized by Israel in the Six-Day War in 1967, was returned to Egypt as part of the peace settlement.

Disappointment with the peace treaty plus deep divisions in the Israeli government and the general population over the Palestinian issue left Arab-Israeli peace negotiations stalled. Foreign Minister Shimon Peres worked diligently early in 1987 to convene an international peace confer-

409

Syrian forces move into Beirut, Lebanon, in February at the request of Lebanese
leaders to halt street fighting that had brought the country close to anarchy.

ence. Peres even held secret meetings with Jordan's King Hussein I in which the two leaders agreed on a framework for such a conference, including representation by a Palestinian delegation. But Prime Minister Shamir, leader of the Likud bloc in Israel's coalition government, refused to go along with Peres' proposal.

Although Peres, leader of the Labor Party, found widespread support for a peace conference in other nations and—according to a May public opinion survey—among 60 per cent of Israelis, Likud opposition doomed the attempt to failure. United States support for the conference was also lacking because of U.S. anger over revelations of Israeli spying in the United States and Israel's involvement in arms shipments to Iran.

Palestinian Resistance. The 20th anniversary of Israel's occupation of the West Bank and the Gaza Strip was marked by an escalation in Palestinian resistance. The worst unrest in Gaza since the 1967 occupation broke out on December 9. Palestinian youths throwing stones and bottles clashed daily with heavily reinforced Israeli security forces.

The violence quickly spread to the West Bank and East Jerusalem and eventually to Arab areas within Israel. At least 22 Palestinians were killed. On December 21, 2 million Arabs in Israel and the occupied territories began a commercial strike to protest the Israelis' use of lethal force against the demonstrators. On December 22, the UN Security Council passed a resolution strongly deploring Israel's harsh riot-control methods. The vote was unanimous, with the United States abstaining.

Continued Terrorism. In early 1987, after a lull lasting several months, terrorists in Beirut, Lebanon, resumed their deadly game of kidnapping foreigners. Two West German businessmen were abducted in January. Also that month, terrorists kidnapped four professors—three Americans and an Indian—from the campus of Beirut University College. A previously unknown organization, Islamic Jihad (Holy War) for the Liberation of Palestine, claimed responsibility for the action.

The abductions followed the arrival in Beirut of Terry Waite, the envoy of the archbishop of Canterbury, on a hostage-rescue mission. Waite himself disappeared on January 20.

One of the West German hostages was released in September, as was a South Korean diplomat, both reportedly in return for the payment of huge ransoms by their governments. United States journalist Charles Glass, kidnapped in June, escaped from his captors, reportedly with Syrian help, in August. But the fate and location of the remaining hostages remained unknown at year-end.

Political Changes. The longest tenure of any modern Arab head of state ended on November

7, when Tunisia's Prime Minister Zine al-Abidine Ben Ali overthrew President Habib Bourguiba on grounds of mental incapacity. The 84-year-old Bourguiba, who had been elected president for life in 1975, had been Tunisia's only president since the country gained its independence from France in 1956. But his rigid opposition to the Islamic resurgence movement, his refusal to allow a multiparty system to develop, and recent arbitrary appointments and dismissals of Cabinet officials had alienated supporters and caused concern over the country's future.

Egypt held multiparty elections in April. The National Democratic Party retained its solid majority, but an alliance of three parties, including the Muslim Brotherhood, an Islamic fundamentalist organization, won 60 seats in the People's Assembly. Another broadening of the democratic process took place in Turkey, as voters in September approved an end to a constitutional ban on political activity by 200 former politicians. Parliamentary elections held in November were the first such elections held without military supervision since a 1980 military coup.   William Spencer

See also IRAN-CONTRA AFFAIR and articles on the various Middle Eastern countries. In the Special Reports section, see UNDERSTANDING ISLAM. In WORLD BOOK, see MIDDLE EAST and individual Middle Eastern country articles.

MINING is the most dangerous of all occupations in the United States, according to the federal government's first conclusive study of occupational deaths, released on July 26, 1987. The National Institute for Occupational Safety and Health (NIOSH) in Atlanta, Ga., conducted the study.

Miners have an annual on-the-job fatality rate of 30.1 per 100,000 workers, NIOSH said. This is about three times as high as the national average of 9 deaths per 100,000 workers. NIOSH found that an average of 315 mining deaths occur each year. The second most dangerous occupation, according to the study, is construction, with 23.1 deaths per 100,000. The safest is wholesale trade, with only 1 death per 100,000 each year.

Mine Fined. The United States Mine Safety and Health Administration on May 11 imposed fines totaling $111,470—the largest in the agency's history—against the owner and operator of a Utah coal mine where 27 workers died in a fire on Dec. 19, 1984. The agency found that the mine's owner—Utah Power & Light Company—and the mine's operator at the time of the disaster, Emery Mining Corporation, had committed safety violations that contributed to the disaster. The fire was at the Wilberg Mine near Orangeville, Utah.

Platinum Found. The United States Geological Survey (USGS) on September 17 reported that ore from gold mines near Fairbanks, Alaska, also contains substantial amounts of platinum. Platinum is a rare metal used in industrial processes, in dentistry, and for jewelry. The agency, which is part of the U.S. Department of the Interior, said there may be a strip of platinum-bearing ore near Fairbanks that could be mined profitably.

The platinum discovery, the first ever recorded in the area, could help decrease U.S. dependence on foreign sources of platinum, according to the USGS. The Soviet Union and South Africa have 98 per cent of the world's known platinum deposits that can be mined economically.

The United States took another step to develop its own platinum supply in 1987. In March, the nation's first platinum mine began operating 80 miles (130 kilometers) southwest of Billings, Mont. The mine is owned by the Stillwater Mining Company, a partnership of one Canadian and two U.S. firms.

Gold Merger. On May 6, three of Canada's largest gold-mining firms agreed to merge, creating the largest gold-mining company in North America. The companies—Placer Development, Limited; Dome Mines, Limited; and Campbell Red Lake Mines, Limited—produced a total of 825,000 troy ounces (25,660 kilograms) of gold in 1986.

Strike Ends. Gold miners and coal miners in South Africa ended that nation's longest mine strike on August 30 after failing to obtain the wage increases and other benefits they sought. The strike, which began on August 9, involved more than 300,000 black miners and as many as 44 mines.

The National Union of Mineworkers, which represents South Africa's black miners, initially sought a 30 per cent increase in wages and improvements in other benefits. But after mine owners fired at least 40,000 strikers, the union agreed to a wage increase of 15 to 23 per cent, an increase it had rejected only four days earlier. The union warned mine owners, however, that the strike was only "a dress rehearsal" for further action in 1988. The strike cost mine owners an estimated $225-million in lost production. Miners lost an estimated $2.5 million a day in wages.

Australian Deal. On June 30, Australia and China agreed to develop a new iron ore mine at Mount Channar in Western Australia. The agreement involves the China Metallurgical Import and Export Corporation and Hamersley Iron Limited. The companies agreed to joint ownership of the mine and to sharing of start-up costs. Production is expected to begin in 1990.   Michael Woods

In WORLD BOOK, see MINING.

MINNESOTA. See STATE GOVERNMENT.
MISSISSIPPI. See STATE GOVERNMENT.
MISSOURI. See STATE GOVERNMENT.
MONGOLIA. See ASIA.
MONTANA. See STATE GOVERNMENT.

MONTREAL. The year 1987 was Montreal's first year under the leadership of Mayor Jean Doré, who was elected and sworn in as mayor in November 1986. Doré replaced Jean Drapeau, Montreal's mayor for nearly three decades.

Doré's rule marked a more open administration than that of Drapeau. In one of his first acts as mayor, Doré symbolically opened the doors to city hall. For security reasons, the front doors of the building had been kept closed, except for official receptions. In addition, citizens were encouraged to attend council meetings and were allowed to ask questions for the first time. And in late 1987, the administration opened a series of 13 neighborhood city halls to give citizens easier access to municipal government.

But Doré's first year as mayor was marred by a number of political mistakes. For instance, on July 14, civic services came to a standstill during a massive rainstorm that flooded thousands of Montreal houses. City storm sewers, which had not been maintained for years, could not handle the flow of water. Doré, who was criticized for retreating to his holiday cottage at Val Morin, in the Laurentian Mountains north of Montreal, later admitted that the move was "an error in judgment."

Charges of police brutality also hurt Doré's administration. More than a dozen suicides were reported in city jails during the year, leading a civilian review board to look into the situation.

Condominium Dispute. In June, a dispute erupted over the redevelopment of an area of Montreal called Overdale. This two-block area of rooming houses and small hotels was bought by a company called Grinch Investments. A plan to tear down the structures and replace them with a $34-million (Canadian dollars; $1 = U.S. 77 cents as of Dec. 31, 1987) condominium development was approved by the Doré administration before any of the area's residents learned of the plan. The administration then canceled the plan but changed its mind again and reapproved the project after the developer promised to build alternate housing in the area for needy residents and subsidize that housing for several years.

Taxes. In December, the City Council started debate on property tax proposals for 1988. Although the proposals were not nearly as drastic as feared, they would still raise taxes by as much as 15 per cent in a single year for some homeowners. Business tax rates, on the other hand, actually dropped to about 13 per cent of rental value from about 16 per cent, a move aimed at continuing the building boom that had benefited much of the city in the 1980's.

Montreal's Economy continued to improve from the low point of the late 1970's, when a combination of recession and political turmoil led a number of industries to leave Montreal. For the first time in the 1980's, the unemployment rate slipped below the 9 per cent mark.

The Port of Montreal continued to improve its performance, with general cargo up by approximately 5 per cent. The city's aerospace industry received large orders for the assembly of fighter aircraft for the Canadian armed forces, pushing employment up to prerecession levels. Only the shipbuilding industry seemed to suffer, as the sole remaining shipyard in the city was on the brink of closing for lack of orders.

Controversy over Public Signs continued to divide the community. Residents of the English-speaking districts of Montreal complained about and, in some cases, defied a 1977 law requiring public signs to be in French only. Tourist officials pointed out that the French signs confused many tourists, especially visitors from the United States.

Quebec Prime Minister Robert Bourassa promised to change the sign laws to allow some English to appear in public in the Montreal area, a promise that earned him support from the English-speaking districts of Montreal. Once elected, however, he backed away from his promise because of heavy opposition from French-Canadian nationalists. At year-end, the controversy over the sign laws was still unresolved.   Kendal Windeyer

See also CANADA; QUEBEC. In WORLD BOOK, see MONTREAL.

MOROCCO. King Hassan II met with Algeria's President Chadli Bendjedid on May 4, 1987, in an attempt to resolve the conflict in Western Sahara. Since 1976, Polisario Front guerrillas, supported by Algeria, have been fighting for independence from Morocco, which claims Western Sahara.

The meeting was organized by King Fahd ibn Abd al-Aziz Al Saud of Saudi Arabia and was held in tents near Oujda, on the Moroccan-Algerian border. Fahd's tent straddled the border as a symbol of his neutrality in the conflict. Fahd offered Hassan $260 million a year in aid to rebuild Morocco's war-shattered economy. In return, Fahd asked Hassan to allow the Saharans to decide their future through a United Nations-sponsored referendum. But Hassan refused, insisting that the area is historically part of his country.

Hassan and Bendjedid agreed on one point—an exchange of prisoners. About 100 Algerians were exchanged for 150 Moroccan soldiers who had been detained after crossing the border into Algeria in pursuit of Polisario guerrillas.

Sand Wall. In April, Morocco completed the sixth section of a 2,000-mile (3,200-kilometer) sand wall—a fortified defense line—enclosing most of Western Sahara. The new section extends 340 miles (550 kilometers) along the territory's southern border with Mauritania to the Atlantic Ocean. This section is designed to deny the Poli-

King Hassan II of Morocco touches his daughter, covered by a veil, during her wedding ceremony in June, as members of the royal family look on.

sario Front access to the sea. In the past, the guerrillas mounted attacks on neutral fishing boats to generate outside pressure on Morocco.

Rebel Attacks. Polisario raiders crossed the wall to make a number of attacks in 1987. In July and August, guerrillas reported overrunning several Moroccan outposts, taking prisoners and capturing equipment such as tanks and personnel carriers. In April, the rebels reported that they had shot down a Moroccan F-5E fighter-bomber.

Despite the heavy cost of the conflict—$1 million a day—the Moroccan people continued to back King Hassan in his determination to hold onto Western Sahara. In July, the opposition Party for Progress and Socialism issued a resolution at its annual congress commending the army for its "heroic role" in Western Sahara and urging Algeria to stop obstructing the settlement process.

The Economy. Economic development was slowed by the adverse effects of rising world oil prices early in 1987, poor harvests, and the cost of the Saharan war. Agricultural output dropped by about 50 per cent. Revenues from phosphate, Morocco's major export, fell 5 per cent. But exports of finished goods rose 20 per cent as low labor costs and tax incentives increasingly attracted foreign investment. William Spencer

See also AFRICA (Facts in Brief Table). In WORLD BOOK, see MOROCCO.

MOTION PICTURES. The year 1987 proved to be a bright one for the motion-picture industry in the United States. For the first time in history, film rentals by U.S. theaters broke the $4-billion mark. The 1987 box-office total reached a record $4.2 billion, due both to a surplus of successful motion pictures and to increased admission prices. Some New York City theaters raised the price of a movie ticket to $7.

The outlook was also bright for theater construction. The major theater chains—including American Multi-Cinema, Loews Theaters, United Artists Theaters, and General Cinema Corporation—announced plans to build larger and more elaborate theaters, in contrast to the no-frills "crackerbox cinemas" that had been the rule during the 1970's. The National Association of Theatre Owners, an organization of film exhibitors, stated that the total number of motion-picture screens hit a new high of 22,721 in 1987—20,637 indoor screens and 2,084 at drive-in theaters. The figure did not include approximately 170 additional screens expected to open by year's end.

The Colorization Controversy continued to rage in the United States. On May 12, 1987, director, writer, and actor Woody Allen, actress Ginger Rogers, and directors Sydney Pollack, Milos Forman, and Elliot Silverstein appeared before Congress to protest *colorization*, the use of computers to add color to vintage black-and-white films. Allen referred to the process as a "mutilation" and called colorized films "cheesy, artificial symbols of one society's greed." Nevertheless, on June 19, the government recognized the legitimacy of colorization under present copyright laws.

Films from Top Directors. Allen's anticolorization pleas may have gone unheeded by Congress, but he had a good year artistically with the bittersweet, nostalgic *Radio Days*. His film *September*, in which Elaine Stritch gave a memorable performance as Mia Farrow's aging mother, was less successful. Steven Spielberg's *Empire of the Sun* gave further evidence of the director's new concentration on storytelling values rather than special effects. The film told the story of an 11-year-old British boy separated from his parents during the Japanese occupation of the international district of Shanghai, China, from 1941 to 1945. Four years after 1983's *Terms of Endearment*, writer-director James L. Brooks enjoyed another critical and commercial success with *Broadcast News*, a romantic comedy about network journalism that seemed destined for several Academy Award nominations.

Joel and Ethan Coen's *Raising Arizona* proved there is a place for idiosyncratic talents in Hollywood. *Matewan*, about an infamous 1920 struggle between striking coal miners and company en-

forcers, reinforced the reputation of its director, independent filmmaker John Sayles. Australian director Fred Schepisi had both critical and box-office success with *Roxanne*, starring Steve Martin. Martin also wrote the screenplay, a witty retelling of French playwright Edmond Rostand's *Cyrano de Bergerac* (1897). It tells the story of a man with a long, ugly nose who helps an inarticulate companion woo the woman he himself loves.

Cinema Sex was much in evidence in 1987. The biggest surprise hit of the year was *Fatal Attraction*, which grossed $126 million by the end of 1987. The movie, in which respectable married attorney Michael Douglas is hounded by his former lover Glenn Close, was a conventional if voluptuously filmed variation of a theme explored in 1971 in Clint Eastwood's *Play Misty for Me*.

Fatal Attraction became the focus of conversations at many social gatherings as well as the inspiration for numerous newspaper editorials. Some viewers interpreted the film as a cautionary fable, evidence that the epidemic of AIDS (acquired immune deficiency syndrome) had brought the sexual revolution to a standstill. Whatever the reason, *Fatal Attraction* obviously struck a responsive chord with 1987 moviegoers.

Dirty Dancing, another movie with a sexual theme, also proved a surprise hit. The film, star-

Albert Brooks, Holly Hunter, and William Hurt, left to right, star as a TV news team in *Broadcast News,* written and directed by James L. Brooks.

From left, Charles Martin Smith, Kevin Costner, Sean Connery, and Andy Garcia play federal agents who take on the mob in the 1987 hit *The Untouchables.*

ring Patrick Swayze and Jennifer Grey, told a nostalgic story of a sheltered young woman's sexual awakening at a Catskills summer resort in the early 1960's.

One of 1987's most controversial films was Alan Parker's *Angel Heart,* in which Mickey Rourke played a luckless private investigator caught in a demonic scheme masterminded by the Devil himself, played by Robert De Niro. The film featured an explicit sex scene between Rourke and Lisa Bonet, who had played Bill Cosby's teen-aged daughter on the popular—and wholesome—television series "'The Cosby Show." The Motion Picture Association of America (MPAA) originally gave *Angel Heart* an X rating. The studio cut some offensive scenes, submitted the film a second time, and received another X rating. A third submission to the MPAA, with more cuts, earned the desired R classification. Despite the ratings furor, the film was not successful at the box office.

Rourke found more favor with his portrayal of an alcoholic in *Barfly,* costarring Jack Nicholson and a resurgent Faye Dunaway. De Niro received more popular acclaim for his performance as mobster Al Capone in Brian DePalma's *The Untouchables,* one of the few films to be equally popular with audiences and critics.

For Jack Nicholson, 1987 proved to be a banner year. Although *The Witches of Eastwick,* a broad ad-

aptation of John Updike's 1984 best seller, received mixed reviews, it proved popular with moviegoers. *Ironweed,* in which Nicholson and Meryl Streep played tragic Depression Era figures, was expected to win critical and commercial favor.

Other Veteran Actors also returned to the limelight in 1987. Italian actor Marcello Mastroianni was widely heralded for his performance as an aging rake in Soviet director Nikita Mikhalkov's *Dark Eyes.* Legendary American actresses Bette Davis and Lillian Gish received strong notices for *The Whales of August,* which brought the two stars together for the first time in their careers, with support lent by Ann Sothern and Vincent Price.

***Ishtar* and Other Disasters.** The year's most famous flop was the extravagant $50-million comedy *Ishtar,* starring Warren Beatty and Dustin Hoffman as third-rate nightclub entertainers innocently entangled in Middle East politics. Directed by Elaine May, the film got a few favorable reviews along with the bad ones, but it grossed only a meek $15 million. Another noteworthy box-office disaster was *Who's That Girl?,* which proved once again that pop star Madonna's quirky charisma may not transfer to the motion-picture screen. Sylvester Stallone's arm-wrestling opus, *Over the Top,* also met with indifference.

Successes. Timothy Dalton, the newest James Bond, made a modest impression on American

Director Woody Allen tells a Senate subcommittee
in May about his opposition to *colorization,* a
process used to add color to black-and-white films.

audiences with *The Living Daylights,* which was
much more successful in other countries. Ironically, Dalton's debut as Bond arrived almost simultaneously with the successful release of *The
Untouchables,* which featured a celebrated performance by former Bond star Sean Connery.

After three unsuccessful film roles, television
idol Tom Selleck came up with a movie hit with
the amusing *Three Men and a Baby.* Barbra Streisand, in her first film since 1983's *Yentl,* appeared
to have a winner with the dramatic *Nuts,* in which
she played a hostile prostitute attempting to prove
her sanity in a court hearing. In *Beverly Hills Cop
II,* Eddie Murphy had a box-office—if not a critical—success with a sequel to his 1985 hit *Beverly
Hills Cop.* The new film, 1987's top-grossing movie
at $154 million, again featured Murphy as a
street-smart Detroit cop who shakes up swanky
Beverly Hills, Calif.

War Movies continued in popularity in 1987.
Oliver Stone's 1986 antiwar film *Platoon* won the
Academy Award for best picture in 1987 and
found favor with audiences in its national release
during the year. Stanley Kubrick made a long-
awaited return to filmmaking with *Full Metal
Jacket,* his first film since the 1980 horror story *The
Shining. Full Metal Jacket,* about the dehumanizing
of troops in Vietnam, found champions among
both critics and audiences. British director John

Irvin's *Hamburger Hill* also found support. *Good
Morning, Vietnam,* a comedy directed by Barry
Levinson and starring Robin Williams, opened in
late December to enthusiastic reviews.

The British Motion-Picture Industry, which
staged a comeback in 1986, continued to thrive in
1987 with such saucy dramas as *Wish You Were
Here* and *Prick Up Your Ears.* Director James Ivory
and producer Ismail Merchant brought out their
adaptation of E. M. Forster's novel *Maurice,* about
a British gentleman's reconciliation with his homosexual tendencies. The novel was completed in
1914 but not published until 1971. The film version won neither the praise nor the audiences
that the Ivory-Merchant version of Forster's 1908
novel *A Room with a View* had in 1986.

John Boorman's autobiographical film *Hope and
Glory* won some of 1987's most glowing reviews.
The film presented the London Blitz—Germany's
all-out air attack on London in 1940 and 1941,
during World War II—as a liberating experience
for a youngster living in the city's grim suburbs.

On the International Scene, French director
Claude Berri's *Jean de Florette* proved to be the
most popular French film worldwide since *La Cage
aux Folles* (1979). *Jean de Florette,* released during
the summer of 1987, was the first entry in a two-
part adaptation of Marcel Pagnol's 1962 novel
L'Eau des Collines (The Water of the Hills). It traced
the downfall of an honest but misguided farmer,
whose destruction is hastened by a greedy land-
owner who lusts after his farm. French actor Gérard Depardieu won considerable praise as the
tragic title character, and veteran entertainer Yves
Montand was rewarded with possibly the finest
critical notices of his long career for his portrayal
of the cunning schemer. The second part of Berri's epic, *Manon of the Spring,* told the story of Florette's avenging daughter. Montand again played
the provincial villain, with Emmanuelle Béart as
Depardieu's daughter.

French director Louis Malle compensated in
1987 for the disappointments of 1984's *Crackers*
and 1985's *Alamo Bay* with the critically endorsed
*Au Revoir, Les Enfants (Goodbye, Children). Au Re-
voir,* a partly autobiographical film, takes place in
a French Roman Catholic boarding school, where
three Jewish children hide from the Nazis during
the final months of World War II.

Italian directors Paolo and Vittorio Taviani's
Good Morning, Babylon offered an affectionate but
muddled examination of the early days of Hollywood. But most critics rated the film as not up to
the standards of the earlier Taviani masterpieces
Padre Padrone (1977) and *The Night of the Shooting
Stars* (1982).   Philip Wuntch

See also AWARDS AND PRIZES (Arts Awards);
DEATHS (Close-Up); MATLIN, MARLEE; NEWMAN,
PAUL. In WORLD BOOK, see MOTION PICTURE.

MOZAMBIQUE. The droughts, floods, and cyclones that struck Mozambique in the mid-1980's contributed to the country's persistent famine and economic woes in 1987. Continuing military strife and the lingering effects of misguided government policies caused even more suffering.

Civil War. According to a United Nations study, drought and 11 years of internal warfare severely affected the lives of 3.5 million Mozambicans, forcing 1 million to 1.5 million from their homes and farms. Many refugees sought sanctuary in Zimbabwe and Malawi.

The source of conflict was the Mozambique National Resistance (Renamo), a rebel guerrilla organization, allegedly backed by South Africa, trying to overthrow the government. The viciousness of the Renamo attacks on peasants rallied international support for Mozambique's ruling party, the Front for the Liberation of Mozambique (Frelimo). Renamo forces launched attacks on numerous isolated villages and disrupted the delivery of food relief throughout 1987. It was reported that 424 civilians were slain by Renamo forces near Homoíne in July, and that 211 men, women, and children were killed in a Renamo ambush of a bus convoy near Taninga in October.

Renamo soldiers continued their attacks on Mozambique's railroad lines, port facilities, and roads in 1987. Destruction of transportation forced neighboring landlocked countries to use the more expensive railroad and port facilities of South Africa. In early 1987, Zimbabwe, Zambia, Malawi, and Tanzania began to post troops to Mozambique to guard railroad links to the Mozambican ports of Beira, Nacala, and Maputo.

Economy. The first full year of Joaquím Alberto Chissano's presidency brought a definite shift away from Mozambique's former Marxist policies. Chissano had in November 1986 succeeded Samora Moisés Machel, whose socialist strategies for Mozambique's development had contributed to the country's economic crisis. Chissano's new economic policies conformed to conditions set in January 1987 by the International Monetary Fund. Chissano relaxed price controls on agricultural products, devalued the currency, and began eliminating government-owned businesses.

Chissano also moved to strengthen diplomatic and economic bonds with the West. In May, he met with Great Britain's Prime Minister Margaret Thatcher in London and Pope John Paul II in Rome. United States President Ronald Reagan and members of the U.S. Congress hosted Chissano in Washington, D.C., in October.

More than 40 international relief agencies and foreign governments aided starving Mozambicans in 1987. J. Gus Liebenow and Beverly B. Liebenow

See also AFRICA (Facts in Brief Table). In WORLD BOOK, see MOZAMBIQUE.

MULRONEY, M. BRIAN (1939-), began his fourth year as prime minister of Canada in 1987. Mulroney's personal popularity, which had plummeted following his record-breaking electoral victory in 1984, improved slightly during 1987. A poll taken in October showed that he was favored by 19 per cent of Canadians as the political leader who would make the most effective prime minister—an increase of 3 percentage points since April. This was the first time that Mulroney had improved his popular support in the three years of his government.

Mulroney had positioned himself as the dominant figure in presenting his government's accomplishments. Although these were substantial, the prime minister seemed to gain little credit from them. Among the achievements of the year was a comprehensive and controversial free-trade pact with the United States agreed upon in October; an agreement reached in April that, when ratified by the federal government and the 10 provinces, will bring Quebec into the 1982 Canadian constitution; and sweeping tax reform proposals unveiled in June. David M. L. Farr

See also CANADA. In WORLD BOOK, see MULRONEY, MARTIN BRIAN.

MUSIC, CLASSICAL. See CLASSICAL MUSIC.
MUSIC, POPULAR. See POPULAR MUSIC.
NAMIBIA. See AFRICA.

NATIONAL PTA membership increased by 5.6 per cent in 1987—the biggest gain in 27 years—raising the number of members to more than 6 million. Speaking at the National PTA convention in Dallas in June, new PTA President Manya S. Ungar of Scotch Plains, N.J., attributed the swelling membership rolls to the growing desire of parents to take an active role in their children's education. Ungar said the theme of her administration would be "The National PTA: Because children are the future." The PTA cooperated with *Redbook* magazine to produce a back-to-school guide for parents, which appeared in the magazine's September issue.

In September, the PTA received a $109,000 grant from the Centers for Disease Control in Atlanta, Ga., to encourage parental support for school programs on AIDS (acquired immune deficiency syndrome). Other PTA activities in 1987 included the second annual Child Safety and Protection Month (November), the second annual "School Is What We Make It" campaign, and the third annual National PTA Drug and Alcohol Awareness Week. Joan Kuersten

In WORLD BOOK, see NATIONAL CONGRESS OF PARENTS AND TEACHERS; PARENT-TEACHER ORGANIZATIONS.
NAVY. See ARMED FORCES.
NEBRASKA. See STATE GOVERNMENT.
NEPAL. See ASIA.

NETHERLANDS introduced rules on April 15, 1987, to stem the flow of refugees seeking asylum in the country and to speed up the procedures for ruling on refugee cases. The influx of refugees had brought the Dutch immigration service to a standstill and strained government resources. The new rules allowed officials at borders and airports to turn back refugees who either passed through or had sought asylum in another Western nation. The time taken to check on individuals seeking asylum plummeted from approximately three months to about two days. All refugees refused asylum were given the right of appeal.

Gulf Force. The Netherlands announced on August 21 that it would be prepared to send minesweepers to the Persian Gulf in a joint operation to protect gulf shipping. Iran, which was at war with Iraq, apparently had laid mines in the gulf. The Netherlands' decision to send minesweepers was subject to further talks with European allies.

Economic Goals. The center-right coalition government led by Prime Minister Ruud Lubbers continued to apply the policies set after its reelection in May 1986. Main economic goals were to reinforce and broaden the economic recovery, to cut unemployment, and to maintain a low level of inflation.

The government was on target with its objective of keeping wage hikes low. Smaller contributions to social security and a tiny inflation rate of 0.2 per cent helped to keep wage increases in the private sector down to 1.5 per cent in 1987.

Call for Restraint. The Organization for Economic Cooperation and Development (OECD), an association of 24 industrialized nations, warned the Netherlands in July that the only way to balance the national budget was to cut government spending. The OECD predicted that the nation's budget deficit would rise by 7.5 per cent of national income in 1987 because of declines in the price of natural gas sold by the Netherlands and a depreciation of the United States dollar, making Dutch goods more expensive in the United States. The OECD stressed that the Netherlands must improve the functioning of markets, make the economy more flexible, and restore adequate incentives to engage in business.

Health Care. The report of a government commission on health care on March 26 recommended the introduction of national health insurance that would cover most medical services, with supplementary insurance to be paid for voluntarily by insured individuals. The health-care commission also said that the Netherlands should reduce the number of hospital beds by 12,000, or 18 per cent, by 1990.   Kenneth Brown

See also EUROPE (Facts in Brief Table). In WORLD BOOK, see NETHERLANDS.

NEVADA. See STATE GOVERNMENT.

NEW BRUNSWICK. Canada's longest-serving provincial premier, Richard B. Hatfield, saw his hopes for a fifth term in office shattered as his Progressive Conservative (PC) party was routed in an election on October 13. Hatfield and his entire cabinet went down to defeat as the opposition Liberals captured every seat in the 58-seat legislature. It was only the second time in Canadian history that a party had won all the seats in a provincial legislature. Before the election, the PC's held 37 seats, the Liberals had 20 seats, and the New Democratic Party held the remaining seat.

The Liberal Leader, sworn in as premier on October 27, was Frank J. McKenna, a 39-year-old criminal lawyer (see MCKENNA, FRANK JOSEPH). McKenna had projected a fresh, vigorous image throughout the campaign, offering few specifics except to emphasize the importance of creating jobs in a province with the second-highest unemployment rate in Canada.

McKenna's 21-member cabinet included 7 ministers without previous legislative experience. He named a woman, Aldéa Landry, to the second most important cabinet position. Landry, a lawyer, was appointed president of the Executive Council and minister responsible for intergovernmental affairs—one of the highest positions achieved by a woman in Canadian provincial politics.

The Issue that apparently defeated Hatfield, though it was never brought out publicly by the Liberals during the campaign, was the premier's unconventional life style. Hatfield's image had been damaged by his alleged use of drugs, based on the discovery of marijuana in his suitcase in 1984. Although he was later acquitted on a charge of possession of the drug, the incident discredited Hatfield among New Brunswick's largely rural and conservative voters. The premier's expensive visit to a West German health spa and his 35 trips to New York City during one year, all undertaken with government or party funds, further tarnished his reputation.

Hatfield made many contributions to his province during his 17 years in office. His administration successfully modernized public services, especially education and health care, in a province that had been backward in this area. He also declared New Brunswick an officially bilingual province, thus recognizing French-speaking regions of the province. About 37 per cent of the people in New Brunswick have French ancestors, and about 16 per cent speak only French.   David M. L. Farr

See also CANADA. In WORLD BOOK, see NEW BRUNSWICK.

NEW HAMPSHIRE. See STATE GOVERNMENT.

NEW JERSEY. See STATE GOVERNMENT.

NEW MEXICO. See STATE GOVERNMENT.

NEW YORK. See NEW YORK CITY; STATE GOVERNMENT.

NEW YORK CITY. United States Congressman Mario Biaggi, Democratic representative since 1969 from the Bronx, one of New York City's five boroughs, was sentenced on Nov. 5, 1987, to 30 months in prison and fined $500,000 on bribery charges. Biaggi was found guilty of accepting a $3,000 Florida vacation from a former Brooklyn Democratic leader, Meade Esposito, in exchange for helping a troubled client of Esposito's insurance firm. Esposito, Biaggi's codefendant, was given a suspended prison term and fined $500,000.

The Biaggi trial was one of six major trials to dominate New York City in 1987. Biaggi's lawyer, Barry Slotnick, was more successful on June 16, when he won an acquittal on major charges for Bernhard H. Goetz, the so-called subway vigilante. Goetz, who is white, admitted shooting four black youths who he said approached him in a menacing way on a Manhattan subway car in December 1984. Goetz, who had been charged with attempted murder and assault, was sentenced on October 19 to six months in jail for carrying an unlicensed gun in the subway incident.

John Gotti, reputed leader of the most powerful crime organization in the city, was acquitted along with six codefendants on March 13 of racketeering and conspiracy charges.

Two other prominent figures were also found innocent. In October, real estate broker John Zaccaro, the husband of 1984 Democratic vice presidential candidate Geraldine Ferraro, was cleared of charges that he extorted payments from a cable television company. And in May, former Secretary of Labor Raymond J. Donovan was acquitted of fraud and larceny charges stemming from his part in a subway construction contract.

Three white teen-agers from Howard Beach, a section of the borough of Queens, were convicted on December 21 of manslaughter after a two-month trial. They were held responsible for the Dec. 20, 1986, death of a black man whose car had become disabled. Witnesses said the youths chased the car's three occupants with baseball bats and wooden clubs. The man who died was killed when he fled onto a highway and was hit by a car.

Scandals. On October 7, a federal grand jury indicted Bess Myerson, a former Miss America and, until April, the city's cultural-affairs commissioner. The indictment charged that Myerson gave a city job to the daughter of a state Supreme Court judge, Hortense W. Gabel. In return for the favor, the indictment said, the judge lowered the alimony payments of contractor Carl A. Capasso, a close friend of Myerson's. Gabel and Capasso were also indicted.

On April 1, three weeks after resigning as Bronx borough president, Stanley Simon, who had held that job since 1979, was indicted by a federal grand jury for extorting $50,000 from a

The barge *Mobro,* its cargo of trash refused by six states and three nations, sits in New York Harbor in June. The trash was burned in September.

Bronx military contractor. He was the second borough president in 14 months to resign because of a scandal. Queens borough President Donald Manes had resigned in early 1986 and later committed suicide. Bronx voters elected Councilman Fred Ferrer as Simon's successor.

Schools. Nathan Quinones, chancellor of the New York City school system, the nation's largest, announced in August that he was resigning his position, effective Jan. 1, 1988. Quinones had faced criticism over administrative shortcomings in the schools, high dropout rates, and lack of job skills among many high school graduates. Minneapolis (Minn.) School Superintendent Richard R. Green was chosen to succeed Quinones.

The Homeless. In late 1987, the administration of Mayor Edward I. Koch began a controversial program to remove mentally disturbed homeless people from the streets—often against their will—and hospitalize them during the winter. Although most homeless people accepted the hospitalization plan, the case of one person who refused to comply with the new regulation attracted national attention. Joyce Brown, 40, persuaded a judge she could cope with street life. But two appeals courts stayed the judge's ruling. In December, Brown remained hospitalized. Owen Moritz

See also CITY. In WORLD BOOK, see NEW YORK CITY.

NEW ZEALAND. Voters reelected the Labour Party government headed by Prime Minister David R. Lange to a second three-year term in the general election held on Aug. 15, 1987. With the victory, Lange became the first Labour prime minister since 1946 to win reelection in New Zealand. The Labour Party increased its majority in the 97-seat Parliament by winning 58 seats. In the previous 95-seat Parliament, it had 56 seats. The National Party won the remaining 39 seats. The Democratic Party lost its 2 seats to the National Party.

Post Changes. Following the election, Lange reshuffled his Cabinet. He relinquished the post of minister of foreign affairs to assume the post of minister of education. Russell Marshall, the former minister of education, was named minister of foreign affairs.

The election results also caused a major reshuffle in the National Party. Sir Robert Muldoon, former prime minister, lost his role as spokesman following the party's defeat.

Economy. The Labour government continued its attempts to boost New Zealand's economy by reorganizing a number of government departments into state-owned corporations so that they function as businesses paid by consumer dollars rather than by tax dollars. Inflation and interest rates fluctuated throughout the year but remained at high levels. The unemployment rate continued to rise and by the end of the year, about 8 per cent of the country's labor force was out of work. The New Zealand dollar remained relatively stable in 1987. Its strength reflected New Zealand's continuing attractiveness to foreign investors.

The 1987-1988 budget presented on June 18 provided for a surplus of 379 million New Zealand dollars ($NZ 1 = U.S. 66 cents as of Dec. 31, 1987). This budget surplus, the first in 35 years, was achieved largely by the planned sale of the government's shares in New Zealand Steel Limited in October and by the sale of shares in other government enterprises, including the national airline, Air New Zealand. The budget forecast an approximate 9 per cent increase in government expenditures and a 22 per cent increase in revenue.

Quake Hits. A major earthquake occurred on March 2 in the Bay of Plenty off the North Island. The quake caused total property damage estimated at $NZ 60 million.

Ban Passed. New Zealand's policy of banning nuclear-powered or nuclear-armed ships from its ports became law on June 4. Parliament approved the measure by a vote of 39 to 29. In 1986, the ban caused the United States to end its military obligations to New Zealand under the ANZUS mutual defense treaty. David A. Shand

See also ASIA (Facts in Brief Table). In WORLD BOOK, see NEW ZEALAND.

NEWFOUNDLAND. Premier Brian Peckford, though heading a Progressive Conservative provincial administration, disregarded party loyalty in 1987 and unleashed a bitter attack on Canada's Progressive Conservative federal government. The federal government had signed a controversial secret treaty in Paris on January 24. The pact, which was intended to pave the way for settlement of a maritime boundary dispute between Canada and France in the Gulf of St. Lawrence, offered France new access to the rich northern cod fishery off Newfoundland.

Peckford, angered at not being consulted over the agreement, accused the federal government of selling out the interests of the Newfoundland fishing industry. He took his fight to a special meeting of provincial premiers on February 9, and on September 17, he withdrew Newfoundland's advisers from the delegation negotiating with France.

The 23,000 members of the Newfoundland Fishermen's Union voted strongly on May 4 to affiliate with the Canadian Auto Workers union, most of whose members work in Ontario. The fishing union had been a branch of the United States-based United Food and Commercial Workers International Union. The Newfoundland fishing union had become disgruntled with the U.S. union's management. David M. L. Farr

In WORLD BOOK, see NEWFOUNDLAND.

NEWMAN, PAUL (1925-   ), won the Academy of Motion Picture Arts and Sciences Award for best actor on March 30, 1987. The award honored his portrayal of a former pool hustler in *The Color of Money*. He had been nominated for best actor six times before and in 1986 got an honorary Academy Award for career achievement.

Newman was born in Cleveland on Jan. 26, 1925. He attended Kenyon College in Gambier, Ohio; Yale University's School of Drama in New Haven, Conn.; and Actors Studio in New York City. In the early 1950's, Newman began his professional career, working in television and theater. He made his film debut in *The Silver Chalice* (1955). Most of Newman's early work was well received by both the public and critics. In 1958, he was named "outstanding actor of the year" at the Cannes Film Festival in France.

Newman was nominated for an Academy Award for his performance in *Cat on a Hot Tin Roof* (1958). His other best actor nominations were for his work in *The Hustler* (1961), *Hud* (1963), *Cool Hand Luke* (1967), *Absence of Malice* (1981), and *The Verdict* (1982). A film Newman produced and directed, *Rachel, Rachel*, was nominated for best picture of 1968.

Newman married actress Joanne Woodward in 1958. They have three daughters, and Newman has two from a previous marriage. Jinger Griswold

NEWSMAKERS OF 1987 included the following:

Keeping It Together. August 16 marked the beginning of a 25-year period during which the world might shake itself apart, according to one interpretation of ancient Maya and Aztec calendars. To prevent this earth-shattering event from occurring, thousands of the planet's human inhabitants attempted on the morning of the fated day to focus their collective will to create a "harmonic convergence" that would calm the world. The 2,000 people who showed up in New York City's Central Park, for example, employed a variety of focusing techniques. Some hummed. Others meditated silently. Occasionally, a conch shell sounded. Did the attempt succeed? So far, it does not seem to have failed.

I'm OK, You're OK, the Task Force Is OK. A new kind of government entity popped into existence in March—the 25-member California Task Force to Promote Self-Esteem and Personal and Social Responsibility. The group was established by state law, with a three-year budget of $735,000. Its task is to study research linking low self-esteem to such chronic social problems as crime, alcoholism, and drug abuse, then to recommend government programs to enhance self-esteem.

Garbage Out, Garbage In. On March 22, a tugboat pulled the garbage barge *Mobro* out of New York City laden with 3,186 short tons (2,890 metric tons) of business refuse, cardboard, paper, and rubber—much of it from the town of Islip, N.Y. Islip authorities had refused to let the trash be buried in its landfill because the landfill was full. A contractor from Alabama bought the trash to sell in North Carolina, where it was to be converted to methane gas for use as a fuel. The tugboat hauled the *Mobro* to North Carolina, but the deal fell through because the contractor had not obtained a permit from the state. The trash then traveled in search of a resting place as far south as the Central American country of Belize. That country, two other nations, and six states turned it away. The *Mobro* story finally ended where it began. By May 16, the barge was back in New York City with an invitation to return to Islip. On July 10, a New York state environmental official announced a plan to burn the trash in Brooklyn and to bury the ash in the Islip landfill. On September 1, the first bales were unloaded and burned.

Pitch and Switch. Jim Abbott, 19, who pitched for the United States in the 1987 Pan American Games in Indianapolis, has an unusual style. After releasing the ball with his left hand, he switches his mitt to that hand. Why? Because he was born with no right hand. Abbott is not only a fine example of using what you have, he is also an excel-

President Reagan and Republican statesman Alf Landon celebrate Landon's 100th birthday three days early on September 6. Landon died on October 12.

The Walt Disney movie *Snow White and the Seven Dwarfs* was released again in 1987, its 50th birthday. *Snow White* was the first full-length cartoon film.

lent pitcher—as Nicaragua's team would attest. He shut them out.

Cage Rampage. Lynne Lorenzen, an 18-year-old basketball player at Ventura High School in Iowa, racked up 54 points in a February game, bringing her total for four years of play to 6,265 points— more than any high school player in the United States had ever scored. And that was on an off night for Lorenzen. The 6-foot 2-inch (188-centimeter) senior averaged 65 points per game.

Record Appearance. One of the oldest records in professional sports fell on June 13, 1987, when Sachio Kinugasa, third baseman for the Toyo Carp, stepped onto the diamond in Hiroshima, Japan, to play in his 2,131st consecutive game. Kinugasa broke the record of 2,130 consecutive games set by Lou Gehrig of the New York Yankees in 1939.

Foreign Competition. An American became very big in a traditional Japanese sport in May 1987. Salevaa Atisanoe, who hails from Hawaii and wrestles under the name Konishiki, became the first non-Japanese in the history of sumo wrestling to attain the ranking of *ozeki* (champion). The 526-pound (239-kilogram) Konishiki moved within one ranking of the top—*yokozuna* (grand champion), which only 61 wrestlers have attained.

Pucker Power. Joel Brandon captured the 10th International Whistle-Off in Carson City, Nev., wowing the judges with a variety of classical, pop,

jazz, and novelty selections. To protect his prize-winning "instrument," said Brandon after the contest, "I have to stay away from too much kissing— but I can hug."

Big Bug. Laine Snyder, 12, of Hollywood, Fla., in July won the Great American Roach-Off, a search for the state with the biggest roaches. Snyder entered a behemoth measuring 2.08 inches (5.28 centimeters) in length, topping some 2,000 entries from 40 states.

And Now, Flying Roaches. Asian cockroaches, which probably traveled by ship from Southeast Asia to Florida in 1984, by early 1987 had established themselves in an area of about 450 square miles (1,170 square kilometers) around Tampa. Experts said there were up to 100,000 flying roaches per acre (0.4 hectare) in one 14-acre (5.7-hectare) area. This translates into about 210 of the bustling little bugs per square yard (0.8 square meter). The roach is attracted by light, breeds rapidly, does not flee from people, and "hitchhikes" in cars, boats, and planes.

Pipe Nightmare. A tenant on the 15th floor of an apartment building in Hamilton, Canada, lost his pet boa constrictor in May. On August 9— *about three months later*—Laurie Lamothe, who lives in a 12th-floor apartment, noticed two little eyes peering at her from the bottom of her toilet. Lamothe immediately spread word of her visitor.

She became an overnight celebrity, her apartment transformed into a virtual open house for the Society for the Prevention of Cruelty to Animals (SPCA), the news media, and plumbers. On August 12, an SPCA official managed to remove the snake's body—it apparently had drowned—from an 11th-floor drainpipe.

Safe Passage. Lord Skelmersdale, Great Britain's undersecretary of the environment, on March 13 officially opened an unusual tunnel under the Henley roadway in Hambleden, England. The tunnel is about 10 inches (25 centimeters) in diameter and was built for toads. Lord Skelmersdale dedicated the tunnel just in time for the local toads' mating season, when thousands of the amphibians try to hop from dry winter grounds across the busy highway to mating ponds. Before the tunnel, many toads had been killed by automobiles on the journey.

Monkeying with the Controls. A monkey named Yerosha—Russian for *troublemaker*—introduced a bit of "free enterprise" to the Soviet space program in October. High above earth in a space capsule, Yerosha freed his left arm from a restraining cuff and began playing with buttons on the craft's control panel. The Soviets did not say whether Yerosha disrupted the flight, but the capsule landed thousands of miles from its destination.

Soothing the Savagery. A two-year-old recording of "Dear Mr. Jesus," a gospel song about child abuse, in November and December made a national singing star of a 9-year-old Texas girl, Sharon Batts. The song had lackluster sales until a disk jockey in Tampa played it shortly before Thanksgiving. The words struck a rich lode of emotion in a society just becoming aware of the full extent of child abuse. Word of the song spread, and by mid-December "Dear Mr. Jesus" was being played by hundreds of stations.

Girl Saved from Well. As a nationwide television audience looked on at about 8 P.M. on October 16, tired rescue workers in Midland, Tex., pulled 18-month-old Jessica McClure out of an abandoned water well into which she had fallen while playing in her aunt's backyard 58½ hours earlier. Jessica had been stuck in a sitting position at a depth of 22 feet (6.7 meters). To get her out, workers drilled another shaft parallel to the well, then bored a horizontal tunnel to the well. Jessica came through the ordeal in remarkably good shape. Surgeons operated on her badly bruised right foot and managed to save everything but one toe.

Mother and Daughter Know Best. When *Chicago Sun-Times* advice columnist Ruth Crowley died in 1955, a young woman named Esther (Eppie) Lederer took over her job. Lederer used the same pen name Crowley had used—Ann Landers. In March 1987, Lederer left the *Sun-Times* to work for the rival *Chicago Tribune*, so the *Sun-Times* conducted

About 250,000 people crowd onto the Golden Gate Bridge in San Francisco on May 24, 1987, to celebrate that structure's 50th anniversary.

a contest to replace her. One of the two winners was Diane Crowley, Ruth's daughter, a lawyer in Springfield, Mass. The other winner was Jeffrey Zaslow, a reporter for *The Wall Street Journal*.

Top Ticket. Donald R. Woomer, Sr., a self-employed plasterer in Hollidaysburg, Pa., did not go to work on October 15. He did not have to. Woomer and his companion, Linda K. Despot, a bookkeeper, learned that morning that they had won $46 million in the Pennsylvania lottery—the largest jackpot ever pocketed in a North American lottery.

Never Too Late. Hulda Crooks of Loma Linda, Calif., scaled Mount Fuji, Japan's highest peak, on July 24. "It's wonderful," she said at the summit. The climber herself was something of a wonder. She was 91 years old.

Scrape with Disaster. British businessman Richard Branson and Swedish balloonist Per Lindstrand on July 3 completed the first crossing of the Atlantic Ocean in a hot-air balloon. Their flight almost ended in disaster, however. About 37 hours after taking off from Maine, the balloon scraped the ground in Northern Ireland, then bounced along the chilly waters between Ireland and Scotland. The two men jumped. A helicopter picked up Branson quickly, but Lindstrand swam for more than two hours before he was spotted and rescued.

Physics student Robert Garisto in February 1987 found an error in Sir Isaac Newton's great science book, *Principia,* published in 1687.

Not Quite a Solo. Eighteen-year-old Tania Aebi of New York City went out sailing by herself on May 28, 1985. She returned—still by herself—on Nov. 6, 1987, having sailed around the world. Unfortunately, Aebi missed breaking a couple of records for solo sailing because she had a friend aboard on an 80-mile (130-kilometer) stretch of the Pacific Ocean.

Made to Be Broken. Computer analyst Lois McCallin on Jan. 21, 1987, set a distance record for human-powered flight over a closed course, pedaling the *Eagle,* an experimental aircraft, 10 miles (16 kilometers) through the air at Edwards Air Force Base in California. The next day, medical student Glenn Tremml flew the *Eagle* 37.2 miles (59.9 kilometers), breaking McCallin's record as well as the open course record.

If They Could See Her NOW. Mary Alexander (Molly) Yard, who was elected president of the National Organization for Women (NOW) on July 18, describes herself as a born feminist. Born some 70 years ago as the third child and third daughter of missionary parents in China, Yard recalled, "My father's Chinese friends said that was a fate worse than death—to have daughters and no sons."

Poet Honored. Richard P. Wilbur on April 17 became the second poet laureate of the United States, succeeding Robert Penn Warren, who stepped down after one year because of poor health. Wilbur's book *Things of This World* won the 1957 Pulitzer Prize for poetry. The new laureate is known for his technical skill and his use of mythical themes in poetry as well as for his excellent translations of comedies written by French playwright Molière.

Wrong, Isaac. A 23-year-old physics student at the University of Chicago in February 1987 detected a minor error made by a giant of science 300 years previously. Robert Garisto discovered that English genius Sir Isaac Newton had used an incorrect value for an angle in a calculation published in *Philosophiae Naturalis Principia Mathematica* (1687), usually called just *Principia,* one of the greatest works in the history of science. Garisto said that he planned to continue his studies of German physicist Albert Einstein's general theory of relativity. Asked whether he expected to find errors in Einstein's work, he replied, "Give me a break."

Honors for a Star. A famous student graduated with honors at Princeton University in New Jersey in June 1987. Escorted by bodyguards, she led her class commencement procession past photographers from as far away as Japan. "I've proven something to myself. I didn't expect to get honors, but I worked as hard as I could from day one," said the graduate, actress Brooke Shields. Jay Myers

NEWSPAPER ownership in the United States continued to become more concentrated in 1987 as newspaper chains expanded their holdings. Ralph Ingersoll II, through Ingersoll Publications Company, on August 6 paid an astonishingly high price—estimated to exceed $125 million—for the *Morristown* (N.J.) *Daily Record*, whose circulation is only 60,000. On August 31, Ingersoll paid $318-million for the five medium-sized newspapers owned by the Horvitz Newspapers chain.

William Dean Singleton's MediaNews Group Incorporated bought two big-city newspapers in a single week. On September 10, MediaNews bought *The Houston Post* from the Toronto Sun Publishing Corporation for $150 million plus a share of revenue increases for the next five years. On September 14, MediaNews bought *The Denver Post* from the Times Mirror Company for $95 million.

Detroit Pact Debates. In federal hearings held from August 3 to 23, two huge chains battled the U.S. Department of Justice over the future of newspaper competition in Detroit. At issue was a joint operating agreement between *The Detroit News,* owned by Gannett Company, the largest U.S. newspaper chain, and the *Detroit Free Press,* owned by Knight-Ridder Newspapers, Incorporated. Federal law allows a failing newspaper to combine operations and split profits with its competitor. The two papers, however, must continue to compete in news coverage.

Both the Justice Department and Administrative Law Judge Morton Needleman recommended that U.S. Attorney General Edwin Meese III reject the operating agreement. Knight-Ridder said it had lost so much money on the *Free Press* that it would be forced to shut the paper down if an agreement were not approved. Media observers expected Meese to decide the case in early 1988.

Times Folds. Gannett on February 14 ceased publication of a 103-year-old daily, *The Louisville* (Ky.) *Times. The Times* was published in the afternoon. Gannett also publishes *The Courier-Journal,* a morning newspaper in Louisville.

Credibility. A Gallup Poll found that 63 per cent of Americans think daily newspapers are believable. On the other hand, 33 per cent said newspapers are not believable, compared with 15 per cent in a poll conducted in 1985.

According to the 1987 poll, 75 per cent of Americans believe that the press tends to invade people's privacy. Privacy became a media issue on May 3, when *The Miami* (Fla.) *Herald* reported that Gary Hart, a candidate for the Democratic presidential nomination, spent a night with a woman who was not his wife. The story forced Hart to drop out of the race, but he reentered it in December (see DEMOCRATIC PARTY).   Mark Fitzgerald

See also AWARDS AND PRIZES (Journalism Awards). In WORLD BOOK, see NEWSPAPER.

NICARAGUA. Hard-pressed economically and with scarce resources devoted to the military, Nicaraguan President Daniel Ortega signed a Central American peace accord on Aug. 7, 1987, along with the presidents of four other Central American nations. Following the accord, Ortega loosened restrictions on the Nicaraguan press and agreed to indirect negotiations for a cease-fire with *contra* rebels supported by the United States.

Contras. The Administration of President Ronald Reagan remained firm in its support of the contras. On March 9, the leading political moderate in the contra leadership, Arturo Cruz, resigned. Cruz said he had found it impossible to implement reforms.

The image of the contras—who have often been accused of human rights violations—was further tarnished on April 28 with the killing of Benjamin E. Linder, a mechanical engineer from Portland, Ore. Linder was slain by contras while working with an armed crew on a hydroelectric project in northern Nicaragua. The government charged that Linder was executed after being wounded.

In 1986, Reagan Administration officials had thwarted a congressional ban on military aid for the contras by diverting profits to them from secret U.S. arms sales to Iran. In the spring of 1987, Congress opened hearings to investigate the mat-

A *contra* leads a patrol of antigovernment troops in Nicaragua in February 1987. A peace accord in August raised hope for an end to the fighting.

ter. As the hearings continued, the Reagan Administration delayed requesting new military funding. See IRAN-CONTRA AFFAIR.

Peace Accord. Under the terms of the August 7 peace accord, all outside aid for rebel groups was to end. The accord also called for an end to press censorship, a cease-fire, and amnesty for rebels. In September, the Nicaraguan government began complying with the provisions on press freedom nearly a month before the required date by lifting its ban on the opposition newspaper, *La Prensa,* and a Roman Catholic radio station.

In October, the government reported that it had reached an amnesty agreement with Miskito Indian rebels who live on Nicaragua's east coast. The rebels had broken away from the main contra leadership, though they still received aid from the U.S. Central Intelligence Agency.

Then, in early November, the government said it would begin indirect negotiations with the contras. On November 6, the government chose Miguel Cardinal Obando y Bravo, head of the Roman Catholic Church in Nicaragua and an outspoken critic of the government, to act as intermediary.

In late December, the contras staged the largest military offensive in their five-year-old rebellion, briefly occupying three towns in northeastern Nicaragua. Also in late December, the U.S. Congress approved $8.1 million in nonmilitary aid for the contras, though $4.5 million of that amount could be used to transport previously purchased weapons. The congressional vote was influenced by a Sandinista defector, Major Roger Miranda Bengoechea, who said that Nicaragua planned to maintain a large reserve army. At year-end, cease-fire talks were at an impasse.

Soviet Relations. The Soviet Union appeared to put some distance between itself and the Nicaraguan regime in 1987. Government officials said the Soviets had told them that they were not willing to shore up Nicaragua's economy, as they have done for Cuba since a U.S. embargo was imposed in the 1960's. On May 30, 1987, Nicaragua announced that the Soviet Union was cutting back oil shipments to 40 per cent of Nicaragua's crude oil needs from 80 per cent. The Soviet decision was reportedly made in anger over Nicaragua's resale of Soviet oil to obtain *hard currencies* (currencies maintained at fixed values in foreign exchange).

By August 1987, the Soviet cutback and the failure to increase other economic aid was having a big impact on the Nicaraguan economy. Nicaraguan Vice President Sergio Ramírez Mercado made an open appeal to "friendly and supportive countries" to send oil to Nicaragua to make up for the loss of Soviet aid. Nathan A. Haverstock

See also LATIN AMERICA (Facts in Brief Table). In WORLD BOOK, see NICARAGUA.

NIGER. See AFRICA.

NIGERIA. Oil, which has been the major reason for Nigeria's prosperity, was the main cause of the country's economic crisis in 1987. Declining world prices for oil reduced Nigeria's oil-export earnings to $6.5 billion in 1987, down from $24 billion in 1980. Nigeria's disagreement with Middle Eastern members of the Organization of Petroleum Exporting Countries (OPEC) over oil prices and production quotas prompted Nigeria in January 1987 to host the founding of a competing group, the African Petroleum Producers' Association. Eight other oil-producing countries joined with Nigeria to form the association.

Economic Austerity. Reduced export revenues and a foreign debt of $20 billion forced the military government of President Ibrahim Babangida to continue its austerity program in 1987. During the year, restrictions were placed on the importation of cars, televisions, refrigerators, and wheat. People were encouraged to use locally produced corn and cassava to make bread. A lack of imported spare parts, however, hurt manufacturing. Unemployment and shortages in basic goods increased, and food riots occurred in several cities.

The government tried to curb inflation and increase exports by devaluating the naira, Nigeria's unit of currency. The value of the naira dropped from 1 naira to U.S. $1 to 4 naira to U.S. $1 after the devaluation.

Religious Conflict. Tensions caused by language and cultural differences among Nigeria's more than 250 ethnic groups have subsided since the civil war of the late 1960's. But religious conflict has continued, and in March 1987 it erupted into violence. In the predominantly Muslim north, riots broke out in the cities of Kafanchan, Kaduna, and Zaria between Muslims and Christians. Dozens of churches and mosques and several Christian schools were burned. At least 15 people died. In response to the strife, the government established an advisory Council on Religious Affairs to encourage respect for all religions.

Return to Civilian Rule. Speculation about Nigeria's political future led the government in April to ban the popular *Newswatch* magazine. The ban was lifted in August after the Armed Forces Ruling Council (AFRC) under President Babangida pledged itself to restore civilian rule in 1992. Previously, the Babangida regime had promised that the transition would take place in 1990. The new government is to be modeled after the United States presidential system, with a two-house legislature and competing political parties.

In August, the AFRC moved its headquarters to Nigeria's future capital city, Abuja, 300 miles (480 kilometers) north of the present Nigerian capital, Lagos. J. Gus Liebenow and Beverly B. Liebenow

See also AFRICA (Facts in Brief Table). In WORLD BOOK, see NIGERIA.

NIXON, RICHARD MILHOUS (1913-   ), 37th President of the United States, met with President Ronald Reagan at the White House on April 28, 1987, to discuss arms control. Earlier, Nixon and his second secretary of state, Henry A. Kissinger, had coauthored an article that raised questions about Reagan's arms-control policies.

Writing in the *Los Angeles Times* on April 26, Nixon and Kissinger urged the President to link the proposed removal of intermediate-range missiles from Europe with reductions in the Communist bloc's numerically superior conventional military forces. Reagan, however, made no such link in negotiations with the Soviet Union leading to the December 8 signing of a treaty eliminating medium-range missiles.

On May 20, Nixon was installed in Paris as one of only 15 foreign associates of the prestigious Academy of Fine Arts. Nixon was chosen for the honor because he encouraged American contributions to French arts projects through tax deductions. In March, Nixon delivered a eulogy at a memorial service for Woody Hayes, the former Ohio State University football coach.

Nixon, 74, underwent prostate surgery in June. In February, his wife, Pat, had a small malignant tumor surgically removed from the inside of her mouth.   Frank Cormier and Margot Cormier

In WORLD BOOK, see NIXON, RICHARD M.

President Oscar Arias Sánchez of Costa Rica speaks to reporters in October after learning that he had won the 1987 Nobel Peace Prize.

NOBEL PRIZES in peace, literature, economics, and the sciences were awarded in 1987 by the Norwegian Storting (parliament) in Oslo and by the Royal Academy of Science, the Caroline Institute, and the Swedish Academy of Literature, which are in Stockholm, Sweden.

The Peace Prize was awarded to Oscar Arias Sánchez, 46, the president of Costa Rica and the chief architect of a regional peace accord designed to end the civil wars in Nicaragua, El Salvador, and Guatemala. The accord was signed by the presidents of those three countries, Arias, and the president of Honduras on August 7. The peace plan called for democratic reforms, cease-fires, and amnesties as well as an end to foreign support for rebels and their use of foreign territory.

The Nobel committee praised Arias for his "outstanding contribution to the possible return of stability and peace to a region long torn by strife and civil war." The committee also expressed the hope that the prize would speed up the carrying out of the peace plan. See LATIN AMERICA.

The Literature Prize went to Joseph Brodsky, 47, a Russian poet who was expelled from the Soviet Union in 1972. Now a U.S. citizen, Brodsky was lauded for his "all-embracing authorship, imbued with clarity of thought and poetic intensity."

Although Brodsky spent 18 months in a Soviet labor camp—for failure to hold a steady job—he was not a political dissident. His banishment from the Soviet Union may have had more to do with the aggressive individuality and sensuality expressed in his poems than with his political beliefs.

Born into a Jewish family in Leningrad, Brodsky was quickly recognized as a major talent in the Soviet Union, though his works have never been officially published there. His first volume of poems in English translation was published in 1973. *A Part of Speech,* his second volume, appeared in 1980.

The Economics Prize was given to Robert M. Solow, 63, of the Massachusetts Institute of Technology (M.I.T.) in Cambridge for developing a mathematical model to identify and measure the factors that make economies grow. In a series of articles published from 1956 to 1960, Solow argued that technological progress is more important to a country's long-term economic growth than are increases in capital and labor. The Nobel committee noted that Solow's model had "an enormous impact on economic analysis." Until Solow's pioneering work, most economists believed that an increase in capital was the most important factor in economic growth.

The Physics Prize was shared by K. Alex Müller, 60, of Switzerland, and J. Georg Bednorz, 37, of West Germany for their breakthrough in superconductivity. The two scientists, who work at the

International Business Machines Corporation Research Laboratory in Zurich, Switzerland, found a material that can transmit electricity without losing current to resistance at a temperature higher than scientists had thought possible.

The scientists' findings, published in January 1986, triggered an avalanche of research. The development of superconducting materials could have such important commercial applications as more efficient electrical generators and transmission lines, faster computers, and high-speed trains. See PHYSICS (Close-Up).

The Chemistry Prize went to two American scientists and a French researcher. The winners were Donald J. Cram, 68, of the University of California at Los Angeles; Charles J. Pedersen, 83, who until his retirement in 1969 worked for E. I. du Pont de Nemours & Company; and Jean-Marie Lehn, 48, of the Louis Pasteur University in Strasbourg, France. They were honored for their work in developing molecules that can "recognize" one another and "choose" which other molecules they will combine with. This principle is currently used in medical testing.

Pedersen was recognized for laying the foundations for an area of research known as "host-guest" chemistry with his discovery of compounds that form complexes with particular *ions* (electrically charged atoms or groups of atoms). Lehn and Cram built on his studies by producing synthetic molecules that, to a certain extent, perform the same functions as enzymes.

The Physiology or Medicine Prize was awarded to Susumu Tonegawa, 48, a Japanese-born molecular biologist working at M.I.T., for his work on the body's immune system. Tonegawa was the first Japanese scientist to win the physiology or medicine prize.

Tonegawa was honored for unlocking the puzzle of how genes change to produce a seemingly endless number of different antibodies, each targeted at a specific disease-producing agent. His work could help scientists improve the effectiveness of vaccines, find cures for autoimmune diseases—in which the body attacks itself—and reduce the risk of rejection of organ transplants.

1986 Winners. The winners of Nobel Prizes in 1986 were Holocaust survivor Elie Wiesel for peace, Nigerian poet and playwright Wole Soyinka for literature, Dudley R. Herschbach and Yuan T. Lee of the United States and John C. Polanyi of Canada for chemistry, James McGill Buchanan of the United States for economics, Ernst Ruska and Gerd Binnig of West Germany and Heinrich Rohrer of Switzerland for physics, and Rita Levi-Montalcini, who is a citizen of both the United States and Italy, and Stanley Cohen of the United States for physiology or medicine.   Barbara A. Mayes

In WORLD BOOK, see NOBEL PRIZES.

NORTH, OLIVER LAURENCE (1943-   ), testified before the United States Congress in July 1987 to explain his role in secret U.S. arms sales to Iran and the illegal diversion of profits to Nicaraguan rebels known as *contras*. See IRAN-CONTRA AFFAIR.

During his testimony, North—a lieutenant colonel in the Marine Corps and former staff member of the National Security Council (NSC)—said he acted with the approval of his superiors. North admitted lying to investigators and falsifying or shredding important documents. Many people who watched the televised hearings were impressed by what they saw as North's forthright, patriotic manner.

North was born in 1943 in San Antonio. After graduation from the U.S. Naval Academy in Annapolis, Md., in 1968, North served as an infantry platoon commander in Vietnam, winning the Silver Star, Bronze Star, and two Purple Hearts. In 1969, North returned to the United States to teach military tactics to Marine officers.

In 1981, North joined the NSC. He was fired in November 1986 because of the arms sales to Iran.

North married the former Betsy Stuart in 1968. They have four children.   Jinger Griswold

NORTH ATLANTIC TREATY ORGANIZATION (NATO). See EUROPE.

NORTH CAROLINA. See STATE GOVERNMENT.

NORTH DAKOTA. See STATE GOVERNMENT.

NORTHERN IRELAND. After months of protests in 1987, Northern Ireland's two Protestant unionist parties were forced to recognize that their campaign against the Anglo-Irish Agreement was a failure. The agreement, signed by the governments of Great Britain and the Republic of Ireland in 1985, gave Ireland a voice in the affairs of Northern Ireland. The two Protestant parties— the Official Unionist Party (OUP) and the more strident Democratic Unionist Party (DUP)—had demanded a referendum on the agreement, which they feared would lead to domination by Ireland, a Roman Catholic nation. The parties appealed to Queen Elizabeth II, but their pleas fell on deaf ears. A campaign by local Unionist councilors to refuse to hold council meetings collapsed as the result of a split between the OUP and the DUP.

On July 2, a task force set up by both parties issued a report that restated their opposition to the Anglo-Irish Agreement. But the report also urged a reopening of dialogue with both the British government and the Roman Catholic minority in Northern Ireland to discuss sharing power between Protestants and Roman Catholics.

Protest Dropped. On September 14, DUP leader Ian R. K. Paisley and OUP leader James Molyneaux dropped their boycott of British government ministers and met with Tom King, secretary of state for Northern Ireland, for the first time in

NORTHWEST TERRITORIES. A plan to divide into two separate territories the vast Northwest Territories, which cover 1.3 million square miles (3.4 million square kilometers), failed to come to pass in 1987. The plan stalled because leaders of Native groups could not agree on the location of the boundary. After years of wrangling, the Inuit (Eskimo), who are largely located in the eastern part of the territories, and the Dene Indians, *métis* (persons of mixed Indian and white ancestry), and whites of the western part of the territories reached a tentative agreement on January 15.

The provisional settlement, which would have included the oil- and gas-rich Beaufort Sea area in the western territory, was subject to approval by the 51,000 residents of the territories and the federal and territorial governments. The disposition of the Beaufort Sea had been a key issue in the partition talks. But other obstacles arose as discussions continued. On March 1, it was announced that agreement could not be reached on the disposition of an area of about 60,000 square miles (155,000 square kilometers) in the central Arctic. The Inuit and the Dene and métis leaders were unable to resolve the dispute, and a March 31 deadline for drawing the boundary between the two territories passed. David M. L. Farr

See also CANADA. In WORLD BOOK, see NORTHWEST TERRITORIES.

NORWAY. The minority Labor government of Prime Minister Gro Harlem Brundtland barely survived a vote of no confidence in the Storting (parliament) on June 12, 1987. The two members of the right wing Progress Party voted with the government, giving it a one-vote margin of victory over the center-right opposition. If the government had lost, it would have had to resign.

The opposition had criticized the Labor Party's inability to cut Norway's 10 per cent annual rate of inflation and to slash state spending. The government needed to take such measures to compensate for a 20 per cent loss in revenues caused by a collapse in the price of oil in 1986. Norway exports oil pumped from wells in the North Sea.

Closer to EC. Norway moved closer to joining the European Community (EC or Common Market) in 1987. Norway had decided in a *referendum* (vote of the people) in 1972 not to join the EC. In 1987, however, with the establishment of new Norwegian delegations to the EC, and EC representation in Oslo, Norway's capital, political observers predicted Norway's early application to join the EC.

Arms Sale Dispute. Johan Jørgen Holst, minister of defense, went to Washington, D.C., on June 23 in an effort to lessen the damage caused by a long-running arms-sale scandal that had soured relations with the United States. Holst's trip followed

Bodies lie outside a destroyed building in Enniskillen, Northern Ireland, after an IRA bomb exploded on November 8, killing 11 people.

more than a year. But Paisley and Molyneaux remained opposed to the task force's recommendation, and other unionist members suspected them of stalling.

On October 7, Peter Robinson, deputy leader of the DUP and one of the authors of the July report, resigned because the parties' leadership ignored the report's recommendations.

Job Discrimination. More companies in the United States in 1987 began refusing to do business with companies in Northern Ireland unless they accepted the MacBride Principles, which ban job discrimination against Roman Catholics in Northern Ireland. Four Irish activists, led by 1974 Nobel Peace Prize winner Sean MacBride, drafted the guidelines in 1985. The British government also took a tougher stance on discrimination. On Sept. 15, 1987, King unveiled a new code that would cancel government contracts with firms that did not comply with the MacBride Principles.

Bombing. The worst bombing in Northern Ireland in years rocked the town of Enniskillen on November 8. Eleven people were killed when the bomb exploded in a community center. The outlawed Irish Republican Army (IRA) later admitted setting the bomb, which the group said was intended to kill security forces. Ian J. Mather

See also IRELAND. In WORLD BOOK, see NORTHERN IRELAND.

Troops take part in winter maneuvers on a Norwegian island in March during a North Atlantic Treaty Organization exercise involving 14,000 people.

a criminal investigation by the Norwegian government into charges that a state-owned armaments manufacturer, Kongsberg Vaapenfabrikk S.A., had sold militarily useful technology to the Soviet Union. The sale violated rules set by the Coordinating Committee on Multilateral Export Controls, which is made up of Japan and all the members of the North Atlantic Treaty Organization (NATO), except Iceland.

The investigation had been sparked by U.S. claims that the Norwegian company and a Japanese firm, Toshiba Corporation, had sold technology that enabled the Soviets to produce submarines that were harder to track than previous models. Kongsberg argued that Norway's Ministry of Trade had cleared the sale. Such sales also require clearance by Norway's Ministry of Foreign Affairs, however, because of their military implications.

Relations with Great Britain worsened over environmental factors, especially acid rain fallout from British factories and Britain's proposal to build a nuclear reactor and nuclear-reprocessing plant at Dounreay, Scotland. Norway feared that the reactor would increase the amount of radioactive material in the North Sea, harming Norwegian fisheries.   Kenneth Brown

See also EUROPE (Facts in Brief Table). In WORLD BOOK, see NORWAY.

NOVA SCOTIA. William J. (Billy Joe) MacLean, a former Nova Scotia cabinet minister who was expelled from the legislature in October 1986 after pleading guilty to falsifying expense accounts, recaptured a seat in a special election on Feb. 24, 1987. The government had tried to bar MacLean from seeking reelection for five years. But MacLean appealed to the courts, and the ban was overturned on January 6. Running as an independent, MacLean won a narrow victory over three opponents. All but two of the members of the legislature boycotted the ceremony when MacLean took his seat on March 12.

On April 10, the government presented a budget that called for no major changes in taxation. The budget promised to reduce the deficit by $16 million to $185 million (Canadian dollars; $1 = U.S. 77 cents as of Dec. 31, 1987) for the current year. It also introduced a stock savings plan allowing investors in smaller Nova Scotia companies a 30 per cent tax credit.

The Canadian branch of the United Automobile Workers failed in its bid to unionize three Michelin tire plants in Nova Scotia. The results of a vote, announced on January 17, showed that a clear majority of the 3,000 workers voted against unionization.   David M. L. Farr

In WORLD BOOK, see NOVA SCOTIA.

NUCLEAR ENERGY. See ENERGY SUPPLY.

NUTRITION. In June 1987, scientists reported for the first time that a large reduction in the level of cholesterol in the blood may prevent *atherosclerosis*, a disease in which fatty deposits thicken and harden the walls of the arteries. Atherosclerosis can cause heart attacks because the fatty substances block arteries that carry oxygen and nutrients to the heart.

The two-year study, conducted by researchers at the University of Southern California School of Medicine in Los Angeles, involved 162 men between the ages of 40 and 59 who had undergone *coronary by-pass surgery*, a procedure that uses veins from the leg to by-pass blocked arteries and provide a new blood supply to the heart. Eighty men were given daily doses of two drugs—colestipol hydrochloride and niacin. (Niacin is considered a vitamin when taken in milligram amounts. But when large doses—3 to 12 grams—are taken daily, niacin is considered a drug.) The men were also put on a diet that was low in fat—only 22 per cent of their total calories per day—and low in cholesterol—less than 125 milligrams per day. The remaining 82 men received *placebos* (inactive substances) and were placed on a less restrictive diet.

The researchers found that the men who received the drugs and followed the strict diet had significant reductions in total blood cholesterol levels, and in *low-density lipoproteins* ("bad" cholesterol). *High-density lipoproteins* (called "good" cholesterol because they may actually slow down the process of atherosclerosis) increased in the men in the diet and drug treatment group. Those in the treatment group also experienced a significantly slower development of atherosclerosis than did the men who received placebos and followed a less strict diet. In addition, about 16 per cent of the men who received the drugs showed an actual reduction in arterial blockage, compared with only about 2 per cent of those taking placebos.

The researchers noted, however, that colestipol and high doses of niacin should be taken only under close medical supervision.

Cholesterol Recommendation. In October 1987, a federal health panel called for regular testing of blood cholesterol for everyone over the age of 20. Cholesterol levels of less than 200 milligrams per deciliter of blood are considered desirable; levels of 200 to 239 are borderline-high; and levels of 240 and above are high-risk. The panel recommended that physicians treat people at risk with strict diets and, in some cases, drugs. As many as 25 per cent of all adults in the United States may be in need of treatment.

Alcohol and Breast Cancer. There may be a link between moderate alcohol consumption and breast cancer, according to two studies published in the May 7, 1987, issue of *The New England Journal of Medicine.* One study conducted by a research group at Harvard Medical School in Boston found that women who had three or more alcoholic drinks per week ran a 30 to 60 per cent greater risk of developing breast cancer than did women who did not drink. The findings were based on a four-year study of questionnaires completed by more than 89,000 women between the ages of 34 and 59.

In the second report, scientists at the National Cancer Institute and other agencies of the National Institutes of Health in Bethesda, Md., analyzed data from the First National Health and Nutrition Examination Survey of more than 7,000 women between the ages of 25 and 74. The researchers found that drinking any amount of alcohol may cause a 50 to 100 per cent increase in the risk of breast cancer. The greatest risk, according to the report, was among those women who consumed more than three drinks per week.

The researchers noted that these studies do not prove that alcohol consumption causes breast cancer. They do suggest, however, that women who are at risk of developing breast cancer—women who have a family history of the disease; obese women; or women who first became pregnant after the age of 25—should limit their alcohol intake. Jean Weininger

See also FOOD; HEALTH AND DISEASE. In WORLD BOOK, see CHOLESTEROL; FOOD; NUTRITION.

OCEAN. In early 1987, scientists on board the Ocean Drilling Program's research drill ship, the *JOIDES Resolution*, encountered the worst sailing weather since the research program began in January 1985. The *JOIDES Resolution* withstood gale-force winds and 30-foot (9-meter) waves in the turbulent South Atlantic Ocean during an expedition to take samples from the ocean floor.

The drill ship took core samples from several sites in waters up to 15,000 feet (4,600 meters) deep. The core samples indicated that millions of years ago, a volcanic rise off the tip of South America separated the lowest depths of the Weddell Sea from the Atlantic Ocean. Then, about 38 million years ago, the rise began to split apart, eventually opening like a giant underwater gate that allowed dense water from the Weddell Sea to flow north into the Atlantic. Today these cold, dense waters flow as far north as New Jersey.

Scientists aboard the *JOIDES Resolution* also learned when Antarctica came to be circled by the Antarctic Circumpolar Current, which is made up of the coldest and most dense water in the world. Scientists have long known that the land masses of South America and Antarctica were connected about 200 million years ago. During that period, warm surface waters from the subtropical Atlantic, Indian, and Pacific oceans flowed south to the Antarctic land mass, warming its climate. Core

Dishes from the *Titanic* are undamaged after lying for 75 years on the floor of the North Atlantic Ocean, where they were found in 1987.

samples taken by the drill ship provided evidence that South America and Antarctica separated between 20 million and 25 million years ago. This allowed a cold ocean current to circle the continent for the first time.

Giant Iceberg. The National Science Foundation reported in November that a huge iceberg broke loose from the Ross Ice Shelf in Antarctica, dramatically altering the frozen shoreline. The iceberg was estimated to be 100 miles (160 kilometers) long, the largest sighted in recent history.

Return to the *Titanic*. In July, a deep-sea diving crew from the French Institute for Research and Exploration of the Sea began to recover artifacts from the wreckage of the British luxury liner *Titanic*. The salvage operation on the *Titanic*—which sank in 1912, killing about 1,500 passengers—was widely criticized as a form of grave robbery. But the French divers and the British investors who financed the expedition insisted that they were careful to treat both the wreck and its artifacts with reverence and respect. They pledged that although *Titanic* artifacts would be exhibited worldwide, none would be sold. The expedition prompted United States senators to pass a bill in August that would prohibit bringing *Titanic* artifacts into the United States for profit.

Dolphin Deaths. In July and August, the carcasses of nearly 400 bottle-nosed dolphins washed onto beaches from New Jersey to Virginia. Laboratory tests revealed that the animals—who were extremely thin and had skin and mouth sores and enlarged organs—died of shock and heart failure. Many of the dolphins had signs of bronchial pneumonia as well. On August 19, marine pathologists reported that the dolphins died of a bacterial infection that may have killed them because they were weakened by exposure to pollution or a virus.

El Niño predictions made in 1986 by researchers studying oceanic patterns in the Pacific Ocean turned out to be fairly accurate. *El Niño* is a warm ocean current that appears off the coast of Peru every three or four years and causes widespread disturbances in global climate patterns. Oceanographers at Columbia University's Lamont-Doherty Geological Observatory in Palisades, N.Y., and at Florida State University in Tallahassee predicted that a moderate or weak El Niño could develop during the winter of 1986 to 1987. Oceanic observations in early 1987 did, in fact, show signs of the early stages of an El Niño, but the threat diminished by May.   Arthur G. Alexiou

In WORLD BOOK, see OCEAN.

OHIO. See STATE GOVERNMENT.

OKLAHOMA. See STATE GOVERNMENT.

OLD AGE. See SOCIAL SECURITY. In the Special Reports section, see THE GRAYING OF AMERICA.

OLYMPIC GAMES. In 1987, North Korea continued to demand that it be allowed to co-host the 1988 Summer Olympic Games to be held in Seoul, South Korea. Plans proceeded smoothly for the 1988 Olympic Winter Games in Calgary, Canada.

At first, North Korea insisted that it stage at least 8 of the 24 sports in the Summer Olympics. North Korea rejected a 1986 offer by the International Olympic Committee (IOC) that would have permitted North Korea to host two sports (archery and table tennis) and parts of two others (a preliminary round of soccer and the start of the men's cycling road race).

In July 1987, South Korea—acting through the IOC—agreed to add women's volleyball and the entire men's cycling road race to its previous offer. Again, North Korea rejected the proposal, demanding all of the soccer competition. South Korea rejected that idea and prepared to stage all of the Summer Games. North Korea repeatedly threatened to lead a Soviet-bloc boycott of the Summer Games, but the threat had little support from the Soviet-bloc nations.

The IOC continued to relax the standards of amateurism by approving professional tennis players for the 1988 Summer Games under certain conditions.   Frank Litsky

In WORLD BOOK, see OLYMPIC GAMES.

OMAN. See MIDDLE EAST.

ONTARIO. Ontario's voters gave resounding approval to the Liberal Party under Premier David Peterson in a provincial election held on Sept. 10, 1987—resulting in the first Liberal majority in Ontario in 50 years. Holding 51 seats in the Legislative Assembly before the election, the Liberals increased their standing to 95 of the 130 members of the Assembly. (There were six unfilled seats before the election—one vacancy and five newly created seats.) The Liberals won 47.5 per cent of the vote, carrying every major city in the province.

The New Democratic Party (NDP) won 19 seats, a loss of 4 from its strength before the election. The NDP cooperated with the Liberals from 1985 to 1987 while the latter party formed a minority government. But by taking second place in the September election and 25.6 per cent of the popular vote, the NDP became the official opposition in the legislature. The Progressive Conservative (PC) Party, which had governed Ontario for 42 years until 1985, fell from 50 seats to 16 seats. The PC's share of the popular vote was 24.6 per cent. Larry Grossman, who led the PC Party in Ontario for two years, lost his own seat in Toronto and announced on September 11 that he would step down as party leader.

Peterson made the federal government's proposed free-trade agreement with the United States a major theme in his campaign. He stressed that without strong protection for the automobile industry, a free-trade pact posed a threat to Ontario, the automaking center of Canada. The NDP opposed free trade, but the PC's supported it.

Budget. Liberal Treasurer Robert Nixon presented the provincial budget on May 20. With a thriving provincial economy, the treasurer was able to bring the deficit under $1 billion (Canadian dollars, with $1 = U.S. 77 cents as of Dec. 31, 1987) for the first time since the 1981 recession. No new taxes were proposed. Provincial revenues were forecast at $33.86 billion and expenditures at $34.84 billion.

Catholic School Funding. On June 25, the Supreme Court of Canada ruled unanimously that controversial legislation involving public support for all levels of Roman Catholic high schools through grade 13 was constitutional. Previously, public funding had been available up to only grade 10. The court ruled that the Ontario legislation marked a valid extension of rights guaranteed to Roman Catholic schools by Canada's 1867 federal constitution.   David M. L. Farr

See also TORONTO. In WORLD BOOK, see ONTARIO.

OPERA. See CLASSICAL MUSIC.

OREGON. See STATE GOVERNMENT.

The Duke and Duchess of York, right, aided by Ontario Premier David Peterson and the duchess's attendant, go canoeing during a July tour of Ontario.

PACIFIC ISLANDS. Two military coups in Fiji in 1987 culminated in the establishment of a republic and the severance of a 113-year-old link with Great Britain. The first coup occurred after a coalition of the Fiji Labor Party and the primarily Indian National Federation Party won a general election held from April 4 to 12. The coalition, led by 52-year-old Timoci Bavadra, an ethnic Fijian, won 28 seats in the country's 52-seat House of Representatives.

The victory by Bavadra's coalition temporarily ended the government of Prime Minister Ratu Sir Kamisese Mara, who had ruled Fiji since the country gained independence in 1970. Nineteen of the coalition's 28 seats were won by ethnic Indians, whose ancestors had been brought to Fiji from India as plantation laborers. After Bavadra appointed Indians to nearly half of his Cabinet positions, ethnic Fijians protested that they were being dispossessed in their own land.

On May 14, Lieutenant Colonel Sitiveni Rabuka and 10 other Fijian soldiers invaded the House of Representatives in Suva, Fiji's capital, and captured the Cabinet members, including Prime Minister Bavadra. They were detained for several days. Meanwhile, Ratu Sir Penaia Ganilau, the governor general, assumed emergency powers under the Constitution and appointed a council of ministers chaired by Rabuka to run the country. Rabuka, previously the third highest officer in Fiji's army, was promoted to command the army.

Talks on Fiji's constitutional future dragged on until September. Although most Fijians insisted that Indians should never have another opportunity to control the government, a compromise seemed possible until Rabuka led a second coup on September 25 and announced that he had taken over Ganilau's executive authority.

Three Weeks of Confusion followed. On October 1, Rabuka said he had revoked the 1970 Constitution. On October 6, he declared Fiji a republic. Ganilau, however, still claimed to be in charge. Finally, on October 15, Ganilau asked Queen Elizabeth, who was attending a meeting of Commonwealth leaders in Vancouver, Canada, to relieve him of his post. Fiji's membership in the Commonwealth lapsed at that meeting.

Rabuka acted as Fiji's head of government until December 5, when he appointed Ganilau president of the new republic. Mara, who insisted that he had no part in the coups, was reinstalled as prime minister. Rabuka, promoted to brigadier general on November 12, became minister of home affairs in Mara's largely civilian Cabinet.

France Seeks Friends. Tahiti's best-known politician, Gaston Flosse, resigned as president of

Facts in Brief on Pacific Island Countries

Country	Population	Government	Monetary Unit*	Foreign Trade (million U.S. $) Exports†	Imports†
Australia	16,297,000	Governor General Sir Ninian Martin Stephen; Prime Minister Robert Hawke	dollar (1.4 = $1)	22,900	26,000
Federated States of Micronesia	79,600	President John Haglelgam	U.S. dollar	no statistics available	
Fiji	717,000	President Ratu Sir Penaia Ganilau; Prime Minister Ratu Sir Kamisese Mara	dollar (1.5 = $1)	240	447
Kiribati	65,000	President Ieremia Tabai	Australian dollar	3	23
Marshall Islands	34,000	President Amata Kabua	U.S. dollar	no statistics available	
Nauru	9,000	President Hammer DeRoburt	Australian dollar	93	14
New Zealand	3,372,000	Governor General Sir Paul Reeves; Prime Minister David R. Lange	dollar (1.5 = $1)	5,750	6,200
Papua New Guinea	3,997,000	Governor General Sir Kingsford Dibela; Prime Minister Paias Wingti	kina (1 = $1.14)	920	969
Solomon Islands	304,000	Governor General Sir Baddeley Devesi; Prime Minister Ezekiel Alebua	dollar (1.9 = $1)	70	83
Tonga	104,000	King Taufa'ahau Tupou IV; Prime Minister Prince Fatafehi Tu'ipelehake	pa'anga (1.4 = $1)	7	41
Tuvalu	8,000	Governor General Tupua Leupena; Prime Minister Tomasi Puapua	Australian dollar	1	3
Vanuatu	145,000	President Ati George Sokomanu; Prime Minister Walter H. Lini	vatu (101 = $1)	18	52
Western Samoa	167,000	Head of State Malietoa Tanumafili II; Prime Minister Va'ai Kolone	tala (2.1 = $1)	16	63

*Exchange rates as of Dec. 1, 1987, or latest available data. †Latest available data.

Fijian army leader Sitiveni Rabuka, shown in island dress, led coups in May and September but returned Fiji to civilian rule in December.

French Polynesia's territorial government on February 7 to work full time in his other post of French secretary of state for the South Pacific. His task, to win friends for France in the region, was complicated by the year's events.

Turmoil in New Caledonia. New Caledonia's original Melanesian inhabitants, called Kanaks, maintained their demands for independence from France. Most Kanaks boycotted a referendum on September 13 to determine the country's political future. French residents voted overwhelmingly in the referendum for continued French rule. On December 4, the United Nations General Assembly voted 69 to 29, with 47 abstentions, to urge France to give New Caledonians self-rule.

Envoy Expelled. Vanuatu expelled the French ambassador and a senior French official in October for allegedly giving money to an opposition political party. It was the third expulsion of a French ambassador since Vanuatu gained its independence from Britain and France in 1980.

Anger over *Rainbow Warrior.* French agent Alain Mafart, who was being held on Hao Atoll in French Polynesia, was evacuated to Paris for medical reasons in December 1987. New Zealand Prime Minister David R. Lange called the transfer of Mafart "a blatant and outrageous" breach of a 1986 French-New Zealand agreement. Mafart had been sentenced to 10 years in prison in New Zealand for bombing the Greenpeace ship *Rainbow Warrior* in Auckland Harbor in 1985 but was transferred to French custody on Hao under the 1986 agreement.

Tahiti Riot. Hundreds of French paramilitary police were flown to Tahiti, the largest island in French Polynesia, after a riot erupted in Papeete, the capital, on October 25. The riot began when police evicted 500 striking dockworkers from the port area. The government declared the first state of emergency in the island's history. Property damage was put at $48 million.

Palau Violence. A fatal shooting and other acts of violence occurred in Palau's capital, Koror, on Sept. 7, 1987, as the Palau Supreme Court was about to begin a hearing into the legality of a referendum held on August 4 to determine the country's relationship with the United States. In the referendum, Palauans voted 5,964 to 2,201 to drop a provision in their Constitution closing their 343 islands to nuclear-powered ships and weapons of the United States. In five earlier referendums since 1983, the Palauans had insisted on the antinuclear provision. Their change of heart occurred after 900 of 1,330 government workers were laid off in July 1987 because the local government ran out of money. Robert Langdon

In WORLD BOOK, see PACIFIC ISLANDS.
PAINTING. See ART.

PAKISTAN suffered from terrorism and military attacks by the Afghan government and its Soviet sponsors along the Afghanistan border during 1987. The trouble seemed to be intended to dissuade Pakistan from continuing to support the Afghan resistance movement.

A series of air raids by planes from Afghanistan struck Pakistani frontier villages in late February and again in late March, killing more than 260. A few smaller attacks occurred later in the year, and Afghan artillery occasionally shelled Pakistani villages. Most attacks were aimed at Pakistani villages through which Afghan resistance supply routes passed.

Terrorist Bombings—which had occurred for years in the North-West Frontier Province and Baluchistan—spread during 1987 to the Punjab and Sind provinces. Pakistani officials said this showed that the Afghan secret police were intensifying efforts to intimidate Pakistan. Some bombs were intended for Afghan resistance leaders in Pakistan, but terrorists also placed many bombs in public places to kill civilian Pakistanis.

The largest terrorist bombing occurred in Karachi on July 14, when 75 people were killed. President M. Zia-ul-Haq blamed Afghanistan for the attack but said Pakistan would not change its policies. By October, terrorists had killed about 250 people and wounded 1,000.

435

PALEONTOLOGY

Internal Discord. Karachi was also torn during 1987 by a continuation of two years of violent clashes between members of the Pathan ethnic group and Mohajir immigrants from India. Battles from late 1986 through 1987 killed about 500.

The political opposition to Zia remained fragmented and ineffective throughout 1987. The main opposition group, the Pakistan People's Party, lost its first major challenge to the ruling Pakistan Muslim League in local elections on November 30.

Nuclear Bomb Development. The head of Pakistan's nuclear research program, Abdel Qadeer Khan, was quoted on March 1 as saying that Pakistan possessed a nuclear device. He later denied this, but in a United States magazine interview published on March 30, Zia acknowledged that his country now had the capability to build a nuclear bomb. On December 17, a Pakistani was convicted in the United States of trying to illegally export special steel used for building nuclear weapons.

Despite this conflict with U.S. opposition to nuclear proliferation, the U.S. Congress decided on December 17 to begin a new $4-billion funding program for military and economic aid to Pakistan. The aid was intended to support Pakistan's policy on Afghanistan.   Henry S. Bradsher

See also AFGHANISTAN; ASIA (Facts in Brief Table). In WORLD BOOK, see PAKISTAN.

PALEONTOLOGY. A large collection of fossilized dinosaur nests with eggs containing unhatched dinosaurs was found in June 1987 in Alberta, Canada. The nests, which were discovered by scientists from the Tyrrell Museum of Paleontology in Drumheller, Alta., are only the third discovery of dinosaur nests. Other nests have been found in Montana and in the Gobi Desert in China. Paleontologists reported that the fossilized eggs were laid by *hadrosaurs* (duck-billed dinosaurs) about 73 million years ago.

Frog in Amber. The discovery of an ancient, remarkably well-preserved frog encased in *amber* (the hardened resin of pine trees) was reported in September by paleontologists George O. Poinar, Jr., and David C. Cannatella of the University of California at Berkeley. The frog, which is about 1 inch (2.5 centimeters) long, was found in the Dominican Republic. It is about 35 million to 40 million years old.

One of only three ancient *vertebrates* (animals with backbones) found preserved in amber, the fossil is also the only known specimen of a frog fossilized in this manner. The scientists speculated that the frog had been carried to the nest of a predatory bird but was entombed in a blob of resin before it was eaten. The scientists reported that the discovery of the frog, along with several other animals from the area also found entombed in amber, indicates that a diverse group of animals occupied the Caribbean islands earlier than had been believed.

Early Life. The discovery of fossils of bacteria that are among the earliest evidence of life on earth was reported in July by paleontologists J. William Schopf and Bonnie M. Packer of the University of California at Los Angeles. The fossils were found in rocks from Australia dated from 3.3 billion to 3.5 billion years old. The scientists reported that the bacteria are similar to modern blue-green algae that produce oxygen as a by-product of photosynthesis. The discovery suggests that oxygen-producing organisms appeared earlier than scientists had believed.

Oldest Land Animals. Evidence of the oldest known land-dwelling animals was reported in January by geologists Gregory J. Retallack and Carolyn R. Feakes of the University of Oregon in Eugene. In rock dated to about 440 million years ago, the scientists found cylindrical fossilized burrows about 0.08 to 0.83 inch (2 to 21 millimeters) in diameter. The rock, from central Pennsylvania, apparently was soil at that time. The scientists speculated that the multilegged arthropods that probably made the burrows may have been among the first creatures on land because the burrows are some 20 million to 25 million years older than any previous evidence for animal life on land.

Abrupt Extinctions. A mass extinction that occurred about 200 million years ago was abrupt, not gradual, as scientists had believed. That conclusion—based on a study of four collections of fossils found in Nova Scotia, Canada—was reported in August by a team of scientists headed by paleontologist Paul E. Olsen of the Lamont-Doherty Geological Observatory in Palisades, N.Y.

The fossils, dated as earliest Jurassic Period—about 200 million years ago—represent a variety of animals, including reptiles and fish, that lived in various freshwater and land environments. The scientists found that by 200 million years ago, at the beginning of the Jurassic Period, many of the animals common in the preceding Triassic Period had disappeared. Scientists had previously thought that the Triassic-Jurassic extinctions had occurred over a period of 15 million to 20 million years. Olsen's group, however, found that the extinctions were relatively abrupt, occurring in less than 850,000 years.

The researchers also speculated that the extinctions may be related to the impact of a meteor that crashed into what is now Quebec, Canada, at about the same time. Some scientists believe that a meteor impact 65 million years ago caused another mass extinction in which the dinosaurs were among the creatures wiped out.   Carlton E. Brett

In WORLD BOOK, see DINOSAUR; PALEONTOLOGY.

436

PAN AMERICAN GAMES. The 1987 Pan American Games became a multisport battle between the United States and Cuba. The United States won most of the honors, and Cuba was second best among the record total of 38 nations.

The games were held from August 8 to 23 in Indianapolis, with a record total of 4,453 athletes competing in 31 sports. The U.S. team included such outstanding athletes as track-and-field stars Jackie Joyner-Kersee and Carl Lewis, and diver Greg Louganis, and all did well.

U.S. Stars. Joyner-Kersee tied the women's world record of 24 feet 5½ inches (7.45 meters) in the long jump. Lewis won with 28 feet 8½ inches (8.75 meters), the sixth longest jump ever. Louganis won the men's 3-meter and 10-meter diving for the third straight Pan American Games.

In most sports, the United States sent its best athletes. In swimming, however, the best U.S. athletes were competing in the simultaneous Pan Pacific Games. Nevertheless, the second-string U.S. men and women won gold medals in 27 of the 32 swimming events.

In track and field, the United States won 13 of the 20 events for men and 13 of the 18 for women. In gymnastics, U.S. athletes won the all-around and team titles for both men and women. Cuba dominated boxing, baseball, fencing, and

Denise Parker of Utah competes in archery in August at the Pan American Games where, at 13, she became the youngest U.S. gold medalist ever.

weight lifting. Brazil was the best in judo, soccer, and men's basketball.

U.S. Disappointments. The United States endured disappointments, too. Its men's basketball team was upset by Brazil, 120-115, in the final. Its boxers won only 1 of the 12 finals; Cubans won 10. The world's best high hurdler, Greg Foster of Chino Hills, Calif., fell in the men's final. The most heralded female gymnast at the games, Kristie Phillips of Houston, fell off the balance beam twice. The young U.S. baseball team upset the veteran Cubans in preliminary competition, 6-4, only to lose to Cuba in the final, 13-9.

Medal Totals. The United States set Pan American records of 168 gold medals and 369 total medals. Cuba and Canada were next in gold medals (75 and 30 respectively) and in total medals (175 and 162).

Silvia Poll, a 16-year-old swimmer from Costa Rica, won eight medals (three gold). Scott Johnson, a gymnast from Lincoln, Nebr., also won eight medals (four gold). José Luís Lozano, a roller-skating racer from Argentina, won five gold.

Problems off the Field. Six athletes from five nations were disqualified after urine tests showed they had taken banned drugs. They included Bill Green of Torrance, Calif., the silver medalist in the hammer throw. Green said he was innocent and appealed the decision.   Frank Litsky

PANAMA. Political protests became frequent in 1987 as many Panamanians grew increasingly unhappy with what they considered a corrupt and repressive government. At the center of the storm was General Manuel Antonio Noriega Morena, commander of the Panamanian Defense Forces.

On June 8, Noriega's former second-in-command—Colonel Roberto Díaz Herrera, who had been forced to retire the previous week—turned on his former commander and leveled several accusations against him. Colonel Díaz said that during the 1984 presidential elections, he and Noriega were responsible for vote fraud that denied victory to Arnulfo Arias Madrid. Díaz further implicated Noriega in drug trafficking; the 1981 death of Brigadier General Omar Torrijos Herrera; and the 1985 murder of Hugo Spadafora, an outspoken critic of the military. Many of Díaz' charges against Noriega had also been made by United States intelligence agencies.

Díaz' allegations led to four days of angry protests and violence. Panama's government imposed a "state of urgency" on June 11, during which many civil and political rights were suspended.

Noriega Denied the Charges, saying they were part of a campaign by the U.S. government to topple him. The state of urgency ended on June 30. One of the first acts of protest that day was by Noriega supporters outside the U.S. Embassy in Panama City, the capital. The demonstrators caused damage estimated at $106,000. The United States suspended all military and economic aid to Panama. On July 30, after Panama paid for the damage, the U.S. Department of State said the aid suspension was being reviewed.

Protests against Noriega, organized by the opposition National Civil Crusade, became heated in July. On the first day of a two-day general strike on July 27 and 28, security forces staged a raid on Díaz' home, arresting him and 45 supporters. Leaders of the Civil Crusade went into hiding. The government also closed down three newspapers and an independent radio station.

Following his arrest, Díaz withdrew his accusations, but many believed that he did so under duress. In November, another former military leader, General Rubén Darío Paredes, said he believed many of Díaz' original charges and predicted a "bloody confrontation" unless Noriega went into exile. On December 23, Díaz was sentenced to five years in prison for crimes against state security. The next day, he was expelled from Panama and flew to Venezuela.   Nathan A. Haverstock

See also LATIN AMERICA (Facts in Brief Table). In WORLD BOOK, see PANAMA.

PAPUA NEW GUINEA. See ASIA; PACIFIC ISLANDS.
PARAGUAY. See LATIN AMERICA.
PENNSYLVANIA. See PHILADELPHIA; STATE GOV'T.

PERU. During 1987, Peruvian President Alan García Pérez tried to juggle demands from the military, the workers, and international creditors. Judging from a September opinion poll that showed his popularity declining to 47 per cent—from 78 per cent in 1986—he did not juggle well.

Curbing the Military. To reassert civilian control over a military organization that often dealt in politics, García Pérez dismissed Peru's air force commander on April 2 for lobbying against unification of the armed forces. The unification, enacted on April 1, reduced military representation in the cabinet to one officer, from three, and consolidated the joint chiefs of staff and the armed forces' three branches into a single, civilian-directed defense ministry.

Peru's military leaders were against the change, particularly because it occurred as leftist rebels belonging to Sendero Luminoso (Shining Path) were stepping up terrorist attacks, including assassinations and bombings, in Lima, Peru's capital city. The leftist rebellion, in its seventh year in 1987, has cost an estimated 10,000 lives.

The Economy. The first national work stoppage since García Pérez assumed the presidency in July 1985 took place on May 19. The Communist-led General Confederation of Peruvian Workers staged the strike to protest the government's economic program. It followed a strike of state petroleum workers, which García Pérez declared illegal on April 22.

Two major lenders announced in early June that further loans to Peru would be suspended because of overdue payments on Peru's foreign debt. The lenders were the World Bank, an agency of the United Nations, and the Inter-American Development Bank, funded mainly by the United States government. In spite of mounting anger from Peru's creditors abroad, García Pérez persisted in linking payments on the foreign debt to Peru's export earnings.

With increasing financial problems, including a predicted inflation rate of 100 per cent in 1987, Luis Alva Castro, Peru's prime minister and finance minister, resigned on June 22. The move was said to be in preparation for a presidential bid in 1990. For García Pérez, the resignation represented a further loss of support from within his ruling American Popular Revolutionary Alliance.

On July 28, García Pérez announced plans to nationalize 10 banks, 17 insurance companies, and 6 finance companies. He claimed the move was necessary to break the stranglehold of a small group of speculative financiers on the national economy.   Nathan A. Haverstock

See also LATIN AMERICA (Facts in Brief Table). In WORLD BOOK, see PERU.

PET. See CAT; DOG.

PETROLEUM AND GAS. Concern about attacks on oil tankers and production facilities in the Persian Gulf by warring Iran and Iraq intensified efforts to construct overland pipelines in the region in 1987. John S. Herrington, secretary of the United States Department of Energy (DOE), said on October 6 that new pipelines eventually would carry more than 50 per cent of the oil exported from the gulf area, significantly reducing the importance of the gulf for oil transport. Oil tankers plying the gulf in 1987 carried about 9 million barrels per day (bpd) to markets in Europe, Japan, and the United States.

Iraqi Pipelines. In an effort to restore its oil exports to prewar levels, Iraq on September 20 signed a contract for the construction of a $1-billion pipeline to carry crude oil across Saudi Arabia to a terminal on the Red Sea. The pipeline—620 miles (1,000 kilometers) long—will have a capacity of 1.65 million bpd when completed in 1989. Iraq's oil minister said the new pipeline will increase the country's export capacity to prewar levels of about 3.6 million bpd, compared with 2.7 million bpd in 1987. The pipeline will carry oil to the Saudi oil port of Yanbu. On July 29, Iraq opened a pipeline linking oil fields near the southern city of Al Basrah with Turkey.

OPEC Disarray. Bickering within the Organization of Petroleum Exporting Countries (OPEC)

The *Gas Prince*, the first reflagged Kuwaiti tanker escorted through the Persian Gulf by the U.S. Navy to arrive in Japan, unloads its cargo in August.

during 1987 prevented the 13-member oil cartel from curbing production or forestalling a widely predicted decline in world oil prices. On June 28, all OPEC members except Iraq agreed to limit their combined oil production to a total of 16.6 million bpd until the end of 1987, an increase over the 15.8 million bpd limit set at the organization's previous meeting in December 1986. Iraq refused to sign the agreement because its quota did not equal that of Iran. By September 1987, however, the pact was being widely flouted, with OPEC members producing an estimated 20 million bpd.

For the first half of 1987, oil prices remained above the official price of $18 per barrel, despite the oil surplus, partly because of tensions in the Persian Gulf. But by August, prices had fallen as OPEC members discounted their surplus oil to attract buyers.

On December 14, OPEC agreed to cut production to a total of 15.1 million bpd for the first six months of 1988. The cartel also maintained the $18-per-barrel price, despite an attempt by Iran to raise the price to $20 per barrel. Iraq again refused to sign the pact in protest against Iran's quota and announced it would continue to pump twice its own quota. Iraq's actions and the expected continuation of cheating by other OPEC members led oil industry analysts to predict a surplus of 2 million bpd.

OPEC's failure to reduce overall production caused oil prices to drop quickly in late December 1987. Many analysts predicted that prices would tumble to $15 per barrel by spring 1988.

Texaco Settlement. A bitter legal battle between Texaco Incorporated and the Pennzoil Company ended on Dec. 19, 1987, with Texaco agreeing to pay Pennzoil $3 billion in cash. The dispute began in 1984, when Texaco acquired the Getty Oil Company for $10.1 billion, shortly after Pennzoil reached what it considered a binding agreement to buy 43 per cent of Getty. Pennzoil subsequently sued Texaco and was awarded more than $10.5-billion in damages. Texaco, the third largest U.S. oil company, filed for bankruptcy on April 12, 1987, after failing to reach a compromise with Pennzoil on reducing the size of the damage award. The action allowed Texaco to continue operating and prevented Pennzoil from taking any action to seize the firm's assets. Texaco was the largest U.S. firm ever to enter bankruptcy proceedings. As part of its agreement with Pennzoil, Texaco was to pay its creditors $2.5 billion in order to emerge from bankruptcy.

Reserves. The DOE reported on September 8 that proven reserves of both crude oil and natural gas in the United States declined in 1986. Reserves of crude oil dropped by 5.4 per cent or 1.5 billion barrels, leaving the United States with 26.9 billion barrels of oil in offshore and onshore fields. The DOE blamed the decline on falling oil prices that discouraged exploration for new oil fields and drilling of new wells. The department noted, for example, that the discovery of new oil fields added only 48 million barrels to U.S. reserves in 1986—the smallest amount since the DOE began monitoring reserves in 1976. Reserves added by extending old oil fields were also the lowest ever recorded by the department. Proven reserves of natural gas also declined in 1986 for the fifth consecutive year. But the decline was slight, only about 0.9 per cent, leaving the United States with 191.6 trillion cubic feet (5.36 trillion cubic meters) of known gas.

Foreign Dependence. Projections issued by the DOE on Aug. 12, 1987, indicated that the United States would grow increasingly dependent on imported oil during 1988, as domestic production of crude oil continued to decline. Imports were expected to reach 6.0 million bpd in 1988, a 6 per cent increase from the 1987 average of 5.7 million bpd and the highest level of oil imports since 1980.

Offshore Drilling. The U.S. Department of the Interior on July 2, 1987, instituted a five-year program to open millions of acres of offshore land for oil and gas drilling. Although the plan would defer leasing on about 46 per cent of the outer continental shelf, environmental groups criticized the program for opening previously restricted environmentally sensitive areas off New England, Florida, and the Pacific Northwest to development. Nine environmental groups filed suit in August to block the plan. The oil industry criticized the program for being too restrictive.

Prudhoe Productivity. The Prudhoe Bay oil field in Alaska on March 5 produced its 5 billionth barrel of oil, surpassing East Texas as the most productive oil field in the United States. Officials of the Standard Oil Production Company, which owns a majority interest in Prudhoe Bay, said that about half of the field's 10 billion barrels of oil had been removed since production began in 1977. Beginning in 1988, oil production is expected to decline by about 10 per cent per year. The East Texas field, in contrast, has produced 4.9 billion barrels of oil since 1930.

Canadian Gas. Canada on April 9, 1987, approved the export of 140 billion cubic feet (3.9 billion cubic meters) of natural gas per year to customers in the Northeastern United States. The approval, granted by Canada's National Energy Board, permitted a total sale of 2.1 trillion cubic feet (588 billion cubic meters) of natural gas, worth about $2 billion, over a 15-year period.

Soviet Production. Natural gas fields in the Soviet Union may become more critical to future world energy supplies than all the oil fields of the Persian Gulf countries, according to a September prediction by the International Gas Union (IGU), an organization representing gas industries in 46 countries. John Kean, president of the IGU, said that natural gas reserves in just two Siberian fields contain an estimated 33.5 trillion cubic feet (9.3 billion cubic meters) of natural gas—40 per cent of the world's total. Kean said that Soviet exports of natural gas are already providing as much as 25 per cent of Western Europe's energy needs.

Monthly oil production in the Soviet Union set a world record of at least 12.6 million bpd during May, according to *Oil & Gas Journal,* a respected industry publication. The Soviet government newspaper *Izvestia (News)* on May 18 reported the successful use of two nuclear explosions to increase production in an oil field in central Russia just west of the Ural Mountains. The underground explosions, each equivalent to about 20,000 short tons (18,000 metric tons) of TNT, transformed a number of small underground oil deposits into one large reservoir from which oil could be recovered economically. In August, a Soviet official reported that the government had set off three such underground explosions in 1987.   Michael Woods

In the Special Reports section, see STORMY DEBATE OVER ACID RAIN. In WORLD BOOK, see GAS; PETROLEUM.

PHILADELPHIA. The celebration of the 200th birthday of the United States Constitution in 1987 was centered in Philadelphia, the city where the document was written. On September 17—the anniversary of the signing of the Constitution—humid, showery weather failed to dampen the spirits of celebrants, who had come by the thousands from all parts of the United States. The city put on a grand show: a parade of 20,000 marchers, an all-day picnic with continuous entertainment near Independence Hall, an address by President Ronald Reagan, fireworks, and a dramatic nighttime lighting of the Benjamin Franklin Bridge, which spans the Delaware River. See Close-Up.

Mayoral Election. W. Wilson Goode, a Democrat and Philadelphia's first black mayor, won a narrow victory over former Mayor Frank L. Rizzo, who had switched to the Republican Party, in the November 3 election. Goode received 51 per cent of the votes to Rizzo's 49 per cent. Goode overcame criticisms of his first term—particularly complaints that the city's streets were unclean and that he erred when he allowed the police to bomb the home of a radical group in 1985. That bombing caused a fire that left 11 people dead and destroyed most of three city blocks.

Rizzo, a former city police commissioner and two-term mayor from 1972 to 1980, was hampered in the campaign by scrutiny of his record in

Celebrating the Miracle at Philadelphia

Philadelphia was where it all had happened 200 years before, and in 1987 Philadelphia led the celebration of the 200th anniversary of the Constitution of the United States. The Commission on the Bicentennial of the United States Constitution, the federal agency coordinating the 1987 observance, listed more than 1,300 "designated bicentennial communities" throughout the United States. But the festivities centered on Philadelphia, where the 55 delegates to the Constitutional Convention of 1787 labored, producing results that George Washington, later the first President of the United States, called "little short of a miracle."

During 1987, more than 10 million visitors poured into the city to celebrate what has become known as the miracle at Philadelphia. The Constitution gala centered on four major events:

■ Memorial Day weekend, when representatives from the 13 original states met to commemorate the official opening of the Constitutional Convention on May 25, 1787. The 1987 festivities included fife-and-drum bands and a festival of traditional foods and crafts of the colonial era.

■ The Fourth of July weekend, featuring parades, fireworks, outdoor concerts, and a hot-air balloon race.

■ July 16, when more than 200 U.S. senators and representatives met in Philadelphia to commemorate the Great Compromise of July 16, 1787. The compromise, reached after seven weeks of bitter debate that threatened to break up the convention, provided for equal representation of all states in the Senate, but representation based on population in the House of Representatives.

■ Sept. 17, 1987, the bicentennial of the actual signing of the Constitution. Philadelphia mounted one of the largest parades ever held, a six-hour procession highlighted by re-creations of floats from the Grand Federal Procession of 1788, the parade celebrating the Constitution's ratification.

At 4 P.M., the hour when the Constitution is believed to have been signed, former Chief Justice of the United States Warren E. Burger, chairman of the federal Commission on the Bicentennial of the United States Constitution, pulled a rope connected to a full-sized replica of the Liberty Bell. As the bell began to toll, 1,500 doves and pigeons were released into the air as a symbol of peace. Bells in many other cities and towns throughout the United States were rung at the same time. Speeches, other ceremonies, and entertainment filled the day, which ended with a dazzling display of fireworks over the Delaware River.

Other bicentennial offerings in Philadelphia could be enjoyed throughout 1987. At the landmark Second Bank of the United States, an exhibition called "Miracle at Philadelphia" displayed five rooms of original documents, artworks, and multimedia presentations about the Constitutional Convention. An exhibition at Old City Hall featured an original copy of England's Magna Carta, a document approved in 1215 that established many legal and political rights eventually incorporated in the Constitution.

Perhaps most of all, visitors flocked to Independence Hall, the red brick building where the Founding Fathers met behind closed doors during the sweltering summer of 1787. There, with the windows shut and draped against eavesdroppers, the delegates argued, shouted, compromised, and sweated through the hottest summer in nearly 40 years. The summer of 1987 followed suit, serving up plenty of steamy days to help Philadelphia visitors relive the experience of the Founding Fathers.

One of the most popular attractions during the bicentennial celebration was one of the most simple. It was a plain speaker's platform called "America's soapbox" across the street from Independence Hall. Throughout the year, eager visitors climbed onto the soapbox to exercise their right to free speech—one of the rights guaranteed by the Constitution.　Sara Dreyfuss

See also CONSTITUTION OF THE UNITED STATES.

A huge parade in Philadelphia on Sept. 17, 1987, marks the 200th anniversary of the signing of the United States Constitution.

A group of federal and city dignitaries observe ceremonies honoring the bicentennial of the Constitution in Philadelphia in May.

office. Critics charged that Rizzo was a racist mayor who condoned the use of harsh measures by the city's police department.

As the hard-fought campaign moved into its final weeks, Goode refrained from attacking Rizzo, choosing instead to emphasize his own accomplishments as mayor. Rizzo, in contrast, lambasted Goode at virtually every turn.

Corrupt Judges. Throughout 1986, the Federal Bureau of Investigation (FBI) conducted electronic surveillance of the city's roofers union headquarters. In 1987, the FBI alleged that many Philadelphia judges had accepted cash gifts from the union. One judge was convicted of extortion. Another judge, accused of demanding $5,600 to fix 14 cases, was awaiting trial at year-end. A third, charged with extorting $1,300 from a lawyer and $300 from the union, also awaited trial.

A state board that monitors judicial behavior recommended to the Pennsylvania Supreme Court in August that nine Philadelphia judges be removed from office for accepting cash gifts from the union. Action was pending at year-end.

The FBI Probe also resulted in the conviction on racketeering charges of Stephen J. Traitz, Jr., leader of the 4,300-member roofers union, and 12 other present or former members of the union. A jury returned the guilty verdicts on November 23. The defendants were charged with extorting money from contractors, systematically attempting to bribe about 50 public officials, and collecting debts for Nicodemo (Little Nicky) Scarfo, the city's reputed organized-crime leader.

Scarfo, who has allegedly headed the Philadelphia area's major crime family since 1981, was tried separately on charges of trying to extort $1-million from a prominent developer, Willard G. Rouse III. Scarfo was sentenced on August 5 to 14 years in prison and fined $150,000. Two of Scarfo's accomplices, City Councilman Leland M. Beloff and Beloff's aide Robert N. Rego, were convicted in the same trial. The three men had demanded the $1-million payoff from Rouse in return for legislation to clear the way for a massive development along the city's waterfront.

Beloff and Rego were also charged with extorting money from two other developers. Beloff received a 10-year prison term, and Rego was sentenced to 8 years. Beloff, who later resigned his council post, appealed his conviction. Meanwhile, he awaited trial on a vote-fraud indictment.

Scarfo, too, faced other charges. On December 12, a federal jury acquitted him and four other defendants of drug-conspiracy charges. But Scarfo remained in prison for extortion, and he also awaited trial on murder charges. Howard S. Shapiro

See also CITY. In WORLD BOOK, see PHILADELPHIA.

PHILIPPINES. Small groups of rebellious soldiers made three unsuccessful attempts to seize power from President Corazon Aquino during 1987. The largest effort occurred on August 28, when about 2,000 troops led by Colonel Gregorio Honasan attacked the presidential palace and occupied key military camps around Manila, the capital. The fighting killed 53 people. Most of the mutineers, including Honasan, were eventually captured.

The rebel soldiers—and opposition politicians—had complained that Aquino's government treated soldiers poorly and did not adequately support their fight against Communist guerrillas. They also charged Aquino with being unduly influenced by leftists and with running an inefficient regime.

Aquino fought back. "All those who have openly challenged my power, my authority and resolve, have suffered for it," she said on October 20. On the same day, the armed forces asked the Philippine Senate to vote to improve soldiers' living standards, revive use of the death penalty for serious crimes, increase the penalty for rebellion, and take other steps to solve military and security problems. In a related development, the United States blocked former President Ferdinand E. Marcos in January and July from apparent attempts to return and seize power.

Lawless Atmosphere. The Communist guerrillas' New People's Army (NPA) intensified fighting

Philippine President Corazon Aquino surveys an honor guard at army headquarters in early September, a week after soldiers there attempted a coup.

during 1987, marking the failure of efforts to negotiate a peaceful resolution to the civil unrest.

Aquino's attempt to negotiate an end to another
rebellion—by Muslim separatists in the southern
islands—also failed, though fighting was limited.

Vigilante groups—most of them formed to fight
the NPA—sprang up in some areas. Private individuals and their neighbors organized some
groups, but authorities worried that landlords and
politicians used the need to counter the NPA as
an excuse for creating private armies.

Two unexplained murders added to the atmosphere of lawlessness. Cabinet secretary Jaime Ferrer was assassinated on August 2, and leftist leader
Leandro Alejandro was shot on September 19.

Philippine Voters approved a new constitution
by more than 3 to 1 in a direct election on February 2. The new Constitution, which restored the
political system Marcos set aside in 1973, called for
a strong presidency and a two-chamber Congress.
The set of laws allowed the president one six-year
term and confirmed Aquino—who took power
when Marcos went into exile after a disputed election in 1986—as president until June 30, 1992.

Voters elected a national Congress on May 11.
A coalition of Aquino supporters won 162 of 200
seats in the House of Representatives and 22 of 24
Senate seats. Jovito Salonga, the winner of the
most votes nationwide for the Senate, became

president of the Senate, the third most powerful
office after the presidency and vice presidency.

Vice President Salvador H. Laurel broke politically with Aquino and resigned his second post as
foreign secretary on September 16. After a cabinet
reorganization announced on the same day,
Aquino dropped two close aides who had been accused of leftist leanings.

Land Reform. One of the most important of the
302 decrees that Aquino issued—before her
power to do so lapsed when Congress opened session on July 27—established an Agrarian Reform
Council. The council's mission was to break up
large landholdings and distribute parcels to land-
less peasants and tenant farmers in an effort to
reduce rural poverty and thus limit the appeal of
Communism. Although some Filipinos complained that the measure was inadequate, many
wealthy landlords vowed to fight it. Aquino
charged Congress with working out the details.

Economy. After several years of declining national output, the economy grew by 5.1 per cent
in the first half of 1987, helped by a construction
boom and higher prices for sugar and coconut exports. Average wages fell in terms of buying
power, however, and the unemployment rate rose
to 14.2 per cent by April.   Henry S. Bradsher

See also ASIA (Facts in Brief Table). In WORLD
BOOK, see PHILIPPINES.

443

PHOTOGRAPHY. In the world of 35-millimeter (mm) photography, 1987 was the year of the autofocus camera. Following the lead of Minolta's groundbreaking Maxxum line, a number of manufacturers introduced their own 35-mm autofocus single-lens reflex (SLR) cameras. Many photographers enthusiastically embraced autofocus technology, insisting that with most subjects it is faster and more accurate than manual focusing. Other photographers, however, were critical of autofocus systems, saying they are error-prone and limited in their capabilities. No other 35-mm innovation in recent years—including the autoexposure technology that has been almost universally accepted by amateur photographers and professional photojournalists alike—has been as controversial as automatic focusing.

Autofocus SLR's divide the image formed by the lens into two parts, then project each half of the image onto an electronic component called a *charge-coupled device* (CCD). The CCD converts the twin images into electronic signals, which it instantaneously relays to a miniature built-in computer. The computer analyzes the signals and then sends instructions to a tiny motor that adjusts the lens to the correct focus.

Among the year's new crop of autofocus cameras, the Canon EOS 650 and the professional-level EOS 620, introduced in February at the Photographic Marketing Association convention in Chicago, were noteworthy. What distinguishes the EOS system is that the focusing motor is incorporated into the lens rather than the camera body, as in other makes of autofocus cameras. Besides eliminating a possibly trouble-prone mechanical linkage between the camera body and the lens, Canon's design produces fast and quiet focusing.

Another notable autofocus camera in 1987 was the Pentax SF1, also introduced at the February convention. The SF1 includes a built-in pop-up electronic flash and a large liquid-crystal display panel that provides a complete status report on the camera. Both those features have become increasingly common in SLR's and appeared on a number of models introduced during the year.

In April, Nikon unveiled the simplest autofocus SLR to date. The N4004 is as uncomplicated to use as a 35-mm point-and-shoot camera but offers a number of sophisticated features, including interchangeable lenses, found only on SLR's.

Many professional photographers have been reluctant to accept autofocus cameras because of the limited number of compatible lenses available for them. But some manufacturers have dealt with that problem by offering autofocus zoom lenses in a broad range of focal lengths. Both Vivitar and Kalimar introduced 28- to 200-mm autofocus lenses in 1987, giving photographers virtually all commonly used focal lengths in a single lens.

Compact 35's. Compact point-and-shoot autofocus cameras continued to dominate the market in 1987, with manufacturers showing remarkable inventiveness in their designs. Unlike autofocus SLR's, compact models focus by emitting a beam of infrared light that is reflected back to a sensor connected to a lens-focusing mechanism. But because the light beam is aimed at the center of the scene, it can cause incorrect focus when the subject is off-center. The Chinon Auto 3001/MAF, introduced in September, solves this problem by emitting three light beams, aimed at the right, left, and center of the scene. Focus is adjusted to make the closest part sharp.

Film. Although color films continued to be at the cutting edge of film technology in 1987, several new black-and-white films were introduced during the year in answer to a dramatic revival in black-and-white photography. Fuji unveiled a fine-grain ISO-400 black-and-white film called Neopan, and Kodak expanded its T-Max black-and-white line, offering both T-Max 100 and T-Max 400 (ISO 100 and 400, respectively) in larger formats. These films incorporate the "tabular" grain technology that Kodak uses in its fast color negative films. Tabular grain allows films to be made more light-sensitive without increasing the size of the silver particles in the emulsion. Steve Pollock

In WORLD BOOK, see CAMERA; PHOTOGRAPHY.

PHYSICS headlines in 1987 announced developments concerning three superlatives: the discovery of a celestial object known as a supernova, the United States government's decision to build a gigantic atom smasher to be called the Superconducting Super Collider (SSC), and a dramatic breakthrough in the field of superconductivity. The superconductivity breakthrough may have been the most exciting development. Following a remarkable discovery in 1986, physicists in early 1987 became locked in a dramatic race to develop ever-better *superconductors,* materials that carry electricity without resistance. New superconductors had the potential to revolutionize everything from the generation and transmission of electrical power to the design of personal computers. See Close-Up.

Supernova. University of Toronto astronomer Ian K. Shelton on the night of February 23 photographed a new object in a galaxy known as the Large Magellanic Cloud. When he discovered the image of the object a few hours later, he contacted the Central Bureau for Astronomical Telegrams in Cambridge, Mass., alerting astronomers around the world to turn their telescopes toward the starlike pinpoint of light. Astronomers identified the object as a *supernova,* a gigantic exploding star—the brightest seen since 1604—and named it Supernova 1987A.

Superconductivity Research Heats Up

An obscure branch of physics exploded spectacularly into the public view in early 1987, stirring our imaginations with dreams of such futuristic devices as electric trains traveling at astonishing speeds while suspended in midair above their tracks, and gigantic coils of wire that could store tremendous amounts of electric power—forever. Newspapers reported results of physics experiments almost daily.

For decades, research on *superconductivity*—the remarkable property of some materials to conduct electricity without resistance when cooled to very low temperatures—had been marked by extremely slow progress. On Jan. 27, 1986, there was a sign that this research was about to accelerate to a blinding speed. On that day, two scientists at the International Business Machines Corporation (IBM) Research Laboratory in Zurich, Switzerland, made what turned out to be a historic discovery. Physicist K. Alex

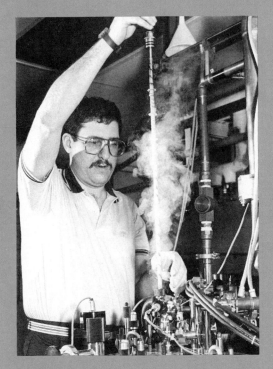

A physicist experiments with a wire that carries electricity without resistance at a near-record temperature—a frigid −290°F. (−179°C).

Müller and crystallographer J. Georg Bednorz found that a ceramic material made of the elements barium, lanthanum, copper, and oxygen became superconducting at a *critical temperature* of about −406°F. (−243°C), about 12 Fahrenheit degrees higher than the critical temperature of any superconductor known.

One problem with superconductivity had been that the gains made possible by the loss of electrical resistance were offset by the expense of cooling the materials to extremely low temperatures. The only substance that could do this at all economically was liquid helium, which was costly and required expensive plumbing.

Superconductors that could be cooled by liquid nitrogen, whose boiling point is −321°F. (−196°C), would be much more economical because liquid nitrogen costs much less, and is much less expensive to use, than liquid helium. The critical temperature of the ceramic material was far below −321°F., but its conductivity had not been thoroughly investigated.

Superconductivity had been discovered in 1911 by Dutch physicist Heike Kammerlingh Onnes. He observed the phenomenon in a copper wire cooled to −452°F. (−269°C). By 1973, physicists had discovered many other superconducting substances but had succeeded in pushing the critical temperature up to only −418°F. (−250°C). There the record remained until Müller and Bednorz came along.

A group of scientists in Japan verified the IBM researchers' results near the end of 1986, setting off a race to develop variations of the ceramic material that would become superconducting at or above the boiling point of liquid nitrogen. Physicist Paul C. W. Chu of the University of Houston was among the first to succeed. In February, he and his colleagues reported development of a new compound of barium, yttrium, copper, and oxygen that became superconducting at −283°F. (−175°C). In the weeks that followed, Chu and others announced evidence—but not proof—of superconductivity at higher and higher temperatures.

As 1987 drew to a close, however, there had still been no convincing proof of a critical temperature higher than Chu's −283°F. And initial optimism about the benefits of the materials that superconduct when cooled with liquid nitrogen had given way to caution. Questions remained, for example, about whether the materials—which are brittle—could be fashioned into useful wire.

Even so, the discovery of "high temperature" superconductivity by Müller and Bednorz was a breakthrough. Recognition came to the two men on Oct. 14, 1987, when they were awarded the 1987 Nobel Prize for physics.   Paul Raeburn

In less than two weeks, physicists made another startling finding. Examination of data recorded at underground laboratories on opposite sides of Earth revealed that a shower of subatomic particles called *neutrinos* originating in the supernova had passed through Earth on February 23. These were the first detections of neutrinos known to have originated outside the solar system.

The detections helped physicists understand what becomes of dying stars. According to commonly accepted theories, massive stars collapse when they run out of the nuclear fuel that sustains them. The collapsed material shrinks until it becomes dense enough to explode in a blinding flash called a supernova. The theories say that supernova explosions release neutrinos, but until Supernova 1987A, physicists had no proof of this. The supernova of 1604 occurred long before scientists had even thought of neutrinos. See ASTRONOMY.

Superconducting Super Collider. On Aug. 7, 1987, more than 200 members of the House of Representatives introduced legislation to authorize the construction of the SSC, which would be the largest and most expensive scientific instrument ever constructed. The machine would be built into an oval tunnel 53 miles (85 kilometers) in circumference, and would cost about $4.4 billion.

Plans call for the machine to accelerate two beams of protons to nearly the speed of light (186,282 miles [299,792 kilometers] per second), and to a combined energy of 40 trillion electron volts. (One electron volt is the amount of energy an electron gains when it moves across an electric field of 1 volt.)

Some 10,000 superconducting electromagnets will steer the beams around the tunnel and direct the beams into violent head-on collisions. Physicists expect many of the collisions to re-create the intense energies believed to have existed in the first few instants after the universe was created in a gigantic explosion known as the *big bang*. Collisions occurring at such energies would create subatomic particles never before observed, enabling physicists to probe even more deeply into the interior of the atom.

One major reason for building the SSC is to determine whether there exists a group of subatomic particles called *Higgs bosons*. The discovery of Higgs bosons would represent a giant step toward physicists' goal of unifying the fundamental forces of nature.

By late 1987, the SSC had received the support of the Administration of President Ronald Reagan. The U.S. Department of Energy had begun the process of selecting a site.   Paul Raeburn

In the Special Reports section, see THE DEATH OF A STAR. In the WORLD BOOK SUPPLEMENT section, see PHYSICS. In WORLD BOOK, see PARTICLE ACCELERATOR.

POETRY. Two eminent poets, Derek Walcott and John Ashbery, brought out new work in 1987. Walcott's *The Arkansas Testament* shows the poet's increasing ability to draw from his experience in the United States as well as his Caribbean origins as a source for poetry. In these poems, more understated than usual for Walcott, he often returns to the balladlike, four-line stanza he used in much of his early work. In *April Galleons,* Ashbery explores, elegantly but elusively, the difficulty of fixing meaning in poetic language.

Roots of Common Experience. C. K. Williams in *Flesh and Blood* and Alan Shapiro in *Happy Hour* write a poetry more rooted than Ashbery's in common experience. Williams' book is a sequence of eight-line poems, often grouped together by theme. Williams is especially adept at revealing the tensions of city life, where people often come suddenly into disturbing closeness with strangers and are not sure how to respond.

Shapiro's poetry, which can be funny even at its most serious, reveals the complications of family, marriage, and friendship. In one of the best poems, "Extra," a middle-aged woman hopes briefly for a fresh start in her marriage when her husband suddenly becomes considerate of her after she has a heart attack. Shapiro reveals, with both sympathy and unsentimental clarity, the motives in both husband and wife that make such a fresh start improbable.

Lyric Poetry. Jorie Graham's *The End of Beauty* and Mark Halliday's *Little Star* both challenge, in different ways, the usual notions of lyric poetry. Graham divides her poems into short sections that interrupt the flow of her language, and she often uses extremely abstract diction. Halliday writes in a conversational, breezy free verse that is close to prose—as if he were trying to test how many of its resources poetry could give up and still remain poetry.

Irish Poets. The Irish poet Seamus Heaney produced *The Haw Lantern,* in which he continues his meditation on the relationship between his double inheritance of language—Irish Gaelic and English—and his sense of Irish identity. Paul Muldoon, another Irish poet who had recently begun to be recognized in the United States as comparable to Heaney in stature, brought out a new *Selected Poems, 1968-1986.*

Other Notable Collections of past work include Gwendolyn Brooks's *Blacks,* Donald Finkel's *Selected Shorter Poems,* and Margaret Atwood's *Selected Poems II,* covering the years 1976 to 1986. Collections of new work of interest included Amy Clampitt's *Archaic Figure,* Robert Duncan's *Grouped Work II: In the Dark,* Howard Nemerov's *War Stories: Poems About Long Ago and Now,* and William Stafford's *An Oregon Message.*   Paul Breslin

In WORLD BOOK, see POETRY.

446

POLAND attempted in 1987 to take a long and risky step down the path of economic and political reform. On November 29, the government held a *referendum* (vote of the people) on a drastic reorganization plan intended to:
- reduce the number of ministries, departments, and individual bureaucrats involved in the central government's control of the economy,
- free state-owned business enterprises from most government controls,
- raise prices and wages to world market levels,
- expand private enterprise, and
- end subsidies of unprofitable enterprises.

Risky Proposal. Such a reorganization held risks for Poland's leader, Wojciech Jaruzelski, because the liquidation of unprofitable enterprises would likely increase unemployment and because prices inevitably must rise more rapidly than wages, thereby lowering the standard of living. The government tried to reassure the Polish people, promising to remain committed to a policy of full employment and to prevent a slump in the standard of living. Nevertheless, consumers disturbed by rumors of drastic increases in prices began panic buying of food and other items.

Price Hikes. The government announced on November 14 that the prices of consumer items would soar an average of 40 per cent in 1988. Prices of heavily subsidized items would skyrocket, with fuel prices and rent doubling or tripling, and prices of food more than doubling on average.

The government said that it was raising prices to "heal the market over two or three years and to arrest inflation." Poland's inflation rate was about 20 per cent.

Measures Defeated. In the November 29 vote, the Polish people unexpectedly rejected the reforms. Only 67 per cent of the country's eligible voters turned out for the referendum. To be approved, the referendum needed "yes" votes by 51 per cent of the eligible voters, not just a majority of those voting. The proposal for economic reforms was defeated because only 44 per cent of eligible voters approved it. A second referendum question, about limited and unspecified political reforms, received only 46 per cent approval.

After the results were announced, a government spokesman said the government would not abandon its plans for economic reforms. He said the referendum was about only the pace and extent of reform, not about whether there should be reform. But on December 5, the government announced that the planned price hikes on food would be spread over three years instead of taking effect all at once.

Major Visits. Poland received two guests of outstanding political significance in 1987—Pope John Paul II and United States Vice President George H. W. Bush. The pope, who was born in Poland, visited from June 8 to 14, in his third return to his homeland. Bush visited from September 26 to 29, shortly after the United States announced that it would exchange ambassadors with Poland—a step toward the reestablishment of diplomatic ties.

Farm Fund Revived. A surprising aftermath of the papal visit was a revitalization of the Roman Catholic Church's agricultural fund—a means of injecting Western capital into Polish farming. In 1986, the Catholic primate of Poland, Josef Cardinal Glemp, had abandoned efforts to set up such a fund after four years of wrangling with the government about taxation and control of the fund. In July 1987, the government approved a plan calling for a Church Agricultural Committee to administer a fund that would pay for water-supply equipment for private farmers.

Economic Data released for the first half of 1987 showed industrial output up by 3.1 per cent and housing construction ahead by 2.3 per cent, compared with the figures for the first six months of 1986. Wage hikes continued to outstrip gains in productivity, however, and prices rose 19 per cent in the first six months of 1987, twice the rise expected for the entire year. Foreign debts stood at about $35 billion.   Eric Bourne

See also EUROPE (Facts in Brief Table). In WORLD BOOK, see POLAND.

POLLUTION. See ENVIRONMENTAL POLLUTION.

POPULAR MUSIC. Technological advancement in audio and video recordings, record-breaking pop acts, and high profiles for heavy metal and new age music highlighted 1987. Business boomed as sales of compact disk (CD) players rose rapidly and record companies issued many new albums and reissued old albums on CD. New technology included *CD video*, which combines video and high-quality *digital* (computerized) audio, and *super-VHS video* (S-VHS), which achieves extremely good video quality due to high-speed playing and recording.

Humanitarian Efforts. Paul Simon and 24 South African musicians who performed on his 1986 *Graceland* album played eight benefit concerts in 1987 to aid South African and American children and black education. Madonna performed a benefit concert for AIDS (acquired immune deficiency syndrome) research on July 13 in New York City's Madison Square Garden. In October, A & M Records released a superstar Christmas album called *A Very Special Christmas,* benefiting the handicapped children's Special Olympics. Steve Van Zant's album *Freedom—No Compromise* included songs about apartheid and the struggle of the American Indian.

The Soviet Union was visited by many American musicians, due to Soviet leader Mikhail S. Gorbachev's policy of openness to cultural exchange

Rock star Madonna sings to a sellout crowd of 77,000 at Wembley Stadium in London in August during her Who's That Girl world tour.

between the United States and his country. In the Rock for Peace concert on July 4 in Moscow, American musicians—including James Taylor and Santana—performed with Russian musicians as a climax to a peace march of 420 Soviet and American citizens protesting the nuclear arms race. During the summer, Billy Joel played six concerts in the Soviet Union to a total of more than 300,000 people.

Women Artists burned up the charts in 1987. In June, Whitney Houston's second album, *Whitney,* was the first album by a female to debut at the number-one spot on *Billboard*'s top pop albums chart (see HOUSTON, WHITNEY). In March, Janet Jackson's album *Control* became the second album ever—after *Thriller,* recorded by Jackson's brother Michael—to produce five "top-five" hits— songs in the top five places on the chart of best-selling recordings. In January, Madonna's "Open Your Heart" became her 10th straight top-five single, the longest series of top-five hits since the Beatles had 15 in the 1960's.

Black Musicians continued to play leading roles in the recording industry in 1987. In addition to the chart successes of Whitney Houston and Janet Jackson, Michael Jackson's long-awaited album *Bad* debuted at the number-one spot on *Billboard*'s chart for best-selling albums. Other black artists with top-selling albums were Jody Watley, Smokey Robinson, L. L. Cool J, and Freddie Jackson.

In the 14th annual American Music Awards on January 26, the big winners were two black artists—Houston with five awards and Lionel Richie with four. At the New York Music Awards in April, black musicians Run/D.M.C., Gregory Abbott, and Cameo each received four awards.

Despite the conspicuous success of some black artists, the National Association for the Advancement of Colored People in April published a study showing widespread racial discrimination in the music industry. Furthermore, the Recording Industry Association of America convened a subcommittee of black executives to make recommendations on possible affirmative action policies for the industry.

Dance Music grew musically and commercially. Among the most popular dance music artists were Kraftwerk, Mel and Kim, Company B, and Lisa Lisa & Cult Jam. In February, the Beastie Boys' *Licensed to Ill* became the first rap album to top the pop albums chart. (Rap recordings feature a kind of rhythmic talking to music.)

Jazz continued to receive industry support, as Columbia Records joined the growing list of major labels revitalizing their jazz catalogs. Industry veteran Mel Fuhrman acquired tapes of unreleased music by jazz great Duke Ellington and began issuing a series of 10 CD's. Some of the best-selling jazz albums were by George Howard, Dexter Gordon, Najee, Stanley Jordan, Kenny G., and Michael Brecker.

Jazz festivals in 1987 were artistic and commercial successes. For example, the 18th annual Louisiana Jazz and Heritage Festival, held from April 24 through May 3 in New Orleans, featured more than 300 performers and drew a crowd of nearly 300,000.

New Age Music, often described as impressionistic music designed to help create relaxation and a meditative spirit, rose sharply in popularity in 1987. The increasing popularity of new age and jazz music programs was a hot topic at the National Association of Broadcasters' Radio '87 convention in Anaheim, Calif., in September. MTV network's VH-1 cable channel added a programming block of new age video called New Visions.

Mainstream Rock also flourished in 1987, particularly in the heavy metal style. Pop metalists Bon Jovi released *Slippery When Wet*, which topped the pop albums chart for 7 weeks and the music video chart for 28 weeks. Bon Jovi also helped pave the way for a metal explosion in which seven other metal acts had top-10 hits—Whitesnake, Poison, Motley Crue, Def Leppard, Europe, Cinderella, and Ozzy Osbourne and Randy Rhoads.

Music Video. Paul Simon won best video for "You Can Call Me Al" and best male performance for "Boy in a Bubble" at the Music Video Awards ceremony on May 15 at the International Music and Media Conference in Montreux, Switzerland. Peter Gabriel's "Sledgehammer," a smash hit in 1986, also was a big winner in 1987 with nine awards at the MTV Video Music Awards in September in Los Angeles.

Hit Songs and Albums. The number-one hit songs of 1987 included Gregory Abbott's "Shake You Down," Huey Lewis and the News' "Jacob's Ladder," Starship's "Nothing's Gonna Stop Us Now," U2's "With or Without You," and Heart's "Alone." Los Lobos' "La Bamba"—from the number-one album *La Bamba,* the soundtrack from the movie about the life of 1950's rocker Richie Valens—also captured a top spot on the charts.

The Grateful Dead, one of the best-loved bands in the 1960's, finally had a top-10 album, *In the Dark,* with a hit single, "A Touch of Grey." Some of the other outstanding albums of the year were by Ireland's U2, former Beatle George Harrison, Rolling Stone Mick Jagger, R.E.M., Hüsker Dü, Fleetwood Mac, Bruce Springsteen, the Cars, Neil Young, and Pink Floyd.

Oldies were big money-makers in 1987. Four albums recorded by the Beatles—reissued on CD's—soared to the top 10 on *Billboard*'s CD chart in March. Also, MCI Home Video released the Beatles' *Help* and *The Making of A Hard Day's Night.* Other releases of oldies included reissues of Tur-

Pop singer Billy Joel gives a rousing, crowd-pleasing performance during one of his July concerts in Moscow's Olympic Sports Complex.

tles albums, four repackagings of Elvis Presley songs to commemorate the 10th anniversary of Presley's death, and a four-record set called *The Otis Redding Story.*

Country Music flourished in 1987. Randy Travis, who had a 1987 hit album, *Always and Forever,* was the big winner at the 22nd annual Academy of Country Music awards show at Knott's Berry Farm in Buena Park, Calif., in April. Travis was honored as top vocalist, his album *Storms of Life* was named album of the year, and his song "On the Other Hand" was voted single of the year.

Big country hits in 1987 included George Strait's *Ocean Front Property,* the first album to debut at number one on the country albums chart, and the long-awaited *Trio* by Emmylou Harris, Dolly Parton, and Linda Ronstadt, which was number one for five weeks on the country albums chart. Reba McEntire, The Judds, Dwight Yoakam, and Hank Williams, Jr., also released best-selling albums in 1987.

Deaths in 1987 included jazz artists Buddy Rich, Maxine Sullivan, Kid Thomas, Sammy Kaye, Jaco Pastorius, and Woody Herman; blues artist Paul Butterfield; songwriter Boudleaux Bryant; and reggae artist Peter Tosh.   Jerry M. Grigadean

See also AWARDS AND PRIZES (Arts Awards). In WORLD BOOK, see COUNTRY MUSIC; JAZZ; POPULAR MUSIC; ROCK MUSIC.

POPULATION. On July 11, 1987, the United Nations (UN) Fund for Population Activities symbolically proclaimed a newborn boy in Zagreb, Yugoslavia, as the world's 5 billionth living inhabitant. The world's exact population is difficult to assess, however, and some statisticians disagreed with the UN proclamation, saying that the 5-billion mark had been reached in 1986. Most experts agreed, however, that global population exceeded 5 billion by the end of 1987.

Growth Rates. In 1987, the overall rate of population growth remained steady at 1.6 per cent, indicating an increase of about 220,000 people every day. The growth rate of individual countries varied widely, with the highest rates in the developing nations. On the African continent, for example, population grew by 3.1 per cent, while growth rates in North America and Europe were only 1.5 per cent and 0.3 per cent, respectively.

Life Expectancy at birth continued to be much lower in the developing nations than in industrial countries. In many African nations, life expectancy at birth was only about 45 years. In Australia, Canada, and the United States, on the other hand, life expectancy averaged 75 years. Japan had the world's highest life expectancy—77 years—and Kampuchea had the world's lowest—31 years.   Jinger Griswold

In WORLD BOOK, see POPULATION.

PORTUGAL. Prime Minister Aníbal Cavaço Silva's Social Democrat Party won a landslide victory in general elections on July 19, 1987, taking 148 seats in the 250-seat parliament. Cavaço Silva's right-of-center minority coalition government had fallen on April 3, losing a parliamentary vote on a *censure motion,* one that requires a government to step down. The motion carried by a vote of 134 to 108. The center-left Democratic Renewal Party of former President Antonio dos Santos Ramalho Eanes introduced the motion, and the Socialists and Communists backed it.

New Legislation. After the election, Cavaço Silva said that he would push for legislation blocked in the last parliament, notably a bill to make it easier to hire and fire workers. Laws passed after the 1974 revolution that brought democracy to Portugal severely restricted firings. The Social Democrats claimed these laws discouraged investment and made job creation difficult.

Cavaço Silva presented his new program to parliament on August 26. Through this program, he said, the government intended to sell all the state-owned businesses, except public utilities and transportation companies. The prime minister's goal was to reduce the national debt, as a percentage of *gross national product* (GNP), to half its 1987 level by 1990. (GNP is a nation's total output of goods and services.)

Cavaço Silva also undertook to revise the land reform law passed after the Communist Party led workers in occupying most of the land in the southern Alentejo region south of Lisbon in 1974 and established marketing cooperatives there. In addition, he planned to implement Portugal's controversial Internal Security Law, setting up an agency to gather information on individuals and organizations, and giving security forces more power. All laws passed since 1974 would be reexamined, he promised.

Royal Visit. Great Britain's Prince and Princess of Wales visited Portugal from January 11 to 14 to commemorate the 600th anniversary of the marriage of King John I of Portugal to Princess Philippa, from the English county of Lancashire. The wedding was the first fruit of a treaty signed in 1386 to bind England and Portugal in "perpetual and real league [alliance]."

Macao Handover. Officials of Portugal and China signed an agreement on April 13, 1987, that will transfer administration of the territory of Macao to China on Dec. 20, 1999. The territory consists of the city of Macao, which occupies a peninsula on the southeast coast of China, and three small islands. Portugal established a colony in Macao in 1557.   Kenneth Brown

See also EUROPE (Facts in Brief Table). In WORLD BOOK, see PORTUGAL.

POSTAL SERVICE, UNITED STATES. Postal officials in 1987 once again sought an increase in the price of postage. In May, the Board of Governors of the United States Postal Service proposed an average 16 per cent hike in rates for all classes of mail. The price of a first-class stamp would rise from 22 cents to 25 cents. The Postal Rate Commission was expected to approve the rate hike by mid-1988.

The Postal Service recorded a deficit of $223-million in the 1987 fiscal year. Deputy Postmaster General Michael S. Coughlin said the service faced about $2 billion in added operating costs over a two-year period.

Tisch Sets Goals. Postmaster General Preston R. Tisch, who took office in 1986 as the Postal Service grappled with the ill effects of a series of scandals, told a Minneapolis, Minn., audience in June 1987, "My goal is to do whatever is needed to establish the Postal Service as the leading service enterprise in America."

Although pushing for higher rates for most types of mail, Tisch advocated reducing the charge for Express Mail service. In 1987, the Postal Service had 10 per cent of the overnight-delivery market, and Tisch said he hoped for a 15 per cent share of that market in six or seven years. Tisch also called for a new class of discounted business mail that customers would mark with computer bar codes to speed the sorting process.

Union Contract. In July, the Postal Service reached agreement with its major unions on new 40-month contracts. The contracts increased wages about 2 per cent per year and provided limited cost-of-living adjustments.

New Board Chairman. On January 6, the Board of Governors elected John N. Griesemer, a Missouri businessman and a board member since 1985, as its chairman. He succeeded John R. McKean, who agreed to step down after the Office of Government Ethics criticized his role in encouraging the board to hire a law firm with ties to his San Francisco accounting firm. McKean remained a board member until resigning in May after being accused of wrongdoing by the General Accounting Office (GAO). The GAO alleged that McKean had improperly used $97,793 in Postal Service funds to pay his lawyer when he testified for Attorney General Edwin Meese III at Senate confirmation hearings in 1984.

On August 26, President Ronald Reagan said he would nominate Ira D. Hall, Jr., an International Business Machines Corporation executive, to succeed Peter E. Voss on the Board of Governors. Voss resigned as vice chairman of the board in 1986 after pleading guilty to kickback charges in a postal scandal. Frank Cormier and Margot Cormier

In WORLD BOOK, see POST OFFICE; POSTAL SERVICE, UNITED STATES.

President Reagan and Soviet leader Mikhail S. Gorbachev walk through the White House grounds on the first full day of their December summit meeting.

PRESIDENT OF THE UNITED STATES Ronald Reagan was beleaguered during much of 1987 as he tried to shake off the ill effects of the Iran-contra affair, a White House scandal—uncovered in 1986—involving arms sales to Iran and the funneling of profits from those sales to *contra* rebels in Nicaragua. See IRAN-CONTRA AFFAIR.

Reagan found some respite from his troubles at a December summit meeting in Washington, D.C., with Soviet leader Mikhail S. Gorbachev. Gorbachev arrived on December 7 to join Reagan in signing a treaty that called for eliminating all land-based intermediate-range nuclear missiles, mainly in Europe, over a three-year period. It was the first superpower agreement to dismantle an entire class of missiles—those with a range of 300 to 3,400 miles (480 to 5,500 kilometers).

The Soviets agreed to destroy about 1,600 warheads on SS4, SS20, SS12, and SS23 missiles, while the United States would scrap about 400 warheads on Pershing II and ground-launched cruise missiles. Elaborate and unprecedented on-site inspection procedures would guarantee that both nations complied with the terms of the pact. Ratification of the treaty by the U.S. Senate seemed likely in 1988.

Both Reagan and Gorbachev expressed their satisfaction with the results of their meeting, the first superpower summit on U.S. soil since 1973.

For the Soviet leader and his stylish wife, Raisa, the Washington visit was a clear public relations success, as they wooed government and private-sector leaders as well as curbside crowds along their way.

Reagan and Gorbachev agreed to meet in Moscow in 1988, and they ordered their respective negotiators in Geneva, Switzerland, to speed up the work on a proposed new treaty that would limit the two superpowers to 4,900 nuclear missile warheads each. The United States currently has about 8,000 warheads, and the Soviets have 10,000.

The President and Gorbachev sidestepped Soviet objections to Reagan's Strategic Defense Initiative (SDI), the "Star Wars" space-based missile defense plan. And they remained far apart on such topics as human rights, including Jewish emigration from the Soviet Union, and regional conflicts, particularly in Afghanistan, Angola, Nicaragua, and the Persian Gulf.

Reagan and Gorbachev had talked about limiting intermediate-range missiles in Europe at their 1986 summit in Reykjavík, Iceland. But Soviet insistence that Reagan limit SDI as a precondition to an arms accord led to a collapse of the talks. On Feb. 28, 1987, however Gorbachev announced that he was willing to negotiate an agreement on intermediate-range missiles "without delay" and without demanding curbs on SDI development.

By October, an agreement seemed so imminent that Secretary of State George P. Shultz went to Moscow to set a date for a treaty-signing summit in Washington. Then Gorbachev stunned him—and the world—by saying on October 23 that he could not attend a summit without some steps being taken to resolve differences over SDI. But the Soviet chief quickly changed his mind, and summit plans were announced on October 30.

Nuclear Testing was another area of superpower jockeying. Gorbachev unilaterally halted underground atomic tests in August 1985 but warned in 1986 that the moratorium would end after the first U.S. nuclear test of 1987. The United States set off an underground blast at a Nevada testing ground on February 3, and the Soviets conducted their first test in 18 months on February 26.

On April 17, the United States announced an unprecedented U.S.-Soviet agreement to conduct underground nuclear tests at each other's test sites. The exchange of tests, set for 1988, would allow each nation to calibrate the monitoring systems it uses to measure earth tremors caused by atomic explosions. Thus, by refining their monitoring capabilities, the two superpowers would be able to verify that all explosions are within agreed-on limits.

Persian Gulf. The Soviet Union also figured prominently, if indirectly, in a Reagan Administration decision to broaden the U.S. military presence in the Persian Gulf, where the continuing war between Iran and Iraq threatened to disrupt the oil shipments of other gulf nations. When Kuwait sought ways to protect its oil shipments, the Soviet Union responded with an offer to lease Kuwait three Soviet oil tankers, under the assumption that the Iranians would hesitate to attack Russian-owned vessels.

Eager to prove the friendship of the United States to Kuwait and its Arab neighbors, and unwilling to leave the Persian Gulf to the Soviets, the Reagan Administration made countermoves. It sent warships deep into the gulf, hoping to deter Iranian attacks on friendly merchant vessels, and it also negotiated a shipping agreement with Kuwait. The Kuwaitis were permitted to fly the American flag on 11 of their oil tankers, thus putting the vessels under the direct protection of the U.S. Navy.

On May 17, the U.S.S. *Stark*, a guided missile frigate, was patrolling in the gulf when it was struck and set afire by two missiles fired by an Iraqi warplane. Thirty-seven U.S. sailors died in the incident. Iraq apologized, saying the attack was a mistake. The *Stark*'s commanding officer, Captain Glenn R. Brindel, and its chief weapons officer, Lieutenant Basil E. Moncrief, Jr., were reprimanded and allowed to resign from the Navy rather than be court-martialed for failure to take

defensive measures. Brindel later claimed that some of the ship's sophisticated defensive electronic systems failed to perform properly.

Congress Questions Gulf Policy. After the attack on the *Stark*, many Democrats in Congress demanded that Reagan delay plans to reflag Kuwaiti tankers and give them Navy protection. He rejected the idea, however. In a largely symbolic gesture, the House of Representatives voted 222 to 184 on July 8 to call for a 90-day delay on the reflagging policy. Only 22 Republicans voted with the majority. A day later, Senate Democrats were unable to muster enough votes to pass a similar resolution.

The reflagging went forward, but not without incident. On July 24, one of the first reflagged supertankers to be escorted by the Navy through the gulf struck an underwater mine that ripped a hole in its hull. There were no casualties, but the Navy, watching helplessly, was embarrassed.

For almost two months thereafter, Navy-guarded tanker convoys moved through the gulf without incident. The prevailing view among U.S. officials was that the Navy's show of force had been a success. Then, on September 21, U.S. helicopter crews using night-vision equipment spotted an Iranian amphibious landing craft dropping mines into the gulf. The helicopters attacked the vessel with machine-gun and rocket fire, killing 5 Iranians and capturing 26 others who abandoned ship. The Navy later sank the Iranian ship and began searching for ways to clear the gulf of mines. Remarkably, the Navy's plans for the Persian Gulf had not included provisions for minesweeping.

More Incidents Followed. United States helicopter gunships on October 8 attacked four Iranian patrol boats that had fired at an American surveillance helicopter over international waters. One boat was sunk, and two others disabled.

On October 16, an Iranian Silkworm missile ripped through the superstructure of a U.S.-flagged Kuwaiti tanker, *Sea Isle City*, injuring the American captain and 17 other crew members. Because the vessel was entering Kuwait's main oil terminals at the time, it was under Kuwaiti rather than U.S. naval protection. But on October 19, four Navy destroyers made what Reagan called "a prudent yet restrained response" to the attack by shelling and destroying two connected oil platforms in the central Persian Gulf that Iran had reportedly been using for military operations. Navy commandos also destroyed radar and communications gear on another platform. Iranians on the platforms were warned in time to flee.

Although Congress showed scant enthusiasm for the Persian Gulf convoys, the Senate on September 18 voted 50 to 41 against invoking the 1973 War Powers Resolution in the gulf. The law was designed to give the legislative branch a role

President Reagan tells the members of the Tower Commission on February 26 that he will study their report on the Iran-contra affair, issued that day.

in deciding whether to pursue undeclared wars, such as the long conflict in Vietnam that ended in 1975.

For much of the year, congressional Democrats sought to place limits on Reagan's flexibility in dealing with arms control, SDI, and nuclear testing. House-Senate conferees finally reached a compromise on November 17. The agreed-on measure barred further moves by the Reagan Administration during the 1988 fiscal year to exceed weapons limits imposed in the unratified Strategic Arms Limitation Treaty of 1979 (SALT II). It also blocked SDI tests that might violate the 1972 Treaty on Limitation of Antiballistic Missile Systems and continued a moratorium on tests of antisatellite weapons in space.

Aid to the Contras. In the wake of the Iran-contra affair, it appeared doubtful that Congress would approve further military aid to the contra guerrillas fighting the Marxist government of Nicaragua—a major item in Reagan's foreign policy. Congress did vote for $3.5 million in new "humanitarian" aid for the contras but postponed a vote on $270 million in new military aid until 1988. An additional $8.1 million in humanitarian aid was included in the $604-billion spending bill passed by Congress on December 22.

On August 4, Reagan surprised many Democrats by enlisting the new Speaker of the House,

Representative James C. Wright, Jr. (D., Tex.), as cosponsor of a Central American peace initiative. Reagan and Wright called on Central American countries, including strife-torn Nicaragua and El Salvador, to negotiate their differences, stop aiding guerrilla forces in neighboring nations, stop accepting outside military aid, and move toward democracy.

The Reagan-Wright effort was upstaged three days later as the presidents of Costa Rica, El Salvador, Guatemala, Honduras, and Nicaragua met in Guatemala under the leadership of Costa Rica's President Oscar Arias Sánchez and signed a peace agreement of their own. Although similar in some respects to the Reagan-Wright plan, the Guatemala accord did not require Nicaragua to cut its military ties with Cuba and the Soviet Union.

Wright quickly embraced the Central American peace effort, which won the Nobel Peace Prize for Arias in October, but Reagan was more restrained in his reaction. Nicaragua and its neighbors began making limited moves to carry out the agreement, but the ultimate fate of the plan was left in doubt until early 1988, when it was scheduled to fully take effect. Frank Cormier and Margot Cormier

See also CABINET; CONGRESS OF THE UNITED STATES; REAGAN, RONALD WILSON; UNITED STATES, GOVERNMENT OF THE. In WORLD BOOK, see PRESIDENT OF THE UNITED STATES.

PRINCE EDWARD ISLAND. Premier Joseph A. Ghiz and his Liberal government, elected in April 1986, carried out an active legislative program during 1987—their first full year in office. Seventy-seven bills were passed, compared with an annual average of 41 during the previous five years. One of the most controversial issues was an amendment requiring the use of seat belts in automobiles—a change that ended Prince Edward Island's status as the only Canadian province declining to make the use of seat belts mandatory.

Ghiz, in keeping with the conservative social mood of the agricultural province, joined a campaign protesting the performance of a musical based on the life of rock star Elvis Presley at the annual summer festival held in the capital city of Charlottetown. The disputed play, *Are You Lonesome Tonight?*, was performed after the board of Charlottetown's Confederation Centre of the Arts backed the director in his desire to expand the range of productions and the length of the center's season.

In a special election on September 14, the Liberals won a seat from the Progressive Conservatives (PC's). The victory gave the Liberals 22 seats in the 32-seat legislature, leaving the PC's with 10 seats.   David M. L. Farr

See also CANADA. In WORLD BOOK, see PRINCE EDWARD ISLAND.

Guards stand outside the burning federal penitentiary in Atlanta, Ga., in November, after Cuban inmates seized the facility.

PRISON. Cuban inmates rioted at federal detention centers in Oakdale, La., on November 21, 1987, and Atlanta, Ga., on November 23. The inmates seized control of the two facilities, setting fire to prison buildings and seizing more than 100 hostages. The take-overs were prompted by an announcement by the United States Department of State that many of the detainees would be returned to Cuba. The inmates—many of whom had criminal records or histories of mental illness that normally would have barred them from legal entry into the United States—fled Cuba in a 1980 boat lift and came to the United States along with thousands of other Cuban refugees.

On November 29, eight days after the Oakdale take-over, the inmates there released their hostages and signed an agreement with government negotiators. The agreement promised that the government would conduct reviews on a case-by-case basis before deciding about deportations. On December 4, under a similar agreement, inmates at the Atlanta facility surrendered their hostages, 11 days after the take-over at that prison.

The U.S. Prison Population reached a record high of 570,519 inmates by June 30, 1987. This was up more than 4 per cent from the 546,659 inmates who were in state and federal prison systems at the end of 1986. Overall, the inmate population increased 65.7 per cent from 1980 to 1986,

according to the Bureau of Justice Statistics (BJS) of the U.S. Department of Justice.

As a result of the growing number of inmates in U.S. prisons, crowding remained a major problem in corrections. In the first six months of 1987, an additional 1,000 beds were needed every week to house new inmates, according to the BJS. In 1986, 21 state agencies used emergency release programs, allowing some inmates to be released before completion of their sentences in order to relieve crowding. During 1987, 36 states were operating under court orders because the federal courts had previously found them to be operating prisons under conditions that violated the Eighth Amendment to the United States Constitution, which forbids "cruel and unusual punishments."

Inmates with AIDS (acquired immune deficiency syndrome) aroused new concerns in prisons in 1987. From July 1983 through September 1986, there were 1,193 confirmed cases of inmates with AIDS in U.S. prisons. During that time, 463 inmates died of the disease. Of those deaths, 231 occurred in 1986. Measures for dealing with the AIDS problem varied among prisons and included setting aside separate housing units for AIDS inmates, testing new inmates for exposure to the AIDS virus, training health-care workers and correctional officers to handle AIDS patients, educating carriers of the AIDS virus and others about the spread and prevention of the disease, and distributing condoms to help prevent the spread of AIDS among inmates.

Death Penalty. As of Dec. 20, 1987, 1,982 inmates, including 20 women, awaited execution in the United States, an increase of about 8 per cent since the end of 1986. Twenty-five prisoners had been executed during 1987.

On April 22, the Supreme Court of the United States ruled that the death penalty is constitutional despite statistical evidence that killers of whites are more likely to receive death sentences than are killers of blacks. The court upheld a death sentence imposed in Georgia against a black man convicted of killing a white policeman. The defendant had charged that the Georgia capital punishment system was biased by racism, according to a statistical study. The court ruled that the study was insufficient proof that the defendant himself had been the victim of such bias.

Beds. In 1986, 14,691 new beds were added to existing prison facilities, at an average cost of $13,135 per bed. Forty new facilities provided an additional 15,548 beds, at an average cost of $48,739 per bed. In 1986, it cost an average of $41.70 a day per inmate to operate a correctional system.   B. Scott Baum

In WORLD BOOK, see PRISON.

PRIZES. See AWARDS AND PRIZES; NOBEL PRIZES.

PROTESTANTISM. Television evangelists in the United States made headlines in 1987—some of them sensational. On January 4, Pentecostal evangelist Oral Roberts announced to his television followers that unless they donated $8 million by March 31 to a medical fund he had started, God would call him "home." Although Roberts received the $8 million he requested, he was criticized by other evangelists who thought his fundraising tactic gave TV evangelism a bad name.

PTL Scandal. Television evangelism received an even worse blow in March. A group of TV evangelists, including Jerry Falwell and Jimmy Swaggart, charged that Jim Bakker, head of an evangelistic and entertainment organization called PTL (Praise the Lord or People That Love) in Fort Mill, S.C., was involved in a number of scandals. On March 19, Bakker admitted that he had had an extramarital sexual encounter with Jessica Hahn, a church secretary, in 1980, and that the PTL leadership had agreed to pay Hahn $265,000 to keep her quiet about the encounter. But as Bakker resigned from the ministry, he accused other TV evangelists of plotting to take over PTL, which includes the 2,300-acre (930-hectare) Heritage USA theme park.

Following Bakker's resignation, PTL leaders named Falwell to run the organization temporarily. Falwell engaged in strenuous fund-raising ac-

tivities that he said were necessary to prevent the PTL from going bankrupt. Jim Bakker; his wife, Tammy Faye; and their supporters accused Falwell of a "hostile take-over." In May, Falwell charged that Bakker also had homosexual encounters while head of the PTL and had taken some of the organization's funds when he resigned. Bakker denied the charges. The media dubbed the exchange of accusations the "holy war."

On June 12, the PTL filed for bankruptcy, two days after the U.S. Justice Department, the Internal Revenue Service, and the Postal Service launched criminal inquiries into PTL operations and the Bakkers' finances. Falwell and other evangelists said that all the media attention to the Bakkers had led to a loss of public support for television evangelism. In autumn, Falwell and the entire replacement PTL board resigned.

The PTL scandal also led the public—and the media—to express concern about the incomes and life styles of other prominent television evangelists, including Falwell, Swaggart, and Robert Schuller. Critics charged that while asking their followers to sacrifice money for the sake of the church, many of these ministers adopted luxurious life styles or failed to give a public account of their own finances.

In November, Falwell announced that he would step down as head of the Moral Majority, a conservative political organization that he founded in 1979, and as head of the Liberty Federation, a larger organization that has included the Moral Majority since 1986. Falwell said he would devote his time to his Baptist church in Lynchburg, Va., his TV ministry, and other activities.

Presidential Bids. Protestant ministers were back in the political news in 1987. On October 1, television evangelist Pat Robertson announced his candidacy for the Republican presidential nomination. See ROBERTSON, PAT.

In September, Robertson said he had collected pledges from 3.3 million Americans who supported his candidacy. Mobilizing his supporters through Assemblies of God and other churches, Robertson surprised other Republican candidates by winning a Republican Party caucus in Michigan in August 1986 and by placing first in a straw poll in Iowa in September 1987.

On September 29, Robertson resigned as chairman and chief executive officer of the Christian Broadcasting Network. He also resigned as a Southern Baptist minister to silence criticism and ensure the separation of church and state in his campaign.

But Robertson was not the first Protestant clergyman to announce his political aspirations in 1987. On October 10, Jesse L. Jackson, a Baptist minister, officially declared that he would run for the Democratic presidential nomination in 1988.

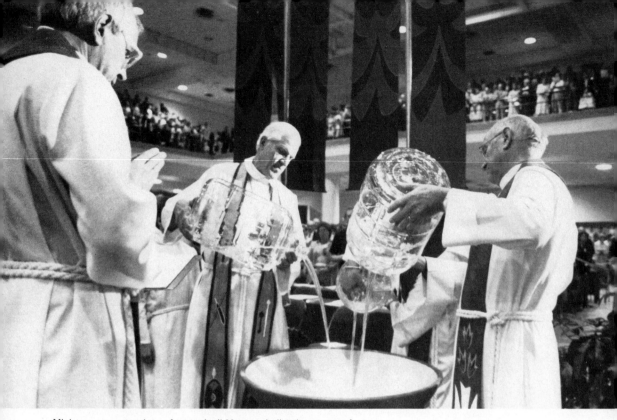

Ministers pour water into a font on April 30 to symbolize the merger of three Lutheran branches to form the fifth largest U.S. Protestant church.

Although political experts said Jackson's chances to win were slim, he was a front-runner in several polls during the year. See JACKSON, JESSE L.

Leaders Meet Pope. On September 11, 30 Protestant leaders, representing—among others—Episcopal, United Methodist, Lutheran, and black denominations, held a conversation and worship service with Pope John Paul II in Columbia, S.C.

Fundamentalist Faction. The Southern Baptist Convention (SBC), the largest Protestant denomination in the United States, continued to live a troubled existence in 1987. During the year, a fundamentalist faction of the SBC placed many of its members on various executive and seminary church boards. These leaders made increasing demands on employees and pastors for loyalty to doctrines that they claimed were essential to Baptist faith. Chief among these doctrines is the belief in the *inerrancy* (freedom from error) of the Bible. SBC moderates believe that the Bible is authoritative as God's word but need not be regarded as free of error in historical, geographical, and other matters.

At its annual meeting in St. Louis, Mo., on June 16, the SBC continued its move to the fundamentalist right. The Peace Committee, a group formed to bring together the convention's fundamentalists and moderates, issued a report at the meeting proposing that all staff and faculty hired by Southern Baptist seminaries believe in the inerrancy of the Bible. But moderates regained some control in November when they defeated fundamentalists in state conventions in Georgia and North Carolina.

Homosexuals and AIDS. The issues of homosexuals in the clergy and the type of ministry that should be given to patients with AIDS (acquired immune deficiency syndrome), many of whom are homosexuals, were prominent topics among Protestants in 1987. On August 24, in Dover, N.H., a jury of United Methodist Church clergy found Rose Mary Denman, pastor of two parishes in Conway, N.H., in violation of a church regulation that prohibits publicly professed homosexuals in the clergy. Denman had challenged the 1984 church law in 1985. The jury suspended her ministry but did not expel her from the church.

Merger Completed. After several years of negotiation, three Lutheran groups voted on April 30 to approve a merger that would create the fifth largest Protestant church body in the United States. The action by the three groups—the Lutheran Church in America (LCA), the American Lutheran Church, and the Association of Evangelical Lutheran Churches—created the Evangelical Lutheran Church in America. The new church has approximately 5.3 million members. On May 1, Herbert W. Chilstrom, bishop of LCA's Minneapolis, Minn., synod, was elected the church's first presiding bishop. The new church, which will be headquartered in Chicago, officially came into being on Jan. 1, 1988.

The merger was not without its controversy, however. A small number of conservative Lutherans, disturbed by the absence of the word *inerrancy* in the new church's constitutional clause on Biblical faith, began to form new denominations or to join small existing ones.

Other News. Among Protestant newsmakers in 1987 was William Sloane Coffin. Coffin, a well-known peace activist in the 1960's and early 1970's, during the Vietnam War, on July 19 announced his resignation as minister of Riverside Church in New York City to become president of SANE/Freeze, an antinuclear organization.

On June 16, the Presbyterian Church (U.S.A) announced that it would move its headquarters to Louisville, Ky. The church's main offices are currently in New York City and Atlanta, Ga.

The United Church of Christ published a new *Book of Worship* in 1987. The new book was more formal than previous editions. It also was the first to use language that represented both men and women equally.   Martin E. Marty

See also RELIGION. In WORLD BOOK, see PROTESTANTISM and articles on Protestant denominations.

PSYCHOLOGY. The link between psychological stress and physical health grew stronger in 1987. Researchers continued to find evidence that stress can weaken the body's disease-fighting immune system, leaving a person more susceptible to infection. In the May issue of the *Journal of Personality and Social Psychology,* psychologist Arthur A. Stone and his colleagues at the State University of New York in Stony Brook reported that even daily mood swings may influence the immune system.

To simulate the way the body protects itself against a virus, Stone administered a harmless protein to 30 dental students once a day for 10 weeks. During this period, the researchers measured the levels of antibodies produced by the students to fight the foreign protein, and obtained reports from the students on their daily moods.

Stone and his colleagues found that on days when students reported they had bad moods, their bodies produced fewer antibodies, and on days when students were in a good mood, antibody production increased. Previous studies have confirmed the link between stress and sickness, but Stone and his colleagues said their study goes even further by suggesting that happiness may play a role in keeping people healthy.

The Cycle of Child Abuse. The question of whether abused children grow up to become abu-

Frank Cotham, *The Wall Street Journal,* permission, Cartoon Features Syndicate
"I suspect your problem is stress-related."

sive parents was addressed in 1987 by Edward Zigler, a child psychologist at Yale University in New Haven, Conn. In the April issue of the *American Journal of Orthopsychiatry*, Zigler and his colleague Joan Kaufman reported that many previous studies on child abuse overestimated the number of abused children who become abusive parents.

Zigler and Kaufman analyzed the research on child abuse and found that though some abused children do become abusive parents, they are the exception, not the rule. Only about 30 per cent of these people become child abusers themselves. Although this figure is about six times higher than the rate of child abuse among parents who were not abused as children, it is still not as high as many people have estimated, the researchers said.

Zigler and Kaufman suggested that it is time researchers look at the conditions that cause abused children to continue the cycle of child abuse as adults. Their review of previously conducted studies revealed several factors that may help stop the cycle of abuse. First, abuse is less likely to be repeated by people who, as children, had the loving support of a parent or foster parent. Second, adults who have a supportive relationship with a spouse or lover and who have few stressful events in their lives have a better chance of being nonabusive, even if they were abused as children. Finally, Zigler and Kaufman said people who are aware of having a history of abuse as children may resolve not to be abusive parents.

Look-Alike Couples. The old wives' tale that married couples who grow old together gradually come to resemble each other may actually be true, according to psychologist Robert B. Zajonc of the University of Michigan in Ann Arbor. In the December 1987 issue of *Motivation and Emotion*, he reported the results of a study that shows how people who share a life could grow to look alike.

Zajonc and his colleagues collected photographs of 12 Midwestern couples. Half of the pictures were taken at about the time the couples married. The rest were taken after the couples had been married for 25 years. Students were then asked to study the photographs and pick the men and women who most resembled each other. When the students tried to match the pictures of individuals who were newlyweds, they succeeded only by chance. But when asked to match the pictures of individuals who had lived together for 25 years, they were much more successful.

Zajonc suggested that people unconsciously mimic the facial expressions of their spouses. Over a long period of time, these shared expressions would tend to sculpt the faces of both individuals, giving them similar patterns of wrinkles and facial muscles. Robert J. Trotter

See also MENTAL ILLNESS. In WORLD BOOK, see PSYCHOLOGY.

PUBLIC HEALTH. President Ronald Reagan on May 31, 1987, urged wider use of blood tests—including voluntary testing of marriage-license applicants—to prevent further spread of the virus that causes AIDS (acquired immune deficiency syndrome). AIDS is a disorder of the body's disease-fighting immune system. As of Dec. 28, 1987, about 49,700 AIDS cases and 27,900 AIDS-related deaths had occurred in the United States since the disease was identified in 1981.

President Reagan called for "urgency, not panic" in dealing with the AIDS epidemic, and "compassion, not blame" in dealing with its victims. The President also announced two new federal programs for mandatory AIDS testing. He said he had approved adding AIDS to the list of infectious diseases for which aliens and immigrants can be denied entry into the United States. The President also ordered the U.S. Department of Justice to develop a testing program for inmates of federal prisons.

On July 23, 1987, Reagan appointed 12 members of a 13-member commission to advise him on AIDS. The commission's chairman, W. Eugene Mayberry, chief executive officer of the Mayo Clinic in Rochester, Minn., had been appointed in June. On October 7, Mayberry and two other members of the panel resigned. Reagan named another member, retired Navy Admiral James D. Watkins, to succeed Mayberry as chairman.

Routine Testing. On August 13, the United States Centers for Disease Control (CDC) in Atlanta, Ga., recommended that physicians routinely test certain patients for exposure to the AIDS virus. The CDC said tests should be performed on patients who have sexually transmitted diseases; on drug abusers who use needles; on prostitutes; and on other people in high-risk categories. The CDC emphasized that a patient should have the right to refuse an AIDS test.

Cancer-Causing Food? A major study published on May 20 urged adoption of stricter standards in the United States to protect the public from traces of potentially cancer-causing insecticides, herbicides, and fungicides in the food supply. The study, conducted by the National Academy of Sciences (NAS), found that existing regulations and laws permit relatively high levels of some cancer-causing chemicals to reach consumers in a variety of foods, such as beef, oranges, and lettuce. The NAS, which is based in Washington, D.C., is an independent organization that advises the U.S. government on science and technology.

The NAS study recommended adopting standards that would expose consumers to no more than a "negligible" risk of developing cancer from pesticides in the food supply. The NAS said the new standards would result in a lifetime risk of no more than 1 case of cancer per 1 million people.

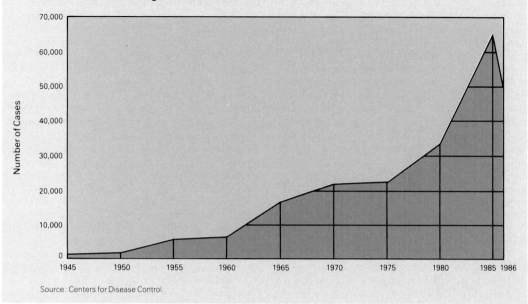

Salmonella Poisoning in the United States

Source: Centers for Disease Control.

Cases of salmonella, a type of food poisoning, have soared in the United States since 1945. The jump in 1985 was due to a major Midwest outbreak.

Fewer Puffs. Canadian Minister of National Health and Welfare Jake Epp on April 22 proposed a far-reaching program to reduce cigarette smoking in Canada, which he described as the country's "leading preventable health problem."

The new program would ban tobacco advertising in newspapers, magazines, billboards, and posters. It would also restrict smoking in government buildings, in banks, and on Canadian airline flights of less than two hours duration. Other provisions would prohibit tobacco companies from using brand names in sponsoring sports and cultural events.

The CDC reported on September 10 that cigarette smoking among adults in the United States had declined to the lowest levels ever reported. According to the CDC study, 26.5 per cent of adults questioned in 1986 said they smoked cigarettes, a decline of 4 percentage points from 1985.

Smokeless Cigarette. On Sept. 14, 1987, the R. J. Reynolds Tobacco Company of Atlanta announced that it had developed a cigarette that could reduce concerns about "passive smoking"— smoke inhaled by nonsmokers. The new cigarette produces virtually no smoke, odor, or ash. But critics questioned whether it would be safer than conventional cigarettes. Michael Woods

See also HEALTH AND DISEASE; MEDICINE. In WORLD BOOK, see PUBLIC HEALTH; SMOKING.

PUBLISHING houses in 1987 were shaken by takeovers and changes of top executives. Rupert Murdoch's News Corporation shocked the industry by the size of its $300-million bid for Harper & Row Publishers, Incorporated, which it bought on March 30. On May 18, Robert Maxwell's British Printing and Communications Corporation topped even that with a $1.7-billion offer to buy Harcourt Brace Jovanovich Incorporated. A defiant Harcourt resisted with a $2.9-billion recapitalization plan. By borrowing so much money, the company became unattractive to buyers.

Women Advanced to the top in publishing in 1987 as never before. On August 24, in the most publicized move, Joni Evans, president of the trade division of Simon & Schuster, Incorporated, became publisher at rival Random House, Incorporated. Nancy Evans (no relation) became president and publisher of the Doubleday Publishing division of Bantam Books in January. Also in January, Carole Baron was named to the same post at Bantam's Dell Publishing Division.

Tariffs Vanish, Royalties Appear. Publishers were cheered by Canada's decision to remove the 10 per cent tariff, or import tax, on United States books sold in that country. The decision took effect on February 19.

Authors were elated when Farrar, Straus & Giroux, Incorporated, announced in March that it would become the first publisher to pay *royalties* on *remaindered copies,* leftover copies that are sold below the cost of printing them. (A royalty is a percentage of a book's sales revenues. Most publishers pay authors by means of royalties.) Farrar, Straus said it would pay a royalty of 5 per cent on the net amount of remaindered sales.

Best Sellers. Americans appeared to be of two minds in their reading in 1987, with fiction bestseller lists made up almost exclusively of light works and nonfiction lists including some serious books that were surprising successes. Chief among the serious works was *The Closing of the American Mind,* a critical look at higher education by University of Chicago professor of social thought Allan Bloom. The nonfiction list included one best seller that some believed was in the wrong category: *Communion,* a book in which author Whitley Strieber said he was carried off into space by aliens who performed experiments on his mind and body.

In fiction, Americans preferred escapist fare written by old favorites. Horror writer Stephen King had best sellers with *The Eyes of the Dragon* and *Misery.* Romance author Danielle Steel scored with *Fine Things* and *Kaleidoscope.* Adventure writer Tom Clancy also had two best sellers, *Red Storm Rising* and *Patriot Games.*   Mark Fitzgerald

In WORLD BOOK, see PUBLISHING.

PUERTO RICO. King Juan Carlos I and Queen Sophia of Spain arrived in Puerto Rico for a two-day visit on May 24, 1987. Thousands of Puerto Ricans turned out to greet the king and queen. This was the first visit ever to the island by reigning monarchs of Spain, which established its first settlement in Puerto Rico in 1508. The royal visitors participated in a conference to plan a celebration in 1992 of the 500th anniversary of Italian navigator Christopher Columbus' landing in the Americas.

In the aftermath of the Dec. 31, 1986, fire that engulfed the Dupont Plaza Hotel in San Juan and resulted in 97 deaths, investigators determined that the fire was caused by arson. By Jan. 29, 1987, three workers on the hotel staff had been charged with murder, arson, and other crimes. The three employees pleaded guilty and were sentenced on June 22 to prison terms ranging from 75 to 99 years.

After a slump, Puerto Rico's all-important tourism business recovered during 1987. Business investment revived, too, as firms announced plans to expand operations on the island to take advantage of tax exemptions restored by Governor Rafael Hernández Colón.   Nathan A. Haverstock

See also LATIN AMERICA (Facts in Brief Table). In WORLD BOOK, see PUERTO RICO.

PULITZER PRIZES. See AWARDS AND PRIZES.

QUEBEC. Robert Bourassa, Quebec's Liberal prime minister, won a significant personal victory in 1987 with the signing of a historic agreement that allowed Quebec to endorse the new Canadian constitution of 1982. Bourassa had worked with the federal government and the other nine provinces on the pact—the Meech Lake accord of April 20, 1987. The document outlined conditions under which Quebec would accept the constitution, a step the province had refused to take when the constitution was proclaimed. (Quebec opposed the constitution on the ground that it would impair the province's rights and power.) On June 3, Canada's Prime Minister Brian Mulroney and the leaders of the 10 provinces signed the agreement. See CANADA.

The Quebec National Assembly approved the accord 95 to 18 on June 23, the first provincial legislature to ratify the agreement formally. Bourassa, who proudly called the accord one of Quebec's "greatest political victories in two centuries," made it clear that Quebec would not consider any major changes in the document.

The vote followed a 35-hour debate on the subject. During the debate, the opposition Parti Québécois—which had worked for years to make Quebec an independent French-speaking nation—lost an amendment that would have given Quebec full legislative powers over linguistic matters.

Economy. The Liberal government, in power since late 1985, eased its fiscal restraint in spending estimates for 1987-1988. Spending for the fiscal year would total $30.1 billion, up 5.9 per cent from the previous year. (Canadian dollars; $1 = U.S. 77 cents as of Dec. 31, 1987.)

The provincial budget was presented on April 30, one week ahead of schedule, after a Montreal radio station released parts of it on its 6 P.M. evening news program. To forestall any effects of the premature release on stock exchange trading, the minister of finance, Gerard D. Lévesque, presented the budget to the Assembly at 11 P.M. on the same evening. A deficit of $2.7 billion was forecast.

Quebec's Major Automobile Plant, owned by General Motors of Canada Limited—the Canadian unit of the U.S.-based General Motors Corporation—and situated at Ste.-Thérèse, Que., received a $220-million government-aid package on March 31. The Canadian and Quebec governments each contributed $110 million to a 30-year, interest-free loan to be used to modernize the 21-year-old assembly plant. The company guaranteed 3,500 production jobs until 1994.

Lévesque Mourned. Quebec mourned the death on November 1 of René Lévesque, prime minister of Quebec from 1976 to 1986.   David M. L. Farr

See also MONTREAL. In WORLD BOOK, see QUEBEC.

RADIO. Modifying an earlier ruling, the Federal Communications Commission (FCC)—which regulates radio and television stations in the United States—in November 1987 said that stations would be free to air "indecent" material between midnight and 6 A.M. without fear of FCC actions. In the last two years, radio broadcasters in particular had come under increasing public pressure because some disk jockeys had gained popularity by use of "shock radio"—vulgar, often sexually oriented comments and stunts.

In April, the outcry against shock radio caused the FCC to warn broadcasters that it would begin imposing a broader definition of indecency. That warning came in response to broadcasts at three FM stations—KPFK in Los Angeles, WYSP in Philadelphia, and KCSB in Santa Barbara, Calif.

Obscene Broadcasting has never been allowed, and the FCC did not quite define what it meant by "indecent." But in its modified ruling in November, the commission said that in the early morning hours, controversial material would have "safe harbor" from FCC reprisals, because it was unlikely that many young children would be listening to radio or watching television at that time without parental permission.

Fairness Doctrine. A bill in Congress that would have made an FCC rule called the Fairness Doc-

trine a law was vetoed by President Ronald Reagan on June 20. The rule, long disliked by broadcasters, required television and radio stations to air all sides of controversial issues. On August 4, the FCC voted unanimously to abolish the policy. Some members of Congress vowed to renew efforts to enact the policy into law.

Programming Formats. Radio continued to be dominated by rock-oriented stations in the United States in 1987. Also continuing a trend, FM radio stations drew many more listeners than stations on the AM band, which often devoted their formats to news, talk shows, and sports.

Keillor Leaves Home. In February, Garrison Keillor, host of the program "A Prairie Home Companion," announced he would discontinue the show in June. The program, broadcast on Saturday nights from St. Paul, Minn., since 1974, was distributed to 4 million weekly listeners by public stations nationwide. "A Prairie Home Companion" was a fond celebration of Americana that recounted, in Keillor's folksy narrative style, the tales of a fictional town called Lake Wobegon, Minn. It was a place, he said, "where the women are strong, the men are good-looking, and all the children are above average." P. J. Bednarski

See also POPULAR MUSIC. In WORLD BOOK, see RADIO.

Garrison Keillor, left, and other performers broadcast the final installment of the popular radio show "A Prairie Home Companion" in June.

RAILROAD companies in the United States saw earnings drop in 1987. Railroads earned about $572 million in the first half of 1987, down from $707 million in the first half of 1986. Rail traffic for the first 50 weeks of 1987 was an estimated 909 billion ton-miles, compared with 846 billion ton-miles for the same period in 1986. On National Railroad Passenger Corporation (Amtrak) trains, ridership was 20,441,179, up about 1.6 per cent from 1986.

Railroad Sales and Mergers. On June 30, the Interstate Commerce Commission (ICC), the U.S. government agency that regulates commercial transportation across state lines, refused to reconsider its 1986 decision rejecting the proposed merger of the Atchison, Topeka & Santa Fe and the Southern Pacific (SP) railroads. The ICC rejected the proposed merger in 1986 on the grounds that it would reduce competition. The ICC was asked to reopen the case because the Santa Fe Southern Pacific Corporation—the parent company that was set up in 1983 pending the approval of the merger—had taken steps to reduce the anticompetitive consequences of the merger. The ICC said, however, that it was still concerned about the reduction in competition.

As a result of the ICC ruling, Santa Fe Southern Pacific Corporation decided to sell the SP railroad. On December 28, the firm said it had agreed to sell the SP to Rio Grande Industries Incorporated for about $1.8 billion. At least two rival groups also wanted to buy the SP, however, and any deal would require ICC approval.

On March 26, the U.S. government sold its 85 per cent interest in Consolidated Rail Corporation (Conrail), a railroad serving the Northeast and Midwest, to private investors for $1.65 billion. The sale set a record for an initial public offering.

Conrail Crash. On January 4, three Conrail locomotives collided with an Amtrak passenger train in Chase, Md. The crash, which killed 16 people, was the worst in Amtrak's history. After the crash, federal investigators found that a safety warning device in the lead Conrail locomotive was turned off. Blood and urine tests of the train's operators revealed traces of marijuana.

These findings sparked the Senate in October to approve a bill requiring a drug-testing program for all public transportation employees whose jobs have some impact on safety. Rail labor unions, however, called the proposed legislation unconstitutional and—even before congressional action—took their own action on this issue. In August, the United Transportation Union announced an agreement with CSX Corporation, owner of the nation's third largest rail system, that calls for increased testing of employees who are suspected of using alcohol or drugs.   David M. Cawthorne

In WORLD BOOK, see RAILROAD.

REAGAN, RONALD WILSON (1911-   ), the 40th President of the United States, was forced to make major changes in his top White House staff in 1987. Following the disclosure of the Iran-contra affair in late 1986, Reagan came under strong pressure to replace his chief of staff, former Treasury Secretary Donald T. Regan. With first lady Nancy Reagan reportedly prominent in the anti-Regan camp, Regan resigned under pressure on February 27. President Reagan then appointed former Senate Republican leader Howard H. Baker, Jr., of Tennessee to the post. In accepting the job, Baker abandoned tentative plans to seek the 1988 Republican presidential nomination.

Other Staff Changes. Another highly visible post, that of White House spokesman, changed hands on February 2 when Larry Speakes left to join Merrill Lynch & Company, a financial services firm in New York City. Marlin Fitzwater, former press secretary to Vice President George H. W. Bush, replaced him. Patrick J. Buchanan resigned on February 3 as White House communications director. Reagan chose John O. Koehler, a former Associated Press executive, to succeed him, but Baker later reorganized the staff, forcing Koehler out of the position. Thomas C. Griscom, a longtime Baker associate, assumed the post on April 1.

Other changes in Reagan's top staff included the resignation of White House political director Mitchell E. Daniels, Jr., who was succeeded by Frank J. Donatelli; and the appointment of Gary L. Bauer to domestic policy adviser. Reagan named Army Lieutenant General Colin L. Powell as his sixth national security adviser in seven years.

Former Aide Scandals. Two long-time Reagan aides had serious legal problems in 1987. Michael K. Deaver, once Reagan's closest personal assistant, was indicted on March 18 on perjury charges that stemmed from his lobbying activities after he resigned as White House aide in 1985. On Dec. 16, 1987, a federal court jury convicted Deaver on three counts of lying under oath. His sentencing was scheduled for February 1988. Lyn Nofziger, a former White House political director and a Reagan associate since 1965, was indicted on July 16, 1987, on charges that his private lobbying efforts violated federal ethics laws. His trial was set for 1988.

Reagan, the Oldest Chief Executive in U.S. history at age 76, had prostate surgery on January 5. A team of seven physicians from the Mayo Clinic in Rochester, Minn., performed the operation at the Bethesda (Md.) Naval Hospital. They found no evidence of prostate cancer.

Reagan, who had major surgery for intestinal cancer in 1985, had minor surgery on January 4 and June 26 to remove noncancerous *polyps* (tumors) from his intestines. He also had cancerous tissue removed from his nose on July 31.

First lady Nancy Reagan returns to the White House from the hospital on October 22, five days after undergoing breast-cancer surgery.

Family Matters. Surgeons removed Nancy Reagan's left breast on October 17 following the discovery of a small, cancerous tumor. After the operation at the Bethesda Naval Hospital, the surgeons said tests showed the cancer had not spread. On October 26, while recuperating from the operation, the first lady was informed of the death of her 91-year-old mother, Edith L. Davis.

The first lady remained actively involved in her antidrug campaign in 1987. On June 8, she broke off from her husband's trip to an economic summit in Venice, Italy, to visit Sweden, where she toured drug-treatment facilities.

Maureen Reagan, daughter of the President and his first wife, actress Jane Wyman, became co-chairman of the Republican National Committee in January. Michael Reagan, adopted son of Reagan and Wyman, sold rights to an autobiographical book to Zebra Books in January. Literary agent Scott Meredith said Michael's account of his relations with his father would be "more on the unfavorable than on the favorable side, but essentially balanced."

On April 14, 1987, the Reagans reported that they paid federal income taxes of $92,460, or 27.5 per cent, on a 1986 adjusted gross income of $336,640. They listed $30,487 in charitable contributions. Frank Cormier and Margot Cormier

In WORLD BOOK, see REAGAN, RONALD WILSON.

RELIGION. Religious leaders made news in 1987 through controversies surrounding television evangelists in the United States and through the efforts of Pope John Paul II to tighten his control over the Roman Catholic Church. The pope also provoked Jewish leaders during the year by meeting with Austria's President Kurt Waldheim, the center of controversy regarding his service in the German army during World War II (1939-1945).

Two TV Evangelists in the United States were key figures in embarrassing episodes. Pentecostal evangelist Oral Roberts told TV viewers on January 4 that God would take his life if a special $8-million fund-raising drive fell short of its goal. The money was raised, but Roberts was criticized by many for his money-raising technique.

The other episode surrounded Jim Bakker, founder of the PTL (Praise the Lord or People That Love) organization. Bakker resigned from the PTL after he admitted on March 19 that he had had an extramarital sexual encounter with Jessica Hahn, a church secretary, in 1980 and that PTL leadership had paid Hahn to keep her quiet. In June, the PTL filed for bankruptcy, and the U.S. Department of Justice, along with other federal agencies, launched criminal investigations into the finances of the PTL.

New Code. These developments prompted calls for reform and for financial forthrightness in the

U.S. Membership Reported for Religious Groups with 150,000 or More Members*

African Methodist Episcopal Church	2,210,000
African Methodist Episcopal Zion Church	1,195,173
American Baptist Association	250,000
American Baptist Churches in the U.S.A.	1,576,483
Antiochian Orthodox Christian Archdiocese of North America	280,000
Armenian Church of America, Diocese of the	450,000
Assemblies of God	2,135,104
Baptist Bible Fellowship, International	1,405,900
Baptist Missionary Association of America	228,125
Christian and Missionary Alliance	238,734
Christian Church (Disciples of Christ)	1,106,692
Christian Churches and Churches of Christ	1,051,469
Christian Methodist Episcopal Church	718,992
Christian Reformed Church in North America	219,988
Church of God (Anderson, Ind.)	188,662
Church of God (Cleveland, Tenn.)	505,775
Church of God in Christ	3,709,661
Church of God in Christ, International	200,000
Church of Jesus Christ of Latter-day Saints	3,860,000
Church of the Brethren	155,967
Church of the Nazarene	530,912
Churches of Christ	1,623,754
Conservative Baptist Association of America	225,000
Episcopal Church	2,504,507
Evangelical Lutheran Church in America	5,326,500
Free Will Baptists	205,546
General Association of Regular Baptist Churches	300,839
Greek Orthodox Archdiocese of North and South America	1,950,000
International Church of the Foursquare Gospel	186,213
International Council of Community Churches	200,000
Jehovah's Witnesses	752,404
Jews	5,814,000
Lutheran Church—Missouri Synod	2,630,588
National Baptist Convention of America	2,668,799
National Baptist Convention, U.S.A., Inc.	5,500,000
National Primitive Baptist Convention	250,000
Orthodox Church in America	1,000,000
Polish National Catholic Church	282,411
Presbyterian Church in America	188,083
Presbyterian Church (U.S.A.)	3,007,322
Progressive National Baptist Convention, Inc.	521,692
Reformed Church in America	340,359
Reorganized Church of Jesus Christ of Latter Day Saints	192,077
Roman Catholic Church	52,893,217
Salvation Army	432,893
Seventh-day Adventists	666,199
Southern Baptist Convention	14,613,618
Unitarian Universalist Association	173,167
United Church of Christ	1,676,105
United Methodist Church	9,192,172
United Pentecostal Church, International	500,000
Wisconsin Evangelical Lutheran Synod	416,473

*A majority of the figures are for the years 1986 and 1987. Source: National Council of the Churches of Christ in the U.S.A., *Yearbook of American and Canadian Churches* for 1988.

$2-billion-a-year religious broadcasting industry in the United States. On September 11, National Religious Broadcasters, an organization based in Morristown, N.J., approved a new code that sets standards of fiscal accountability and ethical guidelines for religious broadcasters.

Pope John Paul II attracted attention in 1987 when he began an 11-day trip to the United States and Canada on September 10. During his visit, the pope told U.S. bishops that dissent from the church's teachings is not compatible with being a "good Catholic" and that it poses an obstacle to receiving the sacraments.

Jewish-Catholic Relations. Tensions between Jews and the Vatican increased in 1987. Some U.S. Jewish leaders boycotted a meeting with the pope in Miami on September 11 to protest the pontiff's reception of Austria's President Waldheim in the Vatican on June 25. Waldheim has been implicated in the deportation and killings of Jews during World War II. Those who did attend the meeting with the pope, however, described it as constructive.

Matters were made worse again on October 24, when Joseph Cardinal Ratzinger, the head of the Vatican's Sacred Congregation for the Doctrine of the Faith, was quoted in a conservative Italian weekly magazine as suggesting that Judaism finds its theological fulfillment in Christianity. The cardinal's remarks appeared to contradict the pope's earlier assurances to a delegation of rabbis and Jewish leaders that he considered them his "elder brothers in the faith of Abraham." Although the Vatican tried to clarify the cardinal's comments, its seeming internal confusion prompted Jewish leaders in November to postpone a conference that was to have taken place in December between American Catholics and Jews.

Woman Leader. The National Council of Churches (NCC), a council of major Protestant and Eastern Orthodox denominations in the United States, made history on November 4 when it elected a woman minister as president. Patricia A. McClurg, a Presbyterian, became president of the NCC on Jan. 1, 1988.

Other News. Throughout 1987, a number of religious groups took up political crusades ranging from legal and moral assistance to victims of AIDS (acquired immune deficiency syndrome) to the movement that gives sanctuary to Central American refugees. Two ordained Baptist ministers—Jesse L. Jackson, a Democrat, and Pat Robertson, a Republican—announced their candidacy for the 1988 U.S. presidential nomination.   Bruce Buursma

See also EASTERN ORTHODOX CHURCHES; JACKSON, JESSE; JEWS AND JUDAISM; PROTESTANTISM; ROBERTSON, PAT; ROMAN CATHOLIC CHURCH. In the Special Reports section, see UNDERSTANDING ISLAM. In WORLD BOOK, see RELIGION.

REPUBLICAN PARTY (GOP) leaders in January 1987 chose the Superdome in New Orleans as the site of the party's 1988 presidential nominating convention. At a meeting of the Republican National Committee (RNC) in Washington, D.C., the site selection committee picked New Orleans over Kansas City, Mo., for the Aug. 15 to 18, 1988, gathering.

During the January meeting, Maureen Reagan, daughter of President Ronald Reagan, was elected cochairman of the RNC, at a salary of $70,000 a year. After some Republicans objected, she insisted she had not asked her father for the job but had earned it through "27 years of breaking my back for the GOP."

A number of GOP leaders at the meeting criticized the spending habits of Republican campaign committees. Targets included two $5,000-a-month consulting contracts. One was with Maureen Reagan, before she got her full-time job, and the other was awarded to Michelle Laxalt, daughter of former Senator Paul Laxalt of Nevada, outgoing RNC general chairman. The National Republican Senatorial Campaign Committee was hit for paying $257,000 in staff bonuses the day after Republicans lost control of the Senate in 1986.

Contributions Decline. Talk about loose spending led early in 1987 to a sharp drop in contributions to the RNC and to the GOP Senate and House of Representatives campaign committees. As a consequence, the RNC fired 40 of its 275 staff employees on July 15 and terminated contracts with 10 politically influential consultants.

Cash flow at the RNC dropped to $17.1 million in the first half of 1987, from $22.5 million in the same half of 1985. Receipts by the Senate campaign committee plunged to $10.7 million in the first half of 1987, from $23 million two years earlier. During the same period, the House campaign committee's income dropped to $6.1 million from $9.6 million.

Embarrassing Lawsuit Settlement. The RNC suffered further embarrassment on July 23 when it agreed to obtain federal court clearance in advance for any future "ballot security programs"—systematic challenges to voter eligibility in heavily Democratic areas. Democrats alleged that the challenges were aimed at harassing black voters.

The agreement settled a $10-million suit brought against the RNC by the Democratic National Committee as a result of a GOP effort to purge voter rolls in Louisiana in 1986. A Republican memo obtained by the Democrats said the effort "could keep the black vote down considerably." The Democrats charged that the Republican tactic violated federal civil rights laws.

President Reagan meets with Vice President Bush, right, and Senator Robert J. Dole—the front-runners in the GOP presidential race—at the White House in July.

Presidential Race. Vice President George H. W. Bush was the acknowledged front-runner in a six-man competition for the 1988 Republican presidential nomination. Bush benefited from his high national office and his close association with a popular Republican President. At the same time, he may have suffered from fallout from the Iran-contra affair and the October stock market crash, both of which tarnished the image of the Reagan Administration.

Senate Republican leader Robert J. Dole of Kansas ranked second in polling on prospective Republican nominees, with United States Representative Jack F. Kemp of New York a distant third. Dole appeared to be ahead of Bush in Iowa, one of the early 1988 caucus-primary states, but Bush enjoyed a commanding lead among Southern Republicans.

Others seeking the GOP nomination were evangelist Pat Robertson, who resigned his ministry to make the race; Pierre S. (Pete) du Pont IV, former governor of Delaware; and Alexander M. Haig, Jr., former secretary of state and White House chief of staff. See the individual biographies on each of the candidates.

Former Senator Laxalt withdrew from the race for the GOP nomination. Jeane J. Kirkpatrick, former United States ambassador to the United Nations, declined to enter.

Before formally entering the campaign, Robertson dealt Bush a surprise setback on September 12 when well-organized followers turned out to give Robertson a big straw-poll upset at a major Republican fund-raiser in Des Moines, Iowa. Seen as a first test of competing political organizations, the vote by party contributors gave Robertson 34 per cent of the straw vote to 25 per cent for Dole. Bush, who had been expected to win, placed third with 23 per cent.

Campaign Heats Up. President Reagan scheduled an October 20 White House meeting with the six Republican rivals to urge that, in their campaigns, they adhere to the "11th commandment" that "thou shalt speak no ill of a fellow Republican." But the meeting was canceled because the President had to deal with the aftermath of the October 19 stock market collapse. Reagan reportedly was concerned about personal clashes involving candidates and staff aides. For example, Robertson called Bush "a whiny loser," Bush accused Robertson of using "kamikaze" tactics, and Dole suggested that Bush's patrician upbringing and manners took him out of the "American mainstream." Frank Cormier and Margot Cormier

See also DEMOCRATIC PARTY; ELECTIONS. In WORLD BOOK, see REPUBLICAN PARTY.

RHODE ISLAND. See STATE GOVERNMENT.

RHODESIA. See ZIMBABWE.

ROADS. See TRANSPORTATION.

ROBERTSON, PAT (1930-   ), a television evangelist, announced his candidacy for the Republican presidential nomination on Oct. 1, 1987. He called for a return to "fundamental moral values."

Marion Gordon Robertson, nicknamed Pat, was born on March 22, 1930, in Lexington, Va. His father, A. Willis Robertson, was a Democratic senator from Virginia from 1946 to 1967. Pat Robertson received a bachelor's degree from Washington and Lee University in Lexington in 1950, and a law degree from Yale University Law School in New Haven, Conn., in 1955. In 1959, he received a Master of Divinity degree from New York Theological Seminary in New York City, and he was ordained a minister of the Southern Baptist Convention in 1961.

Robertson founded the Christian Broadcasting Network (CBN) in 1960. He served as CBN president until 1986, when he became CBN's chief executive officer. He founded CBN University in Virginia Beach, Va., in 1977 and serves as its chancellor. In September 1987, Robertson cut his ties with CBN and resigned from the ministry because of public concern over the separation of church and state in his presidential campaign.

Robertson supported school prayer and a balanced federal budget. He opposed abortion.

Robertson is married to Adelia (Dede) Elmer. They have four children. Mary A. Krier

ROH TAE WOO (1932-   ), chairman of South Korea's ruling Democratic Justice Party, was elected to the South Korean presidency on Dec. 16, 1987. He was scheduled to succeed President Chun Doo Hwan when Chun's term expires in February 1988. Many South Koreans opposed Roh (pronounced *Noh*) after he won his party's nomination on June 10, 1987. In violent street demonstrations, they demanded direct elections and a more democratic government. See KOREA, SOUTH.

On June 29, Roh made a surprising endorsement of the protesters' demand for direct elections. He also urged Chun to release political prisoners, allow freedom of the press, and increase regard for human rights. Chun agreed to the reforms, and Roh was widely praised. Nonetheless, antigovernment protests continued.

Roh was born in Taegu, Korea, on Dec. 4, 1932. In 1955, he graduated from the Korea Military Academy and began an army career during which he attained the rank of general. After the 1979 assassination of South Korean President Park Chung Hee, Roh helped Chun seize the presidency. Chun then named Roh head of the country's Defense Security Command. In 1981, Roh retired from the military.

Roh is married to Kim Ok Sook. They have two children. Jinger Griswold

ROMAN CATHOLIC CHURCH. The Vatican in 1987 restated its position that dissent from official Roman Catholic teaching by members of the Roman Catholic Church is unacceptable. Pope John Paul II took this message directly to Catholics in September, when he began a highly publicized 11-day visit to the United States and Canada.

The trip, which began on September 10, took the pope to Miami, Fla.; Columbia, S.C.; New Orleans; San Antonio; Phoenix; Los Angeles; Monterey, Calif.; San Francisco; and Detroit. Before returning to Rome, he flew to Fort Simpson, Canada, to meet with Indian and Eskimo groups.

During the flight from Rome to Miami, the pope told reporters accompanying him that dissent among Catholic Americans is a "serious problem" but that it involves only a minority of followers. He said Catholics should follow "the teachings of our Lord as expressed through the church."

Four days earlier, in New Orleans, the pope told a group of 60,000 young people to observe the church's teaching regarding sex. "Jesus and His church hold to God's plan for human love, telling you that sex is a great gift of God that is reserved for marriage," he said.

Vatican's Stand on Reproduction. On March 10, 1987, the Vatican released a document denouncing medical procedures involved in artificial human reproduction, such as *in vitro fertilization*, a technique in which male and female sex cells are united in a test tube or other artificial environment. The 40-page document, published by Joseph Cardinal Ratzinger, head of the Vatican's Sacred Congregation for the Doctrine of the Faith, carried the authority of Pope John Paul II.

The document—*Instruction on Respect for Human Life in Its Origin and on the Dignity of Procreation: Replies to Certain Questions of the Day*—was based on traditional Roman Catholic teachings about sex and reproduction. It stressed the need to support human life from the first moment of conception. It also stated that sexual intercourse between married people is the only appropriate method of human reproduction because it gives a "special character" to the transmission of life.

Besides in vitro fertilization, the document also disapproved of prenatal diagnosis in cases where the discovery of defects in an unborn child might lead to abortion; the production of "spare" human embryos for experimentation or sale; the freezing of human embryos; and the use of sperm or *ova* (eggs) for fertilization that are supplied by a person other than the husband or wife. The Vatican also condemned the use of surrogate mothers—women who bear children for other couples.

The document disapproved of *artificial insemination* (a procedure in which sperm is inserted into a woman's reproductive tract in a laboratory) unless it occurs between a married couple and is not

Wearing a fringed robe, Pope John Paul II emerges from a tepee in Fort Simpson, Canada, on September 20 to celebrate a Mass for Indians.

a substitute for sexual intercourse. It said that the procedure presented a "rupture between genetic parenthood, gestational parenthood, and responsibility for [the child's] upbringing."

According to the document, all people must respect human embryos and give them the same regard accorded "any other human person" because they possess human rights. Processes that allow parents to select the sex of their child are unacceptable because people must be respected, regardless of their sex.

The statement encouraged—and consoled—married couples who are unable to have children, and approved fertility drugs and some other medical techniques to cure infertility. The document said, however, that marriage does not give people a right to offspring and that parents should not consider a child the "object of ownership."

The Vatican urged scientists to continue their efforts to find the causes of—and remedies for—sterility. It also urged governments to ban the medical procedures condemned by the church.

Curran to Court. On January 9, Charles E. Curran, a Catholic priest and theologian from Rochester, N.Y., was formally suspended from all teaching duties by the Catholic University of America in Washington, D.C. The university's action followed a decision by the Vatican in August 1986 to ban Curran from teaching in any Catholic college or university because his position on moral issues went against traditional Catholic teachings.

Although Curran said on Jan. 15, 1987, that he would respect the university's decision, he filed suit in the District of Columbia Superior Court on February 27, claiming that the university had denied him his rights as a tenured professor.

Seattle Issue Resolved. On May 27, Pope John Paul II returned full authority to Archbishop Raymond G. Hunthausen of Seattle. Since January 1986, Archbishop Hunthausen had shared his duties with Auxiliary Bishop Donald Wuerl. Bishop Wuerl was assigned to Seattle after a Vatican investigation found Archbishop Hunthausen's positions on birth control, homosexuals, and nuclear arms at odds with the church's policy. The Vatican's action against Archbishop Hunthausen generated strong protest in the United States.

The pope's decision to restore Archbishop Hunthausen's authority was based on the recommendation of a special commission of three bishops, which found that the division of authority in the Seattle archdiocese did not work well. As part of the settlement, the Vatican appointed Bishop Thomas J. Murphy of the Great Falls-Billings diocese in Montana as assistant to Hunthausen.

Catholic-Jewish Controversies. Relations between the Roman Catholic Church and the world's Jewish community experienced two problems in 1987. The first involved John Cardinal O'Connor,

archbishop of New York, and his visit to Israel in the first week in January. Cardinal O'Connor had intended to make an official call on Israel's government leaders in Jerusalem. The Vatican intervened, however, saying that the cardinal's visit to government offices in Jerusalem in any official capacity was in conflict with church policy. The Vatican does not recognize Jerusalem as Israel's capital. It believes that Jerusalem should be an international holy city with no link to any state.

Cardinal O'Connor did see Israel's President Chaim Herzog and Foreign Minister Shimon Peres during his visit. The meetings took place in their homes—not in government offices. Cardinal O'Connor said the meetings were acts of courtesy.

While in Jerusalem, Cardinal O'Connor also visited Yad Vashem, a monument to the 6 million Jews killed in Europe during World War II. A comment that he made during a speech at the monument—that the Holocaust was an "enormous gift Judaism has given the world"—provoked some Jewish leaders in the United States. On January 10, a coalition of more than 50 Jewish organizations in New York City published a statement criticizing Cardinal O'Connor's comment as well as the Vatican's policy on Jerusalem, which prevents diplomatic relations between the *Holy See* (the offices of the pope) and Israel.

Waldheim Meeting. The second event that strained relations between the Roman Catholic Church and the Jewish community occurred on June 25, when Pope John Paul II met with Austria's President Kurt Waldheim in the Vatican. Waldheim had been a German army officer during World War II and had been implicated in the deporting, abusing, and killing of Jews. Waldheim had denied the charges. Jewish leaders around the world protested the pope's willingness to meet with him. They also objected to the pope's formal greeting, which did not mention Waldheim's alleged war record but instead complimented him on his work for peace as United Nations secretary-general from 1972 to 1982.

To ease the tension caused by these events, the pope met with a group of Jewish leaders at Castel Gandolfo, Italy, his summer residence, on September 1. He heard their complaints and concerns over his meeting with Waldheim and other issues. At the end, both sides agreed that anti-Semitism should be deplored and that Adolf Hitler's destruction of Jews should be denounced as anti-Semitic, unchristian, and in violation of the values of both Christian and Jewish traditions.

Later in September, Pope John Paul II told reporters that he had met with Waldheim because Waldheim was the head of a democracy that had ancient ties to the Holy See. Owen F. Campion

In WORLD BOOK, see ROMAN CATHOLIC CHURCH.

ROMANIA suffered in 1987 from undiminished austerity at home and a loss of prestige abroad. Behind the suffering were a continuing economic crisis brought on by years of overambitious planning and the government's poor record on human rights—particularly the harassment of various Christian faiths.

Both houses of the United States Congress included in a pending trade bill provisions that would suspend for six months Romania's most-favored-nation trading status, which had committed the United States to use its lowest tariff rates on all Romanian products. Romania had held this status since 1975. United States President Ronald Reagan wanted to maintain Romania as a most favored nation because it had loosened its policies on the emigration of Jews and ethnic Germans.

As a result of Romania's human rights record, the nation's leader, Nicolae Ceauşescu, also lost international standing. Heads of major Western nations were in no hurry to visit Romania. Ceauşescu's own travels continued, but only to Asian and African countries.

Gorbachev Visits. Soviet leader Mikhail S. Gorbachev visited Romania from May 25 to 27. In a speech on May 26 in Bucharest, Romania's capital, he indirectly criticized Romania's sterile economy and Ceauşescu's practice of promoting members of his family to high government posts. Gorbachev's criticisms, however, seemed to make no impression on Ceauşescu.

Nonetheless, Romania's growing isolation from the West compelled it to move closer to Moscow in both trade and dependence on Soviet raw materials. This isolation also led to an increase in the number of Soviet engineers and other specialists who were heavily involved in Romania's energy, steel, and oil industries.

Tension with Hungary rose in early 1987 over growing complaints by 2 million ethnic Hungarians living in the Transylvania and Banat regions of Romania. This minority group claimed that the Romanian government suppressed their right to Hungarian identity and restricted their contacts with Hungary.

In February, Romania accused Hungary of falsifying the history of Transylvania in a way unfavorable to Romania. On April 2, Hungary strongly denounced Romania.

Riots broke out in November in Bucharest, Brasov, and other Romanian cities. The rioters reportedly were protesting wage cuts and the prospect of energy and food shortages.   Eric Bourne

See also EUROPE (Facts in Brief Table). In WORLD BOOK, see ROMANIA; TRANSYLVANIA.

ROWING. See SPORTS.

RUSSIA. See UNION OF SOVIET SOCIALIST REPUBLICS (U.S.S.R.).

RWANDA. See AFRICA.

SAFETY. Disastrous plane crashes in 1987 helped make the safety of air travel an important public concern in the United States. On August 16, 156 people were killed in Detroit after a Northwest Airlines jetliner failed to gain altitude during take-off and crashed on a busy highway. Only one passenger, a 4-year-old girl, survived. On November 15, a Continental Airlines DC-9 crashed upon take-off during a snowstorm at Denver's Stapleton International Airport. At least 28 people were killed.

The number of near-collisions in midair was also a major air-safety concern of 1987. During the first seven months of the year, 610 near-misses were recorded, 31 per cent more than were recorded in the first seven months of 1986. In the Los Angeles area, near-misses were especially frequent, with three times more incidents in 1987 than in 1986. Even United States President Ronald Reagan was personally affected on August 13, when a small plane flew close to a White House helicopter carrying Reagan to his ranch in Santa Barbara, Calif.

In May, the U.S. National Transportation Safety Board (NTSB) reported an "erosion of safety" in the skies and urged the Federal Aviation Administration (FAA) to take strong corrective measures. Five days later, the FAA inaugurated a computer-

Accidental Deaths in the United States

	1985-1986*		1986-1987*	
	Number	Rate†	Number	Rate†‡
Motor Vehicle	46,500	19.4	47,600	19.5
Home	20,200	8.4	20,200	8.2
Public	19,400	8.1	18,900	7.7
Work	11,700	4.9	10,700	4.4
Total§	93,500	39.0	93,500	38.2

*For 12-month period ending June 30.

†Deaths per 100,000 U.S. population.

‡12-month projection based on 1987 data only.

§The total does not equal the sum of the four classes because *Motor Vehicle* includes some deaths listed under *Work* and *Home.*

Source: National Safety Council estimates.

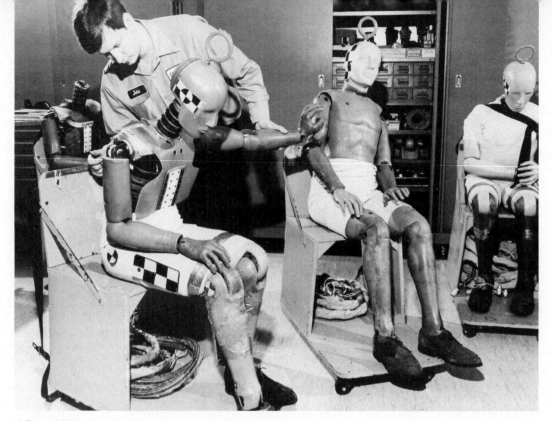

A General Motors technician adjusts a sophisticated new test dummy, called Hybrid III, that will be used in head-on-collision tests of vehicles.

ized traffic control system that allowed air-traffic controllers at FAA headquarters in Washington, D.C., to monitor all planes using the system from coast to coast. Congress and other groups pressed the FAA for even more action, however.

On December 22, Congress voted to ban smoking on commercial airline flights of two hours or less, as of April 23, 1988. The danger of on-board fires was a factor leading to the bill.

Highway Safety. Travel by motor vehicle became potentially more hazardous in the United States after April 1987, when Congress overruled President Reagan's veto of a bill allowing states to raise interstate highway speed limits in rural areas to 65 miles (105 kilometers) per hour. After the bill became law on April 2, many states raised speed limits. Representative James J. Howard (D., N.J.), who sponsored the 1974 law establishing the 55 limit, said the new law could lead to thousands of additional deaths during its five-year period.

According to a 1987 report by the NTSB, the highway death toll for 1986 reached 45,840, an increase of more than 2,000 over the previous year. Because of an increase in travel, however, fatalities per 100 million miles (160 million kilometers) driven remained the same at 2.5.

Vehicle Defects continued to be a problem in 1987, especially for Ford Motor Company. In September, Ford made its second largest vehicle recall

ever, offering to repair 4.3 million 1986, 1987, and 1988 cars, vans, and light trucks. Fuel-line defects had caused about 230 engine fires that injured 16 people.

All-Terrain Vehicles. In December, U.S. manufacturers of three-wheel all-terrain vehicles announced that they would stop selling the motorcyclelike vehicles, which had been linked to hundreds of deaths. Sales of four-wheelers, considered safer, would continue, but the industry began a campaign to inform owners of both types of vehicles about possible dangers.

On-the-Job Hazards. In 1987, the U.S. Occupational Safety and Health Administration (OSHA) toughened enforcement of workplace safety regulations, penalizing companies that failed to record job-related injuries and illnesses. OSHA—which in 1985 imposed only $23,000 in fines—levied nearly $11 million in fines from April through July of 1987. Targets of the safety crackdown included Chrysler Corporation, Caterpillar Incorporated, General Dynamics, and Ford.

In September, OSHA ordered a 90 per cent decrease in the legal limit for workers' exposure to benzene fumes, which have been linked to leukemia and other blood diseases.   Arthur E. Rowse

See also AVIATION. In WORLD BOOK, see SAFETY.

SAILING. See BOATING.

SASKATCHEWAN—its economy weakened by falling prices for wheat, oil, potash (a fertilizer), and uranium—faced a deficit three times higher than expected in 1987. Premier Grant Devine's Progressive Conservative government, reelected in 1986, responded by cutting as many as 2,000 public service jobs and freezing the salaries of other civil servants for the next two years. The provincial budget, introduced on June 17, revealed that the spending cuts, coupled with tax increases, would reduce the projected deficit for the fiscal year 1988 (April 1, 1987, through March 31, 1988) to $577 million (Canadian dollars; $1 = U.S. 77 cents as of Dec. 31, 1987). In the previous fiscal year, it had totaled $1.2 billion.

On August 21, the United States Department of Commerce imposed preliminary penalty duties of up to 85.2 per cent on imported Canadian potash. The ruling was a devastating blow to the Saskatchewan potash industry, which supplies American farmers with as much as 85 per cent of their potash needs. The province retaliated on September 1 by introducing legislation giving it the power to control production in Saskatchewan potash mines. Supporters of the bill predicted that reducing production would pressure the United States government into removing the duties. David M. L. Farr

In WORLD BOOK, see SASKATCHEWAN.

A flag-waving crowd greets Queen Elizabeth II in Canora, Saskatchewan, one of the stops during her five-day October visit to the province.

SAUDI ARABIA. Saudi Arabia's policy of avoiding direct confrontation with other Middle Eastern powers while using its vast wealth for political and economic leverage was severely tested in 1987 by a clash with Iran. The Saudis, who have consistently supported Iraq in its war with Iran, had previously refrained from criticizing Iran. But a clash between Saudi security forces and Iranian religious pilgrims in Mecca during the annual pilgrimage, or *hajj*, in July embroiled the two countries in a bitter public dispute.

The Saudis, as hosts for the pilgrimage—the high point of the Islamic year—had warned Iran's 155,000 pilgrims not to hold political demonstrations as they had in recent years. Nevertheless, on July 31, thousands of Iranian pilgrims staged a public protest criticizing Saudi Arabia for its alliance with "godless" Iraq and its support for United States intervention in the Persian Gulf conflict. According to Saudi reports, when security forces attempted to disperse the crowd, the Iranians began burning automobiles and attacking other pilgrims as well as Saudi security forces. When Saudi police moved in, the Saudis said, the crowd began a panic-stricken retreat.

After order was finally restored, 275 Iranians lay dead, along with 85 Saudi policemen and 42 pilgrims from other countries. Saudi reports said that many of the dead had been trampled in the panic, a position supported by the United States and most Arab countries. The Iranians, however, accused the Saudis of firing on peaceful, unarmed pilgrims at the instigation of the United States. After the incident, demonstrators in Teheran, Iran, sacked the Saudi Embassy, and Saudi officials expelled Iranian pilgrims.

In October, the government urged the United Nations (UN) General Assembly to take action to force Iran to comply with a resolution passed on July 20 by the UN Security Council demanding an end to the Iran-Iraq war. Also in October, the United States agreed to sell the Saudis $1 billion worth of arms, including fighter planes and equipment for tanks and artillery.

The Economy. The first budget formally adopted since 1985 was approved in January. The 1986 budget had been postponed because of the global oil crisis. The 1987 budget set expenditures at $43 billion, a 6 per cent reduction. A 5 per cent increase in the oil production quota set by the Organization of Petroleum Exporting Countries—to 4.3 million barrels per day—ensured higher revenues. In September, Saudi Arabia surpassed Egypt as the Arab world's principal wheat producer, with an annual output of 2.5 million metric tons (2.7 million short tons). William Spencer

See also MIDDLE EAST (Facts in Brief Table). In the Special Reports section, see UNDERSTANDING ISLAM. In WORLD BOOK, see SAUDI ARABIA.

Canada's Governor General Jeanne M. Sauvé, left, and External Relations Minister Monique Landry walk on China's Great Wall in March.

SAUVÉ, JEANNE MATHILDE (1922-   ), who as Canada's governor general represents the country's head of state, Queen Elizabeth II, visited China from March 16 to 25. The governor general toured Chinese cities and met with the country's leaders, including President Li Xiannian, whom she had escorted during his visit to Canada in 1985. During Sauvé's visit, agreements totaling $60 million (Canadian dollars; $1 = U.S. 77 cents as of Dec. 31, 1987) were signed, providing Canadian development assistance for several projects, including management education, language training, and coastal city development.

The governor general's tour of the Far East also included a visit to Hong Kong. There, she laid wreaths at two cemeteries where Canadian soldiers who died in defense of the British colony during World War II (1939-1945) are buried. Sauvé went on to Thailand, where she received an honorary degree from a university in Bangkok.

In November, Sauvé represented Canada in Bridgetown, Barbados, at ceremonies marking the 21st anniversary of independence for the Caribbean country. The governor general also traveled extensively throughout Canada during 1987, undertaking official duties.   David M. L. Farr

See also CANADA. In WORLD BOOK, see SAUVÉ, JEANNE MATHILDE.

SCHOOL. See EDUCATION.

SCOTLAND. The victory of Prime Minister Margaret Thatcher's Conservative Party in the parliamentary election on June 11, 1987, once again left Scotland in an unusual position. Although the country is governed by Britain's Conservative government, the majority of Scotland's 72 seats in Parliament are held by members of the opposing Labour Party. The Labour Party captured 50 of Scotland's parliamentary seats in the June election, while the Conservative Party held onto only 10 seats. The remaining 12 seats were divided between members of the Alliance Party and the Scottish National Party.

The shortage of Conservative seats created problems for Malcolm Rifkind, secretary of state for Scotland. Rifkind had difficulty in finding enough Conservative members of Parliament to appoint as ministers to the Scottish Office (the Scottish equivalent of ministries, based in Edinburgh) and as members of the Scottish Grand Committee, which monitors the Scottish Office.

Taxes. The British government announced plans to introduce a new tax program in Scotland. The new tax would replace the local property tax with a tax levied equally on all adults. Although most Scots agreed that the new tax would be more fair, many were indignant that the tax would go into effect in Scotland before the rest of Great Britain. Scotland was to begin paying the new tax

Led by a piper and followed by a bulldozer, Scottish workers protest the closing of a Caterpillar Incorporated plant near Glasgow on January 31.

in April 1989. In England and Wales, the tax reform was to be phased in over the next four years.

Guinness Take-Over. Scandal—and a subsequent investigation—erupted in January over brewery giant Arthur Guinness & Sons PLC's purchase of Distillers Company Limited, one of Scotland's largest firms. An investigation of the 1986 purchase was launched following charges that Guinness had planned to artificially raise the price of its shares to support its take-over of Distillers.

Concern over the purchase again rumbled through Scotland in April, when London-based Guinness said it would not honor a pledge it made during the take-over to relocate the headquarters of the merged companies in Scotland. On October 2, Guinness announced a compromise in which it would set up a separate company in Scotland called United Distillers to handle the company's whisky and other liquor business. Guinness's head office, however, would remain in London.

BBC Raid. On January 31, the Strathclyde Police raided the Glasgow headquarters of the British Broadcasting Corporation (BBC) and removed videotapes of a film that contained information on Britain's Zircon spy satellite project. The government declared that the film violated the Official Secrets Act. BBC Scotland produced the film, one part of a six-part television series on secrecy in British public life called "The Secret Society."

The raid generated protests throughout Scotland and raised questions about the legality of the search warrant, which permitted the police to confiscate videotapes and documents on the other "Secret Society" films. The Zircon episode had not been shown on BBC television by year-end.

Oil Industry. After a fall in crude oil prices in 1986, Scotland's oil industry rebounded in 1987, due in part to a surge of oil development along the coast. In May, the government announced that 51 new drilling licenses had been granted in the Moray Firth and off the east coast of the Shetland Islands.

In August, British Petroleum joined Conoco Incorporated, Enterprise Oil, and Sante Fe in a North Sea investment project. The project, which could bring 2,500 jobs to northeastern Scotland, will develop the Miller oil field and construct a pipeline to transport untreated gas ashore. The partnership hoped to have government approval of the project by 1988.

In September, Shell Oil Company and Esso received government approval for the development of the Kittiwake oil field in the North Sea. The project could result in 6,000 jobs. Doreen Taylor

See also GREAT BRITAIN. In WORLD BOOK, see SCOTLAND.

SCULPTURE. See ART.

SENEGAL. See AFRICA.

SESSIONS, WILLIAM STEELE (1930-), a United States District Court judge in San Antonio, was sworn in on Nov. 2, 1987, as director of the Federal Bureau of Investigation (FBI). He succeeded William H. Webster, who was named head of the Central Intelligence Agency.

Sessions was born on May 27, 1930, in Fort Smith, Ark. He spent most of his boyhood in Kansas City, Mo. After serving in the U.S. Air Force for five years, rising to the rank of captain, he attended Baylor University in Waco, Tex. He received a bachelor's degree in 1956 and a law degree in 1958.

In 1969, after practicing law in Waco for 10 years, Sessions joined the U.S. Department of Justice in Washington, D.C. In 1971, he was named U.S. attorney for the Western District of Texas.

Sessions was named a federal district judge in El Paso, Tex., in 1974. When Judge John H. Wood, Jr., of San Antonio, chief judge of the Western District of Texas, was assassinated in 1979, Sessions was appointed to succeed him. He then presided in the trial of Wood's killers. During his career on the bench, Sessions earned a reputation for being tough but fair.

An avid outdoorsman, Sessions has climbed to the base camp of Mount Everest twice. He and his wife, Alice, have four children. David L. Dreier

SEYCHELLES. See AFRICA.

SHIP AND SHIPPING. Surplus cargo space continued to take its toll on the world's shipping lines in 1987. As a result, shipping rates remained depressed, though increased United States exports improved rates on eastbound shipments in the Atlantic Ocean.

To offset the decline in revenue, *rate conferences*—groups of ocean carriers allowed to set shipping rates—agreed to rate hikes. On March 1, the Trans-Pacific Freight Conference and the Japan/Atlantic and Gulf Freight Conference increased rates 15 per cent. The North Europe-U.S. Atlantic Conference followed suit on May 1 and increased rates 4 to 8 per cent. But pressure from shipping lines that are not members of rate conferences reduced the impact of the increases.

On February 11, the U.S. Interstate Commerce Commission, a federal agency that regulates railroads, approved CSX Corporation's 1986 purchase of Sea-Land Corporation for $742 million. CSX is a transportation company that owns two railroads in the United States. Sea-Land is a U.S. steamship company that operates a fleet of 56 container vessels. The transaction marks the first time a railroad has acquired a steamship line.

Shipbuilding. Even though the shipping industry suffered from overcapacity in 1987, some of the world's biggest shipping lines began ordering larger vessels during the year. American President Lines, Maersk Line, and Neptune Orient Line each ordered ships capable of holding more than three thousand 20-foot (6-meter) containers. The orders were spurred—in part—by construction subsidies that allowed shipping lines to purchase the ships at extremely reasonable prices. The boom in shipbuilding, however, was expected to aggravate the industry's overcapacity problem.

In terms of tonnage under construction, South Korea overtook Japan in 1987 as the largest shipbuilder in the world.

Labor. The Federal Maritime Commission (FMC) decided in August that the 50-mile rule was discriminatory and should be stricken from industry tariffs. The rule requires that members of the International Longshoremen's Association (ILA) be used to load and unload all containers that hold cargo belonging to more than one shipper if the shippers are located within 50 miles (80 kilometers) of the port.

The FMC decision prompted a strong reaction from the ILA. In September, the ILA asked for new contract talks to seek an alternative that would avoid cuts in jobs or wages.

Thomas W. (Teddy) Gleason, president of the ILA for 24 years, retired in July. He was replaced by John M. Bowers on August 1.   David M. Cawthorne

In WORLD BOOK, see SHIP.
SHOOTING. See HUNTING; SPORTS.
SIERRA LEONE. See AFRICA.

SIMON, PAUL (1928-   ), a United States senator from Illinois, announced his candidacy for the 1988 Democratic presidential nomination on May 18, 1987. Simon, whose trademark is a bow tie, portrays himself as a fiscal conservative who is an old-line liberal Democrat on social issues.

Simon was born on Nov. 29, 1928, in Eugene, Ore. At age 16, he entered the University of Oregon in Eugene but transferred to Dana College in Blair, Nebr.

Simon left school in 1948 to take over a failing weekly newspaper in Troy, Ill., a small town near St. Louis, Mo. As editor, Simon gained a reputation as a crusader against local corruption. He eventually owned a chain of 14 weeklies. Simon is also the author of 11 books.

In 1954, after a two-year stint in the U.S. Army, Simon was elected to the Illinois House of Representatives. He was reelected three times. In 1962, he won election to the Illinois Senate, winning reelection in 1966. He ran successfully for lieutenant governor of Illinois in 1968. In 1974, Simon was elected to the first of five terms in Congress. He was elected to the Senate in 1984.

In 1960, Simon married attorney Jeanne Hurley, also an Illinois state legislator at the time. They have a daughter and a son.   Barbara A. Mayes
SINGAPORE. See ASIA.
SKATING. See HOCKEY; ICE SKATING; SPORTS.

SKIING. Swiss men and women won almost all the skiing honors during the 1986-1987 season. In the world Alpine championships, they took all five gold medals for women and three of the five for men. In the annual World Cup series, they won all five titles for women and four of the five for men. They also produced the most successful skier of the year in Pirmin Zurbriggen.

World Championships. In the biennial championships, held from Jan. 27 to Feb. 8, 1987, in Crans-Montana, Switzerland, the host nation set records with 8 gold medals and 14 total medals. The closest nation in total medals was Austria with 4.

Zurbriggen won the men's giant slalom and super giant slalom. He finished second in the downhill to Peter Müller of Switzerland and second in the combined to Marc Girardelli, an Austrian who skied for Luxembourg. Frank Wörndl of West Germany won the slalom.

In women's competition, Maria Walliser won the downhill and super giant slalom, Erika Hess the slalom and the combined, and Vreni Schneider the giant slalom. The only American medalist, male or female, was Tamara McKinney of Olympic Valley, Calif. She won the bronze in the women's combined, which consisted of special races in slalom and downhill, and earlier in the year she won two World Cup slaloms.

Switzerland's Pirmin Zurbriggen, winner of the overall skiing title in 1987, races past a gate en route to winning a giant slalom in January.

World Cup. Except for an August 1986 stop in Argentina, the season ran from November 1986 to March 1987 in Europe, the United States, and Canada. Zurbriggen won 11 races and took the overall title easily with 339 points to 190 for Girardelli, the runner-up. Zurbriggen also won the season competition in downhill, giant slalom, and super giant slalom. The only championship he missed was the slalom, won by Bojan Krizaj of Yugoslavia.

Zurbriggen's four season titles equaled the record of Jean-Claude Killy of France in 1967, the year the World Cup began. Only four titles were available then because the super giant slalom had not been invented.

The Swiss women won 22 of their 33 World Cup races. They swept the first five positions in the overall standing, led by Walliser with 269 points. The discipline champions were Walliser in the super giant slalom, Walliser and Schneider tied in giant slalom, Michela Figini in downhill, and Corinne Schmidhauser in slalom. The leading non-Swiss was McKinney, sixth with 127 points.

Nordic. In the world championships held from February 11 to 21 in Oberstdorf, West Germany, Norway won 10 and Sweden won 8 of the 39 medals. Thomas Wassberg of Sweden gained two gold and two silver medals in cross-country. Frank Litsky

In WORLD BOOK, see SKIING.

SOCCER. The Dallas Sidekicks, a team that was about to disband for financial reasons after the 1985-1986 season, won the 1986-1987 championship of the Major Indoor Soccer League (MISL), North America's most important soccer league.

In the MISL's ninth season, the 11 teams played 52 regular-season games each from November 1986 to May 1987. In the Western Division, the Tacoma Stars finished seven games ahead of the Kansas City Comets. In the Eastern Division, the Cleveland Force finished one game ahead of the Baltimore Blast, with Dallas in third place.

Dallas upset Baltimore and Cleveland en route to the play-off finals, where it was the underdog against Tacoma. Dallas won the championship series on June 20, 4 games to 3.

In January and February, the league interrupted its season to allow six teams to play the visiting Dynamo Moscow. The visitors, who had won the Soviet first division outdoors 11 times, were inexperienced in indoor soccer. They lost every game, though three were lost by only one goal.

Olympics. In preliminary competition, the United States Olympic team eliminated Canada, 3-2, in a two-game, total-goal series. The United States won the deciding game, 3-0, on May 30 in St. Louis, Mo.

The United States advanced to a home-and-home round-robin tournament with El Salvador and Trinidad and Tobago, with the winner to advance to the 1988 Olympics. The United States all but assured itself of that berth by defeating Trinidad and Tobago, 4-1 and 1-0, and El Salvador, 4-2. Its second game against El Salvador was scheduled for May 1988.

European. In a two-week span in May 1987, Porto of Portugal, Ajax Amsterdam of the Netherlands, and I. F. K. Göteborg of Sweden won the major tournaments for European clubs. Porto defeated Bayern Munich of West Germany, 2-1, on May 27 in Vienna, Austria, for the European Champions Cup, the most important such competition.

Ajax Amsterdam captured the European Cup Winners Cup with a 1-0 victory over Lokomotiv Leipzig of East Germany on May 13 in Athens, Greece. After the game, celebrations by many of the 8,000 touring Ajax fans turned into violence.

I. F. K. Göteborg won the Union of European Football Associations Cup. It defeated Dundee United of Scotland, 2-1, in the two-game, total-goal finals, which ended on May 20 in Dundee. Four days before that game, Dundee was upset by St. Mirren, 1-0 in overtime, in the Scottish Football Association Cup final.

Coventry City won England's major tournament, the English Football Association Cup, by upsetting Tottenham 3-2 in overtime in the final on May 16 in Wembley. Frank Litsky

In WORLD BOOK, see SOCCER.

SOCIAL SECURITY. Trustees of the United States social security system reported on March 31, 1987, that the system promised to remain strong financially into the next century. They also said that the Medicare Hospital Insurance Trust Fund could remain solvent until the year 2002.

But the trustees—three Cabinet members and two private citizens—cautioned that early corrective action was essential to avoid potentially drastic changes later. To keep the hospital insurance program going for the next 25 years, they said, benefits would have to be reduced by 13 per cent or contributions increased by 15 per cent. The hospital insurance program is financed by a 1.45 per cent payroll tax on most workers, collected by the Social Security Administration.

Payroll Deductions. Effective on Jan. 1, 1988, earnings subject to social security payroll taxes were to increase to $45,000, up from $43,800 in 1987, in line with an increase in average wages paid during 1987. The maximum per-worker tax was to rise as a result to $3,379.50 from $3,131 in 1987.

Increase in Benefits. Also to take effect on Jan. 1, 1988, was a 4.2 per cent increase in social security benefits under the cost-of-living adjustment (COLA) program. The Social Security Administration estimates that benefit payments rise by $2 billion for each percentage point of inflation.

Skyrocketing Premiums. Older and disabled Americans participating in the Medicare program were to pay sharply higher premiums starting on Jan. 1, 1988. The increased premiums were to cover Part B of the Medicare program, which includes doctor bills, laboratory fees, and outpatient hospital services. Part A of the program covers inpatient hospital bills.

Because of a continuing escalation of health care costs, monthly premiums were to increase to $24.80 from $17.90, the biggest jump since the Medicare program was established in 1965. The premiums are designed to pay 25 per cent of the cost of Part B, with the remainder provided by general U.S. Treasury revenues.

Congress throughout its 1987 session wrestled with various proposals to further expand the Medicare program to protect participants against "catastrophic" medical costs. On February 12, President Ronald Reagan announced he would propose legislation—developed under the direction of Secretary of Health and Human Services Otis R. Bowen—that would ensure that individuals paying premiums for Medicare's optional medical insurance would pay no more than $2,000 a year in out-of-pocket expenses for hospital and doctor bills. Final congressional action was delayed until at least 1988.   Frank Cormier and Margot Cormier

In WORLD BOOK, see SOCIAL SECURITY.

SOMALIA. See AFRICA.

SOUTH AFRICA. Opposition of South Africa's black majority to the policy of *apartheid* (racial segregation) continued in 1987. The government of State President Pieter Willem Botha on June 10 extended for another year a state of emergency that gave the police extraordinary power in dealing with protests.

According to the United States Lawyers' Committee for Civil Rights Under Law, an estimated 25,000 people in South Africa have been arrested without charges and held for indefinite periods since the protests escalated in September 1984. Many of those detained were under 18 years of age. The list included journalists, church leaders, and educators who ignored censorship restrictions on the discussion and reporting of detentions and race-related incidents of violence.

The Protests have focused on the refusal of the white minority government to allow the black majority, who make up about 73 per cent of the population, to share fully in South Africa's politics and economy. Unlike whites, Asians, and *Coloreds* (persons of mixed race), blacks are denied the title of citizen and are not permitted to vote in national elections.

The Botha government in September 1987 proposed the creation of a National Statutory Council that would allocate 9 of its 30 seats to blacks residing in urban areas. Because the council would have no real legislative or executive power, black leaders overwhelmingly rejected the proposal. One opponent was Zulu Chief Mangosuthu Gatsha Buthelezi, who occasionally supports the Botha government on key issues.

Government measures in dealing with the media and opposition political leaders—as well as restrictions on church services, funerals, and other public meetings that focused on dissent—have been effective. The reported incidents of anti-apartheid violence diminished in 1987. Rent strikes and school boycotts in black areas, however, continued. Fighting continued between rival black political groups, including riots in Pietermaritzburg at year's end that led to the deaths of about 200 black youths.

The African National Congress (ANC), the major black political organization, observed its 75th anniversary on Jan. 8, 1987. The ANC's international standing was enhanced in January when its current president, Oliver Tambo, was received in Washington, D.C., by U.S. Secretary of State George P. Shultz and members of the U.S. Congress. The ANC's status within South Africa itself was strengthened when 61 white South African business leaders, educators, and lawyers met with 17 ANC and other black leaders in Dakar, Senegal, in July. The ANC modified its stance on the use of violence and its previous demands for nationalization of major industries.

Defying an order to return to work, striking South African miners
rally in August at the Vaal Reefs gold mine west of Johannesburg.

The Botha government was reported to have
made informal contacts with the ANC, which has
been banned since 1960. Although the most
prominent ANC leader, Nelson Mandela, remained in prison, the government in November
1987 released another ANC leader, Govan Mbeki,
"for reasons of age and poor health." Mbeki, who
had been jailed in 1964 along with Mandela on
charges of treason, was restricted in his right to
travel and make public statements.

The Economy. South Africa's Central Bank forecast a 3 per cent growth rate for the nation in
1987. The balance of trade remained favorable.
Much of this success was due to the rising price of
gold on the world market and the demands of industrialized states for the other minerals that
South Africa exports. Some countries, including
Israel and Japan, have increased their trade with
South Africa, while others are responding to the
call for economic *sanctions* (penalties).

Black labor unions, which were illegal until the
late 1970's, called several strikes during 1987. In a
three-month strike by transport workers, which
began in March, the union won many of its demands on wages, hiring, and job security. In a
strike by more than 300,000 coal- and gold-mine
workers in August, on the other hand, the union
gained few concessions. More than 35,000 strikers
lost their jobs, and all the strikers lost income. The

Institute for Industrial Relations, a private South
African group, estimated the loss in revenue to industry to have exceeded $225 million. The strike
triggered walkouts in the diamond-mining, steel,
and other major industries, thus seriously disrupt-
ing the economy.

Foreign Pressure. Efforts to use economic sanctions against South Africa to change its apartheid
policy continued in 1987. Dozens of United States
and European companies sold their branch operations to South African business interests. A deficit-reduction bill passed by the U.S. Congress on
December 22 contained a provision eliminating
the right of American companies to subtract taxes
paid to South Africa from their U.S. tax bills.

Overall, results of sanctions were mixed. Late in
the year, Zimbabwe and Zambia gave up their efforts to end economic ties with South Africa. Lacking British support, the Commonwealth—an association that includes Great Britain and the
countries of the former British Empire—failed to
secure unanimity in imposing sanctions.

Elections. Early in 1987, the ruling National
Party faced division within its ranks, with some
party officials resigning to protest the slow pace of
apartheid reform. Other party members, who
were opposed to any change in apartheid, were
joining the ranks of the Conservative Party of
South Africa or the Reconstituted National Party.

SOUTH AMERICA

Hoping to enlarge its majority, the Botha regime called an election in May—two years early—for the House of Assembly, the all-white chamber of the three-house Parliament. Despite receiving a smaller percentage of the popular vote than it did in the 1981 election, the National Party won 123 of 166 contested seats, a gain of 3. The moderate Progressive Federal Party lost 7 of its 26 seats. The Conservative Party of South Africa captured 22 seats, up from 17, thus replacing the Progressive Federals as the official opposition party.

Regional Politics. Relations with southern African nations were strained by the continuing war in Namibia and by South African support of rebel movements in Angola and Mozambique. In June, an investigative commission appointed by the South African government reported that the 1986 airplane crash that killed Mozambique's President Samora Moisés Machel was caused by an inept Soviet flight crew. Mozambique disputed the findings, still charging that South Africa was involved in the crash.   J. Gus Liebenow and Beverly B. Liebenow

See also AFRICA (Facts in Brief Table); ANGOLA; MOZAMBIQUE. In WORLD BOOK, see SOUTH AFRICA.

SOUTH AMERICA. See LATIN AMERICA.
SOUTH CAROLINA. See STATE GOVERNMENT.
SOUTH DAKOTA. See STATE GOVERNMENT.

SPACE EXPLORATION. The Soviet Union outpaced the United States in both manned space flight and launch capabilities in 1987. While United States astronauts remained grounded, a Soviet cosmonaut broke the record for consecutive days in space. Cosmonauts worked in—and outside—a large space station. The Soviets also successfully tested what is now the world's largest rocket, the Energia, capable of orbiting payloads weighing up to 110 short tons (100 metric tons).

U.S. Returns to Space. On the plus side for the United States, the National Aeronautics and Space Administration (NASA) returned to service three of the four types of large rockets grounded by failures in the first half of 1986. The Atlas-Centaur rocket orbited a Navy communications satellite on Dec. 4, 1986, in a mission that had been delayed since May by concern over failures of other U.S. boosters. An Air Force Titan rocket sent a secret military payload into space on Feb. 11, 1987. This was the first Titan flight since a Titan exploded five seconds after liftoff in April 1986.

A NASA Delta rocket orbited the *GOES-H* weather satellite on Feb. 26, 1987, completing a network capable of continuously monitoring the world's weather. Another Delta launched a communications satellite for Indonesia on March 20.

The space shuttle orbiter *Atlantis* rolls in March 1987 to an inspection building at the John F. Kennedy Space Center in Florida.

This chain of successes ended on March 26 when lightning struck an Atlas-Centaur booster about 1 minute after liftoff from Cape Canaveral, Fla. Controllers destroyed the booster to prevent it from falling on populated areas.

U.S. Shuttle. NASA announced on May 20 that it had pushed back the launch date of the next space shuttle from Feb. 18, 1988, to June 2, 1988. Reasons for the postponement included a need to test the liquid-fuel main engines and the redesigned seals and joints for the solid-fuel boosters. Leaks in the seals caused the explosion on Jan. 28, 1986, that killed all seven members of the *Challenger* crew. On May 27 and Aug. 30, 1987, NASA successfully tested its redesigned boosters and found that the seals between their sections did not leak. On December 29, however, NASA said that it would postpone the June launch indefinitely because a motor component had failed during a December 23 test firing of the boosters.

U.S. Space Station. NASA intends to use shuttle boosters to orbit components of a large space station that the United States plans to construct by the mid-1990's. In September 1987, a committee of the National Research Council recommended that NASA develop more powerful solid rocket motors to enable the shuttle to lift heavier loads into orbit, thereby reducing the number of flights required to build the station.

The committee also concluded that the initial cost of the station will be $17 billion to $22 billion, as much as $6.8 billion more than NASA had estimated. The station is an international effort undertaken by the United States, Canada, Japan, and the 13-nation European Space Agency (ESA).

Soviets Fly Ahead. Meanwhile, the Soviet Union continued to expand its space station, *Mir. Mir* was launched in February 1986, but it had been vacant since July 1986. On Feb. 6, 1987, the Soviets launched two cosmonauts aboard a large new spacecraft, *Soyuz TM-2*. Two days later, the cosmonauts—Yuri Romanenko and Alexander Laveikin—boarded *Mir*.

On March 31, the Soviets launched an unmanned module called *Kvant* (*Quantum*), which was intended to dock automatically with *Mir* on April 5. The cosmonauts were to conduct research in astrophysics in the module. *Kvant* failed to dock because a cover mistakenly had been left on its docking port. On April 12, the cosmonauts walked in space and removed the cover. Soviet ground controllers then docked the two craft.

On May 21, the unmanned supply tanker *Progress 30* docked automatically with *Kvant*. This marked the first time in history that four vehicles were linked in space. With the *Soyuz TM-2* docked to one end of *Mir*, *Kvant* to the other, and *Progress 30* linked to *Kvant*, the assembly exceeded 100 feet (30 meters) in length.

A Soviet spacecraft with two cosmonauts aboard blasts off on Feb. 6, 1987, for the space station *Mir*, launched by the Soviets in 1986.

Space Rescue. In July, Soviet officials reported that Laveikin had developed abnormal heart rhythms, and the Soviets launched a rescue mission. Cosmonauts Alexander Viktorenko and Alexander Alexandrov, accompanied by Syrian cosmonaut Mohammed Faris, lifted off on July 22. On July 30, Laveikin, Viktorenko, and Faris returned to Earth, leaving Alexandrov aboard *Mir* with Romanenko.

On December 21, cosmonauts Vladimir Titov, Musa Manarov, and Anatoly Levchenko lifted off to relieve the two men. Alexandrov and Romanenko returned to Earth with Levchenko on December 29, while Titov and Manarov remained aboard *Mir*. Romanenko had set a new endurance record of 326 days in space.

Soviet Boosters. The Soviets used a Proton rocket on July 25 to launch the largest civilian spacecraft ever orbited. Experts described it as about the size of a school bus and weighing more than 15 short tons (13.5 metric tons). Called *Cosmos 1,870*, it carried instruments to survey Earth and identify potential resources.

The Proton was the world's most powerful operational rocket until the May 15 test flight of the Energia. The Soviets planned to use Energia to launch large space-station modules, heavy military payloads, the planned Soviet space shuttle, and perhaps missions to the moon or Mars.

U.S.-Soviet Cooperation. The United States and the Soviet Union on April 15 signed an Agreement Concerning Cooperation in the Exploration and Use of Outer Space. The pact covers 16 projects in five areas: space biology and medicine, astronomy and astrophysics, exploration of the solar system, solar physics, and earth sciences.

Ariane. The ESA on September 15 used an Ariane-3 rocket to launch two communications satellites. This launch was the agency's first success since March 1986. The 1987 flight opened the way for Ariane to orbit a backlog of commercial satellites. Orbiting these payloads could earn $2.45 billion for Arianespace, ESA's commercial branch, between 1987 and 1991.

The Soviet Union sent delegations to the United States, France, Japan, and other nations in 1987 to offer the services of its Proton booster. For $30-million, the Soviets promised to put a 4,000-pound (1,800-kilogram) payload into orbit.

Japan used its large H-1 booster to orbit an engineering test satellite on August 27. A smaller N-2 rocket orbited an astronomy satellite on February 4 and an Earth-survey satellite on February 19.

In March, India tried to launch a scientific satellite. But the booster rocket failed and sent the payload into the Indian Ocean.   William J. Cromie

In WORLD BOOK, see COMMUNICATIONS SATELLITE; SPACE TRAVEL.

SPAIN. Socialist Prime Minister Felipe González Márquez faced a wave of strikes and student demonstrations in 1987. The students demanded more money for universities, more scholarships, and an end to special entrance examinations. They also complained that there were no jobs awaiting them. Spain has an unemployment rate of 45 per cent for people 16 to 24 years old.

Economics Minister Carlos Solchaga Catalán urged employers on February 12 to keep wage increases down to 5 per cent and told them not to give in to strike threats. As he spoke, automobile workers and coal and copper miners were striking, and airline and rail strikes loomed.

Censure Motion. On March 30, González defeated a censure motion brought before the Cortes (parliament) by the right wing Popular Alliance, the largest opposition party. The vote was 194 against the censure motion to 67 for it, with 71 abstentions.

As parliament voted, dairy farmers blocked roads to protest milk quotas set by the European Community (EC or Common Market), which Spain had joined on Jan. 1, 1986. Physicians, students, and transportation workers announced new strikes and protests.

More Strikes. On April 7, 1987, subway workers went on strike, medical students disrupted trading on the Barcelona stock exchange, and 8,000 rural physicians began a two-day strike. Communist-dominated labor unions led general strikes on April 10 and 17.

González threatened to introduce legislation regulating strikes "to ensure maintenance of services essential to the community." An uneasy truce followed a meeting on May 28 with Communist labor union leader Marcelino Camacho.

Lost Votes. On June 10, the Socialists paid a heavy price for the unrest, losing votes in elections for representation in the European Parliament (the EC's legislative branch), and for local and *regional* offices. (A region is a group of provinces.) The Socialists lost majorities in 21 big cities and in 7 of the 13 regions holding elections.

Basque Agreement. The national government agreed on February 23 to form a coalition government of Socialists and members of the Basque National Party in the Basque region. But the separatist group Basque Homeland and Liberty (ETA) continued its bombings and terrorist attacks.

U.S. Bases. Thousands of protesters marched to Torrejon air base near Madrid on March 15, calling for an end to the United States military presence in Spain. Two days later, U.S. Secretary of Defense Caspar W. Weinberger denied that there were any plans to relocate Spanish-based U.S. fighter-bombers.   Kenneth Brown

See also EUROPE (Facts in Brief Table). In WORLD BOOK, see SPAIN.

SPORTS. Drug problems, especially the use of cocaine, continued to plague the sports world in 1987. The most notable case involved 22-year-old baseball player Dwight Gooden, who was earning $1.5 million a year pitching for the New York Mets.

Gooden tested positive after volunteering for a drug test and entered a rehabilitation facility the week before the season opened in April. He spent a month there and another month regaining his pitching form before he returned to the Mets. He had a successful season, with a 15-7 record and a 3.21 earned-run average.

In January, the National Basketball Association (NBA) banned guards Lewis Lloyd and Mitchell Wiggins of the Houston Rockets for two years after drug tests showed they had used cocaine. Walter Davis, a guard with the Phoenix Suns, said he had become involved with cocaine again and returned to a rehabilitation facility.

Drug Programs. Of the major professional sports organizations, only the NBA had a comprehensive drug program agreed to by the league and players. The National Football League was allowed to test once in preseason and thereafter only for reasonable cause. Baseball had no formal agreement, but its policy was to treat and continue to pay first-time offenders who turned themselves in.

Awards. Jackie Joyner-Kersee of Long Beach, Calif., was voted the James E. Sullivan Memorial Award by the Amateur Athletic Union as the outstanding amateur athlete in the United States. She was honored for her two world heptathlon records in 1986. A panel from the United States Olympic Committee named Joyner-Kersee as the sportswoman of the year and swimmer Matt Biondi of Moraga, Calif., as sportsman of the year.

Among the Winners in 1987 were the following:
Cycling. Stephen Roche of Ireland won the world men's professional road-racing title, the Tour de France, and the Tour of Italy. Among the women, Jeannie Longo of France captured the world road-racing title, the Tour de France, and the Coors Classic. In the world championships held from August 25 to September 6 in Vienna, Austria, the only American winner was Rebecca Twigg-Whitehead of Pasadena, Calif., in the women's pursuit.

Diving. Greg Louganis of Boca Raton, Fla., retained his men's springboard title in the World Cup competition held from April 23 to 26 in Amersfoort, the Netherlands. The other champions were from China—Tong Hui in men's platform, Gao Min in women's springboard, and Xu Yanmei in women's platform. Louganis won the U.S. 3-meter and 10-meter outdoor titles but finished second in all three national indoor competitions.

Fencing. In the world championships held from July 17 to 26 in Lausanne, Switzerland, the individual winners were Mathias Gay of West Germany in men's foil, Elisabeta Tufan of Romania in women's foil, Jean-François Lamour of France in sabre, and Volker Fischer of West

Little League baseball makes its debut in Israel in April, with such teams as the Jerusalem Schleppers, the Tira Tigers, and the Tel Aviv Indians.

Germany in epee. The leading American was Peter West-brook of New York City, 14th in sabre.

Marathon. Rosa Mota of Portugal won two of the year's major prizes, the Boston Marathon on April 20 and the world championship on August 29 in Rome. The men's winners included Douglas Wakiihuru of Kenya in the world championships, Ahmed Saleh of Djibouti in the World Cup, Toshihiko Seko of Japan in the Boston Marathon, and Ibrahim Hussein of Kenya in the New York City Marathon.

Rowing. The United States won the men's eight-oared title, its first since 1974, in the world championships held from Aug. 24 to 30, 1987, in Bagsvaerd, Denmark. Romania took the women's title, beating the United States by 1.66 seconds. The Harvard men and the University of Washington women won the U.S. college titles.

Wrestling. The Soviet Union dominated the world championships held from August 19 to 29 in Clermont-Ferrand, France, taking 6 of the 10 gold medals in freestyle and 4 of 10 in Greco-Roman. The freestyle champions included John Smith of Stillwater, Okla., in the 62-kilogram (137-pound) class and Mark Schultz of Villanova, Pa., in the 82-kilogram (180-pound) class.

Other Champions

Archery, world champions: men, Vladimir Esheyev, Soviet Union; women, Ma Xiangjun, China.

Australian Rules Football, Victorian Football League champion: Carlton Blues.

Badminton, world champions: men, Yang Yang, China; women, Han Aiping, China.

Biathlon, world champions: men's 10-kilometer and 20-kilometer, Frank-Peter Rötsch, East Germany; women's 5-kilometer, Yelena Golovina, Soviet Union; 10-kilometer, Sanna Groenlid, Norway.

Billiards, world champions: three-cushion, Torbjorn Blomdahl, Sweden; snooker, Steve Davis, Great Britain.

Bobsledding, world champions: two-man, Ralph Pichler, and four-man, Hans Hiltebrand, both Switzerland.

Canoeing, world 1,000-meter and 10,000-meter kayak champion: Greg Barton, Homer, Mich.

Casting, U.S. all-around champion: Steve Rajeff, Poulsbo, Wash.

Court Tennis, world champion: Wayne Davies, New York City.

Cricket, World Cup champion, Australia.

Croquet, U.S. champion: John C. Osborne, New York City.

Cross-Country, world champions: men, John Ngugi, Kenya; women, Annette Sergent, France.

Curling, world champions: men, Glen Howard, Penetanguishene, Canada; women, Pat Sanders, Victoria, Canada.

Darts, world champion: Jerry Umberger, New Philadelphia, Pa.

Field Hockey, Champions Trophy (women): the Netherlands.

Frisbee, U.S. open overall champions: men, Scott Zimmerman, Arcadia, Calif.; women, Wende Coates, San Diego.

Gymnastics, world all-around champions: men, Dmitri Bilozerchev, Soviet Union; women, Aurelia Dobre, Romania.

Handball, U.S. four-wall champions: men, Naty Alvarado, Hesperia, Calif.; women, Rosemary Bellini, New York City.

Hang Gliding, U.S. champion: Howard Osterlund, Los Gatos, Calif.

Horseshoe Pitching, world champions; men, Dale Lipovsky, Bloomington, Minn.; women, Sandy McLachlin, Dresden, Canada.

Iceboating, DN Class world champion: Mike O'Brien, Lake Hopatcong, N.J.

Judo, world 156-pound (71-kilogram) champion: Mike Swain, San Jose.

Lacrosse, U.S. champions: college, Johns Hopkins; club, Long Island, N.Y.

Lawn Bowling, national open champions: men, Orville Artist, Walnut Creek, Calif.; women, Harriet Bauer, Seattle.

Luge, world champions: men, Markus Prock, Austria; women, Kerstin Schmidt, East Germany.

Modern Pentathlon, world champions: men, Joel Bouzou, France; women, Irina Kiselyeva, Soviet Union.

Motorcycle Racing, world 500-cc moto-cross champion: Georges Jobe, Belgium.

Paddle Tennis, U.S. champions: men, Scott Freedman, Culver City, Calif.; women, Kathy May Paben, Pacific Palisades, Calif.

Parachute Jumping, U.S. combined champions: men, Cliff Jones, West Point, N.Y.; women, Terry Vares, Fort Bragg, N.C.

Platform Tennis, U.S. doubles champions: Hank Irvine, Short Hills, N.J., and Greg Moore, Morristown, N.J.

Polo, world champion: Argentina.

Racquetball, U.S. champions: men, Mike Yellen, Southfield, Mich.; women, Lynn Adams, Costa Mesa, Calif.

Racquets, world champion: John Prenn, Great Britain.

Rhythmic Gymnastics, world all-around champion: Blanka Panova, Bulgaria.

Rodeo, U.S. all-around champion: Lewis Feild, Elk Ridge, Utah.

Roller Skating, U.S. champions: men's freestyle, Gregg Smith, Seven Hills, Ohio; women's freestyle, Pam Jefferson, Bellingham, Wash.; men's banked-track speed, Dante Muse, Des Moines, Iowa; women's banked-track speed, Crissy Brown, Tampa, Fla.

Rugby, World Cup champion: New Zealand.

Shooting, U.S. International Championships, small-bore rifle: three-position, Dan Durben, Colorado Springs, Colo.; prone, William Beard, Indianapolis.

Sled Dog Racing, world champion: Gary Edinger, Kennan, Wis.

Softball, U.S. fast-pitch champions: men, Pay 'n Pak, Bellevue, Wash.; women, Orange County (Calif.) Majestics.

Squash Racquets, U. S. Open men's champion, Jansher Kahn, Pakistan; U.S. women's champion, Alicia McConnell, Bala-Cynwyd, Pa.

Squash Tennis, U.S. champion: Gary Squires, Darien, Conn.

Surfing, world champions: men, Tommy Curren, Santa Barbara, Calif.; women, Frieda Zamba, Flagler Beach, Fla.

Synchronized Swimming, World Cup champion: Carolyn Waldo, Beaconsfield, Canada.

Table Tennis, world champions: men, Chiang Chia Liang, China; women, Ho Che Li, China.

Tae Kwon Do, world heavyweight champions: men, M. Arndt, West Germany; women, Lynnette Love, Oxon Hill, Md.

Team Handball, world Group B champions: men, Soviet Union; women, Bulgaria.

Triathlon, Ironman champions: men, Dave Scott, Davis, Calif.; women, Erin Baker, New Zealand.

Volleyball, U.S. champions: men, Molten, Torrance, Calif.; women, Chrysler Californians, Pleasanton, Calif.

Water Polo, World Cup champion: Yugoslavia.

Water-Skiing, world overall champions: men, Sammy Duvall, Windermere, Fla.; women, Deena Brush, West Sacramento, Calif.

Weight Lifting, super-heavyweight champions: world, Aleksandr Kurlovich, Soviet Union; U.S., Mario Martinez, Salinas, Calif.   Frank Litsky

See also articles on the various sports. In WORLD BOOK, see articles on the various sports.

SRI LANKA. The government's efforts to end four years of guerrilla warfare—which has taken 6,000 lives—were marked by failure in 1987. Even the introduction of thousands of Indian troops as peacekeeping forces could not stop the bloodshed. The unrest involved militant members of Sri Lanka's Tamil ethnic minority, who sought political separation from the Sinhalese ethnic majority.

President J. R. Jayewardene's attempts to find a political solution to the conflict in early 1987 were halted by a wave of Tamil terrorist attacks between April 17 and 22 that killed more than 350 people, including about 110 victims of a bus-station bombing in Colombo, the capital. In late May and early June, Sri Lanka's army responded with a drive to destroy the rebels' base camps near Jaffna, in Sri Lanka's northern peninsula.

Indian Involvement. India—which housed a rebel sanctuary and rebel arms supply centers and training areas—denounced Sri Lanka's military drive. India also intensified its efforts to find a political solution to the unrest. Indian officials brought Velupillai Prabakaran—leader of the Liberation Tigers of Tamil Eelam, the strongest rebel group—to New Delhi on July 24 for talks with Indian Prime Minister Rajiv Gandhi. Warning that India might withdraw support essential to the rebels, Gandhi persuaded Prabakaran to agree to a peace plan. On July 29, Gandhi flew to Colombo and signed an agreement with Jayewardene.

The July 29 Pact provided for a cease-fire, the surrender of rebels' weapons, and amnesty for the rebels. The agreement also joined Sri Lanka's northern province, where Tamils were a majority, with the eastern province, where Tamils made up about 40 per cent of the population. The new political unit would be partially self-governing. On July 30, Indian troops began landing in Sri Lanka to collect rebel weapons while Sri Lankan soldiers in rebel areas were confined to barracks.

Opposition. Colombo was rocked by violent protests from some Sinhalese, who were opposed to the pact because they resented any yielding to Tamil demands or any Indian role in Sri Lanka. During demonstrations and riots, 59 people died. Jayewardene also faced opposition to the agreement within his United National Party.

Opponents of the agreement tried to assassinate Jayewardene in the parliament building on August 18. Although he escaped injury, 2 people were killed and 15 others, including Prime Minister R. Premadasa and the national security minister, were wounded. The attack was blamed on the People's Liberation Front, a Sinhalese Marxist group that had tried unsuccessfully to seize power in 1971. The group later killed more than 40 officials in an attempt to disrupt the government.

Fierce Tigers. The prospect of competition for political control of the north and east caused the

Coffins hold the bodies of victims of an April terrorist bombing that blasted a crowded bus station in Colombo, Sri Lanka, killing about 110.

Liberation Tigers of Tamil Eelam to attack smaller Tamil guerrilla organizations. The Tigers killed some 75 Tamil people in rival villages in mid-September and sought complete control of the north and east.

Sri Lankan soldiers detained 17 Tigers in Jaffna on October 3. Two days later, 12 of the 17 committed suicide rather than be taken to Colombo for interrogation. In revenge, the Tigers murdered 12 soldiers and police officers they had been holding prisoner. They also killed at least 175 Sinhalese in other attacks.

On October 6, the Tigers stated formally that they now opposed the July 29 agreement. The next day, India said its 11,000 troops in Sri Lanka would try to restore order. Indian soldiers, reinforced by additional troops, began a drive to clear the Tigers from their stronghold in and around Jaffna.

In two weeks of savage fighting, hundreds of civilians were reported killed. On October 25, after more than 170 Indian troops were killed and 500 were wounded, India claimed it had eliminated the last Tiger lair in Jaffna. But an estimated 1,200 Tigers, including Prabakaran, were believed to have escaped into the jungle. They continued fighting.

Henry S. Bradsher

See also ASIA (Facts in Brief Table). In WORLD BOOK, see SRI LANKA.

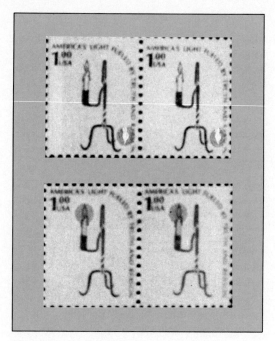

The sellers of 86 U.S. $1 invert stamps, including the 2 at top, were revealed in September 1987 as CIA employees. The other 2 stamps are correctly printed.

STAMP COLLECTING. A previously unnamed "Virginia business firm" where 95 inverted United States $1 stamps were reportedly discovered in 1986 was identified as the Central Intelligence Agency (CIA) in September 1987. According to the Bureau of Engraving and Printing, a CIA employee in March 1986 purchased the stamps—showing a candle and candleholder and inscribed with the words "America's Light Fueled by Truth and Reason"—for normal agency use. Several CIA employees noticed that the candle flame was upside down in relation to the candle.

Eighty-six of the invert stamps were sold in April 1986 to a New Jersey stamp dealer, for an undisclosed sum, by two CIA employees who claimed they worked for a private Virginia company. Three of the stamps were later resold at public auctions—for $5,500, $17,600, and $23,100. The remaining 83 stamps were sold privately, and 1 was subsequently donated to the National Postage Stamp Collection at the Smithsonian Institution. The CIA employees involved were disciplined for their actions.

One sheet of 400 of the invert stamps had been printed. The whereabouts of the remaining 314 stamps was still unknown at year-end.

New U.S. Stamps. The U.S. Postal Service released a pane of fifty 22-cent wildlife commemorative stamps during CAPEX '87, an international stamp exhibition held in Toronto, Canada, from June 13 to 21, 1987. The stamps feature a variety of North American animals. The Postal Service offered special pictorial cancellations from 10 U.S. national parks, dated June 15, the first day the wildlife stamps were on sale in the United States.

During the year, the Postal Service also issued 22-cent stamps commemorating American author William Faulkner, Italian opera singer Enrico Caruso, and the statehood anniversaries of Delaware, Michigan, and Pennsylvania.

Collectors voted the 22-cent stamp collecting booklet and the 33-cent AMERIPEX postal card as the most popular and the best-designed issues, respectively, of 1986 in polls conducted by *Linn's Stamp News* and *Stamp Collector*.

Phosphor Tagging. A special issue of the current 22-cent stamp depicting the American flag flying over the U.S. Capitol was printed with a new *phosphor-tagging* technique in 1987 to investigate its effect on mail-handling equipment. Phosphor tagging is the application of phosphors—substances that glow when exposed to ultraviolet light or other forms of radiation—to the paper on which stamps are to be printed. Tagging enables optically activated mail-handling equipment to automatically position letters for canceling.

Previous phosphor coatings were abrasive to perforating equipment and made it difficult for canceling ink to penetrate the stamp. These problems are avoided by applying the tagging over the central image only, leaving the borders clear. The phosphor-tagged stamps can be identified by a small black *T* printed beneath the Capitol steps.

Auction Sales. At a New York City auction held from March 10 to 12 by Christie's Robson Lowe galleries, a British 1858-1879 one-penny red stamp from the extremely rare printing plate number 77 sold for $82,500. The price is believed to be a record for a British stamp of the 1800's.

In a March 20, 1987, sale—also held by Christie's Robson Lowe—a U.S. 1851 dull-red 3-cent stamp sold for $7,500, more than 1,000 times its catalog value. The stamp, which features a portrait of George Washington, was exceptional only in that it was *on cover* (affixed to its original envelope) and had full upper-right corner sheet margins completely intact. The stamp's catalog value is $7.

The fifth Boker German States sale in Wiesbaden, West Germany, on March 15, 1987, brought more than $3 million for just 306 lots of stamps, an average of about $10,000 per lot. A cover stamped with a superb block of four 1862 ½-shilling arms-issue stamps of the city-state of Lübeck sold for 920,000 Deutsche marks (about $506,000).   Paul A. Larsen

In WORLD BOOK, see STAMP COLLECTING.

STATE GOVERNMENT. State legislatures adjusted tax rates in response to changing economic conditions in 1987. The states as a whole reported a surplus of $2.3 billion for fiscal year 1987 (which ended on June 30 in most states). The National Governors' Association reported in September that 6 states had lowered their taxes in 1987 and 33 states had adopted a total of $6.1 billion in new taxes.

Florida and Texas accounted for about half the new taxes. Florida needed more revenue because explosive population growth had strained such public services as highway construction and maintenance, law enforcement, and welfare.

Texas needed to make up for losses caused by sharp declines in the price of oil. These decreases not only eroded the state's tax base but also pushed up unemployment to record levels, further straining the state budget.

Services Tax. In Florida, a novel tax law that took effect on July 1 touched off a national controversy. Florida's Constitution prohibits a state tax on personal income, traditionally a major source of state tax revenues, so the legislature had to look elsewhere for a new source of revenue. On April 23, the lawmakers enacted a 5 per cent tax on services, and Governor Bob Martinez signed the bill into law the same day. No state had ever taxed services on so large a scale.

The most controversial part of Florida's new law was a tax on advertising. The law taxed not only advertising produced and placed within the state but also ads that were produced outside Florida and placed nationally. National advertising was taxed on the basis of the proportion of the ads that appeared in Florida.

Advertising agencies, advertisers, broadcasters, and magazine publishers protested strongly. Major advertisers and two television networks blacked out certain advertisements in Florida and ran antitax commercials instead.

Martinez finally called the legislature into special session to repeal the tax law. On October 8, the legislature passed a bill eliminating the tax on the placement of advertising but not the tax on advertising production. Martinez vetoed the bill because he favored total abolition of the tax.

On December 10, the legislature passed a total repeal of the service tax, and Martinez signed it the next day. The tax ended on Jan. 1, 1988, and the state sales tax was to rise on February 1 from 5 per cent to 6 per cent to make up lost revenue.

Other Increases. Major tax hikes also passed in Indiana, Minnesota, Missouri, and Oklahoma in 1987. North Dakota, South Dakota, and Utah raised their sales tax rates. Minnesota imposed sales taxes on more items.

To fund highways, at least 15 states raised gasoline taxes, and 9 raised automobile registration fees. And California broke a 50-year tradition of free highways, deciding to build three toll roads.

Tax Relief. Most states passed along to certain groups of taxpayers the windfalls from federal income tax reform. The federal Tax Reform Act of 1986 increased the level of income subject to federal tax. Some state income taxes are based on this federal taxable income, so states that retained their income tax rates stood to receive higher tax revenues.

At least 19 states dropped lower-income people from state tax rolls and increased standard deductions and personal exemptions. Nine states lowered top individual tax rates and reduced the number of tax brackets, enabling them to better compete for business and industry.

Not Enough Money. Alaska, Texas, and Louisiana reported deficits for fiscal year 1987. Illinois imposed spending cuts after the legislature rejected a tax hike proposed by Governor James R. Thompson. As a result of the cuts, more than 500 state employees lost their jobs, and Illinois's 12 public universities raised student tuition rates.

More Than Enough. Delaware, New Hampshire, Oregon, and Wyoming enjoyed budget surpluses of 10 per cent or more. California and Massachusetts collected more revenues than permitted by law and debated how to return the extra money to taxpayers.

Selected Statistics on State Governments

State	Resident population*	Governor†	Legislature† House (D)	(R)	Senate (D)	(R)	State tax revenue‡	Tax revenue per capita‡	Public school expenditures per pupil§
Alabama	4,083,000	Guy Hunt (R)	89	16	30	5	$ 2,997,000,000	$ 740	$ 2,610
Alaska	525,000	Steve Cowper (D)	24	16	8	12	1,856,000,000	3,480	8,840
Arizona	3,386,000	Evan Mecham (R)	24	36	11	19	3,196,000,000	960	2,780
Arkansas	2,388,000	Bill Clinton (D)	91	9	31	4	1,827,000,000	770	2,800
California	27,663,000	George Deukmejian (R)	44	36	24	15#	30,878,000,000	1,140	3,750
Colorado	3,296,000	Roy Romer (D)	25	40	10	25	2,344,000,000	720	4,130
Connecticut	3,211,000	William A. O'Neill (D)	92	59	25	11	3,837,000,000	1,200	5,550
Delaware	644,000	Michael Castle (R)	19	22	13	8	883,000,000	1,390	4,780
Florida	12,023,000	Bob Martinez (D)	75	45	25	15	9,120,000,000	780	4,060
Georgia	6,222,000	Joe Frank Harris (D)	153	27	46	10	4,917,000,000	810	3,170
Hawaii	1,083,000	John Waihee (D)	40	11	20	5	1,491,000,000	1,400	4,370
Idaho	998,000	Cecil D. Andrus (D)	20	64	16	26	745,000,000	740	2,560
Illinois	11,582,000	James R. Thompson (R)	67	51	31	28	9,801,000,000	850	3,980
Indiana	5,531,000	Robert D. Orr (R)	48	52	20	30	4,458,000,000	810	3,380
Iowa	2,834,000	Terry E. Branstad (R)	59	41	30	20	2,459,000,000	860	3,740
Kansas	2,476,000	Mike Hayden (R)	51	74	16	24	1,912,000,000	780	4,140
Kentucky	3,727,000	Wallace G. Wilkinson (D)	72	28	29	9	3,216,000,000	860	3,110
Louisiana	4,461,000	Charles E. (Buddy) Roemer III (D)	84	21	34	5	3,630,000,000	810	3,240
Maine	1,172,000	John R. McKernan, Jr. (D)	86	65	20	15	1,101,000,000	940	3,650
Maryland	4,535,000	William Donald Schaefer (D)	124	17	43	4	4,670,000,000	1,050	4,660
Massachusetts	5,855,000	Michael S. Dukakis (D)	126	33#	32	8	7,668,000,000	1,310	4,860
Michigan	9,200,000	James J. Blanchard (D)	64	46	18	20	9,314,000,000	1,020	3,950
Minnesota	4,246,000	Rudy Perpich (D)	83	51	47	20	4,898,000,000	1,160	4,240
Mississippi	2,625,000	Ray Mabus (D)	113	9	45	7	1,917,000,000	730	2,530
Missouri	5,103,000	John Ashcroft (R)	111	52	21	13	3,608,000,000	710	3,350
Montana	809,000	Ted Schwinden (D)	49	51	25	25	617,000,000	750	4,070
Nebraska	1,594,000	Kay A. Orr (R)	(unicameral) 49 nonpartisan				1,119,000,000	700	3,440
Nevada	1,007,000	Richard H. Bryan (D)	29	13	9	12	1,048,000,000	1,090	3,770
New Hampshire	1,057,000	John H. Sununu (R)	133	267	8	16	484,000,000	470	3,390
New Jersey	7,627,000	Thomas H. Kean (R)	30	49	23	17	8,360,000,000	1,100	6,120
New Mexico	1,500,000	Garrey E. Carruthers (R)	47	23	21	21	1,462,000,000	990	3,540
New York	17,825,000	Mario M. Cuomo (D)	94	56	26	35	22,747,000,000	1,280	6,300
North Carolina	6,413,000	James G. Martin (R)	82	38	42	8	5,580,000,000	880	3,470
North Dakota	672,000	George A. Sinner (D)	45	61	27	26	616,000,000	910	3,210
Ohio	10,784,000	Richard F. Celeste (D)	60	39	15	18	9,062,000,000	840	3,770
Oklahoma	3,272,000	Henry Bellmon (R)	70	31	31	17	2,960,000,000	900	2,270
Oregon	2,724,000	Neil Goldschmidt (D)	34	29	17	13	1,931,000,000	720	4,240
Pennsylvania	11,936,000	Robert P. Casey (D)	103	100	24	26	10,683,000,000	900	4,750
Rhode Island	986,000	Edward D. DiPrete (R)	80	20	38	12	886,000,000	910	4,570
South Carolina	3,425,000	Carroll A. Campbell, Jr. (R)	92	32	37	9	2,887,000,000	850	3,010
South Dakota	709,000	George S. Mickelson (R)	22	48	11	24	404,000,000	570	3,210
Tennessee	4,855,000	Ned R. McWherter (D)	61	38	23	10	3,272,000,000	680	2,840
Texas	16,789,000	William P. Clements (R)	94	56	24	7	11,125,000,000	670	3,580
Utah	1,680,000	Norman H. Bangerter (R)	27	48	8	21	1,365,000,000	820	2,460
Vermont	548,000	Madeleine M. Kunin (D)	75	75	19	11	500,000,000	920	4,460
Virginia	5,904,000	Gerald L. Baliles (D)	65	33**	31	9	4,847,000,000	840	3,810
Washington	4,538,000	Booth Gardner (D)	61	37	25	24	5,219,000,000	1,170	3,810
West Virginia	1,897,000	Arch A. Moore, Jr. (R)	78	22	27	7	1,849,000,000	960	2,960
Wisconsin	4,807,000	Tommy G. Thompson (R)	54	45	20	13	5,492,000,000	1,150	4,700
Wyoming	490,000	Mike Sullivan (D)	20	44	11	19	795,000,000	1,570	6,230

*1987 estimates (source: U.S. Bureau of the Census).
†As of December 1987 (source: state government officials).
‡1986 figures (source: U.S. Bureau of the Census).

§1986-1987 figures per pupil in average daily attendance
  (source: National Education Association).
#One independent.
**Two independents.

At a governors' meeting in February were, from left, Thompson of Illinois, Clinton of Arkansas, Sununu of New Hampshire, and Castle of Delaware.

Education. Several states pumped more dollars into their educational systems in an attempt to create a more knowledgeable work force, which, in turn, would enhance economic development. Mississippi funded educational reforms passed previously and raised teachers' pay. North Carolina raised its corporate income tax to fund education. Indiana enacted tax hikes for a major education program. Illinois and North Carolina exempted savings bonds from state taxes to encourage parents to save for their children's education.

Insurance. Kentucky held a special session in October to increase the amount that employers must pay to the *workers' compensation program,* a state insurance program for individuals injured on the job. Kentucky's workers' compensation fund was in debt. Maine's Governor John R. McKernan, Jr., called a special session in October, resulting in the state reducing disability benefits on future injuries.

A crisis in medical liability insurance continued to plague several states. Florida's highest court in April 1987 voided a 1986 law setting a maximum amount that courts could award for pain and suffering caused by medical malpractice. Doctors walked out of hospitals in protest against the court's decision, and the major insurer of doctors raised its rates by more than 40 per cent. At least 15 states set upper limits on damage awards for pain and suffering.

AIDS. State legislatures in 1987 considered more than 400 bills dealing with the spread of AIDS (acquired immune deficiency syndrome). Illinois enacted 13 AIDS bills, including the nation's second—after Louisiana—requiring marriage-license applicants to take a test for an AIDS *antibody,* a substance whose presence in the blood indicates infection with the AIDS virus. A few other states required AIDS tests for prison inmates and convicted prostitutes, or set criminal penalties for carriers who knowingly infect others.

Drinking and Drugs. Wyoming in 1987 became the only state that had not raised the drinking age to 21, resulting in the loss of 5 per cent of its federal highway aid for fiscal 1987.

Crackdowns on illegal drugs were legislated in Connecticut, Louisiana, Maine, Nevada, and New Jersey. Nevada taxed the sale of illegal drugs, making those convicted of drug trafficking liable for taxes on their drug sales. Such taxes are intended not to raise money but to provide an additional legal weapon against drug dealers.

Random drug tests for workers were banned by legislation in Connecticut, Minnesota, and Vermont, and by court decisions in Georgia and New York. At least five more states restricted smoking in public places.

Family Issues. During the year, more than half the states considered bills requiring the state or private employers to offer leaves of absence to new parents. Five states passed such bills. Maine and Rhode Island provided incentives for private employers to provide child care assistance for their workers. Louisiana became the first state to ban contracts for *surrogate parenthood,* in which one woman bears a child for another woman.

Science Project. Federal plans to build a gigantic atom smasher at federal expense generated a flurry of activity in states that wished to have this machine built on—or under—their soil. The machine, called the Superconducting Super Collider (SSC), would be built inside a ring-shaped tunnel 53 miles (85 kilometers) in circumference. The SSC would cost about $4.4 billion.

Welfare Reform Measures passed in several states, as state and federal governments searched for ways to spend their welfare dollars more effectively. One approach that found favor in state legislatures was to use these funds to train welfare recipients for jobs, enabling the recipients to work their way off the welfare rolls. New York, Pennsylvania, and other states funded job-training programs in 1987. The state of Washington devised a program to replace welfare with job training and state-sponsored employment.   Elaine Stuart Knapp

See also ELECTIONS. In WORLD BOOK, see STATE GOVERNMENT and articles on the individual states.

STEEL INDUSTRY. A worldwide slump in the steel industry in 1987 and fierce competition for export sales caused economic problems for big steel companies in the United States, Japan, and several European countries. Most of the competition came from cheaply produced steel from such countries as South Korea and Taiwan.

On June 2, the American Iron and Steel Institute (AISI) said that U.S. steel firms lost $4.2 billion in 1986, the biggest loss in the industry's history. The AISI, the chief association of U.S. steel producers, said that difficulty in competing with imported steel was the single biggest factor in the loss. It said that imports accounted for about one-third of all steel used in the United States and that 33 countries had increased steel exports to the United States during 1986.

The AISI reported on May 12, 1987, that imports had contributed to a major decline in U.S. steel-production capacity. Between 1980 and 1986, plant closings reduced raw steel production capacity from 154 million short tons (140 million metric tons) to 128 million short tons (116 million metric tons). United States production capacity was expected to decline further by the end of 1987, to 112 million short tons (102 million metric tons). Actual steel production during the first seven months of 1987 totaled 49.4 million short

Workers resume operations at a USX steel mill in Illinois in February after approving a contract ending a six-month steel strike, the longest in history.

tons (44.8 million metric tons), a decline of 4 per cent from the same period in 1986.

Japan's Steel Woes. Increased foreign competition forced two huge Japanese steel companies to make major cutbacks in operations in 1987. On February 13, Nippon Steel Corporation, the world's largest steel producer, said "an unprecedented crisis" would force closing of older blast furnaces and a 29 per cent reduction in employment by 1990. Nippon also announced an accelerated effort to diversify its operations.

On February 17, Kawasaki Steel Limited said it would eliminate 5,300 jobs by 1989 and reduce the salaries of its executives by an additional 18 per cent—on top of a 12 per cent cut instituted in January 1986—in an effort to reduce production costs. All five of Japan's leading steel producers announced on May 29, 1987, that they had lost money during 1986.

The Japan Iron and Steel Federation reported on Aug. 27, 1987, that Japan's steel exports had declined for 11 consecutive months. Shipments to China, Japan's biggest overseas customer, fell by 53 per cent because of rising competition from South Korea and Taiwan.

French Losses. France's two state-owned steel companies on May 4 announced plans to merge in an effort to cut huge operating losses. The two firms, Sacilor and Usinor, reported a total loss of $2.1 billion in 1986. Officials said that the merger would reduce losses by the new company, to be called Usinor Sacilor, by 40 per cent.

Labor Agreement. The United Steelworkers of America and USX Corporation, the largest U.S. steel producer, reached agreement on Jan. 17, 1987, to end the longest steel strike in history. Workers returned to USX plants on February 2 after union members ratified the four-year agreement. The strike, which began on Aug. 1, 1986, had idled about 22,000 workers. The union agreed to reductions in wages and benefits and the elimination of about 1,300 jobs. In return, USX pledged to spend about $500 million to modernize its Monongahela Valley Works near Pittsburgh, Pa., and agreed to a profit-sharing plan. Later in February 1987, USX announced it would reduce its steelmaking capacity by 27 per cent.

Pension Payments. The U.S. Pension Benefit Guaranty Corporation on September 22 ordered LTV Corporation, the second largest U.S. steel firm, to resume making payments to its pension plans. The federal agency had assumed $2.3 billion in company pension liabilities in January after determining that LTV—which declared bankruptcy in 1986—had insufficient money to make the payments. The agency said that LTV had become a profitable corporation again and could resume its own pension payments.   Michael Woods

In WORLD BOOK, see IRON AND STEEL.

STOCKS AND BONDS. In the 1800's, when someone asked railroad tycoon and stock manipulator Jay Gould what the stock market was going to do, Gould replied, "The market, sir, will fluctuate." And that was the story of 1987. For the first three quarters of the year, all fluctuations seemed directed upward—but disaster struck in October.

The Dow Jones Industrial Average (the Dow)—the best-known index of stock prices, which tracks the common stock prices of 30 well-established industrial corporations—had closed 1986 at 1,895.95 and then began breaking records. The Dow passed 2,000 on Jan. 8, 1987, 2,200 on February 5, 2,500 on July 17, and 2,700 on August 17.

The year's peak stock prices came on August 25, when the Dow closed at 2,722.42, nearly 44 per cent higher than it began the year. The Dow slid under 2,600 again on September 3, however, marking the end of a five-year bull market.

The stock market crashed on Monday, October 19, a day that became known as Black Monday, when the Dow fell 508.00 points to hit the year's low, 1,738.74. This was not only a record one-day point loss but also a huge percentage loss—22.6 per cent of the Dow's value. The drop dwarfed even Black Tuesday—Oct. 29, 1929—when the Dow fell 12.9 per cent. In late October 1987, the Dow briefly climbed above 2,000 again before settling back to 1,938.83 at the end of December.

The Standard & Poor's 500 Index (S&P 500), which tracks the prices of most stocks on the New York Stock Exchange (NYSE) as well as the blue-chip stocks tracked by the Dow, also set records in 1987, passing 300 on March 23 and 320 on August 6, and peaking at 336.77 on August 25 for a 39 per cent gain from the end of 1986. The S&P 500 increase was smaller than the Dow's, indicating that the Dow's blue-chip stocks had been gaining value more rapidly than other stocks. By September 8, the S&P 500 had fallen below 320 again.

On October 19, 604 million shares were traded on the NYSE, and the S&P 500 lost 57.86 points, or 20.5 per cent, to hit 224.83. By the end of October, the S&P 500 briefly rose above 250 again before settling at 247.08 at year-end.

Repercussions of Black Monday. The crash of October 19 almost caused the bottom to fall out of financial markets worldwide. In London, the Financial Times-Stock Exchange 100 share index lost almost 22 per cent of its value on October 19 and 20. On October 20, Tokyo's Nikkei index dropped 15 per cent, and in Canada the Toronto Stock Exchange fell 25 per cent. Stock exchanges in Hong Kong and New Zealand did not open.

In the United States, the events of Tuesday, October 20, were nearly as shocking as those of Black Monday due to the financial crisis affecting brokers known as *specialists*. Although by 10:30 A.M. the Dow had gained more than 200 points from

The Dow's Roller Coaster Ride

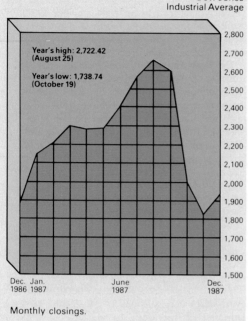

Dow Jones
Industrial Average

Year's high: 2,722.42
(August 25)

Year's low: 1,738.74
(October 19)

2,800
2,700
2,600
2,500
2,400
2,300
2,200
2,100
2,000
1,900
1,800
1,700
1,600
1,500

Dec. Jan.   June   Dec.
1986 1987   1987   1987

Monthly closings.

NYSE closed two hours early each day for the next week to handle the flood of trading.

The Bond Market was much less turbulent than the stock market in 1987. Interest rates on five-year Treasury bonds opened the year at 6.8 per cent, as did rates for tax-free municipal bonds. Both rates began to rise in April, with interest rates on Treasury bonds peaking at 8.6 per cent in May. In July, Treasury bond rates began a sharp rise, reaching 9.8 per cent during the week that ended on October 16.

The Fed's move to put reserves into the banking system involved buying bonds, which raised bond prices and lowered their yields. Five-year Treasury bond interest rates dropped to 8.2 per cent by the end of October and finished the year at 8.4 per cent. In October, the drop for 30-year Treasury bond yields was even more dramatic—from 10.1 per cent to 8 per cent in two weeks. During the first nine months of 1987, investors purchased bonds at a rate of $256 billion per year, but stock financing came to a virtual halt after Black Monday. In November, only 5 companies went public and issued stock for the first time, though more than 200 companies had filed for permission to do so.
                                      Donald W. Swanton

In the Special Reports section, see WILD DAYS ON WALL STREET. In WORLD BOOK, see BOND; INVESTMENT; STOCK, CAPITAL.

the close on Monday, a sudden wave of sell orders nearly shut down the entire market. When an order to buy or sell stock arrives on the floor of the NYSE, it is taken to a specialist, a broker who guarantees to "make a market" for several stocks by offering to buy or sell on his or her own account if there is no customer at that moment. Because many specialists had bought large quantities of stock on Monday, when sell orders outnumbered buy orders, they ran short of cash on Tuesday. When banks refused to lend more money, many specialists stopped trading. Only a few stocks could be traded, and the market seemed headed for a shutdown.

Officials at the Federal Reserve System (the Fed) came to the rescue. On Tuesday morning, Fed officials announced that "The Federal Reserve, consistent with its responsibility as the nation's central bank, affirmed today its readiness to serve as a source of liquidity to support the economic and financial system." The Fed pressured banks to make loans to specialists and provided banks with the monetary reserves they needed to do so.

Specialists who had stopped trading began again by 1 P.M., and by the end of the day, 608 million shares had changed hands. The Dow rose a record-breaking 102.27 points or nearly 6 per cent. The next day, October 21, the Dow rose 186.84 points, its second straight record gain. The

SUDAN. The effort to preserve a civilian democratic government in Sudan in the face of staggering economic and political problems nearly collapsed in August 1987, when the country's coalition government fell. The crisis was triggered by the withdrawal from the coalition of the Democratic Unionist Party (DUP), one of the two largest parties that made up the coalition government formed in April 1986. The withdrawal stemmed from the election of a representative of the majority Umma Party to one of two DUP seats on the country's ruling five-member Supreme Council.

Prime Minister Sadiq el Mahdi formed a caretaker government on Sept. 7, 1987, without the DUP. But the military leaders who led the 1985 coup against former President Gaafar Mohamed Nimeiri and ruled until they restored civilian government in 1986 threatened to take over again unless el Mahdi provided more effective leadership.

Civil Strife. The rebel Sudanese People's Liberation Army (SPLA) scored some significant military gains in 1987. Most government forces in the South were totally isolated in garrison towns. The rebels have been fighting since 1983 for the abolition of Islamic law imposed by Nimeiri over the largely non-Muslim South, as well as for a larger role for southerners in the national government. In October, the SPLA scored a major success, ambushing four troop trains near Aweil.

In December, the government held peace talks in London with the SPLA. The talks, which were the first known contact between the two sides since July 1986, ended without an agreement.

The real tragedy of the civil war was its impact on civilians. Unable to defeat the SPLA in combat, the government played on tribal and religious hatred by arming Muslim tribesmen. In March 1987, Muslim Rizeigat tribesmen massacred some 1,500 Christian Dinkas in Darfur province.

Stymied Relief Efforts. The war also prevented foreign relief agencies from delivering emergency food supplies to starving Sudanese in the South. The problem was compounded by SPLA raids on food-distribution centers. In March, for example, SPLA soldiers stole United States-supplied sorghum from a Red Cross feeding camp located in rebel-held territory. In September, the government ordered all 16 foreign relief agencies to leave Sudan, charging them with cooperating with the SPLA.

Relations with Egypt, which had been chilled since Nimeiri's overthrow, improved in 1987. In March, the two countries signed a "brotherhood charter" providing for closer cooperation in foreign affairs, defense, and social and economic matters.   William Spencer

See also AFRICA (Facts in Brief Table). In WORLD BOOK, see SUDAN.

SUPREME COURT OF THE UNITED STATES. In its 1987 term, which ended on June 26, the Supreme Court of the United States issued significant rulings on the job rights of women and minority groups, possible racism in the imposition of the death penalty, and the teaching of creationism in public schools. The 1987 term also marked the debut of William H. Rehnquist, the court's leading conservative, as chief justice. And for the last half of 1987, the court had just eight members.

Three Nominees. On June 26, the last day of the term, Associate Justice Lewis F. Powell, Jr., 79, announced his retirement. President Ronald Reagan moved swiftly to try to replace Powell, who was widely viewed as a pivotal vote in cases involving controversial issues such as abortion and minority rights. On July 1, Reagan nominated Robert H. Bork, a member of the U.S. Court of Appeals for the District of Columbia Circuit.

Confirmation hearings were held in October by the Democratic-controlled Senate. Many of Bork's critics charged that he held ultraconservative positions on a number of issues, such as freedom of speech and the right of privacy, that placed him outside the mainstream of legal thinking. Bork responded that in recent years he had changed his mind on many issues, moving to a more liberal stance. He was rejected by the Senate, 58 to 42, on October 23. See BORK, ROBERT HERON.

On October 29, Reagan nominated Douglas H. Ginsburg, a conservative judge on the same U.S. appeals court as Bork, for the Supreme Court seat. Ginsburg withdrew his name from consideration a few days later after admitting that he had smoked marijuana on several occasions earlier in his life.

On November 11, Reagan nominated a conservative jurist with more moderate views—Anthony M. Kennedy, a judge for 11 years on the Ninth Circuit Court of Appeals in Sacramento, Calif. Kennedy's nomination was still pending at year-end. See KENNEDY, ANTHONY M.

Women, Minorities, and Jobs. During the 1987 term, the Supreme Court continued to give employers and states considerable flexibility in carrying out *affirmative action* plans—the preferential hiring and advancement of women and members of minority groups to correct past discriminatory employment practices. On March 25, the court provided employers with new protection from reverse-discrimination charges when they promote women and minority-group members to jobs traditionally held by white males.

In a 6 to 3 opinion, the court upheld an affirmative action plan adopted in 1979 by Santa Clara County in California to increase the number of women, minority, and handicapped employees in its work force. Paul E. Johnson, an employee of the Santa Clara County Transportation Agency, had sued the agency. Johnson claimed that by its promotion of Diane Joyce—instead of him—to the position of road dispatcher, the agency had violated the 1964 Civil Rights Act, which forbids race or sex discrimination in employment.

The high court also continued to give federal courts broad authority to correct the consequences of past discrimination. While the court in the past had rejected the use of quotas, it nevertheless upheld a 1983 district court order that required the Alabama State Police Department to promote one black officer for every white officer promoted. In a 5 to 4 decision on February 25, the Supreme Court declared that the discriminatory conduct of the department created a "profound need" for affirmative action.

Capital Punishment. The Supreme Court ruled on April 22 that racial disparities in the imposition of the death penalty are insufficient grounds for challenging the constitutional validity of capital punishment laws. The 5 to 4 decision was harshly criticized by civil rights advocates.

The ruling stemmed from a challenge by Warren McCleskey, a black man sentenced to death in Georgia for murdering a white police officer. McCleskey charged that Georgia's capital sentencing process discriminates against blacks. To support his claim, he cited a study, encompassing more than 2,000 murder cases that occurred in

Judge Robert H. Bork testifies at Senate hearings in September on his
Supreme Court nomination, which the Senate rejected in October.

Georgia during the 1970's, indicating that killers of whites in Georgia were more likely than killers of blacks to receive the death sentence. The high court's opinion accepted the validity of the study but called it "insufficient to support an inference that any of the decision makers in McCleskey's case acted with discriminatory purpose."

In Another Criminal Law Ruling, the court rejected a challenge to pretrial dentention provisions of the 1984 Bail Reform Act. In a 6 to 3 opinion on May 26, the court ruled that concern for public safety can outweigh a defendant's right to bail. The 1984 law permits federal judges to order pretrial detention, without bail, of suspects who are considered a threat to the community.

Religion in the Classroom. Since the early 1960's, the Supreme Court, invoking the First Amendment's ban on the "establishment of religion" in the United States, has refused to permit state-ordered prayer and Bible reading in public school classrooms. Relying on such precedents, the court on June 19 struck down a Louisiana law that required public schools to give equal treatment to the teaching of creationism and evolution. Creationism is the view that a Supreme Being created the world and all its creatures, including human beings, essentially as they are today, perhaps only thousands of years ago. Evolution is the widely taught theory that all animals and plants are the descendants of simple organisms that evolved over billions of years into increasingly numerous and more complex forms.

Writing in a 7 to 2 opinion, Justice William J. Brennan, Jr., said that the First Amendment "forbids alike the preference of a religious doctrine or the prohibition of theory which is deemed antagonistic to a particular dogma." Therefore, Brennan noted, "Because the primary purpose of [Louisiana's] Creationism Act is to advance a particular religious belief, the act endorses religion in violation of the First Amendment."

Other Important Rulings by the Supreme Court in 1986 included the following decisions:
- A 7 to 2 ruling on March 3 that a key civil rights law—Section 504 of the 1973 Rehabilitation Act—protects persons with contagious diseases, such as tuberculosis and AIDS (acquired immune deficiency syndrome), from discrimination in federally funded programs.
- A 7 to 0 ruling on May 4 that the states may require all-male private clubs to admit women.
- A 7 to 2 ruling on June 23 that Congress has the power to deny federal highway funds to states that fail to enact a minimum drinking age of 21 years old.

Glen R. Elsasser

See also COURTS. In WORLD BOOK, see SUPREME COURT OF THE UNITED STATES.
SURGERY. See MEDICINE.

SURINAME. A three-party opposition coalition swept the Nov. 25, 1987, elections in Suriname in what observers called a stunning rebuke of the country's seven-year-old military dictatorship. The Front for Democracy and Development captured at least 40 of the 51 seats in the newly established National Assembly. On Jan. 12, 1988, the Assembly elected a civilian president, agricultural economist Ramsewak Shankar. He was scheduled to take office on January 25, replacing Commander of the National Army Désiré D. Bouterse.

Bouterse, a former sergeant major who promoted himself upon seizing power in 1980, had presided over an oppressive regime. Soon after he had 15 of his political opponents summarily executed in 1982 on suspicion of plotting a coup, the Netherlands suspended $100 million in annual aid. The United States quickly followed suit and withdrew a promised $1.5 million.

Since then, Bouterse has ruled virtually without foreign or domestic support. One of his former bodyguards mounted a rebellion with a few hundred guerrillas in July 1986. During 1987, the rebels shut down a bauxite refining plant and threatened a hydroelectric dam that supplies 25 per cent of Suriname's electricity. Nathan A. Haverstock

See also LATIN AMERICA (Facts in Brief Table). In WORLD BOOK, see SURINAME.

SWAZILAND. See AFRICA.

SWEDEN. Police arrested four members of the Kurdish Workers' Party on Jan. 20, 1987, in connection with the assassination of Prime Minister Olof Palme in 1986. The police said the Kurds were their principal suspects in the killing. Stockholm prosecutor Claes Zeime, however, told a press conference that there was not enough evidence to hold the four men. A month earlier, five other Kurds had been freed for lack of evidence.

Police believed that Palme was murdered because the government had imprisoned two Kurds for killing a party defector in Sweden in 1985. The Kurdish Workers' Party, founded in Turkey in the 1970's, is committed to establishing an independent Kurdish nation on the borders of Iran, Iraq, and Turkey. Sweden ruled in 1984 that the party was a terrorist group.

Prosecutor Quits. Zeime collapsed with an asthma attack on Jan. 26, 1987, and was taken off the case. Calls mounted for a public inquiry into Palme's assassination, like the Warren Commission's investigation of the 1963 murder of United States President John F. Kennedy. A plan submitted to the Swedish government on Feb. 2, 1987, recommended disbanding the police team hunting Palme's killer and replacing Stockholm police chief Hans Holmer. On February 4, Prime Minister Ingvar Carlsson announced that national authorities would take over the investigation.

Film Dispute. Olle Berglund, head of a state-run television channel, accused the United States on February 13 of trying to block the screening of a Soviet documentary film called *Who Killed Olof Palme?* The film charged that the U.S. Central Intelligence Agency and international right wing forces were accomplices in the murder. On March 10, police increased the reward offered for information on the killing from $80,000 to $800,000.

Tension between Sweden and the United States eased later in the year. On September 9, Carlsson became the first Swedish prime minister to visit the White House since 1961.

Police Guard. On June 8, 1987, Sweden mounted its biggest security operation since Palme's funeral for the Stockholm visit of Nancy Reagan, wife of U.S. President Ronald Reagan. Nancy Reagan toured several drug treatment clinics to study their antidrug programs. Police clashed with demonstrators outside her hotel, arresting 90 people.

Export Hike Pushed. The 24-nation Organization for Economic Cooperation and Development (OECD) recommended in April that Sweden change its pattern of economic growth. The OECD said Sweden should curb domestic consumption and increase net exports. Kenneth Brown

See also EUROPE (Facts in Brief Table). In WORLD BOOK, see SWEDEN.

SWIMMING. The United States unveiled two teen-aged world record-breakers in 1987 in Janet Evans and Dave Wharton. They helped the Americans dominate their major competitions of the year—the Pan Pacific Games, the Pan American Games, and the World University Games.

The 15-year-old Evans, from Placentia, Calif., weighed only 95 pounds (43 kilograms). She set two world freestyle records for women in the United States long-course championships, held from July 27 to 31 in Clovis, Calif. They were the 800 meters in 8 minutes 22.44 seconds on July 27 and the 1,500 meters in 16 minutes 0.73 second on July 31. On December 20, in the United States Open in Orlando, Fla., Evans set a world record of 4 minutes 5.45 seconds for the 400-meter freestyle. The previous record of 4 minutes 6.28 seconds, by Tracey Wickham of Australia, had stood since 1978. The 800-meter record was lowered to 8 minutes 19.53 seconds by Anke Möhring of East Germany at the European championships, held from Aug. 16 to 23, 1987, in Strasbourg, France.

The 18-year-old Wharton, of Warminster, Pa., lowered the world record for the men's 400-meter individual medley to 4 minutes 16.12 seconds on August 14 at the Pan Pacific Games, held from August 13 to 16 in Brisbane, Australia. In the European championships, Tamas Darnyi of Hungary reduced Wharton's record to 4 minutes 15.42 sec-

Greg Louganis of the United States displays the form that enabled him to sweep the gold medals in diving at the Pan American Games in August.

SWITZERLAND. The center-right coalition that has ruled Switzerland since 1959 kept its overwhelming majority in parliamentary elections on Oct. 18, 1987. The four parties in the coalition won 159 of the 200 seats in the National Council, 7 fewer than in the last election, in 1983. The chief gainer in 1987 was the environmentalist Green Party, which won 11 seats, an increase of 8.

Swiss Army Knifed. *The Dream of Slaughtering the Sacred Cow,* a television program beamed from West Germany in June 1987, angered many Swiss. The film criticized one of Switzerland's most cherished institutions, its 650,000-man army. Every able-bodied Swiss man between the ages of 20 and 50 trains regularly as a "citizen soldier" and keeps an automatic rifle at home.

Marcos Fortune. Switzerland's highest court ruled on July 1 that Swiss judicial authorities may assist the Philippine government in its efforts to secure an estimated $1 billion in assets held in the name of former Philippine President Ferdinand E. Marcos, his family, and his associates. Authorities in Zurich, Geneva, and Fribourg, Switzerland, then set about determining whether the Marcos assets, frozen by the Swiss cabinet in March 1986, had been acquired legally by the deposed Philippine leader. Kenneth Brown

See also EUROPE (Facts in Brief Table). In WORLD BOOK, see SWITZERLAND.

onds on August 19 and also set a world record of 2 minutes 0.56 second for the 200-meter individual medley on August 23.

Other Records. During 1987, 10 world records were broken and 1 equaled. Matt Biondi of Moraga, Calif., tied his 1986 record of 22.33 seconds for the 50-meter freestyle on July 30 in the U.S. championships. Tom Jager of Collinsville, Ill., lowered it to 22.32 on August 13 in Brisbane.

International Competition. The United States won 24 of the 32 events in the Pan Pacific Games, 27 of 32 swimming events from August 9 to 15 at the Pan American Games in Indianapolis, and 9 of 32 swimming events from July 9 to 14 at the World University Games in Zagreb, Yugoslavia.

Kristin Otto of East Germany won five gold medals in the European championships, Silvia Poll of Costa Rica won eight medals—including three golds—in the Pan American Games, and Noemi Lung of Romania won five golds—and a total of seven medals—in the World University Games.

U.S. Championships. At the National Collegiate Athletic Association (NCAA) championships in March and April, Pablo Morales of Santa Clara, Calif., won three NCAA titles for Stanford University in California. Morales broke John Naber's record of 10 NCAA individual titles set between 1974 and 1977. Frank Litsky

In WORLD BOOK, see SWIMMING.

SYRIA. President Hafiz al-Assad worked diligently throughout 1987 to counter his country's image as a major sponsor of international terrorism. In February, at the invitation of Lebanon's Muslim leaders, he sent 7,000 Syrian troops into Beirut to serve as a peacekeeping force. About 25,000 Syrian troops were already stationed in northern and eastern Lebanon under a 1976 agreement. The Syrians also took steps to halt the drug trade originating in Lebanon's Bekaa Valley, banning the cultivation of marijuana and the opium poppy.

One of Assad's goals in sending Syrian forces to Beirut was to secure the release of foreign hostages. Syrian intervention was reportedly instrumental in the escape of kidnapped American journalist Charles Glass on August 18. Syria also helped arrange the release of West German engineer Alfred Schmidt on September 7.

Further evidence of Assad's determination to polish his country's image abroad included the closing of the office of the Abu Nidal Palestinian terrorist group in Damascus, Syria's capital, in June. Assad also signed an agreement with Turkey in July to deny sanctuary to Kurdish and Armenian guerrillas fighting the Turkish government. The guerrillas had previously been able to escape across the border into Syria.

As a result of these efforts, the United States restored full diplomatic relations with Syria in

September and lifted restrictions imposed in 1986 on U.S. oil company operations there. In July, West Germany released $80 million in aid frozen in November 1986. Also in July, all the nations of the European Community (EC or Common Market) except Great Britain ended a nine-month ban on high-level exchanges with Syria.

Regional Affairs. Assad met with President Saddam Hussein of Iraq in April in an attempt to patch up the two countries' long-standing quarrel. Although nothing positive emerged from the meeting, Assad later warned leaders of Iran, with whom Syria is allied in the war with Iraq, that he would not tolerate any permanent occupation of Arab territory. (Iraq is an Arab nation, but Iran is not.) Assad also halted sales of spare parts to Iran. But Syria's $2-billion debt to Iran kept Assad from breaking the alliance entirely.

Economic Prospects Rose as Syria's diplomatic isolation eased and foreign aid resumed. Oil production increased as the new Thayyem oil field near Dayr az Zawr in southwestern Syria went into production. Its output expanded Syria's total production to 200,000 barrels per day. An 8 per cent increase in grain production enabled the country to reduce grain imports, thus saving much foreign exchange.   William Spencer

See also MIDDLE EAST (Facts in Brief Table). In WORLD BOOK, see SYRIA.

TAIWAN. The administration of Taiwan's President Chiang Ching-kuo took many steps in 1987 to expand its program of liberalization into political and economic activities. Chiang's political party, the Kuomintang, continued to be Taiwan's ruling faction, but it permitted more lively and open debate of official policies.

In 1987, the Legislative Yuan, Taiwan's lawmaking body, for the first time included legislators who belonged to the opposition—12 members of the Democratic Progressive Party (DPP). The DPP was created in 1986, when Taiwan began to relax its ban on opposition political parties. Throughout 1987, the DPP lawmakers and some younger Kuomintang members aroused Taiwan's legislature, which was previously a quiet and inactive council.

End to Martial Law. On June 23, the legislature passed a national security law to replace martial law, which had been in force since 1949. Opposition members protested that the new law was not liberal enough. With the new law in place, Chiang lifted martial law on July 15. The action reduced the military's influence while expanding the power of Taiwan's civil administration and judiciary. It also increased civil rights. At the same time, the Defense Ministry announced that the sentences of 237 civilians convicted of martial law offenses would be reduced and their civil rights restored.

Relations with China. After an internal party dispute, the Kuomintang announced on October 14 that Taiwan residents would be allowed to visit relatives in China for the first time in 38 years. Taiwan's Prime Minister Yu Kuo-hua insisted, however, that Taiwan's official policy remained firm on the "three no's" regarding relations with the Communists in China—no contact, no negotiations, and no compromise.

Foreign Currency Exchange controls were relaxed on July 15 to allow citizens to possess or spend foreign currency. Previously, all foreign money had to be exchanged for local currency, and each citizen could send only about $5,000 per year out of the country. But due to strong economic growth, Taiwan had foreign currency reserves of $62 billion at the end of June, and the value of its currency had risen 31 per cent in 21 months compared with the United States dollar.

President Chiang—who at age 77 suffered poor health and partial blindness—said on September 24 that he had begun using a wheelchair at official meetings. To help him run the Kuomintang, Chiang named Minister of Education Lee Huan as the party's secretary-general on July 4. Vice President Lee Teng-hui was considered Chiang's likely successor.   Henry S. Bradsher

See also ASIA (Facts in Brief Table). In WORLD BOOK, see TAIWAN.

TAKESHITA, NOBORU (1924-   ), secretary-general of Japan's ruling Liberal Democratic Party, became the prime minister of Japan on Nov. 6, 1987. Takeshita (pronounced *tah KEHSH tah*) was the designated successor to Yasuhiro Nakasone, who had served as prime minister since 1982.

Observers described Takeshita as a quiet and thoughtful man who would probably continue many of Nakasone's policies during his two-year term. He announced plans to tackle two of Japan's most important domestic issues—high land prices and the nation's export-dependent economy.

The son of a politician, Takeshita was born on Feb. 26, 1924, in the Shimane prefecture, a rice-growing region in western Japan. In 1944, Takeshita joined Japan's air corps. He was being trained as a *kamikaze pilot* (suicide bomber) when World War II ended in 1945. In 1947, Takeshita graduated from Waseda University in Tokyo and began to teach English at a junior high school.

Takeshita began his political career in 1951, when he won a seat in Shimane's legislative assembly. In 1958, he was elected to Japan's Diet (parliament). He won reelection 10 times. Takeshita held Cabinet posts under three prime ministers, serving as chief Cabinet secretary, construction minister, and, from 1982 to 1986, finance minister.

Takeshita married the former Naoko Endo in 1946. They have three daughters.   Jinger Griswold

TANZANIA. Reform measures introduced in 1986 under President Ali Hassan Mwinyi's economic austerity program showed results in 1987. For the first time in 10 years, Tanzania's economy grew faster than its population. Increased prices paid to farmers stimulated agricultural production. Cotton crops more than doubled 1985 production. Corn, which had to be imported in previous years, became a surplus crop in 1987 and was exported to neighboring countries. Some shortage of important products—such as sugar, salt, and soap—continued, but with less frequency. International confidence in Mwinyi's free-market policies was evident. In July, 21 nations agreed to refinance Tanzania's $3.4-billion foreign debt.

Energy. Tanzania also made strides in developing its own energy sources. With assistance from China, Tanzania began work on its first coal mine. The mine, located in Kiwira, is expected to provide a significant source of energy for industrial and residential use when it begins production in 1988. In July 1987, new oil reserves were discovered off the coast of Tanzania's Pemba Island.

Power Play. On October 31, former President Julius K. Nyerere was reelected chairman of Chama Cha Mapinduzi (CCM), Tanzania's ruling political party. When Nyerere turned the presidency over to Mwinyi in 1985, he promised that he would also turn over the post of CCM chairman, giving Mwinyi full political authority. Nyerere chose to retain the post, however.

Throughout 1987, Nyerere was openly critical of Mwinyi's free-market economic policies and of the International Monetary Fund (IMF), a United Nations agency. He was especially critical of the reforms that the IMF insisted Tanzania follow to qualify for an $800-million loan granted in 1986 to pay off interest on its foreign debt. In February 1987, Nyerere warned Tanzania against abandoning the principles of socialism he introduced 20 years ago in a development plan called the Arusha Declaration.

Transportation. Efforts of southern African nations to cut their economic ties with South Africa over that country's policy of *apartheid* (racial separation) led to an increased use in 1987 of the Tazara Railway. The 1,155-mile (1,860-kilometer) Tazara links Tanzania and Zambia. Instead of shipping minerals and agricultural goods to ports in South Africa in 1987, Zambia, Malawi, Zaire, and Zimbabwe used the Tazara Railway to ship goods to the Tanzanian port of Dar es Salaam.

In 1987, Tanzania began a $100-million rehabilitation program of the Dar es Salaam port. Plans called for doubling the port's load capacity to 4 million short tons (3.6 million metric tons) by 1990. J. Gus Liebenow and Beverly B. Liebenow

See also AFRICA (Facts in Brief Table). In WORLD BOOK, see TANZANIA.

TAXATION. After declaring that taxes would be raised to help cut the United States federal deficit only "over my dead body," President Ronald Reagan was prodded by worried fellow Republicans to accept a tax hike in late 1987. The pressure to raise taxes came in the wake of the October 19 stock market crash, which produced global demands for the United States to reduce its federal budget deficit.

After months of resisting the idea of working closely with Congress to cut the deficit, Reagan agreed on October 20 to meet with Republican and Democratic congressional leaders to fashion a compromise involving both new revenues and spending cuts. Following a month of difficult negotiations, the leaders on November 20 agreed to call for adding $23 billion to federal revenue over two years through higher taxes.

The Tax Increase for the 1988 fiscal year, which began Oct. 1, 1987, was fixed at $9 billion. Reagan and congressional leaders proposed that the revenue be raised without altering income tax rates, imposing sales or consumption taxes, or cutting back on the automatic indexing of income taxes to offset inflation. At the insistence of the Reagan Administration, the negotiators agreed that no provision of the tax legislation could result in lower taxes that were more than offset by increases elsewhere. On December 21, Congress voted to raise the $9 billion by extending the 3 per cent telephone excise tax for three years and by increasing taxes for some corporations and wealthy individuals.

Computers Aid IRS. The Internal Revenue Service (IRS) began 1987 with a new nationwide effort to fight tax evasion. Estimating that in every year 3 million Americans fail to file tax returns, the IRS said 2 million delinquents pay up when dunned. To collect taxes from the remaining 1 million evaders, the IRS in January began a computerized process of preparing returns and assessing taxes against nonfilers.

The IRS expected to collect at least $2 billion plus penalties and interest from 300,000 nonfilers in 1987, and it projected that the total could climb in 1988 to $3.25 billion from 500,000 individuals.

In 1987, the IRS expanded another computerized innovation, which permits tax preparers to file returns claiming refunds by computer link-up with the IRS. About 80,000 taxpayers in 7 areas filed returns by computer in 1987, and the IRS expected 500,000 returns from 16 areas in 1988. The IRS says electronic filing reduces errors and cuts the cost and time of processing.

Complicated W-4. To conform to the Tax Reform Act of 1986, which began taking effect in 1987, the IRS produced a new W-4 tax-withholding form. The form was so complex, however, that it had to be redrafted. A somewhat simplified ver-

Internal Revenue Service Commissioner Lawrence B. Gibbs explains the revised W-4 income tax form to congressional subcommittees in February.

Association and the National Association of State Budget Officers reported that $4.6 billion of the state tax windfall, or 81 per cent, was returned to taxpayers through changes in state tax laws.

Those states making provisions for a full return of the windfall were Arizona, California, Connecticut, Delaware, Georgia, Hawaii, Iowa, Maine, Minnesota, New York, Ohio, Oregon, Virginia, West Virginia, and Wisconsin. States planning to keep the windfall were Alabama, Idaho, Illinois, Indiana, Kansas, Louisiana, Massachusetts, Mississippi, Missouri, Montana, New Mexico, North Carolina, Oklahoma, and Utah. Colorado and Maryland would keep part of the windfall, and at year-end, Kentucky and Michigan had not acted.

On July 29, the National Conference of State Legislators reported that 31 states raised taxes in the first seven months of the year while nine states cut taxes. (The survey did not include Alabama and Massachusetts.) F. John Shannon, executive director of the Advisory Commission on Intergovernmental Relations, noting strong antitax sentiment at the federal level, explained the state tax hikes by saying, "State governors and legislators operate in a much more disciplined environment. They don't have the luxury of taking the easy way out." Frank Cormier and Margot Cormier

See also STATE GOVERNMENT. In WORLD BOOK, see INCOME TAX; TAXATION.

TELEVISION. The three major television networks—the American Broadcasting Companies (ABC), CBS Inc., and the National Broadcasting Company (NBC)—continued to dominate viewer habits in 1987, but not as they had even a decade before. Half of the homes in the United States had cable television, and the proliferation of home videocassette recorders led to more viewers renting recent movies instead of watching network programming.

NBC Strike. About 2,800 employees who were members of the National Association of Broadcast Employees and Technicians (NABET) on June 29 struck NBC, which for three years had been the industry leader in ratings. But the network, now under the ownership of General Electric Company, filled in for striking workers with management and other nonunion employees. On October 24, with little to show for their work stoppage, NABET employees settled with the network. But NBC said it would lay off several hundred workers, claiming the strike had taught the network it could function with fewer employees.

During 1987, members of the Writers Guild of America struck CBS and ABC. But fewer employees were affected and the strikes were of shorter duration than the NABET strike.

Fairness Doctrine. Broadcasters scored a major victory in 1987 when the Federal Communications

sion, the W-4A, was distributed by mid-1987, but the IRS estimated that as many as 18 million people failed to file either form by the Oct. 1, 1987, deadline.

Inadequate Taxpayer Assistance. On April 8, the General Accounting Office (GAO), a congressional watchdog agency, reported to the House of Representatives Committee on Government Operations that more than one-third of the people who call the IRS with tax-law questions are given inaccurate or incomplete answers. GAO employees, posing as taxpayers in need of advice, had used IRS taxpayer-assistance phone lines to ask questions the GAO said were answered correctly only 63 per cent of the time. IRS representatives gave incorrect responses to 22 per cent of the questions and incomplete answers to 15 per cent. Some members of Congress doubted the ability of the IRS to handle queries in the 1988 tax-filing season, when the most sweeping tax-code changes in 30 years begin to take full effect.

State Revenues. One result of the Tax Reform Act of 1986 was a potential $6-billion windfall for the majority of states whose tax laws are patterned after federal law. The act increased the level of income the federal government can tax. Because some state income taxes are based on this federal taxable income, state tax revenue rose in many states. On Sept. 28, 1987, the National Governors'

Commission (FCC), with President Ronald Reagan's blessing, abolished a policy called the Fairness Doctrine. That FCC rule, which dated from the 1940's and was long abhorred by broadcasters, required television and radio stations to air all sides of controversial issues. Critics said the policy violated broadcasters' First Amendment rights. (The First Amendment to the United States Constitution guarantees freedom of speech and of the press.) Critics also charged that the threat of penalties for violating the FCC rule had caused broadcasters to avoid covering some issues at all.

A bill in Congress that would have made the Fairness Doctrine a law was vetoed by Reagan on June 20. On August 4, the FCC voted unanimously to abolish the Fairness Doctrine. But a few members of Congress vowed to renew efforts to enact the policy into law.

Profits Versus Quality. In April, the House of Representatives Subcommittee on Telecommunications and Finance, chaired by Representative Edward J. Markey (D., Mass.), called the head of each network to testify before the subcommittee about profits and program quality. Each network's chief executive denied that his network was sacrificing quality in favor of increased profits. The hearings marked the first time the networks had consented to such inquiries.

Television News. Much of television's news coverage in 1987 centered around the congressional hearings on the Iran-contra affair—the selling of arms to Iran and the diversion of the profits to the Nicaraguan rebels called *contras*. Each of the major networks and public television stations aired much of the coverage live.

CBS gave up on its poorly rated "Morning Program" less than a year after the show began as competition to the more popular "Today" show on NBC and "Good Morning America" on ABC. In late November, CBS unveiled its new morning show, "CBS This Morning."

On the Entertainment Side of television, there were some well-publicized departures. Valerie Harper, star of an NBC situation comedy called "Valerie," left because of contract disputes with producers. Harper was replaced by Sandy Duncan for the 1987-1988 season, and the show was retitled "Valerie's Family." At Fox Broadcasting Company—a network that was established in 1986 and was trying to position itself as "the fourth network"—comedienne Joan Rivers in May was removed, due to poor ratings, from the late-night talk show she had hosted for less than a year.

Fox put together a line-up of programs for two nights—Saturday and Sunday—beginning in the spring of 1987, with hopes of gradually adding

Dabney Coleman pursues Megan Gallagher on "The 'Slap' Maxwell Story," an ABC comedy about an irrepressible and self-centered sportswriter.

The impish Pee-wee Herman cavorts with an armchair that hugs and other whimsical props on his popular CBS television show, "Pee-wee's Playhouse."

more programs. Fox affiliate stations were independent stations that were not aligned with NBC, ABC, or CBS. Some Fox shows, including "Married with Children" and "The Tracey Ullman Show," pleased some critics, and actor George C. Scott drew attention for his role in a comedy called "Mr. President." But Fox was hardly competitive with the major networks in ratings.

Ratings and People Meters. During the 1986-1987 prime-time television season and continuing into the 1987-1988 programming schedule, NBC held a commanding lead in ratings over ABC and CBS. The method of measuring the ratings itself became news in September, when viewership was calculated using a new measuring device called *people meters*. These devices, which require participating viewers to punch a series of buttons on a remote-control device each time they watch television, were thought to give advertisers more accurate information about the ages and types of viewers watching television than the previous measuring procedure. In the old method, a device called a *black box* recorded when a television set was turned on and what channel it was tuned to but did not monitor who in the household was actually watching.

New and Noteworthy Programs of the 1987-1988 season included CBS's "Tour of Duty," which marked the first attempt to depict the Viet-

nam War in a weekly series; ABC's "Dolly," starring Dolly Parton, an effort to revive the old variety show format; "Frank's Place," on CBS, starring Tim Reid in a show that was called a "dramedy"— a cross between comedy and drama—and ABC's "thirtysomething," a drama about a young, affluent married couple that appeared to be an attempt to capture the so-called yuppie viewer.

Some hit shows from previous seasons continued to draw audiences. NBC's "The Cosby Show" was television's hit show for the fourth straight year, though there was evidence that its popularity was waning. The game show "Wheel of Fortune" continued to be enormously popular, as was one of the show's personalities, Vanna White.

In May, one of television's most celebrated programs, NBC's "Hill Street Blues," broadcast its final episode. A staple on the network since 1981, the show's realism and ensemble cast—an approach that was subsequently adopted by a number of new programs—led to dozens of awards.

Movies and Miniseries. Popular made-for-television movies and miniseries included *Out on a Limb* on ABC, a two-part movie about actress Shirley MacLaine's spiritual beliefs; *LBJ: The Early Years* on ABC; and NBC's *Nutcracker: Money, Madness, and Murder*, starring Lee Remick.

Kris Kristofferson starred in ABC's "Amerika," a heavily promoted 14½-hour miniseries that por-

Top-Rated U.S. Television Series

The following were the most-watched television series for the 31-week regular season—Sept. 21, 1986, through April 19, 1987—as determined by the A. C. Nielsen Company.

1. "The Cosby Show" (NBC)
2. "Family Ties" (NBC)
3. "Cheers" (NBC)
4. "Murder, She Wrote" (CBS)
5. "The Golden Girls" (NBC)
6. (tie) "60 Minutes" (CBS)
   "Night Court" (NBC)
8. "Growing Pains" (ABC)
9. "Moonlighting" (ABC)
10. "Who's the Boss?" (ABC)
11. "Dallas" (CBS)
12. "Nothing in Common" (NBC)
13. "Newhart" (CBS)
14. "Amen" (NBC)
15. "227" (NBC)
16. (tie) "CBS Sunday Movie" (CBS)
    "Matlock" (NBC)
    "NBC Monday Night Movies" (NBC)
19. (tie) "Kate & Allie" (CBS)
    "NFL Monday Night Football" (ABC)
21. "NBC Sunday Night Movie" (NBC)
22. (tie) "My Sister Sam" (CBS)
    "L.A. Law" (NBC)
24. "Falcon Crest" (CBS)
25. (tie) "Dynasty" (ABC)
    "Highway to Heaven" (NBC)

trayed life in the United States several years after a Soviet take-over. Farrah Fawcett starred as troubled heiress Barbara Hutton in *Poor Little Rich Girl* for NBC, and Jacqueline Bisset and Armand Assante were lavishly costumed for *Napoleon and Josephine: A Love Story* on ABC.

The Public Broadcasting Service (PBS) aired the complete works of Sir William S. Gilbert and Sir Arthur S. Sullivan—the team that wrote the most popular operettas in the history of the English theater—and a pleasant new anthology series, "Trying Times." PBS's "Masterpiece Theatre" presented Sir Laurence Olivier in *Lost Empires* and Ben Kingsley in *Silas Marner*.

Cable Television's Home Box Office (HBO) aired "Vietnam War Story," an anthology of Vietnam dramas, and *Mandela*, a powerful work about the jailed South African leader, starring Danny Glover. The child-oriented Disney Channel presented *The Boy Who Loved Trolls*, while Showtime featured Jack Lemmon in playwright Eugene O'Neill's *Long Day's Journey into Night*. The sports-oriented Entertainment and Sports Programming Network (ESPN) began airing a limited number of National Football League games, a first for cable television.　　　　　　　　　　　　　　P. J. Bednarski

See also AWARDS AND PRIZES. In WORLD BOOK, see TELEVISION.

TENNESSEE. See STATE GOVERNMENT.

TENNIS. Ivan Lendl, a Czechoslovak who lives in Greenwich, Conn., and Pat Cash of Australia won the major tennis titles for men in 1987. In the four grand-slam tournaments for women, Martina Navratilova of Fort Worth, Tex., won two and was the runner-up in two. But the 31-year-old Navratilova yielded her number-one world ranking to 18-year-old Steffi Graf of West Germany. See GRAF, STEFFI.

Men. Lendl beat Mats Wilander of Sweden in baseline duels in two of the four grand-slam finals. The more important match was the United States Open, which Lendl won, 6-7, 6-0, 7-6, 6-4, on September 14 in Flushing Meadow, N.Y., in 4 hours and 47 minutes. The U.S. Open was played on a hard surface. On June 7 in Paris, Lendl defeated Wilander for the French Open championship on a clay court, 7-5, 6-2, 3-6, 7-6, in 4 hours and 23 minutes.

The Wimbledon final on July 5 in England was played on grass, and the 11th-seeded Cash beat Lendl, 7-6, 6-2, 7-5. In 1986, Cash needed a special invitation to play at Wimbledon because, after health problems, his world ranking had dropped to 413th.

Cash lost the Australian Open final on grass to Stefan Edberg of of Sweden, 6-3, 6-4, 3-6, 5-7, 6-3, on January 25 in Melbourne. In the U.S. Open, Cash was upset in the first round.

Other Stars. At age 34, Jimmy Connors of Belleville, Ill., a former Wimbledon and U.S. Open champion, reached the semifinals of both tournaments. At age 19, Boris Becker of West Germany, who won the Wimbledon men's singles title in 1985 and 1986, was upset in the second round.

In 1986, John McEnroe of Douglaston, N.Y., was the world's ranking player before he took a six-month vacation from tennis because he was tired after years of high-pressure competition. In 1987, McEnroe failed to regain his previous level of play, though his temper was as hot as ever. During the third round of the U.S. Open, he was fined $7,500 for outbursts against match officials and received an automatic two-month suspension.

Women. Navratilova's year started badly. Hana Mandlikova of Czechoslovakia defeated her, 7-5, 7-6, in the Australian Open final on January 24, and Graf beat her, 6-4, 4-6, 8-6, in the French Open final on June 6. Navratilova double-faulted on match point in each of those finals.

Entering Wimbledon, Graf had won all seven of her tournaments during the year. Navratilova had been winless in her six tournaments, having lost in four finals and two semifinals. Navratilova's fortunes changed when she beat Graf, 7-5, 6-3, in the Wimbledon final on July 4 for a record sixth consecutive title there. It was her eighth Wimbledon singles title overall, tying Helen Wills Moody's record. On September 12, Navratilova beat Graf, 7-6,

6-1, for her second straight U.S. Open title and her fourth in five years.

In August, Graf took over first place in the women's computer rankings. By November, her points standing clinched the number-one ranking. Navratilova had held that honor for almost five years except for a six-month span in 1985.

Graf dominated the European circuit by winning the singles titles at the French, Italian, and German opens. She finished the year with 11 tournament victories, a 75-2 record, and $1.1 million in prize money. Graf also helped West Germany win the Federation Cup.

Davis Cup. Paraguay upset the United States, 3 matches to 2, in March in Asunción, Paraguay, as the crowd threw stones and yelled obscenities at the U.S. players. The defeat meant the United States had to beat West Germany in July in Hartford, Conn., or be forced to qualify for Davis Cup competition in 1988, instead of entering automatically. But West Germany won, 3-2, partly because Becker outlasted McEnroe.

Meanwhile, India upset Australia's defending champions, 3-2, in the semifinals of the main competition. That sent India against Sweden in the final, held from December 18 to 20 in Göteborg, Sweden. Sweden won, 5-0.   Frank Litsky

In WORLD BOOK, see TENNIS.

TEXAS. See HOUSTON; STATE GOVERNMENT.

THAILAND celebrated the 60th birthday of King Bhumibol Adulyadej on Dec. 5, 1987. The occasion was festive because, under the Buddhist traditions observed in Thailand, the completion of five 12-year periods of life is especially favorable.

Political Turmoil. In January, the Democrat Party, the largest political party in Thailand's governing coalition, was torn by a dispute that threatened the government's stability. Rebels in the Democrat Party—which in 1986 won 100 of the 347 seats in the House of Representatives—challenged their party leader, Deputy Prime Minister Bhichai Rattakul. The rebels blamed Bhichai for failing to help the party win more cabinet seats and accused him of embezzlement. In a showdown on January 10, Bhichai retained his leadership, however.

Prime Minister Prem Tinsulanonda, who headed the ruling coalition but did not belong to any party, remained above the squabble. The parliamentary opposition's efforts to censure Prem for a series of scandals collapsed on April 22.

In February, a possible successor to Prem, army commander General Chaovalit Yongchaiyuth, stirred controversy with talk of a "peaceful revolution." Chaovalit advocated political, economic, and social changes to benefit the Thai people, and he contemptuously compared members of the parliamentary coalition with trading companies trying to protect their business interests.

Steffi Graf, 18, of West Germany begins a serve in the French Open, which she won in June by defeating Martina Navratilova in the final.

Former Prime Minister Kukrit Pramoj charged that Chaovalit—who had been credited with masterminding a strategy that reduced the threat of Communist rebellion—was now trying to implement Communist-style policies. In response, an anti-Communist paramilitary unit founded by Chaovalit angrily demonstrated outside Kukrit's house on April 5.

Thailand and the United States on January 9 signed an agreement to set up military stockpiles in Thailand over the next five years. The supplies, mainly ammunition, would be available for either country in a crisis. In 1987, U.S. forces also staged occasional military maneuvers in Thailand.

Economic Growth was stronger than the government had predicted. Officials had expected a 5 per cent increase in national output but revised the estimate to 6 per cent. Agricultural production declined in 1986, but in 1987 production grew by an estimated 3 per cent, despite a drought that reduced rice crops. Exports during the first nine months of 1987 surpassed exports for all of 1986.

Foreign investment boomed, helping Thailand develop industries to balance its traditional dependence on agriculture. Exports of manufactured goods ranging from wigs to diesel engines helped pay for more imports.   Henry S. Bradsher

See also Asia (Facts in Brief Table). In World Book, see Thailand.

THATCHER, MARGARET HILDA (1925-   ), became the first British leader since 1827 to be elected to a third consecutive term as prime minister of Great Britain when her party won the parliamentary election on June 11, 1987. Thatcher's Conservative Party defeated the Labour Party with 42 per cent of the vote. See Great Britain.

Thatcher said she would continue her program to reduce government control over Britain's economy. She proposed what she called "substantial and radical" changes during her new term, including replacing local property taxes with a tax levied equally on all adult citizens.

Margaret Hilda Roberts was born on Oct. 13, 1925, in the small town of Grantham in Lincolnshire, England. She earned a B.S. degree in natural science from Somerville College at Oxford University in 1947 and later earned an M.A. degree from Oxford. In 1953, she became a *barrister* (a lawyer who can plead in any court).

Thatcher was elected to the House of Commons in 1959. She was appointed secretary of state for education and science in 1970. In 1975, she became leader of the Conservative Party.

Thatcher became Great Britain's first woman prime minister in May 1979. She was elected to her second term in 1983.

Thatcher married businessman Denis Thatcher in 1951. They have two children.   Mary A. Krier

THEATER. Broadway staged a healthy comeback in 1987. For the first time in three years, both theater attendance and the number of new productions rose. Most important, many of the new shows became instant hits.

Several factors contributed to this new state of health. First, United States playwrights emerged from an artistic slump to create a number of important, well-received plays. Second, imports from London proved successful. Third, advances in theater technology—sound, lighting, and set design—added to the appeal of musical productions. Finally, theaters outside New York City produced more original plays and musicals, assuring the commercial theater of fresh material.

Strong Start. As early as April, it was clear that Broadway was rebounding from its recent slump. Most of the major theaters were either filled or booked, and several new shows had already proved to be hits.

Broadway Bound, the latest of Neil Simon's autobiographical plays—this one about growing up in the Brooklyn borough of New York City—settled in after its December 1986 opening for a long run.

Another domestic play, August Wilson's *Fences*, also won immediate acclaim when it opened in March 1987. This heart-warming play about a black family in Pittsburgh, Pa., featured a powerhouse performance by James Earl Jones as a garbage collector struggling to support and understand his family in the changing social world of the late 1950's.

Great Britain's Royal Shakespeare Company arrived in the spring with an exquisitely styled production of *Les Liaisons Dangereuses*. Christopher Hampton's sophisticated romantic drama followed the erotic adventures of characters created in 1782 by French novelist Pierre Choderlos de Laclos.

Other Noteworthy Plays that opened earlier in 1987 included A. R. Gurney, Jr.,'s *Sweet Sue*, about the midlife romance of a woman whose state of confusion was represented by having two actresses—Mary Tyler Moore and Lynn Redgrave—share the role; Larry Shue's *The Nerd*, a light comedy about the social perils of having a colossal jerk for a friend; and Tina Howe's *Coastal Disturbances*, about the summer romance of an up-and-coming artist and an easygoing lifeguard.

A major revival also appeared early in 1987. A new production of George Bernard Shaw's *Pygmalion* (1912) featured British stage and film star Peter O'Toole—in his Broadway debut—as Professor Henry Higgins.

Blockbusters. What really perked up Broadway in 1987, however, were the March openings of two blockbuster musicals from London. *Starlight Express*, which featured music by Andrew Lloyd Webber—the British composer of *Evita* (1978) and *Cats* (1982)—was an upbeat child's adventure story

With roller skates representing their wheels, actors playing locomotives compete in a cross-country race on stage in *Starlight Express.*

about a steam train that beats out more modern engines in a cross-country race. But its real achievement was a fantastic $2.5-million high-tech set designed by John Napier. Actors on roller skates tore around a multitiered race track that switched course by means of some of the most complex stage machinery ever seen on Broadway. But many critics dismissed the $8-million musical as merely a showcase for expensive stage tricks.

Operatic grandeur was the style of *Les Misérables*, a ponderous but successful musical extravaganza based on the 1862 novel by French writer Victor Hugo. Through the innovative staging of Trevor Nunn and John Caird, a large acting ensemble portrayed one man's long quest for personal justice against the backdrop of the second French Revolution, in the 1830's.

Although both *Les Misérables* and *Starlight Express* were British imports, the lavish "Broadway treatment" of both shows represented the theater's increasing reliance on spectacular productions. Despite critical warnings that such extravaganzas often stress technological stagecraft over basic theatrical art, audiences continued to support such spectacles, which, in fact, helped put Broadway back on its feet financially. Before it opened, *Starlight Express* had an advance ticket sale of $5.6 million, while the advance for *Les Misérables* was a record-breaking $11.2 million.

Up, Up, and Away. With two major musicals and some new plays already open and drawing well by the end of April, the remainder of the 1987 season had nowhere to go but up. And up it went, with *Burn This*, a romantic drama by Lanford Wilson. The contemporary love story was ignited by John Malkovich's fiery performance as a crude roughneck who falls in love with a delicate dancer played by Joan Allen.

Into the Woods, the eagerly awaited new musical by Stephen Sondheim and James Lapine, was a highly fanciful and beautifully staged story about fairy-tale characters who go into an enchanted woods on old-fashioned errands and come out with modern-day emotional problems. The show pleased some critics but disappointed others.

There were no critical reservations about the revival of *Anything Goes* at the Lincoln Center for the Performing Arts. In a sparkling-fresh treatment by director Jerry Zaks, this 1934 Cole Porter musical, starring Patti LuPone, so delighted audiences that it quickly transferred to a Broadway theater.

Other productions that kept Broadway and off-Broadway theaters lighted in 1987 included *Sherlock's Last Case*, a light-hearted view of the great detective and his faithful Watson, played by Frank Langella and Donal Donnelly; and a revival of *Cabaret* (1966) with Joel Grey repeating his role as the emcee of a sleazy 1930's Berlin nightclub.

Political Drama. Although American playwrights trend to produce little political drama nowadays, American audiences enjoy British imports in this category. Offerings in 1987 included *Breaking the Code*, Hugh Whitemore's drama about British intelligence efforts in World War II (1939-1945); *Serious Money*, Caryl Churchill's dark comedy about corruption and greed on the London Stock Exchange; and *Bouncers*, John Godber's fierce social comedy about working-class youth in northern England.

Regional Theater also showed increased vitality in 1987. For the first time in five years, income at nonprofit regional theaters grew faster than operating expenses.

The La Jolla Playhouse in California, under the direction of Des McAnuff, presented Lee Blessing's *A Walk in the Woods*, in which a Soviet diplomat and his American counterpart discuss nuclear armaments. McAnuff had in 1986 mounted the production at the Yale Repertory Theater in New Haven, Conn. In 1987, that theater also jointly premiered, with the Los Angeles Theater Center, a new play by the science editor of *Pravda*, a Soviet newspaper. *Sarcophagus* by Vladimir Gubaryev presented a liberal Russian view of the perils of nuclear arms.

Another Russian theater artist, Yuri Lyubimov, the former director of Moscow's Taganka Theater, made his American directing debut at the Arena Stage in Washington, D.C., with an avant-garde version of Russian writer Fyodor Dostoevsky's 1866 novel *Crime and Punishment*.

Other Important Premieres. The Mark Taper Forum in Los Angeles, which observed its 20th anniversary season in 1987, presented *Burn This* prior to the play's Broadway opening. The Old Globe Theatre in San Diego hosted *Into the Woods* before that musical went to Broadway.

At the Alley Theatre in Houston, George Segal starred in *Henceforward...*, the most recent of several comedies by popular British playwright Alan Ayckbourn to receive its American premiere at this theater. Another respected British playwright, Tom Stoppard, was represented regionally when the Long Wharf Theatre in New Haven premiered *Dalliance*, his comedy-drama about social pretense in 1890's Vienna, Austria. Another play from Great Britain—*Ourselves Alone* by Irish playwright Anne Devlin—received its first American showing at Washington's Arena Stage. Devlin wrote of three women living in Northern Ireland who try to cope with their men's involvement in the war there.   Marilyn Stasio

See also AWARDS AND PRIZES (Arts Awards); WILSON, AUGUST. In WORLD BOOK, see DRAMA; THEATER.

TOGO. See AFRICA.

TORNADO. See DISASTERS.

TORONTO, Canada's largest urban area and main financial center, was a paradox of prosperity and poverty in 1987. Signs of flourishing growth and development in the city coexisted with the specter of homelessness and hunger for many people.

Toronto continued to grow at a phenomenal rate, with housing starts 50 to 60 per cent ahead of 1986—itself a good year. Throughout the city's center, new glass and metal office towers were rising, and more were on the drawing boards—leaving only a handful of buildings more than 25 years old in the area. Another indication of Toronto's prosperity in 1987 was an unemployment rate of 4.4 per cent—half the national average.

Poverty and Prosperity. But despite these signs of a flourishing economy, the Metro Social Planning Council estimated that as many as 10,000 people in Metropolitan Toronto were in need of shelter, a third of them women and children. The city's 21 crowded shelter hostels regularly had to turn away homeless people. (Metropolitan Toronto is a grouping of five neighboring boroughs and the City of Toronto. Its chief governing body is the Metropolitan Council of the Municipality of Metropolitan Toronto—popularly called Metro.)

Hunger was also a concern in Toronto in 1987. During the week before Canada's Thanksgiving Day in October, welfare agencies launched a city-wide campaign for nonperishable food donations to supply 140 centers that distribute free food packages. The agencies estimated that the campaign enabled them to help 50,000 people who would otherwise have gone hungry.

Ironically, such deprivation was related to Toronto's prosperity. Employment opportunities attracted thousands of jobless people from such depressed areas as Canada's Atlantic Provinces, where unemployment ranged as high as 30 per cent. But many who found jobs were unable to find decent family housing in Toronto at prices they could afford. And many who found homes had their budgets strained by soaring rents.

Toronto's hectic growth also sent commercial land prices sky-high. Downtown land that was valued at $400 to $500 per square foot (0.9 square meter) in 1980 was priced at $1,200 or more per square foot in 1987 (Canadian dollars; $1 = U.S. 77 cents on Dec. 31, 1987).

Political Controversy. The tension in Toronto between prosperous economic interests and social concerns was underscored by a yearlong debate over the future of a controversial development project on Toronto's Lake Ontario shore. The development, called Harbourfront, is on waterfront land donated to the city by the federal government. Plans for the project called for demolishing an area of warehouses, railway sidings, docks, and grain elevators and converting it into parkland and social, cultural, and recreational facilities.

Development of the 90-acre (36-hectare) site was to be financed by limited commercial and residential projects. Those projects, in turn, were to generate leasing revenues to fund Harbourfront's social and commercial amenities.

But critics charged that the area was becoming overwhelmed by commercial development, including expensive high-rise condominiums, shops, and a luxury hotel. Many also were concerned over secrecy surrounding deals made with private developers. In March, the City of Toronto announced it would conduct a review of the Harbourfront project. And in April, the federal government put a general freeze on further construction, pending a review of development plans.

School Strike. Elementary-school teachers went on strike on September 22, leaving 157,000 children without classes until October 14. The main issue in the dispute was paid "preparation time"— time needed to prepare classwork, mark papers, and interview parents. The teachers originally demanded 200 paid minutes a week for preparation, while the six area school boards offered no pay for preparation. The settlement was an even compromise, giving the teachers 100 minutes of paid preparation time each week.   Robert Duffy

See also ONTARIO. In WORLD BOOK, see TORONTO.

TOYS AND GAMES. Retail toy sales in the United States continued to grow slowly in 1987, with an increase of just under 5 per cent over 1986 sales. For the second consecutive year, there were no hot-selling items or new product trends. Lack of consumer interest in new products and late shipments of some of the new, high-tech toys had a negative effect on the industry.

Hopping Fun. One of the few best-selling new toys in 1987 was PoGo Bal, a variation on the pogo stick, manufactured by Hasbro Incorporated of Pawtucket, R.I. PoGo Bal is a flat, circular disk that has a rubber ball attached to the top and to the bottom. A person stands on the platform, hugs the top ball with his or her feet, and hops.

Traditional Toys, such as dolls, stuffed animals, and board games, continued to do well in 1987. Two of the year's most popular products were Barbie, the 28-year-old fashion doll made by Mattel Incorporated of Hawthorne, Calif., and Hasbro's G.I. Joe, a plastic action figure. Both Barbie and G.I. Joe were given updated accessories. Barbie became the lead singer in her own rock band, and G.I. Joe became a space traveler with his own space vehicle launch complex.

Interactive Toys. Controversy arose during the year over toys that interact with television shows. The Captain Power line of toys, introduced in

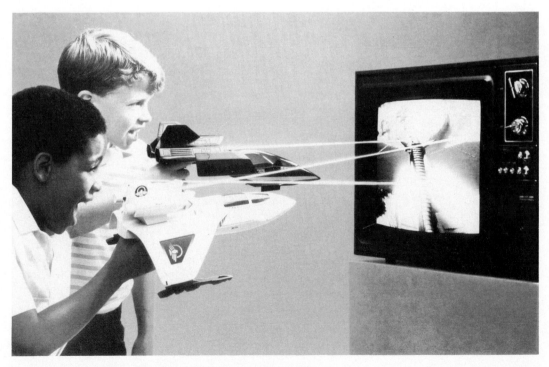

Captain Power toys introduced by Mattel in 1987 enable children to interact with the "Captain Power and the Soldiers of the Future" television show.

1987 by Mattel, is designed to be played during the "Captain Power and the Soldiers of the Future" television show, which premiered in the fall. During a segment in the show, children shoot light beams at characters on the TV from handheld spaceships and the characters appear to shoot back. Although the technology was hailed as a breakthrough, some parents and consumer groups charged that the toys encourage violence and hinder imaginative play.

Other High-Tech Toys introduced in 1987 included PXL 2000, a children's video camcorder from Fisher-Price Toys of East Aurora, N.Y. The camcorder records black-and-white images on the standard audio cassettes used in tape recorders. It plugs into a television set—rather than a videocassette recorder (VCR)—for playback. Jill, a doll from Playmates Toys Incorporated of La Mirada, Calif., can pose multiple-choice questions to a child. The child's response results in an appropriate answer, story, or song from Jill.

Holograms—lifelike, three-dimensional images made on flat surfaces—appeared in the toy industry during the year. The holograms were incorporated into the faces or shields of action figures, such as SuperNaturals from Tonka Toys of Minnetonka, Minn.   Diane P. Cardinale

In World Book, see Doll; Game; Toy.

TRACK AND FIELD. For the second time in the sport's history, world outdoor championships were held in track and field in 1987. For the first time, world indoor championships were held. The year will also be remembered for the world record that Ben Johnson set and for the end of Edwin Moses' nearly 10-year winning streak in the 400-meter hurdles.

In addition to Johnson of Canada and Moses of Newport Beach, Calif., the year's outstanding men were Said Aouita of Morocco, Patrik Sjöberg of Sweden, and Sergei Bubka of the Soviet Union. Among the outstanding women were Jackie Joyner-Kersee of Long Beach, Calif.; Stefka Kostadinova of Bulgaria; Silke Gladisch of East Germany; and Tatyana Samolenko of the Soviet Union.

The world outdoor championships were held from August 29 to September 6 in Rome, with 1,500 men and women from 165 nations. The only previous outdoor championships took place in 1983. The first indoor championships were staged from March 6 to 8 in Indianapolis, with 410 athletes from 84 nations.

Three nations dominated. Outdoors, the leaders in gold medals were East Germany (10), the United States (9), and the Soviet Union (7). Indoors, the leaders were the Soviet Union (6), the United States (5), and East Germany (5).

World Outdoor Track and Field Records Established in 1987

Men

Event	Holder	Country	Where set	Date	Record
100 meters	Ben Johnson	Canada	Rome	Aug. 30	:09.83
2,000 meters	Said Aouita	Morocco	Paris	July 16	4:50.81
5,000 meters	Said Aouita	Morocco	Rome	July 22	12:58.39
High jump	Patrik Sjöberg	Sweden	Stockholm, Sweden	June 30	7 ft. 11¼ in. (2.42 m)
Pole vault	Sergei Bubka	Soviet Union	Prague, Czechoslovakia	June 23	19 ft. 9¼ in. (6.03 m)
Shot-put	Alessandro Andrei	Italy	Viareggio, Italy	Aug. 12	75 ft. 2 in. (22.91 m)
Javelin throw (new javelin)	Jan Zelezny	Czechoslovakia	Nitra, Czechoslovakia	May 31	287 ft. 7 in. (87.66 m)

Women

Event	Holder	Country	Where set	Date	Record
100-meter hurdles	Ginka Zagorcheva	Bulgaria	Drama, Greece	Aug. 8	:12.25
High jump	Stefka Kostadinova	Bulgaria	Rome	Aug. 30	6 ft. 10¼ in. (2.09 m)
Long jump	Jackie Joyner-Kersee	U.S.A.	Indianapolis	Aug. 13	24 ft. 5½ in. (7.45 m)†
Triple jump	Li Huirong	China	Tokyo	Oct. 11	46 ft. ¾ in. (14.04 m)*
Shot-put	Natalya Lisovskaya	Soviet Union	Moscow	June 7	74 ft. 3 in. (22.63 m)
Javelin throw	Petra Felke	E. Germany	Leipzig, E. Germany	July 29	258 ft. 10 in. (78.90 m)

m = meters; *unofficial record; †tied world record.

Ben Johnson of Canada, right, sets a world record of 9.83 seconds in the 100-meter dash in August, defeating Carl Lewis of the United States.

26.44 seconds) and set world records for 2,000 meters (4 minutes 50.81 seconds) and 5,000 meters (12 minutes 58.39 seconds). Sjöberg won the world championship in the high jump at 7 feet 9½ inches (2.37 meters) and set world records indoors at 7 feet 10¾ inches (2.41 meters) and outdoors at 7 feet 11¼ inches (2.42 meters).

Bubka won world championships in the pole vault indoors and outdoors, each at 19 feet 2¼ inches (5.85 meters). He raised the world records to 19 feet 7 inches (5.97 meters) indoors and 19 feet 9¼ inches (6.03 meters) outdoors.

Three women won two gold medals each in the outdoor championships. Joyner-Kersee won the heptathlon with 7,126 points and the long jump at 24 feet 1¾ inches (7.36 meters). Gladisch won the 100 meters (10.90 seconds) and 200 meters (21.74 seconds). Samolenko took the 1,500 meters (3 minutes 58.56 seconds) and 3,000 meters (8 minutes 38.73 seconds). Kostadinova won both the outdoors and indoors world championships in the women's high jump, both with world records—6 feet 8¾ inches (2.05 meters) indoors and 6 feet 10¼ inches (2.09 meters) outdoors.

Other Americans who won world individual titles outdoors were Calvin Smith in the 200 meters (20.16 seconds) and Greg Foster in the 110-meter hurdles (13.21 seconds). Frank Litsky

IN WORLD BOOK, see TRACK AND FIELD.

Outstanding Races. The memorable race in the outdoor championships was the 100-meter dash on August 30, matching Johnson and his main rival, Carl Lewis of Houston. Johnson, with an explosive start, beat Lewis by a meter in 9.83 seconds. That time was one-tenth of a second faster than the 1983 world record set by Calvin Smith of Bolton, Miss., in the thinner air of Colorado Springs, Colo.

The full one-tenth-second improvement was considered a staggering achievement. The only comfort for Lewis was a victory on September 5 in the world-championship long jump with 28 feet 5½ inches (8.67 meters).

Another memorable race during the year came on June 4 in Madrid, Spain, when Moses' winning streak was ended by another American, Danny Harris of Perris, Calif. Moses had won 107 consecutive finals for a total of 122 races, including 15 preliminaries. His previous loss had been on Aug. 26, 1977, against Harald Schmid of West Germany. The world championships matched the three men on Sept. 1, 1987. Moses won the 400-meter hurdle event in 47.46 seconds, barely holding off Harris and Schmid, who both finished in 47.48. At year's end, at age 31, Moses was the world champion again.

Other World Championships. Aouita won the world championship at 5,000 meters (13 minutes

TRANSIT systems in United States cities showed a slight decline in ridership in 1987. According to the American Public Transit Association (APTA), a Washington, D.C.-based trade association that represents public mass-transit systems, ridership from January to May 1987 dipped 0.98 per cent below 1986 levels. Major cities reporting declines included Indianapolis, where the number of passengers dropped 5.8 per cent; Detroit, 5.5 per cent; Minneapolis-St. Paul, Minn., 4.2 per cent; and Baltimore, 3.3 per cent.

Some transit systems had ridership increases, however. In Washington, D.C., for example, the number of transit system riders rose 3.8 per cent. Other cities showing ridership increases were Boston, 2.3 per cent; Philadelphia, 2.4 per cent; and Houston, 2.1 per cent.

Extensions of Transit Systems were started or completed in several U.S. cities during 1987. On March 12, the northeast line of a new 18.3-mile (29.5-kilometer) light-rail passenger system opened in Sacramento, Calif. (Light-rail systems use electrically powered railroad passenger cars that run on street-level tracks.) The second leg of the line began operation on September 5.

A 6-mile (9.7-kilometer) extension of the Baltimore subway system opened on schedule on July 10. The extension increased the line to 14 miles (22.5 kilometers). Baltimore officials estimated

A trolley car, riding on the first part of a line that may eventually connect Sacramento, Calif., and its suburbs, begins operation in March.

that the extension will add 7,500 to 10,000 additional riders daily to the system.

The Orange Line, Boston's 86-year-old elevated-train system, shut down permanently on May 1. The following day, the city opened its new 4.7-mile (7.6-kilometer) subway, also called the Orange Line. The subway links downtown Boston with the city's southwest suburbs. The $743-million project, the largest in Massachusetts history, took nine years to complete.

New Projects. In January, construction began on a 91.1-mile (146.6-kilometer) rail system in Dallas. The $9.7-billion project is expected to be completed in 23 years.

Governor Rudy Perpich of Minnesota in June signed a bill that permits the construction of a 14-mile (23-kilometer) light-rail passenger line between downtown Minneapolis and the suburbs of St. Louis Park, Hopkins, and Minnetonka. The line is expected to be in operation by 1991.

Seattle broke ground on March 6 for a tunnel that will handle buses that run on both diesel and electric power. The tunnel, the first of its kind in the United States, is expected to be completed in 1990. On June 10, residents of Cobb County, Georgia, northwest of Atlanta, voted to establish a 10-route bus line serving the area by Jan. 1, 1988. Start-up and operating costs were to be covered in part by a $5.2-million grant from the Urban Mass

Transportation Administration (UMTA); a $2-million grant from the Georgia Department of Transportation; and funds from a license tax on local businesses. Cobb County leaders said the new bus line would be run by a private operator rather than by the Metropolitan Atlanta Rapid Transportation Authority.

The first subway in Africa opened on Sept. 27, 1987, in Cairo, Egypt. The 10-mile (16-kilometer) line has six stops, all underground.

Federal Funding. Congress on April 2 overrode President Ronald Reagan's veto to approve legislation that provides $87.5 billion for highway and mass-transit projects. The Surface Transportation and Uniform Relocation Assistance Act of 1987, which replaces a law that expired in September 1986, earmarks $18.9 billion for mass-transit systems over the next five years.

UMTA Action. Ralph L. Stanley, UMTA's administrator, resigned on May 31, 1987. He was a strong opponent of federal funding for mass-transit projects. Alfred A. DelliBovi, the former deputy administrator, succeeded Stanley in December. Earlier in the year, the Reagan Administration proposed a 56 per cent cut in funding for the Urban Mass Transportation Administration as part of its 1987 fiscal year budget.   David M. Cawthorne

In WORLD BOOK, see Bus; ELECTRIC RAILROAD; SUBWAY; TRANSPORTATION.

TRANSPORTATION companies in the United States showed mixed results in earnings and traffic during 1987. Net income for the trucking industry rose an estimated 3.5 per cent above 1986 levels. Shipping lines continued to suffer from lagging demand, and mass transit systems showed a slight decline in ridership. Railroad freight traffic for the first 10 months of the year was slightly above 1986 levels.

Frank Smith of Transportation Policy Associates, a consulting firm in Washington, D.C., estimated U.S. transportation revenue at $295 billion for 1987, up 5 per cent from 1986. Intercity freight on the United States mainland, measured in ton-miles, was 2.6 trillon.

Dole Departs. Elizabeth Hanford Dole resigned as secretary of transportation on Oct. 1, 1987, to work on the presidential campaign of her husband, Senator Robert J. Dole (R., Kans.). She became secretary in February 1983, and her tenure in that post was the longest in U.S. history.

On Oct. 8, 1987, President Ronald Reagan nominated James H. Burnley IV, deputy transportation secretary, to succeed Dole. He was sworn in on December 3. See BURNLEY, JAMES HORACE, IV.

New Rules. In June, the Department of Transportation (DOT) began establishing national standards that states will use to issue driver's licenses to bus drivers and truckdrivers. On August 21, in response to concern about aviation safety, the DOT proposed a regulation that would require commercial planes with more than 20 passenger seats to install collision-warning equipment.

Legislation. On April 2, Congress overrode President Reagan's veto of a five-year, $87.5-billion bill for highway construction and mass transit projects. The legislation also permitted states to raise speed limits on rural interstate highways from 55 miles per hour (mph), or 89 kilometers per hour (kph), to 65 mph (105 kph).

Drug Testing. The collision of three Conrail locomotives and an Amtrak passenger train on January 4 in Chase, Md., that killed 16 people focused attention on drug use among transportation employees. Tests by two laboratories found traces of marijuana in the systems of the engineer and the brakeman. On October 31, the Senate approved a bill that would require drug and alcohol tests of all transportation employees who have jobs that affect the safety of passengers.

Random drug testing of DOT employees began in 1987, according to a November 4 announcement by the DOT. The department became the first civilian government agency to carry out such a program. David M. Cawthorne

See also AUTOMOBILE; AVIATION; RAILROAD; SHIP AND SHIPPING; TRANSIT; TRUCK AND TRUCKING. In WORLD BOOK, see TRANSPORTATION.

TRINIDAD AND TOBAGO. See LATIN AMERICA.

TRUCK AND TRUCKING. Earnings for the trucking industry in the United States decreased in 1987. Net income for the first six months of the year was down about 25 per cent from 1986 levels, according to the American Trucking Associations (ATA). Revenues climbed about 2.5 per cent, while expenses increased by more than 3.7 per cent.

The ATA reported that rate discounts—along with cost increases—were behind the decline in earnings. During the year, costs for general supplies rose 9 per cent above 1986 levels. Insurance costs increased by about 8 per cent, while labor costs increased 6 per cent.

Railroad Acquisitions. Action in 1987 by the Interstate Commerce Commission (ICC), the U.S. government agency that regulates the trucking and railroad industries, permitted two railroad holding companies to acquire trucking firms. In September, the ICC gave the Union Pacific Corporation, owner of the Union Pacific Rail System, the go-ahead to acquire Overnite Transportation Company, one of the largest U.S. trucking firms, for $1.2 billion.

In May, a federal court reaffirmed an ICC decision to approve Norfolk Southern Corporation's acquisition of North American Van Lines, one of the largest household-goods movers in the United States. Earlier, the court ruled that the ICC had misinterpreted antitrust law and ordered it to reconsider its approval of the acquisition.

Taxes. On June 23, the Supreme Court of the United States ruled that a tax levied by the state of Pennsylvania on out-of-state trucking companies was unconstitutional. The ruling ensured that similar taxes imposed by other states will be revoked because they discriminate against trucking companies that are not based in those states.

Highway Funding. On April 2, Congress overrode President Ronald Reagan's veto to approve a five-year, $87.5-billion funding bill for highway construction and mass transit projects. The bill also permitted states to raise speed limits from 55 miles per hour (mph), or 89 kilometers per hour (kph), to 65 mph (105 kph) on rural interstate highways.

New Laws. During the year, the U.S. government moved to enforce a 1986 law that instructs the Department of Transportation (DOT) to set blood-alcohol standards for drivers of heavy-duty trucks and buses by Oct. 1, 1988. In November 1987, the National Academy of Sciences recommended a zero blood-alcohol standard for all drivers whose vehicles weigh more than 26,000 pounds (11,800 kilograms). On July 1, a federal law went into effect that prohibits truckdrivers—and other drivers—from carrying driver's licenses from more than one state. David M. Cawthorne

See also TRANSPORTATION. In WORLD BOOK, see TRUCK.

TRUDEAU, PIERRE ELLIOTT (1919-   ), who resigned as prime minister of Canada in 1984, broke
a three-year political silence with a scathing attack
on the Meech Lake constitutional accord—an
agreement that sought to bring Quebec into the
1982 constitution. The accord was fashioned by
Canada's Prime Minister Brian Mulroney and the
10 provincial premiers on April 30, 1987. In a
public statement issued in May and in an appearance before a parliamentary committee on August
27, Trudeau claimed that the accord weakened
the powers of the federal government by subject-
ing it to "remote control" by the provinces.

Trudeau denounced Mulroney for making
concessions to the provinces in return for their
recognition of Quebec as a "distinct society." Trudeau argued that the new designation might result
in the Quebec government placing French linguistic and cultural issues ahead of the individual liberties guaranteed for all Canadians in the 1982
constitution. He also warned that under the
Meech Lake accord there was a danger that the
federal government would become merely a tax
collector, unable to promote national social programs. But in spite of Trudeau's impassioned attack, the document was approved by the House of
Commons on October 26.   David M. L. Farr

See also CANADA. In WORLD BOOK, see TRU-
DEAU, PIERRE E.

Zine al-Abidine Ben Ali, Tunisia's new leader,
speaks to parliament on November 7 after deposing
ailing 84-year-old President Habib Bourguiba.

TUNISIA. Habib Bourguiba, who had ruled Tunisia as president since the country won its independence from France in 1956, was deposed on
Nov. 7, 1987. Prime Minister Zine al-Abidine Ben
Ali, a former army general, then appointed himself president of Tunisia. Ben Ali said he acted because of the 84-year-old Bourguiba's mental deterioration.

Extremist Crackdown. Ben Ali, the former interior minister, was the chief architect of Bourguiba's crackdown on Islamic extremists in 1987. In
March, security forces arrested 40 leaders of the
outlawed Islamic Tendency Movement (MTI),
Tunisia's largest extremist group. The 40 leaders,
along with 50 other militants, went on trial in August, charged with the bombing of four hotels that
month in which 13 people were wounded and
with plotting to overthrow the government with
Iranian help. Thirty-seven of the accused were
tried in absentia.

On September 27, the Court for State Security
pronounced death sentences on 7 defendants
found guilty of direct involvement in the bombings, none of whom were MTI leaders, and acquitted 14. The remaining extremists received
sentences ranging from 2 years to life imprisonment. In October, the only two of the condemned
people in custody were hanged. The death sentences of the remaining condemned defendants,

who had been tried in absentia, were commuted
to life imprisonment.

Bourguiba's orders to retry and hang 10 to 15
of the militants contributed to his downfall. Government officials feared that new trials would
plunge the country into religious warfare.

Tightened Control. In 1987, Bourguiba also
clamped down on legal dissent. In January, he dis-
banded the long-established Tunisian General
Union of Labor, a labor federation, and incorporated its membership into the ruling Socialist Des-
tour Party. Also in January, Bourguiba closed
down the newspaper of the opposition Social
Democratic Movement and jailed party leader
Ahmed Mestiri for defaming the government.

The Economy. The phosphate industry, Tunisia's major export earner, laid off 2,800 workers
in April. The move was taken to cope with a 40
per cent drop in world phosphate prices.

The government's austerity program, begun in
1986, started to show some results. Reduced subsidies for food staples, though unpopular, helped
cut the foreign debt by $50 million. A 25 per cent
devaluation in the dinar encouraged tourism and
increased the value of money sent home by Tu-
nisians working abroad.   William Spencer

See also AFRICA (Facts in Brief Table). In the
Special Report section, see UNDERSTANDING ISLAM.
In WORLD BOOK, see TUNISIA.

TURKEY. Triple by-pass heart surgery in February 1987 failed to slow Prime Minister Turgut Ozal as he moved to reinstate full democracy in Turkey. Ozal hoped that holding elections a year early for the Grand National Assembly, Turkey's parliament, would improve Turkey's chances for membership in the European Community (EC or Common Market).

The elections—held on November 29—capped several months of disputes over election procedures. On September 6, a bare majority—50.24 per cent—of Turkish voters agreed to end prematurely a 10-year ban on political activity by 200 former politicians, including former Prime Ministers Süleyman Demirel and Bülent Ecevit. The ban was imposed after a 1980 military coup. Ozal campaigned against lifting the ban, arguing that the former leaders were responsible for the violence and the economic problems of the late 1970's that had led to the coup.

On September 6, even before the results of the referendum were known, Ozal scheduled new elections for November 1. The election was delayed, however, when Turkey's highest court on October 10 struck down as unconstitutional a section of the law under which the elections were to be held. This section permitted nomination of candidates by political party leaders, rather than by primary election, as done previously.

Opposition forces then attempted to postpone the election until spring 1988. On Oct. 17, 1987, however, Ozal mustered enough support in the Assembly for a new law setting November 29 as election day. The law also expanded the number of seats in the Assembly from 400 to 450.

In the election—the first parliamentary elections held since 1980 without military supervision—Ozal's Motherland Party expanded its majority in the Assembly, winning 292 of the 450 seats. The party won only 36 per cent of the popular vote, however, compared with 45 per cent in 1983.

Kurdish Guerrillas escalated their fight for an independent Kurdish state in eastern Turkey in 1987 with raids on villages and army posts. The guerrillas killed some 400 people, most of them civilians. On July 19, the Turkish government lifted martial law in the last four provinces in eastern Turkey where it had been in effect. But after Kurdish guerrillas ignored an amnesty offer in March, the government imposed emergency rule over eight eastern provinces.

The Economy. Despite foreign debts of $9 billion and a 25 per cent inflation rate, Turkey continued to attract foreign investors. The budget, approved in January by the Assembly, set a reduced deficit of $1.2 billion, which would be covered by internal borrowing.   William Spencer

See also MIDDLE EAST (Facts in Brief Table). In WORLD BOOK, see TURKEY.

UGANDA. Peace returned to many areas of Uganda in 1987. The government of President Yoweri Museveni, however, continued to encounter resistance in both the north and the east. Several thousand rebels were killed in skirmishes during the year, but hundreds of others responded to an amnesty offer by the government in June.

The greatest opposition came from the Acholi ethnic group, who remained loyal to deposed President Milton Obote. About 4,000 "holy spirit" soldiers were led by an Acholi priestess, Alice Lakwena. Half of those troops were killed in government attacks on Cwero, Gulu, and Soroti at midyear. In December, Lakwena was arrested and jailed in Kenya for entering the country illegally.

Economy. Uganda's economic recovery in 1987 was hindered by an inflation rate of almost 200 per cent. The average monthly wage was only $8, and farmers received so little for their crops that many moved to the cities. During the year, the government devalued the Uganda shilling by 77.5 per cent to curb inflation and boost exports.

AIDS (acquired immune deficiency syndrome) reached epidemic proportions during 1987. In Kampala, the capital, an estimated 16,000 people were stricken.   J. Gus Liebenow and Beverly B. Liebenow

See also AFRICA (Facts in Brief Table). In WORLD BOOK, see UGANDA.

UNEMPLOYMENT. See ECONOMICS; LABOR.

UNION OF SOVIET SOCIALIST REPUBLICS (U.S.S.R.). Communist Party General Secretary Mikhail S. Gorbachev emerged in 1987 as a resolute and energetic reformist pushing the Soviet Union toward what many political observers saw as a second Russian revolution. The year also marked the 70th anniversary of the first revolution—the upheaval that established Communist rule in Russia.

Gorbachev pursued a reform movement based on two concepts—*perestroika* (economic and social restructuring) and *glasnost* (openness in the flow of information). Both concepts represented a softening of the *Stalinist* tradition. (Stalinism is a type of Communism characterized by ruthless oppression of opposition. It is named after Joseph Stalin, who began his rise to power as dictator of the Soviet Union in 1922 and ruled until his death in 1953.) See Close-Up.

Domestic reform was one of Gorbachev's two major goals. The other was an arms control agreement with the United States. In 1986, he met twice with United States President Ronald Reagan. The two leaders reached tentative agreement on a treaty banning intermediate-range nuclear missiles, followed by a 50 per cent cut in long-range strategic weapons, before talks broke down over a disagreement on U.S. development of a space-based antimissile system.

Mathias Rust, 19, of West Germany, leans against an airplane he flew from
Finland through Soviet defenses and landed in Moscow's Red Square on May 28.

In February 1987, Gorbachev dropped his demand that the United States limit development of the space-based system. In December, Gorbachev traveled to Washington, D.C., and on December 8 the two leaders signed a treaty eliminating medium-range nuclear missiles.

Gorbachev Won an Endorsement of his program of rapid, radical reform of economic planning and management on June 26, 1987, at a meeting of the Communist Party Central Committee. This organization handles the party's work between party congresses—large gatherings that are normally convened every five years.

Also at the Central Committee meeting, Gorbachev placed more of his staunchest supporters in the Politburo, the Communist Party's policy-making body. Three new full members and one *candidate,* or nonvoting, member were Gorbachev's close allies. The appointments increased the number of full Politburo members to 14.

Gorbachev's Reform Program called for major structural changes in the economy by 1990, the end of the current five-year economic 'plan. A drastic law reducing regulation of state-owned business enterprises—the centerpiece of the program—was to take effect on Jan. 1, 1988. This law would put 60 per cent of such enterprises on a self-financing basis. Managers would have more power to make plans and to set wage scales. This

added authority would, in turn, make managers more accountable to higher authorities.

Gorbachev intended to reduce the power of the three giant bureaucracies clogging the bloodstream of Soviet economic life: Gosnab, which controls raw materials; Gosplan, the committee in charge of planning, from the highest levels of management to the factory floor; and Goskomtsen, which sets prices.

Resistance to Reform. Despite Gorbachev's triumph at the Central Committee meeting, there was still a great deal of doubt that he could overcome two strains of resistance to reform—both legacies of Stalinism. One strain was a conservative adherence to traditional policies among political diehards. The other was apathy among ordinary Soviet people unused to democratic processes.

But glasnost made progress. Radio and television broadcasters in the Soviet Union became increasingly frank in their comments on current problems. Cinemas and theaters showed old, long-forbidden motion pictures and plays about the past.

Gorbachev Condemned Stalin on Nov. 2, 1987, in a speech marking the celebration of the 1917 revolution. Gorbachev said that Stalin had committed "enormous and unforgivable crimes."

Western historians have condemned Stalin harshly for two campaigns. The *forced collectiviza-*

tion of agriculture from 1929 to the early 1930's involved the combining of privately owned plots into large collective farms controlled by the government. To crush opposition to collectivization, Stalin sent several million peasant families to prison labor camps.

During Stalin's *Great Purge* of the mid-1930's, secret police arrested an estimated several million people who posed real or supposed threats to Stalin's power, including thousands of Communist Party members. After a series of major purge trials from 1936 to 1938, the government executed many former associates of Lenin. They included Nicholas (or Nikolai) Bukharin, who had tried to slow the pace of collectivization.

Gorbachev expressed sympathy with Bukharin's ideas. He did not, however, acknowledge the millions believed to have died as a result of the Great Purge.

Khrushchev Praised. Gorbachev's November 1987 speech also praised Nikita S. Khrushchev, Soviet leader from 1953 until his removal in 1964, for exposing Stalin's excesses, pushing for economic reform, and trying to improve relations with the United States. Gorbachev's speech was a major step toward restoring official respect to Khrushchev, long ignored in Soviet ruling circles.

Yeltsin Fired. The local Communist Party organization in Moscow on Nov. 11, 1987, removed Boris N. Yeltsin as its chief. On October 21, Yeltsin had criticized the national leadership at a meeting of the Communist Party Central Committee. According to the Soviet press agency Tass, Yeltsin "went so far as to say that restructuring was giving virtually nothing to the people."

Gorbachev had installed Yeltsin in the Moscow post in December 1985. Two months later, Yeltsin had become a candidate member of the Politburo. Political observers had considered him to be a major supporter of perestroika and glasnost. After his ousting from the Moscow post, Yeltsin was appointed first deputy chairman of the newly organized State Committee for Construction.

Nationalism. Outbreaks of national feeling among some of the Soviet Union's non-Russian peoples posed problems for the Kremlin—and for glasnost in 1987. In July, several hundred Tartars gathered in Moscow's Red Square to demand the creation of a new *autonomous* (self-governing) Tartar republic in their homeland—the Crimea, a peninsula on the Black Sea. The Crimea had been an autonomous republic until 1945. Moscow abolished the republic on the grounds that Crimean Tartars had collaborated with German occupation troops during World War II. The Soviets resettled the Crimean Tartar population of about 250,000 in Asia and repopulated the Crimea with ethnic Russians and Ukrainians. The Crimea became part of the Ukrainian S.S.R. in 1954.

In the capitals of the three Baltic republics of Estonia, Latvia, and Lithuania, there were demonstrations on Aug. 23, 1987, the 48th anniversary of a treaty that cost these lands their independence. In 1939, the Soviet Union and Nazi Germany signed a pact that paved the way for the Soviets to annex the three states in 1940.

On Oct. 17 and 18, 1987, in Yerevan, the capital of the Armenian S.S.R., several thousand people protested openly with demands for nuclear-ecology safeguards inspired by the 1986 Chernobyl disaster. They also demanded respect for the rights of ethnic Armenians living in the neighboring Azerbaijan S.S.R.

Talks with Allies. During an April visit to Czechoslovakia, Gorbachev said that Soviet reforms were not an arbitrary model for the other nations of the Council for Mutual Economic Assistance (COMECON), the Soviet trading bloc. But he made clear that the COMECON nations were expected to study Soviet practice.

Gorbachev shrewdly adjusted his remarks to the conditions in the various COMECON nations. In a low-key visit in late May to East Germany—economically the most prosperous of these nations—he showed no desire to interfere with success. Earlier the same month in Romania, however, he gave COMECON's most economically inefficient—and most antiglasnost—regime a prod toward reform. Visits to Moscow by Poland's leader Wojciech Jaruzelski in April, and Hungary's new Prime Minister Károly Grósz in June, revealed Gorbachev's attraction to more reformist regimes.

Cease-Fire Urged. The Soviets made a steady effort to improve relations with the Persian Gulf states. While maintaining a close alliance with Iraq, the Soviets pressed both Iraq and Iran to accept a United Nations (UN) plan for a cease-fire in their seven-year war. Signs of new Soviet thinking about the UN itself were capped by an announcement on October 15 that Russia would pay its debt of $197 million to the UN for peacekeeping operations of which it had disapproved.

The Soviet Economy improved in many segments but not in the most crucial—agriculture. After an unusually severe winter followed by spring floods, the 1987 grain harvest seemed likely to be at least 30 million metric tons (33 million short tons) below the bumper 1986 crop.

Unemployment. One of Gorbachev's reforms called for eliminating the payment of government subsidies to unprofitable business enterprises and for the closing of businesses that lose money consistently. Some 5,000 enterprises were in line for an immediate shutdown.

Gorbachev acknowledged that millions of workers would lose their jobs because of this reform, and he called for the creation of job retraining programs for these workers.

The Promise of Gorbachev's Glasnost

When Mikhail S. Gorbachev became leader of the Soviet Union in March 1985, he told the Soviet people he planned to revitalize the country and bring new life to the Soviet economy. A little more than two years later, in June 1987, the Communist Party Central Committee set its seal of approval on the most far-reaching reform program the Soviet Union has seen in more than 60 years.

The program—designed by Gorbachev—encourages state-owned enterprises to become more competitive and independent; reduces the Soviet government's control over the distribution and prices of goods; and permits limited private enterprise. But neither the Soviet people nor the rest of the world expected that as part of this economic reform, Gorbachev would relax the government's censorship of the media and encourage *glasnost* (openness) in Soviet society.

Gorbachev, however, made glasnost the slogan for his reform. It has become a part of the vocabulary of the Soviet people as well as of international politics. The Soviet leader's evident sincerity about it has confounded skeptics. Moreover, the new atmosphere of openness has given Moscow more credibility with the West, making it a more comfortable partner in world affairs.

Glasnost does not, though, mean unlimited liberty of expression. Instead, Gorbachev is seen as skillfully using it as a weapon against opponents of reform. The media now are allowed considerable freedom to expose the backwardness of the Soviet economy and the problems deeply rooted within Soviet society, such as official misuse of power and privilege, corruption, and alcohol and drug abuse. Glasnost has begun to tear the veil that concealed incompetence and a lack of initiative.

Under this new openness, the Soviet government has permitted more examination of the horrendous acts of Joseph Stalin, who began his rise to power as dictator of the Soviet Union in 1922 and ruled until his death in 1953. During those years, millions of people who opposed his policies were killed or imprisoned. The media reflected only Stalinist thought, and noncon-

formist literature was ruthlessly suppressed by Soviet authorities.

With Stalin's death, the worst repression ended. Censorship and government control over the media and arts, however, continued—in varying degrees of harshness—under Stalin's successors.

But with glasnost, the whole situation appears to be changing. Books by Soviet writers that were once banned are now being published. It was announced in early 1987 that *Children of the Arbat*, Anatoli Rybakov's novel about the evils of Stalin's regime, would be published by the end of the year. And *Dr. Zhivago*, the famous novel by Nobel Prize-winning author Boris Pasternak about a Russian physician who experiences the turmoil of the Bolshevik Revolution, was scheduled to appear in print in 1988, 31 years after it was published in the West.

Contact between the Soviet Union and the West is increasing under glasnost. Doors are opening for the exchange of technological and marketing know-how and of motion pictures and performers. In 1987, Soviet theaters began showing more Western motion pictures, by such directors as Italy's Federico Fellini, Mexico's Luis Buñuel, and Sweden's Ingmar Bergman. The authorities have also adopted a more lenient attitude toward rock music, permitting Western rock musicians such as Billy Joel, as well as Soviet rock groups, to perform before large audiences. And on television, Soviet viewers are getting more—and relatively accurate—insights into Western life.

Some people see these changes as a turning point in the Soviet system. Other people, including some Soviet officials and leaders of some

Face to face with Soviet citizens, leader Mikhail Gorbachev, in the tweed overcoat, discusses his program of *glasnost* (openness).

Communist countries, see glasnost and Gorbachev's economic reforms endangering the position of the Communist Party. They said that the new openness encourages dissent and that the economic reforms may "open a door" to capitalism.

But glasnost—and *perestroika*—a Russian word meaning *rebuilding* or *restructuring*—do not signal the dismantling of the Soviet system or a move toward capitalism. On the contrary, Gorbachev's economic program is a practical attempt to use capitalism's superiority in marketing and management to boost the Soviet Union economy, which Gorbachev says is in a near-crisis state. He warned his more impetuous glasnost supporters not to go overboard, however. The Soviet leader is aware that radical changes that happen too quickly or go too far—such as the economic reforms in Czechoslovakia in the 1960's, and the Solidarity labor movement in Poland in the early 1980's—can result in problems.

Gorbachev's reforms may bring the Soviet Union closer to Western ideas. But however revolutionary the results, glasnost should be seen as a development firmly rooted in Soviet life. As Gorbachev stressed from the start, "We are going about our reforms in accordance with our own socialist choice . . ." and ". . . on the basis of our notions about social values [and the] Soviet way of life."

Some Soviet experts compare glasnost and perestroika with the New Deal, an economic program implemented by United States President Franklin D. Roosevelt in the 1930's to pull the United States out of the Great Depression. The New Deal set in motion some radical political and economic changes, but it did not change the basic political and social structure of the United States.

For example, as part of a movement to get more people involved in the political process, Soviet authorities proposed to allow two candidates to run for party as well as political offices in 1988. But the Soviet Union is not installing a two-party political system. The Communist Party will continue to be the country's only party. Glasnost may allow even more latitude and diversity in ideas, but it will not allow the advocacy of ideas that are contrary to the interests of a socialist state.

At this point Gorbachev has a long battle ahead of him. Many Westerners and Soviets wonder how far he will take glasnost. But even more important, will the Soviet people, after years of uninspired and unchallenging rule, have the drive to respond to Gorbachev's vision? This may well be glasnost's—and Gorbachev's—greatest challenge.   Eric Bourne

A Communist Party newspaper in Azerbaijan reported in April that some 250,000 people were already "temporarily without work," and other regions reported layoffs. These were the first admissions in the Soviet Union that one of the Communist Party's prime boasts—guaranteed full employment—was in jeopardy.

Chernobyl. Former top officials at the Chernobyl nuclear power station in the town of Pripyat, near Kiev, went on trial on July 7 for acts that resulted in the world's worst nuclear accident in 1986. Plant director Victor Bryukhanov and two engineers were sentenced to 10 years in a labor camp. Three other officials drew shorter sentences.

Young Pilot Penetrates Defenses. Mathias Rust, a 19-year-old West German amateur pilot, flew a single-engine plane unimpeded from Finland across Soviet airspace and landed in Moscow's Red Square on May 28. The flight brought a swift reaction from the Kremlin. Gorbachev fired Defense Minister Sergei L. Sokolov and the chief of the Soviet air forces. Gorbachev seized the chance to appoint a reform-minded ally, General Dimitri T. Yazov, to the defense ministry post. On September 4, Rust was sentenced to four years in a labor camp for the stunt.   Eric Bourne

See also EUROPE (Facts in Brief Table). In WORLD BOOK, see RUSSIA or UNION OF SOVIET SOCIALIST REPUBLICS.

UNITED NATIONS (UN) peacekeeping efforts in 1987 were highlighted by attempts to end the war between Iran and Iraq. On July 20, the Security Council unanimously adopted a resolution demanding that both sides cease fire, withdraw their forces to internationally recognized boundaries, free prisoners of war, and—with the help of United Nations Secretary-General Javier Pérez de Cuéllar—seek to settle their differences. (The permanent members of the Security Council are China, France, Great Britain, the Soviet Union, and the United States. The nonpermanent members during 1987 were Argentina, Bulgaria, Congo, Ghana, Italy, Japan, the United Arab Emirates, Venezuela, West Germany, and Zambia.)

The document also states that the Security Council adopted the resolution under Articles 39 and 40 of the UN Charter. Those articles authorize the Security Council to call for an international boycott or even the use of armed force against any country threatening or breaking international peace.

Reactions to the Resolution. Iraqi UN Ambassador Ismat T. Kittani, present as an invited nonmember of the Council, thanked its members for adopting the resolution. Iran boycotted the meeting, however; and at a news conference the next day, its UN ambassador, Said Rajaie-Khorassani, declared that the United States had pushed

Singer Harry Belafonte, good-will ambassador for the United Nations Children's Fund (UNICEF), watches dancers perform in Senegal in March.

through the resolution to legitimize "illegal policies and practices in the Persian Gulf." But he did not flatly reject the resolution.

On August 11, Iran's Foreign Minister Ali Akbar Velayati sent the secretary-general a note from his government charging that the United States was putting pressure on the Security Council to adopt a new resolution against Iran. The note, transmitted through the Iranian UN mission, said that the UN should declare Iraq the aggressor in the war, that Iraq should pay Iran for losses suffered in the fighting, and that the UN should conduct a thorough study of the conflict and formulate a final solution.

Secretary-General Tries for Peace. Between September 11 and 15, Pérez de Cuéllar visited the Persian Gulf area, where he spent four days sounding out Iran and Iraq on possibilities for ending the war as demanded by the July resolution. At a September 16 news conference at UN Headquarters in New York City, Pérez de Cuéllar said he had given Iran and Iraq a plan for carrying out the cease-fire resolution.

Iran's Deputy Foreign Minister Mohammad Larijani on December 2 discussed the resolution with Pérez de Cuéllar at UN Headquarters. Iraq's Foreign Minister Tariq Mikhayl Aziz followed suit on December 3. The two meetings failed to produce a settlement.

Afghanistan. On September 29, Pérez de Cuéllar reported to the General Assembly that negotiations toward a settlement of the conflict in Afghanistan had reached an advanced stage. The Soviet Union had invaded Afghanistan in 1979 to halt a rebellion against that nation's Communist government. The rebellion was still going on as 1987 drew to a close. The United Nations had been involved in negotiations as a result of resolutions passed by the General Assembly in previous years.

Pérez de Cuéllar said that his personal representative for the negotiations, Diego Cordovez of Ecuador, in late 1986 had sounded out leaders in Afghanistan, Pakistan, and Iran about the possibility of talks. Cordovez persuaded the Afghan and Pakistani foreign ministers to meet in Geneva, Switzerland, in February and March 1987 and in Paris in September. Pérez de Cuéllar said the talks decreased the political friction between the two nations. Pakistan has served as a sanctuary for Afghan rebels.

The General Assembly began its 42nd annual session on September 15. East Germany's Deputy Foreign Minister Peter Florin was elected president for the session.

United States President Ronald Reagan addressed the General Assembly as it began its annual policy debate on September 21. Reagan declared that Iran should accept the UN cease-fire resolution; that the Soviet Union should withdraw from Afghanistan; and that Nicaragua should enjoy "real, free, pluralistic, constitutional democracy," which he said Nicaragua's government was denying the people. Reagan also said he was pleased that he and Soviet Foreign Minister Eduard A. Shevardnadze had discussed cuts in nuclear arms during the previous week. According to Reagan, the United States and the Soviets were agreed in principle on a treaty that would eliminate a whole class of nuclear weapons. The treaty was signed on December 8. See ARMED FORCES.

Shevardnadze Told the Assembly on September 23 that this arms agreement meant that "for the first time in history, the idea of nuclear disarmament is close to the beginning of fulfillment." Answering Reagan's remarks on Nicaragua, however, he said it was heartless to recruit and arm mercenaries, call them "freedom fighters," and pay them to kill. Shevardnadze also said the situation in the Persian Gulf was dangerous and might get out of control.

Kaye Honored. The UN on October 21 conducted a program in memory of American comedian and actor Danny Kaye, a long-time fundraiser for the UN Children's Fund (UNICEF). Kaye died in March at age 74. Pérez de Cuéllar told the gathering that Kaye had drawn attention to the plight of children everywhere.

M'Bow Bows Out. The executive board of the UN Educational, Scientific and Cultural Organization (UNESCO) on October 18 elected a new director general, Federico Mayor Zaragoza, a Spanish biochemist. Mayor defeated the current director general, Amadou-Mahtar M'Bow of Senegal, who dropped out of the race before the final ballot. M'Bow had held the post since 1974.

The new director general said that one of his goals was to persuade the United States and Great Britain to rejoin UNESCO. The two countries had left the organization to protest against what they termed inefficient management, wasteful spending, and a bias against the West.

At a general convention of UNESCO on Nov. 7, 1987, the organization confirmed the election of Mayor. Shortly after the confirmation, M'Bow moved to increase UNESCO's staff and to grant permanent contracts to senior staff members. Mayor's first act after being sworn in on November 16 was to freeze hiring and promotions.

Food Agency Head Reelected. The Food and Agriculture Organization (FAO) of the UN on November 9 reelected Edouard Saouma of Lebanon to a third six-year term as director general. Saouma defeated Moise Mensah of Benin, 94 votes to 59. The United States, Great Britain, Canada, and other industrialized nations opposed Saouma because of FAO practices they considered wasteful. France and West Germany backed him.

Superpowers Pledge to Pay. The Soviet Union on October 15 announced that it would pay all the money it owed the UN. The Soviet debt, dating back to 1973, amounted to about $245 million, of which $197 million was for peacekeeping operations of which the Soviet Union had disapproved.

On Oct. 15, 1987, the UN was owed $997 million by its members. The United States owed the largest amount, $414.2 million.

Pérez de Cuéllar told the United States that about 6,500 UN staffers might not get paid in December unless the United States paid $87 million of its 1987 UN general budget assessment. The United States had paid only $10 million of its $212-million assessment for the year. On November 23, the United States agreed to pay at least $90 million in December.

War Crimes Files Opened. On November 6, the UN opened its files on 40,000 individuals suspected of committing war crimes during World War II (1939-1945). The files had been available to governments carrying out investigations or prosecutions, but a government could obtain a file only by submitting the name of the suspected individual whose file it wanted. Under the new rules, nongovernment researchers, such as historians and journalists accredited by member nations, could look through the files.   William M. Oatis

In WORLD BOOK, see UNITED NATIONS.

UNITED STATES, GOVERNMENT OF THE. The first trillion-dollar budget in the history of the United States was proposed by President Ronald Reagan on Jan. 5, 1987. The record budget put Reagan on a collision course with Democrats in Congress, who for the first time in his presidency controlled both the Senate and the House of Representatives.

The $1,024.3-billion spending plan rejected new taxes, called for increased outlays for defense and foreign aid, and proposed deep cuts in a broad range of domestic programs, ranging from school-lunch programs to medical care for the aged. Democrats were virtually united in their opposition to the Reagan budget, and many House Republicans, too, were unwilling to vote for the domestic-program cuts proposed by the President.

The budget clash resulted in a stalemate between the White House and Congress that seemed beyond compromise until October 19, the day the U.S. stock market crashed. In the wake of the crash, the President came under pressure from Republicans who feared their party might be blamed for the financial crisis, and from foreign governments and financial institutions that had been critical of the Reagan Administration's record deficit spending. Giving ground at last, the President agreed to a bipartisan summit meeting with members of Congress to solve the budget dilemma. In addition, he agreed to consider selected tax increases, which he earlier had vowed would take effect only "over my dead body."

Reducing the Deficit. The federal budget deficit totaled $148 billion in the fiscal year that ended on Sept. 30, 1987, down from a record $220.7-billion a year earlier—a reduction that was due largely to a one-time revenue windfall stemming from the Tax Reform Act of 1986. A much higher deficit seemed in store for fiscal 1988.

After a month of difficult negotiations, Reagan and a bipartisan panel of congressional leaders announced on November 20 that they had reached agreement on the outlines of a plan to reduce the federal deficit by $76 billion over two years. "We are sending the right message at the right time," said Reagan. Of the two-year total, increased taxes would account for $23 billion. The Congressional Budget Office estimated that the plan would result in a fiscal 1988 deficit of $149 billion. The Administration's more optimistic economic assumptions forecast a $130-billion shortfall.

Few members of Congress were satisfied with the compromise. Many critics said the budget cuts and tax increases were too small, considering the size of the deficit. Still, on December 22, Congress passed $603.9 billion in spending authority to fund the federal government through Sept. 30, 1988. A companion bill raised taxes by $9 billion and reduced the deficit by about $33.2 billion. Reagan signed both bills on December 22.

The alternative to adopting the compromise was to leave budget-cutting to the 1985 Gramm-Rudman deficit reduction law. This legislation—named for two of its sponsors, Senators Phil Gramm (R., Tex.) and Warren B. Rudman (R., N.H.)—had been stripped of its provisions for automatic across-the-board spending cuts by a 1986 decision by the Supreme Court of the United States. But Congress voted in September 1987 to provide a new mechanism for automatic cuts if Congress and the President are unable to agree on other means of reaching annual deficit targets. The legislation also eased the spending-reduction goals specified in the 1985 law and delayed the requirement for a balanced budget by two years, to 1993.

While Congress debated the deficit-reduction compromise, it knew failure to agree on the budget would mean that defense and domestic spending would be hit with automatic cuts of $11.5 billion each, for a total of $23 billion. By contrast, the compromise pared only $5 billion from defense and $6.6 billion from domestic programs.

Cabinet. There were wholesale changes in Reagan's Cabinet in 1987. With the resignation on November 5 of Secretary of Defense Caspar W. Weinberger, the only remaining member of the President's original Cabinet was Samuel R. Pierce,

Jr., secretary of housing and urban development. Frank C. Carlucci III, Reagan's national security adviser, was confirmed as Weinberger's successor. Carlucci's deputy, Army Lieutenant General Colin L. Powell, became national security chief.

Secretary of Commerce Malcolm Baldrige was fatally injured on July 25 when a horse he was riding near Walnut Creek, Calif., fell on him while he practiced for a rodeo. He was succeeded by C. William Verity, Jr., former chairman of Armco, Incorporated, a steel company.

Secretary of Transportation Elizabeth Hanford Dole resigned on October 1 to work in the presidential campaign of her husband, Senator Robert J. Dole (R., Kans.). She was succeeded by Deputy Secretary James H. Burnley IV. Secretary of Labor William E. Brock III resigned on November 1, also to join the Dole campaign. As Brock's successor, Reagan nominated Ann Dore McLaughlin, a public relations executive and former deputy secretary of the interior, who took office as labor secretary on December 17.

William J. Casey, hospitalized with a brain tumor, resigned on January 29 as director of the Central Intelligence Agency (CIA). He died on May 6. Deputy Director Robert M. Gates was nominated to succeed Casey. Gates, however, withdrew his name when it became likely that the Senate would delay action on his nomination pending the completion of its inquiry into the Iran-contra affair, the arms-sale scandal that rocked the White House in 1986 and 1987. William H. Webster, director of the Federal Bureau of Investigation (FBI), became CIA chief in May. His replacement as FBI director was former U.S. District Judge William S. Sessions of San Antonio.

The Supreme Court moved onto center stage with the retirement on June 26 of Justice Lewis F. Powell, Jr., 79, a conservative who cast the pivotal vote in a series of 5 to 4 decisions that thwarted Reagan Administration policies involving abortion, job hiring practices, and separation of church and state. Nominated to succeed him was Judge Robert H. Bork of the U.S. Court of Appeals for the District of Columbia, a former law professor at Yale University in New Haven, Conn.

The Senate Judiciary Committee held televised hearings on the nomination, which was strongly opposed by civil rights activists, organized labor, and some women's groups. The hearings focused on Bork's extensive writings, including articles taking issue with a number of major Supreme Court decisions involving civil rights and privacy. On October 23, the Senate rejected the nomination 58 to 42—the biggest losing margin for any Supreme Court nominee in history.

Reagan's second choice was Douglas H. Ginsburg, 41, a conservative jurist who had served on the same court as Bork for less than a year. But

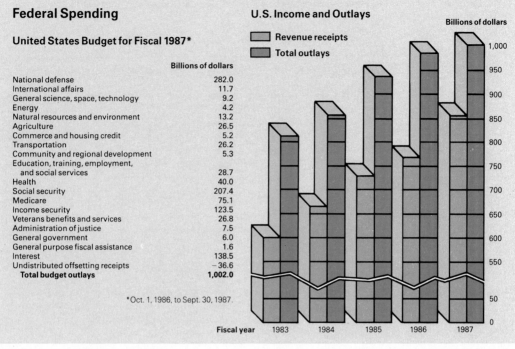

Federal Spending

United States Budget for Fiscal 1987*

	Billions of dollars
National defense	282.0
International affairs	11.7
General science, space, technology	9.2
Energy	4.2
Natural resources and environment	13.2
Agriculture	26.5
Commerce and housing credit	5.2
Transportation	26.2
Community and regional development	5.3
Education, training, employment, and social services	28.7
Health	40.0
Social security	207.4
Medicare	75.1
Income security	123.5
Veterans benefits and services	26.8
Administration of justice	7.5
General government	6.0
General purpose fiscal assistance	1.6
Interest	138.5
Undistributed offsetting receipts	−36.6
Total budget outlays	**1,002.0**

*Oct. 1, 1986, to Sept. 30, 1987.

U.S. Income and Outlays

Billions of dollars

- Revenue receipts
- Total outlays

Fiscal year: 1983, 1984, 1985, 1986, 1987

Source: U.S. Department of the Treasury.

the nomination was withdrawn on November 7 after Ginsburg admitted smoking marijuana several times while he was a Harvard Law School professor. On November 11, Reagan announced his third nominee, Anthony M. Kennedy, a federal appeals court judge from California described as a moderate conservative. Senate hearings on Kennedy's nomination began on December 14. His confirmation, which seemed certain, was still pending at year-end.

Spies. United States government problems with spies continued in 1987. The biggest spy scare involved charges that Marine guards at the U.S. Embassy in Moscow had given Soviet agents free access to the building. Although the Marine Corps was unable to confirm the most serious allegations, one guard—Sergeant Clayton J. Lonetree—was charged with trading government secrets for sex with a Soviet woman. Lonetree was convicted by court-martial in August and given a 30-year prison sentence. He appealed the conviction and sentence.

Cuban Immigrants. On November 20, the State Department announced the revival of a lapsed 1984 immigration agreement with Cuba. Under the terms of the pact, the United States agreed to accept more than 20,000 Cuban immigrants each year. Cuba, in exchange, was to allow the return of about 2,600 convicts and mental patients, many

detained in federal institutions since leaving Cuba in a refugee boat lift in 1980.

Within 24 hours, more than 1,000 Cuban inmates, fearing deportation, seized control of a federal detention center at Oakdale, La., taking hostages and burning much of the prison. Rioting by Cubans then spread to a federal penitentiary in Atlanta, Ga., where more hostages were taken and buildings set afire.

On November 29, the Cubans at the Oakdale facility released their hostages and signed an agreement with federal negotiators. The agreement promised that the government would not conduct mass deportations but would review the detainees on a case-by-case basis. On December 4, the Cubans at the Atlanta prison signed a similar agreement.   Frank Cormier and Margot Cormier

See also CONGRESS OF THE UNITED STATES; IRAN-CONTRA AFFAIR; PRESIDENT OF THE UNITED STATES; SUPREME COURT OF THE UNITED STATES. In WORLD BOOK, see UNITED STATES, GOVERNMENT OF THE.

UNITED STATES CONSTITUTION. See CONSTITUTION OF THE UNITED STATES; PHILADELPHIA (Close-Up).

URUGUAY. See LATIN AMERICA.

UTAH. See STATE GOVERNMENT.

VANUATU. See PACIFIC ISLANDS.

VENEZUELA. See LATIN AMERICA.

Major Agencies and Bureaus of the U.S. Government*

Executive Office of the President

President, Ronald Reagan
  Vice President, George H. W. Bush
  White House Chief of Staff, Howard H. Baker, Jr.
  Presidential Press Secretary, James S. Brady
  Assistant to the President for National Security Affairs—Colin L. Powell
  Council of Economic Advisers—Beryl W. Sprinkel, Chairman
  Office of Management and Budget—James C. Miller III, Director
  Office of Science and Technology Policy—William R. Graham, Jr., Director
  U.S. Trade Representative, Clayton K. Yeutter

Department of Agriculture

Secretary of Agriculture, Richard E. Lyng
  Agricultural Cooperative Service—Randall E. Torgerson, Administrator
  Agricultural Marketing Service—J. Patrick Boyle, Administrator
  Agricultural Research Service—Terry B. Kinney, Jr., Administrator
  Agricultural Stabilization and Conservation Service—Milton J. Hertz, Administrator
  Animal and Plant Health Inspection Service—Donald Houston, Administrator
  Economic Research Service—John E. Lee, Jr., Administrator
  Extension Service—Myron Johnsrud, Administrator
  Farmers Home Administration—Vance L. Clark, Administrator
  Federal Crop Insurance Corporation—E. Ray Fosse, Manager
  Food and Nutrition Service—S. Anna Kondratas, Administrator
  Forest Service—F. Dale Robertson, Chief
  Soil Conservation Service—Wilson Scaling, Chief

Department of Commerce

Secretary of Commerce, C. William Verity, Jr.
  Bureau of Economic Analysis—Allan H. Young, Director
  Bureau of the Census—John G. Keane, Director
  Economic Development Administration—Orson G. Swindle III, Assistant Secretary
  International Trade Administration—Bruce Smart, Undersecretary
  Minority Business Development Agency—James H. Richardson Gonzales, Director
  National Bureau of Standards—Ernest Ambler, Director
  National Oceanic and Atmospheric Administration—J. Curtis Mack II, Acting Administrator and Undersecretary
  Patent and Trademark Office—Donald J. Quigg, Commissioner

Department of Defense

Secretary of Defense, Frank C. Carlucci III
  Secretary of the Air Force—Edward C. Aldridge, Jr.
  Secretary of the Army—John O. Marsh, Jr.
  Secretary of the Navy—James H. Webb, Jr.
  Joint Chiefs of Staff—
    Admiral William J. Crowe, Jr., Chairman
    General Larry D. Welch, Chief of Staff, Air Force
    General Carl E. Vuono, Chief of Staff, Army
    Admiral Carlisle A. H. Trost, Chief of Naval Operations
    General Alfred M. Gray, Jr., Commandant, Marine Corps

Department of Education

Secretary of Education, William J. Bennett
  Office of Bilingual Education and Minority Languages Affairs—Alicia Coro, Director

Department of Energy

Secretary of Energy, John S. Herrington
  Economic Regulatory Administration—Chandler L. van Orman†, Administrator
  Federal Energy Regulatory Commission—Martha O. Hesse, Chairman
  Office of Energy Research—Robert O. Hunter, Jr.†, Director

Department of Health and Human Services

Secretary of Health and Human Services, Otis R. Bowen
  Family Support Administration—Wayne A. Stanton, Administrator
  Health Care Financing Administration—William L. Roper, Administrator
  Office of Human Development Services—Sydney Olson, Deputy Assistant Secretary

Public Health Service—Robert E. Windom, Assistant Secretary
  Alcohol, Drug Abuse, and Mental Health Administration—Donald Ian Macdonald, Administrator
  Centers for Disease Control—James O. Mason, Director
  Food and Drug Administration—Frank E. Young, Commissioner
  National Institutes of Health—James B. Wyngaarden, Director
  Surgeon General of the United States, C. Everett Koop
Social Security Administration—Dorcas R. Hardy, Commissioner

Department of Housing and Urban Development

Secretary of Housing and Urban Development, Samuel R. Pierce, Jr.
  Federal Housing Commissioner—Thomas T. Demery
  Government National Mortgage Association—vacant

Department of the Interior

Secretary of the Interior, Donald P. Hodel
  Bureau of Indian Affairs—Ross O. Swimmer, Assistant Secretary
  Bureau of Land Management—Robert F. Burford, Director
  Bureau of Mines—T. S. Ary †, Director
  Bureau of Reclamation—C. Dale Duvall, Commissioner
  National Park Service—William Penn Mott, Jr., Director
  U.S. Fish and Wildlife Service—Frank H. Dunkle, Director
  U.S. Geological Survey—Dallas L. Peck, Director

Department of Justice

Attorney General, Edwin Meese III
  Bureau of Prisons—J. Michael Quinlan, Director
  Drug Enforcement Administration—John C. Lawn, Administrator
  Federal Bureau of Investigation—William S. Sessions, Director
  Immigration and Naturalization Service—Alan C. Nelson, Commissioner
  Solicitor General—Charles Fried
  U.S. Marshals Service—Stanley E. Morris, Director
  U.S. Parole Commission—Benjamin F. Baer, Chairman

Department of Labor

Secretary of Labor, Ann Dore McLaughlin
  Bureau of Labor Statistics—Janet L. Norwood, Commissioner
  Employment and Training Administration—Roger D. Semerad, Administrator
  Employment Standards Administration—Fred W. Alvarez, Assistant Secretary
  Occupational Safety and Health Administration—John A. Pendergrass, Administrator

Department of State

Secretary of State, George P. Shultz
  U.S. Representative to the United Nations, Vernon A. Walters

Department of Transportation

Secretary of Transportation, James H. Burnley IV
  Federal Aviation Administration—T. Allan McArtor, Administrator
  Federal Highway Administration—Ray A. Barnhart, Administrator
  Federal Railroad Administration—John H. Riley, Administrator
  Maritime Administration—John A. Gaughan, Administrator
  National Highway Traffic Safety Administration—Diane K. Steed, Administrator
  Saint Lawrence Seaway Development Corporation—James L. Emery, Administrator
  U.S. Coast Guard—Admiral Paul A. Yost, Jr., Commandant

Department of the Treasury

Secretary of the Treasury, James A. Baker III
  Bureau of Alcohol, Tobacco and Firearms—Stephen E. Higgins, Director
  Bureau of Engraving and Printing—Robert J. Leuver, Director
  Bureau of the Public Debt—William M. Gregg, Commissioner
  Internal Revenue Service—Lawrence B. Gibbs, Commissioner
  Office of the Comptroller of the Currency—Robert L. Clarke, Comptroller
  Treasurer of the United States—Katherine D. Ortega
  U.S. Customs Service—William von Raab, Commissioner
  U.S. Mint—Donna Pope, Director
  U.S. Savings Bond Division—Katherine D. Ortega, National Director
  U.S. Secret Service—John R. Simpson, Director

*As of Jan. 1, 1988.

Supreme Court of the United States

Chief Justice of the United States, William H. Rehnquist
Associate Justices
William J. Brennan, Jr. John Paul Stevens
Byron R. White Sandra Day O'Connor
Thurgood Marshall Antonin Scalia
Harry A. Blackmun Anthony M. Kennedy†

Congressional Officials

President of the Senate pro tempore—John C. Stennis
Senate Majority Leader—Robert C. Byrd
Senate Minority Leader—Robert J. Dole
Speaker of the House—James C. Wright, Jr.
House Minority Leader—Robert H. Michel
Congressional Budget Office—Edward M. Gramlich, Acting Director
General Accounting Office—Charles A. Bowsher, Comptroller General of the United States
Library of Congress—James H. Billington, Librarian of Congress
Office of Technology Assessment—John H. Gibbons, Director

Independent Agencies

ACTION—Donna M. Alvarado, Director
Agency for International Development—Alan Woods, Administrator
Central Intelligence Agency—William H. Webster, Director
Commission on Civil Rights—Clarence M. Pendleton, Jr., Chairman
Commission of Fine Arts—J. Carter Brown, Chairman
Commodity Futures Trading Commission—Wendy Lee Gramm†, Chairman
Consumer Product Safety Commission—Terrence M. Scanlon, Chairman
Environmental Protection Agency—Lee M. Thomas, Administrator
Equal Employment Opportunity Commission—Clarence Thomas, Chairman
Farm Credit Administration—Frank W. Naylor, Jr., Chairman
Federal Communications Commission—Dennis R. Patrick, Chairman
Federal Deposit Insurance Corporation—L. William Seidman, Chairman
Federal Election Commission—Thomas J. Josefiak, Chairman
Federal Emergency Management Agency—Julius W. Becton, Jr., Director
Federal Home Loan Bank Board—M. Danny Wall, Chairman
Federal Mediation and Conciliation Service—Kay McMurray, Director
Federal Reserve System Board of Governors—Alan Greenspan, Chairman
Federal Trade Commission—Daniel Oliver, Chairman
General Services Administration—Terence C. Golden, Administrator
Interstate Commerce Commission—Heather J. Gradison, Chairman
National Aeronautics and Space Administration—James C. Fletcher, Administrator
National Endowment for the Arts—Francis S. M. Hodsoll, Chairman
National Endowment for the Humanities—Lynne V. Cheney, Chairman
National Labor Relations Board—Donald L. Dotson, Chairman
National Railroad Passenger Corporation (Amtrak)—W. Graham Claytor, Jr., Chairman
National Science Foundation—Erich Bloch, Director
National Transportation Safety Board—James E. Burnett, Jr., Chairman
Nuclear Regulatory Commission—Lando W. Zech, Jr., Chairman
Office of Personnel Management—Constance J. Horner, Director
Peace Corps—Loret Miller Ruppe, Director
Postal Rate Commission—Janet D. Steiger, Chairman
Securities and Exchange Commission—David S. Ruder, Chairman
Selective Service System—Samuel K. Lessey, Jr., Director
Small Business Administration—James Abdnor, Administrator
Smithsonian Institution—Robert McC. Adams, Secretary
Tennessee Valley Authority—Marvin T. Runyon, Chairman
U.S. Arms Control and Disarmament Agency—William Burns†, Director
U.S. Information Agency—Charles Z. Wick, Director
U.S. International Trade Commission—Susan Wittenberg Liebeler, Chairman
U.S. Postal Service—Preston R. Tisch, Postmaster General
Veterans Administration—Thomas K. Turnage, Administrator

†Nominated but not yet confirmed.

VICE PRESIDENT OF THE UNITED STATES

VERITY, C. WILLIAM, JR. (1917-   ), a retired steel company executive, was sworn in as United States secretary of commerce on Oct. 19, 1987. He succeeded Malcolm Baldrige, who was killed in a horse-riding accident on July 25.

Calvin William Verity, Jr., known as Bill, was born on Jan. 26, 1917, in Middletown, Ohio. He graduated from Yale University in New Haven, Conn., in 1939 with a degree in economics.

After working for a New York City advertising agency for a year, Verity returned to Middletown to work for Armco Incorporated. His grandfather founded the company, one of the largest U.S. steelmakers. Verity was elected president and chief executive officer of Armco in 1965 and chairman in 1971, a post he held until his retirement in 1982.

From 1979 to 1984, Verity served as cochairman of the U.S.-U.S.S.R. Trade and Economic Council, a private organization of U.S. executives and Soviet trade officials that seeks to expand trade between the two nations. In 1981, President Ronald Reagan appointed him to head the President's Task Force on Private Sector Initiatives, a panel that sought ways for private charity to fill gaps left by cuts in federal spending.

Verity and his wife, Margaret, live in Middletown. They have three grown children. Sara Dreyfuss
VERMONT. See STATE GOVERNMENT.

VETERANS. President Ronald Reagan on June 1, 1987, signed into law a new GI Bill that provides benefits for United States military personnel, veterans, and members of the reserves. The new law made permanent an educational benefits program that would have expired on Dec. 31, 1989.

VA Fined. On Jan. 8, 1987, U.S. District Court Judge Marilyn Hall Patel in San Francisco ordered the Veterans Administration (VA) to pay more than $100,000 in fines and legal fees for destroying documents and making evasive responses in a suit brought by veterans exposed to radiation during and after World War II. Judge Patel said the VA displayed a "callous disregard for all processes of the court."

Veteran Deaths. On February 13, *The Journal of the American Medical Association* published a study by the U.S. government that found that veterans of the Vietnam War were much more likely to die during their first five years as civilians than their contemporaries who had served elsewhere. According to the study, much of the difference was due to the greater incidence of drug overdoses, automobile accidents, and suicides among Vietnam veterans. Frank Cormier and Margot Cormier

In WORLD BOOK, see VETERANS ADMINISTRATION; VETERANS' ORGANIZATIONS.
VICE PRESIDENT OF THE UNITED STATES. See BUSH, GEORGE H. W.

VIETNAM elected a new National Assembly on April 19, 1987. Voters selected 496 Assembly members from a field of 829 candidates. In mid-June, the Assembly accepted the resignations of Council of State Chairman Truong Chinh and Council of Ministers Chairman Pham Van Dong. Vo Chi Cong, a former deputy head of the National Liberation Front in South Vietnam, became Council of State chairman. The new Council of Ministers chairman was Pham Hung, who had directed North Vietnam's forces in the war against South Vietnam from 1967 to 1975.

Communist Party General Secretary Nguyen Van Linh, Vietnam's most powerful leader, began in 1987 to write a column in the Communist Party newspaper in which he clearly pinpointed the party's failures, often embarrassing officials who opposed reforms. The newspaper editors also urged a move toward change, writing on September 26 that "the percentage of degenerate and deviant" party members remained high and that "many individuals still obstinately continue with their old ways and refuse to improve."

Economic Problems were severe in 1987. A 1985 attempt to liberalize Vietnam's unsuccessful, centrally planned economic system was labeled a failure in 1987. The system had caused annual inflation rates of 700 to 1,000 per cent and depressed living standards by 30 to 50 per cent. In April, officials tried to introduce more free enterprise, but the economy was slow to respond.

According to Pham Hung, drought cut rice production 1 million metric tons (1.1 million short tons) below the targeted goal of 19.2 million metric tons (21.2 million short tons). A prominent medical official in May said that malnutrition was widespread in Vietnam. Refugees leaving the country reported some starvation.

No Answer on MIA's. The approximately 1,790 United States servicemen still missing in action (MIA) from the Vietnam War remained unaccounted for in 1987, despite Vietnam's 1985 promise to resolve the issue within two years. A U.S. delegation headed by retired General John W. Vessey, Jr., and Vietnamese officials led by Foreign Minister Nguyen Co Thach held talks on the issue in Hanoi on August 1 to 3. They agreed "to accelerate progress toward accounting for" the missing and "to address certain urgent humanitarian concerns of Vietnam." It was the first time the United States was willing to link humanitarian aid to the MIA problem.   Henry S. Bradsher

See also ASIA (Facts in Brief Table). In WORLD BOOK, see VIETNAM.

VIRGINIA. See STATE GOVERNMENT.

VITAL STATISTICS. See CENSUS; POPULATION.

Vietnamese and U.S. officials in Hanoi in August discuss the return of remains of U.S. soldiers killed during the Vietnam War.

WALES. A political scandal made headlines in Wales in 1987. The scandal surrounded Keith Best, a 38-year-old lawyer and Conservative member of Parliament for the Isle of Anglesey, an island off the northwest coast of Wales.

In March, it was revealed that Best had made six applications for shares in British Telecom—the company that operates most of Great Britain's telephone system—when the British government sold the company to the private sector in 1984. The rules of the share offer allowed each prospective buyer to make only one application. The scandal caused Best to withdraw from the general election on June 11.

On September 30, Best was convicted of dishonestly making multiple share applications. He was sentenced to four months in prison and fined 3,000 pounds (about $4,900). The Court of Appeal on October 5, however, ruled that the prison sentence was too harsh. Best was freed, but his fine was increased to 4,500 pounds (about $7,300).

Election Results. Many speculated that the Best scandal caused the Conservative Party to lose the Anglesey seat in the June election. Ieuan Wyn Jones of the Plaid Cymru, the Welsh nationalist party, captured the seat.

Despite the fact that Prime Minister Margaret Thatcher's Conservative Party won its third consecutive election in Britain, the Conservatives suffered a setback in Wales. The party lost 5 seats, reducing the number of its members of Parliament to 8. The opposing Labour Party reasserted some of its traditional dominance in Wales by winning 24 seats in the election. Plaid Cymru won 3 seats to equal their highest representation ever in Parliament, and the Liberal-Social Democratic Party Alliance held onto its 3 seats.

Edwards Resigns. Nicholas Edwards, secretary of state for Wales for eight years, resigned from the House of Commons before the election because of poor health. It was later announced that he would be made a life peer, with the rank of baron, and take a seat in the House of Lords.

Peter Walker, a Conservative, succeeded Edwards as secretary of state on June 13, 1987. Walker, a Cabinet member since 1970, had served as secretary of state for energy and secretary of state for agriculture. Some people criticized his appointment by Prime Minister Thatcher because he had no previous connections with Wales. Others argued that Walker's status and experience would benefit the country.

Unemployment. There were signs of continuing improvement in the Welsh economy in 1987. One of the most important indicators—the level of unemployment—showed a decline during the first nine months of 1987. Nevertheless, approximately 150,000 people in Wales were unemployed in September, more than 13 per cent of the work force.

College Controversy. Financial problems beset the University College at Cardiff, one of the colleges of the University of Wales. The college's debts led to a hastily arranged merger in August with the University of Wales Institute of Science and Technology, also located in Cardiff.

Magazine Ends? The Welsh Arts Council decided to withdraw its grant to the 150-year-old Welsh-language magazine *Y Faner* (*The Banner*) in 1988. The decision caused fear that the magazine would fold. The matter was still unresolved at year's end.

The Eisteddfod. At the Royal National Eisteddfod of Wales, held in August in Porthmadog, John Griffith Jones, an industrial chemist, captured the Crown, one of the two chief poetry prizes. The Chair—the other poetry prize—went to Ieuan Wyn of Bethesda.

Other News. Welsh golfer Ian Woosnam won the European Order of Merit in 1987. Woosnam won a number of major tournaments during the year, including the Madrid Open in April and the Scottish Open in July.

Welsh playwright and actor Emlyn Williams died on September 25. Williams, 81, was the author of *The Corn Is Green* (1938).   Patrick Hannan

See also GREAT BRITAIN. In WORLD BOOK, see WALES.

WASHINGTON. See STATE GOVERNMENT.

WASHINGTON, D.C. Federal investigators in 1987 conducted several wide-ranging probes into charges of corruption within the District of Columbia government. Mayor Marion S. Barry, Jr., who began a third four-year term in January 1987, repeatedly denied any wrongdoing. Barry said he was not a target of the investigations, which he charged were a racially motivated assault on his predominantly black administration.

One investigation focused on alleged favoritism in the awarding of city contracts and on whether two city contractors had attempted to buy the silence of convicted cocaine dealer Karen K. Johnson. Johnson was called before a federal grand jury in October to testify on her personal relationship with Mayor Barry. And on May 22, former Washington Deputy Mayor Alphonse G. Hill pleaded guilty to charges of income tax evasion and of defrauding the city government by steering contracts to a friend's firm.

In May, the Federal Bureau of Investigation (FBI) raided the homes or offices of another city official, two city contractors, and an associate of Barry's to collect evidence in the ongoing contracting probe. The FBI also looked into charges that some vice squad officers in the District of Columbia police department kept drugs and money seized from drug suspects. As a result of that investigation, U.S. Attorney Joseph E. diGenova in

September announced dismissal of the 300 to 400 drug cases that were based on vice squad evidence.

Prison Crowding. Faced with overcrowded conditions at the city's prison facilities, the Washington City Council on June 16 approved an early-release law. The law gives the mayor broad powers to free prisoners to meet court-ordered limits on the inmate population. Prisoners convicted of nonviolent crimes could have their sentences reduced by up to 90 days to make them eligible for parole. Barry invoked the new law on July 3, initiating early release of hundreds of inmates.

Meanwhile, plans for a new 800-bed prison in southeast Washington were stalled when the United States Senate Appropriations Committee voted on September 17 to postpone the project until three alternative sites were examined.

Mental Hospital. St. Elizabeths Hospital, a 132-year-old mental hospital in southeast Washington, was transferred from federal to district jurisdiction on October 1. The change of management ended years of negotiations over who should control the facility.

Bottle Bill. District voters on November 3 rejected a proposal to charge deposits on cans and bottles of beverages sold in the city. The initiative, defeated by a 55 to 45 per cent margin, had been backed by environmentalists and civic groups as a means of combating litter. The measure was opposed by a beverage industry coalition.

Statehood. The U.S. House of Representatives Committee on the District of Columbia voted 6 to 5 on June 3 to approve legislation granting statehood to the district. The District of Columbia's delegate to the House, Walter E. Fauntroy, a Democrat—who can vote in committee but not on the House floor—announced in November that he would call for a vote on the statehood bill by the full House of Representatives in early 1988. The measure would also have to be approved by the Senate and signed by the President.

The proposed state of New Columbia, covering less than 70 square miles (180 square kilometers), would be by far the smallest state in the Union. Areas of Washington where U.S. buildings and monuments are located would remain under federal control.

Train Derailment. A CSX Corporation freight train derailed in northeast Washington on the night of September 5, ripping up two CSX tracks as well as parallel tracks of the city's Metro rapid-transit system. There were no injuries, but the derailment severed service on the Metro system's Red Line for three days.   Sandra Evans

See also CITY. In WORLD BOOK, see WASHINGTON, D.C.

A worker clears a path in front of the U.S. Supreme Court Building in January after 26 inches (66 centimeters) of snow fell on Washington, D.C.

524

WATER. On Oct. 1, 1987, officials at the United States Bureau of Reclamation, an agency of the Department of the Interior, announced that beginning in 1988, its mission will change from developing water and other natural resources to managing existing water resources. The bureau was established by the Reclamation Act of 1902 to irrigate farmlands—and in the process "reclaim" Western states from the desert. In its first 85 years, the agency irrigated millions of acres by building reservoirs, power plants, aqueducts, canals, and dams, including such engineering landmarks as Hoover Dam, on the Arizona-Nevada border, and Shasta Dam, in California.

By 1987, however, most rivers in the Western United States were dammed, and most suitable farmland was irrigated. The benefits of constructing more dams and canals would probably be outweighed by the costs of such projects and their harmful effect on the environment. The bureau has been criticized for unnecessary irrigation projects that use tax money to provide cheap water for growing crops that were already in oversupply.

Starting in 1988, the bureau will manage ground-water supplies, restore aquatic environments, clean up polluted water, and in other ways improve the quality of U.S. water supplies.

Hetch Hetchy Reservoir. On Aug. 5, 1987, U.S. Secretary of the Interior Donald P. Hodel proposed the draining of California's Hetch Hetchy Reservoir to open more of Yosemite National Park to tourists. Hetch Hetchy Reservoir, which provides San Francisco with water and hydroelectric power, was created in the early 1900's when engineers dammed the Tuolumne River. The river flooded Hetch Hetchy Valley, the beautiful "twin" of the magnificent Yosemite Valley.

The creation of the reservoir caused one of the bitterest and best-known battles over the environment in U.S. history. First suggested in 1900, the project was opposed by John Muir, the father of modern environmentalism and founder of the Sierra Club. Muir and other opponents of the reservoir argued that nature has a right to exist unchanged and that the beauty of Hetch Hetchy Valley should be preserved. Supporters of the reservoir argued that natural resources such as the valley should be developed wisely to benefit people. The debate ended in 1913, when Congress approved the damming of the Tuolumne.

Hodel's 1987 plan was to remove the dam, drain the reservoir, and allow the valley to return to a natural state. Some environmentalists welcomed his proposal and said that the restored valley would provide an alternate attraction for tourists who now crowd the adjacent Yosemite Valley. San Francisco officials, led by Mayor Dianne Feinstein, opposed the plan, however. They pointed out that the Hetch Hetchy Reservoir and aqueduct system supplies valuable hydroelectric power and water to 2 million people and said that replacement of the water system could cost $6 billion.

Clean Water Act. On February 4, Congress overwhelmingly approved the 1987 Clean Water Act over President Ronald Reagan's veto. The act, which Reagan called a "budget buster," was identical to a bill the President had vetoed in 1986.

In 1972, the first Clean Water Act was enacted to make U.S. lakes and waterways "swimmable and fishable." The statute expired in 1981.

The 1987 Clean Water Act provided $18 billion for grants and loans to construct and expand sewage-treatment plants and $2 billion for other water-pollution control projects. The new act included a provision to control rain-water runoff from cities and farms—a major source of water pollution. The statute also strengthened requirements to remove hazardous waste from water and gave the U.S. Environmental Protection Agency new authority to prosecute and penalize polluters. Legislators hoped the act would result in improved water quality in the Great Lakes, Chesapeake Bay, San Francisco Bay, New York Harbor, Long Island Sound, Delaware Bay, and other areas.   Iris Priestaf

In the Special Reports section, see STORMY DEBATE OVER ACID RAIN. In WORLD BOOK, see WATER.

WEATHER. The first half of 1987 was marked by persistently higher than normal temperatures over most of Canada and the Northern United States. Average temperatures were as much as 10 Fahrenheit degrees (5.6 Celsius degrees) above normal, and record high temperatures were reached in many locations during the six-month period. Alaska's temperatures were above normal from January through March.

The Pacific coastal states were unusually dry during most of the first nine months of 1987. An area extending from southern California and Nevada up to Canada received less than one-third of its normal rainfall. Portions of the Pacific Northwest experienced their worst drought on record. Low stream levels threatened three of the area's main industries—salmon fishing, logging, and winter-wheat farming. For the second consecutive year, extreme summer dryness also developed along the southern Appalachian Mountains from Virginia to Georgia.

The Hurricane Season was relatively mild in 1987. Hurricane Emily made an unexpected strike on Bermuda in September, however. It was Bermuda's first hurricane in 21 years. In October, Hurricane Floyd briefly threatened Florida before passing harmlessly into the Atlantic Ocean.

Deadly Twisters. On February 28, a tornado cut a swath up to 2 miles (3.2 kilometers) wide and 20

miles (32 kilometers) long through several small communities in southeast Mississippi. Seven people were killed, and at least 145 injured.

On the evening of May 22, a massive tornado swept through the town of Saragosa, Tex., killing 30 people and injuring more than 100. The Red Cross reported that 55 homes were destroyed and 40 others severely damaged.

On July 31, several tornadoes hit a suburb of Edmonton, Canada, killing 26 people and injuring nearly 300. It was Canada's most costly natural disaster.

Winter Storms. As 1987 began, snow and high tides battered the Northeastern United States. On January 2, authorities in four states urged residents of exposed coastal areas to take shelter inland as a storm advanced slowly up the East Coast. The storm was accompanied by heavy snow, screaming winds, and beach-scouring waves and high tides. In late 1986, the same storm caused six deaths and millions of dollars of damage in the Southeast. The high-tide menace was caused by several celestial phenomena, including the January 3 occurrence of a *syzygy* (alignment of the sun, moon, and earth). On January 11 and 12, a second coastal storm dumped more than 20 inches (50 centimeters) of snow on Moncton and Fredericton, Canada, and in late January, record snow-

falls and ice storms crippled Canada's Maritime Provinces.

February brought generally mild conditions to most of the United States. International Falls, Minn., recorded its warmest February since record-keeping began in the 1890's. The only outbreak of severe cold sent thermometers in northern Vermont to $-34°F$. ($-37°C$) on February 14. This outbreak followed a severe coastal storm that brought 28 inches (71 centimeters) of snow to portions of Newfoundland, Canada, raising the region's seasonal total to nearly 60 inches (150 centimeters).

Europe's Big Chill. The mild winter of 1986-1987 in North America contrasted sharply with the record cold that hit northern Europe for the second consecutive year. January temperatures averaged 22 Fahrenheit degrees (12 Celsius degrees) below normal. About 265 deaths—at least 77 in the Soviet Union alone—were blamed on the cold weather. For several weeks, ice closed Baltic Sea ports. In London, Big Ben's hammer mechanism froze, silencing the famous bell in the Houses of Parliament clock tower. At the London Zoo, lions had to be housed indoors for the first time in recent memory. In Finland, temperatures sank to a record $-33°F$. ($-36°C$). Below normal temperatures and extensive cloudiness and rain continued

Flooding brings Chicago traffic to a halt in August. A record 8.98 inches (22.8 centimeters) of rain fell on the Chicago area in 13 hours.

through the spring and early summer over most of central Europe.

Summertime Extremes. In late June, lightning caused at least 70 fires that destroyed more than 8,000 acres (3,200 hectares) of tinder-dry forests in California. In Utah, 7,000 acres (2,800 hectares) were destroyed by lightning-sparked fires.

The week of July 26 brought a severe heat wave to the Northern Plains. In portions of the Dakotas, Minnesota, and Iowa, temperatures averaged 12 Fahrenheit degrees (6.7 Celsius degrees) above normal. The *apparent temperature* (a comfort index that represents the combined effects of humidity and temperature) reached 120°F. (49°C).

A deadly heat wave also scorched Bulgaria, Greece, Turkey, and Yugoslavia in July. Greece, which recorded temperatures as high as 113°F. (45°C), was hardest hit. As many as 1,000 Greeks, most of them elderly and infirm, died during 10 days of record-breaking temperatures.

On August 13 and 14, 8.98 inches (22.8 centimeters) of rain fell on Chicago within 13 hours, causing severe flooding. More rain on August 25 boosted the month's total rainfall, measured at the Chicago-O'Hare International Airport, to a record 14.18 inches (36.02 centimeters).

Bangladesh was devastated by flooding after the summer monsoons brought the heaviest rainfall in 75 years. Property damage totaled $1.5 billion. The official death toll was 1,000; unofficial estimates were as high as 5,000. The normal monsoons by-passed much of India, however, causing a severe drought.

Fall Storms and Heat Wave. In early autumn, colder than normal temperatures returned to the Northeastern United States. Portions of Pennsylvania recorded their coldest October in 100 years. On October 4, an early snowstorm crippled Albany, N.Y., with up to 20 inches (50 centimeters) of wet, heavy snow that felled trees and downed power lines.

By contrast, October 5 was the hottest day on record in many California coastal cities. The temperature in Monterey, Calif., soared to 105°F. (41°C); in Los Angeles it reached 103°F. (39°C); and in downtown San Francisco the temperature peaked at 102°F. (39°C). San Francisco's temperature was the highest since record-keeping began 113 years earlier.

The worst storm in several decades swept across southern England on October 15 and 16, bringing winds of more than 100 miles (160 kilometers) per hour to the outskirts of London. Nineteen people were killed by collapsing buildings and falling trees.

Welcome Rain. On November 1, Yakima, Wash., had its first measurable rainfall in 104 days. The rain ended the region's worst forest fire in 40 years, which burned for 10 weeks, blackening about 95,000 acres (38,000 hectares) of southern Oregon's Siskiyou National Forest.

The drought in the southern Appalachians, however, continued to worsen. By November, hundreds of forest fires had erupted there, causing smoke pollution as far away as New York City.

A Mid-December Storm left a trail of heavy snows and 73 deaths in the Southwestern and Midwestern states. El Paso, Tex., was blanketed with 22 inches (56 centimeters) of snow—twice as much as ever recorded there in a single storm.

Ozone Debate. For years, scientists in Antarctica have reported a thinning of the earth's atmospheric layer of ozone, a form of oxygen. The ozone protects plant and animal life by absorbing much of the sun's harmful ultraviolet light.

Measurements of Antarctic ozone taken in 1987 alarmed scientists, some of whom attributed the ozone depletion to the use of chemicals called *chlorofluorocarbons* (CFC's), which are used as refrigerants and aerosol propellants. Other scientists think the depletion was caused by natural changes in atmospheric circulation patterns. In spite of the scientific debate, international officials agreed in September to restrict production of CFC's. See ENVIRONMENTAL POLLUTION. Alfred K. Blackadar

In the Special Reports section, see STORMY DEBATE OVER ACID RAIN. In WORLD BOOK, see METEOROLOGY; WEATHER.

WEBSTER, WILLIAM HEDGCOCK (1924-   ), director of the Federal Bureau of Investigation (FBI), took office as director of the United States Central Intelligence Agency (CIA) on May 26, 1987. Webster promised that the CIA would cooperate with Congress in carrying out spying activities abroad. Webster's predecessor at the CIA, William J. Casey, had been accused of often withholding information from Congress.

Webster was born on March 6, 1924, in St. Louis, Mo. He graduated in 1947 from Amherst College in Massachusetts and received a law degree in 1949 from Washington University in St. Louis.

In 1970, after a 21-year career as a lawyer in St. Louis, Webster was appointed a U.S. district judge for the eastern district of Missouri. Three years later, he was named to the U.S. Court of Appeals for the Eighth Circuit, which includes Missouri.

In 1978, President Jimmy Carter named Webster FBI director. Earlier, it had been revealed that the law-enforcement agency had been involved in many illegal activities, including burglaries and spying on American citizens. Webster is credited with modernizing the FBI and restoring its image.

Webster was widowed in 1984. He has three children. David L. Dreier

WEIGHT LIFTING. See SPORTS.

WELFARE. On Feb. 24, 1987, during a meeting of the National Governors' Association in Washington D.C., governors of 49 states endorsed a plan to overhaul the public welfare system to emphasize job training and work requirements for many welfare participants. The only dissenting vote was by Wisconsin Governor Tommy G. Thompson, a Republican. Both houses of Congress labored on welfare reform during the year but were unable to agree on legislation before adjournment.

Poverty. The poverty rate in the United States edged downward in 1986 for the third straight year, the U.S. Bureau of the Census reported on July 30, 1987. Median family income increased for the fourth year in a row, outpacing inflation by a significant margin.

The Census Bureau said 32.4 million Americans, or 13.6 per cent of the population, had incomes below the official poverty level in 1986. The poverty level was defined as an annual cash income of $11,203 or less for a family of four.

The poverty rate was down from 14 per cent in 1985 (33.1 million Americans). The poverty rate was 22.4 per cent in 1959, when such figures first were computed, and dropped to about 11.5 per cent in the 1960's. But, as a result of inflation and recession, the poverty rate rose sharply in the late 1970's and early 1980's to a peak of 15.2 per cent in 1983. About 22 per cent of children under 6 years old were living in poverty in 1986, a slight decline from the previous year.

Income Gap. Median family income was $29,458 in 1986, 4.2 per cent higher than the 1985 level, after adjusting for inflation. Gordon W. Green, Jr., an official of the Census Bureau's population division, said the four-year rise in median income was the largest sustained increase since the 1960's. But there appeared to be a widening income gap between whites and blacks and between the highest and lowest income levels. The upper 20 per cent of income levels received 46.1 per cent of all family income in 1986—the highest proportion ever recorded—up from 44.2 per cent in 1980. The lowest 20 per cent of income levels received 3.8 per cent of all family income in 1986, down from 4.1 per cent in 1980.

The National Urban League—an organization that works to end racial discrimination—blamed the Administration of President Ronald Reagan for a widening income gap between white and black Americans. According to the group's annual report on "The State of Black America," released on Jan. 14, 1987, per-capita black income averaged 56 per cent of white income in 1985, down from 62 per cent in 1975.

Noncash Assistance. A Census Bureau report in March 1987 said 1 of every 6 American households in 1985 received some form of noncash government benefit based on need, including food stamps, Medicaid, reduced-price school lunches, and subsidized housing. The total market value of the benefits was $56 billion.

Homeless Aid. On Feb. 12, 1987, President Reagan signed a bill earmarking $50 million of federal disaster relief funds to help the homeless in the United States. Although the Reagan Administration had opposed the bill, both houses of Congress approved it by wide margins. On July 1, Congress approved a supplemental appropriations bill for the 1987 fiscal year that included an additional $355 million for the homeless.

Deferrals of Social Services. In a controversial action, the White House announced on January 28 that President Reagan was deferring the spending of $265 million voted by Congress for such activities as education and the transportation of food to the homeless to help finance a 3 per cent pay increase for government employees. The announcement was made just eight days after a three-judge panel of the U.S. Court of Appeals ruled that the President did not have the right to defer spending enacted by Congress. On April 4, the General Accounting Office, an agency of Congress, said that Reagan acted illegally but that it did not have "authority to compel release of the funds."   Frank Cormier and Margot Cormier

In WORLD BOOK, see WELFARE.

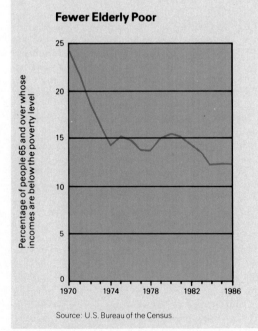

Fewer Elderly Poor

Percentage of people 65 and over whose incomes are below the poverty level

Source: U.S. Bureau of the Census.

The percentage of elderly poor in the United States has been dropping since 1970, primarily due to increases in social security benefits.

WEST INDIES. Prime ministers of six tiny nations in the eastern Caribbean—the former British colonies St. Vincent and the Grenadines, St. Lucia, Dominica, Grenada, Antigua and Barbuda, and St. Christopher and Nevis—and of Montserrat, a British dependency, agreed on May 31, 1987, to work toward union and the formation of a single nation. The English-speaking islands have a combined population of about 600,000 and a gross domestic product of $620 million.

The Bahamas. Prime Minister Lynden O. Pindling easily won reelection on June 19 for a fifth five-year term, despite a well-organized campaign to portray his Progressive Liberal Party as riddled with corruption and involved in drug trafficking. The United States government helped publicize use of the islands as a transit point for cocaine and marijuana headed for the United States. But popular resentment against U.S. meddling in domestic politics helped the 57-year-old Pindling stay in office, according to local observers.

Jamaica's tourism industry continued to recover from a decline brought on by political violence in the 1970's. In the first seven months of 1987, tourism revenues were up 14.2 per cent over the same period in 1986.   Nathan A. Haverstock

See also HAITI; LATIN AMERICA (Facts in Brief Table). In WORLD BOOK, see WEST INDIES.

WEST VIRGINIA. See STATE GOVERNMENT.

WILSON, AUGUST (1945-   ), won the Pulitzer Prize for drama in April 1987 for *Fences*, a play about an embittered black garbage collector in the 1950's and his tormented relationships with his wife and son. *Fences* is the fourth in a projected series of 10 plays about the black experience in the United States in each decade of the 1900's.

Wilson, who was born in Pittsburgh, Pa., dropped out of school in the ninth grade. While working at a series of menial jobs, he wrote plays, short stories, and poems.

In 1978, Wilson moved to St. Paul, Minn. At the urging of the director of a black theater company there, he wrote *Jitney*, the first play in his series. Set at a cab station in Pittsburgh, the drama premiered in that city in 1982. Other plays in the series include *Fullerton Street*, which has never been staged, *Joe Turner's Come and Gone* (1986), and *The Piano Lesson* (1987).

Wilson's box-office breakthrough occurred in 1984 with the Broadway opening of *Ma Rainey's Black Bottom*. It won the New York Drama Critics Circle Award for best new play.

Wilson is married to Judy Oliver. He has a daughter by a previous marriage.   Barbara A. Mayes

WISCONSIN. See STATE GOVERNMENT.
WYOMING. See STATE GOVERNMENT.
YEMEN (ADEN). See MIDDLE EAST.
YEMEN (SANA). See MIDDLE EAST.

YOUTH ORGANIZATIONS. On Feb. 12, 1987, the Boy Scouts of America (BSA) kicked off a national drug-abuse prevention program called "Drugs: A Deadly Game." Through the program, the BSA distributed educational materials to its members. Teachers and other youth leaders received training materials and educational videotapes.

In 1987, Boy Scout residence camps opened to Cub Scouts for the first time. Cub Scouts—boys in second, third, and fourth grades—participated in a four-day and three-night adventure program. The BSA created four new merit badges in 1987 and introduced a revised Webelos Scout book for fourth- and fifth-grade Cub Scouts.

Boys Clubs of America (BCA) in 1987 launched "Outreach '91," a five-year plan designed to increase both the number of young people the BCA serves and the quality of the organization's service. A committee of club leaders proposed that the BCA change its name to Boys & Girls Clubs of America to better reflect the youth population served by the clubs. The proposal was scheduled to be voted on at the 1988 national conference.

The BCA also created two service projects in 1987. "Operation Secure" was designed to help young people protect themselves from crime and violence at home, at school, and on the street. "Smart Moves" teaches boys and girls to avoid drug and alcohol abuse and to delay sexual activity. In September, Ken McBride of Salem, Ore., was named the BCA's 1987-1988 National Youth of the Year.

Camp Fire councils in some areas continued to provide child care for preschoolers and school-age children in 1987. Camp Fire also advocated increased public funding for child care services and the establishment of legal standards for child care.

In 1987, more than 35,000 children and teen-agers took part in Camp Fire's new peace education programs, "A Gift of Peace" and "In Pursuit of Peace." In March, a Camp Fire national board member presented a peace resolution to the children of China. In November, Camp Fire held its biennial Congress in Phoenix.

4-H Clubs in 1987 continued their efforts to address contemporary social issues faced by today's teen-agers. Members of 4-H, many of whom live in cities, towns, and suburbs as well as on farms, developed projects on such nonagricultural issues as substance abuse, teen-age suicide, early pregnancy, and stress. The club also continued to respond to the economic crisis of U.S. farming families by helping young people learn more about competitiveness, profitability, and alternate opportunities in American agriculture.

During the summer, approximately 4,500 teen-agers traveled to Washington, D.C., to participate in an educational program about governmental processes. At the 66th National 4-H Congress,

First lady Nancy Reagan—herself a former
Brownie—helps Girl Scouts celebrate their
organization's 75th anniversary in March.

ber, Betty F. Pilsbury was elected to serve as national president for a second term.

Girls Clubs of America (GCA) in 1987 inaugurated the Girl Hero Award to recognize young women of achievement. The 1987 awards were presented to basketball player Cheryl Miller and television stars Justine Bateman and Tina Yothers. The GCA also introduced the Sports Resource Kit, an aid to planning effective sports programs for girls aged 6 to 18.

Operation SMART, designed to encourage girls to pursue careers in mathematics and science, received a $221,000 grant from the Ford Foundation in 1987. Polly Nou, a 17-year-old Kampuchean refugee from San Leandro, Calif., won the GCA's $2,500 Career Key Scholarship Award.

Junior Achievement created a permanent National Business Hall of Fame exhibit at the Museum of Science and Industry in Chicago in 1987. Funded by private business, the $1-million, computer-controlled exhibit honors more than 100 business leaders who played important roles in the economic development of the United States.

Junior Achievement's new Outreach Project began in Michigan's Upper Peninsula in late 1987. The project was designed to bring the organization to students in rural areas.   Jinger Griswold

In WORLD BOOK, see entries on the individual organizations.

held in Chicago from December 5 through 10, some 1,700 outstanding 4-H members were honored for their achievements.

Future Farmers of America (FFA) held its 60th annual convention in November 1987. At the convention, Vice President George H. W. Bush addressed more than 22,000 FFA members and supporters. Franklin Howey, Jr., of Monroe, N.C., was named Star Farmer of America, and Dan Ruehling of Belle Plaine, Minn., was named Star Agribusinessman of America.

The FFA created two programs in cooperation with the U.S. Information Agency in 1987—World Agri-Science Studies and Congress-Bundestag. Both programs enable U.S. students to study agriculture in Europe.

Girl Scouts in the United States celebrated their 75th anniversary in 1987. During the year, more than 4.5 million visitors to the Smithsonian Institution in Washington, D.C., viewed an exhibit that traced Girl Scout history. The U.S. Postal Service acknowledged the anniversary by issuing a 22-cent commemorative stamp. As part of the yearlong celebration, Girl Scouts organized food drives, planted trees, removed graffiti, built playgrounds, and performed other community services.

In 1987, a new blue uniform for Cadette and Senior Girl Scouts was introduced. At the 1987 National Council, held in Portland, Ore., in Octo-

YUGOSLAVIA in 1987 plunged into its deepest economic recession since the end of World War II in 1945. Financial scandal also rocked the country's banking system and reached the highest levels of the ruling Communist Party.

At the eye of the financial storm was Agrokomerc, a major agricultural and industrial company located in Bosnia and Hercegovina, one of the six republics that make up Yugoslavia. Investigations during the summer of 1987 revealed that the company's ambitious investments were based on the issue of worthless, unsecured promissory notes valued at $750 million.

On September 4, police arrested the company's director and 24 associates on charges of undermining the country's economic system. The political reverberations of the scandal led on September 12 to the resignation of Hamdija Pozderac, a Bosnian, as vice president of the Presidency—a nine-member council that serves as Yugoslavia's chief policymaking body. In December, the Communist Party expelled two members of its Central Committee for their part in the scandal.

Economic Control Debated. Yugoslav economists had long criticized the degree of independence—regardless of national interest—allowed the governments and Communist parties of Yugoslavia's six republics and two areas called *autonomous regions*. The Agrokomerc affair uncovered a hodgepodge of freewheeling financial procedures involving Communist leaders, semi-independent business enterprises, and millions of dollars worth of phony operations. The Federal Assembly (parliament) debated constitutional amendments that would permit stronger central control of the economy, but no vote was scheduled until 1988.

Price Hikes. The government took drastic steps on November 14 in an attempt to stem Yugoslavia's inflation rate of 135 per cent. The steps included increases of 30 to 70 per cent in prices of consumer goods and services, a freeze on wages and the new prices until June 30, 1988, and the introduction of a personal income tax. When food shops in Belgrade, Yugoslavia's capital, opened on Nov. 15, 1987, thousands of shoppers poured in and bought huge quantities of groceries before the shopkeepers could mark them up. Throughout the country, workers reacted angrily, striking for higher pay in at least 40 plants during the first week after the price increases.

Ethnic Conflict continued in Kosovo Province in the Republic of Serbia. Most residents of Kosovo are ethnic Albanians, many of whom want to upgrade Kosovo to the status of a republic. On Oct. 25, 1987, the Presidency ordered special antiriot forces into the province.   Eric Bourne

See also EUROPE (Facts in Brief Table). In WORLD BOOK, see YUGOSLAVIA.

YUKON TERRITORY enjoyed an economic boom during 1987, spurred by a reopened lead and zinc mine at Faro that returned to production in January 1986. During 1987, the mine shipped about 50,000 short tons (45,000 metric tons) of processed ore per month. Also in operation were a new gold mine at Mount Skukum, near the territory's capital of Whitehorse, and *placer mining* activities at several locations. (Placer mining is the washing of loose sand or gravel for gold or other minerals.)

Overall, the Yukon economy was expected to grow by about 25 per cent in 1987. Tourist traffic increased by about 10 per cent, and plans were underway to reopen as a tourist route the narrow-gauge White Pass and Yukon Railway from Skagway to Whitehorse. The railway was the lifeline of the territory until it was closed with the shutdown of the Faro mine in 1982. Another new commercial venture was the establishment of the territory's first domestic reindeer herd near Whitehorse.

The governing New Democratic Party (NDP) won a special election on February 2. This increased the NDP's strength by 1 seat to 9 seats and gave the party its first majority in the 16-seat legislature. The Progressive Conservatives held 6 seats, and the Liberals retained 1.   David M. L. Farr

See also CANADA. In WORLD BOOK, see YUKON TERRITORY.

ZAIRE. After decades of domestic and international strife, Zaire in 1987 was realizing the full potential of its wealth in diamonds, tin, copper, cobalt, manganese, and other minerals. Minerals account for 90 per cent of Zaire's foreign trade. Even though global prices for some minerals had fallen, Zairian mines increased their production.

But Zaire's economic growth was hindered by a $5.9-billion foreign debt, more than 65 per cent of which was owed to West European governments. Zaire's creditors agreed in May to schedule repayment of the debt over a 15-year period. To reduce expenses, the regime of President Mobutu Sese Seko sold 10 government-owned businesses in 1987. Acknowledging the importance of agriculture to the economy, the regime set 1990 as the target date for achieving self-sufficiency in food and improving all phases of agricultural production. In July, state-owned farms were turned over to private farmers' unions.

Mobutu strengthened ties with several other African states in 1987. To assist Chad in its struggle against Libya, he consented to the training of more than 2,000 Chadian troops in Zaire. Zaire also signed border agreements with Zambia, Angola, and Uganda. J. Gus Liebenow and Beverly B. Liebenow

See also AFRICA (Facts in Brief Table). In WORLD BOOK, see ZAIRE.

ZAMBIA. See AFRICA.

ZIMBABWE. In August 1987, Zimbabwe's Parliament voted to eliminate the seats reserved for whites in its two houses. The white minority—now roughly 100,000 out of a total population of more than 9 million—had been guaranteed representation under the 1980 Lancaster House Agreement. That pact, signed in London, ended the civil war in Zimbabwe—formerly called Rhodesia.

Until 1987, whites were given 20 of the seats in the 100-member House of Assembly and 10 of the seats in the 40-member Senate. The change had long been urged by Prime Minister Robert Gabriel Mugabe, who had been trying to reduce white influence in government. White citizens were still eligible for election to Parliament and remained an important force in Zimbabwe's economy.

Other Constitutional Changes were recommended by Mugabe in September. He suggested that Parliament confer more power on the office of president—now largely a ceremonial post held by Canaan Banana—and eliminate the office of prime minister. Mugabe made it clear that he intended to become the first president elected for a six-year term under the new system.

On December 22, Mugabe and opposition leader Joshua Nkomo agreed to merge their political parties and establish a single-party state. The new party is called the Zimbabwe African National Union-Patriotic Front, the name of Mugabe's party. Mugabe became the merged party's first secretary and Zimbabwe's executive president, effective December 31. He was expected to assign a secondary leadership role to Nkomo, former leader of the Zimbabwe African People's Union.

Foreign Affairs. Landlocked Zimbabwe in 1987 maintained over 12,000 troops in Mozambique, its neighbor to the east, helping to guard a 185-mile (300-kilometer) railroad line between Harare and the Mozambican port of Beira. The rail link has often been disrupted by South African-supported rebels opposing the government of Mozambique. The Beira line greatly reduces Zimbabwe's dependence on the longer and more costly South African transport links to world markets.

Mugabe, as head of the nonaligned movement, a group of 102 Third World nations and organizations, has been a leading advocate of global economic sanctions against South Africa for its racial policies. In July, Mugabe and President Kenneth David Kaunda of Zambia agreed on a joint economic boycott of South Africa. But they dropped that plan a few weeks later after analysts predicted that sanctions would cause Zimbabwean bankruptcies, shortages of essential goods, and other problems.   J. Gus Liebenow and Beverly B. Liebenow

See also AFRICA (Facts in Brief Table). In WORLD BOOK, see ZIMBABWE.

ZOOLOGY. A team of scientists reported in June 1987 that research findings indicate that people were directly and indirectly responsible for the extinction of two-thirds of the birds native to the Hawaiian islands. The extinctions occurred following the Polynesian settlement of the islands about 2,000 years ago.

The researchers, from the Smithsonian Institution in Washington, D.C., and five other institutions in the United States, found a collection of small bone fossils from a variety of bird species. The fossils were well preserved in a lava formation on the island of Maui. Using a new high-precision method of dating bone fossils, the scientists traced the history of bird species on the island over a period of 8,000 years. No dramatic changes occurred until human beings settled the island. Then, in a brief period, about 23 species of birds disappeared. At the time of Polynesian settlement, lizards, rodents, and land snails also were introduced. These animals undoubtedly contributed to the devastation by competing with native species for resources and by preying on them.

Frolicking Fish. Coelacanths, a primitive species of fish that was once thought to be extinct, have been observed for the first time in their natural surroundings, West German scientists reported in September 1987. Using a research submarine, the

"Independence" day came on July 5 for this pilot whale, hoisted aboard ship
for its return to sea after a six-month convalescence at a Boston aquarium.

scientists, led by zoologist Hans Fricke of the Max Planck Institute for Comparative Physiology in Seewiesen, West Germany, photographed several coelacanths. The photographs showed the fish performing headstands and swimming belly up and backwards. The West German scientists observed the fish and their unusual behavior at depths of about 660 feet (200 meters) near the Comoros Islands in the Indian Ocean.

Coelacanths belong to a group of primitive fish believed to represent an important evolutionary link with land animals. These fish have a bone structure that appears to represent a transition to the legs of land animals. Coelacanths have existed for more than 300 million years. They were known only from fossils until a fisherman netted a coelacanth off South Africa in 1938.

One Jump Ahead. An unusual example of animal mimicry was reported in April by two teams of scientists working independently of each other. *Mimicry* is a form of natural protection in which an animal closely resembles another animal or its surroundings. Usually, an animal will mimic some poisonous species. For example, the viceroy butterfly resembles the monarch butterfly, which is poisonous to birds. Taking no chances, bird predators avoid both species, even though the viceroy butterfly is safe to eat.

The rare case of mimicry reported in April involved the tephritid fruit fly, which mimics one of its natural enemies, the jumping spider. The fruit flies have striped wings that resemble markings on the legs of the jumping spider. When a fly is startled, it lifts its wings and performs a jerky dance. This dance is similar to one performed by the jumping spider when it signals its claim to a territory. When a spider sees this signal, it stops stalking the fly and flees. Ordinary house flies that do not show the striped wing pattern or wing-lifting behavior, however, are readily captured.

Researchers from Simon Fraser University in Burnaby, Canada, showed that the striped pattern on the wings of the fruit flies was necessary to divert the spider. When they obliterated the stripes on some fruit flies with ink, spiders captured many of these flies.

Biologists from Princeton University in New Jersey and the University of Georgia in Athens drew the same conclusions when they tested another species of fruit fly and 11 species of jumping spiders. The scientists transplanted wings from houseflies to fruit flies and vice versa. Fruit flies with housefly wings were readily attacked. Houseflies with fruit-fly wings were also attacked because the stripes were not displayed properly. Both the striped pattern and the wing-lifting dance were required for full protection.   Clyde Freeman Herreid II

See also PALEONTOLOGY; ZOOS. In WORLD BOOK, see ZOOLOGY.

ZOOS and aquariums throughout North America delighted millions of visitors with an array of impressive new exhibits in 1987. The National Zoo in Washington, D.C., focused attention on creatures without backbones when it opened its Invertebrate Animal Hall on May 7. Invertebrates, such as corals, mollusks, starfish, worms, sponges, and insects, make up about 99 per cent of the animal kingdom.

In the new building, visitors can examine a northern Pacific habitat with an underwater cliff populated by flowerlike anemones and sea stars. Another exhibit features a Caribbean coral reef inhabited by spiny lobsters, tubeworms, banded coral shrimp, and sea urchins. The new hall is designed to increase awareness of invertebrate behavior. Viewers can watch the primitive aquatic propulsion system of the *chambered nautilus* (a sea animal related to the octopus whose body is covered with a coiled shell), and the highly organized society of leaf-cutter ants. Microscopes are provided for glimpses of tiny animals that are invisible to the naked eye.

On April 16, the Metro Toronto Zoo in Canada opened a full-scale replica of the ruins of a Maya temple in Central America. The ruins sit in a jungle clearing complete with a series of waterfalls that tumble into a nearby lake. The simulated relic of an ancient civilization offers visitors dramatic views of jaguars, *tapirs* (bulky, long-nosed relatives of horses), *capybaras* (the world's largest rodents), spider monkeys, flamingos, macaws, and Coscoroba swans.

Savanna in Pittsburgh. On May 21, the Pittsburgh (Pa.) Zoo opened its newly completed African savanna to the public. The 4-acre (1.6-hectare) exhibit immerses visitors in the landscape so that they feel they are sharing it—safely—with such animals as zebras, *elands* (antelopes), elephants, giraffes, ostriches, and crowned cranes. A meandering path winds through shrubs, grasses, and other plants that resemble African vegetation. Brooks, waterfalls, and a 100,000-gallon (380,000-liter) pond serve as natural barriers, providing views that are unobstructed by fences or bars. Animal shelters are concealed behind hills or vegetation.

Dolphin Theater. The Brookfield Zoo near Chicago ushered visitors into a completely revamped Seven Seas Panorama on June 6. The new facility, an updated version of the aquatic mammal exhibit that opened more than 20 years earlier, boasts a 2,000-seat theater where visitors can enjoy acrobatic performances by bottle-nosed dolphins in an 800,000-gallon (3-million-liter) pool of salt water. After the show, the dolphins can be observed from a large underwater viewing gallery.

Penguins and Puffins. Sea World of Florida in Orlando opened Penguin Encounter, the largest and most technically advanced exhibit of its kind

An 11-week-old snow leopard cub, one of two born on June 9, glances up at its mother, Olga, at the Bronx Zoo's Himalayan Highlands in New York City.

in the world, in July. A moving sidewalk carries visitors past a 4,000-square-foot (370-square-meter) Antarctic environment inhabited by more than 300 penguins of six species. When not waddling around on the artificial ice shelf, the birds dive and swim in a pool that holds 160,000 gallons (600,000 liters) of salt water. A daily "storm" deposits 6,000 pounds (2,700 kilograms) of snow on the ice shelf. The exhibit also has a sea-and-cliff habitat for *alcids*—birds such as puffins, murres, and auklets that are the Arctic counterparts of penguins but are not related to them.

Special Births. Hopes were high on June 23, when Ling-Ling, a giant panda at the National Zoo, gave birth to a 4-ounce (110-gram) cub. Although the tiny cub seemed healthy, it died four days later, probably because of an infection in its abdominal cavity.

A Ruppell's griffon vulture chick hatched on February 28 at the Milwaukee County Zoo—apparently the first time this species has bred in North America. On May 24, Washington Park Zoo in Portland, Ore., announced its 24th elephant birth. The Oregon institution has produced more elephant babies than any other zoo in the world. Between July 2 and 9, 18 *broad-snouted caimans*—crocodilians from South America—hatched at the Bronx Zoo, the first time this endangered species has reproduced in captivity.

High-Tech Breeding. Some births in 1987 were the result of experimental techniques. These techniques—successful for the first time—could aid in the breeding of endangered species. The National Zoo tested *in vitro fertilization*—a technique in which male and female sex cells are united in a test tube or other artificial environment—on domestic cats. The sperm from one male cat was used to fertilize *ova* (eggs) from three female cats. In April, five kittens were born. The Cincinnati Wildlife Research Federation—which consists of the Cincinnati (Ohio) Zoo, Kings Island Wild Animal Habitat, and the University of Cincinnati College of Medicine—implanted cat embryos that had been frozen and stored into five female cats. In July, the cats gave birth to a total of 17 kittens.

Rarities. In 1987, American zoos gave the public opportunities to enjoy some animals that are rarely seen, either in zoos or in the wild. In July, the Cincinnati Zoo became the second zoo in the world to have a colony of naked mole rats from Africa. The London Zoo is the only other institution where these small, hairless, bucktoothed rodents may be seen.

During the year, the government of China lent four giant pandas to U.S. zoos. The Bronx Zoo in New York City and the San Diego Zoo each received two of the animals.   Eugene J. Walter, Jr.

In WORLD BOOK, see ZOO.

Answers to the Quiz

1. Indianapolis.
2. *Platoon.*
3. Gary Hart.
4. **b.** (Richard G. Hatcher of Gary, Ind.)
5. Three. (Bettino Craxi, Amintore Fanfani, and Giovanni Goria)
6. Praise the Lord and People That Love.
7. The process of adding color to black-and-white motion pictures.
8. A West German teen-ager flew a small plane from Finland to Moscow, penetrating Soviet air defenses, and landed near the Kremlin.
9. The Teamsters Union.
10. Lutheran.
11. Quebec.
12. On the grounds that the books unconstitutionally promoted what the judge called "the religion of secular humanism."
13. Dennis Conner.
14. Oral Roberts.
15. Vincent van Gogh.
16. He completed an around-the-world wheelchair tour to raise funds for spinal-cord research.
17. Los Angeles.
18. **c.** (Boland)
19. Southern Methodist University.
20. Cumming, Ga., near Atlanta.
21. 1. d.; 2. a.; 3. b.; 4. c.
22. Martina Navratilova.
23. Superconductors.
24. President Kurt Waldheim of Austria.
25. Senator Robert J. Dole (R., Kans.).
26. Robert H. Bork, who became the 12th Supreme Court nominee rejected outright by the Senate.
27. AIDS (acquired immune deficiency syndrome).
28. A *supernova* (exploding star) called 1987A in the Large Magellanic Cloud.
29. Secretary of Commerce Malcolm Baldrige.
30. The National Basketball Association decided to add teams in those cities.
31. To prevent frost damage.
32. **b.** (openness).
33. Sugar Ray Leonard.
34. Disconnecting the odometers on cars test-driven by Chrysler executives.
35. Texaco Incorporated.
36. Governor Evan Mecham of Arizona.
37. Prime Minister Margaret Thatcher of Great Britain.
38. "A Prairie Home Companion."
39. Ben Johnson of Canada.
40. Fiji.
41. Stock prices plummeted on the New York Stock Exchange.
42. Lebanon (Prime Minister Rashid Karami).
43. South Korea.
44. Senator Paul Simon (D., Ill.).
45. Mecca, Saudi Arabia.
46. A lieutenant colonel in the U.S. Marines, fired from the National Security Council staff in November 1986, who testified before the Iran-contra hearings in July 1987.
47. Philadelphia.
48. *Les Misérables.*
49. The Philippines and Haiti.
50. Australia (Hawke) and New Zealand (Lange).

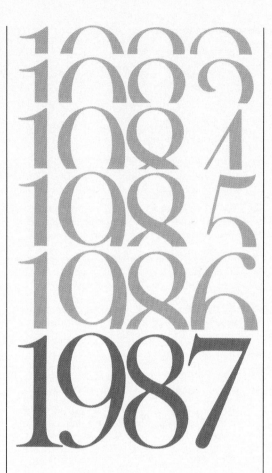

World Book Supplement

1987

To help WORLD BOOK owners keep their encyclopedias up to date, the following revised articles are reprinted from the 1988 edition of the encyclopedia.

See "Physics," page 556.

E. R. Degginger

Antarctica's rugged coast features jagged mountain peaks and glacier-filled valleys. As glaciers flow into the sea, chunks of ice break off to form icebergs like those shown above.

Antarctica

Antarctica, *ant AHRK tih kuh* or *ant AHR tih kuh,* is the ice-buried continent that covers and surrounds the South Pole. This nearly barren land forms the coldest and iciest region in the world. It is slightly colder than the region around the North Pole. The North Pole is located in the Arctic Ocean. But the South Pole lies near the center of the Antarctic continent, on a high windy plateau of ice and snow.

Antarctica covers about 5,400,000 square miles (14,000,000 square kilometers). It is larger than either Europe or Australia. But Antarctica would be the smallest continent if it did not have its icecap. This icy layer, over 2 miles (3.2 kilometers) thick, increases Antarctica's surface area and also makes it the highest continent in terms of average elevation. The average elevation of Antarctica is 7,500 feet (2,300 meters) above sea level.

Ian W. D. Dalziel, the contributor of this article, is Professor of Geological Sciences at the University of Texas, Austin. He has directed research expeditions to Antarctica and has written numerous articles about Antarctic geology.

Stormy waters of the southern Atlantic, Indian, and Pacific oceans isolate Antarctica from the other continents. Ships must steer around towering icebergs and break through huge piles of ice to reach the continent. On land, gigantic glaciers move slowly downhill toward the sea.

Temperatures in Antarctica rarely reach above 32° F. (0° C). Scientists recorded the world's lowest temperature, −128.6° F. (−89.6° C), at Vostok Station, on July 21, 1983. Strong, bitter winds also chill the air. Antarctica's inland plateau has one of the driest climates on earth. It receives no rain and hardly any new snow each year.

Only a few small plants and insects can survive in Antarctica's dry interior. But various animals thrive in the

Facts in brief

Area: About 5,400,000 sq. mi. (14,000,000 km²). *Greatest distance*—Antarctic Peninsula to Wilhelm II Coast, about 3,450 mi. (5,550 km). *Coastline*—about 19,800 mi. (31,900 km).

Elevation: *Highest*—Vinson Massif, 16,864 ft. (5,140 m) above sea level. *Lowest*—sea level.

Physical features: *Chief mountain ranges*—Antarctic Peninsula, Ellsworth, Prince Charles, Transantarctic, Whitmore. *Chief glaciers*—Amundsen, Beardmore, Lambert, Scott. *Chief ice shelves*—Amery, Filchner, Larsen, Ronne, Ross.

Interesting facts about Antarctica

The krill—a small, shrimplike animal—is a key source of food in the Antarctic region. Such animals as fish, birds, and seals feed on krill and are, in turn, eaten by larger animals. Swarms of krill form huge red masses in coastal waters during the day and glow bluish-green at night.

Antarctica's wandering pole, officially called the *south magnetic pole,* moves at least 5 miles (8 kilometers) a year. This is the south pole indicated by compass needles.

Ross Ice Shelf
1841
1600
1912
1909
1952
1980

Thick ice buries most of Antarctica. The continent's deepest ice is more than 10 times the height of the Sears Tower, the world's tallest building.

Antarctica's deepest ice
15,700 feet (4,800 meters)

Plant fossils found in Antarctica reveal that the continent once had a warm, ice-free climate with trees and other leafy plants.

First to reach the South Pole was Roald Amundsen, a Norwegian explorer. His expedition set off from Antarctica's Bay of Whales on Oct. 19, 1911, and reached the pole on Dec. 14, 1911.

Sears Tower
Chicago, Illinois
1,454 feet (443 meters)

WORLD BOOK illustrations by Paul D. Turnbaugh

surrounding waters, including fish, krill, penguins, seals, whales, and many kinds of flying birds. The continent has deposits of coal and metal ores. Geologists have found evidence that petroleum may be present in the seabed offshore. None of Antarctica's mineral resources have been developed.

Long before Antarctica was discovered, ancient Greek philosophers believed that a continent covered the southern end of the earth. Antarctica was first sighted in 1820. During the mid-1800's, explorers sailed along its coast and learned that it was large enough to be called a continent. Inland exploration began in the early 1900's. The Norwegian explorer Roald Amundsen reached the South Pole in 1911. In a dramatic race, he arrived there five weeks ahead of a British expedition led by Captain Robert F. Scott.

During the mid-1900's, U.S. Navy officer Richard Byrd commanded air expeditions that increased scientific interest in Antarctica. In 1959, 12 countries signed a treaty to use the continent mainly for research.

Today, scientists maintain year-round research stations in Antarctica. Activities on the continent encourage international cooperation and the sharing of scientific knowledge. Several countries have claimed parts of the continent in the hope of controlling mineral resources

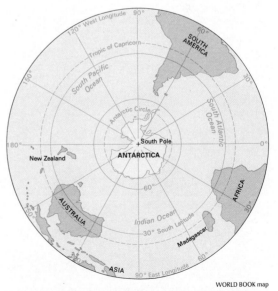

WORLD BOOK map

Antarctica is the continent that covers the South Pole. It borders the southern Atlantic, Indian, and Pacific oceans.

found there. The United States, the Soviet Union, and many other nations refuse to recognize these claims.

Land and climate

Ice and snow cover 98 per cent of the Antarctic continent. High mountain peaks and a few other bare rocky areas make up the only visible land. Underneath the ice, Antarctica has mountains, lowlands, and valleys—much like the landforms of other continents.

The southern parts of the Atlantic, Indian, and Pacific oceans meet to form a body of water often called the Antarctic Ocean or Southern Ocean. Scientists define the Antarctic Ocean's northern limit at about 55° south latitude, near the center of the Antarctic Convergence. The Antarctic Convergence is an irregular band of water about 25 miles (40 kilometers) wide. Within it, cold southern waters meet warmer, saltier northern waters.

Antarctica originally belonged to a land mass that included Africa, Australia, India, and South America. By about 140 million years ago, the land had begun to break apart. The parts gradually drifted to their present locations, and Antarctica became a separate continent.

Many millions of years ago, Antarctica was an ice-free continent. Scientists have found fossils of trees and of dinosaurs and small mammals that once lived there. Glaciers began to form in the polar regions about 30 million years ago. They slowly advanced over parts of the earth during a period known as the Ice Age. Although the Ice Age ended about 10,000 years ago, ice sheets still cover Antarctica and Greenland.

The Antarctic icecap is a thick layer of ice and snow that buries most of the continent. It formed from layers of snow pressed together over millions of years. Air between the grains of snow was pushed out or trapped in bubbles as the bottom layers hardened into ice.

Today, the Antarctic icecap forms the largest body of fresh water or ice in the world. Its volume of $7\frac{1}{4}$ million cubic miles (30 million cubic kilometers) represents about 70 per cent of the world's fresh water. If the ice melted, the earth's oceans would rise and flood coastal cities around the world.

The icecap's thickest parts are located over deep basins that dip far below sea level. In those areas, the icecap is up to 15,700 feet (4,800 meters) thick. At its highest points, over mountain ranges, the icecap rises as high as 13,500 feet (4,100 meters) above sea level.

The weight of the icecap causes the ice to spread outward and slide toward the coasts. Ice near the coasts moves as much as 490 feet (200 meters) a year. Glaciers in narrow valleys move even faster. In some areas, the icecap breaks and forms *crevasses* (cracks) more than 100 feet (30 meters) deep.

Land regions. The Transantarctic Mountains cross the entire continent. Several ranges make up the Transantarctic chain. Some peaks rise more than 14,000 feet (4,300 meters). The Transantarctic chain has the largest of the ice-free, rocky areas known as *dry valleys*. These valleys were carved by glaciers that once occupied them and later retreated. Snow that falls in dry valleys is swept away by winds. Some of the valleys have lakes.

The Transantarctic Mountains divide Antarctica into two natural land regions: (1) East Antarctica and (2) West Antarctica.

East Antarctica faces the Atlantic and Indian oceans and covers more than half the continent. The region consists of rocks that are more than 570 million years old. The rocks form what geologists call a Precambrian shield.

Mountains, valleys, and glaciers mark the coast of East Antarctica. A deep, long crack in the earth's surface known as a *rift valley* cuts into the coastline from the Indian Ocean to the Prince Charles Mountains.

The central part of East Antarctica is a plateau about 10,000 feet (3,000 meters) above sea level. Winds on the plateau blow the snow into ridges, called *sastrugi,* up to

Mount Erebus, Antarctica's most active volcano, towers above Ross Island. In the foreground, a scientist builds an igloo from blocks of snow as part of his survival training.

Ice-free areas called *dry valleys* appear where Antarctica's glaciers have retreated and wind prevents snow from collecting. About 98 per cent of the continent lies beneath ice and snow.

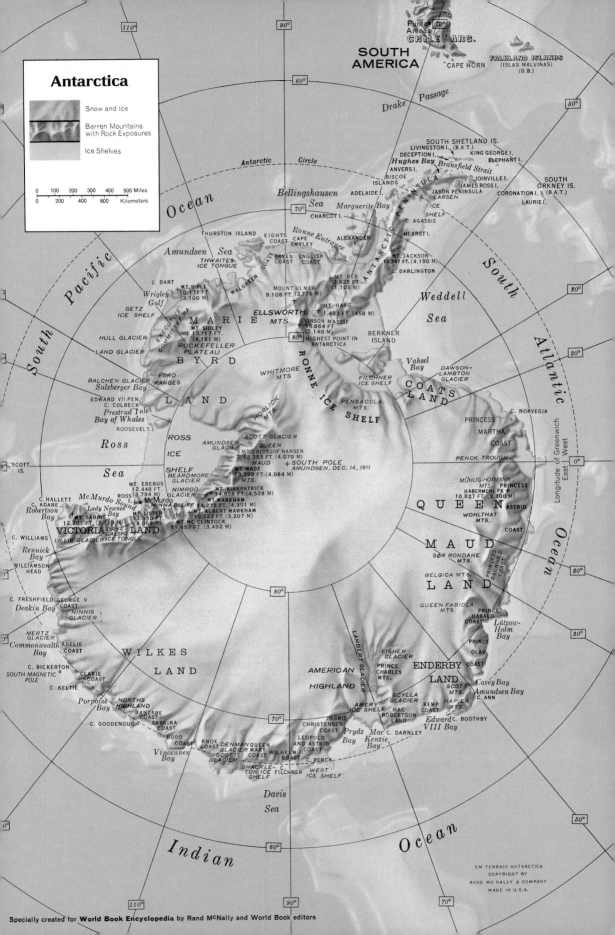

Antarctica

Snow and Ice

Barren Mountains
with Rock Exposures

Ice Shelves

| 0 | 100 | 200 | 300 | 400 | 500 Miles |
| 0 | 200 | 400 | 600 | Kilometers |

Punta Arenas
CHILE / ARG. 70°

SOUTH AMERICA

CAPE HORN

FALKLAND ISLANDS
(ISLAS MALVINAS)
(G.B.)

50°

Drake Passage

60°

SOUTH SHETLAND IS.
LIVINGSTON I. (B.A.T.)
DECEPTION I.   KING GEORGE I.
Hughes Bay   ELEPHANT I.
ANVERS I.   Bransfield Strait
BISCOE   JOINVILLE I.
ISLANDS   JAMES ROSS I.   SOUTH
ADELAIDE I.   JASON PENINSULA   ORKNEY IS.
LARSEN   CORONATION I. (B.A.T.)
CHARCOT I.   ICE   LAURIE I.
Marguerite Bay   SHELF
CHARCOT I.   C. AGASSIZ

Antarctic Circle

Bellingshausen Sea

70°

Ocean

THURSTON ISLAND
EIGHTS
COAST
CAPE
SMYLEY
Ronne Entrance
ALEXANDER I.
HEARST I.

Amundsen Sea
THWAITES
ICE TONGUE
WALGREEN COAST
BRYAN COAST
ENGLISH COAST
MT. JACKSON
13,747 FT. (4,190 M)
C. DARLINGTON

C. DART
MT. SIPLE
10,171 FT.
(3,100 M)
Wrigley Gulf
MOUNT ULMER
9,108 FT. (2,776 M)
MT. REX
3,625 FT.
(1,105 M)

Weddell Sea

30°

GETZ ICE SHELF
EXECUTIVE COMMITTEE RA
MARIE
ELLSWORTH MTS.
MT. HAAG
1,483 FT. (458 M)
VINSON MASSIF
16,864 FT.
(5,140 M)
HIGHEST POINT IN
ANTARCTICA

BERKNER ISLAND

20°

HULL GLACIER
MT. SIDLEY
13,717 FT.
(4,181 M)
LAND GLACIER
ROCKEFELLER
PLATEAU
BYRD
80°

WHITMORE MTS.
RONNE ICE SHELF
FILCHNER
ICE SHELF

Vahsel Bay
DAWSON-
LAMBTON
GLACIER

COATS LAND

C. NORVEGIA

BALCHEN GLACIER
Sulzberger Bay
FORD RANGES
LAND
HORLICK MTS.
PENSACOLA MTS.

PRINCESS MARTHA COAST

PENCK TROUGH

0°

EDWARD VII PEN.
C. COLBECK
Prestrud Inlet
Bay of Whales
ROOSEVELT I.

ROSS ICE SHELF
AMUNDSEN GLACIER
SCOTT GLACIER
QUEEN MAUD
MT. FRIDTJOF NANSEN
13,353 FT. (4,070 M)
SOUTH POLE
AMUNDSEN, DEC. 14, 1911

MÜHLIG-HOFMANN MTS.
HABERMEHL PK
10,827 FT. (3,300 M)
PRINCESS ASTRID COAST

East   West

Longitude of Greenwich

SCOTT IS.

Ross Sea

ROSS SEA
BEARDMORE GLACIER
NIMROD GLACIER
MT. WADE
13,399 FT. (4,084 M)
MT. KIRKPATRICK
14,856 FT. (4,528 M)
MT. MARKHAM
14,275 FT. (4,351 M)
ALBERT MARKHAM
10,522 FT. (3,207 M)

WOHLTHAT MTS.

QUEEN

ASTRID

20°

MT. EREBUS
12,448 FT.
ROSS (3,794 M)
I.
McMurdo
McMurdo Sound
Lady Newnes Bay
MT. SABINE
12,201 FT. (3,719 M)
MT. LISTER
13,350 FT.
(4,069 M)
MINNA BLUFF
MT. MC CLINTOCK
11,457 FT. (3,492 M)
C. HALLETT
C. ADARE
Robertson Bay

QUEEN FABIOLA MTS.
BELGICA MTS.
MAUD
SØR RONDANE MTS.
PRINCESS
RAGNHILD COAST

30°

C. WILLIAMS
Rennick Bay
WILLIAMSON HEAD
VICTORIA DRY LAND
TALOS
LILLIE GLACIER ICE TONGUE

LAND

PRINCE HARALD COAST
Lützow-Holm Bay
PRINCE OLAV COAST

C. FRESHFIELD GEORGE V COAST
Deakin Bay
NINNIS GLACIER
MERTZ GLACIER
Commonwealth Bay
ADELIE COAST
C. BICKERTON
SOUTH MAGNETIC POLE
CLARIE COAST
C. KELTIE

WILKES LAND

LAMBERT GLACIER
FISHER GLACIER
PRINCE CHARLES MTS.
SCYLLA GLACIER
MAC ROBERTSON LAND
AMERY ICE SHELF
KEMP COAST
NAPIER MTS.

AMERICAN HIGHLAND

ENDERBY LAND

Casey Bay
Amundsen Bay
C. ANN
SCOTT MTS.
Edward C. BOOTHBY
VIII Bay

Porpoise Bay
NORTHS HIGHLAND
BANZARE COAST
SABRINA COAST
C. GOODENOUGH
BUDD COAST
Vincennes Bay
KNOX COAST
DENMAN GLACIER
SCOTT GLACIER
SHACKLE-
TON ICE
SHELF
QUEEN MARY COAST
WILHELM II COAST
C. FILCHNER
C. PENCK

INGRID CHRISTENSEN COAST
LEOPOLD AND ASTRID COAST
Prydz Bay
Mac Kenzie Bay
C. DARNLEY

WEST ICE SHELF

Davis Sea

70°

Indian   80°   *Ocean*

90°

60°

CM TERRAIN ANTARCTICA
COPYRIGHT BY
RAND McNALLY & COMPANY
MADE IN U.S.A.

Specially created for **World Book Encyclopedia** by Rand McNally and World Book editors

6 feet (1.8 meters) high. The South Pole lies on the plateau, about 300 miles (480 kilometers) east of the Transantarctic Mountains. This pole, also known as the *south geographic pole,* is the southernmost point of the earth, where all lines of longitude meet.

East Antarctica also has the *south magnetic pole,* the southern point indicated by compass needles. It may move as much as 5 to 10 miles (8 to 10 kilometers) in a year. In the 1980's, it was off the coast of Wilkes Land. For a description of other south poles, see **South Pole.**

West Antarctica borders the Pacific Ocean. It contains hardly any of the old rock of East Antarctica. West Antarctica developed later as part of the Ring of Fire, a string of volcanoes encircling the Pacific Ocean. Much of the region lies below sea level. The Antarctic icecap fills deep basinlike areas of land. If the icecap melted, West Antarctica would become a group of islands.

The Antarctic Peninsula is a mountainous, S-shaped finger of land that points toward South America. In fact, the peninsula forms a continuation of the Andes Mountain chain of South America. Several islands lie near the peninsula. The South Shetland Islands to the west include Deception Island, an active volcano.

West Antarctica includes several other mountain ranges and volcanoes. Vinson Massif, the highest point in Antarctica at 16,864 feet (5,140 meters), stands in the Ellsworth Mountains near the peninsula. An ice-filled rift valley separates the Transantarctic Mountains from Ross Island. Mount Erebus, Antarctica's most active volcano, lies on the island. This majestic volcano rises 12,448 feet (3,794 meters). From time to time, it spurts pieces of volcanic rock into the air.

Coastal waters. Two large gulfs cut into Antarctica at opposite ends of the Transantarctic Mountains—the Ross Sea and the Weddell Sea. Smaller bays indent the coastline. Various channels separate offshore islands from the mainland. For example, the Bransfield Strait separates the South Shetland Islands from the mainland.

Broad, flat sheets of the icecap called *ice shelves* float in several of Antarctica's bays and channels. The Ross Ice Shelf, the largest one, measures about 2,300 feet (700 meters) thick at the inner edge and about 660 feet (200 meters) thick at the outermost edge.

In summer, the outer edges of the ice shelves break away and form immense, flat icebergs. These icebergs are larger, smoother, and more evenly shaped than icebergs in other parts of the world. Scientists have measured Antarctic icebergs with an area as huge as 5,000 square miles (13,000 square kilometers). Other icebergs form when a chunk of ice breaks off the lower end of a coastal glacier and flows into the water. This process, called *calving,* is also common in Greenland.

Each winter, the surface of the Antarctic Ocean freezes into a thin sheet of ice. In summer, this sheet breaks into pieces called *ice floes.* Winds and waves push the floes against one another, forming thick masses known as *pack ice.* Some pack ice piles up in ridges against the shore. In winter, pack ice extends as far as 1,000 miles (1,600 kilometers) from the coast.

Climate. Antarctica's climate varies from extremely cold, dry conditions on the inland plateau to milder, moister conditions along the coasts. Many people call the plateau a "polar desert." It has only about 2 inches (5 centimeters) of snowfall each year. Annual coastal rain

and snowfall averages 24 inches (61 centimeters).

The Antarctic winter lasts from May through August. Summer lasts from December through February. July temperatures range from −40° F. (−40° C) to −94° F. (−70° C) inland and from −5° F. (−15° C) to −22° F. (−30° C) on the peninsula's coast. January temperatures range from 5° F. (−15° C) to −31° F. (−35° C) inland and reach 32° F. (0° C) on the coast. Northern islands may have summer temperatures of 50° F. (10° C).

Icy winds make the Antarctic air feel even colder. Winds that sweep downward from the plateau can average 44 miles (70 kilometers) per hour. Gusts often reach the coast at 120 miles (190 kilometers) per hour.

Natural resources

Plant life. Few plants grow in Antarctica, because of the ice-covered land and the harsh climate. The most common plants are mosses and lichens. These plants cling to rocky areas, mostly on the coasts. Some survive farther inland by bunching together to conserve water. Scientists have discovered rows of black, white, and green lichens growing in tiny cracks in dry valleys.

Only two flowering plants grow in Antarctica. Both live on the northern part of the Antarctic Peninsula. One is a grass that forms dense mats on sunny slopes. The other, an herb, grows in short cushionlike bunches.

Simpler organisms known as *algae* grow on snow, in lakes, and on ice surrounding the continent. Some algae look like pink or green snow. Small plants and algae also drift on the surface of the Antarctic Ocean.

Animal life. Only a few insects and other tiny animals spend their entire lives on the Antarctic mainland. The continent's largest land animal is a wingless *midge,* a type of fly no more than $\frac{1}{2}$ inch (12 millimeters) long. Most land animals live at the edges of the continent. To avoid freezing to death, some lice, mites, and ticks cling to mosses, the fur of seals, or the feathers of birds.

Unlike the continent, the Antarctic Ocean has abundant wildlife. The most common animal of the ocean is *krill,* a small, shrimplike creature that feeds on tiny floating plants. Many other Antarctic animals depend on krill for food, and several countries catch and sell krill as a protein-rich food for people. The *squid*—a soft, boneless sea animal—also is eaten by many Antarctic animals. In addition, about 100 kinds of fish live in the ocean, including Antarctic cod, icefish, and plunderfish.

Several kinds of whales migrate to Antarctica for the summer. Those that feed on krill are blue whales, fin whales, humpback whales, minke whales, right whales, and sei whales. The blue whale is the largest animal that has ever lived. This rare giant grows up to 100 feet (30 meters) long. Antarctic whales that eat fish and squid include killer whales, southern bottlenose whales, southern fourtooth whales, and sperm whales. Killer whales also hunt seals, penguins, and smaller whales.

Various kinds of seals live in Antarctica. They spend most of their lives in the water, where they swim, dive, and catch food. Most of them nest on the coasts. The Antarctic fur seal nests on nearby islands. The largest seal in the world is the southern elephant seal, which feeds on squid. The males may reach a length of 21 feet (6.4 meters). Weddell seals and Ross seals eat fish and squid. Crabeater seals and Antarctic fur seals eat krill. Leopard seals hunt other seals as well as penguins.

Animal life in Antarctica Antarctica's coastal waters have plentiful wildlife, though only tiny animals can survive in the harsh interior. Seals and birds nest on the coast and nearby islands, and whales migrate to the area for the summer. Many of these animals have extra layers of fat to keep warm in the cold, icy climate.

WORLD BOOK illustration by Paul D. Turnbaugh

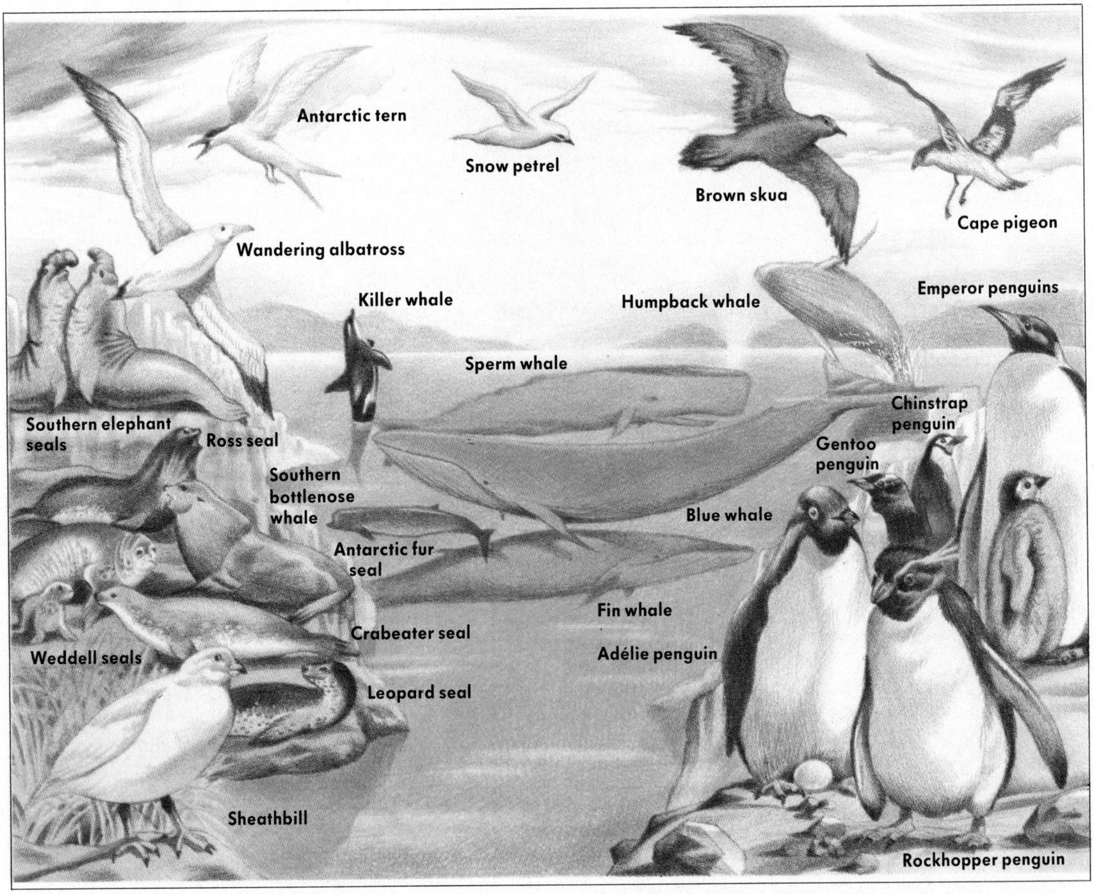

Antarctic tern

Snow petrel

Brown skua

Cape pigeon

Wandering albatross

Killer whale

Humpback whale

Emperor penguins

Sperm whale

Chinstrap penguin

Gentoo penguin

Southern elephant seals

Ross seal

Southern bottlenose whale

Blue whale

Antarctic fur seal

Fin whale

Crabeater seal

Adélie penguin

Weddell seals

Leopard seal

Sheathbill

Rockhopper penguin

During the 1800's and early 1900's, hunters greatly reduced the number of whales and Antarctic fur seals. Today, international wildlife laws prohibit or restrict the killing of these animals.

Penguins are the animals most often associated with Antarctica. These birds cannot fly, and they waddle awkwardly on land. But they are skillful swimmers. They streak through the ocean, diving for fish and other food. Four kinds of penguins breed on the continent. Playful Adélie penguins, the most common kind, build nests of pebbles on the coasts. The tall, quieter emperor penguin grows to about 4 feet (1.2 meters). After the female emperor penguin lays an egg on ice, the male rests the egg on his feet and warms it with the lower part of his belly. Chinstrap penguins and gentoo penguins nest on the Antarctic Peninsula and on islands. Others, including king penguins, macaroni penguins, and rockhopper penguins, nest only on islands north of Antarctica.

More than 40 kinds of flying birds spend the summer in Antarctica. Many types nest on land but spend most of their time diving for food. These birds include albatrosses, prions, and a large group of sea birds known as petrels. Other birds, such as cormorants, gulls, skuas, and terns, return to land more frequently. Some of them

steal food from the nests of other birds. Some land birds, such as sheathbills, nest on the peninsula. Others, including pintails and pipits, nest on islands.

Mineral resources. Geologists have found small copper deposits in the Antarctic Peninsula. East Antarctica has traces of chromium, gold, iron, lead, manganese, molybdenum, and zinc. Coal beds lie within the Transantarctic Mountains. Scientific drilling and coring operations have revealed the possibility of petroleum reserves in the Ross Sea and the Bransfield Strait.

Most of Antarctica's minerals occur in amounts too small to be mined efficiently. Icebergs, rough waves, and strong winds hamper drilling operations at sea. In addition, many scientists fear that large-scale mining would harm Antarctica's environment. However, researchers also hope to find ways to use the icecap as a source of fresh water. For example, large icebergs might someday be towed to desert lands.

Exploration

Discovery of a new continent. People wrote about a southern continent centuries before Antarctica was discovered. Ancient Greek philosophers supposed that a land mass at the earth's southern end was needed to balance the weight of the northern lands. The name Antarctica later came from two Greek words meaning *opposite the bear*. The Bear is a constellation seen from the northernmost region of the earth.

During the A.D. 100's, the Egyptian geographer Ptolemy gave this undiscovered continent the Latin name *Terra Australis Incognita* (unknown southern land). He believed the land was populated and fertile. But many people thought a region too hot for human beings surrounded the equator and blocked the way south. That idea discouraged southern exploration for many years.

In 1772, English navigator James Cook began his search for the southern continent. The British navy instructed Cook to sail as far south as possible. In January 1773, he crossed the Antarctic Circle, an imaginary line circling the earth at about 66° south latitude. A year later, Cook reached a "farthest south" position of 71° 10' south latitude. Huge ice blocks prevented him from going farther, however, and he never sighted land. The expedition sailed around the world at far southern latitudes, demonstrating that any unseen continent was limited to the vicinity of the South Pole.

Cook's voyage also revealed southern waters filled with seals and whales. During the 1800's, many hunters explored the area. In 1819, a British sealer named William Smith discovered the South Shetland Islands.

Nobody knows who first saw the Antarctic continent. Many historians divide the credit among three men who made separate voyages in 1820. In January of that year, Captain Fabian von Bellingshausen of the Russian Imperial Navy reported reaching a point only 20 miles (32 kilometers) from the Antarctic Peninsula. Some historians believe that he saw land but thought it was ice.

That same month, Captain Edward Bransfield of the British navy journeyed south of the South Shetland Islands and probably saw the Antarctic Peninsula. In November, an American sealer named Nathaniel Brown Palmer reported seeing land during a sealing expedition in the same area. Some geographers later called the peninsula Graham Land in honor of James Graham, who headed the British navy in Bransfield's time. Others called it Palmer Land. The United States and the nations of the British Commonwealth finally agreed to the term Antarctic Peninsula in 1964.

Historians also are unsure of who first set foot on Antarctica. Some believe that an American sealer named John Davis went ashore at Hughes Bay on the tip of the peninsula in 1821. But Davis did not know if he had reached the continent or an island. Whalers made the first known landing on the continent in the late 1800's.

In 1823, a British sealer named James Weddell sailed south in search of hunting waters. He reached about 74° south latitude, farther than earlier voyagers had sailed, and found what is now called the Weddell Sea.

Early exploration. More than 75 years passed before explorers proved that the South Pole is located on land. During that time, scientific interest in the Antarctic region increased.

In 1831, an English whaler named John Biscoe became the first to spot land in East Antarctica. This area lies opposite India. Biscoe named it Enderby Land after the whaling company that owned his ship.

In 1837, the king of France sent Lieutenant Jules Dumont d'Urville to claim some southern lands for France.

D'Urville's first attempt led him to discover what is now called Joinville Island, off the tip of the Antarctic Peninsula. He began his next Antarctic voyage from Tasmania, an island near Australia. In January 1840, he sighted icy cliffs rising along the East Antarctic coastline. Many small penguins dotted the pack ice that blocked his way to the land. D'Urville named both the land and the penguins after his wife, Adélie.

About the same time that d'Urville sighted land, Lieutenant Charles Wilkes of the U.S. Navy headed an expedition to perform scientific research. Wilkes's most important contribution to the study of Antarctica was his coastal exploration. His ship moved from Adélie Land toward Enderby Land, tracing more than 1,500 miles (2,400 kilometers) of coastline. This distance showed that Antarctica was large enough to be called a continent.

From 1839 to 1843, the British explorer James Clark Ross made several discoveries. Ross was the first person to go beyond the pack ice surrounding Antarctica. He sailed into the gulf that is now called the Ross Sea. Ross also discovered an island with two volcanoes, which he named after his ships, *Erebus* and *Terror*. He found the gulf barricaded by a towering sheet of ice, now known as the Ross Ice Shelf.

In 1895, a Norwegian businessman named Henryk Johan Bull made the first known landing on the Antarctic mainland. He and his whaling crew went ashore at Cape Adare, a point on the Ross Sea facing New Zealand.

The first inland exploration of Antarctica took place from 1901 to 1904. Robert Falcon Scott of the British navy led a team of explorers and scientists to the Ross Sea. In November 1902, Scott and two other men headed south across the Ross Ice Shelf. But illness, harsh weather, and lack of food forced them to rejoin the team earlier than planned. Another group moved up a glacier through the Transantarctic Mountains and reached the edge of the icy inland plateau.

Ernest Shackleton, a member of Scott's team, returned to Antarctica in 1907. Part of his expedition headed for the south magnetic pole, the southern point indicated by compass needles. They reached it in January 1909. The main group headed for the south geographic pole, the meeting point of lines of longitude. Food shortages forced the men to turn back early. However, they had arrived within 97 miles (156 kilometers) of the pole, close enough to prove that the pole was located on land rather than beneath a frozen sea.

Race to the pole. At the opposite end of the earth, Arctic explorers reached the North Pole in 1909. In June 1910, Captain Scott left London, hoping to win for Great Britain the honor of reaching the South Pole first. In October, while Scott was in Australia, he received a telegram from the Norwegian explorer Roald Amundsen. The telegram informed Scott that Amundsen, too, was going to Antarctica. Amundsen originally had hoped to be the first North Pole explorer. He switched his goal when he heard that the North Pole had been reached.

The race to the South Pole became one of the most famous events in the history of Antarctica. Amundsen and Scott never met, but both knew that they were racing for the same prize.

Amundsen and his four assistants began crossing the Ross Ice Shelf from the Bay of Whales on Oct. 19, 1911. To reach the inland plateau, they had to carve their own

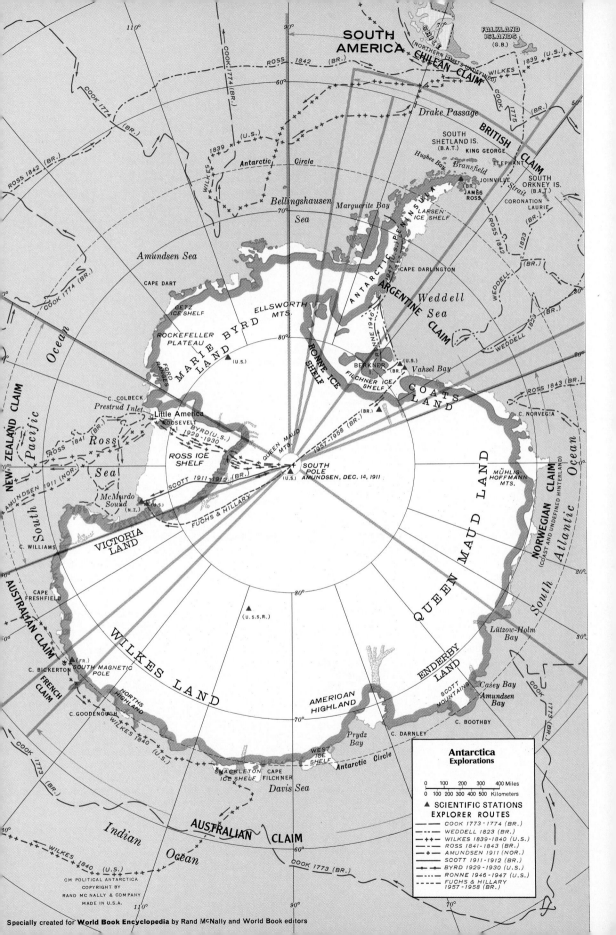

SOUTH AMERICA

FALKLAND ISLANDS (G.B.)

CHILEAN CLAIM

Drake Passage

BRITISH CLAIM

SOUTH SHETLAND IS. (B.A.T.) KING GEORGE ELEPHANT

Hughes Bay Bransfield JOINVILLE SOUTH ORKNEY IS. (B.A.T.)

Antarctic Circle

Bellingshausen Sea

Marguerite Bay

JAMES ROSS

CORONATION LAURIE

LARSEN ICE SHELF

Amundsen Sea

CAPE DART

CAPE DARLINGTON

ARGENTINE CLAIM

Weddell Sea CLAIM

GETZ ICE SHELF

ELLSWORTH MTS.

ROCKEFELLER PLATEAU

MARIE BYRD LAND

RONNE ICE SHELF

BERKNER

FILCHNER ICE SHELF

Vahsel Bay

COATS LAND

C. COLBECK

Prestrud Inlet

Little America
ROOSEVELT

ROSS ICE SHELF

BYRD (U.S.) 1929-1930

QUEEN MAUD MTS.

1957-1958 (BR.)

C. NORVEGIA

QUEEN MAUD LAND

MÜHLIG-HOFFMANN MTS.

NORWEGIAN CLAIM (COAST AND UNDEFINED HINTERLAND)

Ross Sea

SCOTT 1911-1912 (BR.)

SOUTH POLE
AMUNDSEN, DEC. 14, 1911

FUCHS & HILLARY

McMurdo Sound

VICTORIA LAND

NEW ZEALAND CLAIM

Pacific Ocean

South Pacific

C. WILLIAMS

CAPE FRESHFIELD

AUSTRALIAN CLAIM

C. BICKERTON SOUTH MAGNETIC POLE (FR.)

FRENCH CLAIM

C. GOODENOUGH

NORTHS HIGHLAND

WILKES LAND

WILKES 1840 (U.S.)

SHACKLETON ICE SHELF CAPE FILCHNER

Davis Sea

AUSTRALIAN CLAIM

Indian Ocean

WILKES 1840 (U.S.)

COOK 1773 (BR.)

Lützow-Holm Bay

ENDERBY LAND

SCOTT MOUNTAINS

Casey Bay

Amundsen Bay

C. BOOTHBY

AMERICAN HIGHLAND

C. DARNLEY

Prydz Bay

WEST ICE SHELF

Antarctic Circle

South Atlantic Ocean

CM POLITICAL ANTARCTICA
COPYRIGHT BY
RAND McNALLY & COMPANY
MADE IN U.S.A.

Antarctica
Explorations

0 100 200 300 400 Miles
0 100 200 300 400 500 Kilometers

▲ SCIENTIFIC STATIONS
EXPLORER ROUTES

COOK 1773-1774 (BR.)
WEDDELL 1823 (BR.)
WILKES 1839-1840 (U.S.)
ROSS 1841-1843 (BR.)
AMUNDSEN 1911 (NOR.)
SCOTT 1911-1912 (BR.)
BYRD 1929-1930 (U.S.)
RONNE 1946-1947 (U.S.)
FUCHS & HILLARY 1957-1958 (BR.)

COOK 1774 (BR.)

ROSS 1842 (BR.)

COOK 1774 (BR.)

WILKES 1839 (U.S.)

ROSS 1842 (BR.)

WILKES 1839 (U.S.)

COOK 1775 (BR.)

WEDDELL 1823 (BR.)

ROSS 1842 (BR.)

ROSS 1843 (BR.)

ROSS 1841 (NOR.)

AMUNDSEN 1911 (NOR.)

COOK 1774 (BR.)

COOK 1773 (BR.)

Popperfoto

Bettmann Archive

A dramatic race to the South Pole began late in 1911. Norwegian explorer Roald Amundsen, *left,* reached the pole on December 14, five weeks before British navy Captain Robert F. Scott, *above center.* Amundsen's group traveled on skis and had dogs pull their supply sleds. The men all returned safely. Scott and his men died on the way back, not long after this photograph was taken.

route along an unexplored glacier in the Queen Maud Mountains. The men journeyed on skis and wore light, warm furs. Fifty-two Eskimo dogs pulled their four sleds carrying food and supplies. Amundsen marked his route and food storage areas with mounds of snow. He shot the weakest dogs for food, when they were no longer needed to pull the sleds.

Scott set out with 15 other men on Nov. 1, 1911, from Cape Evans, Ross Island. This location was about 60 miles (97 kilometers) farther from the pole than Amundsen's starting point. However, Scott's expedition reached the plateau by way of the Beardmore Glacier, a known route. Scott used motor-powered sleds to carry some supplies. Ponies and dogs pulled other sleds. But the ponies and motor sleds bogged down in the soft snow. The men had to drag the sleds, and food soon ran low. Scott crossed the plateau accompanied by four men.

Amundsen's group arrived at the South Pole on Dec. 14, 1911. They used special navigating instruments to calculate their position. Amundsen left his tent, a Norwegian flag, and a message for Scott at the pole. The group returned to their base on Jan. 25, 1912, with only 11 dogs, but with all five men in good health.

Scott's group reached the pole on Jan. 17, 1912, greeted by Amundsen's flag. Cold, hunger, and exhaustion had severely weakened the explorers. They photographed themselves at the pole and began their return. All five men perished on the way. Two of them died after they were injured on the trail. In late March, a long blizzard forced Scott and his two remaining assistants to camp only 11 miles (18 kilometers) away from food and supplies. A search party found their frozen bodies inside the tent eight months later.

Exploration by air provided a new way to study Antarctica. In 1928, the Australian explorer Sir Hubert Wilkins surveyed the Antarctic Peninsula and nearby islands

in the first airplane voyage over Antarctic land.

In November 1929, the U.S. Navy officer Richard E. Byrd led the first flight over the South Pole. A Norwegian pilot, Bernt Balchen, flew Byrd's crew from the Bay of Whales to the pole and back. The flight lasted less than 16 hours. This journey was part of an expedition that Byrd supervised from 1928 to 1930. In a second expedition from 1933 to 1935, Byrd and his assistants traveled by plane and tractor over the Antarctic interior. They studied the icecap, the earth's magnetism, cosmic rays, weather, and geology.

In 1935, the U.S. engineer Lincoln Ellsworth and the English-born pilot Herbert Hollick-Kenyon took off from Dundee Island, north of the Antarctic Peninsula, hoping to make the first flight across the continent. Near the Weddell Sea, they discovered what are now called the Ellsworth Mountains. Their plane had to land four times because of storms and a fuel shortage. They finally completed the crossing on foot at the Bay of Whales.

In 1946 and 1947, Byrd commanded the U.S. Navy's Operation Highjump, the largest Antarctic expedition by a single country. Operation Highjump sent 4,700 men, 13 ships, and 23 airplanes and helicopters to Antarctica. The expedition members discovered new land, including 26 islands. They photographed about 1,400 miles (2,300 kilometers) of previously unexplored coastline.

That same year, Captain Finn Ronne led a private U.S. air expedition to West Antarctica. Ronne explored areas of the Weddell Sea that had never been seen. The crew included Ronne's wife, Edith, and Jennie Darlington, the wife of his chief pilot. They were the first women to spend a winter on the continent.

International cooperation. Scientific knowledge of Antarctica increased worldwide during the International Geophysical Year (IGY), a program in which scientists carried out research and shared their findings. The IGY

Exploration by air greatly expanded knowledge of Antarctica's geography. In 1929, Richard E. Byrd of the United States Navy first flew over the South Pole. Byrd later led expeditions for the U.S. government in this Fokker trimotor plane.

Granger Collection

began on July 1, 1957, and ended on Dec. 31, 1958.

During the IGY, 12 countries established more than 50 scientific stations on Antarctica and nearby islands. These countries were Argentina, Australia, Belgium, Chile, France, Great Britain, Japan, New Zealand, Norway, the Soviet Union, the Union of South Africa, and the United States. The United States set up a station at the South Pole, plus five coastal stations and one other inland station. The Soviet Union built a station at a point it named the Pole of Inaccessibility. This station lies at the point farthest from all coasts.

IGY researchers in Antarctica studied such topics as earthquakes, gravity, magnetism, oceans, and solar activity. *Meteorologists* (scientists who study weather) determined air pressure, humidity, temperature, and wind direction and prepared Antarctica's first complete weather charts. Other scientists measured the thickness of the icecap and studied the shape of the land.

During the IGY, British geologist Vivian Fuchs headed the first land crossing of the continent. The Commonwealth of Nations organized the expedition, which covered 2,158 miles (3,473 kilometers). Fuchs left on Nov. 24, 1957, from the shore of the Weddell Sea, with dogs and snow tractors. A team led by New Zealand explorer Sir Edmund Hillary placed food and supplies along the second part of the trail. Hillary met Fuchs at the South Pole in January 1958. Fuchs reached McMurdo Sound in the Ross Sea on March 2, 1958.

Antarctic claims. Seven of the 12 countries that built Antarctic bases for the IGY claim parts of Antarctica. The parts are shaped like pie slices, with the South Pole at the center. The Australian government claims two slices that face Australia. France claims a strip covering Adélie Land. Other claims come from Argentina, Chile, Great Britain, New Zealand, and Norway.

The five remaining countries, including the United States, have never claimed land in Antarctica and do not recognize Antarctic claims. However, they reserve the right to make such claims.

In 1959, officials of the 12 countries signed the Antarctic Treaty. The treaty, which took effect in 1961, is a 30-year agreement that allows people to use Antarctica only for peaceful purposes, such as exploration and scientific research. Scientists must share any knowledge that results from their studies. The treaty forbids military forces to enter Antarctica, except those assisting scientific expeditions. It also outlaws the use of nuclear weapons and the disposal of radioactive wastes in Antarctica.

Since the Antarctic Treaty took effect, several additional countries have set up scientific programs in Antarctica and have joined the treaty. Members have also added laws to protect Antarctic plants and animals. The treaty delays the settlement of Antarctic claims and forbids countries to change the size of their claims. Member countries may inspect the bases of other countries for signs of treaty violations.

Michael Parfit

McMurdo Station, a United States research base on Ross Island, has Antarctica's largest community. About 1,000 people live there during the warmer months. Great Britain, the Soviet Union, and a number of other nations also maintain research stations in Antarctica.

Antarctica today has more than 30 year-round scientific stations on the continent and nearby islands. The National Science Foundation maintains the three U.S. stations: (1) Amundsen-Scott South Pole Station, (2) McMurdo Station on Ross Island, and (3) Palmer Station on Anvers Island near the Antarctic Peninsula. Other major stations belong to Australia, Great Britain, Japan, New Zealand, the Soviet Union, and West Germany.

McMurdo Station has Antarctica's largest community. About 1,000 scientists, pilots, and other specialists live there each summer. Fewer than 200 people stay for winter. A water plant collects and desalts seawater from McMurdo Sound. Powerful ships called *icebreakers* plow through the ice and arrive with people and supplies. The station also has runways and a helicopter pad.

Summer activities in Antarctica vary. Geologists collect rock samples from the ice-free dry valleys of the Transantarctic Mountains. On the coasts and at sea, researchers observe animal behavior. Winter restricts scientists to such activities as recording weather data and studying earthquakes and solar radiation.

Some Antarctic studies concern all the continents. Significant research deals with *ozone,* a form of oxygen. Ozone is most concentrated in a layer that varies in altitude from about 14 to 19 miles. This layer protects all living things from certain harmful rays of the sun. In the mid-1980's, scientists discovered that the ozone layer above Antarctica is becoming less concentrated. Evidence pointed to manufactured compounds called *fluorocarbons* as a major cause of this "ozone hole." See **Ozone.**

Many scientists believe that research in Antarctica can answer important questions about the past, present, and future of the earth. The future of Antarctica itself may depend on whether the Antarctic Treaty is renewed when it expires in 1991. Several countries agree that the treaty serves as a model for peaceful international relations and cooperation.   Ian W. D. Dalziel

Related articles in *World Book* include:

Amundsen, Roald	Icecap
Antarctic Circle	International Geophysical
Antarctic Ocean	Year
Byrd, Richard E.	Palmer, Nathaniel B.
Cook, James	Ross, Sir James C.
Ellsworth, Lincoln	Scott, Robert F.
Enderby Land	Shackleton, Sir Ernest H.
Exploration (Polar exploration)	South Pole
Fuchs, Sir Vivian E.	Victoria Land
Glacier	Wilkes, Charles
Iceberg	Wilkins, Sir Hubert

Outline

I. Land and climate
   A. The Antarctic icecap   C. Coastal waters
   B. Land regions   D. Climate
II. Natural resources
   A. Plant life   C. Mineral resources
   B. Animal life
III. Exploration
   A. Discovery of a new   D. Exploration by air
      continent   E. International cooperation
   B. Early exploration   F. Antarctic claims
   C. Race to the pole   G. Antarctica today

Questions

What is the largest land animal in Antarctica?
Who was the first explorer to reach the South Pole? When did he reach it?
What are the two natural land regions of the continent?
How did the Antarctic icecap form?
What are the most common plants in Antarctica?
What is the Antarctic Treaty?
How does Antarctica compare in size with the other continents?
What are ice shelves?
How does the climate of inland Antarctica differ from that of the coasts?
What are some of Antarctica's mineral resources?

Additional resources

Hosking, Eric J. *Antarctic Wildlife.* Facts on File, 1982.
Parfit, Michael. *South Light: A Journey to the Last Continent.* Macmillan, 1985.
Reader's Digest Editors. *Antarctica: Great Stories from the Frozen Continent.* Reader's Digest Services, 1985.
Shapley, Deborah. *The Seventh Continent: Antarctica in a Resource Age.* Resources for the Future, 1985.

Michael Parfit

A researcher at the South Pole checks data gathered by a telescope. Antarctica's unpolluted atmosphere enables scientists to obtain an especially clear view of the sky. The dome of the Amundsen-Scott South Pole Station appears in the background.

© Alvis Upitis, The Image Bank

© Steve Dunwell, The Image Bank

© Alvis Upitis, The Image Bank

A mathematician teaching problem solving　　**Engineers designing machinery**　　**A bank teller directing funds**

The uses of mathematics are wide-ranging. For example, mathematics may be used to solve scientific problems, design industrial projects, and carry out business transactions.

Mathematics

Mathematics is one of the most useful and fascinating divisions of human knowledge. It includes many topics of study. For this reason, the term *mathematics* is difficult to define. It comes from a Greek word meaning "inclined to learn."

Most of the basic mathematics taught in school involves the study of number, quantity, form, and relations. *Arithmetic,* for example, concerns problems with numbers. *Algebra* involves solving *equations* (mathematical statements of equality) in which letters represent unknown quantities. *Geometry* concerns the properties and relationships of figures in space.

The most important skills in mathematics are careful analysis and clear reasoning. These skills can help us solve some of the deepest puzzles we must face. Mathematics is based upon logic. Starting from widely accepted statements, mathematicians use logic to draw conclusions and develop mathematical systems.

The importance of mathematics

The work of mathematicians may be divided into *pure mathematics* and *applied mathematics.* Pure mathematics seeks to advance mathematical knowledge for its own sake rather than for any immediate practical use. For example, a mathematician may create a system of geometry for an imaginary world where objects have more dimensions than just length, width, and depth. Applied mathematics seeks to develop mathematical techniques for use in science and other fields.

Joseph W. Dauben, the contributor of this article, is Professor of History and History of Science at Herbert H. Lehman College and the Graduate Center of the City University of New York. He is the author of The History of Mathematics from Antiquity to the Present. *The drawings in this article were prepared for* World Book *by Zorica Dabich.*

The boundary between pure and applied mathematics is not always clear. Ideas developed in pure mathematics often have practical applications, and work in applied mathematics frequently leads to research in pure mathematics.

Nearly every part of our lives involves mathematics. It has played an essential role in the development of modern *technology*—the tools, materials, techniques, and sources of power that make our lives and work easier.

In everyday life, we use mathematics for such simple tasks as telling time from a clock or counting our change after making a purchase. We also use mathematics for such complex tasks as making up a household budget or figuring our income tax. Cooking, driving, gardening, sewing, and many other common activities involve mathematical calculations. Mathematics is also part of many games, hobbies, and sports.

In science. Mathematics is an essential part of nearly all scientific study. It helps scientists design experiments and analyze data. Scientists use mathematical formulas to express their findings precisely and to make predictions based on these findings.

The physical sciences, such as astronomy, chemistry, and physics, rely heavily on mathematics. Such social sciences as economics, psychology, and sociology also depend greatly on statistics and other kinds of mathematics. For example, some economists create mathematical models of economic systems. These models are sets of formulas used to predict how a change in one part of the economy might affect other parts.

In industry. Mathematics helps industries design, develop, and test products and manufacturing processes. Mathematics is necessary in designing bridges, buildings, dams, highways, tunnels, and other architectural and engineering projects.

In business, mathematics is used in transactions that involve buying and selling. Businesses need mathematics to keep records of such things as inventory and employees' hours and wages. Bankers use mathematics to handle and invest funds. Mathematics helps insurance companies calculate risks and compute the rates charged for insurance coverage.

Branches of mathematics

Mathematics has many branches. They may differ in the types of problems involved and in the practical application of their results. However, mathematicians working in different branches often use many of the same basic concepts and operations. This section discusses several of the main kinds of mathematics.

Arithmetic includes the study of whole numbers, fractions and decimals, and the operations of addition, subtraction, multiplication, and division. It forms the foundation for other kinds of mathematics by providing such basic skills as counting and grouping objects, and measuring and comparing quantities. See **Addition; Arithmetic; Division; Multiplication; Subtraction.**

Algebra, unlike arithmetic, is not limited to work with specific numbers. Algebra involves solving problems with equations in which letters, such as x and y, stand for unknown quantities. Algebraic operations also use negative numbers and *imaginary numbers* (the square roots of negative numbers). See **Algebra; Square root** (Square roots of negative numbers).

Geometry is concerned with the properties and relationships of figures in space. *Plane geometry* deals with squares, circles, and other figures that lie on a plane. *Solid geometry* involves such figures as cubes and spheres, which have three dimensions.

About 300 B.C., Euclid, a Greek mathematician, stated the definitions and assumptions of the system of geometry that describes the world as we usually experience it. But later mathematicians developed alternative systems of geometry that rejected Euclid's assumption about the nature of parallel lines. Such *non-Euclidean geometries* have proven useful, for example, in the theory of relativity—one of the outstanding achievements of scientific thought. See **Geometry.**

Analytic geometry and trigonometry. Analytic geometry relates algebra and geometry. It provides a way to represent an algebraic equation as a line or curve on a graph. It also makes it possible to write equations that exactly describe many curves. For example, the equation $x = y^2$ describes a curve called a *parabola.*

Trigonometry is used widely by astronomers, navigators, and surveyors to calculate angles and distances when direct measurement is impossible. It deals with the relations between the sides and angles of triangles, especially *right triangles* (triangles that have a 90° angle). Certain relations between the lengths of two sides of a right triangle are called *trigonometric ratios.* Using trigonometric ratios, a person can calculate the unknown angles and lengths in a triangle from the known angles and lengths. Formulas involving trigonometric ratios describe curves that physicists and engineers use to analyze the behavior of heat, light, sound, and other natural phenomena. See **Trigonometry.**

Calculus and analysis have many practical uses in engineering, physics, and other sciences. Calculus provides a way of solving many problems that involve motion or changing quantities. *Differential calculus* seeks to determine the rate at which a varying quantity changes. It is used to calculate the slope of a curve and the changing speed of a bullet. *Integral calculus* tries to

find a quantity when the rate at which it is changing is known. It is used to calculate the area of a curved figure or the amount of work done by a varying force. Unlike algebra, calculus includes operations with *infinitesimals* (quantities that are not zero but are smaller than any assignable quantity). See **Calculus.**

Analysis involves various mathematical operations with infinite quantities and infinitesimals. It includes the study of *infinite series,* sequences of numbers or algebraic expressions that go on indefinitely. The concept of infinite series has important applications in such areas as the study of heat and of vibrating strings. See **Series** (Working with infinite series).

Probability and statistics. Probability is the mathematical study of the likelihood of events. It is used to determine the chances that an uncertain event may occur. For example, using probability, a person can calculate the chances that three tossed coins will all turn up heads. See **Probability.**

Statistics is the branch of mathematics concerned with the collection and analysis of large bodies of data to identify trends and overall patterns. Statistics relies heavily on probability. Statistical methods provide information to government, business, and science. For example, physicists use statistics to study the behavior of the many molecules in a sample of gas. See **Statistics.**

Set theory and logic. Set theory deals with the nature and relations of *sets.* A set is a collection of items, which may be numbers, ideas, or objects. The study of sets is important in investigating most basic mathematical concepts. See **Set theory.**

In the field of logic—the branch of philosophy that deals with the rules of correct reasoning—mathematicians have developed *symbolic logic.* Symbolic logic is a formal system of reasoning that uses mathematical symbols and methods. Mathematicians have devised various systems of symbolic logic that have been important in the development of computers.

History

Early civilization. Prehistoric people probably first counted with their fingers. They also had various methods for recording such quantities as the number of animals in a herd or the days since the full moon. To represent such amounts, they used a corresponding number of pebbles, knots in a cord, or marks on wood, bone, or stone. They also learned to use regular shapes when they molded pottery or carved arrowheads.

By about 3000 B.C., mathematicians of ancient Egypt used a *decimal system* (a system of counting in groups of 10) without place values. The Egyptians pioneered in geometry, developing formulas for finding the area and volume of simple figures. Egyptian mathematics had many practical applications, ranging from surveying fields after the annual floods to making the intricate calculations necessary to build the pyramids.

By 2100 B.C., the people of ancient Babylonia had developed a *sexagesimal system*—a system based on groups of 60. Today, we use such a system to measure time in hours, minutes, and seconds. Historians do not know exactly how the Babylonian system developed. They think it may have arisen from the use of weights and measures based on groups of 60. The system had

(Text continued on page 553)

Solving problems for fun

The following problems all require the use of important mathematical skills, including careful analysis of situations and reasoning to reach solutions. Try to solve the problems and then compare your work with the solutions provided.

1. *Which salary would you choose?* Your boss offers you one of two salary arrangements. "Which would you prefer," she asks, "a salary starting at $16,000 a year with an $800 increase each year, or one starting at $8,000 for a half year with a $200 increase each half year?" Which choice offers the higher salary?

Make a chart to show the two choices of salary over a number of years.

Year	Choice 1	Choice 2
First year	$16,000	$8,000 + $8,200 = $16,200
Second year	$16,800	$8,400 + $8,600 = $17,000
Third year	$17,600	$8,800 + $9,000 = $17,800
Fourth year	$18,400	$9,200 + $9,400 = $18,600

Choice 2 gives you $200 more each year than choice 1 does.

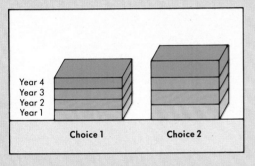

3. *A little pile of paper.* Imagine that you have a huge sheet of paper only $\frac{1}{1,000}$ inch (0.025 millimeter) thick. You cut the sheet in half and put one piece of paper on top of the other.

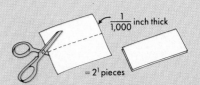

$\frac{1}{1,000}$ inch thick

$= 2^1$ pieces

You cut these two pieces in half and put the resulting four pieces together in a pile. Then you cut the pile of four pieces in half and put the resulting eight pieces in a pile. Suppose that you continue in this manner until you have cut the pile in half 50 times, each time piling up the resulting pieces. How high do you think the final pile would be?

2 × 2

$= 2^2$ pieces

After the first cut, you have 2 pieces. After the second cut, you have 2 × 2, or 2^2 pieces. Following the third cut, you have 2 × 2 × 2, or 2^3 pieces. Therefore, after the 50th cut, you should have 2^{50} pieces. Two multiplied by itself 50 times is about 1,126,000,000,000,000. Because there are 1,000 pieces of paper to the inch, divide by 1,000 to find the number of inches in the pile. Next, divide the number of inches by 12 to find the number of feet in the pile. Then divide the number of feet by 5,280 to find the number of miles. You may be surprised to find that the pile of paper is about 17,770,000 miles (28,600,000 kilometers) high!

2. *Find the counterfeit.* You have nine rare and valuable coins. Although they appear to be identical, you know that one is counterfeit and weighs less than the others. Using a balance scale only twice, how can you find the fake coin?

First, divide the coins into three groups of three coins.

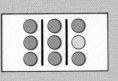

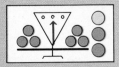

Weigh one group against another. If they balance, then the fake, or light, coin is in the group you have not weighed.

If the two groups of coins do not balance, then the fake coin is in the lighter group on the scale.

Next, take the group of three coins that contains the fake.

Weigh two coins from this group against each other. If they balance, then the coin you have not weighed is the fake.

If the two coins do not balance, then the lighter coin on the scale is the counterfeit.

4. *Where to start?* From what point or points on the earth's surface could you walk 12 miles (19 kilometers) due south, then walk 12 miles due east, then walk 12 miles due north, and find yourself back at your starting point?

The usual answer to this old riddle is the North Pole. But the earth actually has an infinite number of points from which you could begin such a walk.

In theory, the equator forms a circle of latitude around the middle of the earth. As one goes north or south from the equator, the circumference of the circles of latitude gets progressively smaller until you reach the poles. Near the South Pole, there is a circle of latitude exactly 12 miles in circumference. Twelve miles north of this first circle is a second circle of latitude. You can start your walk at any point on this outer circle. You walk 12 miles south and find yourself on the inner circle. Then you walk 12 miles east around this circle—that is, you walk once around the earth, which is only 12 miles in circumference at this latitude. You then walk 12 miles north and arrive back at your starting point.

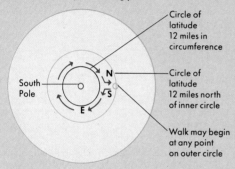

Circle of latitude 12 miles in circumference

South Pole

Circle of latitude 12 miles north of inner circle

Walk may begin at any point on outer circle

An infinite number of other points also can serve as your starting place. There are circles of latitude closer to the South Pole that have a circumference of 6 miles, 3 miles, 2 miles, and so forth. By starting at any point 12 miles north of any of these circles, you could take the walk described. Suppose, for example, you start 12 miles north of the circle of latitude that has a circumference of 1 mile. First you walk 12 miles south. Then you walk 12 miles east—that is, you go around the inner circle 12 times. Then, after walking north for 12 miles, you will arrive at your starting point on the outer circle.

5. *Whose turn to win?* Your friend Rachel challenges you to a game. There are six marbles in a bowl. At a turn, a player may take either one or two marbles. The player who takes the last marble wins the game. Rachel offers to let you take the first turn. If you accept, who wins?

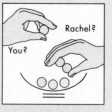

Rachel?

You?

Assume that each player will always make the best move. The winner will take the winning turn when either one or two marbles are left. Therefore, the winner will be the player who leaves the opponent three marbles. If you make the first move and take one marble, Rachel can take two—leaving three for you and winning on her next turn. If, on the first move, you take two marbles, then Rachel can take one—again leaving three for you and winning on her next move. If you accept her kind offer to take the first turn, Rachel will win the game!

6. *The well-dressed doctors.* Doctors Black, Brown, Gray, Green, and White are seated around a circular table, discussing golf. Each doctor wears a suit of a color that corresponds to the name of one of the other doctors. Each suit is of a different color. Based on the following clues, what is the name of the doctor wearing the black suit? (1) The doctor in the black suit sits two places to the left of Dr. Gray. (2) The doctor in the green suit is two places to Dr. Green's right. (3) The doctor in the brown suit sits on Dr. Brown's left. (4) Dr. Black sits to the right of the doctor wearing the white suit.

Draw a circle and label the seating positions A, B, C, D, and E, moving clockwise around the circle. Assign Dr. Gray to position A. It will also help to set up a chart to show the information in the clues. The information provided by clue 1 is shown in the chart below.

Position	Name	Suit color
A	Gray.	Not gray. Not black.
B	Not Gray.	Not black.
C	Not Gray. Not Black.	Black.
D	Not Gray.	Not black.
E	Not Gray.	Not black.

Based on clue 2, you can conclude that the doctor in green does not sit two places to Dr. Gray's right, at position D. In addition, Dr. Green does not occupy position E, because the doctor in black, not green, sits two seats to the right, at position C. Reasoning in this manner, fill in the chart with the information provided by clues 2, 3, and 4.

The completed chart should indicate that the doctor at B cannot be Drs. Gray, Black, or Brown. If you assume that Dr. Green is at B, he or she must wear gray. Then, according to clue 2, the doctor at E wears green and

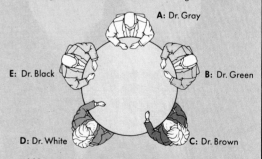

A: Dr. Gray

E: Dr. Black

B: Dr. Green

D: Dr. White

C: Dr. Brown

could be Dr. White or Dr. Black. If Dr. Black is at E, then, according to clue 4, Dr. Gray wears white. This leaves the brown suit for the doctor at D. Then, according to clue 3, Dr. Brown occupies C. This leaves only Dr. White, who must occupy D. Therefore, the doctor in the black suit is Dr. Brown.

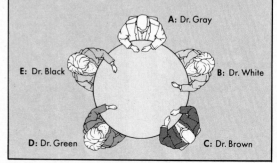

A: Dr. Gray

E: Dr. Black

B: Dr. White

D: Dr. Green

C: Dr. Brown

important uses in astronomy, and also in commerce, because 60 can be divided easily. The Babylonians went well beyond the Egyptians in algebra and geometry.

The Greeks and Romans. Ancient Greek scholars became the first people to explore pure mathematics, apart from practical problems. They made important advances by introducing the concepts of logical deduction and proof in order to create a systematic theory of mathematics. According to tradition, one of the first to provide mathematical proofs based on deduction was the philosopher Thales, who did his work in geometry about 600 B.C.

The Greek philosopher Pythagoras, who lived about 550 B.C., explored the nature of numbers, believing that everything could be understood in terms of whole numbers or their ratios. However, about 400 B.C., the Greeks discovered *irrational numbers* (numbers that cannot be expressed as a ratio of two whole numbers), and they recognized that Pythagorean ideas were incomplete. About 370 B.C., Eudoxus of Cnidus, a Greek astronomer, formulated a theory of proportions to resolve problems associated with irrational numbers. He also developed the *method of exhaustion,* a way of determining areas of curved figures, which foreshadowed integral calculus.

Euclid, one of the foremost Greek mathematicians, wrote the *Elements* about 300 B.C. In this book, Euclid constructs an entire system of geometry by means of abstract definitions and logical deductions. During the 200's B.C., the Greek mathematician Archimedes extended the method of exhaustion. Using a 96-sided figure to approximate a circle, he calculated a highly accurate value for *pi* (the ratio of a circle's circumference to its diameter). About A.D. 150, the Greek astronomer Ptolemy applied geometry and trigonometry to astronomy in a 13-part work on the motions of the planets. It became known as the *Almagest,* meaning *the greatest.*

The Romans showed little interest in pure mathematics. However, they applied mathematical principles in such fields as commerce, engineering, and warfare.

Arab mathematics. Scholars in the Arab world translated and preserved the works of ancient Greek mathematicians and made their own original contributions as well. A book written about 825 by the Arab mathematician al-Khowarizmi described a numeration system developed in India. This decimal system, which used place values and zero, became known as the Hindu-Arabic numeral system. Al-Khowarizmi also wrote an influential book about algebra. The word *algebra* comes from the Arabic title of this book.

In the mid-1100's, a Latin translation of al-Khowarizmi's book on arithmetic introduced the Hindu-Arabic numeral system to Europe. In 1202, Leonardo Fibonacci, an Italian mathematician, published a book on algebra that helped promote this system. Hindu-Arabic numerals gradually replaced Roman numerals in Europe.

Arab astronomers of the 900's made major contributions to trigonometry. During the 1000's, an Arab physicist known as Alhazen applied geometry to optics. The Persian poet and astronomer Omar Khayyam wrote an important book on algebra about 1100. In the 1200's, Nasir Eddin al-Tusi, a Persian mathematician, created ingenious mathematical models for use in astronomy.

The Renaissance. During the 1400's and 1500's, European explorers sought new overseas trade routes,

Important dates in mathematics

c. 3000 B.C. The Egyptians used a system based on groups of 10 and developed basic geometry and surveying techniques.
c. 370 B.C. Eudoxus of Cnidus developed the method of exhaustion, foreshadowing integral calculus.
c. 300 B.C. Euclid constructed a system of geometry by means of logical deduction.
Mid-1100's A translation of al-Khowarizmi's book on arithmetic introduced the Hindu-Arabic numeral system to Europe.
1614 John Napier published his discovery of logarithms, an aid in simplifying calculations.
1637 René Descartes published his discovery of analytic geometry, proposing mathematics as the perfect model for reasoning.
Mid-1680's Sir Isaac Newton and Gottfried Wilhelm Leibniz published their independent discoveries of calculus.
Early 1800's Karl F. Gauss, Janos Bolyai, and Nikolai Lobachevsky separately developed non-Euclidean geometries.
Early 1820's Charles Babbage began to develop mechanical computing machines.
1854 George Boole published his system of symbolic logic.
Late 1800's Georg Cantor developed set theory and a mathematical theory of the infinite.
1910-1913 Alfred North Whitehead and Bertrand Russell published *Principia Mathematica,* which argues that all mathematical propositions can be derived from a few axioms.
Early 1930's Kurt Gödel showed that in any system of axioms, there are statements that cannot be proven.
Late 1950's and 1960's New mathematics was introduced in classrooms in the United States.
1970's and 1980's Computer-based mathematical models came into wide use in studies in business, industry, and science.

stimulating the application of mathematics to navigation and commerce. Mathematics also played a part in artistic creativity. Renaissance artists applied principles of geometry and created a system of linear perspective that gave their paintings an illusion of depth and distance. The invention of printing with movable type in the mid-1400's resulted in speedy and widespread communication of mathematical knowledge.

The Renaissance also brought major advances in pure mathematics. In a book published in 1533, a German mathematician known as Regiomontanus established trigonometry as a field separate from astronomy. French mathematician François Viète made advances in algebra in a book published in 1591.

Mathematics and the scientific revolution. By 1600, the increased use of mathematics and the growth of the experimental method were contributing to revolutionary advances in knowledge. In 1543, Nicolaus Copernicus, a Polish astronomer, published an influential book in which he argued that the sun, not the earth, is the center of the universe. His book sparked intense interest in mathematics and its applications, especially to the study of the motions of the earth and other heavenly bodies. In 1614, John Napier, a Scottish mathematician, published his discovery of *logarithms,* numbers that can be used to simplify such complicated calculations as those used in astronomy. Galileo, an Italian astronomer of the late 1500's and early 1600's, found that many types of motion can be analyzed mathematically.

In a book published in 1637, French philosopher René Descartes proposed mathematics as the perfect model for reasoning. His invention of analytic geometry illustrated the exactness and certainty that mathematics can provide. Another French mathematician of the 1600's, Pierre de Fermat, founded modern number theory. He and French philosopher Blaise Pascal explored probability theory. Fermat's work with infinitesimals helped lay a foundation for calculus.

The English scientist Sir Isaac Newton invented calculus in the mid-1660's. He first mentioned his discovery in a book published in 1687. Working independently, the German philosopher and mathematician Gottfried Wilhelm Leibniz also invented calculus in the mid-1670's. He published his findings in 1684 and 1686.

Developments in the 1700's. A remarkable family of Swiss mathematicians, the Bernoullis, made many contributions to mathematics during the late 1600's and the 1700's. Jakob Bernoulli did pioneering work in analytic geometry and wrote about probability theory. Jakob's brother Johann also worked in analytic geometry and in mathematical astronomy and physics. Johann's son Nicolaus helped advance probability theory. Johann's son Daniel used mathematics to study the motion of fluids and the properties of vibrating strings.

During the mid-1700's, Swiss mathematician Leonhard Euler advanced calculus by showing that the operations of differentiation and integration were opposites. Beginning in the late 1700's, French mathematician Joseph L. Lagrange worked to develop a firmer foundation for calculus. He was suspicious of relying on assumptions from geometry and, instead, developed calculus entirely in terms of algebra.

In the 1800's, public education expanded rapidly, and mathematics became a standard part of university education. Many of the great works in mathematics of the 1800's were written as textbooks. In the 1790's and early 1800's, French mathematician Adrien Marie Legendre wrote particularly influential textbooks and did work in calculus, geometry, and number theory. Important calculus textbooks by French mathematician Augustin Louis Cauchy were published in the 1820's. Cauchy and Jean Baptiste Fourier, another French mathematician, made significant advances in mathematical physics.

Karl Friedrich Gauss, a German mathematician, proved the fundamental theorem of algebra, which states that every equation has at least one root. His work with imaginary numbers led to their increased acceptance. In the 1810's, Gauss developed a non-Euclidean geometry but did not publish his discovery. Working separately, Janos Bolyai of Hungary and Nikolai Lobachevsky of Russia also developed non-Euclidean geometries. They published their discoveries about 1830. In the mid-1800's, Georg Friedrich Riemann of Germany developed another non-Euclidean geometry.

During the early 1800's, the works of German mathematician August Ferdinand Möbius helped develop a study in geometry that became known as *topology.* Topology explores the properties of a geometrical figure that do not change when the figure is bent or stretched. See **Topology.**

In the late 1800's, German mathematician Karl Theodor Weierstrass worked to establish a more solid theoretical foundation for calculus. In the 1870's and 1880's, his student Georg Cantor developed set theory and a mathematical theory of the infinite.

Much exciting work in applied mathematics was performed in the 1800's. In Great Britain, Charles Babbage developed early mechanical computing machines, and George Boole created a system of symbolic logic. During the late 1800's, French mathematician Jules Henri Poincaré contributed to probability theory, celestial mechanics, and the study of electromagnetic waves.

Philosophies of mathematics in the 1900's. Many mathematicians of the 1900's have shown concern for the philosophical foundations of mathematics. In order to eliminate contradictions, some mathematicians have used logic to develop mathematics from a set of *axioms* (basic statements considered to be true). Two British philosophers and mathematicians, Alfred North Whitehead and Bertrand Russell, promoted a philosophy of mathematics called *logicism.* In their three-volume work, *Principia Mathematica* (1910-1913), they argued that all *propositions* (statements) in mathematics can be derived logically from just a few axioms.

David Hilbert, a German mathematician of the early 1900's, was a *formalist.* Formalists consider mathematics to be a purely formal system of rules. Hilbert's work led to the study of imaginary spaces with an infinite number of dimensions.

Beginning in the early 1900's, Dutch mathematician Luitzen Brouwer championed *intuitionism.* He believed people understand the laws of mathematics by *intuition* (knowledge not gained by reasoning or experience).

In the early 1930's, Austrian mathematician Kurt Gödel demonstrated that for any logical system, there are always theorems that cannot be proven either true or false by the axioms within that system. He found this to be true even of basic arithmetic.

Mathematicians have made major advances in the study of abstract mathematical structures during the 1900's. One such structure is the *group.* A group is a collection of items, which may be numbers, and rules for some operation with these items, such as addition or multiplication. Group theory is useful in many areas of mathematics and such fields as subatomic physics.

Since 1939, a group of mathematicians, most of whom are French, have published an influential series of books under the pen name Nicolas Bourbaki. This series takes an abstract approach to mathematics, using axiom systems and set theory.

New areas of mathematical specialization have arisen during the 1900's, including systems analysis and computer science. Advances in mathematical logic have been essential to the development of electronic computers. Computers, in turn, enable mathematicians to complete long and complicated calculations quickly. Since the 1970's, computer-based mathematical models have become widely used to study weather patterns, economic relationships, and many other systems.

Trends in teaching mathematics. Before the 1950's, most mathematics courses in elementary, junior high, and high schools in the United States stressed the development of basic computational skills. During the late 1950's and the 1960's, *new mathematics* was introduced. New mathematics is a way of teaching mathematics that stresses understanding concepts rather than memorizing rules and performing repetitious drills. In the 1970's and 1980's, educators continued to use new mathematics, but they gave added emphasis to problem solving and computational skills.

At the college level, educators have moved away from teaching mathematics in the same way to all students. Instead, colleges and universities offer more courses in specialized applications of mathematics in such fields as economics, engineering, and physics.

Careers

A strong background in mathematics is excellent preparation for a wide variety of careers in business, education, government, and industry. Students who wish to study mathematics in college should take high school courses in algebra, geometry, trigonometry, and calculus, if available. These courses also are useful preparation for study in architecture, engineering, and physics.

In college, the basic courses for a major in mathematics include advanced calculus, differential equations, abstract algebra, numerical analysis, number theory, theories of real and complex variables, probability, and statistics. Courses in logic and computer programming also are useful in preparing for many careers.

Mathematicians teach at all levels. High school mathematics teachers must have at least a bachelor's degree in mathematics. Many mathematicians with a doctor's degree teach at colleges and universities.

Large numbers of mathematicians work in business or industry. Those with a bachelor's degree may find work as accountants, computer operators, and statisticians. Many people who have earned a master's or doctor's degree in mathematics conduct research for the communications, energy, manufacturing, or transportation industries. Some mathematicians serve as consultants who apply their training to industrial problems. Mathematicians also work in the computer industry as programmers or as systems analysts who determine the most efficient use of a computer in any given situation. Insurance companies employ mathematicians as actuaries to calculate risks and help design policies.

Mathematicians also work for government agencies. They analyze census data, gather information about the economy, plan space flights, analyze military needs, and perform other services.   Joseph W. Dauben

Related articles in *World Book* include:

American mathematicians

Banneker, Benjamin	Rittenhouse, David
Bowditch, Nathaniel	Steinmetz, Charles P.
Gibbs, Josiah W.	Von Neumann, John
Peirce, Charles S.	Wiener, Norbert

British mathematicians

Babbage, Charles	Russell, Bertrand
Napier, John	Turing, Alan M.
Newton, Sir Isaac	Whitehead, Alfred North

French mathematicians

Châtelet, Marquise du	Laplace, Marquis de
Descartes, René	Legendre, Adrien M.
Fermat, Pierre de	Pascal, Blaise
Lagrange, Joseph L.	Poincaré, Jules H.

German mathematicians

Bessel, Friedrich	Kepler, Johannes
Clausius, Rudolf J. E.	Leibniz, Gottfried W.
Gauss, Karl F.	

Other mathematicians

Archimedes	Fibonacci, Leonardo	Pythagoras
Bernoulli (family)	Huygens, Christian	Thales
Eratosthenes	Omar Khayyam	Torricelli, Evangelista
Euclid	Ptolemy	
Euler, Leonhard		

Applied mathematics

Accounting	Engineering	Mechanical drawing
Bookkeeping	Insurance	Navigation
Budget	Interest	Surveying
Discount	Map	Weights and measures
Econometrics	Measurement	

Branches of mathematics

Algebra	Geometry	Topology
Arithmetic	Probability	Trigonometry
Calculus	Statistics	

Mathematical machines and devices

Abacus	Calculator	Slide rule
Adding machine	Computer	Vernier

Other related articles

Algorithm	New mathematics	Progression
Chisanbop	Number and numeral	Series
Determinant		Set theory
Game theory	Number theory	Square root
Infinity	Numeration systems	Systems analysis
Integer	Permutations and combinations	
Maya (Communication and learning)		

Outline

I. **The importance of mathematics**
  A. In everyday life   C. In industry
  B. In science   D. In business
II. **Branches of mathematics**
  A. Arithmetic   E. Calculus and analysis
  B. Algebra   F. Probability and statistics
  C. Geometry   G. Set theory and logic
  D. Analytic geometry and trigonometry
III. **History**
IV. **Careers**

Questions

What type of system do we use when measuring time in hours, minutes, and seconds?
Which two men independently invented calculus?
What did Euclid accomplish in his book the *Elements*?
How does analytic geometry relate algebra to geometry?
Which branch of mathematics got its name from the title of a book by al-Khowarizmi?
How does *pure mathematics* differ from *applied mathematics*?
What do mathematicians do as consultants to companies?
How were Hindu-Arabic numerals introduced to Europe?
How does trigonometry help astronomers, navigators, and surveyors?
Which branch of mathematics would you use to calculate the chances that three tossed coins will all turn up heads?

Additional resources

Level I
Burns, Marilyn. *Math for Smarty Pants*. Little, Brown, 1982. Includes trivia, puzzles, and problems for both math haters and math lovers.
Srivastava, Jane J. *Number Families*. T. Y. Crowell, 1979.
Stenmark, Jean K., and others. *Family Math*. Regents of Univ. of California, 1986.

Level II
Buxton, Laurie. *Mathematics for Everyone*. Schocken, 1984.
Kline, Morris. *Mathematics and the Search for Knowledge*. Oxford, 1985.
Richards, Stephen P. *A Number for Your Thoughts: Facts and Speculations About Numbers from Euclid to the Latest Computers*. S. P. Richards, 1982.

Scanning the tracks of subatomic particles

Fermilab

Boeing Aerospace Company

Studying atomic structure to find new superconductors

Sandia National Laboratories

Developing protective coatings for metals

Research in physics explores the structure and behavior of matter and attempts to answer questions about energy. The work of physicists includes developing theories, performing experiments, and improving manufacturing processes and products.

Physics

Physics is the science devoted to the study of matter and energy. Physicists try to understand what matter is and why it behaves the way it does. They seek to learn how energy is produced, how it travels from place to place, and how it can be controlled. Physicists are also interested in how matter and energy are related to each other and how they affect each other over time and through space.

The word *physics* comes from a Greek word meaning *natural things*. Knowledge obtained from the study of physics is important in other sciences, including astronomy, biology, chemistry, and geology. There is also a close connection between physics and practical developments in engineering, medicine, and technology. For example, engineers design automobiles and airplanes according to certain principles of physics. Laws and the-

---

Stanley Goldberg, the contributor of this article, is a Consultant-Planner at the Smithsonian Institution's National Museum of American History. He is the author of Understanding Relativity: Origins and Impact of a Scientific Revolution.

ories of physics have enabled engineers and scientists to put satellites into orbit and to receive information from space probes that travel to distant regions of the solar system. Research in physics has led to the use of radioactive materials in the study, diagnosis, and treatment of certain diseases. In addition, theories and principles of physics explain the operation of many modern home conveniences, from vacuum cleaners to videotape recorders.

What physicists study

Physicists try to answer basic questions about the world, how it is put together, and how it changes. Some physicists, called *experimental physicists,* perform carefully designed experiments and then compare their results to what was predicted to happen. Such predictions come from laws and theories developed by another group of physicists, called *theoretical physicists.* These laws and theories are almost always expressed in the language of mathematics, a basic tool of physics.

The subjects studied by physicists consist of two broad categories, *classical physics* and *modern physics.* These two categories differ primarily in emphasis. Classical physics deals with questions regarding motion and energy. It is composed of five basic areas: (1) mechanics,

(2) heat, (3) sound, (4) electricity and magnetism, and (5) light. Modern physics concentrates on scientific beliefs about the basic structure of the material world. Its major fields include (1) atomic, molecular, and electron physics; (2) nuclear physics; (3) particle physics; (4) solid-state physics; and (5) fluid and plasma physics.

Mechanics is the study of bodies at rest and in motion. For example, it describes how force acts upon an object to produce acceleration. The mechanics of bodies in motion is sometimes referred to as *dynamics.* The mechanics of bodies at rest is called *statics.* One branch of mechanics, known as *fluid mechanics,* deals with the behavior of liquids and gases. Principles of mechanics are used in describing such types of motion as planetary orbits and the paths of other moving objects. They are also important to designers of bridges and other structures, containers, roads, and various kinds of vehicles. See **Mechanics; Dynamics; Statics.**

Heat. The study of heat is called *thermodynamics.* It involves investigating how heat is produced, how it is transmitted from one place to another, how it changes matter, and how it is stored. Heat energy can be transformed into other kinds of energy, and other kinds of energy can be transformed into heat energy. For example, when coal is burned, the chemical energy that binds its molecules is partially transformed into heat. Thermodynamics also includes *cryogenics,* the study of material at very low temperatures. Principles of thermodynamics are essential for understanding all types of heat engines, which include diesel, gasoline, and steam engines, as well as refrigerators and freezers. See **Heat; Thermodynamics.**

Sound. The study of sound is called *acoustics.* Sound consists of vibrations that are produced by an object and which travel through a medium, such as air, water, or the walls of a building. Understanding sound is important for designing auditoriums, hearing aids, tape recorders, phonographs, and speakers. The study of sound also includes *ultrasonics,* which deals with vibrations that have frequencies too high for human beings to hear. See **Acoustics; Sound.**

Electricity and magnetism are so closely related that scientists often refer to the two of them together as *electromagnetism.* The motion of electric charges can produce magnetic effects, and magnetic forces can pro-duce electrical effects. Knowledge of this relationship has led to the development of huge electric generators and such electronic devices as radios, televisions, and computers. See **Electricity; Electromagnetism; Electronics; Magnet and magnetism.**

Light. The study of light is called *optics.* Optics has two major branches, *physical optics* and *geometrical optics.* In physical optics, physicists study the nature of light and the physical processes by which it is *emitted* (given off) from bodies and transmitted from place to place. Geometrical optics is the study of how light travels from place to place, and how the direction of travel is affected by different materials. Such study is important in understanding the lenses and mirrors which are used in telescopes, microscopes, and eyeglasses. See **Light; Optics.**

Atomic, molecular, and electron physics are concerned with understanding the structures of molecules and atoms. In particular, they concentrate on the behavior, arrangement, motion, and energy states of the electrons that orbit atomic nuclei. Studies in atomic, molecular, and electron physics have revealed much about the structure of matter. For example, scientists have determined that substances differ from one another in the arrangement of the atoms of their molecules. Because of this difference, the way that each substance absorbs and emits electromagnetic energy is unique. As a result, scientists are able to identify a substance on the basis of its electromagnetic activity alone. This method of identifying substances has important applications in medicine and in certain industrial situations where minute amounts of a material are involved. See **Atom; Electron; Molecule.**

Nuclear physics involves the study of the structure and properties of the atomic nucleus. It focuses on radioactivity, fission, and fusion. *Radioactivity* is the process by which certain nuclei spontaneously give off high-energy particles or rays. Radioactive materials are used to treat cancer and diagnose illnesses, and to trace chemical and physical processes. *Fission* is the process in which an atomic nucleus splits into two nearly equal parts, releasing a huge amount of energy. It provides the energy for atomic bombs and nuclear reactors. *Fusion* is the process in which the nuclei of two atoms join together to form the nucleus of a heavier element. It oc-

Major branches of physics

Acoustics studies the production and properties of sound.
Atomic physics examines the structure, properties, and behavior of the atom.
Biophysics applies the tools and techniques of physics to the study of living things and life processes.
Cryogenics is the study of extremely low temperatures.
Electrodynamics analyzes the relationship between electrical and magnetic forces.
Fluid physics deals with the behavior and movement of liquids and gases.
Geophysics is the study of the earth and its atmosphere and waters by means of the principles of physics.
Health physics involves the protection of people who work with or near radiation.
Mathematical physics is the study of mathematical systems that stand for physical phenomena.
Mechanics deals with the behavior of objects and systems in response to various forces.

Molecular physics examines the structure, properties, and behavior of molecules.
Nuclear physics is concerned with the structure and properties of the atomic nucleus, and with nuclear reactions and their applications.
Optics is the study of the nature and behavior of light.
Particle physics, also called *high-energy physics,* analyzes the behavior and properties of elementary particles.
Plasma physics is concerned with the study of highly *ionized* gases—that is, gases that have been separated into positively and negatively charged particles.
Quantum physics includes various areas of study based on *quantum theory,* which deals with matter and electromagnetic radiation, and the interactions between them.
Solid-state physics, also called *condensed-matter physics,* examines the physical properties of solid materials.
Thermodynamics is the study of heat and other forms of energy, and of the conversion of energy from one form to another.

curs primarily with hydrogen and other light elements. Fusion, which releases even more energy than does fission, produces the energy of the hydrogen bomb. See **Nuclear physics.**

Particle physics. Physicists have discovered that the protons and neutrons within atomic nuclei are formed of still more elementary particles. Particle physicists conduct research by using devices called *particle accelerators.* These devices can raise subatomic particles to very high speeds. When these particles have reached speeds very close to the speed of light, they are allowed to collide with ordinary matter. Physicists then study the fragments that result from the collisions and measure their energy. In this way, they hope to understand how elementary particles are joined together to make protons, neutrons, and other subatomic particles. See **Particle accelerator; Particle physics.**

Solid-state physics, also called *condensed-matter physics.* Solids may be classified according to how the electrons and nuclei of the different atoms that make them up interact with each other. Physicists who study solids are interested in how the properties of these materials are affected by such factors as temperature and pressure. For example, at extremely low temperatures, some solids lose all electrical resistance, thereby becoming *superconductors.* Research on the electronic structure of solids is especially important in understanding the behavior of *semiconductors,* which serve as the basis of modern electronic devices. See **Semiconductor; Solid-state physics; Superconductivity.**

Fluid and plasma physics. The modern physics of fluids is built on the principles of classical fluid mechanics. Understanding the behavior and movement of fluids is important for the design and construction of automobiles, ships, airplanes, and rockets, as well as for the study of weather. Plasma physics concerns the study of gases called *plasmas.* If enough energy is introduced into a gas, the gas becomes *ionized* (separated into positively and negatively charged particles). The resulting gas is a plasma. Plasmas are used in neon lights and fluorescent lamps. Physicists are studying how plasmas might be controlled and used to produce fusion energy to generate electricity. See **Hydraulics; Mechanics; Plasma.**

History

Through the centuries, physics has been closely linked to developments in technology and to advances in mathematics, astronomy, and other sciences. The use of the word *physics* in its current sense was first recorded in the 1700's.

The beginnings of physics date back to prehistoric times. Stonehenge and the other huge rock structures prehistoric people built indicate that they had some knowledge of mechanics. Such knowledge would have been necessary for them to transport these rocks and to place them on top of one another. In addition, there is some evidence that prehistoric people may have used these rock structures to mark significant moments in the seasonal cycle of the sun and moon.

The first people to leave written records of their discoveries and inventions were the Sumerians, Babylonians, and Egyptians. By around 3000 B.C., the Sumerians had developed a number system, and they used algebraic formulas for following and predicting movements of the stars, sun, moon, and planets. Similar developments occurred in Egypt and Babylonia. The Egyptians also developed practical geometric techniques for use in construction and land surveying.

The Greeks appear to have been the first people to develop general theoretical systems of mathematics and natural science. Beginning about 600 B.C., they developed a general understanding of the principles of geometry. The Greek mathematician Euclid organized these principles into a unified system about 300 B.C.

The Greeks were keen observers of the physical world. In the 300's B.C., the philosopher Aristotle provided proofs, based on physical evidence, of the spherical shape of the earth. In the 200's B.C., the astronomer Eratosthenes calculated the circumference of the earth, and Aristarchus, another astronomer, estimated the relative distances to the moon and sun. Also during the 200's B.C., the inventor and mathematician Archimedes discovered several basic scientific principles and developed a number of measuring techniques.

In the A.D. 100's, Ptolemy, an astronomer in Egypt, developed a model for predicting the positions of the sun, moon, stars, and planets. Like Aristotle and other Greek philosophers, Ptolemy viewed the earth as the center of the universe. Ptolemy's system served as a guide for predicting the motion of the heavenly bodies for nearly 1,500 years.

The Middle Ages began in about the 400's with the fall of the Roman Empire. At that time, records of Greek scientific discoveries were lost to western Europe. From about 400 to 1000, western Europeans had little interest in scientific learning. Most educated people felt that religion, rather than scientific investigation, should provide the answers to questions about the universe.

Much of the Greek written tradition in science was preserved during the early Middle Ages by people in the Middle East. These people translated many of the Greek works into Arabic. Arabic scholars wrote commentaries on these texts, made astronomical observations to correct Ptolemy's system of astronomy, and performed experiments in optics and mechanics.

Trade between the Arab cultures of the East and the Christian cultures of the West increased during the 1000's. As a result, Greek scientific documents were reintroduced into the West, this time as translations from Arabic to Latin. At first, the science of Aristotle and other Greeks was rejected by the church. But during the 1200's, Saint Albertus Magnus, Saint Thomas Aquinas, and other religious scholars successfully reconciled Aristotelian physical science with church principles.

During the 1100's and 1200's, there was also increasing interest in scientific observation and experiments. For example, various writings, including those of the English scholars Robert Grosseteste and Roger Bacon, proposed effective methods for scientific research.

Practical inventions in agriculture and other fields also sparked scientific inquiry in Europe during the Middle Ages. In China and other Asian countries, scientific activity and invention flourished during this period. However, unlike in the West, science and technology had little influence on each other.

The Renaissance is the name given to the period in Europe that extended from about the early 1300's to about 1600. It was a time of social, economic, political, and intellectual excitement that produced many new approaches in both the arts and the sciences.

In the 1300's, at Oxford University and the University of Paris, such scholars as Richard Swineshead and Nicole Oresme investigated the problem of the description of motion. During the 1400's and 1500's, the famous Italian painter and inventor Leonardo da Vinci also conducted studies of motion and hydraulics.

In 1543, the Polish astronomer Nicolaus Copernicus published a revolutionary astronomical system in which he placed the sun—instead of the earth—at the center of the universe. Copernicus proposed that the earth was one of the planets, all of which orbited the sun. At the time, almost no one accepted his point of view. Catholic and Protestant leaders alike felt that his system was in conflict with their religious beliefs. There were also serious scientific objections to the system. Acceptance of the Copernican system required a complete rethinking of the whole basis of physical science. Such a rethinking did in fact occur over the next 150 years, primarily through the work of such major figures as Galileo, Johannes Kepler, and René Descartes.

Beginning in 1609, the Italian astronomer and physicist Galileo built a number of telescopes for observing the heavens. While none of Galileo's observations with his telescopes proved the Copernican system, they did call traditional views into question. Galileo also perfected the idea of the laboratory experiment in his study of the motion of falling bodies. He showed that a person could gain an understanding of the way objects fall toward the earth by assuming that, in the absence of disturbing influences, all the objects accelerate at the same constant rate.

In the early 1600's, the German astronomer and mathematician Johannes Kepler used the observations of others to construct a new and accurate model of the solar system. In the mid-1600's, René Descartes, a French philosopher and mathematician, challenged the long-standing assumption that an absence of motion was the natural state of all objects. Instead, he proposed that objects have *inertia*—that is, they maintain whatever their state of motion unless otherwise disturbed.

The work of Galileo, Kepler, and Descartes reflects a change in attitude that occurred during the Renaissance. People had begun to believe that the physical world was governed by natural laws, and that it was possible to discover those laws. The path to such discovery was now seen to begin with careful measurements carried out, if possible, under controlled laboratory conditions.

Newton. By the 1600's, a great deal of scientific activity was underway. The climax of this increased activity was the publication, in 1687, of *Mathematical Principles of Natural Philosophy,* by the brilliant English scientist, Sir Isaac Newton. In this work, Newton showed how both the motions of heavenly bodies and the motions of objects on or near the surface of the earth could be explained by four simple laws. These laws were Newton's three laws of motion and his law of universal gravitation.

Newton's laws of motion summarized and extended the work of Galileo and Descartes. His law of universal gravitation explained both Galileo's law of falling bodies and Kepler's laws of planetary motion. In order to conduct some of his research and calculations, Newton invented a new form of mathematics, called *calculus.* Another mathematical scholar, Gottfried Wilhelm Leibniz of Germany, independently developed calculus about the same time. See **Calculus.**

In addition to his theoretical discoveries, Newton constructed the first reflecting telescope. Using prisms, he performed ingenious experiments on light that led him to propose that white light was a mixture of all colors. In 1704, he published a particle theory of light. This theory competed with another theory of light that had been proposed by the Dutch physicist Christian Huygens in 1678, but not published until 1690. Huygens had

Important dates in physics

300's B.C. Aristotle formed theories in many areas of physics.
200's B.C. Archimedes discovered the law of the lever and laws for the behavior of liquids.
A.D. 100's Ptolemy pictured the earth as standing still, with the sun, moon, planets, and stars moving in circles around it.
c. 1270 Roger Bacon conducted studies in optics.
1543 Nicolaus Copernicus wrote that the earth and planets move in circles around the sun.
c. 1600 Galileo discovered important laws in many fields of physics, especially mechanics.
1687 Sir Isaac Newton published his laws of motion.
1690 Christian Huygens published a wave theory of light.
1798 Benjamin Thompson, Count Rumford, stated that the motion of particles in a substance produced heat.
1801-1803 Thomas Young revived the wave theory of light.
1803 John Dalton first proposed his atomic theory about the structure of matter.
Early 1830's Michael Faraday and Joseph Henry independently produced electricity with magnetism.
1847 James P. Joule found that heat and energy are interchangeable at a fixed rate.
1864 James Clerk Maxwell published his electromagnetic theory of light.
1887 The Michelson-Morley experiment disproved the existence of the ether.
1895 Wilhelm K. Roentgen discovered X rays.
1896 Antoine Henri Becquerel discovered natural radioactivity.

1898 Marie Curie and her husband, Pierre, isolated the radioactive element radium.
1900 Max Planck published his quantum theory.
1905 Albert Einstein published his special theory of relativity.
1911-1913 Ernest Rutherford and Niels Bohr proposed "planetary system" models of the atom.
1915 Einstein announced his general theory of relativity.
1924 Louis de Broglie put forth the wave theory of the electron.
1925-1926 Erwin Schrödinger and Werner Heisenberg separately developed systems for organizing quantum physics.
1930 Paul A. M. Dirac predicted the existence of the *positron,* a positively charged electron.
1932 Sir John D. Cockcroft and Ernest T. S. Walton built the first particle accelerator.
1938 Otto Hahn and Fritz Strassman achieved fission of the uranium atom.
1942 Enrico Fermi and associates achieved the first controlled nuclear chain reaction.
1947 John Bardeen, Walter H. Brattain, and William Shockley invented the transistor.
1960 Theodore H. Maiman built the first laser.
1964 Murray Gell-Mann and George Zweig proposed the existence of quarks as fundamental particles.
1974 Burton Richter and Samuel C. C. Ting discovered a type of subatomic particle called the *psi particle* or *J particle.*
1983 Researchers led by Carlo Rubbia discovered two types of subatomic particles—the *W particle* and the *Z particle.*

argued that light traveled in the form of waves, rather than particles. But during the 1700's, most scientists accepted Newton's particle theory.

Developments in the 1800's. The Industrial Revolution, which had begun in Great Britain in the 1700's, led to the production of scientific instruments that were extremely accurate for their time and which enabled scientists to perform more complicated experiments. As scientific research grew more complex, people began specializing in more narrowly defined areas of study. Three areas of particular interest in the 1800's were heat and energy, light, and electricity and magnetism.

Developments in the study of heat and energy. At the beginning of the 1800's, it was widely believed that heat existed in the form of a fluid, called *caloric*. But by the middle of the century, scientists had come to view heat not as a fluid, but as a form of energy. That is, they had learned that heat is able to do work. In the 1840's, James Joule, an English physicist, showed how to calculate how much work a given quantity of heat could do. About the same time, a number of physicists, including Lord Kelvin of Great Britain and Hermann von Helmholtz of Germany, independently proposed the law of conservation of energy. This law states that energy cannot be created or destroyed, only transformed from one kind to another. See **Energy** (The conservation of energy).

By the mid-1800's, heat energy also came to be interpreted as the mechanical movement of the atoms of which everything was made. This interpretation was based on the atomic theory proposed in 1803 by John Dalton, an English chemist.

Developments in the study of light. From 1800 to 1803, the English physicist Thomas Young published a series of papers, based on experiments he had done, that revived the theory that light existed in the form of waves. From about 1815 to 1819, Augustin Fresnel, a French physicist, provided still more evidence. By 1850, the wave theory of light was almost universally accepted, replacing Newton's particle theory.

The wave theory of light led physicists to propose the existence of a material called the *ether.* They reasoned that if light traveled in waves and could travel through a vacuum, there had to be some medium present to support the waves. They concluded that all space, including vacuums, was filled with the ether. They interpreted light energy as simply the vibration of the ether, in the form of waves. See **Ether.**

Developments in the study of electricity and magnetism. In 1800, Count Alessandro Volta of Italy announced his invention of the first electric battery. This invention opened the way for new methods of studying electrical effects. About 1820, two physicists, André Marie Ampère of France and Hans Christian Oersted of Denmark, showed that electricity and magnetism were related. In the early 1830's, the English physicist Michael Faraday and the American physicist Joseph Henry independently demonstrated how to produce electricity in a changing magnetic field. Their demonstrations showed that mechanical energy could be converted into electrical energy and suggested the principles behind the generator and the motor.

In the 1860's, the Scottish physicist and mathematician James Clerk Maxwell developed a theory that interpreted visible light as the movement of electromagnetic waves. Maxwell predicted the possible existence of similar electromagnetic waves that were invisible. Heinrich Hertz, a German physicist, detected such invisible *radio waves* in the late 1880's. Hertz's discovery eventually led to the development of radio, radar, and television. But it also suggested that light, electricity, and magnetism were related. All three were viewed as resulting from waves in the ether. Such waves are sometimes referred to as *electromagnetic radiation.*

The beginning of modern physics. Near the end of the 1800's, many physicists were convinced that the work of physics was nearly over. They believed that almost all the laws governing the physical universe had been discovered. Some of them believed that all physi-

Archimedes, a Greek inventor, discovered several basic principles of physics during the 200's B.C. He also developed a number of measuring techniques.

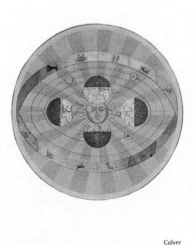

The astronomical system proposed by Polish astronomer Nicolaus Copernicus in 1543 placed the sun, not the earth, at the center of the universe.

Galileo in Italy discovered the law of falling bodies and the law of the pendulum. In 1609, he began building telescopes to observe the heavens.

cal laws would one day be expressed in a few simple equations.

A few problems remained to be solved, however. One such problem involved determining the source of electromagnetic radiation. Scientists knew that under the right conditions, each chemical element radiates a unique combination of visible, infrared, and ultraviolet light, called *line spectra*. At the time, the atom was considered to be the most fundamental unit of matter in the universe. But to some physicists, the line spectra phenomenon suggested that the atom might itself be composed of still more fundamental units.

The dream of explaining all physical phenomena with one small set of basic laws was not realized. Instead, various discoveries began to reveal that such phenomena were more complex than scientists had thought. In 1895, for example, Wilhelm Roentgen of Germany discovered X rays. In 1896, the French physicist Antoine Henri Becquerel discovered *natural radioactivity,* the spontaneous emission of radiation from atoms. In 1897, the English physicist Joseph J. Thomson discovered the first subatomic particle, later called the *electron.* In 1898, French physicists Marie Curie and her husband, Pierre, isolated the radioactive element radium. Such developments signaled that, rather than being nearly over, the work of physics had only begun.

Quantum theory. The early 1900's brought revolutionary developments in physics. Scientists looked for inconsistencies in the classical physics of Newton and others, and discovered new interpretations of observed events.

In 1900, the German physicist Max Planck published his quantum theory of energy transfer to explain the spectrum of light emitted by certain heated objects. He stated that energy is not given off continuously, but in the form of individual units called *quanta.* In 1905, Albert Einstein, the German-born American physicist, proposed a new particle, later called the *photon,* as the carrier of electromagnetic energy. Einstein said that light, in spite of its wave nature, must be composed of these energy particles.

In 1913, the Danish physicist Niels Bohr explained in terms of quanta how atoms absorb and radiate energy. In 1924, Louis de Broglie, a French physicist, proposed that electrons could also exhibit wave properties. In the mid-1920's, two physicists, Erwin Schrödinger of Austria and Werner Heisenberg of Germany, produced separate, but equivalent, systems for organizing all earlier quantum physics. The combined ideas of Schrödinger and Heisenberg have since been developed as the field of *quantum mechanics.* See **Quantum mechanics.**

Einstein and relativity. During the 1800's, physicists tried unsuccessfully to measure the speed of the earth relative to the ether. According to classical physics, the ether was motionless. In the early 1880's, Hendrik A. Lorentz, a Dutch physicist, explained the failure of these experiments by assuming that the ether was partially dragged along as the earth moved through it. Two American physicists, Albert A. Michelson and Edward W. Morley, developed an instrument that made far more precise measurements than earlier devices. Their experiments helped destroy the ether theory. In 1887, Michelson and Morley demonstrated that the earth's movement around the sun had no effect on the speed of light. Their finding could be understood only by assuming that the ether near the surface of the earth moved at the same speed as the earth. However, this assumption contradicted the results of many other experiments.

The contradiction was not resolved until 1905. That year, Albert Einstein analyzed the measuring process itself and, as a result, proposed his special theory of relativity. The theory begins with two *postulates* (fundamental principles). The first postulate states that for all observers moving uniformly relative to each other, the laws of physics have the same form. The second postulate states that for all observers, the speed of light is *invariant* (has the same value). One conclusion from these postulates is that mass and energy are related. Einstein

Granger Collection

Sir Isaac Newton of England stated laws of motion and gravitation during the late 1600's. He also demonstrated that white light is made up of all colors.

UPI/Bettmann Newsphotos

Wilhelm Roentgen of Germany discovered X rays in 1895. The use of X rays helped doctors diagnose illness and injury and revolutionized medicine.

Brown Brothers

Marie Curie of France made many advances in the study of radioactivity. In 1898, she and her husband, Pierre, isolated the radioactive element radium.

expressed this relationship in his famous equation $E = mc^2$. In this equation, E stands for energy, m for mass, and c^2 for the speed of light multiplied by itself.

Einstein also attempted to replace classical gravitational theories with a more exact statement of the laws of gravitation. In 1915, he announced his general theory of relativity. This theory begins by assuming that the effects of gravity on objects are identical to the effects of nongravitational forces acting on objects. Gravity is no longer viewed as a property of objects interacting with each other, but of objects interacting with space itself. The theory predicted that the path of a light beam will be affected by nearby massive objects. This prediction was confirmed in 1919. The theory also predicted the existence of *gravitational waves* that travel at the speed of light. However, these waves have not yet been detected. See **Relativity.**

Uncovering the secrets of the atom. The discovery that atoms have an internal structure prompted physicists to probe further into these tiny units of matter. In England, Ernest Rutherford developed a model of the atom in 1911. In this model, the dense positive charge resided in a small, spherical core called the nucleus, and the electrons traveled around this nucleus. Bohr proposed modifications of the model in 1913. That year, an American, Robert Millikan, obtained an accurate measurement of the electron's charge. See **Atom.**

The discovery of other subatomic particles continued after this early work. In 1932, James Chadwick, an English physicist, conducted experiments that suggested that the atomic nucleus was composed of two kinds of particles: positively charged protons and neutral neutrons. In 1935, Hideki Yukawa, a Japanese physicist, proposed that other particles, which he called *mesons,* exist in the atomic nucleus (see **Meson**).

In 1938, two German physicists, Otto Hahn and Fritz Strassman, discovered nuclear fission by splitting uranium atoms. Scientists quickly realized that, as Einstein's $E = mc^2$ formula indicated, the process of fission could liberate enormous quantities of energy. In 1942, during World War II, the Italian-born physicist Enrico Fermi and his coworkers at the University of Chicago achieved the first controlled fission chain reaction. In 1945, near the end of the war, American scientists and engineers produced the first bombs that relied on nuclear fission for their explosive power. Two such atomic bombs were dropped on Japan in August 1945. See **Nuclear energy** (The development of nuclear energy); **Nuclear weapon.**

Advances in the mid-1900's. After 1945, the picture of the atom grew more complicated as physicists discovered more and more subatomic particles. In 1955, the American physicists Owen Chamberlain and Emilio Segrè discovered the *antiproton* (a negatively charged proton). In 1964, the American physicists Murray Gell-Mann and George Zweig proposed the existence of *quarks* as fundamental particles. Protons and neutrons are composed of different combinations of quarks. Strong evidence for the existence of the quark resulted from the discovery of the *psi particle,* a type of subatomic particle also called the *J particle,* by the Americans Burton Richter and Samuel C. C. Ting. See **Antimatter; Psi particle; Quark.**

Research in the mid-1900's also led to important advances in technology. In 1947, American physicists invented the transistor. This tiny device revolutionized the electronics industry. In the early 1960's, researchers in atomic and optical physics produced light-amplifying devices called lasers. Lasers have become valuable tools in such areas as communications, industry, and nuclear energy research. See **Laser; Transistor.**

Physics today. Physics continues to be one of the most active and important sciences. Ongoing research into the nature of matter has led to important discoveries. For example, researchers in West Germany discovered an important elementary particle, the *gluon,* in 1979. Gluons, which are a type of *boson,* carry the powerful *strong force.* This force, also called the *strong interaction,* binds the atomic nucleus together. In 1983, a

UPI/Bettmann Newsphotos

Albert Einstein proposed the special theory of relativity in 1905. It revised ideas of time and space and provided the basis for releasing the atom's energy.

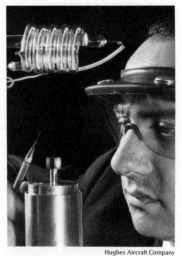

Hughes Aircraft Company

Theodore H. Maiman of the United States built the first laser, a ruby laser, and first operated it in 1960. A laser amplifies light into a powerful beam.

Brookhaven National Laboratory

Samuel C. C. Ting, *above,* and Burton Richter of the United States discovered a new type of elementary particle—the *psi,* or *J, particle*—in 1974.

research team led by Carlo Rubbia of Italy discovered two more subatomic particles—the *W particle* and the *Z particle.* Physicists predict that these particles are a source of the *weak force,* also called the *weak interaction.* This force controls the disintegration of atomic nuclei—the process at work in radioactivity.

Physicists believe that there may be an underlying unity among three of the basic forces of the universe: the strong force, the weak force, and the electromagnetic force that holds electrons to the nucleus. Theories that attempt to establish this underlying unity are referred to as *grand unified theories* (GUT's). Researchers are also testing *supergravity* theories, which would include the fourth fundamental force, gravitation. Such theories illustrate how physicists have again begun to express the hope that a few basic laws will unify all our knowledge about how the world works. See **Grand unified theories.**

Physics also continues to make important contributions to technology. For example, advances in electronics have resulted in the development of extremely sophisticated computers. Lasers and *optical fibers* (glass or plastic filaments that carry light) have led to improvements in communication systems and medical technology (see **Fiber optics**). Physicists have begun developing ceramiclike materials that can act as superconductors at much higher temperatures than the superconductors of the past. Advances in superconductivity could one day lead to such applications as efficient and economical power generators, high-speed trains that float on magnetic fields, and improved medical imaging systems.

Careers in physics

Education and training. A person who plans to pursue physics as a career should take science and mathematics courses in high school. The formal training of physicists begins in college. Physics students must learn calculus, modern algebra, and other forms of higher mathematics. They also take basic courses in chemistry. After a year or two of introductory course work, physics majors begin to specialize, taking more advanced courses in the various subfields of physics. Many of these courses include intensive laboratory work.

Most physics majors continue their education beyond the bachelor's degree. A majority pursue doctor's degrees. A key part of a physicist's training includes learning to ask questions that suggest new approaches to understanding how the world works.

Employment. More than half the physicists in the United States are engaged in research and development activities. Many industries employ physicists in their research departments. These people often work in *applied physics,* which generally involves improving manufacturing processes or products. Many physicists are employed by colleges and universities. They generally divide their time between teaching and research.

Today, physics research often requires the use of highly specialized and expensive instruments and equipment, such as high-energy particle accelerators. In the United States, special laboratories with this type of equipment are funded by government agencies (see **National laboratory**). In Europe, the nations that belong to the European Organization for Nuclear Research built the CERN physics laboratories in Geneva, Switzerland.

Although the U.S. national laboratories and the CERN laboratories have their own staffs, physicists from around the world may apply to use the facilities in their research.   Stanley Goldberg

Related articles in *World Book* include:

American physicists

Alvarez, Luis W.	Michelson, Albert A.
Anderson, Carl D.	Millikan, Robert A.
Bardeen, John	Nier, Alfred O. C.
Bethe, Hans A.	Oppenheimer, J. Robert
Brattain, Walter H.	Purcell, Edward M.
Bridgman, Percy W.	Rowland, Henry A.
Dempster, Arthur J.	Shockley, William
Dunning, John R.	Szilard, Leo
Einstein, Albert	Teller, Edward
Feynman, Richard P.	Thompson, Benjamin
Gell-Mann, Murray	Townes, Charles Hard
Gibbs, Josiah W.	Van Allen, James A.
Goddard, Robert H.	Van de Graff, Robert J.
Henry, Joseph	Wigner, Eugene Paul
Lamb, Willis E., Jr.	Wood, Robert W.
Langley, Samuel P.	Wu, Chien-shiung
Lawrence, Ernest O.	Yang, Chen Ning
Lee, Tsung Dao	Zworykin, Vladimir K.
Mayer, Maria G.	

British physicists

Appleton, Sir Edward	Jeans, Sir James H.
Aston, Francis W.	Joule, James P.
Boyle, Robert	Kelvin, Lord
Bragg, Sir William H.	Maxwell, James C.
Cavendish, Henry	Moseley, Henry G. J.
Chadwick, Sir James	Newton, Sir Isaac
Cockcroft, Sir John D.	Rutherford, Ernest
Crookes, Sir William	Thomson, Sir Joseph J.
Dalton, John	Tyndall, John
Dirac, Paul A. M.	Watson-Watt, Sir Robert A.
Faraday, Michael	Wheatstone, Sir Charles
Hooke, Robert	Wilson, Charles T. R.

French physicists

Ampère, André M.	Curie, Pierre
Becquerel (family)	De Broglie, Louis Victor
Carnot, Nicolas L. S.	Foucault, Jean B. L.
Châtelet, Marquise du	Gay-Lussac, Joseph L.
Coulomb, Charles A. de	Joliot-Curie, Irène
Curie, Marie Sklodowska	Pascal, Blaise

German physicists

Born, Max	Jordan, Ernst P.
Clausius, Rudolf J.	Laue, Max T. F. von
Fahrenheit, Gabriel D.	Mayer, Julius R. von
Geiger, Hans	Mössbauer, Rudolf L.
Hahn, Otto	Nernst, Walther H.
Heisenberg, Werner	Ohm, Georg S.
Helmholtz, Hermann L. F. von	Planck, Max K. E. L.
Hertz, Gustav	Roentgen, Wilhelm K.
Hertz, Heinrich R.	Strassman, Fritz
Jensen, J. Hans	

Italian physicists

Avogadro, Amedeo	Marconi, Guglielmo
Fermi, Enrico	Torricelli, Evangelista
Galileo	Volta, Count
Galvani, Luigi	

Other physicists

Alfvén, Hannes O. G.	Huygens, Christian
Basov, Nikolai G.	Kapitsa, Pyotr
Bohr, Niels	Lorentz, Hendrik A.
Boltzmann, Ludwig	Mach, Ernst
Gamow, George	Meitner, Lise
Herzberg, Gerhard	Oersted, Hans C.

Pauli, Wolfgang
Piccard (Auguste)
Prokhorov, Alexander M.
Raman, Sir Chandra-
    sekhara V.
Sakharov, Andrei D.

Schrödinger, Erwin
Siegbahn, Karl M. G.
Van der Waals, Johannes D.
Yukawa, Hideki
Zeeman, Pieter

Atomic, nuclear, and particle physics

Alpha particle
Antimatter
Antineutron
Antiproton
Atom
Baryon
Beta particle
Boson
Cosmic rays
Crooks tube
Electron
Fission
Fusion
Gamma rays

Gluon
Hadron
Ion
Irradiation
Isotope
Lepton
Meson
Molecule
Muon
Neutron
Nuclear energy
Nuclear physics
Nuclear reactor
Nuclear weapon

Parity
Particle physics
Photon
Proton
Psi particle
Quantum electro-
    dynamics
Quark
Radiation
Radioactivity
Transmutation of
    elements
Upsilon particle
X rays

Electricity

See the **Electricity** article and its list of *Related articles.*

Electronics

See the **Electronics** article and its list of *Related articles.* See also the following articles:

Electric field
Frequency modula-
    tion
Geiger counter
Kilohertz
Mass spectroscopy

Megahertz
Remote control
Short waves
Sniperscope
Teletypesetter
Transducer

Ultrahigh fre-
    quency waves
Van de Graaff gen-
    erator
Very high fre-
    quency waves

Heat

See the **Heat** article and its list of *Related articles.* See also the following articles:

Distillation
Dust explosion
Freezing point
Melting point
Pyrometry

Regelation
Spontaneous combustion
Sublimation
Superconductivity

Light

See the **Light** article and its list of *Related articles.*

Magnetism

See the **Magnet and magnetism** article and its list of *Related articles.*

Mechanics

Aerodynamics
Adhesion
Antigravity
Ballistics
Bernoulli's principle
Capillarity
Cohesion
Condensation
Dyne
Efficiency
Falling bodies, Law
    of
Foot-pound
Force
Friction

Gas
Gravity, Center of
Horsepower
Hydraulics
Inclined plane
Inertia
Lever
Liquid
Manometer
Mechanics
Momentum
Motion
Osmosis
Pascal's Law

Pendulum
Pneumatics
Power
Pressure
Pulley
Screw
Siphon
Surface tension
Torque
Vacuum
Velocity
Viscosity
Wedge
Work

Sound

See the **Sound** article and its list of *Related articles.*

Other related articles

Astronomy
Dark matter

Geophysics
Grand unified theories

Gravitation
Interference
Matter

Quantum mechanics
Relativity
Solar energy

Solar wind
Solid-state physics
Waves

Outline

I. **What physicists study**
   A. Mechanics
   B. Heat
   C. Sound
   D. Electricity and magnet-
      ism
   E. Light
   F. Atomic, molecular, and
      electron physics
   G. Nuclear physics
   H. Particle physics
   I. Solid-state physics
   J. Fluid and plasma physics
II. **History**
III. **Careers in physics**
   A. Education and training
   B. Employment

Questions

What is the difference between the work of a theoretical physicist and that of an experimental physicist?

What did Galileo demonstrate in his study of the motion of falling bodies?

When did physicists achieve the first controlled fission chain reaction? What was the significance of this development during World War II?

What are some examples of developments in engineering and technology that involve the principles of physics?

What are grand unified theories? What distinguishes supergravity theories from grand unified theories?

What are the two postulates of Einstein's special theory of relativity?

What technological advances resulted from physics research in the mid-1900's? How have these advances been important?

How did Arabic scholars contribute to the development of physics during the Middle Ages?

What are quanta? Who first proposed the idea of quanta?

What did Michelson and Morley demonstrate in their 1887 experiment?

Additional resources

Apfel, Necia H. *It's All Elementary: From Atoms to the Quantum World of Quarks, Leptons, and Gluons.* Lothrop, 1985. Suitable for younger readers.

Crease, Robert P., and Mann, C. C. *The Second Creation: Makers of the Revolution in Twentieth-Century Physics.* Macmillan, 1986.

Hobson, Art. *Physics and Human Affairs.* Wiley, 1982.

Segrè, Emilio. *From Falling Bodies to Radio Waves: Classical Physicists and Their Discoveries.* W. H. Freeman, 1984.

Taffel, Alexander. *Physics: Its Methods and Meanings.* 5th ed. Allyn & Bacon, 1986.

Trefil, James S. *The Unexpected Vista: A Physicist's View of Nature.* Scribner, 1983.

Dictionary Supplement

This section lists important words
from the 1988 edition of THE
WORLD BOOK DICTIONARY. This dictionary, first published in 1963, keeps
abreast of our living language with a
program of continuous editorial revision. The following supplement has
been prepared under the direction of
the editors of THE WORLD BOOK EN-
CYCLOPEDIA and Clarence L. Barnhart, editor in chief of THE WORLD
BOOK DICTIONARY. It is presented as
a service to owners of the dictionary
and as an informative feature to subscribers to THE WORLD BOOK YEAR
BOOK.

A a

ac|u|pinch (ak′yə pinch′), *n.* a method of relieving a muscle cramp by pinching the upper lip just under the nose for 20 to 30 seconds: *Although doctors are at a loss to explain the reasons for acupinch's success, they agree that it works* (Reader's Digest). [< *acu*(pressure) + *pinch*]

an|gi|o|plas|ty (an′jē ō plas′tē), *n.* a surgical procedure for clearing a passage in an artery, especially by threading a small balloon through the artery and inflating it to clear blood clots and fatty deposits: *Increasingly, balloon angioplasty is being used as an alternative to coronary bypass surgery* (New York Times). [< Greek *angeîon* receptacle + *-plastia* a molding] —**an′gi|o|plas′tic,** *adj.*

a|nom|a|lon (ə nom′ə lon), *n. Nuclear Physics.* a hypothetical fragment of a nucleus traveling an unusually short distance after colliding with a target nucleus: *These relatively small anomalons surprised scientists who ... believed that anomalons, if they exist, would be much larger particles* (Marc Kusinitz). [< *anoma l*(ous) + *-on*]

ARM (ärm), *n. U.S.* adjustable rate mortgage (a mortgage with an interest rate that changes periodically during the term of the loan): *ARMs with caps [limits on rate increases or decreases] provide greater payment predictability and security for the borrower* (Consumers' Guide).

aus|tral[2] (ou strä′), *n.* the monetary unit of Argentina, equal to 100 centavos. It replaced the peso in 1986. [< American Spanish (Argentina) *austral* < Spanish *austral* southern < Latin *austrālis*]

autologous, *adj.* **2** donated by a person and preserved for his own future use: *autologous blood. Self-donated (autologous) transfusions prevent your contracting an infectious disease, such as AIDS or hepatitis* (Woman's Day).

B b

blush wine, a table wine slightly paler and drier than a rosé. *Blush wines, which are an attempt to make something akin to white wines out of surplus red grapes ... bear names such as "white zinfandel" and "cabernet blanc"* (Frank J. Prial).

boo|bird (bü′bérd′), *n. U.S. Slang.* a sports fan who boos members of the team he roots for when they play poorly: *A pox on all you boobirds who don't appreciate a team which, good or bad, always has the fan on the edge of the seat* (Los Angeles Times).

boutique farm, a farm that specializes in raising exotic crops and livestock: *Elsewhere around the country, boutique farms are producing game birds, ducks, and free-range chickens (which are allowed to roam and forage for natural food to add flavor and improve texture)* (Time).

building sickness, = sick building syndrome: *Surveys show that building sickness is far more common in air-conditioned than in naturally ventilated buildings* (Economist).

bump|out (bump′out′), *n. U.S.* an addition that increases the space of a room in an office, apartment, or house without adding significantly to the outside dimension of a structure: *... bumpouts can be virtually room-size, large enough to be called an addition* (New York Times).

C c

cam|o (kam′ō), *adj., n.* —*adj.* having the colors of military camouflage, especially on clothing: *a camo shirt or jacket. The Notesaf Tablet Holder, of nylon pack cloth, black, green, or camo* (Whole Earth Review). —*n.* a garment or other item with a camouflage pattern: *Most camo is made of denim or canvas material* (Outdoor Life). [< *camo*(uflage)]

chem|i|ga|tion (kem′ə gā′shən), *n.* the irrigation of crops with chemicals, such as fertilizers and pesticides: *Chemigation is usually done with ... special piping to drip small amounts of chemicals at the base of plants* (Sylvan H. Wittwer). [< *chem-* + (irr)*igation*]

col|or|i|za|tion (kul′ə rə zā′shən), *n.* the act or process of making a color photograph or motion picture from black-and-white images by using a computer that is programmed to assign various colors to different shades of black-and-white images: *John Huston ... denounced the colorization of his classic film, "The Maltese Falcon"* (New York Times).

compatibility, *n.* **5** the ability of computer software or hardware to be used with different models or systems without adaptation: *The TRS-80 Model 4 ... desktop computer offers compatibility with existing Model III software and a wide range of advanced features* (Popular Computing).

com|put|er|a|cy (kəm pyü′tər ə sē), *n.* = computer literacy: *The next great revolution in thought lies in ... "computeracy," as he prefers to call it, because the term computer literacy "conveys the erroneous conception that literacy—the use of the alphabet—and computeracy are basically the same"* (Christopher Lehman-Haupt).

contextualism, *n.* **2** *Architecture.* the principle that a structure should fit naturally into its surroundings: *Because of Modern architecture's disregard for contextualism, Modernist structures frequently seem at odds with neighboring buildings* (Robert Campbell).

crack|head (krak′hed′), *n. U.S. Slang.* a person addicted to crack (free-based cocaine): *Men between the ages of 20 and 35 [comprise] more than half the nation's so-called crackheads* (Time).

cruzado, *n.* **1** the monetary unit of Brazil, equal to 100 centavos. It replaced the cruzeiro in 1986.

cry|o|bank (krī′ō bangk′), *n., v.* —*n.* a place for storage of any of various products or organs of the body at extremely low temperature: *The Southern California Cryobank [is] a sperm bank* (Washington Post). —*v.t.* to preserve in a cryobank: *The methodology for cryobanking human semen has undergone continuous refinement* (Patient Care).

D d

deep pocket, *Informal.* **1** a person or company with strong financial resources: *A "deep pocket" is an entity that is perceived to have large assets and insurance ... The requirement that deep pockets pay damages if codefendants cannot is called the "doctrine of joint and several liability"* (Christian Science Monitor). **2** Usually, **deep pockets,** a large amount of capital; strong financial resources: *By bringing in a partner with deep pockets, ... the company was in a position to offer a more attractive deal* (New York Times).

E e

ear candy, *U.S. Slang.* smoothly arranged and pleasant-sounding popular music: *Synthesizers ... fulfill pop music's never-ending quest for fresh ear candy* (Time). *The British trio ... produces some fairly highbrow synthesized ear candy* (Stereo Review).

e|mer|gi|cen|ter (i mèr′jē sen′tər), *n. U.S.* a walk-in clinic for treating minor medical emergencies: *The emergicenter [is] a cross between a hospital emergency room and a family doctor's office ... generally located in shopping centers or along highways* (U.S. News & World Report).

F f

fifth force, *Physics.* a hypothetical force in nature intermediate in range between the gravitational and electromagnetic forces, which are infinite in range, and the strong and weak nuclear forces, which do not extend beyond the radius of an atomic nucleus: *The fifth force ... is quite weak, and is in practice detectable only on scales of about 200 metres, at which it appears as a modification of the usual gravitational force* (New Scientist).

flops (flops), *n.* a unit of speed in the operation of a computer, often used in combination, as in *megaflops* (one million flops) and *gigaflops* (one billion flops): *Already the Cray 2 has busted out of the "megaflops" realm ... Its peak is 1.2 billion flops* (Business Week). [< *f*(loating) *l*(ogical) *o*(perations) *p*(er) *s*(econd)]

fun|some (fun′səm), *adj.* having or loving fun; given to amusement: *She signed on to replace Jennilee Harrison as the third member of the funsome threesome in "Three's Company"* (Maclean's).

fuzzy logic, a form of logic which tries to take into account ill-defined or vague terms such as "very," "somewhat," and "mostly": *Fuzzy logic ... avoids the abrupt changes that might result from the either-or, all-or-nothing judgments inherent in classical logic* (Kevin McKean and Tom Dworetzky). —**fuzzy logician.**

G g

gateway drug, a soft drug, such as alcohol, that often leads the user to turn to hard drugs: *Marijuana is often a gateway drug for other illicit use, specifically cocaine and heroin* (New York Times).

gauge particle, *Nuclear Physics.* any of a group of elementary particles whose function is to transmit forces between other particles: *When the Sun lights the earth, the energy is transmitted ... by photons, the gauge particles of electromagnetism. And when the Earth attracts the Moon, the two exchange gravitons, the gauge particles for gravity* (John Schwartz).

glas|nost (gläs nôst'), *n.* a policy of open and public discussion of domestic issues encouraged by the Soviet government: *No explosion of glasnost in Moscow is going to allow Western scholars on-site inspection of all of Lenin's notes* (William Safire). [< Russian *glasnost'* public notice]

H h

har|mo|lod|ic (här'mə lod'ik), *adj., n.* —*adj.* combining harmonies, melodies, and rhythms in new, unconventional ways: *The "harmolodic" system ... broke down traditional harmonies and rhythms* (New York Times). —*n.* a harmolodic style or composition: *On "Consume" ... he's polyrhythmic, approximating the harmolodics of James "Blood" Ulmer and Ornette Coleman* (Washington Post). [< *harmo*(ny) + (me)*lodic*]

Higgs boson (higz), *Nuclear Physics.* a hypothetical particle with a spin of 0, thought to be the carrier of a force that generates the masses of all the fundamental particles: *The fact that in the standard model the Higgs boson is responsible for all observed masses implies that, even if in the end there is no such thing as a Higgs boson, there is at least a common source for all masses* (Scientific American). [< Peter W. *Higgs*, a British physicist of the 1900's, who proposed it]

hind|cast (hīnd'kast', -käst'), *v.i.,* **-cast** or **-cast|ed, -cast|ing.** to provide weather information based on the record of past atmospheric conditions: *By "hindcasting" from historical data, he says the company can tell a potential offshore bidder, for example, how fierce the worst storms will be at projected drilling sites* (Forbes).

home|school|ing (hōm'skü'ling), *n.* the teaching of children by their parents, especially as an alternative to sending them to school: *This survey of home-schoolers in Australia ... offers useful explanations for those who are curious or skeptical about homeschooling* (John Holt). —**home'school'er,** *n.*

hothouse, —*v.t. Education.* to begin teaching (children) at a very early age in order to stimulate or advance their mental development: *As the debate over the "superbaby" phenomenon intensifies, researchers have coined a verb form to describe it: "hothousing"* (New York Times).

I i

icon, *n.* **3** a picture or drawing representing a command to a computer, as for example the picture of a garbage can representing the command to erase a file: *When the user inserts a program disk into the computer, [there] appears on the computer's display screen ... an icon, or sketch, of each program on the disk* (Howard Bierman).

K k

kludge (klüj, kluj), *v.t.,* **kludged, kludg|ing.** *Slang.* to produce (a computer system, design, or the like) by clumsy improvisation: *A good design ... is beautiful, and people who do design can tell*

whether someone kludged it or whether they knew what they were doing (Washington Post). [origin uncertain]

L l

lith|o|trip|ter (lith'ō trip'tər), *n.* a device that disintegrates stones in the kidney or gall bladder by means of high-energy shock waves directed against the stones outside the body: *The lithotripter ... crushes kidney stones without any kind of incision* (Lawrence K. Altman). [< *litho-* + Greek *thrýptein* to crush, pulverize + English *-er*[1]]

-lock, combining form. complete stoppage; paralysis; jam: *Crowds brimmed the streets conquering gridlock, boat-lock, a taxi strike cablock* (New York Times). *Ever since "gridlock" had become a popular way of describing a standstill traffic jam, another new form, "pedlock," had come along to describe a pileup and immobilization of pedestrians* (Walter Kerr).

low jinks, *Informal.* irreverent or coarse behavior; vulgar jokes or pranks: *Shakespeare's comedy about the befuddlement of lovers and the low jinks of carousers...* (David Richards). [patterned on high jinks]

M m

messenger particle, *Physics.* any pointlike subatomic particle that transmits a fundamental force of nature. The graviton, the photon, the gluon, and the weakon are messenger particles: *The four forces are transported across the space between particles by pointlike quanta, or bundles of energy, which serve as messenger particles* (Robert H. March).

mid|dle|scence (mid'ə les'əns), *n.* = middle age: *Psychologists sometimes refer to this stage of life as "middle-scence" in an effort to explain how the shift from early adulthood to middle age parallels the shift from childhood to puberty* (McCall's). [< *middle* (age) + *-escence,* as in *adolescence*] —**mid|dle|scent,** (mid'ə les'ənt), *adj.*

mi|nox|i|dil (mə nok'sə dil), *n.* a drug used in the treatment of high blood pressure, found also to have the property of stimulating hair growth when applied as a lotion to bald spots in certain individuals: *Dermatologists are not sure how minoxidil works, though ... scientists have found that the drug causes improved blood flow to the scalp* (Chris A. Raymond). [< (a)*min*(e) + *oxid*(e) + (an)*il*(ine)]

mod|er|a|cy (mod'ər ə sē), *n.* the holding of moderate opinions, especially in politics; moderateness: *[He] seems to think that moderacy is the only test to be applied to the candidates* (London Times).

mul|ti|task|ing (mul'ti tas'king, -täs'-), *n.* the performance of two or more tasks concurrently by a computer: *The trend in microcomputers has been to machines that can ... handle several software applications simultaneously, a trick called multitasking* (Peter H. Lewis). Compare **single-tasking.**

munch|a|ble (mun'chə bəl), *adj., n. Informal.* —*adj.* suitable for eating as a snack: *"Empty" calories? True. That's*

what makes ... Planter's Cheese Curls so munchable and yet so steadfastly unsatisfactory (Tom Shales). —*n.* Usually, **munchables.** light food; snack: *They called it the Great Cookie War when two giant companies promoted their newest munchables in Kansas City* (Economist).

mu|ni (myü'nē), *n., pl.* **-nis.** *U.S. Informal.* a bond issued by a city or municipality; municipal bond: *[Henry] Bloch points out that munis are safe, and enormously liquid, and they can be bought in denominations as low as $1,000* (Time). [< *muni*(cipal bond)]

N n

ne|o|ism (nē'ō iz'əm), *n.* newness as a value in politics, art, and the like: *Neoism is being pushed—not by [art] critics, who are generally hostile, but by a few shrewd collectors with a financial stake in its success* (New York magazine). —**ne'o|ist,** *n., adj.*

O o

op|tron|ic (op tron'ik), *adj.* = optoelectronic: *France's Thomson-CSF is developing an optronic surveillance system ... The optronic section housing the camera has provisions for a laser designator* (Aviation Week & Space Technology).

ORV (no periods), off-road vehicle.

ORV|er (ō'är've̅'ər), *n. U.S. Informal.* the owner or driver of an off-road vehicle: *The road was ordered closed by the state, denying ORVs access to the beach and ... ORVers have protested* (Charles A. Bergman).

P p

PCP 1 phencyclidine. **2** pneumocystis carinii pneumonia (a type of pneumonia occurring in patients with severe diseases of the immune system, especially AIDS): *Patients are said to have AIDS if they have one of several diseases, mainly PCP and Kaposi's sarcoma* (Donald P. Francis).

perp (pėrp), *n. U.S. Slang.* a person who has committed a crime: *Police are notorious for creating new words by shortening existing ones, such as "perp" for perpetrator* (Fort Wayne Journal Gazette).

pho|ti|no (fō tē'nō), *n., pl.* **-nos.** *Nuclear Physics.* a hypothetical particle which, according to the theory of supersymmetry, is a weakly interacting form of the photon: *If there are a large number of photinos floating around the cosmos, the sun's gravity would continually draw some of them to its interior* (Science News). [< *phot*(on) + *-ino* (as in *neutrino*)]

pin|strip|er (pin'strī'pər), *n. U.S. Informal.* a business executive: *The airline ... has to attract more business travelers if*

Pronunciation Key: hat, āge, câre, fär; let, ēqual, tėrm; it, īce; hot, ōpen, ôrder; oil, out; cup, pút, rüle; child; long; thin; ᴛʜen; zh, measure; ə represents a in about, e in taken, i in pencil, o in lemon, u in circus.

it hopes to survive. "Pinstripers are not buying our product, for very good reasons," Burr acknowledges (Business Week). [because of the popularity of pinstriped suits among business executives]

poison pill, *U.S.* any means of finance used by a company to make it too costly for a hostile company to acquire it through a tender offer: *Tin parachutes . . . are also a form of a poison pill, which are conditions established by a corporate board to make a takeover prohibitively expensive* (Alison Leigh Cowan).

PUVA (pü′və), *n.* a method of treating psoriasis by the use of a particular drug (psoralen) combined with exposure to ultraviolet light: *Nearly 75 per cent of patients undergoing PUVA treatment get rid of almost all their psoriasis* (Lynne and Stanford Lamberg). [< P(soralen) U(ltra) v(iolet) A]

Q q

qua|si|crys|tal (kwā′sī kris′təl, -zī-; kwä′sē-, -zē-), *n. Physics.* a form of solid matter having unit cells like crystals but lacking the regular repeating pattern of crystalline ions: *Quasicrystals are much harder to (plastically) deform than ordinary solids; also, electronic and vibrational properties are . . . intermediate between those of crystals and glasses* (Paul J. Steinhardt).

R r

race|walk (rās′wôk′), *n., v. —n.* a race in walking for speed or against time: *Carl Schuler . . . took sixth in the . . . Olympic 50-kilometer racewalk* (Washington Post). *—v.i.* to compete in a racewalk: *As Mr. Jacobson sees it, even if one doesn't racewalk, adopting the form of a racewalker can produce more benefits than other walking styles* (New York Times Magazine). **—race′walk′er,** *n.*

S s

SDI or **S.D.I.,** 2 Strategic Defense Initiative (a system of computer-controlled defense using lasers and nuclear ballistic missiles in space to intercept and destroy enemy missiles before they reach their targets): *Opponents point out that even if both nations had an SDI, the situation would be unstable because of the temptation for one nation to strike first* (R. M. Lawrence).

sick building syndrome, a condition of ill health caused by absorbing toxic fumes or other pollutants found in some modern airtight buildings; building sickness: *Office workers in new buildings with sealed windows are coming down with what doctors call "sick building syndrome"—eye, nose and throat irritation, headaches, dizziness, nausea, diarrhea, and rashes* (U.S. News & World Report).

sin|gle-task|ing (sing′gəl tas′king, -täs′-), *n.* the sequential performance of two or more tasks by a computer: *Single-tasking operating systems must process sequentially, and multitasking systems . . . rapidly go from one process to another, appearing to perform many tasks at once* (Byte).

slep|ton (slep′ton), *n. Nuclear Physics.* a hypothetical constituent of a fermion corresponding to any particle in the class of leptons: *Supersymmetric theorists are forced to invent a doubling of the known spectrum of particles, and they have had to make up lots of new names for the unseen "sparticles," such as the spin-0 supersymmetric . . . "squarks" and "sleptons"* (New Scientist).

spin, *n.* 7 *U.S. Figurative.* a way of regarding something; slant; angle: *Americans know how to put a positive spin on the most explosive event* (Los Angeles Times). *As the President's political fortunes have slipped, aides . . . are trying to alter the "spin" of news coverage, especially analyses* (U.S. News & World Report).

squark (skwôrk), *n. Nuclear Physics.* a hypothetical constituent of a fermion corresponding to a quark in the class of hadrons: *According to supersymmetry . . . the hypothetical fermionic partners of quarks and leptons are generically called squarks and sleptons* (John Schwartz).

standard model, *Physics.* the prevailing theory that describes the basic constituents of matter and the fundamental forces by which they interact: *According to the standard model, all matter is made up of quarks and leptons, which interact with one another through four forces: gravity, electromagnetism, the weak force, and the strong force* (Martinus J.G. Veltman).

string, *n.* 13 *Physics.* a basic unit of matter consisting of a one-dimensional curve with zero thickness and a length of about 10^{-35} meter: *The graviton is a closed string—its ends joined to form a loop . . . somewhat like a long, narrow strip of paper that has been given a half twist and then had its ends taped together* (Robert H. March).

su|per|string theory (sü′pər string′), *Physics.* any theory based on supersymmetry in which the basic units of matter are strings (one-dimensional curves): *We presented a superstring theory containing both open and closed strings . . . free from anomalies and infinities* (John H. Schwarz).

sur|ro|ga|cy (sėr′ə gə sē), *n.* the quality or condition of being a surrogate, especially a surrogate mother: *Unlike the New Jersey court case involving a surrogate mother, . . . there was no controversy surrounding Anne's surrogacy* (Christian Science Monitor).

surrogate mother, 1 a woman who gives birth to a child through artificial insemination by a man who is not her husband: *A court in New Jersey . . . gave custody to the contractual parents after the surrogate mother, who took $10,000 to become pregnant, changed her mind* (New Scientist). 2 Also called **surrogate gestational mother,** a female who carries until birth the surgically implanted fertilized egg or embryo of another female. **—surrogate motherhood.**

T t

tele|pres|ence (tel′ə prez′əns), *n.* the feeling of the operator of a remote-control device that he is present at the operation: *A one-to-one relationship between a person's hand and the manipulator grip is no longer adequate; rather, what is now needed is an entire system of peripheral activities to give the operator "telepresence"* (Nuclear News).

tele|work (tel′ə wėrk′), *n.* work done at one's home or other place away from an office or central work site: *The phenomenon of working at home rather than in an office—often called "telework". . . is expected to increase greatly in the years ahead* (Phoenix Gazette). **—tel′e|work′er,** *n.*

tin parachute, a contract guaranteeing continued wages and benefits to the rank and file when control of a company is transferred to new owners: *Unlike golden parachutes for executives, which must be disclosed publicly, tin parachutes are often kept secret—at least until a hostile bidder appears on the scene* (New York Times). [patterned after golden parachute]

trans|ac|ti|vate (tran zak′tə vāt, -sak′-), *v.t.,* **-vat|ed, -vat|ing.** to cause (a cell) to undergo transactivation: *The supposition is that the transactivating proteins . . . are the transforming proteins of the viruses* (Science). **—transac′ti|va′tor,** *n.*

trans|ac|ti|va|tion (tran′zak tə vā′shən, -sak′-), *n. Genetics.* a process by which a viral gene causes the host cell to transcribe a protein which in turn induces the cell to reproduce large amounts of the virus's components: *The gene found in the AIDS virus—called "TAT" for transactivation and transcription activation—can adjust its own production, increasing 500 to 1,000 times* (Philip J. Hilts). [< trans(cription) activation]

V v

vid|e|ot (vid′ē ət), *n. U.S. Slang.* 1 a person who watches too much television: *. . . frightened at the rapid change television has effected on the collective psyche of America—a country he described as a nation of 'videots'* (Listener). 2 a television executive: *The idea of a tennis match for $250,000 or nothing must have been so tempting to the videots* (Washington Post). [< vide(o) + (idi)ot]

W w

wait|ron (wā′tron), *n. U.S.* a waiter or waitress (used to eliminate the reference to the subject's sex): *After the waitron had taken their order, Mr. Warner asked her for a glass of water* (Ron Alexander). [< waitr(ess) + -on, Greek neuter suffix]

week|night|ly (wēk′nīt′lē), *adj.* occurring on weeknights: *Social scientists grind out studies on the style and content of his weeknightly 8 p.m. newscast* (Time).

window, *n.* 6 a rectangular area occupying all or part of a computer display screen: *Windows can be laid side by side or they can overlap. Overlapping windows can be thought of as a stack of papers on a desk, with the window "on top" being the currently active display area* (Carol A. Ogdin).

work front, an area or sphere where a particular kind of work is done; a field of activity: *The work of the chairman and vice-chairman of the Revolutionary Committee has been clearly defined according to different work fronts* (Listener).

Index

How to Use the Index

This index covers the contents of the 1986, 1987, and 1988 editions of THE WORLD BOOK YEAR BOOK.

Each index entry is followed by the edition year and the page number, as:

Bon Jovi: popular music, 88-449

This means that information about this rock group is on page 449 in the 1988 edition of THE YEAR BOOK.

An index entry that is the title of an article appearing in THE YEAR BOOK is printed in capital letters, as: **GEOLOGY.** An entry that is not an article title, but a subject discussed in an article of some other title, is printed: **Hominid.**

The "See" and "See also" cross-references are to other entries within the index. Clue words or phrases are used when two or more references to the same subject appear in the same edition of THE YEAR BOOK, as:

Crash of '87: bank, 88-220; Japan, 88-372; stock market, Special Report, 88-145; stocks and bonds, 88-489

The indication "il." means that the reference is to an illustration only. An index entry in capital letters followed by "WBE" refers to a new or revised WORLD BOOK ENCYCLOPEDIA article in the supplement section, as:

ANTARCTICA: WBE, 88-538

A

coins, 86–262; Korea, North, 87–365; soccer, 88–475; women's sports, Special Report, 87–66
Omaha: city, 88–258, 87–252, 86–254
Oman: Middle East, 88–409, 87–396, 86–400
Ondaatje, Michael: Canadian literature, 88–245
ONTARIO, 88–433, 87–425, 86–427; geology, 86–334; hospital, 87–346; Peterson, David R., 86–432
OPEC (Organization of Petroleum Exporting Countries): Europe, 87–316. See also **PETROLEUM AND GAS.**
Opera. See **CLASSICAL MUSIC.**
Operation Greylord: Chicago, 88–252, 87–246; courts, 86–275
Optical disk: computer, 87–263
Orchestra. See **CLASSICAL MUSIC.**
Oregon: state govt., 88–486, 87–480, 86–480
Organ transplantation: hospital, 88–351; medicine, 87–391
Organization of African Unity (OAU): Africa, 87–179, 86–184
Organization of American States (OAS): Latin America, 88–382
Organization of Petroleum Exporting Countries. See **OPEC.**
Organizations. See **YOUTH ORGANIZATIONS;** names of specific organizations.
Organized crime: crime, 88–283, 87–275; Philadelphia, 87–434
Original intention: Constitution, Special Report, 87–99
Orser, Brian: ice skating, 88–355
ORTEGA, DANIEL, 86–427; ils., 88–283, 87–522, 86–278; Nicaragua, 88–425, 86–418
Ortega Clouthier, Manuel: Mexico, 88–405
Orthodox Church in America: religion, 88–464, 87–457, 86–457
"Oscar" Awards: awards, 88–214, 87–214, 86–214
Osteoporosis: women's sports, Special Report, 87–70
Otter: conservation, 88–275
Otto, Kristin: swimming, 88–494
Ottoman Empire: art, 88–197
Outsourcing: automobile, 88–210
Over-the-counter market: stock market, Special Report, 88–147
Overthrust Belt: national parks, Special Report, 87–110
Oxford Illustrated Literary Guide to Canada, The: Canadian literature, 88–245
Ozal, Turgut: Turkey, 88–511, 87–505
Ozick, Cynthia: literature, 88–390
Ozone: chemistry, 88–249; city, 88–260; environmental pollution, 88–317; national parks, Special Report, 87–111; weather, 88–527

P

PACIFIC ISLANDS, 88–434, 87–426, 86–428; Australia, 88–202
Pacific Northwest Ballet: dancing, 88–286
Packaging: food, 88–329
Paddle tennis: sports, 88–482, 87–477, 86–476
PAGE, GERALDINE, 87–428; deaths, 88–292
Painting: art, 87–196; art restoration, Special Report, 87–132; visual arts, 86–513
Paisley, Ian R. K.: Northern Ireland, 88–428
PAKISTAN, 88–435, 87–428, 86–430; Afghanistan, 88–178, 87–177; Asia, 88–201, 87–202, 86–200; India, 88–358, 87–350; Islam, Special Report, 88–44
Palau: Pacific Islands, 88–435, 87–426
PALEONTOLOGY, 88–436, 87–429, 86–430. See also **ANTHROPOLOGY; ARCHAEOLOGY; Fossil; GEOLOGY.**
Palestine. See **ISRAEL; JORDAN; MIDDLE EAST.**
Palestinians: Israel, 88–368, 86–362; Jordan, 86–366; Middle East, 88–410, 86–399
Palme, Olof: Sweden, 88–493, 87–487, 86–487
PAN (National Action Party): Mexico, 88–405, Special Report, 87–156
PAN AMERICAN GAMES, 88–437; Latin America, 88–385
Pan Pacific Games: swimming, 88–493
PANAMA, 88–437, 86–431; Latin America, 88–383, 87–371, 86–375
Panda: zoos, 88–534
Papua New Guinea: Pacific Islands, 88–434, 87–427, 86–429
Parachute jumping: sports, 88–482, 87–477, 86–476
PARAGUAY, 87–430; Latin America, 88–383, 87–371, 86–375
Parallel processing: computer, 87–262, 86–265

Parents and Teachers, National Congress of. See **NATIONAL PTA.**
Park Chong Chol: Korea, South, 88–377
Park Service, National: national parks, Special Report, 87–102
Parker, Denise: il., 88–437
Parkinson's disease: medicine, 88–403
Parks Canada: national parks, Special Report, 87–108
Parliament. See **CANADA; GREAT BRITAIN.**
Parthenios III: Eastern Orthodox, 88–303
Parti Québécois: Montreal, 86–403; Quebec, 87–452, 86–453
Particle accelerator: physics, 88–446
Pass laws: South Africa, 87–470, 86–471
Passive smoking: public health, 88–459
Pawley, Howard: Manitoba, 88–398, 87–387
PAZ ESTENSSORO, VÍCTOR, 86–431; Bolivia, 88–230, 87–229, 86–228
PBS (Public Broadcasting Service). See **TELEVISION.**
Peabody Broadcasting Awards: awards, 88–216, 87–216, 86–215
Peckford, Brian: Newfoundland, 88–420
Pedersen, Charles J.: Nobel Prizes, 88–428
Peggy Sue Got Married: il., 87–403
Pelli, Cesar: architecture, 88–191
Penguin Encounter: zoo design, Special Report, 87–60; zoos, 88–533
Penkovsky, Oleg: espionage, Special Report, 87–40
Pennsylvania: Philadelphia, 88–440, 87–433, 86–434; state govt., 88–486, 87–480, 86–480
Pennzoil Company: courts, 87–274; petroleum, 88–439
Pension fund: stock market, Special Report, 88–152
Pentagon: U.S. govt., 86–508. See also **ARMED FORCES.**
People Express, Inc.: aviation, 88–212, 87–212
People meter: television, 88–499
People Mover: Detroit, 88–297, 86–291; transit, 87–502
People's Republic of China. See **CHINA.**
Peres, Shimon: Israel, 88–368, 87–358, 86–362, 85–357; Middle East, 86–401
Perestroika: Close-Up, 88–515; U.S.S.R., 88–511
Perestroika: New Thinking for Our Country and the World: literature, 88–390
Pérez de Cuéllar, Javier: il., 86–181; United Nations, 87–507
Pérez Rodríguez, Roberto Martín: Cuba, 88–284
Perlmutter, Nathan: deaths, 88–292
Perry, William: football, 86–326
Pershing IA missile: Germany, West, 88–338
Persian Gulf: armed forces, 88–193; Europe, 88–320; Iran, 88–364; Middle East, 88–406; Netherlands, 88–418; petroleum, 88–438; President, 88–452
Person, Chuck: basketball, 88–226
Personal computer: computer, 88–267; WBE, 86–555
PERU, 88–438, 87–430, 86–432; archaeology, 87–189; García Pérez, Alan, 86–333; Latin America, 88–383, 87–371, 86–375
Pesticide: environmental pollution, 87–311, 86–311
Peterson, David: Ontario, 88–433
PETROLEUM AND GAS, 88–438, 87–431, 86–432; consumerism, 87–272; courts, 87–274; environmental pollution, 88–318; manufacturing, 87–389; Mexico, Special Report, 87–146. See also **ENERGY SUPPLY** and articles on specific countries, provinces, and cities.
Petroleum Exporting Countries, Organization of. See **OPEC.**
PGA (Professional Golfers' Association). See **GOLF.**
pH scale: acid rain, Special Report, 88–53
Pham Hung: Vietnam, 88–522
PHILADELPHIA, 88–440, 87–433, 86–434; architecture, 86–192; city, 88–258, 87–252, 86–254; zoos, 87–525, 86–526
Philately. See **STAMP COLLECTING.**
Philby, Harold: espionage, Special Report, 87–40
PHILIPPINES, 88–442, 87–434, 86–436; Aquino, Corazon, 87–188; Asia, 88–201, 87–202, 86–200
Phoenix: city, 88–258, 87–252, 86–254
Phomvihan, Kaysone: Laos, 88–381
Phonograph. See **CLASSICAL MUSIC; POPULAR MUSIC; Recordings.**
Phosphor-tagging: stamps, 88–484
Photocopying: Canadian Library Association, 87–241

PHOTOGRAPHY, 88–444, 87–436, 86–437; Canadian literature, 86–243; electronics, 86–306; visual arts, 86–514
Physical examinations: medicine, 88–403
PHYSICS, 88–444, 87–437, 86–438; WBE, 88–556. See also **NOBEL PRIZES.**
Physiology: Nobel Prizes, 87–420, 86–421
Piano, Renzo: il., 88–198
Picasso, Pablo: art, 88–196; visual arts, 86–513
Pilsbury, Betty F.: youth organizations, 88–530
Pindling, Lynden O.: West Indies, 88–529
Piño Díaz, Rafael del: Cuba, 88–283
Pinochet Ugarte, Augusto: Chile, 88–253, 87–248, 86–249
Pipeline: petroleum, 88–438
Piquet, Nelson: auto racing, 88–210
Pit bull: dog, 88–300
Pitt, David G.: Canadian literature, 88–245
Pittman-Robertson Act: hunting, 88–354
Pittsburgh: city, 88–258, 87–252, 86–254; zoos, 88–533
Plaid Cymru: Wales, 88–523
Plant. See **BOTANY; FARM AND FARMING; GARDENING.**
Plasma: star death, Special Report, 88–136
Plastics: chemistry, 87–245
Platform tennis: sports, 88–482, 87–477, 86–476
Platinum: mining, 88–411, 87–399
Platoon: motion pictures, 88–416
PLO (Palestine Liberation Organization): Jews and Judaism, 87–362; Jordan, 88–375, 87–363, 86–366; Lebanon, 87–374; Libya, 88–388; Middle East, 87–398, 86–399
POETRY, 88–446, 87–438, 86–439; newsmakers, 88–424; Warren, Robert Penn, 87–515. See also **CANADIAN LITERATURE; LITERATURE FOR CHILDREN.**
PoGo Bal: toys and games, 88–505
Poindexter, John M.: Cabinet, U.S., 87–236; Iran-contra affair, 88–366; President, 87–445
Poirot, Hercule: detective fiction, Special Report, 88–116
Poison gas: environmental pollution, 86–310; geology, 87–330
POLAND, 88–447, 87–439, 86–439; Europe, 88–321, 87–314, 86–315
Pole vault. See **TRACK AND FIELD.**
Police procedural: detective fiction, Special Report, 88–126
Polisario Liberation Front: Africa, 87–179; Morocco, 88–412, 87–401, 86–405
Polish National Catholic Church of America: religion, 88–464, 87–457, 86–457
Political parties. See **Communist Party; DEMOCRATIC PARTY; REPUBLICAN PARTY; and** names of other parties.
Political prisoners: civil rights, 86–257; Cuba, 88–284; Israel, 86–361
Politics: aging in America, Special Report, 88–110
Politics of the Imagination, The: Canadian literature, 88–245
Polk Memorial Awards: awards, 88–216, 87–215, 86–215
Poll, Sylvia: Pan American Games, 88–437; swimming, 88–494
Pollard, Anne Henderson: armed forces, 88–195
Pollard, Jonathan Jay: armed forces, 87–196; crime, 88–282, 86–277; Jews and Judaism, 88–373
Pollution: acid rain, Special Report, 88–52; coal, 87–259; national parks, Special Report, 87–101. See also **CONSERVATION; ENERGY SUPPLY; ENVIRONMENTAL POLLUTION; Water pollution.**
Polo: sports, 88–482, 87–477, 86–476
Pope. See **John Paul II; ROMAN CATHOLIC CHURCH.**
POPULAR MUSIC, 88–447, 87–440, 86–440; awards, 88–214, 87–214, 86–214; Houston, Whitney, 88–353
POPULATION, 88–450, 87–443, 86–442; city, 88–256. See also specific continents, countries, regions.
Population, U.S. See **CENSUS; CITY.**
Pornography: Canadian Library Association, 88–244; crime, 87–276
Portland, Ore.: city, 88–258, 87–252, 86–254
PORTUGAL, 88–450, 87–443, 86–443; Europe, 88–321, 87–314, 86–315; Spain, 86–474
Possum Magic: literature for children, 88–393
POSTAL SERVICE, U.S., 88–450, 87–444, 86–444; labor, 88–379
Potash industry: Saskatchewan, 88–471
Poverty: child welfare, 88–252; city, 88–256, 87–251, 86–252; education, 88–309; welfare, 88–528, 87–519, 86–520

Acknowledgments

The publishers acknowledge the following sources for illustrations. Credits read from top to bottom, left to right, on their respective pages. An asterisk (*) denotes illustrations and photographs that are the exclusive property of THE YEAR BOOK. All maps, charts, and diagrams were prepared by THE YEAR BOOK staff unless otherwise noted.

4	© Alain Nogues, Sygma; © D. Hallinam, FPG; © David Strick, Black Star
5	Rich Frishman; Michael Parfit
9	© J. L. Atlan, Sygma
10	Bruce Gilbert, *New York Newsday*
12	© Sipa Press
13	AP/Wide World
14	Jacques Langevin, Sygma
15	© Patrick Robert, Sygma; © Sygma
16	© J. L. Atlan, Sygma
17	© Daniel Simon, Gamma/Liaison; Anheuser-Busch Inc., St. Louis; © Tony Scott, Sygma; © Ken Franckling, LGI
18	Sotheby's, Inc., New York
20	Focus on Sports; © Patrick Piel, Gamma/Liaison
21	Anglo-Australian Observatory; Sandro Tucci, © *Time* Magazine; © Daniel Forster, Duomo
22	AP/Wide World; © Douglas Kirkland, Sygma; © *Editores Nacionales* from Sygma
23	© Peter Turnley, Black Star; Dirck Halstead, © *Time* Magazine; © Dan Helms, Duomo; David J. Cross, © *Time* Magazine
24	Ron Dirito, Sygma; © Sygma; © J. L. Atlan, Sygma
25	© Piers Cavendish, Reflex from Picture Group; © Felici, Gamma/Liaison; © Dennis Brack, Black Star
26	© Adam J. Stoltman, Duomo; Sherbell/Price from Picture Group
27	© David Madison, Duomo; © *Detroit Free Press* from Black Star; © Selwyn Tait, Black Star
28	© Dan Helms, Duomo; © Tom Mihaler, Sygma; © Torregano, Sipa Press
29	Maria R. Bastone, AFP; © David Woo, *Dallas Morning News* from Sygma; Focus on Sports; © J. L. Atlan, Sygma
30	© Paul Efird, *Gwinnett Daily News* from Picture Group; © John Chiasson, Gamma/Liaison; Toshi Matsumoto, Sygma
31	© Stephen Ferry, Gamma/Liaison
33	Bob Gurecki, Agence France-Presse
34	Ropland and Sabrina Michaud, Woodfin Camp, Inc.
35	Jean Gaumy, Magnum
37	Topkapi Saray Museum Library
38	Arabian American Oil Company; Ronald Sheridan's Photo-Library; Michael Coyne, Black Star
40	Mohamed Amin, Camerapix; Roland and Sabrina Michaud, Woodfin Camp, Inc.
41	C. J. Collins, Photo Researchers
42	Mohamed Amin, Camerapix
44	Steve McCurry; Carl Purcell
45	Alain Nogues, Sygma
46	Art—Eileen Mueller Neill*
47	Henri Bureau, Sygma; Gamma/Liaison; Bersuder, Sipa Press; Franklin, Sygma
50	Grant Heilman
51	Roger M. Cheng, State University of New York Atmospheric Sciences Research Center; Michos Tzovaras, Art Resource
53-54	George Kelvin*
56-59	© Ted Spiegel, Black Star
60	Winston Fraser; © Diana Walker, Gamma/Liaison
61	© Ted Spiegel, Black Star
64	© Charles Feil, FPG; Tennessee Valley Authority
66	National Library of Australia; Photographic Library of Australia
68	Art—Lydia Halverson*; photo—Mitchell Library, Sydney
70	Art—Lydia Halverson*; photo—National Library of Australia
71	National Library of Australia
72	Art—Lydia Halverson*; photo—Art Gallery of New South Wales
73	John Sands Promotional Products, Sydney
74	Art—Lydia Halverson*; photos—Historic Memorials Collection, Parliament House, Canberra; Dixson Galleries, Sydney
75	Mitchell Library
76	Art—Lydia Halverson*; photo—Mitchell Library
77	National Library of Australia
78	Art—Lydia Halverson*; photos—National Library of Australia; Mitchell Library
79	Australian War Memorial, Canberra
80	Art—Lydia Halverson*; photos—Art Gallery of New South Wales; Australian War Memorial, Canberra
81	Australian Consulate-General, New York
82	Photographic Library of Australia; © Carl Roessler, Bruce Coleman Inc.; Twentieth Century Fox from Shooting Star
83	© D. Hallinan, FPG
84	© Tom McHugh, Photo Researchers
86	© Rick Smolan, Sygma
88	© Cary Wolinsky, Stock, Boston; © Michael Coyne, Black Star
89	© David Liddle, Horizon; © David Austen, Black Star
90	© David Moore, Black Star
91	© Oliver Strewe, Wildlight

92	© Robert Frerck; © J. Guichard, Sygma, Photographic Library of Australia
93	© Simon Cowling, Horizon
94	Promotion Australia; Photri from Marilyn Gartman
95	© Philip Hayson, Photographic Library of Australia
96	© Gamma/Liaison
98	© Mike Yamashita, Woodfin Camp, Inc.
103	© Alex Webb, Magnum; © Jeff Lowenthal, Woodfin Camp, Inc.
105	© Timothy Eagan, Woodfin Camp, Inc.; © Melissa Grimes-Guy, Photo Researchers; © David Strick, Black Star
106	© Jim Balog, Black Star
107	© Timothy Eagan, Woodfin Camp, Inc.
109	© Len Barbiera, The Stock Shop; © Robert Isear, Science Source from Photo Researchers
110	© John Ficara, Woodfin Camp, Inc.
112	Tom Herzberg*
116	Rich Frishman; *World Book* photo
117	Universal from Shooting Star; Martha Swope
118	Special Collections, University of Minnesota; Movie Still Archives; Culver; Frank Goodman Associates
122	Culver; Movie Still Archives; Culver; Pulp Magazine Collection, Popular Culture Library, Bowling Green State University, Ohio
126	*World Book* photo
128-129	David Malin and Ray Sharples, Anglo-Australian Telescope Board
131	Vera A. Lentz, Visions; University of Toronto
134	Rob Wood, Stansbury, Ronsaville, Wood Inc.*
135	Anglo-Australian Telescope Board
136-139	Rob Wood, Stansbury, Ronsaville, Wood Inc.*
140	California Institute of Technology and Carnegie Institute of Washington from Hale Observatories; Rob Wood, Stansbury, Ronsaville, Wood Inc.*
141	Michael Marten, Science Photo Library
142	Rob Wood, Stansbury, Ronsaville, Wood, Inc.*
144	Charles Feil, After Image
147	Bettmann Archive; Bob Gurecki, Agence France-Presse
148	Michael Hagel*
153	Bettmann Archive; Maria R. Bastone, Agence France-Presse
154	© John Moss, Black Star; © David Stoecklein, West Stock
155	© John McGrail 1986. All rights reserved
159	Granger Collection
160	Art—Kristin Nelson*; photos—Gernsheim Collection, Harry Ransom Humanities Center, University of Texas at Austin; *The Illustrated London News*
161	Historical Society of Pennsylvania
162	Art—Kristin Nelson*
163	Granger Collection; Bettmann Archive
164-165	Kristin Nelson*
166	Art—Kristin Nelson*; photos—National Museum of American History, Smithsonian Institution; Detail of *Dancing (fancy)* from Stanford Museum of Art, Muybridge Collection
167	Bruce Torrence Hollywood Historical Collection; Bettmann Archive
168	Art—Kristin Nelson*; photos—*San Francisco Examiner*
169	Special Collections, University of Minnesota
170	Art—Kristin Nelson*; photo—Granger Collection
171	Kristin Nelson*
173	AP/Wide World
174	John Chiasson, Gamma/Liaison; Reuters/Bettmann Newsphotos
175	AP/Wide World; Tom Peterson, NYT Pictures
176	© 1987 Chrysalis Visual Programming, Ltd./© 1987 The Coca-Cola Company. "Coca-Cola," "Coke," and the Dynamic Ribbon device are trademarks of The Coca-Cola Company.
177	Agence France-Presse
179	F. Gaillarde, Gamma/Liaison
182	Camerapix
183	Reuters/Bettmann Newsphotos
184	*Edmonton Journal* from Picture Group
185	Catherine Leroy, Sipa Press
186	American Library Association
187	William Claiborne, *The Washington Post*
188	The Institute of Human Origins
190	Walter Coker, University of Florida
191	© Timothy Hursley
193	AP/Wide World
194	U.S. Navy
195	AP/Wide World
196	John Chiasson, Gamma/Liaison
197	AP/Wide World
198	John Chiasson, Gamma/Liaison
200-202	AP/Wide World
203	UPI/Bettmann Newsphotos
204	AP/Wide World
205	National Optical Astronomy Observatories

A Preview of 1988

January

					1	2
3	4	5	6	7	8	9
10	11	12	13	14	15	16
17	18	19	20	21	22	23
24	25	26	27	28	29	30
31						

1 **New Year's Day.**

5 **Twelfth Night,** traditional end of Christmas festivities during the Middle Ages.

6 **Epiphany,** 12th day of Christmas, celebrates the visit of the Three Wise Men to the infant Jesus.

18 **Martin Luther King, Jr., Day,** honoring the slain civil rights leader, is celebrated on the third Monday in January, according to law. The actual anniversary of his birth is January 15.

26 **Australia Day** marks Captain Arthur Phillip's landing in 1788 where Sydney now stands.

31 **Super Bowl XXII,** the National Football League's championship game, in San Diego.

February

	1	2	3	4	5	6
7	8	9	10	11	12	13
14	15	16	17	18	19	20
21	22	23	24	25	26	27
28	29					

1-28 **Black History Month** in the United States.

2 **Ground-Hog Day.** Legend says six weeks of winter weather will follow if the ground hog sees its shadow.

8 **Boy Scouts of America Birthday Anniversary** marks the founding of the organization in 1910.

12 **Abraham Lincoln's Birthday,** observed in most states.

13-28 **Winter Olympic Games** in Calgary, Canada.

14 **Valentine's Day,** festival of romance and affection.

15 **George Washington's Birthday,** according to law, is celebrated on the third Monday in February. The actual anniversary is February 22.

16 **Mardi Gras,** celebrated in New Orleans and many Roman Catholic countries, is the last merrymaking before Lent.

New Hampshire Primary Election, first U.S. presidential primary.

17 **Ash Wednesday,** first day of Lent for Christians, begins the period of repentance that precedes Easter.

Chinese New Year begins year 4686, the Year of the Dragon, on the ancient Chinese calendar.

29 **Leap Year Day.**

March

	1	2	3	4	5
6	7	8	9	10	11	12
13	14	15	16	17	18	19
20	21	22	23	24	25	26
27	28	29	30	31		

1-31 **Red Cross Month.**

3 **Purim,** Jewish festival commemorating how Esther saved the Jews from the tyrant Haman.

6-12 **Girl Scout Week** marks the group's 76th birthday.

13-20 **Camp Fire Birthday Week** marks the 78th anniversary of the group.

17 **St. Patrick's Day,** honoring the patron saint of Ireland.

19 **St. Joseph's Day,** Roman Catholic feast day honoring the husband of the Virgin Mary.

Swallows Return to San Juan Capistrano, California, from their winter homes.

20 **First Day of Spring,** 4:39 A.M. E.S.T.

27 **Palm Sunday** marks Jesus Christ's last entry into Jerusalem, where people covered His path with palm branches.

31 **Maundy Thursday,** Christian celebration of Christ's commandment to love others.

April

					1	2
3	4	5	6	7	8	9
10	11	12	13	14	15	16
17	18	19	20	21	22	23
24	25	26	27	28	29	30

1 **Good Friday** marks the death of Jesus on the cross. It is a public holiday in many countries and several states of the United States.

2 **Passover,** Jewish festival that celebrates the exodus of the Jews from bondage in Egypt.

3 **Easter Sunday,** commemorating the Resurrection of Jesus Christ.

Daylight-Saving Time begins at 2 A.M.

11 **Academy Awards Night,** when the Academy of Motion Picture Arts and Sciences presents the Oscars.

15 **Income Tax Day** in the United States.

17-23 **National Library Week.**

19 **First Day of Ramadan,** the Islamic holy month, observed by fasting.

27 **Professional Secretaries Day** acknowledges the contributions of secretaries in business, government, and other fields.

30 **World Expo 88,** world's fair with the theme "Leisure in the Age of Technology," through October 30 in Brisbane, Australia.

May

1	2	3	4	5	6	7
8	9	10	11	12	13	14
15	16	17	18	19	20	21
22	23	24	25	26	27	28
29	30	31				

1 **May Day,** observed as a festival of spring in many countries and as a holiday honoring workers in socialist and Communist countries.

8 **Mother's Day.**

Rogation Sunday, fifth Sunday after Easter, when Roman Catholics bring their animals to church for a special blessing.

12 **Ascension Day,** or Holy Thursday, 40 days after Easter, celebrates the ascent of Jesus Christ into heaven.

21 **Armed Forces Day** honors all branches of the armed forces in the United States.

22 **Pentecost,** or Whitsunday, the seventh Sunday after Easter, commemorates the descent of the Holy Spirit upon the 12 disciples.

Shavuot, Jewish Feast of Weeks, marks the revealing of the Ten Commandments to Moses on Mount Sinai.

23 **Victoria Day,** in Canada, marks the official birthday of the reigning monarch.

29 **Trinity Sunday,** the eighth Sunday after Easter, honors the union of the Father, the Son, and the Holy Spirit.

30 **Memorial Day,** by law, is the last Monday in May.

Stratford Festival of drama through mid-October in Stratford, Canada.

June

			1	2	3	4
5	6	7	8	9	10	11
12	13	14	15	16	17	18
19	20	21	22	23	24	25
26	27	28	29	30		

6 **D-Day** commemorates the Allied landing in Normandy in 1944, during World War II.

14 **Flag Day.**

14-17 **Royal Ascot,** famous series of thoroughbred horse races in Ascot, England.

19 **Father's Day.**

20 **First Day of Summer,** 11:57 P.M. E.D.T.

All-England (Wimbledon) Tennis Championship, through July 3 in Wimbledon, near London.

23 **Midsummer Day,** summer celebration in many European countries.

July

						1	2
3	4	5	6	7	8	9
10	11	12	13	14	15	16
17	18	19	20	21	22	23
24	25	26	27	28	29	30
31						

1 **Canada Day,** in Canada, celebrates the Confederation of the provinces in 1867.
Halfway Point of 1988, when the year is half over.

4 **Independence Day,** in the United States, the anniversary of the day on which the Continental Congress adopted the Declaration of Independence in 1776.

12 **Baseball All-Star Game,** Cincinnati, Ohio.

14 **Bastille Day,** in France, commemorates the uprising of the people of Paris against King Louis XVI in 1789 and their seizure of the Bastille, a hated Paris prison.

15 **St. Swithin's Day.** According to legend, if it rains on this day, it will rain for 40 more.

18-21 **Democratic National Convention** in Atlanta, Ga.

24 **Tishah be-Av,** Jewish holy day, marks the destruction of the first and second temples in Jerusalem in 587 B.C. and A.D. 70.

25 **Puerto Rico Constitution Day.**

August

	1	2	3	4	5	6
7	8	9	10	11	12	13
14	15	16	17	18	19	20
21	22	23	24	25	26	27
28	29	30	31			

6 **Hiroshima Day,** memorial observance for victims of the first atomic bombing in Hiroshima, Japan, in 1945.

14 **Edinburgh International Festival** of music, dance, and theater, through September 3 in Edinburgh, Scotland.

15 **Feast of the Assumption,** Roman Catholic and Eastern Orthodox holy day, celebrates the ascent of the Virgin Mary into heaven.

15-18 **Republican National Convention** in New Orleans.

19 **National Aviation Day** commemorates the birthday of pioneer pilot Orville Wright in 1871.

26 **Women's Equality Day** commemorates the enactment of the 19th Amendment in 1920 giving women the vote.

30 **United States Open Tennis Championship** through September 11 in Flushing Meadow, N.Y.

September

				1	2	3
4	5	6	7	8	9	10
11	12	13	14	15	16	17
18	19	20	21	22	23	24
25	26	27	28	29	30	

5 **Labor Day** in the United States and Canada.

11 **National Grandparents Day** honors grandfathers and grandmothers.

12 **Rosh Ha-Shanah,** or Jewish New Year, beginning the year 5749 according to the Jewish calendar.

17 **Summer Olympic Games** through October 2 in Seoul, South Korea.
Citizenship Day celebrates the rights and duties of U.S. citizens.

21 **Yom Kippur,** or Day of Atonement, the most solemn day in the Jewish calendar.

22 **First Day of Fall,** 3:29 P.M. E.D.T

26 **Sukkot,** or Feast of Tabernacles, begins—Jewish festival that originally marked the harvest season.

30 **End of the Fiscal Year** for the United States government.

October

						1
2	3	4	5	6	7	8
9	10	11	12	13	14	15
16	17	18	19	20	21	22
23	24	25	26	27	28	29
30	31					

2-8 **National 4-H Week.**

4 **Simhat Torah,** Jewish festival of rejoicing in God's law, marks the end of the annual cycle of Scripture readings.

9 **Leif Ericson Day,** honoring early Norse explorer of North America.

10 **Columbus Day** commemorates Christopher Columbus' landing in America in 1492. The actual anniversary is October 12.
Thanksgiving Day in Canada.

11 **Pulaski Day** honors Casimir Pulaski, Polish general who fought in the Revolutionary War in America.

15 **Sweetest Day,** when sweethearts exchange cards and gifts.

24 **United Nations Day** commemorates the founding of the United Nations in 1945.

30 **Standard Time Resumes** at 2 A.M.

31 **Halloween.**
United Nations Children's Fund (UNICEF) Day.
Reformation Day, celebrated by Protestants, marks the day in 1517 when Reformation leader Martin Luther posted his Ninety-Five Theses.

November

	1	2	3	4	5
6	7	8	9	10	11	12
13	14	15	16	17	18	19
20	21	22	23	24	25	26
27	28	29	30			

1 **All Saints' Day,** observed by the Roman Catholic Church.

5 **Guy Fawkes Day,** in Great Britain, marks the failure of a plot to blow up King James I and Parliament in 1605.

8 **Election Day** in the United States.

11 **Veterans Day** in the United States.
Remembrance Day in Canada.

13-19 **American Education Week.**

14-20 **National Children's Book Week.**

20-27 **National Bible Week,** an interfaith drive to promote reading and study of the Bible.

24 **Thanksgiving Day** in the United States.

27 **Advent** begins, first of the four Sundays in the season before Christmas.

30 **St. Andrew's Day,** feast day of the patron saint of Scotland.

December

				1	2	3
4	5	6	7	8	9	10
11	12	13	14	15	16	17
18	19	20	21	22	23	24
25	26	27	28	29	30	31

4-11 **Hanukkah,** or Feast of Lights, eight-day Jewish festival that celebrates the defeat of the Syrian tyrant King Antiochus IV in 165 B.C.

6 **St. Nicholas Day,** when children in many European countries receive gifts.

10 **Nobel Prize Ceremony** in Stockholm, Sweden.
Human Rights Day marks the anniversary of the adoption of the Universal Declaration of Human Rights in 1948.

13 **St. Lucia Day,** in Sweden, celebrates the return of light after the darkest time of the year.

15 **Bill of Rights Day** in the United States marks the ratification of that document in 1791.

21 **First Day of Winter,** 10:28 A.M. E.S.T.

24 **Christmas Eve.**

25 **Christmas Day.**

26 **Kwanzaa,** black American holiday based on a traditional African harvest festival, through January 1.
Boxing Day, holiday in Canada and Great Britain when mail carriers and others who perform services receive Christmas boxes.

31 **New Year's Eve.**